# Sex Matters

## The Sexuality and Society Reader

SECOND EDITION

**Mindy Stombler**

**Dawn M. Baunach**

**Elisabeth O. Burgess**

**Denise Donnelly**

**Wendy Simonds**

Georgia State University

PEARSON

Boston   New York   San Francisco
Mexico City   Montreal   Toronto   London   Madrid   Munich   Paris
Hong Kong   Singapore   Tokyo   Cape Town   Sydney

*To Jackie Boles, for creating a departmental atmosphere*
*where we can talk—and laugh loudly—about sex.*

*Senior Series Editor:*  Jeff Lasser
*Series Editorial Assistant:*  Erikka Adams
*Senior Marketing Manager:*  Kelly May
*Editorial-Production Service:*  Omegatype Typography, Inc.
*Composition Buyer:*  Linda Cox
*Manufacturing Buyer:*  JoAnne Sweeney
*Electronic Composition:*  Omegatype Typography, Inc.
*Cover Administrator:*  Linda Knowles

For related titles and support materials, visit our online catalog at www.ablongman.com.

Between the time website information is gathered and then published, it is not unusual for some sites to have closed. Also, the transcription of URLs can result in typographical errors. The publisher would appreciate notification where these errors occur so that they may be corrected in subsequent editions.

ISBN 0-205-48544-8

Printed in the United States of America

10  9  8  7  6  5  4  3  2        10  09  08  07  06

**Photo credits:**  p. 56, David Hiller, courtesy of the Kinsey Institute; p. 120, Ed Cunicelli; p. 183, Charles Harrington, Cornell University Photography; p. 397, Michelle Litvin; p. 559, Margaret Benes.

# Contents

chapter **5**    **The Sexual Body**    **245**

# Preface

Ours is a sex-saturated society. We hear of sex drive, sex toys, sex machines, sex slaves, sex scandals, sex gods, sex crimes, and sexaholics. Sex permeates every aspect of our lives from advertising to politics to our relationships with others. Yet we rarely consider the historical, legal, and cultural contexts of sexuality. Many people take the current state of sexual attitudes and practices in our society for granted, as if they are natural, and thus, unchangeable. Understanding contemporary sexual matters requires considering how sexuality varies across time and place and how it is modeled, molded, and even manipulated by those around us. Consider, for instance, the influence of social contexts as you read the following scenarios:

- Imagine that you've chosen to have sex for the first time. How do you know what to do? How do you plan on pleasing your partner? Yourself? Do you turn for guidance to books or magazines, pornographic videos, or the wall of the public bathroom? What makes you excited? Nervous? Will you practice safe sex?

- Imagine that you and your partner do things together that you've never heard about before but make you feel transported, ecstatic, or orgasmic. Or imagine you feel nothing much during your encounters or that you feel disgusted or that you're not even sure if you have "had sex." Imagine that you want to stop but your partner won't. What would you do? Whom would you tell?

- Imagine that you and your partner are the same sex. Would you feel comfortable showing affection in public? Can you imagine a cultural context in which you wouldn't have to worry about others' reactions? Can you imagine how dating someone of the same sex might be beneficial to you?

- Imagine that an evening of partying ends in an unplanned one night stand. You or your partner become pregnant. Would you see the pregnancy as something to celebrate? To ignore? To hide? To terminate? Would your family and friends share your feelings? Would their reaction be the same if you were 15 or you were 45? What if your partner were much older or younger than you? Or of a different race, ethnicity, or religion?

- Imagine that you've made a careful decision to refrain from sexual activity. What circumstances might compel such a decision? Would it be hard to maintain your resolve? Or imagine, by contrast, that you've sought out as much sexual activity as you can find. Either way, who would support your decision to be celibate or sexually adventurous? Who might challenge it? How would these responses be different, depending on your age, your gender, or your social status?

## Sexuality and Society

If you vary the time, the place, or the cultural setting of the scenarios, you'll find that your feelings, the decisions you would make, and the reactions of those around you will probably change. These variations occur because the social norms governing sexual behavior are continually in flux. Other social factors, such as your religious beliefs, level of education, economic status, ethnicity, gender, and age, influence sexual activity and its meaning. All of the following are influenced by society: what counts as a sex act, how often we have sex, what is considered erotic, where we have sex, the age when we begin having sex, with whom we have sex, what we do when we are having sex, how often we desire sex, our reasons for having or avoiding sex, whether we pay others or get paid for sex, and whether we coerce our sexual partners. Although often characterized as a purely biological and often uncontrollable phenomenon, sex is, in fact, social. The readings we have selected portray sex as a social issue influenced by culture, politics, economics, media, education, medicine, law, family, and friends.

## Sex Matters

Our title reflects the content of the book in two ways. First, we have included research articles and essays on a variety of sexual matters. Second, the title supports our assertion that sex, and the study of sexuality, *matters*. There is much to learn about sexuality. Despite the prevalence of sexual matters in public life and the media, as well as its private significance, scholars researching sexuality have difficulty getting institutional and financial support. Funding agencies, politicians, and many academics do not take sexuality seriously.

Yet the study of sexuality is burgeoning, as evidenced by the proliferation of courses on sexuality in colleges and universities throughout the United States. This book applies social theory and methods to the study of sexuality. Thus, research-oriented articles dominate our collection. This empirical focus is enhanced in each chapter by the Spotlight on Research feature, which profiles the work of eleven sex researchers. Each of these interviews echoes the fact that sex really does matter.

## Themes of This Book

Each of our chapters highlights the dual themes of social construction and social control. In other words, society—composed of social institutions and the individuals within them—constructs our understanding of sexuality and influences our behaviors, attitudes, and sexual identities. The readings illustrate that some social institutions and some members of society have more power

to control and define a society's sexual agenda than others. At the same time, social control is usually met with social resistance, and we offer readings that feature examples of successful individual and cultural resistance to societal expectations and oppression.

Chapter 1, "Categorizing Sex," explores how society constructs sexual categories. We challenge readers to question what should count as having sex, a topic with wide-ranging legal and health implications. Readings on intersexuality and transsexuality encourage us to consider the viability of our current categories of "male" and "female," what it takes to change one's sex, and who controls sex assignment and reassignment. Other readings question current methods of categorizing sexual orientation and sexual identity. What does it mean to be straight, gay, lesbian, or bisexual? Is sexual identity a matter of behavior, erotic attraction, or self-definition? What role does community play in the construction of our sexual identities? Although existing categories can be helpful for understanding commonalities, they also collapse a wide variety of experiences and feelings into inflexible and essentialized divisions. As the readings show, sexual categories vary across societies, cultures, and time.

Chapter 2, "Investigating Sexuality," presents historical and contemporary sex research and theory and considers ethical, political, and methodological issues involved in conducting sex research. The readings introduce the unique challenges of conducting sex research. The association of sex with privacy creates a level of anxiety and reluctance among would-be research participants that is unmatched in other areas of research. For example, the cultural unwillingness to see adolescents as sexual beings discourages parents from allowing minors to participate in sex research. Differing religious teachings on sexuality add to the controversial nature of sex research. The protest efforts of fundamentalist religious groups have successfully limited governmental support of art, health, and research programs that involve sexuality. Furthermore, because sexuality has historically been viewed as too trivial to merit social research, funding agencies are reluctant to support sex research.

Chapter 3, "Representing Sex" presents a variety of interpretations of the ways that U.S. culture depicts sexualities and sexual activities. For example, media (books, songs, magazines, videos, Internet, etc.) both reflect and create ideas about sexuality. Cultural representations of sexuality impact viewers or readers in a variety of ways by telling powerful stories about appropriate sexual activity and what happens to individuals who deviate from cultural expectations. Cultural representations tell us about who we are, where we've been, and where we're going. The critical perspectives presented in the readings demonstrate the varieties of possible interpretations of representations.

Chapter 4, "Learning about Sex," describes the diverse sources of education about sexuality and examines how these sources shape people's sexual practices and identities. The readings explore how young people are socialized to understand sex and sexuality. Ironically, although talking (or even thinking) about sex may be considered inappropriate, the articles indicate that from a young age we all absorb many sexual messages. Young people learn appropriate and inappropriate sexual behaviors and attitudes from their families, peers, churches, schools, and the media. These messages about sexuality are often used to control sexual behavior, and the degree and methods of social control are tied to a person's gender, sexual orientation, class, race, and culture.

Chapter 5, "The Sexual Body," addresses how we eroticize bodies, body parts, and bodily functions and explores how notions of the erotic can encourage us to manipulate our bodies. Societal discourse both celebrates and stigmatizes the body and its functions. What is sexy about a person's body? Most people can come up with distinct body types or features that are appealing or unappealing to them. Yet these ideas about

what is sexy and what is not are culturally constructed. For instance, U.S. culture sexualizes women's breasts, whereas other cultures regard breasts only as sites of nourishment and nurturing for children. Cultural constructions of the sexual body also function as a form of social control—shaping how we feel about our own bodies, framing our interactions with others, and even forcing us to manipulate our bodies, both voluntarily and involuntarily, to meet cultural expectations. The articles in this chapter explore many traditional ideas about sexuality that emphasize the gendered and racialized nature of the sexual body.

Chapter 6, "Sexual Practices," examines how people behave sexually. As you read the articles in this section, think about how social norms, laws, religion, families, friends, and partners influence our sexuality and shape our behavior. Also, think about the tremendous diversity in sexual practices reflected in these articles. These readings cover a range of sexual practices such as national patterns of sexual behavior, monogamy, the "down low," crosscultural sexual variations, and sexual desire after age 50. Although how we enact our sexuality varies tremendously, these readings demonstrate what can happen when we vary from expected and accepted ways of acting sexually. Finally, these articles also remind us that sexuality is important from the cradle to the grave; regardless of our age, we remain sexual beings.

The articles in Chapter 7, "Procreative Issues," demonstrate how heterosexual experiences can lead to a range of life-defining or incidental experiences, depending on the place, time, society, and power relations that circumscribe it. For example, purchasing contraception was not a legal right until 1954, and then only for married couples. Also consider the social arrangements for birthing babies, which shifted over the course of the twentieth century from a woman-centered home-based activity to a medically managed procedure, as physicians professionalized and worked to drive midwives out of business. Of all the social institutions with the power to influence procreative matters, law and medicine wield immense influence, even though we might not feel their presence until we remember—or test—their limits.

Chapter 8, "Sexual Disease," illustrates how society treats sexually transmitted infections—commonly called *sexually transmitted diseases* (STDs)—quite differently from other communicable diseases. Sexually transmitted infections (STIs) are the only major group of diseases categorized by their method of transmission, rather than by their symptoms or the parts of the body they affect. People infected with STIs are stigmatized, creating a shield of secrecy in which some people deny to themselves that they have an STI, fail to tell their partners, and avoid seeking treatment. The stigma and perceptions of risk surrounding STIs affect the resources government and medical agencies opt to dedicate to fight them. For example, when AIDS was first discovered, it was seen as a "gay" or "African" disease and received little attention. In spite of intense efforts by gay activists, AIDS was considered a national emergency only when it began infecting white, middle-class heterosexual Americans. Regardless of how much we learn about sexually transmitted infections, fears associated with them continue to be a powerful tool in the control of sexuality.

Chapter 9, "Social Control of Sexuality," illustrates how sexuality is managed and directed by forces both internal and external to individuals. Whereas much research on sexuality emphasizes individual responsibility, in this section we explore the social factors that influence sexual attitudes and behaviors. Social institutions such as the law, medicine, and the military control sexual behavior through systems of rewards and punishments. Interpersonal interactions further constrain sexual choices through means such as harassment and labeling. This chapter explores how the mechanisms of social control are often turned against certain groups and how the social control of sexuality is a powerful weapon of oppression. Some selections highlight how social control is a two-way street, with the forces of control and resistance in constant conflict.

Although people like to think of sex as an intimate—and ideally pleasant—activity, it can be used as a weapon of violence and control to humiliate, degrade, and hurt. The readings in Chapter 10, "Sexual Violence," deal with various types of sexual assault, rape of sex workers, date or acquaintance rape, the rape of men, rape in prison, and rape during war. The articles presented in this section also illustrate the diversity of sexual violence. Although women are the primary targets of sexual violence, no group is exempt. Sexual violence cuts across all social categories. The articles presented here contain graphic and appalling information: it is our hope that readers will not simply be shocked, but rather become motivated to take steps toward ending sexual violence.

Chapter 11, "Commercial Sex," explores the commodification of sexuality. Despite numerous laws regulating the sale of sexual services, it continues to be both a profitable business and a source of abuse. We address the tensions between the freedom to express sexuality through commercial avenues and the exploitation and control of sexuality through its sale. The readings examine who profits financially from the sex industry, who works in the sex industry, and who consumes its products.

## Acknowledgments

Revising this book for the second edition was a challenge and a treat. We would like to thank the folks at Allyn and Bacon for their trust and support throughout the revision. It was great working with Jeff Lasser, our editor, once again. Thanks to Erikka Adams and Heather McNally for fielding our many questions. Thanks also to Shannon Foreman and the team at Omegatype Typography for their wonderful job on the production of this book. We also extend our thanks to the following reviewers, who helped shape the book: Deanna McCaughey, Louisville; Barbara Risman, North Carolina State University; Amy Sueyoshi, San Francisco State University; Colin Williams, Indiana University-Purdue University Indianapolis; and Kassia Wosick-Correa, University of California, Irvine.

We are grateful to the researchers and scholars who took time out of their busy schedules to be interviewed for the Spotlight on Research features. Their dedication to the field of sex research, their humor in the face of monetary and political challenges, and their willingness to share personal experiences make us optimistic about the future of sex research. We want to thank the authors who wrote original pieces for the second edition. Their contributions make the book bigger and better (not that size matters . . . ).

We edited this book in an incredibly supportive environment. Our colleagues in the Department of Sociology at Georgia State University provided unequivocal support for "Team Sex." The department, and particularly chair Donald Reitzes, provided a great deal of practical support by providing graduate student assistance and expense money. Of course this supportive department could not function, nor could Team Sex, without the assistance of Quanda Miller, Selma Poage, Dracy Blackwell, and Tiffanie Bailey. Elisabeth Sheff offered insight on substantive matters. We received crucial assistance from Ryan Burgeson, Marni Kahn, Mikel Walters, Jennifer Chandler, and Elroi Waszkiewicz, who conducted library searches, transcribed interviews, and completed other critical support functions. Mikel Walters put a great deal of time and effort into the Sextistics sections, and Ryan Burgeson compiled the contributor's list. We appreciate Elizabeth Cavalier and Elroi Waszkiewicz's efforts to compile this book's wonderful instructor's manual as well.

Thanks to our families and friends for their encouragement and support. In particular, Mindy would like to thank her six-year-old son, Moey Rojas, for the scintillating conversations about sex, and her parents Lynne and Milton Stombler, and her husband, Carl Rojas, for their support. Dawn thanks Jeff Mullis. Elisabeth appreciates the support of Leila Burgess-Kattoula, Ehsan Kattoula, Charles O. Burgess, and Elisabeth C. Burgess. Denise truly values the graduate students in her gender and sexuality seminars for their insights and questions, her sons Keegan and Nick for their love and patience, and her friends—both near and far—for the diversions they offered. Wendy thanks Jake and Ben Simonds-Malamud, Gregg Rice, and Bumble and Hinky Simonds for their sweetness.

We would be remiss if we did not acknowledge that we have done this revision in spite of the deaths of loved ones, divorce and breakups, depression, the demands of infants and children of all ages, an increasing variety of chronic conditions, minute raises, the horrible Atlantic traffic, the sad state of the world, and general futility of it all!

This book would not have been possible without the many hundreds of undergraduate sexuality students who pass through our department each year. We appreciate their letting us know their favorite readings, for fearlessly voicing their opinions, and for asking tough questions.

This project is truly an example of collaborative feminist work. With Mindy Stombler as the team's "dominatrix," and the constant mutual support among all team members, creating this book often felt more like fun than work. Not only did we enjoy meetings, but our frequent loud laughter provoked the insane jealousy of our colleagues at Georgia State. We hope you have as much fun reading this book as we had putting it together.

# About the Contributors

**Mindy Stombler, Ph.D.,** is a senior lecturer of sociology at Georgia State University. Her research interests include the construction of collective identity in fraternity culture, focusing on black and white fraternity little sister programs and gay fraternities. Her research on gay fraternities examines how men negotiate the dual identities of being gay and being Greek and how men in gay fraternities reproduce hegemonic masculinity. Her latest research project examines power relations and oral sex.

**Dawn M. Baunach, Ph.D.,** is an associate professor of sociology at Georgia State University. Her research interests include inequality and stratification, gender and sexuality, work and occupations, and social demography. In collaboration with Dr. Burgess, she is currently studying the sexual attitudes and behaviors of undergraduate students, including the fluidity of sexuality, homophobia, and sexual disclosure.

**Elisabeth O. Burgess, Ph.D.,** is an associate professor of sociology and affiliated with the Gerontology Institute at Georgia State University. Her research interests focus on changes in intimate relations over the life course, including involuntary celibacy, sexuality and aging, and intergenerational relationships. Currently she is collaborating with Dr. Baunach on research based on a survey of the sexual attitudes and behaviors of undergraduate students. In addition, Dr. Burgess writes on theories of aging and attitudes toward older adults.

**Denise Donnelly, Ph.D.,** is an associate professor of sociology at Georgia State University. Her research interests include sexless marriages, involuntary celibacy, services to battered women, culturally competent approaches to ending violence, and peace in Northern Ireland.

**Wendy Simonds, Ph.D.,** is an associate professor of sociology at Georgia State University. She is author of *Abortion at Work: Ideology and Practice in a Feminist Clinic* (Rutgers, 1996), *Women and Self-Help Culture: Reading between the Lines* (Rutgers, 1992), coauthor with Barbara Katz Rothman of *Centuries of Solace: Expressions of Maternal Grief in Popular Literature* (Temple, 1992), and coauthor with Barbara Katz Rothman and Bari Meltzer of *Laboring On: Birth in Transition in the U.S.* (Routledge, forthcoming). She is currently working on a project entitled Queers on Marriage.

## The Authors

**Melissa Abramovitz** is a freelance writer living in San Luis Obispo, California.

**Alan Guttmacher Institute** is a nonprofit organization focused on sexual and reproductive health research, policy analysis, and public education. Located in New York City and Washington, D.C., the Institute publishes *Perspectives on Sexual and Reproductive Health, International Family Planning Perspectives, The Guttmacher Report on Public Policy,* and special reports on topics pertaining to sexual and reproductive health and rights.

**Tamara Addison** (see Malamuth)

**Allison Kavanagh Alavi** is a sociologist working in Atlanta, Georgia.

**Dennis Altman** is a professor in the school of social sciences at LaTrobe University in Melbourne, Australia.

**Michael Amico** is a member of the class of 2007 at Dartmouth College and editor-in-chief of *queer,* an international intercollegiate journal for undergraduates.

**Linda J. Beckman** is a professor in the California School of Professional Psychology at Alliant International University in Alhambra, California.

**Aaron Belkin** is an associate professor of political science at the University of California in Santa Barbara and the director of the Center for the Study of Sexual Minorities in the Military.

**Dinesh Bhugra** is dean of the Royal College of Psychiatrists in the United Kingdom and professor of mental health and cultural diversity at the Institute of Psychiatry in London.

**Timothy J. Biblarz** is an associate professor and director of graduate studies in the department of sociology at the University of Southern California in Los Angeles.

**Hanne Blank** is a writer, historian, and public speaker currently working on *Virgin: The Untouched History* (Bloomsbury, 2006).

**Pamela Block** is a clinical associate professor in the occupational therapy program at the State University of New York in Stony Brook. Her research interests include multiple marginalization and the intersections of gender, race, poverty, and disability.

**Heather Boonstra** is a senior public policy associate in the Alan Guttmacher Institute's Washington, D.C. office, responsible for promoting the institute's sexual and reproductive health agenda in federal law and policy.

**Keith Boykin** is one of the nation's leading commentators on race, sexuality, and politics. A former White House aide to President Clinton, Mr. Boykin is also a *New York Times* bestselling author, lawyer, educator, and activist.

**Allan M. Brandt** is the Kass Professor of the History of Medicine at Harvard University in Cambridge, Massachusetts.

**Daniel Brook** is a Philadelphia-based freelance journalist whose work has appeared in *Harper's* and *Mother Jones*.

**Vern L. Bullough** is a visiting professor in the department of nursing at the University of Southern California in Los Angeles.

**Centers for Disease Control and Prevention** is one of the thirteen major operating components of the Department of Health and Human Services, which is the principal agency in the U.S. government for protecting the health and safety of all Americans and for providing essential human services.

**Anjani Chandra** is a researcher at the Centers for Disease Control and Prevention.

**Greta Christina** is a freelance writer living in the San Francisco Bay area. Ms. Christina is editor of *Pay for It: A Guide by Sex Workers for Their Clients*.

**Patricia Hill Collins** is an author and professor of sociology at the University of Maryland in College Park.o

**David W. Coon** is an associate professor in the department of social and behavioral sciences at the Arizona State University West Campus in Phoenix.

**Mubarak Dahir** is a Palestinian-American born in Jerusalem to Muslim and Southern Baptist parents. Mr. Dahir writes and lectures on gay and Middle Eastern issues and is the current editor of the *Express Gay News,* the lesbian and gay newspaper of Fort Lauderdale, Florida.

**Robert Darby** is an independent scholar and cultural historian with an interest in the history of sexuality and sexual medicine. He is author of *A Surgical Temptation: The Demonization of*

*the Foreskin and Rise of Circumcision in Britain* (University of Chicago Press, 2005). Mr. Darby resides in Canberra, Australia, where he manages a website, www.historyofcircumcision.net, devoted to the same topic.

**Clive M. Davis** is a professor emeritus of psychology at Syracuse University in New York.

**Phillip W. Davis** is an associate professor of sociology at Georgia State University in Atlanta.

**John D. DeLamater** is a professor of sociology at the University of Wisconsin in Madison and current editor of *The Journal of Sex Research.* His ongoing research focuses on sexual behavior and satisfaction in a sample of over 5,000 persons aged 62 to 67.

**Kathleen Dolan** is an assistant professor of sociology at North Georgia College and State University in Dahlonega.

**Philip Elmer-DeWitt** is an assistant managing editor for *TIME Magazine* living in Brooklyn, New York.

**Rana A. Emerson** is a doctoral candidate in sociology at the University of Texas in Austin.

**Cynthia Enloe** is a professor of government at Clark University in Worcester, Massachusetts.

**Eve Ensler** is a writer, producer, and director, most notably of *The Vagina Monologues.*

**Jeffrey Escoffier** writes on sexuality, gay history and politics, and social theory. His most recent book is *Sexual Revolution* (Thunder's Mouth Press, 2003), an anthology of important writing on sex from the 1960s and 70s. He is also author of *American Homo: Community and Perversity* (University of California Press, 1998) and *John Maynard Keynes* (Chelsea House, 1995).

**Yen Le Espiritu** is a professor and chair of ethnic studies at the University of California in San Diego.

**Elizabeth Fee** is chief of the history of medicine division of the National Library of Medicine at the National Institutes of Health and adjunct professor of history and health policy at the Johns Hopkins University in Baltimore, Maryland.

**Katherine Frank** is a postdoctoral fellow in the department of sociology at the University of Wisconsin in Madison and a faculty associate at the College of the Atlantic in Bar Harbor, Maine. Her research focuses on the boundaries of monogamy for married American couples, and she is currently working on an ethnography of the swinging community.

**Tad Friend** is a staff writer for *The New Yorker.*

**John H. Gagnon** is a professor emeritus of sociology at the State University of New York in Stony Brook. Some of his main research interests include sexual conduct, social control, and AIDS research.

**Ina May Gaskin** is the executive director of the Farm Midwifery Center in Summertown, Tennessee. She is author of *Spiritual Midwifery* and *Ina May's Guide to Childbirth.*

**Nicola Gavey** is an associate professor of psychology at the University of Auckland in New Zealand. She is author of *Just Sex? The Cultural Scaffolding of Rape* (Routledge, 2005).

**Gloria González-López** is an assistant professor of sociology at the University of Texas in Austin.

**Judith Gordon** was, before her death, a nursery school teacher and journalist.

**Sol Gordon** is a professor emeritus of psychology at the University of California in Davis.

**Jamison Green** is an author, educator, and consultant specializing in transgender and transsexual social, legal, and healthcare issues and policy. Mr. Green is currently working on a Ph.D. in law, researching how medical expert witness testimony is used in cases where one's gender is at issue. He is the author of *Becoming a Visible Man* (Vanderbilt University Press, 2004).

**Nora Ellen Groce** is an associate professor in the global health division at the Yale School of Public Health with adjunct appointments in the Yale Department of Anthropology and the Yale Institute for Social and Policy Studies.

**Kate Haas** is a lawyer living in California.

**S. Marie Harvey** is an associate professor of public health at the University of Oregon, directs the Research Program on Women's Health at the Center for the Study of Women in Society, and is a founder of the Pacific Institute for Women's Health in Los Angeles, California.

**Jo Jones** is a researcher at the Centers for Disease Control and Prevention.

**Suzanne Kessler** is a professor of psychology and dean of the School of Natural and Social Sciences at the State University of New York in Purchase. She is coauthor of "Transgendering" in *Handbook of Gender and Women's Studies,* edited by M. Evans, K. Davis, and J. Lorber (Sage, 2006).

**Laura Kipnis** is a professor in the radio-television-film department at Northwestern University in Evanston, Illinois.

**Sheila Kitzinger** lectures to midwives in many different countries. She is an honorary professor at Thames Valley University and teaches in the midwifery master's program at the Wolfson School of Health Sciences. She also teaches workshops on the social anthropology of birth and breastfeeding and on unhappiness after childbirth for birth educators and postnatal counselors.

**Deborah Kolben** is a writer living in New York City where she is a staff reporter at *The New York Sun.* Her articles have appeared in *The Financial Times, The Guardian,* and *New York Daily News.*

**Mary Koss** is a professor in the Meland Enid Zuckerman Arizona College of Public Health at the University of Arizona and principal investigator of the RESTORE Program—a victim-driven, community collaboration that offers an alternative justice intervention for selected sex crimes.

**David M. Latini** is an assistant professor in the Scott Department of Urology at Baylor College of Medicine in Houston, Texas, and the Houston Center for Quality of Care and Utilization Studies at the Michael E. DeBakey VA Medical Center.

**Edward O. Laumann** is the George Herbert Mead Distinguished Service Professor of Sociology at the University of Chicago.

**Alice Leuchtag** is a freelance writer, social worker, counselor, college instructor, and researcher. Active in the civil rights, peace, socialist, feminist, and humanist movements, she has helped organize women in Houston to oppose sex trafficking.

**Jacob Levenson** is a Nieman Fellow at Harvard University in Cambridge, Massachusetts, and author of *The Secret Epidemic: The Story of AIDS and Black America* (Pantheon, 2004).

**Meika Loe** is an assistant professor of sociology and women's studies at Colgate University in Hamilton, New York.

**Jacquelyne Luce** is a medical anthropologist, currently based at the Policy, Ethics, and Life Sciences Research Institute (PEALS) in Newcastle, United Kingdom. She has conducted research on lesbian and bisexual women's narratives of assisted conception, adoption, and pregnancy loss; pregnant performativity; and midwifery. Her current work focuses on women's and men's experiences of embryo donation for preimplantation, genetic diagnosis, and stem cell related research.

**Neil M. Malamuth** is a professor and chair of the communication studies department and professor of psychology and women's studies at the University of California in Los Angeles.

**Tamara Malamuth (Addison)** is a lecturer in the department of psychology at the University of California in Los Angeles.

**Rona Marech** is a staff reporter for *The Baltimore Sun*.

**Michel Marriott** is a staff reporter for the *New York Times*.

**Naomi B. McCormick** was a professor of psychology at the State University of New York in Plattsburgh and a professor of psychology, family studies, and women's studies at the University of Northern Iowa. She is the author of *Sexual Salvation: Affirming Women's Sexual Rights and Pleasures* (Greenwood Press, 1994).

**Chet Meeks** is an assistant professor of sociology at Georgia State University in Atlanta. His primary research interest is the relationship between gay, lesbian, and queer politics and social theory. His current work examines the moral underpinnings of lesbian, gay, and queer organizing and politics in the United States beginning in the mid-twentieth century.

**Robert T. Michael** is a professor at the Harris School of Public Policy at the University of Chicago.

**Stuart Michaels** is a lecturer and the assistant director of the Center for Gender Studies at the University of Chicago.

**Melinda Mills** is a doctoral candidate in sociology at Georgia State University in Atlanta.

**William D. Mosher** is a project officer of the National Survey of Family Growth.

**Jeffery S. Mullis** is a lecturer in the department of sociology at Emory University in Atlanta, Georgia.

**Adina Nack** is an assistant professor of sociology at California Lutheran University in Thousand Oaks.

**Joane Nagel** is a professor of sociology at the University of Kansas in Lawrence.

**Sumie Okazaki** is an associate professor and the director of clinical training at the University of Illinois in Urbana-Champaign.

**Richard Parker** is a professor and chair of the department of sociomedical sciences in the Mailman School of Public Health at Columbia University in New York City.

**Fred Pelka** is a freelance writer and researcher. Mr. Pelka is the author of the *ABC-CLIO Companion to the Disability Rights Movement* and a 2004 Guggenheim Fellow.

**Lewis Perdue** is a *New York Times* bestselling author of twenty books that have sold more than four million copies. His works include *Perfect Killer* and *The Da Vinci Legacy, Daughter of God*. Mr. Perdue has taught journalism at the University of California in Los Angeles and Cornell University.

**June Machover Reinisch** served as director of the Kinsey Institute from 1982 until 1993. Now residing in New York City, Dr. Reinisch is president of R2 Science Communications, Inc. and the director of the Muse Foundation of the Museum of Sex.

**Frank Rich** is a columnist for the *New York Times* and a senior writer for the *New York Times Magazine*, living in New York City.

**Matt Richtel** is a staff reporter for the *New York Times*.

**Dorothy E. Roberts** is the Kirkland and Ellis Professor at the Northwestern University School of Law, with joint appointments in the departments of African American studies and sociology; a faculty fellow of the Institute for Policy Research; and faculty affiliate of the Joint Center for Poverty Research.

**Susan Rose** is a professor and chair of the department of sociology at Dickinson College in Carlisle, Pennsylvania.

**Joshunda Sanders** is currently a reporter for *The Austin-American Statesman* in Austin, Texas. Her writings have appeared in anthologies such as *Secrets and Confidences: The Truth about Women's Friendships* and *My Soul to His Spirit.*

**Stephanie A. Sanders** is an associate professor of gender studies at Indiana University in Bloomington and associate director of The Kinsey Institute.

**Steven Seidman** is a professor emeritus in the department of sociology at the State University of New York in Albany.

**Elisabeth Sheff** is an assistant professor of sociology at Georgia State University in Atlanta.

**Russell P. Shuttleworth** is an Ed Roberts post-doctoral fellow in disability studies at the Institute of Urban and Regional Development at the University of California in Berkeley.

**Morgan Sill** received her M.A. degree in public health from the University of Michigan; she currently resides in Minnesota.

**Annie Sprinkle** is a former prostitute and porn star turned Ph.D. sexologist, educator, and multimedia artist. Ms. Sprinkle is a self-described "Utopian Entrepreneur" and author of *Dr. Sprinkle's Spectacular Sex—Make Over Your Love Life.*

**Judith Stacey** is a professor of sociology and gender and sexuality at New York University. Her research examines changes in family, sexuality, and society, with a current focus on gay family issues.

**Karen Sternheimer** is a lecturer in the department of sociology at the University of Southern California in Los Angeles.

**Erika Summers-Effler** is an assistant professor of sociology at the Notre Dame University in South Bend, Indiana.

**Leora Tanenbaum** is an author, journalist, and columnist living in New York City.

**Melissa Travis** is a graduate student in sociology at Georgia State University in Atlanta.

**Donna Walton** is a research instructor in counseling at George Washington University in Washington, D.C.

**Jane Ward** is an assistant professor of sociology at the University of California in Riverside. She is currently working on the manuscript for her upcoming book, *Doing Diversity in Queer L.A.: How the Mainstream Obsession with Diversity Is Transforming Social Movements.*

**Jennifer K. Wesely** is an assistant professor of criminology and criminal justice at the University of North Florida in Jacksonville. Her work addresses gender, body, power, and identity in such contexts as exotic dancing, domestic violence, homelessness, sports, and the outdoors.

**Kassia Wosick-Correa** is an instructor of sociology at the University of California in Irvine, at Irvine Valley College, and at Chapman University. She is currently researching how monogamous and consensual nonmonogamous relationships negotiate love, commitment, and sexual intimacy. Her main foci are sexual identities, gender, sexual behavior, and intimate relationships.

# chapter 1

# Categorizing Sex

Spotlight on Research

*An interview with . . .*

## Paula C. Rodríguez Rust

Paula C. Rodríguez Rust, Ph.D., specializes in research on sexual orientation diversity. She is the author of two books, *Bisexuality in the United States: A Social Science Reader* (Columbia University Press, 2000) and *Bisexuality and the Challenge to Lesbian Politics* (NYU Press, 1995). Dr. Rodríguez Rust is the principal investigator of the International Bisexual Identity, Community, Ideology and Politics (IBICIP) Study. Her work has been published in a variety of journals and edited volumes. She is currently involved in school-related diversity education in New Jersey.

### What led you to begin studying sexuality?

*Our cultural schizophrenia regarding sexuality makes it both interesting and challenging to study sexuality. Sexuality is all around us—in ads, on television— but it's supposed to be private. I love a challenge; what better challenge than to conduct research about a topic that we are not even supposed to talk about publicly?*

*But it's more than that. To explain how I ended up studying sexuality, first I have to explain why I chose to study sociology. My parents are an electrical engineer and a physician. Growing up, I learned that everything in the world was reducible to the physical, observable world—all properties of matter could be explained by their molecules, and all disease could be explained by looking inside the human body. In 1979, I stepped out of college for a year. While traveling in Israel, I met a cultural anthropologist. She told me about the South Foré, a people that had been plagued by a fatal disease called Kuru. Soon after a person died from the disease, their female relatives often became sick. The medical doctors could not figure out how the disease was being transmitted, nor what organism was causing it. Then, she said, an anthropologist discovered a South Foré tradition in which the female relatives would eat the brain of a deceased person. That is how the doctors discovered that the disease was located in the brain; once they knew that, they found the cause of the disease and slowed its spread. [See http://anthro.palomar.edu/medical/med_4.htm for medical and historical facts about Kuru.] It fascinated me that a biological process—something physical, concrete, observable—could only be explained once culture—something intangible, human, social—was understood. I had never looked at the world this way before, and it opened up an entirely new perspective to me. When I returned to college, I chose to major in sociology/anthropology (a combined department at Oberlin at the time), but I didn't like looking at bones much so I ended up in sociology instead of anthropology.*

*A few years before that, at age 17, I had come out as a lesbian. Suddenly, from the perspective of a lesbian, the world looked very different. Things I had taken for granted were no longer true. I had never realized before how completely our social world assumes heterosexuality; when I assumed I was a heterosexual, that had not been a problem for me, so I'd never noticed it. Now, as a lesbian, I had a very different position vis-à-vis that world—outside it. The shift in perspective fascinated me; how could I have been so blind before, and what else would I discover if I continued looking at the world with different eyes?*

*I enjoy looking at things from new perspectives. We think we understand our world until we look at it from a different perspective. The cultural anthropologist in Israel showed me a different perspective, and coming out as a lesbian showed me a different perspective. My work on sexuality, and bisexuality in particular, has been an effort to develop new perspectives and share them with other people.*

### How do people react when they find that you study sexuality?

*These days they're very surprised. At the moment, I'm writing at home without an affiliation to a university or college. After receiving tenure at two different institutions, my partner and I moved to New Jersey. I decided to continue my research, but without an academic position. So most of the people I meet are the parents of my children's friends, and the people in the self-defense classes I teach. They have no idea I have "another life." I think in general people are interested. They're often not quite sure what to say next, because "and what do you do?" is supposed to be a very casual conversational question and they don't expect the answer "I study sexuality," but usually they end up asking lots of questions.*

### What ethical dilemmas have you faced in studying sexuality?

*My dilemmas have been more political than ethical. When I conducted research for my dissertation in the mid-1980s, the Institutional Review Board required that I obtain signed consent forms from my interviewees. Normally, the fact of participating in a face-to-face interview would be sufficient to indicate consent, but because the topic of the study was a stigmatized form of sexuality, the IRB apparently felt they needed some extra protection. Ostensibly, IRBs are in place to protect research subjects. The irony in the case of my research was that getting signed consent forms would mean that I had to collect and have on record people's names, which was not in the interests of my subjects, for exactly the same reason—i.e., that I was studying stigmatized sexuality!*

*To some extent, the fact that I study my own minority community has been a bit of a dilemma. My first book,* Bisexuality and the Challenge to Lesbian Politics, *is about lesbians' attitudes toward bisexual women in the 1980s. The attitudes I explored included the lack of trust and antipathy many lesbians felt toward bisexual women whom they thought of as traitors. I identify strongly as a lesbian feminist myself—I attended the Michigan Womyn's Music Festival during the first few years before it moved to its current location, I still have some of my old flannel shirts, and I still carry a Swiss Army knife. Parts of that book are worded very carefully, because I thought it important for lesbians to examine our own prejudices, but I did not want to paint a negative picture of our community to outsiders who would not be sensitive to the complex politics inside the lesbian community.*

### What do you think is the most challenging thing about studying sexuality?

*I challenge myself to continually try to find new ways of looking at things. Finding assumptions to question can be a challenge, because what makes them assumptions is the fact that we're not aware we're making them. In more concrete terms, one challenge has been managing the relationship between my own life and my research. Clearly, my interest in sexuality and my scientific perspectives on sexuality are related to my own personal experiences. So, one challenge has been balancing the need for scientific rigor with an acknowledgment of that connection in my work. Should I write in the first person or in the third? Should I mention in the preface to* Bisexuality and the Challenge to Lesbian Politics *that my interest in lesbians' attitudes toward bisexuals began when I noticed myself condemning myself for a brief attraction to a man? On one hand, researchers should strive to be objective, and not let personal biases cloud their research. On the other hand, anyone who thinks their own personal experiences do not inform their research—no matter what they are studying—is merely blind to that influence. From the questions we ask, to the interpretations we make of our findings, our own personal experiences affect our scientific research. To fail to acknowledge that connection means to fail to be scientific.*

### Why is it important to do sex research?

*It's important because there is still a great deal of prejudice based on sexual differences in the world. There is still discrimination. There is still mental cruelty. I still can't marry my partner. Women who are sexually assaulted still feel ashamed. Transgendered and intersexed children are still not understood by their peers and teachers. Women's rights to control their own bodies are still threatened. We need to keep the light shining on these issues, so that we keep moving forward faster than we move backward.*

### If you could teach people one thing about sexuality, what would it be?

*The things I'd like to teach people go way beyond sexuality. Never look at anything from only one perspective. Question your own assumptions. Try to understand others from their perspectives, not from your own—what's natural or necessary for you might not be for others.*

### Is there anything else you'd like to add?

*When I was in graduate school, and I chose to study lesbian and bisexual women, my faculty advisors were very supportive but I know that they were afraid I was committing career suicide. I went out on a limb, and it could very well have meant that I would never get a job in my field. Turns out, it was just a few years later that bisexuality came out of the shadows for two reasons: the bisexual movement became very public, and the discovery of the routes of HIV transmission made bisexuality epidemiologically relevant. Suddenly I was right at the forefront of research on a topic that lots of people were very interested in; and there were very few of us at that forefront. Today, when graduate students ask me whether they should choose a "safe" topic or a topic that they're really interested in, I point out that "safe" topics are probably safe because they've already been thoroughly researched. If I'd chosen a safe topic, I might still be studying that safe—boring—topic. As it is, I'm doing something I still find very interesting. Ask yourself, what do you have that is unique that you can offer the world?*

—Interviewed by Denise Donnelly

# Are We Having Sex Now or What?

Greta Christina

When I first started having sex with other people, I used to like to count them. I wanted to keep track of how many there had been. It was a source of some kind of pride, or identity anyway, to know how many people I'd had sex with in my lifetime. So, in my mind, Len was number one, Chris was number two, that slimy awful little heavy metal barbiturate addict whose name I can't remember was number three, Alan was number four, and so on. It got to the point where, when I'd start having sex with a new person for the first time, when he first entered my body (I was only having sex with men at the time), what would flash through my head wouldn't be "Oh, baby, baby you feel so good inside me," or "What the hell am I doing with this creep," or "This is boring, I wonder what's on TV." What flashed through my head was "Seven!"

Doing this had some interesting results. I'd look for patterns in the numbers. I had a theory for a while that every fourth lover turned out to be really great in bed, and would ponder what the cosmic significance of the phenomenon might be. Sometimes I'd try to determine what kind of person I was by how many people I'd had sex with. At eighteen, I'd had sex with ten different people. Did that make me normal, repressed, a total slut, a free-spirited bohemian, or what? Not that I compared my numbers with anyone else's—I didn't. It was my own exclusive structure, a game I played in the privacy of my own head.

Then the numbers started getting a little larger, as numbers tend to do, and keeping track became more difficult. I'd remember that the last one was *seventeen* and so this one must be *eighteen*, but then I'd start having doubts about whether I'd been keeping score accurately or not. I'd lie awake at night thinking to myself well, there was Brad, and there was that guy on my birthday, and there was David and . . . no, wait, I forgot that guy I got drunk with at the social my first week at college . . . so that's seven, eight, nine . . . and by two in the morning I'd finally have it figured out. But there was always a nagging suspicion that maybe I'd missed someone, some dreadful tacky little scumball that I was trying to forget about having invited inside my body. And as much as I maybe wanted to forget about the sleazy little scumball, I wanted more to get that number right.

It kept getting harder, though. I began to question what counted as sex and what didn't. There was that time with Gene, for instance. I was pissed off at my boyfriend, David, for cheating on me. It was a major crisis, and Gene and I were friends and he'd been trying to get at me for weeks and I hadn't exactly been discouraging him. I went to see him that night to gripe about David. He was very sympathetic of course, and he gave me a backrub, and we talked and touched and confided and hugged, and then we started kissing, and then we snuggled up a little closer, and then we started fondling each other, you know, and then all heck broke loose, and we rolled around on the bed

From "Are We Having Sex Now or What?" by Greta Christina, from *The Erotic Impulse*, edited by David Steinberg, copyright © 1992 by David Steinberg. Used by permission of Jeremy P. Tarcher, an imprint of Penguin Group (USA) Inc.

groping and rubbing and grabbing and smooching and pushing and pressing and squeezing. He never did actually get it in. He wanted to, and I wanted to too, but I had this thing about being faithful to my boyfriend, so I kept saying, "No, you can't do that, Yes, that feels so good, No, wait that's too much, Yes, yes, don't stop, No, stop that's enough." We never even got our clothes off. Jesus Christ, though, it was some night. One of the best, really. But for a long time I didn't count it as one of the times I'd had sex. He never got inside, so it didn't count.

Later, months and years later, when I lay awake putting my list together, I'd start to wonder: Why doesn't Gene count? Does he not count because he never got inside? Or does he not count because I had to preserve my moral edge over David, my status as the patient, ever-faithful, cheated-on, martyred girlfriend, and if what I did with Gene counts then I don't get to feel wounded and superior?

Years later, I did end up fucking Gene and I felt a profound relief because, at last, he definitely had a number, and I knew for sure that he did in fact count.

Then I started having sex with women, and, boy, howdy, did *that* ever shoot holes in the system. I'd always made my list of sex partners by defining sex as penile-vaginal intercourse—you know, screwing. It's a pretty simple distinction, a straightforward binary system. Did it go in or didn't it? Yes or no? One or zero? On or off? Granted, it's a pretty arbitrary definition, but it's the customary one, with an ancient and respected tradition behind it, and when I was just screwing men, there was no compelling reason to question it.

But with women, well, first of all there's no penis, so right from the start the tracking system is defective. And then, there are so many ways women can have sex with each other, touching and licking and grinding and fingering and fisting—with dildoes or vibrators or vegetables or whatever happens to be lying around the house, or with nothing at all except human bodies. Of course, that's true for sex between women and men as well. But between women, no one method has a centuries-old tradition of being the one that counts. Even when we do fuck each other there's no dick, so you don't get that feeling of This Is What's Important, We Are Now Having Sex, objectively speaking, and all that other stuff is just foreplay or afterplay. So when I started having sex with women the binary system had to go, in favor of a more inclusive definition.

Which meant, of course, that my list of how many people I'd had sex with was completely trashed. In order to maintain it I would have had to go back and reconstruct the whole thing and include all those people I'd necked with and gone down on and dry-humped and played touchy-feely games with. Even the question of who filled the all-important Number One slot, something I'd never had any doubts about before, would have to be re-evaluated.

By this time I'd kind of lost interest in the list anyway. Reconstructing it would be more trouble than it was worth. But the crucial question remained: What counts as having sex with someone?

It was important for me to know. You have to know what qualifies as sex because when you have sex with someone your relationship changes. Right? *Right?* It's not that sex itself has to change things all that much. But knowing you've had sex, being conscious of a sexual connection, standing around making polite conversation with someone while thinking to yourself, "I've had sex with this person," that's what changes things. Or so I believed. And if having sex with a friend can confuse or change the friendship, think how bizarre things can get when you're not sure whether you've had sex with them or not.

The problem was, as I kept doing more kinds of sexual things, the line between *sex* and *not-sex* kept getting more hazy and indistinct. As I brought more into my sexual experience, things were showing up on the dividing line demanding my attention. It wasn't just that the territory I labeled *sex* was expanding. The line itself had swollen, dilated, been transformed into a vast gray region. It had become less like a border and more like a demilitarized zone.

Which is a strange place to live. Not a bad place, just strange. It's like juggling, or watchmaking, or playing the piano—anything that demands complete concentrated awareness and attention. It feels like cognitive dissonance, only pleasant. It feels like waking up from a compelling and realistic bad dream. It feels like the way you feel when you realize that everything you know is wrong, and a bloody good thing too, because it was painful and stupid and it really screwed you up.

But, for me, living in a question naturally leads to searching for an answer. I can't simply shrug, throw up my hands, and say, "Damned if I know." I have to explore the unknown frontiers, even if I don't bring back any secret treasure. So even if it's incomplete or provisional, I do want to find some sort of definition of what is and isn't sex.

I know when I'm *feeling* sexual. I'm feeling sexual if my pussy's wet, my nipples are hard, my palms are clammy, my brain is fogged, my skin is tingly and super-sensitive, my butt muscles clench, my heartbeat speeds up, I have an orgasm (that's the real giveaway), and so on. But feeling sexual with someone isn't the same as having sex with them. Good Lord, if I called it sex every time I was attracted to someone who returned the favor I'd be even more bewildered than I am now. Even *being* sexual with someone isn't the same as *having* sex with them. I've danced and flirted with too many people, given and received too many sexy, would-be-seductive backrubs, to believe otherwise.

I have friends who say, if you thought of it as sex when you were doing it, then it was. That's an interesting idea. It's certainly helped me construct a coherent sexual history without being a revisionist swine: redefining my past according to current definitions. But it really just begs the question. It's fine to say that sex is whatever I think it is; but then what do I think it *is*? What if, when I was doing it, I was *wondering* whether it counted?

Perhaps having sex with someone is the conscious, consenting, mutually acknowledged pursuit of shared sexual pleasure. Not a bad definition. If you are turning each other on and you say so and you keep doing it, then it's sex. It's broad enough to encompass a lot of sexual behavior beyond genital contact/orgasm; it's distinct enough *not* to include every instance of sexual awareness or arousal; and it contains the elements I feel are vital—acknowledgment, consent, reciprocity, and the pursuit of pleasure. But what about the situation where one person consents to sex without really enjoying it? Lots of people (myself included) have had sexual interactions that we didn't find satisfying or didn't really want and, unless they were actually forced on us against our will, I think most of us would still classify them as sex.

Maybe if *both* of you (or all of you) think of it as sex, then it's sex whether you're having fun or not. That clears up the problem of sex that's consented to but not wished-for or enjoyed. Unfortunately, it begs the question again, only worse: now you have to mesh different people's vague and inarticulate notions of what is and isn't sex and find the place where they overlap. Too messy.

How about sex as the conscious, consenting, mutually acknowledged pursuit of sexual pleasure of *at least one* of the people involved. That's better. It has all the key components, and it includes the situation where one person is doing it for a reason other than sexual pleasure—status, reassurance, money, the satisfaction and pleasure of someone they love, etc. But what if *neither* of you is enjoying it, if you're both doing it because you think the other one wants to? Ugh.

I'm having trouble here. Even the conventional standby—sex equals intercourse—has a serious flaw: it includes rape, which is something I emphatically refuse to accept. As far as I'm concerned, if there's no consent, it ain't sex. But I feel that's about the only place in this whole quagmire where I have a grip. The longer I think about the subject, the more questions I come up with. At what point in an encounter does it *become* sexual? If an interaction that begins nonsexually turns into sex, was it sex all along? What about sex with someone who's asleep? Can you have a situation where one person is having sex and the other isn't? It seems that no matter what definition I come up with, I can think of some real-life experience that calls it into question.

For instance, a couple of years ago I attended (well, hosted) an all-girl sex party. Out of the twelve other women there, there were only a few with whom I got seriously physically nasty. The rest I kissed or hugged or talked dirty with or just smiled at, or watched while they did seriously physically nasty things with each other. If we'd been alone, I'd probably say that what I'd done with most of the women there didn't count as having sex. But the experience, which was hot and sweet and silly and very, very special, had been created by all of us, and although I only really got down with a few, I felt that I'd been sexual with all of the women there. Now, when I meet one of the women from that party, I always ask myself: Have we had sex?

For instance, when I was first experimenting with sadomasochism, I got together with a really hot woman. We were negotiating about what we were going to do, what would and wouldn't be ok, and she said she wasn't sure she wanted to have sex. Now we'd been explicitly planning all kinds of fun and games—spanking, bondage, obedience—which I strongly identified as sexual activity. In her mind, though, *sex* meant direct genital contact, and she didn't necessarily want

to do that with me. Playing with her turned out to be a tremendously erotic experience, arousing and stimulating and almost unbearably satisfying. But we spent the whole evening without even touching each other's genitals. And the fact that our definitions were so different made me wonder: Was it sex?

For instance, I worked for a few months as a nude dancer at a peep show. In case you've never been to a peep show, it works like this: the customer goes into a tiny, dingy black box, kind of like a phone booth, puts in quarters, and a metal plate goes up; the customer looks through a window at a little room/stage where naked women are dancing. One time, a guy came into one of the booths and started watching me and masturbating. I came over and squatted in front of him and started masturbating too, and we grinned at each other and watched each other and masturbated, and we both had a fabulous time. (I couldn't believe I was being paid to masturbate—tough job, but somebody has to do it . . . ). After he left I thought to myself: Did we just have sex? I mean, if it had been someone I knew, and if there had been no glass and no quarters, there'd be no question in my mind. Sitting two feet apart from someone, watching each other masturbate? Yup, I'd call that sex all right. But this was different, because it was a stranger, and because of the glass and the quarters. Was it sex?

I still don't have an answer.

---

## Would You Say You "Had Sex" If . . . ?

**Stephanie A. Sanders**
**June Machover Reinisch**

. . . The current public debate regarding whether oral sex constitutes having "had sex" or sexual relations has suffered from a lack of empirical data on how Americans as a population define these terms.[1,2] The data reported here were originally collected in 1991 for their relevance to sexual history information gathering and to specifi-

cally examine the need for behavioral specificity to avoid possible confusion.[3] These findings also serve as an indication of attitudes regarding definitions of having "had sex" among college students [at a large Midwest State university] assessed prior to current media publicity about this issue. . . .

Almost everyone agreed that penile-vaginal intercourse would qualify as having "had sex." Approaching this level of common perspective and yet importantly different is the fact that while 81% of participants counted penile-anal intercourse as having "had sex," 19% did not. In contrast, few individuals considered deep kissing (nearly 2%) or breast contact (nearly 3%) as having "had sex" with a partner. . . . Approximately 14% to 15% indicated that manual stimulation of the genitals (either given or received) would constitute having "had sex." Only 40% indicated that they would say they had "had sex" if oral-genital contact was the most intimate behavior in which they engaged (60% would not). For the behaviors less frequently included as having "had sex," men were slightly more likely to incorporate them into the "had sex" category. . . .

Among the behaviors assessed, oral-genital contact had the most ambivalent status. Overall, 60% reported that they would not say they "had sex" with someone if the most intimate behavior engaged in was oral-genital contact. Additionally, we found evidence of belief in "technical virginity." Compared with others, those who had experienced oral-genital contact but had never engaged in penile-vaginal intercourse were less likely to consider oral-genital contact as having "had sex." . . .

The virtually universal endorsement of penile-vaginal intercourse as having "had sex" in contrast with the diverse opinions for other behaviors highlights the primacy of penile-vaginal intercourse in American definitions of having "had sex." The lack of consensus with respect to what constitutes having "had sex" across the sexual behaviors examined herein provides empirical evidence of the need for behavioral specificity when collecting data on sexual histories and identifying sexual partners.

## NOTES

1. *The Starr Report Referral to the United States House of Representatives Pursuant to Title 28, United States Code §595(c).* Available at: http://icreport.house.gov/icreport. Submitted by the Office of the Independent Counsel, September 9,1998.

2. Baker, P., Marcus, R. Experts scoff at perjury loophole proposed for Clinton. *Washington Post.* August 15, 1998:A6.

3. Reinisch, J. M., Sanders, S. A., Ziemba-Davis, M. The study of sexual behavior in relation to the transmission of human immunodeficiency virus: caveats and recommendations. *Am Psychol.* 1988;43:921–927.

*Source:* Sanders, Stephanie A. and June Machover Reinisch. 1999. "Would You Say You 'Had Sex' If . . . ?" *Journal of the American Medical Association* 281: 275–277. Reprinted by permission. © 1999 American Medical Association.

# Who Will Make Room for the Intersexed?

Kate Haas

## Introduction

Between 1.7 and 4% of the world population is born with intersex conditions, having primary and secondary sexual characteristics that are neither clearly male nor female.[1] The current recommended treatment for an infant born with an intersex condition is genital reconstruction surgery to render the child as clearly sexed either male or female.[2] Every day in the United States, five children are subjected to genital reconstruction surgery that may leave them with permanent physical and emotional scars.[3] Despite efforts by intersexed people to educate the medical community about their rejection of infant genital reconstruction surgery, the American medical community has not yet accepted the fact that differences in genital size and shape do not necessarily require surgical correction.[4]

Genital reconstruction surgery may involve removing part or all of the penis and scrotum or clitoris and labia of a child, remodeling a penis or creating a vaginal opening.[5] While the initial surgery is typically performed in the first month of a child's life, genital reconstruction surgery is not only performed on infants.[6] Older children may be subjected to multiple operations to construct "functional" vaginas, to repair "damaged" penises, and to remove internal sex organs.[7] Personal accounts written by intersexed adults indicate that some children have been subjected to unwanted surgery throughout their childhood and teenage years without a truthful explanation of their condition.[8]

Genital reconstruction is rarely medically necessary.[9] Physicians perform the surgeries so that intersexed children will not be psychologically harmed when they realize that they are different from their peers.[10] Physicians remove external signs that children are intersexed, believing that this will prevent the child and the child's family from questioning the child's gender.[11] However, intersexed children may very well feel more confused about their gender if they are raised without any explanation about their intersex condition or input into their future treatment options.[12] The medical community's current practice focuses solely on genital appearance, discounting the fact that chromosomes also affect individuals' gender identities and personalities.[13]

Operating on children out of a belief that it is crucial for children to have genitals that conform to male/female norms ignores the fact that even the best reconstruction surgery is never perfect.[14] Genital reconstruction surgery may result in scarred genitals, an inability to achieve orgasm, or an inability to reproduce naturally or through artificial insemination.[15] The community-held belief that an individual's ability to engage in intercourse is essential, even without orgasm or reproductive capability, seems to govern the decision to perform genital surgery on many otherwise healthy, intersexed children.[16]

Despite the intersex community's rejection of genital reconstruction surgery, no U.S. court has

From Haas, Kate. 2004. "Who Will Make Room for the Intersexed?" *American Journal of Law and Medicine* 30(1): 41–68. Reprinted by permission of the American Society of Law, Medicine and Ethics.

examined the legality of performing these operations without the individual child's consent.[17] By contrast, Colombian courts have heard three such cases and have created a new standard for evaluating a parent's right to consent to genital reconstruction surgery for their minor children.[18] In response to the Colombian rulings and pressure from intersex activists, the American Bar Association recently proposed a resolution recommending that physicians adopt the heightened informed consent procedures required by the Colombian Constitutional Court decisions.[19]

This Article questions whether genital reconstruction surgery is necessary in the Twenty-first Century. [The next section] discusses the history and current preferred "treatment" for intersex conditions. . . . [The following sections analyze] the protection that current U.S. law could provide to intersexed children [and explore] how international law may influence decisions regarding the treatment of intersexed children.

## A History of Collusion: Destroying Evidence of Ambiguous Genitals

The term "intersex" is used to describe a variety of conditions in which a fetus develops differently than a typical XX female or XY male.[20] Some intersexed children are born with "normal" male or female external genitals that do not correspond to their hormones.[21] Others are born with a noticeable combination of male and female external features, and still others have visually male or female external characteristics that correspond to their chromosomes but do not correspond to their internal gonads.[22] Individuals who are considered intersexed may also be born with matching male chromosomes, gonads, and genitals but suffer childhood disease or accident that results in full or partial loss of their penis.[23] The loss of a penis may lead physicians to recommend that a boy be sexually reassigned as female.[24] Although the conditions differ, the commonality of intersexed people is that their gonads, chromosomes, and external genitalia do not coincide to form a typical male or female.[25] The current American medical treatment of intersexuals is to alter the individual's internal and external gonads to sex them as either clearly male or clearly female.[26]

Medical "treatment" of intersexuals has only been practiced in the United States since the 1930s.[27] During that period, the medical community determined that intersexed people were truly male or female but had not fully developed in the womb.[28] Hormone treatments and surgical interventions were meant to complete the formation of an intersexed adult into a "normal" man or woman.[29] By the 1950s, physicians were able to identify most intersex conditions at birth and began operating immediately on intersexed children to eliminate any physical differences.[30]

Prior to the treatment of intersexuality in the United States, intersexed Americans were treated as either male or female according to their dominant physical characteristics.[31] This strict male/female delineation is not used in all countries though. Other cultures have treated intersexuals differently, either as a third sex, neither male nor female, or as natural sexual variations of the male or female sex.[32] Alternatively, some societies still accept intersexed people without clearly defining their sex at birth.[33]

For instance, within small communities in the Dominican Republic and Papua New Guinea, there is a hereditary intersex condition known as 5-alpha reductase deficiency that occurs with a relatively high frequency.[34] This condition causes male children to be born with very small or unrecognizable penises.[35] During puberty, the children's male hormones cause their penises to grow and other secondary male sexual characteristics to develop.[36] Most of these children are raised as girls and begin living as men when they reach puberty.[37] These communities have accepted these intersexuals without genital reconstruction surgery.[38] In the United States, however, a child with the same condition would likely be surgically altered at birth, raised as a girl and treated with hormones to prevent the onset of male physical development.[39]

Genital reconstruction surgery became standard practice in the United States through the efforts of John Money, a Johns Hopkins University professor.[40] Money introduced the theory that children are not born with a gender identity, but rather form an understanding of gender through their social upbringing.[41] He based this theory on early research done with intersexed children who were surgically altered at birth and raised as either male or female.[42] Money's research found that children who were born with exactly the same genetic makeup and physical appearance fared equally well when raised as either females or males. He concluded that chromosomes did not make any difference in gender differentiation, and that children could be successfully reared as either sex irrespective of their anatomy or chromosomal make-up.[43] Money attempted to prove his theory by demonstrating that a "normal" male child could be successfully raised as a female with Bruce Reimer.[44]

In 1972, Money made public his experimental sex reassignment surgery on a twenty-two-month-old male child named Bruce Reimer who had been accidentally castrated during a routine circumcision.[45] The doctor who examined Reimer shortly after the accident believed that he would be unable to live a normal sexual life as an adolescent and would grow up feeling incomplete and physically defective.[46] Money's solution was to perform a sex change operation on baby Bruce and to have his parents raise him as a girl named Brenda. During Brenda's childhood, Money removed all of "his" internal reproductive organs. As Brenda approached puberty "she" was given female hormones to trigger breast development and other female secondary characteristics.[47] By removing Brenda's gonads, Money destroyed Brenda's reproductive capability. However, Money believed that by changing Brenda's sex, he would make it possible for her to engage in intercourse and marry.[48]

Early reports of Money's experiment claimed that the operation was successful and that Brenda was a happy, healthy girl.[49] Money's research was published throughout the world, convincing doctors that gender was a societal construct, and therefore intersexed children could be raised unconditionally as either male or female.[50] He believed that the only way to ensure that both the family and the child would accept the child's gender was if the child's genitals looked clearly male or female. Based on this theory, babies born with ambiguous genitals or small penises and baby boys who were accidentally castrated were surgically altered and raised as females.[51] Similarly, children born with mixed genitalia, gonads, and chromosomes were surgically altered to fit the definition of a "normal" male or female.[52] Following U.S. lead, other countries also began to practice routine genital reconstruction surgery on intersexed infants.[53]

Despite the widespread use of genital reconstruction surgery, there is no research showing that intersexuals benefit psychologically from the surgery performed on them as infants and toddlers.[54] No follow-up studies were ever done on adult intersexuals who underwent genital reconstruction surgery as children.[55] In the late 1980s, researchers attempting to disprove Money's gender identity theory began searching for Brenda, the subject of Money's highly publicized research.[56] The boy who was raised as a girl was now living as a man and had changed his name to David.[57] In 1997, Milton Diamond and Keith Sigmundson published an article rebutting the results of Money's famous gender research.[58] The publicity caused by Diamond and Sigmundson's article led to a biography of Reimer by John Colapinto. When Colapinto interviewed Reimer in 1997, Reimer admitted that he had always been certain that he was not a girl, despite being deceived by his doctor and his family.[59]

Reimer suffered emotional duress at all stages of his development, despite the corrective surgery that was meant to make him "normal." In his biography of Reimer, Colapinto describes the painful experiences that Reimer suffered throughout his childhood and teenage years.[60] During her childhood, Brenda did not fit in with her peers and felt isolated and confused.[61] As early as kindergarten, other children teased Brenda about her masculinity and failure to adopt "girl's play."[62] Although her kindergarten teacher was not initially told of her sex change, the teacher reported realizing that Brenda was very different from other girls.[63]

In addition to her failure to fit in socially, Brenda was constantly reminded that she was different by her parents and Dr. Money. During her visits to Johns Hopkins, Money would often force her to engage in sexual role-play with her twin brother in order to enforce that she was a girl and he was a boy.[64] Her genitals were scarred and painful as a child and she hated to look at them.[65] She became suspicious that something terrible had been done to her, primarily due to the frequent doctor's visits with John Money. During these visits, Dr. Money and his associates questioned Brenda about her genitals and her gender identity.[66] Rather than enforcing her gender identity, the medical intervention compounded the trauma caused by her medical condition.

One particularly traumatic procedure inflicted on intersexed children was not discussed in the biography of David Reimer. Intersexed children who have artificially created vaginas must undergo vaginal dilation procedures throughout their early childhood.[67] In order to ensure that the newly created vaginal opening does not close up, the child's parents must insert an object into the child's vagina on a daily basis.[68] This procedure has sexual implications that may be emotionally traumatic for many children.

As a teenager, Reimer rejected his assigned sex and refused to take his female hormones. He reported engaging in typically male behavior throughout his teens. He dressed as a male, chose a trade school for mechanics, and even began urinating standing up.[69] When Reimer's parents finally told him that he was born male, he immediately chose to adopt a male identity and changed his name to David.[70] He had a penis constructed and implanted, and underwent breast reduction surgery to rid himself of the breasts de-veloped through estrogen therapy.[71] There is no procedure that can replace the gonads that were removed as part of Reimer's sex reassignment surgery. There is also no cure for the deception that he experienced upon learning that his parents and doctors had lied to him about many aspects of his life.[72] The trauma of learning about his condition caused David to attempt suicide on several occasions.[73]

David is now married and has adopted his wife's children.[74] His story reads as a happy ending to many people. However, David could have avoided the gender dysphoria, loss of reproductive capability, and many years of therapy that resulted from genital reconstruction surgery. These experiences are not atypical in the intersexed community. According to many intersexed activists, the comfort of being raised in a clear gender role does not outweigh the pain of deception or the physical side effects associated with the surgery.[75]

Despite the emotional and physical scars that people like David Reimer face from genital reconstruction surgery, the majority of American physicians continue to encourage early childhood surgery.[76] In some cases, physicians have insisted on performing genital reconstruction surgery on teenagers without their consent.[77]

In 1993, an intersexed activist named Cheryl Chase began a support and advocacy group for intersexed adults called the Intersex Society of North America ("ISNA").[78] Chase was born with a large clitoris, which was removed when she was an infant.[79] When she was eight years old, her internal gonads were removed without her knowledge or consent.[80] Because of the surgery, she is no longer capable of having her own children or obtaining orgasm.[81] Today, Chase and other advocates are vocal about their hope for a moratorium on the invasive treatment of intersexed children.[82]

ISNA members have contributed significantly to the debate over genital reconstruction surgery by providing personal insight into the effects of surgery on intersexed adults. As of the late 1990s, more than 400 intersexed individuals from around the world contacted ISNA and recounted stories similar to Ms. Chase's.[83] According to ISNA, sex change operations and genital normalizing surgeries should not be performed on children until the child has the ability to consent personally to the operation.[84]

At this point, there is insufficient proof that intersexed adults who are not operated on fair any worse than intersexed adults who have had genital reconstruction surgery as children.[85] The only research that has been done on intersexed adults who have not been surgically altered also comes from John Money. In the 1940s, prior to his well-known study on Reimer, Money interviewed many intersexed adults about their gender identity and upbringing.[86] To his surprise, he found that intersexed adults who had not undergone genital reconstruction surgery had a gender identity comparable to other adult males and females.[87] Unfortunately this research was done as part of Money's doctoral thesis and was never published. . . .[88]

### Making Room for Intersexuals in the United States

The United States does not currently provide any procedural protection for intersexed children. In the United States, doctors are not required to receive the consent of intersexed children before performing genital reconstruction surgery.[89] Neither are parents routinely given sufficient information to make an informed decision on their child's behalf.[90] Currently, the United States lacks even the standard for informed consent. . . .[91]

Thus far, there has been no legal challenge brought on behalf of intersexed children in the United States. Intersexed adults who have inquired about suing their doctors for performing genital reconstruction surgery that altered their gender have met resistance.[92] Intersexed adults have been told that because the doctors followed standard medical practice when they performed the surgery, the doctors are not liable for medical malpractice.[93]

. . . [T]he U.S. Constitution does not have specific provisions protecting a child's right to bodily integrity. However, the Constitution has been interpreted to protect privacy rights, including the right to marry and reproduce, and the right to bodily integrity generally.[94] Common law also provides some protection for children when there is no "informed" consent, or when a parent's consent or lack of consent to medical treatment is found to be contrary to the child's best interest.[95] In addition to case law supporting the need for informed consent and the best interest of the child, there are recent federal and state statutes protecting female children from genital mutilation.[96] Thus, while no intersexed Americans have successfully sued a physician or hospital for conducting early genital reconstructive surgery, they may have grounds to sue based on female genital mutilation laws, the constitutional right to privacy and lack of informed consent by their parents.

### Constitutional Protection for Intersexuals: Leaving Room for an Open Future

The U.S. Constitution protects individuals from overreaching government power through the Fourteenth Amendment, which states "No state shall make or enforce any law which shall abridge the privileges or immunities of citizens of the United States, nor shall any state deprive any person of life, liberty, or property, without due process of law. . . ."[97] The U.S. Supreme Court has interpreted the Fourteenth Amendment as protecting individuals from government action that infringes upon certain "fundamental rights" considered "implicit in the concept of ordered liberty."[98]

The Supreme Court has found that the right to bodily autonomy, the right to choose whether or not to reproduce, the right to marry, and the right to make decisions about how to raise children are all fundamental privacy rights.[99] The government may not violate a person's liberty by infringing any of these rights without first proving in a court of law that there is a compelling state interest that must be served, and that the method that the government is using is narrowly tailored to achieve a compelling governmental interest.[100]

Historically, children have not been accorded the same constitutional rights as adults. A child's parents and the government are allowed to restrict some rights that would be held fundamental for an adult.[101] The Supreme Court has also recognized a fundamental right to family privacy, according parents a high degree of respect regarding decisions they make about their child's upbringing.[102] This includes the choices parents make regarding their children's medical care.[103] Despite the Fourteenth Amendment right to family privacy, the parents' rights must be weighed against the children's rights to be protected against harm. The doctrine of parens patriae articulates the government's interest in protecting the rights of vulnerable individuals from harm.[104]

The doctrine of parens patriae allows the government to interfere with parents' choices about how to raise their children when the children may be harmed because of the parents' actions or inactions.[105] Generally, the government interferes with parental decisions under laws prohibiting parental abuse or neglect.[106] In the case of intersexed children, the government may have reason to override the parents' decision to perform surgery if the surgery would harm the child. . . .

### Bodily Integrity: If It Works, Don't Fix It

Included in the Fourteenth Amendment right to privacy is the right to bodily autonomy, which protects individuals from intrusion by the government into their health care decisions.[107] This right includes the right to choose to forego medical treatment, even if foregoing treatment may result in death.[108] For the most part, children are not accorded the right to choose medical treatment or to choose to forego medical treatment without parental consent, despite the fact that it has been found to be a fundamental right.[109] The reason that parents are allowed to consent for children is that a child may not be able to understand fully the consequences of their own consent because of their age or inexperience.[110]

There are several exceptions to the rule requiring parental consent to treatment. . . . These exceptions take into account the fact that parents do not always act in their child's best interest, and a child may suffer abuse or psychological harm if required to seek parental consent to certain treatments. The right to choose whether or not to undergo genital reconstruction surgery should be an exception to the general rule allowing parental consent to treatment of minors. Genital reconstruction surgery is a personal choice that children should be allowed to make on their own in certain circumstances, or, at a minimum, in conjunction with their parents. It is difficult for many children to learn about their intersexuality. However, it is also hard for children to learn to cope with pregnancy, drug addiction, mental illness, or their HIV positive status. In contrast to intersex conditions, all of the above medical conditions are free of parental consent requirements under certain circumstances.

Genital reconstruction surgery is arguably the ultimate infringement of an individual's bodily autonomy. Genital reconstruction surgery can cause a child significant psychological and physical harm.[111] For these reasons, parents should not be allowed to make the decision to alter surgically their child's genitals without the child's consent absent clear and convincing evidence that it is in the child's best interest. If the state participates by allowing the procedure to be performed at a state hospital or by ordering the procedure over the child's objection, then there may be a constitutional violation of the child's right to bodily autonomy under the Fourteenth Amendment.

### Reproduction: Gonads Cannot Be Replaced

The right to choose whether or not to reproduce is a fundamental right and, accordingly, certain restrictions are placed on the government's right to interfere with decisions bearing on reproduction.[112] For example, all minors regardless of age have the right to seek an abortion without undue burden from the state, though the state may act to ensure that a woman's decision is informed.[113] Therefore, even when state law requires minors to receive parental consent before seeking an abortion, minors are permitted a judicial bypass, allowing them the right to prove to a court that they are mature enough to make the decision to have an abortion without parental consent.[114] Children may also have the right to seek contraception, treatment for pregnancy, and childbirth without parental consent.[115]

Because reproduction is a fundamental right, parents are limited in their ability to consent to sterilization procedures for their children. Generally, sterilization is raised in the context of a parent who wants to sterilize a handicapped child to protect the child from the harm of a dangerous pregnancy. If there is an objection made by the child or an advocate for the child, then a court cannot order the procedure against the child's objections without affording the child due process.[116] The child must be appointed an independent guardian *ad litem,* and receive a fair trial at which the court must determine by clear and convincing evidence that the operation to remove the child's gonads will be in the child's best interest.[117]

As with all people, some intersexed adults do not have the ability to reproduce even without genital reconstruction surgery.[118] Others will retain their full reproductive capacity even after the surgery is performed.[119] However, some intersexuals have the ability to reproduce either naturally or artificially and are denied that right by the removal of their gonads and other reproductive organs. For those children whose gonads are removed to complete their physical transformation, their fundamental right to reproduce has been violated. For example, a child born with male chromosomes and sexed at birth as female will have her gonads removed, thus, effectively sterilizing her. . . .

### Marriage: Determining Gender Determines Sexuality

Genital reconstruction surgery may inhibit or completely interfere with a child's fundamental right to marry. In the United States, there are currently no states in which it is legal to marry someone of the same sex.[120] In 1993, several gay couples challenged the prohibition against same-sex marriages under the Hawaii Constitution.[121] The Hawaii Supreme Court ruled in favor of the plaintiffs and allowed the first gay couples to marry legally.[122] In reaction to the ruling, the Hawaii state legislature immediately amended their own constitution to prohibit same-sex marriages.[123] The federal government reacted to the first gay marriages by passing the Defense of Marriage Act, which allows states to refuse to recognize same-sex marriages that are legally valid in another state.[124] Given that 3% of the world population does not fit into a clearly defined sex and still engage in marriage and child birth, it would be wise to re-think this prohibition.

However, given the laws as they currently stand, genital reconstruction surgically defines an intersexed person as male or female, thus, prohibiting them from marriage to a person of their "same" gender. Intersexuals are in a unique position before they undergo genital reconstruction surgery because they can petition the court to change their legal gender from female to male or male to female without having to undergo a sex change operation. They must prove that they are intersexed, that they have unclear genitals, and that they identify as the opposite sex, and their birth certificate may be altered.[125]

Once an intersexed person has undergone genital reconstruction surgery making his or her genitals clearly male or female, he or she cannot then choose to change his or her birth certificate without having a second round of surgeries performed.[126] For example, if a child born with male chromosomes or mixed chromosomes is surgically assigned a female gender at birth, that individual would be prohibited from marrying a female later in life without first undergoing another sex change operation.[127] In this case, if the initial gender reconstruction surgery had not been performed, this person would be considered a male, not a homosexual female, and thus would have a fundamental right to marry.

By choosing a gender for the child and performing reconstruction surgery at birth, the doctors may be infringing on an individual's ability to marry as an adult. The imposition of additional surgery to change their assigned sex would add such high financial and emotional costs on the individual that it may prohibit some, otherwise qualified, intersexuals from marrying.

### Taking a First Step: Informing Parents That Their Child Is Intersexed

Physicians must receive informed consent from all patients before they treat them for any medical condition.[128] If physicians fail to obtain informed consent from their patients, they may be liable for medical malpractice.[129] Under the informed consent doctrine, a patient may even choose to refuse life saving treatment after weighing their treatment options.[130] The informed consent doctrine originated in the tort doctrine of battery, which includes intentionally touching a person in a way that they find harmful or offensive.[131] The surgical removal of part or all of a child's genitals must only be done after receiving informed consent or it may be considered battery.

Absent a recognized exception allowing children to consent to their own medical treatment, parents will generally be allowed to give or withhold consent for medical treatment on behalf of their children. In the United States, genital reconstruction surgery is not currently a procedure that children are allowed to consent or object to without their parents' participation. For informed consent to be valid, the parents must be informed of the nature and consequence of their child's medical condition, as well as the various treatment options available. . . .

[P]arents of intersexed children are not given enough information to make a truly informed decision about their child's treatment.[132] Some parents are not told that their child is intersexed, but instead that their child is a girl or boy with "unfinished" genitals that the doctor will repair with surgery.[133] Physicians may also tell the parents that their baby will have "normal" genitals after surgery.[134] Surgery may make the child's

genitals look more clearly male or female, but it will also leave scarring and possibly diminish sexual functions.[135] Generally, more than one surgery is needed to alter completely the genital appearance, and the average number of surgeries is three or more.[136] Surgery and check-ups will continue through the child's early years and may be extremely stressful for the child and his or her parents.[137]

Additionally, parents must understand that while surgery will make intersexed children look more similar to their peers, it will not change their chromosomes. Even with hormone therapy, many intersexed youth will endure gender dysphoria.[138] They may feel confused about their gender despite having genitals that look clearly male or female. Intersexed adults may decide that their assigned gender is not their gender of choice. This might prompt the desire for additional, more complicated surgeries to perform a complete sex change operation.[139] Most of these facts are not presented to the parents of intersexed children at the time that they approve genital reconstruction surgery.[140] If parents are encouraged to consent to surgery without being told of the risks and side effects, their consent is not truly informed. . . .

### Genital Mutilation: Equal Protection for Intersexed Children

Intersex children may also have a claim for medical malpractice based on violation of the law prohibiting female genital mutilation.[141] In 1996, Congress passed the Criminalization of Female Genital Mutilation Act.[142] Five states have also individually criminalized female genital mutilation.[143]

The process of removing or altering the genitalia of intersexed children is a form of genital mutilation as defined by the statute.[144] The law prohibits anyone from authorizing or performing an operation on a female child to remove all or part of her genitals for other than health reasons.[145] The statute explicitly covers ritual circumcisions, even if the child herself believes in the religious or cultural significance of the procedure.[146] In section 116(c), the law specifically states that no account shall be taken of the effect of any belief that has led the person or their family to demand the operation.[147] This Act holds the physician liable even if the family believed that the operation would be in the child's best interest and it was standard practice in their ethnic or religious community.[148]

According to the Act, the only way that genital operations can be legally performed on female children in the United States is if the doctor can show that under section 116(b)(1), it is necessary for the health of the person on whom it is performed. . . .[149]

When an intersexed child is operated on to normalize his or her genitals, it is also part of a cultural tradition. Parents want their child to look like other children in Western countries, or as close to "normal" as possible.[150] In some Native American cultures, India, the Dominican Republic, and Papua New Guinea, intersexed people are accepted in society and occupy a specific cultural and social position.[151] In those cultures it would not be considered beneficial to the child to alter the child's genitals.

In the United States, intersexed children are operated on in order to make them look like other children who are not intersexed. Although some medical conditions might endanger intersexed children and therefore make the operations beneficial, this is not usually the case.[152] Most doctors who agree with genital operations for intersexed children claim that the surgery is necessary to protect their mental health.[153] However, no studies have been done that support the question of whether or not genital reconstruction and hormones actually protect the mental health of the patient any better then counseling and education. . . .[154]

The congressional findings on the practice of female genital mutilation in the United States are particularly relevant to the issue of genital surgery on intersexed children. In particular, Congress found that female genital mutilation harms women both physically and psychologically.[155] They found that the practice violates both federal and state constitutional and statutory laws.[156]

The damaging physical and psychological effects of genital reconstruction surgery are identical to the effects of ritual female circumcision. In both cases, the surgery may result in pain, scarring, and the inability to achieve orgasm.[157] Congressional findings that females should not be subjected to the loss of any part of their genitalia for cultural reasons is directly applicable to intersexed children.

The Act indicates that parents do not have the right to give consent to nonessential genital surgery and doctors do not have the right to perform such surgery even if it will make the children assimilate with their ethnic and religious community.[158] The statute only applies to female children.[159] If taken as such, the statute may violate equal protection.[160] However, the Act does not define "female" by genetic make-up or external characteristics. Arguably, most intersexed children fall under one definition of "female" or another. Thus, intersexed children who have their clitoris reduced or other genital parts removed seem to have a strong claim of assault under the Female Genital Mutilation Act.

### Sexual Diversity and the International Community

The United States should consider international standards for the treatment of children when considering the legality of genital reconstruction surgery. One of the main standards by which to judge the international consensus on children's rights is the Convention on the Rights of the Child.[161] The United States was one of only two United Nations member countries that did not sign the Convention on the Rights of the Child.[162] Despite the fact that the United States has not signed the Convention, it is an internationally accepted standard that should be considered by U.S. healthcare practitioners.

The Convention recognizes the rights of children independent of their parents by allowing them to veto parents' decisions on issues of health, education, and religious upbringing.[163] The Convention specifically states that a child should have input into all decisions affecting him or her.[164] Because the decision to alter a child's genitals will forever change the course of the child's life, particular care should be taken to involve the child in this decision.

The second international agreement that is relevant to the treatment of intersexuals is the Nuremberg Code, signed by the United States after World War II.[165] The Nuremberg Code prohibits countries from conducting experimental medical treatments on patients without their express informed consent.[166] Since genital reconstruction surgery has only been in practice during the last thirty years and no studies have been done to prove the procedures effectiveness, critics argue that genital reconstruction surgery is still experimental.[167] If the procedure is an experimental procedure, then the level of consent required should be higher.

Other countries look to the U.S. medical establishment in developing standards of care.[168] It is important for intersexed children around the world that doctors within the United States make a concerted effort to provide parents and children with all available knowledge regarding intersex conditions before making the recommendation to perform genital reconstruction surgery.

## Conclusion

. . . [F]uture legal decisions in the United States and abroad should prohibit hospitals from performing childhood genital reconstruction surgery when it is not medically necessary. The current insistence on genital "normalizing" surgery can be explained by our society's obsession with physical appearance and our fear of people who are "different."[169] However, as the Americans with Disabilities Act and other anti-discrimination laws integrate more and more people with different physical characteristics and abilities, society will begin to accept physical differences as a natural and positive part of being human.[170] At the point that our society makes room for the intersexed

through laws prohibiting gender reassignment surgery and unnecessary genital reconstruction surgery on children, then people will begin to acknowledge the existence of intersexuals. When faced with the fact that 3% of the population has chromosomes, genitals, and sexual characteristics that are different, teachers will need to modify sex education courses. Ideally, children will learn that every individual has unique sexual characteristics that help make up their gender identity and sexual preference. Through open discussions of growth and sexual development, intersexed children will learn that they are not alone, and others will learn that intersexuality is a common condition that may effect someone they know.[171]

### NOTES

1. ANNE FAUSTO-STERLING, SEXING THE BODY: GENDER POLITICS AND THE CONSTRUCTION OF SEXUALITY 51 (2000) (reporting that 1.7% of the population may be intersexed); Julie A. Greenberg, *Defining Male and Female: Intersexuality and the Collision Between Law and Biology*, 41 ARIZ. L. REV. 265, 267 (1999) (reporting that Johns Hopkins sex researcher John Money estimates the number of people born with ambiguous genitals at 4%). Historically, people with intersex conditions were referred to as "hermaphrodites" but this word has been rejected as embodying many of the misperceptions and mistreatment of intersexed people. Raven Kaldera, *American Boyz Intersexuality Flyer*, at http://www.amboyz.org/intersection/flyerprint.html (last visited Mar. 27, 2004).

2. Hazel Glenn Beh & Milton Diamond, *An Emerging Ethical and Medical Dilemma: Should Physicians Perform Sex Assignment Surgery on Infants with Ambiguous Genitalia?*, 7 MICH. J. GENDER & L. 1, 3 (2000); Fausto-Sterling, *supra* note 1, at 45; see *infra* note 4.

3. Emi Koyama, *Suggested Guidelines for Non-Intersex Individuals Writing About Intersexuality and Intersex People*, at http://isna.org/faq/writing-guidelines.html (last visited Mar. 27, 2004). *But see* Beh & Diamond, *supra* note 2, at 17 (estimating the number of sex reassignments in the United States at 100 to 200 annually).

4. Kishka-Kamari Ford, *"First Do No Harm"— The Fiction of Legal Parental Consent to Genital-*

*Normalizing Surgery on Intersexed Infants*, 19 YALE L. & POL'Y REV. 469, 471 (2001).

5. FAUSTO-STERLING, *supra* note 1, at 61–63.

6. *Id.* at 45; Ford, *supra* note 4, at 471; Sentencia No. SU-337/99 (Colom.), *available at* http://www.isna.org/Colombia/case1-part1.html (last visited Mar. 27, 2004) [hereinafter Ramos]. There are currently no published English translations of the three Colombian cases referred to in this Article. E-mail from Cheryl Chase, founding director of Intersex Society of North America ("ISNA") (Mar. 19, 2002) (on file with the author).

7. FAUSTO-STERLING, *supra* note 1, at 62, 84–85.

8. *Id.* at 84. Fausto-Sterling recounts the story of a twelve-year-old intersexed girl named Angela Moreno who lost her ability to orgasm after having her enlarged clitoris removed without her consent. She was told that she had ovarian cancer and was going to have a hysterectomy performed. Later she discovered she never had ovaries. Instead, she had testes that were also removed during the procedure. *Id.*

9. *Id.* at 63–65; Ford, *supra* note 4, at 476–77.

10. Fausto-Sterling, *supra* note 1, at 63–65; Ford, *supra* note 4, at 476–77. According to Ford, "medical professionals admit that it is the psychosocial problem of intersex that makes it an emergency." *Id.*

11. FAUSTO-STERLING, *supra* note 1, at 64–65; Beh & Diamond, *supra* note 2, at 51.

12. *See* FAUSTO-STERLING, *supra* note 1, at 84; Beh & Diamond, *supra* note 2, at 2; JOHN COLAPINTO, AS NATURE MADE HIM: THE BOY WHO WAS RAISED AS A GIRL 143–50, 212–13 (2000). In his book, Colapinto vividly describes the gender dysphoria and sexual confusion of David Reimer, a boy raised as a girl after his penis was destroyed during a botched circumcision. *Id.* at 143–50. This biographical account of Reimer's life was written with the cooperation and participation of Reimer himself who sat for more than 100 hours of interviews and allowed the author access to all of his confidential files and medical records. *Id.* at xvii. Colapinto also discusses other children who have suffered extreme gender dysphoria growing up without being informed of their condition. One fourteen-year-old girl described in the book dropped out of high school and threatened suicide if she could not have reconstructive surgery to make her a boy. Testing revealed that she was intersexed, having male chromosomes and female external genitalia. *Id.* at 212.

13. COLAPINTO, *supra* note 12, at 32; FAUSTO-STERLING, *supra* note 1, at 46. Fausto-Sterling cites Johns Hopkins researcher John Money, "From the sum total of hermaphroditic evidence, the conclusion that emerges is that sexual behavior and orientation as male or female does not have an innate, instinctive basis." *Id.*

14. FAUSTO-STERLING, *supra* note 1, at 85–87.

15. *Id.* at 58, 80, 85–87.

16. *Id.* at 57–58. Doctors consider a penis adequate if, as a child is able to stand while urinating and, as an adult is able to engage in vaginal intercourse. *Id. See also* Ford, *supra* note 4, at 471 (stating the "penis will be deemed 'adequate' at birth if it is no less than 2.5 centimeters long when stretched").

17. Ford, *supra* note 4, at 474.

18. Julie A. Greenberg & Cheryl Chase, *Colombia's Highest Court Restricts Surgery on Intersex Children*, at http://www.isna.org/colombia/background.html (last visited Mar. 27, 2004) (synthesizing in English the three Colombian cases to which this Article will refer).

19. E-mail from Alyson Meiselman, Liaison Representative of NLGLA (Aug. 19, 2002) (on file with author). The American Bar Association ("ABA") resolution was proposed by the International Law and Practice Section regarding surgical alteration of intersexed infants. The memorandum was drafted for the ABA Commission on Women in the Profession. *Id.* The resolution will be voted on by the House of Delegates at the August 2003 ABA meeting in San Francisco, California. E-mail from Alyson Meiselman, Liaison Representative of NLGLA (April 29, 2003) (on file with author). A draft of the proposed resolution is available at http://www.kindredspiritlakeside.homestead.com/P_ABA.html (last visited Mar. 27, 2004).

20. FAUSTO-STERLING, *supra* note 1, at 36–39, 48–54.

21. *Id.*

22. *Id.* at 48–54. The most common forms of intersexuality are: Congenital Adrenal Hyperplasia, which affects children with XX chromosomes and is otherwise referred to as "female pseudo-hermaphrodite"; Androgen Insensitivity Syndrome, which affects children with XY chromosomes and is also referred to as "male pseudo-hermaphrodite"; Gonadal Dysgenesis, which predominantly affects children with XX chromosomes; Hypospadias, which affects children with XX chromosomes; Turner Syndrome, which affects children with XO chromosomes and causes these children to lack some feminine characteristics such as breast growth and menstruation; and Klinefelter Syndrome, which affects children with XXY chromosomes and causes

these children to lack some external male characteristics. *Id.*

23. *Id.* at 66.

24. Beh & Diamond, *supra* note 2, at 3; *see* Colapinto, *supra* note 12, at 32.

25. FAUSTO-STERLING, *supra* note 1, at 51.

26. *Id.* at 56–63; Beh & Diamond, *supra* note 2, at 3.

27. FAUSTO-STERLING, *supra* note 1, at 40.

28. *Id.*

29. *Id.*

30. *Id.* at 44–45.

31. *Id.* at 40.

32. *Id.* at 33.

33. *Id.* at 109. For example, the Dominican Republic and Papua New Guinea acknowledge a "third type of child," however, they still recognize only two gender roles. *Id.*

34. *Id.*

35. *Id.*

36. *Id.*

37. *Id.*

38. *Id.*

39. *Id.*

40. COLAPINTO, *supra* note 12, at 39. Colapinto quotes Dr. Benjamin Rosenberg, a leading psychologist specialized in sexual identity, as saying, "Money was 'the leader—the front-runner on everything having to do with mixed sex and hermaphrodites. . . .'" *Id.*

41. *Id.* at 32–35; Ford, *supra* note 4, at 471.

42. COLAPINTO, *supra* note 12, at 32.

43. *Id.* at 32–35.

44. *Id.* at 50, 67–68, 70.

45. *Id.* at 65. John Money presented the case at the annual meeting of the American Association for the Advancement of Science on December 28, 1972.

46. *Id.* at 16.

47. *Id.* at 131.

48. *Id.* at 50. Money envisioned Brenda marrying a man and engaging in vaginal intercourse. *Id.*

49. *Id.* at 65–71.

50. *Id.* "The twins case was quickly enshrined in myriad textbooks ranging from the social sciences to pediatric urology and endocrinology." *Id.* at 70.

51. Ford, *supra* note 4, at 471–73; Beh & Diamond, *supra* note 2, at 3.

52. Ford, *supra* note 4, at 471; Beh & Diamond, *supra* note 2, at 3.

53. COLAPINTO, *supra* note 12, at 75.

54. Summary of Sentencia No. SU-337/99 (Colom.), at 4 [hereinafter Ramos Summary] (on file with author). The Colombian Court asked for follow-up studies on intersexed children and was not able to obtain any. *Id.*; COLAPINTO, *supra* note 12, at 233–35. There have been several cases of genetic males raised as females that were not followed until recently. *Id.* at 273–75; *see also* FAUSTO-STERLING, *supra* note 1, at 80–91 (providing statistics and personal accounts of intersexuals who received surgery during childhood).

55. Ramos Summary, *supra* note 54, at 4.

56. COLAPINTO, *supra* note 12, at 208–09. Milton Diamond, an outspoken opponent of John Money put out an advertisement searching for Brenda in the 1980s. With the help of Keith Sigmundson, he tracked down the subject of Money's famous study. *Id.* at 199, 208–09.

57. *Id.* at 208.

58. *Id.* at 214. The article was published in the *Archives of Pediatrics and Adolescent Medicine* in March 1997. *Id.*

59. *Id.* at 216.

60. *Id.* at 60–63, 145–50.

61. *Id.*

62. *Id.* at 60–63

63. *Id.* Due to Reimer's negative behavior at school, she was referred to a guidance counselor in the first grade. Brenda's parents then allowed her doctor to speak with her guidance counselor and her teacher about her condition. *Id.* at 63–64.

64. *Id.* at 87.

65. *Id.* at 92.

66. *Id.* at 80.

67. Ramos Summary, *supra*, note 54, at 9; Kaldera, *supra* note 1.

68. Kaldera, *supra* note 1.

69. COLAPINTO, *supra* note 12, at 190–95.

70. *Id.* at 180–85.

71. *Id.* at 184.

72. *Id.* at 267. The Reimer family moved after Brenda's sex change operation and her parents created stories about other parts of their family history in order to hide the truth from her. *Id.* at 100–01, 106, 267.

73. *Id.* at 188.

74. *Id.* at 195.

75. *Id.* at 218–20; Alice Dreger, *Why Do We Need ISNA?,* ISNA NEWS, May 2001, *at* http://isna.org/newsletter/may2001/may2001.html. Because of the private nature of the topic many intersexed adults are

hesitant about talking of their experiences. *Id.;* FAUSTO-STERLING, *supra* note 1, at 85. The ISNA website provides links to personal accounts written by intersexed adults, press releases, medical information, and other resources.

76. FAUSTO-STERLING, *supra* note 1, at 45–50.

77. *Id.* at 84.

78. *Id.* at 80; Intersex Society of North America, ISNA NEWS, Feb. 2001, *at* http://isna.org/newsletter/feb2001/feb2001.html.

79. FAUSTO-STERLING, *supra* note 1, at 80.

80. *Id.*

81. *See Id.* at 81; ABCNews.com, *Intersex Babies: Controversy Over Operating to Change Ambiguous Genitalia,* Apr. 19, 2002, at http://abcnews.go.com/sections/2020/DailyNews/2020_intersex_020419.html; COLAPINTO, *supra* note 12, at 217–18.

82. Colapinto, *supra* note 12, at 220.

83. *Id.* at 218.

84. *Id.* at 220; Intersex Society of North America, ISNA's Amicus Brief on Intersex Genital Surgery, Feb. 7, 1998, *available at* http://isna.org/colombia/brief.html.

85. COLAPINTO, *supra* note 12, at 233–34; FAUSTO-STERLING, *supra* note 1, at 94–95.

86. COLAPINTO, *supra* note 12, at 233–35.

87. *Id.* at 234. The study included interviews with ten intersexed adults who had not been operated on as infants. The study found that genital appearance only plays a small part in a person's formation of gender identity.

88. *Id.*

89. Beh & Diamond, *supra* note 2, at 38–39.

90. Ramos Summary, *supra* note 54, at 4.

91. Glenn M. Burton, *General Discussion of Legal Issues Affecting Sexual Assignment of Intersex Infants Born with Ambiguous Genitalia,* § IIG, *at* http://www.isna.org/library/burton2002.html (last visited Mar. 27, 2004).

92. Beh & Diamond, *supra* note 2, at 2.

93. *See* Helling v. Carey, 519 P.2d 981, 983 (Wash. 1974). A physician may be negligent even if they follow customary medical practice. *Id.; see* Burton, *supra* note 91, § IIA. Burton writes that the American Board of Pediatrics added an addendum to their 1996 recommendation for early surgical intervention acknowledging the recent debate over infant genital reconstruction surgery. *Id.*

94. Loving v. Virginia, 388 U.S. 1, 12 (1967) (holding that the right to marry is fundamental); Skinner

v. Oklahoma, 316 U.S. 535, 541 (1942) (holding that the right to reproduce is fundamental); Rochin v. California, 342 U.S. 165, 172–73 (1952) (holding that the right to bodily integrity is fundamental).

95. *See* Parham v. J.R., 442 U.S. 584, 606–07 (1979) (holding that a parent can involuntarily commit a minor child for mental health treatment as long as the treatment is determined to be in the child's best interest by an independent medical determination). The Court stated that there should be an independent examination to determine that parents were not using the hospital as a "dumping ground." *Id.* at 598. *See also In re* Rosebush, 491 N.W.2d 633, 640 (1992) (recognizing the best interest standard applies for determining whether life saving treatment should be provided for a minor child against the parent's wishes).

96. *E.g.,* 18 U.S.C. § 116 (2000).

97. U.S. CONST. amend. XIV, § 1.

98. Gideon v. Wainwright, 372 U.S. 335, 342 (1963).

99. Washington v. Glucksberg, 521 U.S. 702, 720 (1997); Planned Parenthood of Southeastern Pa. v. Casey, 505 U.S. 833, 851 (1994) ("Our law affords constitutional protection to personal decisions relating to marriage, procreation, contraception, family relationships, child rearing, and education." (citing Carey v. Population Services International, 431 U.S. 678 (1977))).

100. *Washington,* 521 U.S. at 721 ("The 14th Amendment 'forbids the government to infringe . . . 'fundamental' interests at all, no matter what process is provided, unless the infringement is narrowly tailored to serve a compelling state interest.'" (quoting Reno v. Flores, 507 U.S. 292, 302 (1993))).

101. *Casey,* 505 U.S. at 899. Although the Court reaffirmed that women have a constitutional right to seek an abortion without undue burden, a state may require minors to seek a parent's consent for an abortion provided that there is an adequate judicial bypass procedure. *Id.* In an earlier case, the Supreme Court stated "our cases show that although children generally are protected by the same constitutional guarantees against governmental deprivations as are adults, the State is entitled to adjust its legal system to account for children's vulnerability and their needs for 'concern, . . . sympathy, and . . . paternal attention.'" Bellotti v. Baird, 443 U.S. 622, 635 (1979).

102. Lassiter v. Dep't of Social Services of Durham County 452 U.S. 18, 39 (1981); *see* Wisconsin v. Yo-

der, 406 U.S. 205, 232–34 (1972); Pierce v. Society of Sisters of the Holy Names of Jesus and Mary, 268 U.S. 510, 534–35 (1925); Meyer v. Nebraska, 262 U.S. 390, 399 (1923).

103. Parham v. J.R., 442 U.S. 584, 602–04 (1979) ("The fact that a child may balk at hospitalization or complain about a parental refusal to provide cosmetic surgery does not diminish the parents' authority to decide what is best for the child.").

104. *Id.* "The court is not without constitutional control over parental discretion in dealing with children when their physical or mental health is jeopardized." *Id.* at 603. "The parent's interests in a child must be balanced against the State's long-recognized interests as parens patriae." Troxel v. Granville, 530 U.S. 57, 88 (2000). *See also* Prince v. Massachusetts, 321 U.S. 158 (1944). In *Prince,* the Supreme Court examines the parents' right to have their child distribute religious material on the street *Id.* The Court allowed the state to limit parent's power in this regard stating, "Parents may be free to become martyrs themselves. But it does not follow they are free, in identical circumstances, to make martyrs of their children before they have reached the age of full and legal discretion when they can make that choice for themselves." *Id.* at 170.

105. Elizabeth J. Sher, *Choosing for Children: Adjudicating Medical Care Disputes Between Parents and the State,* 58 N.Y.U. L. REV. 157, 169–70, 170 n.57 (1983); Jennifer Trahan, *Constitutional Law: Parental Denial of a Child's Medical Treatment for Religious Reasons,* 1989 ANN. SURV. AM. L. 307, 309 (1990). Trahan has divided the medical neglect cases into three categories: those where the child's death is imminent; those where there is no imminent harm; and those where the child is endangered but death is not imminent. *Id.* at 314–15. In most cases, courts will interfere when death is imminent and where the child is endangered even where death is not imminent. However, when there is no risk of imminent death, the parent's religious rights and privacy rights are weighed against the state's parens patriae rights. *Id. See also In re* Richardson, 284 So.2d 185, 187 (1973) (denying parents' request to consent to son's kidney donation for the benefit of his sister where it was not found to be in the son's own best interest).

106. Child Abuse Prevention and Treatment Act of 1996, Pub. L. No. 93-247, 88 Stat. 4 (codified in sections of 42 U.S.C. §§ 5101-5116i (2000)); Adoption and Safe Families Act of 1997, Pub. L. No. 105-89,

111 Stat. 2117 (1997); *see Lassiter,* 452 U.S. at 34 (citing various statutes in support of decision to uphold a termination of parental rights).

107. Rochin v. California, 342 U.S. 165, 172–73 (1952).

108. Cruzan v. Director, Mo. Dep't of Health, 497 U.S. 261 (1990).

109. Parham v. J.R., 442 U.S. 584, 603 (1979); Lawrence Schlam & Joseph P. Wood, *Informed Consent to the Medical Treatment of Minors: Law & Practice,* 10 HEALTH MATRIX 141, 142 (2000); *see* Andrew Popper, *Averting Malpractice by Information: Informed Consent in the Pediatric Treatment Environment,* 47 DEPAUL L. REV. 819 (1998).

110. Schlam & Wood, *supra* note 109, at 147–49.

111. FAUSTO-STERLING, *supra* note 1, at 81.

112. Eisenstadt v. Baird, 405 U.S. 438, 453 (1972). The Court stated that it is the right of the individual to decide "whether to bear or beget children." *Id.*

113. Planned Parenthood of Southeastern Pa. v. Casey, 505 U.S. 833, 899–901 (1994).

114. Planned Parenthood of Central Mo. v. Danforth, 428 U.S. 52 (1976); Bellotti v. Baird, 443 U.S. 622 (1979).

115. *Casey,* 505 U.S. at 833 (abortion); Carey v. Population Serv. Int'l, 431 U.S. 678 (1977) (contraception); *see also* Schlam & Wood, *supra* note 109, at 166.

116. Estate of CW, 640 A.2d 427 (Pa. Super. Ct. 1994).

117. *Id.; see In re* Guardianship of Hayes, 608 P.2d 635 (Wash. 1980). In limited circumstances, parents can consent for their incompetent children to be sterilized to protect them from harmful pregnancies. *Id.* at 638. However, there are strict procedural guidelines that the court follows before allowing parental consent. *Id.* at 639. The following guidelines must be followed: (1) the child must be represented by a disinterested guardian ad litem; (2) the child must be incapable of making her own decision about sterilization; and (3) the child must be unlikely to develop sufficiently to make an informed judgment about sterilization in the foreseeable future. *Id.* at 641. Even after the court establishes the listed criteria, the parent or guardian seeking an incompetent's sterilization must prove by clear, cogent, and convincing evidence that there is a need for contraception. *Id.* First the judge must find that the individual is physically capable of procreation. *Id.* Second the judge must find that she is likely to engage in sexual activity at the present or in the near future under circumstances

likely to result in pregnancy. *Id.* Finally the judge must determine that the nature and extent of the individual's disability, as determined by empirical evidence and not solely on the basis of standardized tests, renders him or her permanently incapable of caring for a child, even with reasonable assistance. *Id.*

118. Reproductive rights will not be infringed for those intersexed children who are incapable of producing sperm or eggs or who do not have a functional uterus.

119. Reproductive rights will also not be infringed for intersexed children who have clitoral reduction surgery and do not have their gonads or uterus removed.

120. However, in Vermont, same-sex couples may seek a civil union, pursuant to Vt. St T.15 § 1201. These civil unions may not be recognized by other states. *See* William C. Duncan, *Civil Unions in Vermont: Where to Go From Here?*, 11 WIDENER J. PUB. L. 361, 373–76 (2002). In addition, the Massachusetts Supreme Judicial Court held in *Goodridge v. Dep't of Public Health,* that barring an individual from the protections, benefits, and obligations of civil marriage solely because that person would marry a person of the same sex violates the Massachusetts Constitution and stayed the judgment for 180 days to permit the Legislature to take action. 798 N.E.2d 941 (Mass. 2003).

121. Baehr v. Lewin, 852 P.2d 44 (Haw. 1993); Baehr v. Miike, No. 91-1394, 1996 WL 694235 (Haw. Cir. Ct. Dec. 3, 1996).

122. *Lewin,* 852 P.2d at 67.

123. HAW. CONST. art. 1, § 23; *see also* Baehr v. Miike, No. 91-1394, 1996 WL 694235 (Cir. Ct. Haw. Dec. 3, 1996). The Hawaii Constitution was amended by voter referendum shortly before the decision was rendered in *Baehr v. Miike.* David Orgon Coolidge, *The Hawai'i Marriage Amendment: Its Origins, Meaning and Fate,* 22 U. HAW. L. REV. 19, 82, 101 (2000).

124. Defense of Marriage Act, 28 U.S.C. § 1738C (1996).

125. Lynn E. Harris, *Born True Hermaphrodite, at* http://www.angelfire.com/ca2/BornHermaphrodite (last visited Mar. 27, 2004). The Superior Court, County of Los Angeles, granted the two-part request of Lynn Elizabeth Harris, Case No. 437625, changing the name and legal sex on her birth certificate from Lynn Elizabeth Harris to Lynn Edward Harris, and from female to male, respectively. *Id.*

126. *See In re* Estate of Gardiner, 22 P.3d 1086 (Kan. Ct. App. 2001). Most court cases discussing the legality

of changing birth certificates, names or gender identification only consider chromosomes as one factor in determining a person's legal gender. *Id.* The main factor that courts consider is the genitalia of the individual requesting a legal change of status. *Id.* In this case involving a male to female transsexual, the court discusses intersex conditions extensively in explaining the difficulty in determining legal gender. *Id.*

127. Burton, *supra* note 91, § IIIC. Burton cites Littleton v. Prange, 9 S.W.3d 223 (Tex. App. 1999). In *Littleton v. Prange,* a male to female transsexual legally changed her birth certificate to female and married. 9 S.W.3d at 224–25. However, the court found that she was not a legal spouse because she was born male and thus was unable to sue for the wrongful death of her husband. *Id.* at 225–26.

128. Cruzan v. Mo. Dep't of Health, 497 U.S. 261, 269 (1990). "This notion of bodily integrity has been embodied in the requirement that informed consent is generally required for medical treatment. Justice Cordozo, while on the Court of Appeals of New York, aptly described this doctrine: Every Human being of adult years and sound mind has a right to determine what shall be done with his own body; and a surgeon who performs an operation without his patient's consent commits an assault, for which he is liable in damages." *Id.*

129. *Id.*

130. *See Id.* at 279.

131. *See* Washington v. Glucksberg, 521 U.S. 702, 725 (1997).

132. Beh & Diamond, *supra* note 2, at 47–48.

133. FAUSTO-STERLING, *supra* note 1, at 64–65.

134. Beh & Diamond, *supra* note 2, at 47; Ford, *supra* note 4, at 483–84.

135. Ford, *supra* note 4, at 483.

136. FAUSTO-STERLING, *supra* note 1, at 86.

137. Ford, *supra* note 4, at 485.

138. *Id.* at 484.

139. *Id.*

140. *See* Beh & Diamond, *supra* note 2, at 48–52.

141. 18 U.S.C. § 116 (2000).

142. *Id.*

143. Bruce A. Robinson, *Female Genital Mutilation in North America & Europe, at* http://www.religious tolerance.org/fem_cira.htm (last updated Jan. 22, 2004). "FGM has . . . been criminalized at the state level in California, Minnesota, North Dakota, Rhode Island, and Tennessee." *Id.*

144. 18 U.S.C. § 116.

145. *Id.*

146. *Id.*

147. *Id.* § 116(c).

148. *Id.* § 116.

149. *Id.* § 116(b)(1).

150. FAUSTO-STERLING, *supra* note 1, at 48, 51.

151. *Id.* at 109.

152. *Id.* at 52, 55, 58. Intersexed children with Congenital Adrenal Hyperplasia may develop problems with salt metabolism, which could be life threatening if not treated with cortisone. *Id.* at 52. Some intersexed babies may have an increased rate of urinary tract infections possibly leading to kidney damage. *Id* at 58.

153. Beh & Diamond, *supra* note 2, at 46; FAUSTO-STERLING, *supra* note 1, at 58.

154. Ramos Summary, *supra* note 54, at 4; Kaldera, *supra* note 1, at 4.

155. 18 U.S.C. § 116.

156. Pub. L. No. 104-208, div. C, § 645(a), 110 Stat. 3009–709 (1996) (codified as amended at 18 U.S.C. § 116 (2000)). "The Congress finds that—(1) The practice of female genital mutilation is carried out by members of certain cultural and religious groups within the United States; (2) the practice of female genital mutilation often results in the occurrence of physical and psychological health effects that harm the women involved; (3) such mutilation infringes upon the guarantees of rights secured by Federal and State law, both statutory and constitutional; (4) the unique circumstances surrounding the practice of female genital mutilation place it beyond the ability of any single State or local jurisdiction to control; (5) the practice of female genital mutilation can be prohibited without abridging the exercise of any rights guaranteed under the first amendment to the Constitution or under any other law; and (6) Congress has the affirmative power under section 8 of Article 1, the necessary and proper clause, section 5 of the fourteenth Amendment, as well as under the treaty clause, to the Constitution to enact such legislation." *Id.*

157. FAUSTO-STERLING, *supra* note 1, at 85–86.

158. See 18 U.S.C. § 116.

159. *Id.*

160. Craig v. Boren, 429 U.S. 190, 197–98 (1976). Equal protection claims brought on the basis of gender must meet intermediate scrutiny; thus, the government must show that there is a legitimate state interest in treating the sexes differently, and that this statute is substantially related to a legitimate government interest. *Id.*

161. *Convention on the Rights of the Child,* G.A. Res. 44/25, U.N. GAOR, 44th Sess., Supp. No. 49, at 167, U.N. Doc. A/44/49 (1989), *available at* http://www.un.org/documents/ga/res/44/a44r025.htm.

162. *Id.* The other country that did not sign the convention was Somalia. *See* Office of the United Nations High Commissioner for Human Rights, *Status of the Ratification of the Convention on the Rights of the Child* (Nov. 4, 2003), *available at* http://www.unhchr.ch/html/menu2/6/crc/treaties/status-crc.htm.

163. *Convention on the Rights of the Child, supra* note 161.

164. *Id.*

165. *Trials of War Criminals Before the Nuremberg Military Tribunals Under Control Council Law No. 10 (1946–1949)* [*Nuremberg Code*], *available at* http://www1.umn.edu/humanrts/instree/nuremberg.html [hereinafter *Nuremberg Code*]; Grimes v. Kennedy Krieger Institute, Inc. 782 A.2d 807 (2001). This case discusses experimental research on children in the United States without informed consent. *Id.* at 811. The court in that case stated, "The Nuremberg Code is the most complete and authoritative statement of the law of informed consent to human experimentation. It is also part of international common law and may be applied, in both civil and criminal cases, by state, federal and municipal courts in the United States." *Id.* at 835 [internal quotations omitted]. The court refers to the text of the Nuremberg Code to support its conclusion that the consent to the research was invalid, "The voluntary consent of the human subject is absolutely essential. This means that the person involved should have legal capacity to give consent; should be so situated as to be able to exercise free power of choice, without the intervention of any element of force, fraud, deceit, duress, over-reaching, or other ulterior form of constraint or coercion; and *should have sufficient knowledge and comprehension of the elements of the subject matter involved as to enable him to make an understanding and enlightened decision.*" *Id.*

166. *Nuremberg Code, supra* note 164.

167. In *Ramos,* the court explores the experimental nature of the surgery and its possible violation of the Nuremberg Code. Ramos Summary, *supra* note 54, at 6.

168. COLAPINTO, *supra* note 12, at 75.

169. Cf. Ryken Grattet & Valerie Jenness, *Examining the Boundaries of Hate Crime Law: Disabilities and the 'Dilemma of Difference,'* 91 J. Crim. L. & Criminology 653 (2001) (exploring the susceptibility of minority groups to hate crimes).

170. Americans with Disabilities Act of 1990 [ADA], 42 U.S.C. § 12101, (2000). The ADA was enacted in the face of discrimination against individuals with disabilities in all areas of life. *Id.* The purpose of the ADA is to ensure inclusion of individuals with disabilities in employment, education, public accommodations, and government services. *Id.*

171. Fausto-Sterling, *supra* note 1.

## Defining Genitals: Size Does Matter

**Suzanne Kessler**

The size of an infant's genitals is important to physicians who "manage" the sex assignment of intersexed infants. In her book entitled *Lessons from the Intersexed,* Suzanne Kessler explores how physicians use size to determine the appropriateness of genitals:

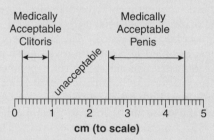

*Ranges of Medically Acceptable Infant Clitoral and Penile Lengths*

"How big must a clitoris be before physicians decide it is too large? . . . In spite of there being a table of standards, physicians are more likely to refer to the average clitoris in food terminology, such as a pea or a small bean. In general, medical standards do not allow clitorises larger than .9 centimeters (about 3/8 of an inch). . . . When is a penis too small? In general, medical standards permit infant penises as small as 2.5 centimeters (about one inch) to mark maleness, but usually not smaller. [Boys with penises smaller than 2.5 centimeters may be reassigned as girls based on the assumption that] a male infant needs a penis of a certain size in order to be accepted by family and peers. [The figure shown here] indicates standard clitoral and penile lengths for infants, revealing that intermediate area of phallic length that neither females nor males are permitted to have."

*Source:* Kessler, Suzanne, *Lessons from the Intersexed*, copyright © 1998 by Suzanne J. Kessler. Reprinted by permission of Rutgers University Press.

# Sex and

# the Trans Man

Jamison Green

I've been asked to speak to thousands of college students, professionals, and corporate staff members on the subject of transsexualism and I've found that audience members are frequently confused [about] the difference between transgender and transsexual. I use the words transgender and transsexual to describe specific human behaviors or conditions: transgender means "across gender" and it describes people whose sex and gender identity or expression are not aligned the way most people experience themselves as male or female. Many people have the ability to break gender boundaries and function outside of the stereotypes that generally define men and women. Transgender people may appear androgynous, whether they choose to do so or whether their appearance or characteristics are involuntary, or they may have the ability to express more than one gender, like some cross-dressers or drag performers can do. Some transgender people feel that the best way for them to manage their gender variance is to medically (and legally, if possible) change their sex. I (and most medical authorities) call this subset of transgender people transsexual people. This is the category to which I belong.

I was transgendered as a child and young adult. I was born with a female body, but the spirit that informed that body was masculine, so much so that, as a child, even when I was wearing a dress people couldn't tell what sex I was. I thought I should have been born male, but people expected me to be a girl, so I did the best I could without completely erasing my personality. So for a long time people thought I was a "tomboy," and that I would "grow out of it;" but I knew I was different. I knew I wasn't really a girl, but I didn't know how to express that to other people around me without sounding like I didn't think very highly of women. On the contrary, I thought girls and women were wonderful; I just didn't know how I could possibly become one, in spite of my female body. I tried to just be a human being with a female body, but the older I got, the less comfortable I felt having people perceive me as something in between.

Not all transgender or transsexual people have experiences that are identical to mine, a man born with a female body (alternatively labeled a female-to-male—or FTM—transsexual, or trans man). And I believe that people who are either natively "in-between" or who choose to live an androgynous life should be free to do so. No one should be forced to change his or her sex; but for some people, changing their sex is a necessary process if they are to make personal progress in their life.

It took me until I was well into my thirties before I figured out that it was actually possible to change one's sex from female to male, and to gather the courage to do it. In those days (the early 1980s), there was very little information available about surgical sex reassignment, and every step of the way felt like an experiment. One of the first things I noticed when I began to take testosterone was a tremendous increase in libido about a week after my first injection. Testosterone does several things to one's body: causes body and facial hair growth, activates genes for male-pattern baldness (if present), increases red blood cells, increases serum (blood) cholesterol, increases muscle density, causes the vocal cords to thicken (and changes the voice), changes the texture of the skin, increases metabolism (makes one feel warmer and increases perspiration), changes body odor, can contribute to weight gain if proper diet and exercise are not maintained, and causes the genital organs to increase in size (in some individuals, the clitoris can become the size of a small penis, with a glans and coronal ridge and erectile tissue that nearly doubles its size on arousal). Most of these changes take place over a period of months or even years (every body is different), but in most female-to-male transsexual people, increased libido is the first change they perceive. I thought it felt pretty good myself!

Some people wonder how going through surgical sex reassignment changes your sexual orientation. Sexual expression is, in large part, reactive; that is, it is dependent upon who is one's partner or "object choice." Certainly, one can have sexual interests that are never expressed because of inhibition, lack of opportunity, or deliberate (or unconscious) repression. This is true for anyone. There's a theory (but no large scale studies have ever been done on this topic to prove the theory) that FTM transsexual people are sexually attracted to women. Some theorists have even conjectured that trans men are simply homophobic lesbians, or women who feel that only men should be able to love women, so if they love women they must be men. It's probably possible to find some trans men who feel this way, but not all trans men who are attracted to women are so constrained by social convention. There are definitely trans men who are attracted to men, too, just like there are very feminine women who are attracted to other very feminine women, and masculine men who are attracted to masculine men. It's important to realize that a lot of assumptions people make about how gender expression indicates sexual orientation are simply logical errors caused by

heterocentrism, something (very much like racism or sexism) that many people don't even realize they use to filter their social observations.

One of the remarkable things that I've found is that people's sexual orientation and sexual expression can actually change in ways that are unexpected and surprising. Because of the number of people who have transitioned (both FTM and MTF, or from male-to-female) who have told me about changes in their sexual orientation that they were not expecting to happen, I have to conclude that human beings do not have control of their own sexual orientation. One example from among my acquaintances is the trans man who started life as a heterosexual woman who anticipated that once he transitioned to a male body he would simply be a gay man. However, it didn't turn out that way: he found that he didn't really like gay men, and he kept finding himself attracted to women (and women were making advances toward him, too!). Another example is the trans man who was a committed lesbian who seemed to have a lot of resentment toward men who, surprisingly, became a gay man once he could completely express his masculinity through a male body. Ironically, this man, like many trans men, has never had genital reconstruction. He manages to engage in gay male sex without having a penis. How does he do that? He does it creatively, and erotically, with a full command of his masculine self-expression. The idea that you have to have a penis to be a man—gay *or* straight—is another fallacy. We don't always think through the logic of our assumptions about sex, gender, or sexuality.

Some trans people have a strong need to have their genitals match their gender, though, and that is no better or worse than not caring whether your gender and genitals line up the way people expect. There should not be a value judgment about whether anyone is more real than anyone else because their genitals are a certain shape or size. In an enlightened society, there is no reason to judge people on this, or any other, physical basis. For those trans men who require genital reconstruction, there are several technical options, each of which has advantages and drawbacks. The least expensive technique, called metaoidioplasty (sometimes spelled metoidioplasty), involves using the inner labia and clitoral hood to "finish" the testosterone-elongated clitoral shaft along the underside, and raising it about one centimeter upward on the body so it is in a more penile position and can better extend forward when erect. This process retains full erotic sensation and the ability to achieve erection through engorgement of the native erectile tissues, but also results in a penis that is relatively small, usually from two to four inches in length when erect. Another issue to consider is that while techniques are advancing, urinary extension through the penis may still result in painful and expensive complications. The most technically advanced (and expensive) alternative that can create a penis of a moderately realistic size uses muscle tissue from (usually) the forearm, which can be disfiguring. This alternative also requires implants to achieve erection, and the penis never changes size, even on arousal. A scrotal sac is formed from the labia majora, which is homologous tissue (technically, the same tissue that forms the scrota), and the testes are prosthetic implants that do not produce sperm. So when trans men who have had genital reconstruction have orgasm, they do not ejaculate through the penis. They may have some fluid emission upon orgasm from the glands that remain inside the opening of the vagina, which in most cases is constricted or completely closed off. So when it comes to constructing penises, if size matters, erectile capacity suffers. That's the trade-off. Either way, trans men can have very interesting bodies.

Hormones, in particular, definitely have an effect on the nature of one's orgasm. And that is the only generalization it is safe to make about trans men's sexual response: hormones do change it. There is usually an increase in libido, or interest in sexual expression, but the type of stimulation one prefers may change, or the ability to have multiple orgasms may change. In my case, before taking testosterone I required very little stimula-

tion and would have multiple orgasms. Once I started taking testosterone, I began to enjoy increased stimulation for a longer period of time, and I have one orgasm, and that's that for at least an hour. Another friend of mine had exactly the opposite experience: prior to taking testosterone he would only have a single orgasm, but once he started his hormonal transition he found he was capable of multiple orgasms. Many trans men find themselves more interested in using sex toys like dildos and vibrators, or experimenting with different modes of sexual expression such as sadomasochism or bondage and discipline, but this can depend, too, on the interests of their partner(s). Many trans men have very conventional sexual lives, and feel no need to experiment. Every body is different! Some trans men who have vaginas enjoy the experience of vaginal penetration, while others who still have them may ignore them completely. And some trans men do not have vaginas, depending on whether they have had genital reconstruction, and how that reconstructive surgery was done. For the most part, those trans men who have had genital surgery retain erotic sensation and orgasmic capacity, though the type of stimulation they enjoy will usually change somewhat. How it changes is such an individual matter that it is impossible to describe.

Sex for trans men is as rich and varied and diverse as sex can be for any other type of person. For each of us, whether we are trans or non-trans, the way or ways in which we manifest our gender, our gender identity, and/or our sexual orientation is an individual matter that is a blend of factors, including our family, our culture, our biology—including our hormones, our instincts, our personality, our social experience/history, and our beliefs and expectations.

One other question people frequently ask about sex for trans people is this: is sex better as a man or as a woman? My answer is, first of all, because of my transgender status, I don't think I ever experienced sex the way most women do. I didn't experience myself as a woman, and I never had missionary position sex with a man. I enjoyed sex with women, and my female partners often told me that they experienced me as a man sexually, even though they knew I had a female body. But the real answer to the question is that sex is better when you are connected to your body. For me, once I had a male body, I was more fully present in my body, and I can say that I have really enjoyed sex better in this body. The best sex isn't dependent on being a man or a woman. The size or shape of your genitals (or your partner's!) aren't what make sex good; what makes for good sex is being present in your body, really engaging with another person, and consciously giving and receiving sexual energy and pleasure. That's what's important.

# Straight Dude Seeks Same: Mapping the Relationship between Sexual Identities, Practices, and Cultures

Jane Ward

In January of 2005, I discovered the following personal ad in the Casual Encounters section of Craigslist Los Angeles, an online community bulletin board:

*Let's Stroke It Together NOW! All (Str8) Guys to Str8 Porn, Hot:*
*I have done this now about 20 times and it never fails to amaze me how hot it can get. Nothing gay here at all, just two guys, watching hot porn, stroking until just before the point of no return and stopping. It hits the ceiling when we finally pop. Something about two guys stroking it together touches most guys and they feel comfortable after about 3 minutes, then it's heaven. Testosterone city!*

When I read this ad for the first time, I was at a meeting with queer feminist colleagues, all of whom, including myself, marveled at the suggestion that the ad was anything but gay. At best, we imagined that this man was sexually repressed; at worst, we imagined his life "in the closet" and the pain caused by so much internalized homophobia. Yet as we scanned through three days of Craigslist postings, we discovered dozens of similar ads in which straight men were soliciting sex with other men.

The ads point to the complex and often seemingly contradictory relationship between sexual identities, sexual practices, and sexual cultures. Is there really "nothing gay here at all"? What are the social and political stakes of arguing that there is or isn't something gay about sex between straight-identified men? And why were my friends and I (as queer) so invested in owning a cultural space that is so decidedly intent on identifying

with heterosexuality? Metrosexuality discourses and television shows such as *Queer Eye for the Straight Guy* have inundated us with knowledge about the pairing of heterosexual sex and ostensibly queer culture (Miller 2005). However, sociological knowledge about how same-sex sexuality lives and flourishes within "heterosexual culture" has generally been limited to the study of total institutions, such as prisons and the military, in which heterosexual sex is presumably unavailable (Kaplan 2003, Schifter 1999). In response to these questions and the lack of sociological research that engages them, I decided to conduct a small pilot study of the "STR8 dude" community on Craigslist in order to explore a different side of queer heterosexuality—gay sex for the straight guys, or what I call "dude sex." Research assistants and I collected and coded 118 Craigslist ads in which straight-identified men solicited sex with other men.[1] The findings of the study point not only to the ways in which heterosexuality is constructed and authenticated among men who have sex with men, but also to the limitations of current sociological analyses of these kinds of sexual relationships. Despite the temptation to view the men who post on Craigslist as closeted or to invoke other ideas about repressed homosexuality, I emphasize here the theoretical and political importance of reading their ads as they wish them to be read—as one among myriad manifestations of *heterosexuality.*

Like Blackness in the 19th century, homosexuality is often implicitly subject to a one-drop rule, in which any same-sex sexual experience muddies the waters of heterosexuality at best, and marks one as either an open or repressed homosexual, at worst. Even to the extent that we allow for the identity "bisexual," this identity is also frequently suspect as a form of repressed homosexuality (Hutchins and Ka'ahumanu 1991). On the one hand, the one-drop system maintains heterosexual privileges by policing the boundaries of heterosexuality and homosexuality and ensuring that the smallest indiscretion can become cause for harassment, isolation, or violence. Even those carefully prescribed social contexts in which we allow heterosexuals to engage in queer transgression, presumably without being severely stigmatized (e.g., adolescent boys "experimenting," college women making out at parties for male onlookers) are accompanied by shame and self-doubt that can only be assuaged by disclaimers about developmental theories or drunkenness. On the other hand, to "own" all same-sex sexuality as queer terrain has also been a useful political strategy for the lesbian and gay movement, and one that has been supported by scholarship on sexuality. From Kinsey's (1948) sexual identity scale to Adrienne Rich's (1980) lesbian continuum, many theorists of sexual identity have asserted that almost *everyone* engages in some form of same-sex desire and practice, and that variation is largely a matter of degree or quantity. Continuum models of sexual identity lay the groundwork for resisting the gay/straight binary, yet do so by illustrating that many people who call themselves "straight" might actually be closer to the gay end of the continuum. In the end, it appears we are all invested, for different reasons, in calling as many people and behaviors "gay" as possible, a practice that leaves the gay/straight binary intact.

As Eve Sedgwick explains in *Epistemology of the Closet* (1992), the notion of "the closet" implies a real or essential "gay self" that is waiting to be revealed. It implies some truth of sexuality that exists outside of the social process of its naming and confession. Similarly, continuum models of sexuality tend to rank people as more or less gay or straight based on the quantity of their same-sex desires and practices, overlooking the social context in which sexuality is given form and shape. Are straight women who "get it on" when they get drunk at parties "more gay" than lesbian couples I know who, for many reasons, rarely ever have sex anymore? Are the straight dudes on Craigslist "more gay" than a man who comes out in his late 50s and spends several years finding a sexual partner? According to social constructionist theory, it is difficult to answer these questions because homosexuality and heterosexuality do not refer to essential aspects of the self or some quantifiable set of sexual practices, but to the culturally and historically specific language used to explain and regulate sexuality (Almaguer 1993, Blackwood and Wieringa 1999, Fausto-Sterling 2000, Foucault 1978, Seabrook 1999). In other words, gay and straight are what we decide they are, and how we make these decisions varies across time and place.

### Gay Sex versus Dude Sex

The erotic culture of dude sex highlights the ways that "gay" and "straight" cannot be reduced to sexual practice, especially in a time when the queer eye (aesthetic tastes, fashion, and the ability to make a fine risotto) is marketed for mass consumption. In contrast with the logic that gay and straight are opposite ends of a behavioral and gender-based binary, the STR8 dudes who post on Craigslist view "gay" as a *chosen* identity that is not particularly linked to *who* is having sex, or *what* sexual acts are involved. Instead, being gay is about *how* sex is done. Among STR8 dudes, "gay" is a *cultural* phenomenon with which one can identify or disidentify, a form of gender expression, and a community affiliation—not a description of one's sexual practice. In a clever turn, STR8 dudes on Craigslist assert that it is willingness to consume queer culture that makes others queer—and conversely, it is commitment to the symbols of heterosexual masculinity that keeps them straight. The following ads, representative of dozens of others, illustrate how STR8 dudes authenticate their heterosexuality while soliciting sex with other men.

*STR8 for STR8 Dudes:*
*I'm STR8 looking to mess around with another STR8 dude from time to time. Discreet and looking for more than one time hook-time hookups so if you respond, have the balls to follow through with this ad and meet up.*

*STR8 Bud Smoke-n-Stroke (420):*
*Any other hot straight dudes wanna smoke out, kick back and jack off to some hot porn? Like to kick it with another bro and work out a load together? . . . We'll just be jacking only—no making out, no touching, no anal bullshit. And smoking out!!!*

*STR8 Drunk Dude Looking to Get Off:*
*Hi there, Looking to lay back, have some beers, etc. and watch some STR8 porn this evening. I'm 5.10, brown hair, brown eyes white dude.*

Authentic heterosexuality is established in part by demonstrating one's disinterest in presumably gay activities ("anal bullshit"), as well as one's interest in hyper-masculine activities. STR8 dudes are often drunk or stoned, they watch heterosexual porn, and they maintain a clear emotional boundary between them that draws upon the model of adolescent friendship, or the presumably harmless, "proto-sexual" circle jerk.[2] Reference to "being buddies" and "having the balls" to have sex with another dude also helps to reframe dude sex as a kind of sex that bolsters, rather than threatens, the heterosexual masculinity of the participants. Only those who are "man enough" will want dude sex or be able to handle it. Yet what is perhaps the most important evidence of heterosexuality provided by STR8 dudes in their posts, and at the heart of STR8 dudes' culture of desire, is the discursive presence (and yet literal absence) of women in their sexual encounters. Unlike in similar websites for gay men, women are a central part of STR8 dudes' erotic discourse. In some cases, women are referenced as acceptable or preferable but unavailable sex partners, reinforcing that dude sex is an insignificant substitute for "real" sex:

*Laid back STR8 guy seeks same for j/o [jerk off] buddy:*
*Easygoing STR8 Caucasian male seeks same—looking for a buddy to stroke with who enjoys STR8 porn and sex with women but who is cool and open minded. I'm not gay but do like to show off and have done some bi stuff in the past. Interested in jerk off only. I'm in shape and attractive, and this is no big deal to me. Don't have girlfriend right now and wanted to get off today so hit me back if interested.*

In an alarming number of other cases, violence against women is advertised as a central part of the sexual encounter. STR8 dudes explain that while masturbating together, they will talk about women's bodies and imagine sex with women. The desire to act out the gang rape of a woman is also common, although not always explicit, such as in the following ad:

*Whackin Off to Porn:*
*STR8 porn. Gang bang. STR8, bi-curious masculine white guy lookin for a masculine guy. Get into stroking bone with a bud, talkin' bout pussy and bangin' the bitch.*

While the phrases "gang bang" and "bangin' the bitch" are used in this ad, it is unclear who the object of the gang bang will be. In most ads, heterosexual porn and *talk* about women's bodies serves the function of incorporating the objectification of women into dude sex. In a few ads, however, such as the following, women were represented by blow-up dolls that dudes would have sex with in lieu of an available woman.

*Any Straight/Bi Guys Want to Help Me Fuck My Blow-up Doll???:*
*Come on guys . . . we can't always pick up the chick we want to bone right??? So let's get together and fuck the hell out of my hot blow-up doll. Her mouth, her pussy, and her ass all feel GREAT. Just be cool, uninhibited, horny, and ready to fuck this bitch. It's all good here. . . .*

In some cases, women are invited to observe dude sex, yet even in these cases, it is the sex between the two STR8 dudes that is the event. While women are present in the encounter, they reinforce the heterosexuality of the men involved, even as their role is clearly voyeuristic and ancillary:

> *Wanna Bang a STR8 Dude in Front of His Girl:*
> *This is a fantasy of mine, and hey it's new years,*
> *why not? I'd like to bang a STR8 guy in the ass*
> *in front of his chick. I'd even bang a STR8 dude 1*
> *on 1 if you want. I'm not into guys that sound/act*
> *like chicks. I'm really not into guys, I just think it's*
> *kinky/hot to do this.*

The link between dude sex and the gang rape of women suggests that we may read dude sex as a sexualized form of (heterosexual) male bonding that is facilitated by misogyny and violence against women. Gang rapes, not typically viewed as homosexual sex, nonetheless involve men cheering on and witnessing the orgasms of other men. Like in the Craigslist ads, women's bodies are the objects of violence, while the expression of agentic sexuality occurs among and between the men involved. This pattern suggests that dude sex is a sexual and often violent expression of heterosexual masculinity and heterosexual culture, quite distinct from gay male culture in which misogyny typically manifests as the invisibility, rather than the objectification, of women (Ward 2000). Marilyn Frye (1983), in her analysis of drag queens, argues "What gay male affectation of femininity seems to be is a serious sport in which men may exercise their power and control over the feminine, much as in other sports. . . . But the mastery of the feminine is not feminine. It is masculine." Similarly, we might consider that while dude sex makes use of and masters homosexual sex, this deployment of homosexual sex in the service of heterosexuality is not homosexuality. It is heterosexuality, or, to be more accurate, it is heterosexual culture. Indeed, there may be "nothing gay here at all."

### Gay Men Pretending to Be Straight?

In her recent book *Black Sexual Politics* (2004), Patricia Hill Collins examines the sub-culture of men on the DL (down low)—Black men who have sex with men but don't identify as gay or bisexual and are typically married or have girlfriends. Benoit Denizet-Lewis, the journalist who first wrote about the down low phenomenon in the *New York Times Magazine*, describes the DL as a reaction to the (white) racialization of gay male culture. Denizet-Lewis (in Collins 2004, p. 173) explains: "Rejecting a gay culture that they perceive as white and effeminate, many Black men have settled on a new identity, with its own vocabulary and customs and its own name: Down Low. There have always been men—Black and white—who have had secret sexual lives with men. But the creation of an organized, underground subculture made up of Black men who otherwise live straight lives is a phenomenon of the last decade." Men on the DL also meet in specialized websites and chat rooms, and like the STR8 dudes on Craigslist, they neither identify as gay nor wish to participate in gay male culture. While Denizet-Lewis suggests that the DL culture is a response to a racial system in which homosexuality is perceived as a "white thing" and Black masculinity is linked to fatherhood, it's important to note the existence of other Black identities, such as "same-gender loving," that simultaneously take pride in same-gender relationships *and* Blackness by rejecting the centrality of whiteness in gay culture.[3] In other words, being on the DL is not the only way to have sex with men while asserting one's Blackness; instead, it reflects a particular desire to participate in Black hyper-masculinity, relationships with women, and heterosexual culture.

Yet Patricia Hill Collins consistently reads men on the DL as closeted and gay, referring to them as "a new subculture of gay men" and arguing that, "for men on the DL, masculinity that is so intertwined with hyper-heterosexuality renders an openly gay identity impossible" (p. 207). While I agree with Collins' contention that the DL identity reflects a particularly complex positionality informed by race, gender, and sexual desire, I want to complicate the suggestion that men on the DL are closeted gay men who cannot come out because they are constrained by homophobia and racism. Such arguments obscure the processes through which Black men *do* assert nonheterosexual identities even in the face of homophobia and racism, as well as obscure the authentic pleasure that DL men take in heterosexual culture, heterosexual identity, and relationships with women.

Recent analyses of men on the DL reflect the temptation to invoke the closet as a means of understanding all same-sex sexuality that is not willing to call itself "gay" (see also King 2004). In part this is due to the ideology of the contemporary lesbian and gay rights movement, in which many queers themselves assert basic rights based on the premise that sexual identity is biologically determined and just waiting to be discovered, revealed, outed. Seduced by this logic myself, my first reaction to the STR8 dudes' ads was to perceive the men who wrote them as closeted gay men, and my second reaction was to perceive them as "real" gay men pretending to be straight in order to satisfy a fetish for "real" straight men. After hearing from many gay male friends about their desire to seduce straight men, I became attentive to the possibility that the Casual Encounters section of Craigslist might be a place in which gay men seduce one another by posing as straight. While the vast majority of the ads gave no indication of familiarity with gay culture, and generally expressed disdain for it, some posts seemed to hold the tell-tale signs of "undercover" gay men, such as the following:

*Do You Like Stroking Your Dick with Another STR8 Guy? I Got STR8 Porn!:*
*Looking to host in West LA, laid back, chill watchin extremely hot porn, all kinds. Pullin' out your cock when you get your woody, start playing with it more, take off your clothes and watch porn jackin all the way, watchin your buddy or buddies get horned up and on fire. The testosterone is in the air, you see him rapidly jerkin and stopping, you do the same thing, for however long it feels good. Looking at him stroke is hot for you, the same for him. Fi-*

*nally you can't hold back, he can't either, he shoots right before you and seeing his dick surt [sic] all that cum makes your orgasm all the more intense. THE RULES ARE THERE ARE NO RULES!!! GAY GUYS THIS IS PROBABLY NOT YOUR CUP OF TEA, no clones, baseball capped generic guys here, real guys, real passion, real woodies.*

While the long and indulgent description of the sex itself is somewhat distinct from the other more minimalist and emotionless ads, what brought my attention to this post was the reference to "clones," "cup of tea," and "real passion." The latter are simply language choices that seemed out of sync with the macho tenor of the other ads, however the reference to "clones"—a queer insider term popular in the 1970s to describe straight-acting gay men—suggests an intimate familiarity with gay male culture. Ironically, the very expression of desire for "real" straight men (and not straight-acting gay men) is what casts suspicion on the authentic heterosexuality of this STR8 dude. In other words, what is suspicious in this ad is neither the sex it describes, nor the meaning it attributes to the sexual encounter. Instead it is the cultural reference to queer worlds of knowledge that makes me think that, indeed, there is "something gay" in this particular ad!

## Conclusions: The Significance of Culture

Academic discussion regarding the social construction of sexual identities often revolves around whether we might privilege sexual practice as the unit of analysis, or whether scholars of sexuality are better served by focusing our attention on the meanings and identities that social actors assign to sexual practices. In the Casual Encounters section of Craigslist, neither sex itself nor the self-identifications of the men who post there are useful guides for delineating the boundaries of queer and non-queer, or establishing political alliances with queer stakeholders. From a queer perspective, to de-queer the sex described on Craigslist is to give up the epistemological pleasure of self-righteous knowing, owning, outing, and naming. In the face of homophobia and heterosexism, the self-righteous pleasure of honing one's "gaydar" is one of few queer luxuries. Yet this study suggests that de-queering various forms of same-sex sexuality may be a quicker route to queer liberation than one that builds solidarity around sex acts. Instead, shared *culture*—including aesthetic preferences, a sense of collective identity, and participation in a community of resistance—may better help us determine whom we "own" as queer scholars and activists. While I am not inclined to want to swell the ranks of heterosexuals or argue that fewer people engage in same-sex desire than we think, this study does point to the theoretical and political usefulness of disowning or "sending back home" (to heterosexual culture) the STR8 dudes who have the "balls" to have sex with one another.

Such a project accomplishes three important interventions. First, this analysis invites us to give name to new identities and practices that aren't predicated on the idea of essential, hidden gayness, and that demonstrate the multiplicity and richness of queer as well as heterosexual sexual expressions. Building upon Sedgwick's call to transcend theories of the closet, which privilege and reify sexual practices, we may then map same-sex sexuality across identities, cultures, and space.

Second, what are straight and gay if not sexual practices? I suggest we view these distinctions as primarily sociocultural categories, or cultural spheres that people choose to inhabit in large part because they experience a cultural fit. Some men like to have sex with men in the bathrooms of gay bars after dancing to techno music, others like to have sex with men while watching straight porn and talking about bitches. Because the only thing these experiences have in common are sex acts between men, we might view heterosexuality, then, as a system of erotic relations and a cultural experience that appeals to people who choose to be straight. Conversely, we might view queerness as a system of erotic relations and a cultural experience that appeals to people who choose to be queer.

Lastly, where is the power in this analysis and what does this mean for the queer movement? In social movement context, redefining queer and non-queer as cultural affiliations implies that queer "rights" serve to protect not everyone who engages in same-sex sexuality, but all those who are excluded from, and alienated by, hegemonic STR8 culture—gender freaks, all kids in gay–straight alliances, all people who are or are willing to be part of this thing we call "gay." Such an approach refuses biological determinism, the essentialism of the closet, and distinctions between "us" and "them" rooted in the gay/straight binary. But perhaps more importantly, if it's not same-sex sexual practices that bind us, we must examine and take responsibility for the cultural spheres that we produce. Queer culture becomes not simply the outgrowth of resistance to oppression—although it certainly is this—but an available repertoire of aesthetic distinctions, personal preferences, and comforts we call home: dyke haircuts, techno music, drag shows, queer jokes, leather, and so on. To view queerness as constitutive of these pleasures, as opposed to some agreed upon set of rights linked to sexual practices, will keep queerness intact regardless of movement gains or losses.

## NOTES

The research described in this article was supported by an Investigator Development grant to the author from the Wayne F. Placek Fund of the American Psychological Foundation.

1. This pilot study was approved by the Internal Review Board at the University of California, Riverside. Research assistants and I collected and coded 118 ads, which represented all of the ads placed during a nine-day period (from January 6 through January 15, 2005) in which straight-identified men solicited sex with other men. We collected and coded ads until we determined that we had coded enough ads to identify the primary and recurring discursive methods used by STR8 dudes on Craigslist to construct and authenticate their heterosexuality.

2. While many ads focus on masturbation, 65% of ads coded in this study expressed desire for, or openness to, oral or anal sex.

3. Same-gender loving is a concept created by and for black men and women in same-gender relationships. The term has been embraced as one that rejects the white origins of the identities "gay" and "lesbian," and focuses more on the practice and culture of "loving" people of the same gender. See www.fobrothers.com, "a reference-based online community for the same-gender loving black man."

## REFERENCES

Almaguer, Tomás. 1993. "Chicano Men. A Cartography of Homosexual Identity and Behavior." In Abelove, Barale & Halperin (eds.) *The Lesbian and Gay Studies Reader*. New York: Routledge.

Blackwood, Evelyn and Saskia Wieringa. 1999. *Female Desires and Transgender Practices across Cultures*. New York: Columbia University Press.

Collins, Patricia Hill. 2004. *Black Sexual Politics: African Americans, Gender, and the New Racism*. New York: Routledge.

Fausto-Sterling, Anne. 2000. In *Sexing the Body: Gender Politics and the Construction of Sexuality*. New York: Basic Books.

Foucault, Michel. 1978. *The History of Sexuality: An Introduction*. New York: Vintage Books.

Frye, Marilyn. 1983. "Lesbian Feminism and Gay Rights." In *The Politics of Reality: Essays in Feminist Theory*. New York: Crossing Press.

Hutchins, Loraine and Lani Ka'ahumanu (eds.). 1991. *Bi Any Other Name: Bisexual People Speak Out*. New York: Alyson Publications.

Kaplan, Danny. 2003. *Brothers and Others in Arms: The Making of Love and War in Israeli Combat Units*. New York: Harrington Park Press.

King, J. K. 2004. *On the Down Low: A Journey Into the Lives of "Straight" Black Men Who Sleep With Men*. New York: Broadway.

Levine, Martin. 1998. *Gay Macho: The Life and Death of the Homosexual Clone*. New York: New York University Press.

Miller, Toby. 2005. "A Metrosexual Eye on Queer Guy." *GLQ: A Journal of Lesbian and Gay Studies*. Volume 11, Number 1, pp. 112–117.

Rich, Adrienne. 1980. "Compulsory Heterosexuality and Lesbian Existence." *Signs: Journal of Women in Culture and Society*. Volume 5, Number 4, pp. 631–660.

Schifter, Jacobo. 1999. *Macho Love: Sex Behind Bars in Central America*. New York: Harrington Park Press.

Seabrook, Jeremy. 1999. *Love in a Different Climate: Men Who Have Sex With Men in India*. New York: Verso.

Sedgwick, Eve Kosofsky. 1992. *Epistemology of the Closet*. Berkeley: University of California Press.

Ward, Jane. 2000. "Queer Sexism: Rethinking Gay Men and Masculinity." In Peter Nardi (ed.) *Gay Masculinities*. Thousand Oaks, CA: Sage Publications.

# Why Are We Gay?

Mubarak Dahir

Everybody has an idea: It's genetics—we're born that way. It's our mothers and testosterone in the womb. It's the environment as we were growing up. One thing we know for sure: The possible explanations raise as many questions as they answer, particularly: What would happen if we found the one true answer? and, Would we change if we could?

Mark Stoner pins it on the clarinet. Ever since Stoner, a 41-year-old creative director for an advertising agency in Lancaster, Pa., realized that three out of four of his childhood friends who played the clarinet grew up to be gay, he has taken note of who among his adult gay friends once played the instrument. What he calls an "exhaustive but unscientific" survey covering two decades indicates that "there is an extremely high correlation between playing the clarinet and being gay," he says.

"My theory is that most boys want to play the trumpet," the former woodwind player says, only partly in jest. "But the more sensitive boys wind up with the clarinet, and we're the ones who turn out gay."

Stoner's theory, of course, is offered tongue-in-cheek. But in the past decade or so, researchers from disparate fields spanning genetics, audiology, and behavioral science have amassed bits and pieces of evidence that they believe indicate what may determine sexual orientation. If they're right, our sexual orientation may well be fixed long before any maestro blows his first note.

But despite some compelling studies that indicate that the propensity to be gay or lesbian is determined before birth—either genetically or through biological processes in the womb—most researchers today agree a complex combination of genetics, biology, and environmental influences work together to make the determination. Just how much is predetermined by the forces of genes and how much is shaped by influences such as society and culture remain unclear—and hotly debated. So too does the corollary question of whether sexual orientation is somehow an innate trait and thus fixed for life or whether it is malleable and thus changeable over time.

More than scientific curiosity hangs in the balance. For years the gay and lesbian political establishment has leaned, at least to some degree, on the argument that sexual orientation is inborn and permanent and thus should not be a basis for discrimination. The tactic has proved incredibly successful. Polls repeatedly indicate that Americans who believe sexual orientation is either genetic or biological are much more likely to support gay and lesbian civil fights than those who believe it is determined primarily by environmental influences.

In a Gallup Poll conducted in May [2001] half of those surveyed said they believe homosexuality is genetic, and half said it is environmental. In a 1977 Gallup Poll, respondents pointed to the environment over genetics by more than a 4-to-1 ratio. The poll calls this shift in perception "one of the more significant changes in American public opinion on gay and lesbian issues." It is clearly accompanied by increasing tolerance

From Dahir, Mubarak. 2001. "Why Are We Gay?" *The Advocate* 842: 30–39. Reprinted from The Advocate. © 2001 by Mubarak Dahir. Used by permission of LPI Media.

toward gays and lesbians. In May [2001], 52% of Gallup respondents said homosexuality is an "acceptable alternative lifestyle," compared with 38% in 1977. And a majority, 54%, agreed that "homosexual relations between consenting adults should be legal," compared with 43% in 1977.

"The question of whether or not gayness is immutable is rather crucial in the political arena," says Simon LeVay, a neuroscientist who in 1991 found structural differences between the brains of gay men and heterosexual men. "The American public will have a different attitude toward gay rights depending on whether they believe being gay is a matter of choice or not. You can argue all you want that it shouldn't be that way, but that's the fact. If science can show sexual orientation is a deep aspect of a person's being, there is potential for immense good. But it does mean the science gets politicized."

Politics aside, scientists insist there is commanding research to show that sexual orientation is largely influenced by genetics. "There's no debate on that from any reasonable scientist. The evidence for it stands fast," says Dean Hamer, a molecular biologist at the National Institutes of Health and an early pioneer in research linking sexual orientation to genes. In 1993, Hamer was the first to report finding a specific slice of DNA that could be linked to homosexuality.

He first studied the family histories of 114 gay men and discovered that many male relatives on the mother's side of the family were also gay. Since men always inherit an X chromosome from their mothers, the study suggested a genetic link between the X chromosome and homosexuality. Hamer then scrutinized the DNA of 40 pairs of gay brothers and found that 33 of them shared a specific region on a portion of the X chromosome.

His work supported earlier evidence pointing to a genetic link to homosexuality. In 1991, J. Michael Bailey, a psychology professor at Northwestern University, and Richard Pillard, a psychiatrist at Boston University School of Medicine, examined a group of gay men, 56 of whom had an identical twin, 54 of whom had a fraternal twin brother, and 57 of whom had a brother by adoption. Among those with an identical twin, in 52% of the cases the twin was also gay. Among fraternal twin brothers, in 22% of cases both twins were gay. Just 11% of those who had a brother by adoption reported that the brother was gay. Another study by Bailey and Pillard found similar patterns in lesbians.

Overall, a person with a gay identical twin is at least 10 times more likely to be gay. A man with a gay brother is anywhere from three to seven times more likely to also be gay. And a woman with a lesbian sister is anywhere from four to eight times more likely to also be lesbian. "All this shows that sexual orientation is largely genetic," Pillard says.

Hamer says genes provide about 50% of the influence on sexual orientation. Pillard wouldn't give a fixed percentage, although he said he believes it is "substantially" greater than 50%. Other scientists have estimated the genetic contribution could be as high as 70%.

However strong the influence of genes, it is not 100%. "We're never going to find the 'gay gene,'" Hamer says. "There's no switch that turns it on or off. It's not that simple."

He and other researchers agree that the remaining influences are a complex mixture of biological developments and environmental stimuli. But how much power each wields is as yet unknown.

Evidence is mounting, however, for the argument that much of the remaining influence comes from prenatal biological phenomena. LeVay, for example, found a size difference between gay men's and straight men's hypothalamuses—a part of the brain believed to affect sexual behavior. His "hunch," he says, is that gay men's brains develop differently than straight men's because they are exposed to higher levels of testosterone during pregnancy.

"There's growing evidence to support the idea that biological and developmental factors before birth exert a strong influence on sexual orientation," LeVay says.

A host of biological indicators of homosexuality boost the theory. For example, research from the University of Liverpool in England has shown that gay men and lesbians are more likely than straights to be left-handed and that lesbians have hand patterns that resemble a man's more than a straight female's. Dennis McFadden, a scientist at the University of Texas at Austin, has reported that lesbians' auditory systems seem to develop somewhere between what is typical for heterosexual men and women. According to studies done by Marc Breedlove, a psychologist at the University of California, Berkeley, there is a direct correlation between the lengths of some fingers of the hand and gayness. And what gay man doesn't relish the study that found that gay men tend to be better endowed than their straight counterparts?

The common thread in many of these findings is the belief that differences in prenatal development are responsible for the variances in anatomy—and in sexual orientation as well. Like LeVay, Breedlove attributes his finding of finger-length differences between gay and straight men to the level of fetal exposure to testosterone. "There is a growing body of research to support the theory that different hormone levels can cause the brain to differentiate one way or the other—to be straight or gay," LeVay adds.

But it remains murky just how much and just how strongly these biological factors shape sexual orientation. "I honestly can't be sure how to interpret the differences I found in brain structure," LeVay says.

Which leaves open the final, and most controversial, possibility: How much is sexual orientation determined by a person's environment?

Even the most ardent geneticists and biologists aren't willing to discount a role for external stimuli. "I certainly wouldn't rule out that life experiences can play a role in sexual orientation," LeVay says.

Historically, determining the "causes" of homosexuality was left entirely to the domain of psychology, which attempted to explain homosexuality with theories of mental maladjustment.

Perhaps ironically, today it is often psychologists and psychiatrists who argue most arduously against the environmental influence on gayness.

"I've spent 30 years studying psychology, and I don't see any environmental differences that affect a person's sexual orientation," says Richard Isay, a psychiatry professor at Cornell University and author of the book *Becoming Gay.*

Psychiatrist Richard Pillard agrees. "I strongly believe that at birth the wiring in the brain tells us if we are gay or straight," he says.

Isay says that "all the tired old postulations"—that homosexuality is caused by, for instance, an overprotective mother, a distant father, or a sexual molestation or trauma in childhood—have been "completely discredited" by the mental health profession. What the environment affects, he says, is "how you express your sexuality. Very, very few mental health professionals hold on to the notion that environment molds sexual orientation, and there's just no real evidence to support that."

However, numerous researchers point to what LeVay categorizes as the "oodles of data" that sexuality appears to be more fluid in women than in men, suggesting that, for some people at least, sexual orientation may not be genetically or biologically predetermined but heavily influenced by factors such as culture, customs, politics, and religion.

It's no secret why the long-standing debate over environmental influences is so critical and so contentions: If environmental stimuli can "make" us gay, can't other such stimuli then "make" us straight?

The latest firebomb thrown into this discussion is the now highly contested report by Columbia University psychiatrist Robert Spitzer, who in [2001] disclosed results of a study in which he claimed that 66% of the gay male participants and 44% of the lesbians who were "highly motivated" could change not just their sexual behavior but their sexual orientation. The study has come under harsh criticism from psychologists and psychiatrists for its methodology, particularly for relying on data provided solely by phone-interviewed subjects recruited primarily from religiously biased "ex-gay" organizations.

"There's no question in my mind that what Spitzer reported was not a change in sexual orientation but simply a change in sexual behavior," Isay says.

But Spitzer is sticking to his guns. While he admits that "the kinds of changes my subjects reported are highly unlikely to be available to the vast majority" of gay men and lesbians, "there is a small minority of people in which sexual orientation is malleable." He estimates that perhaps 3% of gays and lesbians can change their sexual orientation. "It would seem that reparative therapy is sometimes successful," he says. He brushes aside questions about his methodology of relying too heavily on the self-reporting of obviously self-interested parties. "I talked to 200 people on the phone. Some may be exaggerating [their changes], but I can't believe the whole thing is just made up."

Spitzer, who was among those who worked to get homosexuality removed as a mental disorder from the American Psychiatric Association in 1973 and who has long been a supporter of gay rights, says his work has come under attack "because it challenges both the mental health professionals and the gay activists on their party line. I would hope my work causes people in both camps to rethink their dogma."

Spitzer also acknowledges that his research is being "twisted by the Christian right" for political purposes and says that was never the intention of his work. But science, he says, "will always be manipulated by people on both sides of the political debate."

Spitzer's study notwithstanding, gay and lesbian activists applaud the mounting scientific evidence regarding the origins of sexual orientation. But even though most results would likely be considered favorable to the gay and lesbian political agenda, activists remain cautious about basing too much political strategy on scientific findings.

"We welcome research that helps us understand who we are," says David Smith, a spokesman for the Human Rights Campaign, a gay lobbying group based in Washington, D.C. "And we've seen a growing body of evidence to indicate there are genetic and biological influences on sexual orientation. But we believe the studies shouldn't have a bearing on public policy. Gay, lesbian, bisexual, and transgendered people should have equal rights regardless of the origins of sexual orientation."

And Shannon Minter, a senior staff attorney at the National Center for Lesbian Rights in San Francisco, is "skeptical that science can ever fully answer the questions to something as humanly complex as sexual orientation. Sure, it's interesting and worth studying, but I'd be careful about jumping to too many conclusions either way."

Mark Stoner shares Minter's ambivalence about finding "the answer" and her wariness that human sexuality can be easily tabulated and measured in the lab.

"It's interesting cocktail chatter, but I don't particularly care what made me gay," says Stoner, who has two older brothers and thus may be a personal example of one theory that links having older brothers with higher levels of prenatal testosterone and thus a greater chance of being gay. "I don't think we'll ever be able to boil it down to a finite set of variables. It's probably genetic and biological and environmental and cultural and social and a whole lot more that we can't squeeze into comfortable definitions. There are always going to be exceptions to whatever rules the scientists discover."

As if to underscore his point, Stoner adds a footnote to his clarinet theory: "Over all the years of doing my survey, I did find one gay trumpet player."

# Identity and Community: The Social Construction of Bisexuality in Women

Kassia Wosick-Correa

My friend thinks that it would be so much easier for me if I could choose one—if I could say I am lesbian or say that I am straight. And I think it would be easier for *her*. It doesn't make it easier for me, it makes it worse.

—*Lili, age 30*

Identity can be defined as an individual's psychological relationship to particular social category systems (Frable 1997). Establishing an identity of some sort provides visibility; it denotes one's position as either similar or different. Identity is also a primary indicator of status, and is consequently an important tool in achieving social acceptance, creating social networks, and also fulfilling political agendas (Goffman 1963; Bernstein 1997). When identities are constructed based on ascribed characteristics such as gender, race, and sexuality, individuals often experience those identities as inherent to their personal experience. Since individuals often essentialize these identities, it is difficult for many to comprehend the role *society* has in constructing the meanings of these identities, a process sociologists refer to as "social construction."

Sexual identity has been constructed in a binary structure of "straight" or "gay," a significant problem for those who are sexually attracted to both genders. Bisexuality is often regarded as a transition to homosexuality or an experimental phase rather than a separate sexual orientation. Bisexuals find themselves positioned in a sort of paradox: identifying as gay or straight does not adequately characterize the full spectrum of their sexual desires and behaviors, yet avoiding labels such as gay or straight results in searching for a socially defined identity somewhere in between.

Collins (2000) argues this feeling of being in-between is similar to the experience of biracial individuals, and suggests researchers study them in relation to one another "because of the unique developmental problems biracial and bisexual individuals encounter, such as confusion regarding their identity, a tendency to identify with one aspect of their identity, or accepting a bi-identity" (222). Collins' research on biracial Japanese-Americans suggests that biracials respond to the pressures of identity negotiation with *self-evaluation, masking identities,* and *shifting identities.* The process of *self-evaluation* includes questioning one's racial composition as well as exploring the possibility of identifying with more than one racial identity. *Masking* one's identity consists of attempting to "pass" as a member of a certain racial category, and also refers to encouraging others' assumptions of being monoracial. *Shifting* one's identity refers to maximizing part of one's identity in order to move between two monoracial groups simultaneously. According to Collins, biracials both mask and shift identities in the racial identity negotiation process.

Similar to Collins' findings on biracial self-identity, Ault (1996) examines how bisexual women negotiate the clearly defined binary structure of sexual orientation. Many of Ault's bisexual research participants allowed other people to assume they were heterosexual (masking) because of their male partners, whereas other respondents denied their bisexual identity (shifting) in order to establish solidarity with lesbians and queer communities.

One reason many bisexuals have sought refuge among gays and lesbians is the perception that bisexuality is stigmatized in the same fashion as homosexuality. In order to alleviate stigma and feelings of marginalization, gays and lesbians have formed communities based on shared sexual identities for support. Research suggests, however, that the self-identified bisexual experiences a certain level of stigma from the gay and lesbian community as well as the heterosexual community (Paul 1984; Ault 1996). Bisexuals are perceived as indecisive, unable to form committed relationships, or are simply in a transitional phase of sexual orientation (Ault 1996; Oswald 2000; Klein 2002).

Many individuals do choose to adopt a bisexual identity. Both Collins (2000) and Ault (1996) found that those who attempt to do so use a variety of strategies in their identity negotiation process. Few researchers have examined exactly how the binary structure of sexual identity influences the negotiation of bisexual identity among women. In order to answer this question, this research examines both identity negotiation as well as participation in different communities for identity support.

Research acknowledges the role of community in establishing and supporting social identities (Troiden 1988; Weston 1991). The definition of what is actually considered a community, however, has remained a complex and problematic issue in contemporary sociology. Community usually refers to a group of people who identify with each other on the basis of certain social characteristics, shared experiences and some social interaction. This social interaction often aids in both the creation as well as maintenance of one's identity. Communities also provide the foundation for generating and maintaining shared social identities. However, just as community has the power to *include* those with shared identities, it also has the power to *exclude* those who deviate from shared identities.

Contemporary research indicates that there are bisexual communities that are emerging as separate from gay and lesbian communities. These communities provide support and resources for other bisexuals in ways that the gay and lesbian community cannot (Klein 1978; Collins 2000). In addition, many bisexuals have turned to the polyamory community[1] for inclusion and support of their participation in nonmonogamy. However, there is minimal research on how a bisexual community or a polyamory community affects bisexual identity. The question, therefore, is not only how identity develops in relation to the binary structure of gay/straight, but also what is the impact of various types of communities on the development and maintenance of bisexual identity among women?

This article explores how the binary structure of sexual identity and participation in different types of communities impacts bisexual women. Based upon 24 in-depth interviews, I examine how bisexual women respond to the gay/straight dichotomy in their sexual identity negotiation process and explore different types of communities bisexual women participate in for support.

## Methods

This study is based on 24 in-depth interviews with self-identified bisexual women gathered from area LGBT centers and bisexual discussion groups throughout southern California. The interviews included questions that focused on the participant's previous sexual experiences, coming out experiences, current relationship(s), and participation in different communities. Each participant was assured that her identity would remain confidential, thus pseudonyms are used in the results of this study. The common themes of experiencing self-evaluation, masking identities, and shifting identities in the negotiation of bisexual identity, utilizing community in the identity negotiation process, and participation in different types of community (gay and lesbian, bisexual, polyamory) guide the discussion of the research results.

## Results and Discussion

### Fluidity: Case Studies of Self-Evaluation, Masking Identities, and Shifting Identities

Data show that bisexual women go through periods of self-evaluation when constructing their sexual identities. Almost all of the interviewees referred to having difficulty at some point in their identity development with the idea of being, needing, or wanting to be either straight or gay. Some respondents had previously identified as lesbian, stating that if they liked women, they must be gay. This thinking is certainly a product of the binary straight/gay structure; there is no room for "in-between." In addition, many of the respondents sometimes masked their identity in order to gain acceptance from either gays and lesbians or heterosexuals, depending on the social context. These findings are consistent with other research that found that although many women are attracted to both men and women, the idea that one must identify as either straight or gay restricts using the label bisexual (Ault 1996; Oswald 2000).

Interviewees also reported identifying as bisexual in certain situations and as lesbian in other situations. Some interviewees described how they "played up" their relationships with women in order to gain legitimacy with other lesbians, and many allowed others to assume they were lesbian. This finding is consistent with Collins' (2000) research that suggests one way biracials cope with negotiating identity is to shift according to the social context. In order to better understand how bisexual women use self-evaluation, masking identities, and shifting identities in the negotiation of their bisexual identity, let us examine the experiences of two study participants, Luna and Connie.

Luna is a 27-year-old woman who has been married to her male partner, who identifies as bisexual and gender-queer, for over two years. She expressed having crushes on both boys and girls when she was young, although she never used any labels to define her sexuality until she was older. Luna grew up in a fundamentalist Christian home, stating that her parents never talked about sex, and gave clear messages that homosexuality was wrong. She described her experience coming out to her parents:

I originally came out as bisexual socially when I was 18, and a few years later I came out to my parents as gay. I guess I thought that since I had to tell them something, it was probably the easiest thing to tell them I was gay. That was going to be the least amount of conversation. I guess a part of it is that if bisexuals have a choice, then they can choose to live the way my parents think they should live. So coming out to them as gay eliminated that potential of choice.

Luna stated that she knew her parents could not understand bisexuality, and decided that shifting her identifying to lesbian was the best decision for both her and them. I asked Luna if she identified to others besides her parents as a lesbian:

I think because I was dating a woman when I started graduate school, people *assumed* I was a lesbian. So all of the people that I met saw me as a lesbian until I specifically told them differently. I never hid my relationship with my girlfriend at the time, but I also didn't actively go out of my way to tell people I was bisexual and not a lesbian. I never really disclosed my bisexuality partly because I figured I'd be more ostracized by other lesbians, and partly because I had a sense that bisexuality makes people really uncomfortable. And I think there was a sense, too, that I was really frustrated with the idea of being bisexual and there was a part of me that really wished I were a lesbian and it would just be easier that way. I wouldn't have to think about things and have to work them out in my own life.

The above story speaks to the pressure and expectations of a binary sexual identity structure. Luna felt frustration with the idea of falling "in-between" what it means to be straight and what it means to be gay. She stated that she went through periods of thinking she was in fact a lesbian, but her attraction to both women and men prevented her from identifying as gay. Her periods of self-evaluation coincided with her intermittent desire to be a lesbian out of sheer convenience. This desire is not uncommon; a number of the women interviewed in this study expressed how easy it would be to "just be a lesbian" both personally and socially.

Throughout the interview, Luna shared other experiences of how the binary structures of sexuality and gender seem to weigh on both herself and her marital relationship. For example, in order to negotiate restrictive language, Luna and her spouse avoid labels that reinforce polarized identities, and often refer to their sexuality as queer and/or pansexual to avoid dual gender language. Because Luna's marital partner identifies as gender-queer, Luna also subverts the binary gender structure by carefully choosing pronouns that are gender-ambivalent such as partner or spouse when referring to him (which she would not say, because "him" refers to a man).

Luna also allowed others to make assumptions about her sexuality based on the gender of her partner. Keeping silent about one's sexual orientation in the face of assumption is a common strategy in negotiating bisexual identity. However, some of the interviewees stated that silence was precisely the reason that bisexuality is not more visible, and speaking out about their bisexuality is an important way to challenge the assumptions of either/or. Connie's experience, however, illustrates that negotiating silence about sexuality can be more difficult than anticipated.

Connie is a 46-year-old woman who has been married to her heterosexual husband for almost seventeen years. Connie has identified as bisexual since before she got married, and her husband knows about her sexuality and is very supportive. She maintains that she is equally attracted to men and women, and emphasized that monogamy is important to her. I asked Connie why she still maintains her bisexual identity even though she is married and monogamous:

> I think it's important because we are social creatures and we do have to identify. It's a way of making sense of the universe. I love men, and I love women. I still fantasize about women, and I don't want to say that I'm not that way anymore because it's re-

pressive and is a big part of me. It's my makeup, it's my genetics, and it's a part of me that's never going to go away. And I need to be around other people who feel the same way . . . it's like, "Oh, my people!"

Connie is not out as bisexual to many of her friends and family. She stated that she is currently going through a sort of second coming out, due in part to her child growing older and a renewed desire to have personal space. She has recently been attending bisexual support groups and trying to find books and literature on bisexual issues.

> I've become angry because I felt like I was spending so much energy suppressing the fact that I am attracted to women, and there was no one to talk to. I started feeling guilty and a lot of shame. I was avoiding issues that wouldn't go away. I felt like I couldn't talk to any of my friends about it [being bisexual]. I want to be around other people that understand. I'm frustrated that I couldn't be honest with my friends about being bisexual. I wasn't able to be my real self. I really constructed my image in a way that was really skewed, totally heterosexual. I hated it. So I started to do something about it. I started to come out to my close friends. The goal is not so I can run off and have an affair, the goal is accepting that part of me.

Many of the interviewees stated that keeping silent about their bisexuality is like lying to their friends and family about their true selves. Yet many women described their difficulties with being vocal about their bisexual identity. The assumption that one is either straight or gay makes coming out as bisexual more labor intensive; in Connie's situation, although her bisexual identity is important to her, her stereotypical heterosexual image makes it harder for her to come out to friends and family as bisexual. She expressed that it was time, however, to overcome that difficulty of being out as bisexual because of her growing frustration and anger. Her solution was to get socially involved with other bisexuals and lesbians.

> I finally said I need to deal with being out and my bisexuality is not going away. I'm doing it for my husband and my child as well. I realized I needed

to develop friendships and spend time and be with other people that are bisexual and gay/lesbian identified. My attraction to women is still very strong in me. I need to be around other people that identify like me. I have been a real pain in the ass lately because of it. I checked out the local gay/lesbian center and got into a bisexual group and a lesbian talk group with a psychotherapist who identifies as bisexual. I am just kind of getting my feet wet again and meeting people like me.

Almost all of the interviewees shared Connie's desire to socialize with other bisexuals and/or gays and lesbians. Many women stated that especially among bisexuals, they did not have to curb their language when talking about attractions to both men and women. Results indicate that this self-censoring with regard to expressing sexual attraction occurred both with heterosexuals and gays and lesbians.

Managing this self-censorship is an important component in the negotiation of bisexual identity. The interviewees were asked about what helped in the adoption, use, and maintenance of their bisexual identity. Many of them stated that they found support through friends who were bisexual or gay/lesbian, and surrounded themselves with open-minded individuals who provided acceptance. In addition, most of the respondents referred to participation in some form of community for resources and support for their bisexuality.

### Identity Negotiation: The Use of Communities

This study's findings indicate that there are three different types of communities through which bisexual women find support, information, and social interaction. Some of the women stated they felt included in more than one of these communities, commenting that each provided a different level of support for their bisexual identity as well as their current relationship situation. Many of the interviewees, however, preferred some communities and felt completely rejected by others.

These three communities vary in their ability to challenge the boundaries of a polarized sexual identity structure as well as to offer alternatives to monogamous relationships. The *gay and lesbian community* is the least radical when attempting to challenge the straight/gay dichotomy. In addition, monogamy is still highly regarded in many gay/lesbian circles. The *bisexual community*, however, is more radical in resisting the dominant binary sexual structure. Not only does the bisexual community challenge the gay/straight binary, it also attempts to challenge the gender dichotomy through less rigid boundaries of gender and sex. However, many interviewees stated that the bisexual community emphasizes monogamy. The most radical is the *polyamory community*, which challenges the dichotomies of gender and sexual identity, and more importantly offers relationship alternatives to monogamy for people regardless of sexual orientation.

### Reinforcing Boundaries: The Gay and Lesbian Community

Bisexuals sometimes engage in same sex relations; thus many have attempted to form allegiance with gays and lesbians in an effort to create solidarity in opposition to heterosexuality. In this study, fifteen of twenty-four (63%) respondents stated they felt comfortable in the gay and lesbian community. Most of the interviewees at one point or another looked to the gay and lesbian community for resources and support in the development of their sexual identity.

Despite many interviewees articulating a certain level of inclusion in gay and lesbian communities, most expressed ambivalence when describing their experiences within the community. Linda, a 30-year-old bisexual woman involved in a long-term relationship with a lesbian partner, considered herself a part of the gay and lesbian community.

I consider myself a member of the gay and lesbian community and I don't see bisexuals as being separate from gays and lesbians. I figure we are all queer. That's a term many people find pejorative, but we are family. I always figure we are all family; we are all in this together. We are in the minority compared to most of society because we are not 100 percent straight.

Later in the interview, however, Linda described a memorable experience participating in a predominately lesbian social group. She said that she was not going to announce her bisexual identity to the group members at meetings because they were lesbians.

> Needless to say it wasn't something I was going to shout from the rooftop that "hey guess what, I'm bisexual." I thought how nice would it be to be in a group where people feel like they could be themselves? So I thought, I can finally be myself, I can be out. I thought, how ironic would that be to be in the closet in a gay-oriented group? I didn't think that I would have to experience that. But I did. I felt like I had to be in the closet with my straight friends about the fact that I wasn't straight and I felt like I had to be in the closet with my gay and lesbian friends about the fact that I was bi.

Rejection or hostility from the gay and lesbian community based on one's bisexual identity is an experience shared by almost all of the interviewees. This finding is consistent with other research on bisexuals; although many do feel they are a part of a gay and lesbian community, they continue to report negative experiences (Ault 1996; Rust 2000). In addition to relaying experiences of personal overt rejection, all twenty-four interviewees stated they have heard negative stereotypes of bisexuals perpetuated in both the gay and lesbian and straight communities. Many of the stereotypes surrounded the relationship between lesbians and bisexual women. Each interviewee quoted verbatim common stereotypes of bisexuals as: fence sitters, perverts, indecisive, indiscriminate, non-existent, confused, in denial, promiscuous, and greedy. Samantha, a 28-year-old bisexual woman married to a man, described a number of these stereotypes.

> I think some people think that bisexuals are greedy because they want both. Or because they can't de-

cide. I think that probably the biggest stereotype is that people don't believe that there is bisexuality. You are either gay or straight and that those people are just confused or sick. I have heard jokes about not being able to choose or being greedy or whatever. In a way I laugh because it's kind of true. I feel like it's not so much that I am driven to be a bisexual person, it's that I have that option. I can exercise it just like anyone else in the world.

Almost all of the interviewees stated that the generation and perpetuation of stereotypes of bisexuals and bisexuality has at one time or another influenced their identification as bisexual to others in both the gay and lesbian community as well as the straight community. Results indicate, however, that bisexual women somewhat expect stereotypes from the straight community, and are often surprised when they hear negative comments about bisexuals from the gay and lesbian community. Maggie is a 24-year-old who has always felt more comfortable around gays and lesbians because of her bisexuality, yet told of a negative experience while at a lesbian/gay social gathering.

> They [lesbians] were okay with me being at the gathering until they found out I was bi. Their reaction was hostile, almost really angry. I have actually had a lot of lesbians be angry with me when they found out I was married [to a man]. Not even women I was dating—I was just trying to cultivate friendships. But also a lot of lesbians were really on me about it, saying that I was actually really a lesbian, and just hiding. They said that I was using my marriage to closet myself because there isn't as much stigma. Like I can just hide away and have my little life and do this on the side. I guess they felt that I wasn't as gay as them.

Even Marion, a single woman in her early fifties who definitely felt like she was a member of the gay and lesbian community, says: "I do not confess to the lesbian community that I am bisexual. I don't need any more rejection. If I did confess, they would reject me."

The experiences of Maggie and Marion highlight how many bisexual women turn to the gay and lesbian community for inclusion and participation in social functions, yet ultimately resist disclosing their sexual orientation in order to maintain that inclusion and acceptance. My findings indicate that bisexual women do turn to the gay and lesbian community for support in establishing and developing their sexual orientation.

However, the gay and lesbian community many bisexual women look to for acceptance and support of their bisexual identity often requires the same censorship encountered in the straight community with regard to disclosing bisexual identity. What other possible communities, therefore, are bisexual women accessing for acceptance and support?

### Challenging Boundaries: The Bisexual Community

There is considerable disagreement as to whether there is actually a specifically *bisexual* community. Rust (1992) suggests that self-identified bisexual women are in fact pulling away from the lesbian community and creating a community based on their shared bisexual identity. Bisexual activists have long argued that there is a sub-community of the gay and lesbian community geared toward bisexuals, yet few have successfully pursued gaining its recognition in mainstream America (Hutchins and Ka'ahumanu 1991).

In addition to disagreement over the existence of a bisexual community, many also dispute the necessity of a specific community for bisexuals. Many researchers and activists state that solidarity and support as well as social and political achievements would be better realized through unified efforts; further dividing the sexual orientation minority population would be more of a detriment than an advantage.

Part of the difficulty in assessing the existence as well as the necessity of a bisexual community stems from the various definitions of community. I asked each interviewee if they thought a gay and lesbian community exists. All twenty-four (100%) participants responded that there is in fact an established gay and lesbian community. Many re-

ferred to the geographic areas of Hillcrest, West Hollywood, and Long Beach as physical gay and lesbian communities, highlighting gay-friendly businesses, bars, pride parades, and other social events for gays and lesbians. Each interviewee was subsequently asked if she felt there is a bisexual community. Eleven of twenty-four (46%) respondents stated that they felt there is in fact a separate bisexual community. Whereas all participants asserted without hesitation that there is an established gay and lesbian community, when asked about a bisexual community, some of the participants prefaced their response by asking my definition of community. Julia, a 26-year-old who is currently dating a man and a woman, hesitated when I asked her if she thinks there is a bisexual community. She replied no, offering her definition of community.

> Community to me means a bunch of people gathering together for a common purpose to provide support together either in friendship or in advocacy or people who feel the need to bond together with a common thread.

Many other interviewees echoed Julia's definition of community. Other definitions included having a common characteristic that unifies people, engaging in regular physical interactions, communicating with one another via the Internet, and having activist organizations to lead a group deemed a community. Those who did feel a bisexual community exists described it as small, concentrated in certain geographic areas, and slowly increasing in numbers and visibility. In addition, a few of the interviewees cautioned that bisexuals did not form their own community because of rejection from the gay and lesbian community. Linda, the previously introduced woman who is involved with the gay and lesbian community, feels that there is a specifically bisexual community because people want to be with others who are similar.

> I think there is a separate community, but I don't think that they are separate because they are totally shunned by the gays and lesbians. I think that it is

just a matter of people who are similar want to be around other people who have similar feelings and similar situations. Like when I was married to my husband: I was in a relationship and had a situation with someone else as well and that's not the norm. And for society in general, to be able to find other people who have similar life situations, it's just nice to hang out together.

The results of this study indicate that there are many benefits for the bisexual woman to engage in what may be considered a bisexual community. Julia gave a response similar to Linda's when I asked her what advantages there are in communicating with others who are similar.

There are a lot of people who have "been there, done that," and there's a lot of experience to be gained from listening to what other people have gone through and their realizations about themselves, and it's a good place to say, "I can really identify with that." That's helpful to me.

Stella, a 38-year-old, is currently dating two men. She is actively involved in a variety of gay and lesbian organizations as well as coordinating and participating in specifically bisexual groups and functions. Stella explains why she prefers to socialize with bisexuals.

I found that bi community is really important to me. I liked hanging out with bisexual people. I don't need support so much any more, but I like being around people who have the same issues that I do and that I can relate to. It's nice. And I also like dating bi people. Both socially and dating-wise, that's the pool of people I feel most comfortable with and like best. Having a good bi community in a social sense has been really important to me and I don't want to leave it. At least so far it has been more important to me to do the work and have the parties go on than to say the hell with it. I'm still feeling if it is important enough to you, you have to do it yourself.

The experiences of Linda, Julia, and Stella illustrate how interaction with other bisexuals has a positive effect on supporting as well as affirming one's bisexuality. Many of the interviewees stated that when socializing with other bisexuals, they felt like there was more freedom to reveal their sexual attractions or their involvement with men and/or multiple relationships than if they were socializing with gays and lesbians or heterosexuals. Almost all of the respondents indicated that they felt more comfortable around other bisexuals because they did not have to hide their bisexual identities or censor their language or discussions. For example, Lindsey, a 20-year-old bisexual woman who has a boyfriend, discussed how out of place she felt in a gay/lesbian support group. She stated that she consequently sought out other bisexuals for socializing, and experienced a more supportive atmosphere: "I like to be able to talk about my boyfriend and in the same breath talk about women I'm attracted to and have people not look confused."

Lili, a 30-year-old single bisexual woman, shared an experience that echoes Lindsey's comfort around other bisexuals.

I went to this lesbian women's group and I didn't really feel that I identified with anyone there. I like the bisexual group better. I just feel like it's more open and non-judgmental. Nobody there cares what your sexual orientation is. It's one of those places where I can feel like I am attracted to women but nobody is concerned if I have acted on it. You can be attracted to women or more attracted to men, a lesbian, a gay man, or someone straight who is just curious and nobody cares. You can move at your own pace and you are not judged.

Lindsey and Lili both expressed their preference of participating in groups of other bisexuals rather than gays and lesbians. Whereas Lindsey and Lili share similar attitudes toward being with other bisexuals, they disagree on the existence of a bisexual community. Lindsey does not believe there is a bisexual community.

It doesn't seem like there's a community. I mean, it's like asking if there's a stamp collecting community. There are stamp collectors, and they come together for stamp collecting conventions, but you don't think of them as a community.

Lili, however, does believe there is a bisexual community.

Yes, there is a bisexual community. We have a group down here in San Diego that is really active, and we are always having meetings and social functions. We also participated as a group in the San Diego Pride Parade in July. There are a lot of us here.

This study's findings indicate that socializing with other bisexuals is beneficial to one's bisexual identity. Bisexuals are able to be more open about their sexual identity and engagement in relationships when they are interacting with other bisexuals. Therefore, the idea that one must identify as either gay or straight is challenged in the bisexual community.

The bisexual community, however, is only somewhat radical in challenging the relationship structure of monogamy. Many of the interviewees stated that although they consider themselves monogamous, there is a certain amount of pressure to remain monogamous. This could be an attempt at dispelling both gay/lesbian and straight myths of bisexual promiscuity and inability to commit. Further, many of the interviewees who are in polyamorous relationships stated similar concerns over the bisexual community promoting monogamy. For these women, a polyamory community offered them a level of support not found in the bisexual community.

## Questioning Boundaries:
## The Polyamory Community

In addition to the participants in this study seeking support and guidance from the gay/lesbian and bisexual communities, many respondents who identify as polyamorous stated that they found support from polyamory groups not only for nonmonogamous relationships but also their bisexuality. Polyamory can be characterized by a number of different open or closed relationship models that include but are not limited to primary/secondary partners, multiple primary partners, and multiple non-primary partners (Labriola 1999: 225).

Of those who identified as both bisexual and polyamorous, many referred to receiving support from the polyamory community in addition to the gay/lesbian and bisexual communities. Julia, who is currently dating a man and a woman, began checking out Internet mailing lists devoted to bisexuals to see what others were saying about bisexuality. She has since moved to participating in those mailing lists devoted to polyamory. I asked her if she was still a part of the bisexual mailing lists: "I am actually on the poly lists now. There is kind of an interweaving of the bis and the polys, so I get my share of both being on the poly list."

Anita, a 31-year-old, is currently dating several men and women. I asked Anita why she prefers to socialize with other polys:

> I didn't have a real sense of community with lesbians or bis where I used to live. Here I definitely feel like I am part of a community because of the poly community.

Sylvie, also a 31-year-old, is married to a man and is dating other women and men. Sylvie said that she liked being a part of a polyamory community because it met her needs for support and inclusion: "The bisexual community here is not very cohesive. I am actually much more involved in the poly community. I get support for my bisexuality and my open relationships."

Julia, Anita, and Sylvie all commented that although the poly community is comprised of individuals who identify as straight, gay, lesbian, and bisexual, poly community members are very open-minded and supportive of many different labels and identities. Other interviewees stated that few challenged or questioned their bisexual identity in the poly community; one goal of the poly community is to challenge conventional ideas of sex, sexuality, and gender, although some scholars argue that this is more complicated than community reports would indicate (Sheff 2005).

In addition, many of the interviewees stated that part of their motivation in seeking support from a more specifically polyamorous community is that monogamy is still heavily emphasized in both the gay/lesbian and bisexual communities, although more so in the lesbian community. In addition, finding other people involved in polyamory was important to all of the participants who identified as polyamorous because of the potential difficulties encountered with non-monogamy. My results indicate that the polyamory community is the most radical in challenging not only the relationship structure of monogamy but also the dichotomies of sexuality and gender.

## Conclusion

The results of this study show that in response to the binary structure of sexual identity, bisexual women go through periods of self-evaluation, and also mask and shift their identities according to the social context. According to the data, bisexual women feel limited by the restrictive nature of a gay/straight binary. By adopting a bisexual identity, many seek to resist such limited categories; however, according to a few of the interviewees, bisexual identity is also limiting in certain ways. Through comparing the binary structures of gender and sexuality, the process of negotiating a bi identity is better understood as challenging a socially established dichotomy rather than being confused or indecisive.

The data from this study also indicate that bisexual women look to different communities for support and guidance in their identity negotiation process. The emergence of polyamorous and bisexual communities has given bisexual women additional or alternative resources for support, guidance, and information about bisexuality. I find that the three different types of communities bisexual women participate in for support vary in how radically they challenge the gay/straight binary as well as the relationship structure of monogamy. The gay/lesbian community is the least radical, lacking in its resistance of the gay/straight binary as well as acceptance of polyamory. The bisexual community is somewhat radical, because it challenges the gay/straight binary yet still accepts monogamy. The polyamory community is the most radical, because it has the ability to challenge the binary structures of gender and sexual-

ity while actively acknowledging nonmonogamy as a valid relationship option.

Bisexual women are continually challenging the socially constructed categories of sexual identity, and although some do so simply by adopting a bi identity, others find the process of challenging restrictive identity boundaries more difficult. Communities that are supposed to help in the identity negotiation process with support and shared experiences end up limiting those who do not fit the community's mold. Future research must examine the role communities play not only in the construction and support of identity, but also in terms of the boundaries and restrictions they put on those individuals who challenge community norms.

**NOTE**

1. Polyamory is often referred to as the ability or desire to have more than one relationship partner or lover simultaneously, openly, and consensually. Members of the poly community may identify as straight, gay, lesbian, bisexual, or avoid sexual labels.

**REFERENCES**

Ault, Amber. 1996. "Ambiguous Identity in an Unambiguous Sex/Gender Structure: The Case of Bisexual Women." *The Sociological Quarterly,* 37 (3): 449–463.

Bernstein, Mary. 1997. "Celebration and Suppression: The Strategic Uses of Identity by the Lesbian and Gay Movement." *American Journal of Sociology,* 103 (3): 531–565.

Collins, J. Fuji. 2000. "Biracial-Bisexual Individuals: Identity Coming of Age." *International Journal of Sexuality and Gender Studies,* 5 (3): 221–253.

Frable, D. E. S. 1997. "Gender, Racial, Ethnic, Sexual, and Class Identities." *Annual Review of Psychology,* 48, 139–163.

Goffman, Erving. 1963. *Stigma: Notes on the Management of Spoiled Identity.* New Jersey: Prentice-Hall.

Hutchins, Loraine, and Ka'ahumanu, Lani, eds. 1991. *Bi Any Other Name: Bisexual People Speak Out.* Boston: Alyson Publications.

Klein, Fritz. 1978. *The Bisexual Option.* New York: Arbor House.

Klein, Fritz. 2002. E-mail to the author. 11 Jan 2002.

Labriola, Kathy. 1999. "Models of Open Relationships." Pp. 217–225 in *The Lesbian Polyamory Reader,* edited by M. Munson and J. Stelboum.

Oswald, Ramona Faith. 2000. "Family and Friendship Relationships After Young Women Come Out as Bisexual or Lesbian." *Journal of Homosexuality,* 38 (3): 65–83.

Paul, Jay P. 1984. "The Bisexual Identity: An Idea without Social Recognition." *Journal of Homosexuality,* 9 (2–3): 45–63.

Rust, Paula C. 1992. "The Politics of Sexual Identity: Sexual Attraction and Behavior among Lesbian and Bisexual Women." *Social Problems,* 39 (4), November 1992: 366–387.

Rust, Paula C. 1993. "Coming Out in the Age of Social Constructionism: Sexual Identity Formation among Lesbian and Bisexual Women." *Gender and Society,* 7 (1): 50–77.

Rust, Paula C. 2000. "Bisexuality: A Contemporary Paradox for Women." *Journal of Social Issues,* 56 (2): 205–221.

Sheff, Elisabeth. 2005. "Polyamorous Women, Sexual Subjectivity, and Power." *Journal of Contemporary Ethnography* 34 (3): 251–283.

Stryker, Sheldon. 2000. "Identity Theory." Pp. 1253–1258 in *Encyclopedia of Sociology,* 2nd ed., vol. 2, edited by E. Borgatta and R. Montgmery.

Troiden, Richard R. 1988. *Gay and Lesbian Identity: A Sociological Analysis.* New York: General Hall.

Weston, Kathleen. 1991. *Families We Choose: Lesbians, Gays, Kinship.* New York: Columbia University Press.

## Nuances of Gay Identities Reflected in New Language

**Rona Marech**

First, there was the term "homosexual," then "gay" and "lesbian," then the once taboo "dyke" and "queer."

Now, all bets are off.

With the universe of gender and sexual identities expanding, a gay youth culture emerging, acceptance of gays rising and label loyalty falling, the gay lexicon has exploded with scores of new words and blended phrases that delineate every conceivable stop on the identity spectrum—at least for this week.

Someone who is "genderqueer," for example, views the gender options as more than just male and female or doesn't fit into the binary male-female system. A "trannydyke" is a transgender person (whose gender is different than the one assigned at birth) attracted to people with a more feminine gender, while a "pansexual" is attracted to people of multiple genders. A "boi" describes a boyish gay guy or a biological female with a male presentation; and "heteroflexible" refers to a straight person with a queer mind-set.

The list of terms—which have hotly contested definitions—goes on: "FTM" for female to male, "MTF" for male to female, "boydyke," "trannyboy," "trannyfag," "multigendered," "polygendered," "queerboi," "transboi," "transguy," "transman," "half-dyke," "bi-dyke," "stud," "stem," "trisexual," "omnisexual," and "multisexual."

"The language thing is tricky," said Thom Lynch, the director of the San Francisco Lesbian, Gay, Bisexual, Transgender Community Center. "I feel sorry for straight people."

Tricky, maybe, but also healthy and empowering, said Carolyn Laub, the director of the Gay-Straight Alliance Network, which links gay and lesbian student clubs in the state.

"We in society and in our generation are developing new understandings of sexual orientation and gender identities and what that means to us," she said. "We don't really have enough language to describe that; therefore, we have to create new words."

For those back in the linguistic dark ages still wondering what's wrong with "homosexual," the evolution of queer identity language has progressed something like this: "Homosexual" sounded pathological and clinical, so activists went about creating their own words, starting with "gay" and "lesbian." That was well and good, but terms like "dyke" and "queer" had an appealing spiki-ness and served double-duty by stripping the sting from words that had heretofore been considered unspeakably nasty.

The adjustment took time for some: As recently as 2002, visitors at the San Francisco community center routinely complained about a sign proudly pronounc-ing it "the queerest place on Earth," Lynch said. But in the Bay Area, in the age of "Queer Eye for the Straight Guy," that sort of sensitivity is beginning to seem almost quaint. Even some straight people have adopted the word because they have gay parents or an affinity for gay culture.

These days, "queer" is especially handy because it's vague enough to encompass just about everyone. The word and its newfangled linguistic cousins have be-come indispensable as the transgender population in the Bay Area has grown exponentially—into the tens of thousands, advocates say—and sexual identities have become increasingly complicated.

"If you're not a man or woman, words like 'gay' or 'lesbian' don't fit you anymore," said Sam Davis, founder of United Genders of The Universe, a support group and speakers bureau. "The words from just a few years ago aren't adequate to talk about who we are, where we're coming from and who we like."

. . . A lot of the identity fluidity, name mania and word invention is bubbling up from the next generation of queer youth.

"Now that community resources are in place and public acceptance has increased, it's more feasible for adolescents to come out during adolescence," said Cait-lin Ryan, a researcher at San Francisco State University who has studied lesbian, gay and bisexual youth. "What we're getting in the LGBT community is the power of youth. It's their expression and exuberance and energy and also their contribution to the culture."

It makes sense that youth, in particular, are coming up with new words and trying them on, considering that "identity development is one of the most important de-velopmental tasks of adolescence," she said.

Growing acceptance of gays and lesbians has also encouraged idiosyncrasy, Ryan said. "Identities are very personal. That was much less true 20 years ago, when identity was more around community. Now that there's a community, a vibrant one with resources, there's more room for personal identity. Before, the tribe was so much more important," she said.

To further complicate matters, race and ethnicity af-fect who is using which words. Some people of color prefer the word "stud" to "butch," meaning a masculine-identified lesbian. Which makes someone who falls between a stud and a femme—a more "feminine" lesbian—a "stem."

And genderbending and genderqueerness aren't as prevalent among people of color, said Mateo Cruz, who's Latino and a staff member at the Pacific Center, Berke-ley's LGBT center.

In these communities, "queer" and the terms it spawned have a reputation of being "white," so some shy away from them in favor of "same-gender-loving people" or "men who sleep with men," or—among Spanish-speakers—"homosexual," which is also a Span-ish word.

"A lot of the stereotypes of what a 'queer' person is supposed to be, especially in mainstream media, is always a white person," said Solomon, who is African American. "A lot of issues people of color have with their families is their parents are saying, 'If you're gay, then you want to be white.' Because that's all they see. So yeah, 'queer' is not a word that a lot of people of color use."

No wonder Cruz sometimes grows frustrated when he leads discussions about appropriate language in anti-homophobia workshops. It can take an hour for his savviest students to list the "hundreds" of words they know for gay, lesbian, bisexual and transgender people. Then the discussion about what the words mean, who can use them and whether they're polite, often drags on ad nauseam.

When Cruz's coding system—circles, big X's and dot-ted lines to connote cool, uncool, and sometimes-cool terms—inevitably breaks down, he throws up his hands.

"However people self-identify," he tells students, "we have to respect."

### What it all means

Definitions of many words in the gay lexicon are hotly contested. Here is a sample:

Genderqueer: Someone who views the gender options as more than just male and female or who doesn't fit into the binary male-female system.

Transgender: An umbrella term for transgression of the binary gender system. May include surgical, hormonal or nonhormonal changes that result in a gender identity different from the one assigned at birth.

Pansexual: Someone attracted to people of multiple genders.

Trannydyke: A transgender person attracted to people with a more feminine gender.

Trannyfag: A transgender person attracted to people with a more masculine gender.

Boi: A boyish gay guy or a biological female with a boyish presentation.

Heteroflexible: A straight person with a queer mind-set.

*Source:* Marech, Rona. 2004. "Nuances of Gay Identities Reflected in New Language: 'Homosexual' Is Passé in a 'Boi's' Life." *San Francisco Chronicle* Online. Copyright 2004 by the *San Francisco Chronicle*. Reproduced with permission of the *San Francisco Chronicle* via Copyright Clearance Center.

## Sextistics

### Did You Know?

- Compared to urban teens, suburban teens are more likely to report that teens who have oral sex are still virgins (45 percent and 60 percent respectively).[1]
- Approximately 4 percent of men and women aged 15 to 44 describe themselves as homosexual or bisexual. However, 11 percent of women aged 15 to 44 reported having had at least one sexual experience with another woman, and 6 percent of men aged 15 to 44 reported having had anal or oral sex with another man.[2]
- "[Forty-eight percent] of self-identified gay and bisexual college students became aware of their sexual identity in high school;"[3] 26 percent became aware of their sexual identity in college.[4]
- The term *heterosexuality* initially referred to people who had sexual inclinations for both sexes.[5]
- One in approximately 100 newborns has genitalia that differs from medical standards for male or female.[6]
- Over one of every 1,000 infants receives surgery to "normalize" their genitalia.
- The Intersex Society of North America (ISNA) "is devoted to systematic change to end shame, secrecy, and unwanted genital surgeries." Founded in 1993, they have over 1,000 supporters.[7]
- Estimations of a transsexual population are often flawed. Some estimates only count individuals who have undergone genital surgery. Others count gender identity disorder diagnoses. Both measures underestimate the population.

*—Compiled by Mikel Walters*

**NOTES**

1. NBC News. 2005. "NBC News, People Magazine Commission Landmark National Poll." MSNBC, January 19. Retrieved November 21, 2005 from www.msnbc.com.

2. Ibid.

3. Sexuality Information and Education Council of the United States. 2001. "Lesbian, Gay, Bisexual and Transgender Youth Issues." Retrieved November 21, 2005 from www.siecus.org.

4. Rust, Paula. 2002. "Bisexuality: The State of the Union." *Annual Review of Sex Research* 13:180.

5. Blackless, Melanie, Anthony Charuvastra, Amanda Derryck, Anne Fausto-Sterling, Karl Lauzanne, and Ellen Lee. 2000. "How Sexually Dimorphic Are We?" *American Journal of Human Biology* 12:151–166.

6. Ibid.

7. Intersex Society of North America. 2006. "Our Mission." Retrieved January 16, 2006 from www.isna.org.

2

# *Investigating Sexuality*

*An interview with . . .*

### Julia R. Heiman

Julia R. Heiman, Ph.D., a leader in the field of sex research, is the sixth director of The Kinsey Institute for Research in Sex, Gender, and Reproduction at Indiana University, Bloomington. Heiman, who joined the university on June 1, 2004, is also a professor in the Psychological and Brain Sciences Department with a joint appointment in the Psychiatry Department in the IU School of Medicine in Indianapolis.

**So, to start off the interview, what got you interested in the study of sexuality in the first place?**

*In 1971, in the early stages of my graduate career, I was working for the summer with a professor named James Geer, who was a faculty member in the Psychology Department at Stony Brook. He had been studying emotions such as fear and their psychophysiological components for many years. Masters and Johnson's sexual treatment book,* Human Sexual Inadequacy, *had just been published. Dr. Geer was interested in figuring out if there was something there that psychophysiologists should study, and basically gave me the choice of doing something in the fear research area or in the sexuality research area. I picked sexuality [because] at the time almost no one else in the lab (except Ray Rosen) was working on it while several people were working on fear research. That started my whole interest in the psychophysiology of sexuality. Jim Geer, along with an engineer named George Sintchak, developed the vaginal photoplethysmograph, and that allowed the physiological measurement of sexuality to be a possibility. This meant that a study that looked at a combination of social, psychological, and physiological variables could be done. I did the second study using the vaginal photoplethysmograph. This was a comparison between men and women's [sexual] responses that became my dissertation. To this day, I remain interested in those basic questions—the subjective and physical experience of sexuality—what that means to people in terms of their problems and health, and to our understanding of humanity. So, some of the reason that I got into sexuality research was my own doing, and a great deal of it was timing of persons and events that made it possible.*

### How do you tell people that you study sexuality? How do they react?

*Well, that's an interesting question, and it varies, as you can imagine. If I am talking to other social or psychosocial researchers, they're usually interested and usually wondering how sexuality studies might relate to their own work. As you go to some of the other disciplines, it varies. Some people think it's quaint, while others think it's odd. Some think it's not quite science. If you tell the general public, they can have reactions all over the place. They can feel like, "Well, that's a little strange," or they can feel like, "Oh well, that allows me to ask you every single question I ever had about sexuality. I'd better start right now!" But, in general, if you as a person doing sexuality research are comfortable with it, interested in it, and feel it's important, most people will pick up on that, and they'll want to know more.*

### Of the projects that you've done over your academic career, which was the most interesting, and why?

*I would say those projects that surprised me or didn't turn out quite the way I expected were the most interesting. For example, when we looked at differences between genders in patterns of [sexual] responding, we didn't find that many. Another instance would be the study I did on adding romantic content to erotic content in films. There were few differences in arousal when the romantic content was added. Sexual content was what made people aroused. The fact is that sexual response is pretty robust, and the tendency is to respond. Another thing that I found very, very interesting is that the more important data, when you are talking about sexuality, concerns variability rather than similarity. Means (averages) are fine, but when you have a group—for example women responding to sexual fantasy—there is a mean, but the interesting information is really that responses go from very weak to very strong. This focus on variability was introduced by Alfred Kinsey, and contains an important message about our sexuality. That doesn't mean that all variability is always healthy, but it does mean that variability is part of the human condition when it comes to sex.*

**What are the biggest ethical dilemmas that you've faced? Could you tell us about one particularly thorny dilemma, and how you solved it?**

*There are certain kinds of film content that I, though I see the legitimacy of showing it, am hesitant to use. For instance, showing people a really aggressive rape scene and getting their reactions to it can make them worried or anxious. I think this type of work needs to be done in order to understand and treat problematic sexual behaviors, but you have to make sure that you are studying it in the most serious and careful way possible, so as not to harm the participants. Sometimes the only way we can study difficult and unpleasant topics is by studying difficult and unpleasant topics. But, you need to be extremely alert to ethical considerations, and make sure that you have someone else (such as the Institutional Review Board) look over and approve your protocols. You also need to be careful about your own sensitivities about what is ethical, and make sure that you are fully informing respondents of risk, and giving them every possible opportunity to decide whether or not to participate, and not communicating biases inadvertantly.*

**What are the most challenging things about studying sexuality?**

*I think of several aspects. For one, measurement continues to be a struggle. Looking for new methods that might better measure what we are interested in. There are lots of mediocre measures available. We have to acknowledge the weaknesses of the measures, and make sure we agree with why they should be used, or take the time to develop new ones of our own. Another issue is seriously working across disciplinary lines and incorporating different disciplinary perspectives. Political sensitivity is another issue. Sex research is so politicized that even though individual researchers may not consider themselves to be political, the topic is, and you may have to deal with—or at least be very careful with—these issues. Finally, I think we need to find better ways to translate our research to the general public so they can understand and benefit from it.*

**What's it like being the Director of the Kinsey Institute?**

*Well, I've only been doing this for fifteen months, so I'm still feeling new in this job. What is most stimulating is that the Institute is an extremely unique and unusual and truly interdisciplinary gathering place. [In addition to those studying the psychological and physiological aspects of sexuality], we have people coming in who are scholars of history or gender, and they find things to work on in our archives. We have a huge collection of manuscripts and materials, art and photography, and they use these to do scholarly studies of various aspects of sexuality. Of course, we also have people doing ongoing empirical studies, developing new ideas and grants. All of this makes the Institute alive and vibrant. One of the important things for the field of sexuality is to have a place like the Kinsey Institute where interdisciplinary research can take place. It has a history that goes back more than fifty years and that has survived a lot of controversy. You wouldn't expect a place like the Kinsey Institute to be in such a conservative state [Indiana], and yet the atmosphere here works well for sex research ideas.*

**How have things changed since the Kinsey film came out last year?**

*I was coming into this job just as the Hollywood feature film,* Kinsey, *was about to be launched, and our focus was being prepared for how we were going to handle the publicity and the media—especially if it was negative. On balance, the reaction has been more positive than negative. There were no disasters that happened as a result of the film. We did get attacked by a small group that is very anti-sex research—that will say anything to discredit sexuality research—and they campaigned in some cities. As the movie gained attention, we kept the website open and answered questions. We also went around to various cities and presented the film and talked about where sex research is today. We made a number of new contacts and new friends. We seem to have a lot more supporters now as a result.*

**Ok, a final question—if you could teach people one thing about sexuality, what would that be?**

*Oh, not just one! How about a multi-part answer? First, I think we need to understand what influences sexual feelings and desires and behaviors, because it's really part of understanding what humans are about. Second, it is important to understand what your own sexuality is about and how it changes over time. There is a lot of room for variability without it being a problem or difficulty for one's self or others. Every culture decides for itself what is normal and abnormal, but to act like the variation in sexuality should not be there, or can be eliminated, is probably naïve. Finally, how do we help citizens develop a concept of sexual health that fosters respect for body and person?*

—Interviewed by Denise Donnelly

# Alfred Kinsey
# and the Kinsey Report

Vern L. Bullough

The more I study the development of modern sexuality, the more I believe in the importance and significance of Alfred Kinsey. Although his research was on Americans, it came to be a worldwide source of information about human sexuality and set standards for sex research everywhere. In America and much of the world, his work was a decisive factor in changing attitudes toward sex. Within the field of sexuality, he reoriented the field, moving it away from the medical model and medical dominance, to one encompassing a variety of disciplines and approaches. In short, his work has proved revolutionary.

To understand what Kinsey wrought, one must look at the field of sexuality when Kinsey began his studies. One must also look briefly at Kinsey as an individual to understand his accomplishments.

## Sex Research, 1890–1940

The modern study of sexuality began in the nineteenth century, and these early studies were dominated by physicians. It was assumed that since physicians were the experts on body functions, they should be the experts regarding sexual activities. In a sense, this was a divergence from

the past, when sexuality had been regarded almost entirely as a moral issue. And although there were still moral issues involved, physicians were also judged as qualified to speak on these issues as well. Although few physicians had any specialized knowledge on most sexual topics, except perhaps for sexually transmitted diseases, this did not prevent them from speaking with authority on most aspects of human sexuality.

Havelock Ellis, one of the dominant figures in promoting sexual knowledge in the first third of the twentieth century, said that he sought a medical degree primarily because it was the only profession in which he could safely study sex. Inevitably, most of the so-called experts were physicians. Equal in influence to Ellis was Magnus Hirschfeld, another physician. Both Ellis and Hirschfeld compiled what could be called sexual histories, as Kinsey later compiled. Ellis, however, acquired almost all of his histories from correspondence of volunteers and, as far as I know, never interviewed anyone. Hirschfeld, later in his career, compiled many case histories based on interviews, but early on he depended mainly on historical data and personal knowledge. Unfortunately. Hirschfeld used only a small portion of his data in his published books, and before he could complete a comprehensive study of sexuality, his files were destroyed by the Nazis (Bullough, 1994).

Although some of the data physicians reported about sex was gathered from their own practices, these were usually interpreted in terms of traditional views and were supplemented by historical materials or reports of anthropologists to increase their authenticity. Simply put, most physicians

From Bullough, Vern. 1998. "Alfred Kinsey and the Kinsey Report: Historical Overview and Lasting Contributions." *Journal of Sex Research* 35: 127–131. Copyright 1998 by the Society for the Scientific Study of Sexuality. Reproduced with permission of the Society for the Scientific Study of Sexuality via Copyright Clearance Center.

writing about sex were influenced more by the zeitgeist of the time rather than by any specialized base of knowledge. A few early physician investigators, such as the American obstetrician Robert Latou Dickinson (Dickinson & Beam, 1931, 1934), had over 1,000 case studies, but most had only a handful. As the twentieth century progressed, the ordinary physician probably was regarded as the easiest available authority on sex, but most of the medical writings on sexual topics came from psychiatrists, particularly those who were psychoanalytically trained (Bullough, 1997). Unfortunately, even the most comprehensive sex studies undertaken by psychiatrists, such as that of George Henry, were flawed by the assumptions of the investigators interpreting data. For example, they assumed that homosexuals were ill. Moreover, whether the answers to their questions were valid for determining differences with heterosexuals is uncertain, as there was a lack of any comparative study of heterosexuals (Henry, 1941).

Still, assumptions about medical expertise remained. When the Committee for Research in the Problems in Sex (CRPS), the Rockefeller-funded grant-giving body operating under the umbrella of the National Research Council, began to explore the possibilities of carrying out surveys of sexual behavior, they first sought out physicians. For example, Adolf Meyer of Johns Hopkins University was commissioned to complete a study of attitudes of medical students, but failed to complete his work. The only social scientists funded in the first 20 years of the CRPS were psychologists, although anthropological consultants and members of other fields provided occasional input. Lewis Terman, for example, was given funds to carry out studies on attitudes toward sex and marriage. Though his and similar studies were valuable, they depended on questionnaires rather than interviews to gather their data (Terman, Buttenweiser, Ferguson, Johnson, & Wilson 1938), and the sexual part of their studies was secondary to other interests. Even though one of the major reasons the CRPS had been created in 1921 was to complete such general studies, the committee

members were either unwilling or unable to find a person to carry out this kind of study. I suspect that the first factor was more important than the second: There is considerable evidence to indicate that the committee members were uncomfortable with studies on actual sexual behavior and much preferred to fund what might be called bench (i.e., laboratory-based) scientists to social scientists. I should add that this attitude was not shared by the Rockefeller Foundation or John D. Rockefeller, Jr.: both funded other survey projects dealing with sex, including that of Katherine Bement Davis (1929).

Funding for research projects when Kinsey began his work operated much more according to an old-boy network than it does today. There was little advertisement of fund availability and individuals were invited to apply, had to be nominated to apply, or had to have a connection. Certain universities and individuals dominated the disbursement of the money available. To an observer [today] examining most of the research grants given for sex research, the relationships look almost incestuous.

Unfortunately for the committee, sex activity could not be studied exclusively in the laboratory or even in the field by observing animals or gathering historical data. There had been nongrant-supported popular studies of sex, but their samples were not representative and the questionnaires were poorly designed. Moreover, in keeping with its reliance on academia, the committee seemed reluctant to give its imprimatur to individuals conducting such studies. What was needed was a person willing to blaze new trails, dispassionately examining sex without the preconceived notions of most of the physicians then involved in writing about sex. The qualified individual or individuals needed an academic connection, preferably one with an established reputation for scientific studies.

### Kinsey Comes on the Scene

It was in this setting that Kinsey entered the scene. He was the right person at the right time;

that is, a significant amount of money was available for sex research and there was an interest within the CRPS for some general kind of survey of American sex behavior. Who was Kinsey?

In terms of overall qualification, Kinsey's best asset was that he was a bench scientist, a biologist with a Ph.D. from Harvard, and an internationally known expert on gall wasps. But he was also a broad-based scientist. Unlike most research scientists today, who often are part of a team, researchers in the 1930s in the United States were self-dedicated and carried a major teaching load. Kinsey, for example, simultaneously taught general biology, published two editions of a popular introductory general biology text, two editions of a workbook, and a general text on methods in biology, and carried out major research. His entry into sex seems to have been serendipitous, taking place after he had completed his studies on gall wasps. Professors at the University of Indiana had discussed the possibility of an introductory cross-discipline course on marriage, then a topic beginning to receive some attention in academic circles. Kinsey was not only involved in such discussions but took the lead. In 1938, he was invited to coordinate and direct the new course on marriage and family. As a sign of the time, the course was taught by an all-male faculty from a variety of disciplines, including law, economics, sociology, philosophy, medicine, and biology.

Before the appearance of courses on marriage and family, the academic discussion of human sexuality had been confined to lectures in the hygiene-type courses that had been established on many campuses in the second decade of the twentieth century, largely through the efforts of the American Social Hygiene Association. The approach to sex of these hygiene classes was quite different from that of the marriage and family courses, as they generally emphasized the dangers of sexually transmitted diseases and masturbation. In a sense, these hygiene-type courses were conceived to preserve sexual purity, whereas the sexual portions of marriage and family courses

provided information, following the outlines of the better sex manuals of the time.

Kinsey went even further in his discussion of sexuality than the sex-positive marriage manuals, and soon clashed with Thurman Rice, a bacteriology professor who had written extensively on sex, primarily from the point of view of eugenics. For many years, Rice had delivered the sex lectures in the required hygiene course, where the males were separated from the females when he gave his lectures. Kinsey deliberately had not included Rice in his recruited faculty, which probably furthered Rice's antagonism. Rice was typical of an earlier generation of sex educators in that he considered moral education an essential part of sex education. He believed and taught that masturbation was harmful, condemned premarital intercourse, and was fearful that Kinsey's course on marriage was a perversion of academic standards. For example, he charged Kinsey with asking some of the women students about the length of their clitorises. To show that his accusations were based on more than gossip, Rice demanded the names of students in Kinsey's class so that he could verify such classroom voyeurism. Rice opposed Kinsey's questioning of students because he believed that sexual behavior could not and should not be analyzed by scientific methods because it was a moral topic, not a scientific one. Rice's perspective thus was perhaps typical of the hygiene approach to sex.

Kinsey had probably been doing at least some of the things that Rice mentioned because he had approached sex as a taxonomist—as one interested in classifying and describing—as a dispassionate scientist and not as a reformer or politician. In a sense, he was a political innocent. He believed that science could speak for itself, and he criticized his faculty colleagues who took any kind of political stand. He refused to join organizations that he felt had any kind of political agenda, including the Society for the Scientific Study of Sexuality (SSSS) in its early years.

There is, however, much more to Kinsey's interest in sex than the dispassionate scientist. In his personal life, he was not inhibited about body functions. Even before starting his course on marriage, he had sought information about the sex life of his students. His openness about sex (see Jones, 1997: 1997a) was what Rice objected to.

It might well be that when Kinsey began teaching the sex course, he was undergoing a kind of midlife crisis, feeling that he had come to know all he wanted to know about gall wasps and needing to explore new fields. Sex to him represented an unexplored new field where comparatively little was known, and where there was much information to be gleaned. He began his study as he had that of gall wasps: finding out what was known and, in the process, building up a personal library of serious books on sex (hardly any of these had found their way into university libraries) and reading extensively. He also sought first-hand information by questioning his students about topics such as their age at first premarital intercourse, frequency of sexual activity, and number of partners.

All this gave fodder to Rice and his allies, including a number of parents who, perhaps at Rice's urging, complained about the specific sexual data given in the course and particularly about questions that Kinsey asked of his students. The president of the university, Herman Wells, a personal friend of Kinsey who had appointed him coordinator of the course, counseled him and gave him two options: to continue to teach the course and give up some of his probing of student lives, or to devote more time to his sex research and not teach the course. Because Kinsey had already begun to extend his interviews off campus, the answer was perhaps inevitable. Although Kinsey continued to teach courses in biology, his load was reduced, and much of his life came to be devoted to sex research.

Because Kinsey was already well connected to the scientific establishment, his initial efforts to study sex received encouragement from the CRPS. He received an exploratory grant from them in 1941, during which time he would be evaluated as to suitability for a larger grant.

George W. Corner, a physician member and later the chair of the CRPS, visited Kinsey as one of the grant investigators to determine whether Kinsey deserved further funding. He was tremendously impressed and reported that Kinsey was the most intense scientist he had ever met. He added that Kinsey could talk about little besides his research. According to Corner (1981), Kinsey was an ideal person for a grant to study sex:

> He was a full professor, married with adolescent children. While carrying on his teaching duties in the zoology department he worked every available hour, day and night, traveling anywhere that people would give him interviews. He was training a couple of young men in his method of interviewing. Dr. Yerkes and I submitted separately to his technique. I was astonished at his skill in eliciting the most intimate details of the subject's sexual history. Introducing his queries gradually, he managed to convey an assurance of complete confidentiality by recording the answers on special sheets printed with a grid on which he set down the information gained, by unintelligible signs, explaining that the code had never been written down and only his two colleagues could read it. His questions included subtle tricks to detect deliberate misinformation. (p. 268)

Important to the continuation of the grant was the support of the university administration and its president, which Kinsey received despite sniping by some fellow faculty members such as Rice and others who regarded Kinsey's interest in sex with suspicion. As Corner's reference to Kinsey's family indicates, the committee wanted to make certain that the researcher had no special agenda except, perhaps, to establish some guides to better marriages. Kinsey satisfied them on this account and was well aware that any indication otherwise might endanger his grant. Thus, his own sex life remained a closed book, only to be opened by later generations of scholars (Jones, 1997). The CRPS came to be so committed to Kinsey that by the 1946–1947 academic year, he was receiving half of the committee's total budget.

Before the interviews stopped with Kinsey's death, about 18,000 individuals had been interviewed, 8,000 by Kinsey himself. Kinsey strongly believed that people would not always tell the truth when questioned about their sexual activities and that the only way to deal with this was through personal interviews in which the contradictions could be explored. He did not believe that self-administered questionnaires produced accurate responses: He regarded them as encouraging dishonest answers. He also recognized that respondents might lie even in a personal interview, but he provided a variety of checks to detect this and believed his checks were successful. Subjects were usually told that there were some contradictions in their answers and were asked to explain them. If they refused to do so, the interview was terminated and the information not used. Kinsey was also aware of potential bias of the interviewer. He sought to overcome this bias by occasionally having two people conduct the interviews at different times and by relying mainly on four interviewers, including himself, to conduct the study. If there was a bias, it came to be a shared one. The questions, however, were so wide-ranging that this too would limit much of the potential for slanting the data in any one direction. Following taxonomic principles, he wanted to gather data from as many subjects as possible, and he hoped initially to conduct 20,000 interviews and later to conduct 80,000 more. He did not live to achieve this. Before he died, the funding sources had dried up for such research, and other methods based on statistical sampling grew more popular.

### What Kinsey Did

Kinsey's major accomplishment was to challenge most of the assumptions about sexual activity in the United States. In so doing, he aroused great antagonism among many who opposed making sexual issues a matter of public discussion and debate. One reason for the antagonism is that he brought to public notice many sexual practices that previously had not been publicly discussed. Although Kinsey prided himself as an objective scientist, it was his very attempt to establish a taxonomy of sexual behaviors—treating all activities as more or less within the range of human behavior—that got him into trouble. Karl Menninger, for example, said that "Kinsey's compulsion to force human sexual behavior into a zoological frame of reference leads him to repudiate or neglect human psychology, and to see normality as that which is natural in the sense that it is what is practiced by animals" (quoted in Pomeroy, 1972, p. 367).

Most sex researchers today accept the fact that total objectivity in our field is probably impossible. Some of Kinsey's difficulty resulted from his belief that he could be totally objective. He did not realize that the way he organized his data sometimes could challenge his objectivity, even though the organization seemed logical. For example, Kinsey developed a seven-point bipolar scale, which was one of the standard methods of organizing data in social science research at that time. He did not trust people's self-classification as homosexual or heterosexual. Therefore, he decided that regardless of how they might have classified themselves, the only objective indicator that he could use was to define sex in terms of outlet—namely, what activity resulted in orgasms.

In most seven-point scales, the extremes are represented by 0 and 6 (or by 1 and 7, depending upon the number with which the scale starts). Most people tend to respond using the middle of the scale. When one rates heterosexual orgasm as 0 and homosexual orgasm 6, a logical decision in terms of taxonomy, he in effect weights the scale by seeming to imply that exclusive heterosexuality is one extreme and exclusive homosexuality the other. Although his data demonstrated that far more people were identified as exclusively heterosexual than as any other category, his scale also implied that homosexuality was just another form of sexual activity, something that I think Kinsey believed was true. For his time and place this was revolutionary. His discussion of homosexuality and its prevalence resulted in the most serious attacks upon him and his data (Kinsey, Pomeroy, & Martin, 1948).

Kinsey was a trailblazer, openly and willingly challenging many basic societal beliefs. It was not only his dispassionate discussion of homosexuality that roused controversy, but also his tendency to raise questions that society at that time preferred to ignore. In his book on males, for example, he questioned the assumption that extramarital intercourse always undermined the stability of marriage and held that the full story was more complex than the most highly publicized cases led one to assume. He seemed to feel that the most appropriate extramarital affair, from the standpoint of preserving a marriage, was an alliance in which neither party became overly involved emotionally. Concerned over the reaction to this, however, he became somewhat more cautious in the book on females. He conceded that extramarital affairs probably contributed to divorces in more ways and to a "greater extent than the subjects themselves realized" (Kinsey, Pomeroy, Martin, & Gebhard, 1953, p. 31).

Kinsey was interested in many different sexual behaviors, including that between generations (i.e., adults with children or minors). One of his more criticized sections in recent years is the table based on data he gathered from pedophiles. He is accused of not turning these people over to authorities, although one of the major informants was already serving time in jail for his sexual activities when interviewed. Kinsey gathered his data wherever he could find it, but he also reported on the source of his data. His own retrospective data tended to show that many individuals who experienced intergenerational sex as children were not seriously harmed by it, another statement that got him into trouble.

Kinsey is also criticized for his statistical sampling. Although his critics (even before his studies were published) attempted to get him to validate his data with a random sample of individuals, he refused on the grounds that not all of those included in the random sample would answer the questions put to them and that, therefore, the random sample would be biased. It is quite clear that Kinsey's sample is not random and that it overrepresents some segments of the population, including students and residents of Indiana. Part of the criticism, however, is also due to the use and misuse of the Kinsey data without his qualifications. This is particularly true of his data on same-sex relationships, which are broken down by age and other variables and therefore allowed others to choose the number or percentage of the sample they wanted to use in their own reports.

Another assumption of American society that Kinsey also challenged was the asexuality of women. This proved the issue of greatest controversy in his book on females. A total of 40% of the females he studied had experienced orgasm within the first months of marriage, 67% by the first six months, and 75% by the end of the first year. Twenty-five percent of his sample had experienced orgasm by age of 15, more than 50% by the age of 20, and 64% before marriage. On the other hand, he also reported cases in which women failed to reach orgasm after 20 years of marriage. In spite of the controversies over his data on orgasms, it helped move the issue of female sexuality on to the agenda of the growing women's movement of the late 1960s and the 1970s, and to encourage further studies of female sexuality.

In light of the challenges against him, Kinsey ignored in his writings what might be called sexual adventurers, paying almost no attention to swinging, group sex, and alternate lifestyles such as sadism, masochism, transvestism, voyeurism, and exhibitionism. He justified this neglect by arguing that such practices were statistically insignificant. It is more likely that Kinsey was either not interested in them or not interested in exploring them. He was also not particularly interested in pregnancy or sexually transmitted diseases. However, he demystified discussion of sex insofar as that was possible. Sex, to him, was just another aspect of human behavior, albeit an important part. He made Americans and the world at large aware of just how big a part human sexuality played in the life cycle of the individual and how widespread many kinds of sexual activities were.

Kinsey was determined to make the study of sex a science, a subject that could be studied in colleges much the same way that animal reproduction was, with succeeding generations of researchers adding to the knowledge base. He succeeded, at least in the long run. He had a vision of the kind of studies that still needed to be done, some of which were later done by his successors at Indiana and elsewhere, but he himself died before he could do them and the funds dried up.

Another of his significant contributions was to establish a library and to gather sources about sexuality from all over the world. He blazed a trail for future sex researchers: The library he established at Indiana University served as an example that helped many of us to persuade other university libraries to collect works from this field. Although there are now several impressive collections of this kind in the country, Kinsey's collection is still tremendously important.

In sum, Kinsey was the major factor in changing attitudes about sex in the twentieth century. His limitations and his personal foibles are appropriately overshadowed by his courage to go where others had not gone before. In spite of the vicious attacks upon him during his last few years of life, and the continuing attacks today, his data continue to be cited and used (and misused). He changed the nature of sexual studies, forced a reexamination of public attitudes toward sex, challenged the medical and psychiatric establishment to reassess its own views, influenced both the feminist movement and the gay and lesbian movement, and built a library and an institution devoted to sex research. His reputation continues to grow, and he has become one of the legends of the twentieth century. . . .

## REFERENCES

Bullough, V. L. (1994). *Science in the bedroom: a history of sex research*. New York: Basic Books.

Bullough, V. L. (1997). American physicians and sex research. *Journal of the History of Medicine, 57*, 236–253.

Corner, G. W. (1981). *The seven ages of a medical scientist*. Philadelphia: University of Pennsylvania Press.

Davis, K. B. (1929). *Factors in the sex life of twenty-two hundred women*. New York: Harper.

Dickinson, R. L., & Beam, L. (1931). *A thousand marriages*. Baltimore: Williams and Wilkins.

Dickinson, R. L., & Beam, L. (1934). *The single woman*. Baltimore: Williams and Wilkins.

Henry, G. (1941). *Sex variants: a study of homosexual patterns* (2 vols.). New York: Hoeber.

Jones, J. H. (1997, August 2 & September 1). Annals of sexology: Dr. Yes. *New Yorker*, pp. 99–113.

Jones, J. H. (1997a), *Kinsey: A Public/Private Life*. New York: Norton.

Kinsey, A., Pomeroy, W., & Martin, C. (1948). *Sexual behavior in the human male*. Philadelphia: Saunders.

Kinsey, A., Pomeroy, W., Martin, C., & Gebhard, P. (1953). *Sexual behavior in the human female*. Philadelphia: Saunders.

Pomeroy, W. B. (1972). *Dr. Kinsey and the Institute for Sex Research*. New York: Harper and Row.

Terman, L., Buttenweiser, P., Ferguson. L., Johnson, W. B., & Wilson, D. P. (1938). *Psychological factors in marital happiness*. New York: McGraw-Hill.

# Survey of Sexual Behavior of Americans

Edward O. Laumann, John H. Gagnon, Robert T. Michael, and Stuart Michaels

**M**ost people with whom we talked when we first broached the idea of a national survey of sexual behavior were skeptical that it could be done. Scientists and laypeople alike had similar reactions: "Nobody will agree to participate in such a study." "Nobody will answer questions like these, and, even if they do, they won't tell the truth." "People don't know enough about sexual practices as they relate to disease transmission or even to pleasure or physical and emotional satisfaction to be able to answer questions accurately." It would be dishonest to say that we did not share these and other concerns. But our experiences over the past seven years, rooted in extensive pilot work, focus-group discussions, and the fielding of the survey itself, resolved these doubts, fully vindicating our growing conviction that a national survey could be conducted according to high standards of scientific rigor and replicability. . . .

The society in which we live treats sex and everything related to sex in a most ambiguous and ambivalent fashion. Sex is at once highly fascinating, attractive, and, for many at certain stages in their lives, preoccupying, but it can also be frightening, disturbing, or guilt inducing. For many, sex is considered to be an extremely private matter, to be discussed only with one's closest friends or

intimates, if at all. And, certainly for most if not all of us, there are elements of our sexual lives never acknowledged to others, reserved for our own personal fantasies and self-contemplation. It is thus hardly surprising that the proposal to study sex scientifically, or any other way for that matter, elicits confounding and confusing reactions. Mass advertising, for example, unremittingly inundates the public with explicit and implicit sexual messages, eroticizing products and using sex to sell. At the same time, participants in political discourse are incredibly squeamish when handling sexual themes. . . . We suspect, in fact, that with respect to discourse on sexuality there is a major discontinuity between the sensibilities of politicians and other self-appointed guardians of the moral order and those of the public at large, who, on the whole, display few hang-ups in discussing sexual issues in appropriately structured circumstances. . . .

The fact remains that, until quite recently, scientific research on sexuality has been taboo and therefore to be avoided or at best marginalized. While there is a visible tradition of (in)famous sex research, what is, in fact, most striking is how little prior research exists on sexuality in the general population. Aside from the research on adolescence, premarital sex, and problems attendant to sex such as fertility, most research attention seems to have been directed toward those believed to be abnormal, deviant, criminal, perverted, rare, or unusual, toward sexual pathology, dysfunction, and sexually transmitted disease—the label used typically reflecting the way in which

From Laumann, Edward O., et al. 2000. *The Social Organization of Sexuality: Sexual Practices in the United States*. University of Chicago Press. Reprinted by permission.

the behavior or condition in question is to be regarded. "Normal sex" was somehow off limits, perhaps because it was considered too ordinary, trivial, and self-evident to deserve attention. To be fair, then, we cannot blame the public and the politicians entirely for the lack of sustained work on sexuality at large—it also reflects the prejudices and understandings of researchers about what are "interesting" scientific questions. There has simply been a dearth of mainstream scientific thinking and speculation about sexual issues. We have repeatedly encountered this relative lack of systematic thinking about sexuality to guide us in interpreting and understanding [our] many findings. . . .

In order to understand the results of our survey, the National Health and Social Life Survey (NHSLS), one must understand how these results were generated. To construct a questionnaire and field a large-scale survey, many research design decisions must be made. To understand the decisions made, one needs to understand the multiple purposes that underlie this research project. Research design is never just a theoretical exercise. It is a set of practical solutions to a multitude of problems and considerations that are chosen under the constraints of limited resources of money, time, and prior knowledge.

## Sample Design

The sample design for the NHSLS is the most straightforward element of our methodology because nothing about probability sampling is specific to or changes in a survey of sexual behavior. . . .

Probability sampling, that is, sampling where every member of a clearly specified population has a known probability of selection—what lay commentators often somewhat inaccurately call random sampling—is the sine qua non of modern survey research (see Kish 1965, the classic text on the subject). There is no other scientifically acceptable way to construct a representative sample and thereby to be able to generalize from the actual sample on which data are collected to the population that that sample is designed to represent. Probability sampling as practiced in survey research is a highly developed practical application of statistical theory to the problem of selecting a sample. Not only does this type of sampling avoid the problems of bias introduced by the researcher or by subject self-selection bias that come from more casual techniques, but it also allows one to quantify the variability in the estimates derived from the sample. . . .

### Sample Size

How large should the sample be? There is real confusion about the importance of sample size. In general, for the case of a probability sample, the bigger the sample, the higher the precision of its estimate.[1] This precision is usually measured in terms of the amount of sampling error accruing to the statistics calculated from the sample. The most common version of this is the statement that estimated proportions (e.g., the proportion of likely voters planning to vote for a particular candidate) in national political polls are estimated as being within ±2 or 3 percent of the overall population figure. The amount of this discrepancy is inversely related to the size of the sample: the larger the sample, the smaller the likely error in the estimates. . . .

In order to determine how large a sample size for a given study should be, one must first decide how precise the estimates to be derived need to be. To illustrate this reasoning process, let us take one of the simplest and most commonly used statistics in survey research, the proportion. . . . For example, what proportion of the population had more than five sex partners in the last year? What proportion engaged in anal intercourse? With condoms? Estimates based on our sample will differ from the true proportion in the population because of sampling error (i.e., the random fluctuations in our estimates that are due to the fact that they are based on samples rather than on complete enumerations or censuses). If one drew repeated samples using the same methodology, each would produce a slightly different estimate. If one looks at the distribution of these *estimates,* it turns out that they will be normally distributed (i.e., will follow the famous bell-shaped curve known as the Gaussian or normal distribution) and centered around the true proportion in the population. The larger the sample size, the tighter the distribution of estimates will be.

This analysis applies to an estimate of a single proportion based on the whole sample. In deciding the sample size needed for a study, one must consider the subpopulations for which one will want to construct estimates. For example, one almost always wants to know not just a single parameter for the whole population but parameters for subpopulations such as men and women, whites, blacks, and Hispanics, and younger people and older people. Furthermore, one is usually interested in the intersections of these various breakdowns of the population, for example, young black women. The size of the interval estimate for a proportion based on a subpopulation depends on the size of that group in the sample (sometimes called the *base "N,"* i.e., the number in the sample on which the estimate is based). It is actually this kind of number that one needs to consider in determining the sample size for a study.

When we were designing the national survey of sexual behavior in the United States for the NICHD [National Institute of Child Health and Human Development], we applied just these sorts of considerations to come to the conclusion that we needed a sample size of about 20,000 people. . . .

First, let us consider the cooperation or response rate. No survey of any size and complexity is able to get every sampling-designated respondent to complete an interview. Individuals can have many perfectly valid reasons why they cannot participate in the survey: being too ill, too busy, or always absent when an effort to schedule an interview is made or simply being unwilling to grant an interview. While the face-to-face or in-person survey is considerably more expensive than other techniques, such as mail or telephone

surveys, it usually gets the highest response rate. Even so, a face-to-face, household-based survey such as the General Social Survey successfully interviews, on the average, only about 75 percent of the target sample (Davis and Smith 1991). The missing 25 percent pose a serious problem for the reliability and validity of a survey: is there some systematic (i.e., nonrandom) process at work that distinguishes respondents from nonrespondents? That is, if the people who refuse to participate or who can never be reached to be interviewed differ systematically in terms of the issues being researched from those who are interviewed, then one will not have a representative sample of the population from which the sample was drawn. If the respondents and nonrespondents do not differ systematically, then the results will not be affected. Unfortunately, one usually has no (or only minimal) information about nonrespondents. It is thus a challenge to devise ways of evaluating the extent of bias in the selection of respondents and nonrespondents. Experience tells us that, in most well-studied fields in which survey research has been applied, such moderately high response rates as 75 percent do not lead to biased results. And it is difficult and expensive to push response rates much higher than that. Experience suggests that a response rate close to 90 percent may well represent a kind of upper limit.

Because of our subject matter and the widespread skepticism that survey methods would be effective, we set a completion rate of 75 percent as the survey organization's goal. In fact, we did much better than this; our final completion rate was close to 80 percent. We have extensively investigated whether there are detectable participation biases in the final sample. . . . To summarize these investigations, we have compared our sample and our results with other surveys of various sorts and have been unable to detect systematic biases of any substantive significance that would lead us to qualify our findings at least with respect to bias due to sampling.

One might well ask what the secret was of our remarkably high response rate, by far the highest of any national sexual behavior survey conducted so far. There is no secret. Working closely with the NORC [National Opinion Research Center] senior survey and field management team, we proceeded in the same way as one would in any other national area probability survey. We did not scrimp on interviewer training or on securing a highly mobilized field staff that was determined to get respondent participation in a professional and respectful manner. It was an expensive operation: the average cost of a completed interview was approximately $450.

We began with an area probability sample, which is a sample of households, that is, of addresses, not names. Rather than approach a household by knocking on the door without advance warning, we followed NORC's standard practice of sending an advance letter, hand addressed by the interviewer, about a week before the interviewer expected to visit the address. In this case, the letter was signed by the principal investigator, Robert Michael, who was identified as dean of the Irving B. Harris Graduate School of Public Policy Studies of the University of Chicago. The letter briefly explained the purpose of the survey as helping "doctors, teachers, and counselors better understand and prevent the spread of diseases like AIDS and better understand the nature and extent of harmful and of healthy sexual behavior in our country." The intent was to convince the potential respondent that this was a legitimate scientific study addressing personal and potentially sensitive topics for a socially useful purpose. AIDS was the original impetus for the research, and it certainly seemed to provide a timely justification for the study. But any general purpose approach has drawbacks. One problem that the interviewers frequently encountered was potential respondents who did not think that AIDS affected them and therefore that information about their sex lives would be of little use.

Gaining respondents' cooperation requires mastery of a broad spectrum of techniques that successful interviewers develop with experience, guidance from the research team, and careful field

supervision. This project required extensive training before entering the field. While interviewers are generally trained to be neutral toward topics covered in the interview, this was especially important when discussing sex, a topic that seems particularly likely to elicit emotionally freighted sensitivities both in the respondents and in the interviewers. Interviewers needed to be fully persuaded about the legitimacy and importance of the research. Toward this end, almost a full day of training was devoted to presentations and discussions with the principal investigators in addition to the extensive advance study materials to read and comprehend. Sample answers to frequently asked questions by skeptical respondents and brainstorming about strategies to convert reluctant respondents were part of the training exercises. A set of endorsement letters from prominent local and national notables and refusal conversion letters were also provided to interviewers. A hotline to the research office at the University of Chicago was set up to allow potential respondents to call in with their concerns. Concerns ranged from those about the legitimacy of the survey, most fearing that it was a commercial ploy to sell them something, to fears that the interviewers were interested in robbing them. Ironically, the fact that the interviewer initially did not know the name of the respondent (all he or she knew was the address) often led to behavior by the interviewer that appeared suspicious to the respondent. For example, asking neighbors for the name of the family in the selected household and/or questions about when the potential respondent was likely to be home induced worries that had to be assuaged. Another major concern was confidentiality—respondents wanted to know how they had come to be selected and how their answers were going to be kept anonymous.

### Mode of Administration: Face-to-face, Telephone, or Self-Administered

Perhaps the most fundamental design decision, one that distinguishes this study from many others, concerned how the interview itself was to be conducted. In survey research, this is usually called the *mode* of interviewing or of questionnaire administration. We chose face-to-face interviewing, the most costly mode, as the primary vehicle for data collection in the NHSLS. What follows is the reasoning behind this decision.

A number of recent sex surveys have been conducted over the telephone. . . . The principal advantage of the telephone survey is its much lower cost. Its major disadvantages are the length and complexity of a questionnaire that can be realistically administered over the telephone and problems of sampling and sample control. . . . The NHSLS, cut to its absolute minimum length, averaged about ninety minutes. Extensive field experience suggests an upper limit of about forty-five minutes for phone interviews of a cross-sectional survey of the population at large. Another disadvantage of phone surveys is that it is more difficult to find people at home by phone and, even once contact has been made, to get them to participate. . . . One further consideration in evaluating the phone as a mode of interviewing is its unknown effect on the quality of responses. Are people more likely to answer questions honestly and candidly or to dissemble on the telephone as opposed to face to face? Nobody knows for sure.

The other major mode of interviewing is through self-administered forms distributed either face to face or through the mail.[2] When the survey is conducted by mail, the questions must be self-explanatory, and much prodding is typically required to obtain an acceptable response rate. . . . This procedure has been shown to produce somewhat higher rates of reporting socially undesirable behaviors, such as engaging in criminal acts and substance abuse. We adopted the mixed-mode strategy to a limited extent by using four short, self-administered forms, totaling nine pages altogether, as part of our interview. When filled out, these forms were placed in a "privacy envelope" by the respondent so that the interviewer never saw the answers that were given to these questions. . . .

The fundamental disadvantage of self-administered forms is that the questions must be much simpler in form and language than those that an interviewer can ask. Complex skip patterns must be avoided. Even the simplest skip patterns are usually incorrectly filled out by some respondents on self-administered forms. One has much less control over whether (and therefore much less confidence that) respondents have read and understood the questions on a self-administered form. The NHSLS questionnaire (discussed below) was based on the idea that questions about sexual behavior must be framed as much as possible in the specific contexts of particular patterns and occasions. We found that it is impossible to do this using self-administered questions that are easily and fully comprehensible to people of modest educational attainments.

To summarize, we decided to use face-to-face interviewing as our primary mode of administration of the NHSLS for two principal reasons: it was most likely to yield a substantially higher response rate for a more inclusive cross section of the population at large, and it would permit more complex and detailed questions to be asked. While by far the most expensive approach, such a strategy provides a solid benchmark against which other modes of interviewing can and should be judged. The main unresolved question is whether another mode has an edge over face-to-face interviewing when highly sensitive questions likely to be upsetting or threatening to the respondent are being asked. As a partial control and test of this question, we have asked a number of sensitive questions in both formats so that an individual's responses can be systematically compared. . . . Suffice it to say at this point that there is a stunning consistency in the responses secured by the different modes of administration.

### Recruiting and Training Interviewers

We firmly believed that it was very important to recruit and train interviewers for this study very carefully. In particular, we worried that interviewers who were in any way uncomfortable with the topic of sexuality would not do a good job and would adversely affect the quality of the interview. We thus took special steps in recruiting interviewers to make it clear what the survey was about, even showing them especially sensitive sample questions. We also assured potential recruits that there would be no repercussions should they not want to work on this study; that is, refusal to participate would not affect their future employment with NORC. None of these steps seemed to hinder the recruitment effort. In general, interviewers like challenging studies. Any survey that is not run of the mill and promises to be of current public relevance is regarded as a good and exciting assignment—one to pursue enthusiastically. In short, we had plenty of interviewers eager to work on this study. Of course, a few interviewers did decline to participate because of the subject matter.

## The Questionnaire

The questionnaire itself is probably the most important element of the study design. It determines the content and quality of the information gathered for analysis. Unlike issues related to sample design, the construction of a questionnaire is driven less by technical precepts and more by the concepts and ideas motivating the research. It demands even more art than applied sampling design requires.

Before turning to the specific forms that this took in the NHSLS, we should first discuss several general problems that any survey questionnaire must address. The essence of survey research is to ask a large sample of people from a defined population the *same set of questions*. To do this in a relatively short period of time, many interviewers are needed. In our case, about 220 interviewers from all over the country collected the NHSLS data. The field period, beginning on 14 February 1992 and ending in September, was a time in which over 7,800 households were contacted (many of which turned out to be ineligible for the study) and 3,432 interviews were completed. Central to

this effort was gathering comparable information on the same attributes from each and every one of these respondents. The attributes measured by the questionnaire become the variables used in the data analysis. They range from demographic characteristics (e.g., gender, age, and race/ethnicity) to sexual experience measures (e.g., numbers of sex partners in given time periods, frequency of particular practices, and timing of various sexual events) to measures of mental states (e.g., attitudes toward premarital sex, the appeal of particular techniques like oral sex, and levels of satisfaction with particular sexual relationships).

The basic problem in writing a questionnaire thus becomes the construction of a formal protocol that combines the specific wording of questions as well as instructions and skip patterns that allow the interviewer to take all the respondents over the same material. As much as possible, each respondent should be asked the same questions in the same words and in the same order since variations in wording and order are known to affect the responses that one gets (cf. Bradburn, Sudman, et al., 1979; Groves 1989). There are two ways to approach this problem. One approach is to make the questionnaire very simple, treating each question as a separate summary statement that can be answered independently of all other questions. This is what one must do in a self-administered questionnaire. It is also almost always the practice in questionnaires that focus on attitudes.

The problem that we faced in writing the questionnaire was figuring out how best to ask people about their sex lives. There are two issues here that should be highlighted. One is conceptual, having to do with how to define sex, and the second has to do with the level or kind of language to be used in the interview.

Very early in the design of a national sexual behavior survey, in line with our goal of not reducing this research to a simple behavioral risk inventory, we faced the issue of where to draw the boundaries in defining the behavioral domain that would be encompassed by the concept of sex.

This was particularly crucial in defining sexual activity that would lead to the enumeration of a set of sex partners. There are a number of activities that commonly serve as markers for sex and the status of sex partner, especially intercourse and orgasm. While we certainly wanted to include these events and their extent in given relationships and events, we also felt that using them to define and ask about sexual activity might exclude transactions or partners that should be included. Since the common meaning and uses of the term *intercourse* involve the idea of the intromission of a penis, intercourse in that sense as a defining act would at the very least exclude a sexual relationship between two women. There are also many events that we would call sexual that may not involve orgasm on the part of either or both partners.

Another major issue is what sort of language is appropriate in asking questions about sex. It seemed obvious that one should avoid highly technical language because it is unlikely to be understood by many people. One tempting alternative is to use colloquial language and even slang since that is the only language that some people ever use in discussing sexual matters. There is even some evidence that one can improve reporting somewhat by allowing respondents to select their own preferred terminology (Blair et al., 1977; Bradburn et al., 1978; Bradburn and Sudman 1983). Slang and other forms of colloquial speech, however, are likely to be problematic in several ways. First, the use of slang can produce a tone in the interview that is counterproductive because it downplays the distinctiveness of the interviewing situation itself. An essential goal in survey interviewing, especially on sensitive topics like sex, is to create a neutral, nonjudgmental, and confiding atmosphere and to maintain a certain professional distance between the interviewer and the respondent. A key advantage that the interviewer has in initiating a topic for discussion is being a stranger or an outsider who is highly unlikely to come in contact with the respondent again. It is not intended that a longer-term bond

between the interviewer and the respondent be formed, whether as an advice giver or a counselor or as a potential sex partner.[3]

The second major shortcoming of slang is that it is highly variable across class and education levels, ages, regions, and other social groupings. It changes meanings rapidly and is often imprecise. Our solution was to seek the simplest possible language—standard English—that was neither colloquial nor highly technical. For example, we chose to use the term *oral sex* rather than the slang *blow job* and *eating pussy* or the precise technical but unfamiliar terms *fellatio* and *cunnilingus*. Whenever possible, we provided definitions when terms were first introduced in a questionnaire—that is, we tried to train our respondents to speak about sex in our terms. Many terms that seemed clear to us may not, of course, be universally understood; for example, terms like *vaginal* or *heterosexual* are not understood very well by substantial portions of the population. Coming up with simple and direct speech was quite a challenge because most of the people working on the questionnaire were highly educated, with strong inclinations toward the circumlocutions and indirections of middle-class discourse on sexual themes. Detailed reactions from field interviewers and managers and extensive pilot testing with a broad cross section of recruited subjects helped minimize these language problems.

## On Privacy, Confidentiality, and Security

Issues of respondent confidentiality are at the very heart of survey research. The willingness of respondents to report their views and experiences fully and honestly depends on the rationale offered for why the study is important and on the assurance that the information provided will be treated as confidential. We offered respondents a strong rationale for the study, our interviewers made great efforts to conduct the interview in a manner that protected respondents' privacy, and we went to great lengths to honor the assurances that the information would be treated confidentially. The subject matter of the NHSLS makes the issues of confidentiality especially salient and problematic because there are so many easily imagined ways in which information voluntarily disclosed in an interview might be useful to interested parties in civil and criminal cases involving wrongful harm, divorce proceedings, criminal behavior, or similar matters.

## NOTES

1. This proposition, however, is not true when speaking of nonrandom samples. The original Kinsey research was based on large samples. As noted earlier, surveys reported in magazines are often based on very large numbers of returned questionnaires. But, since these were not representative probability samples, there is no necessary relation between the increase in the sample size and how well the sample estimates population parameters. In general, nonprobability samples describe only the sample drawn and cannot be generalized to any larger population.

2. We ruled out the idea of a mail survey because its response rate is likely to be very much lower than any other mode of interviewing (see Bradburn, Sudman, et al., 1979).

3. Interviewers are not there to give information or to correct misinformation. But such information is often requested in the course of an interview. Interviewers are given training in how to avoid answering such questions (other than clarification of the meaning of particular questions). They are not themselves experts on the topics raised and often do not know the correct answers to questions. For this reason, and also in case emotionally freighted issues for the respondent were raised during the interview process, we provided interviewers with a list of toll-free phone numbers for a variety of professional sex- and health-related referral services (e.g., the National AIDS Hotline, an STD hotline, the National Child Abuse Hotline, a domestic violence hotline, and the phone number of a national rape and sexual assault organization able to provide local referrals).

## REFERENCES

Blair, Ellen, Seymour Sudman, Norman M. Bradburn, and Carol Stacking. 1977. "How to Ask Questions About Drinking and Sex: Response Efforts in Measuring Consumer Behavior." *Journal of Marketing Research* 14: 316–321.

Bradburn, Norman M., and Seymour Sudman. 1983. *Asking Questions: A Practical Guide to Questionnaire Design.* San Francisco: Jossey-Bass.

Bradburn, Norman M., Seymour Sudman, Ed Blair, and Carol Stacking. 1978. "Question Threat and Response Bias." *Public Opinion Quarterly* 42: 221–234.

Groves, Robert M. 1989. *Survey Errors and Survey Costs.* New York: Wiley.

Kish, Leslie. 1965. *Survey Sampling.* New York: Wiley.

## *Doing It Differently: Women's and Men's Estimates of Their Number of Lifetime Sexual Partners*

**Mindy Stombler and Dawn M. Baunach**

A recent national survey of sexual practices found that men report having more than three times as many sexual partners as women over the course of their lifetimes (David, Smith, and Marsden 2001). Theoretically, heterosexual men's and women's estimates should be the same because for each new female partner a man adds to his "lifetime account," a woman adds a new male partner to her "lifetime account." The discrepancy between women's and men's estimates remains even when researchers define *sexual partners* very specifically and account for possible sampling problems (such as undersampling female sex workers). What explains the gender gap in claims people make about numbers of sexual partners?

One possibility is that women and men misrepresent their number of lifetime sexual partners to others. Our society tends to hold a double standard regarding the sexual behavior of women and men. Men who have a great deal of sexual experience generally are not subject to shame (and in some circles their behavior is lauded), whereas women with "too many" lifetime partners are stigmatized. Attempts to give interviewers the socially approved response (called *social desirability bias*) may lead women to intentionally underreport their numbers or men to inflate theirs.

Another possibility is that people misrepresent their behaviors to themselves. If women discount partners for whom they feel little affection, such partners could slip from memory, thereby erroneously lowering their reported lifetime account. Women and men also rely on different estimation strategies. Women tend to enumerate (actually count), whereas men tend to give rough estimates (Brown and Sinclair 1999; Weiderman 1997). Weiderman (1997) notes a clear tendency for men reporting larger numbers of lifetime sexual partners to choose numbers that end in 0 or 5. Men prefer "round" numbers rather than exact counts.

The number of sexual partners that women and men report does become more similar when researchers shorten the time frame for estimation to the past year or the past five years (see the table below), indicating that both men and women estimate more accurately over a shorter period of time. In addition, the cultural meaning that we attach to our accumulated lifetime number of sexual partners carries more weight than, say, the number of partners we might have in a year. Taking the double standard into account, it might be in women's best interest to carefully consider their number of lifetime sexual partners and in men's best interest to round up.

| | MEAN NUMBER OF SEXUAL PARTNERS | | RATIO |
|---|---|---|---|
| | Women (n = 1,313) | Men (n = 1,029) | Men : Women |
| Lifetime | 5.36 | 17.00 | 3.17 |
| Last Five Years | 1.46 | 2.08 | 1.42 |
| Last Year | .89 | 1.25 | 1.40 |

*Source:* General Social Survey, 2000.

## REFERENCES

Brown, Norman R., and Robert C. Sinclair. 1999. "Estimating number of lifetime sexual partners: Men and women do it differently." *The Journal of Sex Research,* 36: 3 (292–297).

Davis, James Allan, and Tom W. Smith. 1991. *General Social Surveys, 1972–1991: Cumulative Codebook.* Chicago: National Opinion Research Center.

Weiderman, Michael. 1997. "The truth must be in here somewhere: Examining the gender discrepancy in self-reported lifetime number of partners." *The Journal of Sex Research,* 34: 4 (375–386).

# Racism and Research:

# The Case of the Tuskegee Syphilis Study

Allan M. Brandt

In 1932 the U.S. Public Health Service (USPHS) initiated an experiment in Macon County, Alabama, to determine the natural course of untreated, latent syphilis in black males. The test comprised 400 syphilitic men, as well as 200 uninfected men who served as controls. The first published report of the study appeared in 1936 with subsequent papers issued every four to six years, through the 1960s. When penicillin became widely available by the early 1950s as the preferred treatment for syphilis, the men did not receive therapy. In fact on several occasions, the USPHS actually sought to prevent treatment. Moreover, a committee at the federally operated Center for Disease Control decided in 1969 that the study should be continued. Only in 1972, when accounts of the study first appeared in the national press, did the Department of Health, Education, and Welfare halt the experiment. At that time seventy-four of the test subjects were still alive; at least twenty-eight, but perhaps more than 100 had died directly from advanced syphilitic lesions. In August 1972, HEW appointed an investigatory panel which issued a report the following year. The panel found the study to have been "ethically unjustified," and argued that penicillin should have been provided to the men.

From Brandt, Allan. 1978. "Racism and Research: The Case of the Tuskegee Syphilis Study." © The Hastings Center. Reprinted by permission. This article originally appeared in the Hastings Center Report, Vol. 8, No. 6 (1978).

This article attempts to place the Tuskegee Study in a historical context and to assess its ethical implications. Despite the media attention which the study received, the HEW *Final Report*, and the criticism expressed by several professional organizations, the experiment has been largely misunderstood. The most basic questions of *how* the study was undertaken in the first place and *why* it continued for forty years were never addressed by the HEW investigation. Moreover, the panel misconstrued the nature of the experiment, failing to consult important documents available at the National Archives which bear significantly on its ethical assessment. Only by examining the specific ways in which values are engaged in scientific research can the study be understood.

## Racism and Medical Opinion

A brief review of the prevailing scientific thought regarding race and heredity in the early twentieth century is fundamental for an understanding of the Tuskegee Study. By the turn of the century, Darwinism had provided a new rationale for American racism. Essentially primitive peoples, it was argued, could not be assimilated into a complex, white civilization. Scientists speculated that in the struggle for survival the Negro in America was doomed. Particularly prone to disease, vice, and crime, black Americans could not be helped by education or philanthropy. Social Darwinisms analyzed census data to predict the virtual extinction of the Negro in the twentieth century, for they believed the Negro race in

America was in the throes of a degenerative evolutionary process.

The medical profession supported these findings of late nineteenth- and early twentieth-century anthropologists, ethnologists, and biologists. Physicians studying the effects of emancipation on health concluded almost universally that freedom had caused the mental, moral, and physical deterioration of the black population. They substantiated this argument by citing examples in the comparative anatomy of the black and white races. As Dr. W. T. English wrote: "A careful inspection reveals the body of the negro a mass of minor defects and imperfections from the crown of the head to the soles of the feet. . . ." Cranial structures, wide nasal apertures, receding chins, projecting jaws, all typed the Negro as the lowest species in the Darwinian hierarchy.

Interest in racial differences centered on the sexual nature of blacks. The Negro, doctors explained, possessed an excessive sexual desire, which threatened the very foundations of white society. As one physician noted in the *Journal of the American Medical Association,* "The negro springs from a southern race, and as such his sexual appetite is strong; all of his environments stimulate this appetite, and as a general rule his emotional type of religion certainly does not decrease it." Doctors reported a complete lack of morality on the part of blacks:

> Virtue in the negro race is like angels' visits—few and far between. In a practice of sixteen years I have never examined a virgin negro over fourteen years of age.

A particularly ominous feature of this overzealous sexuality, doctors argued, was the black males' desire for white women. "A perversion from which most races are exempt," wrote Dr. English, "prompts the negro's inclination towards white women, whereas other races incline towards females of their own." Though English estimated the "gray matter of the negro brain" to be at least a thousand years behind that of the white races,

his genital organs were overdeveloped. As Dr. William Lee Howard noted:

> The attacks on defenseless white women are evidences of racial instincts that are about as amenable to ethical culture as is the inherent odor of the race. . . . When education will reduce the size of the negro's penis as well as bring about the sensitiveness of the terminal fibers which exist in the Caucasian, then will it also be able to prevent the African's birth-right to sexual madness and excess.

One southern medical journal proposed "Castration Instead of Lynching," as retribution for black sexual crimes. "An impressive trial by a ghost-like kuklux klan [sic] and a 'ghost' physician or surgeon to perform the operation would make it an event the 'patient' would never forget," noted the editorial.

According to these physicians, lust and immorality, unstable families, and reversion to barbaric tendencies made blacks especially prone to venereal diseases. One doctor estimated that over 50 percent of all Negroes over the age of twenty-five were syphilitic. Virtually free of disease as slaves, they were now overwhelmed by it, according to informed medical opinion. Moreover, doctors believed that treatment for venereal disease among blacks was impossible, particularly because in its latent stage the symptoms of syphilis become quiescent. As Dr. Thomas W. Murrell wrote:

> They come for treatment at the beginning and at the end. When there are visible manifestations or when harried by pain, they readily come, for as a race they are not averse to physic; but tell them not, though they look well and feel well, that they are still diseased. Here ignorance rates science a fool. . . .

Even the best educated black, according to Murrell, could not be convinced to seek treatment for syphilis. Venereal disease, according to some doctors, threatened the future of the race. The medical profession attributed the low birth rate among blacks to the high prevalence of venereal disease which caused stillbirths and miscarriages. Moreover, the high rates of syphilis were thought to lead to increased insanity and crime. One doctor writing at the turn of the century estimated that the number of insane Negroes had increased thirteen-fold since the end of the Civil War. Dr. Murrell's conclusion echoed the most informed anthropological and ethnological data:

> So the scourge sweeps among them. Those that are treated are only half cured, and the effort to assimilate a complex civilization driving their diseased minds until the results are criminal records. Perhaps here, in conjunction with tuberculosis, will be the end of the negro problem. Disease will accomplish what man cannot do.

This particular configuration of ideas formed the core of medical opinion concerning blacks, sex, and disease in the early twentieth century. Doctors generally discounted socioeconomic explanations of the state of black health, arguing that better medical care could not alter the evolutionary scheme. These assumptions provide the backdrop for examining the Tuskegee Syphilis Study.

## The Origins of the Experiment

In 1929, under a grant from the Julius Rosenwald Fund, the USPHS conducted studies in the rural South to determine the prevalence of syphilis among blacks and explore possibilities for mass treatment. The USPHS found Macon County, Alabama, in which the town of Tuskegee is located to have the highest syphilis rate of the six counties surveyed. The Rosenwald Study concluded that mass treatment could be successfully implemented among rural blacks. Although it is doubtful that the necessary funds would have been allocated even in the best economic conditions, after the economy collapsed in 1929, the findings were ignored. It is, however, ironic that the Tuskegee Study came to be based on findings of the Rosenwald Study that demonstrated the possibilities of mass treatment.

Three years later, in 1932, Dr. Taliaferro Clark, Chief of the USPHS Venereal Disease Division and author of the Rosenwald Study report, decided that conditions in Macon County merited renewed attention. Clark believed the high prevalence of syphilis offered an "unusual opportunity" for observation. From its inception, the USPHS regarded the Tuskegee Study as a classic "study in nature,"[1] rather than an experiment. As long as syphilis was so prevalent in Macon and most of the blacks went untreated throughout life, it seemed only natural to Clark that it would be valuable to observe the consequences. He described it as a "ready-made situation." Surgeon General H. S. Cumming wrote to R. R. Moton, Director of the Tuskegee Institute:

> The recent syphilis control demonstration carried out in Macon County, with the financial assistance of the Julius Rosenwald Fund, revealed the presence of an unusually high rate in this county and, what is more remarkable, the fact that 99 per cent of this group was entirely without previous treatment. This combination, together with the expected cooperation of your hospital, offers an unparalleled opportunity for carrying on this piece of scientific research which probably cannot be duplicated anywhere else in the world.

Although no formal protocol appears to have been written, several letters of Clark and Cumming suggest what the USPHS hoped to find. Clark indicated that it would be important to see how disease affected the daily lives of the men:

> The results of these studies of case records suggest the desirability of making a further study of the effect of untreated syphilis on the human economy among people now living and engaged in their daily pursuits.

It also seems that the USPHS believed the experiment might demonstrate that antisyphilitic treatment was unnecessary. As Cumming noted: "It is expected the results of this study may have a marked bearing on the treatment, or conversely the non-necessity of treatment, of cases of latent syphilis." . . .

## Selecting the Subjects

Clark sent Dr. Raymond Vonderlehr to Tuskegee in September 1932 to assemble a sample of men with latent syphilis for the experiment. The basic design of the study called for the selection of syphilitic black males between the ages of twenty-five and sixty, a thorough physical examination including x-rays, and finally, a spinal tap to determine the incidence of neuro-syphilis. They had no intention of providing any treatment for the infected men. The USPHS originally scheduled the whole experiment to last six months; it seemed to be both a simple and inexpensive project.

The task of collecting the sample, however, proved to be more difficult than the USPHS had supposed. Vonderlehr canvassed the largely illiterate, poverty-stricken population of sharecroppers and tenant farmers in search of test subjects. If his circulars requested only men over twenty-five to attend his clinics, none would appear, suspecting he was conducting draft physicals. Therefore, he was forced to test large numbers of women and men who did not fit the experiment's specifications. This involved considerable expense since the USPHS had promised the Macon County Board of Health that it would treat those who were infected, but not included in the study. Clark wrote to Vonderlehr about the situation: "It never once occurred to me that we would be called upon to treat a large part of the county as return for the privilege of making this study. . . . I am anxious to keep the expenditures for treatment down to the lowest possible point because it is the one item of expenditure in connection with the study most difficult to defend despite our knowledge of the need therefor." Vonderlehr responded: "If we could find from 100 to 200 cases . . . we would not have to do another Wassermann on useless individuals. . . ."

Significantly, the attempt to develop the sample contradicted the prediction the USPHS had made initially regarding the prevalence of the disease in Macon County. Overall rates of syphilis fell well below expectations; as opposed to the USPHS projection of 35 percent, 20 percent of those tested were actually diseased. Moreover, those who had sought and received previous treatment far exceeded the expectations of the USPHS. Clark noted in a letter to Vonderlehr:

> *I find your report of March 6th quite interesting but regret the necessity for Wassermanning [sic] . . . such a large number of individuals in order to uncover this relatively limited number of untreated cases.*

Further difficulties arose in enlisting the subjects to participate in the experiment, to be "Wassermanned," and to return for a subsequent series of examinations. Vonderlehr found that only the offer of treatment elicited the cooperation of the men. They were told they were ill and were promised free care. Offered therapy, they became willing subjects. The USPHS did not tell the men that they were participants in an experiment; on the contrary, the subjects believed they were being treated for "bad blood"—the rural South's colloquialism for syphilis. They thought they were participating in a public health demonstration similar to the one that had been conducted by the Julius Rosenwald Fund in Tuskegee several years earlier. In the end, the men were so eager for medical care that the number of defaulters in the experiment proved to be insignificant.

To preserve the subjects' interest, Vonderlehr gave most of the men mercurial ointment, a non-effective drug, while some of the younger men apparently received inadequate dosages of neo-arsphenamine. This required Vonderlehr to write frequently to Clark requesting supplies. He feared the experiment would fail if the men were not offered treatment. . . .

The readiness of the test subjects to participate of course contradicted the notion that blacks would not seek or continue therapy.

The final procedure of the experiment was to be a spinal tap to test for evidence of neuro-syphilis. The USPHS presented this purely diagnostic exam, which often entails considerable pain and complications, to the men as a "special treatment." Clark explained to Moore:

> We have not yet commenced the spinal punctures. This operation will be deferred to the last in order not to unduly disturb our field work by any adverse reports by the patients subjected to spinal puncture because of some disagreeable sensations following this procedure. These negroes are very ignorant and easily influenced by things that would be of minor significance in a more intelligent group.

The letter to the subjects announcing the spinal tap read:

> Some time ago you were given a thorough examination and since that time we hope you have gotten a great deal of treatment for bad blood. You will now be given your last chance to get a second examination. This examination is a very special one and after it is finished you will be given a special treatment if it is believed you are in a condition to stand it. . . .
>
> REMEMBER THIS IS YOUR LAST CHANCE FOR SPECIAL FREE TREATMENT. BE SURE TO MEET THE NURSE.

The HEW investigation did not uncover this crucial fact: the men participated in the study under the guise of treatment.

Despite the fact that their assumption regarding prevalence and black attitudes toward treatment had proved wrong, the USPHS decided in the summer of 1933 to continue the study. Once again, it seemed only "natural" to pursue the research since the sample already existed, and with a depressed economy, the cost of treatment appeared prohibitive—although there is no indication it was ever considered. Vonderlehr first suggested extending the study in letters to Clark and Wenger:

> At the end of this project we shall have a considerable number of cases presenting various complications of syphilis, who have received only mercury and may still be considered untreated in the modern sense of therapy. Should these cases be followed over a period of from five to ten years many interesting facts could be learned regarding the course and complications of untreated syphilis.

"As I see it," responded Wenger, "we have no further interest in these patients *until they die*." Apparently, the physicians engaged in the experiment believed that only autopsies could scientifically confirm the findings of the study.

Bringing the men to autopsy required the USPHS to devise a further series of deceptions and inducements. Wenger warned Vonderlehr that the men must not realize that they would be autopsied:

> There is one danger in the latter plan and that is if the colored population become aware that accepting free hospital care means a post-mortem, every darkey will leave Macon County and it will hurt [Dr. Eugene] Dibble's hospital.

The USPHS offered several inducements to maintain contact and to procure the continued cooperation of the men. Eunice Rivers, a black nurse, was hired to follow their health and to secure approval for autopsies. She gave the men non-effective medicines—"spring tonic" and aspirin—as well as transportation and hot meals on the days of their examinations. More important, Nurse Rivers provided continuity to the project over the entire forty-year period. By supplying "medicinals," the USPHS was able to continue to deceive the participants, who believed that they were receiving therapy from the government doctors. Deceit was integral to the study. When the test subjects complained about spinal taps one doctor wrote:

> They simply do not like spinal punctures. A few of those who were tapped are enthusiastic over the results but to most, the suggestion causes violent shaking of the head; others claim they were robbed of their procreative powers (regardless of the fact that I claim it stimulates them).

Letters to the subjects announcing an impending USPHS visit to Tuskegee explained: "[The doctor] wants to make a special examination to find out how you have been feeling and whether the treatment has improved your health." In fact, after the first six months of the study, the USPHS had furnished no treatment whatsoever.

Finally, because it proved difficult to persuade the men to come to the hospital when they became severely ill, the USPHS promised to cover their burial expenses. The Milbank Memorial Fund provided approximately $50 per man for this purpose beginning in 1935. This was a particularly strong inducement as funeral rites constituted an important component of the cultural life of rural blacks. One report of the study concluded. "Without this suasion it would, we believe, have been impossible to secure the cooperation of the group and their families."

Reports of the study's findings, which appeared regularly in the medical press beginning in 1936, consistently cited the ravages of untreated syphilis. The first paper, read at the 1936 American Medical Association annual meeting, found "that syphilis in this period [latency] tends to greatly increase the frequency of manifestations of cardiovascular disease." Only 16 percent of the subjects gave no sign of morbidity as opposed to 61 percent of the controls. Ten years later, a report noted coldly, "The fact that nearly twice as large a proportion of the syphilitic individuals as of the control group has died is a very striking one." Life expectancy, concluded the doctors, is reduced by about 20 percent.

A 1955 article found that slightly more than 30 percent of the test group autopsied had died *directly* from advanced syphilitic lesions of either the cardiovascular or the central nervous system. Another published account stated, "Review of those still living reveals that an appreciable number have late complications of syphilis which probably will result, for some at least, in contributing materially to the ultimate cause of death." In 1950, Dr. Wenger had concluded, "We now know, where we could only surmise before, that we have contributed to their ailments and shortened their lives." As black physician Vernal Cave, a member of the HEW panel, later wrote, "They proved a point, then proved a point, then proved a point."

During the forty years of the experiment the USPHS had sought on several occasions to ensure that the subjects did not receive treatment

from other sources. To this end, Vonderlehr met with groups of local black doctors in 1934, to ask their cooperation in not treating the men. Lists of subjects were distributed to Macon County physicians along with letters requesting them to refer these men back to the USPHS if they sought care. The USPHS warned the Alabama Health Department not to treat the test subjects when they took a mobile VD unit into Tuskegee in the early 1940s. In 1941, the Army drafted several subjects and told them to begin antisyphilitic treatment immediately. The USPHS supplied the draft board with a list of 256 names they desired to have excluded from treatment, and the board complied.

In spite of these efforts, by the early 1950s many of the men had secured some treatment on their own. By 1952, almost 30 percent of the test subjects had received some penicillin, although only 7.5 percent had received what could be considered adequate doses. Vonderlehr wrote to one of the participating physicians, "I hope that the availability of antibiotics has not interfered too much with this project." A report published in 1955 considered whether the treatment that some of the men had obtained had "defeated" the study. The article attempted to explain the relatively low exposure to penicillin in an age of antibiotics, suggesting as a reason: "the stoicism of these men as a group; they still regard hospitals and medicines with suspicion and prefer an occasional dose of time-honored herbs or tonics to modern drugs." The authors failed to note that the men believed they already were under the care of the government doctors and thus saw no need to seek treatment elsewhere. Any treatment which the men might have received, concluded the report, had been insufficient to compromise the experiment.

When the USPHS evaluated the status of the study in the 1960s they continued to rationalize the racial aspects of the experiment. For example, the minutes of a 1965 meeting at the Center for Disease Control recorded:

*Racial issue was mentioned briefly. Will not affect the study. Any questions can be handled by saying these people were at the point that therapy would no longer help them. They are getting better medical care than they would under any other circumstances.*

A group of physicians met again at the CDC in 1969 to decide whether or not to terminate the study. Although one doctor argued that the study should be stopped and the men treated, the consensus was to continue. Dr. J. Lawton Smith remarked, "You will never have another study like this; take advantage of it." A memo prepared by Dr. James B. Lucas, Assistant Chief of the Venereal Disease Branch, stated: "Nothing learned will prevent, find, or cure a single case of infectious syphilis or bring us closer to our basic mission of controlling venereal disease in the United States." He concluded, however, that the study should be continued "along its present lines." When the first accounts of the experiment appeared in the national press in July 1972, data were still being collected and autopsies performed.

## The HEW Final Report

HEW finally formed the Tuskegee Syphilis Study Ad Hoc Advisory Panel on August 28, 1972, in response to criticism that the press descriptions of the experiment had triggered. The panel, composed of nine members, five of them black, concentrated on two issues. First, was the study justified in 1932 and had the men given their informed consent? Second, should penicillin have been provided when it became available in the early 1950s? The panel was also charged with determining if the study should be terminated and assessing current policies regarding experimentation with human subjects. The group issued their report in June 1973.

By focusing on the issues of penicillin therapy and informed consent, the *Final Report* and the investigation betrayed a basic misunderstanding of the experiment's purposes and design. The HEW report implied that the failure to provide penicillin constituted the study's major ethical misjudgment; implicit was the assumption that

no adequate therapy existed prior to penicillin. Nonetheless medical authorities firmly believed in the efficacy of arsenotherapy for treating syphilis at the time of the experiment's inception in 1932. The panel further failed to recognize that the entire study had been predicated on nontreatment. Provision of effective medication would have violated the rationale of the experiment—to study the natural course of the disease until death. On several occasions, in fact, the USPHS had prevented the men from receiving proper treatment. Indeed, there is no evidence that the USPHS ever considered providing penicillin.

The other focus of the *Final Report*—informed consent—also served to obscure the historical facts of the experiment. In light of the deceptions and exploitations which the experiment perpetrated, it is an understatement to declare, as the *Report* did, that the experiment was "ethically unjustified," because it failed to obtain informed consent from the subjects. The *Final Report*'s statement, "Submitting voluntarily is not informed consent," indicated that the panel believed that the men had volunteered *for the experiment*. The records in the National Archives make clear that the men did not submit voluntarily to an experiment; they were told and they believed that they were getting free treatment from expert government doctors for a serious disease. The failure of the HEW *Final Report* to expose this critical fact—that the USPHS lied to the subjects—calls into question the thoroughness and credibility of their investigation.

Failure to place the study in a historical context also made it impossible for the investigation to deal with the essentially racist nature of the experiment. The panel treated the study as an aberration, well-intentioned but misguided. Moreover, concern that the *Final Report* might be viewed as a critique of human experimentation in general seems to have severely limited the scope of the inquiry. The *Final Report* is quick to remind the reader on two occasions: "The position of the Panel must not be construed to be a general repudiation of scientific research with human subjects." The *Report* assures us that a better designed experiment could have been justified:

> It is possible that a scientific study in 1932 of untreated syphilis, properly conceived with a clear protocol and conducted with suitable subjects who fully understood the implications of their involvement, might have been justified in the pre-penicillin era. This is especially true when one considers the uncertain nature of the results of treatment of late latent syphilis and the highly toxic nature of therapeutic agents then available.

This statement is questionable in view of the proven dangers of untreated syphilis known in 1932.

Since the publication of the HEW *Final Report,* a defense of the Tuskegee Study has emerged. These arguments, most dearly articulated by Dr. R. H. Kampmeier in the *Southern Medical Journal,* center on the limited knowledge of effective therapy for latent syphilis when the experiment began. Kampmeier argues that by 1950, penicillin would have been of no value for these men. Others have suggested that the men were fortunate to have been spared the highly toxic treatments of the earlier period. Moreover, even these contemporary defenses assume that the men never would have been treated anyway. As Dr. Charles Barnett of Stanford University wrote in 1974, "The lack of treatment was not contrived by the USPHS but was an established fact of which they proposed to take advantage." Several doctors who participated in the study continued to justify the experiment. Dr. J. R. Heller, who on one occasion had referred to the test subjects as the "Ethiopian population," told reporters in 1972:

> I don't see why they should be shocked or horrified. There was no racial side to this. It just happened to be in a black community. I feel this was a perfectly straightforward study, perfectly ethical, with controls. Part of our mission as physicians is to find out what happens to individuals with disease and without disease.

These apologies, as well as the HEW *Final Report,* ignore many of the essential ethical issues which the study poses, The Tuskegee Study reveals the persistence of beliefs within the medical profession about the nature of blacks, sex, and disease—beliefs that had tragic repercussions long after their alleged "scientific" bases were known to be incorrect. Most strikingly, the entire health of a community was jeopardized by leaving a communicable disease untreated. There can be little doubt that the Tuskegee researchers regarded their subjects as less than human. As a result, the ethical canons of experimenting on human subjects were completely disregarded.

The study also raises significant questions about professional self-regulation and scientific bureaucracy. Once the USPHS decided to extend the experiment in the summer of 1933, it was unlikely that the test would be halted short of the men's deaths. The experiment was widely reported for forty years without evoking any significant protest within the medical community. Nor did any bureaucratic mechanism exist within the government for the periodic reassessment of the Tuskegee experiment's ethics and scientific value. The USPHS sent physicians to Tuskegee every several years to check on the study's progress, but never subjected the morality or usefulness of the experiment to serious scrutiny. Only the press accounts of 1972 finally punctured the continued rationalizations of the USPHS and brought the study to an end. Even the HEW investigation was compromised by fear that it would be considered a threat to future human experimentation.

In retrospect the Tuskegee Study revealed more about the pathology of racism than it did about the pathology of syphilis; more about the nature of scientific inquiry than the nature of the disease process. The injustice committed by the experiment went well beyond the facts outlined in the press and the HEW *Final Report.* The degree of deception and damages have been seriously underestimated. As this history of the study suggests, the notion that science is a value-free discipline must be rejected. The need for greater vigilance in assessing the specific ways in which social values and attitudes affect professional behavior is clearly indicated.

## NOTES

1. In 1865, Claude Bernard, the famous French physiologist, outlined the distinction between a "study in nature" and experimentation. A study in nature required simple observation, an essentially passive act, while experimentation demanded intervention which altered the original condition. The Tuskegee Study was thus clearly not a study in nature. The very act of diagnosis altered the original conditions. "It is on this very possibility of acting or not acting on a body," wrote Bernard, "that the distinction will exclusively rest between sciences called sciences of observation and sciences called experimental."

## EDITOR'S NOTE

On May 16, 1997 President Bill Clinton apologized to the participants in the Tuskegee Study. He acknowledged that the U.S. government had done "something that was wrong—deeply, profoundly, and morally wrong."

# Sexuality and
# Social Theorizing

Denise Donnelly, Elisabeth O. Burgess, and Wendy Simonds[1]

## Introduction

Many of us don't think of sexuality and theorizing as two things that go together, but theories can be very useful in helping us understand sexuality. Theories are simply ways of viewing and organizing the world and of making sense of what happens. Sociologists use theories to understand, explain, predict, question, or change social behaviors and trends. Theories about sex vary dramatically across time and place, and reflect the social and moral thinking of the day.

In addition to helping us understand the history and context of sexuality, theories also provide explanations for sexual attitudes and behavior: why there are differences in how people think about sex or how people behave sexually, how societal norms and laws regarding sex arise and are enforced, and how and why change takes place. Sexuality is important in most of our lives, yet many people don't understand it, are uncomfortable talking about it, and don't know where to go to get their questions answered. Sexuality theories can provide explanations and answers, but no one theory is appropriate for addressing all questions and concerns about sexuality. Thus, we are especially interested in the ways in which sociological theories help us understand the social construction and social control of sexuality.[2]

We'll begin by reviewing what some early thinkers (called sexologists) had to say about sexuality. Then, we'll examine the utility of sociological theory for studying sex, and end with some current theories, questions, and challenges. As you'll see, theories about sexuality are constantly offered, challenged, revised, and rejected. Throughout the reading, we'll be asking "What relevance does theory have for helping us understand the social construction and control of sexuality?"

## Laying the Groundwork: The Sexologists

We're probably all familiar with Sigmund Freud, sometimes called "The Father of Modern Psychoanalysis," who felt that sexuality was a driving force in human behavior (Freud [1938] 1995), but there were other important early thinkers as well. For example, at the end of the nineteenth century (prior to most of Freud's work), Richard von Krafft-Ebing ([1871] 1965) cataloged types of sexual deviance, and later on, Havelock Ellis (1942) pondered the differences between normal and abnormal sexuality and appealed for tolerance of a wide array of sexual behaviors.[3]

Freud, the most theoretical of the early sexologists, based his observations on the people he treated, who were mainly wealthy Victorians. Freud believed that sex was a basic drive that motivated most people, and that sexuality was formed early in life. He theorized that, as toddlers, young boys fell in love with their mothers (the "Oedipus complex") and that young girls fell in love with their fathers (the "Electra complex"). He suggested that each wanted the same-sex parent out of the way. He introduced the terms "penis envy" and "castration anxiety," arguing that young girls envied boys' penises, and that young boys were anxious about keeping theirs, for they feared that their fathers would castrate them to win the rivalry over their mothers. According to Freud, in order to resolve these issues and become healthy heterosexual adults, children had to learn to identify with their same-sex parents. Freud also made many controversial statements about women's sexuality, including his supposition that women have two types of orgasms (clitoral and vaginal), with the vaginal being superior, and that recollections of sexual abuse are simply the fantasies of neurotic young women who fantasize about their fathers and crave excitement in their lives.[4]

Some of the ideas of Freud and his contemporaries may seem very outdated by today's standards, but these sexologists still influence the ways in which scholars think about sexuality and the ways therapists treat sexual problems. The work of these early sexologists resisted the social control of sexuality by challenging state and religious definitions of normal and abnormal sexual practices and contributed to the social construction of sexuality by openly discussing sexual variability, the origins of homosexuality, and the relation of women to sexuality. While their perspectives may lack the social and historical sophistication of later theories, their ideas have persisted through the years.

In the United States during the mid-twentieth century, the study of sexuality shifted from theorizing to research. Using models drawn from the biomedical sciences, researchers such as Alfred Kinsey (Kinsey, Pomeroy, and Martin 1948; Kinsey, Pomeroy, Martin, and Gebhard 1953) and William Masters and Virginia Johnson (1966; 1970), provided an empirical base for testing the ideas and theories of earlier scholars. Although they were primarily researchers, their findings have influenced the ways in which Americans think about sexuality today.[5]

## The Contributions of Twentieth-Century Sex Researchers to Sexual Theorizing

Alfred Kinsey is probably the best known of the twentieth-century sex researchers. His curiosity about human sexuality led him and his team to survey 12,000 Americans and to write *Sexual Behavior in the Human Male* (1948) and *Sexual Behavior in the Human Female* (1953). His books created a huge controversy and were even banned in some areas. This negative publicity increased the visibility of his work, exposing his ideas on sexuality to hundreds of thousands of average Americans. He challenged the conservative ways in which sexuality was constructed by documenting the range of sexual practices among Americans and discussing numerous taboo topics including female orgasm, masturbation, and homosexuality. Moreover, Kinsey argued that "normal and abnormal" and "good and bad" were labels created to control sexuality. He illustrated the wide diversity in sexual expression in the United States and noted the discrepancies between public standards for sex and private expressions of sexuality. The research of Kinsey and his peers raised questions about the theories of Freud and the early sexologists, and laid the groundwork for more recent theories such as postmodernism and queer theory, which we discuss later.[6]

From the mid-sixties to the mid-eighties, Masters and Johnson (1966; 1970) further challenged social constructions of sexuality by observing volunteers engaging in masturbation and coitus in their labs, while hooked up to monitors. Although their samples were not representative, their data and theories on human sexual response are still used by clinicians today.[7] For example, they demonstrated that the clitoris is the seat of the orgasm (in direct contradiction to Freud's earlier theorizing) and documented similarities and differences in male and female sexual response. Masters and Johnson also argued that couples' sexual problems were not caused by neuroses or disorders, but instead resulted from poor communication, marital conflict, or a lack of information. Their findings greatly influence the ways in which both scholars and the general public think about and theorize sexuality today by questioning prior theories and providing an empirical basis for many of our later theories.

## Sociological Theories and Sexuality

Our discussion of theorizing about sexuality will focus on differences between "traditional" sociological theories and those—such as feminism and postmodernism—that emerged in reaction to these perspectives. Traditional sociological theories include structural functionalism, conflict theory, symbolic interactionism, and exchange theory. Although most classical sociological theory (written in late nineteenth and early twentieth centuries) did not explicitly address issues of sexuality, those who wrote on the subject usually did so within the context of marriage, emphasizing the social control of intimate relations. For instance, Marx ([1888] 1978) and Durkheim ([1897] 1979) analyzed the regulatory practices of marriage, while Max Weber called sexual love "the greatest irrational force of life" ([1915] 1958: 343). Weber saw religious forces as seeking to diminish love's power through regulation—again, referring to marriage. Other lesser-known theorists of this era, such as Marianne Weber, Charlotte Perkins Gilman, and Anna Julia Cooper, examined marriage as a gendered form of social control over sexuality.

Structural-functionalism, or systems theory,[8] strongly influenced social thought and policy in the post–World War II years. According to structural functionalists, society was organized into parts (or structures), each of which had a specific function to fill. When each was performing its function, the system would run smoothly. In families, for example, men were supposed to be wage earners and administrators, while women were supposed to be housewives, mothers, and caretakers. The structural functionalists argued that things worked best when each person knew her or his role and stuck to it (Parsons and Bales 1955). Regarding sexuality, they argued that men were "naturally" the aggressors, and were always ready and willing to have sex, while women were "naturally" more reticent and submissive, and

had to be coaxed into sexual situations. Men continually pushed the boundaries, while women constantly enforced them. Women had "pure" natures, while men were more experienced sexually, and expected to be "worldly." According to structural functionalism, the system functioned best only when heterosexuals married, had children together, and raised them in two-parent families. From this traditional perspective, sociologists viewed homosexuals and others who did not fit into the nuclear family model as "dysfunctional" or "deviant." Examples include Albert J. Reiss's writing on street hustlers (1961), and Laud Humphreys's ethnographic exploration of sex in public restrooms (1970).

Structural-functionalism and deviance theories dominated sociology and influenced the social construction and control of sexuality into the 1970s. Social movements—for civil rights, sexual rights, women's rights, and gay/lesbian rights—led to questioning of the status quo, and eventually raised questions that led to theoretical change. What about men who weren't sexually aggressive or promiscuous, and women who were? Were they really "dysfunctional" as the theory suggested, or were they simply part of a normal range of behaviors (as Kinsey's analysis indicated)? Was the system really running smoothly, or was it simply supporting the largely white, male, middle-class status quo? Where did single mothers, people of color, gays and lesbians, and those who enjoyed nonmarital sex fit in? Because of these questions, sociological theorizing about sexuality took several turns.

Conflict theorists (Buss and Malamuth 1996; Eisenstein 1978) argued that the systems surrounding marriage, family, and sexuality were not running smoothly at all, and that the norms of the day were oppressive to many people. Anyone who fell outside a very narrow range of behaviors was penalized and often ostracized as well. At best, these nonconformists were considered deviants, and punished with social stigma. At worst, they were arrested, jailed, institutionalized, or even killed because of their sexuality. In many states, this social control extended to laws against having sex with someone of the same sex, someone of a different racial or ethnic group, or someone to whom you were not married (D'Emilio and Freedman 1997).

Conflict theorists also asked questions about sexual rights and freedoms and examined how arrangements of the day (such as marriage) were benefiting some people (men), while hurting others (women) (Eisenstein 1978). They questioned the status quo and pushed for social change, arguing that as long as sexual practices were conducted between consenting adults, they shouldn't be considered dysfunctional, abnormal, or illegal; and that current sexual arrangements were in need of examination and, potentially, elimination. Contemporary applications of conflict theory are also evident in global and political economy approaches to sexuality (Altman 2001) that examine "how economic and political transformations have shaped sexual experiences, identities, politics, and desires" (Gamson and Moon 2004: 56).[9]

While conflict theorists challenged norms, systems, and stability, they often neglected any examination of the interpersonal level. Indeed, not all people wanted to be "freed" from conformity and stability, and some stayed in sexual relationships because of love and commitment, despite elements of institutional oppression (Simmel 1964). And while the conflict theorists explained change very well, they sometimes lacked explanations for stability. On the whole, conflict theories did a better job of explaining structural and systematic sexual oppression than they did of explaining individual behaviors. In contrast, symbolic-interaction and exchange theories—which we review next—emphasized the individual level of analysis.

Symbolic interaction theorists were less concerned with social structures and institutions, and more concerned with how individuals interacted sexually (Plummer 2003). These theorists examined the meanings attached to sexual behaviors and how behavior changes based on interactions with others (Goffman 1959). Symbolic interac-

tion helps explain the social construction of sexuality—why people interpret others as they do, why misunderstandings occur, and how individuals form opinions about themselves as sexual beings. However, because the symbolic interaction theorists focus on microlevel interactions (between dyads or small groups), they tend to underestimate the role of social institutions and structures in controlling sexual behavior.

One theory that emerged from the symbolic interactionist perspective was social constructionist theory (Berger and Luckmann 1966). Proponents of this perspective argued that through interaction, individuals create shared meanings that are reinforced by norms, laws, and social institutions. Social construction theory helps us understand why people label some components of sexuality "right" and others "wrong," and why there is so much pressure to conform to sexual norms (Plummer 2003).

Another direction taken by symbolic interaction theory was sexual scripting theory (Gagnon and Simon 1973; 1987). These theories, based on an acting analogy (Goffman 1959), suggest that humans have scripts for sexual behavior that tell us who to be attracted to, how to behave sexually, and even how to feel about our sexual experiences. Sexual scripts exist on the social level, the interpersonal level, and the individual level. Cultural scripts are contained in the broader norms of a society and define what is legal or illegal, permissible or not permissible. Interpersonal scripts tell us how to act with partners and how to respond to certain situations, while individual (or intrapsychic) scripts influence how we view ourselves and evaluate our sexuality.

Taking a slightly different perspective, exchange theorists argued that sexuality was in many ways a transaction or trade. Unlike the structural functionalists who focused on maintaining stability, the exchange theorists posited that relationships are only stable so long as people feel they are getting a fair deal (Thibault and Kelly 1967). If the balance tilts too far in their partner's favor, they may withhold sex, have an affair, begin using pornography, or even withdraw from the relationship entirely in an attempt to tip the balance of power back in their own favor (Donnelly and Burgess 2006). One early exchange theorist was Waller (1938), who suggested that in a heterosexual relationship, women exchange their looks, youth, and sexuality for a man's status, money, and security. The couple bargain with each other—and the one who has the least interest in continuing the relationship has the upper hand. Much popular wisdom contained in "self-help" books (such as Robin Norwood's 1990 book, *Women Who Love Too Much*) is still based on these notions.

Critics of exchange theory point out that like conflict theory, it strips the role of love, emotion, and sacrifice from understanding romantic and sexual relationships. Exchange theorists assume that individuals act in rational, utilitarian ways (attempting to maximize rewards and minimize costs), and that they are always motivated by self-interest. Moreover, they assume that value can be attached to all aspects of a relationship, and that people actually measure the quantity and quality of sexual interactions. A final critique of this theory is that, like symbolic interaction, it pays little attention to the larger social context in which exchanges take place.

In sum, traditional sociological theories tended not to place sexuality at the center of their theorizing, but rather addressed sexuality within the context of families, couples, relationships, and deviance. While these theories may help us understand the social control and construction of sexuality, they tend to describe, rather than question, existing social arrangements. Challenges to these ways of thinking about sex often came from other disciplines and from countries outside the United States.

## Challenges and Alternatives to Traditional Sociological Theorizing

With the emerging sexual freedom of the 1970s, sexual research and theorizing became less taboo.

Although it was still marginal to most of mainstream sociology, some theorists began to place sexuality at the center of their inquiries. These new perspectives challenged sociologists' silence with regard to issues of sex and sexuality and pushed the boundaries of traditional social sciences. Although they posed a wide variety of questions, we focus on those asked by three groups: feminists, postmodernists, and queer theorists. These theorists draw on ideas and explanations from a variety of disciplines across the humanities and social sciences. While it is impossible to address all the contributions of these three theoretical perspectives, we will introduce a few of the key themes for understanding the social construction and control of sexuality. First, we'll examine the challenges posed by feminist theories.

By feminist theory, we mean a variety of (often competing) perspectives, or feminisms.[10] At the heart of these perspectives is the idea that patriarchal (male-run) societies are oppressive to women, and that women must have both freedom and choice if they are to contribute to society and become fully participatory adults. Feminists identify "the personal as political," meaning that the troubles women face as a result of sexism are not simply individual private issues (such as an abusive male partner), but rather part of a larger public problem (domestic violence) best solved through political change (Weedon 1999). Three key contributions of feminist theory include feminist discussions of the gendered nature of sexuality; heterosexuality as a form of social control; and the notion of intersectionality.

First, feminists question the ways in which sexuality has been constructed, and note that these constructions favor men in a variety of ways. At the intersection of gender and sexuality, for example, they point out that men control women's sexuality by defining it in masculine and heterosexual terms (Rich 1980). All women are presumed to be heterosexual, men are presumed to be the initiators of sex, and the sex act itself is defined in terms of male performance (Tiefer 1995). Traditionally, "sex" meant that a man inserted his penis into a woman's vagina, and other forms of sexuality were seen as "not quite sex." When the man ejaculated, "sex" was over. Moreover, feminists questioned the usefulness of the very categories we use for sex and gender, illustrating that gender itself is a social construction and that using biological essentialist arguments[11] about "women's natural place" is also a means of social control (Elshtain 1981; Epstein 1988).

Feminist theory about sexual violence, such as rape and sexual harassment, explored how violence is a tool of social control by men, and pointed out that restrictions on abortion, birth control, and sexual expression were oppressive to women and denied them choice (Brownmiller 1976; Kelly 1988; Russell 1998). Some feminists (Dworkin 1987; 1989; MacKinnon 1989) theorized that because of the power differentials between men and women, all heterosexual sex had an element of force behind it. They saw heterosexual sex and rape as existing on a continuum, with the common element being male control of female sexuality. In contrast, a coalition of sex-positive feminist theorists campaigned for the recognition of women's agency in sexuality, and began to organize groups such as dancers and prostitutes into professional unions and organizations (see Nagle 1997).

A second strand of theory emerged from the work of lesbian feminists who theorized that the institution of heterosexuality and restrictive notions about "normal" sexuality limit what counts as sexual. Adrienne Rich (1980) argued that heterosexuality is central to patriarchy and, thus, not a choice but rather a form of social control of women. Moreover, she theorized that there is not a clear distinction between lesbians and heterosexual women but instead argued women's experiences can be understood on a lesbian continuum. This continuum describes the range of women's experiences with other women, including identifying with them, bonding with them, and sharing sexual experiences.

As feminism promised to give "voice" to women, many asked "whose voice?" For example, Gayle S. Rubin (1984) argued that feminist theories of sex must account for the oppression of all sexual minorities, not just women. She posited that the state and other social institutions reinforce an erotic hierarchy that defines "normal" sexual behavior, emphasizing heterosexual, marital, monogamous, vanilla sex,[12] and demonizing other sexual practices. Not always popular with mainstream feminists, these theories drew on many of the same ideas as postmodern and queer theories that we discuss later.

Marginalized groups of women, such as women of color, poor women, women with little or no formal education, and women from non-Western nations, argued that the majority of feminist theorizing ignored their standpoints and assumed that white middle class women's experiences represented everyone (hooks 1981; 1984; Lorde 1984; Moraga and Anzaldúa 1983; Mohanty, Russo, and Torres 1991). For example, African American feminist theorists (sometimes called "womanists") argued that while white women may suffer because of their gender status, the color of their skin gives them privilege to be protected sexually and depicted as virginal or pure. In contrast, black women have been seen as sexually accessible and their history has been one of rape and exploitation by both white and black men (Davis 1983; Hill Collins 2004; hooks 1984; Wyatt 1997).

Initially, critics of white feminist thought focused primarily on racial differences, arguing that the standpoint of African American women was ignored in feminist theorizing, but eventually sociologists such as Patricia Hill Collins (1991; 2004) pointed out that intersectionality—the ways in which a *variety* of statuses and characteristics intersect—needed to be taken into account when thinking about female sexuality. Intersectionality theory contended that not only does one's race affect the ways sexuality is experienced and perceived, but so does one's class, age, ability, sexual orientation, and nation. Essentially, there can be no single perspective on black women's sexuality, poor women's sexuality, or the sexuality of women in non-Western nations.

While feminists critiqued the gender order, postmodernists questioned the usefulness of grand theories to explain the social world and wondered whether it was meaningful to search for universal, all-encompassing truths about society.[13] They argued that there was no "right" way of seeing or describing the world, and that no two people shared the same reality. They posited that ideas about right and wrong and good and bad had no inherent meanings, but were simply social constructions that had emerged from modern society. They questioned the concept of modernity itself, and wondered if modern society, with its emphasis on science, positivism, and progress, was really beneficial to humanity.

Moreover, the postmodernists recommended that we not take the social order at face value, but instead work to deconstruct existing structures (such as language, law, or sexuality) by examining their various components (such as history, discourse, and interaction). In contrast to earlier theorists, postmodernists emphasized that the power to control and construct sexuality does not lie with one central entity (such as government), but is constantly negotiated by a variety of ways of talking or thinking about a topic, coming from a variety of groups (such as religion, activist movements, or the legal system).

Applying these ideas to sexuality, postmodern theorists argued that sexuality has been produced in socially and culturally specific ways. Michel Foucault (1978) examined the construction of sexuality by analyzing a variety of discourses and sexual practices. In the *History of Sexuality,* he rejected "the repressive hypothesis" that blamed the Victorians for the shame and guilt that people in many Western societies felt about sexuality, and instead examined the influence of the scientific discourse on these constructions of sexuality. He rejected the dominant belief that modern industrial societies, such as the Victorians, "ushered in an age of increased sexual repression" (49). Rather, he argued that multiple sources of power

(for instance, religion, medicine, education, law) dominated our understandings of sexuality and sought to manipulate sexual attitudes and practices according to their own (often very profitable) agendas. He went on to say that scientific disciplines, such as psychology and medicine, control sexualities, but while they inform us, they also dominate us. Individuals internalize the norms set by scientists, and monitor their own behavior in an effort to conform to the scientific constructions of sexuality.

Postmodern perspectives have appealed to a wide variety of scholars, and some feminist postmodernists felt that feminism and postmodernism could be complementary. For example, both groups questioned concepts such as objectivity, universality, and reason, claiming that what is considered objective in a given culture at a particular time in history reflects the interests of those in power. Moreover, both feminists and postmodernists have worked to avoid the tendency to construct theories based on the experiences of privileged groups of women (Flax 1990; Nicholson 1990).

Although the deconstruction of modern ideas about sexuality is a useful theoretical exercise, critics maintain that it is more of an intellectual exercise than an explanatory framework. They note that while postmodernism critiques and deconstructs modernity and objectivity, it suggests no alternatives and provides no agenda for social change. While postmodern perspectives have gained some acceptance in sociology (Mirchandani 2005), the larger contribution of this perspective has likely been its influence on queer theory.

Drawing on the energy of the gay and AIDS movements of the 1980s and the academic perspectives of postmodernism, feminism, and gay and lesbian studies, queer theorists (Seidman 1996; Stein and Plummer 1996; Sullivan 2003) challenged the identities seen as normative and natural in our culture, insisting they were instead, "arbitrary, unstable, and exclusionary" (Seidman 1996: 11).[14] For example, queer theorists argued that sexuality is structured as a "binary opposition" (meaning that our culture has constructed heterosexuality and homosexuality as opposites), with heterosexuality given the label of good and homosexuality the label of bad or immoral. These labels are then used for social control, as evidenced by the passage of laws against same-sex marriage and adoption. Additionally, focusing on some identities and not others silences or excludes the other experiences. Part of the queer theorists' project is to continually question and deconstruct current beliefs about sexual, gender, and sex identities. By questioning binary social categories such as male or female, masculine or feminine, and heterosexual or homosexual, queer theorists demonstrate how these sexual categories and identities are actually fluid and not necessarily natural. Rather, they argue that current categorizations of sexuality, gender, and sex are tied to power, and that some institutions and groups have more power to define what is sexually acceptable than others do. Queer theorists believe transsexuals, the intersexed, and those immersed in drag culture are boundary crossers, challenging rigid categories of sex, gender, and sexual identity (c.f. Butler 1990; Currah 2001).

When they speak of "queering" sexuality, queer theorists are not talking about making everyone gay or lesbian. Instead, they are questioning (or "queering") existing sexual arrangements that privilege heterosexual, coupled, monogamous adults. This queering reveals the biases our ideas are constructed on, and demonstrates how certain groups benefit from current constructions of sexual identities. In general, queer theorists argue that it is important to separate the sexual behaviors that people participate in from the moral judgments of those with power in a society.

For all its contributions to sexuality theory, queer theory does not appeal to everyone and some scholars question its usefulness for sociological inquiry. For instance, Namaste (1996) and Green (2002) question the explanatory power of queer theory and argue that their focus on the abstract ignores the social realities of real sexual

beings. Furthermore, Gamson and Moon (2004) debate the value of queer theory for addressing traditional sociological problems such as systems of oppression, and suggest that contributions of social theories, such as intersectionality and political economy, are more useful for sociological research.

Feminists, postmodernists, and queer theorists challenge the boundaries on which much of sexual theorizing takes place, while also building on some aspects of earlier theories and ideas. The common thread among the theories presented in this section is that current arrangements are socially constructed and must be questioned. They posit that old ideas about sexuality may not be useful or relevant, and indeed act as a form of social control—silencing, excluding, and even harming groups of people.

As you might imagine, these theories are confusing to many students, and aren't necessarily that popular with "mainstream" society. Most people take existing structures (institutions, norms, and conventions) surrounding sexuality at face value, and rarely think to question (or deconstruct) them. People assume that existing patterns of behavior exist because that is what works best for society, and that to go against these rules, beliefs, and norms would be to invite chaos. Even when people violate these widely held prohibitions, such as the ones against premarital sex or adultery, they often still feel that as a whole, these rules benefit society. Moreover, these norms are upheld and enforced by social institutions such as religion, family, education, the legal system, and the economy. To question them feels—and may well be—dangerous.

### Can Theory Help Us Understand Sexuality?

So, back to our original question—can social theories help us understand sexuality? We think so. Although each of the theories presented here is based on a different assumption and operates at a different level, they all provide us with ways of understanding the sexual behavior of individuals and groups, the development of social norms, and the underpinnings of social policies regarding sexuality. These theories invite us to ask interesting questions and to push the boundaries of our knowledge. The most liberatory theories, in our view, are the ones that reject notions of normalcy, resist moralizing, and question biological or essentialistic views of sexual behavior. Rather than providing answers, such theories delight in muddying the waters and raising new questions. Will we ever have a theory that explains all aspects of sexuality? Probably not. But by theorizing about sex, we broaden our understandings of ourselves and of the world around us. And, it very well may be that the most interesting parts of sexuality are in the questions, not in the answers!

## NOTES

1. The authors would like to thank Mindy Stombler and Dawn M. Baunach, who were integral in defining the structure and content of this article and providing valuable perspectives on theory and sexuality and essential editorial advice. In addition, we acknowledge the assistance of Elisabeth Sheff, Elroi Waszkiewicz, Elizabeth Cavalier, Amy Palder, Robert Adelman, and Chet Meeks, who read earlier versions of this article and participated in numerous theoretical debates on sexuality.

2. By social construction we mean the process by which people create ideas, meanings, categories, and values through interaction. Social control refers to a system of rewards and punishments intended to control or influence others' behavior.

3. The field of sexology and the scientific study of sexuality emerged in the late nineteenth century. Sigmund Freud, Richard von Krafft-Ebing, and others were integral to the development of sex research and our understanding of sexuality. These scholars and others in the late nineteenth and early twentieth centuries were trained in the medical profession and, thus, approached issues of sexuality using a medical model. The ideas of these early sex researchers contributed to our theoretical understanding of sexuality in more ways than we can discuss in this essay. For more on the history of sex research see Bullough (1995), and for the

classic writings of this era see Bland and Doan (1998) and Barreca (1995).

4. The latter was a revision to his earlier theory. Initially, he believed that sexual abuse was real, but because of his colleagues' disbelief, Freud revised his theory and marked his patient's recollections of child sexual abuse down to "fantasy."

5. For more on Kinsey, see Reading 7 in this book. For additional information on sex research during the twentieth century see Ericksen (1999) and Bullough (1995).

6. During the first half of the twentieth century several other researchers conducted sex surveys of specific populations, including Katherine Bement Davis's research on female sexuality (1929) and Evelyn Hooker's work on male sexuality (1956; 1957; 1958), and expanded our understanding of sexual variation and the social construction of sexual deviance.

7. Teifer (1995) provides a thorough critique of Masters and Johnson's sample and their findings about the human sexual response cycle.

8. For many scholars, the distinction between these theories is the level of analysis. Structural-functionalism addresses the structural or societal level of analysis and systems theory explores the microlevel issues of families and individuals.

9. See also Reading 53 in this book.

10. Additionally, the term *feminism* covers theory, belief systems, and political action. Many times it is difficult to distinguish among them because the boundaries between academic perspectives and practices are not always clear.

11. Biological essentialism argues that women are naturally different from men because of their ability to become mothers, and that these differences mean that women are better suited to certain roles and men to others.

12. *Vanilla sex* refers to standard heterosexual practices, and excludes such variations as sadomasochism (BDSM), fetish, and kink.

13. The ideas of postmodernism and poststructuralism are intertwined and trace their roots to French philosophers such as Foucault (1978) and Lyotard (1984). As with feminism, there are many variations and conflicting perspectives on these theories. In this article we are focusing on postmodernism.

14. Like the feminists and postmodernists, queer theorists do not always agree or even acknowledge the same texts. In addition to Foucault, discussed previously,

Judith Butler (1990; 1993) and Eve Sedgewick (1990) produced works widely acknowledged to be central to queer theory. In this article we emphasize sociological interpretations of queer theory.

## REFERENCES

Altman, Dennis. 2001. *Global Sex*. Chicago: University of Chicago Press.

Barreca, Regina, ed. 1995. *Desire and Imagination: Classic Essays in Sexuality*. New York: Meridian.

Berger, Peter L. and Thomas Luckmann. 1966. *The Social Construction of Reality*. New York: Doubleday.

Bland, Lucy and Laura Doan, ed. 1998. *Sexuality Uncensored: The Documents of Sexual Science*. Chicago: University of Chicago Press.

Brownmiller, Susan. 1976. *Against Our Will: Men, Women, and Rape*. New York: Bantam Books.

Bullough, Vern. 1995. *Science in the Bedroom: A History of Sex Research*. New York: Basic Books.

Buss, David M. and Neil Malamuth. 1996. *Sex, Power, Conflict: Evolutionary and Feminist Perspectives*. London: Oxford University Press.

Butler, Judith. 1990. *Gender Trouble: Feminism and the Subversion of Identity*. New York: Routledge.

Butler, Judith. 1993. *Bodies that Matter: On the Discursive Limits of "Sex."* New York: Routledge.

Currah, Paisley. 2001. "Queer Theory, Lesbian and Gay Rights, and Transsexual Marriages." In *Sexual Identities, Queer Politics* (pp. 178–199), edited by Mark Blasius. Princeton, NJ: Princeton University Press.

Davis, Angela Y. 1983. *Women, Race, & Class*. New York: Vintage Books.

Davis, Katherine Bement. 1929. *Factors in the Sex Life of Twenty-Two Hundred Women*. New York: Harper.

D'Emilio, John D. and Estelle B. Freedman. 1997. *Intimate Matters, Second Edition*. Chicago: University of Chicago Press.

Donnelly, Denise and Elisabeth O. Burgess. 2006. Involuntary Celibacy in Long-Term Heterosexual Relationships. Unpublished Manuscript.

Durkheim, Emile. [1897] 1979. *Suicide: A Study in Sociology*. New York: Free Press.

Dworkin, Andrea. 1987. *Intercourse*. New York: Free Press.

Dworkin, Andrea. 1989. *Pornography: Men Possessing Women*. New York: Dutton.

Eisenstein, Zillah. 1978. "Developing a Theory of Capitalist Patriarchy and Socialist Feminism." *Capitalist Patriarchy and the Case for Socialist Feminism*, by Zillah Eisenstein. New York: Monthly Review Press.

Ellis, Havelock. 1942. *Studies in the Psychology of Sex, Volumes 1 and 2*. New York: Random House.

Elshtain, Jean Bethke. 1981. *Public Man, Private Woman*. Princeton, NJ: Princeton University Press.

Epstein, Cynthia Fuchs. 1988. *Deceptive Distinctions: Sex, Gender, and the Social Order*. New Haven, CT: Yale University Press and Russell Sage Foundation.

Ericksen, Julia A. 1999. *Kiss and Tell: Surveying Sex in the Twentieth Century*. Cambridge, MA: Harvard University Press.

Flax, Jane. 1990. "Postmodern and Gender Relations in Feminist Theory." In *Feminism/Postmodernism* (pp. 39–63), edited by Linda J. Nicholson. New York: Routledge.

Foucault, Michel. 1978. *The History of Sexuality: An Introduction, Volume 1*. New York: Vintage Books.

Freud, Sigmund. [1938] 1995. *The Basic Writings of Sigmund Freud*. Translated by A. A. Brill. New York: Modern Library.

Gagnon, John H. and William Simon. 1973. *Sexual Conduct: The Social Sources of Human Sexuality*. Chicago: Aldine.

Gagnon, John H. and William Simon. 1987. "The Sexual Scripting of Oral Genital Contacts." *Archives of Sexual Behavior* 16:1–25.

Gamson, Joshua and Dawne Moon. 2004. "The Sociology of Sexualities: Queer and Beyond." *Annual Review of Sociology* 30:47–64.

Goffman, Irving. 1959. *The Presentation of Self in Everyday Life*. New York: Anchor.

Green, Adam Isaiah. 2002. "Gay but not Queer: Toward a Post-Queer Study of Sexuality." *Theory and Society* 31:521–545.

Hill Collins, Patricia. 1991. *Black Feminist Thought: Knowledge, Consciousness, and the Politics of Empowerment*. New York: Routledge.

Hill Collins, Patricia. 2004. *Black Sexual Politics: African Americans, Gender, and the New Racism*. New York: Routledge.

Hooker, Evelyn. 1956. "A Preliminary Analysis of Group Behavior of Homosexuals." *Journal of Psychology* 42:217–225.

Hooker, Evelyn. 1957. "The Adjustment of the Male Overt Homosexual." *Journal of Projective Techniques* 21:18–31.

Hooker, Evelyn. 1958. "Male Homosexuality in the Rorschach." *Journal of Projective Techniques* 23:278–281.

hooks, bell. 1981. *Ain't I a Woman: Black Women and Feminism.* Boston: South End Press.

hooks, bell. 1984. *Feminist Theory: From Margin to Center.* Boston: South End Press.

Humphreys, Laud. 1970. *Tearoom Trade: Impersonal Sex in Public Places.* Chicago: Aldine.

Kelly, Liz. 1988. *Surviving Sexual Violence.* Boston: Cambridge University Press.

Kinsey, Alfred C., Wardell B. Pomeroy, and Clyde E. Martin. 1948. *Sexual Behavior and the Human Male.* Philadelphia: Saunders.

Kinsey, Alfred C., Wardell B. Pomeroy, Clyde E. Martin, and Paul H. Gebhard. 1953. *Sexual Behavior and the Human Female.* Philadelphia: Saunders.

Krafft-Ebing, Richard von. [1871] 1965. *Psychopathia Sexualis: A Medico-Forensic Study.* Translated by Harry E. Wedeck. New York: Putnam.

Lacan, Jacques. [1972–1973] 1998. *On Feminine Sexuality: The Limits of Love and Knowledge.* Translated by Bruce Fink. New York: Norton.

Lyotard, Jacques. [1979] 1984. *The Postmodern Condition: A Report on Knowledge.* Translated by G. Bennington and B. Massumi. Minneapolis: University of Minnesota Press.

Lorde, Audre. 1984. *Sister Outsider: Essays and Speeches.* Trumansburg, NY: Crossing Press.

MacKinnon, Catherine A. 1989. *Toward a Feminist Theory of the State.* Cambridge, MA: Harvard University Press.

Marx, Karl. [1888] 1978. "Manifesto of the Communist Party." In *The Marx-Engels Reader, Second Edition* (pp. 469–500), edited by Robert C. Tucker. New York: W.W. Norton.

Masters, William H. and Virginia Johnson. 1966. *Human Sexual Response.* Boston: Little, Brown.

Masters, William H. and Virginia Johnson. 1970. *Human Sexual Inadequacy.* Boston: Little, Brown.

Mirchandani, Rekha. 2005. "Postmodernism and Sociology: From Epistemological to Empirical." *Sociological Theory* 23:86–115.

Mohanty, Chandra Talpade, Ann Russo, and Lourdes Torres. 1991. *Third World Women and the Politics of Feminism.* Bloomington: Indiana University Press.

Moraga, Cheríe and Gloria Anzaldúa. 1983. *This Bridge Called My Back: Writings by Radical Women of Color.* New York: Kitchen Table/Women of Color Press.

Nagle, Jill, ed. 1997. *Whores and Other Feminists.* London: Routledge.

Namaste, Ki. 1996. "'Tragic Misreadings': Queer Theory's Erasure of Transgender Subjectivity." In *Queer Studies: A Lesbian, Gay, Bisexual, and Transgender Anthology* (pp. 183–203), edited by Brett Beemyn and Mickey Eliason. New York: New York University Press.

Nicholson, Linda J., ed. 1990. *Feminism/Postmodernism.* New York: Routledge.

Norwood, Robin. 1990. *Women Who Love Too Much.* New York: Pocket Books.

Parsons, Talcott and Robert F. Bales. 1955. *Family, Socialization and the Interaction Process.* Glencoe, IL: Free Press.

Plummer, Ken. 2003. "Queers, Bodies, and Postmodern Sexualities: A Note on Revisiting the 'Sexual' in Symbolic Interaction." *Qualitative Sociology* 26:515–530.

Reiss, Albert J., Jr. 1961. "The Social Integration of Queers and Peers." *Social Problems* 9:102–120.

Rich, Adrienne. 1980. "Compulsory Heterosexuality and Lesbian Existence." *Signs: Journal of Women in Culture and Society* 5:631–660.

Rubin, Gayle S. 1984. "Thinking Sex: Notes for a Radical Theory of the Politics of Sexuality." In *Pleasure and Danger: Exploring Female Sexuality* (pp. 267–319), edited by Carole S. Vance. New York: Routledge.

Russell, Diana. 1998. *Dangerous Relationships: Pornography, Misogyny, and Rape.* Thousand Oaks, CA: Sage.

Sedgwick, Eve. 1990. *Epistemology of the Closet.* Berkeley: University of California Press.

Seidman, Steven, ed. 1996. *Queer Theory/Sociology.* Malden, MA: Blackwell Publishers.

Simmel, Georg. 1964. *Conflict and the Web of Group Affiliations.* New York: Free Press.

Stein, Arlene and Ken Plummer. 1996. "'I Can't Even Think Straight': 'Queer' Theory and the Missing Sexual Revolution in Sociology." In *Queer Theory/Sociology* (pp. 129–144), edited by Steven Seidman. Oxford, UK: Blackwell.

Sullivan, Nikki. 2003. *A Critical Introduction to Queer Theory*. New York: New York University Press.

Thibaut, J. and H. Kelley. 1967. *The Social Psychology of Groups*. New York: John Wiley & Sons.

Tiefer, Leonore. 1995. *Sex Is Not a Natural Act and Other Essays*. Boulder, CO: Westview Press.

Waller, Willard Walter. 1938. *The Family: A Dynamic Interpretation*. New York: Dryden.

Weber, Max. [1915] 1958. "Religious Rejections of the World and Their Directions." In *From Max Weber: Essays in Sociology* (pp. 323–362), edited by H. H. Gerth and C. Wright Mills. New York: Oxford University Press.

Weedon, Chris. 1999. *Feminism, Theory, and the Politics of Difference*. Oxford, UK: Blackwell.

Wyatt, Gail Elizabeth. 1997. *Stolen Women: Reclaiming Our Sexuality, Taking Back Our Lives*. New York: John Wiley and Sons.

# (How) Does the Sexual Orientation of Parents Matter?

**Judith Stacey and Timothy J. Biblarz**

Today, gay marriage is taking on an air of inevitability" (*Detroit News*, "Middle Ground Emerges for Gay Couples," October 4, 1999, p. A9). So observed a U.S. newspaper from the heartland in September 1999, reporting that one-third of those surveyed in an *NBC News/Wall Street Journal* poll endorsed the legalization of same-sex marriage, while 65 percent predicted such legislation would take place in the new century (Price 1999). During the waning months of the last millennium, France enacted national registered partnerships, Denmark extended child custody rights to same-sex couples, and the state supreme courts in Vermont and in Ontario, Canada ruled that same-sex couples were entitled to full and equal family rights. Most dramatically, in September 2000 the Netherlands became the first nation to realize the inevitable when the Dutch parliament voted overwhelmingly to grant same-sex couples full and equal rights to marriage. As the new millennium begins, struggles by nonheterosexuals to secure equal recognition and rights for the new family relationships they are now creating represent some of the most dramatic and fiercely contested developments in Western family patterns.

It is not surprising, therefore, that social science research on lesbigay family issues has become a rapid growth industry that incites passionate divi-sions. For the consequences of such research are by no means "academic," but bear on marriage and family policies that encode Western culture's most profoundly held convictions about gender, sexuality, and parenthood. As advocates and opponents square off in state and federal courts and legislatures, in the electoral arena, and in culture wars over efforts to extend to nonheterosexuals equal rights to marriage, child custody, adoption, foster care, and fertility services, they heatedly debate the implications of a youthful body of research, conducted primarily by psychologists, that investigates if and how the sexual orientation of parents affects children.

This body of research, almost uniformly, reports findings of no notable differences between children reared by heterosexual parents and those reared by lesbian and gay parents, and that it finds lesbigay parents to be as competent and effective as heterosexual parents. Lawyers and activists struggling to defend child custody and adoption petitions by lesbians and gay men, or to attain same-gender marriage rights and to defeat preemptive referenda against such rights (e.g., the victorious Knight Initiative on the 2000 ballot in California) have drawn on this research with considerable success (cf. Wald 1999). Although progress is uneven, this strategy has promoted a gradual liberalizing trend in judicial and policy decisions. However, backlash campaigns against gay family rights have begun to challenge the validity of the research.

In 1997, the *University of Illinois Law Review Journal* published an article by Wardle (1997), a Brigham Young University law professor, that

From Stacey, Judith and Timothy J. Biblarz. 2001. "(How) Does the Sexual Orientation of Parents Matter?" *American Sociological Review* 66: 159–183. Reprinted by permission of the American Sociological Association and the authors.

impugned the motives, methods, and merits of social science research on lesbian and gay parenting. Wardle charged the legal profession and social scientists with an ideological bias favoring gay rights that has compromised most research in this field and the liberal judicial and policy decisions it has informed. . . . The following year, Wardle drafted new state regulations in Utah that restrict adoption and foster care placements to households in which all adults are related by blood or marriage. Florida, Arkansas, and Mississippi also have imposed restrictions on adoption and/or foster care, and such bills have been introduced in the legislatures of 10 additional states (Leslie Cooper, ACLU gay family rights staff attorney, personal communication, September 27, 2000). In March 2000, a paper presented at a "Revitalizing Marriage" conference at Brigham Young University assailed the quality of studies that had been cited to support the efficacy of lesbigay parenting (Lerner and Nagai 2000). Characterizing the research methods as "dismal," Lerner and Nagai claimed that "the methods used in these studies were sufficiently flawed so that these studies could not and should not be used in legislative forums or legal cases to buttress any arguments on the nature of homosexual vs. heterosexual parenting" (p. 3). Shortly afterward, Gallagher (2000), of the Institute for American Values, broadcast Lerner and Nagai's argument in her nationally syndicated *New York Post* column in order to undermine the use of "the science card" by advocates of gay marriage and gay "normalization."

We depart sharply from the views of Wardle and Gallagher on the merits and morals of lesbigay parenthood as well as on their analysis of the child development research. We agree, however, that ideological pressures constrain intellectual development in this field. In our view, it is the pervasiveness of social prejudice and institutionalized discrimination against lesbians and gay men that exerts a powerful policing effect on the basic terms of psychological research and public discourse on the significance of parental sexual orientation. The field suffers less from the overt

ideological convictions of scholars than from the unfortunate intellectual consequences that follow from the implicit hetero-normative presumption governing the terms of the discourse—that healthy child development depends upon parenting by a married heterosexual couple. . . .

We take stock of this body of psychological research from a sociological perspective. We analyze the impact that this hetero-normative presumption exacts on predominant research strategies, analyses, and representations of findings. After assessing the basic premises and arguments in the debate, we discuss how the social fact of heterosexism has operated to constrain the research populations, concepts, and designs employed in the studies to date. . . .

### The Case Against Lesbian and Gay Parenthood

Wardle (1997) is correct that contemporary scholarship on the effects of parental sexual orientation on children's development is rarely critical of lesbigay parenthood. Few respectable scholars today oppose such parenting. However, a few psychologists subscribe to the view that homosexuality represents either a sin or a mental illness and continue to publish alarmist works on the putative ill effects of gay parenting (e.g., Cameron and Cameron 1996; Cameron, Cameron, and Landess 1996). Even though the American Psychological Association expelled Paul Cameron, and the American Sociological Association denounced him for willfully misrepresenting research (Cantor 1994; Herek 1998, 2000), his publications continue to be cited in amicus briefs, court decisions, and policy hearings. For example, the chair of the Arkansas Child Welfare Agency Review Board repeatedly cited publications by Cameron's group in her testimony at policy hearings, which, incidentally, led to restricting foster child placements to heterosexual parents (Woodruff 1998).

Likewise, Wardle (1997) draws explicitly on Cameron's work to build his case against gay parent rights. Research demonstrates, Wardle maintains, that gay parents subject children to disproportionate risks; that children of gay parents are more apt to suffer confusion over their gender and sexual identities and are more likely to become homosexuals themselves; that homosexual parents are more sexually promiscuous than are heterosexual parents and are more likely to molest their own children; that children are at greater risk of losing a homosexual parent to AIDS, substance abuse, or suicide, and to suffer greater risks of depression and other emotional difficulties; that homosexual couples are more unstable and likely to separate; and that the social stigma and embarrassment of having a homosexual parent unfairly ostracizes children and hinders their relationships with peers. Judges have cited Wardle's article to justify transferring child custody from lesbian to heterosexual parents.

Wardle (1997), like other opponents of homosexual parenthood, also relies on a controversial literature that decries the putative risks of "fatherlessness" in general. . . . Wardle, like Blankenhorn, extrapolates (inappropriately) from research on single-mother families to portray children of lesbians as more vulnerable to everything from delinquency, substance abuse, violence, and crime, to teen pregnancy, school dropout, suicide, and even poverty.[1] In short, the few scholars who are opposed to parenting by lesbians and gay men provide academic support for the convictions of many judges, journalists, politicians, and citizens that the sexual orientation of parents matters greatly to children, and that lesbigay parents represent a danger to their children and to society. . . .

## The Case for Lesbian and Gay Parenthood

Perhaps the most consequential impact that heterosexism exerts on the research on lesbigay parenting lies where it is least apparent—in the far more responsible literature that is largely sympathetic to its subject. It is easy to expose the ways in which the prejudicial views of those directly hostile to lesbigay parenting distort their research (Herek 1998). Moreover, because anti-gay scholars regard homosexuality itself as a form of pathology, they tautologically interpret any evidence that children may be more likely to engage in homoerotic behavior as evidence of harm. Less obvious, however, are the ways in which heterosexism also hampers research and analysis among those who explicitly support lesbigay parenthood. With rare exceptions, even the most sympathetic proceed from a highly defensive posture that accepts heterosexual parenting as the gold standard and investigates whether lesbigay parents and their children are inferior.

This sort of hierarchical model implies that *differences* indicate *deficits* (Baumrind 1995). Instead of investigating whether (and how) differences in adult sexual orientation might lead to meaningful differences in how individuals parent and how their children develop, the predominant research designs place the burden of proof on lesbigay parents to demonstrate that they are not less successful or less worthy than heterosexual parents. Too often scholars seem to presume that this approach precludes acknowledging almost any differences in parenting or in child outcomes. . . .

Rethinking the "no differences" doctrine, some scholars urge social scientists to look for potentially beneficial effects children might derive from such distinctive aspects of lesbigay parenting as the more egalitarian relationships these parents appear to practice (Patterson 1995; also see Dunne 2000). More radically, a few scholars (Kitzinger 1987, 1989; Kitzinger and Coyle 1995) propose abandoning comparative research on lesbian and heterosexual parenting altogether and supplanting it with research that asks "why and how are lesbian parents oppressed and how can we change that?" (Clarke 2000:28, paraphrasing Kitzinger 1994:501). While we perceive potential advantages from these agendas, we advocate an alternative strategy that moves beyond hetero-normativity without forfeiting the fruitful potential of comparative research. . . . Moreover, while we welcome research attuned to potential strengths as well as vulnerabilities of lesbigay parenting, we believe that knowledge and policy will be best served when scholars feel free to replace a hierarchical model, which assigns "grades" to parents and children according to their sexual identities, with a more genuinely pluralist approach to family diversity. . . .

### Problems with Concepts, Categories, and Samples

The social effects of heterosexism constrain the character of research conducted on lesbigay parenting in ways more profound than those deriving from the ideological stakes of researchers. First, as most researchers recognize, because so many individuals legitimately fear the social consequences of adopting a gay identity, and because few national surveys have included questions about sexual orientation, it is impossible to gather reliable data on such basic demographic questions as how many lesbians and gay men there are in the general population, how many have children, or how many children reside (or have substantial contact) with lesbian or gay parents. Curiously, those who are hostile to gay parenting tend to minimize the incidence of same-sex orientation, while sympathetic scholars typically report improbably high numerical estimates. Both camps thus implicitly presume that the rarer the incidence, the less legitimate would be lesbigay claims to rights. One could imagine an alternative political logic, however, in which a low figure might undermine grounds for viewing lesbigay parenting as a meaningful social threat. . . .

Across the ideological spectrum, scholars, journalists and activists appear to presume that the normalization of lesbigay sexuality should steadily increase the ranks of children with lesbian and gay parents. In contrast, we believe that normalization is more likely to reduce the proportion of such children. Most contemporary lesbian and gay parents procreated within heterosexual marriages that many had entered hoping to es-

cape the social and emotional consequences of homophobia. As homosexuality becomes more legitimate, far fewer people with homoerotic desires should feel compelled to enter heterosexual marriages, and thus fewer should become parents in this manner.

On the other hand, with normalization, intentional parenting by self-identified lesbians and gay men should continue to increase, but it is unlikely to do so sufficiently to compensate for the decline in the current ranks of formerly married lesbian and gay parents. . . .

A second fundamental problem in sampling involves the ambiguity, fluidity, and complexity of definitions of sexual orientation. . . . What defines a parent (or adult child) as lesbian, gay, bisexual, or heterosexual? Are these behavioral, social, emotional, or political categories? Historical scholarship has established that sexual identities are modern categories whose definitions vary greatly not only across cultures, spaces, and time, but even among and within individuals (Katz 1995; Seidman 1997). . . . What about bisexual, transsexual, or transgendered parents, not to mention those who re-partner with individuals of the same or different genders? Sexual desires, acts, meanings, and identities are not expressed in fixed or predictable packages.

Third, visible lesbigay parenthood is such a recent phenomenon that most studies are necessarily of the children of a transitional generation of self-identified lesbians and gay men who became parents in the context of heterosexual marriages or relationships that dissolved before or after they assumed a gay identity. These unique historical conditions make it impossible to fully distinguish the impact of a parent's sexual orientation on a child from the impact of such factors as divorce, re-mating, the secrecy of the closet, the process of coming out, or the social consequences of stigma. . . .

Fourth, because researchers lack reliable data on the number and location of lesbigay parents with children in the general population, there are no studies of child development based on random, representative samples of such families. Most studies rely on small-scale, snowball and convenience samples drawn primarily from personal and community networks or agencies. Most research to date has been conducted on white lesbian mothers who are comparatively educated, mature, and reside in relatively progressive urban centers, most often in California or the Northeastern states. . . .

In short, the indirect effects of heterosexism have placed inordinate constraints on most research on the effects of gay parenthood. We believe, however, that the time may now be propitious to begin to reformulate the basic terms of the enterprise.

## Reconsidering the Psychological Findings

Toward this end, we examined the findings of 21 psychological studies . . . published between 1981 and 1998 that we considered best equipped to address sociological questions about how parental sexual orientation matters to children. . . . To evaluate this claim, we selected for examination only studies that: (1) include a sample of gay or lesbian parents and children and a comparison group of heterosexual parents and children; (2) assess differences between groups in terms of statistical significance; and (3) include findings directly relevant to children's development. The studies we discuss compare relatively advantaged lesbian parents (18 studies) and gay male parents (3 studies) with a roughly matched sample of heterosexual parents. . . . The authors of all 21 studies almost uniformly claim to find no differences in measures of parenting or child outcomes. In contrast, our careful scrutiny of the findings they report suggests that on some dimensions—particularly those related to gender and sexuality—the sexual orientations of these parents matter somewhat more for their children than the researchers claimed. . . .

Our discussion here emphasizes findings from six studies we consider to be best designed to iso-

late whatever unique effects parents' sexual orientations might have on children. . . .

## Children's Gender Preferences and Behavior

. . . The findings demonstrate that, as we would expect, on some measures meaningful differences have been observed in predictable directions. For example, lesbian mothers in R. Green et al. (1986) reported that their children, especially daughters, more frequently dress, play, and behave in ways that do not conform to sex-typed cultural norms. Likewise, daughters of lesbian mothers reported greater interest in activities associated with both "masculine" and "feminine" qualities and that involve the participation of both sexes, whereas daughters of heterosexual mothers report significantly greater interest in traditionally feminine, same-sex activities (also see Hotvedt and Mandel 1982). Similarly, daughters with lesbian mothers reported higher aspirations to nontraditional gender occupations (Steckel 1987). . . .

Sons appear to respond in more complex ways to parental sexual orientations. On some measures, like aggressiveness and play preferences, the sons of lesbian mothers behave in less traditionally masculine ways than those raised by heterosexual single mothers. However, on other measures, such as occupational goals and sartorial styles, they also exhibit greater gender conformity, than do daughters with lesbian mothers (but they are not more conforming than sons with heterosexual mothers) (R. Green et al., 1986; Steckel 1987). Such evidence, albeit limited, implies that lesbian parenting may free daughters and sons from a broad but uneven range of traditional gender prescriptions. It also suggests that the sexual orientation of mothers interacts with the gender of children in complex ways to influence gender preferences and behavior. Such findings raise provocative questions about how children assimilate gender culture and interests—questions that the propensity to downplay differences deters scholars from exploring. . . .

### Children's Sexual Preferences and Behavior

. . . A significantly greater proportion of young adult children raised by lesbian mothers than those raised by heterosexual mothers in the Tasker and Golombok (1997) sample reported having had a homoerotic relationship (6 of the 25 young adults raised by lesbian mothers—24 percent—compared with 0 of the 20 raised by heterosexual mothers). The young adults reared by lesbian mothers were also significantly more likely to report having thought they might experience homoerotic attraction or relationships. The difference in their openness to this possibility is striking: 64 percent (14 of 22) of the young adults raised by lesbian mothers report having considered same-sex relationships (in the past, now, or in the future), compared with only 17 percent (3 of 18) of those raised by heterosexual mothers. Of course, the fact that 17 percent of those raised by heterosexual mothers also report some openness to same-sex relationships, while 36 percent of those raised by lesbians do not, underscores the important reality that parental influence on children's sexual desires is neither direct nor easily predictable.

If these young adults raised by lesbian mothers were more open to a broad range of sexual possibilities, they were not statistically more likely to self-identify as sexual, lesbian, or gay. . . . The only other comparative study we found that explores intergenerational resemblance in sexual orientation is Bailey et al. (1995) on gay fathers and their adult sons. This study also provides evidence of a moderate degree of parent-to-child transmission of sexual orientation.

Tasker and Golombok (1997) also report some fascinating findings on the number of sexual partners children report having had between puberty and young adulthood. Relative to their counterparts with heterosexual parents, the adolescent and young adult girls raised by lesbian mothers appear to have been more sexually adventurous and less chaste, whereas the sons of lesbians evince the opposite pattern—somewhat less sexually ad-

venturous and more chaste. . . . In other words, once again, children (especially girls) raised by lesbians appear to depart from traditional gender-based norms, while children raised by heterosexual mothers appear to conform to them. . . .

### Children's Mental Health

Given historic social prejudices against homosexuality, the major issue deliberated by judges and policy makers has been whether children of lesbian and gay parents suffer higher levels of emotional and psychological harm. Unsurprisingly, therefore, children's "self-esteem and psychological well-being" is a heavily researched domain. . . . [T]hese studies find no significant differences between children of lesbian mothers and children of heterosexual mothers in anxiety, depression, self-esteem, and numerous other measures of social and psychological adjustment. The roughly equivalent level of psychological well-being between the two groups holds true in studies that test children directly, rely on parents' reports, and solicit evaluations from teachers. The few significant differences found actually tend to favor children with lesbian mothers.[2] Given some credible evidence that children with gay and lesbian parents, especially adolescent children, face homophobic teasing and ridicule that many find difficult to manage (Tasker and Golombok 1997; also see Bozett 1989:148; Mitchell 1998), the children in these studies seem to exhibit impressive psychological strength.

Similarly, across studies, no relationship has been found between parental sexual orientation and measures of children's cognitive ability. Moreover, to our knowledge no theories predict such a link. Thus far, no work has compared children's *long-term* achievements in education, occupation, income, and other domains of life. . . .

### Parental Behavior toward Children's Gender and Sexual Development

The scattered pieces of evidence cited above imply that lesbigay parenting may be associated with a broadening of children's gender and sexual repertoires. Is this because lesbigay parents actively attempt to achieve these outcomes in their children? Data . . . provide little evidence that parents' own sexual orientations correlate strongly with their preferences concerning their children's gender or sexual orientations. For example, the lesbian mothers in Kweskin and Cook (1982) were no more likely than heterosexual mothers to assign masculine and feminine qualities to an "ideal" boy or girl, respectively, on the well-known Bem Sex Role Inventory. However, mothers did tend to desire gender-traits in children that resembled those they saw in themselves, and the lesbians saw themselves as less feminine-typed than did the heterosexual mothers. This suggests that a mother's own gender identity may mediate the connection between maternal sexual orientation and maternal gender preferences for her children.

Also, in some studies lesbian mothers were less concerned than heterosexual mothers that their children engage in gender "apropriate" activities and play, a plausible difference most researchers curiously downplay. . . .

### Parenting Practices: Developmental Orientations and Parenting Skills

. . . First, studies find the nonbiological lesbian co-mothers (referred to as lesbian "social mothers" in Brewaeys et al. [1997]) to be more skilled at parenting and more involved with the children than are stepfathers. Second, lesbian partners in the two-parent families studied enjoy a greater level of synchronicity in parenting than do heterosexual partners. . . .

These findings imply that lesbian co-parents may enjoy greater parental compatibility and achieve particularly high quality parenting skills, which may help explain the striking findings on parent/child relationships. . . .

We believe (as do Brewaeys et al. 1997; Chan, Brooks, et al. 1998; Chan, Raboy, and Patterson 1998; Flaks et al. 1995) that the comparative strengths these lesbian co-parents seem to exhibit have more to do with gender than with sexual orientation. Female gender is probably the source of the positive signs for parenting skill, participation in child rearing, and synchronicity in child evaluations. . . .

In our view, these patterns reflect something more than a simple "gender effect," however, because sexual orientation is the key "exogenous variable" that brings together parents of same or different genders. Thus, sexual orientation and gender should be viewed as *interacting* to create new kinds of family structures and processes—such as an egalitarian division of child care—that have fascinating consequences for all of the relationships in the triad and for child development (also see Dunne 1999, 2000; Patterson 1995). Some of the evidence suggests that two women co-parenting may create a synergistic pattern that brings more egalitarian, compatible, shared parenting and time spent with children, greater understanding of children, and closeness and communication between parents and children. The genesis of this pattern cannot be understood on the basis of either sexual orientation or gender alone. Such findings raise fruitful comparative questions for future research about family dynamics among two parents of the same or different gender who do or do not share similar attitudes, values, and behaviors.

We know little thus far about how the sexual orientation of nonresidential fathers may be related to their relationships with their children . . . (and even less about that for custodial fathers). The Bigner and Jacobsen studies (1989, 1992) find similarity in parenting and in father/child relations among heterosexual nonresidential fathers and gay nonresidential fathers. Bozett (1987a, 1987b, 1989) found that in a small sample of children with gay fathers, most children had very positive feelings toward their fathers, but they also worried that peers and others might presume that they, too, had a gay sexual orientation (Bozett did not include a control group of children with heterosexual fathers).

### Parental Fitness

. . . [E]vidence to date provides no support for those, like Wardle (1997), who claim that lesbian mothers suffer greater levels of psychological difficulties (depression, low self-esteem) than do heterosexual mothers. On the contrary, the few differences observed in the studies suggest that these lesbian mothers actually display somewhat higher levels of positive psychological resources.

Research on a more diverse population, however, might alter the findings of difference and similarity. . . . For example, the ethnographic evidence suggests that people of color with homoerotic practices often value racial solidarity over sexual solidarity. . . . If, as it appears, racial/ethnic solidarities deter disproportionate numbers of people of color from coming out, they might suffer greater psychological and social costs from living in the closet or, conversely, might benefit from less concern over their sexual identities than do white gay parents. We also do not know whether lesbian couples of different racial/ethnic and social class contexts would display the same patterns of egalitarian, compatible co-parenting reported among the white lesbian couples.

### No Differences of Social Concern

[Our] findings . . . show that the "no differences" claim does receive strong empirical support in crucial domains. Lesbigay parents and their children in these studies display no differences from heterosexual counterparts in psychological well-being or cognitive functioning. Scores for lesbigay parenting styles and levels of investment in children are at least as "high" as those for heterosexual parents. Levels of closeness and quality of parent/child relationships do not seem to differentiate directly by parental sexual orientation, but indirectly, by way of parental gender. Because every relevant study to date shows that parental sexual orientation per se has no measurable effect on the quality of parent–child relationships or on children's mental health or social adjustment, there is no evidentiary basis for con-

sidering parental sexual orientation in decisions about children's "best interest." In fact, given that children with lesbigay parents probably contend with a degree of social stigma, these similarities in child outcomes suggest the presence of compensatory processes in lesbigay-parent families. Exploring how these families help children cope with stigma might prove helpful to all kinds of families. . . .

Less research has explored questions for which there are stronger theoretical grounds for expecting differences—children's gender and sexual behavior and preferences. . . . Children with lesbigay parents appear less traditionally gender-typed and more likely to be open to homoerotic relationships. In addition, evidence suggests that parental gender and sexual identities interact to create distinctive family processes whose consequences for children have yet to be studied.

### *How the Sexual Orientation of Parents Matters*

We have identified conceptual, methodological, and theoretical limitations in the psychological research on the effects of parental sexual orientation and have challenged the predominant claim that the sexual orientation of parents does not matter at all. We argued instead that despite the limitations, there is suggestive evidence and good reason to believe that contemporary children and young adults with lesbian or gay parents do differ in modest and interesting ways from children with heterosexual parents. Most of these differences, however, are not causal, but are indirect effects of parental gender or selection effects associated with heterosexist social conditions under which lesbigay-parent families currently live.

First, our analysis of the psychological research indicates that the effects of parental gender trump those of sexual orientation (Brewaeys et al. 1997; Chan, Brooks, et al. 1998; Chan, Raboy, and Patterson 1998; Flaks et al. 1995). A diverse array of gender theories (social learning theory, psychoanalytic theory, materialist, symbolic interactionist) would predict that children with two same-gender parents, and particularly with co-mother parents, should develop in less gender-stereotypical ways than would children with two heterosexual parents. . . . Children who derive their principal source of love, discipline, protection, and identification from women living independent of male domestic authority or influence should develop less stereotypical symbolic, emotional, practical, and behavioral gender repertoires. Indeed, it is the claim that the gender mix of parents has no effect on their children's gender behavior, interests, or development that cries out for sociological explanation. . . .

Second, because homosexuality is stigmatized, selection effects may yield correlations between parental sexual orientation and child development that do not derive from sexual orientation itself. For example, social constraints on access to marriage and parenting make lesbian parents likely to be older, urban, educated, and self-aware—factors that foster several positive developmental consequences for their children. On the other hand, denied access to marriage, lesbian co-parent relationships are likely to experience dissolution rates somewhat higher than those among heterosexual co-parents (Bell and Weinberg 1978; Weeks, Heaphy, and Donovan forthcoming, chap. 5). Not only do same-sex couples lack the institutional pressures and support for commitment that marriage provides, but qualitative studies suggest that they tend to embrace comparatively high standards of emotional intimacy and satisfaction (Dunne 2000; Sullivan 1996; Weeks et al. forthcoming). . . .

Most of the differences in the findings discussed above cannot be considered deficits from any legitimate public policy perspective. They either favor the children with lesbigay parents, are secondary effects of social prejudice, or represent "just a difference" of the sort democratic societies should respect and protect. Apart from differences associated with parental gender, most of the presently observable differences in child "out-

comes" should wither away under conditions of full equality and respect for sexual diversity. . . . Because lesbigay parents do not enjoy the same rights, respect, and recognition as heterosexual parents, their children contend with the burdens of vicarious social stigma. Likewise, some of the particular strengths and sensitivities such children appear to display, such as a greater capacity to express feelings or more empathy for social diversity (Mitchell 1998; O'Connell 1994), are probably artifacts of marginality and may be destined for the historical dustbin of a democratic, sexually pluralist society.

Even in a utopian society, however, one difference seems less likely to disappear: The sexual orientation of parents appears to have a unique (although not large) effect on children in the politically sensitive domain of sexuality. The evidence, while scanty and underanalyzed, hints that parental sexual orientation is positively associated with the possibility that children will be more likely to attain a similar orientation—and theory and common sense also support such a view. Children raised by lesbian co-parents should and do seem to grow up more open to homoerotic relationships. This may be partly due to genetic and family socialization processes, but what sociologists refer to as "contextual effects" not yet investigated by psychologists may also be important. Because lesbigay parents are disproportionately more likely to inhabit diverse, cosmopolitan cities—Los Angeles, New York and San Francisco—and progressive university communities—such as Santa Cruz, Santa Rosa, Madison, and Ann Arbor (Black, Gates, et al. 2000)—their children grow up in comparatively tolerant school, neighborhood, and social contexts, which foster less hostility to homoeroticism. Sociology could make a valuable contribution to this field by researching processes that interact at the individual, family, and community level to undergird parent–child links between gender and sexuality.

Under homophobic conditions, lesbigay parents are apt to be more sensitive to issues surrounding their children's sexual development and to injuries that children with nonconforming desires may experience, more open to discussing sexuality with their children, and more affirming of their questions about sexuality (Mitchell 1998; Tasker and Golombok 1997). It therefore seems likely, although this has yet to be studied, that their children will grow up better informed about and more comfortable with sexual desires and practices. However, the tantalizing gender contrast in the level of sexual activity reported for sons versus daughters of lesbians raises more complicated questions about the relationship between gender and sexuality. . . .

We recognize the political dangers of pointing out that recent studies indicate that a higher proportion of children with lesbigay parents are themselves apt to engage in homosexual activity. In a homophobic world, anti-gay forces deploy such results to deny parents custody of their own children and to fuel backlash movements opposed to gay rights. Nonetheless, we believe that denying this probability capitulates to heterosexist ideology and is apt to prove counterproductive in the long run. It is neither intellectually honest nor politically wise to base a claim for justice on grounds that may prove falsifiable empirically. Moreover, the case for granting equal rights to nonheterosexual parents should not require finding their children to be identical to those reared by heterosexuals. Nor should it require finding that such children do not encounter distinctive challenges or risks, especially when these derive from social prejudice. . . . Inevitably, children share most of the social privileges and injuries associated with their parents' social status. If social prejudice were grounds for restricting rights to parent, a limited pool of adults would qualify.

One can readily turn the tables on a logic that seeks to protect children from the harmful effects of heterosexist stigma directed against their parents. Granting legal rights and respect to gay parents and their children should lessen the stigma that they now suffer and might reduce the high rates of depression and suicide reported among closeted gay youth living with heterosexual par-

ents. Thus, while we disagree with those who claim that there are no differences between the children of heterosexual parents and children of lesbigay parents, we unequivocally endorse their conclusion that social science research provides no grounds for taking sexual orientation into account in the political distribution of family rights and responsibilities. . . .

## NOTES

1. The extrapolation is "inappropriate" because lesbigay-parent families have never been a comparison group in the family structure literature on which these authors rely (cf. Downey and Powell 1993; McLanahan 1985).

2. Patterson (1994) found that children ages 4 to 9 with lesbian mothers expressed more stress than did those with heterosexual mothers, but at the same time they also reported a greater sense of overall well-being. Patterson speculates that children from lesbian-mother families may be more willing to express their feelings—positive and negative—but also that the children may actually experience more social stress at the same time that they gain confidence from their ability to cope with it.

## REFERENCES

Bailey, J. Michael, David Bobrow, Marilyn Wolfe, and Sarah Mikach. 1995. "Sexual Orientation of Adult Sons of Gay Fathers." *Developmental Psychology* 31:124–29.

Baumrind, Diana. 1995. "Commentary on Sexual Orientation: Research and Social Policy Implications." *Developmental Psychology* 31:130–36.

Bell, Alan P. and Martin S. Weinberg. 1978. *Homosexualities: A Study of Diversity among Men and Women.* New York: Simon and Schuster.

Bigner, Jerry J. and R. Brooke Jacobsen. 1989. "Parenting Behaviors of Homosexual and Heterosexual Fathers." *Journal of Homosexuality* 19:73–86.

———. 1992. "Adult Responses to Child Behavior and Attitudes toward Fathering: Gay and Nongay Fathers." *Journal of Homosexuality* 23:99–112.

Black, Dan A., Gary Gates, Seth Sanders, and Lowell Taylor. 2000. "Demographics of the Gay and Lesbian Population in the United States: Evidence from Available Systematic Data Sources." *Demography* 37:139–54.

Bozett, Frederick W. 1987a. "Children of Gay Fathers." Pp. 39–57 in *Gay and Lesbian Parents,* edited by F. W. Bozett. New York: Praeger.

———. 1987b. "Gay Fathers." Pp. 3–22 in *Gay and Lesbian Parents,* edited by F. W. Bozett. New York: Praeger.

———. 1989. "Gay Fathers: A Review of the Literature." Pp. 137–62 in *Homosexuality and the Family,* edited by F. W. Bozett. New York: Haworth Press.

Brewaeys, A., I. Ponjaert, E. V. Van Hall, and S. Golombok. 1997. "Donor Insemination: Child Development and Family Functioning in Lesbian Mother Families." *Human Reproduction* 12:1349–59.

Cameron, Paul and Kirk Cameron. 1996. "Homosexual Parents." *Adolescence* 31:757–76.

Cameron, Paul, Kirk Cameron, and Thomas Landess. 1996. "Errors by the American Psychiatric Association, the American Psychological Association, and the National Educational Association in Representing Homosexuality in Amicus Briefs about Amendment 2 to the U.S. Supreme Court." *Psychological Reports* 79:383–404.

Cantor, David. 1994. *The Religious Right: The Assault on Tolerance and Pluralism in America.* New York: Anti-Defamation League.

Chan, Raymond W., Risa C. Brooks, Barbara Raboy, and Charlotte J. Patterson. 1998. "Division of Labor among Lesbian and Heterosexual Parents: Associations with Children's Adjustment." *Journal of Family Psychology* 12:402–19.

Chan, Raymond W., Barbara Raboy, and Charlotte J. Patterson. 1998. "Psychosocial Adjustment among Children Conceived Via Donor Insemination by Lesbian and Heterosexual Mothers." *Child Development* 69:443–57.

Clarke, Victoria. 2000. "Sameness and Difference in Research on Lesbian Parenting." Working paper, Women's Studies Research Group, Department of Social Sciences, Loughborough University, Leicestershire, UK.

Downey, Douglas B. and Brian Powell. 1993. "Do Children in Single-Parent Households Fare Better Living with Same-Sex Parents?" *Journal of Marriage and the Family* 55:55–72.

Dunne, Gillian A. 1999. "What Difference Does 'Difference' Make? Lesbian Experience of Work and Family Life." Pp. 189–221 in *Relating Intimacies,* edited by J. Seymour and P. Bagguley. New York: St. Martin's.

———. 2000. "Opting into Motherhood: Lesbians Blurring the Boundaries and Transforming the Meaning of Parenthood and Kinship." *Gender and Society* 14:11–35.

Flaks, David K., Ilda Ficher, Frank Masterpasqua, and Gregory Joseph. 1995. "Lesbians Choosing Motherhood: A Comparative Study of Lesbian and Heterosexual Parents and Their Children." *Developmental Psychology* 31:105–14.

Gallagher, Maggie. 2000. "The Gay-Parenting Science." *New York Post.* March 30, p. 3.

Green, Richard, Jane Barclay Mandel, Mary E. Hotvedt, James Gray and Laurel Smith. 1986. "Lesbian Mothers and Their Children: A Comparison with Solo Parent Heterosexual Mothers and Their Children." *Archives of Sexual Behavior* 15:167–84.

Herek, Gregory M. 1998. "Bad Science in the Service of Stigma: A Critique of the Cameron Group's Survey Studies," Pp. 223–55 in *Stigma and Sexual Orientation: Understanding Prejudice against Lesbians, Gay Men, and Bisexuals,* edited by G. M. Herek. Thousand Oaks, CA: Sage.

———. 2000. "Paul Cameron Fact Sheet" (Copyright 1997–2000 by G. M. Herek). Retrieved (http://psychology.ucdavis.edu/rainbow/html/facts_cameron_sheet.html).

Hoeffer, Beverly. 1981. "Children's Acquisition of Sex-Role Behavior in Lesbian-Mother Families." *American Journal of Orthopsychiatry* 51:536–44.

Hotvedt, Mary E. and Jane Barclay Mandel. 1982. "Children of Lesbian Mothers." Pp. 275–91 in *Homosexuality, Social, Psychological, and Biological Issues,* edited by W. Paul. Beverly Hills, CA: Sage.

Katz, Jonathan Ned. 1995. *The Invention of Heterosexuality.* New York: Dutton.

Kitzinger, Celia. 1987. *The Social Construction of Lesbianism.* London, England: Sage.

———. 1989. "Liberal Humanism as an Ideology of Social Control: The Regulation of Lesbian Identities." Pp. 82–98 in *Texts of Identity,* edited by J. Shotter and K. Gergen. London, England: Sage.

———. 1994. "Should Psychologists Study Sex Differences? Editor's Introduction: Sex Differences Research: Feminist Perspectives." *Feminism and Psychology* 4:501–506.

Kitzinger, Celia and Adrian Coyle. 1995. "Lesbian and Gay Couples: Speaking of Difference." *The Psychologist* 8:64–69.

Kweskin, Sally L. and Alicia S. Cook. 1982. "Heterosexual and Homosexual Mothers' Self-Described Sex-Role Behavior and Ideal Sex-Role Behavior in Children." *Sex Roles* 8:967–75.

Lerner, Robert and Althea K. Nagai. 2000. "Out of Nothing Comes Nothing: Homosexual and Heterosexual Marriage Not Shown to be Equivalent for Raising Children." Paper presented at the Revitalizing the Institution of Marriage for the 21st Century conference, Brigham Young University, March, Provo, UT.

McLanahan, Sara S. 1985. "Family Structure and the Reproduction of Poverty." *American Journal of Sociology* 90:873–901.

Mitchell, Valory. 1998. "The Birds, the Bees . . . and the Sperm Banks: How Lesbian Mothers Talk with Their Children about Sex and Reproduction." *American Journal of Orthopsychiatry* 68:400–409.

O'Connell, Ann. 1994. "Voices from the Heart: The Developmental Impact of a Mother's Lesbianism on Her Adolescent Children." *Smith College Studies in Social Work* 63:281–99.

Patterson, Charlotte J. 1994. "Children of the Lesbian Baby Boom: Behavioral Adjustment, Self-Concepts and Sex Role Identity." Pp. 156–75 in *Lesbian and Gay Psychology: Theory, Research, and Clinical Applications*, edited by B. Green and G. M. Herek. Thousand Oaks, CA: Sage.

———. 1995. "Families of the Lesbian Baby Boom: Parents' Division of Labor and Children's Adjustment." *Developmental Psychology* 31:115–23.

Price, Deb. 1999. "Middle Ground Emerges for Gay Couples." *Detroit News*, October 4.

Seidman, Steven. 1997. *Difference Troubles: Queering Social Theory and Sexual Politics*. New York: Cambridge University Press.

Steckel, Alisa. 1987. "Psychosocial Development of Children of Lesbian Mothers." Pp. 75–85 in *Gay and Lesbian Parents*, edited by F. W. Bozett. New York: Praeger.

Sullivan, Maureen. 1996. "Rozzie and Harriet?: Gender and Family Patterns of Lesbian Coparents." *Gender and Society* 10:747–67.

Tasker, Fiona L. and Susan Golombok. 1997. *Growing Up in a Lesbian Family*. New York: Guilford.

Wald, Michael S. 1999. "Same-Sex Couples: Marriage, Families, and Children, An Analysis of Proposition 22, The Knight Initiative." Stanford Institute for Research on Women and Gender, Stanford University, Stanford, CA.

Wardle, Lynn D. 1997. "The Potential Impact of Homosexual Parenting on Children." *University of Illinois Law Review* 1997:833–919.

Weeks, Jeffrey, Brian Heaphy, and Catherine Donovan. Forthcoming. *Families of Choice and Other Life Experiments: The Intimate Lives of Non-Heterosexuals*. Cambridge, England: Cambridge University Press.

Woodruff, Robin. 1998, Testimony re: "Subcommittee Meeting to Accept Empirical Data and Expert Testimony Concerning Homosexual Foster Parents." Hearing at the Office of the Attorney General, September 9, 1998. Little Rock, AK. Available from the authors on request.

## *Funding Sex Research*

**Mindy Stombler**

Getting funding for sex research has always been challenging. In the 1950s, Alfred Kinsey and his colleagues lost funding from the Rockefeller Foundation following publication of their controversial report on women's sexuality. More recently, the National Health and Social Life Survey (1994)—the closest we've come to a national sexual "census"—lost federal funding following opposition by Representative William Dannemeyer and Senator Jesse Helms. The researchers were forced to dramatically reduce the scope of their project, after conservatives in Congress lobbied against funding sexuality research.[1] Other grant-seekers report that they find themselves in a very defensive position. According to James Wagoner, president of Advocates for Youth, "For

20 years it was about health and science, and now we have a political ideological approach. . . . Never have we experienced a climate of intimidation and censorship as we have today."[2]

In 2003, there was a strong Congressional effort to block the funding of four National Institutes of Health (NIH) grants. These grants had already been judged as outstanding by peer scientists in an independent review process. The grants called for research on sexual risk taking and its link to sexual arousal, the sexual habits of older men, Asian sex workers, and sexual and gender identity among American Indians. Conservative politicians argued that the government had no business funding such inappropriate topics. Efforts to block the funding were narrowly defeated by two votes in the House.[3] Although some scientists will continue to apply for large government grants, others are becoming increasingly discouraged and are turning to alternative sources. Aside from the federal government, sources for funding sex research include a handful of private institutions and universities, whose resource pools are often more limited.[4] This lack of available funding reduces the scope of the sex-related research projects that do get carried out. For example, a recent extensive sex survey conducted by the CDC (see the box in Chapter 6 entitled "Sexual Behavior and Health") had to cap its sample at age 44, ignoring the sexual behaviors of the older generation that brought us the sexual liberation movement. [5]

As conservative politicians fight to reduce funding available for sex research, researchers feel pressured to focus on topics for which funding is available, such as pharmaceutical research. This trend necessarily narrows the breadth of researchable topics to those connected to potential profit making. Geoffrey Miller, a psychologist, claims that his research on kissing (why couples kiss less the longer they remain involved) is valuable for society but not necessarily fundable: "kissing could help couples rejuvenate a marriage and reduce divorce rates . . . but it's less threatening and more profitable to study orgasms."[6] In fact, Mark Schwartz of the Masters and Johnson clinic claims that the survival of the study of sexual behavior is a result of the HIV/AIDS epidemic and the development of Viagra "because the pharmaceutical companies suddenly became very interested in the fact that they can make huge amounts of money off the genitals."[7] Leonore Tiefer, a sex researcher interviewed in

Chapter 5, cautions sex researchers about their over reliance on pharmaceutical money, insisting it contributes to a medical model of sexuality where all sexual problems can be fixed with a pill.[8]

Following the AIDS crisis and the public's concern with teen pregnancy rates, researchers who studied sexually transmitted infections (STIs) and reproductive health had a decent chance of being funded. But today, even these researchers have their share of challenges. Recently scientists who study HIV/AIDS and other STIs claim they have been warned by government officials to avoid the use of certain key words in their grant applications. Grants that include terms like "sex workers," "men who sleep with men," "anal sex," "needle exchange," "prostitute," "gay," "homosexual," and "transgender" are rumored to face additional scrutiny in an already fiercely competitive arena.[9]

Frustrated by the increasing interference of politicians, researchers—and even federal agency directors—have been fighting back. For example, scientists from a range of disciplines have formed the Coalition to Protect Research (CPR), an organization "committed to promoting public health through research [and promoting the idea that] sexual health and behavior research is essential to providing a scientific foundation for sound public health prevention and intervention programs." [10] Organizations like this and the Society for the Scientific Study of Sexuality (SSSS) call for politicians to respect the scientific peer review process and to actively fund sex research.

## NOTES

1. Senator Helms and Representative Dannemeyer were also leaders in the successful effort to de-fund the American Teenage Study, a project designed to study "patterns of adolescent sexual and contraceptive behavior and the cause of these patterns" (106). In Udry, J. Richard. 1993. "The Politics of Sex Research." *The Journal of Sex Research* 30 (2):103–110.

2. Navarro, Mireya. 2004. "Experts in Sex Field Say Conservatives Interfere with Health and Research." *The New York Times.* July 11.

3. McCain, Robert Stacy. 2003. "Sex and Child Health: Critics Wonder Why NICHD Funds Studies." *The Washington Times:* A02.

4. American Experience: Kinsey, Online Forum, Day 2. February 15, 2005. Retrieved December 12, 2005 from www.pbs.org/wgbh/amex/kinsey/sfeature/sf_forum_0215.html.

5. Hunter, Jennifer. 2005. "Sex Study Spurns Generation of Love." *Chicago Sun-Times*. October 5:63.

6. Clark, Justin. 2005. "Sex: The Big Turnoff." *Psychology Today*. Jan/Feb.

7. Clay, Rebecca. 2003. "Sex Research Faces New Obstacles." *APA Online*. Retrieved December 12, 2005 from www.apa.org/monitor/apr03/obstacles.html.

8. Tiefer, Leonore. 1995. *Sex is Not a Natural Act and Other Essays*. Boulder, CO: Westview Press.

9. Goode, Erica. 2003. "Certain Words Can Trip up AIDS Grants, Scientists Say." *New York Times*. Section A, Column 6, National Desk:10.

10. Coalition to Protect Research (CPR).Retrieved December 16, 2005 from www.cossa.org/CPR/cpr.html.

# The Reluctant Polyamorist: Conducting Auto-Ethnographic Research in a Sexualized Setting

Elisabeth Sheff

It is 3:00 a.m. I am lying half naked on a sea of cushions on my living room floor. "Rick," my partner with whom I have been madly in love for 10 years, is lounging beside me wearing nothing but his boxers. There is some soft-core "chick porn" on the television, and we are sharing a bottle of wine. Our kids are asleep in their bedrooms. It is the first time we have spent more than 20 minutes awake and alone together in at least 10 days, maybe more. We kiss, enjoying the relaxing moment.

I hear a sound and, grabbing my shirt, turn as the door opens. Our good friend "Dylan" enters the front door. She has recently split up with her husband and has a key to our house for those nights when she is couch surfing. We are used to her coming in late at night, but we have never been in this position when she entered before. I blush and say something inane.

"Oh, I've seen this one before. It's a good one," Dylan says, settling on the pillow beside me. "Hey guys, what's up?" she asks, smiling, and then guffaws, "This part is so stupid—like anyone would ever really do that!" We sit and watch the movie for a while, our cuddling becoming steadily more sensual. It is not, however, going the way it had in my fantasy of this moment, this event. Instead of captivating and erotic, it feels awkward and uncomfortable to me. I begin to develop a stomachache. A few minutes later I realize I need to pee, rise from the pillow pile and head to the bathroom, feeling distinctly queasy. I muse to myself, "Teaching that class tonight just wore me out. Makes sense, though. I've been up since yesterday at 7:00 a.m. and the baby woke me up twice last night. No wonder I'm exhausted."

I return to the living room to find the two of them on the pillows, heads turned towards me, smiling. "I'm bushed, you guys. I think I'm just gonna go to bed. Goodnight," I say, blowing them a kiss and heading into the bedroom I share with Rick. A few moments later, Rick enters the room. "Are you okay, honey? What's up?" he asks, sitting on the edge of the bed. "I'm just wiped out, babe, I just want to go to sleep. Everything's fine. I'm really okay with this," I say. "I'm not so sure that this is a good idea," Rick says, frowning. "I think I'll just tell Dylan we're going to sleep and she can have her usual couch." I respond "No, honey. I'm really fine with this. Go ahead."

We chat for a few minutes, Rick asking me several more times if I am sure that this is okay with me. I am certain, at least, that it is time to try it. We have been moving at a glacial speed towards a polyamorous relationship for 10 years now, and neither of us has ever before come *even close* to actually having sex with someone else. I am tired of hanging on the verge for so long and ready for something, anything, to happen. At least I think I am, I hope I am. I want to be, that is for sure. We had always imagined that it would be both of us together with the same woman, but suddenly that does not seem as appealing as it did before. "I *am* sure about this, honey." I tell Rick, "Get out there and have sex with Dylan!" He hesitates for a second, and then says "Okay, if you're *sure* that you're sure," and, kissing me, rises to go. "Do we have any more condoms?" he asks. "This one is expired." "Under the bathroom sink, next to the tampons," I reply. He says "Thanks, babe," and leaves the room.

I lie in the dark room for a moment, wondering if this really is a good idea. I have been extremely nervous about this for a long time, worried that I will feel jealous or insecure. I anticipate lying awake, listening for sounds coming from the next room. Instead, I fall asleep almost instantly and wake sometime later to find Rick climbing in bed with me, followed soon after by Dylan. The three of us assume spoon position and fall back to sleep.

I wake the next morning and they have both gone to work. I do not teach on Fridays, so I was able to stay in bed until the baby woke up. I wander in to the kitchen and see that they have each left notes, asking me how I am and to give them a call later. "How *am* I?" I wonder, and gingerly check in with myself, feeling strangely as if I'm inspecting a limb to see if it is broken. I find that I'm fine. Not pretending to be fine, but actually *feeling* fine. I'm shocked. I had expected an intense, dramatic reaction. Instead I feel serene, just normal (well, as normal as I get, anyway). I probe a bit deeper into my feelings. *Really?* Actually fine? I find that I truly am, and marvel at the fact that this event that had seemed so monumental for such a long time is, in fact, rather anticlimactic. Almost mundane even. "Amazing!" I think to myself and, shifting the baby to the other hip, start the coffee.

*        *        *

In this article I detail my qualitative, ultimately auto-ethnographic research practices exploring subcultural groups involved in polyamory. Polyamory is a form of relationship in which people have multiple romantic, sexual, and/or affective partners. It differs from swinging with its emphasis on long-term, emotionally intimate relationships; and from adultery with its focus on honesty and (ideally) full disclosure of the network of sexual relationships to all who participate in or are affected by them. Both men and women have access to additional partners in polyamorous relationships, distinguishing them from those engaged in polygamy, a relational form in which men have multiple wives but women have a single husband.

Very little sociological research has examined polyamory. Other than my own work (Sheff 2005), the scant extant scholarship (Rubin 2001) mentions it only in passing and provides no in-depth analysis of participants' experiences. The relatively unknown nature of polyamorous practices and communities makes qualitative, and especially ethnographic, research an appropriate methodological choice. Ethnography is a form of research that usually involves participant observation and interviews to reveal collective understandings among populations related to the phenomena under study, and is a favorite among researchers examining sexual minorities.

My roles in this complex setting ranged from "peripheral" to "complete" member (Adler and Adler 1987) over the seven years I was actively associated with several polyamorous communities. I originally approached the group in February of 1997 to investigate the potential impact of polyamory on my own relationship. My partner "Rick" introduced the idea of the two of us engaging in a triadic relationship with another woman shortly after we met in 1993, before we were aware of the term polyamory or of an organized community of practitioners. He saw a long-term, romantic triad as the fulfillment of his dream of living in an alternative family, and he thought that a triadic relationship would fit me well because I identify as bisexual. He did not understand how a bisexual person could be satisfied with a single partner, and worried that I would miss sexual contact with women were he and I monogamous.

I was 23 when I met Rick, and had been in few prior relationships. Those relationships I had had were painful, adolescent experiences. I had been in love once before, but it was "bush league" compared with the love I felt for Rick. While his focus on non-monogamous relationships was a source of discomfort for me, so many other areas of our relationship were so wonderful that I continued our association.

My initial reaction to Rick's desire to open our relationship was almost complete rejection of the idea. I felt hurt that he wanted additional lovers, fearing that it meant that he saw me as too fat or insufficiently skilled as a lover. Rick's attempts to comfort me offered some small solace, especially his assertion that he had always been non-monogamous and his desire for other lovers was not specific to his relationship with me.

Rick and I discussed opening our relationship to another woman regularly for several years. As the marathon conversation wore on, I began to place greater stock in his assurances that he was completely committed to me. I also found Rick's arguments in favor of polyamory increasingly compelling. While I was not eager to try multiple-partner relating, I sincerely wished to remain in my relationship with Rick, and this topic was clearly of great import to him.

One bleak winter evening during my second semester of graduate school, I heard two people interviewed on National Public Radio. They were discussing their practice of polyamory, the exact sort of relationship Rick had been advocating. An Internet search revealed that the radio interviewees hosted support groups and informational meetings in my local area. Rick and I attended several large group meetings and potluck picnics, and I became increasingly interested in these friendly, open-minded people and their unconventional lifestyles. They appeared nonjudgmental of my hesitation to engage in polyamorous relationships, and I discovered that I had many other areas of mutual interest with them.

During this early phase, Rick and I primarily attended sporadic organized polyamorous events and began slowly to socialize occasionally with local polyamorists. About once a month, Rick and I would attend a polyamorous event, such as an informational community meeting in the library, a support group, or a potluck party. I began to understand how these relationships worked for some people, and conversations with Rick took on a completely new tone of possibility now that we had role models actually practicing multiple-partner relationships. My social role in the setting had become one of friend/seeker, someone who

sought to explore polyamory in order to decide whether to participate. Our sporadic attendance at polyamorous functions and socializing with local polyamorists went on for roughly a year prior to my transition to an active research role.

## The Shift into Active Research

The more time I spent with the polyamorists, the more I liked them. As I became more familiar with setting members, I recognized the potential for sociological analysis of this previously unexamined group. About a year and a half after my introduction to the local polyamorous community, I took a graduate ethnography course and chose the polyamorists as a subject, embarking on "opportunistic" research (Riemer 1977) that was later to become "auto-ethnographic" (Hayano 1979).

My initial role of friend/seeker easily expanded to include a research component. Setting members were comfortable with me because they already knew that I was a graduate student. They willingly participated in the research, explaining concepts and allowing me to ask questions during support group meetings. I frequently asked openly research-oriented questions, though I initially refrained from taking notes in front of setting members. I became increasingly close with several local polyamorists, whom I found like-minded and friendly. At this point, I began to attend the monthly meeting for polyamorous women.

The transition from civilian to researcher was sometimes challenging; occasionally I felt uncomfortable in groups, knowing that I would later take notes on the interactions and that some group members might have been unaware of my status as a researcher. Fox felt similar discomfort when she felt compelled to "tread a line between overt and covert roles" in her investigation of a punk social scene (1987: 341; see also Adler 1985; Henslin 1972). Although I enjoyed socializing with polyamorists, I remained "acutely aware of differences between members and [myself]" and thus retained a peripheral membership role (Adler and Adler 1987: 39).

Eventually I established an amorous relationship with "Steve," a man I had interviewed the previous year but with whom I had not socialized since then. With that relationship I made the transition to a complete membership role characterized by full immersion in the scene as a "native" who shared a "common set of experiences, feelings, and goals" with those in my setting (Adler and Adler 1987: 67). Ironically, it was at this transition to complete membership status that I disengaged almost completely from the local polyamorous community. I had completed data collection and was analyzing my results, so I had no further need for regular contact with respondents. Rick and Steve clashed personally and developed intense animosity over time, and I had increasing difficulty managing the conflict between these two important people in my life. I withdrew even more from the research setting, in part because I was overwhelmed with the emotional discord involved in my multiple-partner relationship and spent so much time in intense discussions with both Rick and Steve, as well as personal and couple's counseling, that I had no time left for community interaction.

While some people are able to navigate the complexities of multiple-partner relating and gain tremendous benefits, Rick and I did not turn out to be among them. The whole episode damaged our relationship considerably and we verged on splitting up for some time. Eventually Rick and I realized that we needed to flee the difficulties of our disastrous polyamorous attempt if our relationship was to survive, so we sold our house and moved to another state where a university had offered me a job. I had no more contact with Steve.

## Methodological Challenges in the Field

I experienced some difficulties in this sexualized research setting. First, my field observations were colored by and limited to my own experi-ence. While this is true of all ethnographers, my discomfort with the sexualized settings and potential for sexual interaction severely limited my knowledge of the sexual component of the community.

For instance, at one social event, a clothing optional pool party, I spent the vast majority of my time socializing and eating rather than floating naked in the pool. My primary contacts at that party were the others nearby, who were also socializing and eating. Although I was not aware of any overt public sexuality, I could not clearly see what was happening in the deep end of the pool, and I left the party rather early. It is likely that the party was at least partially populated by people engaged in a far more active sexuality than that of which I was aware. Instead, I focused on "sociability almost to the exclusion of sexuality" (Warren and Rasmussen 1977; see also Warren 1974) and thus did not collect data about the semi-public sexual interactions that were most likely happening at the party.

Second, I had developed unequal relationships with men and women in the setting. My friendships with women were far more emotionally intimate than my friendships with men, from whose potential unwanted sexual advances I felt the need to protect myself. I was also known as a feminist in polyamorous subcultures, a fact that may have impacted the information I received in interviews, especially from men who might have hesitated to reveal politically incorrect information or attitudes.

Third, issues of participant self-selection may have skewed my sample. I interviewed people who had the time, money, and geographical proximity to attend polyamorous groups and social functions. Polyamorists usually communicated logistical details (date, time, and location) for the majority of the gatherings I attended or heard about primarily through emails and websites. Similarly, those with enough time and money to attend a weekend retreat in a remote California location, or with Internet access to receive my email calls for interviews, comprised the sample of people with whom I was able to speak when I traveled to the California Bay Area to collect data. Thus, my sample was composed almost exclusively of a specific class of people who could afford home computers and Internet access, and had the leisure time to interact with others via email, peruse polyamorist websites, or attend weekend conferences. While this email method of recruitment gave me access to a wider range of people than I would otherwise have had, they were mostly the same *type* of person, namely those who own and are comfortable using computers. These people tended to be overwhelmingly white, middle- or upper-middle class, and university educated. This issue could be mitigated, however, since this population appeared to compose the vast majority of members of the communities that I studied. Nonetheless, I fear that I was unable to access marginal polyamorists, especially those without computer access.

A final difficulty involved my Human Subjects Committee (a board that approves and monitors research involving human subjects) agreement. I was prohibited from speaking with anyone younger than eighteen years of age. Thus, this research reflects the view of parents involved in polyamorous relationships, but the views of the children are largely absent. Some parents did report on their children's feelings and thoughts, but this second-hand reporting is obviously incomplete.

## Comparison with Other Types of Sex Research

My discomfort with being viewed as a potential sexual partner mirrored that of other researchers who have examined sexual minorities and similarly reported difficulties navigating settings with "considerable sexual tension and display" (Warren and Rasmussen 1977: 25). Golde (1970: 6) observed that women in field research settings tend to be perceived as sexually provocative, especially when they are unmarried. My long-term partnership was the equivalent of quasi-marriage, but

conferred no "protection" (Warren and Rasmussen 1977) on me in this multiple-partner setting.

My ongoing concern with protecting my partners' and my own privacy is also a common theme among ethnographers, especially those who engage in participant observation with sexual minorities or members of other "deviant" groups. Fine (1993: 380) acknowledges this tension between disclosure and privacy, explaining that "the question is whether we can preserve our privacy while we reveal the impact and relevance of our behavior, both public and private." This question was especially salient for me as I discussed my personal involvement in the setting, and I asked Rick to read the introduction to this article before I decided to submit it.

In establishing a romantic relationship with one of my respondents, I joined the dubious and often covert ranks of ethnographic researchers who have romantic or sexual relationships in the field. Some obscure this fact and it emerges only posthumously (e.g., Malinowski 1967). Others mention it briefly but accord it little analysis (e.g., Turnbull 1986). Another segment discusses it as an integral component of their research (e.g., Irwin 2003). A minority make sexual interaction in the field the focal point of their ethnography (e.g., Ronai and Ellis 1989). The majority of researchers who discuss sexuality in the field, however, tend to focus on their experiences of sexual harassment rather than their own sexual relationships (e.g., Conway 1986).

There is undoubtedly a large contingent of researchers who engage in romantic or sexual relationships in their field settings and refrain from mentioning it at all because sexual contact stigmatizes academics, especially women academics (Whitehead and Price 1986: 302). These relationships may offer some redemptive value, however, as Goffman's (1989: 129) observation indicated (with a heterocentrism characteristic of his generation), a researcher knows she or he is incorporated into the research setting when "the members of the opposite sex [in the setting] become attractive to you."

## Findings

In this section I focus on two specific areas of findings: gender and family. The vast majority of polyamorists espouse gender equality, and many are even able to maintain it to varied degrees. Some women reported feeling more free to be themselves in a polyamorous community:

> Women with multiple lovers are usually called sluts, bitches, very derogatory, very demeaning in sexual context. Whereas men who have multiple lovers—they're studs, they're playboys, they're glorified names, where with a woman it's very demeaning. So to be a woman and have multiple partners, it's been very empowering and claiming some of that back, saying I have just as much right to be a sexual person with many lovers as men do . . . without the shame and the guilt.

Many men similarly reported a feeling of freedom that accompanied the greater gender role flexibility available to them in polyamorous settings. One polyamorous man observed of other men he knew from his local polyamorous community that:

> Their vibe is more free. They don't have as much societal baggage. They don't seem to like talking about bitches, drinking beer, and pissing on things. They are more intellectual and sensitive, like artists and musicians.

While many valued gender equality, it did not always work out as they had anticipated. Some women, especially those who were bisexual (which was almost all of them) felt objectified by men who wanted to have sex with multiple women simultaneously. One woman remarked that:

> Well, it gets real old, forever dealing with the hot bi babe fantasy. I mean, I would love to be in a triad with two men devoted to me, who wouldn't? But my personal ad online as a single woman looking for two men gets only responses from f/m [female/male] couples who want a third. I am soooooo damn sick of that!

Things were not always so perfect for polyamorous men, however. Several men lamented the fact that they did not receive enough attention in their triadic sexual encounters with two women simultaneously. Women also tended to have an easier time finding multiple partners than did most men. A respondent once said to me:

> It is a poly phenomenon that often the woman in the couple is kind of reluctant and is dragged kicking and screaming into poly. Then when the man is done with his experimentation the woman often finds that it suits her character and stays with it. It is almost like acquiring a skill, once she's got it, it becomes part of how she wants to live her life. It can be real confronting when the man wants to become involved in the poly lifestyle and then finds out that it is really much easier for a woman to establish relationships, and not only do they establish them easier, they tend to get more intimate and deeper faster, cause that is what women are good at. Speaking generally, women like that kind of stuff. So the men can become very uncomfortable.

Both polyamorous women and men experienced some benefits from their involvement in multiple-partner relationships, though each group also paid a price for their sexual freedom. Loss of control over partners' sexual interactions with others and the potential for a fantasy to go awry when actually lived out sometimes tarnished the luster of these relationships for some polyamorists.

Polyamorists also deal with a number of issues related to their families. Much like people who choose to be open about their involvement in same-sex relationships, many polyamorists have to decide whether to come out to their families of origin and meet with the same varied reactions that many others who come out have experienced. Some are completely accepted by their families and embraced as a family unit themselves at gatherings with their parents and siblings. One respondent related a story about her mother's 80th birthday party, a major event for their extended family, who came from all over the United States and Japan to attend. The respondent, her wife, and their two husbands had anticipated blending in with the rest of the attendees, because a group ostensibly composed of two couples was so common. She said she was:

> Focused on my mom's birthday. You know, I did not feel a need to make a statement about 'We are here together' or something like that. And I could not believe it, she was up on stage thanking everyone for coming and she called us all up and she said 'I want to introduce you to my children' and that was it. Everyone knows that me and my sister are her only *biological* children, so some of them had no idea what she was talking about. But now we were all her kids and that was that! I was really touched; for her to do that meant a lot to me.

Polyamorous parents also deal with decisions around coming out to their children and the potential impact of that revelation. For instance, polyamory could affect child custody if an ex-spouse finds out and raises the issue in court. Again paralleling people in same sex relationships, some polyamorists have lost custody of their children because of their involvement in multiple partner sexual relationships.

Many polyamorists see multiple parents as a great benefit to both the children and other parents as well. One respondent observed that:

> There's more attention for the kids. I really think it takes five adults to have one child, and I say that without any kind of humor. It takes five adults and one of those adults is just around to take care of mom. Anyway, it's big time stuff and our culture treats monogamy and heterosexual relationships as the only way to be. And lesbian and gay people who are fighting for the right to marry and I'm looking at them going I just don't get it. It takes more [people] than that!

Others felt greater difficulty parenting in polyamorous relationships than they did or imagined they would in monogamous partnerships. For instance, one respondent related a story in which her son, upset by the departure of his mother's boyfriend, lamented, "I know he is breaking up with you, but why does he have to break up with me too?"

Polyamory is a challenging and complex relational style, and researching this community of sexual minorities was difficult and complex as well. My ethnographic experience changed my life and forced me to confront my own deeply-held views and insecurities. While I no longer identify as polyamorous and feel considerable reluctance to try multiple-partner relating again, I see polyamory as a legitimate relational style that gives some people the freedom to honestly have multiple partners. Many of my respondents reported that becoming polyamorous had dramatically changed their lives for the better. Some even saw it as an innate sexual orientation against which they had struggled for years before "coming out" as polyamorous.

Similarly, many polyamorists felt the desire to redefine relational norms and roles to better fit their needs, though some found that real life did not work out the way the relationships did in their fantasies. Inclusion of polyamorous people enriches the spectrum of recognized relationship styles and augments sociological understanding of sexuality. Similarly, awareness of the polyamorous possibility may allow some people to conceive of new modes of relationship previously unimagined. It is this proliferation of choice that could contribute to social change.

## REFERENCES

Adler, P. 1985. *Wheeling and Dealing*. New York: Columbia University Press.

Adler, P. and Adler, P. 1987. *Membership Roles in Field Research*. Newbury Park, CA: Sage.

Conway, M. 1986. "The Pretence of the Neutral Researcher" in Whitehead and Conway (Eds.), *Self, Sex, and Gender in Cross-Cultural Fieldwork*. Urbana: University of Illinois Press.

Fine, G. 1993. "Ten Lies of Ethnography." *Journal of Contemporary Ethnography*, 22:267–294.

Fox, K. 1987. "Real Punks and Pretenders: The Social Organization of a Counterculture." *Journal of Contemporary Ethnography*, 16(3).

Goffman, E. 1989. "On Field Work." *Journal of Contemporary Ethnography*, 18:123–132.

Golde, P. 1970. "Introduction" in Golde (Ed.) *Women in the Field*. Chicago: Aldine.

Hayano, D. 1979. "Auto-Ethnography, Problems, and Prospects." *Human Organization,* 38:99–104.

Henslin, J. 1972. "Studying Deviance in Four Settings: Research Experiences with Cabbies, Suicides, Drug Users, and Abortionees" in Douglas (Ed.), *Research on Deviance.* New York: Random House.

Irwin, K. 2003. "Saints and Sinners: Elite Tattoo Collectors and Tattooists as Positive and Negative Deviants." *Sociological Spectrum,* 23:27–57.

Malinowski, B. 1967. *A Diary in the Strict Sense of the Term.* London: Routledge and Kegan Paul.

Riemer, J. 1977. "Varieties of Opportunistic Research." *Urban Life,* 5:467–477.

Ronai, C. and Ellis, C. 1989. "Turn-Ons for Money." *Journal of Contemporary Ethnography,* 18(3).

Rubin, R. 2001. "Alternative Family Lifestyles Revisited, or Whatever Happened to Swingers, Group Marriages and Communes?" *Journal of Family Issues,* 22(6):711–727.

Sheff, E. 2005. "Polyamorous Women, Sexual Subjectivity, and Power." *Journal Contemporary Ethnography,* 34(3):251–283.

Turnbull, C. 1986. "Sex and Gender: The Role of Subjectivity in Field Research" in Whitehead and Conway (Eds.), *Self, Sex, and Gender in Cross-Cultural Fieldwork.* Urbana: University of Illinois Press.

Warren, C. 1974. *Identity and Community in the Gay World.* New York: John Wiley.

Warren, C. and Rasmussen, P. 1977. "Sex and Gender in Field Research." *Urban Life,* 6.

Whitehead, T. and Price, L. 1986. "Sex and the Fieldwork Experience" in Whitehead and Conway (Eds.), *Self, Sex, and Gender in Cross-Cultural Fieldwork.* Urbana: University of Illinois Press.

## Sextistics

### Did You Know?

- The Society for the Scientific Study of Sexuality (SSSS), founded in 1957, currently has more than 1,000 members, including anthropologists, biologists, educators, historians, nurses, physicians, psychologists, sociologists, theologians, therapists, and others professionals.[1]
- Richard von Krafft-Ebing coined the term *masochism* by using the name of Leopold von Sacher-Masoch, who wrote of his masochistic desires in his novel *Venus in Furs*. Krafft-Ebing is also credited for coining that term *sadism* after the Marquis de Sade, an eighteenth-century writer imprisoned for the explicitness of his work.[2]
- Dr. Magnus Hirschfeld opened the world's first sexological institute in 1919. Located in Berlin, the Institute for Sexual Science promoted sex education, contraception, marriage counseling, and gay and women's rights. In 1933, the Nazis destroyed the Institute's library, burning most of Hirschfeld's collection.[3]
- Together, William H. Masters and Virginia E. Johnson developed scientific instruments to measure sexual response. During their decade-long study, they observed 700 men and women while engaged in coitus or masturbation. Masters and Johnson were married in 1971 and divorced in 1993.[4]
- The print media response to the Kinsey Report *Sexual Behavior in the Human Female* in 1953 was generally favorable with one notable exception: *Cosmopolitan*.[5]
- Laura Linney, who played Clara McMillen, the wife of Alfred Kinsey, was nominated for an Academy Award in 2005 for her role in the movie *Kinsey*.[6] It grossed over $10 million in the United States alone.[7]

*—Compiled by Mikel Walters*

### NOTES

1. The Society of the Scientific Study of Sexuality. 2005. "About SSSS." Retrieved December 14, 2005 from www.sexscience.org.
2. Bullough, Vern. 1994. *Science in the Bedroom: A History of Sex Research.* Basic Books.
3. Ibid.
4. Kolodny, Robert C. 2001. "In Memory of William H. Masters." *Journal of Sex Research* 38: 274–276.
5. The Kinsey Institute of Research in Sex, Gender, and Reproduction. "Facts about *Kinsey, the Film.*" Retrieved December 2, 2005 from http://kinseyinstitute.org/about/Movie-facts.html.
6. Academy of Motion Picture Arts and Sciences. 2005. "77th Academy Awards Nominees and Winners." Retrieved January 30, 2006 from www.oscars.org/77academyawards/nomswins.html.
7. MovieWeb. 2005. "*Kinsey* (2004)." Retrieved January 16, 2006 from www.movieweb.com/movies/film/90/590/summary.php.

# chapter 3

# Representing Sex

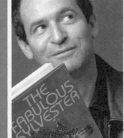

*An interview with . . .*

## Joshua Gamson

Joshua Gamson, Ph.D., is Professor of Sociology at University of San Francisco. His research and teaching focus on the sociology of culture, with an emphasis on contemporary Western commercial culture and mass media, social movements, and the history, theory, and sociology of sexuality. He is the author of *Claims to Fame: Celebrity in Contemporary America* (California, 1994); *Freaks Talk Back: Tabloid Talk Shows and Sexual Nonconformity* (Chicago, 1998); and *The Fabulous Sylvester: The Legend, The Music, The Seventies in San Francisco* (Henry Holt, 2005).

**What led you to begin studying sexuality?**

*I didn't know it at the time, but studying sexuality began for me as part of what some scholars have called "identity work." I was a 23-year-old graduate student at UC Berkeley, and I'd decided it was time to figure myself out a bit better, and a big part of that seemed to be figuring out my sexuality a bit better. I knew that the Bay Area was a great place to do that, given the history of sexual subcultures—gay ones, especially—but somehow I didn't want to just take myself out exploring. So I decided to study it, come at my personal life from the outside in, as it were. When I had a statistics paper to do, I made it about public opinion about homosexuality, for instance. When I took a graduate seminar in partici-pant observation research, I eventually decided on a field site that would get me into San Francisco, among gay and lesbian people: the AIDS activist group ACT UP. That turned into a very rewarding research experience, and to do it I had to teach myself some of the literature on sexuality-based social movements, so it fed my head. But it also fed my identity. That work moved me into a part of the gay community that I liked, felt comfortable in, and identified with; it helped me see myself as gay, and to actually experience gayness without shame or apology. It was a case of personal identity leading to intellectual pursuit and then back to personal identity. That back and forth continues to this day.*

### How do people react when they find that you study sexuality?

*It depends on which people are doing the reacting, I suppose. Back when I started, my more senior colleagues would generally seem mystified, as if they couldn't quite figure out what there was to study about sexuality. Some, I'm certain, didn't and still don't think it's a legitimate area of study, but I think a lot of people just didn't know how to have a conversation about studying sexuality. That's rarely the case any more, partly because over the last decade the field has become much more established and much less marginalized in sociology—and partly because sexuality has been such a significant political and public policy focal point. Younger people seem to think it's kind of cool that I study sexuality, or cool that there is such a field of study. Then there are always those who want to joke about how much fun the "research process" must be.*

### Which of your projects have you found most interesting? Why?

*My two book projects were the most interesting to me, for sure. The book on TV talk shows,* Freaks Talk Back, *was interesting to me for a whole slew of reasons. I found it really interesting to investigate how the everyday produc-tion routines—the kinds of things talk show producers think about, talk about, worry about, and do all the time to get a show made—affected LGBT topics. Usually, when scholars and activists talk about "cultural visibility," they have only a vague sense of what kinds of institutional and organizational processes shape that visibility, and I felt like I was pushing past that vagueness. I was also really interested in the experiences of guests, and learned a lot about sexuality politics from that—in particular, the internal struggle over who best represents "gayness," which is very much a class-based divide. I became very interested in how complicated media visibility was for sexually-stigmatized and gender-nonconforming populations: How gay and lesbian respectability was shored up on the shows by demeaning or stereotyping transgender and bisexual guests; how the exposure of class and race diversity among LGBT populations only really came about through the extraordinarily exploitative, confess-accuse-pull hair kind of shows, like Springer. Media visibility has really changed since then, but that project tuned me in to dynamics of gay visibility I still see all around me.*

*My most recent book,* The Fabulous Sylvester, *was interesting in a whole other kind of way. It's a sort of combination biography (of the 1970s openly gay, sometimes cross-dressing, African American disco star, Sylvester) and cultural history (of San Francisco's gay subcultures, in which Sylvester lived and through which he rose to fame; and of AIDS, from which Sylvester died). So it was interesting partly because it was a different sort of project, more narrative and less analytical scholarly. It was interesting to me because it put me into contact with Sylvester's life and friends, and his story is just beautiful, and beautiful largely because his sexuality was such an integrated part of who he was—he was never closeted, and he suffered quite a bit for that, but he eventually became an international disco star by putting gay "fabulousness" to music, while refusing to be reduced to, or by, sexuality, and by never apologizing for being gay and sexual. I also loved delving into 1970s gay liberation cultures, which were so creative and novel and important, and which have been largely lost to AIDS, assimilation, and fear.*

### What ethical dilemmas have you faced in studying sexuality?

*I haven't really experienced ethical dilemmas, frankly. I'm not studying sexual behavior, and I've never studied covert sexual populations, so I've never had concern about revealing things that might hurt the subjects. I always tell people I'm a researcher, and give them the option of not participating, or of participating without having their name used, and sometimes people take me up on that. When I'm interviewing, they always have the option of having me turn off the tape recorder. The closest I've come to an ethical dilemma is in dealing with the question of how what I write might be used by others, such as journalists or policymakers who have an anti-gay agenda—which is, of course, totally out of my control. I don't think I've ever made a decision to censor myself for fear that the wrong people would use it in a way that damages those to whom I'm loyal and allied, but I certainly am careful how I frame and phrase things.*

### What do you think is the most challenging thing about studying sexuality?

*The most challenging thing for me is that it's a constantly moving target. Again, I don't study sexual behaviors, but instead sexual identities, movements, politics, cultures, and cultural representations. One can easily be at the end of a project and find the phenomenon entering some radically different new phase, so that one has to be ready to always rethink and revise. (Maybe that's one of the rea-*

*sons I enjoyed doing the Sylvester book, since it was more historical.) Media visibility is a good example: Ten years ago, when I finished the talk show book, the issue was still that LGBT people were mainly invisible on television or restricted to narrow stereotypes; the issues now, after Ellen, Will and Grace, Queer as Folk, The L Word, Queer Eye, and so on, are quite different. The talk show study, over the course of just a few years, went from being a statement about the limits and paradoxes of LGBT media visibility to being an account of a historical moment. A study of same-sex marriage laws now, to take another example, is going to face the same sort of difficulty; things are changing so rapidly in legislation and law related to sexuality. That's not an insurmountable challenge, and I'd rather study something that is active and volatile than something inert. But sexual cultures and politics don't stand still for their snapshot.*

### Why is it important to do sex research?

*Most basically, because sex is an important part of human existence, and it's been so smothered by shame and negativity that there's still plenty that's not well understood. Although it hasn't always been the case, and I suspect won't be forever, sexuality has also become a significant basis for people's identities and self-understandings, and it affects their life chances and life paths in various ways—where they wind up living, what kinds of jobs they can and can't get. And sexuality is one of several significant bases of social inequality, and therefore is a very significant arena of politics. These are things that need to be understood, both just because more knowledge is better than less, and because sexualities research can help us figure out what needs to be changed and how to change it—the research can inform the pursuit of social justice.*

### If you could teach people one thing about sexuality, what would it be?

*That it's both more significant and less significant than it's been made out to be: Sexuality is not just a phenomenon of nature, and not just "personal," but a phenomenon of society, and political; at the same time, at the root of all of this politics is just sex, just the fun and sometimes funny things people do with their bodies, together and alone.*

—Interviewed by Denise Donnelly

## "Where My Girls At?"

## Negotiating Black Womanhood in Music Videos

Rana A. Emerson

**W**hile much has been written about the significance and impact of hip-hop culture on the lives of Black youth, young Black women, until very recently, have failed to be located as substantial producers, creators, and consumers of hip-hop and Black youth culture (George 1998; Perkins 1996; Rose 1994; Watkins 1998). Most of the contemporary research and criticism has focused on the experience of young men of African descent and, with rare exceptions, has implicitly and often explicitly identified Black popular culture, specifically hip-hop culture, with masculinity (George 1998; Perkins 1996; Rose 1991, 1994).

Yet, African American women have a significant presence in hip-hop and Black popular culture, and in music videos, where they appear as dancers; models; and, most significantly, as performers. At the same time, the hip-hop genre and the music videos that are used to promote records and performers have been harshly critiqued for the antiwoman (specifically anti-Black woman) messages and images contained within them. Critics have pointed out that many discourses in hip-hop culture reproduce dominant and distorted ideologies of Black women's sexuality (hooks 1992; Morgan 1999; Perkins 1996).

Nevertheless, despite the misogynistic representations of Black womanhood that pervade

From Emerson, Rana A. 2002. "'Where My Girls At?' Negotiating Black Womanhood in Music Videos." *Gender & Society* 16(1): 115–135. Reprinted by permission of Sage Publications.

music videos, the 1990s witnessed the emergence of Black women performers, producers, writers, and musicians who have also made the music video into a site for promotion, creativity, and self-expression. Black women performers, songwriters, and producers, including Erykah Badu, Missy "Misdemeanor" Elliott, and Lauryn Hill, have profoundly affected hip-hop culture as well as the wider sphere of popular culture. While most music videos, including those of some Black women performers, exacerbate the exploitation of the Black woman's body and perpetuate stereotypes of Black womanhood, Badu, Elliott, and Hill depict themselves as independent, strong, and self-reliant agents of their own desire, the masters of their own destiny.

The medium of the music video, the primary promotional vehicle for the recording industry today, is an especially rich space to explore the ways in which race, gender, class, and sexuality intersect in the construction and proliferation of ideologies of Black womanhood in the mass media and popular culture. This study explores Black women's representation in music video through the analysis of a sample of videos by African American women singers, rappers, and musicians produced and distributed at the end of the 1990s.

Most of the previous studies of Black women's representation in music videos have, on one hand, either focused on the hegemonic and stereotypical imagery and discourses of Black femininity or, on the other hand, exaggerated the degree of agency that Black female performers in music video have by emphasizing the resistant and counterhegemonic elements of the music video representations. Instead, this study demonstrates that in the cultural productions of Black women, music videos in this case, hegemonic and counterhegemonic themes often occur simultaneously and are interconnected, resulting in a complex, often contradictory and multifaceted representation of Black womanhood.

## Literature Review

The vast majority of representations of Black women in popular culture are firmly grounded in the dominant ideologies surrounding Black womanhood in American society. Patricia Hill Collins (1991a) described these ideologies as controlling images that are rooted in the maintenance of hegemonic power and serve to justify and legitimize the continued marginalization of Black women. The media and popular culture are primary sites for the dissemination and the construction of commonsense notions of Black womanhood. Music videos, which have been criticized for their objectifying and exploitative depictions of women of all races and ethnicities (Aufderheide 1986; Dines and Humez 1995; Frith, Goodwin, and Grossberg 1993; Hurley 1994; Kaplan 1987; Stockbridge 1987; Vincent 1989; Vincent, Davis, and Boruszkowski 1987), often represent Black women according to the controlling images discussed by Hill Collins. The images that are seen most often are the hypersexualized "hot momma" or "Jezebel," the asexual "mammy," the emasculating "matriarch," and the "welfare recipient" or "baby-momma" (a colloquial term for young, unwed mothers). . . .

This study improves on the previous research on Black female music video performance because it problematizes the often-unexamined notion of resistance. Overall, this study furthers the inclusion of Black female youth in the conversation surrounding hip-hop culture by recognizing the active participation of Black female performers and audiences within it (McRobbie 1991, 1993, 1997; McRobbie and Nava 1984). In this way, it serves to question the identification of hip-hop culture with Black masculinity and Black male youth by demonstrating that music videos also serve as sites for expressing the lived experiences of Black female youth. . . .

## Method

I collected a purposive sample of 56 music videos that featured Black women performers using the method of "theoretical sampling" (Lindlof 1995; Strauss 1987). The videos were tape-recorded from the daily broadcast programming of cable networks BET, MTV, and VH1 and were collected during the week of 7 January 1998. The majority of the Black women's videos collected in the sample (38) were taped from BET. Fewer videos by Black women artists were collected from MTV (13) and VH1 (5). According to *Billboard* magazine, for the week ending 11 January 1998, 11 videos featuring Black women artists were in heavy rotation on BET, while MTV featured 5 and VH1 included 2. The sample included those videos in heavy rotation on all three channels, plus all other videos played during the time period that met the criteria. . . .

Videos were purposively sampled and chosen on the basis of the following characteristics: They featured Black female performers (defined as singers, rappers, or other musicians), who were either lead performers or appeared as guests in the videos of other performers (excluding background dancers and singers) regardless of race and gender. An additional criterion for selection was that the performers whose videos I included self-identified as having African or African American heritage. I judged this by observing the signifiers of race in the marketing of the artist, the signs and indicators of Black culture apparent in their work, and my knowledge of this self-identification obtained from outside sources such as interviews and other journalistic accounts.

The videos included in this analysis mirror *Billboard* magazine's rotation playlists for MTV, VH1, and BET. The rotation, or frequency, at which a video is shown, is determined by a number of factors including the promotional efforts of the record company, the anticipation of the release, and ongoing sales of the single or album. . . .

The coded variables were as follows: the camera's gaze or point of view; the mode of address or the gender of those being "spoken to" in the video; presentation and performance of gender roles; physicality and the body; relationships between women; relationships with men; the presence and degree of female anger, rage, or aggression; the presence of violence; expression of female sexual desire; what sexual behavior, if any, is present; images of motherhood; the number and gender composition of group members; the presence of dance in the video; sound; the type of narrative (if any) in the video; the type of image the artist is projecting; intertextuality or references to other videos, songs, or other media; apparent signifiers of Blackness; class or occupational markers; geographic setting; and age.

Those coding categories that occurred most frequently across the sample of videos or appeared to have the most impact and significance within a critical subgroup of videos were identified as the key themes and issues. To assess the relative importance of these factors, I selected 20 music videos in the sample (indicated by bold italics in Table 13.1), which exhibited the most salient emergent themes. I conducted a close reading and textual analysis of the visual images, the narrative and representations, and the accompanying musical tracks and lyrics of each of these 20 videos to confirm, contextualize, and further clarify the observations made during the first stage of the analysis. . . .

## *Stereotypes and Controlling Images*

. . . Several stereotypes emerge in the ways Black women's videos are programmed, as well in the content of the videos themselves. First, the videos emphasize Black women's bodies. Second, they construct a one-dimensional Black woman-

hood. Finally, the presence of male sponsors in the videos and a focus on themes of conspicuous consumption and romance further exhibit the types of social constraints faced by young Black women.

### The Body

The first way that patterns of social constraint emerge is in the emphasis on the body. It is clear that female rap and rhythm and blues (R&B) performers are required to live up to dominant notions of physical attractiveness and measure up to fairly rigid standards of beauty. The most striking example of this is the lack of variety in body size and weight. This was surprising, considering the conventional wisdom that the Black community possesses alternative beauty standards that allow for larger body types. . . . [T]he majority of the videos I coded (30) featured artists who would be considered thin by most standards, while only 9 featured performers who would be considered overweight. The only women who are larger than the ideal are Missy "Misdemeanor" Elliott, Angie Stone, and a member of the group Xscape. . . .

### One-Dimensional Womanhood

For the most part, the portrait of Black womanhood that emerges from the video analysis is flat and one-dimensional. Black women are not represented in their full range of being. They are not multifaceted but are reduced to decorative eye candy. Black women performers are not allowed to be artists in their own right but must serve as objects of male desire. In the videos, only three of the featured artists were older than 30 (Janet Jackson, Whitney Houston, and Aretha Franklin). Indubitably, this reflects the youth-oriented nature of popular culture.

Pregnant women and mothers, as well as women older than 30, are not desirable as objects of the music video camera's gaze, reinforcing the sense that only women who are viewed as sexually available are acceptable in music videos. Only two of the videos depicted motherhood: Erykah Badu is visibly pregnant in *Tyrone*, and Joi is

**Table 13.1**  *List of Videos Selected*

| TITLE | ARTIST | YEAR |
|---|---|---|
| *All Cried Out* | Allure featuring 112 | 1997 |
| *Everyday* | Angie Stone and Devox | 1997 |
| *A Rose Is Still a Rose* | Aretha Franklin featuring Lauryn Hill | 1997 |
| ***I've Got This Feelin'*** | ***Bobby Brown, with Whitney Houston*** | *1997* |
| *Morning* | Bridgette McWilliams | 1997 |
| ***Retrospective for Life*** | ***Common and Lauryn Hill*** | *1997* |
| ***Give It to You*** | ***Da Brat*** | *1995* |
| ***No, No, No*** | ***Destiny's Child featuring Wyclef Jean*** | *1997* |
| *Reality* | Elusion | 1997 |
| ***Too Gone Too Long*** | ***En Vogue*** | *1997* |
| *MyLovin' (You're Never Going to Get It)* | En Vogue | 1992 |
| *Don't Let Go* | En Vogue | 1996 |
| ***Givin' Him Something He Can Feel*** | ***En Vogue*** | *1993* |
| ***Tyrone*** | ***Erykah Badu*** | *1997* |
| ***On and On*** | ***Erykah Badu*** | *1997* |
| *Killing Me Softly* | Fugees | 1996 |
| *Anytime Anyplace* | Janet Jackson | 1994 |
| *Together Again* | Janet Jackson | 1997 |
| *Got Till It's Gone* | Janet Jackson | 1997 |
| *Together Again* (Deeper Remix) | Janet Jackson | 1997 |
| *Love Will Never Do Without You* | Janet Jackson | 1990 |
| *The Party Continues* | Jermain Duprie featuring Da Brat | 1997 |
| ***Ghetto Superstar*** | ***Joi*** | *1997* |
| ***Swing My Way*** | ***KP and Envyi*** | *1997* |
| *Young Sad and Blue* | Lysette | 1997 |
| ***Honey*** | ***Mariah Carey featuring Puff Daddy and Mase*** | *1997* |
| *Butterfly* | Mariah Carey | 1997 |
| *Breakdown* | Mariah Carey featuring Bone Thugs and Redman | 1997 |
| *The Roof* | Mariah Carey featuring Mobb Deep | 1997 |
| *Seven Days* | Mary J. Blige featuring George Benson | 1997 |
| ***I'm Not Gonna Cry*** | ***Mary J. Blige*** | *1997* |
| *I Can Love You* | Mary J. Blige featuring Lil' Kim | 1997 |
| ***All I Need*** | ***Method Man and Mary J. Blige*** | *1995* |
| ***Beep Me 911*** | ***Missy Elliot featuring 702*** | *1997* |
| ***Sock It to Me*** | ***Missy Elliot featuring Da Brat and Lil' Kim*** | *1997* |
| *Am I Dreaming* | Ol' Skool featuring Xscape and Keith Sweat | 1997 |
| *So Long* | Phaija | 1997 |
| *Don't Stop the Music* | Playa featuring Missy Elliot | 1997 |
| *All about the Benjamins* | Puff Daddy featuring the Lox, Lil' Kim, and B.I.G. | 1997 |

*(continued)*

**Table 13.1**  *Continued*

| TITLE | ARTIST | YEAR |
|---|---|---|
| *It's All about the Benjamins* | *Puff Daddy featuring The Lox, Lil' Kim, Dave Grohl, and Fuzzbubble* | *1997* |
| *I'll Be Missing You* | Puff Daddy, Faith Evans, and 112 | 1997 |
| **Man Behind the Music** | **Queen Pen featuring Teddy Riley** | **1997** |
| *All My Love* | Queen Pen featuring Eric Williams of Backstreet | 1997 |
| *We Getz Down* | Rampage featuring 702 and Billie Lawrence | 1997 |
| **R U Ready** | **Salt n' Pepa** | **1997** |
| *Wannabe* | Spice Girls | 1997 |
| *Say You'll Be There* | Spice Girls | 1997 |
| *Rain* | SWV | 1997 |
| *Silly* | Taral Hicks | 1998 |
| *Firm Biz* | The Firm (Nas, ZA, and Foxy Brown) | 1997 |
| *Luv 2 Luv Ya* | Timbaland and Magoo featuring Shaunte | 1997 |
| **Red Light Special** | **TLC** | **1994** |
| *You're Making Me High* | Toni Braxton | 1997 |
| *Unbreak My Heart* | Toni Braxton | 1996 |
| *What about Us* | Total featuring Missy Elliot | 1997 |
| **DJ Keep Playing** | **Yvette Michelle** | **1997** |

NOTE: Titles in bold italics indicate videos that were used in both content and textual analysis.

shown with her infant daughter in her video, *Ghetto Superstar*.

Sexual diversity is another element of Black womanhood that is conspicuously absent and also reflects the desirability of perceived sexual availability for men. None of the videos featured performers who were lesbian or bisexual, nor did they show even implicit homosexual or bisexual themes. This was interesting in light of the emergence of critically acclaimed and commercially popular bisexual and lesbian artists, most notably, Me'Shell Ndgeocello (whose most controversial video *Leviticus: Faggot* was censored by BET). As can be gleaned from the frequently homophobic rhetoric in hip-hop and R&B songs, sexual difference and nonconformity are still not legitimized in Black popular culture. As a result, it is not particularly surprising that bisexual and lesbian themes do not emerge in a sample of popular Black women's music videos. . . .

## Black Women's Agency: Countering Controlling Images

Despite the continuing objectification and exploitation of Black women in music videos, I found evidence of contestation, resistance, and the assertion of Black women's agency in many others (*n* = 25) as well. This agency emerged through the identification with signifiers of Blackness; an assertion of autonomy, vocality, and independence; and expressions of partnership, collaboration, and sisterhood with other Black women and Black men.

### Signifiers of Blackness: Black Aesthetic, Black Context

In these videos, Blackness does not carry a negative connotation. Instead, it is the basis for strength, power, and a positive self-identity. Darker skin is privileged among Black women artists, actresses, models, and dancers in the videos. Thirty of the videos featured women with darker complexions or a combination of lighter and darker skinned women. This was an especially interesting finding after the controversies of the 1980s and 1990s about the frequent use of light-skinned women in music videos, which was criticized for valuing a white standard of beauty (Morgan 1999). In contrast, the videos examined in this study evinced a Black aesthetic in which standards of beauty, while problematic in themselves, were nevertheless based on a more African aesthetic.

The prevalence of a clear hip-hop sensibility supports the valuation of Black culture. Twenty of the videos were coded as being evocative of an urban hip-hop style. What emerges from these observations is the construction of a clear Black aesthetic. In fact, it becomes obvious that these videos exhibit an essentially Black universe. Although this was not specifically coded, white people appeared rarely if ever in the videos. When they do appear, they tend to be minor characters. . . .

### Autonomy, Vocality, and Independence

Despite the predominance of traditional gender roles in the music videos, Black women performers are frequently depicted as active, vocal, and independent. This vocality is most frequent within the context of traditional relationships, where the performers express discontent with, and contest, the conditions faced by Black women in interpersonal relationships.

Instead of exhibiting representations of physical violence and aggression, sometimes found in men's videos, this sample of videos demonstrates the significance of verbal assertiveness. Speaking out and speaking one's mind are a constant theme. Through the songs and videos, Black women are able to achieve voice and a space for spoken expression of social and interpersonal commentary.

A video by Erykah Badu, *Tyrone*, is the most conspicuous example of this theme. The lyrics, in which Badu dismisses a neglectful lover who prefers the company of his shiftless, unemployed friends, demonstrate her ability to get out of a bad relationship in which her sexual, emotional, and financial needs are not being met. Her words are underscored by her performance style. Badu is at center stage wearing African attire, including her signature headdress, and standing next to an ankh, an ancient Egyptian symbol of life. As she sings, her gestures, inflections, and facial expressions underscore the meaning of the song and increase her rapport with the very enthusiastic women in the audience. The "Tyrones" of the world know who they are, and the women they are involved with have an example of the most expedient and effective way of dealing with them. Badu clearly speaks her mind and asserts her own interests forcefully.

Although they are not clearly and unequivocally rejecting the desirability and basic dynamics of heterosexual relationships, Black women in these videos assert their own interests and express dissatisfaction with the unequal state of Black men-women interpersonal relations. Black women also express their own agency and self-determination through direct action. What emerges is the ability of a Black woman to define her own identity and life outcomes.

### Sisterhood, Partnership, and Collaboration

Although Black women assert independence, they do not accomplish their goals alone. In these videos, Black women look to each other for support, partnership, and sisterhood. Collaborations between women artists are a constant and recurring theme throughout the videos and suggest a sense of community and collectivity. This shows that women need each other for guidance and support to succeed and survive in the recording industry and the world at large. Within these collaborations, unlike the male sponsorships discussed above, the spotlight is shared, and the guest star does not overshadow the featured artist.

The most interesting video in which this occurs is *Sock It to Me*, in which Missy Elliott collaborates with the rappers Lil' Kim and Da Brat. It has an outer-space, fantasy theme, and in the visual narrative, Missy and rapper Lil' Kim appear in red and white bubble space suits as explorers on a mission. As soon as they land on an uncharted planet, they are pursued by an army of monstrous robots under the control of the evil "mad scientist," portrayed by Missy's collaborator and producing partner Timbaland. They are chased throughout the rest of the video through space and on various barren planets. The chase scenes are interspersed with scenes of Missy, as she dances in the forefront of a troupe of dancers wearing futuristic attire. Missy also appears solo, seemingly suspended in space as she sings the track of the song. Just as Missy and Kim appear to be in danger of succumbing to Timbaland's goons, fellow rapper, Da Brat, during her rap sequence on the music track, comes to the rescue on a jet ski–type spacecraft. They speed off through space, fighting off the mad scientist's crew, and arrive safely at Missy's mothership, prominently marked with the letter *M*.

Throughout the chase sequences, the viewer's identification remains squarely with Missy and Kim, solidified by the close-up shots of their frightened facial expressions as they flee the goons and the (albeit short-lived) satisfaction apparent on their faces when they mistakenly believe that they have escaped their pursuers.

The extended chase scene signifies the continued quest to escape the threat of male dominance. It symbolizes the agency of women who refuse to be subsumed or annihilated by male dominance, as represented by the monstrous troops of the male mad scientist. The sisterhood that is implied by the camaraderie between Missy and Lil' Kim, their ability to escape Timbaland's evil troops, and the fact that they are rescued by another woman, Da Brat, further demonstrates the collective power of Black women to help each other be self-sufficient and not dependent on men.

Overall, what emerges from this combination of agency, voice, partnership, and Black context is a sense of the construction of Black woman–centered video narratives. Within these narratives, the interests, desires, and goals of women are predominant and gain importance in contrast to those in which they are exploited and subsumed.

Black women are quite firmly the subjects of these narratives and are able to clearly and unequivocally express their points of view.

### *Ambivalence and Contradiction: Negotiating Black Womanhood*

In this section, I discuss the ambivalent and contradictory relationship that young Black women appear to have with Black popular culture and how those contradictions are reflected in the music videos in this sample. In this regard, music videos exemplify a tension between the structural constraints of race and gender on one hand and women's resistance and self-affirmation on the other.

Every day, young Black women face conflicting messages about their sexuality and femininity, as well as their status both in the Black community and society at large. They must figure out how they should construct and assert their identity as Black women. Therefore, it is not surprising that within the cultural productions of young Black women, themes of contradiction and ambivalence would emerge.

While it sometimes appears that these artists are directly reflecting and capitulating to oppressive social forces, this seeming compromise can be interpreted more accurately as ambivalence regarding contradictory messages about Black female sexuality, namely, the coexistence of hypersexual images and the denigration and denial of the beauty of the Black female body. In response to these contradictory notions of Black womanhood, Black women performers frequently reappropriate often explicit images of Black female sexuality. This strategy of self-representation as sexual may, on one hand, be interpreted as a sort of false consciousness that reflects an acceptance of the controlling images of Black womanhood. However, I argue that instead, these sometimes explicit representations of Black women's sexuality actually exemplify a process of negotiating those contradictory and often conflicting notions and, more significantly, represent an attempt to use the space of the music video to achieve control over their own sexuality. The four themes that I located that indicate this process include collaboration between Black men and women, representation of a multidimensional sexuality, returning the gaze, and the indeterminate gaze. . . .

### Multidimensional Sexuality: Reappropriating the Black Female Body

Most of the artists portray themselves with a highly stylized and glamorous image. Wearing designer gear, these women singers present themselves as sexy and provocative. In 21 of the videos, the artist was depicting a glamorous image, while in 17 they were coded as having a sexual image. This emphasis on appearance and physical attraction confirms the notion of the excessive sexuality of the Black woman. It supports the ideological controlling image of the hypersexual "sapphire" or "jezebel," effectively undermining Black womanhood and humanity.

However, in the videos analyzed, glamour and style are not the only salient attributes possessed by Black women artists. Instead, a sexualized image often occurs simultaneously with themes of independence, strength, a streetwise nature, toughness, and agency. Most of the time, the same artists express themselves in a single video as sexy and savvy, glamorous and autonomous. Fifteen of the videos depict artists having an independent image, and 13 are streetwise and tough. Many of these videos were also coded as glamorous and sexual.

What seems to emerge is a contradiction between the complex and often unconventional representations of Black women artists and the appearance of objectified and clearly one-dimensionally sexualized Black women dancers. Fifteen of the videos were coded as featuring female background dancers. For the most part, when these dancers appear on screen, they are scantily clad and move in a highly suggestive manner. Male dancers, in contrast, only appear in 8 of the 56 videos and are rarely explicitly sexualized. In Da Brat's *Give It to You*, which takes place at what appears to be a hip-hop industry party, Da Brat's tough and streetwise, even boyish, image

contrasts sharply with the appearance of scantily clad female "groupies" who are mingling and dancing in the crowd. Missy Elliott's *Beep Me 911* is set in what seems to be a pornographic peep show. Missy and 702 dance among go-go dancers who appear to be life-sized marionettes, as Timbaland and Magoo observe through a glass barrier. Missy is demanding that her lover tells her what's up by beeping her, to tell her why "you're playing on me." She asserts her own interests, the fulfillment of her own physical and emotional desires, which is ironic considering that her demands are being articulated in a context of male sexual pleasure and satisfaction.

The fact remains that sex sells. In the entertainment industry, there is a call for bodies, namely, female bodies, to be on display to stimulate record sales. If it is not the artist herself, then models and dancers serve this purpose. Women remain the object of sexual desire, the selling point, and the bodies on display.

On the other hand, the juxtaposition and combination of sexuality, assertiveness, and independence in these videos can also be read as the reappropriation of the Black woman's body in response to its sexual regulation and exploitation. What emerges is an effort on the part of the Black female artist to assert her own sexuality, to gain her own sexual pleasure.

Whether this indicates compromise or capitulation to objectification and exploitation is not definitively clear. It is difficult to reach a conclusion on this solely from the data gathered from textual analysis. One would need to investigate the creative production decision-making process. However, the results of this analysis and interpretation indicate that trade-offs are made in the construction of an artist's image. Black womanhood, as expressed through Da Brat and Missy's performances, is the result of a process of negotiation in which objectification of the female body must be present in order for the performer to gain a level of autonomy, to gain exposure. While this seems on the surface like "selling out" to the dictates of patriarchy and the marketplace, I would argue that instead, it affirms the multidimensional nature of Black womanhood. A woman does not need to alienate her sexuality to be assertive, nor must she be a one-dimensional sex object. She can be allowed to express her sexuality, her body, and her own life simultaneously. In these texts, the Black woman is constructed, through this seeming contradiction, as being able to assert the pursuit of pleasure without sacrificing her humanity.

### Returning the Gaze:
### Sexuality on a Woman's Terms

An interesting manifestation of the phenomenon of contradiction and ambivalence is the pattern of a reversal and returning of the gaze. A critical mass of videos feature men as objects of women's desire, where men's bodies are the center of the camera's gaze. What also occurs in these videos is a reversing of traditional gender roles in which men are objectified. Simultaneously, women remain the object of the camera's gaze as well. In *Swing My Way,* KP and Envyi pursue a male love interest in a club. In *You're Making Me High,* Toni Braxton and actresses Erika Alexander, Vivica Fox, and Tisha Campbell rate male visitors on a numerical scale as they appear in an elevator, while Toni's *Unbreak My Heart* features Black male supermodel Tyson Beckford. TLC (group members T-Boz, Left Eye, and Chilli) are the only women players (and the only fully clothed individuals) in a sexy game of strip poker in *Red Light Special,* and Janet Jackson's *Love Will Never Do Without You* centers the well-chiseled Black body of Djamon Hounsou and the buffed white body of actor Antonio Sabato Jr. alongside her own washboard abs. What all of these videos have in common is the construction of the male body, and particularly the Black male body, as the object of Black female pleasure. The male body is not merely looked at; rather, it is actively pursued. These women clearly and unequivocally express what they want, how and when they want it, and that they frequently get it.

What results is a space where the erotic can become articulated on a woman's terms. When videos featuring themes of sexual desire and fulfillment were coded, signifiers of mutual sexual

fulfillment predominated, and women's sexual fulfillment was more often portrayed than for men. Although women were usually visually constructed as the source of male pleasure, when issues of sexual pleasure were articulated either in the lyrical or visual text, or both, the importance of female sexual desire became key. This construction of a sphere of erotic agency does not simply symbolize the subjectivity of the individual Black woman but also results in the construction of agency at the social and cultural level. It results in a space for an articulation of themes of freedom and liberty.

A long-standing theme in Black popular culture and the African American performance tradition has been the connection and interrelatedness of themes of sexuality to those of freedom (Davis 1998; Gilroy 1993). Angela Davis (1998) cites Audre Lorde's theory of "The Erotic as Power" in describing the ways in which the lyrics and performances of Black women artists included associations of sexuality as freedom and social commentary. In describing Billie Holliday's performance of "Some Other Spring," Davis elucidates how Holliday reappropriated the concept of love and sexual desire to symbolize liberty and autonomy:

> In a more complex racial and cultural context, she was able to carry on a tradition established by the blues women and blues men who were her predecessors: the tradition of representing love and sexuality as both concrete daily experience and as coded yearning for social liberation. (1998, 173)

Within the context of racial and sexual oppression and marginalization, love and sexuality have come to signify not only interpersonal relationships but also Black women's struggles for liberation and freedom at a broader level.

### The Indeterminate Gaze

The address and gaze in these videos were frequently indeterminate. It was difficult to ascertain where the camera's gaze was intended to originate and to whom the video images and narrative were addressed. While clearly not ungendered, the gaze and address were frequently also neither male nor female. Both the male and female audience member or viewer appears to be constructed within these texts. The camera objectifies the Black female body in a traditional manner, while the lyrics of the song are addressed to a male subject. However, it becomes apparent that men are not the only intended audience. There appears to be a space constructed within the text that allows for Black women viewers to place themselves as subjects of the text, of the narrative.

A mélange of visual and aural strategies contribute to the construction of this indeterminate gaze. In these videos, the camera positioning, artist performance, and narrative structure are combined with visual omniscience. In addition, an indeterminate point of view and frequently non-gender-specific song lyrics contribute to the possibility of a multigendered and even ungendered gaze within music video texts. The Black female performers are not just looking at and talking to men but looking at and speaking with women as well. The unspecified and omniscient point of view constructed by camera positioning supports this by allowing both men and women to see themselves as subjects of the song and video.

The most compelling examples of this phenomenon occur in videos by the group En Vogue. In *Giving Him Something*, a remake of the Aretha Franklin R&B classic, En Vogue performs in a club for an all-male audience. They move seductively, gyrate their hips, and sing provocatively of "giving him something he can feel so he knows my love is real." The men in the audience are responding viscerally, biting their knuckles, and swooning. This scenario is interesting because while the group members are clearly objectified on stage and are explicitly sexualized, it is clear that they are gaining pleasure reciprocally along with a certain level of power over these men who are virtually losing control of their faculties as a result of their performance. Second, the men in the audience are extremely attractive themselves and are the objects of the camera's gaze. What is important here is that not only are men gaining pleasure from viewing the video, but women, as the viewers, are as well. This is not a mere role reversal but an example of an articulation of mutual

pleasure and enjoyment. The Black woman is the agent of her own pleasure as well as the vehicle for the fulfillment of the man's desire. She is not just the object but also becomes the subject. As in the gaze reversal videos discussed above, not only does she give sexual pleasure, she also pursues, receives, and accepts it.

Informed by the context of the gender politics of Black male and female relationships, this construction of the unfixed, multiple gaze serves to level the sexual playing field. En Vogue, Toni Braxton, and TLC are not simply on display for men (although they surely are); their videos also place men on display for them and their fellow women viewers. In addition, and significantly, the simultaneous existence of their sexuality and independence contests inequality in man–woman relationships. As a result, instead of being the object of exploitation, the Black woman performer is able to construct a subject position for herself and her women viewers. While this is not articulated as a complete role reversal, which would ostensibly alienate male audiences, it is instead expressed as a mutual pursuit of sexual pleasure and satisfaction.

## Conclusion

Despite the potentially limiting aspects of the frequently contradictory and stereotypical themes in music videos, I demonstrated that a more nuanced and complex depiction of Black womanhood emerges in the representations of Black woman performers.

My findings support and enhance the current literature in Black feminist theory. Whereas in *Black Feminist Thought* Hill Collins (1991a) demonstrated how the controlling images of Black womanhood are disseminated and legitimized through social institutions, my study extends her notion by showing how popular entertainment serves as a space for the proliferation of these controlling images. Hill Collins (1991a, 1991b) described the ways that Black women have countered these hegemonic notions of Black femininity through their culture, focusing on literature and performance in the Blues tradition. I show how Black women also are able to articulate other key themes of self-valuation, self-determination, and a critique of the interlocking nature of oppression. The themes of returning the erotic gaze and reappropriating the Black female body add an additional dimension to Black feminist theory by showing how Black women may use the sphere of culture to reclaim and revise the controlling images, specifically "the Jezebel," to express sexual subjectivity.

Of course, the conclusions drawn as a result of a textual content analysis of music videos are necessarily limited by the absence of inquiry into the production and reception of music videos and by the lack of a more comprehensive survey of the cultural landscape in which they exist. As a result, this study is not a complete analysis of the social context of Black female representation in music videos, and further investigation into Black women's reception and interpretation of music videos, as well as their role as cultural producers in the entertainment industry, is recommended.

## REFERENCES

Aufderheide, Pat. 1986. Music videos: The look of the sound. *Journal of Communication* 36:58–77.

Davis, Angela Yvonne. 1998. *Blues legacies and Black feminism: Gertrude "Ma" Rainey, Bessie Smith, and Billie Holiday.* New York: Pantheon Books.

Dines, Gail, and Jean Humez. 1995. *Gender, race and class in media.* Thousand Oaks, CA: Sage.

Frith, Simon, Andrew Goodwin, and Lawrence Grossberg. 1993. *Sound and vision: The music video reader.* New York: Routledge.

George, Nelson. 1998. *Hip hop America.* New York: Viking.

Gilroy, Paul. 1993. *The Black atlantic: Modernity and double consciousness.* Cambridge, MA: Harvard University Press.

Hill Collins, Patricia. 1991a. *Black feminist thought: Knowledge, consciousness and the politics of empowerment.* New York: Routledge.

———1991b. Learning from the outsider within: The sociological significance of Black feminist thought. In *Beyond methodology: Feminist scholarship as lived research,* edited by Mary Margaret Fonow and Judith A. Cook. Bloomington and Indianapolis: Indiana University Press.

hooks, bell. 1992. *Black looks: Race and representation.* Boston: South End.

Hurley, Jennifer M. 1994. Music video and the construction of gendered subjectivity (or how being a music video junkie turned me into a feminist). *Popular Music* 13:326–38.

Kaplan, E. Ann. 1987. *Rocking around the clock: Music television, postmodernism and consumer culture.* New York: Methuen.

Lindlof, Thomas R. 1995. *Qualitative communication research methods.* Thousand Oaks, CA: Sage.

McRobbie, Angela. 1991. *Feminism and youth culture: From "Jackie" to "just seventeen."* Boston: Unwin Hyman.

———. 1993. Shut up and dance: Youth culture and changing modes of femininity. *Cultural Studies* 7 (3): 46.

———. 1997. *Back to reality? Social experience and cultural studies.* Manchester, UK, and New York: Manchester University Press.

McRobbie, Angela, and Mica Nava. 1984. *Gender and generation.* London: Macmillan.

Morgan. 1999. *When chickenheads come home to roost: My life as a hip-hop feminist.* New York: Simon & Schuster.

Perkins, William Eric. 1996. *Droppin' science: Critical essays on rap music and hip hop culture.* Philadelphia: Temple University Press.

Rose, Tricia. 1991. Never trust a big butt and a smile. *Camera Obscura* 23:9.

———. 1994. *Black noise: Rap music and Black culture in contemporary America.* Hanover, NH: Wesleyan University Press, University Press of New England.

Stockbridge, Sally. 1987. Music video: Questions of performance, pleasure and address. *Continuum: The Australian Journal of Media and Culture* 1(2). [cited 2 April 1997]. Available from www.mcc.murdoch.edu.au/readingroom/1.2/stockbridge.html.

Strauss, Anselm. 1987. *Qualitative analysis for social scientists.* Cambridge, UK, and New York: Cambridge University Press.

Vincent, Richard C. 1989. Cho's consciousness raised? Portrayal of women in rock videos re-examined. *Journalism Quarterly* 66:155–60.

Vincent, Richard, Dennis K. Davis, and Lilly Ann Boruszkowski. 1987. Sexism on MTV: The portrayal of women in rock videos. *Journalism Quarterly* 64:750–55, 941.

Watkins, S. Craig. 1998. *Representing: Hip hop culture and the production of Black cinema.* Chicago: University of Chicago Press.

# My Meidel Is the Centerfold: Is Playboy's First Jewish Bunny a Role Model?

Deborah Kolben

Growing up, I learned a few things about Jewish girls from the copy of *Truly Tasteless Jokes* my brother kept in our bathroom. In addition to being frigid and cheap, I learned that we love Bloomingdale's, dislike oral sex, and prefer circumcised penises—as the joke goes, we like everything better when it's 20% off. While Jewish men are noted for their keen minds and acerbic wit, Jewish women are hailed as overbearing mother figures with big boobs, bodacious thighs, and a penchant for debilitating headaches—a stereotype perpetuated by Jewish men like Woody Allen and Philip Roth, whose male protagonists admire Jewish women's minds but lust after young shiksa bodies.

Thanks to Lindsey Vuolo, a 20-year-old college student from Pennsylvania who bared her bod in the November 2001 issue of *Playboy,* that stereotype might finally be changing. As the self-proclaimed first-ever synagogue-attending Jewish centerfold, Lindsey finds herself heralding a new generation of young Jewish women seeking appreciation for their bodies as well as their minds. Already busy with school, car-dealership appearances, and magazine signings, Lindsey has also had to schedule time to defend her bunnyhood to the Jewish community, which has had a mixed reception to her naked debut. On a panel organized by Makor, a Jewish cultural center on Manhattan's Upper West Side, she went head-to-head with Shmuley Boteach, the young Hassidic rabbi famed for his book *Kosher Sex* as well as for his post in Michael Jackson's clutch of spiritual advisors. Boteach's objections to pornography stem from Jewish law, *halacha,* which holds that sex and nudity are sanctified and belong behind closed doors. "The issue for Judaism," Boteach writes in *Kosher Sex,* "is that pornography does not enhance the passion and romance between a couple, but rather replaces them by something alien." Unwilling to cow to the rabbi, (who, it should be noted, promoted his own book in *Playboy*) Lindsey stood her ground, explaining that she had done nothing wrong. According to Lindsey, *Playboy* doesn't even count as pornography because to her the word conjures up images of "penetration, urination, and things like that."

In a *New York* magazine article, Lindsey affirmed her decision to pose nude. "I believe that the only regrets in life are the risks you [don't] take. And once people talk to me, they realize I not only have the guts to take my clothes off, but I'm intellectually prepared to defend myself." While Lindsey's defense might be more plucky than brainy, her naked-girl-power message—that it's okay to be smart and sexy—has won her an unlikely fan club among young Jewish women tired of their negative image in pop culture. Liz Budnitz, 26-year-old Berkeley native and Barnard Center for Women employee, attended a progressive Hebrew school that offered an entire class on the stereotypes of Jewish women. Among the subjects discussed were the loud whiny voice, unruly dark hair, and overbearing mother image associated with Jewish women. "All of these contribute to that unsexy stereotype," Budnitz explains. "The beauty ideal in magazines is blond,

From Kolben, Deborah. 2002. My *Meidel* Is the Centerfold: Is *Playboy's* First Jewish Bunny a Role Model?" *Bitch* (May). Reprinted by permission.

thin, making as little noise and taking up as little space as possible. And honey, that ain't Jewish women!"

So who are Jewish women? According to the boob tube we're Fran Drescher, the whiny Nanny; Andrea Zimmerman, *90210*'s frumpy, competitive brainiac; and Kyle's mom on *South Park,* an overbearing kvetcher who inspires the other kids to sing "Kyle's mom is a big fat bitch." Other media favorites include Long Island Lolita Amy Fisher, Hollywood Madam Heidi Fleiss, and, of course Monica Lewinsky, that thong-flashing, gentile-boss-wooing icon. Our public image is that of needy princess, supergeek, controlling matriarch, and conniving whore all rolled into one.

When I called Lindsey on a Friday afternoon to discuss the public image of American Jewish women, she was lying in bed studying for her Communications class at Indiana University of Pennsylvania before heading out to Wolfendale's, the bar where she continues to work—not because she has to, but because the people there "are like family." It was one of these Wolfendale family members who snapped some digital photos of Lindsey and bet her 50 bucks that she was *Playboy* material; Lindsey agreed to the bet but never thought anything would come of it. The daughter of a Bronx-born Jewish mother and an Italian father who converted to Judaism, Lindsey was raised as a Reform Jew and says she feels an even stronger connection to her religion now that she's away from home. Of course, she was concerned about what her parents and rabbi would say about her foray into soft-core, but when she returned home from college, even the ladies at Friday night services were saying *mazel tov.*

Before seeing the November issue of *Playboy,* the only photo I could find of Lindsey was on the Internet—she was 13, wearing a tallis, and reading from the Torah. The transformation from dark-haired young *meidel* to bleached blond with an immaculately groomed muff is a bit disconcerting at first; thanks to *Playboy*'s hair and makeup artists, however, Lindsey resembles every other centerfold, which is to say her lips

are glossy, her body round, and her eyes enticing. Under a photo of Lindsey spread-eagle on a bed wearing three-inch heels is a caption that reads, "Lindsey goes to college in the small town where her grandmother grew up." Beneath the Playmate data sheet where Lindsey has written in wide bubbly letters that she has 34 DD breasts and gets turned on by true love (not *davening* and doctors, as one might expect) is a photo captioned, "My Bat Mitzvah, age 13." And the centerfold shot, set in a wholesome kitchen equipped with a copper teakettle, a bowl of eggs, and a fresh-baked pie, features Lindsey reclining naked on a wooden butcher's block, covered in flour. (A surprising choice, since according to the old joke the only thing Jewish girls make for dinner are reservations).

While there have been other Playmates with names like Greenberg, Lindsey claims to be the first Jewish playmate to flaunt her religion. "I think there might have been Playmates that were kind of half-Jewish and just never really talked about it," she explains. In contrast, Lindsey's *Playboy* spread is all Jewish: In addition to the Bat Mitzvah picture, Lindsey discusses a recent trip to Israel, saying, "Being in Jerusalem was so emotional for me—I broke down and cried."

Addressing the stereotype of Jewish girls as loose, Lindsey refutes assertions of widespread promiscuity. "We're too smart to be easy," she quips. Even so, compared to our Catholic peers—for whom sexual guilt is a given—Jews have surprisingly few issues with sex, religiously speaking. As Boteach writes in his erotic opus, "Unlike other religious traditions, Judaism has never had a prudish or conservative sexual ethic." As in Catholicism, Jewish law governs sexual activity, but the body is sanctified rather than sinful: Ancient rabbis advised men and women on how to pleasure their spouses and, as Boteach notes, "The rabbis made female orgasm an obligation incumbent on every Jewish husband." (A dictum that once caused my gentile male writing professor to exclaim, "No wonder they went to the beds of shiksas!" and may also explain why some Jewish girls developed the unofficial motto, "A little coitus never hoitus.")...

Bradley Hirschfield, a modern orthodox rabbi and vice president of The National Jewish Center for Learning and Leadership, believes Lindsey has been a positive force. "Now you have Jewish men who will go home and masturbate to a Jewish girl for a change," Hirschfield enthuses on Beliefnet, a website devoted to religious discourse. While this might seem a tad disingenuous—after all, most men probably don't care whether the women in the photos they whack off to are Jewish or not—Hirschfield equates Lindsey with progress.... Lindsey shares Hirschfield's sentiments, adding, "Before *Playboy* I was just another Jewish woman," she says. "Now, I'm not Golda Meir or anything, but I hope that I can be a role model for Jewish women."

Lindsey falls along a continuum of progress for Jewish women that began in 1945 when Bess Myerson, a brunette from the Bronx, became the first and only Jewish woman to win the title of Miss America. On the way into the pageant at Atlantic City, an old woman with numbers tattooed on her arm grabbed Myerson and told her, in Yiddish, If you win, it will not only be a sign that we are free, but that we are also beautiful. Though she seems to agree with Hirschfield that the ability to be as sexually objectified as her non-Jewish peers amounts to a giant leap for female Semitic affirmation, Lindsey also realizes that beauty isn't everything. "A lot of people email me," she says in a conversation with Boteach posted on Beliefnet. "I'm a Jewish doctor and I graduated with this degree from Yale." Or, "My son, my Jewish son, one goes to Princeton and the other goes to Stanford..." I've replied to them "Thank you very much for the offer. Thanks for taking the time to tell me how beautiful I looked in my layout, thanks for your support. But I can't date someone because they like the way I look."

# Gay-for-Pay: Straight Men and the Making of Gay Pornography

Jeffrey Escoffier

Situational homosexualities emerge when heterosexually-identified individuals encounter institutional settings that permit or reward homosexual behavior. Simon and Gagnon's (Gagnon and Simon 1973; Simon and Gagnon 1986) theory of sexual scripts allows us to understand situational sexualities as the result of interplays among stereotyped social cues, prescribed role-playing, enabling social conditions, and the converging intra-psychic motivations of participating individuals. Both the norms that regulate sexual behavior and the enabling social conditions that elicit and permit homosexual conduct from heterosexually-oriented participants can be activated using sexual scripts that circulate throughout the culture. Cues and social roles are embedded in culturally available scenarios, while the enabling conditions are often those material circumstances (prisons, barracks, economic need, drug use, or porn studio) that limit or exclude the supply of potential heterosexual sex partners (Escoffier 1999). In contrast to its use in the 1940s and 1950s, I distinguish situational sexuality from sexual behavior as governed by the individual's sexual identity which, over the course of his life, is constantly forged, reinforced, interrupted and reconfigured within and through culture and history.

In many cases, sexual scripts are situationally specific. The "situation," in part, emerges from the characteristics (gender, race, age) of the potential population of sex partners which constrain or normalize a sexual repertoire not normally chosen by the situated individual. Albert Reiss's classic essay "The Social Integration of Queers and Peers" explored a form of homosexual prostitution that took place between young men ("peers") who did not "define themselves either as hustlers or as homosexuals" and homosexual men ("queers") who performed fellatio upon them (Reiss 1961, p. 102). Reiss found that certain norms governed the sexual transactions that occurred between the young men and homosexuals, the most important that it be undertaken "solely as a way of making money: sexual gratification cannot be actively sought as a goal in the relationship." Another was that the transaction between them "must be limited to mouth-genital fellation. No other sexual acts are tolerated" (ibid.). Reiss also found that the young men defined someone as homosexual "not on the basis of homosexual *behavior*, but on the basis of participation in the homosexual *role*, the 'queer' role."

In this article I examine the homosexual activities of a group of men whose primary sexual identities are not gay, yet who regularly perform in gay pornographic videos. These men are widely known in the porn industry and among spectators as "gay-for-pay," the implication being that they would not engage in homosexual conduct were they not paid to do so. Of course, there are many explanations for such behavior. I will argue that this group of men exemplifies "situational homosexuality." There is no irrefutable evidence establishing these men as *really* straight or *actually* gay

From Escoffier, Jeffrey. 2003. "Gay-for-Pay: Straight Men and the Making of Gay Pornography." *Qualitative Sociology* 26: 531–555. Reprinted with kind permission from Springer Science and Business Media.

but in denial. However, all sexual conduct in the video porn industry is to one degree or another an example of situational sexuality inasmuch as the performers are often required to engage in sexual acts for monetary compensation that they would not otherwise choose to perform and with partners for whom they feel no desire.

### The Gay Porn Industry: Identity Politics and Markets

Since the late 1960s, the pornography industry in the United States has grown rapidly. While there is little reliable information about its size or annual revenues, experts estimate that the "adult entertainment" industry—which includes "XXX" videos and DVDs, Internet porn, cable and satellite porn, peep shows, phone sex, live sex acts, sex toys, and porn magazines—takes in somewhere between eight and ten billion dollars per year. That is comparable to Hollywood's annual domestic ticket sales or the annual revenues of professional sports. Again, while there are no reliable estimates, the gay market represents a significant portion of this amount—probably from ten to twenty-five percent (Antalek 1997a; Rich 2001; Thomas 2000).

Until the early 1970s male homosexual pornography was produced and distributed under "black market" conditions. The first commercial male pornographic films were probably made in the late 1960s, but they were few in number (Waugh 1996). Only after the gay movement had gained momentum were companies formed explicitly to produce gay male pornography. The production and distribution of commercial gay pornography took off between 1970 and 1985. Initially, gay pornographic movies were made by amateur filmmakers, and to some degree, many of the films made in this period represented an expression of the filmmaker's own newly "liberated" homosexuality—this was especially true for many of the performers. This development also reflected the liberating effect of the sexual revolution: during the same period, straight erotic films, such as *I Am Curious (Yellow), Deep Throat, The Devil in Miss Jones* and *Last Tango in Paris,* often played in mainstream movie houses. Wakefield Poole's gay *Boys in the Sand* opened in 1973, followed shortly by Jerry Douglas's *Back Row* (1974) and, like straight erotic movies, both films played in mainstream movie houses.

After 1985, production of gay pornography entered a new period in which video technology and extensive ownership of VCRs lowered its cost and made pornography more accessible. It became inexpensive and easy to rent. The new technology also enabled pornography to be viewed privately and at home. The AIDS crisis reinforced the privatized experience, some viewers turning to video porn out of fear of engaging in homosexual activities.

Moreover, starting in the mid 1980s, the gay market developed into a lucrative and dynamic growth sector for many industries, supplying specialty consumer goods to satisfy the aesthetic, social and sexual preferences of homosexuals. The commercial development of gay male pornography also benefited greatly from the growth of the gay market and urban gay communities by supplying erotic images to a growing number of self-accepting gay men. This demand helped shape the business in a number of ways: the standards of physical attractiveness, the repertoire of sexual acts, the production values, and the narrative conventions closely reflected the prevailing attitudes of gay male consumers.

In the early days of gay commercial pornography, it was difficult to recruit performers because homosexual behavior was still highly stigmatized and production was illicit. The performers were frequently recruited by the filmmakers (who were primarily gay) from among friends, casual sexual partners and boyfriends (Douglas 1996a). There was no pre-existing network or agents to recruit performers for gay pornographic films. . . .

Today, the gay pornography industry has a highly developed infrastructure of production companies, distribution networks and technical services, as well as agents and scouts for performers. If the first phase (1970–1985) in the development of commercial gay pornography attracted primarily gay men as performers, the second phase (post-1985) began to attract performers who did not identify as gay or homosexual. One contributing factor is that male performers were better paid in the gay pornography industry than in the straight side of the business. Given the heterosexual focus of straight pornography and the primarily male audience, the industry's female performers are better paid than most of the male performers. The prolific director Chi Chi Larue estimates the number of straight men in gay pornographic videos to be sixty percent. I suspect that this is on the high side, or it may merely reflect her selection of performers for her own work. By the mid 1980s, there was active recruiting of performers by scouts, photographers and others who work in the gay segment of the industry.

## The Spectator of Gay Pornography: Documentary Illusion and Identity Effects

Pornography probably has a more significant role in the life of gay men than it does among comparable groups of heterosexual men. Gay men often turn to gay pornography for cultural and sexual validation. As film critic Richard Dyer has noted, gay pornography contributes to the education of desire—it provides knowledge of the body and of sexual narratives, and examples of gay sexuality and of sexuality within a masculine framework. Since most gay men have become adults without having been socialized in the social and sexual codes of their communities, pornography can contribute to that as well (Dyer 1992).

The pleasure and sexual excitement that viewers of porn experience depend, to some degree, on the patterns of social and sexual interactions (i.e., the narratives, cues and symbols) that circulate in the larger culture (Kipnis 1996; Loftus 2002). The gay spectator's psychological response to the fictive world of pornography

and sexual fantasy—the symbolic conditions of sexual arousal—and the everyday life of social roles, values and social structures is mediated by the ideological and social developments of the gay community; not only do psycho-social elements predominate in the organization of the pornographic materials, but both the immediate social context and wider social environment also influence the sexual response to pornography (Gagnon and Simon 1973, pp. 260–265). Gagnon and Simon, in their analysis of pornography, show that an individual's fantasy life and his capacity for sexual arousal is significantly influenced by cultural context and historical situation. For example, in gay porn condoms are widely used (for many years they have appeared in almost all videos) for anal intercourse, in sharp contrast to their virtual absence in heterosexual pornography. Some gay men find that they are not aroused by the sexual action in "pre-condom" era movies, made before the discovery of AIDS—in this way the ideological and social context clearly influence the potential for sexual excitement.

In the case of video pornography, its effectiveness stems from its ability to satisfy the viewer's expectation that the sex is plausibly "real" in some way—a pornographic film or video is a "document" of sexual pleasure, of successful arousal and orgasm. The viewer's sexual arousal presumes the suspension of *disbelief* in pornography's fictional character. A "documentary illusion" exists in the photographic pornographic genres, which promise to enact certain sexual fantasies and certify them through the "authenticity" of *erections* (although some significance may be lost with the increased use of Viagra and other drugs) and *orgasms*. The psychological as well as the ideological power of pornography is achieved through this certification of sexual fantasy by its "documented" sexual conclusions—visibly displayed orgasms (Patton 1988, pp. 72–77; Williams 1989, pp. 93–119; Barthes 1986).

Viewers' responses and reviews of porn videos often minimize the genre's ambiguous expectations between fantasy/fiction and real sex. The sexual acts portrayed must seem genuinely exciting to the performers in order to arouse the viewer (they must be realistically credible), while also representing fantasies that invoke the culture's sexual scenarios. Reviewers sometimes will stress the "realness." "Ultimately what viewers want to see," one reviewer writes, "is guys *having* sex, not actors *pretending* to have sex. A few times there were some moans and some 'Oh, yeah, fuck me!' that sounded like typical porno soundtrack, but other than that this all seemed very authentic" (Foxxe 1999). . . .

Pornography's *identity effects* are enunciated through the genre's dominant semantic and syntactical conventions: the "standard" narrative sequence (kissing, oral sex, rimming, anal intercourse) of sexual acts, a convincingly energetic performance and, most importantly, the *erections* and visible *orgasms* that authenticate (and narratively close the scene) the embodied forms of homosexual desire. Operating within the "documentary illusion" the erections and the orgasms putatively "prove" to a gay male spectator that these "sexually desirable, masculine, and energetic performers" are *really* gay—thus affirming the gay male identity. An individual video may often deviate from these generic expectations, either through failure to provide a credible performance or by offering new or creative sexual variations.

In addition to its identity effects, gay male porn also has a somewhat paradoxical "hetero/masculinist effect," in which the generic conventions that consolidate and reinforce gay male identity coexist with frequent representations of "straight" men engaging in homosexual acts. In this way gay porn reinforces the incongruity between male homosexual desire—stigmatized, abject—and the heterosexual dominance of the masculine regime of desire. It serves to situate homosexual *desire* within masculine territory irrespective of heterosexual or gay identities (Pronger 1990, pp. 125–176). Thus, the widespread employment of straight performers in gay pornography intensifies the contradiction between *gay male identity* and *homosexuality without identity,*

conferring legitimacy on homosexual *behavior* independent of gay identity.

The creation of a market for gay pornography relies upon the cultural and economic significance of gay identities, and not—however widespread it may be among males—homosexual desire (Bronski 1984, pp. 166–174; Burger 1995; Harris 1997; Chasin 2000). Its expansion into other identity markets continues to reflect a significant trend in the gay pornography business, hence the growing number of videos targeting various demographic or sexual audiences—Latinos, black men and other gay men of color, the leather, S/M and bear subcultures, and all sorts of sexual specialties like spanking, uniforms and other fetishisms (Suggs 1999).

The central ambivalence between *identity* and *behavior* in gay male porn frames the reactions of spectators to—along with their libidinal investments in—porn "stars" (Dyer 1979, pp. 17–19). The gay men who buy or rent and view a video expect the sexual pleasure portrayed to be "authentic" enough to produce an orgasm. For the most part, the orgasm affirms the sexual act leading up to it and contributes to the viewer's own sexual arousal (Patton 1988; Williams 1989). But if the performer isn't gay, then the potential "meaning" of the orgasm is ambiguous. It can mean that orgasm is "acted" (or dramatically fabricated in some sense—"It's really only a heterosexual orgasm!"), or it can mean that even a straight man experienced an orgasm from sex with a man—this is one of the central ambiguities of gay porn (Pronger 1990, pp. 125–154). It potentially undermines the viewer's willingness to suspend disbelief in the fictional aspect of the porn video. Thus, while every pornographic movie made for a gay male market manifestly performs at least two tasks—to sexually stimulate its viewers and, in some way, to affirm their sexual identity—it may also perform a third and more contradictory task: to provide evidence of *homosexuality without identity* (Bech 1997, pp. 17–84). It may do so either narratively, through the inclusion of scenes portraying straight men having credible sex with gay men, or by employing "known" heterosexual (gay-for-pay) performers to credibly represent gay male sexuality.

## The Theory of Sexual Scripts

. . . Gagnon and Simon introduced a thoroughgoing conception of sexual behavior as a learned process, one that is possible not because of instinctual drives or physiological requirements, but because it is embedded in complex social scripts that are specific to particular locations in culture and history. Their approach stressed the significance of individual agency and cultural symbols in the conduct of our sexual activities. . . . No previous theorists of sexuality had interpreted sexual behavior as so completely social. They redefined sexuality from being the combined product of biological drives and social repression into an arena of creative social initiative and symbolic action. . . . In their theory they argue that individuals utilize their interactional skills, fantasy materials and cultural myths to develop "scripts" (with cues and appropriate dialogue) as a means for organizing their sexual behavior (1973; Simon and Gagnon 1986).

Sexual arousal and the performance of sexual acts frequently depend upon the meanings and cues of the social and cultural context. In fact, human sexual behavior is organized by structured expectations and prescribed interactions that are coded like scripts. The theory of sexual scripts as formulated by Gagnon and Simon provides a useful analytical framework for exploring the dynamics of sexual performance in pornographic production. Scripts are metaphors for the narrative and behavioral requirements for the production of everyday social life. In their theory of sexual scripting, Simon and Gagnon (1986) suggest that these "scripts," with cues and appropriate dialogue, which are constantly changing and which reflect different cultural groups, circulate in societies as generic guidelines for organizing social behavior. They distinguish three distinct levels of scripting: *cultural scenarios* provide instruction on the narrative requirements of broad social roles; *interpersonal scripts* are institutionalized patterns in everyday social interaction; and *intrapsychic scripts* are those that an individual uses in his or her internal dialogue with cultural and social behavioral expectations (ibid., pp. 98–104). For example, interpersonal scripts help individuals to organize their self-representations and those of others to initiate and engage in sexual activity, while the intrapsychic scripts organize the images and desires that elicit and sustain an individual's sexual desire. Cultural scenarios frame the interpersonal and intrapsychic scripts in the context of cultural symbols and broad social roles (such as race, gender or class) (Goffman 1976).

Thus the making of pornography, like other forms of sex work, relies upon the learned sexual responses of its participants—much of the sexual behavior shown in pornography is a display of situational sexuality. However, unlike other forms of sex work, gay pornography as a representational genre, which often implicitly reflects as well as affirms an *identitarian* agenda, is explicitly marketed to self-identified gay men. However, the gay male pornography industry routinely recruits men who do not identify as gay or homosexual to perform in gay videos. In addition, non-gay-identified men frequently have used their work in gay pornography to launch lucrative careers as escorts. Nevertheless, the fact that industry gossip about sexual orientations circulates constantly demonstrates how important these issues are to the industry's operation as well as to the audience's response (for examples of this kind of fan discourse see the forums at www.atkol.com). In gay pornographic videos, the ability of actors who are self-defined and otherwise behaviorally heterosexual to perform homosexual acts, maintain erections (both while penetrating or being penetrated) and have orgasms provides the opportunity to explore the construction of situational homosexuality on the gay pornography set.

One distinctive characteristic of video pornography is that it is a dramatic fabrication of sexual activity that also requires demonstrations of "authentic" sexual signs, that is, erections and orgasms. The dramatic fabrication is achieved not only by the performers enacting sexual scenes but also by elaborate editing and montage of the filmed sexual acts themselves. Usually the filming of a sexual scene requires many takes, stops and starts, and requires the performers to regain their erections. The maintenance and refreshing of erections—"wood" in the industry vernacular—is a constant preoccupation of video pornographers.

The gay pornography business, through its employment of men who are heterosexual or who do not self-consciously identify as gay, provides straight actors with social conditions that enable situationally specific sexual behavior. The pornography industry supplies (1) the social and physical space where these sexual activities can take place; it provides (2) other actors who expect to engage in sexual activities with one another; and it offers (3) narratives of sexual activities that invoke the culturally available sexual scripts that elicit and activate the filmed sexual activities. Pornographic video production is obviously a "situation" in which sexual activity can take place: it provides access to sexual experiences for its participants (Simon and Gagnon 1986, pp. 104–107).

## Gay-for-Pay as a Porn Career: Constructing the Persona

It is common practice that when anyone enters the porn industry they adopt a stage name—a *nom de porn*—by which they will be known to viewers. This protects the performer's privacy despite what is often a very visible public presence. In addition to taking the *nom de porn*, the performer must create his "character" as a performer. This persona is a "career script" through which the performer integrates traits of personality, physical characteristics and sexual performance style.

The new "porn star" fashions himself from the cultural myths and social roles that define male sexuality or violate masculine roles, or that affirm homosexual desire or draw upon ethnic or racial beliefs. Performers must obviously also draw

upon their "intrapsychic" fantasies and beliefs. Thus one performer may create his persona as the aggressive, dirty-talking "top" (the one who penetrates). In Rod Barry's case, his persona enables him to play the military man having sex in the barracks, a white trash hillbilly who fucks his cousin Seth but who won't kiss (they are "fucking cousins, not kissing cousins"), or a man who, in his first scene as a "bottom" (the one who is penetrated), "aggressively" urges on the man who tops him (Escoffier 2000). Another performer might create his persona as an exclusive top, a man with a large penis and a man who never kisses—elements drawn from sexual scripts, from both cultural scenarios and intrapsychic fantasies or fears.

Whatever his sexual preferences, when any man seeks employment in gay pornographic video production he must justify his choice from a number of perspectives. Participation in gay pornographic video production is, to some degree, a socially stigmatized activity (especially for those who do not identify as gay), not only because it is a form of sex work and because most people believe that public sexual performance negatively affects those who participate in it, but also because homosexuality is still a stigmatized form of sexuality. Thus, every new entrant into the porn business must give himself *permission* to engage in it (Simon and Gagnon 1986, pp. 109–110; Abbott 2000). Men who identify as heterosexual wanting to work in the gay porn industry must overcome the standard presumption that only gay men would want to perform in gay pornographic films. Obviously, the description of these performers as "gay-for-pay" presumes that the permission they require is primarily economic. But economic permission is often entangled with other reasons, such as curiosity or latent homosexual fantasies, such as in the following example:

*Um, well, I was straight before I found out about gay videos, but I was a straight person with, like, thoughts and feelings. And through my twenties, they got real strong. I almost thought I would try to have an interlude or a contact with a man. I thought about it, yeah, I was, like, one of those straight-curious types. But then I got into gay video, and I decided I can simultaneously make money and fulfill a fantasy. The money's a perfect way to justify going into the sexual world. I guess I consider myself formerly straight and now I'm sexually bi with a life-style of straight" (Paul Morgan, in Spencer 1998).*

Permission for some performers can come from surprisingly odd sources. One performer, who had "danced" in local Latino gay bars in Jackson Heights in New York City, gave one of the more unusual forms of permission:

*Interviewer:* How did you get started in this business?

*Tiger Tyson:* I just went in and did the video *Tiger's Brooklyn Tails* about two years ago. It turned out very successful. I didn't know I was going to become this whole character.

*I:* Did making films come naturally?

*TT:* It was something new, being that I'm bisexual. You could say I lost my virginity on video . . .

*I:* You haven't bottomed on film. Would you?

*TT:* No, never. I would probably turn into a little punk . . . I wouldn't feel right being on the bottom.

*I:* Do you now date guys?

*TT:* No. Actually I'm engaged. She's very supportive . . . I met her at Magic Touch while I was dancing for gay men, and she knows all about the videos. My mother is even supportive . . . that's why I don't bother to think I'm doing something wrong. If my mother doesn't feel disgraced, I feel good about it" (Straube 1999).

Dancing or stripping in gay bars, as Tyson's story suggests, is a common way of entering the world of gay porn, where other dancers or agents will scout for producers of gay videos (De Marco 2002). But many of the young straight men who enter the gay porn industry develop their permission to engage in homosexual activity in a video by using a surprisingly limited number of "scripts." One of the most common narratives that gay-for-

pay performers tell of their entry into the industry is the story of responding to a modeling ad or the approach of a recruiter who misleadingly offers to set up a photo shoot that turns out to be a nude photo shoot or porn audition. Brian Estevez, who worked in the industry in the late 1980s, gives this account of his recruitment:

*Brian Estevez:* They wanted to see my whole body . . . and I thought: "What the fuck is this?" . . . At that point, I began to wonder what was going on and what the deal was. I turned to the old guy and said, "You told me modeling. What is this shit?" He then told me that these guys had big companies and that they made movies. I told him I didn't want to do movies—and then he started talking money and I swear . . . I don't know . . . I guess money manipulated me . . . I didn't want to do it!

*Interviewer:* And then the next step?

*BE:* . . . and I went ahead, even though I'm very straight to this day.

*I:* Now about being straight . . .

*BE:* . . . You know, I grew up very straight—never had *any* homosexual tendencies.

*I:* You didn't connect it in any way to sexual pleasure?

*BE:* I didn't get any sexual stimulation from it. Even to this day, even in a sexual act, even if I have a hard-on and everything—I still didn't connect it to "Wow, this feels good."

*I:* And yet you started in films as a bottom?

*BE:* Well, I didn't have a lot of choice.

*I:* I'd think a straight boy would be a bit put off—that being a top would be more logical . . . more straight.

*BE:* I know—and that's how I felt. I'd much rather be a top, and in my later movies I didn't bottom anymore. It's just when they manipulated me into the business, they manipulated me into being a bottom. They told me that I wasn't big enough or buff enough to play a top role, so I was labeled a bottom—a small, hot guy who gets dick up his ass. After a few times around, I said, "Fuck it—I'm not doing that anymore."

*I:* Was the fact that you were doing it eating away at you?

*BE:* [quietly] Yeah—being a top would have been easier on my ego.

*I:* Did you enjoy it *while* it was happening?

*BE:* No, I didn't, because suddenly, out of nowhere, I was taking these big, hot monster dicks up my ass. It wasn't pretty (Richards 1991).

Estevez's construction of permission to perform in gay porn involves a series of disclaimers: "I'm very straight to this day," "I didn't get any sexual stimulation . . . even if I have a hard-on," and "I didn't have a lot of choice [to bottom]." Elaboration of permission and the construction of a persona often go hand-in-hand. Estevez's account illustrates this when he explains that "they manipulated me into being a bottom. They told me that I wasn't big enough or buff enough to play a top role, so I was labeled a bottom—a small, hot guy who gets dick up his ass . . . being a top would have easier on my ego." Eventually, he refused to bottom, and in his later videos he only topped. However, it is clear from the permission Estevez gives himself and his ambivalence about the roles he performs in gay pornography that his persona is fashioned from other socially prevalent sexual scripts. Particularly noteworthy is his need to disclaim the evidence of erections as signifiers of sexual pleasure in a publication for gay men.

Constructing a persona is an important step for any new entrant in the gay industry, but for the straight performers it is probably the most important step. Gay men can rely to some extent on their private sexual personalities. For the heterosexual man, constructing a persona becomes the basis for navigating the demands of directors, agents, interviewers and audience members, and provides a foundation for determining what sexual acts and roles he will perform. In part, the persona is the self-conscious construction of a "personal" sexual script that draws on the individual's intrapsychic script as well as on grand cultural scenarios. The persona is a sort of sexual resume which the actor constructs around the kind of permission that he gives himself for entering the gay pornography business, but it is also based on the image that he wishes to project of who he is as a sexual performer. The persona is what sociologist Erving Goffman has called (following certain vernacular uses) a "front": " . . . that part of the individual's performance which regularly functions . . . to define the situation for those who observe the performance" (1959, pp. 22–30). The actor's porn persona consists of a hodgepodge of beliefs about gender, sexuality, identity, acceptable sexual scripts that he may engage in, and his repertoire of acceptable sexual acts. Thus the actor's porn persona is a "situational sexual identity" that is constructed to be used within the confines of a porn career and the gay porno business. The persona is important because it enables the performer to have a self-concept that gives him permission to engage in homosexual activity and thus to sustain a credible sexual performance, to have erections and to produce orgasms.

Once the actor has his porn persona, he will use it to negotiate auditions, interviews with the press, street encounters with fans and, most importantly, performances. He will use the persona to answer questions about why he started doing gay pornography (e.g., "I'm in it for the money"), his sexual orientation, his physical assets as a sexual performer (muscles, penis size, a "fuckable" ass), those particular sex acts he will or won't do, and to limit who is cognizant of his career in gay porn, and to provide plausible excuses for any failure to turn in credible performances. Another aspect of a porn persona is whether the actor engages in professionally related activities like escorting or dancing. Usually, people in the industry—agents, directors or journalists—help new entrants develop their porn personas. Often, industry insiders inject a more palpable "marketing spin" into a new actor's persona. Insiders also supply standard terms like "top," "bottom" or "versatile" for roles involving anal intercourse, or more complex terms like "sex pig," "trade" or "straight bottom" to characterize the actors' porn performances.

When a gay-for-pay performer successfully conveys sexual pleasure, fans begin to question the performer's sexual orientation. Frequently a performer will concede that he is in fact bisexual. Describing himself as sexual is at least as common:

*Interviewer:* Obviously, you think of yourself as heterosexual . . .

*Rod Barry:* [interrupting] I wouldn't say "heterosexual." I'd say "sexual."

*I:* What's the difference between being sexual and bisexual?

*RB:* I think bisexual means you're a switch-hitter, you like it both ways. Sexual is you like an orgasm and you don't care how you get it . . . (Douglas 1998a).

Porn personas are intentionally constructed to facilitate work in the porn industry, but they often reflect intrapsychic investments. Rod Barry's description of himself as "sexual" may be more than a justification or permission to engage in homosexual sex. Over the course of his career he has insistently characterized himself as "sexual" or even "omni-sexual" rather than gay or bisexual: "Don't call me gay. Don't call me straight. Don't call me bisexual. Just call me sexual. I can cater to anybody . . . a gay male, a transsexual, or a female," he proclaimed in another interview (Antalek 1997b). He suggests a sexuality for himself that encompasses a wide range of "object choices" and roles (top or bottom); his image may embody an emerging style of masculine sexuality, one envisioned by Foucault: "What these signs and symbols of masculinity are for is not to go back to something that would be on the order . . . of machismo, but rather to invent oneself, to make oneself into the site of production of extraordinarily polymorphous pleasures" (Escoffier 2000; Foucault quoted in Halperin 1995, pp. 89–90).

Virtually every actor who makes a name for himself as a top is challenged to bottom at some point in his career. Rod Barry, a former Marine and one of the top gay-for-pay porn stars in the late 1990s, was frequently asked if he would bottom. He always replied, "Where's the bucks?" The decision to bottom is justified in many ways but, like other aspects of the persona, involves repackaging symbolic resources, social roles and culturally available sexual scripts:

*I:* Was "getting fucked" a big step or just another step?

*RB:* Another step. Obviously, it's a big step, because in the industry, everybody makes a big deal out of it . . . That day was, to me, like any other day. Except for the fact that I was "getting fucked" . . . It's different from what I was doing, but it's just like any other day at the office.

*I:* Did you feel that you were playing a feminine role at that moment?

*RB:* No. No. No. And if you watch the movie, I don't think so, because I'm an aggressive top and I was also an aggressive bottom, playing the same way, like reaching around and grabbing his ass and pulling him: "Do it right!" (Douglas 1998a)

Barry's performance as a bottom was very favorably reviewed by fans and critics. In a review in *Manshots*, director Jerry Douglas wrote: "Either Barry is one hell of an actor or he does delight in bottoming . . . his pleasure seems downright palpable. His energetic response to the rutting, the sparkle in his eyes, his joyous grin, and his rockhard erection all confirm that he is indeed as exciting a bottom as he is a top" (Douglas 1998c, pp. 38–39). . . .

The longer their porn careers, the more actors are under pressure to revise their personas, to expand their repertoire of sex acts, and to put themselves into new situations in order to avoid becoming too predictable, and therefore boring to their fans. An integral dynamic of the porn industry, and for many forms of sex work, is a steady pressure for "fresh meat." . . . Most porn actors are aware of this retrogressive dynamic and try to develop a career strategy for their post-porn careers. Some leave the industry and go into other careers or businesses. Some work behind the scenes in porn, while others increasingly rely on escorting or some other form of sex work—which usually just stretches out the retrogressive dynamic over a longer period. Some performers will try to hold onto their fans by expanding their sexual repertoire—they will bottom or do a gang bang picture. But this progression usually leads to lower budget productions as well. "One interesting thing about this business," director Kristen Bjorn observed, "is that the longer you are in it, the less money you are paid. Once you are an old face, and an old body, forget it. You're through as far as your popularity goes" (De Walt 1998). . . .

## Wood and Money Shots: Sexual Performance as Work

. . . While porn actors, like other sex workers, may exclude certain activities from their repertoire, their sexual behavior is governed by the demands and constraints of the video production context. Heterosexual actors in gay pornography must necessarily engage in homosexual sex acts. However, in the context of video production, three other factors help to define their sexual activities. One is the constant interruption of the homosexual activities in which they engage. A second is the use of various forms of heterosexual pornography—such as straight porn magazines or hetero porn videos shown on television monitors on the sidelines—as aids in maintaining their erections and stimulating orgasm. Third is post-production and editing, which result in the illusion of an "authentic" sexual performance. The finished movie is the combined product of the credible sexual performances of the actors, the director's skill in motivating and preparing the actors to perform the sexual acts filmed, and the success of post-production editing in sustaining the credibility and coherence of the sex portrayed

and minimizing any discrepancies between the actors' personas and their sexual performances.

For the straight actor in gay pornography, it is the on-set performance of homosexual acts that defines his ability to successfully manage the situationally specific sexual demands. Many of these heterosexual actors claim that their first sexual encounter with another man was on the set of a gay porn video. Thus, even before his first homosexual experience, a straight actor must choose his repertoire of sexual acts. Certainly his most significant decision is whether or not he will engage in anal intercourse as a top or as a bottom. The repertoire of sex acts is very much a part of the actor's development of his porn persona. The shaping of his persona is dependent on those sexual scripts—those that exist in the culture at large, his own intrapsychic ones or those he can imagine in his everyday life—in which he is able to invest his energy. Thus, for the straight actor, there is a continuum from the "trade" role, where the actor refuses all "gay" sex roles or reciprocity, to that of "sex pig," where he engages energetically in all aspects of sexual activities, to the "straight bottom" role, in which the straight actor engages primarily as a bottom.

The trade role is the gay porn role in which the actor "presumably" can maintain the most distance from the stigma of being labeled as homosexual but, ironically, the straight bottom is a role that allows the performer to demonstrate that he is not aroused even though he is being penetrated—QED he is not gay. The straight bottom, since he does not even need to produce an erection, requires even less of a libidinal investment than does an actor with a trade persona. However, the straight bottom role may also be adopted when an actor doesn't have the confidence or ability to maintain an erection in order to anally penetrate his, co-star. One such performer, Tim Barnett, during an interview questioning his choice of roles, responded:

*Interviewer:* Since you were relatively new to male-male sex . . . did you lay out any rules? . . .

Was the whole menu of what you [were] going to do discussed, or was it just "You're going to bottom"?

**Tim Barnett:** I think it was more or less discussed when I came out [to Los Angeles].

**I:** The scene was filmed around what you were willing to do?

**TB:** Right. And I'm very versatile . . .

**I:** Was there ever any question . . . whether you would top or if it would be a flip-flop?

**TB:** . . . They wanted me to top Greg or do a flip-flop, and it just never came about . . . I just don't know if I'm comfortable enough with the sex yet that I would be a top.

**I:** It's easier to be a bottom.

**TB:** It's a lot easier to be a bottom (Douglas 1996b).

Despite the relative "ease" of bottoming, the *1996 Adam Gay Video Directory* (Anonymous 1996) was, nevertheless, critical of Tim Barnett's performances: "Tim is a big beefy blonde who just loves to get fucked. Unfortunately, he enjoys giving his co-stars pleasure so much he rarely has time to maintain his own erection." (Here the reviewer maintains the public pretense of Barnett's libidinal investment, attributing his lackluster performance to his focus on giving pleasure to his co-stars.) Even gay actors, like straight actors, may have difficulties staying hard while being penetrated. That can be ignored, if they project some form of libidinal engagement. Without any erections or effective engagement a straight bottom cannot give a credible performance.

Once the actor decides on the acts he is willing to perform, the major practical issue is the enactment of a credible performance of sexual acts. As I have already mentioned, heterosexual actors often use straight porn magazines, straight videos on monitors or "fluffers" (performers who fellate the actor off-camera) to help themselves achieve erections. Tim Barnett, the straight bottom quoted above, was asked if he used the person he was playing opposite to or if he drew on his own private world to get himself aroused. The

actor answered: "Both. It really depends who it is. I really like my nipples played with, and sometimes the other person will be the kind of person I'd like to have playing with my nipples. A lot of times I'll use a magazine" (Douglas 1996a).

Another adaptation is the development of what might be called a "professional" work ethic on the porn set. Still photographer Greg Lenzman discusses one such actor:

*Usually, with the gay-for-pay, there are certain things they will not do or they don't have that energy. But there are some exceptions. Rod Barry, who started off more as a straight—I think he's now moved on to a lot of stages in his video career . . . [H]e will give all for his shoots and is very supportive of other performers. He's a joy to work with on a set, and you just know you're going to have a good scene with Rod Barry. The scene with Rod bottoming for the first time was just like an evolution" (Douglas 1998b).*

Dirk Yates, the director-producer who discovered Rod Barry, concurred:

*He seemed pro from the first day I met him . . . He did twenty-nine scenes in a year. He started right off the bat. And I believe the guy's straight—maybe I'm wrong—but I've never seen such a performer. He would never turn you down on anything" (Lawrence 1999).*

To porn video viewers, an important element is the sexual chemistry of the performers. It is unclear how often this is really the performers' chemistry or the result of editing and post-production work. How do performers who are not gay manage to project the sexual appeal needed to attract viewers? Gay-for-pay performer Rod Barry insists that "porno is all about energy" (Douglas 1998a).

Kristen Bjorn, probably the most successful contemporary director of gay porn, has made a series of videos using predominantly performers who do not identify, in any sense, as gay or homosexual (Jamoo 1997). While most of his actors are Latin American and European (and therefore from societies with different "sexual scripts"), they nevertheless have a large following of American gay men. Both Bjorn and his assistant director, who goes by the name of "the Bear," have discussed the desirability of using straight actors many times. In one interview, the Bear notes:

> . . . *Straight men usually have less of a problem getting erections for still photography as well as video. I believe that they are better prepared to come to work knowing that sexual energy must come from themselves through fantasy, memories, erotic magazines, etc. Gay men often come to work thinking that their work is going to be a realization of a sexual fantasy that they have had for a long time. When they realize that they are not in control of the sexual activity, partners, and duration, they become detached and often bored with it and one another. When a gay model is turned on to another model, it can be great to film. In many cases the models are not that excited by each other, especially after four full days of filming the same sex scene. As one model put it at the end of a scene, "That was the longest trick that I ever had!" Once a gay model has decided that he is not sexually interested in the other models, it seems most difficult to bring him into the action and get him aroused. Straight boys don't seem to be as dependent upon the excitation of the other models nor as concerned whether or not they are exciting their partners. But when a gay model perceives that he is not arousing his partner, as often happens in scenes that involve gay and straight models together, it can make him feel insecure with himself. This affects his ability to get erections and ejaculate. Straight models are not as sensitive to the stimuli that can make or break a gay model's performance (Bear 1999).*

The dynamics between gay men and straight actors is another important factor in the production of credible homosexual performances. Homophobic attitudes on the part of a straight actor often undermine the necessary "sexual chemistry." Gay actors often complain about working with straight performers. As the Bear notes, gay men are much more sensitive to the sexual chemistry between themselves and the straight actors. The identity issue frequently surfaces in gay men's assessment of working with heterosexual actors.

Tommy Cruise, who explicitly identifies as a bisexual and as a bottom, comments:

> *One of the things I hate is working with straight guys, because if they're not attracted to me, then I don't like it. People say, "What is your favorite guy like?" It doesn't matter as long as they like me. That turns me on. If someone wants to fuck me really bad, that just turns me on—because they want me. Don't ask me why, I don't really know. That's what does it for me. It's not very enjoyable for me when I'm with a straight guy. A lot of straight guys, they don't even want me touching them. I'm like, "Why are you even in the business?" I've only worked with two straight guys who were okay—and one of them actually blew my mind. He was the strangest dude I ever saw. He was like, "Okay, time to get a hard-on." Boom, he'd get a hard-on. It's like he's standing there like a friggin' robot. "Okay, time to come." Boom, he comes. He was so on-cue, it was kind of freaky, but he was so good to work with (Douglas 1999).*

Cruise's remarks point to the importance of the straight actor's attitude towards gay men and homosexuality, in addition to his intrapsychic need for his sexual partners to find him attractive. Buddy Jones, a gay man who has performed in several Kristen Bjorn movies, found it enjoyable to work with a straight actor. He reported:

> . . . *It was a turn-on working with a straight boy . . . who was eating my ass and sucking my dick. And he was really good at that, especially the rimming. I was concerned about turning him on while he was fucking me, because I was really turned on. I thought that in his mind he was just working. But then his hard cock was up my ass and his hot cum shot all over me, and it kind of made me wonder if he was really enjoying it (Bear 1999).*

One gay man, Eric Hanson, who performs primarily as a top, says that his favorite co-star is "straight bottom" Kurt Stefano: " . . . He has a great persona about him. I think it's the straight thing going on with him. Straight-acting guys are a total turn-on" (Adams 1998).

By itself, the porn persona is not sufficient for the successful management of sexual performances. . . . Getting wood and producing orgasms are merely the certifying components of sexual performances in pornographic movies. Porn actors must convincingly play the roles of men engaged in sex in other ways in order to sustain a credible homosexual performance. As one porn actor after another iterates in interviews throughout the gay press and pornography magazines, making porn is hard work (no pun intended).

## The Camera Frame: Sexual Scripts and Video Production

. . . For straight performers, the gay porn video set provides highly structured access to homosexual activity. It is a social space dense with sexual cues (Simon and Gagnon 1986, pp. 105–107). Video production organizes the space (both physical and social) where sex will take place. But the making of pornography necessarily invokes the culture's generic sexual scenarios—the sex/gender scripts; racial, class and ethnic stereotypes; the dynamics of domination and submission; and various reversals and transgressions of these codes. Porn video scripts utilize these cultural and symbolic resources. These culturally significant symbolic codes help mobilize the actor's private desires and fantasy life in the service of the video's sexual narrative.

The making of a porn video requires not only the performance of real sexual acts but also the simulation of a coherent sexual "narrative." Real sex acts are usually performed, but the video representation of them is more coherent than the actual sexual activity being filmed. The shooting of any sexual scene is made up of an apparently simple sex act photographed from several different perspectives. In fact, the performed act is interrupted many times to arrange shooting angles and lighting and to allow the actors to "get wood"—to regain their erections.[1] For example, the cameraman crawls under actors fucking doggie-style, then shoots them from above to show penetration of the ass, then from behind

the active party to catch yet another penetration shot of the hard penis going in and out. Then the "money shots" (shots of the actors ejaculating) of all the performers in the scene have to be choreographed, often at the end of many hours of filming. The actors may need help of various kinds to help them ejaculate—heterosexual porno magazines, porn videos on monitors, or manipulation by one of their co-actors such as biting their nipples, inserting a finger in their anus, or kissing them. Thus a 15-to-20-minute sexual scene that the viewer sees is edited and patched together, with soundtrack added, from footage shot over a six or seven hour period. . . .

Ultimately, it is the director's choreography of sexual performances and the effectiveness of the editing process that give pornography its quality as an idealization of sexual performance. Whatever shortcomings commercial pornography exhibits—the repetitiveness of sexual activities, inadequate performances (flaccid erections, lackluster orgasms, bored actors) and shoddy production values—they are exacerbated by the idealization that pornography as a medium promotes. . . .

The director uses the porn actor's persona as the raw material for the sexual plot when choreographing the sexual combinations. Of course, sometimes actors can't successfully manage the persona that they want to project. For example, if a straight performer whose persona presents him as "trade" (i.e., he will not perform oral sex, allow himself to be penetrated, or kiss) can't get an erection, making him unable to penetrate the performer assigned to play bottom, then he and the director must negotiate some modification in order to have a credible sex scene. If he isn't fired and replaced, the actor with the "trade" persona may have to perform outside his persona—perform oral sex or agree to bottom—in order to get paid. In the last couple of years, Viagra has helped in achieving and maintaining erections, but there are still numerous other problems involving an actor's ability to live up to his persona and perform credible sex.

## Conclusion

The making of gay male pornography provides an interesting example of the dynamics of situational homosexuality. Since performing in pornography is a kind of sex work, the performers' sexual conduct is a specific response to their customers' preferences and does not represent the preferred sexual responses of the performer. In other words, the sex that is performed is that for which' the customer is willing to pay (Adams 1999, pp. 102–121).

In gay pornography, the participants have had to develop a "persona" or "front" (a *nom de porn*, sexual histories, a repertoire of sex acts) to negotiate the social demands they must contend with as sexual participants. Like any front, it is more manageable if it is, to some degree, consistent with biographical attributes of the participant. But the persona also provides the performer with a way of invoking the potential cultural scenarios and sexual scripts that are compatible with his intrapsychic scripts (Goffman 1959). The production process of gay pornography creates a *situation* that enables straight men to engage in homosexual sex for money. It is a highly organized commercial space that supplies sex partners, symbolic resources and other erotic stimulants, and a video production technology that can produce coherent and credible sexual narratives and images.

The *identitarian* expectations of gay spectators shape both the making of a pornographic video and their interpretations of the sexual performances. It is commonly presumed that when an actor in a pornographic video has an erection while being penetrated he must be gay. In contrast, I have argued that credible homosexual performance, whether or not it sexually arouses the performer, can take place without conscious identification as a homosexual person or even without spontaneous preference for homosexual forms of activity. Situational homosexualities emerge when heterosexually identified individuals encounter situations that enable or reward homosexual behavior.

Situational homosexuality is socially constructed sexuality. All sexual performance is fundamentally situational and does not always result in long-lasting social psychological commitment to any one form of sexual activity. It is a process that draws on both *intra-psychic scripts* and *cultural scenarios* and integrates them into the *interpersonal scripts* of everyday social life. The theory of sexual scripts presumes that sexual performance is not about discovering and pursing one's intrapsychic desires (the presumptive core sexual self), but about defining and constructing scenarios of desire using cultural scenarios and negotiating interpersonal situations (Gagnon and Simon 1973; Foucault 1997). The men who work in the gay porn industry—whether gay, straight or "sexual"—must all construct scripts in order to perform. In this way they are no different from any person engaging in sexual activity—since all sexual performance is situational.

**NOTE**

1. This has changed to some degree since the introduction of Viagra in 1998. Regaining erections is now much quicker.

**REFERENCES**

Abbott, S. A. (2000). Motivations for pursuing an acting career in pornography. In R. Weitzer (Ed.), *Sex for sale: Prostitution, pornography and the sex industry* (pp. 17–34). New York: Routledge.

Adams, J. C. (1998). The Adams report, www.radvideo.com/news/adamhans.html.

Adams, M. (1999). *Hustlers, escorts, porn stars: The insider's guide to male prostitution in America.* Las Vegas: The Insider's Guide.

Anonymous (1996). Current performers: Tim Barnett. In *1996 Adam Gay video directory* (pp. 7–8). Los Angeles: Knight Publishing.

Antalek, J. (1997a). Porn in the USA. *Q San Francisco*, October/November (//qsf-magazine.com/9711/index.html).

Antalek, J. (1997b). Porn in the USA: Rod Barry. *Q San Francisco*, October/November (//gsfmagazine.com/9711/index.html).

Barthes, R. (1986). The reality effect. In R. Barthes (R. Howard [Trans.]), *The rustle of language* (pp. 141–148). New York: Hill and Wang.

Bear (1999). Interview with Buddy Jones. *Manshots,* 11 (pp. 30–33, 80).

Bech, H. (1997). *When men meet: Homosexuality and modernity.* Chicago: University of Chicago Press.

Bronski, M. (1984). *Culture clash: The making of Gay Sensibility.* Boston: Alyson.

Burger, J. R. (1995). *One-handed histories: The eroto-politics of gay male video pornography.* Binghampton: Harrington Park Press.

Chasin, A. (2000). *Selling out: The gay and lesbian movement goes to market.* New York: St. Martin's Press.

De Marco, J. R. G. (2002). The world of gay strippers. *The Gay and Lesbian Review,* 9, March/April (pp. 12–14).

De Walt, M. (1998). The eye of Kristen Bjorn. *Blueboy,* January (pp. 52–55).

Douglas, J. (1996a). Jaguar Productions: Interview with Barry Knight and Russell Moore. *Manshots,* 8, Part 1: June (pp. 10–15); Part 2: August (pp. 10–15, 72).

Douglas, J. (1996b). Interview with Tim Barnett. *Manshots,* 8, February (pp. 30–33, 72–73).

Douglas, J. (1998a). Interview with Rod Barry. *Manshots,* 10, June (pp. 53–57, 72–73).

Douglas, J. (1998b). Behind the camera: Interview with Greg Lenzman. *Manshots,* 10, August (pp. 10–15, 81–82).

Douglas, J. (1998c). *Beach buns* (review). *Manshots,* 10, November (pp. 38–39).

Douglas, J. (1999). Interview with Tommy Cruise. *Manshots,* 11, October (pp. 66–71, 78–79).

Dyer, R. (1979). *Stars.* London: British Film Institute.

Dyer, R. (1992). Coming to terms: Gay pornography. In R. Dyer, *Only entertainment* (pp. 121–134). London: Routledge.

Escoffier, J. (1999). Non-gay identified: Towards a post-identitarian theory of homosexuality. Paper presented at the annual meeting of the Eastern Sociological Society, March 6.

Escoffier, J. (2000). Dirty white guy: Rod Barry's career from Marine to porn star. Unpublished paper.

Escoffier, J., & Spieldenner, A. (1998). Assessing HIV prevention needs for immigrant men who have sex with men (MSM) in New York City. Grand Rounds, HIV Center for Clinical and Behavioral Studies, Columbia University, School of Public Health, New York, April 30.

Foucault, M. (1997). Sex, power and the politics of identity. In M. Foucault (P. Rabinow [Ed.]), *The essential works of Michel Foucault, 1954–1984, volume I: Ethics, subjectivity and truth* (pp. 165–173). New York: The New Press.

Foxxe, A. (1999). Home bodies. *Unzipped,* August 31 (p. 40).

Gagnon, J. H., & Simon, W. (1973). *Sexual conduct: The social sources of human sexuality.* Chicago: Aldine.

Goffman, E. (1959). *The presentation of the self in everyday life.* New York: Doubleday Anchor.

Goffman, E. (1974). *Frame analysis.* New York: Harper & Row.

Goffman, E. (1976). *Gender advertisements.* New York: Harper & Row.

Halperin, D. (1995). *Saint Foucault.* Cambridge: Harvard University Press.

Harris, D. (1997). The evolution of gay pornography: Film. In D. Harris, *The rise and fall of gay culture* (pp. 111–133). New York: Hyperion.

Jamoo (1997). *The films of Kristen Bjorn.* Laguna Hills: Companion Press.

Kipnis, L. (1996). How to look at pornography. In L. Kipnis, *Bound and gagged: Pornography and the politics of fantasy in America* (pp. 161–206). New York: Grove Press.

Lawrence, D. (1999). *The Dirk Yates collection: Adam Gay video erotica.* Los Angeles: Knight Publishing.

Loftus, D. (2002). *Watching sex: How men really respond to pornography.* New York: Thunder's Mouth Press.

Patton, C. (1988). The cum shot-three takes on lesbian and gay sexuality. *OUT/LOOK,* 1, (pp. 72–77).

Pronger, B. (1990). *The arena of masculinity: Sports, homosexuality and the meaning of sex.* New York: St. Martin's Press.

Reiss, A. (1961). The social integration of queers and peers. Social *Problems,* 9, (pp. 102–120).

Rich, F. (2001). Naked capitalists. *The New York Times Magazine,* May 20, (pp. 51–56, 80–81, 92).

Richards, R. W. (1991). Interview with Brian Estevez. *Manshots,* 3, (pp. 53–58,79).

Simon, W., & Gagnon, J. (1986). Sexual scripts: Permanence and change. *Archives of Sexual Behavior,* 15, 97–119.

Spencer, W. (1998). Interview with Paul Morgan. *Manshots*, 10, December, (pp. 52–57, 72–73).

Stoller, R. J. (1991). *Porn: Myths for the twentieth century.* New Haven: Yale University Press.

Straube, T. (1999). Porn profile: Tiger Tyson. *HX*, May 14, (p. 68).

Suggs, D. (1999). The porn kings of New York. *Out*, June, (pp. 85–89).

Thomas, J. A. (2000). Gay male video pornography: Past, present and future. In R. Weitzer (Ed.), *Sex for sale: Prostitution, pornography and the sex industry* (pp. 49–66). New York: Routledge.

Waugh, T. (1996). *Hard to imagine: Gay male eroticism in photography and film, from their beginnings to Stonewall.* New York: Columbia University Press.

Williams, L. (1989). *Hard core: Power, pleasure and the "frenzy of the visible".* Berkeley: University of California Press.

## What We Know about Pornography

**Clive M. Davis and Naomi B. McCormick**

### What Is Pornography?

The word pornography derives from a Greek word meaning writing about prostitutes. Although there is no widely accepted modern definition, the common element in all definitions is that the material is sexually explicit. Controversy revolves around whether specific depictions are art or smut, good or bad, innocuous or harmful. People often label as pornographic material that violates their own moral standards and use the terms artistic or erotic for sexual materials they find acceptable.

Pornography must be distinguished from obscenity. Obscenity is a legal term identifying material that has been judged by the courts to have violated specific statutes pertaining to sexually explicit material. Central to these statutes is whether the material violates community standards of acceptability and whether it involves minors. Thus, many books, movies, and even advertisements that are acceptable today could have been judged obscene earlier in our history.

### The Effects of Exposure to Sexually Explicit Material

Since the 1960s, research has been conducted to assess the effects of exposure to sexually explicit material. Primary attention has been paid to commercially produced materials intended to generate sexual arousal and/or activity in adult audiences. Three components have been of principal interest: (a) the degree of explicitness, (b) whether the material also contains aggression, and (c) whether it depicts women in demeaning and degrading ways. . . .

### Reactions

People vary in response to sexual materials: Some react negatively to all depictions, whereas others find at least some material acceptable and arousing. Materials that are liked produce more positive emotions and greater sexual arousal than those that are disliked, for both sexes. Nonetheless, sexual arousal may occur even when people are mildly offended. Men tend to respond more positively to the more hard-core and male-dominated material; women tend to react more negatively to this material.

Individuals who hold authoritarian beliefs and have conservative social and religious attitudes tend to experience more sex guilt and react more negatively to explicit materials. Even if they do experience arousal, they judge the material to be undesirable.

Hypermasculine men tend to hold more negative and sexist attitudes toward women. They also are likely to believe that women respond positively to dominant, aggressive men. These men react more positively to scenes of sexual aggression and degrading portrayals of women. Most people, both men and women, respond negatively to this type of material.

### Changes in Sexual Attitudes and Sexual Behavior

Repeated exposure generally increases tolerance of explicit material and to the behaviors depicted, except for those who start out with negative attitudes. Those who are aroused by the material are likely to engage in sexual acts, such as masturbation or coitus, within a few hours of exposure. Repeated short-term exposure results in increased disinterest and satiation, but after a period of no exposure, the impact is regained.

### Attitudes toward Women and Aggressive Behavior

For obvious ethical, moral, and legal reasons, researchers have not conducted experiments to determine whether exposure to material in which high levels of sexual explicitness and violence are both present leads to increased sexual violence. They have, however, looked at whether men with a history of such exposure are more likely to have committed sex crimes. Sex offenders tend to come from restrictive and punitive home environments. Compared to nonoffenders, they have had more undesirable experiences during childhood, including heightened exposure to sexual and physical abuse. Some offenders have had more exposure to explicit materials than other men, but early exposure alone does not increase the risk of becoming a sex offender.

In controlled laboratory research, individuals have been exposed to material containing (a) both aggression and explicit sex, (b) only aggression, and (c) only the sexual material. The results suggest it is exposure to aggression that triggers aggressive behavior. Exposure to sexual material alone does not increase aggression toward women. For most people, aggression and sex are incompatible. For a small percentage of men predisposed to aggression toward women, however, combining sex and aggression does stimulate arousal and aggressive responses.

The impact of exposure to sexist, demeaning material depends on the person's pre-existing attitudes. Under some conditions, those predisposed to negative views become more calloused and accepting of these negative views.

### *Is Pornography Harmful?*

The answer is complex: "It depends." For those who believe that anything fostering more permissive attitudes toward sexuality or that even viewing others engaging in sexual acts is morally wrong, then exposure to explicit sexual material is clearly unacceptable. Others, however, believe that there is nothing wrong with permissive attitudes and being stimulated by explicit materials. Indeed, materials depicting consensual activity have been used in beneficial ways by therapists and educators to reduce anxiety and to improve sexual knowledge, and by individuals and couples to enhance their sexual pleasure. . . .

Exposure to material that contains sexist or violent depictions can promote undesirable attitudes and behaviors. Increased censorship, however, will not be effective in addressing the problems, for three reasons. Firstly, censorship is most often directed toward only the most sexually explicit material, leaving the much more problematic sexist and violent content of R-rated material untouched. Secondly, censorship would not end sexual exploitation or violence. The roots of those behaviors are far deeper in the culture. Sexist, sexually explicit material is more a symptom than a cause of female subordination and sexual violence. Finally, restrictions beyond the existing obscenity laws and protection for minors would create numerous other problems in a free, democratic society. Few sexual scientists judge the evidence as warranting additional restrictions.

### RECOMMENDED READINGS

Davis, C. M., & Bauserman, R. (1993). Exposure to sexually explicit materials: An attitude change perspective. *Annual Review of Sex Research, 4,* 121–209.

Donnerstein, E. L., & Penrod, S. (1987). *The question of pornography: Research findings and policy implications.* New York: Free Press.

Fisher, W. A., & Barak, A. (1991). Pornography, erotica, and behavior: More questions than answers. *International Journal of Law and Psychiatry, 14,* 65–83.

McCormick, N. B. (1994). *Sexual salvation: Affirming women's sexual rights and pleasures.* Westport, CT: Praeger.

*Source:* Davis, Clive M. and Naomi B. McCormick. "What Sexual Scientists Know . . . : About Pornography." *What Sexual Scientists Know* 3(1). Reprinted by permission of the Society for the Scientific Study of Sexuality.

## An Overview of Pornography Studies

**Neil M. Malamuth, Tamara Addison, and Mary Koss**

*Meta-Analytic Studies of Pornography Research*

| META-ANALYTIC STUDY | METHOD | PARTICIPANTS | STIMULUS | DEPENDENT MEASURE | EFFECT SIZE | N | CONCLUSION |
|---|---|---|---|---|---|---|---|
| Allen, Emmers, et al. (1995) | Correlational and Experimental combined | Students | | Attitudes for Sex Aggression | .10* | 4,268 | More pornography use, more support aggression |
| | Correlational only | | All pornography use combined | | .06 | 2,020 | No reliable effect |
| | Experimental only | | Pornography use combined vs. control | | .15* | 2,248 | More pornography use, more support aggression |
| | | | Nonviolent pornography only vs. control | | .13* | 1,048 | Nonviolent pornography increases support for aggression |
| | | | Violent pornography only vs. control | | .11* | 719 | Violent pornography increases support for aggression more than control |
| | | | Studies with both nonviolent pornography and violent pornography | | .16* | 762 | Violent pornography increases support more than nonviolent pornography, though both significant |
| Allen, D'Alessio, & Brezgel (1995) | Experimental | Students | All pornography combined vs. control | Laboratory aggression | .13* | 2,040 | Pornography increases aggression |
| | | | Nudity vs. control | | -.14* | 403 | Nudity reduces aggression |

| META-ANALYTIC STUDY | METHOD | PARTICIPANTS | STIMULUS | DEPENDENT MEASURE | EFFECT SIZE | N | CONCLUSION |
|---|---|---|---|---|---|---|---|
| Allen et al. (2000) | Correlational | Offenders vs. nonoffenders | Nonviolent pornography vs. control | | .17* | 1,229 | Nonviolent pornography increases aggression |
| | | | Violent pornography vs. control | | .22* | 353 | Violent pornography increases aggression |
| | | | Pornography use | Overall measure | .06 | 2,543 | No difference |
| | | | | Frequency of use | –.05 | 1,212 | No difference |
| | | | | Age of first exposure | .03 | 903 | No difference |
| | | | | Sexual "acting out" after pornography use | .23* | 1,261 | Offenders more likely to "act-out" after pornography use (masturbation, consensual sex, or forced sex) |
| | | | All pornography | Physiological sexual arousal | .15* | 2,099 | Offenders more aroused by all pornography combined |
| | | | Consenting pornography | Physiological sexual arousal | –.26* | 625 | Offenders less aroused by consenting sex |
| | | | Violent pornography | Physiological sexual arousal | .39* | 207 | Offenders more aroused by violent pornography |

N = number of participants in total of studies combined.
*Indicates statistical significance of average effect across studies.

Source: Malamuth, Neil M., Tamara Addison, and Mary Koss. 2000. "Pornography and Sexual Aggression: Are There Reliable Effects and Can We Understand Them?" Annual Review of Sex Research 11: 26–91. Reprinted by permission of the Society for the Scientific Study of Sexuality.

# Little White Lies: Race, Dildos, and American Culture

Allison Kavanagh Alavi

You may be wondering what dildos have to do with race in the United States. Dildos, which are objects that are usually plastic or rubber, shaped to resemble penises, and sometimes equipped to vibrate, are one of the many objects that people use to express discourse. *Discourse* is a specific type of practice through which we communicate messages to and about one another. For instance, when you turn on your television and are bombarded with messages about what to wear, how to act, how to understand the events in your community and the world, and how to incorporate all of this information into your daily life, you are hearing and engaging in the practice of discourse. These messages lay the foundation for how we differentiate what is normal from what is abnormal (Foucault 1990). That is, we mold our perception of the world and our system of categorization around the discourse that we encounter in our lives. And it's discourse that pops up everywhere and seeps into the construction of things that seem relatively innocuous—even dildos.

I examine how discourse is used in the construction and packaging of dildos to portray black men as hypersexual and sexually aggressive. Messages of black male hypersexuality are articulated through the construction of black dildos that are larger and more graphic than their white counterparts. Think about this: If someone asked you which racial group has the largest penis, on average, which one would you pick? You would probably say black men, and you would not be alone. However, the average American penis, regardless of race, is about 5.1 inches long (Kimmel and Messner 1998). So why does this myth exist, and more importantly, what are its consequences? To answer this question, I looked at phallic representations within the adult novelty industry (i.e., dildos). My hope was to understand how, where, and why the myth of the super-huge black penis exists and to uncover the racist assumptions that underlie this notion.

## Racist Discourse: Its Roots and Uses

*Q:* What's white and twelve inches?
*A:* Nothing. (From *Ceramic Uncles and Celluloid Mammies* by Patricia A. Turner, 1994: 21.)

The roots of modern racist discourse regarding black male hypersexuality and the super-huge black penis are found in the writings of fourteenth and fifteenth century English authors (Pieterse 1992). These authors promoted ideas of racial deficiency and inadequacy to justify policies of enslavement, colonization, and the brutal treatment of black people. "Proof" of black men's inherent inferiority and dangerous sexual tendencies was provided in these works through assertions that African penises were abnormally large. These authors considered large genitalia unholy, signifying a closeness with animals and filth and a departure from spirituality, humankind, and God. Never mind that these claims lacked anatomical support.

In the United States, white southern slave owners who defended the institution of slavery reassured themselves of the "rightness" of slave ownership by insisting that the slave master was "'enlightened,' 'humane,' and 'Christian,'" and that the slave was a savage creature that 'needed' the direction and control of slavery to discipline his or her sexual urges" (Takaki 1993:113). Fears of interracial sexuality only increased the need to justify the oppression of blacks in the United States. The eugenics policies that emerged early in U.S. history reflected the beliefs of many white people, our "founding fathers" included, who viewed blacks as the "libidinous race" (Takaki 1993:74). These policies forbade the intermingling of the races to ensure that the white race would remain "pure" and superior. Black men, in particular, were targeted by these policies because, as Thomas Jefferson explained, they were thought to prefer the beauty of white women to "those of [their] own species" (Takaki 1993:75).

The late 1800s in the United States were marked by an increase in white hysteria over black sexuality. This fear, in part, represented the insecurities of white southern males during reconstruction who faced a declining economy and vulnerability in the new market. Black men, therefore, became a target for white males who feared a loss of power. The result was the circulation of rape myths and the subsequent lynching of thousands of black men (D'Emilio and Freedman 1988). For example, "between 1889 and 1899 a person was lynched every other day, and in nine cases out of ten the victim was a Black who had been accused of rape" (Pieterse 1992:177).

Today's media have become the sites where discourse about the sexual perversion and dangerousness of black men is articulated. Here we see individuals like Mike Tyson and O. J. Simpson held out for public display as emblems of black male sexual rage and hypermasculinity (hooks 1995).

Media representations of black males tend to portray them as defendants and lawbreakers, while their white counterparts are represented as law-abiding and heroic individuals (Dixon and Linz 2000). These types of representations influence our expectations and make images of black criminality seem normal (Peffley, Shields, and Williams 2000). Consequently, these portrayals go relatively unchallenged even as they subtly

and not so subtly influence policy decisions. For example, racial framing by the media can influence the allocation of resources or the support of policy initiatives that would benefit mostly minority populations. Moreover, these images can result in the brutal treatment and subjugation of a group of people who do not hold the power or resources to counter a discursive attack. Patricia Hill Collins explains that:

> Because the authority to define societal values is a major instrument of power, elite groups, in exercising power, manipulate ideas. . . . They do so by exploiting already existing symbols or creating new ones. These controlling images are designed to make racism, sexism, poverty, and other forms of social injustice appear to be natural, normal, and inevitable parts of everyday life. (2000:69)

Discourse, therefore, is a means of controlling the behavior of individuals or groups by defining what is normal and what is not, what is acceptable and what is not, and who can fill the definition of normal and acceptable. Those who do not want to or cannot conform to the standards set by the dominant group within a society are labeled deviant or abnormal.

Taken together, the history of racist sexual discourse, the media's reliance on racist notions in its portrayal of black men, and the consequential control and institutionalization of racism, marginalize black men and label them as deviant and dangerous. These notions erase the history and reality of racism in the United States and reassure those in power of the rightness and justness of their position.

This is not to say, however, that a marginalized group cannot adopt the discourse targeted against it as a means of empowerment. Just as the gay and lesbian community has reclaimed the symbol of the pink triangle from its past use by Nazis, other groups have also adopted oppressive images and discourse into their identities (Elman 1996). Many cultural products, such as rap music and graffiti, draw on oppressive discourses used to marginalize people's voices to create a body of discourse that undermines dominant discourse and controlling imagery (Rose 1994). For example, [Public Enemy's] "Fight the Power" stood as an anthem against oppression and marginalization throughout the 80s and well into the 90s. This subversion creates a space for self-definition and expression within marginalized communities.

## The Dildo: From Rx to XXX

The social meaning of the dildo has changed over time. Once a treatment for hysteria or womb disease, the dildo has become a purely sexual toy and a lucrative commodity.

Dildo usage to massage the genitals of women to produce an orgasm was a common treatment for hysteria in the seventeenth century. Doctors believed hysteria caused nervous disorders, mental illness, fatigue, and a host of other female afflictions (Maines 1999). Because societies of the West constricted the definition of proper sexual acts to those focused on the penetration of the vagina by the penis, and because masturbation was considered unchaste, the problem of alleviating hysteria through female orgasm was left to science. Medicalizing the female orgasm sanitized it (Maines 1999). However, the old techniques of genital massage were tiresome, time-consuming, and difficult to master. To answer the calls of physicians trying to increase their income, the mechanical vibrator was invented. It did in minutes what might have taken the doctor an hour (Maines 1999). Moreover, now midwives or nurses who monitored the machines could more easily perform the treatment. At last, it seemed doctors had an answer to their problems—or did they?

As technological advancements made the vibrating devices more compact and easier to power and as the price for a device became more affordable, people began purchasing machines for home use. This took the vibrator out of the doctor's office and placed it discreetly into patients' bedrooms (Maines 1999). The advertising industry began to market vibrators for home use and the vibrator began to lose some of its legitimacy as a purely medical device. Following the removal of hysteria as a disease in the mid-twentieth century and the sexual revolution of the 60s and 70s, the dildo or vibrator was exclusively promoted as a sexual toy rather than as a medical device.

## Methodology

In this project, I began with the hypothesis that discourses about black male hypersexuality are reflected in the marketing of dildos within the adult novelty industry, and that these discourses are part of a hegemonic racist discourse found in the United States. But how do you test something like this?

I decided to do a content analysis of adult novelty manufacturers' catalogues. Content analysis is a method of research in which the researcher examines the content of some form of media, such as newspapers, books, catalogues, magazines, television, and movies, to establish "who says what, to whom, why, how, and with what effect" (Babbie 2001:305). I obtained 17 catalogues from nine different manufacturers, which contained a total of 401 useable dildos. I looked at the dildos and their packaging to see if there was a significant difference between light and dark toned dildos. I only looked at dildos that resembled a skin tone and then categorized those tones along a continuum that went from pure white to pure black. Using this method, I determined the relationship between the size and the color of the dildos included in my sample.

## Findings

The darker dildos in my sample were significantly longer, wider, and more graphic than the lighter dildos. The average length of the darker dildos was almost 1.25 inches longer than the lighter ones, and there were far more dark dildos that fell into the category of wide girth. Moreover, the darker dildos were constructed to have more details, such as pubic hair, scrotums, and veins, than the lighter dildos in my sample. These findings support the cultural belief that black men have larger penises than white men. In addition, they suggest that darker skin is associated with more animal or corporal urges. It seems that dildos, much like the Barbie doll, are constructed to reflect the beliefs that we hold about certain groups of people. And the dildos included in my study seemed to provide a caricature of the bodies of a marginalized group in society that does not have a powerful amount of influence on the dominant forms of discourse articulated through social artifacts.

The words used on the packaging to describe the dildos in my sample were perhaps the most interesting element of my study. The following are some examples of the types of phrases used on the packaging of the light and dark dildos included in my sample:

*Dark*
"You Need a Thick, Long and Massive Ebony Cock . . . You want BAM! Huge Realistic Cock"
"Black Thunder 12 Thick Inches"
"Midnight Vibe; Powerful and Soft Jelly Vibes— Midnight G"
"Bad Boyz Know How to Do It! Bad Boyz 8" Vibrating Devil Dong. . . ."

*Light*
"It bends to please"
"Pumping . . . Pleasure Cocks"
"Rotating 9 inches of Thick, Firm Pleasure"
"Experience the Ultimate Cyber Orgasm"
"Exciting Shape"

The phrases used to describe the darker dildos reify notions of black hypersexuality and abnormally large penis size. Words like *bam, massive,* and *devil dong* suggest that there are dangers inherent to black sexuality, in contrast with the words used to describe the lighter dildos included in my study, which emphasize pleasure and eroticism. *Orgasm, pleasure,* and *exciting* do not invoke the same imagery as the words used on the

packaging of the darker dildos. The words used on the packaging of the dildos reinforced the notion that black sexuality is aggressive, hyperactive, and dangerous, whereas white sexuality is sensual, exciting, and enjoyable.

Even more surprising were the words used by the manufacturers in the catalogues to distinguish between different colored dildos. Fifty-three percent of all of the light dildos were described as flesh colored or natural, while 78 percent of all of the darker dildos included in my sample were described as black. This finding indicates the assumption that white people are the norm and that their skin tone is natural, whereas other skin tones represent some deviation from the norm. In other words, white people are just people, while everyone else is raced (Dyer 1997:1).

As far as the colors and patterns on the packaging, I found the strongest association between black packaging and darker dildos. This may indicate that there is another type of marking going on. In our culture, the color black tends to signify evil, death, and danger. By using black as the dominant color of the packaging, darker dildos were marked as something dangerous and perhaps sinful.

## Analysis

I found the clear presence of a discourse that marked darker tones as abnormal and lighter tones as normal to be the strongest evidence that racist discourse has seeped into something as unexpected as a dildo. The use of this discourse in the construction of dildos, whether intentional or not, promotes the idea that black male sexuality is dangerous but controllable and possessible by the women and men who buy these dildos. Moreover, these dildos are constructed to reinforce the stereotype of the "big black cock," which supports the ideas that black men are sexually aggressive. Portraying darker dildos as longer, wider, and more graphic, and using terms and colors to emphasize these things, does not alone instill racist notions of black male sexuality into the minds of the public. Rather, it is the interplay of this construction of darker dildos along with the racist discourse that is rooted in the imperialist history of the West as well as the institutionalization of racism that reify notions of black hypersexuality into our psyches.

## REFERENCES

Babbie, Earl. 2001. *The Practice of Social Research.* 9th ed. Belmont, CA: Wadsworth/Thomson Learning.

D'Emilio, John, and Estelle Freedman. 1988. *Intimate Matters: A History of Sexuality in America.* New York: Harper & Row.

Dixon, Travis, and Daniel Linz. 2000. "Overrepresentation and Underrepresentation of African Americans and Latinos as Lawbreakers on Television News." *Journal of Communication,* Spring: 131–154.

Dyer, Richard. 1997. *White.* New York: Routledge.

Elman, Amy R. 1996. "Triangles and Tribulations: The Politics of Nazi Symbols." *Journal of Homosexuality* 30(3): 1–11.

Foucault, Michel. 1990 [1978]. *The History of Sexuality.* Vol. 1. New York: Vintage.

Hill Collins, Patricia. 2000. *Black Feminist Thought: Knowledge, Consciousness, and the Politics of Empowerment.* 2nd ed. New York: Routledge.

hooks, bell. 1995. "Representing the Black Male Body." In *Art on My Mind: Visual Politics* (pp. 202–212). New York: The New Press.

Kimmel, Michael, and Michael Messner. 1998. *Men's Lives.* 4th ed. Boston: Allyn Bacon.

Maines, Rachel P. 1999. *The Technology of Orgasm: "Hysteria," the Vibrator, and Women's Sexual Satisfaction.* Baltimore, MD: The Johns Hopkins University Press.

Peffley, M., T. Shields, and B. Williams. 1996. "The Intersection of Race and Crime in Television News Stories: An Experimental Study." *Political Communication* 13: 309–327.

Pieterse, J. N. 1992. *White on Black: Images of Africa and Blacks in Western Popular Culture.* London: Yale University Press.

Rose, Tricia. 1994. *Black Noise: Rap Music and Black Culture in Contemporary America.* Middletown, CT: Wesleyan University Press.

Takaki, Ronald. 1993. *A Different Mirror: A History of Multicultural America.* New York: Little, Brown.

Turner, P. A. 1994. *Ceramic Uncles & Celluloid Mammies.* New York: Anchor Books.

# Feeble Excuses: Public Representations
# of Gender, Sexuality, and Disability

Pamela Block

The sexuality of women with cognitive disabilities[1] has been a subject of concern to social service professionals and policy makers in the United States for over a century. Historically, in professional treatises, newspaper accounts, freak shows, literature, and film, women with cognitive disabilities have been portrayed in contradictory ways as both sexually vulnerable and socially threatening, needing professional management and control. Discussions of the "sexual nature" of this group are still present in medical, legal, and popular cultural discourse. This presentation considers [four] examples . . . where the sexual identities of women with cognitive disabilities received national scrutiny. Two of the cases are historical: the life-long institutionalization of "Deborah Kallikak" at the end of the 19th century and the 1927 sterilization of Carrie Buck. [Two] are contemporary: the sterilization of Cindy Wasiek in 1994, and the 1989 Glen Ridge sexual assault of a young woman with a cognitive disability. . . . These examples reveal that implicit cultural assumptions (modern fairy tales) about the sexuality and fertility of women with cognitive disabilities are embedded in United States history, and still very much in evidence today.

Disability, when applied as medical or psychological diagnoses, takes the culturally, socially, and historically derived identity of an individual and subsumes it beneath a designation of pathology. When an individual enters the biomedical and psychosocial service-systems as disabled every other personal characteristic becomes secondary; the person becomes defined by their disability. Whether the disability is physical, mental, or imaginary, labeling a person in this way attaches stigma and results in social exclusion (1,2,3). Disability studies theorists stress the importance of separating the *disability* (physiological condition) from the *impairment* (the social ramifications of the condition) (4,5). For example, having no legs is a physiological condition, but it is the inaccessibility of buildings that creates a barrier and results in exclusion.

Following feminist and other critiques of science (6,7,8,9,10,11,12,13,14), I would call into question the notion of psychiatry or biomedicine as representative of pure empirical science. An illusory shelter of scientific rationalism obscures the fundamentally ideological nature of the "treatment" of individuals with cognitive disabilities and psychiatric illness. . . .

Early twentieth century theories of mental development (and deficiency) in the United States were usually linked to social status. Although "mental deficiency" was considered a medical diagnosis, the decision to label an individual "mentally deficient" was closely tied to structures of power, i.e., ideologies of race, class, and sexuality, theories of modernization and racial degeneracy, and cultural perceptions of urbanization, immigration, masculinity and femininity. The late 1800s and early 1900s was a period of exceler-

From Block, Pamela. 2000. "Sexuality, Fertility, and Danger: Twentieth Century Images of Women with Cognitive Disabilities." *Sexuality and Disability* 18: 239–254. Reprinted with kind permission from Springer Science and Business Media.

ated social change due to immigration and rapid urbanization. Former slaves, rural people, and immigrants (from places other than Western Europe) crowded into the cities (15,16). Elite groups feared that large influxes of people they considered to be of poor mental and physical quality would result in "degeneration" on a national scale. The need to control marginal populations resulted in new prisons and mental institutions, and the development of new professions, such as social work (17). It also resulted in the growth of the eugenics movement.

Throughout this century people with cognitive disabilities in the United States have been constructed in two ways: as social threats that must be segregated in order to protect the social order, or as socially vulnerable, without the skills to survive in a dangerous and rejecting society. The main barrier faced by people with cognitive disabilities has been social exclusion. In the early decades of this century, institutionalization of people with cognitive disabilities was not uncommon. Even today, people with cognitive disabilities have difficulty finding independence outside of segregated programs, not because of their personal limitations, but because they are not wanted (18). Expressions of rejection range from banishment to freak shows, refusals to implement inclusive educational and employment policies, to crimes of violent hatred (5,3).

Although this paper focuses primarily on cultural images of women, it is important to note that powerful images concerning the sexuality of men with cognitive disabilities also exist. Many people believe that men with cognitive disabilities are sexual predators (19). Historically, men with cognitive disabilities were institutionalized for fear of their supposed potential for physical or sexual aggression. There are many recent cases where men with cognitive disabilities have been arrested and convicted on charges of physical and/or sexual assault, and even murder, with no evidence other than a personal confession. Confessions of people with cognitive disabilities are questionable because they are often eager to

please, and easily intimidated. They may attempt to tell questioners what they want to hear and/or simply fail to understand the implications of what they are saying (20). Robert Perske (1991) describes cases where men with cognitive disabilities were convicted and even sentenced to death despite the absence of any corroborating evidence. This was true even in cases where evidence pointing to other suspects existed.

Cultural beliefs concerning the sexual danger presented by men with cognitive disabilities are pervasive. It is common that when a new group home is established for neighbors to voice concerns for the safety of their children. Such fears have been around longer than the story of Frankenstein's monster. Despite popular assumptions that men with cognitive disabilities are likely to be child molesters, the obverse comes closer to the truth. Although girls and women with cognitive disabilities are at higher risk, men and boys of this group are far more likely to experience sexual aggression than boys without disabilities. As is the case for men without disabilities, men and boys with cognitive disabilities who have experienced sexual aggression may, in turn, begin to hurt others. . . .

The stories presented below have a fairy tale quality: They depict demonic succubae, imprisoned women, controlling mothers, extreme poverty, stolen children, demonic changelings, cruel foster parents, evil wizards (doctors, psychologists, and psychiatrists), and human wolves. . . .

### Goddard and the "Kallikaks"

Psychologist Henry H. Goddard was an early-twentieth century eugenics theorist specializing in the detection and treatment of feeble-mindedness. He viewed low intelligence as the rout of all other types of degeneracy, including prostitution, criminality, poverty and alcoholism. His most famous work was the 1913 eugenics family study entitled *The Kallikak Family: A Study in the Heredity of Feeble-Mindedness*. Critiques of Goddard's research revealed that his methods were shoddy at best, and fraudulent at worst (21,22). Although Goddard's conclusions were proved false, the legacy of his work is still visible in the United States and abroad. His persuasive arguments for the large-scale segregation of people considered "feeble-minded," and the custodial training-school model he advocated persisted virtually intact in the United States until the 1980s and still exists in places. In addition, Goddard's theories and his institutional model influenced modern popular-cultural conceptions of people with cognitive disabilities in the United States.

Goddard researched the family history of a 23-year-old woman he called "Deborah Kallikak," a resident of the Training School for Feeble-minded Boys and Girls in Vineland, New Jersey. Goddard coined the term Kallikak from the Greek words *kallos* (beauty) and *kakos* (bad) (22). By tracing Deborah's family history, Goddard claimed to have found a recessive gene for feeble-mindedness passed down by her family for five generations. Goddard classified Deborah as a moron, a term he coined from the Greek word for "foolish." Goddard believed that morons were particularly dangerous to society because there was no physical manifestation of disability. According to historian David J. Smith:

> The label moron came to be widely applied to people who were considered to be "high grade defectives"—those who were not retarded seriously enough to be obvious to the casual observer and who had not been brain-damaged by disease or injury. Morons were characterized as being intellectually dull, socially inadequate, and morally deficient. (22, p. 12)

Morons could be lovely, (as shown in Goddard's book by pictures of Deborah in beautiful dresses and neat hair), but sinister, because they could easily "pass" for normal. "Moronic" traits were intangible: the inability to understand complex emotional or social situations resulting in "regressed behaviors," poor judgment, poor insight, and poor decision making abilities, and an "increased vulnerability to life events,"[2] According

to Goddard, the only way to protect society from degeneration was to segregate feeble-minded individuals and prevent them from marrying and passing their recessive traits to their descendents.

Although Goddard described Deborah as "valuable to the institution" (23, p. 2), he did not hesitate to form conclusions about what her fate might have been if she were allowed to leave Vineland:

> Today if this young woman were to leave the institution, she would at once become prey to the designs of evil men or evil women and would lead a life that would be vicious, immoral, and criminal, though because of her mentality she herself would not be responsible. There is nothing that she might not be led into, because she has no power of control, and all her instincts and appetites are in the direction that would lead to vice. (23, p. 12)

Goddard warned that there were families like the Kallikaks everywhere, multiplying at twice the rate of the rest of the population. He described one such family living in urban misery:

> In one arm she held a frightful looking baby, while she had another by the hand. Vermin were visible all over her. In a room with few chairs and a bed, the latter without any washable covering and filthy beyond description. There was no fire and both mother and baby were thinly clad. They did not shiver, however, nor seem to mind. The oldest girl, a vulgar, repulsive creature of fifteen came into the room and stood looking at the stranger. She had somehow managed to live. All the rest of the children, except the two that the mother was carrying, had died in infancy. (23, pp. 73–4)

According to Goddard, this life could have been Deborah's fate, had she not been safely kept in the custody of the training school.

Eventually, Goddard's research was criticized for his use of lay field-workers who made diagnoses of feeble-mindedness based on observation, interviews, or even decades-old stories told by relatives or neighbors (22). It was not until more than sixty years after Goddard published his study that Stephen J. Gould and his colleague

Steven Selden noticed that the photographs of the supposedly "feeble-minded" branch of the Kallikak family were retouched to make the subjects appear stupid and ominous. In the photos, Deborah's family members were shown in rural settings in front of rough shacks.

*All have a depraved look about them. Their mouths are sinister in appearance; their eyes are darkened slits. But Goddard's books we nearly seventy years old, and the ink has faded. It is now clear that all the photos of the non-institutionalized kakos were phonied by inserting heavy dark lines to give eyes and mouths their diabolical appearance. (21, p. 171)*

Smith was able to find and interview surviving family members who were characterized as feeble-minded in Goddard's book. He found no indication of cognitive disability in any of them. Many graduated from high school or college and worked in professions such as teaching and mechanics. Deborah entered the Vineland training school in 1889 when she was 8 years old. She remained institutionalized until her death at 89 years of age. By today's standards she would never have been institutionalized at all. Despite Goddard's diagnosis of moron, Smith found her academic challenges more indicative of what today would be called a learning disability (22). Goddard used his diagnosis of Deborah in order to promote his theories of "feeble-mindedness" and his institutional model of service provision. Through this model, implemented nationally and abroad, Goddard influenced the lives of thousands of men and women who received this diagnosis and were forced to live in training schools and mental institutions. Additionally, Goddard's representation of the "Kallikak" family as a threatening source of social and genetic degeneration caught the popular imagination. Images of sexually deviant "feeble-minded" families who, for generation after generation have lived in rural or urban degradation are recurrent figures in literature, film, and television. Goddard's theories provided professional legitimacy to cultural assertions that cognitive disability was shameful

and must be hidden. He introduced the notion of "feeble-mindedness" as a pathology that must be extracted from society like a cancer. Through images of degradation and defect, women considered feebleminded were depicted as less than human, yet with an insidious power to corrupt and transform society if they were not removed from it. This position would later be advocated prominently by the United States eugenics movement.

## Eugenics and the Sterilization of Carrie Buck

Eugenics, the science of the genetic improvement of the human race, was influenced by Darwin's theory of the importance of heredity in the evolutionary process, and Mendel's research on the transmission of genetic traits over generations. Meaning to "harness the force of heredity for the improvement of man," eugenics was used to establish race and class distinctions as "natural" and incontrovertible (24,25). The eugenics movement was not homogeneous; it included a variety of different political and scientific views. However, it was the more extreme theories that had the greatest influence on the development of United States national policy.

Deborah Kallikak's case is illustrative of the special treatment women diagnosed as feebleminded received at the hands of professionals. As early as the 1870s "feeble-minded" women were identified as a population in need of control and stewardship (16,26). The government, medical establishment, and society-at-large became wary of the assumed "obsessive sexual nature" of this group (27,28,29,30,31). Distorted sexual stereotypes are typical of many marginalized social groups (32,33), but unlike people stigmatized for their gender, economic status, or race, tens of thousands of "feeble-minded" US citizens were forcibly institutionalized, segregated by sex, and denied the right to have sexual relations and raise families (34,35,36,37). African Americans with disabilities were sometimes turned away from institutions and sent to prison instead (38).

Goddard believed segregation was the ultimate solution to feeble-mindedness and mentioned sterilization merely as a "makeshift" measure until enough facilities could be built (23, p. 117). However, by the 1920s it became apparent that it was too expensive to maintain such a large population in segregated institutions, even when the higher-functioning residents performed tasks to defray the cost of their upkeep (18). Sterilization and parole came to be seen as a more economically viable solution.

Harry H. Laughlin of the Eugenics Record Office drafted a model law, which included a list of ten "socially inadequate" groups targeted for sterilization:

*1) feeble-minded; 2) insane (including psychopathic); 3) criminalistic (including the delinquent and wayward); 4) epileptic; 5) inebriate (including drug habituees); 6) diseased (including the tuberculous, the syphilitic, the leprous, and others with chronic, infectious, and legally segregable diseases); 7) blind (including those with seriously impaired vision; 8) deaf (including those with seriously impaired hearing); 9) deformed (including the crippled); and 10) dependent (including orphans, ne'er-do-wells, the homeless, tramps and paupers) (39).*

In the wording of this law, "the state eugenics agent was empowered to investigate a person's heredity, to make arrests, and to cause the offender to be sterilized" (37, p. 35). Between 1907 and 1931 eugenics laws permitting the involuntary sterilization of criminals, degenerates, and imbeciles were passed in 30 states. Sterilization might entail tubal ligation or even full removal of the uterus, a much more complicated and expensive procedure (37, p. 36).

The sterilization of Carrie Buck in 1927 was the precedent for the large-scale movement throughout the United States to sterilize people diagnosed as mentally deficient. At the time of the court case, Buck, her mother, and her sister were residents of the State Colony for Epileptics and Feeble-minded in Lynchburg, Virginia. It was

later determined that, as with Deborah Kallikak, none of them would be defined today as having cognitive disabilities. Between the ages of 3 and 17, Buck was the "foster-child" (i.e., unpaid servant) of the Dobbs family of Charlottesville, Virginia. According to Buck, she became pregnant in 1923 after being raped by the Dobbs' nephew. The Dobbs family then arranged for Buck, after cursory testing, to be certified as feebleminded and institutionalized—just as her mother had been three years previously.

In 1924, a eugenic sterilization law was passed in Virginia. Alfred Priddy superintendent of the State Colony, attorney Aubrey Strode, working closely with the Eugenic Records Office in New York, decided to use Carrie Buck as a test case to determine the constitutionality of the law. Through the court case Buck vs. Bell, the law allowing eugenic sterilization was upheld by the state of Virginia in 1925 and the United States Supreme Court in 1927 (26). Supreme Court Justice Oliver Wendell Holmes, Jr. wrote:

*She may be sexually sterilized without detriment to her general health and that her welfare and that of society will be promoted by her sterilization. We have seen more than once that the public welfare may call upon the best citizens for their lives. It [the state] would be strange if it could not call upon those who already sap the strength of the State for these lesser sacrifices, often not felt to be such by those concerned, in order to prevent our being swamped with incompetence. It is better for all the world, if instead of waiting to execute degenerate offspring for a crime, or let them starve for their imbecility, society can prevent those who are manifestly unfit from breeding their kind. . . . Three generations of imbeciles are enough. (40)*

Carrie Buck was sterilized in 1927 and released into the community as a domestic servant. Her sister Doris, aged 16, was also sterilized and paroled (26). Doris Buck had been told the operation was an appendectomy and was unaware she was sterilized until 1979 (26, p. 216). She was later part of a successful lawsuit undertaken by the American Civil Liberties Union (ACLU) in

1980 on behalf of the 8,300 people sterilized in Virginia institutions between 1927 and 1974 (26, p. 251). Winifred Kempton and Emily Kahn (1991) reported that between 1907 and 1957 roughly 60,000 individuals, a conservative estimate, were involuntarily sterilized in the United States, many without being told (41, p. 96).

Although the eugenics movement was discredited after World War II because of the extreme measures taken by Nazi Germany, sterilization was still advocated and used (both legally and illegally) in the United States through the 1970s. Although policy makers dropped this strategy for social control, certain doctors and social workers continued to advocate for the practice on an individual level, sometimes with the support and encouragement of the woman's parents. After the 1980s, due to several high profile lawsuits such as the ACLU suit in which Doris Buck participated, doctors became less willing to perform the procedure without a clear legal mandate. Yet sterilization was still considered an option by many families wishing to "protect" their daughters.

## The Sterilization of Cindy Wasiek

The 1994 sterilization of Philadelphia resident Cindy Wasiek, following a seven-year court battle, shows that the nonconsensual sterilization of women with cognitive disabilities is still advocated and practiced, although such practice is sometimes contested (42,43). Cindy Wasiek was described in newspapers as having a mental age of 5, and being "severely retarded." Her mother, Dorothy Wasiek, feared her daughter might be raped and become pregnant. Because of anti-seizure medications, she could not place her daughter on contraceptive medication. She decided that sterilization would be the best way to protect her daughter. The central theme in this story was not Cindy Wasiek's safety, but rather how to allay her mother's fears. Cindy Wasiek's entire life was structured on her mother's fear of her being raped and becoming pregnant. She was even placed in a group home where all residents

and staff were women. Most parents do not have the power to make decisions about the sexuality and fertility of their children. However, parental and public perceptions considered Cindy Wasiek's disability to be so severe that she was prevented from being an active participant in the life decisions that concerned her. Cultural perceptions that people with cognitive disabilities are perpetual children allow parents to influence or control all aspects of their adult lives.

People with disabilities are more likely to experience sexual abuse than the general population, but the chances of Cindy Wasiek being raped and becoming pregnant were statistically remote (44). In any case, sterilization is not a protection from rape or sexually transmitted diseases. Based on the argument that a mother should have the authority to decide what is best for her daughter, Dorothy Wasiek had her daughter sterilized after Supreme Court Justice Souter refused to grant what is ordinarily a routine stay until the court had heard the case (42). Although this was not eugenic sterilization, the opportunity was available because of the continued existence of a law (passed by virtue of the eugenics movement) allowing nonconsensual sterilization. Because of the legacy of the eugenics movement, involuntary sterilization of people with cognitive disabilities remains culturally acceptable in the United States, although it would be unacceptable for use on other marginalized groups. Individuals with cognitive disabilities continue to be denied the rights granted to other United States citizens. Decisions regarding their bodies and their lives continue to be made without their consent.

## Glen Ridge Sexual Assault

On March 1, 1989, exactly one hundred years after Deborah Kallikak was institutionalized at Vineland, New Jersey, a young woman with a cognitive disability was playing ball in a neighborhood park in Glen Ridge, New Jersey. A group of young men from her high school, many of whom had known her for over a decade, came up and promised her a date with a popular high-school athlete if she would accompany them to a nearby house. When they arrived at the house, where two of the young men lived, the woman was told to undress and perform various sexual acts on herself and several of the young men. Eventually, some of them took turns inserting a fungo bat, a broom handle, and a stick into her vagina (45).

In the winter of 1992–1993, when three of these young men were tried for sexual assault, a defending attorney criticized the young woman's mother because "she took no measures to protect young men from her daughter" (46). The defense was attempting to prove that the young woman "craved sex" (47) and was "aggressive in her attitude and approach toward boys" (48). This is the modern legacy of the eugenics scholars who wrote about the "immoral" and "uncontrollable sexual nature" of women with cognitive disabilities. Defense lawyers in sexual-assault cases will sometimes assert that a woman is sexually promiscuous, but how often is the victim presented as a social threat? The defense's statements evoke images not of mere promiscuity, but of a sexually dangerous woman from which young men must be protected. This image was affirmed in the courtroom by a psychiatrist, and outside the courtroom by neighbors who, according to one journalist, "spoke of her as some kind of succubus, with unknowable needs and unfathomable wants" (49).

The young woman grew up with the young men who assaulted her. Her sister stated that, as a child, she was pinched and called "piggy," "dummy," and "retarded" by neighborhood children. Once, she was tricked into eating dog feces by a group of children that included two of the young men on trial (50). Journalist Anna Quindlen wrote:

> They behaved as though she were an inflatable doll, an inanimate object. Subtract the stereotypes about loose girls and uncontrollable male urges, and you come up with a clear picture of what went on in that basement: young men doing a cruel and reprehensi-
> ble thing to a woman they chose specifically because they knew her limitations and tractability. This case isn't about boys being boys. It's about boys being predators. I guess it wasn't much of a leap, from the dog feces to the broomstick. (51)

During the trial, both the prosecution and the defense attempted to use stereotypes about people with cognitive disabilities to their advantage. Instead of focusing on the character and history of the perpetrators, discourse revolved almost exclusively on the young woman's sexuality or vulnerability to abuse. Researcher Bernard Lefkowitz (45) found a pattern where many nondisabled young women in Glen Ridge were abused and harassed by this same group of young male athletes, but these events were never mentioned during the trial. Instead, the defense resurrected images of the disabled woman's obsessive sexuality that, although discredited decades ago, still have a powerful presence in our culture. The imagery used by prosecution was evocative of Goddard's description of Deborah Kallikak. They described the young woman from Glen Ridge as innocent, but yearning for social acceptance and so eager to please that she was incapable of saying "no."

In order to prove she was "mentally defective," the prosecution agreed to forego protection afforded by the rape shield law. Unlike most sexual assault trials, where information on sexual history is barred by law, the young woman's experiences were discussed in minute detail. The defense argued that "the case's complexities forced them to explore the woman's sexual past to prove that she knew what she was doing and wanted it" (52). The prosecutors made no objection, asserting that the woman's sexual history supported their contention that she was "mentally defective," as defined by New Jersey's sexual assault laws, and thus incapable of understanding her right to refuse sexual activity (53).

The jury was persuaded by this argument. In 1993, the three young men were found guilty of sexual assault, and sentenced to remain for an "indeterminate" minimum term of imprisonment in what was described as a "campuslike complex for young offenders" (54). They were immediately free on bail and remained so for the duration of the appeals process. They began serving prison time in 1997.

Both the woman's lawyers and the journalists covering the case continually referred to her pliability, low self-esteem, and passivity. It was repeatedly asserted that her "mental age" was 6 or 8 and that her I.Q. was 64 at most. They were more interested in what she was than in who she was. Without the issue of "mental defect," however, the case would have been difficult, if not impossible, to win. . . .

## Conclusion

It is clear from these stories that despite advances in recent decades, disability remains a stigma in the United States, especially mental disability. . . . In 1889 Deborah Kallikak was imprisoned for life because she was judged too feeble-minded to live in our society. In 1993, the perpetrators of a brutal sexual assault in Glen Ridge received sentences of less than two years. The Wasiek sterilization case revealed that it is culturally acceptable for parents of children with disabilities to make the most intimate and personal decision about the lives and futures of their children. . . .

Despite the many barriers to overcome, the future is hopeful. Women and men with cognitive disabilities in national and international self advocacy movements such as Self Advocates Becoming Empowered are working together to achieve for inclusion into US communities and cultures and equal protection under the law. They are asserting their rights to care, counseling and educational services, and empowering people with cognitive disabilities to assert, protect, and heal themselves.

## NOTES

1. I have chosen to use the term "cognitive disability" to refer to individuals with a diagnosis of mental retardation. While I have yet to find an unproblematic label, this one is more specific and less pejorative than most, and can be translated into other languages with less difficulty than terms such as "developmental" or "intellectual" disability.

2. The traits still form an important part of modern definitions for mental retardation. For a more detailed exploration of the evolution of definitions for mental retardation, see the first chapter of Block 1997.

## REFERENCES

1. Goffman, E: Stigma: Notes on the Management of Spoiled Identity. New Jersey, Prentice Hall, 1963.
2. Mercer, J: Labelling the Mentally Retarded: Clinical and Social System Perspectives on Mental Retardation. Berkeley, University of California Press, 1973.
3. Waxman, B. F: Hatred: The Unacknowledged Dimension in Violence Against Disabled People, Sexuality and Disability 9(3):185–99, 1991.
4. Asch, A., Fine, M: "Introduction: Beyond Pedestals." In Women with Disabilities: Essays in Psychology, Culture and Politics. Philadelphia, Temple University Press, 1988, pp. 1–37.
5. Thompson, R. G: Extraordinary Bodies: Figuring Physical Disability in American Culture and Literature. New York, Columbia University Press, 1997.
6. Fausto-Sterling, A: Life in the XY Corral. Women's Studies International Forum 12(3):319–331, 1989.
7. Fausto-Sterling, A: Myths of Gender: Biological Theories About Women and Men. New York, Basic Books, 1985.
8. Harding, S: The Science Question in Feminism. Ithaca, Cornell University Press, 1986.
9. Haraway, D: A Manifesto for Cyborgs: Science Technology and Socialist Feminism in the 1980s. Socialist Review 80:65–105, 1985.
10. Haraway, D: Situated Knowledges: The Science Question in Feminism and the Privilege of Partial Perspective. Feminist Studies, 14(3):575–596, 1988.
11. Hubbard, R: The Politics of Women's Biology. New Brunswick, Rutgers University Press, 1990.

12. Kuhn, T. S: The Structure of Scientific Revolutions (2nd ed.). Chicago, University of Chicago Press, 1970.

13. Martin, E: The Egg and the Sperm: How Science has Constructed a Romance Based on Stereotypical Male-Female Roles. Signs 16(3):485–501, 1991.

14. Mies, M: Sexist and Racist Implications of New Reproductive Technologies. Alternatives. 12:323–42, 1987.

15. Block, P: Biology, Culture, and Cognitive Disability: Twentieth Century Professional Discourse in Brazil and the United States. Duke University, Unpublished Doctoral Dissertation, 1997.

16. Rafter, N. H: Claims Making and Socio-Cultural Context in the First US Eugenics Campaign. Social Problems, 39(1):17–34, 1992.

17. Rafter, N. H.: White Trash: Eugenics as Social Ideology. Society 26(1):43–49, 1988.

18. Trent Jr., J. W: Inventing the Feeble Mind: A History of Mental Retardation in the United States. Berkeley, University of California Press, 1994.

19. Schilling, R. F., Schinke, S. P: Mentally Retarded Sex Offenders: Fact, Fiction and Treatment. Journal of Social Work and Human Sexuality 7(2):33–48, 1989.

20. Perske, R: Unequal Justice: What Can Happen When Persons with Retardation or Other Developmental Disabilities Encounter the Criminal Justice System. Nashville, Abingdon Press, 1991.

21. Gould, S. J: The Mismeasure of Man, New York; W. W. Norton and Co, 1981.

22. Smith, D. J: Minds Made Feeble: The Myth and Legacy of the Kallikaks. Maryland, Aspen Systems Corp, 1985.

23. Goddard, H. H: The Kallikak Family: A Study in the Heredity of Feeble-Mindedness. New York, The Macmillan Company, 1913.

24. Fairchild, H. P: The Melting Pot Mistake. Boston: Little Brown and Company, 1926.

25. Osborn, F: Preface to Eugenics. New York, Harper & Brothers, 1940.

26. Smith, D. J. and Nelson, K. R: The Sterilization of Carrie Buck. New Jersey, New Horizon Press, 1989.

27. Abramson Paul R. et al: Sexual Expression of Mentally Retarded People: Educational and Legal Implications. American Journal of Mental Retardation 93(3):328–34, 1988.

28. Edmonson, B. et al: What Retarded Adults Believe about Sex. American Journal of Mental Deficiency 84(1):11–18, 1979.

29. Heshusius, L: Sexual Intimacy, and Persons We Label Mentally Retarded: What They Think—What We Think. Mental Retardation 20(4):164–8, 1982.

30. Kempton, W: The Sexual Adolescent Who is Mentally Retarded. Journal of Pediatric Psychology 2(3):104–7, 1977.

31. Sinason, V: Uncovering and Responding to Sexual Abuse in Psychotherapeutic Settings. In Thinking the Unthinkable: Papers on Sexual Abuse and People with Learning Difficulties, H. Brown and A. Craft (eds.). London, FPA Education Unit, 39–49, 1988.

32. hooks, Bell: Selling Hot Pussy: Representations of Black Female Sexuality in the Cultural Marketplace, Black Looks: Race and Representation. Boston, South End Press, 1992.

33. Parker, R. G: Bodies, Pleasures, and Passions: Sexual Culture in Contemporary Brazil. Boston, Beacon Press, 1991.

34. Blank, R. H: Fertility Control: New Techniques, New Policy Issues. New York, Greenwood Press, 1991.

35. Gordon, L: Women's Body, Women's Right. New York, Penguin, 1976.

36. Reilly, P. R: The Surgical Solution: The History of Involuntary Sterilization in the United States. Baltimore, Johns Hopkins University Press, 1991.

37. Shapiro, T. M: Population Control Politics: Women, Sterilization, and Reproductive Choice. Philadelphia, Temple University Press, 1985.

38. Noll, S: Feeble-Minded in Our Midst: Institutions for the Mentally Retarded in the South 1900–1940. Chapel Hill, The University of North Carolina Press, 1995.

39. Laughlin, H: The Legal Status of Eugenical Sterilization, Washington: Eugenics Record Office, 1993. Cited in Rodriguez-Trias, H., Sterilization Abuse. In Biological Woman: The Convenient Myth. R. Hubbard, M. S. Henifin and B. Fried (eds.). Cambridge. Schenkman Publishing Company, Inc. pp. 147–160, 1982.

40. Buck vs. Bell, quoted in 38, p. 3, 1927.

41. Kempton, W., Kahn E: Sexuality and People with Intellectual Disabilities: A Historical Perspective. Sexuality and Disability 9(2):93–111, 1991.

42. Bowden, M: A Fight Over Sterilization May Finally Be Finished. Philadelphia Inquirer, Al, A14, Sat. November 12, 1994.

43. Goldberg, D: Woman's sterilization may end long Pennsylvania legal fight. Washington Post. A:2 col. 5, January 7, 1995.

44. Sobsey, D: Violence and Abuse in the Lives of People with Disabilities: The End of Silent Acceptance. Baltimore, Paul H. Brookes Publishing Co., 1994.

45. Lefkowitz, B: Our Guys: The Glen Ridge Rape and the Secret Life of the Perfect Suburb. Berkeley, University of California Press, 1997.

46. Hanely, R: Prosecutor Mocks Defense in Trial on Sexual Assault. New York Times B6: Col. 5, February 18, 1993b.

47. Hanley, R: Sex-Assault Trial Stresses Woman's Past. New York Times A26: Col. 4, October 31 1992a.

48. Hanley, R: Young Woman Was Aggressive Toward Boys, Psychiatrist Says. New York Times, B5: Col. 5, January 1, 1993a.

49. Junod, T: Ordinary People: Were the Suburban Youths Who Raped a Retarded Girl "Star Athletes" or "Just Typical Kids?" Sports Illustrated 78(12):68, March 23, 1993.

50. Hanley, R: Sister Calls Woman in Assault Case Pliable. New York Times B6: Col. 5, November 11, 1992c.

51. Quindlen, A: 21 Going on 6. New York Times, Sec. 4:17, December 13, 1992.

52. Manegold, C. S: A Rape Case Worries Advocates for the Retarded. New York Times Sec. 4:3, March 14, 1993.

53. Hanley, R: Accuser's Past at Issue in Assault Case. New York Times, late edition B26, November 5, 1992b.

54. Nieves, E: Sentences in Sexual Assault Divide Glen Ridge Jurors. New York Times Sec 1:48, April 25, 1993.

# How the Internet
# Is Shaping Sex

Lewis Perdue

Just as sex has shaped the Internet, the Internet also influences sex and our society in ways which could have very substantial cultural implications, including changes in the community standards definition of obscenity, empowering women working in the sex field and moving adult material from its traditional male orientation to one which caters to women's desires as well.

The Internet has changed obscenity in the United States by untethering the definition of community from the purely physical to one which is bound by bits and bandwidth.

In the United States, pornography and erotica are not illegal, but obscenity is. But trying to define obscenity has been a perennial question for the Supreme Court for more than a century now with no court having supplied the nation with its "final answer."

In a 1964 case, *Jacobellis v. Ohio*, Justice Potter Stewart distilled the essence of the problem when he said, quite candidly, that while he could not define obscenity, "I knew it when I saw it." The Supreme Court later tried to strike a workable compromise in 1973 with *Miller v. California* which created a three-step test: For a work to be judged illegal all three of the following must be present: the average person, applying contemporary community standards, must find that the work, taken as a whole, appeals to prurient interests; second, that it depicts or describes, in a

patently offensive way, sexual conduct as defined by state law; and third, that the work, taken as a whole, lacks serious literary, artistic, political, or scientific value.

In the Miller case, the Supreme Court concluded that obscenity is in the eye of the beholder and varies widely from place to place. What people in Mormon-dominated Utah consider obscene is obviously different from the loose and tolerant folks in San Francisco or New York.

"What the court did not tell us in crafting the [Miller] obscenity test is how the geographic scope of the community is to be analyzed," said Lawrence G. Walters, a Florida-based partner of Weston, Garrou & DeWitt, a national law firm headquartered in Los Angeles which specializes in First Amendment cases. "Is it [the community] the city? The county? How the community is measured becomes exceedingly important . . . where the issue of acceptance of comparable material exists."

Walters noted that in the Miller case, the Supreme Court held that the relevant community was the entire state of California. "We have received rulings in other cases that the community constitutes the county, a tri-county area or the entire state of Florida," he said.

Global media, including the Internet, cable and satellite television have effectively destroyed the ability of courts to define a community using geographic boundaries, Walters said, a view held by all the legal authorities I interviewed.

Indeed, the Third District U.S. Court of Appeals prevented enforcement of the federal Child Online Protection Act (COPA), citing among

From Perdue, Lewis. 2002. "How the Internet Is Shaping Sex." In *EroticaBiz: How Sex Shaped the Internet* (pp. 151–168). Reprinted by permission.

other things, the unconstitutional vagueness of defining community standards in an age when the world is available on any computer or television in any community. "The court clearly said you could not apply local community standards to global media," Walter said.

Walter said that when porn was available only in print or on film or video cassette, "a small community could physically keep the material out through zoning or obscenity prosecution." But the advent of technology, he said, "means that anyone, in any community can have their porn available in the privacy of their own home—something the Supreme Court says is legally protected. Technology allows you to do this without imposing it on others. In America, we like our porn available but not in our faces," Walters continued. "We want access, but we don't want to have to see it in stores or on the street." . . .

Walters said that . . . technology has already altered the way that local juries decide on guilt or innocence in these cases. The state of Florida, he said, recently dismissed obscenity charges against an adult Internet client of his when he raised the community standards issue as a defense.

Walters agreed with other legal experts that the acquittal of a Provo, Utah, video rental store owner on obscenity charges is one of the most telling cases of how technology has changed local community standards.

While San Francisco and Provo show extreme outward differences in their attitudes, a local court case in Provo indicates that the citizens of the two cities are a lot more alike in their proclivities toward pornography than the pious Mormon congregations in Utah would like to admit.

The case started in 1996 when police raided Larry W. Peterman's two small independent Movie Buffs video stores in American Fork and Lehi, Utah. The action was taken after more than 4,000 people in Utah County—which likes to call itself the most conservative county in the United States—signed a petition calling for Peterman's prosecution. Peterman's store was not an adult-oriented book and paraphernalia store, but like

thousands of independent video stores across the United Sates, offered the complete gamut of videos that people wanted to rent. His store had everything from Disney's Dalmatians and Bruce Willis splattering blood and guts across the screen to an adult section in the back with Debbie Doing Everybody. Peterman testified that 11 percent of all rentals were adult in nature, somewhat below the national average of 16 percent. But that number, the court would learn, is deceptively low.

Rather than simply not visit the adult section of the store, the 4,000 pious petitioners pressed for a pornography prosecution to prevent other Provonians from perusing Peterman's pornography.

Prospects didn't look terribly bright for Peterman until one day his attorney, Randy Spencer, was gazing out the courtroom window at the penultimate symbol of Mormon's mammon: Marriott. While Mormons try to keep their flock on the shortest of leashes, they'll never turn away from making a buck off selling forbidden fruit and drink to those who are already headed for Hell: alcohol, coffee and tea as well as video sex are available for paying infidels who stay at a Marriott.

Spencer's investigator, defense witness Richard Gale, testified he checked into the Provo Marriott, set up a tripod and a video camera, and recorded 11 adult movies that were offered over the in-room On Command service. . . . After documenting the cornucopia of sex films available right in the middle of the nation's most conservative county, he then subpoenaed the Marriott's pay-per-view purchase records. . . .

Even though most Marriott guests who tuned into the in-room porn were presumably from beyond the borders of Provo, this is legally irrelevant, according to Walters and other legal experts. What's necessary in defining community standards, they say, is whether the material is available in the community.

But Peterman's defense attorney didn't stop with the video proclivities of Provo's visitors. He then went after local cable and satellite television providers' records on subscriptions and rentals of sex flicks by Provo residents.

What he found was a nearly fathomless pit of hypocrisy: the citizens of Utah County rented far more porn flicks per capita than did people in the rest of the United States. Indeed, Spencer pointed out that satellite channels had sold more than 20,000 adult sex videos during the time period in which Peterman was charged with violating obscenity laws. Not only that, but the 20,000 was roughly twice the per capita number of sales as the rest of the United States. . . .

Despite the fact that this material isn't marketed, revenue-wise, it's one of our biggest money-makers," said Peggy Simons of TCI Cable in her court testimony. TCI has since been purchased by AT&T and has expanded its offerings of adult entertainment.

The difference, of course, is that the Provonians were privately purchasing porn from purveyors who were not visible to the community, thus allowing them pious deniability and the capability of having their porn and prosecute it too.

The jury acquitted Peterman after just 2-½ hours of deliberation. Despite his acquittal, he had already been severely punished by the process. Peterman said the ordeal left him bankrupt and the lengthy prosecution led to his divorce. His foes rejoiced in Peterman's misfortune. According to the *Provo Herald*, "Gayle Ruzicka, president of the local chapter of the national Eagle Forum, also claimed victory. 'We won what we wanted,' she said. 'There are no longer Movie Buffs stores in the county.' "

In addition to changing how we define community standards, the Internet has confused local governments about whether they even have jurisdiction. The city of Tampa, Florida, tried to shut down VoyeurDorm, arguing that the home occupied by 13 scantily clad women and 55 continually webcasting cameras was an adult business improperly located in a residential neighborhood. However, in late September 2001, the 11th U.S. Circuit Court of Appeals sided with VoyeurDorm, saying that the actual "business" was conducted in cyberspace and not at the house.

The court said, "The public does not, indeed cannot physically attend" activities at the house and thus, it "does not fall within the purview of Tampa's Zoning Ordinance."

Perhaps of even more cultural importance are the changes that the Internet is bringing to the uneasy relationship between women and the public conception of how they should relate to sex.

One woman who is doing that in her own quiet profitable way is the adult web's most visible and successful female entrepreneur, Danni Ashe: founder, CEO and number-one talent of her softcore adult content site, Danni's Hard Drive (www.danni.com). Ashe created her site in 1995 after a series of snafus on the topless gentleman's club circuit left her looking for a better way to make a living.

"I had a number of bad experiences as a feature dancer and knew I was going to need to make a change," said Ashe who said that her first online experiences were with Usenet news groups where she found many of her fans congregating. "I really got hooked talking and interacting with people on alt.sex.breast and alt.sex.movies [both are Usernet news groups] and it wasn't long before someone posted a message that said, 'Gee, Danni, you should have a Website!' "

She connected with some Web designers in early 1995 and offered them half of the company if they would build her site. They refused. Had they accepted, they would own a 50 percent share in a company which has 4.3 million page views per day from 33,000 unique visitors. More than 29,000 members pay her $24.95 per month. Those memberships, plus income from hosting other sites and producing video and images in its five state-of-the-art production studios put the company on track to gross $8 million in 2001. Significantly, the company has a profit margin close to 35 percent leaving it with an operating statement that almost any Fortune 500 company would lust for. That level of profitability has allowed Danni.com to develop its own credit card fraud detection systems, in-house digital production facilities and a streaming video system—DanniVision—which easily trumps both RealPlayer and Microsoft Media player for quality and ease of use.

Today, the company has a staff of about 50, a 16,500-square-foot headquarters in West Los Angeles, and hosts sites for more than 300 models, B-movie and adult actresses, amateurs, Penthouse Pets, Playboy Playmates and exotic dancers. And while Danni's Hard Drive is strictly soft, she also hosts hard core sites for other women in the business.

But that's now and not the spring of 1995, when the two Web designers, who had no vision of what might be, demanded hard cash. "So I paid them the $900 they asked me for," Danni said. "But I wasn't getting what I wanted." So she decided to do it herself. While most people take a Bahamian vacation for the sun, seafood, gambling and some steel band music, Danni took an HTML programming manual and Nicholas Negroponte's *Being Digital* and absorbed them both.

When she got back, she reprogrammed the site herself and it was such a hit that she had to give up webmastering in the summer of 1996 to manage the company's growth which was so fast that her husband quit his job in the motion picture industry to help her.

Along the way, she's been covered for being uncovered (profitably) by more business and news publications than any other woman in recent history: *The Wall Street Journal, USA Today, Time, U.S. News and World Report* among the many. The *Guinness Book of World Records* lists her as the most downloaded woman on the Internet. In January 2001, for example, Danni received 59 million page views, twice as popular as Martha Stewart, three times more popular than either Oprah or Britney Spears. In fact, on Feb. 20, 2001, Ashe broke the billion-download mark.

Danni's financial success has proved that the marketplace will pay for something different from the usual extreme hardcore found elsewhere. She will not show, host or allow in her revenue affiliate programs any content she feels is degrading to women, thus indicating that financial power can be the muscle to make changes for the better.

Danni Ashe, however, is just the most visible woman among thousands who run and control their own online adult businesses. Before the advent of the Internet, most of the pornography business was controlled by men; there were very, very few women entrepreneurs. But starting and running an online adult business relies less on large amounts of capital and more on brains, ability and the willingness to work hard, which is why it has so many women webmasters, entrepreneurs and even strippers and porn stars who run and control their own sites, thereby giving them a greater degree of control over the use and promotion of their own bodies than was ever possible in the pre-Internet days. In addition, the adult side of the Internet pays better than other online sectors and is among the most egalitarian industries in the world.

The popular and politically correct view of women in the sex trade from both the religious right and the radical feminist left is that pornography oppresses and exploits women. Both the Pulpit and the Politically Correct say that women involved with pornography are the pawns of pimps; they are powerless "poor little dears" who have fallen on bad times. With no choices left to them, these women have entered the sordid world of sex and degradation from which they need to be rescued because, being women, they are helpless and unable to make responsible decisions about their own lives.

Obviously the attitudes of women in the online adult sector are shaped by their decisions to work in a sex-related business. Like anyone who chooses to work in any vocation whether it be fighter pilot, editor or accountant, these women express attitudes and opinions that justify the decisions they have made. Nevertheless, the fact that there is a legion of female entrepreneurs working in this field—where there had previously been none—is due to an environment fostered by the Internet.

These women are not simply content to go with the online flow, but are determined to use the technology to shape the face of sex and to create a new category of erotica that appeals to women.

While I use the chosen "handles" of the women interviewed, I have met most of them face to face at trade shows and have spoken with them all by phone on numerous occasions.

Not unexpectedly, the numerous performers, webmistresses and other businesswomen I interviewed unanimously derided prevailing attitudes as self-motivated, power-grabbing, outdated, flat-out wrong and unrepresentative of their opinions and needs.

"Andrea Dworkin and others like her don't see the whole picture," said Australian webmistress, KarenJ. "I do believe that trying to ban pornography displays a lack of understanding about human nature. People love sex, they love looking at sex. Trying to ban it is misguided. If feminists want to stop women being exploited they need to *change* pornography, and this is what I think the women working in online porn are doing. We're presenting an alternative that isn't sexist or demeaning—it's more a celebration of sex." Sandra at WEN (Women's Erotic Network, a support site for women who operate adult websites) pointed out that the popularity of amateur sites is also helping to move porn into the realm of reality, where women are treated with more respect.

"Currently, a lot of mainstream porn presents women as objects that need to be penetrated. The language is often derogatory and sometimes the intent is implied to be violent (she needs to be 'pounded' and so on)," said Sandra. "I also believe the obsession with teens reveals a worrying preponderance towards latent pedophilia," she continued.

"Men like to see the mechanics of sex, and often their fantasies may involve domination. However I believe these needs can be catered to without the extreme sexism and objectification that is often presented. I'm certain a lot of men don't really want to see that kind of thing in porn," said KarenJ. "I also believe that the way women are presented in mainstream porn has an effect on the way some men think about and treat women. In

this respect, I tend to agree with feminists who say that porn is harmful to women.

"The other problem with mainstream porn," said KarenJ, "is its ability to mislead about what makes for good sex. If watching porn is your only means of sex education, you're in for an unhappy sex life. In this, I believe that porn provides a huge disservice to men and women alike. Again, I think women's porn can only improve this situation, because at least we're showing what women want."

And what got her into the porn business?

"I was introduced to the world of women's erotica online around March 2000 when I wrote an article on what porn was available on the Internet for women," KarenJ said. "I found Purve [an Australian erotic Website for women run by a woman who goes by the nickname, "CJ"], was impressed with it, and offered my services as a writer to CJ, the owner of Purve. I was amazed that the operator of such a major site was Australian like me. She encouraged me to get into the business, and my first site for women went up in July 2000. I now have nine sites up and running—not many, but I also work as a freelance journalist, and have considered adult sites to be a nice 'hobby.'"

KarenJ is 27, a qualified librarian in Queensland who used to work in the library of the *Sydney Morning Herald*. "I can make money under my own steam, without having to obey time clocks," she says. "No one watches my productivity except myself, and I know when I need to stop and rest. On top of this, I wear my daggiest clothing around, I don't have to commute, and I can do the housework and shopping when necessary.

"I love creating adult sites because it's an outlet for my creativity. I consider myself to be a frustrated novelist, and creating websites is a quicker way of making your writing public, without the hassle of publishers," she said. "I think women's sites require a great deal more creativity than men's sites. Men are just after the pictures, women want to read, be entertained, and feel they're part of a community. To create a women's site that is interesting requires a lot of planning, imagination and a good sense of humor. You need your surfers to identify with you, and you have to make them feel at home.

"I do believe women's porn will change the nature of mainstream porn. I think it will swing the pendulum away from the nastier, sexist side of it, and turn it into something affirming for everyone," she said. "You can't get rid of porn, but you can make it more real, more enjoyable, more equal and positive. I think the Internet is the best forum for this to happen, as it takes porn away from the seedy back streets and puts it into the bedroom."

Adult webmistress Oceania, who lives in Tennessee and creates custom erotic stories for her paying clients, has her own harsh words for both the radical left and religious right and their attempts to ban pornography. "Feminists forget that we are all sexual beings and that one man's porn is not necessarily porn. As for exploitation, everyone—every class, color, race—has been and will continue to be exploited by someone or thing. Just look at advertising and you know that nothing is sacred."

Oceania started her career as a graphic designer in New York City, having graduated from a well-known Manhattan university. She found her way to the adult Web by serendipity.

"I had answered an ad to become the voice-over for a software program for handicapped, mainly sight-impaired, people, so they could touch the screen and navigate the file menus by sound," she said. The software sold well overseas to hospitals and other institutions. My voice got a lot of fan mail from Japan and Russia and Iraq and different places from people who wanted to hear more."

Oceania then built Venetian Dreams (www.venetiandreams.com) which offers stories which she writes and records herself. In addition to reading and listening to existing stories, customers can pay her to write and record a story for them based on their own desires and fantasies.

Laurel, another graphic designer turned adult webmistress who offers thousands of erotic stories in her site, Literotica (www.literotica.com), believes the way that society treats women as a whole is far more degrading than what women find in the world of online sex. "Personally, I think menial office jobs for low pay exploit women (and men) far more than a Hustler centerfold ever could," she said. "When certain feminists make these claims [about women and pornography] they're treating women the same way they claim misogynists do—as mindless, powerless pawns to be manipulated by men. The assumption is that porn is wrong, and the only reason any woman would be involved in the porn industry is if she were coerced or forced into it. Those feminist assumptions ignore the fact that women do it for the same reason they take any job: for the money. The purpose of a job is to make a living, period. We choose a certain career out of all the possible careers because it may appeal to us more than others, but it's still a job. Any job has its good and bad days. Posing nude in a magazine is no more exploitative or humiliating than being chewed out by your boss when you miss a deadline, or being made to work overtime on a project when you'd rather be home with your family. . . ."

Australian Webmistress "CJ," who operates Purve (purve.com) and an associated network of adult sites including sexhit.com, her own traffic revenue program, says: "Those who speak out against pornography may have either had bad experiences sexually or are assuming those who present explicit material must also support rape, child pornography and so on. I hope that by increasing the number of women in this industry, we can show that we are in control of our own paths and that we can help to make positive changes from within the industry. I am a woman and I had several choices of career path. I have always had many opportunities open to me and have chosen to work in an industry which some would say is not a 'choice' and that I am contributing to the degradation of women. I think my achievements show quite the opposite. Women can make a choice to do whatever they choose and to be successful at it."

Like Oceania and Laurel, CJ began as a graphic designer then migrated from corporate positions to the Web, "Because it lets me do what I want to do when I want to do it." On the other hand, she is not as sanguine about the Web's equality for women.

"I don't think there is such a thing as equal in any business, Web or not," CJ said.

"In fact, I think it's a little harder to be equal when you are a female Internet pornographer. In a boardroom you struggle with being taken seriously; in the porn world you struggle to cover your breasts while still remaining a woman. I have breasts. Therefore I must be exposing them for money. I have a brain. Therefore, I must be using it to charge money to view my breasts."

"Your struggles are what you make them," she emphasized. "I've only had a few small instances where I was offended by a sexist comment. Mostly I have been treated extremely well by all who work in this industry. Those who don't show respect for one another usually hear about it rather quickly."

All of the women I interviewed said that they hoped to redefine, or at least expand, the range of erotica offered on the Web by creating a different class of material that appeals more to women and couples. But, like sister webmistress Susanna (www.couples-sex.com), she said that what questions are asked and how people ask them are vital prerequisites to getting an accurate answer.

"By asking 'What do women want?' a lot of people are automatically saying 'Hey, they all have a vagina, they must all like romance novels,'" CJ said. "Women are as diverse, if not a lot more so, in their likes and turn-ons as men". . . .

"From the beginning of our quest for women's erotica, we have argued about 'what women want' as we each have a different formula that is working for our own clientele," she said. "The biggest mistake we have made in this market is throwing all women into a big target audience and saying, 'You are woman, you must be turned on by stories and romance.' My goal is to allow women to feel that it is okay if you get wet while you are watching a guy masturbate, an anal sex scene or reading a romance novel. By creating the cliche 'Women like romance and text over pics' we are telling those who don't fit this 'criteria' that they aren't normal."

"In reality," CJ continued, "what we should be trying to inspire is expression, encouragement, development of a woman's *own* sexuality—which is a personal thing that cannot be defined by a 'target market.' I believe women are more attracted to words because we have told them they should be. The adult market has automatically assumed men like pics and women like stories. Therefore, what has been made available is what has been purchased by women as a whole. Today's market is very different from three years ago when this area took off but there is still that need to throw target markets into a big pot and stir them all around and throw in what we think goes there."

Literotica's Laurel said she finds that women are more interested in words than pictures. "It's not that the women are less visual—though I think we're kind of cultured to not be as visual—but I don't think that it's a natural thing. I think women do enjoy looking, but a lot of what's out there on the Internet isn't geared toward women. It's either gay content that some site has tried to gear toward women, but women know the difference. So it's hard to find good female pictures that aren't either all romance soft focus—you know, lace and all that—or just gay male. Women want their own porn because, you know, they can be just as nasty as anybody."

Laurel sees the romance reader as a key visitor to her site. "We keep the romance; we have the category based for that reason. Women buy romance novels because women are sexual beings."

In fact, Laurel said that the book industry has started to realize that the market she has tapped may be good for them as well. "We're putting out a book of our best writings that's being published right now by a small press, Black Book in San Francisco." In addition, she launched a wireless and PDA oriented content site in early 2001 to take advantage of their growing popularity.

All the women I interviewed applauded to some extent the cybermeritocracy the Internet has engendered.

In 1997, southern Colorado webmistress "Bestat" was running a computer consulting business with her husband. As is all too common, many clients assumed that women weren't technically inclined and thus her husband "fronted" for the duo even on jobs where she was the technical lead. Bestat was holding down an outside clerical job at a mediocre salary when she decided to develop their Web design business and quickly recognized the potential of sex on the Web.

"After all, sex was the only thing making money," she said. "I quickly built a little free site and the sponsor programs immediately started producing pocket change. I quickly realized that no one was doing 'toon' content (cartoon sex) which is why I built my first pay site: cartoonsex. com (www.cartoon-sex.com)."

She now has a network of her own sites, each specializing in things like hentai, adult anime, Vargas-like erotica and more. Combined, her sites get more than 30,000 unique visitors per day and pull in a "six-figure income" that allowed her to quit the mediocre $40,000 per year clerical job she had held. She also found a respect in cyberspace that was denied her in the physical world where people felt that women shouldn't worry their pretty little heads over all that nasty programming stuff.

"There's an equality on the web," Bestat says. "You succeed online based on your ability."

"There are also a lot of adult webmasters who are disabled," said Bestat. "The adult Web allows them to be judged on their work and talent and not on their looks or disabilities. It also allows them to work flexible hours from their homes."

Of course, equality and flexibility exist on the non-adult Web as well, but for most people, there's not enough money to be made to support themselves. "I know a guy who's on the boards [adult webmaster message boards] who was an agoraphobic and was on welfare because he couldn't go outside his house," said Bestat. "He's now off welfare and earning a very good living on the Web."

Not unexpectedly, Bestat has her own strong ideas about those who would try to eliminate pornography: "Well, being an ex-hippie, I am a huge believer in freedom of speech and expression," she said. "I do not believe porn exploits women; many women make an excellent living off this industry both in front of and behind the camera. I also believe in sex as a natural beautiful thing, which unfortunately is not the majority view, or the majority that is vocal in the U.S. at least. I am often amused and disappointed in the feminist outcry against porn, when our society allows people of all ages to watch shootings, maiming, horrific acts of inhumanity and death on a daily basis on TV and in movies and video games. I believe society causes more ill than good with trying to suppress sexual expression; it is like keeping a pride of lions and trying to suppress their urge for meat. By condemning porn and making it 'evil' for a person to express themselves sexually, we create an underground environment that is ripe for fraud, deceit, and exploitation." . . .

Despite the pioneering efforts of these women and their very different sexual perspectives, for now, the very biggest adult websites are still owned by men, mostly because those operations are extensions of more traditional sex businesses such as phone sex, videos, strip clubs and skin magazines. Women have penetrated the business of the adult Internet in only the past five or six years and are hammering away at a mirrored ceiling that looks to be far less obdurate than the glass ceilings blocking women's career paths in corporate America.

For performers—both amateurs and professionals like Danni Ashe—entertaining a paying audience without leaving the comfort and safety of their own home (or a secure production studio with a bed) has made working in the sex industry safer than ever before. In addition, since these women run their own businesses, they control the cash, direct how their bodies will be used and have the ultimate say over the portrayal of their images.

This is not to say that the old sex industry has disappeared. Street prostitutes still get abused and murdered by their pimps and Johns and die in ever-increasing numbers from AIDS. Men and women performing in adult films also risk sexually transmitted diseases despite programs requiring recent medical confirmation that they are STD-free. As a whole, the sex trade is still run by and

for men. But the Internet and the availability of cheap accessible technology has offered women an opportunity they have never had before.

The Internet has allowed women to breathe life into their unconventional ideas about what is sexy. In the process, this is taking porn and erotica in new directions on the Net and off, offering a growing alternative to the traditional for-guys-only orientation that has dominated sex for millennia. . . .

## Sextistics

### Did You Know?

- Among the top twenty most-watched television shows by teens, 70 percent include some kind of sexual content.[1] Within these shows, sex scenes occur at an average rate of five scenes per hour.[2]
- Today only 14 percent of television shows with sexual content include at least one reference to sexual risk or responsibility.[3]
- Only half of all scenes on TV that show vaginal intercourse involve characters who have an established relationship with the other person.[4]
- Teens aged 12 to 17 who heavily viewed sexual content on TV were twice as likely to initiate sexual intercourse than teens who saw the least amount of sexual content.[5]
- In 1995, while modeling for MAC Cosmetics, RuPaul became the first drag queen supermodel.[6]
- In 1896, the short (twenty-second) film, *The May Irwin Kiss,* featured the first film kiss. The graphic depiction of a kiss shocked movie goers and caused one of the first calls for film censorship by the Roman Catholic Church.[7]
- The first transsexual TV character was Officer Mel Brubaker played by Randi Brooks in the 1986 police comedy *The Last Precinct.*[8]
- Lysol was once promoted as a contraceptive douche.[9]
- Vincent Schiavelli played the first openly gay main character in the TV sitcom *The Corner Bar,* airing June 1, 1972.[10]
- The first lesbian kiss on TV was on *L.A. Law*, February 7, 1991. Although over fourteen million people saw this episode, only fifty-one contacted NBC to complain. Some of the complaining viewers were concerned the kiss was too short.[11]
- The first married couple to sleep in the same bed was Mary Kay and John Sterns in *Mary Kay and Johnny* in 1947. They were not only married onscreen, but off screen as well.[12]
- The first sitcom to address abortion was *Maude* during November 1972 when Maude unexpectedly became pregnant. While two CBS stations refused to carry the two-part show, sixty-five million viewers watched the episodes and 24,000 complaint letters were sent to the network.[13]
- In effect from 1930 to 1966, the Hays Code regulated Hollywood movies.[14] These moral restrictions included a ban against films containing sexual content such as lustful kissing or embracing, sexual dancing, miscegenation, and rape.[15]

*—Compiled by Mikel Walters*

**NOTES**

1. Kunkel, Dale, Keren Eyal, Keli Finnerty, Erica Biely, and Edward Donnerstein. 2005. "Sex on TV 4." The Henry J. Kaiser Family Foundation. Retrieved January 30, 2005 from www.kff.org/entmedia/upload/Sex-on-TV-4-Full-Report.pdf.

2.   Ibid.

3.  Ibid.

4.  Ibid.

5.  Ibid.

6.  RuPaul. "Bio/History." Retrieved January 28, 2006 from www.rupaul.com/about.html.

7.  Filmsite.org. 1996. "Sexual or Erotic Films." Retrieved November 21, 2005 from www.filmsite.org/sexualfilms.html.

8.  TVAcres. 2004. "Transexuals on Television and in the Movies." Retrieved November 30, 2005 from http://tvacres.com/sex_taboos_transexuals.html.

9.  Gibbons, Sheila. 2004. "A Brief History of Modern Contraceptive Ads." Planned Parenthood. Retrieved January 20, 2006 from www.plannedparenthood.org/pp2/portal/files/portal/ webzine/artsculture/art-041231-advertisements.xml.

10.  Ibid.

11.  Murphy, R. 2005. "Top 10: TV Firsts." Retrieved November 30, 2005 from www.askmen.com/toys/top_10_100/114_top_10_list.html.

12.  Ibid.

13.  Ibid.

14.  Filmsite.org. 2005. "Sexual or Erotic Films." Retrieved November 21, 2005 from www.filmsite.org/sexualfilms.html.

15.  ArtsReformation.com. 2006. "The Motion Picture Production Code of 1930 (Hays Code)." Retrieved January 30, 2006. from www.artsreformatin.com/a001/hays-code.html.

# chapter 4

# *Learning about Sex*

Spotlight on Research

*An interview with . . .*

## Ritch C. Savin-Williams

Ritch C. Savin-Williams, Ph.D., is chair and professor of human development at Cornell University in Ithaca, New York. His research centers on the psychological strength, resiliency, and well-being of same-sex attracted youths and adults. He is author of *The New Gay Teenager* (Harvard University Press, 2005), *"Mom, Dad, I'm Gay": How Families Negotiate Coming Out* (American Psychological Association, 2001), *". . . And Then I Became Gay": Young Men's Stories* (Routledge, 1998), and the co-editor of *The Lives of Lesbians, Gays, and Bisexuals: Children to Adults* (Harcourt Brace College Publishing, 2001).

### What led you to begin studying sexuality?

*My interest in adolescent development centers on the promotion of resiliency, strength, and coping skills of youths. I am less interested in what places youths at risk as I am in what gives them the ability to do well. Clearly, sexual development during adolescence has been a taboo topic for researchers, except insofar as it is a component of delinquency or a medical, social, or political problem. For example, we know a lot about unsafe sex, but little about the meaning or significance of sexuality for an adolescent's enjoyment of daily life or conception of the future. We know a lot about sexual intercourse but little about other sexual behaviors such as kissing and oral-genital contact. Contraception, pregnancy, sexually transmitted diseases, sexual intercourse debut, number of sex partners, and the linkage of vaginal-penile intercourse to clinical and social problems are common topics of sex researchers; sexual desire, pleasure, physical and emotional intimacies, the meaning of sex, what is sex, and sexual minorities are uncommon. I want to help promote the positive aspects of sexuality for adolescent development.*

**Which of your projects have you found most stimulating?**

*The most fun I have had conducting sexuality research were the intensive, indepth interviews I did with 78 young women with same-sex attractions. These women willingly shared their sexual histories with honesty and insight that humbled me. Their developmental trajectories were so divergent from my own that it was as if I was privy to a new experience of growing up. Their thrilling and heart-wrenching stories about growing up in the 1990s with attractions for other women convinced me that they were the most resilient, healthy, spirited group of youths I had ever encountered.*

**What have you found most challenging about studying sexuality?**

*The most challenging aspect of my work has been convincing adult authorities to end the silence about adolescent sexuality, showing them that it is "okay" to ask youths about their sexual development. Many adults are incredibly anxious about sexuality and they project that discomfort onto younger cohorts. All that I ask is that I be allowed to do my task—to let adolescents speak for themselves; I am merely a conduit and translator, and occasionally an interpreter of their lives.*

**Why is it important to do sex research with adolescents?**

*We know a considerable amount about many aspects of adolescents' lives. Their sexual development is the last frontier. The silence and the medicalization of their sexuality must be ended so that those youths who are embarrassed about their sexuality, who do not feel "normal," and who spend far too many hours chastising themselves for "unpure" thoughts and behavior can be freed from these constraints to live normal, happy lives.*

**What ethical dilemmas have you faced in your research with adolescents? How did you resolve them?**

*University review boards demand parental permission for inclusion of their under-18 child in behavioral research. Few parents want us to ask their children about their sexuality. One approach is thus to retrospectively ask over-18 youths and young adults about their sexual histories. This skirts one dilemma but compounds another—we aren't listening to the sexual lives of adolescents as they live them. So much has transpired in the sexual development of adolescents prior to age 18. Second, sometimes gaining parental permission places youths at-risk for parental censure or chastisement, such as when sexual-minority youths want to talk about their lives as lesbian, gay, or bisexual adolescents, but have not yet disclosed to their parents. Making this case to university review boards has allowed me to interview 16 and 17 year olds—but even this resolution appears to imply that at age 16—but not before—a young person becomes capable of making a decision to share her sexual history.*

**How do people react when they find out that you study sexuality?**

*Envy.*

**If you could teach people one thing about sexuality, what would it be?**

*Sex is great, meant to enjoy and add meaning to one's life.*

—Interviewed by Denise Donnelly

# The Death of the Stork:
# Sex Education Books for Children

Wendy Simonds

## Why Not the Stork?

You may say, "Isn't it easier and less embarrassing to tell them about the stork?" There are several reasons. . . . Even if he doesn't suspect anything at 3, he is surely going to find out the truth or the half-truth when he's 5 or 7 or 9. It's better not to start him off wrong and have him later decide that you're something of a liar. And if he finds out that you didn't dare tell him the truth, it puts a barrier between you, makes him uneasy. He's less likely to ask you other questions later, no matter how troubled he is (Spock and Rothenberg, 1992: 511).

> "Does it feel good when a mommy and daddy make a baby?" he asked.
>
> Joey's father answered, "It feels very nice, especially since you're able to be so close to someone you love."
>
> "Hey," Joey said in an excited voice, "maybe sometime you two can show me how you do it."
>
> Joey's parents smiled and laughed, but Joey knew it was a nice laugh and they weren't making fun of him.
>
> "Joey, when a mommy and daddy make love, it's private, just something for the two of them," said Joey's father.
>
> "Well, when can I do it? When can I make a baby?"
>
> "When you get older, Joey," said Joey's mother. (Brooks and Perl, 1983)

This hokey conversation from *So That's How I Was Born!*, a sex education book aimed at preschoolers, exemplifies the sort of sexual honesty Spock and Rothenberg prescribe advising against the stork story. And certainly everyone believes that honesty is the best policy. But there's more than one way to be honest, and there are multiple truths about sexuality. We educate kids based on our perceptions of social reality, often without questioning norms to which we've grown accustomed. We also educate kids without knowing we're doing it—with offhand remarks or behaviors that we're not aware they notice. When we do intend to teach, we can now select from a variety of texts designed to help us. Parents may choose sex education books because doing so gets them off the hook altogether from discussing sex with their kids, or they may use the books as supplementary material. Several of these books have introductory notes to parents instructing them about instructing their kids. Sex education books for children both represent and shape cultural ideologies about children, sexuality, and procreation.

In my research, I found no sex education books targeted to young children published before the late 1960s. Publishers apparently began to perceive young children as a market for this sort of didactic material as a result of a particular combination of cultural forces that together promoted resistance to authority and more openness about sexual matters in the late 1960s and early 1970s: the student movement, the feminist movement, the gay rights movement (all of which are indebted to the Civil Rights movement); hippie subculture; the so-called sexual revolution; and the human potential movement. Advice books on sexuality for adults also flourished during this time (e.g., see Ehrenreich and English 1986; Simonds, 1992), and sex education programs proliferated in U.S. public schools (Moran 2000). The notion that children should be educated about sex before adolescence developed as cultural views of adolescents *as* sexual became accepted by educators and doctors. Thus, adolescents were in need of sexual education—especially regarding management and control. Moran describes the development of these ideas, beginning at turn of the twentieth century (2000). Patton (1996) writes that the way in which we now conceive of adolescence is "as a time of turmoil between a period of innocence (childhood) and one of accomplished identity and safety (adulthood)" (75). So how do we present sexuality to innocents to prepare them for impending turmoil?

In order to consider this didactic medium systematically and sociologically, I bought all the androgynous (not addressed specifically to one gender) and mainstream press picture books geared toward young children (both preschool aged and preadolescent) about sex currently in print and available through Amazon.com in 2001, along with a few for older kids and a few offering advice to parents about talking about sex with their children. In all, I surveyed ten books for young children, three for adolescents, and four for parents. (These books are arranged by category in the bibliography.) These books span over thirty years; the earliest is a 1979 reprint of a 1968 book, and the most recent book is from 1999.[1]

These books, taken together, address a loose set of problems that parents face in their presumed desire to present a variety of complex, baggage-laden topics to young children in an understandable way without feeling deeply uncomfortable in the process. Talking about sexuality and childbearing with children creates a multifaceted dilemma. Parents are, in essence, attempting to create an openness about a range of topics they may feel unable to be truly open about. First there is the issue of deterrence: How can we present sexuality without making it seem too appealing? What if they want to do it too? Second, how do we avoid frightening children with all the ways

that sexual encounters and their outcomes can be painful, even horrible? How do we balance our desire not to frighten them with our third goal: offering them information that might protect them from sexual dangers and unintended consequences (sexual predators, rape, sexually transmitted diseases, teen pregnancy, abortion, not to mention heartbreak)? Fourth, how do we deal with, acknowledge, respond to evidence of, and instruct them about their own sexuality? And fifth, how do we teach them appropriate contexts for expressions of sexuality?

What are appropriate contexts, after all? In this rest of this essay, I look at how authors of sex books for children contextualize sexuality. These books reify (and occasionally resist) heteronormative, gendered, and medicalized sociosexual conventions through an examination of four general topics: sex and childbirth (which are central in all books), managing childhood sexuality, and alternatives to procreative sex. My primary focus is on the books for young children, I supplement my discussion of these books with interpretations of the books for older children and for parents.

### Changing Bodies

In sex books for kids, authors foreground the primary discussion of procreative sex with brief anatomy lessons. They equate biological sex with gender: There are people with penises and people with vaginas, and this is what makes them boys or girls. Eventually, they grow up into men and women and make babies together utilizing these parts. Laurie Krasny Brown and Marc Brown (1997) preface their presentation of genital difference with a litany of ways in which boys and girls *may* be different (clothes, hairstyles, playing styles, emotions). After each example they write that the difference is "sometimes, but not always" evident. Then they move to anatomy: "Actually the only sure way to tell boys and girls apart is by their bodies. If you're a boy, you have a penis, scrotum, and testicles. If you're a girl, you have a vulva, clitoris, and vagina" (11–12). This text appears alongside illustrations of a naked boy and girl, with labeled body parts. The cartoon girl proclaims, "Look! Our bodies are more alike than different!" Harris and Emberley (1999) include a similar picture, with the text "Most parts of our bodies . . . are the same and look quite the same whether we are female or male. . . . The parts that are different are the parts that make each of us a female or a male" (10).

Authors do not mention the possibility of not being able to tell bodies apart easily, nor do they broach the topic of gender identity that doesn't "match" genitalia, nor do they question the bifurcated social constructs of girl and boy, man and woman. As Joey's mother says in *So That's How I Was Born!* (Brooks and Perl, 1983), "a boy's body isn't better than a girl's body and a girl's body isn't better than a boy's. They're just different from the time they're born and each is special in their own way." In this way, authors proclaim gender difference as essential (rooted in dimorphic biological sex), while also contradictorily claiming the difference doesn't matter. Perhaps introducing sex and gender ambiguity and fluidity would confuse kids. The majority of babies are born genetically dimorphous, after all, and most people appear to grow up relatively comfortable with socially constructed gender divisions. Yet in other cases, it is not the frequency of a phenomenon that determines whether authors will present it; some of these books include discussions of occurrences at least as infrequent as intersexuality or gender-bending identities (e.g., multiple births, home births, adoption), apparently without worrying about the confusion these mentions might cause. Authors seek to demystify some social practices but leave others untouched, and in so doing remain generally conservative and take most cultural norms for granted.

To cite another example, the illustrations and photographs of children and their families in these books only show racially alike families. Though the majority of those pictured are white, illustrators and photographers include children and adults interacting with each other across ra-

cial boundaries. I could find only one clear depiction of an interracial family (Smith and Wheatley, 1997, 14). Harris and Emberley (1999) have a few illustrations that *might* be interracial family groups. Thus, even as authors and illustrators seek to present and promote multicultural interaction, very few depict interracial intimacy.

## *Making Love and Making Babies*

Children do, indeed, ask their parents "Where did I come from?" or "How are babies made?" Thus, many parents find themselves working backward from baby (or pregnancy) to heterosexual sexuality. I suspect that if children initiate conversations about sexuality apart from procreation many parents don't know what to do or say, so they may end up in the procreation story because it's easier for them to deal with than sexuality on its own.

Sexual information conveyed in the books for young children tends to be vague, to reinforce heteronormativity, and to represent penile–vaginal intercourse as the only example of sexual activity in which men and women engage. Sometimes authors omit the act altogether, as in Joanna Cole's *How You Were Born* (1993) and Alastair Smith's *How Are Babies Made?* (1997).

> *In a woman's* body *are egg cells. The egg cell is round. It does* not *have a shell like a chicken's egg. In a man's body are sperm cells. The sperm cells have long tails and can swim. When a sperm and an egg join together, they form a special cell that can grow into a baby. (Cole, 1993, 19)*

> *How does the baby start? A tiny sperm from the man's body has to join up with a little egg from the woman's body. (Smith, 1997, 5)*

When authors do discuss penile–vaginal intercourse, they describe it as pleasurable and functional for both men and women, and portray it taking place within the context of loving relationships:

> *Sexual intercourse may seem gross or nice, scary or funny, weird or cool—or even unbelievable to you.*

*But when two people care for each other, sexual intercourse is very loving. Kids are much too young to have sexual intercourse. (Harris and Emberley, 1999, 29)*

*When a woman and a man who love each other go to bed, they like to hug and kiss. Sometimes, if they both want to, the man puts his penis in the woman's vagina and that feels really good for both of them. Sperm come out through the man's penis. If one tiny sperm meets a tiny egg inside the woman's body, a baby is started, and the man and woman will be the baby's parents. (Gordon and Gordon, 1992)*

None of the authors describes orgasm, though clearly they present the emission of sperm as momentous. Joey's parents (Brooks and Perl, 1983) label the lovers "mommy" and "daddy" before the fact, thus presenting sex as predicated on the goal of future parenthood:

*One of the ways a mommy and daddy show they love one another is by hugging each other very close. In bed, they can get really close when a daddy puts his **penis** inside the special opening between a mommy's legs which is called a **vagina**. The sperm comes out of the daddy's penis and goes into the mommy's vagina, and then the sperm meets the egg and a baby starts. (Brooks and Perl, 1983).*

Andry, Schepp, and Hampton's *How Babies Are Made* (1979) and Baker's *The Birds and the Bees* (1990) are more lackluster than the others in their descriptions of procreative sex:

*The sperm, which come from the father's testicles, are sent into the mother through his penis. To do this, the father and mother lie down facing each other and the father places his penis in the mother's vagina. Unlike plants and animals, when human mothers and fathers create a new baby they are sharing a very personal and special relationship. (Andry, Schepp, and Hampton, 1979)*

*When men and women mate, the penis becomes stiff and is inserted into the vagina, which has become larger and moist, ready to receive it. (Baker, 1990)*

These authors make heterosex sound like a cross between directions for putting together a bookcase and a recipe for baking a cake. (I can't help but imagine the seductive dialogue, "Hey baby, I have some sperm I'd like to send you through my penis! May I insert it?" "Oh yeah, my vagina is large and moist, ready to receive!") Both of these books present humans' procreative method after first laboriously introducing habits of other plant and animal species. Andry, Schepp, and Hampton (1979) interestingly sever this naturalistic connection with other living things, separating humans out by insisting on our emotional superiority ("unlike plants and animals. . . ."). As in the other children's books that stick to humans, they want to show that sex is more than just the casual rubbing together of stamens and pistils. The experts writing for an adult audience endorse this technique of grounding sex in satisfying long-term connection between adults. Spock and Rothenberg (1992) advise, "Parents shouldn't ever let the anatomical and physiological explanation of sex stand alone but always connect it with the idealistic, spiritual aspects" (509).

My favorite among these books for young children is Babette Cole's *Mommy Laid an Egg OR Where Do Babies Come From?* (1993). Cole uses humor throughout the book, both in the prose and in her illustrations, which mix a cartoon family together with raucous childlike stick-figure drawings. The book begins with the cartoon parents misinforming their children, "some babies are delivered by dinosaurs," "you can make them out of gingerbread," and "sometimes you just find them under stones." The children respond with laughter, and say "what a bunch of nonsense!" They proceed to instruct their parents about what procreative sex actually is, all the while pointing to their crude comical illustrations.

*Girl:* "Mommies do have eggs. They are inside their bodies."
*Boy:* "And daddies have seeds in seed pods outside their bodies. Daddies also have a tube. The seeds come out of the pods and through the tube."
*Girl:* "The tube goes into the mommy's body through a hole. Then the seeds swim inside using their tails." (Cole, 1993)

On the page where the boy proclaims "here are some ways . . . mommies and daddies fit together," Cole illustrates his words with childlike drawings of the mommy and daddy cavorting in a variety of imaginative positions while linked at the crotch, including holding balloons, bouncing on a big ball (labeled "space hopper"), and lying on a skateboard. These are raunchy yet clean, because they are children's drawings (and do not depict genitalia, only breasts). The language is crude in a childish way, yet the botanical allegories don't seem embarrassingly goofy, just goofy in a fun way. Sex seems fun for once—not just a pleasant sperm-delivery arrangement. Why else would the participants wear party hats?

In the other four books for young children that include illustrations of sex (the other five do not depict the act), the man is on top in three (Baker, 1990; Harris and Emberley, 1999; Andry, Schepp, and Hampton, 1979), and the man and woman are side by side in one (Gordon, Gordon, and Cohen, 1992). The copulators are all under the covers except in Baker's drawing (which is decidedly unrevealing despite the nudity of the illustrated characters).

### *Having Babies*

The next step after procreative sex in all of these books is pregnancy and birth. After a brief discussion of the growth of the fetus and changes in the mother's body, authors tell how babies are born. They depict childbearing as wonderful, a job to be done together by a mommy and a daddy (who cheers her on). Many authors tell the story of birth from the point of view of the baby, which is apparently the perspective with which they imagine child readers will identify. Authors do not discuss pain in childbirth, although Cole (1993) comes close, referring to contractions as "sharp twinges called labor pangs" (30). Authors portray labor as a biological (muscular) activity, as hard work that a woman does, or both. Birth is described as awesome and wonderful for the parents.

Marc Brown (Brown and Brown, 1997) and Michael Emberley (Harris and Emberly, 1999) both depict women in the lithotomy position (on their backs, with feet in stirrups) surrounded by masked and gowned people. The daddies are also decked out in medical garb, though in Emberley's drawing he doesn't wear a mask. Laura Krasny Brown (1997) writes "When a baby is ready to be born, muscles in the mother's womb begin to tighten and relax, tighten and relax, helping her push out the baby. In most births, the baby comes out the vagina, which stretches to let it pass through" (28). Similarly, the text accompanying Emberley's drawing says:

> When a baby is about to be born, the muscles in the mother's uterus begin to squeeze tight. This is called "labor." "Labor" is another word for "work." A mother's muscles work very hard to push and squeeze the baby out of the uterus and into the vagina. Then the mother's muscles push and squeeze the baby's body through the vagina. The vagina stretches wide as the baby's soft, wet, and slippery body travels through it. (Harris and Emberley, 1999:56–57)

Even though these authors' descriptions of labor and birth sound like they might have been written by midwives, they tend to depict medical management of the process as normal. Three of the ten authors mention alternatives to hospital birth, but none depict it. Joanna Cole (1993) writes: "Your mother and father went to the hospital or childbirth center where you were to be born. If you were born at home, then the doctor or midwife came to your house" (31). The photographs accompanying this text show couples in more casual hospital or birth center settings than the settings depicted in the other books, but none are at home. Sol and Judith Gordon write: "Some babies are born at home. But most women like to go to the hospital for the birth of their baby" (1992). This text is accompanied by a drawing of a woman lying in the lithotomy position in a hospital, a masked woman birth attendant standing between her legs holding a screaming baby up for her (and us) to see. We are positioned behind and above the woman's head, watching the baby come out from her vantage point, but we can also see her face, and she looks happy. We do not see a vaginal view of birth except in Cole's (1993) child drawing, which shows a baby sticking out of a round-blob mother and saying "Hello Mommy!" All other illustrations show babies mediated by medical personnel in medical settings both during and after birth.[2]

### Teaching about Touching

Only two of the sex books for young children explicitly address children's sexuality. Brown and Brown (1997) and Harris and Emberley (1999) attempt to differentiate between touching that is "okay" and "not okay"—that is, between masturbation and sexual abuse. Brown and Brown (1997) write:

> Touching and rubbing your genitals to feel good is called masturbation. Some of us try this; some of us don't. However, it's best to do this private kind of touching off by yourself.
>
> Touching others is just as important. . . . If someone doesn't want to be touched, then respect his or her wishes—don't do it! . . . Everyone needs good touches to feel loved and happy. . . . But no one has the right to touch you in a way that feels wrong or uncomfortable.
>
> If you don't like the way someone touches you, speak up and tell him or her to stop. If that doesn't work, tell your mom or dad or another grownup. Your body belongs to you, and you should say who touches it! (16–19)

Harris (1999) goes into more detail about both masturbation and abuse, and like Brown and Brown, the discussion of masturbation leads into the issue of abuse. The Browns differentiate between self-touches that feel good, touches from others that *are* good, and those that feel wrong or are somehow dislikable. Harris (1999) makes the same points, and goes into more detail about contentiousness over masturbation: "Every fam-

ily has its own thoughts and feelings about masturbation. . . . Some people and some religions think it's wrong to masturbate. But most doctors agree that masturbation is perfectly healthy and perfectly normal, and cannot hurt you or your body" (69). Doctors apparently have the last word and validating authority on the subject. This is ironic, given that well into the twentieth century, sex educators backed up denouncements of masturbation as pathological with medical authority. (See Conrad and Schneider, 1992, 180–181, on nineteenth-century conceptualizations of masturbation as disease; and Moran, 2000, 57, on lasting sex educational prohibitions.)

Harris next defines touches that are not okay: "But if any person touches any part of your body and you do not want them to, say "STOP!"" . . . Sexual abuse happens when someone touches the private parts of a person's body and does NOT have the right to do that" (1999, 70). Harris acknowledges that sexual abuse is "always wrong," that it "can hurt" or "feel gentle," and thus, that it can be "very confusing" (70). He advises, like the Browns, that children tell someone they trust if they experience sexual abuse, and reassures readers that it is "NEVER your fault" (70–71).

Authors writing for older kids and parents all discuss masturbation and sexual abuse in similar terms to those utilized by the Browns and Harris and Emberley. They describe masturbation as normal and generally healthy; they describe sexual abuse as always dangerous. In contrast to the warnings they issue about abusive sex, Spock and Rothenberg (1992) and Westheimer (1998) describe "sex play" between children as generally harmless. Westheimer acknowledges only that this occurs among boys, writing: "Sometimes groups of boys will masturbate together. There's nothing wrong with doing this in privacy" (53).

As for solitary masturbation, Eyre and Eyre (1998) and Spock and Rothenberg (1992) warn against too much of this good thing. Spock and Rothenberg discuss what they call "excessive masturbation," never specifying how often is too much. They do attempt, after raising this specter, to keep parents calm:

> It's important for parents to know that the fear that something will happen or has happened to the genitals is one of the most common causes of excessive masturbation in young childhood.
>
> To tell such children that they'll injure themselves makes matters worse. To tell them that they're bad and that you won't love them any more gives them a new fear. (504)

Even as they introduce this behavior as abnormal, Spock and Rothenberg (1992) reassure parents that sexual exploration is natural, writing:

> I think that whatever your personal beliefs or feelings, you should avoid threatening or punishing your children when they reveal their natural sexuality. . . . It's important to try to say something about how normal and universal the activity is. It's good for children to feel they can ask their parents about sex. (506)

I would imagine this seemingly conflicting advice could be confusing to parents, especially those who themselves have been brought up by parents who disapproved of masturbation.

In a prescripted dialogue between a father and a son who asks "Is masturbation bad?" (meant to be helpful for parents seeking to initiate discussion with their kids) the Eyres (1998) propose replying: "Everyone at least experiments with it. But it can be a problem if it becomes a habit or happens too often" (105). The father then advises the son to "think about how beautiful and awesome it can be with the beautiful and special wife you'll have someday. . . . If you try to do this, you won't feel like masturbating as often, and when you do, at least you'll be thinking about the best kind of sex that will happen someday with your wife" (106). The Eyres propose monogamous married sex fantasies as a fantasy to curb boys' sexual urges. They promote cross-generational sex talk cleansed of eroticism. All authors who write about sexual urges in children stress that they are natural or normal, even as they coach

parents about how to best contain, constrain, and train these impulses.

## Words You May Have Heard

Authors of sex books for young children tend to limit discussion of sexual issues to procreative sex, and occasional mentions of masturbation and child abuse. Authors of sex books for adolescents all cover masturbation and sexual abuse, but beyond this they tend to discuss sexual diversity (anything other than penile–vaginal intercourse) in a very limited way. All but one of the books (Harris and Emberley) I will discuss in this section are addressed to older children or to parents.

Both Joanna Cole (Cole and Tiegreen, 1988) and Sol Gordon (Gordon and Cohen, 1992) mention that the man and the woman, whose bodies "are made so that they fit together" (Cole, 1988, 51), are involved in more than simple penetration. Cole writes, "Having intercourse is also called 'making love' because a man and a woman usually feel so lovingly toward each other when they do it. They hug, kiss, and stroke each other's bodies" (51). Gordon, too, keeps penile–vaginal intercourse central, writing that "before, during and after sexual intercourse, a couple will usually kiss, embrace and stroke each other to show their affection" (1992, 7). Westheimer offhandedly mentions anal and oral sex in her section on AIDS: "some people think they can avoid AIDS by practicing anal intercourse (putting the penis in the anus) or oral sex (putting it in the mouth). They are dead wrong" (Westheimer and deGroat, 1998:74).

Throughout these books, authors depict loving sexual relationships between men and woman as normative. When they do discuss alternatives—gayness, lesbianism, and bisexuality (transgenderedness is never mentioned)—they treat them with a liberal touch, yet cordon these topics off into short sections of their own. These authors advocate tolerance, but are careful to avoid endorsing or advocating nonheterosexual activities. The following are three examples of discussions of "homosexuality." The first two are from books for older children, and the third is from a book for parents:

> Some people prefer to have sexual experiences with persons of their own sex. They are called homosexuals. Most boys and girls have homosexual thoughts occasionally. Some even have homosexual experiences. This doesn't mean that they are homosexual. The people properly called homosexual are those who, as adults, have sexual contacts only with persons of their own sex. . . . Some people enjoy sexual relations with both sexes throughout their adult life. They are called bisexuals. Modern psychologists no longer see homosexual or bisexual behavior between consenting adults as a disorder. (Gordon and Cohen, 1992, 28)

### Why Are Some People Straight and Others Gay?

> Psychologists do not really know what causes a person's sexual preferences. Some believe that whether a person is straight or gay depends on experiences in early childhood. Others think homosexuality might be an inherited, or built-in preference. . . .

### Is Homosexuality a Sickness?

> No. People used to believe that homosexuality was a form of mental illness, but now psychiatrists say that it is not. Homosexuality is just one way people can express love.

### Can Homosexuals Choose Not to Be Gay?

> Homosexuals can choose not to practice homosexuality. . . . But for most gay people, it is probably not possible to choose how they feel inside and which sex they are attracted to. (Cole and Tiegreen, 1988, 75)

### Is It Bad to Be a Homosexual?

> We don't think so, but that's one of those questions that different people have different opinions about. Some people think that you should only have sexual relations with a person of the other sex, and that anybody who doesn't choose to do that is not doing the right thing. In this family we agree with the scientists and doctors who say that a homosexual is just different from a heterosexual, but not bad or

> sick or strange. Certain people who don't approve of homosexuals are sometimes very cruel to them, so many homosexuals are hurt and tend to be very private about their personal lives. That's too bad, we think, because it's very hard and sad to have to hide that you love someone. (Calderone and Ramey, 1982, 87)

Even as they attempt to advocate openmindedness, authors frame sexual nonconformity as deviant by using the clinical term *homosexual*, by discussing lesbian/bisexual/gay sexuality via questions that are pointedly negative, and by emphasizing that it was once officially pathological. By consistently presenting medicine as the arbiter of the current non-pathology of "homosexuality," authors do not question medical authority or effectively critique its past homophobia. Calderone and Ramey's discussion of homophobia, although disapproving, also presents it as a valid point of view. They describe "some people" who think that only straight sex is "the right thing." Authors denounce cruelty and violence, but do not explicitly denounce homophobic beliefs. The Eyres (1998) are overtly homophobic. They discuss "homosexuality" in one paragraph (which precedes a paragraph on AIDS), saying "we shouldn't judge a person who is gay, but it can be a sad situation because it doesn't allow for the birth of children or for the kind of family that a heterosexual couple can have" (97).

Reading these parts of the books I was reminded of Jesse Green's (1999) description of learning about sexuality from the library of his mother, Sally Green, a pioneering sex educator in the 1970s:

> It was the girls I felt I understood, at least in their longings. I quickly learned what this was called; I had looked it up often under "H" and "G," had read in my mother's psychiatric texts the current thinking and statistics on the subject. And though some books described my condition with sympathy, not one was enthusiastic. None told me—as virtually all of them told everyone else—to celebrate my awakening sexuality, but at best to endure it in hopes of a miraculous alteration down the road. (89)

Indeed, many of the authors writing for older kids and adults seek to reassure readers that nonheterosexual urges and experiences can be transitory. Though the categories they introduce have the same essential ring to them as gender does in the books for young kids, authors recognize some flux on the road to a permanent sexual identity. But because authors explain that eventually sexual identity (straight, gay, lesbian, bisexual) is permanent, this changeability comes across as an experimentation phase.

> Are you homosexual? It's difficult to know. Some people don't figure out if they're gay or straight until their late teens or their twenties. Having a crush on, or even kissing or touching, someone of your own sex does not necessarily mean that you're gay. (Westheimer, 1993, 54)

> Because there are so many negative ideas in our society about being gay, young people may panic if they have any feelings or daydreams about people of their own sex. Yet most of them will not end up being gay. Naturally, a small percentage will—about five to ten percent. . . . But most will not. They are simply going through a stage of growing up. (Cole, 1988, 76)

Three of the four books addressed to parents offer advice about what parents should do if they think their kids aren't straight. Ratner and Chamlin (1985) pose the hypothetical question, "Will my son's love of 'dressing up' lead to homosexuality?" And they respond, "No. Many parents discourage boys from playing 'dress-up' and 'house,' but at certain ages, certainly preschool, it's appropriate. Preschoolers actively assume many different roles" (35). They imply that at a certain age, gender-bending will straighten out. Spock and Rothenberg (1992) imply this as well, saying "When parents think that their little boy is effeminate or their little girl too masculine, they may worry that the child will grow up to be a homosexual or lesbian. In fact, the majority of such children will grow up to be heterosexual" (52). However, they then recommend therapy for a boy who wants to play with girls and dolls, and who wants to wear dresses ("I would assume that

something had gotten mixed up in his identification"), as well as for a girl who plays "only with boys" and is "**always** unhappy about being a girl" (52). A girl who prefers to play with boys and who "occasionally" wishes she were a boy, "but also [enjoys] playing with girls" does not concern them (52).

Harris and Emberley (1999) are the only authors of books for young children who explore alternatives to heterosexuality, and they are the only authors in my sample who explain that love and sexual behavior can be multifaceted without invoking the past pathologizing or current acceptance of medical experts: "There are lots of kinds of love—like love between a parent and child, love between friends, love between kids, love between teenagers, and love between grownups. There can be love between a female and a male, or a male and a male, or a female and a female" (31). They go on to explain the terms homosexual, heterosexual, gay, lesbian, and straight, and proclaim "A person's daily life—having friends, having fun, going to work, being a mom or dad, loving another person—is mostly the same whether a person is straight or gay." This text appears with an illustration of a possibly interracial gay male couple and their two kids eating dinner (32). Authors seek to promote harmony across difference by positing that difference is overshadowed by commonalities among people, regardless of sexual identity.

### So What Should We Tell the Kids?

First let me sum up what we do tell the kids in the discourse of didactic books: that the central focus of sexuality is procreative penile–vaginal intercourse; that this form of sexuality is "natural" and good; that participants should be monogamous adults; and that their sexual expression is based in love and enacted in private. Many authors writing for older kids and adults do acknowledge other sorts of sexual behavior, but these discussions are limited and not integrated into presentations of what is clearly the main event. Nonheterosexual activities are marginalized. The books can be seen as precursors to school-based sex education programs, which increase the focus on dangers, often advocate abstinence, and are notoriously heterosexist and devoid of discussions of gendered or sexual power dynamics (e.g., see Raymond 1994; Watney 1991).

When do we tell children that some sex is amazing, some is lovely, some is dull, some becomes repugnant in retrospect, and some is horrible while it's happening? When do we tell them about its potential variety and variability? When do we expose children to a peerlike level of sexual honesty in which we speak to them of the intensity of desire, the fickleness of lust, the pain of rejection? Or do we simply not venture this far into the murky depths of sexuality? Do we just let them find out whatever they'll find out by themselves from people we can only hope will not hurt them or mess up their lives? All the while, we must bear in mind that something we say to them today could be the impetus for therapy later. What truths, warnings, and recommendations do we dare to communicate? In short, our task is absurd and impossible the more we ponder it, yet most of us would agree that to say nothing would be worse than to make some kind of attempt.

So we're back where we started, with Spock and Rothenberg's (1992) admonition against the stork, in favor of the truth. There is no absolute truth about sexuality, so we have to decide what and how we want to discuss sexuality with our children. Sex education books for children and parents are generally a step in the right direction, and are certainly better than nothing, in my view. But they are not as comprehensive or critical or political as they could be.

Imagine sex education books that would present gender and genitals as socially constructed; sexuality could then more easily be conceived by young readers as taking place on a continuum rather than as written in stone. Imagine books that present sex as not only the cause of procreation but also as recreational, as indeed it is for most people engaged in it most of the time. Imagine books that present sexual activities other than penile–vaginal intercourse as satisfying and good for body and soul (or even just for body!). Imagine sex educational books that would acknowledge and contest power dynamics based on gender and sexual categories—books that would urge children to interrogate, rather than reify, these categories. Imagine the sex lives that might develop out of such an antifoundational foundation. Would you buy these books for your children?

## NOTES

1. I figured Amazon's selection would be representative of what you might find by making the rounds at a selection of decent chain or independently owned bookstores, based on my anecdotal experience. I've checked in about two dozen bookstores—chains, privately owned, feminist—around the United States over the past couple of years, and usually there are no more than a few available at any one store.

2. Interestingly, though most of the parents depicted in the birth scenes in these books are white, many of the primary medical personnel (those catching the babies—presumably doctors or midwives) are black women.

## REFERENCES

### Sex Books for Young Children

Andry, Andrew, Steven Schepp, and Blake Hampton (ill.). 1979 (1968). *How Babies Are Made.* Boston: Little, Brown.

Baker, Sue. 1990. *The Birds and the Bees.* Swindon, Bologna, New York: M. Twinn.

Brooks, Robert, and Susan Perl (ill.). 1983. *So That's How I Was Born!* New York: Aladdin.

Brown, Laura Krasny, and Marc Brown. 1997. *What's the Big Secret?: Talking about Sex with Girls and Boys.* Boston: Little, Brown.

Cole, Babette. 1993. *Mommy Laid an Egg OR Where Do Babies Come From?* New York: Chronicle Books.

Cole, Joanna, and Margaret Miller (photo.). 1993 (1984). *How You Were Born.* New York: Mulberry.

Davis, Jennifer, and Laura Cornell (ill.). 1997. *Before You Were Born: A Lift-the-Flap Book.* New York: Workman.

Gordon, Sol, Judith Gordon, and Vivien Cohen (ill.). 1992 (1974). *Did the Sun Shine before You Were Born?: A Sex Education Primer*. Amherst, NY: Prometheus Books.

Harris, Robie H., and Michael Emberley (ill.). 1999. *It's So Amazing!: A Book about Eggs, Sperm, Birth, Babies, and Families*. Cambridge, MA: Candlewick Press.

Smith, Alastair, and Maria Wheatley (ill.). 1997. *How Are Babies Made?* London: Usbourne Publishing.

### Sex Books for Older Children

Cole, Joanna, and Alan Tiegreen (ill.). 1988. *Asking about Sex and Growing Up: A Question-and-Answer Book for Boys and Girls*. New York: Beech Tree.

Gordon, Sol, and Vivien Cohen (ill.). 1992 (1977). *Facts about Sex for Today's Youth*. Amherst, NY: Prometheus Books.

Westheimer, Ruth, and Diane deGroat (ill.). 1998 (1993). *Dr. Ruth Talks to Kids: Where You Came From, How Your Body Changes, and What Sex Is All About*. New York: Aladdin.

### Sex Books for Parents

Calderone, Mary S., and James W. Ramey. 1982. *Talking with Your Child about Sex: Questions and Answers for Children from Birth to Puberty*. New York: Random House.

Eyre, Linda, and Richard Eyre. 1998. *How to Talk to Your Child About Sex*. New York: Saint Martin's Griffin.

Ratner, Marilyn, and Susan Chamlin. 1985. *Straight Talk: Sexuality Education for Parents and Kids 4–7*. New York: Viking.

Spock, Benjamin, and Michael B. Rothenberg. 1992 (1945). *Dr. Spock's Baby and Child Care*. New York: Pocket Books.

### Other Sources

Ehrenreich, Barbara, and Diedre English. 1986. *Re-Making Love: The Feminization of Sex*. Garden City, NY: Anchor Press/Doubleday.

Green, Jesse. 1999. *The Velveteen Father: An Unexpected Journey to Parenthood*. New York: Villard Books.

Moran, Jeffrey P. 2000. *Teaching Sex: The Shaping of Adolescence in the 20th Century*. Cambridge, MA: Harvard University Press.

Patton, Cindy. 1996. *Fatal Advice: How Safe-Sex Education Went Wrong*. Durham, NC: Duke University Press.

Raymond, Diane. 1994. "Homophobia, Identity, and the Meanings of Desire: Reflections on the Cultural Construction of Gay and Lesbian Adolescent Sexuality." In *Sexual Cultures and the Construction of Adolescent Identities*, edited by Janice M. Irvine. Philadelphia: Temple UP.

Simonds, Wendy. 1992. *Women and Self-Help Culture: Reading Between the Lines*. New Brunswick, NJ: Rutgers University Press.

Watney, Simon. 1991. "School's Out." In *Inside/Out: Lesbian Theories, Gay Theories*, edited Diana Fuss (pp. 387–401). New York: Routledge.

## *What Do I Say to My Children?*

### Sol Gordon and Judith Gordon

*Sex educators Sol Gordon and Judith Gordon stress the importance of being an askable parent in their book* Raising a Child Responsibly in a Sexually Permissive World.[1] *Here are their responses to some of the most frequently asked questions:*

### *When Should I Tell?*

The answer is simple: It is time to tell whenever the child asks. If you are an askable parent, your children may come to you with questions about sex from the time they are two or three years old. Young children's questions are sometimes nonverbal. For example, a child may constantly follow you into the bathroom. To encourage them, you could say, "It looks like you're wondering about something—can I guess what it is?"

Some shy children might ask no questions at all, even of the most askable parents. If your child hasn't raised sexuality-oriented questions by age five, you should start the conversation. Read a book with your child. Tell him or her about a neighbor or a relative who is going to have a baby. While it's fine on occasion to make analogies to animals, do not concentrate on them in your explanations. People and animals have very different habits.

### How Explicit Should I Be?

Make it a point to use the correct terminology. Avoid such childish expressions as "pee-pee" or "wee-wee." . . . [P]arents can be explicit without overstating the case or feeling compelled to describe sexual relations to a child who hasn't yet grasped much more basic ideas. It is also wiser to say at the start that a baby has its beginning in the mother's uterus, not the stomach, because a child's imagination can easily picture the fetus being mixed up with the food.

### Is There Such a Thing as Giving Too Much Sex Education Too Soon?

Parents worry a great deal about whether they can "harm" their children with "too much" information or by telling their children things that they won't understand. Let us state again that despite the protests of a few "experts," knowledge is not harmful. It does not matter if the child doesn't understand everything you say. What counts is that you are an askable parent. If the child can trust you

not to be rigid or hostile in your response or to give misinformation, he or she will ask you questions and use you as a source of wisdom and guidance. . . .

### What about Embarrassing Questions in Public?

Children have a great knack for asking the most delicate questions in the supermarket or when special guests have come to dinner. The best approach, no matter how embarrassed you are, is to tell the child that he or she has asked a very good question; if you still have your wits about you, proceed to answer it then and there. In most cases, your guests will silently applaud. If you feel you can't answer the question right away, it is very important to praise the child for asking and to state specifically when you will discuss it. In general, it is better to risk shocking a few grown-ups than to scold or put off your own child.

**NOTE**

1. Gordon, S., and Gordon, J. 2000. *Raising a Child Responsibly in a Sexually Permissive World,* Second Edition (pp. 43–46). Holbrook, MA: Adams Media.

# Fear of Sex: Do the Media Make Them Do It?

**Karen Sternheimer**

When I was twelve I did something I never had done before: I snuck into an R-rated movie. My friend and I told our parents we would be seeing a PG film playing at the same complex and bought tickets for that movie, so when they dropped us off and later picked us up they would have no idea. When the lights went down we walked into another theater to see *Young Doctors in Love,* which promised to feature a racier version of our favorite daytime soaps.

In spite of feeling that any minute an usher would appear and kick us out, it seemed remarkably easy to enter this forbidden zone. But aside from a few more four-letter words, the movie was no different than any television show I'd seen except it was longer. This of course did not stop us from embellishing what we saw when we returned to school on Monday. I was finally part of the group who had seen an R-rated movie, and for a day that felt good.

My story is not unique, of course. At one point most young people take a peek behind the iron curtain of adulthood. Knowledge about sex is often kept from children as long as possible, considered the final frontier separating adults from children. It is a hard-fought battle that is almost never won

From Sternheimer, Karen. 2003. "Fear of Sex: Do the Media Make Them Do It?" In *It's Not the Media: The Truth about Pop Culture's Influence on Children* (pp. 169–192). ISBN 0813341388. Copyright © 2003 by Karen Sternheimer. Reprinted by permission of Westview Press, a member of Perseus Books, LLC, and the author.

by adults, in part because sex permeates our media culture. Sex becomes associated with maturity and with status largely because adults define it that way and our popular culture appears to be obsessed with sex. It only makes sense for young people to be curious, and media culture threatens to satisfy all sorts of sexual curiosities.

Sex is feared almost as much as violence, and the belief that sexuality in media culture will increase teen sexual activity is quite common. . . . Horror stories of teen promiscuity make the media rounds to demonstrate the popular hypothesis that kids now are morally depraved (note stories about equally promiscuous adults aren't considered newsworthy) and imply the media are at fault. Has media culture created a sex-crazed generation? While yes may be the simple answer, this chapter critically assesses common beliefs about media, youth, and sex and demonstrates that the relationship between the three is more complex than we are often told. As we will see, changes in economics and demographic shifts during the past century have driven changes in sexual attitudes and behavior. But sexuality has always been part of coming of age, and parents have always felt anxious about this passage. The declining ability of adults to control children's sexual knowledge has created a high level of fear and that fear is often focused on popular culture. When we take a closer look at how young people make sense of sexuality in media, we see that they are not simply influenced by popular culture, but use sexual representations to create identity and status within their peer groups.

## *Teenage Sex: New Media, New Mores?*

While attending a seminar about issues concerning contemporary youth, a man who appeared to be in his early to mid-fifties said with certainty, "People didn't have sex before marriage back when I was a kid. It just wasn't done." He was very sure of himself and it was clear he wanted to set the younger expert straight. "You weren't there," he told her. "Now things are totally different. Kids today just don't have the same morals."

I wasn't there either, but then again neither was he. The time he spoke of did not exist. The history he remembers is likely television and film history. On that count, he would be right. It just wasn't done—on TV.

Sexual behavior steadily changed throughout the twentieth century. During the "good old days" adults shared many of the same fears that today's parents have, that young people were engaging in behavior they never did at their age, and that kids today have too much freedom and not enough sexual restraint. Chances are, if history is any indicator, in about fifty years people will look back at today as an age of innocence too. When it comes to young people and sexuality, the past has always seemed more innocent because it is viewed through the lens of nostalgia.

Sexuality in media has always been a cause for concern. Film content in the 1920s reflected changes in sexual mores, featuring Rudolph Valentino's passionate kissing and sometimes even female nudity. Hollywood's early stars created scandals just like those in our own era; their wild parties, frequent failed marriages, and sex scandals made conservative groups weary. Movies were a new source of influence that religious leaders feared would bypass the family, school, and religion in importance in young people's lives. Politicians and the Catholic Legion of Decency called for government censorship. Instead, the new film industry guaranteed self-regulation by what came to be known as the Hays Office, led by prominent political figure Will Hays, to monitor movie content and ensure it met the standards of a new code, formally implemented in 1934.[1] As the country took a more conservative turn at the end of the 1920s, the Hays Office restricted film content to what was deemed "wholesome entertainment." This included censoring any content that appeared to criticize "natural or human" laws so as not to incite "the lower and baser element" of American society.[2] Rules governing film production were overtly racist—no interracial relationships were allowed—and any criticism of the status quo was interpreted as a violation of the "moral obligation" of the entertainment establishment. An extremely reactionary ideology of filmmaking was justified in the name of preserving children's "innocence."

The Hays Code dominated film production until 1966. In an attempt to compete with the rise of television, films started presenting sexuality more frankly beginning in the 1960s, particularly as European "New Wave" films by directors like Federico Fellini and Jean Luc Godard helped redefine movies as art. Twenty years later, cable television and videos brought more sexually explicit programming into the home. Sex has become another product of contemporary society, circulating more rapidly and difficult to control and regulate because highly sexualized images attract attention and profit. Adults now have less control over what young people know about sex, which blurs the perceived distinction between adults and children.

Popular culture *is* different today than in the past and provides an easy (but ultimately misguided) answer to explain social changes. We didn't arrive here on the coattails of television or movies; popular culture incorporates and reflects societal issues and values, many of which some people find objectionable. Instead of targeting attention solely on popular culture, we need to first understand the social context of sex in twentieth and twenty-first century America.

## New Century, New Meanings

During a discussion in my juvenile delinquency course a student once volunteered that he was sure teen sex is much more prevalent now than ever before. "We don't hear about teenage pregnancy being a problem during colonial times or anything," he noted.

There is some truth to this statement, particularly because "teenagers" as we now think of them did not exist until about one hundred years ago. Colonial "teens" were likely to be regarded as adults with full familial and economic responsibilities. . . . [C]ross-cultural and historical studies have not found adolescence as we know it to have existed in all societies, suggesting the teenager is more of a social than biological creation.[3] Thus, it is hard to compare the teenagers of today with those of the past. This new phase of life emerged as the outcome of industrialization and the diminished necessity for people in their teens to join the labor force. Previously, the group we now know of as teenagers often functioned as adults: they worked instead of attending school and may have been married with children. The time before adulthood steadily lengthened throughout the twentieth century, as did the gap between sexual maturity and marriage. Socially and sexually we expect teenagers today to function partially as adults and partially as children. The roles and expectations of adolescents today are far different from their counterparts a hundred years ago.

## New Sexual Freedom

It is nearly impossible to understand changes in dating rituals without considering the economic context. Courtship began to change with the rise of industrialization and was marked by the gradual decrease of adult control. In rural life work was concentrated in the home, so supervision of courtship was much simpler: a suitor might call on a potential mate at her home with parents or chaperones very close by. Industrialization led to the growth of cities and took adults away from the home for longer periods of time. The possibility for supervision decreased, as did the amount of space a family might have had in which courtship could take place. Dating thus moved from the parlor to the public sphere, and progressively became more of an independent pursuit with less family intervention. Highly populated cities offered more anonymity and the expansion of suburbs following World War II created even more space for young people to congregate away from adults. The new affluence of the postwar era brought more leisure time for teens, and teenagers could do what they wanted with less fear of getting caught or punished. Economic changes led to higher rates of high school and college attendance, which increased separation between adults and young people. . . .

The 1950s economic boom created the possibility for many people to experience youth as a time of leisure, while a generation before teens were much more likely to be in the labor force. Young people were likely to have fewer responsibilities than their parents had before them, and childhood and adolescence were increasingly seen as time for fun.[4] Dating became associated with recreation rather than procreation, as the search for a spouse became a more distant concern. . . .

[T]echnological changes created more freedom for young people. The widespread availability of electricity at the beginning of the twentieth century enabled nightlife to emerge away from the family home, and the automobile became an important part of American dating. Courtship grew even more difficult to monitor, as having a car provided more privacy, opportunities for sexual experimentation, and the ability to travel even farther from parental supervision. Drive-in restaurants and movies as well as lovers' lanes are examples of semi-private settings where teens went to be away from parental supervision.

Contrary to nostalgia, premarital sex did occur before the so-called sexual revolution of the 1960s; it was the *reaction* to premarital sex that changed. In mid-century, for instance, if sex resulted in pregnancy, it was more likely to remain secret through a quick marriage, a forced adoption, or, for the affluent perhaps, an abortion disguised as another medical procedure.[5] The main difference now is that we are more likely to acknowledge both premarital sex and teen pregnancy compared with in the past, and it is certainly talked about in public forums and in the news media. Teenage girls today are less likely to be pressured into early marriage and more likely to have access to birth control.

Premarital sex and pregnancy have always been part of the contemporary social landscape. . . . Yet we still often hope that people who are sexually mature don't engage in sexual behavior before socially defined adulthood, if not marriage. A full 72 percent of adults responding to the 1998 General Social Survey agreed that teen sex before marriage is "always wrong," yet a large proportion of people engage in sex before their teen years end.[6] In all likelihood many in the survey had premarital sex themselves, but help build a generation gap by insisting teens do as we say, not as we did.

### Asexual Children?

Movies, daytime soap operas, talk shows, and the Internet are often filled with sexualized imagery. If only children were not exposed to so much so soon, popular thinking goes, they would maintain their "innocence" instead of becoming sexually active. . . .

Adults often attempt to deny the importance of sexuality within childhood, because to do otherwise is kind of scary. After all, America was largely founded by Puritans. Sexual innocence serves as a major marker in the way our society presently defines children and distinguishes them from adults. Interestingly, the term "adult" tends to connote sexuality rather than responsibility. "Adult" books and "adult" films indicate sexual content, not emotional maturity. We like to believe that knowledge of sex represents the last remaining dividing line between childhood and adulthood.

But does it really?

Sexual exploration is and has been a big part of childhood, but perceptions of how parents should deal with sexually curious children have shifted during the past century.[7] Before World War II, American child-rearing practices reflected the belief that controlling children's behavior could prevent any "inappropriate" sexual exploration. In the postwar era the influence of Sigmund Freud and Benjamin Spock altered perceptions about sexuality and childhood. Both Freud and Spock considered children inherently sexual, so sexual curiosity was natural, even necessary for healthy development. Unlike the prewar notion that control created a well-adjusted child, postwar advice urged parents to avoid shaming their children lest a fixation develop. Parents were encouraged to provide information about sex, a major shift from prewar practices.

Starting in the early 1970s a backlash against the new openness began.[8] The 1960s tends to get the credit for being a time of sexual freedom, but actually the 1970s was the time when much experimentation happened. This new sexual openness led to fears that a more accepting approach to childhood sexuality had gone too far, that the lack of discouragement in early childhood led to less restraint against premarital sex. But think back to your own "facts of life" talk, if your parents had one with you. If it was anything like mine, it was tense and embarrassing for all parties involved—certainly not a pep talk. Concerns about parents' being "too open" blamed behavioral changes on the availability of information and did not take into account the demographic, economic, and political changes of the twentieth century. Our contemporary ambivalence about sexuality was born, as were complaints that the media make them do it. Today American adults want young people to be both psychologically healthy and sexually restrained, which is why we are at best ambivalent about providing children with information about sex; sex education now is often just abstinence education.

Sexuality, as much as adults may like to convince themselves otherwise, is not only a part of adulthood and adolescence but also a part of early childhood. We often dismiss things like childhood crushes as innocent puppy love, but the reality is that the development of sexual identity is an important component of childhood. Instead of young people simply learning about sex in the media and then acting on what they watch, preteens and teens try to make sense of what they see in the context of their other experiences. Seeing all these images of sex does not necessarily mean that children interpret them by having sexual intercourse, but instead that coming to terms with sexuality in popular culture and their lives is a major part of adolescence and preadolescence as well.

## A Tale of Two Studies

A 2001 Kaiser Family Foundation study of sex on television is a great example of the traditional American approach to understanding sex, youth, and media.[9] The study received a great deal of media attention because it follows the conventional wisdom that there is even more sex on TV than ever, presumed to be a potential danger to youth. This study's assumptions are in direct contrast to a 1999 British study that received no American media attention. The British study critically examines how children make sense of representations of sexuality and romance on television.[10] Comparison of these two studies reveals our tendency to underestimate youth and overstate the power of popular culture.

### Assumptions of the Kaiser Study

While the authors of this study insist that television is not the most important factor in sexual socialization, television is the main focus of their study. Researchers analyzed over a thousand television programs, counting incidents they deemed sexual in nature,[11] . . . yet they interviewed no young people to ascertain how they actually interpret these messages. This method isolates meaning from the context of both the program and the audience, a problem the researchers don't seem to be worried about. Additionally, this study broadly

defines sexual messages to include flirting, alluding to sex, touching, kissing, and implication of intercourse. When the incidents get boiled down into statistics, hugs and handholding appear the same as more explicit representations of sex. . . .

The researchers seem to presume that young viewers will be heavily influenced by television, completely negating young peoples' ability to interpret media images on their own.[12] The authors presume that media are an important source of information about sex for teens, but media sources are not where young people get most of their knowledge. Within the report, authors noted that only 23 percent of teens say they learn "a lot" about pregnancy and birth control from television, while 40 percent have "gotten ideas on how to talk to their boyfriend or girlfriend about sexual issues" from media.[13] We focus on media when other sources are clearly more important because media is the feared spoiler of innocence—it is always there for us to credit with social influence and enables us to overlook the complexity of the history of sexuality and social change. . . .

[T]he authors note almost as an aside that many teens feel they do not get enough information about sex from parents or teachers. Rather than focusing on this point, we belabor the media issue. We fear that popular culture is filling the void that nervous adults have created and beg Hollywood to teach kids about sex more responsibly. Here's an idea: how about we initiate a dialogue about sex ourselves, where young people are not just preached to but heard. We ought to stop whining about what young people shouldn't know and start dealing with what they *do* know. . . .

The authors cite the risky sexual behaviors some adolescents engage in to support the need for their research, but they fail to provide real context.[14] In emphasizing negative behaviors, important statistics get buried. Prime example: the majority of teens under fifteen (80 percent of girls and 70 percent of boys) reported *not* being sexually active.[15] Most of those sexually active reported using condoms, yet the authors of the Kaiser Family Foundation report chose to invert these statistics to tell the negative story. Dangerous behavior is of course important to examine, but perhaps the biggest problem here is that we focus on adolescent risk and fail to put it in the context *of adult* behavior. For instance, the 1998 General Social Survey found that just 20 percent of adults used condoms during their last sexual encounters. By ignoring adults within the media-sex panic we pathologize teen behavior even if it is consistent (or even better than) that of adults.[16]

In sum, this study found that sexual content (as the researchers define it) on television rose from a similar study two years before, but so what? We are left with no information about how young people actually interpret and make sense of these programs. It is important that we find out how young people interpret sexual images in advertising, music, and television in their context, and in their own words. If we are so concerned about teen sexuality we need to talk with them, not just about them, to learn more. The British study did just that.

### Talking "Dirty"

Initiating conversations about sex with children is not just frowned upon, in some situations it is considered morally questionable or even illegal. Likewise, providing sex education in schools is frequently the subject of fierce debate. Maybe that's why studies like the one conducted by the Kaiser Family Foundation only focus on television. Talking about sex is considered indecent where children are concerned, enabling us to maintain the illusion that they can be separated from the rest of the world.

No doubt, this is why the British authors chose a provocative title for their study. . . . "Talking Dirty: Children, Sexual Knowledge and Television" was published in the journal *Childhood* in spring 1999 with no American fanfare. Not surprising, considering that the authors challenge our assumptions about childhood and sexuality at every turn. First, the authors critique the belief

that television is responsible for the loss of childhood "innocence" and argue it is best to find out what children *do* know rather than continue to focus on what adults *want* them to know. To that end, the researchers were more concerned with how the children they studied made sense of the programs they watched, and how they understood the content in the context of their own lives. Unlike the Kaiser Family Foundation study, . . . these researchers were interested in how children negotiated their social roles as children dealing with a subject that is regarded off-limits for them. The research team sought to find out what the children knew and how they made sense of it on their own terms, avoiding value judgments in the process.

Secondly, in contrast with traditional views that we need only pay attention to teenagers when it comes to sex, these researchers talked with six-, seven-, ten-, and eleven-year-olds in small groups, asking them to talk about what programs they liked and disliked. Children were then asked to sort a list of program titles into categories, which enabled researchers to see how the children defined adult content compared with programs that the kids considered appropriate for children, teens, or general audiences. Sex itself was not brought up by researchers but by the children, often used by the kids to define adult programs.

Researchers found that although most children felt that programs with romantic themes were "adult" shows (like *Ricki Lake* and *Blind Date*), the ten- and eleven year-olds were quite familiar with these programs and others like them. Kids reported that adult shows were appealing because they knew that they were supposed to be off-limits. . . . [T]he authors of the *Childhood* study note that claiming interest or knowledge of an "adult" program elevates one's status amongst peers. It was not uncommon for some kids to claim knowledge of a show when they clearly hadn't seen it. Other research has found similar results when studying children's interest in horror films; the more restrictive rating the film earned, the greater mark of status kids attained by watching.[17]

Gender was also central in identifying children's interest in the television programs discussed. The younger boys in particular were likely to deny any interest in shows with kissing or romantic themes. That was "girl stuff," which they wanted no part of. The authors also observed that children feigned shock or disgust about romantic scenes, a response common amongst preadolescents in adult company.

Rather than advance the narrow view that sexual content does something *to* children, this research informs us that it is used *by* children to build peer connections and to make sense of sexuality from a safe distance. Children use adult themes from television to try to demonstrate adult-level competence and knowledge. The researchers concluded that neither television nor audiences "hold anything approaching absolute power. Television obviously makes available particular representations and identities. . . . In defining and debating the meanings of television, readers also claim and construct identities of their own."[18]

In my own research with high school students, I found that sexuality in media is used differently depending on the context: in groups comprised of mostly males, sexuality was collectively defined as the celebration of women as objects, while mainly female groups tended to challenge the objectification of women's sexuality.[19] . . . Interestingly, boys in predominantly female groups tended to agree with their female classmates that [an] ad's use of a scantily clad woman was offensive. The teens I studied clearly demonstrate how the meaning of popular culture is created collectively in the context of peer culture, a negotiation process that goes way beyond simple cause-and-effect.

As the above example demonstrates, sometimes the way people talk about sexuality is a way to bolster their status among their friends. Rather than only criticize the quantity of sexual images in the media, providing more opportunities for young people to critically discuss these images is a way to better understand underlying beliefs about sex and gender. Young people use media imagery in their struggle to fit in with each other while developing individual identities. They also try to fit

into the larger society, where issues of sex, gender, and power are deep seeded.

### Sexuality and Children's Culture

Several recent American studies demonstrate the importance of sexuality within elementary and middle school children's peer groups. Traditionally, studies of children have focused only on social and cognitive development, or on how close kids are to being like adults. However, recent sociological thinking has sought to understand children as creators of their own experiences who need to be understood in their own contexts without only considering them adults in the making.[20] Rather than devise surveys to get answers to the questions adults think are important, these researchers immersed themselves into the daily experiences of children's lives. . . .

These studies detail that young people may borrow issues from adult culture and from the media, but children's culture does not completely emerge from either.[21] Instead, an interactive negotiation process takes place as children seek acceptance and status from their peers. While popular culture is an important part of this undertaking, it is not the all-powerful force many adults fear.

Adults tend to view children as imitators, sponges who soak up the language, behavior, and attitudes of the world around them. But sociologists Patricia and Peter Adler studied children's peer groups for eight years and concluded that we need to recognize the power of preadolescent peer culture. According to their research, children negotiate individual identities while striving to maintain status amongst peers, and sexual themes are interwoven into this process. Adults somehow fail to acknowledge (or remember) that curiosity about sexuality is a big part of growing up.

In her study of elementary school students, sociologist Barrie Thorne discusses how games like "kiss and chase" demonstrate that children are actively involved in the construction of their own sexuality.[22] We might deem this sort of behavior "innocent child's play," but that would ignore how children themselves define their experiences.

I can remember the excitement of chasing a boy I liked; of course I had no clue what I'd do if I caught him. Thorne details how children's play incorporates heterosexual meanings into everyday occurrences and shapes male-female interactions. Accusing someone of "liking" a student of the other sex is used to police boundaries between genders. . . . Also, popular rhymes ("Susie and Bobby sitting in a tree, K-I-S-S-I-N-G") amongst girls highlight the importance of romantic connections within children's games.

Children use popular culture to negotiate meanings from the world around them within their peer groups. . . . In a study of middle school students, researchers found that sexually explicit scenes from movies are often repeated in peer groups in order for the storyteller to solidify his or her rank in the group.[23] . . .

[Y]oung people are not simply influenced by popular culture, they negotiate meaning within the context of their friends and within the larger structure of social power. There *is* a problem when boys must adopt very narrow versions of masculinity to fit in. But if we were to somehow totally succeed in keeping children away from these sorts of films, or even do away with all such representations of sexuality in popular culture, we will have done nothing to address the real issue. The media did not initiate women's objectification, but we see it most clearly there. Popular culture is where we see reflections of power and inequality. It is naïve to think that the next generation only reproduces this shallow form of sexuality because they see it in movies or on TV. They are part of a society where gender inequality is replicated in many social institutions, including education, religion, government, and economics. Our popular culture shows us some of the ugly realities of our society and we focus on media as if that's where these realities originate. . . .

### The Danger of Innocence

The myth of childhood innocence is not simply a benign fantasy, it can be a dangerous one. First of all, it does not match the reality of children's experiences. Secondly, sexually curious or sexually knowledgeable kids are . . . considered damaged, spoiled, and robbed of [their] rightful "childhood" when in fact their knowledge may stem from sexual abuse.[24]

Clinging to the notion of childhood innocence serves to further entice those who exploit children. . . . Abusers are often titillated by innocence, which our cultural construction of childhood unconsciously supports. . . . [W]e must . . . reevaluate how our culture unwittingly contributes to this eroticized definition of childhood innocence.[25] Even though most of us are not pedophiles and do not directly harm children, the insistence on children's inherent innocence can create danger for children. . . .

Adding to the confusion is the manner in which innocence is eroticized, particularly within girls and women. . . . Virginity has served as a sexual commodity for centuries, increasing female value on the marriage market in the past and fueling male fantasies in the present. . . . Innocence serves as a sexual marker denoting increased desirability, reflecting the traditional gender order where women's passivity and lack of experience are prized and reproduce patriarchal power. Beauty pageants are a good example of the contradictions between innocence and sexuality projected onto the female child's body. While young girls in pageants are made to look like women, women are encouraged to look like girls.[26] The teenage female body is fetishized as the ideal against which adult women are measured.

Our culture creates and reinforces inconsistencies, asking us to see children as pure and untainted by the adult world when in fact sexuality is part of the human experience. This of course does not mean people of all ages ought to engage in sexual intercourse, but instead that we must recognize that self-awareness, curiosity, and some knowledge of sex are a part of childhood. When we acknowledge that media alone do not create curiosity and knowledge about sex, we begin to recognize the complexity of children's experiences. Our anxiety is rooted in the fear that adults cannot control children's knowledge or identities.

One of the ways our culture defines childhood is the absence of knowledge of sex, yet its presence in popular culture serves as a reminder that our ideal childhood is merely an illusion. While adult guidance is useful to help young people navigate this terrain, we must also recognize that sexuality is partially rooted in peer culture, which by definition excludes adults.

## More Promiscuous Than Ever?

Just as sexuality seems like a new invention for each generation of teens, the fear of teen sexuality is renewed in each adult generation. . . . Teenage sex is frequently associated with irresponsibility, disease, promiscuity, and unwanted pregnancy. We claim that teens have trouble controlling themselves due to "raging hormones," implying that adolescents are ruled by sexual impulses. Ironically, we blame powerful forces of nature for shaping teen behavior, yet at the same time we condemn young people for this allegedly biological and natural behavior. Meanwhile, we ignore the majority of teens who are responsible or do not engage in sex, and we don't stereotype promiscuous adults as hormone-crazed animals. When it comes to young people and sex, we tend to hear only the negative side of the story. We hear about the kid who makes a sex video and shows all of his friends. The teens frequently on tabloid-style talk shows speak freely of their ample sexual experience. . . . Chastity just isn't dramatic.

Consequently, a false impression exists, created in part by media culture, that young people are sexually out of control at earlier and earlier ages. Even teens themselves think their peers are having sex more than they really are. A survey conducted by the National Campaign to Prevent Teen Pregnancy found that more than half of teens overestimated the percentage of their classmates who are sexually active.[27] Sociologist Mike Males dispels such faulty perceptions in *The Scapegoat Generation: America's War on Adolescents*. Based on his analysis of public health statistics, Males found:

- Between 1970 and 1992 there was just a 7 percent rise in the number of junior high school aged boys claiming to have had sex and a 6 percent rise amongst girls;[28]
- Adult men (aged nineteen to twenty-four) are far more likely than teen boys to father children born to teenaged girls;[29]
- Adult men, not teenaged boys, are most responsible for spreading HIV and other sexually transmitted diseases to girls;[30]
- For 40 percent of girls under fifteen who report being sexually active, their *only* sexual experience was rape.[31]

In addition, Males points out that we must consider any claims of sexual activity with skepticism. In spite of the belief that teens now are far more sexually active than adolescents of previous generations were, any data must be analyzed through the context of the sexual mores of the time. Simply put, people are more likely to *under-report* behavior that is considered deviant and more likely to *over-report* behavior that they perceive as elevating their status amongst peers. The fact that claiming sexual experience is treated differently now than fifty years ago makes accurate comparisons difficult. While boasting may be a factor, we must also consider that surveys rarely distinguish between forced and consenting sex. The small proportions of young teens who report having had sexual experiences quite possibly have been victims of sexual abuse.

The second and third points made above highlight the inadequacy of the term "teenage sex." We overlook the role adults, particularly adult males, play in teen pregnancy and the spread of sexually transmitted diseases. Adult men are responsible for seven out of ten births to girls eighteen and younger.[32] Also, because the HIV infection rate for teen girls is so much higher than for teen boys (a whopping disparity of 8 to 1), it is unlikely that teen boys are responsible for a large proportion of new cases.[33] . . .

Nonetheless, politicians and public health officials try to steer this conversation away from adults and onto teens. In Males' analysis, he found that the teen birth rate can be predicted not by changes in media or pushes for abstinence, but by adult birth rates and poverty rates.[34] It is far easier to blame media than to study the effects of poverty. Studying poverty is dangerous: we uncover structural problems that can't be blamed on individuals; we find reasons to question the viability of our current economic policies. It is much easier to simply charge poor people with personal failure without examining why the link between teen motherhood and poverty is so strong.[35] We let policymakers off the hook and give the media bashers something to complain about.

We are all too eager to point out the bad behavior of a few teenagers and hold them up as symbolic of an entire generation. Imagine if we saw a story on the news about a child molester followed by a commentary on how the middle-aged generation is completely without moral grounding. Of course this would never happen—we would say the molester was a sick individual, different from the rest of us. Yet we never afford young people this same explanation. Teens are accused of participating in risky sexual behavior, allegedly coaxed by sex in media. Adults tend to ignore the fact that a large proportion of young people report very little or no sexual experience, but instead focus on those that do.[36] We also hear very little about the fact that the teen birth rate has been steadily *falling* since 1990 and that the teen abortion rate fell 39 percent between 1994 and 2000.[37]

Finally, and perhaps most significantly, we overlook the role of sexual abuse in the discussion about teens and sex. For many young people, sex is not a choice they have made but it was forced upon them. Adolescents who have been sexually abused as children are also far more likely to engage in riskier sexual practices in the future.[38] Rather than focus so heavily on popular culture leading to sexual activity, we see that *adult* behavior must be taken to task. We need to pay more attention to adults who impregnate, infect, and sexually abuse children and adolescents. They are the problem here, not the media.

## Why Lie?

So how is it that in a society that claims to put young people first, we ignore the good news and highlight the risky behavior of a few? The answer is by no means simple, but one that has become a recurring theme in the way our society has treated disempowered groups. Immigrants, racial ethnic minorities, women, and the poor at varying times in history have been perceived as sexually out of control and in need of tighter social restraint. . . . In the next section we will see the parallels between the treatment of young people now with historical perceptions of immigrants, racial ethnic minorities, women, and the poor.

### Fear, Sex, and Social Control

It is difficult to think of sexuality as anything but personal and individual, but the way we understand sex is socially constructed. Sexuality is a central site where struggles over social power take place.[39] The regulation and control of sexuality have served as ways to maintain dominance over disempowered groups. One such power struggle in the United States has emerged following demographic shifts of the past hundred years. Historically, fears that the population is becoming less Protestant and less white have led to attempts to control the reproduction of immigrant and nonwhite groups. This has been accomplished by policies promoting sterilization, removing girls from their families if juvenile courts believed they were likely to engage in sex, and, more recently, demonizing mothers of color.[40] Due to this fear, during the early part of the century white women's pregnancies were encouraged, and their access to birth control and abortion was restricted. So while sexuality is personal, the uses and meanings attached to the practice are decidedly social and linked with broader systems of power.

### No Sex As a Weapon

The sexuality of groups perceived to be a threat is labeled dangerous and serves to legitimate public policies that restrict members' behavior. Many

African-American men were lynched by whites allegedly protecting white women's virtue; black male sexuality came to be defined as a threat to the racial order. Miscegenation laws were enacted for much the same reason. They were created to prevent a union of a non-white man and a white woman, but were certainly not enforced when slave owners fathered the children of black slave women. This double standard reveals how the dominant group maintains power by controlling the sexuality of the "other." . . .

Measures like California's Proposition 187, which sought to restrict undocumented immigrant children from obtaining an education or medical care, represent the same kind of logic, that our society just cannot afford any more of "those" children. Contrast the "welfare queen" diatribe to the personal and corporate outpourings to multiple-birth families that have five, six, even seven children at once, which they cannot afford. These families appear on news magazine programs and talk shows to speak of their multiple blessings, while policymakers and pundits rail against the huge cost of other people's children. Concerns about promiscuity, pregnancy, and disease have served as a way for dominant groups to assert control over those whom they feel threatened by, whether the threat is real or imagined.

### Gender (Dis)order

In addition to changes in demographics we have been experiencing shifts in the gender order that are closely linked with sexuality. Historically, abstinence has been a female burden, with girls and women supposedly responsible for regulating male sexuality. The social control of women has been secured in recent history by policing female sexuality. . . . Women who enjoyed sex were viewed as deviant and considered threats. Even when women's desire ceased to be considered a medical problem, sexual gratification was defined as a socially undesirable quality, one that might reduce a woman's chances for marriage. This was of course a serious threat in a time when women's

wages rarely enabled them to live independently. Women were socially and economically constrained by the need for male financial support, as well as by the fear of unplanned pregnancy.

The threat of rape has historically been used to keep women from public spaces, supported by the practice of humiliating rape victims in court and not acknowledging marital rape. Women's sexuality has been a double-edged sword: a woman's worth has been tied to her appeal to men, yet rape has historically been blamed on women for being too appealing. The threat of sexual violence, even if not carried out, serves to limit women's movement and freedom.

In recent decades the widespread availability of birth control and shrinkage in the wage gap between men and women have created more personal freedom for women. But the old sexual double standards, that male sexuality is natural and female sexuality is a threat, are still alive in our fears about teens and sex. Concerns about teens' sexual activity reflect shifts in the gender order: attempts to control teen sexuality tend to focus on girls, on pregnancy, on girls' self-esteem and body image, but usually leave male sexuality out of the conversation. . . . So why is *female* sexuality so frightening?

Teenage girls are considered a threat when they seek to become more than just sexual objects—when they act as sexual *agents* we worry. . . . American society still expects girls to hold the keys to chastity, but at the same time they are held up as the ideal form of female desire. Open any fashion magazine and chances are good a teenage girl will be pouting back at you. We see this representation of teenage girls in many forms of popular culture, but it certainly does not originate there; its history lies in our tendency to value women who are young and sexually available for men. Rather than only blaming media culture for this representation of teenage girls, we need to take a closer look at the nature of power, sex, and gender in contemporary American society. Underneath fears of teens having sex are concerns about the changing meaning of gender.

### The Genie Is Out of the Bottle

Societal shifts spurred by economic changes have altered American life, which has made it more difficult to monitor teens. Knowledge of or engagement in sex reveals that the illusion of innocence cannot be sustained, no matter how hard adults may try. Censoring media will not work, nor will less than complete and honest sex education.[41] This includes dealing with the reality of how sexual content is used and understood by young media audiences. No matter how much we may want to turn back the clock we can't. Teen sexuality *is* a threat: it destroys the unsustainable myth that adults can fully control young people's knowledge or their actions. The media are an easy target, but not the root cause of the changes in the attitudes and practice of sexuality in the twenty-first century.

As we have seen, changes throughout the twentieth century have provided young people with the means to become more independent from their parents, rendering their behavior far harder to control. Generally adults look at this as a sad reality, one that will inevitably lead to the breakdown of social order and the decline of American society.

Adults need to recognize that teenagers cannot be fully controlled, nor should this be our goal. . . . [I]nstead we must acknowledge that teenage sexuality is not new nor is it necessarily the threat that adults believe it to be. Education that helps young people deal with the realities of sexuality is needed, beyond doom-and-gloom scare tactics. Most centrally, adults need to let go of the illusion that childhood innocence can be maintained through ignorance. We have to begin by understanding how young people make sense of sex, both in media and in their lives.

### Rethinking Media, Youth, and Sexuality

Sex on TV, in movies, and on the Internet scares lots of adults. Representations of sex in media expose the reality that childhood does not and cannot exist in a separate sphere from adulthood. Ironically, we use sex as the ultimate dividing line between childhood and adulthood, the line in the sand that adults try so hard to maintain and young people try so hard to cross. We define sex as a ticket to adulthood, so we should not be surprised when teens do, too. . . . Sex in popular culture reminds us that we cannot sustain the lengthened version of childhood we have idealized since the mid-twentieth century. The realities of sex dispel myths about childhood and media remind us such myths cannot be upheld.

We often associate changes in sexual behavior with changes in media. Historical shifts are difficult to see and understand, while media are by nature visible and always trying to grab our attention. And yes, frank exploration of sexuality is more prominent in popular culture now than it was at mid-century. But sexuality within popular culture has changed in conjunction with other social changes. Media are not the sole cause, but a messenger, jumping into the social conversation about sex, not starting it. To paraphrase Syracuse University's Robert Thompson's explanation, media do not push the envelope; they merely open the envelope that has been sitting under our noses.[42]

That being said, we should not ignore representations of sexuality in media. They provide useful clues about power and privilege and can launch greater exploration of contested meanings of both sexuality and gender. Rather than seek to censor, we should study media representations to analyze the taken-for-granted nature of relationships and sexuality in our culture. But instead of using these representations for cultural criticism, we often condemn the images and fail to critically challenge what they represent. If we really are concerned about the meanings young people make from such images, we ought to encourage people to critically address them, not simply call for self-censorship.

The truth is there aren't *enough* representations of sex in popular culture: not enough exploration of the depth of emotion that comes with sexual intimacy and not enough representations of regular-looking bodies.[43] Depictions of sex in media offer a prime opportunity to open up important discussions about gender and power within society as well. Of course, if we could have conversations like this there wouldn't be so much fear about sex in media in the first place. Instead of fearing the "negative effects" of sex in media and demanding that it go away, we need to keep learning about how young people make sense of sex in both media and in their lives.

We can choose to cling to old fears and old ways of thinking and try and make ourselves believe in the whimsical myth of innocence. Of course, that will leave us complaining from here to eternity, because the fear is based on faulty beliefs about both media and children. On the other hand we can get real and try to better understand how young people make sense of what they do know, rather than bemoaning *that* they know. The choice is ours: we can either try in vain to put the genie back into the bottle or open our eyes and create a deeper level of understanding of both media and youth.

## NOTES

1. Lyn Gorman and David McLean, *Media and Society in the Twentieth Century: A Historical Introduction* (New York: Blackwell, 2003), pp. 36–40.

2. The Motion Picture Production Code, 1930.

3. James E. Cote and Anton L. Allahar, *Generation on Hold: Coming of Age in the Late Twentieth Century* (New York: New York University Press, 1994), chapter 1.

4. For further discussion see Martha Wolfenstein, "Fun Morality: An Analysis of Recent American Child-Training Literature," in *The Children's Culture Reader,* ed. Henry Jenkins (New York: New York University Press, 1998), p. 199.

5. Rickie Solinger, "Race and 'Value': Black and White Illegitimate Babies, 1945–1965," in *Feminist Frontiers,* fourth edition, eds. Laurel Richardson, Verta Taylor, and Nancy Whittier (New York: McGraw-Hill, 1997), p. 282.

6. National Opinion Research Council, General Social Survey (NORC: University of Chicago, 1998). www.icpsr.umich.edu-GSS-index.html.url.

7. Henry Jenkins, "The Sensuous Child: Benjamin Spock and the Sexual Revolution," in *The Children's Culture Reader,* ed. Henry Jenkins (New York: New York University Press, 1998), p. 209.

8. Jenkins, ibid., p. 225.

9. Kaiser Family Foundation, "Sex on TV," full report online: www.kff.org/contentl2001/3087SexOnTv.pdf.

10. Peter Kelley, David Buckingham, and Hannah Davies, "Talking Dirty: Children, Sexual Knowledge and Television," *Childhood* 6, no. 22 (1999): 221–242.

11. This study replicated a previous study of sex on television by analyzing 1,114 programs from the 1999–2000 season. Authors sought to address whether the frequency of what they defined as sexual messages were increasing, how sexual messages are presented, and whether the risks and responsibilities of sex are portrayed.

12. For discussion about how audiences create varying meanings from texts and are not simply manipulated by messages, see: David Morley, *Television, Audiences and Cultural Studies* (New York: Routledge, 1992); John Fiske, *Understanding Popular Culture* (London: Routledge, 1989); and Ien Ang, *Living Room Wars: Rethinking Audiences for a Postmodern World* (London, Routledge, 1996).

13. Kaiser Family Foundation, ibid., p. 1.

14. Kaiser Family Foundation, ibid., p. 1.

15. Alan Gutmmacher Institute, *Facts in Brief Teen Sex and Pregnancy,* 1999 (online: [www.agi-usa.org]).

16. Mike Males, *Framing Youth: Ten Myths About the Next Generation* (Monroe, Maine: Common Courage Press, 1999), chapter 6.

17. Julian Wood, "Repeatable Pleasures: Notes on Young People's Use of Video," in *Reading Audiences: Young People and the Media,* ed. David Buckingham (Manchester: Manchester University Press, 1993), p. 184.

18. Kelley et al., 238.

19. Karen Sternheimer, "A Media Literate Generation? Adolescents as Active, Critical Viewers: A Cultural Studies Approach" (Ph.D. dissertation, University of Southern California, 1998).

20. For elaboration on this concept, see: William Corsaro, *The Sociology of Childhood* (Thousand Oaks, Calif.: Pine Forge Press, 1997), chapter 1. Alan Prout and Allison James, "A New Paradigm for the Sociology of Childhood? Provenance, Promise, and Problems," in *Constructing and Reconstructing Childhood,* eds. Alli-

son James and Alan Prout (London: Falmer Press, 1997), pp. 7–33. Patricia A. Adler and Peter Adler, *Peer Power: Preadolescent Culture and Identity* (New Brunswick, N.J.: Rutgers University Press, 1998), introduction.

21. Corsaro discusses the concept of "interpretive reproduction" in chapter 2 of the work listed above. He argues that children do not merely reproduce adult culture but re-interpret it to fit their own experiences.

22. Barrie Thorne, *Gender Play* (New Brunswick, N.J.: Rutgers University Press, 1993).

23. Donna Eder, Catherine Colleen Evans, and Stephen Parker, *SchoolTalk: Gender and Adolescent Culture* (New Brunswick, N.J.: Rutgers University Press, 1995), pp. 83–102.

24. Jenny Kitzinger, "Who *Are* You Kidding? Children, Power, and the Struggle Against Sexual Abuse," in *Constructing and Reconstructing Childhood,* eds. Allison James and Alan Prout (London: Falmer Press, 1997), pp. 165–189.

25. For further discussion see James R. Kincaid's provocative book, *Child-Loving* (New York: Routledge, 1992).

26. Giroux discusses beauty pageants in "Stealing Innocence: The Politics of Child Beauty Pageants," in *The Children's Culture Reader,* ed. Henry Jenkins (New York: New York University Press, 1998), p. 277.

27. Results of the National Campaign to Prevent Teen Pregnancy as reported by Lisa Mascaro, "Sex Survey: Teach Teens To Just Say No," *Daily News,* April 25, 2001, p. N1.

28. Mike Males, *The Scapegoat Generation: America's War on Adolescents* (Monroe, Maine: Common Courage Press, 1996), p. 46.

29. Males, ibid., pp. 47–48.

30. Males, ibid., p. 52.

31. Males, ibid., p. 56.

32. Males, ibid., p. 48.

33. Males, ibid., p. 51.

34. Mike Males, *Framing Youth: Ten Myths about the Next Generation* (Monroe, Maine: Common Courage Press, 1999), pp. 214–215.

35. In *Framing Youth,* pp. 182–188 Males discusses the connections between poverty and early pregnancy. He argues that underlying fears of teenage pregnancy is fear of young people of color, and that focusing only on pregnancy enables us to avoid talking about race and class. He concludes it is easier to demonize teen mothers and popular culture than to understand why teen pregnancy is so much more likely amongst the poor. The middle-class privileges many Americans take for granted often do not apply to this disadvantaged group, who are less likely to benefit from public education and whose economic prospects, even *without* children, are rather grim. In sum, Males argues that the teens most at risk of becoming pregnant are the same ones we demonize as we refuse to acknowledge the economic and social challenges they face *prior* to becoming parents.

36. Statistics supporting this point from the Centers for Disease Control and Prevention can be found in the introduction of: Dale Kunkel, Kirstie Cope-Farrar, Erica Biely, Wendy Jo Maynard Farinola, and Edward Donnerstein, *Sex on TV: A Biennial Report to the Kaiser Family Foundation 2001* (Menlo Park, Calif.: Kaiser Family Foundation, 2001).

37. Alan Gutmmacher Institute, *Trends in Abortion in the United States, 1973–2000,* 2003.

38. See Debra Boyer and David Fine, "Sexual Abuse as a Factor in Adolescent Pregnancy and Child Maltreatment," *Family Planning Perspectives* 24 (1992): 4–11.

39. See Michel Foucault, *The History of Sexuality Volume* 1: *An Introduction* (New York: Vintage, 1980).

40. For a discussion of this practice in the beginning of the twentieth century see Steven Schlossman and Stephanie Wallach, "The Crime of Precocious Sexuality," in *Juvenile Delinquency: Historical, Theoretical and Societal Reaction to Youth,* second edition, eds. Paul M. Sharp and Barry W. Hancock (Englewood Cliffs, N.J.: Prentice-Hall, 1998), pp. 41–62. Immigrant girls were often considered delinquent if juvenile courts believed they were *likely* to engage in sex—no proof of actual behavior was necessary.

41. See Debra Haffner, *Beyond the Big Talk: Every Parent's Guide to Raising Sexually Healthy Teens* (New York: Newmarket Press, 2001). Also see Deborah Roffman, *Sex & Sensibility: The Thinking Parent's Guide to Talking Sense About Sex* (Reading, Mass.: Perseus, 2001).

42. Closing speech delivered at the National Media Education Conference in Colorado Springs, Colo., 1998. Thompson noted that television programs tend to be at least a decade behind in terms of presenting social changes. For instance, in spite of the social turbulence of the 1960s, television programs did not reflect the changing social climate until the 1970s.

43. For further discussion, see Naomi Wolf, *The Beauty Myth: How Images of Beauty Are Used Against Women* (New York: Anchor Books, 1991).

# Whorified Virgins:
# Gay Youth and Sex

Michael Amico

Many young gay men are perceived by themselves and others as "whores," but it is a label that other gay youth are consciously rejecting. An earlier generation of gay men embraced sexual liberation as the driving goal of gay liberation itself, and found it empowering to be a "whore" or a "slut." "Sexual objectification is a focus of our quest for freedom," declared "A Gay Manifesto" of the 1970's (by Carl Wittman).[1] But gay youth culture has changed dramatically since then. Gay young people in general have veered toward a more heterosexual definition of their sexual relations. Few would agree with the sentiment expressed in another manifesto of early Gay Liberation, that of Martha Shelley in her classic essay "Gay is Good": "straight roles stink."[2]

Gay youth are not only rejecting the idea of being "whores," they are also consciously drawing on the straight-sex concept of "virginity." Claiming some form of gay virginity does not necessarily mean gay youth want to be virgins—or are—in any traditional sense. It is mainly a reaction against being regarded as a whore. The trouble is, every lesbian, gay, transgender, bisexual, or questioning youth has a different definition of what it means to be a "virgin." How does a gay person lose his or her virginity? What bodily orifices must be penetrated? Is it the giver, receiver, or both who lose their virginity? Do lesbians need a strap-on to get the job done? Do gay men require a penis? These questions stem from the fact that there is no agreement on what constitutes going too far, far enough, the real deal, or "losing one's V-card"—in other words, having sex. Asked if they have lost their virginity, most gay youth will answer with a question on the order of: "What do you consider sex?"

This is a serious dilemma for gay youth, one that has always existed but has rarely been discussed. Unlike their straight counterparts, gay youth are often unable to define themselves as sexual beings, because the familiar definitions of heterosexual sex and virginity do not apply. And yet, many gay youth are adopting heterosexual terms as part of a new wave of integration with their straight friends. The April/May 2005 issue of *YGA* ("Young Gay America"), a national glossy magazine for and about non-straight youth, focused on religion and spirituality.[3] Gay youth are seen as attempting to reconcile their religious beliefs with their mode of sexual expression. In so doing, many find themselves simply co-opting terms such as "virgin" in an attempt to make sense of their sexual expression and its inherent cultural difference from the valorized straight sexual pairing. There is no doubt that a major way for gay youth to assert their claim to self-definition is through sexual expression. Therefore, it is time to ask what it means to have sex *as* a gay person.

Gay youth do not have a place in the heterosexual framework because they are not by definition engaging in straight sex. Since gay people cannot be virgins, they (or at least gay men) are

From Amico, Michael. 2005. "Whorified Virgins: Gay Youth and Sex." *Gay & Lesbian Review* (July–Aug): 34–36. Reprinted by permission of Michael Amico.

assumed to be its opposite: perennial sex fiends, always out to get more action. Gay youth have thus been "whorified." The relentless pursuit of sex is the subtext in TV shows like *The L Word* and *Queer as Folk,* while the mainstream media tends to show gay young people going to clubs or surfing the Web for sex and more sex. Of course, in reality gay teen life is not all about sex. At the same time, sex is a crucial component of a gay person's identity. A puritanical, authoritarian straight voice has instilled fear and caution in the sexual expression of gay young people. No wonder many are turning away from demonized labels such as "whore" or "slut" and embracing the notion of virginity. Gay youth are almost never asked what they think about their sex lives or how they define themselves.

There is a history of gay sex acts that informs both gay sexual expression and those who judge it. As recently as 2003, when the U.S. Supreme Court struck down state sodomy laws in *Lawrence v. Texas,* gay sex acts were illegal in thirteen states. Gay people are thought to be whores because in other people's eyes they are only looking to have sex. In their own eyes they are merely trying to find a safe way to express their sexuality and need for intimacy without being judged.

The assumption that gay sexual expression is necessarily coercive and exploitative was at work in a 2000 case in which Matthew Limon, a mildly retarded eighteen-year-old, was sentenced to seventeen years and two months in a Kansas prison for giving a blow job to a consenting fourteen-year-old boy in his group home.[4] After five years in prison, Limon's case was finally overturned. However, Limon's ongoing legal battle shows that the U.S. still refuses to acknowledge the societal parameters preventing all youth, especially gay youth, from exploring their sexuality and illustrates the lengths to which straight society will sometimes go to abet that prevention. There is no fundamental right to have gay sex in the U.S. Federal and state laws permit a limited number of sex acts as long as they take place in private and occur between two people over the arbitrary age of consent. The moral underpinning of these laws is interpreted as a shared universal value system, even though it is predominantly Christian. No wonder that many of today's gay youth favor having a long-term, monogamous relationship over more sexually open ones; there is no opportunity to fully explore any alternatives.

But even gay youth are vilifying themselves as sluts. A gay man I know was recently feeling bad about not having sex. A gay friend asked him, "If you could sleep with anyone you wanted to, would you do it?" The first man responded, "Yes, immediately." To which the other guy replied, "Well, you shouldn't, because I did it for awhile and it made me feel terrible. I just did it because I didn't respect myself."

Gay youth are necessarily caught in a mainstream culture overdetermined by a pathologizing discourse around gay sex. Historically, gay people have been considered psychologically and behaviorally diseased by heterosexual society because of the sex acts they "commit." So it makes sense that gay youth lack both the opportunity and a language with which to discuss their sexual lives. Constantly dealing with a new and emerging cultural identity, they have no choice but to figure out their sexual status in relation to their straight friends. Of all the labels and identities that heterosexual teens have, gay teens have two that are also used to define heterosexual women's only options: "virgin" and "whore." As the old Italian joke goes: "All women are whores, except my mother. She's a virgin." Since there is no middle ground between these two extremes, gay youth are forced to gravitate toward one identity or the other. And since being gay is typically viewed in purely sexual terms, gay people tend to be marked automatically as whores. Of course, no one is simply a whore or a virgin. However, these two words guide the perception and representation of the gay youth community from within and without. Gay teens never question these two words while even using them to describe themselves.

Without an eager, observant, and considerate audience, gay youth will never be able to discuss their actual lives and sexual desires. This problem with gay identity is compounded by the fact that the representation of gay life in the media is determined by marketing interests that profit from presenting images that conform to popular stereotypes about gay people. The "gay" ads appearing in gay magazines depict bodies that are clearly unattainable for most young people, gay or straight. The token "gay guy" on *The Real World* either has AIDS or is involved in a sex scandal. Pedro from *RW San Francisco* died of AIDS shortly after filming wrapped, while *RW Miami* cast member Danny made headlines last year when he was arrested for exposing himself while cruising a porn theater in Kansas City. Why AIDS and sex scandals? Because that is what most people know as indicative of gay life. Gay youth are not speaking for themselves in a world monopolized by blatant consumerism. Many are having great, enjoyable sex, but what the general public sees on a daily basis is that gay teens who have sex get caught, get sick, and will be forever unsatisfied. Meanwhile, network TV, with shows such as *Will and Grace,* tends to present only squeaky-clean images of gay people while pushing gay sex to the sidelines.

A closer look at the images presented in the mainstream and gay media reveals why many youth are afraid to talk about their sexuality. Gay kids are beaten up at school, abused at home, and made to feel ashamed. In 2003, the major gay teen story was about New York City's Harvey Milk School, which was created for kids who were physically harassed at their previous school.[5] *The Advocate* regularly profiles (i.e., sympathizes with and pities) gay youth in its "Generation Q" commentaries by highlighting their hardships after being thrown out by their parents or the like. The message that these stories convey, however inadvertently, is how horrible it must be for gay teens at school and in their homes each day. Gay youth come to realize that if they reveal their innermost sexual fantasies and fears, they are likely to be perceived as deviant, wasteful whores. So they end up not saying anything at all and realize

it is much better and safer that way. While many older gay men had no trouble discussing their sex lives when they came out thirty years ago, times have changed. AIDS workers have introduced a whole new safe-sex-dominated vocabulary, and the federal government has been pushing "abstinence only" programs for all young people that make sex seem risky and dirty.

Having received all the wrong messages, gay youth tend to look down on peers who are perceived as promiscuous. Gay youth often resist the label of whore by declaring their virginity. I have heard many say, for example, "As long as I don't have anal sex, I'm not a man-whore." But this denial is rooted in a fallacious application of straight sexual procedures to gay ones. When a heterosexual man inserts his penis into a woman's vagina for the first time, he proudly boasts to his friends that he is no longer a virgin. This is not a valid or realistic way of talking about gay sex—even if gay people doggedly insist on substituting the anus for the vagina.

Gay youth do not have sex the way heterosexuals do and often use the concept of virginity to explain away an endless amount of wonderful, exciting, and sometimes confusing physical contact. Virginity functions as a code word for "how far" one goes. In a Dartmouth College dining hall recently, a group of gay male friends and I were talking about the previous night. I asked one of the guys "how far" he went on his date. He pointedly asserted, "I'm still a virgin," even while admitting to engaging in a wide range of sexual activities. In both gay and straight circles, "virginity" is usually used to distinguish foreplay from the real thing. But while the latter is well-defined for heterosexual men, its meaning is not so clear for gay men. For one thing, gay males are capable of playing both the role of penetrator and penetrated in anal sex—and the same is also true of oral sex.

That many gay youth aspire to be "virgins" is a response to the messages they receive about their sexuality—messages from straight adults (most often their disapproving parents), religious zealots, and puritanical moralists in real life and in the mass media. The latest confusing signal comes from the gay community itself: the fight for same-sex marriage endorses the validity of a strictly heterosexual institution, one that links (however archaically) virginity with being single and sex with marriage. The fundamental cultural block to achieving marriage equality for gay people is that the moral and legal codes of the straight world do not want to acknowledge the gay sex that goes along with gay marriage. By legalizing marriage rights for all, the state would effectively be approving all the wondrously kinky sex acts they so ardently fear. For gay youth not intending to get married anytime soon, marriage is obviously not the best way to go about idealizing gay sex. Just as marriage has traditionally been used as a club with which to enforce chastity on heterosexuals, especially women, the push for same-sex marriage seems to enforce a notion of gay sex outside of marriage as whorish. Again we find that if gay people cannot be virgins, they are left with its opposite: whoredom. Legalizing marriage between all sexes would destabilize the hierarchy of sex acts. That would be too scary and too close for comfort for a mainstream society that finds it easier to just label gay people as whores. Whereas virgin is a name readily used by gay youth to fit in with the rest of the world, whore is a name introduced by conservative, authoritarian voices to contain the "spread" of a gay sexual identity.

Since gay sex and even public displays of affection are forbidden, gay youth have little choice but to conceal their sexual practices or misconstrue them as part of some traditional dream of virginity and marriage. The Internet, as the new cruising space for gay youth, is now the prime means of communication about sex because it is safe and anonymous. A cyber identity on AIM (AOL Instant Messenger) allows a young person to fantasize about sex without bodily contact. One can be a whore for talking dirty on-line and be a virgin for not consummating the sex. There is nothing inherently wrong with cybersex. In fact, gay youth have no choice if they are not allowed other places for sexual expression. Since many gay youth have a problem meeting one another in person, the Internet proves a perfect facilitator of a sexual dialogue. And yet, gay youth are looking to be anything but whores. Compared to the older gay male profiles on Manhunt.net, younger gay men are less likely to post a picture of their face, preferring to maintain a fictitious identity that keeps their sexual desires and selves at arm's length. One of my close friends at Dartmouth does not post his picture with his profile on Manhunt. When I asked him why, he told me that people would think he is a whore. Even though they are young and good-looking, such guys want to keep the illusion that they are virgins. They want to get laid but have to pretend to be virgins in order to have sex. If people think they are whores, no one will want to have sex with them (the traditional dilemma for young women).

The notion of virginity fits neatly into young gay lives at a time when political and moral agendas promote abstinence for straight people and offer no support at all for gay sex acts. Thus, personal censorship is running rampant. In combination with a generation gap in gay communities and virginal definitions of sex acts, gay youth are being cut off from an inheritance of a gay history rife with glorious sex.

Most crucially, the invasion of virginity leads to the heterosexual imperative to act according to someone else's rules. That way, gay youth will become indistinguishable from straight youth, everyone will conform, and no one will have to reconcile the inerasable differences between us all. It is easier for the media and educators alike (parents, teachers, and priests) to make believe that all youth, gay and straight, will grow up to *want* the same kind of sex. Sexual relations among gay youth must be seen as valid forms of sexual expression in and of themselves, without comparison to their straight counterparts. This is not *The Real World;* it is the queer world. Gay youth internalize heterosexual relationships and their rules and modes of conduct because that is what they see in the media and experience firsthand with policing adults. Left with little choice, they must either mold their actions to accommodate "straight" ways of conceptualizing and physicalizing relationships or else invent their own methods.

By buying into the language of virginity, gay youth are allowing the straight majority to limit their options and diminish their integrity. Virgin equals un-adult in this equation, so it permanently infantilizes one who cannot lose his or her virginity, preventing him or her from growing into "mature" adulthood. Gay youth today find themselves either whorified (and scared) or virginized (and rendered helpless). What they need to recognize is that virginity has no meaning in a same-sex context. Gay youth must value the sex they have in and of itself.

**NOTES**

1. Carl Wittman, "A Gay Manifesto," *We Are Everywhere: A Historical Sourcebook of Gay and Lesbian Politics,* eds. Mark Blasius and Shane Phelan (New York: Routledge, 1997) 380–88.

2. Martha Shelley, "Gay is Good," *We Are Everywhere: A Historical Sourcebook of Gay and Lesbian Politics,* eds. Mark Blasius and Shane Phelan (New York: Routledge, 1997) 391–93.

3. *YGA,* "The God Issue," Issue 3: April/May 2005.

4. For more information on the Matthew Limon case, see "The Other Matthew" by Michael Bronski in *The Boston Phoenix* (February 20–27, 2003) and the Kansas State Supreme Court decision (*State v. Limon,* 122 P.3d 22 (Kansas 2005)).

5. For more information on the Harvey Milk School, see "A Safe Haven Finds Itself Under Siege" by Michael Winerip in *The New York Times* (August 27, 2003) and "Not So Fast Times at Queermont High" by Michael Bronski in *Z Magazine* (November 2003).

# "We Don't Sleep around Like White Girls Do":
# Family, Culture, and Gender in Filipina American Lives

Yen Le Espiritu

I want my daughters to be Filipino especially on sex. I always emphasize to them that they should not participate in sex if they are not married. We are also Catholic. We are raised so that we don't engage in going out with men while we are not married. And I don't like it to happen to my daughters as if they have no values. I don't like them to grow up that way, like the American girls.

—*Filipina immigrant mother*

I found that a lot of the Asian American friends of mine, we don't date like white girls date. We don't sleep around like white girls do. Everyone is really mellow at dating because your parents were constraining and restrictive.

—*Second-generation Filipina daughter*

. . . [G]ender is a key to immigrant identity and a vehicle for racialized immigrants to assert cultural superiority over the dominant group. In immigrant communities, culture takes on a special significance: not only does it form a lifeline to the home country and a basis for group identity in a new country, it is also a base from which immigrants stake their political and sociocultural claims on their new country (Eastmond 1993, 40). For Filipino immigrants, who come from a homeland that was once a U.S. colony, cultural reconstruction has been especially critical in the assertion of their presence in the United States—a

way to counter the cultural Americanization of the Philippines, to resist the assimilative and alienating demands of U.S. society, and to reaffirm to themselves their self-worth in the face of colonial, racial, class, and gendered subordination. Before World War II, Filipinos were barred from becoming U.S. citizens, owning property, and marrying whites. They also encountered discriminatory housing policies, unfair labor practices, violent physical encounters, and racist as well as anti-immigrant discourse.[1] While blatant legal discrimination against Filipino Americans is largely a matter of the past, Filipinos continue to encounter many barriers that prevent full participation in the economic, social, and political institutions of the United States (Azores-Gunner 1986–87; Cabezas, Shinagawa, and Kawaguchi 1986–87; Okamura and Agbayani 1997). Moreover, the economic mobility and cultural assimilation that enables white ethnics to become "unhyphenated whites" is seldom extended to Filipino Americans (Espiritu 1994). Like other Asians, the Filipino is "always seen as an immigrant, as the 'foreigner-within,' even when born in the United States" (Lowe 1996, 5). Finally, although Filipinos have been in the United States since the middle of the 1700s and Americans have been in the Philippines since at least the late 1800s, U.S. Filipinos—as racialized nationals, immigrants, and citizens—are "still practically an invisible and silent minority" (San Juan 1991, 117). Drawing from my research on Filipino American families in San Diego, California, I explore in this article the ways racialized immigrants claim through gender the power denied them by racism.

From Espiritu, Yen Le. 2001. " 'We Don't Sleep around Like White Girls Do': Family, Culture, and Gender in Filipina American Lives." *Signs* 26: 415–440. Reprinted by permission of the University of Chicago Press.

My epigraphs, quotations of a Filipina immigrant mother and a second-generation Filipina daughter, suggest that the virtuous Filipina daughter is partially constructed on the conceptualization of white women as sexually immoral. This juxtaposition underscores the fact that femininity is a relational category, one that is co-constructed with other racial and cultural categories. These narratives also reveal that women's sexuality and their enforced "morality" are fundamental to the structuring of social inequalities. Historically, the sexuality of racialized women has been systematically demonized and disparaged by dominant or oppressor groups to justify and bolster nationalist movements, colonialism, and/or racism. But as these narratives indicate, racialized groups also criticize the morality of white women as a strategy of resistance—a means of asserting a morally superior public face to the dominant society. . . .

But this strategy is not without costs. The elevation of Filipina chastity (particularly that of young women) has the effect of reinforcing masculinist and patriarchal power in the name of a greater ideal of national/ethnic self-respect. Because the control of women is one of the principal means of asserting moral superiority, young women in immigrant families face numerous restrictions on their autonomy, mobility, and personal decision making. . . .

### Studying Filipinos in San Diego

San Diego, California has long been a favored area of settlement for Filipinos and is today the third-largest U.S. destination for Filipino immigrants (Rumbaut 1991, 220). . . . San Diego has been a primary area of settlement for Filipino navy personnel and their families since the early 1900s. As in other Filipino communities along the Pacific Coast, the San Diego community grew dramatically in the twenty-five years following passage of the 1965 Immigration Act. New immigration contributed greatly to the tripling of San Diego county's Filipino American population from 1970 to 1980 and its doubling from 1980 to

1990. In 1990, nearly 96,000 Filipinos resided in the county. Although they made up only 4 percent of the county's general population, they constituted close to 50 percent of the Asian American population (Espiritu 1995). Many post-1965 Filipino immigrants have come to San Diego as professionals—most conspicuously as health care workers. A 1992 analysis of the socioeconomic characteristics of recent Filipino immigrants in San Diego indicated that they were predominantly middle-class, college-educated, and English-speaking professionals who were more likely to own than rent their homes (Rumbaut 1994). At the same time, about two-thirds of the Filipinos surveyed indicated that they had experienced racial and ethnic discrimination (Espiritu and Wolf, forthcoming).

The information on which this article is based comes mostly from in-depth interviews that I conducted with almost one hundred Filipinos in San Diego.[2] Using the "snowball" sampling technique, . . . I chose participants . . . through a network of Filipino American contacts whom the first group of respondents trusted. To capture the diversity within the Filipino American community, I sought and selected respondents of different backgrounds and with diverse viewpoints. The sample is about equally divided between first-generation immigrants (those who came to the United States as adults) and Filipinas/os who were born and/or raised in the United States. . . . They included poor working-class immigrants who barely eked out a living, as well as educated professionals who thrived in middle- and upper-class suburban neighborhoods. However, the class status of most was much more ambiguous. . . . Reflecting the prominence of the U.S. Navy in San Diego, more than half of my respondents were affiliated with or had relatives affiliated with the U.S. Navy.

My tape-recorded interviews, conducted in English, ranged from three to ten hours each and took place in offices, coffee shops, and homes. My questions were open-ended and covered three general areas: family and immigration history, ethnic identity and practices, and community development among San Diego's Filipinos. . . . Even without prompting, young Filipinas almost always recounted stories of restrictive gender roles and gender expectations, particularly of parental control over their whereabouts and sexuality.

I believe that my own personal and social characteristics influenced the actual process of data collection, the quality of the materials that I gathered, and my analysis of them. As a Vietnam-born woman who immigrated to the United States at the age of twelve, I came to the research project not as an "objective" outsider but as a fellow Asian immigrant who shared some of the life experiences of my respondents. During the fieldwork process, I . . . actively shared with my informants my own experiences of being an Asian immigrant woman: of being perceived as an outsider in U.S. society, of speaking English as a second language, of being a woman of color in a racialized patriarchal society, and of negotiating intergenerational tensions within my own family. . . . These shared experiences enable me to bring to the work a comparative perspective that is implicit, intuitive, and informed by my own identities and positionalities—and with it a commitment to approach these subjects with both sensitivity and rigor. . . .

## "American" and Whiteness: "To Me, American Means White"

In U.S. racial discourse and practices, unless otherwise specified, "Americans" means "whites" (Lipsitz 1998, 1). In the case of Asian Americans, U.S. exclusion acts, naturalization laws, and national culture have simultaneously marked Asians as the inassimilable aliens and whites as the quintessential Americans (Lowe 1996). Excluded from the collective memory of who constitutes a "real" American, Asians in the United States, even as citizens, remain "foreigners within"—"non-Americans." . . . In the case of Filipinos who emigrated from a former U.S. colony, their formation as racialized minorities does not begin in the

United States but rather in a "homeland" already affected by U.S. economic, social, and cultural influences (Lowe 1996, 8). . . .

## Constructing the Dominant Group: The Moral Flaws of White Americans

. . . While much has been written on how whites have represented the (im)morality of people of color (Collins 1991; Marchetti 1993; Hamamoto 1994), there has been less critical attention to how people of color have represented whites. . . . I argue that female morality—defined as women's dedication to their families and sexual restraint—is one of the few sites where economically and politically dominated groups can construct the dominant group as other and themselves as superior. Because womanhood is idealized as the repository of tradition, the norms that regulate women's behaviors become a means of determining and defining group status and boundaries. As a consequence, the burdens and complexities of cultural representation fall most heavily on immigrant women and their daughters. . . .

### Family-Oriented Model Minorities: "White Women Will Leave You"

. . . Many of my respondents constructed their "ethnic" culture as principled and "American" culture as deviant. Most often, this morality narrative revolves around family life and family relations. When asked what set Filipinos apart from other Americans, my respondents—of all ages and class backgrounds—repeatedly contrasted close-knit Filipino families to what they perceived to be the more impersonal quality of U.S. family relations. . . . "Americans" are characterized as lacking in strong family ties and collective identity, less willing to do the work of family and cultural maintenance, and less willing to abide by patriarchal norm in husband/wife relations. . . .

Implicit in negative depictions of U.S. families as uncaring, selfish, and distant is the allegation that white women are not as dedicated to their families as Filipina women are to theirs. Several

Filipino men who married white women recalled being warned by their parents and relatives that "white women will leave you.". . . . For some Filipino men, perceived differences in attitudes about women's roles between Filipina and non-Filipina women influenced their marital choice. A Filipino American navy man explained why he went back to the Philippines to look for a wife:

> My goal was to marry a Filipina. I requested to be stationed in the Philippines to get married to a Filipina. I'd seen the women here and basically they are spoiled. They have a tendency of not going along together with their husband. They behave differently. They chase the male, instead of the male, the normal way of the traditional way is for the male to go after the female. They have sex without marrying. They want to do their own things. So my idea was to go back home and marry somebody who has never been here. I tell my son the same thing: if he does what I did and finds himself a good lady there, he will be in good hands.

Another man who had dated mostly white women in high school recounted that when it came time for him to marry, he "looked for the kind of women" he met while stationed in the Philippines: "I hate to sound chauvinistic about marriages, but Filipinas have a way of making you feel like you are a king. They also have that tenderness, that elegance. And we share the same values about family, education, religion, and raising children." . . .

### Racialized Sexuality and (Im)Morality: "In America, . . . Sex Is Nothing"

Sexuality, as a core aspect of social identity, is fundamental to the structuring of gender inequality (Millett 1970). Sexuality is also a salient marker of otherness and has figured prominently in racist and imperialist ideologies (Gilman 1985; Stoler 1991). Historically, the sexuality of subordinate groups—particularly that of racialized women—has been systematically stereotyped by the dominant groups.[3] At stake in these stereotypes is the construction of women of color as morally lacking in the areas of sexual restraint

and traditional morality. Asian women—both in Asia and in the United States—have been racialized as sexually immoral, and the "Orient"—and its women—has long served as a site of European male-power fantasies, replete with lurid images of sexual license, gynecological aberrations, and general perversion (Gilman 1985, 89). In colonial Asia in the nineteenth and early twentieth centuries, for example, female sexuality was a site for colonial rulers to assert their moral superiority and thus their supposed natural and legitimate right to rule. The colonial rhetoric of moral superiority was based on the construction of colonized Asian women as subjects of sexual desire and fulfillment and European colonial women as the paragons of virtue and the bearers of a redefined colonial morality (Stoler 1991). The discourse of morality has also been used to mark the "unassimilability" of Asians in the United States. At the turn of the twentieth century, the public perception of Chinese women as disease-ridden, drug-addicted prostitutes served to underline the depravity of "Orientals" and played a decisive role in the eventual passage of exclusion laws against all Asians (Mazumdar 1989, 3–4). The stereotypical view that all Asian women were prostitutes, first formed in the 1850s, persisted. Contemporary American popular culture continues to endow Asian women with an excess of "womanhood," sexualizing them but also impugning their sexuality (Espiritu 1997, 93).

Filipinas—both in the Philippines and in the United States—have been marked as desirable but dangerous "prostitutes" and/or submissive "mail-order brides" (Halualani 1995; Egan 1996). These stereotypes emerged out of the colonial process, especially the extensive U.S. military presence in the Philippines. Until the early 1990s, the Philippines, at times unwillingly, housed some of the United States's largest overseas airforce and naval bases (Espiritu 1995, 14). Many Filipino nationalists have charged that "the prostitution problem" in the Philippines stemmed from U.S. and Philippine government policies that promoted a sex industry—brothels, bars, and massage parlors—for servicemen stationed or on leave in the Philippines. During the Vietnam War, the Philippines was known as the "rest and recreation" center of Asia, hosting approximately ten thousand U.S. servicemen daily (Coronel and Rosca 1993; Warren 1993). In this context, *all* Filipinas were racialized as sexual commodities, usable and expendable. A U.S.-born Filipina recounted the sexual harassment she faced while visiting Subic Bay Naval Station in Olongapo City:

> One day, I went to the base dispensary . . . I was dressed nicely, and as I walked by the fire station, I heard catcalls and snide remarks being made by some of the firemen. . . . I was fuming inside. The next thing I heard was, "How much do you charge?" I kept on walking. "Hey, are you deaf or something? How much do you charge? You have a good body." That was an incident that I will never forget. (Quoted in Espiritu 1995, 77)

The sexualized racialization of Filipina women is also captured in Marianne Valanueva's short story "Opportunity" (1991). As the protagonist, a "mail-order bride" from the Philippines, enters a hotel lobby to meet her American fiancé, the bellboys snicker and whisper *puta* (whore): a reminder that US. economic and cultural colonization in the Philippines always forms a backdrop to any relations between Filipinos and Americans (Wong 1993, 53).

Cognizant of the pervasive hypersexualization of Filipina women, my respondents, especially women who grew up near military bases, were quick to denounce prostitution, to condemn sex laborers, and to declare (unasked) that they themselves did not frequent "that part of town." As one Filipina immigrant said,

> Growing up [in the Philippines], I could never date an American because my dad's concept of a friendship with an American is with a G.I. The only reason why my dad wouldn't let us date an American is that people will think that the only way you met was because of the base. I have never seen the inside of any of the bases because we were just forbidden to go there.

Many of my respondents also distanced themselves culturally from the Filipinas who serviced US. soldiers by branding them "more Americanized" and "more Westernized." In other words, these women were sexually promiscuous because they had assumed the sexual mores of white women. This characterization allows my respondents to symbolically disown the Filipina "bad girl" and, in so doing, to uphold the narrative of Filipina sexual virtuosity and white female sexual promiscuity. In the following narrative, a mother who came to the United States in her thirties contrasted the controlled sexuality of women in the Philippines with the perceived promiscuity of white women in the United States:

> In the Philippines, we always have chaperons when we go out. When we go to dances, we have our uncle, our grandfather, and auntie all behind us to make sure that we behave in the dance hall. Nobody goes necking outside. You don't even let a man put his hand on your shoulders. When you were brought up in a conservative country, it is hard to come here and see that it is all freedom of speech and freedom of action. Sex was never mentioned in our generation. I was thirty already when I learned about sex. But to the young generation in America, sex is nothing.

Similarly, another immigrant woman criticized the way young American women are raised: "Americans are so liberated. They allow their children, their girls, to go out even when they are still so young." In contrast, she stated that, in "the Filipino way, it is very important, the value of the woman, that she is a virgin when she gets married."

The ideal "Filipina," then, is partially constructed on the community's conceptualization of white women. She is everything that they are not: she is sexually modest and dedicated to her family; they are sexually promiscuous and uncaring. Within the context of the dominant culture's pervasive hypersexualization of Filipinas, the construction of the "ideal" Filipina—as family-oriented and chaste—can be read as an effort to reclaim the morality of the community. This effort erases the Filipina "bad girl," ignores competing sexual practices in the Filipino communities, and uncritically embraces the myth of "Oriental femininity." Cast as the embodiment of perfect womanhood and exotic femininity, Filipinas (and other Asian women) in recent years have been idealized in U.S. popular culture as more truly "feminine" (i.e., devoted, dependent, domestic) and therefore more desirable than their more modern, emancipated sisters (Espiritu 1997, 113). Capitalizing on this image of the "superfemme," mail-order bride agencies market Filipina women as " 'exotic, subservient wife imports' for sale and as alternatives for men sick of independent 'liberal' Western women" (Halualani 1995, 49; see also Ordonez 1997, 122).

Embodying the moral integrity of the idealized ethnic community, immigrant women, particularly young daughters, are expected to comply with male-defined criteria of what constitute "ideal" feminine virtues. While the sexual behavior of adult women is confined to a monogamous, heterosexual context, that of young women is denied completely (see Dasgupta and DasGupta 1996, 229–31). . . .

## The Construction(s) of the "Ideal" Filipina: "Boys Are Boys and Girls Are Different"

. . . Although details vary, young women of various groups and across space and time—for example, second-generation Chinese women in San Francisco in the 1920s (Yung 1995), U.S.-born Italian women in East Harlem in the 1930s (Orsi 1985), young Mexican women in the Southwest during the interwar years (Ruiz 1992), and daughters of Caribbean and Asian Indian immigrants on the East Coast in the 1990s (Dasgupta and DasGupta 1996; Waters 1996)—have identified strict parental control on their activities and movements as the primary source of intergenerational conflict. Recent studies of immigrant families also identify gender as a significant determinant of parent-child conflict, with daughters more likely than sons to be involved in such conflicts and instances of parental derogation (Rumbaut and Ima 1988; Woldemikael 1989; Matute-Bianchi 1991; Gibson 1995).

Although immigrant families have always been preoccupied with passing on their native culture, language, and traditions to both male and female children, it is daughters who have the primary burden of protecting and preserving the family. Because sons do not have to conform to the image of an "ideal" ethnic subject as daughters do, they often receive special day-to-day privileges denied to daughters (Haddad and Smith 1996, 22–24; Waters 1996, 75–76). This is not to say that immigrant parents do not place undue expectations on their sons; rather, these expectations do not pivot around the sons' sexuality or dating choices.[4] In contrast, parental control over the movement and action of daughters begins the moment they are perceived as young adults and sexually vulnerable. It regularly consists of monitoring their whereabouts and forbidding dating (Wolf 1997). For example, the immigrant parents I interviewed seldom allowed their daughters to date, to stay out late, to spend the night at a friend's house, or to take an out-of-town trip.

Many of the second-generation women I spoke to complained bitterly about these parental restrictions. They particularly resented what they saw as gender inequity in their families: the fact that their parents placed far more restrictions on their activities and movements than on their brothers'. Some decried the fact that even their younger brothers had more freedom than they did. "It was really hard growing up because my parents would let my younger brothers do what they wanted but I didn't get to do what I wanted even though I was the oldest. I had a curfew and my brothers didn't. I had to ask if I could go places and they didn't. My parents never even asked my brothers when they were coming home." . . .

When questioned about this double standard, parents generally responded by explaining that "girls are different":

I have that Filipino mentality that boys are boys and girls are different. Girls are supposed to be protected, to be clean. In the early years, my daughters have to have chaperons and curfews. And they know that they have to be virgins until they get married. The girls always say that is not fair. What is the difference between their brothers and them? And my answer always is, "In the Philippines, you know, we don't do that. The girls stay home. The boys go out." It was the way that I was raised. I still want to have part of that culture instilled in my children. And I want them to have that to pass on to their children.

Even among self-described Western-educated and "tolerant" parents, many continue to ascribe to "the Filipino way" when it comes to raising daughters. As one college-educated father explains,

Because of my Western education, I don't raise my children the way my parents raised me. I tended to be a little more tolerant. But at times, especially in certain issues like dating, I find myself more towards the Filipino way in the sense that I have only one daughter so I tended to be a little bit stricter. So the double standard kind of operates: it's alright for the boys to explore the field but I tended to be overly protective of my daughter. My wife feels the same way because the boys will not lose anything, but the daughter will lose something, her virginity, and it can be also a question of losing face, that kind of thing.

Although many parents discourage or forbid dating for daughters, they still fully expect these young women to fulfill their traditional roles as women: to marry and have children. A young Filipina recounted the mixed messages she received from her parents:

This is the way it is supposed to work: Okay, you go to school. You go to college. You graduate. You find a job. *Then* you find your husband, and you have children. That's the whole time line. *But* my question is, if you are not allowed to date, how are you supposed to find your husband? They say "no" to the whole dating scene because that is secondary to your education, secondary to your family. They do push marriage, but at a later date. So basically my parents are telling me that I should get married and I should have children but that I should not date.

. . . The restrictions on girls' movement sometimes spill over to the realm of academics. Dasgupta and DasGupta (1996, 230) recount that in the Indian American community, while young men were expected to attend faraway competitive colleges, many of their female peers were encouraged by their parents to go to the local colleges so that they could live at or close to home. Similarly, Wolf (1997, 467) reports that some Filipino parents pursued contradictory tactics with their children, particularly their daughters, by pushing them to achieve academic excellence in high school but then "pulling the emergency brake" when they contemplated college by expecting them to stay at home, even if it meant going to a less competitive college, or not going at all. . . .

I argue that these parental restrictions are attempts to construct a model of Filipina womanhood that is chaste, modest, nurturing, and family-oriented. Women are seen as responsible for holding the cultural line, maintaining racial boundaries, and marking cultural difference. This is not to say that parent-daughter conflicts exist in all Filipino immigrant families. Certainly, Filipino parents do not respond in a uniform way to the challenges of being racial-ethnic minorities, and I met parents who have had to change some of their ideas and practices in response to their inability to control their children's movements and choices:

I have three girls and one boy. I used to think that I wouldn't allow my daughters to go dating and things like that, but there is no way I could do that. I can't stop it. It's the way of life here in America. . . . (Professional Filipino immigrant father)

My children are born and raised here, so they do pretty much what they want. They think they know everything. I can only do so much as a parent. . . . When I try to teach my kids things, they tell me that I sound like an old record: They even talk back to me sometimes. . . . The first time my daughter brought her boyfriend to the house, she was eighteen years old. I almost passed away, knocked out. . . . (Working-class Filipino immigrant mother)

These narratives call attention to the shifts in the generational power caused by the migration process and to the possible gap between what parent say they want for their children and their ability to control the young. . . .

### Sanctions and Reactions: "That Is Not What a Decent Filipino Girl Should Do"

I do not wish to suggest that immigrant communities are the only ones in which parents regulate their daughters' mobility and sexuality. Feminist scholars have long documented the construction, containment, and exploitation of women's sexuality in various societies (Maglin and Perry 1996). We also know that the cultural anxiety over unbounded female sexuality is most apparent with regard to adolescent girls (Tolman and Higgins 1996, 206). The difference is in the ways immigrant and nonimmigrant families sanction girls' sexuality. To control sexually assertive girls nonimmigrant parents rely on the gender-based good girl/bad girl dichotomy in which "good girls" are passive, threatened sexual objects while "bad girls" are active, desiring sexual agents (Tolman and Higgins 1996). . . . This good girl/bad girl cultural story conflates femininity with sexuality, increases women's vulnerability to sexual coercion, and justifies women's containment in the domestic sphere.

Immigrant families, though, have an additional strategy: they can discipline their daughters as racial/national subjects as well as gendered ones. That is, as self-appointed guardians of "authentic" cultural memory, immigrant parents can attempt to regulate their daughters' independent choices by linking them to cultural ignorance or betrayal. As both parents and children recounted, young women who disobeyed parental strictures were often branded "non-ethnic," "untraditional," "radical," "selfish," and "not caring about the family." Female sexual choices were also linked to moral degeneracy, defined in relation to a narrative of a hegemonic white norm. Parents were quick to warn their daughters about "bad" Filipinas who had become pregnant outside marriage.[5] As in the case of "bar girls" in the Philippines, Filipina Americans who veered from acceptable behaviors were deemed "Americanized"—as women who have adopted the sexual mores and practices of white women. As one Filipino immigrant father described "Americanized" Filipinas: "They are spoiled because they have seen the American way. They go out at night. Late at night. They go out on dates. Smoking. They have sex without marrying."

From the perspective of the second-generation daughters, these charges are stinging. The young women I interviewed were visibly pained—with many breaking down and crying—when they recounted their parents' charges. This deep pain, stemming in part from their desire to be validated as Filipina, existed even among the more "rebellious" daughters. One twenty-four-year-old daughter explained:

> My mom is very traditional. She wants to follow the Filipino customs, just really adhere to them, like what is proper for a girl, what she can and can't do, and what other people are going to think of her if she doesn't follow that way. When I pushed these restrictions, when I rebelled and stayed out later than allowed, my mom would always say, "That is not what a decent Filipino girl should do. You should come home at a decent hour. What are people going to think of you?" And that would get me really upset, you know, because I think that my character is very much the way it should be for a Filipina. I wear my hair long, I wear decent makeup. I dress properly, conservative. I am family oriented. It hurts me that she doesn't see that I am decent, that I am proper and that I am not going to bring shame to the family or anything like that.

This narrative suggests that even when parents are unable to control the behaviors of their children, their (dis)approval remains powerful in shaping the emotional lives of their daughters (see Wolf 1997). Although better-off parents can and do exert greater controls over their children's behaviors than do poorer parents (Wolf 1992; Kibria 1993), I would argue that all immigrant parents—

regardless of class background—possess this emotional hold on their children. Therein lies the source of their power: As immigrant parents, they have the authority to determine if their daughters are "authentic" members of their racial-ethnic community. . . .

Faced with parental restrictions on their mobility, young Filipinas struggle to gain some control over their own social lives, particularly over dating. In many cases, daughters simply misinform their parents of their whereabouts or date without their parents' knowledge. They also rebel by vowing to create more egalitarian relationships with their own husbands and children. A thirty-year-old Filipina who is married to a white American explained why she chose to marry outside her culture:

> In high school, I dated mostly Mexican and Filipino. It never occurred to me to date a white or black guy. I was not attracted to them. But as I kept growing up and my father and I were having all these conflicts, I knew that if I married a Mexican or a Filipino, [he] would be exactly like my father. And so I tried to date anyone that would not remind me of my dad. A lot of my Filipina friends that I grew up with had similar experiences. So I knew that it wasn't only me. I was determined to marry a white person because he would treat me as an individual.[6]

Another Filipina who was labeled "radical" by her parents indicated that she would be more open-minded in raising her own children: "I see myself as very traditional in upbringing but I don't see myself as constricting on my children one day and I wouldn't put the gender roles on them. I wouldn't lock them into any particular way of behaving." It is important to note that even as these Filipinas desired new gender norms and practices for their own families, the majority hoped that their children would remain connected to Filipino culture.

My respondents also reported more serious reactions to parental restrictions, recalling incidents of someone they knew who had run away, joined a gang, or attempted suicide. A Filipina high-school counselor relates that most of the Filipinas she worked with "are really scared because a lot of them know friends that are pregnant and they all pretty much know girls who have attempted suicide." A 1995 random survey of San Diego public high schools conducted by the Federal Centers for Disease Control and Prevention (CDC) found that, in comparison with other ethnic groups, female Filipino students had the highest rates of seriously considering suicide (45.6 percent) as well as the highest rates of actually attempting suicide (23 percent) in the year preceding the survey. In comparison, 33.4 percent of Latinas, 26.2 percent of white women, and 25.3 percent of black women surveyed said they had suicidal thoughts (Lau 1995).

## Conclusion

Mainstream American society defines white middle-class culture as the norm and whiteness as the unmarked marker of others' difference (Frankenberg 1993). In this article, I have shown that many Filipino immigrants use the largely gendered discourse of morality as one strategy to decenter whiteness and to locate themselves above the dominant group, demonizing it in the process. Like other immigrant groups, Filipinos praise the United States as a land of significant economic opportunity but simultaneously denounce it as a country inhabited by corrupted and individualistic people of questionable morals. In particular, they criticize American family life, American individualism, and American women (see Gabbacia 1994, 113). Enforced by distorting powers of memory and nostalgia, this rhetoric of moral superiority often leads to patriarchal calls for a cultural "authenticity" that locates family honor and national integrity in the group's female members. Because the policing of women's bodies is one of the main means of asserting moral superiority, young women face numerous restrictions on their autonomy, mobility, and personal decision making. This practice of cultural (re)construction reveals how deeply the conduct of private life can be tied to larger social structures.

The construction of white Americans as the "other" and American culture as deviant serves a dual purpose: It allows immigrant communities both to reinforce patriarchy through the sanctioning of women's (mis)behavior and to present an unblemished, if not morally superior, public face to the dominant society. Strong in family values, heterosexual morality, and a hierarchical family structure, this public face erases the Filipina "bad girl" and ignores competing (im)moral practices in the Filipino communities. Through the oppression of Filipina women and the denunciation of white women's morality, the immigrant community attempts to exert its moral superiority over the dominant Western culture and to reaffirm to itself its self-worth in the face of economic, social, political, and legal subordination. In other words, the immigrant community uses restrictions on women's lives as one form of resistance to racism. This form of cultural resistance, however, severely restricts the lives of women, particularly those of the second generation, and it casts the family as a potential site of intense conflict and oppressive demands in immigrant lives.

## NOTES

1. Cordova 1983; Sharma 1984; Scharlin and Villanueva 1992; Jung 1999.

2. My understanding of Filipino American lives is also based on the many conversations I have had with my Filipino American students at the University of California, San Diego, and with Filipino American friends in the San Diego area and elsewhere.

3. Writing on the objectification of black women, Patricia Hill Collins (1991) argues that popular representations of black females—mammy, welfare queen, and Jezebel—all pivot around their sexuality, either desexualizing or hypersexualizing them. Along the same line, Native American women have been portrayed as sexually excessive (Green 1975), Chicana women as "exotic and erotic" (Mirande 1980), and Puerto Rican and Cuban women as "tropical bombshells, . . . sexy, sexed and interested" (Tafolla 1985, 39).

4. The relationship between immigrant parents and their sons deserves an article of its own.

5. According to a 1992 health assessment report of Filipinos in San Francisco, Filipino teens have the highest pregnancy rates among all Asian groups and, in 1991, the highest rate of increase in the number of births as compared with all other racial or ethnic groups (Tiongson 1997, 257).

6. The few available studies on Filipino American intermarriage indicate a high rate relative to other Asian groups. In 1980, Filipino men in California recorded the highest intermarriage rate among all Asian groups, and Filipina women had the second-highest rate, after Japanese American women (Agbayani-Siewert and Revilla 1995, 156).

## REFERENCES

Azores-Gunter, Tania Fortunata M. 1986–87. "Educational Attainment and Upward Mobility: Prospects for Filipino Americans." *Amerasia Journal* 13(1): 39–52.

Cabezas, Amado, Larry H. Shinagawa, and Gary Kawaguchi. 1986–87. "New Inquiries into the Socioeconomic Status of Pilipino Americans in California." *Amerasia Journal* 13(1): 1–21.

Collins, Patricia Hill. 1991. *Black Feminist Thought: Knowledge, Consciousness, and the Politics of Empowerment.* New York: Routledge.

Cordova, Fred. 1983. *Filipinos. Forgotten Asian Americans, a Pictorial Essay, 1763–1963.* Dubuque, Iowa: Kendall/Hunt.

Coronel, Sheila, and Ninotchka Rosca. 1993. "For the Boys: Filipinas Expose Years of Sexual Slavery by the U.S. and Japan." *Ms.*, November/December, 10–15.

Dasgupta, Shamita Das, and Sayantani DasGupta. 1996. "Public Face, Private Space: Asian Indian Women and Sexuality." In *"Bad Girls/Good Girls": Women, Sex, and Power in the Nineties,* ed. Nan Bauer Maglin and Donna Perry, 226–43. New Brunswick, N. J.: Rutgers University Press.

Eastmond, Marita. 1993. "Reconstructing Life: Chilean Refugee Women and the Dilemmas of Exile." In *Migrant Women: Crossing Boundaries and Changing Identities,* ed. Gina Buijs, 35–53. Oxford: Berg.

Egan, Timothy. 1996. "Mail-Order Marriage, Immigrant Dreams and Death." *New York Times,* May 26, 12.

Espiritu, Yen Le. 1994. "The Intersection of Race, Ethnicity, and Class: The Multiple Identities of Second Generation Filipinos." *Identities* 1(2–3):249–73.

———. 1995. *Filipino American Lives*. Philadelphia: Temple University Press.

———. 1997. *Asian American Women and Men: Labor, Laws, and Love*. Thousand Oaks, Calif.: Sage.

Espiritu, Yen Le, and Diane L. Wolf. Forthcoming. "The Paradox of Assimilation: Children of Filipino Immigrants in San Diego." In *Ethnicities: Children of Immigrants in America*, ed. Ruben Rumbaut and Alejandro Portes. Berkeley: University of California Press; New York: Russell Sage Foundation.

Gibson, Margaret A. 1995. "Additive Acculturation as a Strategy for School Improvement." In *California's Immigrant Children: Theory, Research, and Implications for Educational Policy*, ed. Ruben Rumbaut and Wayne A. Cornelius, 77–105. La Jolla: Center for U.S.-Mexican Studies, University of California, San Diego.

Gilman, Sander L. 1985. *Difference and Pathology: Stereotypes of Sexuality, Race, and Madness*. Ithaca, N. Y.: Cornell University Press.

Green, Rayna. 1975. "The Pocahontas Perplex: The Image of Indian Women in American Culture." *Massachusetts Review* 16(4):698–714.

Haddad, Yvonne Y., and Jane I. Smith. 1996. "Islamic Values among American Muslims." In *Family and Gender among American Muslims: Issues Facing Middle Eastern Immigrants and Their Descendants*, ed. Barbara C. Aswad and Barbara Bilge, 19–40. Philadelphia: Temple University Press.

Halualani, Rona Tamiko. 1995. "The Intersecting Hegemonic Discourses of an Asian Mail-Order Bride Catalog: Pilipina 'Oriental Butterfly' Dolls for Sale." *Women's Studies in Communication* 18(1):45–64.

Hamanoto, Darrell Y. 1994. *Monitored Peril: Asian Americans and the Politics of Representation*. Minneapolis: University of Minnesota Press.

Jung, Moon-Kie. 1999. "No Whites: No Asians: Race, Marxism and Hawaii's Pre-emergent Working Class." *Social Science History* 23(3):357–93.

Kibria, Nazli. 1993: *Family Tightrope: The Changing Lives of Vietnamese Immigrant Community*. Princeton, N. J.: Princeton University Press.

Lau, Angela. 1995. "Filipino Girls Think Suicide at Number One Rate." *San Diego Union-Tribune*, February 11, A-1.

Lipsitz, George. 1998. *The Possessive Investment in Whiteness: How White People Profit from Identity Politics*. Philadelphia: Temple University Press.

Lowe, Lisa. 1996. *Immigrant Acts: On Asian American Cultural Politics*. Durham, N. C.: Duke University Press.

Maglin, Nan Bauer, and Donna Perry. 1996. "Introduction." In *"Bad Girls/Good Girls": Women, Sex, and Power in the Nineties*, ed. Nan Bauer Maglin and Donna Perry, xiii–xxvi. New Brunswick, N. J.: Rutgers University Press.

Marchetti, Gina. 1993. *Romance and the "Yellow Peril": Race, Sex, and Discursive Strategies in Hollywood Fiction*. Berkeley: University of California Press.

Matute-Bianchi, Maria Eugenia. 1991. "Situational Ethnicity and Patterns of School Performance among Immigrant and Nonimmigrant Mexican-Descent Students." In *Minority Status and Schooling: A Comparative Study of Immigrant and Involuntary Minorities*, ed. Margaret A. Gibson and John U. Ogbu, 205–47. New York: Garland.

Mazumdar, Suchetta. 1989. "General Introduction: A Woman-Centered Perspective on Asian American History." In *Making Waves: An Anthology by and about Asian American Women*, ed. Asian Women United of California, 1–22. Boston: Beacon.

Millett, Kate. 1970. *Sexual Politics*. Garden City, N. Y.: Doubleday.

Mirande, Alfredo. 1980. "The Chinano Family: A Reanalysis of Conflicting Views? In *Rethinking Marriage, Child Rearing, and Family Organization*, ed. Arlene S. Skolnick and Jerome H. Skolnick, 479–93. Berkeley: University of California Press.

Okamura, Jonathan, and Amefil Agbayani. 1997. "*Pamantasan*: Filipino American Higher Education." In *Filipino Americans: Transformation and Identity*, ed. Maria P. Root, 183–97. Thousand Oaks, Calif.: Sage.

Ordonez, Raquel Z. 1997. "Mail-Order Brides: An Emerging Community." In *Filipino Americans: Transformation and Identity*, ed. Maria P. Root, 121–42. Thousand Oaks, Calif.: Sage.

Orsi, Robert Anthony. 1985. *The Madonna of 115th Street: Faith and Community in Italian Harlem,*

*1880–1950.* New Haven, Conn.: Yale University Press.

Ruiz, Vicki L. 1992. "The Flapper and the Chaperone: Historical Memory among Mexican-American Women." In *Seeking Common Ground: Multidisciplinary Studies,* ed. Donna Gabbacia. Westport, Conn.: Greenwood.

Rumbaut, Ruben. 1991. "Passages to America: Perspectives on the New Immigration." In *America at Century's End,* ed. Alan Wolfe, 208–44. Berkeley: University of California Press.

———. 1994. "The Crucible Within: Ethnic Identity, Self-Esteem, and Segmented Assimilation among Children of Immigrants." *International Migration Review* 28(4):748–94.

Rumbaut, Ruben, and Kenji Ima. 1988. *The Adaptation of Southeast Asian Refugee Youth: A Comparative Study.* Washington, D.C.: U.S. Office of Refugee Resettlement.

San Juan, E., Jr. 1991. "Mapping the Boundaries: The Filipino Writer in the U.S." *Journal of Ethnic Studies* 19(1):117–31.

Scharlin, Craig, and Lilia V. Villanueva. 1992. *Philip Vera Cruz: A Personal History of Filipino Immigrants and the Farmworkers Movement.* Los Angeles: University of California, Los Angeles Labor Center, Institute of Labor Relations, and Asian American Studies Center.

Sharma, Miriam. 1984. "Labor Migration and Class Formation among the Filipinos in Hawaii, 1906–46." In *Labor Immigration under Capitalism: Asian Workers in the United States before World War II,* ed. Lucie Cheng and Edna Bonacich, 579–611. Berkeley: University of California Press.

Stoler, Ann Laura. 1991. "Carnal Knowledge and Imperial Power: Gender, Race, and Morality in Colonial Asia." In *Gender at the Crossroads of Knowledge: Feminist Anthropology in the Postmodern Era,* ed. Micaela di Leonardo, 51–104. Berkeley: University of California Press.

Tafolla, Carmen. 1985. *To Split a Human: Mitos, Machos y la Mujer Chicana.* San Antonio, Tex.: Mexican American Cultural Center.

Tiongson, Antonio T., Jr. 1997. "Throwing the Baby out with the Bath Water." In *Filipino Americans: Transformation and Identity,* ed. Maria P. Root, 257–71. Thousand Oaks, Calif.: Sage.

Tolman, Deborah L., and Tracy E. Higgins. 1996. "How Being a Good Girl Can Be Bad for Girls." In *"Bad Girls/Good Girls": Women, Sex, and Power in the Nineties,* ed. Nan Bauer Maglin and Donna Perry, 205–25. New Brunswick, N. J.: Rutgers University Press.

Villanueva, M. 1991. *Ginseng and Other Tales from Manila.* Corvallis, Oreg.: Calyx.

Warren, Jenifer. 1993. "Suit Asks Navy to Aid Children Left in Philippines." *Los Angeles Times,* March 5, A3.

Waters, Mary C. 1996. "The Intersection of Gender, Race, and Ethnicity in Identity Development of Caribbean American Teens." In *Urban Girls: Resisting Stereotypes, Creating Identities,* ed. Bonnie J. Ross Leadbeater and Niobe Way, 65–81. New York: New York University Press.

Woldemikael, T. M. 1939. *Becoming Black American: Haitians and American Institutions in Evanston, Illinois.* New York: AMS Press.

Wolf, Diane L. 1992. *Factory Daughters: Gender, Household Dynamics, and Rural Industrialization in Java.* Berkeley: University of California Press.

———. 1997. "Family Secrets: Transnational Struggles among Children of Filipino Immigrants." *Sociological Perspectives* 40(3):457–82.

Wong, Sau-ling. 1993. *Reading Asian American Literature: From Necessity to Extravagance.* Princeton, N. J.: Princeton University Press.

Yung, Judy. 1995. *Unbound Feet: A Social History of Chinese Women in San Francisco.* Berkeley: University of California Press.

# Going Too Far?

## Sex, Sin and Social Policy

Susan Rose

What if I want to have sex outside of marriage? I guess you'll just have to be prepared to die.

—*No Second Chance*

The United States leads the industrialized world in teen pregnancy, abortion and sexually-transmitted disease rates—and in legislating and funding abstinence-until-marriage programs as social policy. It also stands out as the only industrialized country still embroiled in a debate about whether creationism should be taught in public schools. These issues help reveal the dynamic interplay between religion and politics in the United States. In examining the role and power of conservative religious groups in shaping domestic and foreign policy, this paper focuses on the issues of reproductive and sexual health, education and family—and the impact they have on young people. . . .

[T]his study presents a comparative analysis of Danish and U.S. approaches to family planning, reproductive health and sexuality education. . . . The case of Denmark is informative because the rates of teen pregnancy and attitudes towards sexuality 50 years ago were not much different than those in the United States. Since the 1970s, however, Denmark has taken a much more pragmatic approach to teen sexuality and sex education. Although Danish and American teens tend to have similar patterns of sexual debut and activity, Danish teens have much lower rates of

teenage pregnancy, abortion and sexually transmitted diseases (STDs). . . . Today the dominant Danish discourse about sexuality and reproductive rights is strikingly different from the dominant discourse in the United States—not because Danes are by nature or nationality "just more open" about sex and Americans "just naturally more prudish"—rather, the debates over sexuality and reproductive rights and responsibility are rooted in different religious, political, economic and community orientations.

## Abstinence-Until-Marriage Programs in the United States

Since 1996, nearly $1 billion in state and federal funding has been allocated for abstinence-only education despite a lack of evidence supporting the effectiveness of this approach (Hauser 2004; Kirby [1997] 2000; Manlove et al. 2004; "New Studies" 2005; "Sex Education" 2002; "Waxman Report" 2004). . . .

Despite the declining teen pregnancy rates during the 1990s, 34 percent of teenage girls get pregnant at least once before they reach age 20, resulting in more than 850,000 teen pregnancies a year—the vast majority of which are unintended. At this level, the United States has the highest rate of teen pregnancy in the fully industrialized world. Roughly 9 million new STIs also occur among teenagers and young adults in the United States annually (Children's Defense Fund 2004; Henshaw 2004; "New Studies" 2005). By law, abstinence-only programs must have as their "exclusive purpose, teaching the social, psychological and health gains to be realized by abstaining from sexual activity." While this is a desirable option for young people, it is also problematic for many. By promoting abstinence-only education that omits complete, medically accurate information, U.S. policy ignores research, public opinion and the experience of other countries about what actually works to prevent teenage pregnancy and STIs.

The Waxman Report (December 2004), which examined school-based sex education curricula, concluded that many young people are receiving medically inaccurate or misleading information, often in direct contradiction to the findings of government scientists. Since 1999, several million children ages 9 to 18 have participated in the more than 100 federally-funded abstinence programs. After reviewing the 13 most commonly used curricula, Congressman Waxman's staff concluded that two of the curricula were accurate but 11 others . . . contain unproved claims, subjective conclusions or outright falsehoods regarding reproductive health, gender traits and when life begins (Connolly 2004; see also "Texas Teens Increased Sex After Abstinence Program" 2005; Waxman 2004).

In May 2002, the House of Representatives passed H.R. 473, the Personal Responsibility, Work and Family Protection Bill, which renewed funding of abstinence-only programs at the level of $50 million a year for the next five years. While there was opposition to the bill by many, including Rep. Lois Capps (D-Calif.) who argued that "abstinence programs are exaggerating the failure rate of condoms" and using "terror techniques to keep teens from having sex," the bill passed . . . with committee Republicans arguing that "it would be impossible to agree on what information is medically accurate."

### Americans Teaching Fear

In abstinence-until-marriage materials, sex is often equated with death, disease and danger, fear surfaces as the primary message and tactic used to persuade young people to steer clear of sex before or outside of marriage. The abstinence-only video, "No Second Chance," used for middle-school Sex Respect audiences, juxtaposes discussions of having sex outside of marriage with images of men dying from AIDS. In "No Second Chance," an evangelical sex educator compares sex outside of marriage—not to the all-American game of baseball—but to playing Russian Roulette. She tells a classroom of young people that: "Every time you have sex, it's like pulling the trigger—the only difference is, in Russian Roulette, you only have one in six chances of getting killed." When one boy asks, "what if I have sex before marriage?" he is told, "Well, I guess you'll just have to be prepared to die. And you'll probably take with you your spouse and one or more of your children." James Dobson's organization, Focus on the Family, distributes "No Second Chance" and its companion, "Sex, Lies, and the Truth." Both have been widely used in public, as well as Christian, schools throughout the United States (Kantor 1994; Mast 1983; "Teaching Fear" 1996). According to the organization's website (1999–2005), "Sex Respect" is now being used in 50 states and 23 countries.

Founder and president of the National Abstinence Clearing House in Sioux Falls, South Dakota, Leslie Unruh uses snakes to teach about STDs and the dangers of using condoms. "As she uncoils her nest of rubber vipers: Herbie Herpes, Wally Wart, Hester Hepatitis, Albert AIDS, Lucy Loss of Reputation—and don't forget—poor Pregnant Peggy Sue, she tells young people about the risks of sex before marriage." (Sternberg 2002) "Condoms," she says, "are overrated. 'We tell them condoms won't protect your heart, that latex won't stop human papilloma virus.'" (See also Brody 2003; quoted in Sternberg 2002.) Another abstinence-only curriculum, *Abstinence Works: A Notebook on Pre-Marital Chastity,* invokes the image of Mother Teresa (Driscol 1990). Displayed on its 1990 cover is a picture of Mother Teresa on one side and a picture of a skeleton on the other. Surrounding them in bold italics are the words:

*Today I set before you Life or Death, Blessing or Curse.
Oh, that you would Choose Life that you and your
children might Live.*

—*Deuteronomy 30:19*

Leslie Kantor, former director of the SIECUS
Community Advocacy Project, conducted an extensive content analysis of abstinence-only sex-
ed programs produced and promoted by Christian Right groups that are used in public schools.
She concluded:

> *These programs omit the most fundamental infor-
> mation on contraception and disease prevention,
> perpetuate medical misinformation, and rely on
> religious doctrine and images of fear and shame in
> discouraging sexual activity.*

Given this introduction to sexuality in increasing numbers of public schools across the United
States (Dailard 2000; Landry et al. 1999), how
are young Americans conditioned to think about
and negotiate their own and others' sexuality?
Once they marry—if they choose to marry—how
will they deal with their sexuality and the sexuality of their spouses? Even within the context of a
heterosexual marriage, how are such negative—
even terrifying images—suddenly transformed?
And what about those who do not live within the
confines of a heterosexual marriage; those who
are gay, lesbian or transgendered; or those who
find themselves without a partner, be it through
death, divorce or never marrying? Where should
the lines between private belief and public policy
be drawn?

The Religious Right represents some 10 percent of the adult American population. Their
concerns about teenage sex and teen pregnancy
clearly resonate with a larger public, but their
solutions do not. Their influence on social policy
is disproportionate to their numbers; the vast
majority of the American public is supportive of sex education. A 2004 report on "Public
Support for Comprehensive Sexuality Education"
indicates that 93 percent of parents of junior
high school students and 91 percent of parents
of high school students believe it is very or some-

what important to have sex education as part
of the school curriculum.[1] And young people?
Eighty-two percent of adolescents ages 15–17
and 75 percent of young people ages 18–24 want
more information on "how to protect yourself
from HIV/AIDS and other STDs," "the different types of birth control that are available," and
"how to bring up sexual health issues such as
STDs and birth control with a partner" (Hoff
2003: pp. 70–71 and 111–112).

The electorate likewise shows support for
comprehensive sexuality education: 63 percent
of voters said they were more likely to vote for a
candidate who supports comprehensive sex education, while only 10 percent of engaged voters
supported abstinence-until-marriage programs
in public schools ("Mobilizing Support" 2002).
While 30 percent of American adults agree with
the statement "the federal government should
fund sex education programs that have 'abstaining from sexual activity' as their only purpose,"
67 percent of adults agree with the statement that
"the money should be used to fund more comprehensive sex education programs that include information on how to obtain and use condoms and
other contraceptives" (*Sex Education in America*
2000: 7). Although 28 percent of American adults
agreed that "providing information about how
to obtain and use condoms and other contraception might encourage teens to have sexual intercourse," 65 percent of adults believed that "not
providing information about how to obtain and
use condoms and other contraception might mean
more teens will have unsafe sexual intercourse"
(*Sex Education in America* 2004:22).

Even conservative Christians tend to support comprehensive sex education. A 1999 survey showed that 8 in 10 conservative Christians
supported comprehensive sex education in high
schools and 7 in 10 supported it in middle schools
(Survey of America's Views 1999). Former President and CEO of SIECUS for 12 years and current
president of "The Religious Institute on Sexual
Morality, Justice and Healing," Deborah Haffner
agrees, arguing that the majority of evangelicals

support comprehensive sex education that includes abstinence as an option.[2]

In spite of millions of dollars in funding, to date, there are no sound empirical data that indicate that abstinence-only programs are effective; in fact, there have been very few evaluation studies of abstinence-until-marriage programs (Kirby 2001; Manlove 2004; "New State Evaluations" 2004). Empirical data also suggest that to the degree that an effect of comprehensive sex education has been identifiable, it has been found to *postpone* initiation of sexual intercourse; reduce the frequency of intercourse and number of sexual partners; increase the use of contraceptives; and reduce pregnancy rates among teens (Kirby [1997]; 2001; Schorr 1998; "Teaching Fear" 1994). Why, then, do abstinence-only approaches appeal to many politicians and policy-makers, even when the majority of Americans support comprehensive sex education? What are the consequences of implementing abstinence-only approaches compared with comprehensive sex education that includes abstinence as a reasonable and often desirable option? No one is debating whether abstinence should be presented as a viable option and reasonable choice. What critics are questioning is how *abstinence-until-marriage* programs came to masquerade as *education* in public schools. . . .

## International Consequences: From Domestic to Foreign Policy

[R]ecent actions to limit reproductive health reveal the ways in which the United States is retreating from its own previous position and that of its traditional allies around the world (LaFranchi 2004). On his first day in office in January 2001, President Bush reimposed the "global gag rule" that had been instituted by President Reagan in 1984 and revoked by President Clinton in 1993. Imposing the United States' position on the abortion practices of other countries, however, reflects neither U.S. law nor U.S. public opinion. It also significantly impedes women's access to family planning and contraceptive services by prohibiting U.S. family planning assistance to hospitals and health clinics in developing countries that also provide abortions or abortion-related information (Cohen 2001).

At the U.N. Children's Summit in May 2002, U.S. Health Secretary Tommy Thompson argued for the teaching of abstinence as the preferred approach to sex education. According to a CBS World News report, "The three-day conference was long on rhetoric about the sanctity of childhood but short on consensus. Delegates at a U.N. session on children haggled . . . over a final declaration with the United States, the Vatican and Islamic states in favor of sexual abstinence and against any hint of abortion for adolescents" (Ireland 2002; U.N. Children's Summit Hits Snag 2002). Susan Cohen, writing for the Guttmacher Institute, reported that: "The United States delegation, siding with the Sudan, Iran, and Iraq" (and sliding perilously close to Bush's "evil axis"), "both stupefied and angered the European (EU) and Latin American delegations which finally voted against the U.S. position." Adrienne Germain, president of the International Women's Health Coalition, bluntly stated:

*This alliance shows the depths of perversity of the [U.S.] position. On the one hand, we're presumably blaming these countries for unspeakable acts of terrorism, and at the same time we are allying ourselves with them in the oppression of women.*

—quoted in Cohen 2002

In its closing statement at the summit, the EU delivered a strong rejoinder to the United States. "Young people should be empowered to make appropriate and safe choices about their sexual behavior." . . .

Likewise, in the seven-day Asian and Pacific Population Conference held in Bangkok in December 2002, the American delegation engaged in an acrimonious debate with all of the other countries over abortion, sex education and methods of birth control (Dao 2002). . . . Rejecting proposals by the Bush Administration, 32 Asian nations reaffirmed the historic agreement reached at the 1994 International Conference on Population and Development (ICPD). They also agreed on an action plan to advance reproductive and sexual health and rights across the region (Caucus for ICPD 2002; Statement by Obaid 2002; "U.S. Fails to Block" 2002).

"It is sad to see the U.S. move from being a leader on these issues, to that of a minority voice," said Ninuk Widyantoro of the Women's Health Foundation in Indonesia:

> *Sexual and reproductive health is one of the most important social issues of the millennium. We know that the U.S. delegation does not even represent the views of the majority of the American people. The current U.S. administration is being held hostage by an extreme conservative minority with little regard for the health, welfare and freedoms of women. . . . We hope that in the future, U.S. delegations . . . will more accurately represent the humanitarian values of the women and men of their nation.*
>
> —quoted in Dao 2001

Such positions have distanced the United States even further from the worldwide consensus on reproductive and sexual health issues that the United States had once been instrumental in shaping. . . .

## Cross-National Data on Teen Sexual Behavior

The United States leads the industrialized world in its high rates of teenage pregnancies, abortions and STDs. Although the U.S. *teen pregnancy rate* has decreased during the past decade, it is still nine times higher than that of the Netherlands, nearly five times higher than in Germany, and nearly four times higher than the rate in France. The *teen birth rate* is also much higher in the United States, nearly 11 times higher than in the Netherlands, nearly five times higher than the rate in France, and nearly four times higher than in Germany.[3] The *teen abortion rate* is nearly eight times higher in the United States than in Germany, nearly seven

times higher than in the Netherlands, and nearly three times higher than in France (Feijoo 2001). Much higher rates for HIV, syphilis, gonorrhea and chlamydia likewise distinguish the United States (Darroch et al. 2001; Feijoo 2001).

Cross-national studies reveal that differential rates in teen pregnancy are influenced by cultural attitudes towards and education about sexuality, the accessibility of health care and contraception, the relationship between religion and politics, and the degree of economic inequality (Jones et al. 1996). With one of the highest rates of infant mortality, child death, child poverty and economic inequality between rich and poor in the industrialized world, the United States is not faring well (Brouwer 1998; Henshaw 2004; Kids Count 2000; "New Studies" 2005; Shapiro 1992; Singh et al. 2000; *State of America's Children* 2004). Rather than deal with these complex and interrelated issues, however, U.S. policy too often addresses teen pregnancy as an isolated social problem and increasingly advises young girls to *"just say no."*

### Just Say No

Abstinence-only advocates advise young people to not have sex; their aim, however, is to curtail sexual activity for anyone not in a heterosexual marriage. Uneasy about teen sexuality, homosexuality, the increase in out-of-wedlock births, and the erosion of the patriarchal, nuclear family, they emphasize the dangers of sex and the hazards of sexual relationships outside of marriage (Gallagher 1999). Fear rather than affirmation, rejection rather than acceptance, and denial rather than knowledge about sexuality tend to dominate abstinence-only materials, and serve as a chilling effect on contemporary American research and social policy.

For example, in 1987 a number of institutes, . . . supported a proposal by Edward Laumann, et al., to undertake an ambitious study of sexuality in America. Scientists . . . "wanted more general studies of sexuality to then examine such issues as teen pregnancy, sexual dysfunction and child abuse." But soon after the contract was awarded, the researchers noted that (America's) "national squeamishness about sex" began to emerge (Michael et al. 1994: 27; Nussbaum 1997). Government officials in particular were squeamish about the inclusion of questions about masturbation—evidenced also in the forced resignation of former U.S. Surgeon General Jocelyn Elders for using the M-word (masturbation). Political battles followed. . . . As a result, the researchers conducted the study through private money; the sample was reduced from 20,000 to 3,500 adults, and no one under the age of 18 was included in the sample (Boonstra 2001; Nussbaum 1997:225). . . .

In contrast to the current U.S. trends in legislating abstinence-only policies, Denmark—and many other countries both in the industrialized and developing world—continue to implement more comprehensive research and sex education programs, believing that it is important to inform and educate young people about sexuality and contraception. They believe that adolescents have a right to information (Alford 2005).

## Attitudes toward Teen Sexuality in the United States and Denmark

### Case Study: The United States

Since the 1960s, Religious Right political groups have waged a campaign against the teaching of comprehensive sex education in public schools. . . . Phyllis Schafly, head of the conservative Eagle Forum, went as far as to argue that exposing children in public schools to sex ed may constitute child abuse (1985). Their position was clear: any discussion about sex belonged in the home, not in the schools.

By the 1980s, however, it was clear that the Religious Right was having little success in removing sex education from the schools.[4] As a result, conservative Christian groups shifted strategies and began to promote "abstinence-only" programs in the public schools. . . . Through a range of educational materials, videotapes and promotional advertising, they have effectively promoted curricula that teach fear and withhold vital information about prevention of AIDS and teen pregnancy.

Programs such as "Sex Respect," "Facing Reality" and curricula developed by Teen Aid initially . . . received federal Title XX funding through the Adolescent Family Life Act (AFLA). . . . The state and federal money used to fund "Sex-Respect" was essential, according to a writer for the *Conservative Digest*:

> . . . *the Adolescent Family Life Act was expressly for the purpose of diverting [federal] money that would otherwise go to Planned Parenthood into groups with traditional values. This noble purpose has certainly been fulfilled here.*
>
> —quoted in (Teaching Fear 1994: 11)

While rates of pregnancy, AIDS and other sexually transmitted diseases remain alarmingly high among America's youth, opponents of sex education have become increasingly successful in censoring vital, life-saving information that has proven effective in dealing with these problems (Kantor 1994).

### Beyond Sex: Teaching Traditional Gender Roles

Central to the sex ed debate is the Religious Right's attempt to preserve patriarchy and to privilege men's rights over women's rights and parental rights over children's rights (Bendroth 1993; Hawley 1994; Howland 1997; Marty and Appleby 1999; Riesebrodt 1993). The idea of equality between men and women is threatening to many advocates of abstinence-only policies. Not only are they working to prevent sex before or outside of marriage, they are also fighting to preserve the traditional, patriarchal family. The pro-marriage movement goes hand-in-hand with this (Gallagher 1999; Stacey 2002) as does the promotion of old-fashioned gender-role norms.

As one reads through the abstinence-only materials, one finds an old and mixed message. It is the story of sex as the tale of predator and prey—and women, beware. Men are considered to be sexual beings, who beyond a certain point, cannot hold back. Therefore, women must. . . .

The Religious Right's concern about sex and sexuality focuses on issues regarding social order and control—especially over women's bodies and desires. The adage that "good girls don't" but "real boys do" continues to engender the double-standard that defines male and female in opposition to one another, although many of the abstinence-only curricula are pushing for abstinence for all pre-marrieds. This framework, however, reveals contradictions. From a conservative Christian perspective, humans are not animals (which is at the crux of the evolution-creation debate), rather they stand only a little lower than the angels. Yet, they are also seen as no different from animals driven by sexual instincts: once aroused, there is no turning back. These distinctions sound very familiar because they are part of the "sexual wisdom" of American culture that goes well beyond the confines of conservative Christian thinking. . . .

The renewed efforts to undermine sex education are not just about sex; they are part of a broader challenge to public education which centers around parents' vs. children's and states' rights.

### Gender and Sexual Politics of the Religious Right

The attempts of the Religious Right in the United States to preserve parental rights over those of children's rights reveal the kind of hostility directed towards women and children. In his critique of the Fourth World Conference on Women, Gary Bauer, president of the Family Research Council, wrote that feminists wanted "to enshrine the 'rights' of adolescents to information and medical services where sex and AIDS were concerned, without 'interference' from parents" and that although, "parents rights were not completely overruled, they were subordinated to 'the best interests of the child.'" Moreover, "these radical women are trying to achieve greater equality between women and men in economic and po-

litical spheres, so that women can better support their families and children" (Bauer 1995). . . .

### Different Discourses: The Danish Approach

The dominant Danish discourse about sexuality and reproductive and teens' rights is strikingly different from the dominant discourse in the United States (Adolescent Sexual Health 2001; see also Heins 2001; "Sexuality Rights" 1995). In Denmark, the rights of adolescents to sexual and reproductive information and choice are framed within the context of a *social democracy* and have been embedded in Danish legislation since 1966. . . .

*Denmark became the first country in the world to grant young people, regardless of age, access to contraception and contraception counseling. . . . It's about human rights: in order for you to act responsibly, you have to have choices—government or parents or whoever the decision makers are cannot demand responsible behavior of teenagers or of the population if they don't give them an opportunity to make their own choices based on sufficient information. . . . We have developed an enabling environment for young people to support themselves in the process of making their sexual identity and realizing themselves as becoming adults—and sexuality is an important part of becoming an adult. . . . Young people have the right to ask and they have a right to be met with respect . . . they shouldn't be let down, they should be supported. (Rasmussen, 1998)*

Rasmussen also argued that progressive social policies recognizing adolescent sexuality have not promoted promiscuity.

*From the outside, (it seems that) we in Denmark have the most liberal system of adolescent sexual and reproductive health and rights. Seen from the inside, however, we don't tend to think that we have a very liberal system. We tend to think that we have a very practical and pragmatic approach to the fact that young people do start having sexual relations somewhere in their teens. In Denmark, actually rather late: around 16.7 for boys and even 16.9 for girls, and it really hasn't changed very much over time. And 80 percent of young people use contraception at first intercourse. That may not be enough but it's a very favorable situation. (See also Knudsen 1999.)*

Historically, dominant Danish attitudes towards sexuality were not so different from mainstream American ones (Centerwall 1995; "Sexual Rights" 1995). Within the past three decades, however, we find Danes much more open about sexuality and contraceptive use than Americans (David et al. 1990). The Danish government has mandated the teaching of comprehensive sex education as part of the general school curriculum. These programs tend to be quite pragmatic and straightforward, without being graphic, which is hard for many Americans to envision.

One of the sex ed videos used in elementary schools, "Where Do Babies Come From," is a cartoon-animated video that presents four children talking, laughing and giggling with one another as they share questions and information about where babies come from. Covering female and male anatomy, menstruation, intercourse and birthing, the video presents a lot of information in a very funny yet direct way. When I showed this to my college class, students said that it was the best—the most informative and the funniest— "documentary" they had ever seen on sex education. The video demystifies sex and invites the audience to laugh with the children and couple, who are loving, affectionate—and yes—sexual with one another. The message reflects the reality that kids are curious and have lots of questions, that talking about sex can be both embarrassing and fun, and that it's as much about feelings, caring and love as it is about biology.

## Young People's Perspectives

Individual interviews and co-ed classroom and small-group discussions (both same sex and co-ed) with approximately 100 Danish and 300 American teens revealed significant differences in how they spoke about sexuality and relationships. The Danish teens tended to talk about sex in terms of mutual pleasure and responsibility whereas the American teens tended to speak in

terms of performance and achievement (as in "feeling inadequate if they didn't *achieve* orgasm"). When asked when "no means no," both Danish boys and girls were quite clear: "when someone says no, that means no." Their language did not assume that the male was the predator and the female the prey who was the one pressured into having sex. For example, one 15-year-old boy in the presence of his male and female classmates said:

> If I don't feel like it, then I want that to be OK. If my girlfriend doesn't like something, well then we try something else. If one of us doesn't want to, then we find another way. Or we go for a walk.

A 15-year-old girl in the same class commented:

> If a girl says no and she really means yes, well then she's the one who misses out—she could have said yes if she wanted to.

In discussions with American teenagers, there was much less consensus. Deciding when "no meant no" was seen as a very confusing judgment call, and there was greater tolerance for—or at least more willingness to not speak out against— sexually aggressive behavior. In the American classrooms, those who came right out and said "if someone says no, that means no" were in the minority. Typically there would be a prolonged conversation about whether a person (always assumed to be a female) was clear in her own mind, whether she really meant no when she said no, how forcefully or frequently she said no, whether she was giving double messages either verbally or non-verbally, what the girl was wearing, and how she was acting when she said no. The same ambivalence or confusion was expressed in small-group discussions and individual interviews as well.

The discourse among American teenagers also was gendered in ways that the Danish discourse about sexual responsibility and responsiveness was not. In the American context, only females were referred to as saying "no" or being ambivalent about having sex; not once was the male pronoun used to speak of someone saying "no." When it came to talking about women's ambivalence, the discussion often led to girls and women being untrustworthy rather than confused or conflicted about what they wanted, or their being unclear in their expression of what they did and did not want. The blame for *mis*communication was placed, as much by other women as by men, on the female. Often the conversation in the American classroom would fall back on: "I have known girls who tease men;" ". . . who say no when they mean yes;" "You can't blame the guys." "If the girl teases a guy, then she has to be ready to get what she gets." "After a certain point, you can't expect a guy to just stop." In the Danish context, both male and female teenagers put responsibility on the individual to say what he or she meant, and they held the individual responsible for *his or her* actions (including contraceptive choices). In the American context, more responsibility and blame was placed on the female especially if something went wrong. . . .

This seemed to be much less of a quandary for the Danish girls interviewed. While some of them had sex that was not particularly pleasurable, they were less likely to have experienced unwanted or forced sex and much more likely to know what they wanted and didn't want. They also were much less likely to confuse love and sexual desire. For the Danish young people and their parents, it was OK to have sex with someone once you turned 16 or 17. Validation did not depend on how much you were in love with the other person, but how responsible you were in making decisions. Becoming sexual was considered a part of normal development, of growing up.

> Love is such a strong word. I have a boyfriend and I care about him. We're having sex and that's OK with my parents. They know. They just want us to be protected. He can sleep over at my house. But, I can't say I love him. Love and hate are such strong words. My parents, and my sisters and my brother— I love them. I've known them all my life. But my boyfriend, I've only known him a few months. We

need to know each other more. It should be really deep when you say that.

> *—17-year-old Danish girl*

> I really love my boyfriend. So I think it's OK I'm having sex with him. But if my parents caught me, they would kill me!

> *—17-year-old American girl*

Lene, the Danish girl, takes love quite seriously. It is not a word to be thrown about easily. Sex, on the other hand, is not a big deal. It's fun, but you need to take care to use protection so you don't get AIDS or an infection. Elena, the American girl emphasizes love. Because she's in love, it's OK to have sex. Elena is both sincere and adamant when she says, "I really love my boyfriend," but then she leans forward and whispers, "But if my parents caught me, they would kill me. If they knew, it would be all over. I don't know why they can't understand how much we love each other."

Another striking contrast between the Danish and American teenagers was their attitude towards alcohol and sex. While the American teenagers reported that they or their friends often drink in order to lower their inhibitions to have sex, the Danish teenagers believed that alcohol and sex were not a good match. A small group of 15- to 17-year-old Danish girls commented:

> It ruins it if you're drunk I think. If the boy's very drunk he can't get it up. He can't get [an] erection and that ruins it a lot. So I think you shouldn't do it if you're drunk. And you forget the condom if you're drunk. It's easier to have good sex if you're not drunk.

A 15-year-old boy concurred,

> If you're drunk, you can't do it very well and it doesn't feel as good. If I really like a girl, I don't drink before we have sex.

The Danish girls were also more open in talking about sexuality, communication and intimacy:

> But I think you have to be comfortable. If you feel totally comfortable and safe with the person, you do more things. So I think you can have sex and all,

but the more safe and the more comfortable you get with the person the more wild the things get the more open you get with your boyfriend.

*—16-year-old Danish girl*

. . . What both Danish and American young people emphasized was their desire for more information and discussion about feelings, emotions and relationships. They wanted more communication with their parents and teachers. Many of them faced problems at home: a parent's alcoholism, abuse, depression that often made that communication difficult.

For example, Laura, an American 14-year-old girl shared her story just after attending an abstinence-only assembly at her rural school in central Pennsylvania. . . .

My Mom got pregnant when she was 16 and had to really struggle. Then when my older sister got pregnant at 16, my Mom was really angry. She wouldn't talk to her about sex or getting pregnant; and she doesn't talk to me. She just yells and tells me "not to do it." You can't have a reasonable conversation with her about it. And now it's really crazy at home with my sister's baby, and everyone crying and screaming. It's nuts. I think we need to know more about sex not less.

Laura felt left in the lurch both at home and at school when it came to sex education. The school counselor who sat in with us agreed: "They deserve more—better." Both American and Danish teenagers wanted parents and teachers to trust them more, respect them more, and teach them more. They believed they needed more, rather than less, information, but it was the American teenagers who pointed to the number of their friends, sisters or school mates who had gotten pregnant as proof. . . .

### Adolescent Rights as Human Rights: The Danish Case

. . . Since the 1960s, with the activism of the labor, women's, and disabilities' movements, young people's rights were also recognized and given a more prominent place in Danish society.

*During the '60s, the Danish Welfare Society . . . realized that young people were equal members of society and should share the same benefits of belonging to society as adults. If we want people to behave responsibly, we have to give them the chance to . . . The government saw the benefits of this—if you give them (young people) the option, you can also demand that they behave responsibly.*

*—Rasmussen*

This was a recurrent theme in interviews with teachers, as well as with sex educators and professionals working in the area of reproductive health. Bjarne Rasmussen, AIDS-Secretariat at the Frederiksberg Hospital . . . explained in a 1998 interview:

*It's important not to cheat young people. . . . To be honest in sexual education, especially in the schools because if the young people find out that you are cheating them, they won't believe you later on. It's very, very important to get a discussion going. It's important to make the young people understand that they make their own choice. They must make an active choice and say 'I want to use contraception' or 'I don't want to use contraception' because they have made the choice and they are involved.*

### Conclusion

Who then is going too far? The Danes in providing information or the Americans in withholding information? While the onset of sexual activity for Danes is similar to that of Americans, both averaging around 16.7 years, Danish teenagers are more likely to use contraception and are much less likely to get pregnant, have an abortion or contract a sexually transmitted disease. There are also proportionately fewer Danish 11 to 14 year olds who have been engaged in sexual activity (B. Rasmussen [1997] 1998). . . .

In the American context, special interest groups vie for power and often have disproportionate influence. This is the case with sexuality education and reproductive health in general. Numerous mainstream organizations, including medical, government, and religious agencies, are supportive of comprehensive sexuality education. Many signed a letter to President Bush stating that they are committed to responsible sexuality education for young people that includes age-appropriate, medically accurate information about both abstinence and contraception, [and] urge [him] to reconsider increasing funding for unproven abstinence-only-until-marriage programs."[5] And while new bills are being introduced to better support comprehensive sexuality education, at the moment, abstinence-only programs continue to dominate the agenda.

Abstinence-only proponents not only provide medical misinformation and promote fear and ignorance, they also fail to plan, fund, and implement effective social policy that could more effectively curb teen pregnancy and the spread of STDs—and provide better economic, educational, and health opportunities for all young people. Experts on teen pregnancy and child welfare . . . convincingly argue that teen pregnancy is less about young girls and their sex lives than about restricted horizons and the boundaries of hope. Yet, the Religious Right continues to blame the "fallen girl/woman," the feminization of men, the decline of two-parent families, homosexuality, and the media for the ills of our society rather than economic and structural forces that perpetuate inequality between men and women, and between the enriched and impoverished classes. In the battle over sexuality and choice, it's girls' and women's bodies, lives, and livelihoods that are all too often sacrificed blamed, marginalized and held accountable for creating the problem of teen pregnancy. . . .

[F]amily planning, reproductive and sexual health, and economic well-being are vital concerns for individuals, communities, and nations. The United States which is the only country that legislates and funds abstinence-only-until marriage programs in public schools, also leads the world in its high rates of teenage pregnancies, abortions, and STDs. Moreover, abstinence-only-until-marriage programs have been taught for over two decades and yet there is still no peer-reviewed research that proves it is effective.[6] While rates of pregnancy, AIDS, and other sexually transmitted diseases remain alarmingly high among America's youth and people in the developing world, opponents of sexuality education and reproductive health are trying to censor vital information and services both at home and abroad.

The Religious Right has not achieved its agenda, but it has produced a chilling effect on comprehensive sexuality education. . . . In the interest of all children, as well as family well-being, we need to take seriously a broad-based approach to both social problems and social policy that is based on empirical evidence and a recognition of the pluralistic society in which we live. This is what democracy is all about. In the final analysis, rather than having gone too far, the United States has not gone nearly far enough in providing reliable information, education and health care to our children.

### NOTES

1. Only 4 percent of parents of junior high school students and 6 percent of parents of high school students believe sexuality education should not be taught in school ("Public Support" 2004).

2. Personal communication, January 2005.

3. Adolescent child-bearing is more common in the United States (22 percent of women reported having a child before age 20) than in Great Britain (15 percent), Canada (11 percent), France (6 percent) and Sweden (4 percent). And the differences are even greater when comparing births to younger teenagers. A greater proportion of U.S. teenagers did not use contraception at either the first or most recent intercourse (25 percent and 20 percent respectively) than that reported in France (11 percent and 12 percent), Great Britain (21 percent and 4 percent), Sweden (22 percent and 7 percent) (Adolescent Sexual Health 2002; Darroch et al. 2001; Feijoo 2001; Jones et al. 1996; "Teenage Sexual and Reproductive 2001).

4. This fieldwork included classroom observations; class, small group, and one-on-one interviews with teenagers; and interviews with parents, teachers, and sex educators. In the case of the Central Pennsylvania School, 240 9th through 12th graders also filled out

surveys in the week following the abstinence-only assemblies sponsored by Heartbeat Community Services. This number included all those in one of four health classes or a quarter of the high school population.

5. In 1981, a national poll indicated that 70 percent of parents favored sex-ed programs in the public schools; a 1985 poll showed 75 percent of adults approving sex-ed in the public high schools, with 52 percent approving of such programs in grades 4 through 8; most respondents also believed that programs should cover a wider range of topics, including teaching about birth control, the biology of reproduction, the nature of sexual intercourse and abortion ("Teaching Fear" 1994).

6. An evangelical psychologist, James Dobson heads up the largest Christian-Right Organization in the United States, Focus on the Family (FOF), with magazines reaching 3 million readers, and a daily radio program reaching more than 5 million people on 3,000 stations worldwide. He is also author of *Dare to Discipline,* one of the leading child care manuals sold in the United States.

## REFERENCES

Allord. S., N. Cheetham and D. Hauser. 2005. *Science and Success in Developing Countries: Holistic Programs That Work to Prevent Teen Pregnancy, HIV & Sexually Transmitted Infections.* Washington, D.C.: Advocates for Youth.

Bendroth, Margaret Lamberts. 1993. *Fundamentalism and Gender, 1875 to the Present.*: Yale University Press.

Boonstra, Heather. 2004. "Abstinence-Promotion and the U.S. Approach to HIV/AIDS Prevention Overseas." *Issues in Brief.* The Alan Guttmacher Institute.

Brouwer, Steve. 1998. *Sharing the Pie: A Citizen's Guide to Wealth and Power.* Henry Holt & Co.

Children's Defense Fund. 2004. "Children's Defense Fund Blasts Withholding of Report on Hunger." Press Release: Oct. 24.

Cohen, Susan. June 2001. "Global Gag Rule: Exporting Antiabortion Ideology at the Expense of American Values." *The Guttmacher Report on Public Policy,* 4(3).

Connolly, Ceci. 2004. "Some Abstinence Programs Mislead Teens, Report Says." *Washington Post,* December 2, A01.

Dailard, Cynthia. April 2000. "Fueled by Campaign Promises, Drive Intensifies to Boost Abstinence-Only Education Funds." *The Guttmacher Report on Public* Policy, 3(2).

Dao, James. 2002. "Over U.S. Protest, Asian Group Approves Family Planning Goals." *New York Times,* December 18.

Darroch, Jacqueline, Singh Susheela, Jennifer J. Frost and the Study Team. November/December 2001. "Differences in Teenage Pregnancy Rates Among Five Developed Countries." *Family Planning Perspectives,* 33(6). The Alan Guttmacher Institute.

David, H. A., J. M, Morgall, M. Olser, et al. 1990. "United States and Denmark: Different Approaches to Health Care and Family Planning." *Studies in Family Planning,* 21:1–19.

Driscoll, Patricia. 1990. *Abstinence Works: A Notebook on Pre-Marital Chastity.* Womanity Publications.

Gallagher, Maggie. 1999. *The Age of Unwed Mothers Is Teen Pregnancy the Problem? A Report to the Nation.* New York: Institute for American Values. (http://www.americanvalues.org/Teen.PDF).

Hauser, Debra. 2004. Five Years of Abstinence-Only-Until-Marriage Education: Assessing the Impact. Washington, DC: Advocates for Youth.

Hawley, John, editor. 1994. *Fundamentalism and Gender.* Oxford University Press.

Heins, Marjorie. 2001. *Not in Front of the Children.* Hill & Wang.

Henshaw, S. K. 2004. *U.S. Teenage Pregnancy Statistics with Comparative Statistics for Women Aged 20–24.* New York: The Guttmacher institute.

Hoff, Tina, et al. 2003. *National Survey of Adolescents and Young Adults: Sexual Health Knowledge, Attitudes, and Experiences.* "National Survey of Adolescents and Young Adults: Sexual Health Knowledge, Attitudes, and Experiences." Henry J. Kaiser Family Foundation.

Howland, Courtney, editor. 1999. *Religious Fundamentalisms and the Human Rights of Women.* St. Martin's Press.

Ireland, Doug. May 27, 2002. "US and Evil Axis—Allies for Abstinence." *The Nation.*

Jones, Elise, et al. 1996. *Teenage Pregnancy in Industrialized Nations.* Yale University Press.

Kantor, Leslie. August/September 1994. "Attacks on Public School Sexuality Education Programs: 1993–94 School Year," *SIECUS Report.*

Kirby, Douglas. 1997. *No Easy Answers: Research Findings on Programs to Reduce Teen Pregnancy.* Washington, D.C. National Campaign Prevent Teen Pregnancy.

———. 2001. *Emerging Answers: Research Findings on Programs to Reduce Teen Pregnancy.* Washington, DC: National Campaign to Prevent Teen Pregnancy.

Knudsen, Lisbeth. 1999. "Recent Fertility Trends in Denmark." *Report 11.* Danish Center for Demographic Research.

Landry, D. J., L. Kaeser and C. L. Richards. 1999. Abstinence promotion and the provision of information about contraception in public school district sexuality education policies. *Family Planning Perspectives* 31(6):280–286.

LaFranci, Howard. 2004. "On Family Planning, U.S. vs. Much of the World: De-emphasis of Contraception Runs Contrary to Global Goals." *Christian Science Monitor.* March 30.

Manlove, Jennifer, Angela R. Papillio and Erum Ikramullah. September 2004. "Not Yet: Programs Designed to Delay First Sex Among Teens." Washington, DC: National Campaign to Prevent Teen Pregnancy

Marty, Martin, and Scott Appleby (eds.). 1993. *Fundamentalisms and Society,* Vol 2. University of Chicago Press.

Mast, Coleen Kelly. 1977. "Sex Respect: The Option of True Sexual Feeling," *Student Handbook* (rev. ed.) 7. 90, Bradley, IL: Respect Incorporated.

Michael, Robert T., John H. Gagnon, Edward O. Laumann and Gina Kolata. 1994. *Sex in America: A Definitive Survey.* Little, Brown.

"Mobilizing Support for Sex Education: New Messages and Techniques." 2002. New York: The Othmer Institute of Planned Parenthood of NYC.

"New State Evaluations Show Federally Funded Abstinence-Only Programs Have Little Effect." September 27, 2004. Washington, D.C.: Advocates for Youth.

"New Studies Signal Dangers of Limiting Teen Access to Birth Control Information and Services: Researchers and Medical Experts Urge New Congress and State Legislatures to Heed Data." January 18, 2005. Media Release. New York: The Guttmacher Institute.

*No Second Chance.* Jeremiah Films.

Nussbaum, Martha. 1997. *Cultivating Humanity: A Classical Defense of Reform in Liberal Education.* Harvard University Press.

"Public Support for Comprehensive Sexuality Education." 2004. *SIECUS Fact Sheet.* (www.siecus.org/pubsfact/fact0017.htm)

Rasmussen, Bjarne. 1997. "Young People's Sexual Behavior," *Danish National Survey and Report.* AIDS Sekretariat, Frederiksberg Hospital, Denmark.

Rasmussen, Bjarne. June 1998. AIDS Sekretariat, Interview with the author.

Rasmussen, Nell. June 1998. Director of the Danish Family Planning Association, Copenhagen, Interview with author.

Riesebrodt, Martin. 1993. *Pious Passion: the emergence of modern fundamentalism in Iran and the United States.* University of California Press.

Schafly, Phyllis, editor. 1985. *Child Abuse in the Classroom.* Crossway Books.

*Sex Education in America: A View from Inside the Nation's Classrooms.* 2000. Menlo Park, CA: The Kaiser Family Foundation.

Schorr, Lisbeth. 1988. *Within Our Reach.* Anchor Press.

"Sex Education: Politicians, Parents, Teachers, and Teens." Issues in Brief. The Alan Guttmacher Institute. (www.agi-usa.org/pubs/ib_2-01.html)

Sex Respect Website (http://www.sexrespect.com/ProgramOrig.html).

Shapiro. 1992. *We're Number One.* Vintage Books.

Singh, Susheela and Jacqueline E. Darroch. 2000. "Adolescent Pregnancy and Childbearing: Levels and Trends in Developed Countries." *Family Planning Perspectives.* 32(1).

Stacey, Judith. July 9, 2001. "Family Values Forever." *The Nation.*

*State of America's Children 2004.* Children's Defense Fund.

Sternberg, Steve. 2002. "Sex Education Stirs Controversy." *USA Today.* July 11.

*Survey of Amenca's Views on Sexuality Education.* 1999. Washington, DC: SIECUS and Advocates for Youth.

"Teaching Fear: The Religious Rights' Campaign Against Sexuality Education." 1996. People for the American Way. (http://www.pfaw.org/pfaw/general/default.aspx?oid=2025&print=yes&units=all).

"Texas Teens Increased Sex After Abstinence Program." January 31, 2005. Houston: Reuters.

"UN Children's Summit Hits Snag." May 10, 2002. (Reuters) CBS World News.

"U.S. Fails to Block Consensus at Bangkok Population Conference." 2002. International Women's Health Coalition. Posted Tuesday, December 17. (http://www.iwhc.org/index.cfm?fuseaction= page&pageID).

The Waxman Report. December 2004. "The Content of Federally Funded Abstinence-Only Education Pro- grams." Prepared for Rep. Henry A. Waxman. U.S. House of Representatives Committee on Government Reform. Minority Staff Special Investigations Division. (http://www.democrats.reform.house. gov/Documents/20041201102153-50247.pdf).

## Did You Know?

- Sixty-two percent of teens say they are most likely to talk about sex with a friend. Forty-one percent say they also talk to their parents.[1]
- In one study, 98 percent of parents felt they had communicated with their teen about alcohol use, drug use, and sex, whereas only 76 percent of teens said these discussions took place.[2]
- Seventy-nine percent of parents want their children to learn about sexual orientation in sexuality education classes at school.[3]
- African American and Latino teens are more likely to rely on their parents for sexual health information than are white teens.[4] However, the same teens also said they learned "a lot" about sexual health issues from TV, movies, magazines, or the Internet.[5]
- Comprehensive sexuality education postpones initiation of sexual intercourse and increases the effective use of contraceptives.[6]
- A 1998 study by the Alan Guttmacher Institute found that among the 70 percent of public school districts that have a policy to teach sexuality education, 86 percent require that abstinence be promoted as either the preferred or only option for teenagers outside of marriage.[7]
- SIECUS, the Sexuality Information and Education Council of the United States, since its inception in 1964, has been at the "forefront of efforts to promote sexuality education for people of all ages, protect sexual rights, and expand access to sexual health." SIECUS affirms that sexuality is a "fundamental part of being human, one that is worthy of dignity and respect."[8]
- The following professional organizations support comprehensive sexuality education: American Medical Association, American Academy of Pediatrics, American Nurses Association, American Psychological Association, The Alan Guttmacher Institute, American Public Health Association, American College of Obstetricians and Gynecologists, and National School Boards Association, as do the editors of this text.

*—Compiled by Mikel Walters*

### NOTES

1. NBC News. 2005. "NBC News, People Magazine Commission Landmark National Poll." MSNBC, January 19. Retrieved November 21, 2005 from www.msnbc.com.

2. Sexuality Information and Education Council of the United States. 2001. "Issues and Answers: Fact Sheet on Sexuality Education." Re-trieved November 21, 2005 from www.siecus.org/pubs/fact/fact0007.html.

3. The Henry J. Kaiser Family Foundation. 2000. "Sex Education in America: The View from Inside the Nation's Classroom." Retrieved January 30, 2006 from www.kff.org/kaiserpolls/pomr012904oth.cfm.

4. Sexuality Information and Education Council of the United States. 2004. "Fact Sheet: Sexuality and Youth in Communities of Color." Retrieved March 1, 2005 from www.siecus.org/pubs/fact/fact0012.html.

5. Ibid.

6. Rose, Susan. 2005. "Going Too Far? Sex, Sin and Social Policy." *Social Forces* 84: 1207–1232.

7. Dailard, Cynthia. 2000. "Fueled by Campaign Promises, Drive Intensifies to Boost Abstinence Only Education Fund." *The Guttmacher Report on Public Policy* 3(2). Retrieved January 30, 2005 from www.guttmacher.org/pubs/tgr/03/2/gr030201.html.

8. Sexuality Information and Education Council of the United States. 2006. "About SIECUS." Retrieved January 28, 2006 from www.siecus.org/about/index.html.

chapter 5

# *The Sexual Body*

Spotlight on Research

*An interview with . . .*

## Leonore Tiefer

Leonore Tiefer, Ph.D., is clinical associate professor of psychiatry at the New York University School of Medicine in New York City and has a private practice in sex therapy and psychotherapy in Manhattan. Recently, Dr. Tiefer has become internationally known as the primary spokesperson for a movement that challenges the medicalization of women's sexual problems by the pharmaceutical industry (for more information, see www.fsd-alert.org). Both the Society for the Scientific Study of Sexuality and the Association for Women in Psychology selected her for their Distinguished Scientific Career Awards in 2004.

### What led you to begin studying sexuality?

*I see sexuality as one of the most interesting and complex topics in all of academia. In the 1960s, I majored in psychology and in psychology grad school (UC Berkeley) I was at first attracted to the subject of learning and conditioning. But after two years of research on learning in rats I felt bored, and I became more interested in physiological psychology—the study of the biological bases of behavior. Frank Beach had a very active research group studying mating behavior in rodents and dogs, and although at that time (he changed later) he wouldn't fund*

*hyped the pleasures and right-wing values have hyped the dangers—and, oddly, both insist that sex is a "natural" result of evolution (or God)—and that learning, practice, reading, reflection, conversation, and research are unnecessary. I believe just the opposite.*

**Is there anything else you'd like to add?**

*Every college and university should have a Department of Sexuality Studies. At the present time it is impossible to get the kind of multidisciplinary education I think every sexologist needs. You have to do it all on your own. As a consequence, few sexologists are well trained. Such departments would employ sexuality scholars who would generate interesting new theory and research. I wish I could be in such a department.*

—Interviewed by Denise Donnelly

reading 24

## The Sorcerer's Apprentice:
## Why Can't We Stop Circumcising Boys?

Robert Darby

People have always eaten people,
What else is there to eat?
If the Juju had meant us not to eat people
He wouldn't have made us of meat.

—Flanders and Swann, "The Reluctant Cannibal"

The pediatrician spent hours resuscitating and assessing the injuries of a boy who had been born unable to breathe, without a pulse, and with a broken humerus and depressed skull fracture resulting from a difficult forceps delivery. He then visited the mother, whose first question was "When can he be circumcised?" Such a sense of priorities indicates the privileged place of male circumcision in modern America and highlights the difficulties in explaining what Edward Wallerstein has called "the uniquely American medical enigma." Why does routine circumcision persist in the United States long after it has been abandoned in the other English-speaking countries that originally took it up? Despite critical statements from the American Academy of Pediatrics and the College of Obstetricians and Gynecologists in 1971, 1975, 1978, 1983, 1989, and 1999, the operation is still performed on well over half of all newborn boys.

The U.S. experience contrasts with that of the other countries in which routine circumcision had once been common. In Britain, the procedure was widely recommended in the 1890s, reached

its peak of popularity in the 1920s (at a rate of about 35 percent), declined in the 1950s, and all but disappeared by the 1960s. In Australia, the incidence of circumcision peaked at over 80 percent in the 1950s, but it declined rapidly in the 1980s after statements by pediatric authorities. Today it stands at about 12 percent. The Canadian pattern is broadly similar, though the decline was slower until the late 1990s, when rates fell sharply. In New Zealand, the procedure was nearly universal between the wars, but fell so precipitately in the 1960s that now fewer than 2 percent of boys are circumcised. We thus face a classic puzzle of comparative sociology: Why did routine circumcision arise in the first place? Why only in Anglophone countries? Why did it decline and all but vanish in Britain and its dominions? Why does it survive in the United States?

Nobody has firm answers to these questions. The rise of circumcision was associated with the "great fear" of masturbation and anxiety about juvenile sexuality; the misidentification of infantile phimosis (the naturally nonretractile state of the juvenile foreskin) as a congenital abnormality; the puritan moralities of the nineteenth century; dread of many incurable diseases, especially syphilis, and the rising prestige of the medical profession, particularly surgeons, leading to excessive faith in surgical approaches to disease control and prevention. Most of these features were common to all European countries, however, and the factors which provoked the Anglophone [pattern] remain obscure. . . . The fall of circumcision in Britain was associated with other medical advances, especially the discovery of antibiotics,

From Darby, Robert. 2005. "The Sorcerer's Apprentice: Why Can't We Stop Circumcising Boys?" Contexts 4(2): 34–39. Reprinted by permission of the University of California Press, www.ucpress.edu. © 2005 by the American Sociological Association.

the decline of anxiety about masturbation, concern about complications and deaths, and the development of a more positive attitude toward sexual pleasure. In 1979, an editorial in the *British Medical Journal* attributed much of the trend to a better understanding of normal anatomical development and the consequent disappearance of fears about childhood phimosis.

The same editorial contrasted the British case with the situation in the United States, where the majority of boys were still circumcised, and many doctors (despite the AAP statement) defended the procedure with some vehemence. It offered no suggestions as to why the experience of the two leading Anglophone powers diverged so sharply after the 1940s, but clues may be found in the relatively low incidence of circumcision in Britain, its concentration among the upper classes, and the fact that even at the height of its popularity it was a minority practice that lasted scarcely more than two generations. In the United States, generous medical insurance policies after World War II allowed more families to take advantage of surgical procedures, and the introduction of Medicaid in the 1960s permitted even the poor to enjoy many of the same services as the rich. The practice thus came to affect the vast majority of U.S. males and to endure for more than two generations, with the result that there were soon few doctors and parents who were familiar with the normal (uncircumcised) penis and thus knew how little management it needed. In Britain, there were always doctors and relatives who had not lost touch with the way things used to be. In my research on Britain and Australia, I found that routine circumcision began as a doctor-driven innovation, became established in the medical repertoire, spread rapidly, and then declined slowly as doctors ceased to recommend it. Since parents had absorbed the advice of the generation before and many fathers had been circumcised themselves, they continued to ask for it. The fundamental reason for the circumcision of boys is a population of circumcised adults.

The American situation remains puzzling: Why has a custom initiated by our Victorian forebears prospered so mightily in the age of medical miracles? Some doctors blame parents for demanding circumcision, while parents accuse physicians of suggesting and even urging the operation, and of not warning them about risks and possible adverse effects. Critically minded doctors call for "the organized advocacy of lay groups . . . rather than the efforts of the medical profession," while others object to the interference of "outsiders" in what they insist is a strictly clinical matter. Wallerstein felt that the practice continued because "medical and popular literature abounds in serious errors of scientific judgment," with the result that the medical profession is reluctant to take a firm or united stand. Although few think there is any real value in circumcision, and many regard it as cruel and harmful, doctors seem mesmerized by the force of parental demand and social expectation. Like the sorcerer's apprentice in *Fantasia,* they watch helplessly as the waters mount, waiting for the master magician to return and restore normality.

There has been remarkably little research into this problem. Circumcision is a highly controversial subject, but most of the debate is over whether it should be done, not on why the practice continues; those who defend it regard it as an unproblematic hygiene precaution or at least a parent's right to choose, and often become annoyed when critics ask them to justify it. Discussion of the issue is hampered by uncertainty as to the incidence of routine circumcision, its social distribution, and the reasons parents want it or agree to have it done. There has certainly been a significant decline in the incidence of circumcision in the United States since the 1970s, but it has been neither steady nor uniform across the country. The rate fell from 85 percent of newborns in the 1970s to 60 percent in 1988, rose again to 67 percent in 1995, then fell slightly to 65 percent in 1999—the last year for which authoritative figures are available. But given the AAP's critical statement in 1999, another substantial reduction might be coming. The incidence of circumcision varies significantly by region, and nearly all the observed reduction has occurred in the West, particularly in California, where the rate fell from 63 percent in 1979 to 36 percent in 1999. In the Northeast, the rate remained constant at about 65 percent over the same period, while in the Midwest and South it actually increased—from 74 to 81 percent and 55 to 64 percent, respectively.

Other variations are found on the basis of ethnic origin and education level. When Edward Laumann and colleagues analyzed data from the National Health and Social Life Survey (covering men aged 18–59) they found that while 81 percent of whites were circumcised, the figure was only 65 percent for blacks and 54 percent for Hispanics. Whereas 87 percent of men whose mothers were college graduates were circumcised, the figure for those whose mothers did not complete high school was only 62 percent. Laumann also found that circumcision was less common among conservative Protestants, but noted that all these differences shrank as the sample got younger, suggesting a trend toward homogeneity. We can thus say that circumcision is rarer among blacks and Hispanics (though more common than it was), and that the same is probably true among non-Muslim Asians, among the less educated, and in the western states. But we cannot know which of these is the decisive variable; it may be that blacks, Hispanics, and Asians tend to be less educated than whites and also to be concentrated in the South and West.

Preventive circumcision has always been an experimental and controversial surgery, never endorsed by the medical profession as a whole. Given the uncertainty of its benefits, the high risk of harm, and the significance of the organ being so dramatically altered, you might expect a few ultranervous adults would elect to have it done to themselves but not for millions to inflict it on their babies. These days only a few diehards seriously believe that circumcision in infancy confers compelling health benefits, and nobody suggests that the practice continues because the inhabitants of

Indiana are healthier than those of California or because Americans in general are healthier than the populations of countries where the practice is rare. Indeed, readily available statistics suggest the opposite. Although per capita health spending is vastly greater in the United States than anywhere else, health outcomes on such key indicators as infant mortality, life expectancy, and the incidence of Sexually Transmitted Diseases (STDs) are significantly worse in the United States than in comparably developed countries where most men retain their foreskins. Far from circumcision being a protection against STDs, as often claimed, Laumann found that circumcised men had more STDs, both bacterial and viral, than the uncut, and the United States has the highest incidence of HIV infection of any country in the developed world except Portugal.

If American health outcomes are no better than those of noncircumcising countries, why does this "health precaution" survive on a mass scale? Robert Van Howe suggests seven lines of inquiry: (1) the foreskin is the focus of myths, misconceptions, and irrationality affecting the medical profession and public alike; (2) a lack of respect for the rights and individuality of children; (3) a contrasting exaggerated respect for the presumed sensibilities of religious minorities who practice circumcision for cultural reasons; (4) the reluctance of physicians to take a firm stand against circumcision and to refuse parental requests; (5) a bias in American medical journals, which tend to favor articles with a pro-circumcision tendency; (6) a failure to subject circumcision to the normal protocols for surgery, such as the need for informed consent, evidence of pathology, and proof of prophylactic benefit; and (7) strong financial incentives to perform the operation, which is generally covered by medical insurance.

To these suggestions might be added the role of the armed forces. During the two world wars, the U.S. military made a concerted effort to circumcise servicemen because it believed this would make them less susceptible to venereal disease. Military discipline forced men to submit to a procedure they would not otherwise have agreed to, and thousands of men were circumcised in their late teens and early 20s. When they returned home and became fathers, doctors began asking whether they wanted their sons circumcised. Remembering the ordeal that they or their buddies had endured from the operation as adults, many said yes, thinking it would avoid the need to do it later when the pain was thought to be worse than in infancy. With two generations circumcised, the foreskinned penis became rare, and few men had the personal experience to refute the rumors told about it.

The importance of financial incentives has been stressed by a number of critics. In their analysis of Medicaid funding, Amber Craig and colleagues found that low and declining rates of circumcision correspond to regions where the procedure is not funded, notably in California, which dropped coverage in 1982. Even more striking is their finding that the higher the rebate, the higher the incidence of circumcision—vivid proof of the power of market signals. Nor do the advantages of circumcision—for doctors—end there. Despite optimistic claims that the rates of injury and death are low, there has never been an adequate assessment of long-term complications, and they are certainly more frequent than most people think. The dirty little secret in pediatric surgery is that badly performed circumcisions, causing discomfort or poor cosmetic outcomes, often necessitating repeat operations and repair jobs, are common; one attorney who specializes in medical malpractice reports that some urologists see at least one such case each week. In this way the division of professional labor ensures that the benefits of circumcision are spread far beyond the original doctors: their mistakes provide work for many colleagues and the disasters add lawyers to the equation.

Yet physicians may not be the major beneficiaries. In the age of biotechnology and tissue engineering, human body parts have a high market value, and baby foreskins are prized as the raw material for many biomedical products, from skin grafts to antiwrinkle cream. The strongest pressure for the continuation of circumcision may not be from doctors or parents at all, but from the hospitals that harvest the foreskins and sell them to commercial partners.

Lack of unanimity and conviction among the medical profession has been stressed by Lawrence Dritsas, who attempts to deconstruct the AAP's unwillingness to make a firm recommendation and its corresponding tactic of throwing the burden of decision onto parents. He quotes an article that offered this explanation:

> *"We are reluctant to assume the role of active advocacy (one way or the other) because . . . the decision is not usually a medical one. Rather, it is based on the parents' perceptions of hygiene, their lack of understanding of the surgical risks, or their desire to conform to the pattern established by the infant's father and their own societal structure."*

He translates this to mean that circumcision is irrational but that, contrary to the usual protocol, "parental wishes become sufficient, while medical necessity, normally a guiding rule for the surgeon's knife, takes a back seat." Dritsas contrasts this hands-off approach with the AAP's ethically based rejection of female genital mutilation (where the possibility of a health benefit is not even entertained). In its position statement on informed consent the AAP says, "Providers have legal and ethical duties to their child patients to render competent medical care based on what the patient needs, not what someone else expresses. . . . The pediatrician's responsibility to his or her patient exists independently of parental desires or proxy consent." Except, it seems, when it comes to male circumcision.

Dritsas is genuinely puzzled by the glaring contradictions in AAP policy and explains them in terms of medical culture and the apprenticeship model of professional training, which does not encourage students to question authority. "For a physician to cease performing circumcisions represents a condemnation of past practice and an admission of error," he writes, and nobody holding the power of life and death wants to be seen as doing that. The doctors are thus in much the same position as the parents themselves, whose unconsidered assumption that the baby will be circumcised is an expression of the authority of their grandparents' physicians who convinced prior generations that it was the thing to do. Dritsas criticizes the stance of the AAP as reminiscent of the response of Pontius Pilate when confronted with the problem of what to do with Jesus. In his view, what they are really saying is that, "as scientific doctors, we find ourselves unable to recommend or deny this procedure; therefore, you will decide, and we shall be your scalpels." This sort of abdication of responsibility contrasts with the proactive stances of pediatric bodies in Britain, Australia, New Zealand, and, most forcefully, Canada, which have seen it as their duty not only to discourage parents from seeking circumcision but, in the end, to refuse to perform the operation.

There must be an explanation for these national differences. The medical profession is not an independent force; its members are subject to the same social pressures that shape the beliefs and condition the actions of everybody else. Several recent commentators have thus argued that circumcision should not be seen as a medical issue at all but as an expression of social norms. At a superficial level this has long been known. In the 1950s Dr. Spock urged circumcision because it would help a boy to feel "regular," and pediatricians since then have noted that "entrenched tradition of custom is probably the greatest obstacle faced by those who would decrease the number of circumcisions done in this country." But it is only recently that the sociological aspect of the question has received serious attention. In a comprehensive survey of the history of modern circumcision and the debate over its "advantages," published in 2002, Geoffrey Miller shows in brilliant detail how late Victorian physicians succeeded in demonizing the foreskin as a source of moral and physical decay. Acting as "norm entrepreneurs" they "reconfigured the phallus," transforming the foreskin from a feature regarded as healthy, natural, and good into one feared as polluted, chaotic, and bad. The incessant quest for novel associations between the foreskin (often expressed as "lack of circumcision") and nasty diseases is a tribute to the lasting success of their enterprise.

As a legal scholar, Miller is surprised at the law's indifferent or often supportive attitude toward what one might expect it to regard as an assault, or at least a mutilation, but he points out that the law is an expression of the surrounding culture and cannot be expected to be too far ahead of prevailing norms. Even so, he considers routine circumcision in the mainstream community to be on the way out. Although still normative, it is in decline and edging toward the critical halfway mark, or "tipping point," where the incidence can be expected to fall precipitously as parents come to believe that their children will now face stigma if they are circumcised. Like foot-binding in China or wife-beating in nineteenth-century Britain, a widely accepted social convention is "likely to collapse as the culture reaches a 'tipping point' and turns against the practice." The increasingly desperate search for new health reasons to circumcise—urinary tract infections (1985), HIV AIDS (1989), and cervical cancer in potential future partners (revived in 2002)—may delay the process, but cannot permanently halt it.

Sarah Waldeck offers a subtle analysis of how norms contribute to a person's behavioral cost-benefit calculations, how the desire to have a child circumcised fits into this assessment, and thus why parents continue to seek it. She is particularly interested in the "stigma" supposedly attached to the uncircumcised penis in a society where most males are cut, and she considers the role of the popular media in perpetuating a stereotype of the foreskin as somehow disagreeable. She also notes that few parents have any clear reasons for wanting their sons circumcised and produce them only when challenged. The most common justifications turn out to be the supposed need to look like the father or peers and not to be teased in the proverbial locker room. If "health benefits" are mentioned at all, they enter as an afterthought or when other arguments fail. Waldeck still subjects the medical case to scientific, legal, and ethical scrutiny, and finds it inadequate to justify the removal of healthy body parts from nonconsenting minors. She concludes with a thoughtful discussion of how the American norm might be changed and suggests three specific strategies: requiring parents to pay for the procedure; requiring doctors who perform the operation to use effective pain control; and tightening the informed-consent process.

As a celebrated German-Jewish philosopher once observed, "The tradition of all the dead generations weighs like a nightmare on the brains of the living." When preventive circumcision was introduced in the late nineteenth century, concepts of medical ethics, informed consent, therapeutic evidence, and the cost-benefit trade-off were rudimentary. Neither the morality nor the efficacy of the procedure was seriously debated, nor was there any study of its long-term consequences; it became established in the medical culture of Anglophone countries by virtue of the authority of its early promoters. No matter how many statistics-laden articles get published in medical journals, circumcision cannot shake off the traces of its Victorian origins. It remains the last surviving example of the once respectable proposition that disease could be prevented by the preemptive removal of body parts, which, though healthy, are thought to be a weak link in the body's defenses. In its heyday, this medical breakthrough, described by Ann Dally as "fantasy surgery," enjoyed wide esteem and included excisions of other supposed foci or portals of infection, such as the adenoids, tonsils, teeth, appendix, and large intestine. Few doubted that if the doctor thought you were better off without any of these, it was your duty to follow his orders.

Because there was no real debate about the propriety or efficacy of preemptive amputation as a disease-control strategy when it was first introduced, those who wanted to remove healthy body parts from children were able to throw the burden of proof onto their opponents. Instead of the advocates having to demonstrate that the gain outweighed the loss, it was up to the doubters to prove that the loss outweighed the gain. The consequence is that what should have been a debate about the introduction of preventive circumcision in the 1890s has turned into a debate about its abolition a century later. Miller and Waldeck are probably right to argue that circumcision will not die out until the uncut penis becomes an acceptable—perhaps the preferred—option. But the transformation of attitudes will not seem so improbable, nor is the task of effecting it so daunting, if we remember that there is no need to invent a new norm, merely to restore the sensibility that governed the Western world before the late nineteenth century. In the 1870s, when Richard Burton remarked that Christendom "practically holds circumcision in horror," the observation was ceasing to be true, but it was certainly the case before Victorian doctors reconfigured the phallus and bequeathed a thorny problem to their successors.

(*Note on terminology*: In this article "circumcision" or "routine circumcision" means circumcision of normal male minors in the absence of any medical indication or valid religious requirement, on the decision of adults, and without the consent of the child.)

## RECOMMENDED RESOURCES

*Lawrence Dritsas. "Below the Belt: Doctors, Debate and the Ongoing American Discussion of Routine Neonatal Male Circumcision." *Bulletin of Science and Technology* 21 (2001):297–311, A brief analysis of the uncertainties, contradictions, and disagreements among American medical professionals.

*Geoffrey Miller. "Circumcision: Cultural-Legal Analysis." *Virginia Journal of Social Policy and the Law* 9 (2002):497–585. Miller shows how Victorian medical men transformed popular images of the penis and set routine circumcision in motion.

Robert Van Howe. "Why Does Neonatal Circumcision Persist in the United States?" In *Sexual Mutilations:*

*A Human Tragedy*, ed. Marylin Milos and George Denniston (Plenum, 1997). A discussion of the main factors behind American exceptionalism.

*Sarah Waldeck. "Using Circumcision to Understand Social Norms as Multipliers." *University of Cincinnati Law Review* 72 (2003):455–526. A searching analysis of routine circumcision as a cultural phenomenon.

*Edward Wallerstein. "Circumcision: The Uniquely American Medical Enigma." *Urologic Clinics of North America* 12 (1985): 123–32. Why doctors and parents prefer health faddism to biological evidence.

*Items marked with an asterisk are available online at the Circumcision Information and Resource Pages website: http://www.cirp.org/library.*

## Female Genital Cutting

### Elisabeth O. Burgess

Cultural norms regarding physical attractiveness, sexual appeal, chasteness, and/or marriageability often encourage the manipulation of women's and girls' bodies. These issues are evident in many times and places; for instance, Wesley (Reading 28) discusses the lengths to which exotic dancers will go in order to maintain their sexual appeal. Manipulation of the female body falls on a continuum from clothing, hairstyles, and make-up on one end, to surgical procedures at the other extreme. It also includes techniques such as breast enhancement surgery, hymen restoration (to "reinstate" virginity), and labia slimming or plumping. Some bodily manipulations are "elective," while others are externally imposed on girls and women by parents and caregivers. One of the most extreme forms of bodily manipulation is female genital cutting.

Female genital cutting (FGC) is the current name for a variety of practices that involve the cutting of female genitalia. These practices have been called everything from *female circumcision* to *female genital mutilation*. The naming of these procedures is meaningful because each carries a value judgment (Walley, 2002; Davis, 2004) and serves to "other" African or non-Western women (Njambi, 2004). The term *circumcision* brings to mind male circumcision (See Darby, Reading 24) and, thus, encourages us to view the procedure as medicalized and less severe in scope. In contrast, to call it *female genital mutilation* suggests that the intent is to harm or torture women. To better represent the problem and consequences of this procedure, many health activists, researchers, and policy makers have adopted the term *female genital cutting,* which allows for more culturally sensitive discussion of the topic and acknowledges the diversity of practices (James and Robertson, 2002).

The World Health Organization (2000a; 2000b) identifies four types of FGC:

1. Removal of part or all of the clitoris.
2. Removal of clitoris and labia minora (also known as *clitoridectomy* or *excision*).
3. Removal of the clitoris, labia minora, and labia majora (also known as *infibulation*). The wound is stitched or covered until it heals. Sometimes a foreign object is placed in the wound to leave a place for the flow of urine and menstrual blood.
4. Other procedures that alter the genitals include, but are not limited to, cauterization, burning, and piercing.

Although rates of FGC are difficult to measure, the World Health Organization (2000a) estimates that between 100 and 140 million girls and women have undergone some variation of FGC, and approximately 2 million girls are at risk of FGC each year. Infibulations are the most severe form of FGC, and represent approximately 15 percent of all cases. While all types of FGC pose health risks, such as infection, infibulation is particularly hazardous. The severity of the surgery and unsanitary conditions often lead to medical complications including infertility; infection; difficulties with urination, menstruation, and childbirth; and even death (World Health Organization, 2000b). If the wound heals properly, the resulting scar tissue and size of the opening may require deinfibulation (tearing or cutting of the scarred tissue) for sexual activity or childbirth. In most cases women are reinfibulated after childbirth (World Health Organization, 2000b; Walley, 2002).

Although the majority of genital cutting occurs in Africa, it also occurs in some parts of Asia and the Middle East.[1] Moreover, FGC has occurred in other times and places. In the Victorian Era, some European and American doctors used clitoridectomy as a cure for masturbation and nymphomania (Sheehan, 1997; Walley, 2002) and Chase (2002) argues that contemporary surgery on intersexed infants[2] is also a form of genital cutting.

In Africa, older women or midwives commonly perform genital cutting procedures on young girls.[3] The cultural belief is that FGC will ensure that girls remain virgins, thus making them desirable brides, and that uncut genitals are unclean and offensive. Also, many men believe that FGC of a female partner enhances male sexual pleasure (James and Robertson, 2002). Some cultures perform FGC as communal initiation rites for girls at puberty. After undergoing the procedure, girls are welcomed into the community of women, often receiving gifts and gaining social status (James and Robertson, 2002; Njambi, 2004). Although some girls risk their lives by leaving their families in an effort to avoid genital cutting,[4] other girls see these ceremonies, which may combine FGC with other rites of passage, as bonding experiences that enhance life-long solidarity (James and Robertson, 2002; Walley, 2002; Njambi, 2004).

Human rights organizations, including UNICEF, the World Health Organization, the United Nations Population Fund, Amnesty International, and numerous feminist organizations condemn FGC and define it as a violation of civil rights, favoring its elimination (World Health Organization, 2000a; Kalev, 2004). As a result, rates of FGC have decreased in some areas and numerous African women and men are working to eradicate FGC (Robertson, 2002). The World Health Organization provides training for nurses, midwives, and health care workers in order to increase awareness of health problems that arise from the practice of FGC (World Health Organization, 2001). In contrast, some FGC-practicing communities favor continuing the less severe FGC practices as long as they are carried out under medical supervision in sanitary conditions.

## NOTES

1. It is also important to recognize that FGC is not the only or even necessarily the most important health and body issue facing women in Africa or the developing world (Robertson, 2002; Njambi, 2004).

2. See Reading 2 by Haas for more on intersexuality.

3. Although infants and adult women may undergo FGC, the majority of cases are girls aged 4 to 10 (Leonard, 2000).

4. Over the past several decades there have been several well publicized cases of women and girls seeking asylum to avoid FCG for themselves or their daughters. (See Njambi, 2004, for a critique of media coverage of these cases.) In many cases, these girls are cut against their will. In other cases, male and female peers ostracize uncut girls.

## REFERENCES

Chase, Cheryl. 2002. "'Cultural Practice' or 'Reconstructive Surgery'? U.S. Genital Cutting, the Intersex Movement, and Medical Double Standards." Pp. 126–151 in Stanlie M. James and Claire C. Robertson. (Eds.) *Genital Cutting and Transnational Sisterhood: Disputing U.S. Polemics*. Chicago: University of Illinois Press.

Davis, Kathy. 2004. "Responses to W. Njabi's 'Dualism and Female Bodies in Representations of African Female Circumcision: A Feminist Critique': Between Moral Outrage and Cultural Relativism." *Feminist Theory, 5* (3), 305–323.

James, Stanlie M. and Claire C. Robertson. 2002. "Introduction: Reimagining Transnational Sisterhood." Pp. 5–15 in Stanlie M. James and Claire C. Robertson. (Eds.) *Genital Cutting and Transnational Sisterhood: Disputing U.S. Polemics*. Chicago: University of Illinois Press.

Kalev, Henriette Dahan. 2004. "Cultural Rights or Human Rights: The Case of Female Genital Mutilation." *Sex Roles, 51,* 339–348.

Leonard, Lori. 2000. "Interpreting Female Genital Cutting: Moving beyond the Impasse." *Annual Review of Sex Research, 11,* 158–190.

Njabi, Wairimu Ngaruiya. 2004. "Dualism and Female Bodies in Representations of African Female Circumcision: A Feminist Critique." *Feminist Theory, 5* (3), 281–303.

Robertson, Claire C. 2002. "Getting beyond the Ew! Factor: Rethinking U.S. Approaches to African Female Genital Cutting." Pp. 54–86 in Stanlie M. James and Claire C. Robertson. (Eds.) *Genital Cutting and Transnational Sisterhood: Disputing U.S. Polemics*. Chicago: University of Illinois Press.

Sheehan, Elizabeth A. 1997. "Victorian Clitoridectomy: Isaac Baker Brown and His Harmless Operative Procedure." Pp. 325–334 in Roger L. Lancaster and Miceala di Leonardo. (Eds.) *The Gender Sexuality Reader: Culture, History, Political Economy.* New York: Routledge.

Walley, Christine J. 2002. "Searching for Voices: Feminism, Anthropology, and the Global Debate over Female Genital Operations." Pp. 17–53 in Stanlie M. James and Claire C. Robertson. (Eds.) *Genital Cutting and Transnational Sisterhood: Disputing U.S. Polemics.* Chicago: University of Illinois Press.

World Health Organization. 2000a. "Fact Sheet, Number 241: Female Genital Mutilation." Retrieved January 15, 2006 from www.who.int/mediacentre/factsheets/fs241/en.

World Health Organization. 2000b. "A Systemic Review of Health Complications of Female Genital Mutilation Including Sequelae in Childbirth." Retrieved January 15, 2006 from www.who.int/mediacentre/gender/other_health/en/systreviewFGM.pdf.

World Health Organization. 2001. "Female Genital Mutilation, The Prevention and the Management of the Health Complications: Policy Guidelines for Nurses and Midwives." Retrieved January 15, 2006 from www.who.int/reproductive-health/publications/rhr_01_18_fgm_policy_guidelines/index.html.

# Little Girls in Women's Bodies: Social Interaction and the Strategizing of Early Breast Development

Erika Summers-Effler

*"Do you think it's any fun to be the biggest kid in the class?"*

*"I don't know," I said. "I never thought about it."*

*"Well, try thinking about it. Think about how you'd feel if you had to wear a bra in fourth grade and how everybody laughed and how you always had to cross your arms in front of you. And about how the boys called you dirty names just because of how you looked."*

From *Are You There God? It's Me, Margaret* (Blume, 1970)

Girls who develop breasts early do not passively endure this developmental event. Rather, early breast developers actively negotiate their environment. The meaning of symbols, including women's breasts, is far from given; it is actively created in interaction with others (Mead, 1934). The meaning girls ascribe to the experience of early breast development very much depends on both the specifics of their social context and their strategies for negotiating interactions about their breasts. In this article, I explore the stories of women who developed breasts before their peers did, women who developed a woman's body when they were still little girls. I report on the analysis of narratives of early breast development from a sociological perspective, with a focus on interactional ritual. I provide a theoretical model for considering the experiences of early developers based in the theoretical tradition that addresses the role of ritual and its resulting emotion in shaping the power and meaning of symbols (Collins, 1990; Durkheim, 1995; Goffman, 1967). In the case of the early breast developer, an interaction ritual approach entails consideration of the role of social interaction and the emotion it produces in shaping the meaning the early developer's breasts have for her. The purpose of this study was to consider how repeated social positioning within specific social contexts generates the strategies early developers use to deal with the social implications of their early breast development. In turn, these strategies help to determine the meaning of their breasts for early breast developers.

## Early Developers

There have been many studies of early physical maturation from a psychological perspective. These studies have conceptualized the impact of early development in primarily two ways: (1) that the experience of early development creates difficulties in adaptation; and (2) that early developers are at particular social and psychological risk because they are forced into adolescence too early and do not have enough time to adjust to their new status (Silbereisen & Kracke, 1997; Wiesner & Ittel, 2002). There is little consistent support for either theory (Alsaker, 1995), as well as few consistent findings across studies (Alsaker, 1995; Simmons & Blyth, 1987; Wiesner & Ittel, 2002). However, research does consistently support these generalizations: early developers engage in sexual

From Summers-Effler, Erika. 2004. "Little Girls in Women's Bodies: Social Interaction and the Strategizing on Early Breast Development." *Sex Roles* 51: 29–44. Reprinted with kind permission from Springer Science and Business Media.

activity earlier than on-time and later maturers (Brooks-Gunn, 1988; Flannery, Daniel, Rowe, & Gulley, 1993; Magnusson, Stattin, & Allan, 1985); early developers have particularly negative body images (Alsaker, 1995; Brooks-Gunn, 1988; Petersen & Crockett, 1985; Williams & Currie, 2000); and early developers have higher rates of depressive symptoms than on-time or late developers (Alsaker, 1992; Nottelman et al., 1987). . . . .

Researchers . . . exacerbate inconsistency in findings by basing studies on objective measures of development without taking into account the importance of individual social context. The body itself does not constitute the problem of early development; rather the social context in which the body changes determines the extent to which the body matters. Pubertal timing effects are likely to be the product of the girls' reactions to the interaction between the timing of puberty relative to that of peers and the responses of people in her environment to that development (Petersen, 1988). We need to look at the process of meaning-making that takes place at the level of the interaction between the girl and her social environment to make sense of the various or different outcomes associated with early maturation. Because the development of breasts has a distinctively social impact, it is important to separate the experience of early breast development from the more general category of early development. An interaction ritual perspective can explain the significance of early breast development in particular by allowing us to consider how the interaction opportunities of the early breast developer may differ from those who develop breasts at an average or slower rate.

### Interaction Ritual Theory

Interaction ritual theory developed from the sociological tradition that addresses the role of ritual and its resulting emotion in shaping the power and meaning of symbols (Collins, 1990; Durkheim, 1912; Goffman, 1967). In the lan-

guage of interaction ritual theory, all focused social interaction is ritual. Emotion is central to the theory, and interaction ritual theory states that emotional energy is gained or lost in focused interaction, whether or not this focus takes place in a formal ritual, such a religious service, or an informal ritual, such as an exchange of pleasantries (Collins, 1990; Goffman, 1967). There are transitory emotions (e.g., joy, shock, anger) but emotional energy is a longer term durable emotional tone that fluctuates as a level across interactions. People are motivated to maximize emotional energy, which they experience as confidence, enthusiasm, and willingness to initiate interactions. People are therefore also motivated to avoid the loss of emotional energy, which feels like depression and low self-esteem (Collins, 1990).

If an interaction builds solidarity, all involved will achieve status and feel included—everyone will experience a boost of emotional energy. If the group excludes one or some, those excluded will feel a loss of status and emotional energy. The feeling associated with loss of status is shame—the physical sensation of *cringing* withdrawal from others and the *cringing* within that accompanies the felt need to hide and conceal the self (Bartky, 1990). Shame sensations and responses are typical physical responses to threat. In the case of shame, the threat is exclusion from one's social network (Scheff, 1990).

Collins (1990) argued that there are also power interaction rituals, where, during a focused interaction, one or some gain power at the expense of one or some who lose it. Those who have more power are in order-giver positions, and those who have less are in order-taker positions (Collins, 1990). Order-takers submit to the will of the order-givers, which results in a gain of emotional energy for those in power and loss for those who are subordinately positioned. Those who gain power will feel a boost in confidence, whereas those who lose it will feel the drain of emotional energy—depression and loss of self-esteem.

We connect the emotions generated in social interaction to symbols associated with the interaction, and this creates the meaning of the symbols for the person who experiences the emotional impact of the interaction. We use these emotionally loaded symbols to strategize about future interactions. If a symbol is associated with an increase in emotional energy, we will seek it out; if it is associated with a loss of emotional energy we will try to avoid the type of interaction associated with that symbol (Collins, 1990). Thus differing emotional responses within an interaction could create different meanings associated with the same symbol—order-givers and order-takers are likely to develop different meanings associated with the symbols involved in a power interaction. Over time the meaning of symbols changes as we move from interaction to interaction, which means that a symbol might represent a gain in emotional energy at one point and a loss at another. The meaning of symbols represents strategies for interaction that change in response to an individual's changing environment. When we have options and can move toward positive interactions, we maintain proactive interaction strategies—we move forward and seek increases in emotional energy. However, when there are limited interactions available to us, and they all potentially generate a loss of emotional energy, we develop defensive strategies to avoid further loss of emotional energy.

We update proactive strategies in response to emotional indicators; a loss of emotional energy generates new meaning for the symbols involved in the interaction, and suggests that we use new and different strategies for participating in interaction. Defensive strategies, on the other hand, anticipate some loss of emotional energy, so we do not necessarily update them when the strategy produces a loss. As a result, defensive strategies can become fixed and resilient once formed. This means that proactive strategies remain much more flexible and responsive to the environment than do defensive strategies. Defensive strategies are born of limited social options; they represent a short-term solution to emotional energy loss, but potentially a long-term drain as they allow

for some emotional energy loss and are not easily updated.

For the purposes of this study, I defined *social position* as the status (inclusion vs. exclusion) and power (order-taker vs. order-giver) outcomes of social interaction. I defined *social context* as the available social interactions in one's environment. The limits of social context are both physical, that is literally the people and types of interactions available (an important constraint for children), and socially constructed through chains of interactions over time, that is through the creation of the meaning for symbols, past experiences set expectations for what interactions are possible and what interactions are likely to be positive or negative. Through the lens of interaction ritual theory, the social impact of early breast maturation is a product of the options for social interaction that are available to the early breast developer (social context), the emotional consequences of the interactions in term of power (order-giver vs. order-taker) and status (inclusion vs. exclusion), and the strategies (proactive vs. defensive) that early breast developers create within the context of their options for social interaction. It is conceivable that early breast development could lead to inclusion or exclusion, power or subordination; we need to look at the circumstances of individuals and their responses to these circumstances to understand the impact of their strategies for coping with early breast development, as well as the meaning of their breasts for these women.

## Social Context

### Developmental Issues

Findings about late childhood provide important clues to aspects of social context that are central to the experience of the early breast developer. Puberty begins with hormonal changes that are generally accompanied by an increase in body fat and the development of breast buds; menarche occurs on average 2 years later (Alsaker, 1995). Although variability is the rule rather than exception for all pubertal processes (Brooks-Gunn,

1988), general trends of rates and order of physical development of boys and girls in puberty mean that the early breast maturing girl is generally not only different from her girlfriends, but way ahead of her male classmates as well (1988).

The transition from child to adolescent has been identified as a period of heightened psychological risk for girls (Brown & Gilligan, 1992). . . . For many girls, it is a time of disconnection, dissociation, and repression. Social comparison is also particularly important at this developmental stage (Alsaker, 1995; Silbereisen & Kracke, 1997), which suggests that visible physical differences may play a particularly important role in social interactions. There is evidence to suggest that girls choose to socialize with those who are at a similar developmental stage; early-maturing girls may have more limited social networks (Brooks-Gunn, & Samelson, 1986), which has implications for loss of status (exclusion) and emotional energy.

### The Feminine Body in Patriarchal Culture

The larger culture offers up particularly powerful symbols that have gained prominence through experience of interactions overtime (Collins, 2001). Once central, these symbols become widely diffused and operate as shortcuts, or pre-packaged strategies, for interactions (Summers-Effier, in press). For contemporary American girls, the development of an adult feminine body, breasts in particular, takes place within a culture where the shape and form of breasts, and women's bodies more generally, are loaded with meaning. Breasts are the most obvious sign of the sexualized adult feminine body. They are fetishized in contemporary Western cultures, and they constitute the defining feature of sexual attractiveness (Latteier, 1998; Yalom, 1997). The rate of plastic surgery on breasts highlights the social importance of breasts (Davis, 1991; Morgan, 1991). As or because breasts play such an important role in social life, breasts cannot but render girls more self-conscious, whether they feel pleasure from a sense of sexual power over men or a sense of inadequacy because of men's scrutiny (Frost, 2001).

However, any power that girls may feel because of their breasts' development is potentially discrediting as well. Latteier (1998) found that women with large breasts are typed as incompetent, immoral, immodest, and not very smart.

The advent of breasts is important because of their public nature and cultural link to sexuality (Brooks-Gunn, 1984). . . . As these girls develop women's bodies, they begin to be seen as sex objects. At the same time, they are confronted with the prevalent view that only "bad girls" have sex (Tolman, 1994). As a result, early breast developers must negotiate a potentially "bad girl" identity, regardless of their behavior.

Bartky (1990) pointed out that contemporary American girls are also developing within a cultural context of the current "tyranny of slenderness," where women are forbidden to become large or massive. The shape a woman's body takes on as she matures—the full breasts and rounded hips—have become distasteful. Girls have been found to have lower opinions of their appearance and weight than boys do both in childhood and adolescence (Mendelson, White, & Mendelson, 1996). Blyth, Simmons, and Zakin (1985) found that the cultural ideal of thinness for women is strong and pervasive among girls in late childhood, and this is particularly detrimental for early-maturers, because the onset of puberty means that they are alone and thus more prominent because of the increase and redistribution of body fat.

### The Process of Sexual Objectification

The early breast developer engages in interaction rituals within developmental and cultural limits. Latteier (1998) suggested that, for a growing girl, the advent of body consciousness often comes with the first appearance of breasts. Bartky (1990) described how self-consciousness arises from sexually objectifying interactions. Sexual objectification happens in interactions where a woman's or girl's sexual parts or sexual functions are separated from the rest of her self and either reduced to the status of mere instruments or regarded as if they were capable of representing her. One way to become sexually objectified is to be the object of a perception, unwelcome and inappropriate, that takes the part for the whole (Bartky, 1990). Bartky (1990) stated that the process of the identification of a person with her sexuality becomes oppressive when such identification becomes habitually extended into every area of her experience. Much of the time, sexual objectification occurs whether women want to be sexually objectified or not. Empirical findings (e.g., McKinley, 1998) support the notion that dominant cultural constructions of the female body encourage women to watch their own bodies as objects and to feel shame when they do not achieve cultural standards; McKinley found that women have higher levels of surveillance, body shame, and discrepancy between their actual and ideal weights than do men. Sometimes this internalization of cultural standards is achieved through day-to-day interactions that do not appear to be threatening on the surface; other times the process is more aggressive, as in cases of sexual abuse, assault, and harassment.

For girls, growing up means becoming massively identified with the body. Therefore the changes during adolescence have inherent difficulties associated with alienation from and objectification of parts of the self and body (Frost, 2001). Attention to breasts is particularly central to the experience of sexual objectification in which the girl learns to become her own internal critic (Frost, 2001)....

Within the perspective of interaction ritual theory, we can identify sexually objectifying interactions as power interactions where the observer reduces the observed to a body or body parts in a way that is discrediting to the rest of the person. It is unlikely that early breast developers, or any woman with breasts for that matter, can avoid being sexually objectified at times. However, just because someone assumes an order-giver position does not mean that the receiving individual will follow the orders. Whether one assumes a subordinate position and submits to sexual objectification or not, follows orders or not, depends

entirely on one's social options. The options available to early breast developers determine whether the dynamics of sexual objectification in social interactions are taken in as part of the interior dialogue of the self. Not every girl who is objectified will submit to this treatment, develop defensive strategies, or even share in the objectified meaning of themselves. Their responses depend on the availability of alternative interactions.

## Method

### Participants

Brooks-Gunn and Petersen (1984) have noted that one of the major problems in conducting research on early development is that researchers more commonly use physiologically oriented markers than socially oriented markers. I avoided this problem by asking self-identified early developers to tell the story of their *experience* of early development. I located women to interview by making announcements in two undergraduate Introduction to Sociology classes in a large selective university in an east coast city, asking resident assistants in dormitories in this same university to ask their neighbors, and asking my personal acquaintances. In all cases I simply stated that I wanted "to hear the stories of women who self-identified as early developers, girls who felt that they began puberty significantly before their peers." ... Thirteen women contacted me, and I listened to and tape-recorded the stories of all 13. [See the following table.] Each woman took somewhere between 1 and 2½ hours to tell her story....

### Procedure

I asked the self-identified early developers to tell the story of their breast development. This procedure is in line with methods for episodic narrative interviews, where informants are asked to tell stories about particular topics (Murry, 2003). Such narratives provide access to the richness of situations, perceptions, and feelings that guide the person in interaction (Stuhlmiller, 2001). Researchers (Polkinghorne, 1988; Sarbin, 1986) have argued that personal stories reveal the way

| NAME | AGE | ETHNICITY | DEVELOPED BREASTS | MENARCHE |
|------|-----|-----------|-------------------|----------|
| Lilly | 25 | Asian American | 8 years old | 10 years old |
| Jen | 18 | White American | 8 years old | 9 years old |
| Sue | 23 | White American | 8 years old | 10 years old |
| Tabitha | 34 | White American | 8 years old | 10 years old |
| Eileen | 21 | White American | 9 years old | 9 years old |
| Rebecca | 22 | White American | 10 years old | 11 years old |
| Sara | 22 | White American | 8 years old | 10 years old |
| Trish | 26 | White American | 7 years old | 9 years old |
| Kerry | 20 | White American | 8 years old | 10 years old |
| Laura | 22 | White American | 9 years old | 10 years old |
| Jenny | 19 | Japanese | 9 years old | 10 years old |
| Jack | 31 | Dutch | 8 years old | 10 years old |
| Grace | 20 | Korean American | 8 years old | 10 years old |

people view their problems and act in response to them, which makes this method particularly well suited for the purposes of exploring social context and interaction strategies.

Although retrospective narratives are necessarily limited because of the narrator's distance from the actual events, that distance has the benefit of allowing a reflexive stance that would not have been possible while the events were in progress (Stuhlmiller, 2001). . . . Thus, in considering the social and emotional implications of breast development, it ultimately makes sense to organize a study around perceived timing rather than any sort of objective measure. Although there is research to suggest that these women's recollection of objective timing is accurate, their perception of the timing is more important to the social experiences that are the focus of this project. . . .

I used all of the narratives to develop three ideal type[s] of strategies for maximizing emotional energy within the context of early breast development: hiding the breasts, using the breasts for popularity with boys, and proactively resisting the subordinate positioning and exclusion associated with the development of breasts. I have selected three accounts of early breast development that allow me to convey a range of experiences and strategies associated with breast development, while staying close to the stories that the women told. As much as I could, I have presented the quotes as part of the integrated stories I heard. Although this lets their voices come through in the analysis, it requires teasing apart themes that are presented as interconnected. I present my data in this way to get at the personal, subjective, meaning-making aspects of early breast development.

## Results

### Social Positioning and Social Context of Early Breast Development

#### Tabitha

Tabitha was 34 years old at the time she told me about her early development. She grew up White in upper middle-class, predominantly White suburbs and in a large eastern Canadian city. She started to develop breasts when she was 8 years old, and she started to menstruate when she was 10 years old. She was well over 5' tall in third grade, and she said that she felt like a physical misfit because of her height even before she started to develop. Tabitha's story runs counter to the generalization that early developers engage in sexual activity earlier than average and late-developing girls. She is one of three women with whom I spoke who described themselves as an early physical developer but a late sexual developer. [Lilly and Sara said this as well.] We can see how the strategies that Tabitha used to negotiate the environment in which she developed breasts contributed to alienation from her body, anger toward men, and discomfort with her own sexuality.

Whereas some women talked of gaining social power because of their larger breasts, Tabitha said she only felt excluded and ashamed because of her different body.

> I started to wear heavy sweaters to cover myself so that no one would see me. I was in total denial—I just didn't want it to be true. You should see my 6th grade class picture. I was 5'11 and 110 lbs. I had this long stringy hair that I was hiding behind. All of the other girls in the picture are wearing little spaghetti strap dresses in bright colors and smiling, and I was seated in this little chair with my knees practically up to my ears because I was way too tall for it, a big thick sweater to try to hide my breasts, jeans that were too short for me, and a miserable expression on my face. That picture pretty much captures my experience in elementary school. I felt big, awkward, and not cute and pretty; I stuck out, and I felt miserable.

Although Tabitha did not tell stories of being teased by her peers, she felt a loss of status (exclusion) because of her changing body. She attempted to control how different she appeared by hiding her body to prevent loss of status. Her description of her sixth grade picture is a depiction of what it felt like to experience the shame of being different; she felt unattractive and miserable as she fought a losing battle to attempt to hide her difference.

Peers figured prominently in the accounts of some of the early breast developers, but Tabitha

primarily told stories of being subordinately positioned and losing power at the hands of adult men because of her larger breasts. She told a story about how sexual harassment by a teacher contributed to her sense of shame and helplessness associated with her body.

> When I was in seventh grade, I had a male science teacher. One day he called me out into the hall. I was confused and anxious because I was always a good kid. We went out into the hall, and I stood against the lockers, backed up against them with him standing in front of me with his arm stretched out and his hand on the lockers right by my head. He said, "Tabitha, I've heard that you've been telling kids that you think that I think that you have a great body." Well I just could have died right there. All I could think of was that he thought that I had done this awful thing, and that I just had to make him believe that I had never said that. I said over and over, "I didn't say that! I swear! I would never never say anything like that!" And then he leaned in on his arm so that his face was close to mine and he said, "Well it's true, I do think that you have a great body." I was so shocked. I don't think that I responded at all. I could have melted into the floor. I turned around and went back into the classroom, and he never said anything about it again, and I never told anyone.

Her teacher used his power to humiliate and objectify her. He was insensitive to her distress and her efforts to preserve her character in what she felt was an attack against it. As she told the story, she was concerned with appealing to his authority, repeatedly claiming her innocence, whereas he carried out an inappropriate interaction over which she had almost no control. Despite her past efforts to be a good student, and her efforts in the interaction to present herself as good and worthy, he reduced her to her body. This interaction left her feeling alone in her shame.

Not only did her teacher sexually objectify and harass her, men routinely grabbed her in public. She talked of getting used to adult men harassing her and of her failed attempts to hide her body.

Men were constantly looking at me, making comments, and touching me. Many many times men on the bus and in public would grab my ass or touch my breasts. I didn't get angry, or even scared, I just accepted that this was what men were like, and this is how I was going to be treated now that I had breasts. It never occurred to me to tell my parents or ask for help, because I thought that there was something about me that was making the men act this way. I tried to control it by wearing bigger and thicker clothes, but it didn't seem to work.

Again and again her breasts were associated with the discrediting and threatening attention she received. Tabitha's story illustrates how when girls have little control over their environment, sexually objectifying interactions will result in the incorporation of the powerful meaning of the significant symbols of the interaction, their breasts, as irresistible, available, and discrediting, into their own understanding of their bodies. Within limited options for avoiding objectifying interactions, the only thing left to control in her environment was herself. Using defensive strategies to attempt to hide and cover her body only further added to her sense of personal responsibility for the treatment she received.

Tabitha split her time between the homes of her mother and father. Her mother talked openly with her about everything, however her father not only neglected to give her emotional support that might have helped her to deal with the difficulties she encountered because of her changing body, he too began to treat her differently once her body began to change. She revealed how her father's treatment of her contributed to her sense of shame and worthlessness.

When I was in fifth grade I remember waking up with a nightmare. My Dad slept in this king-sized bed alone so I started to climb into bed with him. He woke up and freaked out. "What are you doing?! You can't do that! This is totally inappropriate!" It was around then that he started in on telling me how worthless and unlovable I was. It really started at about the same time that I started to develop breasts. He used to embarrass me in front of men

on purpose. I guess my father just didn't know what to do with me when I started to grow breasts.

She keenly felt the diminished power associated with her body as her father used his authority and power to position her subordinately. In ninth grade, she had another experience of inappropriate advances by a teacher, and this time she went to her father. Her father questioned her repeatedly about whether she was certain; he stressed the fact that a man's career was on the line until she backed off and said that she may have misinterpreted what happened. Her treatment at the hands of her father helped to create a sense of a being on her own and of a lack of control over her environment, both of which encouraged turning toward defensive strategies—taking responsibility for her social interactions and attempting to downplay and hide her body.

Tabitha connected her experience of early breast development to both her feeling of anger toward men who found her attractive and her alienation from her body and sexuality.

Now I don't feel intimacy connected to my body or sex. I attach meaning to kissing and handholding, because that's the kind of stuff that men didn't want from me when they would grab at me on the busses. I just don't think of myself as a sexually desirable person. I know that all of these men would grab me and look at me, but that was just my body. If I put any effort in [to what I look like] and I get attention for it, I get really upset. Like I'm not a knockout unless I dress in this way for men. Compliments like that just remind me of how superficial and basic men are. I'm reminded of my father, the teachers, and the strangers in public, and it just leaves a horrible taste in my mouth. I don't feel sexy, and I can't imagine why anyone would think that I was. I just can't think of myself in that way.

Tabitha associated her breasts with not fitting in with peers and with sexual harassment from adults in power, both situations over which she had little control. In her experience, men's sexuality is abusive and objectifying, and, as a result, her own sexuality suggests the danger of being objectified and subjected to the harassment of men. She accepted harassment both as her responsibility and as the inevitable nature of men. In response, she downplayed her body and dissociated herself from her body and sexuality. These strategies created for her the meanings of her larger breasts, of men's sexuality, and of her own sexuality. Even though Tabitha said that she likes her breasts and that she looks "fantastic naked," she believes that her breasts are to be hidden and that men are not to be trusted.

### Kerry

Kerry was 20 years old at the time of the interview. She is White, and grew up in an upper middle-class, predominately White section of a medium-sized midwestern city. Like Tabitha, Kerry started to develop breasts when she was 8 years old, and she experienced menarche when she was 10 years old. Kerry's story of breast development brought her to an entirely different place socially and sexually from Tabitha's. She was one of three women with whom I talked who said that her breasts led to early sexual activity. Her social environment offered different constraints and opportunities, and we can see how her strategizing for positive social positions within these led to early sexual activity and lowered self-esteem.

Kerry's parents were supportive during her development. Her father, a pediatrician who specialized in adolescent medicine, made her feel particularly comfortable. Kerry did not think or believe that her mother was quite as comfortable with her changing body as her father was, but her mother communicated her support. Kerry thought or said that both of her parents felt sorry for her because of her early development.

Although she talked about being teased, Kerry made it clear that even peers who pointed out her physical difference with no intention of teasing made Kerry feel excluded and different. As status is a sense of belonging, her developing breasts represented a loss of status and emotional energy. Although it might appear to an adult observer, or to the adolescents who made the comments, that

her peers were just pointing out the obvious or were just curious, their comments contributed to a loss of emotional energy because they marked her as different, an outsider. Kerry described the emotional effect of this loss of status in the same way as Tabitha did—it made her "miserable."

Kerry talked about feeling alone and vulnerable, and she curtailed her activity and wore big clothes to control how much of her body other people saw.

> Nobody else was developed. I got made fun of all of the time. I hated it. I wouldn't swim. I was miserable. I quit gymnastics because of it. I wouldn't get in a leotard because I had breasts. I quit gymnastics and that was awful because I was really good at gymnastics. I was embarrassed; like I wouldn't wear anything, I was always wearing big clothes. I hated the whole thing; it made me miserable.

Unable to control the impact her changing breasts had on her social circumstances, Kerry went to great lengths to hide them. She not only wore clothes to hide her breasts, she also curtailed physical activities she enjoyed so that people would not see them.

Kerry told of boys who touched her against her will and snapped her bra straps.

> I remember wearing a bra in fourth grade and having people make fun of me. Boys were just really cruel about it. I remember one boy yelling about my breasts across the playground. They saw it, and boys would snap it. It was supposed to be funny but it hurt. Other people laughed, but I didn't.

Snapping bra straps is not just about marking difference; by touching her body against her will and by hurting her, the boys made the loss of power associated with her changing body real, literal. Early development for Kerry meant the loss of both status and power among peers.

Kerry's story changed when she entered the fifth grade. The boys and girls around her started demonstrating romantic interest in the other sex, and she suddenly found herself in a position of power, as she had breasts that the boys found desirable. She described how her body resulted in her popularity, but this attention ultimately undermined her self worth.

> In the end of fourth and fifth grade, it wasn't a problem anymore because my boobs made me very popular. Once I got to fifth grade, I had a lot of boyfriends. It was obvious why, because I was the only girl with boobs. I'm sure the reason why they wanted to date me was because I was so developed and that was the only reason. I was very popular with the boys, and the girls were jealous. They were like, "Oh my God, you are like the hottest girl." And I was like, "no, it's just because of my boobs." I knew it was just because of that, but it was still flattering.

Until boys started showing interest in her, her breasts were nothing but a "problem." They were a social problem because they represented a loss of status with friends and a loss of power at the hand of boys who would snap her bra straps and embarrass her. The boys were interested in her sexually, and the girls were jealous of the boys' attention. This changing social dynamic presented a new opportunity for her to use her breasts to gain social power and emotional energy. It is important to note, however, that although she said that her body was no longer a problem, through the objectifying interactions she came to see her body as nothing more than a desired commodity from which she dissociated herself. This fracturing of her self assured that she would gain only limited self-esteem from the positive attention; she was certain that it had little to do with "her." Even with this new power over the boys, her relationships with girls were still limited as girls continued to treat her differently. The girls were either jealous or scornful; either way she still did not enjoy full status or inclusion.

She clearly articulated the process and impact of objectification. Note that despite all of the supposedly positive attention she received for it, she does not even feel positive about her body.

> Developing early made me do stuff early with boys. Sex and sexual things have always been on my mind. I didn't really like it all the time when I was doing this with guys, but I felt flattered that they were noticing me. But then, I kind of realized it wasn't because of who I am. I don't know why I did it, maybe because it's easier to get guys to accept you if you're having sex with them. Whereas girls are very tough. Being physical with boys gave me confidence, but it didn't make me feel good to know a boy liked me just for my body. In the end I guess I don't even feel that good about my body.

Using her breasts socially was ultimately a losing proposition for Kerry. She had power because boys wanted her, but she had little power in the actual interaction to voice, and get, what she wanted. She told of gaining short-term power (i.e., the order-giving position of deciding who would receive her sexual attention) and status (attention/inclusion) with the boys, but, over the long-term, these sexual interactions drained her emotional energy and self-esteem because the sexual power was simultaneously discrediting and self-alienating. Using this power also made her feel out of control. Her strategy of using her breasts to improve her social position, one of the only strategies available to her for gaining emotional energy in interaction with her peers, led to a downward spiral of emotional energy that had relative peaks but ultimately lowered her level of emotional energy and her self-esteem.

### Laura

Laura is White, and she grew up in a middle-class, mostly White suburb of an east coast city. At the time that we talked, she was 22. Like Tabitha and Kerry, she started to menstruate when she was 10 years old, but she did not develop noticeable breasts until she was 9 years old. Laura's story illustrates the happy ending to the story of early breast development in many respects, not because she did not experience social difficulty, but because she was able to use proactive strategies for maximizing emotional energy rather than defensive strategies for minimizing the loss of emotional energy than defensive strategies for negotiating social interaction about her breasts. Her use of proactive strategies rather than defensive allowed her to avoid feeling responsible for her diminished social position, while encouraging interactions that helped to create even more opportunities for developing proactive strategies. She was the only woman with whom I talked who described her early development of breasts as positive, as something that she would chose to experience again, despite the social awkwardness and teasing. . . .

[Laura] told of how she tried to hide her breasts, and how, with her mother's support, she was able to negotiate interactions pertaining to her social difference so that she was able to diminish her shame.

> I tried to hide my breasts in the fourth and fifth grade. I refused to wear a bra in fifth grade. My Mom was really cool about it though. She was just like, "don't worry." She would bring things home all of the time for me to try on and she would call them undershirts, but later on I realized they were like sports bras. When I got dressed around my friends, I felt like we just all had undershirts on, so my Mom really made it easier for me.

Her unwillingness to wear a bra did not represent rebellion against authority or convention; it was rather a way of denying that she was indeed significantly different from her peers. Her mother's response to her denial demonstrated that she understood the reason for her daughter's refusal, and she worked to create a situation where her daughter could still fit in with the other girls. Laura's mother's efforts buffered Laura in a limited way from the loss of status that her larger breasts represented.

Despite her mother's efforts, Laura still received unwanted attention. She talked about catcalls she received from men.

> I never wore anything tight, but you know, you can see the outline of a person's shape through their clothes. I would sometimes get comments walking downtown from older men. I was like, "I'm not even 13 years old yet!" It was like, "you are so yucky!"

Responses from strangers no doubt had implications for the sexual objectification of her body, but, unlike Tabitha's self-blame for strangers' re-

actions, Laura saw the strangers, rather than herself as "yucky." This difference in responses did not necessarily change the immediate impact of the experience of sexual objectification and subordinate positioning that the two girls shared, but it did have implications for what this interaction meant to them. Although it may appear to be a subtle difference, wearing big clothes to hide a body that elicits sexual responses from men who "cannot help themselves," who are responding directly to the signal of breasts (Tabitha), represents much more self-blame and loss of critical analysis of one's social position than wearing big clothes to hide a body from the yucky men (Laura), who themselves, rather than the breasts, are clearly the source of the problem.

Laura understood that she suffered not directly from her breasts, but because of other people's responses to them. This placed the source of her discomfort in the social interaction, not within her self, and gave her a more powerful position to negotiate interactions pertaining to her difference. Laura described how she entered into conflict with boys to continue playing sports with them.

> I was like, "yes, I have breasts, but they're not going to stop me from doing things I like." I was very much a tomboy and then this happened [breast development], and it was really hard to stay athletic. When you're a girl, and they notice they're like, "why don't you just watch us play." I would say, "no!" I think because I was very stubborn, and I refused to accept that I was going to be left out of stuff because of something that I couldn't control, people began to see that I was still the same old person. My dad was the soccer coach. He also tried to make me feel very comfortable. It let me know that he understood.

Throughout her story, Laura discussed how she got the message repeatedly that her breasts should not be seen to move. She was told she should restrict her activity so that her breasts would be seen in the light in which they were expected to be seen—unmoving, docile, and sexual. Rather than resisting within her self by acquiescing and refusing to run so that the attention and negative feedback would temporarily disappear, she was able to resist on the level of social interaction. She told the boys "no!" and insisted on continuing to play sports. She maintained a proactive strategy for maximizing emotional energy by keeping the situation to be negotiated in the social world rather than within her body.

Her father's understanding of her social position and his support helped to prevent her from internalizing and developing defensive strategies. His connection with her and his acknowledgement of her situation offered status and created space in the environment where she had some control, some option besides turning inward. It is also likely that positive experiences associated with participation in athletics were a source of both power and status that undermined other sexually objectifying interactions. Kerry talked of quitting gymnastics, but it is important to note that gymnastics is about body display as well as performance. A sport that does not emphasize the visual (such as soccer) may undermine the sexual objectification of the body by providing an outlet where the body can remain integrated with the girl's larger identity.

As with the other girls, the time came when breasts equaled sexual attention, which meant an opportunity for social power. For Laura, this potential for social power happened as five elementary schools came together for middle school, so that the one or two girls who developed early in each school were together. She said that they all became fast friends. She talked about how reactions from boys continued to play a central role in her experience of her breasts.

> Lots of guys would come up to me and asked me to go places with them and stuff like that. I guess it made me more popular with the guys, or at least more noticed. The boys were just starting to take interest, but they were interested for the wrong reasons. I wanted nothing to do with it. Back then it was like, "Boobs! Oh my gosh! I got to have them!" The boys had this huge image of boobs being attractive.

Unlike Kerry, Laura was critical at that time of the popularity that the boys offered. She was able to resist using her breasts for social power at the cost of sexual objectification. Laura regained some status when she was able to develop connections to other early developers. It may be that their support enabled her to resist the sexual advances boys were making toward her.

Laura gave her analysis of why the other early developing girls responded the way that they did to their early breast development.

> Some of the girls were trying to hide their breasts as much as they could; these were the girls who were super shy and couldn't deal with the development and any attention they got for it. Other girls were wearing really short skirts and tight shirts and trying to show off their new bodies; these were the girls who used development like a stage. I think on one hand the hiding was about becoming comfortable with their body while the showing off was about accepting a role that they thought they had because they were developed.

Although she presented the strategies for dealing with early development (hiding or flaunting) as either/or alternatives, she herself was able to find comfort with her body and refused the role of sex object. She stated this clearly in the quote below where she said that she would develop breasts early again if she could.

> If I had to do it over again, I would pick to be an early developer. It [developing breasts early] was negative in that it made me feel self-conscious, but when everybody else was going through puberty much later they were very self-conscious and I had already gotten over it when I was younger. I think I had more time to learn to accept my body before we all started dating and that sort of thing, so I was never very negative about it [my body]. I had so much more time to find out who I was, and to be comfortable with who I was, instead of using boys to make me feel better about myself.

At the beginning of her story Laura did hide her body, but then she moved on to describe how she refused to hide herself when she wanted to run and play. She also refused to take advantage of the double-edged power offered to her by the boys who were all too willing to grant her social power at the price of sexual objectification. At the same time, she did not become alienated from her body and sexuality in the same way that Tabitha did. She described herself as starting to date around the same time as most of her peers—no earlier and no later. Early development was a developmental event that she negotiated proactively. Her assessment of her experience was much more global; she compared the social experiences of herself and her peers. This social critique is both product of and continued foundation for proactive emotional energy-maximizing strategies that allowed her to resist her environment rather than to constrain herself.

## Discussion

### Interaction Ritual Approach to Understanding Early Breast Development

The results of this study established the fundamental theoretical point that the *meaning* early breast development has for girls is based in social interaction. As I stated earlier, in interaction ritual theory, the meaning of a symbol is ultimately a strategy for action, a way of negotiating one's social position in a particular environment. We relate to symbols through their relevance for our emotions. We use them as guides to emotional energy. People are motivated to act proactively to maximize emotional energy, but, when there are limited options, this process is subverted, and individuals develop defensive strategies. The individual's social contexts determine what sorts of strategies they are likely to use. Although these early breast developers have limited choices, they are not passive. They strategize within the available framework; the early breast-developing women in this study told stories of trying to improve their situation within the limits of their bodies and their environments. We can see how the relationships between social contexts, social interactions, and the different strategies they generated had various impacts on the women who

used them. We can also see how the power stratification associated with gender is produced and reproduced in face-to-face interaction.

Although the experience of having noticeable breasts is one that cuts across timing of development, these women talked about diminished status among their peers (exclusion) and targeted peer harassment (power-draining interactions). In their stories they suggested that they experienced diminished social positions because they went through breast development early and alone. Both age of onset and the age of onset relative to peers were important in their stories. Age of onset had implications for the sort of reception the early breast developers received for being off time. All of these women stated that in early elementary school they were teased and subjected to friends' curiosity; only in late elementary school did they gain the opportunity to trade on the sexual power of their breasts. It may be that breasts in third and fourth grade were frightening for both boys and girls. There was power in their breasts, but it was latent because they caused so much discomfort among peers. Being first and alone was also important in its own right. Regardless of whether peers and adults teased, sexually harassed, or admired their breasts, being the only one with breasts had implications for loss of status. This noticeable physical difference marked the early breast developers as a type of outsider among their peers in a time when fitting in is particularly important for social life (Alsaker, 1995; Silbereisen & Kracke, 1997). The experience of having breasts is not unique to early breast developers, but the combination of teasing, exclusion, and sexual power may very well be unique.

Breasts were super-saturated with conflicting meaning for these early breast-developing girls (Latteier, 1998; Schmitt, 1986). It is no wonder that large samples and multiple regression models cannot easily represent multiple and conflicting experiences of girls who develop breasts early. Breasts, because they changed these girls' social positions, became objects of negotiation. Although their stories reveal that the meaning of breasts was not uniform across the different local cultures in which these women interacted, breasts uniformly signified adult femininity, which was both empowering and discrediting. The above stories illustrate three ideal types for these women's negotiation of early breast development that I developed based on the analysis of these accounts of early breast development as well as the assumptions of interaction ritual theory. Most of the women told of using defensive strategies that could be categorized as hiding the body and using the body for popularity. As girls they used a combination of these approaches as their social circumstances changed. Laura was the only one who told a story of relying almost entirely on proactive strategies. I include her as an ideal type because her story represents how social circumstances, an athletic history, and accommodating parents can radically alter the interaction strategies, experience, and perception of early breast development.

### Defensive Strategies

When individuals cannot control their environment, and it is full of subordinating interaction rituals, they will turn to defensive strategies and attempt to control their own behavior to avoid the worst of subordinate positioning and further loss of emotional energy. When women are subject to the inevitable and uninvited evaluating gaze of male observers, they learn to evaluate and constrain themselves to avoid interactions that lead to further loss of emotional energy. These early breast-developing women used defensive strategies that were based on controlling that which stigmatized them, their body. Latteier (1998) stated that when girls develop breasts, the

> body is no longer the me of childhood—that bundle of amorphous pleasures and pains, the me that loves to run and jump and eat ice cream. The body becomes my equipment, my display, and something I own, something for which I'm responsible. My body is a quantity to be judged by others who draw conclusions about me based on what they see (p. 15).

The women with whom I spoke built defensive strategies by either downplaying the body or playing up the body so that they could maintain a sense of control over the responses they received. As is characteristic of interaction strategies that are derived from limited social options, both strategies (i.e., hiding and showing off) offered some social advantage at the price of being discrediting in other ways. As Young (1980) pointed out, developing a sense of our bodies and ourselves as beautiful means that we stifle the sensation of our capable, active bodies as strong, and move forward to struggle with the resistance offered up by the physical world. On the other hand, when we insist that our bodies are strong and capable, or at least not available to the male gaze, we risk being considered unattractive, not beautiful.

### Denying Strategies

Despite findings that early developers engage in sexual activity before on time and late developers (Brooks-Gunn, 1988; Flannery et al., 1993; Magnusson et al., 1985), Tabitha's story of early breast development suggests how social circumstances can conspire to produce a radically different outcome: sexual repression and alienation. When a girl turns to a defensive strategy of hiding her body or resigning herself to sexual harassment from men, she can develop and sustain meanings associated with her breasts that are based in shame and anger. Tabitha understood that men and sex are harmful, which undermined notions that her body and sexual activity could be sources of pleasure. Sexual harassment is more likely to lead to a sense of disembodiment than of embodiment and active pleasure (Frost, 2001). As I stated earlier, defensive strategies are likely to be much more resilient than proactive strategies, that is, shame, anger, and disassociative interaction strategies may outlast the sexually harassing interactions, and such was the case for Tabitha. Latteier (1998) found that when women have suffered a good deal of teasing or other negative attention for their breasts in late childhood and early adolescence, they tended not to enjoy breast stimulation. Of course, this outcome may also be true for early breast developers who choose to be sexually active. As Kerry stated, just because she was willing to be sexual with boys did not mean that she enjoyed it.

### Using It Strategies

Smolak, Levine, and Gralen (1993) found that girls who went through puberty early and started dating early were at particular risk for body dissatisfaction and eating disorders. Kerry, as well as the two other women who told stories of having used the sexual power of breasts, had lasting negative feelings about her body. Bartky (1990) pointed out that to succeed in the provision of a beautiful or sexy body gains a woman attention and some admiration, but little real respect and rarely any social power. Using the body for popularity in sexual interactions may produce short-term emotional energy gains, but ultimately the experience can be discrediting and objectifying, which leads to low emotional energy associated with the symbol of the interaction—the body. Meeting feminine attractiveness standards may enhance the power a woman has over her social environment, yet the very fact that she physically matches the cultural stereotype of a feminine woman may also cause her to be taken less seriously by others (Franzoi, 2001). Franzoi (2001) pointed out that the exchange of a woman's direct social power for her perceived beauty and accompanying indirect power is one of the defining features of benevolent sexism, which rewards conforming behavior but ultimately undermines women's power.

Are women who trade on this discrediting power blindly following the dictates of culture against their own best interests? I suggest not. In cases when one does not have direct social power, and one is offered indirect power, why would one not take it? We must consider the social context that limits the options of those who are strategizing to make the best of their situations. In cases of diminished social position, this effort can lead to indirect defensive strategies that ultimately lead

to even lower emotional energy and reaffirmed diminished status. Such is the case in the account that Kerry gave of early dating and sexual activity that contributed to both her immediate popularity and her long-term negative feelings about her body.

### Maintaining Proactive Strategies

Sometimes, despite hostile social circumstances, there are interactions available that enable one to maintain proactive maximizing strategies. It is important to note that almost all of the women told stories of initially using proactive strategies to manage their social difficulties, such as getting angry about initial comments, teasing, or exclusion. However, only some of the girls experienced any success as a result or were supported in their efforts. . . . Brown and Gilligan found that girls who had close, open, and often overtly conflictual relationships with their parents, their mothers in particular, were able to maintain the ability to resist—to be a social critic and to give voice to their own experience. As in the case of Laura, a supportive parent can help to maintain proactive strategies. However, Kerry's story illustrates that sometimes this support from parents still is not enough to prevent the development of defensive strategies. . . .

Proactive interaction strategies are the most desirable because they are the most flexible. When we are able to experience some success using proactive strategies, we maintain a sense of control that enables us to negotiate rocky social terrain. Proactive strategies also frame emotional energy-draining social circumstances as social problems rather than as the problem of those who are experiencing lower status and lower power. This means that proactive strategies in the face of oppressive circumstances offer the greatest potential for social change. Change may only be realized on the face-to-face interaction level, such as Laura's success in being able to play with the boys despite her breasts, but there is a possibility that such strategies could lead to wider social change. Regardless of what level of social life resistance may affect, engaging in resistance is important because it prevents self-blame for problems born of diminished social position.

### Interaction, Sexual Objectification of Breasts, and the Oppression of Women

We construct the meaning of our breasts and other aspects of our bodies through interaction in lived day-to-day experience (Schmitt, 1986). The social dynamics of interaction are the basis for the sexual objectification of women's bodies, as well as our feelings about our selves and the internalized objectification of our bodies. Research by Mendelson et al. (1996) supports the importance of interaction and emotion; they found that women's self-esteem was not related to relative weight, but was associated with feelings about their appearance. Similarly, Franzoi and Chang (2000) found that the aspects of the body that women felt most positive about were those that they could alter cosmetically to be more attractive, however they were also aspects of their appearance that lowered others' perceptions of their competence and dominance. Also, men were more likely to experience their bodies as process, whereas women were likely to view them as objects to be controlled (Franzoi & Chang, 2000). Such findings offer an illustration of interaction ritual theory that suggests that power is not abstract but based in the real ability to generate social interactions that are positive and controllable. When our social context limits our ability to find dependable positive interactions, we try to control ourselves to prevent the further loss of power and status.

For adolescent girls, saying what they think and feel often represents social risks, such as the risk of losing relationships (status) and finding themselves powerless and alone (Brown & Gilligan, 1992). Brown and Gilligan (1992) suggested that as this happens, resistance to their social situation turns inward and manifests as dissociation and not knowing, and undermines their potential for engaging in open conflict. Brown and Gilligan defined resisting as girls using their voices to speak up to oppressive authority. This is similar to what I have identified as proactive emotional energy-maximizing strategies. They noted the confidence and psychological health associated with a connection to one's voice and the ability to resist actively, and they suggested that girls lose these abilities as they transition into adolescence. Proactive maximization strategies then are not only difficult for early breast developers to maintain, but for all girls as they transition into adolescence. Thus it is likely that most girls will resort to some sort of defensive strategy, thereby producing inner personal and interpersonal disturbances that reflect their struggles to control themselves to limit subordinate positioning.

Spadola (1998, p. 33) suggested that almost every adolescent girl "feels that her breasts are not right," that they are too fast or too slow, too big or too small. Women with different timings can feel "off" about their breasts. We can assume that for every early developer that boys or men proposition because of her relatively large breasts, there are late developers whom boys and men ignore because of their lack of noticeable breasts. Why do we always want the breasts we do not have? Why are stories of discomfort so universal? Because through face-to-face day-to-day interaction we learn that breasts are loaded with conflicting meaning; they indicate power and availability, motherhood and sexuality. They mean many things in many different contexts, and any woman is likely to find herself in a social situation where she wishes she had different breasts. For example, the same woman might wish for smaller breasts at work and larger ones at home (Spadola, 1998). Personality attributes are associated with breast size, and the increasing availability of cosmetic surgery to change our breasts, to bring them into alignment with the breasts that we think that we "should" have, only reaffirms our responsibility for having "bad" breasts or the "wrong" breasts. The conflicting ideals for breasts are illustrative of the conflicting demands on women and girls. As Yalom (1997) suggested, how a woman regards her breasts is a good indicator of her personal self-esteem, as well as of the collective status of women in general.

Paying attention to interaction allows us to see the power/status conflicts that are basic to repeated subordinate positioning and how this repeated social positioning in relation to women's bodies creates the larger patterns of power associated with gender (Collins, 2001). When we look at the culture and interactions surrounding women's bodies, we see how women can actively appropriate and recycle oppressive symbols back into the larger culture. These social circumstances reproduce the prevalence of negative body feelings that undermine women's political organizing (McKinley, 1998). However, we are motivated to experience positive social positioning; we are motivated to work against the power of symbols that degrade us when ever possible. This means that oppression is unstable and that there is always room for breaks and resistance. We need to look to the structure of everyday interaction and see not only how the dynamics of face-to-face interactions create and reproduce patterns of oppression, but also how those who are subordinately positioned strategize within their social context [and] are sometimes able to develop strategies that undermine and even destroy oppressive patterns of interaction.

## REFERENCES

Alsaker, F. D. (1992). Pubertal timing, overweight, and psychological adjustment. *Journal of Early Adolescence, 12,* 396–419.

Alsaker, F. D. (1995). Timing of puberty and reactions to pubertal changes. In M. Rutter (Ed.), *Psychosocial disturbances in young people: Challenges for prevention* (pp. 37–82). Cambridge, UK: Cambridge University Press.

Bartky, S. L. (1990). *Femininity and domination: Studies in the phenomenology of oppression.* New York: Routledge.

Blume, J. (1970). *Are you there God? It's me, Margaret.* New York: Bantam Doubleday.

Blyth, D. A., Simmons, R. G., & Zakin, D. F. (1985). Satisfaction with body image for early adolescent females: The impact of pubertal timing with different school environments *Journal of Youth and Adolescence, 14*(3), 207–225.

Brooks-Gunn, J. (1984). The psychological significance of different pubertal events to young girls. *Journal of Early Adolescence, 4,* 315–327.

Brooks-Gunn, J. (1988). Antecedents and consequences of variations in girls' maturational timing. In M. D. Levine & E. R. McAnarney (Eds.), *Early adolescent transitions* (pp. 101–121). Lexington, MA: Lexington Books.

Brooks-Gunn, J., & Petersen, A. C. (1984). Problems in studying and defining pubertal events. *Journal of Youth and Adolescence, 13*(3), 181–196.

Brooks-Gunn, J., & Samelson M. W. M. (1986). Physical similarity of and disclosure of menarcheal status to friends: Effects of age and pubertal status. *Journal of Early Adolescence, 6,* 3–14.

Brown, L. M., & Gilligan, C. (1992). *Meeting at the crossroads: Women's psychology and girls' development.* Cambridge, MA: Harvard University Press.

Collins, R. (1990). Stratification, emotional energy, and the transient emotions, In T. Kemper (Ed.), *Research agendas in the sociology of emotions* (pp. 27–57). New York: State University of New York Press.

Collins, R. (2001). Situational stratification: A micro-macro theory of inequality. *Sociological Theory, 18,* 17–43.

Davis, K. (1991). Remaking the she-devil: A critical look at feminist approaches to beauty. *Hypatia, 6*(2), 21–43.

Durkheim, E. (1995). *The elementary forms of religious life.* New York: Free Press.

Flannery, D. J., Rowe, D. C., & Gulley, B. L. (1993). Impact of pubertal status, timing, and age on adolescent sexual experience and delinquency. *Journal of Adolescent Research, 8*(1), 21–40.

Franzoi, S. L. (2001). Is female body esteem shaped by benevolent sexism? *Sex Roles, 44,* 177–188.

Franzoi, S. L., & Chang, Z. (2000). The sociocultural dynamics of the physical self: How does gender shape body esteem? *Perspectives on Social Problems, 12,* 179–201.

Frost, L. (2001). *Young women and the body.* New York: Palgrave.

Gerth, H. H., & Mills, C. W. (Eds.). (1946). *From Max Weber: Essays in sociology.* New York: Oxford University Press.

Goffman, E. (1967). *Interaction ritual: Essays on face-to-face behavior.* Chicago: Aldine.

Holloway, W. (1989). *Subjectivity and method in psychology: Gender, meaning, and science.* London, UK: Sage.

Latteier, C. (1998). *Breasts: The women's perspective on an American obsession.* New York: Harrington Park Press.

Magnusson, D., Stattin, H., & Allan, V. (1985). Biological maturation and social development: A longitudinal study of some adjustments processes from mid-adolescence to adulthood. *Journal of Youth and Adolescence, 14*(4), 267–283.

Mead, G. H. (1934). *Mind, self, and society.* Chicago: University of Chicago Press.

Mendelson, B. K., White, D. R., & Mendelson, M. J. (1996). Self-esteem and body esteem: Effects of gender, age, and weight. *Journal of Applied Developmental Psychology, 17,* 321–346.

McKinley, N. M. (1998). Gender differences in undergraduates' body esteem: The mediating effect of objectified body consciousness and actual/ideal weight discrepancy. *Sex Roles, 39,* 113–133.

Morgan, K. P (1991). Women and the knife: Cosmetic surgery and the colonization of women's bodies. *Hypatia, 6*(3), 25–53.

Murry, M. (2003). Narrative psychology and narrative analysis. In P. M. Comic, J. E. Rhodes, & L. Yardly (Eds.), *Qualitative research in psychology: Expanding perspectives in methodology and design* (pp. 95–112). Washington DC: APA.

Nottelman, E. D., Susman, E. J., Dorn, L. D., Inoff-Germain, G., Loriaux, D. L., Cutler, G. B., et al. (1987). Relationships among chronological age, pubertal state, height, weight, and serum levels of gonadotropins, sex steroids, and adrenal androgens. *Journal of Adolescent Health Care, 8,* 35–48.

Petersen, A. C. (1988). Adolescent development. *Annual Review of Psychology, 39,* 583–607.

Petersen, A. C., & Crockett, L. J. (1985). Pubertal timing and grade effects on adjustment. *Journal of Youth and Adolescence, 14,* 191–206.

Polkinghorne, D. E. (1988). *Narrative knowing and the human sciences.* Albany: SUNY Press.

Sarbin, T. R. (1986). *Narrative psychology: The storied nature of human conduct.* New York: Praeger.

Scheff, T. J. (1990). *Microsociology: Discourse, emotion, and social structure.* Chicago: University of Chicago Press.

Schmitt, R. L. (1986). Embodied identities: Breasts as emotional reminders. *Studies in Symbolic Interaction, 7*(A), 229–289.

Silbereisen, R. K., & Kracke, B. (1997). Self-reported maturational timing and adaptation in adolescence. In J. Schulenberg, J. L. Maggs, & K. Hurrelmann (Eds.), *Health risks and developmental transitions during adolescence* (pp. 85–109). Cambridge, UK: Cambridge University Press.

Simmons, R. G., & Blyth, D. A. (1987). *Moving into adolescence: The impact of pubertal change and school context.* New York: Aldine de Gruyter.

Spadola, M. (1998). *Breasts: Our most public private parts.* Berkely: Wildcat Canyon Press.

Stuhlmiller, C. M. (2001). Narrative methods in qualitative research. Potential for therapeutic transformation. In K. R. Gilbert (Ed.), *The emotional nature of qualitative research* (pp. 64–79). New York: CRC Press.

Summers-Effler, E. (in press). Sense and context: The role of emotion and culture in the process of the self. *Advances in Group Processes.*

Tolman, D. (1994). Doing desire: Adolescent girls' for/with sexuality. *Gender and Society, 8,* 324–342.

Wiesner, M., & Ittel, A. (2002). Relations of pubertal timing and depressive symptoms to substance use in early adolescence. *Journal of Early Adolescence, 22*(1), 5–23.

Williams, J. M., & Currie, C. (2000). Self-esteem and physical development in early adolescence: Pubertal timing and body image. *Journal of Early Adolescence, 20*(2), 129–149.

Yalom, M. (1997). *A history of the breast.* New York: Ballantine.

Young, I. M. (1980). Throwing like a girl: A phenomenology of feminine body comportment, motility, and spatiality. *Human Studies, 3,* 137–156.

# Fixing the Broken Male Machine

Meika Loe

The quest for manhood—the effort to achieve, demonstrate, and prove masculinity—is rooted deep in American history, starting at least with the nineteenth century's self-made man.[1] But in the early twenty-first century, when gender equity is believed to be increasingly achievable and men are no longer the sole family breadwinners, male power and control are no longer assured. Scholars specializing in masculinity studies have had much to say about male confusion in the roughly thirty years preceding Viagra. Attempts to understand and locate "masculinity in crisis" are varied and incomplete, but crucial to an understanding of the success of the Viagra phenomenon.[2] ...

Today, a new and profitable masculine recovery movement is being generated with the aid of a pharmaceutical drug, and the male body is re-emerging as a site for confidence and control.... Now, millions of men turn to Viagra to reclaim something they lost.... [T]his ... is a silent movement, forged by individuals who may be vaguely aware of other men pursuing "recovery" of potency confidence, and "life" at the same time. But for most of the participants, the recovery process is too personal and too stigmatizing to discuss.

The silence, privacy, and relative invisibility of this movement proved difficult for a sociologist wanting to talk with Viagra consumers. Many

From Meika, Loe. 2004. "Fixing the Broken Male Machine." In *The Rise of Viagra: How a Little Pill Changed Sex in America* (pp. 62–93). New York University Press. Reprinted by permission.

times I asked myself, Where do those who are wanting to recover their potency "hang out," besides in doctors' offices? This question was difficult to answer and left me feeling sympathy for the men who wanted an answer to the same question. Where did men turn who wanted to talk with other men about their experiences with ED or Viagra? In the end, the communities I found that are built around the experience of erectile dysfunction and recovery were support groups and internet chat rooms. The majority of men featured in this chapter were members of male support groups or ED-themed internet chat rooms when they agreed to talk with me. What emerges is a discussion of bodies in need of "fixing."

## Male Bodies in Need of Fixing

In the late twentieth century, masculinities scholars began to write about the connections between manhood and men's bodies. Australian social scientist R. W. Connell wrote, "True masculinity is almost always thought to proceed from men's bodies."[3] Sander Gilman's work revealed how "aesthetic surgeries" such as penile implants can help in the achievement of masculinity. And sociologist Michael Kimmel suggested that the realms of health and fitness have replaced the workplace in the late twentieth century as the next major testing ground for masculinity, where body work inevitably becomes a "relentless test."[4] But few masculinity scholars have taken a critical perspective on current theories of the body as a machine or as a surface imprinted with social symbolism.[5]

Likewise, limited scholarship on male sexual bodies suggests that sexuality, particularly heterosexuality, is a proving ground for masculinity.[6]

Only recently have researchers, particularly feminist social scientists, begun to expand their inquiries to include the medicalization of male bodies.[7] Since Viagra's release, a small number of women social scientists have written about the ways in which this product promises to reinforce "phallocentrism" or, in my words, "erect the patriarchy."[8] In other words, some are concerned that a product like Viagra may hinder ongoing efforts for gender equality. Others are concerned about the new commodification of masculinity and the related proliferation of mass insecurity around manhood.[9] Additionally, medical sociologists Marco and Fishman have written about Viagra's potential for liberatory or disciplinary effects.[10] In contrast, most male scholars who study masculinity have yet to fully take up the question of the new medicalized male body or, more specifically, the Viagra body.[11]

How have men themselves responded to this newfound medical attention? In the following pages, medical professionals and patients use the language of "trouble" and "repair" as they grapple with "deficient" body parts, the concept of manhood, and medical diagnoses. In the process, they expose as constructs that which we take for granted; they imagine their bodies as machines, and they use Viagra as a tool for fixing their broken masculinity. And finally, they discover that Viagra not only solves problems but sometimes produces them as well.[12]

### A Problematic Package

Several years after Viagra's debut, I had a fascinating conversation with a doctor and his long-time patient about sexual dysfunction. Upon hearing about my research, a man I will call Gray had volunteered to help by bringing me to talk to the only expert he knew on Viagra, his doctor.[13] Dr. Bern, an internist in private practice in his sev-

enties, and Gray, a retired business owner in his eighties, had a fifty-year history together.[14] As we sat in Dr. Bern's office in Los Angeles, California, discussing my research project, both men tried to convince me that masculinity was intimately tied to penile functioning.

*DR. BERN:* You see, sexual dysfunction in males is peculiar. I'm sure if someone is a paraplegic and can't walk he would feel psychologically deprived. But beyond the great obvious lack—people who don't see or hear as well, they don't feel like they have lost their manhood, you see. I must tell you, and I'm not a psychiatrist, but I think it is far more prevalent in males than it would be in females. The fact that if women don't have sexual gratification . . . It isn't that they don't miss it, but they don't have the psychological burden that males seem to have. Maybe it's a throwback to the time when the caveman went and dragged a woman out on his shoulder.

*ML:* So sexuality is integral to male identity?

*GRAY:* Absolutely! [My wife and I] talked about it for a long time—well, a couple of weeks before the [prostate] operation itself. We talked about it's possible we may not be able to have sex because the apparatuses they had out didn't necessarily work. So you could go for the rest of your life without having sex. And [the doctor] is so right. You feel part of your manhood is gone.[15]

Doctor Bern uses an evolutionary example to construct contemporary male sexuality as overt, desirous, assertive, and central to masculinity, in contrast to femininity, which is passive and nonsexual. Manhood is seen as the ability to have sexual control of and desire for women. Most importantly, though, Dr. Bern and Gray agreed that the trouble associated with erectile dysfunction involves the psychological burden of the loss of manhood. Most of my male interview subjects, both consumers and practitioners, were in agreement on this point. If the penis is in trouble, so is the man.

You probably wouldn't understand it—it's a big part of manhood. Ever since you're a little boy growing up that's a part of your masculinity. And whether it's right or wrong, and however you deal with it—that's, well, I'm dealing with it and I seem to be okay. If a man gets an erection, or the boys in the shower compare each other, that's your masculinity. A lot of men don't like to admit it. (Phil, fifty-four years old, white, heterosexual, insurance broker)[16]

[Viagra] makes my penis larger, length and width-wise, and that's inherent to the macho thing of men. With impotence, I felt like part of my manhood has been lost. (Byron, seventy years old, white, hetero-sexual, unknown occupation)[17]

After many of these conversations, I began to see that for men like Byron, Phil, and Gray, gender and sexuality may be difficult to separate out. Masculinity requires sexuality, and vice versa.[18] In contrast, femininity has traditionally been con-structed in opposition to masculinity and, thus, sexuality.[19] What these men were telling me was that sexuality, or "erectile health," is compulsory for men, integral to achieving and maintaining manhood. (Implicit here is the requirement that heterosexual desire is compulsory for men.) Or as Australian cultural critic Annie Potts would put it, in a phallus-centered world, "Every man must pump up for phallocracy."[20]

While men may not discuss their masculinity problems openly with a doctor, the comments above and Viagra's recent block-buster success are representative of a new global concern for the "broken," or impotent, male. Some social scien-tists have argued that gender is "accomplished" in daily life through our interactions with others. In other words, we perform and interactively "do" masculinity or femininity through our appear-ance, body language, tone of voice, etc. Following this logic, the "accomplishment" of masculinity is situated, to some extent, in erectile achievement.[21] Fixing the "male machine" and ensuring erectile functioning, for the patients quoted above and countless others, is a way to ensure masculinity. Just as some social scientists have argued that cos-metic surgery is institutional support for women

to successfully accomplish and "do" femininity,[22] Viagra can be seen as a biotechnological tool used to ensure masculinity by fixing the broken male machine.

### The Poorly Functioning Male Machine

As Donna Haraway first argued in her ground breaking essay the "Cyborg Manifesto," we are all "cyborgs." A cyborg is a hybrid creature com-posed of both organism and machine who popu-lates a world ambiguously natural and crafted.[23] Think of Arnold Schwarzenegger in *The Termina-tor,* for example. Today, most medical language about the body reflects the overlap between humans and machines. Medical texts regularly describe bodies using mechanical terminology such as "functioning" and "maintenance." In her research into twentieth-century understand-ings of health and the body, anthropologist Emily Martin found that the human body is commonly compared to a disciplined machine. Like a ma-chine, the body is made up of parts that can break down.[24] Similarly, Elizabeth Grosz argued that in a postmodern world, the body is treated as a mechanic structure in which components can be adjusted, altered, removed, and replaced.[25] Ill-ness, then, refers to a broken body part. Fixing this part ensures the functioning of the machine. The metaphor of the body as a smoothly func-tioning machine is central to the way Viagra has been presented. In this chapter, you will see how doctors and patients use mechanical metaphors to make sense of body and gender trouble, or "bro-ken" masculinity.

Such industrial metaphors are used regularly by Viagra spokesperson Irwin Goldstein, who is known for describing erectile functioning as "all hydraulics" and suggesting that dysfunction re-quires rebuilding the male machine. Following this metaphor, common treatment protocols for erectile dysfunction center on treating the penis, the broken part, separately from the body, the machine. In the new science of sex, penile dys-function can be measured in a variety of ways:

degree of penile tumescence (rigidity), penetrability (ability to penetrate the partner), sustainability of erection, and satisfaction with performance. These measures are figured into Pfizer-distributed "sexual health" scales and questionnaires. While they may not always do so, doctors are encouraged by Pfizer sales representatives to use these resources and to center their sexual health discussions with patients around erectile performance, asking patients to rate their erections in terms of penetrability, hardness, maintenance, and satisfaction levels.

For Pfizer, the focus is on treating the dysfunctional penis. Emphasis is on "optimal" or "maximal" performance—rigidity and sustainability of the erection—which means that anything less than such performance constitutes erectile dysfunction....

Likewise, in the world of science, Goldstein has written that "submaximal rigidity or submaximal capability to sustain the erection" is another way of understanding erectile dysfunction.[26] In other words, "maximal" erectile rigidity and longevity are normal and expected. This understanding of the penis as dysfunctional and fixable (even perfectible) is exemplified in the following statements by two white men in their fifties; Dr. Curt, a urologist in a medical clinic, and Chuck, a heterosexual architect.

> What I do is say [to patients complaining of erectile dysfunction], "Tell me about the erections. When you were twenty years old let's say they were a ten, rock hard. Where would they be now on a scale from one to ten?" So I give them some objectible [sic] evidence that they can give me. They'll say, "Oh, now it's a two." A lot of guys say it's now a seven or eight. I say, "Can you still perform with a seven or eight?" They say, "Yeah, but its not as good as it was." (Dr. Curt, urologist in medical clinic)[27]

> I'd say as far as functioning sexually, I'm probably at 70 percent. I just can't get hard enough to penetrate. Everything works but the erection. If I were to rate my erectile functioning prior to surgery, with now, I'd say it's at 75 percent. It will never be back to 100 percent, I know that. So I'm somewhat sat-

isfied. And the doctors always tell me that this is a long process, and that I need to be patient about getting back to functioning. So I'm in a wait-and-see mode. (Chuck, fifty-three years old, white, heterosexual, architect)[28]

Many patients who are currently looking for treatment for erectile dysfunction inhabit the in-between, "mild ED" arena (in terms of performance rankings from one to ten) and appear to be concerned with restoring their "machine" to a "normal" level of functioning. Despite Chuck's focus on "getting back to functioning," sexual standards have changed, I believe in part as a response to Viagra, and now "normal" is often not enough.[29]

It is important to point out that while many of these discussions are focused on the penis, they may also reflect expectations about normal manhood and aging. As we have learned, to be normal sexually means being normal in terms of gender, and vice versa. Also implicit in these pursuits of "normality" is a sense of denial and rejection of bodily change and perhaps aging. Thus, Chuck may be just as focused on "getting back to" manhood and youth as he is on "getting back to" normal sexual functioning.

## Trouble with Normal

In some cases, Viagra is used by heterosexual and homosexual men who feel that normal penile functioning is not good enough, and extra-normal functioning is now the goal. While these men claim they do not "need" Viagra, they are more satisfied with their performance when they do use it.[30] In the quotations below, Viagra consumers Will and Stanford imply that the pre-Viagra penis is slow, unpredictable, and uncertain, and, thus, problematic.

> [I was] totally surprised in my ability to stay erect without effort and the ability to repeatedly snap to attention. Amazing effect. Sorta magical in a way. (Will, fifty-three years old, white, homosexual, program coordinator)[31]

I noticed that if I get titillated [after using Viagra], then the penis springs to attention. Not atypically. But more facile. It's easier. I don't know if it takes less time. It's more convincing. It's not like maybe I'll get hard and maybe I won't. It's like "Okay, here I am!" (Stanford, sixty-five years old, white, heterosexual, counselor)[32]

For Will and Stanford, the Viagra body may be preferable to the natural body because it is consistent and predictable. While rigidity is the goal, part of optimal penile performance is to appear flexible; thus, the Viagra body is, in part, a flexible body.[33] According to... Emily Martin, flexibility is a trait cherished and cultivated in all fields, including health.[34] In *Flexible Bodies*, Martin shows how the healthiest bodies in the postmodern era are disciplined machines that also exhibit current cultural ideals such as flexibility, fitness, and elasticity. Viagra can be used as a tool to achieve this ideal elastic body—a body that is always "on call."

Interestingly, the Viagra body is both flexible and controlled, in contrast to the cultural stereotype of men as virile and "out of control." Whereas women have historically been called upon to regulate and control male (mostly teenage) hypersexuality, men are now able to regulate, as well as empower, their bodies with the help of a pill. For Stu, the "on-call" Viagra penis will consistently respond when it is needed, whereas the "natural" body is unpredictable, and therefore unreliable.

Erections are a lot more temperamental than people are willing to admit. But we have this image of masculinity and expectations of male sexuality as being virile and always ready to go and be the conqueror. And I think that this pill allows people to finally live out that myth (laughs). That was one of the things I had to learn early on is that I had irrational expectations of sexuality. And that men don't have big erections every time they want to, usually, and that to believe that one did was to set oneself up for disappointment. (Stu, thirty-six years old, white, homosexual, student)[35]

As Stu points out, Viagra exposes the flawed "natural" body and enables a man to achieve mythic, powerful, and controlled masculinity. By appearing "natural," the Viagra body can easily replace the problematic body in order to avoid the inevitable disappointment. In this way, the Viagra body exists somewhere between artificial and natural, and even beyond to super-natural levels.

For many, the promise of Viagra is the fact that it can deliver "optimal" results, pushing the consumer beyond his own conceptions of "normal" functioning. In this way, Viagra comes to be seen as a miracle cure because it not only "fixes" the problem but also makes it "better." Below, Viagra is described as an enhancement drug. . . .

It's pretty amazing if you can take a pill and get a better erection. Or even an erection . . . [Viagra is] the first type of medication like this, and for it to work, I mean, is it a wonder drug? Well maybe some of the antibiotics maybe, or diabetes drugs—those are wonder drugs. But in the sexual area, you could say in terms of sexual activity and all of that, yeah, it's a wonderdrug. (Dr. Tobin, urologist in private practice)[36]. . .

The entire world relies on drugs simply because they work, or solve—or help—physical conditions. Why is Viagra any different if it is able to extend—excuse the pun—the full and most zestful part of being human? (Will, fifty-three years old, white, homosexual, program coordinator)[37]

As the voices above reveal, doctors and patients tend to collaborate in imagining Viagra as a magic bullet that can "extend" the realm of "normal" and push people to the next level: extranormality, or superhumanness. By pushing the boundaries of erectile function, performance, and sexuality, Viagra sets new standards and, ironically, marks countless male bodies as in need of repair. Consequently, millions of men are now convinced that their sexual and masculine performance can be improved with Viagra.

### *Viagra to the Rescue?*

Viagra can also come to the rescue for men who feel that they are not quite masculine enough.

While culture, the media, the economy, or relationships can be a source of "male crisis," such factors are complicated to fix. However, when the problem is located solely in the individual body and treated as a physiological dysfunction, the repair can seem easier. Even clinical psychologists, who acknowledge that the trouble can be psychological, social, or relational, may join medical practitioners in seeing Viagra as a tool for regaining body function and repairing confidence and masculinity. Viagra, as a recent biotechnological innovation and medical treatment, represents progress on the path towards health and freedom.

Some consumers take Viagra hoping to restore or supplement not only "natural" physiological function but also "normal" masculinity and heterosexuality.[38] Others choose not to use Viagra, claiming that Viagra is more problem than solution in that it can produce an artificial and uncontrollable body. This section will reveal how patients and doctors grapple with medical solutions, the promise of Viagra, and the necessity of repairing broken male bodies and masculinities.

In an era of advancing sexual medicine, patients and doctors now collaborate in their judgments about successful medical solutions.[39] Both may agree that Viagra will enhance or fix gender, sexuality, and maybe even health and aging....

Other doctors and consumers construct their own, sometimes counterhegemonic or contrary meanings about medicine and sexual dysfunction. This may mean reframing what is problematic and in need of treatment or redefining popular conceptions of what is "normal" and "natural." Below, I illustrate how the growing relationship between sexuality and medicine becomes accepted, and how the repair of broken sexual bodies becomes associated with quick and efficient medical solutions, to the point where such solutions are taken for granted by all involved. In the process, ideologies about what is natural versus artificial, functional versus dysfunctional, and excessive versus deficient are used to make sense of the troubled and fixable body.

Medicalization, or the increased treatment of previously nonmedical problems with medicines, is generally viewed as an inevitable feature of our contemporary lives. Medical professionals like Drs. Pellis...and Redding do not question what they see as the forward march of medical science. Instead, these practitioners tend to embrace this push towards new knowledge, solutions, and healthier bodies as beneficial, inevitable, and unstoppable.

> It started a long time ago. Sexuality is a mind/body connection. Even Freud said it; one day there will be medical solutions to sexual problems. So he foresaw it as inevitable. (Dr. Pellis, psychiatrist in medical clinic)[40]...

> It's true—science is getting to that point. [Doctors are] better able to help the body in ways it can't help itself. We don't know what else the medications do—just what they do do. But as with guns or anything, it is a tool, and the more medications that come out, the less the coincidence of stigma around mental health seems to occur. (Dr. Redding, psychotherapist in private practice)[41]

As science enables doctors to help "when bodies can't help themselves," medical solutions are increasingly normalized and accepted, and their professions are legitimated. Even among mental health practitioners such as Dr. Redding, quoted above, medications can be seen as "tools" to help professionals do their jobs and cut through the stigma of mental health work.

Then again, for some medical professionals who don't write prescriptions or who work outside of the current medical system, medicalization is a force to be reckoned with. Drs. Blackwood [and] Bern...find themselves becoming defensive as they witness their previously accepted ideas about health and treatment slowly become outmoded.

> Everything is medicalized, and HMOs vote in favor of medication over therapy. I think it's a travesty. I find it very disturbing. (Dr. Blackwood, psychologist in private practice)[42]

> I happen to be a therapeutic nihilist. I'm a firm believer that the less medicine you take for anything,

the better off you are. That doesn't mean I won't use medication. But I don't run and jump in areas. (Dr. Bern, internist in private practice)[43]

. . . These doctors take issue with a health care system and a culture that creates and validates expanding medicine. . . . Such contrary voices appear deviant in a world that generally embraces medical science as unquestioned progress, and even as the path towards health and freedom.[44]

More often than not, medical professionals and journalists couch the discovery and availability of Viagra in the language of scientific progress. After a barrage of Pfizer promotion, media attention, "scientific" reporting on the high prevalence of erectile dysfunction, and the clear popularity of Viagra after its debut in 1998, the medical professionals I interviewed are generally convinced that ED is a "major public health concern" and that Viagra is a "magic bullet" treatment.[45] Employing discourses of scientific advancement, most medical practitioners construct Viagra as a vast improvement over previous treatments for erectile dysfunction, which are now constructed as risky, painful, expensive, time consuming, and complicated. Viagra's success comes in part from this construction as the biotechnological answer to erectile dysfunction that promises the most freedom, simplicity, and expedience, due to its convenient pill form. . . .

> It has really helped a lot of people. I've seen some great successes. And it's certainly much easier to do than the other alternatives—penile injections, prostheses, all of these vacuum devices. The alternatives are all more complicated than simply popping a pill. (Dr. Loud, urologist in private practice)[46]

> Viagra is really great because it is just a pill and as long as it works it's great. And you don't have to stick needles in, or use cumbersome equipment. . . . Instead of going to see a counselor and spending a lot of money and time on a problem that may not necessarily get better with psychotherapy—this way you take a pill and get better. (Dr. Cummings, urologist in medical clinic)[47]

For . . . [Drs. Loud] and Cummings, simply "popping a pill" is constructed as quick, easy, and painless—not nearly as threatening as the other options: chemicals delivered through needles, equipment hooked up to the body, or months of counseling. This sentiment is shared with consumers like Thorn and Scott, who have tried other available options for treating sexual dysfunction, such as pumps and psychological counseling.

> [The vacuum pump] is difficult from a standpoint. . . . It's all the apparatuses, the preparation, and even with the constriction ring which is basically like a tourniquet, I still could not hold a firm enough erection for penetration. So it just didn't work for that effect. It's really tough because it takes all the spontaneity out of it. (Thom, fifty-three years old, white, heterosexual, engineer)[48]

> Viagra is so popular in my belief because it cuts out the "middle man" as it were . . . all the psychosexual counseling that one would have to go through in order to get to the root of the problem. I know what my problem is without some psycho babbler telling me! It's lack of confidence in the size of my penis! (Scott, thirty-seven years old, Welsh, heterosexual, manager)[49]

Thom and Scott are among the millions of men who like Viagra for its spontaneity and ease. Medical solutions have been so successful that sometimes devices and pharmaceuticals appear to be the only options for treatment. Ricardo, a sixty-one-year-old Mexican-American consumer of Viagra, says he's tried every type of treatment and considered every gadget available, seemingly unaware that alternatives to prescription treatments exist (e.g., therapy).[50] "I've tried everything. There's a gadget for everything. . . . Don't forget, years ago we didn't have any of this. I'm really okay—I finally ended up with a pump that works. I tell everybody, 'Man, I'm back!' "[51] Ironically, with recent "advances" in medical technology, the production of seemingly straight-forward and accessible treatments, the availability of medication on-line, and direct-to-consumer advertising, consumers are finally free to cut out the "middle man"—the therapist, doctor, or healthcare practitioner—and just get what they need, quickly and easily. In fact, with the push towards health-care efficiency and insurers' reticence to cover counseling, I have been told that referrals to therapists to treat the psychological dimensions of ED have decreased substantially.[52]

Medicine continues its forward march, impacting bodies and lives in such a way as to blur the line between what is real and what is man made. This tension between "the natural" and "the artificial" is a common theme in my conversations with others about Viagra. Pfizer's most crucial selling point (after constructing a widespread need for Viagra) involves convincing consumers that Viagra not only is the easiest treatment to use but also is as close to "natural" as one can get. A 1999 Pfizer ad reads, "Achieve erections the natural way—in response to sexual stimulation." Not only is a pill simple and efficient, but Viagra enables the body to work normally and "naturally." Following Pfizer's lead, medical professionals construct Viagra as restorative, moving men smoothly and easily from dysfunction to "normal functioning."[53]

> These are distraught, angry, guilty people. . . . We're just trying to restore them to normal. Or just get them to some functioning—to relieve personal distress. (Irwin Goldstein, urologist in sexual dysfunction clinic)[54] . . .
>
> Generally, there's a need for this stuff. Many medications inhibit sexual functioning. And people with diabetes tend to need it. Viagra seems to work quite naturally. And it's selling like crazy. (Long, chain-store pharmacist)[55]

According to those quoted above, Viagra can be understood as a medical treatment for dysfunction, which can restore and relieve distressed and deficient people and bodies. Like these medical professionals, I felt for the men I spoke with, many of whom had admitted their concerns only to their doctors (amazingly not even to their partners) and to me.[56] These men wondered if they were "normal" but suffered in silence because of the shame they associated with their bodies, and because of the lack of close friendship networks to turn to for support.[57] For these men,

admitting to impotence (even to themselves) was like conceding that they were no longer young or masculine in a culture that conflates these identities with sexuality and sexual health. Thus, the project of restoring "normal functioning" cannot be divorced from the achievement of "normal masculinity." In this way, both patients and doctors construct Viagra not only as a treatment for erectile dysfunction but also as a pill that restores masculinity.

## Viagra: A Dose of Masculinity

"Erectile performance," or achievement of an erection with the potential to penetrate and ejaculate, is central to the "accomplishment" of heterosexual masculinity, according to medical definitions of erectile functioning. By defining terms in this way, medicine is actively shaping what is permissible and ideal in terms of gender roles.[58] Male roles and expectations are clearly laid out in Pfizer's 2000 definition of erectile dysfunction; in a brochure designed for doctors ED is described as "the consistent inability of a man to achieve and/or maintain an erection sufficient for satisfactory sexual performance." We are left to assume that successful masculine performance requires a specific and successful penile performance, involving consistency, achievement, and satisfaction. Is this really the case?

In my conversations with male consumers, I asked if Viagra could be seen as a masculinity pill of sorts. Most affirmed this idea, reiterating the link among erections, potency, and masculinity. Below, it is apparent that white, heterosexual, male consumers ranging from twenty-seven to seventy-five years of age have literally bought into the idea of a masculinity pill.

*ML:* Is Viagra a masculinity pill?
*FRED:* (He laughs.) I can't argue with that. Without it you aren't much of anything.
*ML:* What do you mean?
*FRED:* If you have an impotency problem to any degree, you look for something to help it with,

or you abstain completely. If they feel like this is a masculinity problem, I guess they are right. (Fred, seventy-five years old, white, heterosexual, retired Marine)[59] . . .

Viagra to me is a miracle pill! It does boost confidence as well as other things! I suppose it can be called a masculinity pill, for without an erection, I believe that my masculinity is somewhat diminished! (Scott, thirty-seven years old, Welsh, heterosexual, manager)[60] . . .

According to these men, Viagra can be seen as a treatment for lost, "diminished," troubled, or incomplete masculinity. As Fred mentioned above, impotence reveals that a man is "not much of anything." Over and over in my interviews, in the face of erectile difficulty or even deficiency, male consumers cast themselves as incomplete, or "half a man." Taking a dose of Viagra allows men to be "whole" again. . . .

However, even for "complete" men, Viagra appears to offer an "extra boost" of masculinity. In the quotations below, both patients and practitioners describe how men use Viagra to enhance their masculinity—to construct themselves as studs and supermen. Interestingly, these medical professionals acknowledge the fact that patients may not be "sexually dysfunctional" before taking Viagra but may just be curious about having a "better" erection.

Some men, like [my] older clients, used [Viagra] just for that extra hardness. They could always get an erection, but [they would say] "I'm sixty-five and it just don't work like it used to." So they might be a little softer. So they'd use it just to harden things up. So they just felt like studs. (Dr. Pemel, sexual health practitioner in private practice)[61]

It's the superman complex. It's that "faster, shinier, bigger" sort of thing. Men feel they've gotta do/have this: the new TV, the car, and the latest products. You know by the numbers that not all the guys getting [Viagra] have erectile dysfunction. (Wilshore, pharmacist)[62]

I am not a macho type at all, but Viagra certainly has made me feel more masculine and sexy at sixty!

(Pal, sixty years old, white, heterosexual, retired court administrator)[63]

Practitioners also work to perpetuate the relationship between "complete" manhood and "normal" erectile function. Erectile health equals healthy and complete masculinity to many consumers and practitioners. A man who is dysfunctional may be constructed as castrated, lacking a penis, and/or lacking manhood. For example, conference programs for the 1999 conference on "The Pharmacologic Management of Erectile Dysfunction"—underwritten by several pharmaceutical companies with Pfizer as the largest donor—showed on the outside page a profile of a man cut in half who becomes whole on the inside page where "objectives for treatment" were listed. . . .

When erectile functioning decreases, confidence and sense of masculinity tend to disappear as well, and the body reveals this loss in its posture. Below, Bob, a black heterosexual barber in his sixties, and Pemel, a white forty-something sexual health practitioner, shared with me how the image of a "shrinking" man conveys the way erectile dysfunction can visibly take its toll.[64] As I flipped through Bob's booklet, "Keys to Great Sex for Men over Fifty," I showed him the first page, which reads in large letters, "YOUR PENIS SHRINKS 19.8% AS YOU GET OLDER," part of an ad for testosterone treatment. I asked if he believed this.

Yes, that's what prompted me [to buy the treatment]. Oh yeah, you wake up in the morning and you know something is different. Reading this stuff makes you more aware of what is happening. After taking stuff, there is a difference, a change. (Bob, sixty-two years old, black, heterosexual, business owner)[65]

This whole thing psychologically, men being impotent, it's just devastating. It just affects so much. Testosterone levels. The ability to produce muscle in our bodies. I mean, men just shrink when they just don't have a strong erection. So it's interesting. Not that they become waifs, but . . . in the cases I've seen once they start to have more erections, they are more interested, hormonally things are flowing, testosterone is being produced more, and they are kind of feeling bigger and bulkier and more manly in many ways. (Dr. Pemel, sexual health practitioner in private practice)[66]

Here, the norm for males is to be big and bulky, not shrinking and diminutive. This theme of loss came up frequently in conversations with practitioners and consumers, although expressed and constructed in various ways. Many times loss of erectile function is seen as a death. Social scientist Annie Potts, in a critical commentary on "The Hard-On," reminds us that the experience of "the fallen flesh"—or the limp penis causing the body to appear desexed, soft (feminine), and powerless—is a common male horror story because it feminizes the body, rendering the person unidentifiable as a man.[67]...

[Other men] literally compared erectile dysfunction to death. For them, Viagra is constructed as a tool for restoring not only masculinity but also "life" itself.

Sexual dysfunction is no joke. These people have horrible lives, they may lose their relationships, and they come in a fairly desperate condition. Some say they'd rather be dead. Both men and women. And their lives are destroyed. They have nowhere to turn. They are not themselves. All of that. (Irwin Goldstein, urologist in sexual dysfunction clinic)[68]

I'm fifty-five and for some reason I just didn't seem to feel like I was alive and well like I was when I was twenty years old. And you know, I thought that shouldn't be so because that's not the way it is. I've never talked to anybody about that situation, so I told my doctor. For some reason or other I said I'd like to try something to see if I'm still alive or not. And so anyway he says, "Do you want to try this Viagra?" I say I don't like drugs or anything artificial. Maybe my time is over and that should be the end of that. But then I tried [Viagra]. (Joel, fifty-five years old, white, heterosexual, unknown occupation)[69]

...For most of these consumers, an active, erect penis symbolizes normal health, masculinity, and sexuality. A limp penis or absence of virility

appears to symbolize death of the body as well as of manhood. To capture this disinterest in life that comes with erectile failure, Pfizer has chosen the tag line "Love Life Again" to sell its product.

As we have seen, for both male consumers and (usually male) practitioners, communicating about pain, loss, and concerns associated with sexual problems can be difficult, embarrassing, and heavily laden with metaphor, myth, and shame.[70] Phrases such as "it's over" and "I'm no longer alive," along with labels such as "shrinking," "eunuch," and "incomplete" reveal male discomfort with discussing sexuality and convey the degree of importance erectile functioning plays in men's sense of self, masculinity, and health. These men visit doctors with their complaints to investigate ways to fix their selves, their manhood, and their health. In the process, patients look to practitioners and those around them to provide a rationale for their troubles....

## Repair = Trouble

Not all consumers buy into the techno-fix model. Some consumers commented that although Viagra may promise bodily repair or enhancement, it can actually cause more trouble than it's worth. In this section, consumers indicate that Viagra creates problems, not solutions. For Joel and Don, Viagra is constructed as technotrouble, rendering the male body increasingly out of control.

I don't ever want to try [Viagra] again. The thing about it is, the side effects could be very dangerous for someone a little older than I am. Because you do end up with palpitations. Your body is just not your body. So if [your functioning is] not normal, I think it's better to just let it go at that. Or make pills that are much, much weaker. But I wouldn't recommend it for anybody. (Joel, fifty-five years old, white, heterosexual, unknown occupation)[71]

I have tried it. I went a long time and the bottom line is I don't like it. It hasn't done me any good and it had a harmful side effect—heart-burn and indigestion. I'm a little fearful of it. I'm a healthy guy and I don't take any maintenance medicines of any kind. My system seems to be functioning nicely. I think I'll just leave it alone. (Don, sixty-seven years old, white, heterosexual, retired fire captain)[72]

As we saw earlier, some men see Viagra as a tool to create the ideal flexible body. For other consumers, Viagra may produce a body that is overly rigid and inflexible. For them, the Viagra effect is "unnatural" and uncontrollable, and consequently undesirable for both Dusty, a homosexual student, and Stanford, a heterosexual counselor in his sixties.

> Well, I also didn't like it because it was unnatural. Like you were hard and you stayed hard. And I also didn't like the fact that it guaranteed things would be sexual until you weren't hard. I didn't like the idea of being forced into being sexual. You can't do anything nonsexual when you are on it. So basically it guarantees that the entire period you are on it is going to be sexual. (Dusty, seventeen years old, white, homosexual, student)[73]

> The idea that I thought was hilarious at first—that erection that won't go away—is not hilarious at all. In fact it happens and sometimes endangers one's life. (Stanford, sixty-five years old, white, heterosexual, counselor)[74]

For Stanford and, Dusty, Pfizer's Viagra tag line, "Love Life Again," is inappropriate. Instead of regaining an appreciation for life, these men see Viagra as dangerous or even deadly. While priapism or death can occur in rare instances of Viagra use, and even Pfizer admits that Viagra is not for everyone, neither Stanford nor Dusty experienced real bodily danger while taking Viagra. Nonetheless, both take Viagra seriously, remaining cautious and seeming to prefer the natural way to the artificial alternative.

Rather than lose control of their bodies or experience trouble through repair, some men construct alternatives to the pharmaceutical quick-fix model, accepting their bodies as they are or just "leaving it alone." Despite overwhelming evidence that Viagra is associated with the production of normal and/or mythic masculinity, men

like Ollie and Joel work hard at reconstructing masculinity as separate from "erectile health." They insist that heterosexual masculinity can be achieved without the help of Viagra or consideration of erectile potential.

> Oh no, if you don't feel like a man before you take the pill, you're not a man anyways. No, you have to know where you're at. If you have a little misfunction, that's minor. But you have to be a man before you go through that. It's not a macho pill. (Joel, fifty-five years old, white, heterosexual, unknown occupation)[75]

> I've talked to a lot of different men about this. Some cannot live without sex. They feel their sex makes them the man that they are. And I'm not sure how important that is to me. I'm a man anyways. It's about self-esteem. What do you think about yourself to begin with? (Ollie, sixty-four years old, black, heterosexual, printer)[76]

For many, Viagra fits perfectly in a society that is known for pushing the limits of normal. Some men are critical of American culture and Viagra's role in perpetuating the endless pursuit of the quick fix. Hancock and Miles warn of a hedonistic, money-driven, artificial world, where there is a pill for everything. For them, Viagra exists in this world as a crutch or bandaid solution to larger social problems.

> We are willing to take the latest thing that is fast and painless. Also, Americans seem to think happiness is their birthright. They take Viagra to become better, happier. And supermen. All that stuff about self-worth, image, and sex life, it's what people want. . . . And maybe those guys who think they need Viagra just need to chill out and reduce stress in their lives. It's about lifestyle modification more than anything, I think. Maybe we are too lazy and it just takes too long. We want something to work fast. (Hancock, sixty-nine years old, white, heterosexual, retired teacher)[77]

> I think there is a gross overuse of drugs for happiness and well-being. Feeling depressed, get a script for a mood enhancer . . . feeling tired, get a pill for energy . . . want to have better sex, get some blue magic. What about the age-proven solution of re-

moving or reducing the problems or stress factors affecting your life and then seeing if pharmacological agents are still needed? (Miles, forty-five years old, white, heterosexual, paramedic) [78]

Here, Miles and Hancock construct society as drug-infused, producing individuals who are dependent upon pills for health and happiness. They, along with Stu and Ollie, are critical of corporate and biotechnological attempts at constructing needs, desires, and easy markets for products.

How do I express this? This is a . . . capitalist hegemony of our emotions. We live in a state of anomie, or at least we are told that we do, and we're also told what to do about it. Have you seen these commercials? I have files of "The Paxil Christmas" that I cut out of a magazine. This young college-aged woman in a family Christmas portrait and it says, "You can go home this year and have a good time. Paxil." Paxil and Prozac and Zoloft—that's what it was. They ran these ads and marketed them to different age groups and they are telling us what the problem is—creating a problem—and they give us a solution. We all have anxieties and relationship issues, and they do this to make it look like the way to solve your relationship issue is to take Paxil. The way to deal with your crazy family is to take Paxil. That way you don't have to address the relationship issues, substantive issues. I have a big problem with that. (Stu, thirty-six years old, white, homosexual, student)[79]

I think everything we do nowadays is overblown. I just see that society is just driving us crazy, making us jump through hoops and do things we really don't need to do. So a drug for everything . . . I think they—or not they, but the way things are set up, is to make you want to do things. Even if you don't want to do it, you are driven if you pay attention to what's going on. I'm not that kind of person. I won't let you do me that way. You won't be able to drive me that way. I just don't believe in it. (Ollie, sixty-four years old, black, heterosexual, printer)[80]

These men are clearly critical of Viagra's potential to enforce social and gender ideals. They refuse to "buy into" mythic masculinity, and they see through the problematic language used to describe medical progress as well as so-called

widespread public health crises. In this way some men do resist and reframe masculinity, biotechnology, and medical science in ways that make sense to them. Rather than construct their bodies as troubled, with Viagra as a technofix or magical solution, these consumers see Viagra as problematic, contributing to larger social problems. These skeptical voices, however, are easily drowned out by the overwhelming chorus of those who sing Viagra's praises.

## Masculinity, Biotechnology, and Resistance

At the turn of a new century, the desire to "fix" and "erect" male sexuality and power in a male-dominated society appears to be strong. This desire is perhaps a reaction to the gains of women's liberation and sexual empowerment, and as some of the men I spoke with pointed out, we are also living in a time of self-help movements, expanding medicalization, great social change, and personal crisis. Today it is not uncommon to hear about American social problems such as "male betrayal," the "malaise among men," and the "masculinity crisis." Just as Betty Friedan warned against women "buying into" their own victimhood in the 1960s, so now it is argued that men are buying into commercially packaged manhood in many forms, including "amped-up virility" and "technologically-enhanced supermanhood."[81]

When Lewis Carroll wrote *Alice's Adventures in Wonderland* in 1865, the idea of an ingestible tonic that would answer Alice's wishes and make her "grow large" was a magical, fantastical fantasy. Today, we all inhabit this magical reality, surrounded and tempted by endless products packaged in promises of personal transformation. This is the era when the "magic bullet" for sexual energy, confidence, and masculinity comes in the form of a pill. Today, so-called lifestyle drugs of all types are available to anyone with access to the internet and a credit card. And Americans have a newly transformed relationship with biotechnology, one that goes beyond "healing" to "transforming" and "fixing" bodies with the help of reproductive technologies, hormones, implants, surgeries, and other technological innovations.

Today, enhancement technologies are not just instruments of self-improvement or even self-transformation—they are tools for working on the soul.[82] The new player in this enhancement tale is the man who has been told he is sick. With Viagra, a highly successful masculine empowerment campaign is underway, centered around a new, late-twentieth-century tool, a magic blue pill that promises to produce and enhance male "magic wands." The doctor's tools are now turned back on the doctor himself. The male body is constructed as in need of repair, and is a new site for medical and biotechnological innovation and healing. With health and fitness as the new testing ground for masculinity, Viagra enters doctors' and patients' worlds, envisioned as cutting-edge biotechnology and used, I argue, as a cultural and material tool in the production and achievement of "true" manhood. Then again, Viagra can lead to male confidence without even being ingested. One of my informants told me that he purchased Viagra at a time of intense sexual insecurity with a partner but hasn't had a chance to use it. He is hoping that just having it around will make him a more self-confident lover. Others echoed this idea, that simply pills in the medicine cabinet was enough of an assurance.

The implications of constructing the male body as sexually potent, or as a technologically enhanced machine, can be both hurtful and helpful, as medical professionals, Viagra consumers, and their partners have discovered. Here I think of a friend's lesson about the importance of antidepressants: "You can't start a revolution if you're so depressed you can't get out of bed!" Similarly, during the course of this research, practitioners told me that their patients would not be attentive to their partners' sexual needs or desires if they were insecure or paralyzed by their own. Thus Viagra enabled them to be more confident and attentive to themselves as well as to their partners. In this way, it is important to acknowledge that prescription drug use has the potential to enable broad social change.

Nonetheless, social historian Lynne Luciano warns,

> Medicalizing impotence lures men into believing there is a standard for erections to which they must adhere. By quantifying the normal erection—it has to be just hard enough to achieve penetration and last long enough to achieve ejaculation—medicalization forces men to conform to its specifications for masculinity. The results are twofold: first, men, like women, have their sexuality and desirability linked to physical parameters; second, emotion, sexual technique, and the role of one's partner are rendered insignificant. By making the erection the man, science isn't enhancing male sexuality, but sabotaging it.[83]

Like Luciano, many social theorists have recently expressed concern with the state of manhood in America. Sexologist and practicing therapist Wendy Stock points out that to focus on male bodies as Viagra-infused, finely tuned, flexible machines perpetuates a detached, unemotional masculinity. She comments, "Although a common cultural male fantasy is to be able to function like a machine, as the sexual equivalent of the Energizer Bunny, both men and women may lose something if medical interventions allow us to function without the necessity of emotional connection. Is the ability to perform like a sexual machine desirable, individually or on a cultural scale?"[84] Similarly, feminist journalist and social commentator Susan Faludi warns of a "performance culture . . . where people are encouraged to view themselves as commodities that are marketed and fine-tuned with chemicals, whether it's Viagra or Prozac or Botox injections."[85]

Despite such warnings, sexual medicine continues to expand, as experts and marketers find ways to understand and treat a wider and wider range of sexual troubles for men and women. At a major international conference on sexual dysfunction in 2003, definitions and treatments for "rapid ejaculation" and "delayed ejaculation" were being discussed and finalized. For women, delay or absence of orgasm, arousal, or desire is cause for medical intervention. Insurers also intervene, by setting rules about who has access to sexual health treatments, and how many. Meanwhile, performance anxiety will only grow as the definition of "normal" sexuality and masculinity narrows. As sexual medicine gets more and more commonplace, what will be the ramifications for those who don't follow medical protocol? For those who have little interest in sexuality, or in medical models of sexuality? Lynne Luciano poses similar questions, with no clear answers:

> What happens to a man or woman who doesn't want to take drugs to enhance sexuality, who is content to age without the benefit of pills and potions? How far are we willing to go in our public discourse about how much sex is enough, and what constitutes good sex, and how central a role sex should play in relationships? Medical advances and healthier lifestyles offer men hope for longer and more potent sex lives than at any other time in history. But expectations are likely to continue to outpace reality. Not even Viagra can guarantee sexual success for all men, all the time. What it can guarantee is a continuing moral and ethical debate.[86]

The individual stories in this [reading] add up to what I see as a larger, disturbing story about the pressures and requirements for being fully male in American society, and even worldwide. Are we doing our men a service in the Viagra era? As the doctors and patients that I interviewed and quote in this chapter reveal, Viagra can and is being used to enforce and perpetuate an ideal masculinity. In this way consumers collaborate with medical professionals and pharmaceutical companies in an attempt to understand and fix "broken" bodies. Perhaps of more interest, my data also reveal the struggle with the necessity for the Viagra-enhanced body, and what that struggle represents. As men negotiate their relationship to this product, mainstream ideas about sexuality, masculinity, and health are both reinforced and redefined in important ways. For example, some men insist that "doing" masculinity does not require sexual performance. Others are criti-

cal of a society that increasingly promotes and depends upon biotechnology for achieving health and happiness. They have their own ideas about manhood, medicalization, and biotechnology that may or may not fit with Pfizer's. In general, this chapter reveals men complicating manhood by constructing not only corporate corporealities[87] but also "various and competing masculinities" in the Viagra era.[88] As most of us do, the men I spoke with are constantly negotiating social and cultural pressures to be healthy, young, sexual, and in control.

For Pfizer, fixing the broken male machine is supposed to be a simple process with the help of Viagra. The men in this chapter suggest otherwise, pointing out that the bodily "repair" process, the man, and the culture he belongs to are all more complex than Pfizer may acknowledge.

## NOTES

1. Michael Kimmel, *Manhood in America: A Cultural History* (New York: Free Press, 1996).
2. In the 1970s and 1980s, gender scholars began to complicate and problematize normative (and thus prescriptive) white, heterosexual "hegemonic masculinity." For more on hegemonic masculinity, see Robert Connell, *Masculinities* (Berkeley: University of California Press, 1995). Michael Messner, *The Politics of Masculinities: Men in Movements* (Thousand Oaks, CA: Sage Publications, 1997) argues that a singular, reductionist, unified masculinity does not reflect a society in which "at any given moment there are various and competing masculinities." Responding to feminist scholarship, early masculinities scholars argued that patriarchy forces men to oppress themselves and other men. Such scholars inspired many inquiries into male competition, power struggles, and self-objectification. Joseph Pluck's *The Myth of Masculinity* (Cambridge: MIT Press, 1981) suggested that hegemonic masculinity and the promotion of unattainable ideals caused men to experience "sex role strain" in trying to attain the unattainable. In this way, Pluck sparked an interest in male confusion and "crisis" related to out-of-date, inflexible, contradictory, turn-of-the-century sex roles. Similarly, Lynne Segal, in *Slow Motion: Changing Masculinities* (London: Virago, 1990) warned that

lived masculinity is never the seamless, undivided construction it becomes in its symbolic manifestation. She argued that in the late twentieth century, masculinity was not in crisis per se, but it was less hegemonic than before. While contemporary, increasingly visible and complicated masculinities can exist in tension with potentially outdated roles and expectations, this tension can also lead to confusion about manhood and how to "do" it.

3. Connell, *Masculinities*, 45.

4. Kimmel, *Manhood in America*, 332

5. Connell proposes his own model, the "body-reflexive" model, in which the social relations of gender are experienced in the body and are constituted through bodily action. See Connell, *Masculinities*, 60–64.

6. See, for example, Susan Brood, *The Male Body: A New Look at Men in Public and Private* (New York: Farrar, Straus, and Giroux, 1999); Marc Faseau, *The Male Machine* (New York: Dell, 1975); Kimmel and Messner, *Men's Lives*; and Michael Kimmel, *Manhood in America*.

7. See, for example, Annie Potts, "The Essence of the Hard-On," in *Men and Masculinities* (3:1, 2000): 85–103. Also see Leonore Tiefer, "The Medicalization of Impotence: Normalizing Phallocentrism," *Gender and Society* (8, 1994): 363–77, and *Sex Is Not a Natural Act and Other Essays* (San Francisco: Westview Press, 1995).

8. See, for example, Potts, "The Essence of the Hard-On"; Tiefer, *Sex Is Not a Natural Act*; Lynne Luciano, *Looking Good: Male Body Image in Modern America* (New York: Hill and Wang, 2001); and Barbara L. Marshall, " 'Hard Science:' Gendered Constructions of Sexual Dysfunction in the 'Viagra Age,' " *Sexualities* (5:2, 2002):131–58. Phallocentrism refers to the phallus, a male organ that symbolizes power and control.

9. See, for example, Bordo, *The Male Body*.

10. Laura Mamo and Jennifer Fishman, "Potency in All the Right Places: Viagra as a Technology of the Gendered Body," *Body and Society* (7:4, 2001): 13–35.

11. A very limited cohort of scholars, primarily historians, has written about how white men's heterosexual bodies have been normalized and naturalized and, in rare cases, pathologized. See Bordo, *The Male Body*. Also see Vern Burlough, "Technology for the Prevention of 'les maladies produites par la masturbation,' " *Technology and Culture* (28:4, 1987): 828–32; and Kevin Mumford, "Lost Manhood Found: Male Sexual Impotence and Victorian Culture in the United States,"

*Journal of the History of Sexuality* (3:1, 1992). Kevin Mumford explores how male impotence was medicalized, constructed, and cured historically. Starting from advertisements promising male virility and vigor, Mumford traces the "crisis of masculinity" along with modernization and the changing American conceptions of male sexuality and masculinity from the 1830s to the 1920s.

12. All names have been changed to protect the identity of my informants. The twenty-seven male consumers I spoke with are a self-selected group who responded to the interview requests I made through internet postings, newspaper advertisements, practitioner referrals, senior-citizens organizations, personal contacts, and prostate cancer support-group meeting announcements. Those consumers who volunteered for an interview generally had experience with Viagra and had an interest in sharing this experience because it had affected their lives in some way (good or bad). A group of men from a post-prostate-surgery support group agreed to speak with me over the phone under conditions of anonymity and confidentiality about their experiences dealing with surgery-induced ED. Interestingly, all had tried Viagra, and none had had any "success" with it, a fact that turned several of the interviews into "ranting" sessions, which rendered visible how emotionally invested these consumers were in Viagra's promise. Of the twenty-seven male consumers I spoke with, all but two had tried Viagra, and half of these discontinued using Viagra after the initial trial because of unsatisfactory response or preference for a different product. This "take rate" is representative of the larger population of Viagra users nationally; Pfizer's research has shown that over half of those who receive a prescription for Viagra do not request a refill.

13. In addition to being the only Viagra expert known to most men, their doctors are the only person most men feel comfortable talking to about their sexual problems.

14. I also spoke with twenty-two medical practitioners. Six of the twenty-two medical professionals I spoke with are female; sixteen are male. Eight are acclaimed experts in sexual medicine, regularly publishing and delivering lectures on female sexual dysfunction.

15. Dr. Bern, interview with author, tape recording, California: August 2000.

16. Phil, phone interview, tape recording, May 2000.

17. Byron, phone interview, tape recording, May 2000.

18. In *The Male Body,* Susan Bordo explores the link between masculinity and the phallus throughout Western history from Roman phallic gods to St. Augustine's "lustful member" to John Bobbitt's detachable penis to Clinton's not-so-private parts (24–25). Bordo argues that for as long as we can remember, the phallus has embodied our cultural imagination, symbolic of power, permission, defiance, and performance. Annie Potts adds that medicine and sexology produce and perpetuate the idea that an erect penis signifies "healthy" male sexuality—a destructive form of hegemonic masculinity that "ignores the diversity of penile pleasures" (89).

19. The idea that female sexuality can only be awakened by (or responsive to) the male was popular in marriage manuals of the early twentieth century and currently exist in medical discourse about female sexual dysfunction. . . .

20. Potts, "The Essence of the Hard-On," 98. Potts argues that we need an expansive view of male sexuality that need not rely on phallic ambitions. This would require a rethinking of penis power, "a relinquishment of this organ's executive position in sex," and an "embrace of a variety of penile styles: flaccid, erect, and semiflaccid/semierect" (100).

21. For more on gender as an accomplishment, see Candace West and Don Zimmerman, "Doing Gender," *Gender and Society* (1, 1987): 125–51; and Candace West and Sarah Fenstermaker, "Doing Difference," *Gender and Society* (9:1, 1995): 8–38. Also see West and Fenstermaker, *Doing Gender: Doing Difference* (New York: Routledge, 2002).

22. See, for example, Diane Dull and Candace West, "Accounting for Cosmetic Surgery: The Accomplishment of Gender," *Social Problems* (38:1, 1991): 54–71; and Kathy Davis, *Reshaping the Female Body: The Dilemma of Cosmetic Surgery* (New York: Routledge, 1995).

23. Donna Haraway, *Simians, Cyborgs, and Women: The Reinvention of Nature* (New York: Routledge, 1991): 149.

24. See Emily Martin, *Flexible Bodies* (Boston: Beacon Press, 1994).

25. Elizabeth Grosz, *Space, Time, and Perversion: Essays on the Politics of Bodies* (New York: Routledge, 1995): 35.

26. See any of Goldstein's coauthored reports in the *International Journal of Impotence Research*, volumes 10, 11, 12, and 15.

27. Dr. Curt, interview with author, tape recording, California: August 2000.

28. Chuck, phone interview, tape recording, May 2000.

29. Differing markedly in age, health, and reason for using Viagra (and, less markedly, in race, occupation, and sexual orientation), my sample is representative of a diversity of Viagra users. Pfizer identifies its largest market as "men over forty years of age." Pfizer Pharmaceuticals, Inc., *Patient Summary of Information about Viagra,* Fact Sheet, 1999, 2000; and *Uncover Ed,* Pfizer Informational Brochure, March 2000. In my sample of male consumers, diseases, medications, and surgeries were the most frequently cited reasons for trying Viagra. Ten of the twenty-seven male consumers I interviewed experienced erectile difficulties after undergoing prostate surgery. Others blamed erectile dysfunction on age (four), diabetes (one), heart problems (one), and medications (two). Three consumers cited psychological (self-esteem) factors as the main cause of their erectile difficulties. Perhaps of most interest is the significant number of interviewees who denied they had erectile dysfunction (seven), and instead explained that they used Viagra as an assurance or enhancement drug. Pfizer does not officially acknowledge or discuss this population of Viagra users in its promotional or training information, although these users may fall into the "mild ED" and "psychological and other factors" categories.

30. Nora Jacobson found this to be the case with breast implants in her book *Cleavage: Technology, Controversy, and the Ironies of the Man-Made Breast* (New Brunswick, NJ: Rutgers University Press, 2000). Some have suggested that gay males are a ready market for the "enhancement" uses of Viagra, including several of my gay interview subjects. But both gay and straight men in my interview pool expressed interest in the enhancement uses of Viagra.

31. Will, interview with author, tape recording, California: September 2000.

32. Stanford, interview with author, tape recording, California: August 2000.

33. Previous treatments for ED included a liquid injected directly into the penis, which would produce an erection for several hours (Caverject). Viagra is constructed as a superior treatment due to its simple delivery (as a pill) and production of a penis that will wait to become erect until the user is ready.

34. See Martin, *Flexible Bodies.*

35. Stu, interview with author, tape recording, California: October 2000.

36. Dr. Tobin, phone interview, tape recording, May 2000.

37. Will, Ibid.

38. Potts, in "The Essence of the Hard-On" (94), reminds us that the true mark of therapeutic success is restoration of "phallic manhood."

39. This idea comes from Riessman, "Women and Medicalization: A New Perspective," *Social Policy* (14:1, 1983).

40. Dr. Pellis, interview with author, tape recording, California: May 2000.

41. Dr. Redding, interview with author, tape recording, California: May 2000.

42. Dr. Blackwood, phone interview, tape recording, May 2000.

43. Dr. Bern, Ibid.

44. Peter Conrad and Joseph Schneider, *Deviance and Medicalization: From Badness to Sickness* (London: Mosby, 1980); and Riessman, "Women and Medicalization."

45. See Edward Laumann, A. Paik, and R. Rosen, "Sexual Dysfunction in the United States: Prevalence and Predictors," *JAMA* (281:6, 1999): 537–44. . . .

46. Dr. Loud, interview with author, tape recording, California: August 2000.

47. Dr. Cummings, interview with author, tape recording, California: August 2000.

48. Thom, phone interview, tape recording, May 2000.

49. Scott, e-mail interview, e-mail transcript, May 2000.

50. There is a long-standing struggle between therapists and practitioners to locate the source of erectile dysfunction and treat either physiological or psychological manifestations of the problem.

51. Ricardo, phone interview, tape recording, August 2000.

52. Barbara L. Marshall, " 'Hard Science.' "

53. Viagra competitor Enzyte is an over-the-counter product that offers "natural male enhancement," which seems to put Viagra in the "unnatural" (synthetic) category.

54. Irwin Goldstein, phone interview, tape recording, November 2000.

55. Long, interview with author, tape recording, California: October 2000.

56. I never expected to be a stand-in for consumers' doctors. In these cases where consumers asked for advice, I awkwardly assured them that I was not an expert on ED, but judging from my interviews with other male consumers, their experiences sounded normal. If the side effects they mentioned sounded potentially dangerous (like heart palpitations or trouble breathing), I advised them to contact their doctors as soon as possible.

57. Interestingly, several of the men I spoke with, primarily those who had undergone prostate surgery, felt more of a stigma associated with incontinence than with impotence. This is yet another area where millions of men suffer in silence.

58. See Janice Raymond, *Transsexual Empire: The Making of the She-Male* (New York: Atheneum, 1994).

59. Fred, phone interview, tape recording, August 2000.

60. Scott, Ibid.

61. Dr. Pemel, interview with author, tape recording, California: August 2000.

62. Wilshore, interview with author, tape recording, California: May 2000.

63. Pal, email interview, e-mail transcript, August 2000.

64. Bordo, in *The Male Body,* argues that in a culture where "big and bulky" represent male ideals, "shrinkage" is feared, as evidenced in popular culture *(Seinfeld, Boogie Nights,* etc.).

65. Bob, interview with author, tape recording, California: August 2000.

66. Dr. Pemel, Ibid.

67. Potts, "The Essence of the Hard-On," 96.

68. Irwin Goldstein, Ibid.

69. Joel, interview with author, tape recording, California: October 2000.

70. Relationship experts have described this "delicate dance" that couples do when they are dealing with situations like sexual dysfunction. Without open communication between partners, the fear of "failure" can lead to avoidance and alienation, which can only exacerbate the problem.

71. Joel, Ibid.

72. Don, Ibid.

73. Dusty, interview with author, tape recording, California: August 2000.

74. Stanford, Ibid.

75. Joel, Ibid.

76. Ollie, phone interview, tape recording, May 2000.

77. Hancock, phone interview, tape recording, May 2000.

78. Miles, e-mail interview, e-mail transcript, August 2000.

79. Stu, Ibid.

80. Ollie, Ibid.

81. Quoted in Susan Faludi, *Stiffed: The Betrayal of the American Male* (New York: Morrow, 1999): 602.

82. See Carl Elliott, *Better Than Well: American Medicine Meets the American Dream* (New York: Norton, 2003): 53.

83. Luciano, *Looking Good*, 165.

84. Wendy Stock and C. Moser, "Feminist Sex Therapy in the Age of Viagra," in *New Directions in Sex Therapy: Innovations and Alternatives*, P. Kleinplatz, ed. (New York: Brunner-Routledge, 2001): 27.

85. P. J. Huffstutter and Ralph Frammolino, "Lights! Camera! Viagra! When the Show Must Go On, Sometimes a Little Chemistry Helps," *Los Angeles Times*, July 6, 2001, A1.

86. Luciano, *Looking Good*, 204.

87. I have Michael Kimmel to thank for helping me come up with this term.

88. This phrase is borrowed from Michael Messner's *Politics of Masculinities*.

# Myth Information
# vs. the Fat Facts

Hanne Blank

It's probably a symptom of our sexual immaturity as a culture, but sexuality as a public topic nearly always seems to elicit boorishness and generally bad behavior. Despite the fact that no one is really immune to the sting of sexual humiliation (and perhaps because of it) any source of sexual or personal difference ends up being grist for the stereotype and mockery mill. The more stigmatized the difference or the group of people who are the target, the worse the treatment. Since fatness is held in deeper disdain than almost any other sort of physical difference, fat people's sexuality is all too often considered aberrant, disgusting, or just a very crass joke.

Unfortunately, the myths around fat and sex don't just stay in the realm of locker room humor and jokes the guys tell at the bar. Assumptions, presumptions, projections, and outright lies form the preponderance of what most people think they know about fat people and sex, to the point where even those we assume to be in a position to know better (doctors, psychologists, sex columnists) fall back on the hoary old myths.

For instance, in the 1972 edition of *The Joy Of Sex*, one of the "bibles" of the sexual revolution, "obesity" was listed in the "Problems" section, with the implications that fatness is always a problem for people's sex lives, that fatness di-

rectly causes impotence (it doesn't), and that only thin people really had any business having sex. Here's some of what author Alex Comfort had to say about fat people and sex:

> *"Fatness in our culture is unlovely. We know someone whose pretty, fat daughter can only get Middle Eastern boyfriends because of this norm. Renoir's women, who, when naked, look ideal for sex, would look a little too plump if clothed.*
>
> *"What isn't realized is that in men overweight is a physical cause of impotence. If neither this nor the esthetics of it bother you, you may still have to circumvent it. King Edward VII of Britain ('Tum-Tum') had a special couch resembling a gynecological table made to enable him to get on target. Most stout men can manage with the woman astride, backing or facing. If this doesn't work, try lying face-up over the edge of the bed, feet on the floor, while she stands astride. An over-heavy man is a bad problem—Cleopatra could say, "O happy horse, to bear the weight of Anthony," but he didn't weigh 200 pounds. If you are grossly overweight, set about losing it, whether you value your sex life or only your life. That applies to both sexes. Modern girls, though supple, tend to be underweight by the sexual standards of the past, especially for rear-entry positions and for making love on a firm surface."*

One wonders how Comfort could've been so sanguine about knowing a long-dead Roman's weight . . . but more than that, one wonders if he'd ever actually had sex with a fat person, or spoken to any about their sex lives. If the most pertinent examples he could come up with were Renoir paintings (beautiful, but they're paintings, not flesh-and-blood people), a long-dead British ruler (who was in any case a well known lover of

From Blank, Hanne. 2000. "Myth Information vs. the Fat Facts." In *Big Big Love: A Sourcebook on Sex for People of Size and Those Who Love Them* (pp. 14–33). Reprinted with permission from Greenery Press.

fat in all its guises who would sometimes weigh his guests before and after meals), and a Shakespeare play (the speech from which Comfort draws his lines, incidentally, has nothing to do with fatness), he wasn't trying very hard. It wouldn't be too surprising if he didn't try at all, if this section had been something of an afterthought.

But nonetheless, there it was in *The Joy Of Sex*. As a result, this sort of thing has loomed large as an authoritative statement about sex and fat in the minds of an awful lot of people for an awfully long time. It jibes with the "received wisdom" we get about fat people, and therefore few people question it. Doubtless this is why it's been perpetuated in a lot of other sex-advice books and columns. Even well-read, intelligent, thinking folks who question the other received wisdom that has a role to play in their lives tend to buy into opinion and aesthetic judgment when it comes dressed up as fact and fits in with the stereotypes which inform their lives. After all, there are still a lot of people who believe that all Black men have enormous penises (nope), that all Asian men have tiny ones (nope again), that Frenchmen are uniformly impeccably wonderful lovers (sorry, no), that bisexuals are just confused (wrong), and that gay men like sticking live rodents into their rectums (not even kinda). If a prevailing cultural prejudice makes it convenient to put a sexual stereotype on any discriminated-against minority, you can bet it'll have its adherents. The more widespread the discrimination, and the more acceptable that discrimination within the culture, the broader the sexual misinformation and mythology will reach. But stereotypes can be lessened or eradicated, given time, effort, and education.

Unfortunately, we still live in a world where it's still entirely acceptable to say "Oh, all fat women are desperate," "People who are fat are hiding from their sexuality," or "Fat girls love to give head because they're obviously orally fixated." As a result, not too surprisingly, many people behave accordingly, methodically denigrating fat people's sexual integrity, desirability, and worth every step of the way. Sometimes, the people who do this

are fat themselves. They say that "homophobia begins at home," and the same is true of anti-fat prejudice: fat people are taught, and taught very well, to internalize negative stereotypes about fat people. Members of minority groups are not immune from having to overcome their own internalized stereotyping, or from harming themselves or other fellow members of that minority when they don't do so.

In this section, we go head to head with some of the biggest fattest lies about fat people's sexuality. The sexual denigration and/or disenfranchisement of any group of people is an injustice and a denial of the birthright that each of us has, as a human animal, to be happily, healthily, and pleasurably sexual. Read on, and learn the reality behind the stereotypes—what you find out may well surprise you.

**Fat is universally ugly. No one thinks fat people are sexually attractive.**

In a word: bullshit.

Not only are there plenty of people nowadays who find fat people attractive, there always have been. Plenty of wonderful artworks, from the fat fertility goddess statuettes of prehistory to the paintings of artists like Titian, Rubens, Renoir, Cassatt, and the great contemporary painter Botero stand as testament to the fact that not only do some people like to look at fat bodies, some people like them well enough to keep their images around just because they're beautiful. From Lillian "Diamond Lil" Russell to Jessye Norman, Sophie Tucker to Roseanne Barr, and not forgetting the likes of Kate Smith, Camryn Manheim, "Mama" Cass Elliot, Carnie Wilson, Kathy Bates, Wendy Jo Sperber, Anna Nicole Smith, Missy "Misdemeanor" Elliott, Bessie Smith, and Martha Wash, there have always been sexy fat women in the world of entertainment whose abundant bodies have helped keep the fans entranced. And fat men—many of them comic geniuses like John Belushi, John Candy, Dom De Louise, and Oliver Hardy (of Laurel and Hardy fame), but also including other luminaries like Luciano Pavarotti,

Orson Welles, Drew Carey, Brian Dennehy, and John Goodman—have been no slouches at garnering acclaim and interest, both professional and otherwise.

By and large, the notion of fat being "automatically" sexually revolting is a conceit developed by and most prominent in first-world, white, Christian culture. In other cultures, fatness is not regarded in the same ways. Recent research has shown that in many far-flung cultures that are traditionally fat-positive—Fiji was a recent case in point—an obsessive preoccupation with thinness and corresponding increases in the occurrence of eating disorders like bulimia and anorexia come along with the introduction of Western culture, particularly television.

In many cultures, the most traditionally desirable body types are those which are considerably plumper than would be considered conventionally sexy in North America. In these cultures—and within many minority cultural groups in North America as well, most notably much of the African-American and Latino communities—fatter people are much more often expected to be fully participatory sexual beings. Fat American women traveling in the Middle East, Africa, parts of Latin and South America, the Pacific Islands and Micronesia, and other locales often report their surprise when they are treated as sex objects in the same way that thin, big-busted California-tan blondes generally are at home. Fat men often find greater social and sexual acceptance in other cultural settings, too.

Not so long ago, a degree of fatness was a status symbol. In some cultures it still is. Being fat, after all, means you have enough to eat, and that you probably don't have to do backbreaking physical labor to survive. But times change, and in a culture where very few people have to do physical labor much of the time, it becomes a valued commodity to have time to go and do physical exercise as a form of leisure activity. Historically, as it's become easier for most Westerners to lead fairly comfortable and well-nourished lives with a minimum of hard labor involved in the processes

of daily life, it's gotten easier to get fat. Not too surprisingly, it's become less socially and culturally valuable to be so.

Regardless of whether fat is presently fashionable, there are and have always been some people who simply are attracted to fatter bodies. There are countless more who have the potential to be attracted to fatter bodies but who don't necessarily count fatness in the abstract as a specific turn-on. There's no more rhyme or reason to this than there is to any other physical attraction. Some people think fat people are hot. That's just the way it is.

When we see someone, we evaluate their weight and size in the same way that we evaluate height, bone structure, hair color, the size or ratio of certain parts of the body, musculature, face shape, and numerous other factors. Depending on our tastes, we might think that what we see is attractive, repugnant, or nothing special. Just as there are "leg men" and "breast men," women who like men with cleft chins and women who like men with big hands, people who like redheads or goatees or big nipples or bubble butts, there are people who find fatter, plumper, rounder bodies attractive.

Most people are capable of finding a range of body types and shapes attractive. This is an advantage, since human beings are so varied. Most people find that there are limits to the range of things that they find attractive—but where these limits fall depends on the individual. Some people's range of attraction excludes fatter bodies. But some people's range of attraction excludes thin bodies. Yes, Virginia, there are actually people in the world who will turn down an advance made by a thin person because they just don't happen to find thinness at all sexually interesting. One self-identified fat admirer writes: "Sometimes, if a woman is too thin, I fear beforehand that I will have difficulties with erection. So to prevent a mutual disappointment, I may refuse."

And of course, there are a great many people—probably the majority—who are attracted to people for a combination of different factors, and for whom the "intangibles" like intelligence, sense of humor, compassion, political and religious views, supportiveness, and so on are actually just as important as anything physical, if not sometimes more so. Deke Hammel, the owner of *Generous.net,* a size-accepting website that has an extensive online personals board for people of size and those who love them, is an ardent supporter of big people's sexuality, but as he says of himself: "To be honest, I'm not a fat-admirer. I'm a smile fetishist. Both of my wives had smiles that measured in the hundreds of watts. And my second wife wasn't just slender, she was downright skinny. Like sleeping with a bicycle. But if sex is the only reason you're getting married, I don't think the marriage has any chance of surviving."

It's very common for people to become attracted to one another in a nonsexual way first, and to have the sexual side of things develop out of that emotional attachment. This happens with thin people, fat people, old people, young people, differently-abled people, able-bodied people, and everyone in between. Sometimes people think of this negatively, as "Oh, my partner loves me in spite of my size," but the fact of the matter is that there are people of all sizes who are in wonderful, loving, sexy, fulfilling relationships that are not predicated on intense gut-wrenching sexual attraction to physical characteristics. In other words, it's not "in spite of your size," it's "because you're a wonderful loveable person who also happens to be fat." Some of the qualities a partner likes may even be qualities—like compassion, understanding of difference, resilience, and ability to cope with stressful situations—that have been enhanced because of the many difficulties you've faced going through life as a fat person. Being different can teach you a lot, after all. Some of the things you can learn from being different are very attractive to the kinds of people who are looking for more than just another pretty face when they look for a romantic or sexual partner.

**Fat people are fat because they're hiding from their sexuality.**

Being sexual is a human characteristic that exists irrespective of size. Fat people have the same range of sexual preferences, interests, fantasies, libido levels, hang-ups, and persuasions as thin people. Fat people have the same genitalia as thin people, and their genitals work in the same ways. Fat people fall in and out of love, get married and divorced, have affairs, scope out attractive strangers, have one-night-stands, go to sex parties, have long monogamous relationships, and do everything that everybody else does that has to do with sex or sexuality or sexual relationships.

At the same time, it is true that because of the way society generally regards fat people, fat people often don't receive the same amount of generalized sexual attention that thinner people generically do. Because there is a social stigma attached to it, there are fewer people who are willing to be open about finding fat people attractive. This doesn't necessarily mean they don't, just that they're less likely to be public about it. Because of the presumption that fat people are not sexually attractive, there is often less pressure on fat people to package themselves or behave in ways that are generally considered sexually alluring. For example, no one finds it odd if a fat person stays home from the dance, or if there aren't any fat people at a singles' gathering. In fact, people might find it distressing if fat people do show up to these events. Not surprisingly, fat people who show up to these events often feel very pressured, uncomfortably exposed, and set up for failure.

For these reasons and more, it can be very reassuring and comforting to a person who is insecure about their ability to be sexual when they are not expected to be sexual. It minimizes the risk of rejection and other unpleasant experiences. But not participating in the social parts of sexual life is a double-edged sword, providing a certain amount of immediate comfort, but at a price. Insecurity and lack of participation in a full social and sexual life can become a chicken-and-egg problem: insecurity makes it more tempting to hide, and hiding makes it harder to shuck that insecurity. As their insecurity gets worse, some people become fatter, because some people do eat as a response to emotional stress and insecurity, but this is far from universal. The insecurity/hiding cycle is also not limited to fat people. There are a lot of thin people who are different from the mainstream in one way—queer people often go through similar situations—who also experience it.

Generally speaking, people don't become fat because they're afraid of sex—fat people become intimidated by sexuality because they see what the culture holds up as ideals of sexual attractiveness and because it's made clear to them that they don't match up to those ideals. Heaven knows that people in general have enough angst about sex in general that it doesn't take much to make people feel paralyzed. You don't have to be fat to worry that you're not good enough, that you don't know what you're doing, that your penis or breasts are too small to please a partner, and so forth. When you combine those everyday sexual anxieties with the threat of being sexually rejected lock, stock, and barrel because you're fat, it's amazing that more fat people don't completely give up the game. That there are so many sexually vital fat people is testament to their will, self-confidence, and perseverance.

It isn't a fear of sex that makes people fat. People gain weight for a lot of reasons, but mostly fat people are fat because they're fat, just like tall people are tall because they're tall or left-handers are left-handed because they're left-handed, as a result of genetics, upbringing, and dumb luck. Fatness can indeed have negative effects on sexuality because of the way in which fat people are treated in the social and sexual arenas, and negative sexual experiences can lead to emotionally-triggered over-eating, which may or may not result in weight gain. But implying a causal relationship between fear of sex and becoming fat is pretty shaky logic. After all, lots of fat people actually have great sex lives and have no problems being sexual. There are fat people on every point of the spectrum of sexual orientation and behavior right next to their thin brothers and sisters—and getting busy with them, too.

Likewise shaky is the notion that people become fat to put a "wall" between themselves and the outside world. Sure, it's possible for fat people to react to their fat that way, and make their fatness their "space maintainer" between themselves and the demands of the world. People have any lot of ways of doing that. The yen for escape is hardly unique to fat people. Some people sit at home and watch television by themselves all the time. Some people move to distant rural areas and live in homesteader cabins without electricity or phones. Some people become obsessive workaholics. There are those who choose drugs or alcohol to make their worlds more palatable. Some people take an organized spiritual path to remove themselves from the world at large and become monks, nuns, or other spiritual seekers or pilgrims. There's nothing about the desire to wall one's self off from the madding crowd and all its demands that is in any way a specifically "fat" desire. The only difference is that fat people's bodies provide the locus for a temptingly tidy, but usually incorrect, visual metaphor.

### Fat people are desperate, because it's so hard for them to find anyone who will sleep with them.

It'd be a lie to say that fat people are never desperate for a date or for sex. But it'd be a lie to say that thin people never get desperate, either. Even conventionally drop-dead gorgeous, thin, magazine-cover bombshells are sometimes desperate for a date or for sex—people can be as lonely because they're perceived as unattainable and thus unapproachable as they can be if they're seen as undesirable. No one gets to have sex whenever they want it, however they want it, with whomever they want. That's just the way the cookie crumbles.

People of all kinds go through dry spells, have insecurities about whether or not they're desirable, and worry that there's something about them that people secretly find off-putting or unattractive. You'll notice that ad campaigns, particularly for health and beauty aids, are designed to capitalize on these fears with their "Use our product to avoid being unattractive!" messages, implying, of course, that without outside help, your average Joe or Jane is, in their raw state, going to be a hideous mess who couldn't attract so much as an ant at a picnic.

People of all kinds can get a bit neurotic and obsessive when they're insecure about their attractiveness. Insecurity and obsessiveness, in turn, tend more often than not to make people seem less attractive than they would otherwise, thus compounding the problem. When people are told that they're not going to be able to find sexual or romantic partners, that no one will find them attractive, or that they're "losers"—as is the case with most people who are not thin, who are often told these things by family members as well as classmates and co-workers as well as the culture at large—they end up with a significant extra obstacle that they must overcome in order to get on with the business of having full, interesting, active sex and romantic lives with all the usual joys, disappointments, and triumphs.

Part of what makes people (fat or not) feel desperate for love or sexual attention is what might be characterized as a famine mentality. This paradoxical mindset is well summed-up in Auntie Mame's oft-quoted phrase, "Life's a banquet, and some poor suckers are starving to death." In other words, if you believe that any much-desired commodity is critically rare, you'll be fearful of not getting enough (or not getting any at all), no matter how abundant that commodity might really be. Desperate, fearful people are not generally at their best, and they're prone to making bad, panicky decisions. That's human nature.

In sexual situations, this can mean that, out of the fear produced by the famine mentality, people will sometimes agree to things that are not mentally or physically healthy for them. They may think that they'd better go along with what's being offered, since they might not get another chance anytime soon. They may worry that if they don't, their partner might decide to discard them for someone more desirable or just more compliant. If someone thinks they might not get

another chance, or feels that they should put out for whoever's interested since they're convinced that few people ever will be, they're likely to make decisions about sex that they would neither make nor defend under other circumstances. As a result, fear and a "famine mentality" often mean that people end up having rotten sexual experiences when there's no earthly reason for them to have to have sex that isn't the way they want it to be....

Whether by dint of conscious effort, finding a partner whose attentions help break the "no one's ever going to want me" loop, or just the passage of time and increased maturity, there are a lot of fat people who are in no way desperate. One of the most powerful forces in helping people get loose of the "fat and ugly and desperate" cycle is finding friends, family, and philosophies that help reinforce self-confidence and self-worth. Finding sources of support like the ones described here is vital to having a full and self-loving life, and in turn, vital to being able to love and live to the top of your ability....

**Fat men have tiny penises.**

Some do, some don't. Statistically speaking, average hard penis length is about five and a half to six inches. The way men's penises look when they are soft, and the size they appear to have when soft, is not a reliable indicator of how large they may be when they're erect (hand size, foot size, or the size of a man's nose, by the way, are also unreliable guides). Generally, just as fat people's libidos, sexual orientations, desires, and fantasies come in the same range as that of the population as a whole, the same is true of genitalia, whether it's male or female. Some are big, some are small, some are thick, some are thin, experience and statistics both suggest that penis size doesn't necessarily have anything to do with the size of the rest of a man's body.

However, fat men's penises may *appear* to be smaller than thinner men's. There are a couple of reasons this may appear to be the case. A fat man's penis is likely to appear smaller by comparison to the rest of his size simply because of the proportions of things. If belly, hips, and thighs are quite large, an average-sized penis is not going to appear "average sized" because everything else in the vicinity is bigger than "average." Another reason that fat men's penises may seem smaller or shorter is that, just as fatter women can have a fat deposit over the pubic bone, resulting in a considerably bigger mound of venus (or mons veneris) than a thinner woman might have, men also develop fat deposits in the same general place. A pad of fat around the base of the penis may make the penis appear, and in some positions effectively be, shorter than it would be if that fat pad were not present.

For many men, lying on their backs (with or without a pillow under the hips) will let the fat around the base of the penis spread out sideways more than usual, which can reduce the amount of fat padding that is directly around the base of the penis. For this reason, big men often find they achieve their deepest penetration when their partner is on top of them....

**Fat people are sexless.**

Not at all! Fat people have the same wide range of sexualities, libidos, preferences, hang-ups, fantasies, and desires that everybody else does. In willful ignorance of this rather salient fact, the culture in which we live has a tendency to de-sexualize fat people, insisting that they are not sexually attractive, don't have sex easily or well, and they don't "look sexual."

Saying that someone doesn't "look sexual" is saying two things: first that someone doesn't conform to standard ideals of what sexual attractiveness is "supposed to be," and secondly that their body doesn't conform to what a member of a given sex is "supposed" to look like. Our culture currently considers a very slim, almost childlike body shape to be the most sexually attractive body shape. Some commentators have suggested that the preferred feminine body shape of the 1990s is not really female, but that it more closely resembles the body shape achieved by men in drag. This is ironic in light of the fact that sometimes fat

bodies are seen as "between genders" or "devoid of gender," as amorphous, hard to place *à la* the "It's Pat" character in the well-known *Saturday Night Live* skits—and there are some real explanations for why fat bodies can sometimes seem hard to place or hard to conceptualize in terms of gender and what we expect gender to mean.

There is as enormous range of shape diversity in fatter people's bodies, and because the scale is large, it's easy to see. There is a similar diversity in non-fat bodies, but it's not always as noticeable. You can, for instance, find thin women who have small breasts and very pronounced hips—but add fifty pounds, and have a lot of it be carried on the hips and butt, and it becomes that much more noticeable.

When fat is deposited in places like the hips, buttocks, or breasts, it tends to enhance those secondary sexual characteristics. However, bodies can also carry fat deposits in places like the belly and waist, thighs, upper arms, and men's breasts, places in which the fat may obscure, lessen, or take away the sex-linked body shaping that is a big part of how we learn to identify sex and gender and to determine which bodies are sexually attractive. Women who are "hourglass" shaped, with big breasts, big butt and hips, but who have a comparatively narrow waist can carry quite a bit of fat but still be still identifiably female and feminine. Anna Nicole Smith, Marilyn Monroe, and Mae West all capitalized on this classic shape, and that "hourglass" waist-to-bust/hip ratio is part of what gives Camryn Manheim her on-screen appeal, too. Women who are "pearshaped," where the weight is carried mostly from the waist down in the hips, butt, and thighs, still retain the female/feminine visual shape signifier of narrow waist and broad hips, even if their breasts are not proportionately large enough to make them into the "hourglass" silhouette.

An "apple shaped" woman of the same actual weight, who carries her fat mostly in her belly and torso, however, is less likely to be seen as sexually desirable and less likely to be identified as feminine (not the same as female). If her breasts are small, she may be even more confusing to the eye, since fat men often develop small breasts and tend to be "apple shaped" too. This can be an asset to some transgendered women, or to women who enjoy crossdressing, but to many apple-shaped women, it's a source of consternation. The "hourglass" is the way women are "supposed to be" shaped, the quintessential shape that people see and immediately identify as female and feminine. No matter whether a woman is too thin to be curvy, or has her curves in what she might consider to be the "wrong places" to have that overall body shape, she may feel that she looks less than feminine.

Male bodies, on the other hand, are not expected to be rounded and curved in the same fat-padded way that women's are. The lines associated with men's bodies tend to be straighter and whatever curves are there are generally supposed to be muscular. Consequently, the more a fat man's body maintains those straight and muscular lines, the more he will be perceived as masculine and manly. The "teddy bear," "lumber-jack," or "bear" archetype is a fat man who is built on the stereotypical male plan, skeletally speaking: broad shoulders, narrow hips, and usually quite tall. Bears carry their weight in their bellies almost exclusively, and as an adjunct often have a fair amount of body and facial hair, both of which contribute to their being seen as very male and masculine.

However, not all fat men are built like bears. Men who are less broadshouldered, who tend to carry their fat along their sides and back more than in their bellies, or whose fat rides in their lower belly, hips, and thighs tend to become more or less "pearshaped." This body shape is more often seen as female, with its visual connotations of "childbearing hips" and the typically broader woman's pelvis, than it is seen as male. Fat men aren't the only men to be seen as less masculine because of their body shape, though. Very thin-framed men with narrow shoulders are also more likely to seem more androgynous, and very skinny men without much muscle mass often get pasted

with the "98-pound weakling" label no matter how strong they may in fact be.

Breasts are another gender-complicating issue that fat men face. Not all fat men will develop fat deposits in their breasts, but many do. It's perfectly reasonable that this should happen: breasts are breasts because of fat, and women's breasts and men's breasts aren't all that different structurally. Sometimes, enlarged breasts in men are diagnosed as a medical condition called gynecomastia or gynomastia (woman-breastness), but strictly speaking, there's nothing at all medically wrong with most fat men who happen to have fat deposition in their breasts. Basically, they're just another place for the body to store fat, but since people usually equate visible breasts with femaleness, it might be disturbing or confusing to come across a man with who has them.

There are also some hormonal issues that can affect fat men and women. Some of these can result in visible body changes that can create gender confusion. Fat, as a tissue, is one of the sites in the body which produces estrogen. Therefore, the fatter you are, the more estrogen you're likely to have in your body. Higher estrogen has a couple of side effects: first, it means that many fat people's skin is very soft and supple and may feel "satiny" to the touch—an asset to women, but possibly less so for men, for whom very soft skin might be seen as an effeminate trait. In some men, high estrogen may also mean less facial and body hair, giving a baby-faced look. The softness of fat people's bodies is one of the things that a lot of fat admirers find very sensual and attractive.

Sometimes there are other fat-related hormonal conditions that have the opposite effect. Polycystic Ovarian Syndrome (PCOS), a condition that is found in women of all sizes, has a strong propensity to encourage weight gain and to make weight loss difficult or impossible. One of the classic symptoms of PCOS is hirsutism, or excess growth of facial and body hair—a normally-occurring male secondary sex characteristic. Some women who have facial hair decide to shave it, pluck it, or undergo electrolysis.

Other women prefer to let it grow and enjoy their lives as "bearded ladies." It should be noted that not all women with hirsutism have PCOS, and not all women with hirsutism are fat. However, there is a correlation between these conditions in some cases.

Clearly, fat people's bodies can create some serious confusion among the clues people unconsciously use to assign gender and to make assumptions about sexuality, sex drive, and sexual prowess. Does this actually mean that a person's sexuality, sex drive, or sexual prowess is diminished, even in cases where there are hormonal imbalances? Probably not. Perceptions of fat people as sexless have more to do with the power of visual cues than they do with the truth of any individual fat person's sexuality, libido, sexual identity, or sexual prowess.

**Fat people are grateful for any sexual attention at all. They'll do anything you want.**

Don't bet on it. While it is true that people who are routinely sexually disenfranchised often have feelings of sexual insecurity and undesirability, and this sometimes leads to people feeling that they need to "compensate" for their perceived lack of worth or attractiveness by being overly compliant with any partner's wishes, this is not always the case. People with low self-confidence and a low opinion of their own sexual worth are far more likely to subjugate their own desires to those of a partner regardless of what they weigh. This is particularly true of people who have internalized emotional abuse about their worthiness as human beings and as sexual beings.

Many fat people are threatened with a loveless life from childhood and are told that they "won't have a boyfriend/girlfriend" or "won't find a husband/wife" unless they lose weight. This sort of message in childhood alone, but particularly when it is coupled with rejection, abuse from a partner, or repeated experiences of feeling sexually humiliated, can scar just about anyone. Most people do carry around some scars of this ilk, regardless of their size. Life is like that, unfortu-

nately. Most people chalk up their scars to experience, the "school of hard knocks," or perhaps "that man (or woman) who done me wrong." For fat people, though, with all the training we get that our fat makes us horrible human beings who deserve whatever bad comes to us, it becomes awfully easy to assume that any bad relationship or any rejection is due explicitly to our being fat. We lose our sense of what is legitimately related to fatness and what is not.

This is just one way in which it can be very difficult for fat people to identify and establish their personal boundaries. Psychologist Dr. Barbara Altman Bruno remarks that fat people are often likely to have problems establishing and maintaining healthy sexual boundaries because they've often had other people ignore or deliberately crush their own personal and bodily boundaries from the time they were small. Fat kids and teenagers are often forced to subject their bodies and their appetites to other people's ideas of what they should be like. Parents force kids to go on diets and take them to intrusive, often abusive, doctors to be treated for the non-disease of being fat. Parents often withhold affection from their "bad" fat children, whose bodies defy their parents' wishes, in a form of emotional blackmail. Sometimes this is subconscious, and sometimes it is overt. Kids and teenagers feel a lot of media and peer pressure about body image and often end up with eating disorders. People in restaurants and grocery stores often seem to feel quite entitled to comment on a fat kid (or adult) eating in public. And, as we all know, kids on the playground can be ruthless to anyone who is different.

People who are used to having to try to force their own bodies and appetites to conform to other people's notions of what is appropriate are likely not to have very much experience with making decisions to do things that feel authentically right for them. They may not have ever learned to trust their own instincts about their physical appetites and desires, whether food-related or sexual. They may simply assume that they shouldn't ever express their own desires lest it turn out not to be something a partner (or parent, or whomever) wants to hear. Fat people often grow up learning that the way to be accepted is to conform what someone else wants regardless of your own boundaries or comfort level.

Fat people are not alone in fearing that they won't be loved, or alone in feeling that they have to continually try to subjugate their needs and desires to other people's in order not to lose love and acceptance, but it is a problem with particular resonance to the fat community. This kind of codependence plays itself out in all kinds of relationships, but can have particularly disastrous consequences in the sexual arena. It's okay to have boundaries, and perfectly justifiable to insist on having your limits respected, no matter what your size. People who seek out fat partners in the belief that they will have fewer boundaries and can thus be more easily exploited are being predatory. This sort of behavior is simply insupportable.

Often having overcome many obstacles to learn how, many people of size have excellent skills at defining and maintaining personal and sexual boundaries. They know how to express their desires and how to say no to things they're not interested in doing. They know their limits and their capabilities, and aren't afraid to speak up. People usually find that the more confident they are in general, the easier it is to be confident with maintaining sexual boundaries. Don't assume that any fat person is going to be an easier mark or have lower standards than any thin person. Assuming wrong might earn you a tight slap across the face from a justifiably offended fat hand.

## Fat people stink and are filthy, especially their genitals.

Unless there's some sort of illness or infection at work that's causing it, people generally don't smell bad as long as they bring some soap and water into contact with their epidermis on a fairly regular basis. Soap and water work the same way no matter who's using them.

Among Westerners, Americans are notoriously hypersensitive about matters of body odor. We use legendary quantities of scented soaps, antibacterial soaps, antiperspirants, deodorants, scented detergents, and all the rest to try to render our bodies unnaturally antiseptic and scentless. Because of this, we tend to be hyper-reactive whenever we do happen to smell normal bodily scents, and we also tend to stigmatize body odors more highly whenever they happen to come from a person of a class that we don't happen to like too much.

On the average, however, most fat people don't smell any different from anyone else. Fat people wash, use deodorants, and so forth, according to their personal preferences just like everyone else you know. Some fat people do have reach problems. Occasionally this can make it difficult for them to easily wash and/or examine their genitals. However, necessity is the mother of invention, and people come up with ingenious solutions to their problems. Companies like Ample Stuff...provide catalogs of products designed with the needs of big people in mind, many of which are designed to make good hygiene easy for everyone.

## If you sleep with a fat person, you'll get crushed or smothered.

The truth of the matter is that sex with a fat person won't crush you, suffocate you, or smother you any more than eating watermelon seeds will make watermelons grow inside your stomach. Notwithstanding the many jokes, rumors, urban legends, pornographic cartoons, old wives' tales, and other testimonials to the inevitability of a fat person crushing their sexual partners, it just doesn't work that way. Human beings are pretty sturdy. Moreover, having sex with a fat person doesn't put weight on your body in the same way that it would if, for instance, a grand piano fell out of a second story window onto your head. Yes, fat people do weigh more than thin people, but that doesn't mean that they have no control over how or whether they put their weight on their partners. Furthermore, having weight on your body doesn't necessarily hurt or do anyone any harm. Some people rather like the sensation. A few of them even pay rather handsomely for it on the rare occasions when they find a dominatrix who is both physically and mentally equipped to provide it.

It seems odd that no one bats an eyelash at the thought of a 280-pound football player having sex with a tiny hundred-pound cheerleader type, but somehow people are capable of believing that a 280-pound woman could somehow manage to crush a male partner inadvertently during sex and not even know it. This is patently ludicrous. It's just not all that probable that a fat person will do any damage to a sexual partner unless, God forbid, they are actually *trying* to do them harm.

Fat people are just as capable as anyone else of moving out of the way if a partner expresses distress or displeasure (and their partners are just as capable of doing their best to signal their distress and to move out of harm's way if the need arises). Moreover, fat people are fat, not insensible. Skin is sensitive to pressure and touch whether it covers bone, muscle, or fat. You might sit on a penny and not know it was there, sure. But no matter what their size, people do not simply sit on or roll over on top of large objects—especially something as large as another human being—and not notice. People are also notoriously difficult to sit on. As size-acceptance activist and *Fat!So?* author Marilyn Wann said when giving a tongue-in-cheek description of an experiment she and her fat boyfriend conducted to see if they could crush one another during sex: "People just thrash too much when they're suffocating. It's just not very much fun." In all seriousness, it would indeed be rather a remarkable feat to crush someone to death with your own body, and even more remarkable not to notice it....

**Anyone who thinks fat people are sexy has to have some psychological problem.**

While it is often more socially challenging to be in a relationship that isn't the kind of relationship mainstream society holds up as ideal, it's not crazy to want to have a relationship with a person whom you love and find sexy and desirable, no matter what society thinks. Generalizations like "anyone who thinks fat people are sexy has to be crazy . . ." just beg to be debunked by being applied across

the board. Try inserting "Black," "short," "left-handed," "French," "Catholic," "men with small penises," or any generic adjective that refers to a generic group of people into that sentence in place "fat." Pretty illuminating, isn't it?

The moral of the story is simply that not everyone has the same tastes and not everyone wants the same things in their relationships or from their partners. Not sharing your tastes doesn't mean someone "has a psychological problem," it just means that they're different from you. People like what they like for a number of complex reasons. There's no more reason or logic for liking tall skinny blondes with gravity-defying breast implants than there is for liking short plump brunettes with small, firm breasts and meaty, hearty thighs. *De gustibus non est disputandum*—there's no accounting for taste.

**Fat women love to give oral sex because they're orally fixated.**

Why is it that people say this about fat people, but not about cigarette smokers, gum-chewers, people who habitually gnaw the ends of their pens and pencils, or who engage in any of the other classic oral fixation behaviors? Sure, it's tempting—if wildly incorrect—to assume that fat people are fat because they have oral fixations which cause them to eat constantly, but that's just not the case. Some people who are fat probably do have oral fixations, given the laws of probability, but an oral fixation doesn't necessarily lead to becoming fat. Furthermore, oral fixation isn't necessarily a condition that plays itself out sexually. Some fat people (male and female) love giving oral sex. Some fat people don't. Some fat people love receiving oral sex. Some fat people don't. Some fat people would rather read a book than do either one. Same with thinner people.

The upshot is that sometimes, yes, you'll find a fat person who would rather give head than just about anything else, but probably no more or less often than you'd find that proclivity among thinner partners. If you'd like your partner to perform oral sex more often, remember that nothing provides encouragement like a good example!

## Because He Liked to Look at It

### Eve Ensler

This is how I came to love my vagina. It's embarrassing, because it's not politically correct. I mean, I know it should have happened in a bath with salt grains from the Dead Sea, Enya playing, me loving my woman self. I know the story. Vaginas are beautiful. Our self-hatred is only the internalized repression and hatred of the patriarchal culture. It isn't real. Pussys unite. I know all of it. Like, if we'd grown up in a culture where we were taught that fat thighs were beautiful, we'd all be pounding down milkshakes and cookies, lying on our backs, spending our days thigh-expanding. But we didn't grow up in that culture. I hated my thighs, and I hated my vagina even more. I thought it was incredibly ugly. I was one of those women who had looked at it and, from that moment on, wished I hadn't. It made me sick. I pitied anyone who had to go down there.

In order to survive, I began to pretend there was something else between my legs. I imagined furniture—cozy futons with light cotton comforters, little velvet settees, leopard rugs—or pretty things—silk handkerchiefs, quilted pot holders, or place settings—or miniature landscapes—clear crystal lakes or moisty Irish bogs. I got so accustomed to this that I lost all memory of having a vagina. Whenever I had sex with a man, I pictured him inside a mink-lined muffler or a red rose or a Chinese bowl.

Then I met Bob. Bob was the most ordinary man I ever met. He was thin and tall and nondescript and wore khaki clothes. Bob did not like spicy foods or listen to Prodigy. He had no interest in sexy lingerie. In the summer he spent time in the shade. He did not share his inner feelings. He did not have any problems or issues, and was not even an alcoholic. He wasn't very funny or articulate or mysterious. He wasn't mean or unavailable. He wasn't self-involved or charismatic. He didn't drive fast. I didn't particularly like Bob. I would have missed him altogether if he hadn't picked up my change that I dropped on the deli floor. When he handed me back my quarters and pennies and his hand accidentally touched mine, something happened. I went to bed with him. That's when the miracle occurred.

Turned out that Bob loved vaginas. He was a connoisseur. He loved the way they felt, the way they tasted, the way they smelled, but most important, he loved the way they looked. He had to look at them. The first time we had sex, he told me he had to see me.

"I'm right here," I said.

"No, you," he said. "I have to see you." "Turn on the light," I said.

Thinking he was a weirdo, I was freaking out in the dark. He turned on the light.

Then he said, "Okay. I'm ready, ready to see you."

"Right here." I waved. "I'm right here."

Then he began to undress me.

"What are you doing, Bob?" I said.

"I need to see you," he replied.

"No need," I said. "Just dive in."

"I need to see what you look like," he said.

"But you've seen a red leather couch before," I said.

Bob continued. He would not stop. I wanted to throw up and die.

"This is awfully intimate," I said. "Can't you just dive in?"

"No," he said. "It's who you are. I need to look."

I held my breath. He looked and looked. He gasped and smiled and stared and groaned. He got breathy and his face changed. He didn't look ordinary anymore. He looked like a hungry, beautiful beast.

"You're so beautiful," he said. "You're elegant and deep and innocent and wild."

"You saw that there?" I said.

It was like he read my palm.

"I saw that," he said, "and more—much, much more."

He stayed looking for almost an hour, as if he were studying a map, observing the moon, staring into my eyes, but it was my vagina. In the light, I watched him looking at me, and he was so genuinely excited, so peaceful and euphoric, I began to get wet and turned on. I began to see myself the way he saw me. I began to feel beautiful and delicious—like a great painting or a waterfall. Bob wasn't afraid. He wasn't grossed out. I began to swell, began to feel proud. Began to love my vagina. And Bob lost himself there and I was there with him, in my vagina, and we were gone.

*Source: The Vagina Monologues* by Eve Ensler, copyright © 1998 by Eve Ensler; foreword copyright © 1998 by Gloria Steinem. Used by permission of Villard Books, a division of Random House, Inc.

# Exotic Dancing and the Negotiation of Identity:

# The Multiple Uses of Body Technologies

Jennifer K. Wesely

**B**ody technologies are the techniques we engage to change or alter our physical appearance. A continuum of body technologies might range from temporary alterations like makeup or attire on one end to more permanent or invasive changes like cosmetic surgery or drugs on the other. Although all body technologies are artificial, the technologized body passes as natural when it conforms to dominant social expectations of gendered bodies. Indeed, as visible accomplishments writ upon the body, body technologies can be acts of "doing gender" (West and Zimmerman 1987). Scholarship about particular body technologies like cosmetic surgery (Balsamo 1997; Dull and West 1991; Kaw 1998; Morgan 1998) and bodybuilding (Balsamo 1997; Heywood 1998; Holmlund 1997; Wesely 2001) has pointed out the ways that body technologies can both reinforce and challenge "natural" conceptions of gender. For instance, "technologies of femininity refer to those knowledges, practices, and strategies that manufacture and normalize the feminine body: those techniques, actions, and structures deployed to sculpt, fashion, and secure bodily shapes, gestures, and adornments that are recognizably female" (Cole 1993, 86–87)....

Conceptualizing gender as performance suggests that a multiplicity of embodied identities can be created through body technologies. For instance, sex performer Annie Sprinkle blurs boundaries between performance and porn; she parodies pornographic images of her gendered body by revealing the artificiality of its technologized femininity. In one of her early 1990s shows titled *Post Porn Modernist,* Sprinkle invited audience members to examine her cervix with flashlights after she inserted a speculum into her vagina. This speculum as well as a plethora of dildos, elaborate costumes, and makeup are the types of body technologies Sprinkle uses to disturb straightforward interpretations of her as a sex object. . . . Furthermore, in the specific context of the performance piece, she is able to actively choose when, where, and how to adopt a particular identity through her body. Similarly, in her *Anatomy of a Pinup Photo,* Sprinkle is photographed as a porn star but labels each body technology, providing helpful statements like "Mandatory fake beauty mark/Breasts are real but sag. Bra lifts breasts/Hemorrhoids don't show, thank goodness/Gloves cover tattoos for a more All-American girl effect, borrowed from Antionette/I can't walk and can barely hobble/Corset hides a very big belly" (Williams 1997, 373), and so on. By systematically noting the body technologies she uses, Sprinkle unveils her performance of femininity.

Obviously, not all women involved in sex work, whether pornography, prostitution, stripping, peep shows, or other variations, consciously attempt to destabilize gender using body technologies in the way Annie Sprinkle does. They may, for instance, be most concerned with pre-

From Wesely, Jennifer K. 2003. "Exotic Dancing and the Negotiation of Identity: The Multiple Uses of Body Technologies." *Journal of Contemporary Ethnography* 32: 643–669. Copyright 2003 by Sage Publications. Reprinted by permission of Sage Publications Inc.

senting an image that will be financially rewarded by customers (Sweet and Tewksbury 2000a). Yet literature has not examined the multiple layers of identity that are being both created and discarded through the use of body technologies for exotic dancers and what meanings the dancers then derive from these bodies. In fact, only recently has literature about exotic dancing begun to address the matrix of power and body issues that exists (Chapkis 2000, 1997; Lever and Dolnick 2000; Nagle 1997; Wesely 2002; Wood 2000). . . .

The study presented in this article is unique in that it examines the various meanings that body technologies hold for these women and how this relates to their gendered, embodied identities. Many times exotic dancers reproduce a stereotypically feminine and sexualized appearance through their body technologies; nonetheless, it is essential that . . . we look beyond this one-dimensional appraisal. This article addresses the idea that women are not passive recipients of or are limited to one-dimensional identity meanings, but instead engage body technologies for multiple reasons. It incorporates the realization that women's active choices about their bodies and identities might be constrained by the contexts in which they participate. . . . Ultimately, then, I investigate how dancers negotiate and grapple with these different aspects of their lived experiences in relation to their identities and bodies.

## Method

The information for this study was gleaned from ethnographic research conducted from March to November 2000. Qualitative, in-depth interviews with twenty current and former exotic dancers in a southwestern metropolitan area were the primary method of data collection. I also observed at two different clubs, listened to a local radio show featuring interviews with exotic dancers and club managers in the area (some of whom were in this study), and informally spoke with club personnel. . . .

## The Women

In this study, pseudonyms were used in all cases to protect the identities of the interviewees. The race/ethnicity of these women varied widely, and they self-identified as one Hispanic/Hawaiian, one African American, one African American/Hispanic, two Puerto Ricans, one Mexican American, one Filipino/White, one native African, one Costa Rican/Sicilian, and eleven Caucasians. The ages of the women at the time of the interview ranged from eighteen to forty years, with an average of twenty-six years. I interviewed nine current and eleven former dancers, but these categories are quite fluid. For example, several "former" dancers were not dancing at the time but had not ruled out returning to the industry; similarly, some "current" dancers had been "off and on" for years although they were involved in the industry at the time of the interview. The ages they began dancing ranged from fourteen to twenty-nine years, with an average age of nineteen. The average amount of time they were employed as dancers was five years but spanned one and a half months to seventeen years. One woman was a college graduate, one was a high school dropout, five had a high school education, and the rest had some college credit. At the time of the interview, five were currently enrolled in college.

## Discussion of Findings

### "What Can I Change about Myself, to Make Me More Appealing to These Guys?"

Like all women, exotic dancers learn early on of the contemporary ideal of feminine attractiveness. This ideal is difficult, if not impossible, to attain. "Through the pursuit of an ever-changing, homogenizing, elusive ideal of femininity . . . we continue to memorize on our bodies the feel of . . . never being good enough" (Bordo 1993, 166). Contemporary society is bombarded by media images of extremely thin women with large breasts, and for exotic dancers, this "Barbie doll" body is the one that got the most attention from customers. To achieve the successful performance of this body, the stripper's outward appearance is thus carefully and often painfully (re)constructed via body technologies. On one level, this is motivated by the financial reward that is reaped from the display of a successfully sexualized body—money has been found to be the major motivator for dancers in multiple studies (see Ronai and Ellis 1989; Sweet and Tewksbury 2000a; Wood 2000). However, pressure to technologize the body in service to the ideal is reinforced in many other ways in the club.

One manager, Joe, discussed on a radio program how he ran a purportedly "upscale gentleman's club." According to several women I interviewed who worked at his establishment, he forced girls to "weigh-in" and meet his arbitrary weight standards or risk being fired. He even directed them to do drugs to help them lose weight.

> So I remember one time, Joe came in and was like, "Ok, all you fat girls are weighing in. Including you." And I'm like, I'm thick, I'm black, I'm supposed to be big. He's like, "No, including you. You guys are all weighing in." And he told you, "Lose five, or lose ten. This is how much time you have. Lose six." This was also his way of weeding out girls. That's how I got into crystal [metamphetamine]. I'm all, how am I supposed to lose ten pounds in two weeks? He goes, "Why don't you talk to so-and-so?" So I talked to so-and-so and she offered me crystal. She gave me crystal, and that's how it started. That was my weight-loss drug. (Valerie)

If the women had difficulty addressing Joe's demands, he advised them to take illegal and addictive drugs, paving the way for the use of these substances as a body technology designed to keep their weights at the "proper" standards. Indeed, drugs were a body technology that often served as a weight-control mechanism. As Julie said, "Soon as I stopped doing crystal, girl, I gained 30 pounds. Now I do everything in the world to stay fit, but it's just not the same as that 'magical' diet" Their awareness of surveillance by club personnel increased the pressure the women felt to be extremely thin.

> You're always scrutinized by the people you work for. . . . I never saw any overweight dancers. So that was just common knowledge. After awhile they started firing girls that were getting heavier. Lose weight and you can come back. I knew because the "house mother" and manager would walk around and look at the girls. (Irene)

As a result, Irene had liposuction, although she "did not need the liposuction. I think I weighed 125 pounds. But I was so obsessed with being skinny for the job."

It has been suggested that eating disorders like anorexia and bulimia may be related to the objectification of women and the conflation of thinness with ideals of female beauty (McLorg and Taub 1987, 177). Again, this is only exacerbated in a context in which club personnel monitor the women's weight and customers financially reward them for being thin. In addition to drugs and cosmetic surgery, the women used body technologies like eating disorders, laxatives, and obsessive exercising to stay skinny enough to meet (management/customer/societal) standards. Many described starving themselves or eating in tiny amounts. Roxy said, "But I think the key factor is that you just don't eat. And when you do eat, it just leaves your system. And then your body goes into starvation mode." Similarly, Kate recalled,

> I remember trying not to eat so much, because I wanted to be thin. There were times I wouldn't eat for days. . . . I had anorexic issues. I'd eat an egg a day for a week, Diet Pepsi was the only thing I would drink. A lot of girls [at the club] were bulimic.

. . . Samantha's desire to be thin was partly motivated by her perception of the successful or ideal female body and how paying customers are *owed* this body:

> If I go to an out-call right after I eat, I feel like I'm pouchy. Like I got fat a little bit. If I just ate, I tell

them, "I'm sorry, I just ate, my stomach's sticking out a little bit." They're paying a lot of money.

Samantha's apology to the customers revealed her feeling that men who pay "a lot" to see her body had the right to see a fantasy image, which she was obligated to deliver. With thinness essential to this image, an eating disorder became part of the matrix of ways she technologized her body.

The dancers also became hyperaware of how they measured up against other workers and critiqued their own bodies even more harshly. These comparisons and self-evaluations are reflective of Rosenberg's (1979) analyses of social comparisons and reflected appraisals. With their appearance as what Rosenberg (1979) calls the "evaluated characteristic," some of the women became extremely self-critical when they fell short of the lucrative sexualized ideal. "In such an environment there may well be a disconcerting mismatch between the individual's taken for granted self concept, representing his [sic] fundamental framework for dealing with his [sic] world, and the messages about himself [sic] returned by others" (Rosenberg 1979, 125). One example is Marie's recollection: "You have guys give you money and say, if you had [big] boobs, you'd have the perfect body. And you hear those things all the time." Harsh self-critique was often informed by reactions from customers that undermined the women's confidence or made them critical of themselves and their bodies. Indeed, Marie related the above information when sharing why she chose to get breast implants.

Self-critique was also due to the women's own evaluation of themselves in comparison to others. As Rosenberg (1979) points out, "People in general . . . tend to compare their evaluated characteristics with those around them" (p. 125). Gina described an awareness of herself in comparison to the other dancers in the club *and* a sense of what customers will pay for or pay attention to:

When I was performing I was constantly comparing myself to other people. Constantly. 'Cause there's always somebody who looks better. There's always somebody who's got a tighter body, bigger boobs, who's got better looking abs. . . . You become very in tune with how you look and who is making money and how they look. And you know, most of the girls who are making money have dyed blonde hair, and big boobs, and they look like Barbie dolls. . . . It really affected me personally when I would walk up to a guy and he would look me up and down and say, no thanks. . . . I would start feeling down on myself, what's wrong with me, my boobs aren't big enough, my hair's not blonde enough, I'm not tall enough, I'm not thin enough. . . . I'd start picking apart my body. I'd sit in the dressing room, wondering: what can I change about myself, to make myself more appealing to these guys?

Gina's experience bore out a perception of the thin, blonde, busty, tall image as the ideal, to which she compared herself and began to harshly self-critique. Her comparison was also affected by negative customer reactions. Rita commented,

I think it's really hard not to fall into the trap of wanting big tits. . . . Standing next to a girl with double-D tits I feel like, where did mine go? And these girls lay down, and they're sticking straight up like rockets. And they make a lot of money. Almost all the girls have fake tits, in [this state].

Reinforcing Rosenberg's (1979) concepts of social comparisons and reflected appraisals, Rita, like Gina, united comparison ("standing next to a girl") and an awareness of customer responses ("they make a lot of money"). Interestingly, Rita compared her body directly to the cosmetic surgery of others, effectively bypassing the notion that the ideal image in the club was possible without body technology.

Jessie, who is Mexican American, felt that she was less attractive than her coworkers for a number of reasons: "And I'm really self-conscious about my body, because I have three kids. . . . And I'd see all these girls, pretty girls, white girls, flat stomach, boob jobs, and I'm like, oh my gosh." Jessie's quote included skin color as a component of her idealized assessment of physical beauty;

she incorporated "whiteness" into her concept of what she lacks in appeal. This invokes cultural constructions of feminine beauty as white and the exclusion or distortion of nonwhite bodies within this context (hooks 1997). Jessie's inclusion of "white" along with "pretty," "flat stomachs," and "boob jobs" also reflects a construction of whiteness as an aspect of the physical self that can be technologized to more closely approximate the ideal. In a related discussion of Tina Turner, bell hooks (1997) notes that the racist aesthetic of "blonde hair as the epitome of beauty" is often reinforced through the use of wigs and other artificial means—in short, body technologies that reproduce whiteness as the standard of feminine beauty.

As a result of these feelings of inadequacy, comparison, and critique, the exotic dancers employed a number of body technologies to increase their ability to make money and to feel confident and sexy in the exotic dance club; these span quite a spectrum. Even comportment and posture became ways of technologizing the physique; these technologies can be clustered on the more "temporary" side of the continuum. Gina described,

> When you become a dancer, you learn to walk with, you know, your butt stuck out, your boobs, you learn to throw your shoulders back so your boobs are as firm looking as possible. You learn to carry yourself a certain way.

Rita's experience was the same:

> We're not posing naturally. You don't [normally] stick your butt out or your chest out that far, and suck in. But somewhat, but when I dance, out of habit now my body just goes to the shape I want it to be in, and I have my own routine that I go through.

But being the fantasy Barbie doll goes beyond even these aspects of appearance. After all, dolls do not have any body flaws or body hair, and they certainly do not bleed. A hairless pubic area is regulation in a club that, according to one woman, had a sign posted in the dressing room: "Girls are getting too hairy!" The women shaved most, if not all, of their pubic hair. While menstruating, some described the practice of "cut and tuck"—after inserting a tampon, the string is cut and tucked inside the vagina. These types of body technologies helped further the doll-like image of the female body while hiding the realities of biology.

According to the women, the technologies they engaged usually rewarded them financially, which upped the ante and fed into an urgency to further technologize the body. Irene described,

> You get kind of obsessed with body perfect and perfection in the body. I had breast implants put in in the mid-80s. Then, later on, around '91 or '92, I had another set put in, bigger ones. Because the feeling was the bigger your boobs, the more table dances you got.

Skye had breast implants, dyed her hair blonde, wore blue contacts in her brown eyes—all body technologies she felt brought her closer to this Playboy look. "I wish my eyes were [naturally] blue instead of brown. I wish my hair was [naturally] blonde. That's the stripper image. That's how I learned about these things, looking at Playboy magazines. That's how I learned to do it." With pornographic magazines as her instruction manuals, Skye used body technologies to replicate the fantasy image.

During her three years as a dancer, twenty-one-year-old Cory had extensive cosmetic surgery, including hair implants, nose job, cheek implants, chin surgery, breast implants, tummy tuck, and liposuction. She felt that she was at a disadvantage *without* these surgeries and spent about $30,000 achieving the look she wanted.

> Yeah, I didn't think I was beautiful enough to dance. But I wanted to keep on dancing. So I was like, I can make more money if I do this. And I did, but it all started because of dancing. If I wasn't dancing, I wouldn't have done the things I did, never. Never. I don't regret it now, but I think I'll regret it when I get older. My mother tells me that.

It was of little concern to Cory that she may "regret" her cosmetic surgery later. However, she was told by her doctor that she got breast cancer from her huge implants, and they consequently had to be removed. Her main worry was about the resultant appearance of her breasts.

> I was pissed. . . . Basically, I didn't care about the cancer. I care about me not having big boobs. And then once you get a boob job all that skin is stretched. So it was going to go back and it was going to be saggy.

Samantha, who had two nose surgeries and two "boob jobs," had a response not unlike Cory's.

> I got in a car accident, and when I was in the car I never thought about death. All I thought about was, oh my god, I hope nothing happens to my face. I really think if anything ever happens to my face, my body, I would kill myself. This is me, this is all I have. I wouldn't be able to go on with my life.

Samantha's and Cory's statements dramatically reflect how the efforts to maintain a fantasy body are so all-consuming that other aspects of identity are dwarfed in comparison, as well as concerns for health and safety. As dancers, these women relied on their bodies in ways that necessitated their constant critique, attention, and maintenance, leading to more body technologies.

## "He Thought He Owned a Piece of Me"

The buying and selling of the dancers' bodies goes beyond the commodification of the image—it also occurs literally, with customers purchasing various body technologies and giving them to the dancers as "gifts." This happened most often through the buying of costumes and cosmetic surgery. By buying breast implants for a dancer, for instance, the customer takes control of the effort to reshape the woman's body in the fantasy image. At the same time, the women sometimes felt powerful when they convinced customers to pay for body technologies, since they are expensive and garner more business for the dancer.

> I had this guy that used to come into the club, he was my customer, he would give me money all the time. So once I was like, I've always wanted a tummy tuck, just picture me with a tummy tuck.

And he was like, yeah, you'd look so good. I was like, I need the money to do it, and he was like, you want me to get you a tummy tuck? I was like, will you, please? So he did get me a tummy tuck, which costs about $5000. (Cory)

By using persuasive tactics that referred to how she would more fully approximate the fantasy image—"picture me with a tummy tuck"—Cory convinced the customer to pay for her surgery. Julie noted that persuading a customer to pay for breast implants got attention from other dancers, while also piquing suspicion of sexual acts the dancer may have performed to gain such a favor. . . .

Cyclically, the sexualized, fantasy body was used to acquire the capital to afford a particular body technology, and this body technology further contributed to the objectification and instrumental use of the body. Valerie articulated this cycle: "Dancing is like a monkey on your back. It's like a drug addiction. You dance a lot so you can get better costumes so you can make more money so you can get better costumes. . . it's a vicious cycle."

Sometimes the offer of cosmetic surgery was a more obvious manifestation of male coercion. For example, within the context of Angel's life, it was another control tactic by the abuser with whom she lived. As a result of running away from home and a number of other circumstances, at the age of fifteen, Angel was taken in by this terrifying and violent man. Identifying himself as her boyfriend, he often pimped her and forced her to dance, while underage, at the strip club he managed. He wanted to buy Angel breast implants but she refused.

> Chris offered to get me breast implants when I was sixteen. It really made me think, well, how happy am I with my body? And I decided no. I thought, I'm small, they would look funny on me. He said, "We've got an appointment set up for you, how big do you want 'em?"

In this way, cultural norms that refigure women's bodies as objects of consumption for the male gaze are taken to a new and frightening level. Indeed, with the money that the customer (or pimp) pays to remake the woman in his or the fantasy image, he may feel as though this re-creation belongs to him. Not just a consumer of the body with paid rights to gaze, he now literally owns this body....

### "So I'll Ask a Guy, Do You Prefer Blondes?"

When body technologies are channeled into the reproduction of particular images of female attractiveness, they begin to erase visible difference. Although dancers must perform a sexy and appealing personality—a drama of desire—for the customer, their real-life goals and needs are usually not of concern to clientele. Indeed, the customer may not want too much knowledge about a dancer's real life history (Wood 2000). Thus, dancers feel largely differentiated not by in-depth personal characteristics but by their performed, sexualized bodies. Consequently, when their bodies are technologized and commodified so as to emphasize one particular fantasy image, there are even fewer opportunities to be different. Indeed, the women described feeling differentiated from other dancers by only the most superficial of identifiers, like blonde or brown hair. Competition heightened as they moved closer to one standard look because there were almost always several girls who shared external attributes.

For instance, Tasha felt unique because of her hair color. As a result of being a redhead, she was exempt from competition among other dancers. She said, "I was the only redhead there. There was a competition between the blondes and brunettes, but I wasn't in that competition clique or anything." Another way that women were distinguished from other dancers was on the basis of skin color. Although some aspects of Valerie's comments below imply that skin color is a superficial identifier, she also addressed the more complex motives of racism on the part of club management.

The racism was from the managers, preferential treatment. If you worked at a nightclub and you were black, you were pretty damn good looking. If you were average, they wanted nothing to do with you. You were a day girl. You either had a super-great body or you were super good looking. With the white girls, they were less picky . . . but with the black and Hispanic, they were beautiful. A lot of these white girls were really plain, girl-next-door type. But guys like that too. Clubs weren't real big on hiring too many [minorities]. You didn't want six or seven black girls at a small club. You couldn't do it, because that's not what brought in the money. I think the most black girls I ever worked with were six to eight, and that was at a club that held 200 girls. . . It didn't bother me. Nothing bothers me. It was better for me, 'cause if a client wanted a dark skin girl, it was me and the other girl. Not like the white girls, there was some vicious competition.

Valerie began her quote by addressing racist hiring practices. She went on to note that to be hired by the club, black women had to go above and beyond the normal standards of (white) beauty by being exceptionally attractive or sexy. The suggestion that women of color have to work harder than white women to achieve the same level of sexual desirability (by customers) again equates whiteness with the feminine beauty ideal (hooks 1997). Valerie acknowledged that black women are not what "bring in the money." As one of the "exceptional" black women, she expressed that she benefits from being one of the few hired to dance at the club. In her comment "It doesn't bother me," Valerie affected a posture of indifference to the larger implications of the management's discrimination and the customers' alleged desires. Her comments skim the surface of the racism inherent in the preference for white dancers, alluding to an affinity for skin *color* while divorcing this preference, on the part of both management and customers, from its social and cultural meanings. Indeed, Valerie referred to her skin *color* rather than her ethnic identity that exempted her from competition with Caucasian dancers; she suggested that the factors that differentiate the women are literally skin-deep, even when skin color connotes a much more complex identity.

Jessie, who is Mexican American and has a cropped haircut, was bothered when called by the name of a similarly coiffed African American actress all night by a customer:

> You have to be sexual, a fantasy for a guy, basically. I used to have drunk men always tell me something different. This one drunk guy called me Halle Berry. He kept me at his table all night, saying "This is my Halle Berry."

Jessie suggested that the "sexual fantasy" for this customer was Halle Berry, and as a woman of color with a similar haircut, she was enough of an approximation. The most obvious racist implication of the intoxicated customer's comments is the blurring of distinction between people of color, uniting them under one exoticized rubric. This generic "exotic" image was capitalized on by Roxy, who is Puerto Rican, in her description of how she used body technologies to appear to be a different race in the club. She said,

> But as far as the race thing, sometimes I would accentuate that. Like with the makeup, or the [eye]liner. For the exotic image. One guy wanted a party and he wanted two Oriental girls. And there was only one available and [the organizer] was like [to me], well, you're close enough!

In the cases of Jessie and Roxy, haircut and skin color, and makeup and skin color, respectively, became the superficial identifiers that defined them in the club context for the customer. Jessie and Roxy had different reactions to being categorized this way, and it is difficult to truly discern customer motives in each scenario. In Jessie's case, pornographic myths "of black female sexuality created by men in a white supremacist patriarchy" (hooks 1997, 120) may have played a role, although arguably, dancers are expected to appear to be who the customer wants them to be, with or without racist (sexist, classist) implications. The exotic fantasy approximation appears

skin-deep, but deeper motives of racism or hatred may be part of customer preferences.

When grouped together on the basis of superficial visible identifiers, the bodies of women in the club became depersonalized, dehumanized, and commodified. The commodified bodies are easily fragmented into parts and selected auction style to maximize profit.

> So I'll ask a guy, do you prefer blondes, do you prefer real tits, fake tits, legs, tits, what kind of guy are you? You're like, I'm sure we have what you're looking for, we have one of everything. Tell me what you like, I'll send a couple of girls over. You like blondes, I'll send you three or four blondes and you can choose. That's what we're here for. The waitresses will do that, they'll ask them what they like. And they'll say, ok, I need four brunettes, go talk to this guy. (Rita)

Reduced to physical attributes, the individuality of their complex identities is flattened. The women's fragmented parts are categorized by a selection process that is not unlike that regarding an inanimate object such as a car or a sofa. As Rita said, "A guy will just point, I want that one, I want that one in white, or I want the brown-haired one." The women often made choices about their bodies that reinforced this commodification because this proved to be most lucrative for them.

At the same time, the dancers' comments also pointed to deeper, more complex rationales inherent in the choices made about their bodies. In cruel irony, the aspects of their bodies that the women contorted, tucked, removed, implanted, and plucked so as to embody the fantasy image were also often the aspects of their bodies that had originally differentiated them from other dancers. As the body technologies were applied in service to the idealized image, so too did the appearance of the women siphon into the narrow confines of a particular look. In response to this, the amount and severity (in terms of both pain and mutilation) of body technologies employed by the dancers was ratcheted up as they attempted to *feel* more unique while simultaneously *appearing* so to customers. Rita described technologies such as tattoos or piercings as ways of making a dancer appear—and feel—different or unusual.

> There's only so many things you can do to be interesting. That's why girls get tattoos or get pierced. You're standing there [naked] in shoes, what can you do? We all look the same. You've seen one pair [of breasts], you've seen them all. You try to be different, you think, oh, it's going to be my tan or my makeup or my clothes. I hate that.

Within the club, the range of body technologies that are financially rewarding is limited in scope and confounded dancers' attempts to fulfill the fantasy image and yet still be different or feel unique. Rita was frustrated by the failure of particular body technologies—her "tan," "makeup," or "clothes"—to truly differentiate her from the other dancers. She found that tattoos and piercings were used by dancers to counter this failing.... For the women in this study, body technologies sometimes had the effect of neutralizing individuality rather than being a means of its expression. This obstacle contributed to the amount and type of technologies used, as Rita described. This is one level, then, on which dancers engaged particular technologies in an effort to carve out some more significance and meaning for themselves and their bodies.

On another level, while they focused on technologizing their bodies into moneymakers, the women sometimes found this pursuit empty and unsatisfying. This is especially evident in Angel's case. She began by addressing her engagement of the technology of body piercing: "I have lots of piercings. I have my (clit)hood pierced, I got that when I was dancing when I was 16, I thought that would be more exotic. I had my eyebrow pierced, my nose." Angel proposed that her piercings, including her genital piercing, were for the purposes of being "exotic" while working as a dancer. Her implication was that this would differentiate her from others and thus be more appealing to customers. Yet even the clithood piercing, which is probably more unusual and shocking than the piercing of, for instance, the ear lobes, was increasingly common in the strip club. Rita revealed her genital piercing to me by pulling aside her bikini bottom as we talked, seated on stools, in the club where she worked. Skye had twelve piercings all over her body, and other dancers had comparable numbers, including quite a few clithood piercings. The effectiveness of body piercing as a technology that would help the women carve out an individual niche was, in some regards, negated.

Indeed, when I further probed as to why Angel endured so many piercings, she replied,

> I kind of got bored with my body. . . . I would get dry runs on my body. Which are when they give you a tattoo without any ink. I had it done in different spots just to see what it feels like. It doesn't leave a mark, it bleeds. My ankle, it felt really good when I got it [tattooed], because I had always been through so much pain.

Angel's continued quote revealed much more about the multiple reasons for her choices of body technologies. More superficial meanings are peeled back as she segued from talking about her exotic piercings to technologies that she engaged purely for the purpose of physically feeling *something*. Based on her comment "I kind of got bored with my body," there is a sense that in an industry where everything revolves around a preoccupation with female appearance, repeated body technologies generate monotony. And as they continued to use body technologies to approximate an idealized image, the women's bodies became less vitally linked to their identities. This is revealed in Skye's comment about her breast implants, "And since I got my boobs done, they seem like just part of my costume." Yet as Angel demonstrated, body technologies can also recall her to her own body through the physical sensations and pain they elicit. Importantly, Angel's statement touched on the tremendous pain that includes the sexual and other abuses these women may have experienced from childhood on (Wesely 2002). To cope, they develop a numbness that furthers their disassociation from their bodies (Wesely 2002, 2003). The pain Angel experienced from "dry runs" reminded her that she can feel in this very basic, physical way. The salient point here is that body technologies clearly serve multiple purposes for these women. The reasons for choosing body technologies are fluid, engaged at different moments and having a variety of meanings.

### "They Only Look Good in a Strip Club"

Literature about exotic dancing has addressed the ways that dancers deal with identity problems like stigma that result from working in the sex industry (see Sweet and Tewksbury 2000a; Thompson and Harred 1992). These works note that management of stigma and other identity issues may include the segmentation or hiding of the dancer role. Here, I suggest incorporating the ways that body technologies both hinder and assist efforts to manage identity. For instance, for those who have used technologies of a more invasive, permanent nature, it is difficult to leave the fantasy performance from the club behind. They cannot easily disguise this aspect of their dancer personas. Rita described the trouble that dancers with huge breast implants have when transitioning to life outside the club: "In real life, when we're dressing in clothes. . . if you've got huge tits you look awful during the day. They look good only in a G-string in a strip club." The more permanent technologies challenged the ways that dancers tried to segment aspects of body and identity.

At the same time, other body technologies were used to facilitate this process. For instance, many used technologies to erase, eradicate, or separate their dancer personas before, during, and after work. Several would symbolically cleanse themselves of the dancer role after work by showering immediately. Lana said, "I scrub myself after work. Completely. I feel like I leave the club in the shower. When I get home from work I wash the club away." As a site of transition between roles, the skin was a surface upon which symbolic

technologies were engaged. While working, Jessie periodically doused herself with perfume, as if to repel odors of the club that might seep into the core of her being.

> One thing I always did—which was weird to me, but guys would bring it to my attention—but I would pour perfume all over me. I guess I would hate walking out of there smelling like cigarettes and alcohol. Even before I would go home or change into my regular clothes, I would spray myself down. It was just, like, your stomach turns, smelling like cigarettes and alcohol. I think I went through a bottle [of perfume] a week. Every time I went on stage I would squirt myself.

The perfume was a body technology that helped Jessie maintain a symbolic barrier between herself and the club. As a tangible barrier between the internal and the external body realms (Hewitt 1997), the skin is often the site of various body technologies designed to mark identities or transitions between them.

Drugs and alcohol were another body technology that marked the transition into the dancer role while anesthetizing the women to the environment or instilling in them a feeling of power or bravado. In fact, drugs served multiple purposes; as mentioned above, they were often used as a technology for weight loss. The prevalence of drugs found in this study is consistent with previous literature about the exotic dancing environment (see especially Forsyth and Deshotels 1997). "For some workers, limited drug or alcohol use can enhance a worker's sense of power and control by 'building confidence' and easing the shift in character from the sex worker's 'ordinary self' to a 'professional persona'" (Chapkis 2000, 187). This was illustrated by Roxy, who recalled doing drugs immediately before going onstage to perform.

> We would all go to the back room and do lines [of cocaine] together. Like, they're playing your music and you know you have to go on in like five seconds and you're back there wiping your nose. It's kind of like, your brain explodes, but the minute you

inhale through your nostril, it's like it hits the back of your head. You're experiencing it as you go up on the stage.

Roxy's transition into this role literally exploded in her consciousness, propelling her into her dancer persona. Samantha used alcohol for a similar purpose. She worked privately, performing at outcalls at clients' homes. But when she was hired for a bachelor party, she always got intoxicated beforehand. "To go to a bachelor party, I have to drink, because those I cannot handle. I cannot handle a bunch of guys screaming, and going, woooo! I drink before I go. When you drink you can do whatever, it really doesn't matter." Both as a transition into the dancer role and to numb herself, Samantha relied on alcohol. Substances like drugs and alcohol are body technologies that the women engaged to deal with the conflicts of identity they experience.

The women clarified that although drugs and alcohol were effective body technologies in the short term, in the long term, there were complications that compounded rather than alleviated identity issues. Roxy stated, "I was getting drunk all the time. I would do nothing but drink beer, wine. One night I was just laying in bed, bawling, thinking there's got to be more than this." This realization was a turning point, and she began attending church for guidance. Others realized later how drugs took a physical toll on them. Marie noted, "Women stay really sickly thin with those [drugs]. Now, when I walk into the club, I actually see how sick those girls are." Similarly, Julie said, "That all had to do with the drugs, too. How could somebody be good-looking with those great big black bags under the eyes from five nights of not sleeping. It's like, you are ugly, bitch. Dancing and drugs, it was horrible." Mitzi recalled the effects drugs had on her, saying,

> We'd do drugs in high school, college. A couple of years of that in dancing. "Oh, white stuff? Let's put it in our nose!" I look back on pictures of me, skinny girl, with boobs, and I look gray. I just look horrible. I have this big head and skinny body.

…As a body technology, drugs and alcohol served multiple purposes for these women. In the short term, it helped them maintain low weight and made it easier to transition into and maintain the dancer role while sometimes numbing them or providing them with added bravado or feelings of power. Yet in the long term, there were effects on the women that had severe repercussions on their health and psyche. Clearly, body technologies intersected with identity confusions for the women and both helped and hindered their efforts at the management of these complexities.

## Conclusions

In the exotic dance club, body technologies are engaged for a variety of purposes, not the least of which is to perform a highly successful fantasy image. Although body technologies have the potential to destabilize or challenge constructions of gendered bodies and related identity, this is even more difficult in a context that capitalizes on very limited constructions of the fantasy feminine body. Indeed, the women in the study felt tremendous pressure to conform to body constructions that revolve around extreme thinness, large breasts, and other features that conform to a "Barbie doll" image. They used a myriad of body technologies to achieve this look, ranging on a continuum from comportment and posture, shaving, and high heels to invasive technologies like cosmetic surgery and drugs. Devoting considerable energies and finances to these technologies, the women found that they usually pay off in customers' (monetary) reactions.

However, the technologies the women used to achieve the fantasy image moved their physical differences toward a standard of attractiveness that commodified them and erased distinctiveness. In an effort to assert individuality (for both personal and job-related reasons), the dancers also employed body technologies to make themselves stand out. This was a frustrating endeavor for the women, who wanted to both perform the fantasy image successfully and at times be recognized and validated for their own uniqueness and complexity. The corresponding tension that persisted was that the women made choices about their bodies but did so in a context (the sex-work industry) that limited these choices and thus confounded their feelings of agency concerning their bodies and identities. They attempted to use body technologies to manage these identity issues and to segment roles and transition in between them. Nonetheless, some of the technologies, especially permanent ones, added to the incomplete nature of this process.

It is significant that at least for a while, the dancers were so consumed with the exotic dancing context that they would drastically modify their bodies to continue being successful in the industry. At the same time, this is not entirely surprising. After all, "women in the bar play a game that they know well; in some form, they have been forced to play it for years" (Ronai and Ellis 1989, 295). In a society that puts such emphasis on female appearance, women are taught that they must continually make efforts to perfect their looks in keeping with standards of attractiveness (Bartky 1990; Bordo 1993). Using beauty and sexiness has historically been one of the few ways women could achieve any feeling of power (Ronai and Ellis 1989). This attention based on the body translates into very little power in "legitimate" arenas, like social, political, and cultural spheres (Irigaray 1985). Nonetheless, dancers make a living off this social expectation of their bodies.

The women in this study struggled to both be successful in the industry and have their bodies, quite literally, *mean* something to them, to help them make sense of who they are. They clearly engaged body technologies to be competitive in the industry. But they also used body technologies to mark themselves, to numb themselves, to make themselves feel, to prove something, to forget something, and a whole host of other reasons. Furthermore, the same technology may serve multiple purposes, depending on when and how it was used and with what intentions. The ways that the women used body technologies to make

their bodies *mean* something to them goes beyond a dichotomy of complete resistance against or utter collusion with social expectations and norms. Daily, hourly, minute-by-minute, these women were refashioning themselves. How we interact with our bodies is never simple, and even for women who work in an industry that capitalizes on one-dimensional meaning, they are not limited to that one, static meaning. Although there has been quite a bit of literature about stripping over the years, very few studies get at the complexity of this issue; traditionally, scholars have been much more concerned with straightforward understandings of a "deviant" population. By revealing the dancers' negotiations and conflicts as they engaged body technologies, this article carves out a new dimension of study about women who work as exotic dancers....

## REFERENCES

Balsamo, A. 1997. *Technologies of the gendered body: Reading cyborg women.* Durham, NC: Duke University Press.

Bartky, S. 1990. *Femininity and domination.* New York: Routledge.

Boles, J., and A. Garbin. 1974. The strip club and stripper-customer patterns of interaction. *Sociology and Social Research* 58:136–44.

Bordo, S. 1993. *Unbearable weight.* Berkeley: University of California Press.

Chapkis, W. 1997. *Live sex acts: Women performing erotic labor.* New York: Routledge.

Chapkis, W. 2000. Power and control in the commercial sex trade. In *Sex for sale,* edited by R. Weitzer, 181–201. New York: Routledge.

Cole, C. 1993. Resisting the canon: Feminist cultural studies, sport, and technologies of the body. *Journal of Sport & Social Issues* 17:77–97.

Dull, D., and C. West. 1991. Accounting for cosmetic surgery: The accomplishment of gender. *Social Problems* 1:54–69.

Forsyth, C. J., and T. H. Deshotels. 1997. The occupational milieu of the nude dancer. *Deviant Behavior* 18:125–42.

Hewitt, K. 1997. *Mutilating the body: Identity in blood and ink.* Bowling Green, OH: Bowling Green State University Popular Press.

Heywood, L. 1998. *Bodymakers: A cultural anatomy of women's bodybuilding.* New Brunswick, NJ: Rutgers University Press.

Holmlund, C. 1997. Visible difference and flex appeal: The body, sex, sexuality and race in the *Pumping Iron* films. In *Building bodies,* edited by P. Moore, 87–102. New Brunswick, NJ: Rutgers University Press.

hooks, b. 1997. Selling hot pussy: Representations of black female sexuality in the cultural marketplace. In *Writing on the body,* edited by K. Conboy, N. Medina, and S. Stanbury, 113–28. New York: Columbia University Press.

Irigaray, L. 1985. *This sex which is not one* [in French]. Translated by C. Porter. Ithaca, NY: Cornell University Press.

Kaw, E. 1998. Medicalization of racial features: Asian-American women and cosmetic surgery. In *The politics of women's bodies: Sexuality, appearance and behavior,* edited by R. Weitz, 166–83. New York: Oxford University Press.

Lever, J., and D. Dolnick. 2000. Clients and call girls: Seeking sex and intimacy. In *Sex for sale,* edited by R. Weitzer, 85–100. New York: Routledge.

McLorg, P., and Taub, D. 1987. Anorexia nervosa and bulimia: The development of deviant identities. *Deviant Behavior* 8:177–89.

Morgan, K. P. 1998. Women and the knife: Cosmetic surgery and the colonization of women's bodies. In *The politics of women's bodies: Sexuality, appearance and behavior,* edited by R. Weitz, 147–66. New York: Oxford University Press.

Nagle, J., ed. 1997. *Whores and other feminists.* New York: Routledge.

Ronai, C. R., and C. Ellis. 1989. Turn-ons for money: Interactional strategies of the table dancer. *Journal of Contemporary Ethnography* 18:271–98.

Rosenberg, M. 1979. *Conceiving the self.* New York: Basic Books.

Thompson, W., and J. Harred. 1992. Topless dancers: Managing stigma in a deviant occupation. *Deviant Behavior* 13:291–311.

Sweet, N., and R. Tewksbury. 2000a. Entry, maintenance and departure from a career in the sex industry: Strippers' experiences of occupational costs and rewards. *Humanity and Society* 24:136–61.

———. 2000b. "What's a nice girl like you doing in a place like this?" Pathways to a career in stripping. *Sociological Spectrum* 20:325–43.

Wesely, J. 2001. Negotiating gender: Bodybuilding and the natural/unnatural continuum. *Sociology of Sport Journal* 18:162–80.

———. 2002. Growing up sexualized: Issues of power and violence in the childhood and adult lives of female exotic dancers. *Violence Against Women* 8:1186–211.

———. 2003. Where am I going to stop? Exotic dancing, fluid body boundaries, and effects on identity. *Deviant Behavior,* 24:483–503.

West, C., and D. Zimmerman. 1987. Doing gender. *Gender & Society* 1:125–51.

Williams, L. 1997. A provoking agent: The pornography and performance art of Annie Sprinkle. In *Writing on the body,* edited by K. Conboy, N. Medina, and S. Stanbury, 360–79. New York: Columbia University Press.

Wood, E. A. 2000. Working in the fantasy factory: The attention hypothesis and the enacting of masculine power in strip clubs. *Journal of Contemporary Ethnography* 29:5–31.

# The G-Spot

# and Other Mysteries

Elisabeth O. Burgess

*Is there a G-spot?* One common question about female sexuality is whether there is a localized place in the vagina, often referred to as the *G-spot,* which causes especially pleasurable sensations when stimulated. The G-spot, or Grafenberg Spot, was named for Dr. Ernst Grafenberg, a German gynecologist who first described this spot in 1950. Although Grafenberg often is credited with discovering this spot, descriptions of sensitivity in a specific area of the vagina can be found across cultures and historical periods (Sevely & Bennett, 1978; Ladas, Whipple, & Perry, 1982). Yet, contemporary sexologists disagree about the significance of the G-spot and its prevalence in the female population. Those who support the G-spot claim that it is either a bundle of nerves, possibly representing the root of the clitoris, or a gland or series of glands that produce lubrication. Those who believe that the G-spot is a myth argue that there is no anatomical evidence that it exists.

Over the past two decades, the G-spot has gained widespread acceptance by the mass media. Numerous articles on sexual pleasure in the popular press, self-help literature, and on the Internet describe the G-spot and provide instructions on using it for sexual pleasure (see Winks, 1998). These readings frequently cite the book *The G-Spot and Other Recent Discoveries about Human Sexuality* (Ladas et al., 1982) as evidence that all women have G-spots. Ladas and her colleagues (1982) reported that the G-spot is located by applying deep pressure to the anterior vaginal wall. These researchers and other colleagues argue that this spongy mass, about the size of a quarter and the shape of a bean, can be found about halfway up the anterior (or belly) side of the vagina. The mass becomes more rigid or identifiable when a woman is sexually aroused (Perry & Whipple, 1981; Zaviacic & Whipple, 1993; Zaviacic, Zaviacicova, Holoman, & Molcan, 1988). According to self-reports, the G-spot produces orgasms that are "more intense" and "full body" than other female orgasms (Davidson, Darling, & Conway-Welch, 1989; Ladas et al., 1982; Perry & Whipple, 1981). Ladas and her colleagues (1982) report that in a study supervised by Perry and Whipple, a medical professional was able to locate a G-spot in each of over 400 female volunteers (p. 43). Because Ladas and her colleagues found that all women in their study had G-spots, they explain that women who have not been able to locate their G-spot are either not sufficiently aroused or not using the proper technique to locate it.

Although many women believe that the G-spot exists, not all women have heard about the G-spot and many women have not found their own G-spot. A survey of over 1,000 women found that although 85.3 percent of the women surveyed believed that a sensitive area existed in the vagina, only 65.9 percent reported having such an area (Davidson et al., 1989). This survey also found that angle of entry, position of intercourse, and a woman's degree of emotional involvement with her partner affected her ability to orgasm from being stimulated in this area. Because traditional sexual positions such as the "missionary position" fail to stimulate the anterior wall of the vagina, women who explore other sexual practices such as manual stimulation from a partner or vibrator may be more likely to discover a G-spot (Ladas et al., 1982).

In contrast, some researchers strongly dispute the existence of the G-spot. Alzate and colleagues (Alzate, 1985; Alzate & Hoch, 1986) argue that the walls of the vagina are sensitive to touch, but there is no specific area in the vagina that produces orgasm. These authors also argue that there is no anatomical evidence of a G-spot and critique previous research for using small clinical samples and anecdotal evidence. In a recent review of the literature on the G-spot, Hines (2001) calls it a myth and goes on to say that "the widespread acceptance of the reality of the G-spot goes well beyond available evidence" (p. 361). Other prominent sex researchers, including Masters and Johnson (1966), do not discuss the G-spot or an especially sensitive area in the vagina but instead focus on the clitoris as the locus of female orgasms.

Some feminist researchers also dispute the existence of the G-spot, but for different reasons. These scholars fear that the "discovery of the G-spot" and subsequent emphasis on vaginal orgasms support Freudian notions about the female orgasm and privilege heterosexual male-centered models of sexuality. These authors emphasize the clitoris as the primary location of the female orgasm and sexual empowerment for women (Ehnreich, Hess, & Jacobs, 1987; Gerhard, 2003). Other feminist researchers believe that, because of cultural preferences about (hetero)sexual behavior, many women prefer to view the vagina as an important location of orgasmic response. These scholars recognize that orgasm is not merely a physiological response but it is also an emotional and psychological response to sexual stimuli and, as such, orgasms centered in the vagina should not be ignored (Hite, 1976; Schneider & Gould, 1987). However, if such a spot does exist, even supporters such as Ladas (2001) argue that it is harmful to think of the G-spot as the holy grail of female sexuality. The female body contains many potential erogenous zones. Whether individuals find stimulation of these locations pleasurable depends on the social context, the expertise of their partner, and personal preference.

*Do women ejaculate?* Another common debate about the sexual body is whether women ejaculate. For centuries, erotic literature and sex research has alluded to the elusive female orgasm that results in a squirt of liquid from the woman (Belzer, 1981; Sevely & Bennett, 1978). Contemporary researchers disagree as to where it comes from, what it is, and whether it is something that all women are capable of releasing.

Most often associated with G-spot stimulation, female ejaculation is the release of fluid through the urethra at the climax of an orgasm. One common concern about female ejaculation is whether the fluid is urine (a result of incontinence) or whether it is similar to male ejaculate. Self-reports indicate that this fluid is different from urine in smell, consistency, and color (Belzer, 1981; Davidson et al., 1989; Taormini, 2000). Chemical analyses of female ejaculate have been less conclusive. Although Goldberg and his colleagues (1983) found the expelled fluid to be chemically similar to urine, numerous other clinical studies argue that the consistency of this fluid is significantly different from urine (Addiego, Belzer, Moger, Perry, & Whipple, 1981; Belzer, Whipple, & Moger, 1984; Zaviacic, Zaviacicova, Holoman, & Molcan, 1988). Without larger samples of ejaculate, it will be difficult to reach a definitive conclusion about the nature of these fluids.

A related controversy associated with female ejaculation concerns the source of the fluid. The most common theory is that the Skene's glands, which surround the urethra, secrete fluid into the urethra that is then ejaculated upon orgasm. Researchers who support this theory argue that female ejaculate may have a different consistency, at different times, for different women. In addition, reported rates of ejaculation among women vary from 10 percent to over 50 percent (Bullough et al., 1984; Ladas et al., 1983). Only a few women report ejaculating fluid with every orgasm. Although manipulation of the G-spot is not required to produce female ejaculation, women who experience pleasure or orgasms through stimulation of the G-spot are more likely to report experiencing ejaculation (Davidson et al., 1989). Either way, by focusing solely on chemical components of the fluid, researchers are ignoring the role this event plays in sexual satisfaction.

Female ejaculation also has become the subject of several self-help sexuality books and sexuality workshops. According to an article by Taormino (2000), female ejaculation was the subject of one of the workshops at the 2000 Michigan Womyn's Festival. After the workshop, several women participated in the "First Annual Ejaculation Contest," competing in categories such as speed, distance, quantity, and best single-handed job. Although reports based on nonclinical trials do not receive scientific approval, the nature of this contest helps to alter negative stigma associated with female ejaculation.

There are several important implications of this research on female ejaculation. Because female ejaculation is not a widely known phenomenon, women who experience the expulsion of fluids frequently feel shame or anxiety (Davidson et al., 1989). Many women, particularly those who are uncomfortable examining the fluid, assume that any release of fluid is urine and a sign of urinary incontinence. In some cases women may seek and receive medical treatment for urinary incontinence when this is not the problem. If women were aware that the expulsion of fluid was a normal and healthy bodily function, they would feel free to enjoy a pleasurable event rather than perceiving themselves as deviant (Winton, 1989).

## REFERENCES

Addiego, Frank, Edwin G. Belzer, Jill Comolli, William Moger, John D. Perry, & Beverly Whipple. 1981. Female Ejaculation: A Case Study. *The Journal of Sex Research,* 17, 13–21.

Alzate, Heli. 1985. Vaginal Eroticism: A Replication Study. *Archives of Sexual Behavior,* 14, 529–537.

Alzate, Heli, & Zwi Hoch. 1986. The "G-Spot" and "Female Ejaculation": A Current Appraisal. *Journal of Sex and Marital Therapy,* 12, 211–220.

Belzer, Edwin G. 1981. Orgasmic Expulsions of Women: A Review and Heuristic Inquiry. *The Journal of Sex Research,* 17, 1–12.

Belzer, Edwin G., Beverly Whipple, & William Moger. On Female Ejaculation. *The Journal of Sex Research,* 20, 403–406.

Bullough, Bonnie, Madeline David, Beverly Whipple, Joan Dixon, Elizabeth Rice Allgeier, & Kate Cosgrove Drury. 1984. Subjective Reports of Female Orgasmic Expulsion of Fluid. *Nurse Practictioner,* 9, 55–59.

Davidson, J. Kenneth, Carol A. Darling, & Colleen Conway-Welch. 1989. The Role of the Grafenburg Spot and Female Ejaculation in the Female Orgasmic Response: An Empirical Analysis. *Journal of Sex and Marital Therapy,* 15, 102–120.

Ehrenreich, Barbara, Elizabeth Hess, & Gloria Jacobs. 1986. *Re-Making Love: The Feminization of Sex.* New York: Anchor Books.

Gerhard, Jane. 2004. The Politics of the Female Orgasm. In M. Stombler, D. M. Baunach, E. O. Burgess, D. Donnelly, & W. Simonds (Eds.). *Sex Matters: The Sexuality and Society Reader* (pp. 213–224). Boston: Allyn & Bacon.

Hines, Terence M. 2001. The G-Spot: A Modern Gynecological Myth. *American Journal of Obstetrics and Gynecology,* 185, 359–362.

Hite, Shere. 1976. *The Hite Report: A Nationwide Study of Female Sexuality.* New York: Dell.

Goldberg, Daniel C., Beverly Whipple, Ralph E. Fishkin, Howard Waxman, Paul J. Fink, & Martin Weisberg. 1983. The Grafenberg Spot and Female Ejaculation: A Review of Initial Hypotheses. *Journal of Sex and Marital Therapy,* 9, 27–38.

Ladas, Alice. 2001. Review of *Secrets of Sensual Lovemaking* and *The Good Vibrations Guide. Journal of Sex Education and Therapy,* 26, 150–151.

Ladas, Alice, Beverly Whipple, & John Perry. 1982. *The G-spot and Other Recent Discoveries about Human Sexuality.* New York: Plenum.

Masters, W. H., & V. E. Johnson. 1966. *Human Sexual Response.* Boston: Little, Brown.

Perry, John D., & Beverly Whipple. 1981. The Varieties of Female Orgasm and Female Ejaculation. *SIECUS Report,* May–July, 15–16.

Schneider, Beth E., & Meredith Gould. 1987. Female Sexuality Looking Back into the Future. In Beth B. Hess & Myra Marx Ferree (Eds.). *Analyzing Gender: A Handbook of Social Science Research* (pp. 120–153). Newbury Park, CA: Sage.

Sevely, J. L., & J. W. Bennett. 1978. Concerning Female Ejaculation and the Female Prostate. *The Journal of Sex Research,* 14, 1–20.

Taormini, Tristan. 2000. Pucker Up. *Village Voice,* September 5, 45(35), 130.

Winks, Cathy. 1998. *The Good Vibrations Guide: The G-Spot.* San Francisco: Down There Press.

Winton, Mark A. 1989. Editorical: The Social Construction of the G-Spot and Female Ejaculation. *Journal of Sex Education and Therapy,* 15, 151–162.

Zaviacic, Milan, Alexandra Zaviacicova, Igor Karol Holoman, & Jan Molcan. 1988. Female Urethral Expulsions Evoked by Local Digital Stimulation of the G-Spot: Differences in the Response Patterns. *The Journal of Sex Research,* 24, 311–318.

Zaviacic, Milan, & Beverly Whipple. 1993. Update on the Female Prostate and the Phenomenon of Female Ejaculation. *Journal of Sex Research,* 30, 148–151.

## Sextistics

### Did You Know?

- Typically, 60 to 90 percent of male to female transsexuals report they are capable of achieving orgasm following sex reassignment surgery.[1]
- In 1998, Australian physician Helen O'Connell determined the clitoris was twice the size as previous thought.[2]
- There are approximately 8,000 nerve endings in the clitoris.[3]
- In 1998 the Pentagon approved a $50 million to buy Viagra for troops and veterans.[4]
- In 2003, the Wrigley's Corporation announced they patented a chewing gum that enables erections.[5]
- A national study of sexual behavior in the U.S. found that 43 percent of women and 31 percent of men report some form of sexual dysfunction.[6]
- Hymenoplasty, an operation that restores a ruptured hymen (a thin membrane that attaches to the vaginal walls) is increasing in popularity. However, this procedure, like most reconstruction surgeries, is not taught in medical residency.[7]
- An intact hymen is often associated with virginity and a symbol of purity despite the fact that it can rupture without coitus. Although hymenoplasty surgery has recently received public attention, June Reinish of the Kinsey Institute reports that hymen repair techniques have been around for ages; for example, midwives used membranes from animals to disguise a ruptured hymen.[8]
- Nonsurgical methods of penis enlargement are ineffective and are not endorsed by any medical organizations.[9]

*—Compiled by Mikel Walters*

### NOTES

1. Lawrence, Anne. 2005. "Sexuality before and after Male-to-Female Sex Reassignment Surgery." *Archives of Sexual Behavior* 34:135–145.

2. O'Connell, H. E., J. M. Hutson, C. R. Anderson, and R. J. Plenter. 1998. "Anatomical Relationship between the Urethra and Clitoris." *Journal of Urology* 159:1892–1897.

3. Chalker, Rebecca. 2000. *The Clitoral Truth.* Seven Stories Press.

4. New York Times. 1998. "Viagra is a $50 Million Pentagon Budget Item." *New York Times,* October 4. Retrieved January 29, 2006 from http://query.nytimes.com/gst/fullpage.html?sec=health&res=9506E5DE1138F937A35753C1A96E958260.

5. Loe, Meika. 2004. *The Rise of Viagra.* New York University Press.

6. Laumann, Edward O., Anthony Paik, and Raymond C. Rosen. 2001. "Sexual Function in the United States: Prevalence and Predictors." In *Sex, Love, and Health in America: Private Choices and Public Policies* (pp. 352–376), edited by Edward O. Laumann and Robert T. Michael. University of Chicago Press.

7. Chozick, Amy. 2005. "Virgin Territory: U.S. Women Seek a Second First Time.*" Wall Street Journal,* December 15, pp. A1, A14.

8. Ibid.

9. Mayo Clinic. "Beware of Penis-Enlargement Scams." Retrieved January 29, 2006 from http://mayoclinic.com/print/penis/mc00026.

# chapter 6

# Sexual Practices

*An interview with . . .*

## Pepper Schwartz

Pepper Schwartz, Ph.D., is a professor of sociology at the University of Washington in Seattle. She is the author of *The Great Sex Weekend* (Putnam, 1998), *Everything You Know about Love and Sex Is Wrong* (Perigree, 2001), *Finding Your Perfect Match* (Perigree, 2006), and *Ten Talks Parents Must Have with Their Children about Sex and Character* (Hyperion, 2000). Dr. Schwartz has published more than forty scholarly articles, and was the recipient of the 2005 American Sociological Association Award for the Public Understanding of Sociology.

**What led you to begin studying sexuality?**

*I was studying law and society at Yale during the "sexual revolution" and when the first sexuality courses were being taught to undergraduates, I took a job as teaching assistant in one of those classes. When I read the assigned readings I became upset about what I thought was misinformation or missing information—so I decided to study sexuality instead of law and society!*

**Which of your projects have you found most interesting?**

*It's hard to choose. I suppose the most intense project was the 10 years I spent studying heterosexual and homosexual couples that was published as* American Couples *(Morrow, 1983) and in a number of scholarly articles. It included over 12,000 questionnaires and 600 face-to-face interviews. That study (coauthored with Philip Blumstein) took over my life for a decade. The data and the people were utterly fascinating.*

**What have you found most challenging about studying sexuality?**

*Trying to convince academia (and the public) that the study of sexuality is sociologically important for both policy and people's lives.*

**Why is it important to do sex research?**

*It helps us to understand how important social policy concerning sexuality is—and which interests do battle in order to vest their own set of morality and constraints. We need to better understand ourselves, our gender, and the opposite gender. This includes understanding the elemental issues of sexual identity and emotional commitments. When we study sexuality, we learn about others who are different from us and we create empathy and are more likely to understand social justice.*

**Have you faced any ethical dilemmas in your research? How did you resolve them?**

*I have intense and private data on relationships from individual interviews in couple studies. I have been pressured to give that data to one member of the couple in some cases of divorce or breakup. I have resisted it and so far won.*

**How do people react when they find out that you study sexuality?**

*It depends. If I'm seated next to them in an airplane, they stop working and want to talk. Many people call me up and tell me their problems or ask for recommendations for therapists. Some people find it amusing or intimidating. Mostly, they are intrigued and supportive.*

**If you could teach people one thing about sexuality, what would it be?**

*Sexuality is a gift. We need to understand it, rather than be misled by myths and prejudices, in order to avoid shame, guilt, or mistreatment or intolerance of others. We need to honor our own and others' rights to sexual fulfillment, sexual safety, and privacy.*

—Interviewed by Denise Donnelly

# Now for the Truth
# about Americans and Sex

Philip Elmer-Dewitt

Is there a living, breathing adult who hasn't at times felt the nagging suspicion that in bedrooms across the country, on kitchen tables, in limos and other venues too scintillating to mention, other folks are having more sex, livelier sex, better sex? Maybe even that quiet couple right next door is having more fun in bed, and more often. Such thoughts spring, no doubt, from a primal anxiety deep within the human psyche. It has probably haunted men and women since the serpent pointed Eve toward the forbidden fruit and urged her to get with the program.

Still, it's hard to imagine a culture more conducive to feelings of sexual inadequacy than America in the 1990s. Tune in to the soaps. Flip through the magazines. Listen to Oprah. Lurk in the seamier corners of cyberspace. What do you see and hear? An endless succession of young, hard bodies preparing for, recovering from or engaging in constant, relentless copulation. Sex is everywhere in America—and in the ads, films, TV shows and music videos it exports abroad. Although we know that not every zip code is a Beverly Hills, 90210, and not every small town a Peyton Place, the impression that is branded on our collective subconscious is that life in the twilight of the 20th century is a sexual banquet to which everyone else has been invited.

From Elmer-DeWitt, Philip. 1994. "Now for the Truth about Americans and Sex." *Time* 144(16): 62–68. Copyright © 1994, TIME Inc. Reprinted by permission.

Just how good is America's sex life? Nobody knows for sure. Don't believe the magazine polls that have Americans mating energetically two or three times a week. Those surveys are inflated from the start by the people who fill them out: *Playboy* subscribers, for example, who brag about their sex lives in reader-survey cards. Even the famous Kinsey studies—which caused such a scandal in the late 1940s and early '50s by reporting that half of American men had extramarital affairs— were deeply flawed. Although Alfred Kinsey was a biologist by training (his expertise was the gall wasp), he compromised science and took his human subjects where he could find them: in boardinghouses, college fraternities, prisons and mental wards. For 14 years he collared hitchhikers who passed through town and quizzed them mercilessly. It was hardly a random cross section.

Now, more than 40 years after Kinsey, we finally have some answers. A team of researchers based at the University of Chicago has released the long-awaited results of what is probably the first truly scientific survey of who does what with whom in America and just how often they do it.

The findings—based on face-to-face interviews with a random sample of nearly 3,500 Americans, ages 18 to 59, selected using techniques honed through decades of political and consumer polling—will smash a lot of myths. "Whether the numbers are reassuring or alarming depends on where you sit," warns Edward Laumann, the University of Chicago sociologist who led the research team. While the scientists found that the spirit of the sexual revolution is alive and well in some quarters—they found that about 17%

of American men and 3% of women have had sex with at least 21 partners—the overall impression is that the sex lives of most Americans are about as exciting as a peanut-butter-and-jelly sandwich.

Among the key findings:

- Americans fall into three groups. One-third have sex twice a week or more, one-third a few times a month, and one-third a few times a year or not at all.
- Americans are largely monogamous. The vast majority (83%) have one or zero sexual partners a year. Over a lifetime, a typical man has six partners; a woman, two.
- Married couples have the most sex and are the most likely to have orgasms when they do. Nearly 40% of married people say they have sex twice a week, compared with 25% for singles.
- Most Americans don't go in for the kinky stuff. Asked to rank their favorite sex acts, almost everybody (96%) found vaginal sex "very or somewhat appealing." Oral sex ranked a distant third, after an activity that many may not have realized was a sex act: "Watching partner undress."
- Adultery is the exception in America; not the rule. Nearly 75% of married men and 85% of married women say they have never been unfaithful.
- There are a lot fewer active homosexuals in America than the oft-repeated 1 in 10. Only 2.7% of men and 1.3% of women report that they had homosexual sex in the past year.

The full results of the new survey are scheduled to be published next week as *The Social Organization of Sexuality* (University of Chicago; $49.95), a thick, scientific tome co-authored by Laumann, two Chicago colleagues—Robert Michael and Stuart Michaels—and John Gagnon, a sociologist from the State University of New York at Stony Brook. A thinner companion volume, *Sex in America: A Definitive Survey* (Little, Brown; $22.95), written with New York *Times*

science reporter Gina Kolata, will be in bookstores this week.

But when the subject is sex, who wants to wait for the full results? Even before the news broke last week, critics and pundits were happy to put their spin on the study.

"It doesn't ring true," insisted Jackie Collins, author of *The Bitch, The Stud* and other potboilers. "Where are the deviants? Where are the flashers? Where are the sex maniacs I see on TV every day?"

"I'm delighted to hear that all this talk about rampant infidelity was wildly inflated," declared postfeminist writer Camille Paglia. "But if they're saying the sexual revolution never happened, that's ridiculous."

"Positively, outrageously stupid and unbelievable," growled *Penthouse* publisher Bob Guccione. "I would say five partners a year is the average for men."

"Totally predictable," deadpanned Erica Jong, author of the 1973 sex fantasy *Fear of Flying*. "Americans are more interested in money than sex."

"Our Puritan roots are deep," said *Playboy* founder Hugh Hefner, striking a philosophical note, "We're fascinated by sex and afraid of it."

"Two partners? I mean, come on!" sneered *Cosmopolitan* editor Helen Gurley Brown. "We advise our Cosmo girls that when people ask how many partners you've had, the correct answer is always three, though there may have been more."

Europeans seemed less surprised—one way or the other—by the results of the survey. The low numbers tend to confirm the Continental caricature of Americans as flashy and bold onscreen but prone to paralysis in bed. Besides, the findings were pretty much in line with recent studies conducted in England and France that also found low rates of homosexuality and high rates of marital fidelity. (The French will be gratified by what a comparison of these surveys shows: that the average Frenchman and -woman has sex about twice as often as Americans do.)

If the study is as accurate as it purports to be, the results will be in line with the experience of most Americans. For many, in fact, they will come as a relief. "A lot of people think something is wrong with them when they don't have sexual feelings," says Toby, a 32-year-old graduate student from Syracuse, New York, who, like 3% of adult Americans (according to the survey), has never had sex. "These findings may be liberating for a lot of people. They may say, "Thank God, I'm not as weird as I thought."

Scientists, on the whole, praise the study. "Any new research is welcome if it is well done," says Dr. William Masters, co-author of the landmark 1966 study Human Sexual Response. By all accounts, this one was very well done. But, like every statistical survey, it has its weaknesses. Researchers caution that the sample was too limited to reveal much about small subgroups of the population—gay Hispanics, for example. The omission of people over 59 is regrettable, says Shirley Zussman, past president of the American Association of Sex Educators, Counselors and Therapists: "The older population is more sexually active than a 19-year-old thinks, and it's good for both 19-year-olds and those over 59 to know that."

The Chicago scientists admit to another possible defect: "There is no way to get around the fact some people might conceal information," says Stuart Michaels of the Chicago team, whose expertise is designing questions to get at those subjects people are most reluctant to discuss. The biggest hot button, he says, is homosexuality. "This is a stigmatized group. There is probably a lot more homosexual activity going on than we could get people to talk about."

It was, in large part, to talk about homosexual activity that the study was originally proposed. The project was conceived in 1987 as a response to the AIDS crisis. To track the spread of the AIDS virus—and to mount an effective campaign against it—government researchers needed good data about how much risky sexual behavior (anal sex, for example) was really going on. But

when they looked for scientific data about sex, they found little besides Kinsey and Masters and Johnson.

So the National Institutes of Heath issued a formal request for a proposal, tactfully giving it the bland title "Social and Behavioral Aspects of Fertility Related Behavior" in an attempt to slip under the radar of right-wing politicians. But the euphemism fooled no one—least of all Jesse Helms. In the Reagan and Bush era, any government funding for sex research was suspect, and the Senator from North Carolina was soon lobbying to have the project killed. The Chicago team redesigned the study several times to assuage conservative critics, dropping the questions about masturbation and agreeing to curtail the interview once it was clear that a subject was not at high risk of contracting AIDS. But to no avail. In September 1991 the Senate voted 66 to 34 to cut off funding.

The vote turned out to be the best thing that could have happened—at least from the point of view of the insatiably curious. The Chicago team quickly rounded up support from private sources, including the Robert Wood Johnson, Rockefeller and Ford foundations. And freed of political constraints, they were able to take the survey beyond behavior related to AIDS transmission to tackle the things inquiring minds really want to know: Who is having sex with whom? How often do they do it? And when they are behind closed doors, what exactly do they do?

The report confirms much of what is generally accepted as conventional wisdom. Kids *do* have sex earlier now: by 15, half of all black males have done it; by 17, the white kids have caught up to them. There *was* a lot of free sex in the '60s: the percentage of adults who have racked up 21 or more sex partners is significantly higher among the fortysomething boomers than among other Americans. And AIDS *has* put a crimp in some people's sex lives: 76% of those who have had five or more partners in the past year say they have changed their sexual behavior, by either slowing down, getting tested or using condoms faithfully.

But the report is also packed with delicious surprises. Take masturbation, for example. The myth is that folks are more likely to masturbate if they don't have a sex partner. According to the study, however, the people who masturbate the most are the ones who have the most sex. "If you're having sex a lot, you're thinking about sex a lot," says Gagnon. "It's more like Keynes (wealth begets wealth) and less like Adam Smith (if you spend it on this, you can't spend it on that)."

Or take oral sex. Not surprisingly, both men and women preferred receiving it to giving it. But who would have guessed that so many white, college-educated men would have done it (about 80%) and so few blacks (51%)? Skip Long, a 33-year-old African American from Raleigh, North Carolina, thinks his race's discomfort with oral sex may owe much to religious teaching and the legacy of slavery: according to local legend, it was something slaves were required to do for their masters. Camille Paglia is convinced that oral sex is a culturally acquired preference that a generation of college students picked up in the '70s from seeing Linda Lovelace do it in *Deep Throat,* one of the first—and last—X-rated movies that men and women went to see together. "They saw it demonstrated on the screen, and all of a sudden it was on the map," says Paglia. "Next thing you knew, it was in Cosmo with rules about how to do it."

More intriguing twists emerge when sexual behavior is charted by religious affiliation. Roman Catholics are the most likely to be virgins (4%) and Jews to have the most sex partners (34% have had 10 or more). The women most likely to achieve orgasm each and every time (32%) are, believe it or not, conservative Protestants. But Catholics edge out mainline Protestants in frequency of intercourse. Says Father Andrew Greeley, the sociologist-priest and writer of racy romances: "I think the church will be surprised at how often Catholics have sex and how much they enjoy it."

But to concentrate on the raw numbers is to miss the study's most important contribution.

Wherever possible, the authors put those figures in a social context, drawing on what they know about how people act out social scripts, how they are influenced by their social networks and how they make sexual bargains as if they were trading economic goods and services. "We were trying to make people think about sex in an entirely different way, says Kolata. "We all have this image, first presented by Freud, of sex as a riderless horse, galloping out of control. What we are saying here is that sex is just like any other social behavior: people behave the way they are rewarded for behaving."

Kolata and her co-authors use these theories to explain why most people marry people who resemble them in terms of age, education, race and social status, and why the pool of available partners seems so small—especially for professional women in their 30s and 40s. "You can still fall in love across a crowded room," says Gagnon. "It's just that society determines whom you're in the room with."

That insight, applied to AIDS, leads the Chicago team to a conclusion that is sure to get them into trouble. America's AIDS policy, they say, has been largely misdirected. Although AIDS spread quickly among intravenous drug users and homosexuals, the social circles these groups travel in are so rigidly circumscribed that it is unlikely to spread widely in the heterosexual population. Rather than pretend that AIDS affects everyone, they say, the government would be better advised to concentrate its efforts on those most at risk.

That's a conclusion that will not sit well with AIDS activists or with many health-policy makers. "Their message is shocking and flies against the whole history of this epidemic," says Dr. June Osborn, former chair of the National Commission on AIDS. "They're saying we don't have to worry if we're white, heterosexual adults. That gets the public off the hook and may keep parents from talking to their kids about sex. The fact is, teens are at enormous risk for experimentation."

Other groups will find plenty here to make a fuss about. Interracial couples are likely to take offense at the authors' characterization of mixed-race marriages as unlikely to succeed. And right-to-life activists who believe abortion is widely used as a cruel form of birth control are likely to be unconvinced by the finding that 72% of the women who have an abortion have only one.

Elsewhere in the study, the perceptual gulf between the sexes is reminiscent of the scene in *Annie Hall* where Woody Allen tells his psychiatrist that he and Annie have sex "hardly ever, maybe three times a week," and she tells hers that they do it "constantly; I'd say three times a week." In the Chicago study, 54% of the men say they think about sex every day or several times a day. By contrast, 67% of the women say they think about it only a few times a week or a few times a month. The disconnect is even greater when the subject turns to forced sex. According to the report, 22% of women say they have been forced to do sexual things they didn't want to, usually by someone they loved. But only 3% of men admit to ever forcing themselves on women. Apparently men and women have very different ideas about what constitutes voluntary sex.

But the basic message of *Sex in America* is that men and women have found a way to come to terms with each other's sexuality—and it is called marriage. "Our study," write the authors, "clearly shows that no matter how sexually active people are before and between marriages . . . marriage is such a powerful social institution that, essentially, married people are all alike—they are faithful to their partners as long as the marriage is intact."

Americans, it seems, have come full circle. It's easy to forget that as recently as 1948, Norman Mailer was still using the word fug in his novels. There may have been a sexual revolution—at least for those college-educated whites who came of age with John Updike's swinging *Couples,* Philip Roth's priapic *Portnoy* and Jong's *Fear of Flying*—but the revolution turned out to have a beginning a middle and an end. "From the time of the Pill to Rock Hudson's death, people had a sense of freedom, says Judith Krantz, author of *Scruples.* "That's gone."

It was the first survey—Kinsey's—that got prudish America to talk about sex, read about sex and eventually watch sex at the movies and even try a few things (at least once). Kinsey's methods may have been less than perfect, but he had an eye for the quirky, the fringe, the bizarre. The new report, by contrast, is a remarkably conservative document. It puts the fringe on the fringe and concentrates on the heartland: where life, apparently, is ruled by marriage, monogamy and the missionary position. The irony is that the report Jesse Helms worked so hard to stop has arrived at a conclusion that should make him proud. And it may even make the rest of us a bit less anxious about what's going on in that bedroom next door.

—Reported by Wendy Cole/Chicago, John F. Dickerson/New York and Martha Smilgis/Los Angeles

---

### *Sexual Behavior and Health*

**William D. Mosher, Anjani Chandra, and Jo Jones**

This [box] provides reliable national estimates of some basic statistics on certain types of sexual behavior, sexual orientation, and sexual attraction for men and women 15–44 years of age, based on data collected in the United States in 2002. The data are relevant to public health concerns, including efforts to prevent HIV and other sexually transmitted infections, and to demographic and social concerns such as birth and pregnancy rates among teenagers. The data are from the 2002 National Survey of Family Growth (NSFG), and are based on 12,571 in-person interviews with men and women 15–44 years of age.

## Highlights of Findings

### Teens

- At ages 15–19, about 12 percent of males and 10 percent of females had had heterosexual oral sex but not vaginal intercourse. . . . This percent drops to 3 percent for both males and females at age 22–24, when most have already had vaginal intercourse. . . .

### Adults—heterosexual activity

- Among adult males 25–44 years of age, 97 percent have had sexual contact with an opposite-sex partner in their lives; 97 percent have had vaginal intercourse, 90 percent have had oral sex with a female, and 40 percent, anal sex with a female. Among women, the proportions who have had sexual contact with an opposite-sex partner were similar.
- Males 30–44 years of age reported an average (median) of 6–8 female sexual partners in their lifetimes. Among women 30–44 years of age, the median number of male sexual partners in their lifetimes was about four. The findings appear to be similar to previous surveys conducted in the early 1990's.

### Same-sex activity

- Three percent of males 15–44 years of age have had oral or anal sex with another male in the last 12 months (1.8 million). Four percent of females had a sexual experience with another female in the last 12 months. . . .
- The proportion who had same-sex contact in their lifetimes was 6 percent for males and (using a different question) 11 percent for females. . . .
- About 1 percent of men and 3 percent of women 15–44 years of age have had both male and female sexual partners in the last 12 months. . . .

### Sexual orientation

- In response to a question that asked, "*Do you think of yourself as heterosexual, homosexual, bisexual, or something else?*" 90 percent of men 18–44 years of age responded that they think of themselves as heterosexual, 2.3 percent of men answered homosexual, 1.8 percent bisexual, 3.9 percent "something else," and 1.8 percent did not answer the question. . . . Percents for women were similar. . . .

### Sexual attraction

- Survey participants were asked if they were sexually attracted to males, to females, or to both. Among men 18–44 years of age, 92 percent said they were attracted "only to females," and 3.9 percent, "mostly" to females. Among women, 86 percent said they were attracted only to males, and 10 percent, "mostly" to males. The percentage attracted "mostly to males" was 3 percent in a survey conducted in 1992, compared with 10 percent in the 2002 NSFG.

### Selected health measures

- 29 percent of men who have ever had male-male sexual contact were tested for HIV (outside of blood donation) in the last year, compared with 14 percent of men with no same-sex sexual contact.
- 17 percent of men who ever had male-male sexual contact had been treated for a non-HIV sexually transmitted infection (STI), compared with 7 percent of those who had never had male-male sexual contact.
- Among men 15–44 years of age who had at least one sexual partner in the last 12 months, 39 percent used a condom at their most recent sex. Among never married males, this figure was 65 percent, compared with 24 percent of married males. Among males who had ever had sexual contact with another male, 91 percent used a condom at their last sex, compared with 36 percent of men who never had sex with another male.

*Source:* Mosher, William D., Anjani Chandra, and Jo Jones. 2005. "Sexual Behavior and Selected Health Measures: Men and Women 15–44 Years of Age, United States, 2002." *CDC Advance Data from Vital and Health Statistics* 362 (September 15). Available at www.cdc.gov.

# Against Love: A Treatise on the Tyranny of Two

**Laura Kipnis**

Love is, as we know, a mysterious and controlling force. It has vast power over our thoughts and life decisions. It demands our loyalty, and we, in turn, freely comply. Saying no to love isn't simply heresy; it is tragedy—the failure to achieve what is most essentially human. So deeply internalized is our obedience to this most capricious despot that artists create passionate odes to its cruelty, and audiences seem never to tire of the most deeply unoriginal mass spectacles devoted to rehearsing the litany of its torments, fixating their very beings on the narrowest glimmer of its fleeting satisfactions. . . .

Ever optimistic, heady with love's utopianism, most of us eventually pledge ourselves to unions that will, if successful, far outlast the desire that impelled them into being. The prevailing cultural wisdom is that even if sexual desire tends to be a short-lived phenomenon, "mature love" will kick in to save the day when desire flags. The issue that remains unaddressed is whether cutting off other possibilities of romance and sexual attraction for the more muted pleasures of mature love isn't similar to voluntarily amputating a healthy limb: a lot of anesthesia is required and the phantom pain never entirely abates. But if it behooves a society to convince its citizenry that wanting change means personal failure or wanting to start over is shameful or simply wanting more satisfaction

than what you have is an illicit thing, clearly grisly acts of self-mutilation will be required.

There hasn't always been quite such optimism about love's longevity. For the Greeks, inventors of democracy and a people not amenable to being pushed around by despots, love was a disordering and thus preferably brief experience. During the reign of courtly love, love was illicit and usually fatal. Passion meant suffering: the happy ending didn't yet exist in the cultural imagination. As far as togetherness as an eternal ideal, the 12th-century advice manual "De Amore et Amor is Remedio" ("On Love and the Remedies of Love") warned that too many opportunities to see or chat with the beloved would certainly decrease love.

The innovation of happy love didn't even enter the vocabulary of romance until the 17th century. Before the 18th century—when the family was primarily an economic unit of production rather than a hothouse of Oedipal tensions—marriages were business arrangements between families; participants had little to say on the matter. Some historians consider romantic love a learned behavior that really only took off in the late 18th century along with the new fashion for reading novels, though even then affection between a husband and wife was considered to be in questionable taste.

Historians disagree, of course. Some tell the story of love as an eternal and unchanging essence; others, as a progress narrative over stifling social conventions. (Sometimes both stories are told at once; consistency isn't required.) But has modern love really set us free? Fond as we are of projecting our own emotional quandaries back

From Kipnis, Laura. 2001. "Against Love: A Treatise on the Tyranny of *Two.*" *New York Times Magazine* October 14: 99–102. © 2001, Laura Kipnis. Reprinted by permission.

through history, construing vivid costume dramas featuring medieval peasants or biblical courtesans sharing their feelings with the post-Freudian savvy of lifelong analysands, our amatory predecessors clearly didn't share all our particular aspirations about their romantic lives.

We, by contrast, feel like failures when love dies. We believe it could be otherwise. Since the cultural expectation is that a state of coupled permanence is achievable, uncoupling is experienced as crisis and inadequacy—even though such failures are more the norm than the exception.

As love has increasingly become the center of all emotional expression in the popular imagination, anxiety about obtaining it in sufficient quantities—and for sufficient duration—suffuses the population. Everyone knows that as the demands and expectations on couples escalated, so did divorce rates. And given the current divorce statistics (roughly 50 percent of all marriages end in divorce), all indications are that whomever you love today—your beacon of hope, the center of all your optimism—has a good chance of becoming your worst nightmare tomorrow. (Of course, that 50 percent are those who actually leave their unhappy marriages and not a particularly good indication of the happiness level or nightmare potential of those who remain.) Lawrence Stone, a historian of marriage, suggests—rather jocularly, you can't help thinking—that today's rising divorce rates are just a modern technique for achieving what was once taken care of far more efficiently by early mortality.

Love may or may not be a universal emotion, but clearly the social forms it takes are infinitely malleable. It is our culture alone that has dedicated itself to allying the turbulence of romance and the rationality of the long-term couple, convinced that both love and sex are obtainable from one person over the course of decades, that desire will manage to sustain itself for 30 or 40 or 50 years and that the supposed fate of social stability is tied to sustaining a fleeting experience beyond its given life span.

Of course, the parties involved must "work" at keeping passion alive (and we all know how much fun that is), the presumption being that even after living in close proximity to someone for a historically unprecedented length of time, you will still muster the requisite desire to achieve sexual congress on a regular basis. (Should passion fizzle out, just give up sex. Lack of desire for a mate is never an adequate rationale for "looking elsewhere.") And it is true, many couples do manage to perform enough psychic retooling to reshape the anarchy of desire to the confines of the marriage bed, plugging away at the task year after year (once a week, same time, same position) like diligent assembly-line workers, aided by the occasional fantasy or two to help get the old motor to turn over, or keep running, or complete the trip. And so we have the erotic life of a nation of workaholics: if sex seems like work, clearly you're not working hard enough at it.

But passion must not be allowed to die! The fear—or knowledge—that it does shapes us into particularly conflicted psychological beings perpetually in search of prescriptions and professional interventions, regardless of cost or consequence. Which does have its economic upside, at least. Whole new sectors of the economy have been spawned, with massive social investment in new technologies from Viagra to couples' porn: capitalism's Lourdes for dying marriages.

There are assorted low-tech solutions to desire's dilemmas too. Take advice. In fact, take more and more advice. Between print, airwaves and the therapy industry, if there were anyway to quantify the G.N.P. in romantic counsel, it would be a staggering number. Desperate to be cured of love's temporality, a love-struck populace has molded itself into an advanced race of advice receptacles, like some new form of miracle sponge that can instantly absorb many times its own body weight in wetness.

Inexplicably, however, a rebellious breakaway faction keeps trying to leap over the wall and emancipate themselves, not from love itself—

unthinkable!—but from love's domestic confine-
ments. The escape routes are well trodden—love
affairs, midlife crises—though strewn with the
left-behind luggage of those who encountered
unforeseen obstacles along the way (panic, guilt,
self-engineered exposures) and beat self-abashed
retreats to their domestic gulags, even after pledging body and soul to newfound loves in the balmy
utopias of nondomesticated romances. Will all the
adulterers in the audience please stand up? You
know who you are. Don't be embarrassed! Adulterers aren't just "playing around." These are our
homegrown closet social theorists, because adultery is not just a referendum on the sustainability
of monogamy; it is a veiled philosophical discussion about the social contract itself. The question on the table is this: "How much renunciation
of desire does society demand of us, versus the
degree of gratification it provides?" Clearly, the
adulterer's answer, following a long line of vener-
able social critics, would be, "Too much."

But what exactly is it about the actual lived
experience of modern domestic love that would
make flight such a compelling option for so many?
Let us briefly examine those material daily life
conditions.

Fundamentally, to achieve love and qualify for
entry into that realm of salvation and transcen-
dence known as the couple (the secular equivalent
of entering a state of divine grace), you must *be*
a lovable person. And what precisely does being
lovable entail? According to the tenets of modern
love, it requires an advanced working knowledge
of the intricacies of *mutuality*.

Mutuality means recognizing that your partner has needs and being prepared to meet them.
This presumes, of course, that the majority
of those needs can and should be met by one
person. . . .

Meeting those needs is the most effective way
to become the object of another's desire, thus at-
taining intimacy, which is required to achieve the
state known as psychological maturity. (Despite
how closely is reproduces the affective conditions
of our childhoods, since trading compliance for

love is the earliest social lesson learned; we learn
it in our cribs.)

You, in return, will have your own needs met
by your partner in matters large and small. In
practice, many of these matters turn out to be
quite small. Frequently, it is the tensions and
disagreements over the minutiae of daily living
that stand between couples and their requisite
intimacy. Taking out the garbage, tone of voice,
a forgotten errand—these are the rocky shoals
upon which intimacy so often founders.

Mutuality requires *communication*, since in order to be met, these needs must be expressed. . . .
What you need is for your mate to understand
you—your desires, your contradictions, your
unique sensitivities, what irks you. (In practice,
that means what about your mate irks you.)
You, in turn, must learn to understand the mate's
needs. This means being willing to hear what
about yourself irks your mate. Hearing is not a
simple physiological act performed with the ears,
as you will learn. You may think you know how
to *hear*, but that doesn't mean that you know how
to *listen*.

With two individuals required to coexist in
enclosed spaces for extended periods of time,
domesticity requires substantial quantities of
compromise and adaptation simply to avoid
mayhem. Yet with the post-Romantic ideal of
unconstrained individuality informing our most
fundamental ideas of the self, this can prove a
perilous process. Both parties must be willing to
jettison whatever aspects of individuality might
prove irritating while being simultaneously allowed to retain enough individuality to feel their
autonomy is not being sacrificed, even as it is being surgically excised.

Having mastered mutuality, you may now proceed to *advanced intimacy*. Advanced intimacy
involves inviting your partner "in" to your most
interior self. Whatever and wherever our "inside"
is, the widespread—if somewhat metaphysical—
belief in its existence (and the related belief that
whatever is in there is dying to get out) has assumed a quasi-medical status. Leeches once served

a similar purpose. Now we "express our feelings" in lieu of our fluids because everyone knows that those who don't are far more prone to cancer, ulcers or various dire ailments.

With love as our culture's patent medicine, prescribed for every ill (now even touted as a necessary precondition for that other great American obsession, longevity), we willingly subject ourselves to any number of arcane procedures in its quest. "Opening up" is required for relationship health, so lovers fashion themselves after doctors wielding long probes to penetrate the tender regions. Try to think of yourself as one big orifice: now stop clenching and relax. If the procedure proves uncomfortable, it just shows you're not open enough. Psychotherapy may be required before sufficient dilation can be achieved: the world's most expensive lubricant.

Needless to say, this opening-up can leave you feeling quite vulnerable, lying there psychically spread-eagled and shivering on the examining table of your relationship. (A favored suspicion is that your partner, knowing exactly where your vulnerabilities are, deliberately kicks you there—one reason this opening up business may not always feel as pleasant as advertised.) And as anyone who has spent much time in—or just in earshot of—a typical couple knows, the "expression of needs" is often the Trojan horse of intimate warfare, since expressing needs means, by definition, that one's partner has thus far failed to meet them.

In any long-term couple, this lexicon of needs becomes codified over time into a highly evolved private language with its own rules. Let's call this couple grammar. Close observation reveals this as a language composed of one recurring unit of speech: the interdiction—highly nuanced, mutually imposed commands and strictures extending into the most minute areas of household affairs, social life, finances, speech, hygiene, allowable idiosyncrasies and so on. From bathroom to bedroom, car to kitchen, no aspect of coupled life is not subject to scrutiny, negotiation and codes of conduct.

A sample from an inexhaustible list, culled from interviews with numerous members of couples of various ages, races and sexual orientations:

You can't leave the house without saying where you're going. You can't not say what time you'll return. You can't go out when the other person feels like staying at home. You can't be a slob. You can't do less than 50 percent of the work around the house, even if the other person wants to do 100 percent more cleaning than you find necessary or even reasonable. You can't leave the dishes for later, load them the way that seems best to you, drink straight from the carton or make crumbs. You can't leave the bathroom door open—it's offensive. You can't leave the bathroom door closed—your partner needs to get in. You can't not shave your underarms or legs. You can't gain weight. You can't watch soap operas. You can't watch infomercials or the pregame show or Martha Stewart. You can't eat what you want—goodbye Marshmallow Fluff; hello tofu meatballs. You can't spend too much time on the computer. And stay out of those chat rooms. You can't take risks, unless they are agreed-upon risks, which somewhat limits the concept of "risk." You can't make major purchases alone, or spend money on things the other person considers excesses. You can't blow money just because you're in a bad mood, and you can't be in a bad mood without being required to explain it. You can't begin a sentence with "You always. . . ." You can't begin a sentence with "I never. . . ." You can't be simplistic, even when things are simple. You can't say what you really think of that outfit or color combination or cowboy hat. You can't be cynical about things the other person is sincere about. You can't drink without the other person counting your drinks. You can't have the wrong laugh. You can't burn cigarettes when you're out because it embarrasses your mate, even though you've explained the unspoken fraternity between smokers. You can't tailgate, honk or listen to talk radio in the car. And so on. The specifics don't matter. What matters is that the operative word is "can't."

Thus is love obtained.

Certainly, domesticity offers innumerable rewards: companionship, child-rearing convenience, reassuring predictability and many other benefits too varied to list. But if love has power over us, domesticity is its enforcement wing: the iron dust mop in the velvet glove. The historian Michel Foucault has argued that modern power made its mark on the world by inventing new types of enclosures and institutions, places like factories, schools, barracks, prisons and asylums, where individuals could be located, supervised, processed and subjected to inspection, order and the clock. What current social institution is more enclosed than modern intimacy? What offers greater regulation of movement and time, or more precise surveillance of body and thought, to a greater number of individuals?

Of course, it is your choice—as if any of us could really choose not to desire love or not to feel like hopeless losers should we fail at it. We moderns are beings yearning to be filled, yearning to be overtaken by love's mysterious power. . . .

Exchanging obedience for love comes naturally—after all, we all were once children whose survival depended on the caprices of love. And there you have the template for future intimacies.

If you love me, you'll do what I want—or need, or demand—and I'll love you in return. We all become household dictators, petty tyrants of the private sphere, who are, in our turn, dictated to.

And why has modern love developed in such a way as to maximize submission and minimize freedom, with so little argument about it? No doubt a citizenry schooled in renouncing desire instead of imagining there could be something more would be, in many respects, advantageous. After all, wanting more is the basis for utopian thinking, a path toward dangerous social demands, even toward imagining the possibilities for altogether different social arrangements. But if the most elegant forms of social control are those that came packaged in the guise of individual needs and satisfactions, so wedded to the individual psyche that any opposing impulse registers as the anxiety of unlovability, who needs a soldier on every corner? We are more than happy to police ourselves and those we love and call it living happily ever after. Perhaps a secular society needed another metaphysical entity to subjugate itself to after the death of God, and love was available for the job. But isn't it a little depressing to think we are somehow incapable of inventing forms of emotional life based on anything other than subjugation?

## Asexuality

**Melissa Travis**

We live in a society that assumes adults are interested in good sex. However, some people just don't want to have sex. Asexuality is indifference toward sexual activity and may be found in at least one percent of adults (Bogaert 2004).[1] Although some researchers believe that asexuality is a disorder requiring treatment and some consider it a simple disinterest in sex, others consider it a legitimate sexual identity and argue that, like other sexual identities, it is fluid and may change over time (Melby 2005).

What does this all mean? Some asexual people have romantic attractions to others but do not sexually con-

summate their relationships. Others have no romantic attractions or sex drive at all but may engage in sex just to please a partner. Although asexual individuals may not be interested in having sex, some enjoy friendships that contain intimate connections such as cuddling, sleeping in the same bed, massage, and other tender or affectionate interactions. They enjoy the nonsexual intimacy that comes from sharing and being close to another person. But even with their sexual indifference, asexual people can develop jealous feelings toward their friends or partners who are engaged in sexual relationships with someone else (AVEN 2005). Individuals who identify as asexual may join asexuality advocacy groups such as the

Asexuality Visibility and Education Network (AVEN) to discuss their experiences and provide each other support (AVEN 2005).

**NOTE**

1. From a probability sample of over 18,000 participants drawn from British households, Anthony Bogaert (2004: 284) found that 1.05% of respondents (aged 16–59) "reported that they had never felt sexual attraction to anyone at all." He described these respondents as "asexual"

**REFERENCES**

AVEN. 2005. *Asexual Visibility and Education Network.* Retrieved March 19, 2005 from www.asexuality.org/discussion.

Bogaert, Anthony. 2004. "Asexuality: Prevalence and Associated Factors in a National Probability Sample." *Journal of Sex Research* 41:279–287.

Melby, Todd. 2005. "Asexuality Gets More Attention, But Is It a Sexual Orientation?" *Contemporary Sexuality* 39(11): 1, 4–5.

# Mexican Immigrant Women and Sexual Initiation

Gloria González-López

Editor's note: *The following selection is from the book* Erotic Journeys: Mexican Immigrants and Their Sex Lives *(University of California Press, 2005). In this book, Dr. González-López explores the interplay between gender, class, ethnicity, and migration on the sex lives of Mexican immigrant women and men. For this project, Dr. González-López interviewed sixty Mexican immigrants living in Los Angeles, most of them Catholic. She conducted in-depth individual interviews with twenty women and ten men from Mexico City and twenty women and ten men from the state of Jalisco. Informants from Jalisco included individuals from very small towns and villages. All of the informants had lived in Los Angeles for at least five years and they were between the ages of 25 and 45. They all identified themselves as heterosexual during the interviews. This reading focuses on the first sexual experiences of women in her study. González-López (2005) argues "[s]exual purity is socially assembled as a life-enhancing resource; it becomes what I call* capital femenino. *That is, virginity takes on a social exchange value that Mexican women, a subordinate social group in patriarchal society, use to improve and maximize their life conditions and opportunities" (p. 38). Sexual abstinence is also tied to respect for the family,* women's fear of sexism, and, less frequently, to Catholic norms of virginity. Despite cultural prescriptions for virginity before marriage, 70 percent of the women in this study were not virgins when they were married. This reading explores how women are both controlled by and challenge this cult of virginity.

From González-López, Gloria. 2005. "Women and Sexual Initiation: Between Pleasure and Danger." In *Erotic Journeys: Mexican Immigrants and Their Sex Lives* (pp. 50–61). Reprinted by permission of the University of California Press. © 2005 The Regents of the University of California.

. . . For the women in this study, diverse forms of female sexuality are reconfigured along a bipolar continuum joining pleasure and danger.[1] At one extreme, I examine sexual stories that offer the possibility for Mexican women to reclaim sexual autonomy, agency, and pleasure. At the other end, I identify the moral and social contradictions shaping Mexican women's sexuality. A wide variety of mechanisms of social control linked to a woman's loss of virginity emerge between these two extremes. These tendencies are not equally balanced; the danger end of the continuum is over-represented in my data. The sexual behavior described by my respondents includes the following characteristics along the pleasure–danger spectrum:

1. Pleasure. A woman may question the various dynamics controlling her sexuality and may come to reclaim it so that she can experience it freely. The stories shared by the women who identified with this tendency illustrate the ways that women living in patriarchal societies can enjoy their sexuality. The women's testimony also indicates that women have the capability to experience sexual agency and autonomy, and to enjoy sex and erotic desire as positive feelings and opportunities for exploring emotional intimacy with a partner before marriage.

2. Sexual risks and threats. A woman may take a risk in claiming and experiencing sexuality while encountering dangerous situations and experiencing painful repercussions: (a) the risk of pregnancy and, in a worst-case scenario, coerced marriage; (b) guilt for not complying with an ethic of family respect; and (c) feelings of shame, fear, confusion, frustration, ambivalence, worthlessness, and failure, or *fracaso,* as a result of their earliest sexual encounters.

3. Danger. A woman faces the risk of being sexually coerced or victimized and of involuntarily losing her virginity due to sexual violence (i.e., rape, incest). For one-third of the women who had premarital sex, rape and/or incest were their first sexual experiences. That is, 80 percent of women survivors of sexual violence in the study were virgins when they were raped. Their testimonies reveal mechanisms of sexual control and power hidden behind sexualized gender relations.

Each one of these three female heterosexual experience patterns resounds with feminist theorist Lynne Segal's proposal to acknowledge the existence of multiple female heterosexualities. Segal writes: "Once we look for sexual diversity and fluidity, the fluctuating nature of heterosexual encounters or relation-ships [sic] is obvious: some are pleasurable, self-affirming, supportive, reciprocal or empowering; others are compulsive, oppressive, pathological or disabling; most move between the two" (1994, 260).

The sexualities of most of the women that I interviewed do not necessarily move symmetrically between the two extremes identified by Segal. Risk and danger surround the heterosexual encounters of many of these women. Many women born and educated in underdeveloped and developing nations still face multiple sources of gender inequality. Nevertheless, Segal's framework offers an alternative for exploring both the possibilities for Mexican immigrant women to claim their right to sexual autonomy, pleasure, and agency and to identify the social, cultural, and political forces that oppress women involved in heterosexual relationships.

By adopting this continuum, I do not deny women's simultaneous exposure to both pleasure and danger in sex. I use this model exclusively to represent how they interpret their first sexual encounters. Some of the women I interviewed revealed how in some situations pleasure and danger can occur simultaneously. Danger and pleasure are not mutually exclusive and, at times, the former may enhance the latter. For example, some women recalled how as teenagers hiding from or lying to a parent about a boyfriend enhanced their expectation and excitement of an intimate encounter with him. Prohibition enhanced desire; their challenge was to find ways to keep the thrill alive while challenging the proscriptions that kept them from pleasure.

After analyzing the women's sexual narratives, I found Segal's awareness of "the fluctuating nature of heterosexual encounters" and what she calls "relation-ships" fascinating. Her notion of female heterosexualities was also an invitation to listen to the men's stories, in a dialogue of sorts between the two genders.

## Erotic Love, Emotional Pleasure

Not all of the women in this study who had sex before marriage experienced guilt, shame, fear of sexism, or family persecution. A small number, five out of twenty of those who had [voluntary] premarital sex, experienced it in a positive way. They had no regrets. Instead, having sex for the first time had a special meaning: it had been an expression of trust in and deep love for a man:

*Graciela:* I felt good, not nervous or anything, and I never regretted it. . . . I really loved him, I had sex with him because I really loved him.
*Rosalía:* I felt happy because he was my first boyfriend and I did it for the first time with him and felt happy. I have never regretted it.
*Lolita:* Since I trusted him . . . and I loved him . . . I did not feel bad. In other words, I felt good.

Zenaida described her first sexual encounter in a tone of elation: "I felt happy because I adored that man. . . . I never felt nervous because I knew what was happening, and I did not feel afraid either. All I remember is that I felt so happy, and so in love with him. . . ." When I asked if she had noticed a change in the relationship after having sex, she replied, "It got better; we got closer to each other. We had a great time." Oralia's sexual experience was like Zenaida's, exciting and pleasurable: "I never felt bad, quite the contrary, I felt . . . as if he was already a part of me. When I looked at him from the distance, I really rejoiced. [The relationship] got better. Yes, it got better."

What is required for a man educated in a patriarchal society to experience sexuality in ways that are similarly positive? In this study, three men had sexual relations for the first time with women with whom they had developed a steady relationship. Raúl had sex for the first time when he was nineteen or twenty, with a beloved girlfriend who was a year or two younger than him. Tenderly, he described the deep emotional relationship he had with her. Emiliano had intercourse for the first time when he was fifteen. With a wistful sigh, he recalled the woman, who was five years older than him, as *el amor de mi vida* (the love of my life). Daniel, the youngest of the men from Jalisco, had sex with a girlfriend about a year younger than him. He also described their relationship as emotionally meaningful.

A commonality in the life of this manly trio was the influence of education on their personal perceptions of sexuality and gender relations. Raúl explained that by the time he had sex for the first time, he had already found answers to many of his questions about reproduction and human sexuality in his psychology classes at the Colegio de Ciencias y Humanidades—the CCH. CCH is the equivalent of a senior high school at the Universidad Nacional Autónoma de México (UNAM)—the largest public university in the nation, located in Mexico City. Coincidentally, Emiliano reported that although he stopped attending school after he had finished *secundaria*

(the equivalent of ninth grade), his older cousin had become his mentor with regard to human sexuality during his adolescent years. Emiliano reported that his cousin, like Raúl, was completing his education at the CCH. Daniel reported that a middle-school teacher had a powerful influence on his perceptions of sexuality and gender relations. That teacher eventually became the school principal. He was a respected yet controversial figure in Daniel's small town for openly teaching his students about reproduction, human sexuality, and for promoting equal rights between women and men. During our interview, Daniel realized that his teacher had been a substitute for his absent father, who had died when he was a little boy. Raúl, Emiliano, and Daniel echo the experiences of other young Mexicanos. In a study of more than three hundred young Mexican men, Stern et al. (2003) found that some of their informants approached their male cousins and uncles who were attending *preparatoria* or college in order to ask them questions about sexuality. The men's stories also resonate with Hirsch's findings for women: those who embraced views of sexual intimacy within marriage—as opposed to those who were more "reproductive oriented"—had completed higher levels of formal education and had been exposed to school-based sex education programs (2003, 224).

Besides education, the three men shared similar personal histories, which were also a factor in shaping their expansive sexual views. They described loving relationships with the women with whom they experienced sex for the first time. They used the term *nervioso* to describe feelings of anxiety during their first sexual encounters. In their cases, the first sexual experience had intensified emotional bonding and improved the quality of their relationships:

*Raúl:* I felt as if she had become part of my life, and I think that I also became part of her life.
*Emiliano:* It [the relationship] improved a lot, and ah . . . we, we understood each other well; I think it was much better that way. . . . Happy.

I felt good. It surprised me because [I thought] because she is older, she has more experience, and it was not that way. It was very tender and affectionate.

*Daniel:* It [the relationship] became more open; better, with more tranquility and everything. . . . I developed more love for her.

The three men noted that their respective partners had been virgin women, but that they had felt no moral obligation to marry. They rejected the idea that a man's decision to refrain from sexual relations with a girlfriend was a sign of *respeto a la mujer.* Nevertheless, they were aware that unexpected pregnancy might have led to marriage. They asserted that the decision to preserve virginity until marriage was a woman's personal choice and not a moral obligation. None of these men married the women with whom they explored heterosexual desire for the first time, but they remembered those love experiences with nostalgia. Interestingly, the two men from Mexico City continued to engage in sex as part of later dating experiences, a practice that at some point resulted in unexpected pregnancies and coercive marriages with women they were not sure about. Daniel is still single and dreaming of a woman with sexual desire and experience with whom he can explore erotic pleasure, commitment, and love.

For both women and men, the decision to have sex before marriage and experience it with pleasure was a consequence of social awareness (via education) and the recognition of an emotional connection between love and sex. For women in particular, questioning Catholic Church teachings on sexuality was a factor. Zenaida, a college-educated woman from Mexico City, spoke passionately when I asked about religion's influence on a woman's sexuality: "Sexuality, for both men and women, is something personal, it's an intimate issue. [No one should] tell you what you can do and what you cannot do, not even the Church!"

Oralia, who had sex before marriage, saw things differently. While talking about her deep Catholic faith, Oralia said that although she did not regret having sex (and her husband had never complained about it) she had experienced feelings of guilt later in life. "I know I offended God in that way as in many other things," she said. "I know it wasn't right, because He didn't want me to do it. I am sorry because I offended God, but I know He already forgave me and He knows I love my husband and that I would not do it with anybody else."

Unlike Oralia, none of the men in the study reported feelings of guilt and remorse related to religion. The testimony of women like Oralia, and that of the other women, discussed earlier, bring us back to the sex experiences of women who dare to explore pleasure and joy before marriage while trying to disentangle themselves from a web of moral condemnation.

How is the first sexual encounter experienced when it happens before marriage and does not lead to pregnancy? A third of the women who had voluntarily had sex before marriage experienced fear, guilt, confusion, disappointment, shame, physical pain, frustration, and a sense of worthlessness and failure, or *fracaso:*

*Norma:* I felt disappointed because I always thought it was something special, beautiful . . . like everybody had told me.

*Diamantina:* I was scared . . . because I did not know about it, and the next day I was afraid and I could not look him in the face because I was ashamed of myself.

*Deyanira:* I did not like it . . . you know, it hurts and then you bleed and I did not like that at all. . . . He did not do it roughly or anything, but I remember feeling bad.

*Felicia:* I felt very bad and very strange. He did not force me, and I would not know how to explain it to you . . . but I felt strange. I did not know what sex or love was about.

*Idalia:* When I did it the first time I felt worthless. . . . I thought everything was gone for me. I felt *fracasada,* I felt like a failure.

Idalia further explained the meaning of *fracaso* to me: "Well, *yo fracasé,* that means that I failed, that I did not get married, following the custom that says that I have to walk down the aisle [as a virgin]." In relation to premarital sex and pregnancy out of wedlock, *fracaso* was also used by some of the men I interviewed.[2]

In short, having sexual relations before marriage was morally confusing for this subgroup of women.[3] For women who voluntarily experience premarital sex, sexual activity flows between two extremes. At its worst, sex results in pregnancy out of wedlock and leads to coerced marriage. At its best, sexual activity does not result in pregnancy but creates feelings of guilt or regret for not having complied with the ethic of family respect. Although none of the men were faced with a girlfriend's pregnancy as a consequence of their first sexual encounters, some were exposed to coercive marriages later in life when they had to deal with a partner's unexpected pregnancy. In addition, some men felt that they were constantly watched by their families. In that respect, the women and men shared similar risks, but the extreme dangers were reserved for women.

## *Rape of a Virgin*

Being educated in a patriarchal society where a devotion to virginity is still pervasive may magnify the trauma of rape in a virgin woman. Eight women in the study (four from Jalisco and four from Mexico City) described the emotional ordeal of rape in detail. They related the horror, agony, confusion, shame, and guilt that were brought about by the rape, and of the damaging impact rape had had on their lives. The following are condensed accounts of their stories.

*Nora.* A Mexican man she had dated raped her in Los Angeles. Her only daughter was the consequence of this assault. During our interview, she showed anxiety when the topic of virginity came up. Nora had refrained from any sexual activity for twenty-eight years; all her life, she had dreamed of marrying in white. Being raped and becoming pregnant as a result dashed her hopes. At the time of our interview, she was living without benefit of marriage with a Mexican man she described as kind and understanding.

*Victoria.* She remembered vividly the fear of being killed after a man she did not know kidnapped her and took her to his house, where he raped her, when she was an adolescent. She still swallows tears when she sees that her son, the result of the rape, has the rapist's face and gestures. She is married to a man she describes as handsome and good, but who at times complains because she was not a virgin at marriage. He knows her son but not the whole truth about what happened.

*Candelaria.* She came to the United States to escape her rapist, a neighbor who had forced her to have intercourse with him many times over the years, beginning when she was very young. Immediately after she was told that she had given birth to a little girl, Candelaria cried and prayed that her only daughter would never have to go through the same kind of experience. She married an immigrant man she met in Los Angeles. Under the influence of alcohol her husband complains that she was not a virgin when they married. He doesn't know about the rape. She also recalled feeling "embarrassed, ashamed, and confused" after her older brother "touched her in inappropriate ways" more than once when she was ten or twelve.

*Tomasita.* She still cries in silence and confusion, trying to forget the ways in which her uncle sexually abused her when she was five or six years old. She is separated from her last partner and lives with her children.

*Belén.* Her father forced her to have repeated intercourse with him from the time she was nine years old until adolescence. As with many incest survivors, Belén's sexual ordeal did not stop with her father—two cousins also abused her and, as a young adult, Belén was the victim of date rape. She still recalls fears of being rejected by men as the main reason why she maintained a relationship with the boyfriend who raped her and finally married her. They are still together and they live in Los Angeles.

*Irasema.* Unlike the vast majority of the study participants, she described herself as a former "Daddy's girl" who owned a garment shop. She was an upper-middle-class young woman in her native Mexico City. When she was nineteen and riding in a car with her boyfriend, he took an unknown detour and drove to a hotel, where he raped her. She is currently in a relationship with an immigrant man that she described as a great lover, gentle and compassionate.

*Fernanda.* She is extremely protective of the two daughters she is currently raising. She cries and thinks of them as she experiences flashbacks of her uncle molesting her and her younger sister while both were spending Christmas in their relatives' small town. A Latino man who came out of the dark as she walked down the alley leading to the sweatshop where she works in Los Angeles sexually assaulted her. She has had different types of relationships, at times rough and at times marked by love. She is currently unmarried but living with a man.

*Diamantina.* She identified her father's alcoholism as the main reason why he would wake her up at night, touching her genitalia, when she was eight or ten. Similar incidents happened with one of her brothers. She recalled both experiences as a dream, something impossible to believe. She does not know if she "technically" lost her virginity because of those experiences. (The "technical" aspects of virginity were also a concern for Macaria, who had been sexually assaulted with no penetration. At the end of our interview, she asked whether a gynecologist would be able to tell if she was still a virgin or not.) Diamantina ended her story by describing her current relationship as not the best in terms of sexual satisfaction. Her husband works long hours to be a good provider.

The women had been sexually victimized under varying circumstances, and they differed with respect to the quality of their relationships. Yet they all shared certain commonalities. They all had felt morally devastated, devalued, and ashamed after losing their virginity in a violent and offensive way. For some, losing their virginity as a result of rape meant that they had been robbed of their *capital femenino* and engendered fears of not being able "to marry right." Some women experienced bitter regret about having to forfeit the cherished dream "to marry in white." Being raped also meant experiencing shame. Embarrassment and confusion were reasons why the women had not revealed their experiences to their families. Several were afraid of being blamed for their own victimization. Their ultimate concern was to learn what to do as mothers so as to spare their daughters the same fate. Elsewhere, I have examined these stories in more depth with regard to the negative consequences of rape on the women's emotional lives (see González-López, forthcoming).

### Men and Sexual Violence

*Though an appalling number of men do rape, most men do not. It is a fact of great importance, both theoretically and practically, that there are many non-violent men in the world. This too needs explanation, and must be considered in a strategy for peace.*

—R. W. Connell, *The Men and the Boys*

What do the men in this study think about sexual violence against women? When I asked male informants that question, some replied in one sentence while others gave complex answers. The overwhelming majority made the male figure solely responsible for acts of violence against women, while also naming the psychological factors they believed might explain a rapist's behavior: lack of personal control or self-confidence, selfishness, alcohol and drug use, and so on. Men from Mexico City were more likely to attribute sexual violence to sexism, while men from small towns in Jalisco were more passionate and severe in the judgments, using terms such as "beast;" "brutish;" "savage;" and "animal" to condemn rapists. A similar pattern emerged in the men's opinions about husbands who complained about their wives' earlier sexual involvement and the women's fear of sexism. Men from Mexico City were more likely to blame gender inequality for rape than their rural counterparts. This pattern follows my argument about fluid yet systematic variations in masculinity and patriarchy depending on socioeconomic context. Only a minority of the men alleged that a woman's attire and behavior could be held as a cause of rape.

Unlike the women in my sample, only one man reported his first sexual experience as having been abusive. Although he did not elaborate, Vinicio briefly stated that an adult man in his family had attempted to sexually molest him when he was about five years old. Although the vast majority of men did not report sexual abuse, some had been profoundly affected by violence against women. Like Vinicio, they were moved when that subject came up during the interviews. They exhibited the same emotional responses as the women's concerning recriminations from the women's partners for their not being virgins at marriage. For Alejandro, Ernesto, Diego, and Sebastián, sexual violence against the women they love—including mothers, sisters, wives, and daughters—is part of their personal histories.

Alejandro asked me during our interview whether I could provide a professional referral for his wife. He explained she had been raped in her early twenties, while still living in her native town on Mexico's Pacific Coast. He explained that although sex between them was sometimes pleasant, tensions still emerged in moments of intimacy because of the rape she had experienced. "All I do to help her is give her lots of affection and support," he said. One of the reasons why he had learned to be sensitive and caring toward his wife was the rape experience of another woman he has always loved: his mother.

Ernesto, who is forty-three, had migrated from his native Guadalajara to Los Angeles when he was twenty-three. Not long afterward, he had married a Mexican divorcee who was also an immigrant. Early in the marriage, Ernesto learned about her painful past, which eventually led to conflict between them. Like Alejandro's, Ernesto's sex life was negatively affected by the physical, sexual, and emotional violence his wife had experienced. "I do not sleep with her. For a long time, I have not slept with her, I have my own room," he stated with deep concern.

Like Alejandro, Ernesto has also encouraged his wife to seek professional help but without success. Despite his sexual frustrations, he is proud of his behavior as a married man. "I have always been faithful," he said. "I am not like those people who need to be with one woman and then another one. I firmly believe in being faithful to my wife."

Alejandro's family history helped him to develop compassion toward his wife. In the early stages of our interview, we explored the reasons why he believed that women and men should have equal rights. He explained that, while attending elementary school, he had begun to notice conflict between his parents. Although his father was not physically violent toward his mother, Alejandro witnessed the emotional abuse she endured and that made him especially caring toward her, his sisters, and women in general. For both Alejandro and Ernesto, falling in love with and marrying a rape survivor had led to tolerance, acceptance, and self-sacrifice.

Both men's stories resonate with a pattern I discuss elsewhere: the relational nature of gender and sexuality via motherhood (González-López 2003). The mothers in that study taught their daughters about the value of virginity on the basis of their own sexual histories. Similarly, married men like Ernesto and Alejandro who are involved with rape survivors become sensitive toward their partners when women in their families of origin have had similar experiences. The rape of a sister or a daughter had different—but no less painful—consequences on a man's life. Diego, for example, harshly condemned violence against women as he described his own feelings after learning that his sister had been raped:

One of my sisters . . . over there in Mexico, someone took advantage of her. When I learned about it,

I experienced a stunning feeling of impotence. You feel rage, of course. You feel like going to look for him, giving him a lesson, leaving him half dead. You feel so indignant; she is blood of your blood! Someone, an asshole, a coward gets there and abuses her just because he wanted to and she didn't, so all he had was force, right? It demoralizes me not only about my sister but also about all women.

Diego explained that although his parents had an exemplary marriage, his only two sisters had married abusive husbands from whom they were now legally separated. Diego, one of the most eloquent of my informants, firmly condemned violence against women and children. Sebastián whispered that his daughter had been raped at the age of seven or eight by a family relative while still living in Mexico. Now a teenager, the girl was nearby, listening to our conversation. Discreetly, Sebastián reported that his daughter had never exhibited behaviors or attitudes suggesting that she had been raped. Nevertheless, he was bent on protecting her from further abuse.

In short, women whose first experience of intercourse was rape have undergone moral, spiritual, and psychological devastation. This type of gender violence also affects their sons, husbands, brothers, and fathers. From sexual desire to coercive sex, the continuum captures the paradoxes of patriarchal institutions and ideologies that selectively affect women as well as men.

In this [reading] I examined how sexuality is a malleable social process for both genders. A woman's decision to preserve virginity until marriage goes far beyond the values imposed by the Catholic Church. Virginity is socially constructed as a resource that Mexican women can use in their search for marriage opportunities. As *capital femenino*, virginity possesses a social exchange value that women deploy to improve life conditions and expand opportunities. Because marriage is still a means of subsistence and upward social mobility for many Mexican women, virginity increases the likelihood that they will have conflict-free and financially stable marriages. In addition, virginity is a safeguard against risks like pregnancy out of wedlock, family punishment, and sexism. As shown by the testimony in this chapter, women are not alone in their use of sexual purity. Men actively participate in, and some benefit from, the construction of virginity as a social asset.

Women may explore erotic desire, pleasure, and emotional intimacy within loving relationships. Nevertheless, for many in this study, their first sexual contact was tied up with acts of domination. The men's testimony tended to confirm the women's reports of sexual violence, affirming rather than contradicting the feminine voices. The same testimony also revealed that virginity is a social exigency for women, more so than for men. On the other hand, the men's narratives suggest multiple expressions of masculine identity, some of which may promote gender equality. Education and family life in varying socioeconomic contexts (i.e., rural and urban) shape heterosexual masculine identities.

The social processes discussed in this [reading] are continuously being reproduced through negotiation, conflict, and accommodation between women and men. . . .

## NOTES

1. My use of this paradigm is inspired by Carole S. Vance's (1984) examinations of women's sexuality.

2. Amuchástegui (2001), Hirsch (2003), Prieur (1998), Szasz (1997), and others doing sex research in various regions of Mexico have found similar patterns. The terms *fracaso* or *mujer fracasada* were used by many of the women and men to describe the experiences of women who have had sexual relations before marriage and also those of *madres solteras*, that is, single women who get pregnant out of wedlock and do not get married. This commonly used expression is quite revealing: being a *fracaso* means failing to comply with the social and moral expectation of being a virgin before marriage and therefore having the risk of being socially and morally devalued. Juana Armanda Alegría (1974) examines the social and moral burden placed on women who are described as a *fracaso*: society places an existential *fracaso* on them.

3. Women who had intercourse for the first time after getting married did not have an easier experience.

Most reported feeling discomfort, shame, embarrassment, fear, anxiety, or confusion about what "they were supposed to do" before, during, and after their first sexual encounter. Two women from Jalisco had extreme reactions. Salomé did not visit her family for two months after she was married. She was ashamed to see her parents because "they would know she was sexually active." And Beatriz experienced a panic attack on her wedding night. She and her husband sought the professional services of a psychotherapist during their honeymoon on the Pacific Coast.

## REFERENCES

González-López, Gloria. Forthcoming. "Nunca he dejado de tener terror: Sexual Violence in the Lives of Mexican Immigrant Women" In D. Segura and P. Zavella (Eds.) *Women in the U.S.-Mexico Borderlands: Structural Violence and Agency in Everyday Life*. Duke University Press.

González-López, Gloria. 2003. "De madres a hijas: Gendered Lessons on Virginity across Generations of Mexican Immigrant Women." Pp. 217–240 in Pierrette Hondagneu-Sotelo (Ed.) *Gender and U.S. Migration: Contemporary Trends*. University of California Press.

Segal, Lynne. 1994. *Straight Sex: Rethinking the Politics of Pleasure*. University of California Press.

Stern, Claudio, Cristina Feuentes-Zurita, Laura Ruth Lozano-Treviño and Feneke Reysoo. 2003. "Masculinidad y salud sexual y reproductive: Un studio de caso con adolecentes de la Ciudad de Mexico." *Salud Pública de Mexico*, 45: 34–43.

# The Search for Sexual Intimacy
# for Men with Cerebral Palsy

Russell P. Shuttleworth

*"I don't give a flying fuck about the ADA be-cause that's not gonna get me laid!"*

In this [article], I explore the search for sexual intimacy for 14 men with cerebral palsy who live independently in the San Francisco Bay Area. . . . I noted the details of these [sexual] attempts, their successes and failures, what they thought were impediments and what they thought helped. I kept an ethnographic journal while living with and working as a personal assistant for one of the men, a longtime friend, and also included notes from time spent socializing with several other men in the study. I also interviewed 17 relevant others such as wives, girlfriends, ex-girlfriends, parents, siblings, personal assistants (PA's) and physical therapists for their perspectives on these men's sexual situation. The 14 men who make up the primary sample were between the ages of 18 and 51 when I began interviewing them. All of the men live independently in the San Francisco Bay Area. They all have some degree of mobility impairment: 11 men use wheelchairs, one man uses crutches and two men limp when they walk. Eleven have speech impairments, and four of these use augmentative communicative devices such as an alphabet board or computer with speech output. Eleven men were white and

From Shuttleworth, Russell P. 2000. "The Search for Sexual Intimacy for Men with Cerebral Palsy." *Sexuality & Disability* 18: 263–282. Reprinted with kind permission from Springer Science and Business Media.

three were black. Twelve men were heterosexual, one man was gay, and one man was primarily heterosexual but had experienced several short affairs with men. . . .

I first wanted to find out what these men felt were the range of issues in trying to negotiate and establish sexual intimacy with others. Then, I wanted to move on to address their contention with these issues and barriers. Lastly, I wanted to find out what aspects of self and society helped them in some cases to facilitate the establishment of sexual relationships.

## Social and Cultural Issues and Impediments

Although most of the men experienced sexual relationships one or more times in their lives, all of them also mentioned plenty of difficulties. I discerned these issues through an analysis of both topics and themes in subjects' accounts (1, 2). Significant issues included:

• *Socio-sexual isolation during formative years:* Even in mainstream situations, these men experienced isolation from adolescent social contexts in which youths' sexual identities are being formed and when the learning of flirting etiquette is taking place. This often affected their ability to negotiate sexual intimacy as young adults.

• *The parent factor:* Parents almost uniformly sent negative messages to disabled children and adolescents about their possibility of a sexual life and marriage as adults. Even parents who were supportive in every other way fed into this exclusion, albeit often from the need to protect their son from the heartache of what they saw as future rejection.

• *Lack of sexual negotiation models for disabled people:* These men bemoaned the fact that there are no models in the media and few in everyday life that show disabled people how to negotiate romance and sexual intimacy with others. This would include a lack of disability and sexuality education and counseling while growing up.

• *Cultural ideals of attractiveness:* A major impediment mentioned by participants was our society's ideals of attractiveness, which are most explicitly conveyed via the media. Most felt that these unattainable ideals clearly affected their possibilities in establishing sexual intimacy with others.

• *Body image:* Our society's ideals of attractiveness and social expectations of normative functioning and control often contribute to a negative body image. In fact, all but one of the younger men in the study admitted to having a poor body image at one time or another.

• *Embodied responses:* There were five men who told me that they experienced bodily responses to the evaluative gaze of the non-disabled other in the context of negotiating sexual intimacy or in sexual encounters themselves: the exacerbation of spasticity or dysthargic speech, or the manifestation of more serious embodied responses such as hyperventilation and breathing difficulty.

• *Friendship:* For some of the heterosexual men, friendships with women occasionally blossomed into sexual relationships. In fact, this is the avenue that almost all of the men see as offering the best potential for a sexual relationship. Yet, paradoxically, friendship is often experienced as a painful barrier and seen as symbolizing their asexuality. When they try to move a relationship with a female friend to a more romantic and sexual place, she will most often say she just wants to be friends.

### Social Expectations of Normative Functioning and Control

I want to delve a little deeper into several other significant issues in order to give a sense of how research participants experienced and interpreted what they often perceived to be barriers to negotiating and establishing sexual intimacy with others. The majority of men referred to the difficulty that they had with meeting social expectations of normative functioning and control. David,[1] a man who uses an electric wheelchair and has a significant speech impairment, told me, "We fly in the face of this society's emphasis on being in control of one's self." These men feel that negative evaluations in terms of some aspect of control or functioning have more potential to disqualify them within the context of trying to establish sexual intimacy with others than in other areas of life. Dirk, who also uses a wheelchair and has a speech impairment, had this to say:

*D:* I think that all relationships are sort of grounded in unconscious—each person brings certain things to that relationship, one of those things is physical autonomy or, whatever phrase that you want to use. I think that one of the things that, this is something that I've speculated about before, one of the things that makes it difficult for many people to have a really intimate relationship with a person with a substantial disability is that on some level, the person with a disability is a child.

*R:* Is or appears?

*D:* Well, developmentally, physically because they don't have this—they're operating physically on the—not as person, as a being, as a physical being, they don't—they're operating on the level of a kid; of an eight-year-old, of a five-year-old. If you can't go to the bathroom, if you can't feed yourself, if you're uncoordinated, if you're not graceful, those are all attributes of a little kid. Again, I don't think that people are necessarily aware of this stuff consciously but I think that there's a certain discomfort with the idea or, the reality of associating your intimate self with—the intimate self with someone else who isn't where you're at. Because intimacy, part of what intimacy is, is kind of sending the sort of outer, sort of formal self so that your inner—what I call your child self, can come out. That's what makes intimate relationships special, I think.

Two types of social expectations are normative mobility and communication. . . .

### Expectations of Normative Mobility

All except a couple of the men thought that mobility was an issue in trying to establish a relationship with someone or even for connecting in more casual sexual encounters. Those who used wheelchairs often put it in terms of women being turned off by the fact that they were in a wheelchair. The following quote from Ross, a man who has a slight limp, shows how the issue can play out for more mildly impaired men:

*Ro:* I'll be at a party and I'll be sitting there and then you know, someone will start flirting with me or whatever. And it's all good until I go and get up and get a beer. And sometimes I'll do it on purpose, like if it's someone that I am actually interested in, I'll do it on purpose. Like I won't even need a new beer but I'll find some reason to get up because I am kind of putting them to the test.

*R:* So this has happened a number of times in this situation?

*Ro:* Yeah, I definitely think I could have had a lot more sex with a lot more people, except for the fact that they disappear on me. I don't think it was for lack of interest initially, I think a lot of occasions when I could have had sex or whatever, have been sort of changed by their . . .

*R:* Perceptions?

*Ro:* Yeah, their perceptions. They're realizing that I have a disability and when I am just sitting there they don't know.

In the next quote notice how comparison to normative mobility has affected Jim's body image, which directly impacts his attempts at establishing intimate relationships:

> My body image comes directly in my face when I'm dealing in some kind of relationship with a woman. It comes up a lot, so much. Because once again I put pressure on myself saying if I like a woman, I would say how can she like me with my weird ass fucking body and the way I walk. I can go out and lecture and I can do whatever; I do that stuff really good, but when it comes to relationships then that's the dark side of me.

### Expectations of Normative Communication

All but two of the men with speech impairments, at one time or another, have felt that communication presented a barrier to developing intimacy and sexual relationships. For example, listen to what Josh, who uses a head pointer and alphabet board, says:

*J:* It is like I'm trapped inside this body that doesn't work.

*R:* Some things work.

*J:* Russell, you know what I mean. I want to charm girls with my personality, because I know I could . . .

*R:* Feeling trapped—how do you cope with that?

*J:* I really do not know. . . . When I go to campus, I see so many girls that I would try to talk to if I could.

*R:* And you don't think it would work to approach them with your board?

*J:* No. That is why I said it is like I'm trapped.

*R:* Not being able to speak to them?

*J:* Yes, it drives me nuts because I think I am a really nice person, but most people will never get to know that.

Bob considers his dysthargic speech and bodily difference in relation to body image as a major reason for his rejection:

*R:* So, body image is still a struggle?

*B:* Always will be because of the way people look at you. I mean you want to be accepted by the mass majority and being rejected by the mass majority is a major problem. You're rejected because you talk differently, because your body is in a strange position, those are the two major points of acceptance, of being accepted.

### Expectations of Masculinity

Another barrier for these men is our society's male gender role expectations such as putting an arm around a date, initiating a kiss, etc. Josh muses:

> It is funny because if a girl came up to me, would I know what to do? Like I do not kiss very well. Or because my arms are down here [by his sides], I cannot very well try to hold her hand. So what the hell do I do?

During another interview, he said: "I think women like to be touched and hugged; I cannot very well do that. It drives me nuts."

An ex-girlfriend of one of the participants, a man with limited use of his arms said that she was dissuaded from continuing her relationship with him by the social pressures that cast him as an unattractive mate. One example being the comments of her friend, who asked, how could she stand being with a man who couldn't put his arms around her? In Bourdieu's terminology, men and women incorporate a gendered habitus involving gender specific dispositions and bodily practices—culturally constructed, female and male ways of being-in-the-world and of inhabiting the body (3). People with cerebral palsy typically cannot embody gender in some of these ways. In terms of trying to establish intimacy and sexual relationships, you can see how these men feel it affects their sexual situation.

### *Analytic and Interpretive Concepts*

I now want to briefly describe the analytic and interpretive concepts that I employed to make sense out of these men's contention with adversity in their search for sexual intimacy.

### Intersubjectivity

In using the term intersubjectivity, I want to convey the notion that our immediate felt sense of interactions with others is not only affected by others' overt actions (what people appear to actually say and do) but also by their implicit, unspoken evaluations and judgments, which are often manifested in their body language, facial expressions, and negative resistance to our intentions. For example, someone may tell us something, but we sense that this is a facade and that they in fact mean the opposite. How we affect each other in the immediate moment before we step back to reflect, pulls the Cartesian subject out of the constituting mind and into the interaction itself as an intercorporeal phenomenon (4, 5). Thus, rather than being separate subjects, we inhabit an intersubjective world comprised of both explicitly and implicitly conveyed meanings.

### Embodied Sensitivities

Embodied sensitivities are the result of habitual interactions with and responses (and nonresponses) of others in particular context within an implicit background of cultural images and meanings—in this study the images and meanings of disability and desirability. This was an orienting concept for what I seemed to be getting from some of my early interviews: research participants were using metaphors such as "I feel blocked" and "trapped" in reference to not being able to make romantic advances. I saw these metaphors as expressions of an embodied sensitivity to their socio-sexual situation (4, 5, 6).

### Intentional-Felt Sense Structures

As mentioned, our different modes of feeling pleasant or unpleasant signify access or obstruction to our intentions (6), that is, our feelings relate directly to how close our expectations and desires come to being met. For example, we might become sad or angry if the object of our intentions, a person we wish to become close to, ignores us. I mapped the intentional-felt sense structures in subjects' accounts to give me an understanding of subjects' feelings in the face of what was often others' negative resistance (6, 7). I especially wanted to see the ways in which men emerged from their feeling states.

### Lived/Integrative Metaphors

I also looked for lived or integrative metaphors in these men's accounts. As anthropologists such as Becker (8), Low (9), and Kirmayer (10) have shown, metaphors often mediate between lived experience and social processes and cultural meanings. Jackson talks about lived or integrative metaphors, metaphors that in some sense refer to embodiment, as disclosing "the interdependency [and unity] of body and mind, self and world" (11, p. 9). For example, when one of the men kept telling me "I feel blocked" from even attempting to approach a woman or to negotiate a date with a woman, I interpreted this as simultaneously expressing his implicit comparison to hegemonic ideals of attractiveness, an embodied (felt) sense of the others' negative resistance to seeing him in a sexual light, and the grip that both of these had on his self-agency.

### Epiphanies or Turning Points

Social scientists in Western societies have noted that epiphanies or turning points often emerge from crisis situations and "have the potential for creating transformational experiences for the person" (12, p. 15). While similar to the "Aha!" experience that Kasnitz notes as a turning point in her study of leaders in the ILDR Movement (13), the epiphanies noted in this study are much more concerned with the sense of one's self in relation to one's sexuality.

### *Intersubjective Modes*

. . . Analysis of these men's accounts in terms of the above analytic and interpretive framework, revealed three general modes of intersubjectivity in contending with adversity in their interpersonal attempts to find lovers: 1) a mode in which participants feel immobilized; 2) a mode

in which participants risk rejection and attempt to find a lover; 3) a mode in which participants disengage from the context of trying to negotiate intimacy. This schema should be viewed as a dynamic process. All but the least significantly impaired man and a couple of the younger men had moved through these modes and sometimes back and forth especially between the latter two in the course of their lives.

### Immobilization

Some of the disabled men whom I interviewed said that although they may desire to negotiate a casual relationship or friendship in the direction of romance and sexual intimacy, they simply cannot act on their intention. One man likened it to emotionally "freezing up." Disabled men who feel intersubjectively immobilized in this way are characterized by a high internalization of the dominant cultural norms of functioning, ideals of attractiveness and desirability and gender role expectations. In fact, for most of these men, this may be an initial way of contending with their sexual situation. As mentioned, they generally have no or little adolescent experience in the interpersonal etiquette of flirting and dating and there are minimal societal models that inform disabled people how to negotiate sexual intimacy with others. It is thus difficult for them to envision themselves establishing a sexual relationship with another, albeit this is what they might desire. Listen to Carl:

> . . . that's the paradox of my psyche because in one respect I sincerely desire to have sexual contact with a female, but on the other hand I can't imagine myself doing it. So as much as I might want to do it, I think if there was a naked woman standing in front of me and she was like, okay I am here, you can have sex with me . . . I wouldn't do it because I would be scared shitless, I guess because I have never had the little steps that you have that lead up to that point when you are growing up: Like you have a girlfriend, you have a first kiss, you go on a date.

Yet, these men also sense that others do not respond to them as sexual beings in their everyday encounters. Their sense of being desexualized by others ipso facto provides them with evidence of their lack of masculinity, as a quote from Josh exemplifies:

*J:* It is like I don't have any maleness.

*R:* Do you really have a lack of maleness?

*J:* Women see me as asexual.

*R:* When do you feel a lack of maleness? At what times?

*J:* I see how girls look at me and treat me. When girls talk to me they do not seem interested in that way. . . . The feeling they give off. I feel blocked. I know I do not stand a chance. They just want to be my friend.

Frustration, anger, and sometimes hopelessness are common feelings that these men experience as their intentions are felt as blocked before they are even voiced. As mentioned, this felt blockage is comprised of their own comparative engagement with ideal images of masculinity and desirability, the desexualizing context as such which is often implicit in others' demeanor towards them and the grip that these influences have on their self-agency. . . .

Extreme cases of immobilization can result in the gradual closing off of sexual feelings. Carl speaks again:

> I have sort of blocked off that sexual part of me. I don't become stimulated as easily just because—it's almost like it's shut down. . . . I can find a woman attractive but whereas before . . . I could easily become aroused . . . there's almost like a shield now. So I have almost constructed for myself a barrier. . . .

It is as if Carl's intention for intimacy and sexual relations, his sexual self-agency and bodily desire, not finding a conducive interpersonal context, is thwarted before it can even be fulfilled in his imagination. The shield he refers to not only separates him from his sexual feelings, but also blocks him from imagining even the slightest possibility of establishing a sexual relationship with someone.

Burying one's self in school or a career or claiming indifference to their closed off sexuality are typical ways of contending for the disabled men who felt immobilized during interpersonal encounters. Even though it is the others' evaluative gaze that they believe sets in motion their feelings of asexuality and lack of masculinity, these men's metaphors can nevertheless also focus on aspects of themselves as quashing their intentions toward intimacy. Jim, for example, referred to this as the "rising up" of the "dark" or "weak side of me," or Carl, in the quote above, emphasizes his own construction of the barriers that block his agency.

### Engagement

Some men, however, are never immobilized to this degree and others manage to eventually become intersubjectively engaged. While dominant cultural images of desirability and attributions of asexuality may still loom, they have come to understand that the possibility of actual rejection must be faced. Negative resistance to or rejection of their desires and advances is common, which often leads to feelings of frustration, anger and emotional pain. Thus, alternating periods of engagement and social withdrawal in searching for love are typical. When describing unsuccessful attempts to negotiate intimacy, the metaphors that these men use often point less to their own self-agency as being blocked and more to the other as thwarting their negotiations. For example, Jack lamented:

> . . . after I get to know them better and they know me, I will try to make certain advancements and a wall will come; and that's when I get very mad and angry because I don't understand the purpose of that wall, and I don't believe that I'm moving too fast or anything, but I'm often surprised at how fast that wall comes up.

In this instance, one can quite clearly see how becoming angry, Jack's emotional reaction, reveals the frustration of his intention, a denial of access to that space of possibility for an intimate and sexual relationship with another.

Epiphanies of engagement point to a gradual building of confidence, a willingness to try new approaches, and a toughening of one's self in the face of one's circumstances. Dirk said, ". . . it seems to me that my life has been a gradual ascendency, more and more confident." Brent stated that, ". . . when I started becoming sexual, in my early twenties, I was very shy and I'm still very shy. The difference is, when I was that young, I didn't really know about as much or have access to these kind of personal ads and the computer thing and I mean in that sense I've become more aggressive and outgoing." Jack has also changed:

*J:* I'm a lot more bolder now. I think I'm more willing to take a chance.

*R:* So, when you were say in your twenties and even early thirties, you were not as bold?

*J:* Probably not. I think a lot of it has to do with having or going through hard times where I find out that the girl doesn't like me as much as I like her. I think I have been through a number of situations like that. I think it made me stronger. And at the same time, kind of numb because I feel I will never let myself get that bad.

*R:* So, we have two notions here one of strength and the other of numbness.

*J:* Yeah, but it's a good numbness; it's kind of like protection around the heart. Like I will never let anybody get to me the way that they did. In other words, I will always have my guard up, and I will never let anybody into my inner sanctum of my heart, if that makes sense.

## Disengagement

Bob and I were in a popular East Bay restaurant and pub talking about his previous sexual encounters and relationship history when he pointed to the cocktail waitress across the room:

*B:* You see this blonde waitress?

*R:* Yeah.

*B:* I'd be interested in her, but I know where her brain is. She looks like an interesting girl, but

I know what she's looking for. Now 20 years ago, I would have gone up against a brick wall and tried it, but why frustrate yourself, that's the thing. You see that she's cute, but she doesn't see the reverse. No way . . . It's like the American myth and lie: you will be happy and married, but that's not always true. But you have to deal with it. I bet if you asked a woman, any of these girls in the room if they'd go out with a disabled man, right now—there are a total of seven girls in the room right now—I guarantee you only one out of seven would consider it. I guarantee. Why is that? Because we are not even thought of, not even considered as a viable mate. See, we're fighting an uphill battle from the beginning, the older you get, the larger the hill gets, or the steeper the hill is. That's the way, as they get older, they look for different things. Believe me, I've thought about this a long time; that's why I haven't dated for a while.

Bob's comments illustrate withdrawal or disengagement from the interpersonal context of attempting to "score a date." Different from immobilization, disengagement appears to be foremost the desire to avoid frustration. That space of possibility in which negotiations to establish sexual intimacy with others occurs is seen as virtually inaccessible and not worth the effort and risk. In fact, Bob told me he hasn't dated in ten years. Metaphors here still show the other as the primary obstruction in the negotiation process. In his quote, it is the other who Bob feels builds the brick wall. Turning points are cast in negative terms, as one learns from past failures of the futility of trying.

Disengagement can of course be of much shorter duration than ten years. A major component is the felt sense of frustration and wanting to escape that sense, if only for a while. Dirk for example, lamented, "You get a bad response and you shut down." One disengages and retreats from efforts at making an intimate connection with others at least for the time being.

### Facilitatory Aspects of Self and Society

Despite their difficulties, most of the men in this study have experienced long-term, sexually intimate relationships at one time or another in their lives, and there are several who have managed to consistently do this. While part of their success can be attributed to meeting lovers whose criteria are less in line with hegemonic norms and ideals, establishing intimate relationships could also depend on their cultivation of certain facilitatory aspects of self and society.

### Employing Practical Strategies of Interpersonal Connection

Some of these were pretty typical strategies such as flirting, participating in social activities that reflect your interests or hobbies, placing relationship ads in newspapers or on the Internet. But some drew on participants' differences such as making the non-disabled other feel at ease, often using humor that makes light of one's self or one's disability. As Lenny puts it: "Have humor with yourself. . . . Don't take yourself seriously."

Within a friendship or a beginning dating relationship, some of the older men with speech impairments said that using one's race and body to communicate was very important. David said he liked to use his "puppy dog eyes" to draw the other in. Lenny claimed that much of his communication was non-verbal, especially when dates were winding down. Although he did not have much upper limb use, Lenny's feet were incredibly dexterous, decked out as they were with several rings, and he was very efficient in using the keypad on his speech device. His favorite line was asking a woman if she wanted a backrub.

### Cultivating Supportive and Communal Contexts

The cultivation of a supportive context in which one's sexuality is acknowledged and encouraged could also help facilitate the establishment of sexual relationships. While it certainly helps to have this kind of support early on in the family unit, or even to receive some kind of education or counseling on disability and sexuality issues, this was generally not the case for the men I interviewed. It was, thus, left up to them to discover a supportive context in which their sexuality could be nurtured. Several contexts that provided men in this study a space to work on their sexual self-esteem and sexual integration were the Independent Living and Disability Rights Movements, disability related work environments, peer support from other disabled people in general, communes, avant garde artistic communities and cyber space communities such as chat rooms.

Disability related work, disability community activities, and communal living situations, such as communes, dorms, hospitals or summer camps were also places or situations where sexual relationships could develop. David, for example, told me:

> I think I am lucky in a way my disability prevented me from going through that bullshit of dating . . . most of my sexual and/or intimate relationships were mostly with . . . communal living environment, i.e., the rehab hospital, camp, the dormitory . . . college— getting involved with attendants. So I looked at dating, I look at most of the way I met my sexual partners, I feel very fortunate because, you got to know them because they were there, you didn't have to do this whole ritualistic going out on a date routine.

David expresses well what held for the majority. While dating does occur, it usually develops out of a long or growing friendship. While several men have also met lovers through avenues such as singles bars and relationship ads in newspapers or on the Net, most of the men see these contexts as being fraught with the possibility of rejection through comparison to cultural images of desirability and normative evaluations.

### Transgressing the Employer–Employee Boundary in Relationships with Personal Care Assistants

In the quote above, David mentions something else that turned out to be very significant for some of the men in this study. Out of the 11 men who used personal assistants, four developed sexually intimate relationships with their assistant at one time or another, and a couple of men have experienced sexual encounters or full blown relationships with more than one personal assistant over the years. In some cases, these relationships have been very long lasting, and two men are in current relationships with women who were originally their personal assistants. Of the remaining seven men who used personal assistants, two told me they had attempted to negotiate either sexual intimacy or a dating relationship with one or more of their personal assistants; of the five others, four said they had been very attracted to a personal assistant at one time or another in their lives.

Although recognized as a relational space from which sexual intimacy can sometimes develop, the disabled person-personal assistant relation has nevertheless been seen by some people in the Disability Rights Movement as fraught with the potential for exploitation and at the very least boundary confusion (14). Yet, the lack of acknowledgment given by the Disability Rights Movement to the relationship potential here needs to be examined more closely. While the possibility of sexual abuse, the abuse of power, and the exploitation of women's gender role of caring certainly exists, the successful sexual relationships that developed between PA's and the men in the current research should make disabled people think twice before closing off this everyday context as an avenue for romance.

### Expanding the Masculine Repertoire

Several disability studies scholars and researchers have noted the dilemmas that disabled men confront in the face of our society's hegemonic ideals of masculinity such as competitiveness, strength, control, endurance and independence (15, 16, 17, 18). For the men in this study, confronting the dilemma of how to be masculine when one is disabled cannot be divorced from their interpersonal attempts to establish sexual intimacy with others. That is, the dilemma of disabled mas-

culinity is felt most acutely in the relations with those to whom they are sexually attracted. Those men who attempted to conduct themselves in rigid accordance with hegemonic masculine ideals and who measured themselves against these ideals were more apt to remain immobilized or socially withdraw when they fell short; and indeed much of the blame for their failure in love was shouldered by their inability to measure up.

Those men, however, who perceived hegemonic masculinity as less a total index of their desirability and who could sometimes draw on alternative ideals such as interdependence, prioritizing emotional intimacy, becoming friends first and not immediately pushing for a sexual relationship, allowing the other to sometimes make the first move when necessary without feeling less of a man, could better weather rejection and remain open to the possibility of interpersonal connection and sexual intimacy. These ideals and dispositions, which are sometimes associated with femininity, thus take their place alongside more hegemonic masculine ideals and dispositions in subjects' psyches and interpersonal practices. For example, note Fred's insistence on emotional intimacy in a sexual relationship:

*F:* I never wanted just sex.
*R:* What do you want with sex?
*F:* Intimacy.
*R:* How do you define intimacy? What is it?
*F:* Living with people in an intimate way.
*R:* Close?
*F:* Yes.
*R:* What about emotions, do they come into it at all?
*F:* That was why I did not try hookers.

While Fred wants sex, he is very explicit about not wanting "just sex." . . .

### Concluding Thoughts

Foucault and others argue that the constitutive power of sex holds only for modern Western subjects (19, 20, 21). Sexual relations between people obviously occurred before modernity; however, according to the arguments of these constructionists, sex has only recently become a constituent aspect of the self. Foucault, of course, never historically ventured beyond the confines of the West and some anthropologists would certainly argue with his implying an exclusivity for our focus on the sexualized self (22, 23). Yet, one does not have to agree with the exclusionary implications of his argument to apprehend that there does appear to be an increasingly constitutive role for sex in terms of identity and selfhood in the history of the West. In such a context, securing some kind of sexual intimacy, however defined by the individual, becomes a paramount project of self-constitution.

From this perspective, the claiming of sexuality by disabled people (24), against the cultural assumption of their asexuality, is thus also a bid for full subjectivity. This is one reason why the issue of disabled people's sexuality has assumed such political importance in recent years (24, 14). Considered in this light, the efforts of the men in this study to negotiate sexual intimacy take on a particular self-constructive urgency and meaning. The stakes are indeed high. Is it any wonder then, that although facing sexual oppression and sociocultural barriers to sexual intimacy at every turn, which can manifest as an intersubjective process brimming with contention, these men nevertheless continue searching for a lover? And by cultivating some combination of the above aspects of self and society, most have been successful at one time or another in establishing sexual relationships with others. Yet, their too often difficult journey to sexual subjectivity and love means that a critical, disability and sexuality studies must remain committed to interrogating and critiquing the adverse context of disability and desirability that currently exists in our society.[2]

## Acknowledgments

The research in this chapter was assisted by a fellowship from the Sexuality Research Fellowship Program of the Social Science Research Council with funds provided by the Ford Foundation.

## NOTES

1. All names used in this paper are pseudonyms.
2. It should be mentioned that for those disabled people who reside in institutional or quasi-institutional settings such as group homes, this journey becomes even more difficult, fraught as it is with intra-institutional barriers.

## REFERENCES

1. Luborsky, M. R: The identification and analysis of themes and patterns. *In* Qualitative Methods in Aging Research, J. F. Gubrium and A. Sankar (eds.). Thousand Oaks, Sage, 1994.
2. Kaufman, S: The Ageless Self: Sources of Meaning in Later Life. Madison, University of Wisconsin Press, 1986.
3. Bourdieu, P: Outline To A Theory Of Practice. Cambridge, Cambridge University Press, 1977.
4. Merleau-Ponty, M: Phenomenology Of Perception. C. Smith, (trans.) London, Routledge and Kegan Paul Ltd., 1962.
5. Ostrow, J: Social Sensitivity: A Study Of Habit And Experience. New York, State University of New York Press, 1990.
6. Buytendijk, FJ: The phenomenological approach to the problem of feelings and emotions. *In* Feelings And Emotions: The Moosehead Symposium In Cooperation With The University Of Chicago. M. L. Reymert (ed.). New York, McGraw Hill Book Company, 1950, pp. 127–1416.
7. Fell, J. P: The phenomenological approach to emotion. *In* Emotion. D. K. Candland, J. P. Fell, E. Keen, A. I. Leshner, R. M. Tarpy, and R. Plutchik, (contributors). Monterey, Brooks/Cole Publishing Company, 1977, pp. 252–285.
8. Becker, G: Metaphors in disrupted lives: Infertility and cultural constructions of continuity. Medical Anthropology Quarterly 8: 383–410, 1994.
9. Low, S: Embodied metaphors: Nerves as lived experience. *In* Embodiment And Experience: The Existential Ground Of Culture And Self, T. J. Csordas (ed.). Cambridge, Cambridge University Press, 1994, pp. 139–162.

10. Kirmayer, L. J: The body's insistence on meaning: Metaphor as presentation and representation in illness experience. Medical Anthropology Quarterly 6: 323–346, 1992.

11. Jackson, M: Introduction: Phenomenology, radical empiricism, and anthropological critique. *In* Things As They Are: New Directions In Phenomenological Anthropology, M. Jackson (ed.). Bloomington, Indiana University Press, 1996, pp. 1–50.

12. Denzin, N. K: Interpretive Interactionism. Newbury Park, Sage Publications, Inc., 1989.

13. Kasnitz, D: Life event histories and the US Independent Living Movement. *In* Disability and The Life-course, M. Priestley (ed.). Cambridge, Cambridge University Press, in-press.

14. Shakespeare, Tom Gillespie-Sells, Davies, D: The Sexual Politics Of Disability: Untold Desires. New York, Cassell, 1996.

15. Hahn, H: Masculinity and disability. Disability Studies Quarterly 9: 1–3, 1989.

16. Gerschick, T. J., & Miller, A. S: Gender identities at the crossroads of masculinity and physical disability. *In* Toward A New Psychology Of Gender, M. M. Gergen and S. N. Davis (eds.). New York, Routledge, 1996, pp. 455–475.

17. Shakespeare, T: The sexual politics of disabled masculinity. Sexuality and Disability 17: 53–64, 1999.

18. Tepper, Mitchell: Letting go of restrictive notions of manhood: Male sexuality, disability and chronic illness. Sexuality and Disability 17: 37–52, 1999.

19. Foucault, M: The History of Sexuality, Volume I: An Introduction. R Hurley (trans.). New York, Pantheon, 1978.

20. Weeks, J: Sexuality and Its Discontents: Meanings, Myths & Modern Sexualities. London, Routledge & Kegan Paul, 1985.

21. Halperin, D: One Hundred Years of Homosexuality: And Other Essays on Greek Love. New York, Routledge, 1990.

22. Herdt, G., Stoller, R. J: Intimate Communications: Erotics And The Study Of Culture. New York, Columbia University Press, 1990.

23. Freidl, E: Sex: The invisible. American Anthropologist 96: 833–844, 1994.

24. Guldin, A: Claiming Sexuality: Mobility-Impaired People and Sexualities in American Culture. Unpublished MA paper in anthropology, University of Iowa, 1999.

25. Waxman, B., Finger, A: The politics of sex and disability. Disability Studies Quarterly 9: 1–5, 1989.

## What's a Leg Got to Do with It?

**Donna Walton**

What's a leg got to do with it? Exactly what I thought when, during a heated conversation, a female rival told me I was less than a woman because I have one leg.

Excuse me. Perhaps I missed something. How could she make such an insensitive comment about something she had no experience with? Was she some expert on disabilities or something? Was she, too, disabled? Had she—like me—fought a battle with cancer that cost her a limb? For a split second, my thoughts were paralyzed by her insensitivity. But, like a defeated fighter who returns to the ring to regain victory, I bounced back for a verbal round with Ms. Thang.

I am woman first, an amputee second and physically challenged last. And it is in that order that I set out to educate and testify to people like Ms. Thang who are unable to discern who I am—a feisty, unequivocally attractive African-American woman with a gimpy gait who can strut proudly into any room and engage in intelligent conversation with folks anxious to feed off my sincere aura.

It is rather comical and equally disturbing how folks—both men and women—view me as a disabled woman, particularly when it comes to sexuality. They have so many misconceptions. Straight women, for example, want to know how I catch a man, while most men are entertained with the idea that because I have one leg sex with me must be a blast.

I have even been confronted by folks who give me the impression that they think having sex is a painful experience for me. Again, I say, What's a leg got to do with it?

For all of those who want to inquire about my sexual prowess but dare not to, or for those who are curious about how I maintain such positive self-esteem when life dealt me the proverbial "bad hand," this story is for you. But those who have a tough time dealing with reality probably should skip the next paragraph because what I am about to confess is the gospel truth.

I like sex! I am very sexual!! I even consider myself sexy, residual limb and all. You see, I was a sexual being before my leg was amputated 19 years ago. My attitude didn't change about sex. I just had to adjust to the attitudes of others.

For example, I remember a brother who I dated in high school—before my leg was amputated—then dated again five years later. The dating ended abruptly because I realized that the brother could not fathom the one-leg thing. When he and I were home alone, he was cool as long as we got hot and bothered with my prosthesis on. However, whenever I tried to take off my artificial leg for comfort purposes, he immediately panicked. He could not fathom seeing me with one leg.

I tried to put him at ease by telling him Eva's story from Toni Morrison's novel *Sula*—that "my leg just got tired and walked off one day." But this brother just could not deal. He booked.

On the other hand, my experiences with lesbians have varied; they don't all book right away, but some have booked. Not all are upfront with their feelings 'cuz women are socialized to be courteous, emotional, and indirect, sparing one's feelings. Instead, some tend to communicate their discomfort with my missing limb in more subtle ways. For example, one lesbian I dated did not want to take me out to bars, clubs and other social settings. My lop-sided gait was an embarrassment, and the fact that I use a cane garnered unwanted attention for her. Behind closed doors, she did not have any problems with it. How we would be perceived by trendy lesbians was her main concern.

Conversely, I have had positive experiences with lesbians as well. For instance, I have dated and been in love with women who have been affirming and supportive while respecting my difference. My wholeness has been shaped by all of these experiences. Without hesitation, I can now take off my prosthesis, be comfortable hopping around on one-leg and the sex. . . . . . . is still a blast.

How does a woman with one leg maintain such a positive self-esteem in a society where people with dis-

abilities are not valued? Simply by believing in myself. I know you're saying, "That sounds much too hokey." But as I said earlier, this is the gospel truth.

I was 19 years old when my leg was amputated. I was diagnosed with osteogenic sarcoma, bone cancer. During the first five years after my surgery, concentrating on other folks' perceptions of me was the least of my concerns. I was too focused on beating the odds against dying. You see, I was given only a 15% chance of survival—with spiritual guidance and support from my family—I had made the very difficult decision to stop taking my chemotherapy treatments. Doctors predicted that, by halting the dreadful chemotherapy, I was writing my own death certificate. However, through what I believe was divine healing, my cancer was eradicated.

Before this cancerous ordeal, I was not strong spiritually, and my faith was rocked when my leg was amputated because I thought I was to keep my leg. At the time, I could not see past the physical. After my amputation, I was preoccupied with the kinds of crippling thoughts that all the Ms. Thangs of the world are socialized to believe: that I was not going to be able to wear shorts, bathing suits or lingerie; that my womanness was somehow compromised by the loss of a limb.

If you have a disability and are in need of some fuel for your spirit, check out any novel by Toni Morrison (*Sula* is my favorite because of the one legged grandmother, Eva) or Khalil Gibran's *The Prophet.* These resources helped me build self-esteem and deal with my reality.

Ultimately, building positive esteem is an ongoing process. To that end, I am currently producing a motivational video that will outline coping strategies for female amputees.

No matter what your disability or circumstance, you cannot give in to a defeatist attitude. When you do, your battle is lost. There is a way of fighting back. It is called self-esteem.

Believe in yourself, and you will survive—and thrive.

*Source:* Walton, Donna. "What's a Leg Got to Do With It?" *Health Quest Magazine* 3: 51–52. Reprinted by permission of *Health Quest Magazine,* www.healthquestmag.com.

# Tainted Love? Exploring the Contours of Interracial Romance and Resistance to Interracial Intimacy

Melinda Mills

## Discovering Racial Borders

Over a year ago, during a visit in Florida with my parents, I went with them to a local restaurant. The service at this establishment, we thought, left much to be desired in the way of friendliness. Rather than being greeted in a warm, welcoming fashion, we were received rather tepidly. The waitress demonstrated palpable trepidation and hesitation as she cognitively grappled with the appearance of a white woman (my mother), her black husband (my father), and their brown daughter (me). The looks of reservation must have been an omen, an attempt to prepare me for the impending experience of the evening, the racial rude awakening of the day. Although the details of what occurred between being seated, being waited on, and being served remain blurry, one moment of my brief and casual interaction with a waiter lingers. Upon inquiring about the availability of another table (since I kept getting collided into in one way or another), the white male waiter responded with unrighteous indignation, "Well, if you'd just move closer to your husband, you wouldn't be in the way." My husband? In the way? My mind began reeling, my thoughts swirling around the racist, sexist assertion so casually dumped on me in that moment, my body stunned into silence at the casual yet clearly incestuous suggestion, my voice overanxious to announce: "That's my dad, not my husband!" But before I knew it, the waiter had disappeared, leaving me to consider his flippant and callous remarks.

How could I possibly have been misread as the romantic partner of a man at least twice my age,

and seated not directly next to me, but indeed on the complete opposite "side" of the circular table? What information, if any, suggested such a relationship to the waiter, and why was he unable to register the relationship between my mother and father, one that has lasted for over 30 years, and, I am afraid, endured more than its fair share of similarly racist, if not offensive, comments, situations, and experiences such as this?

First, let us consider what constitutes an interracial relationship. If we agree that racial categories continually change across time, space, and place, and yet are stable (and detectable) enough that we can collectively agree upon, for the most part, who is White, Black, Native American/American Indian, Asian/Pacific Islander, and Hispanic/Latino, then an interracial relationship consists of two individuals who identify as one of those races. Furthermore, interracial relationships may also contain multiracial individuals, people who identify as two or more races. I call these relationships "multiracial interracial relationships" in recognition of the multiracial identity of the mixed race individual in such a relationship. Although many nuances exist in our racial identities, we are often pressured to stick to our own kind, to choose racial identities and partners that reflect our physical appearance and presumed racial group membership. Consequently, as discussed below, most people marry people with very similar characteristics, in terms of class, education, age, even skin tone (Coltrane 2000; Kalmjin 1993; Hunter 2005), and when they fail to do so, they are met with resistance, curiosity, and suspicion.

Arguably, those most likely to encounter these forms of social control include the approximately 5 percent of Americans who marry across the color line (U.S. Census Bureau 1998, 2003). Nevertheless, this discouraging statistic on the rate of interracial marriage provides a context for understanding and dare I say, forgiving, the waiter's oversight. With so few intermarried couples to serve as a reference point, it is no wonder that the waiter, by presuming a false romance between father and daughter, misrecognized our familial connections. Or is it? Would the waiter (a metaphor for people at this point) have been more willing to accept an intermarriage of a different racial combination (i.e., White and Asian/Pacific Islander; White and Hispanic/Latino), or an interracial couple, simply out on a casual date, with marriage not posing the inevitable looming "threat" it once did? Is there a qualitative difference between dating and marriage, and if so, does the waiter's hang-up have to with a personal repulsion to visual images of interracial intimacy dancing in his head? Let's see.

### Differential Racial Romance or Reluctance?

The U.S. Census Bureau (2000) reports the following percentages of interracial couples: 51 percent Non-Hispanic White with Hispanic couples, 21 percent White with Asian American/Pacific Islander couples, 12 percent White with Native American couples, 10 percent White with African American couples, and 6 percent all other (Asian with African American, Hispanic with African American, etc.). Amidst these trends, different patterns of intermixing by race and ethnicity exist (by age, gender, class, and other social positions, a discussion of which remains prohibitive given space limitations of this article). I will discuss a few notable trends.

Whites and African Americans remain the racial groups least likely to intermarry, with African American men being more likely to marry outside of their race (13%) than African American

women (2.7%), but both African American men and women tend to marry a white partner when they intermarry (U.S. Census Bureau 2000; Qian 2005). While whites infrequently marry interracially, they are often part of existing interracial couples. As Zhenchao Qian (2005) explains, "although just 4 percent of whites are involved in interracial marriages, 92 percent of all interracial marriages include a white partner" (34). This is partly a result of the large number of white people in the U.S. population and partly a result of white status in the culture (Qian 2005).

Conversely, Native Americans are the most likely of any racial group members to marry outside of their race. Schwartz and Scott (2003: 249) posit, "They are more likely to marry a white person than another Native American person and least likely to marry an African American." A large number of married Native Americans (approximately 3 out of 4) have a non-Native American spouse (Spain 1999). Along similar lines, many Asian Americans intermarry, particularly with whites (about 38%), with Asian American women intermarrying more than Asian American men. This partnering pattern generates much resentment among Asian American men, who wish to marry within their racial group, but expands the pool of eligible partners for Asian American women. Black women express similar sentiments (ones that parallel that of Asian American men) with regards to partner eligibility concerning African American men. The disproportionate incarceration of Black men and the high rates of Black male unemployment, both the result of patterns of structural discrimination, reduce the population of desirable Black male mates for African American women wanting to marry an African American man (Davis 2003). While these patterns may eventually motivate these women to search outside of their racial group for a marital partner, research has yet to reflect such a shift in black women's interest. Finally, Hispanics/Latinos frequently intermarry whites, and "41 percent of married couples of Latina/o [or Hispanic] origin were married to a non-Latina/o [or Hispanic]"

(U.S. Bureau of the Census 2000). As these authors discuss, the varying rates of intermarriage reflect more than the impact of race; gender, class, geographical location, age, and other social factors influence interracial relationship formation and marital patterns (Schwartz and Scott 2003: 251).

### Resisting and Embracing Particular Racial Combinations

Although several combinations of interracial coupling exist, some pairings endure more scrutiny or are more visible than others that fly under the radar. The differences in scrutiny and visibility motivate me to wonder, "If my father was a different race, Asian maybe, and I then was Asian/White, would the waiter have made the same mistake? Would he have expressed a similar resistance to such an interracial family, or would our race mixing have gone relatively unnoticed or remained unimportant?"

I ask these questions to highlight how skin color matters, along with several other social positions, in our everyday lives. With some scholars arguing about the "honorary white" status of light-skinned Asians (i.e., Chinese, Japanese versus Indian, Cambodian) and Latinos (Cuban, Puerto Rican versus Dominican, Guatemalan) who selectively get read as white given their physical, social, cultural assimilation or approximation of whiteness, the statistics that reflect higher rates of intermarriage between these groups (White/Asian; White/Latino) seem unsurprising (Gallagher 2004; Hunter 2005). Additionally, the continual sociocultural devaluation of and distancing from blackness also provides partial explanation for the intermarriage rate of Blacks (which remains the lowest of all racial groups). The lingering polarization between racial groups, once understood as a white/black dichotomy, now exists as a not-black/black one, a strategy clearly operating to differentiate between the haves and the have-nots (or to maintain white/light skinned privilege, and the disadvantage of dark skin) (Dal-

mage 2004a; 2004b; Gans 2003; Herring, Keith, and Horton 2003; Hunter 2005; Yancey 2003). The selective inclusion of racial groups (besides Black) into whiteness can be understood as racial redistricting, a practice that again supports the claim that people work to cement this non-black/black distinction (Gallagher 2004).

### Dating, Mating, and Marriage

Since dating has attracted more scholarly attention in recent decades, sociologists have discovered that individuals increasingly date for sociability, recreation, and entertainment, rather than an immediate shared goal of marriage (Schwartz and Scott 2003; Ramu 1989). Given this potential difference in the value of dating versus marriage, people generally express less reluctance about interracial romance in dating than in marriage. Thus, marriage continues to be a more privileged institution, possibly because this form of commitment comes with changes in individual rights, changes that do not occur during dating. Perhaps they perceive the stakes of dating to be lower, but in any case, according to "a recent survey by George Yancey, more than one-half of African-, Hispanic-, and Asian-American adults have dated someone from a different racial group, and even more of those who have lived in integrated neighborhoods or attended integrated schools have done so. Most dates, of course, are casual and do not lead to serious commitments, and this is especially true for interracial dating" (Qian 2005: 33–34; Yancey 2002). A 1997 *USA Today*/Gallup poll similarly found that a higher number of teens indicate that they support interracial dating over marriage (support that dwindles as people approach 30), whether in theory (30%) or in practice (57%) (Joyner and Kao 2005).

This issue of theory (the hypothetical) versus practice (the actual) highlights a potential disconnect between attitudes and behavior, or more simply, what people say that they might do, and what they actually do. More Americans will socially or publicly support or express no objection to racial intermarriage but few choose to enter such a marriage. Given that almost two out of three of White people express approval of interracial marriage (Tyson 1997), and about 5 percent of all Americans actually racially intermarry, a huge and quizzical gap exists between racial attitudes and behavior. What might explain this disconnect? Here enters yet another American paradox, this one existing in a time of blissfully trumpeted colorblindness.

People quickly disregard or dismiss race as unimportant (love is all that matters) in partner choice where others are concerned, but when the choice is a personal one, people more readily notice racial difference and its importance. As a result, they oppose intermarriage for themselves and close relatives, but not for others. This inconsistency between attitudes and behavior makes further sense when we consider the often severe consequences for crossing the color line. Many people have learned through various forms of social, physical, and cultural regulation, that interracial attraction and intimacy remain taboo. This regulation, often experienced in the form of "border patrolling," attempts to maintain false differences between races and promote the practice of racial homogamy by policing and regulating people's romantic interest in and involvement with racially different others (Dalmage 2000).

Whether subtly or directly communicated or expressed, border patrolling remains indicative or suggestive of the social and sexual taboos against race mixing that exist in this society. But why, decades after the U.S. Congress, in its 1967 *Loving v. Virginia* case, declared anti-miscegenation unconstitutional, have these taboos remained? Why do people who so frequently express support publicly for interracial relationships and unions seldom form and maintain one of their own, particularly to the point of marriage? Why does the "just don't marry one" saying still ring true in a day and age when society seems so tolerant, if not accepting, of interracial romance? Or have things really changed?

First, we must acknowledge the structural forces/factors shaping interracial social contact, factors that help and/or hinder the amount of meaningful social interactions racially different people have in a racially divisive society. Then, we must acknowledge social sexual scripts that rely on and perpetuate stereotypes of various groups. Finally, we must recognize the individual influences that encourage or discourage people to cross the color line: the human agency that people possess in deciding whether to be seduced by potentially harmful and misleading stereotypes or to resist or critique them by crossing racial borders in social, sexual, and/or romantic relationships.

In several different arenas, scholars have illustrated how structural barriers have been erected that prohibit or impose limitations on the kinds of social contact racially diverse groups of people might otherwise have with one another (Hacker 2003; Massey and Denton 1993; Moran 2001). These areas include housing, education, employment, religion, and recreation, just to name a few. Racial residential segregation, for example, whether chosen or subtly enforced, inhibits the sort of meaningful exchanges and sustained social interaction that might eventually evolve into intimate relationships. So these spatial layouts and designs strategically separate people, establish the framework for our friendly social interactions, outline the parameters of our social life, inform who we should consider neighbors, and by extension, friends, lovers, family. But the boundaries put in place and regulated through residential segregation do not stop there. Where people work, worship, recreate, or educate themselves also reflects the racial divisions of this society.

In addition to these prohibitive structural forces, more micro-level barriers exist to discourage sexual, romantic, and marital race mixing. Much like the lyrics in a song made popular in *West Side Story* advised, "stick to your own kind, one of your own kind," we learn through socialization processes and social interaction to heed this cautionary tale. The knitted brows, penetrating stares, and other concerned looks; the surprising questions, such as, "Are you two *together*?" or, "Is *he* your *boyfriend*?" or other expressions of disapproval painfully but powerfully remind people that there is a price to pay for rejecting societal expectations. Failure to follow the rules results in social, sexual, economic, and cultural penalties (ostracism, isolation, marginalization, etc.).

But perhaps we remain painfully aware of the consequences of crossing borders, and do so anyway; perhaps we are intoxicated and fascinated by racial difference, have an insatiable desire for such difference, and the sex keeps us coming back for more. Maybe we're gluttons for punishment; maybe we have fetishes that need to be embraced and explored. Maybe we have been seduced by the constant flow of images celebrating interracial intimacy, or ones that put black booties and white cuties (boobies?) on a pedestal. In the following section, I discuss some of the sexualized "controlling images" (Collins 2000) circulating in the media—images that inform and misinform us, but continually titillate and create or perpetuate social sexual scripts (racist, sexist stereotypes that inform how we understand people's sexuality), such as the myth of the submissive but sexually skillful Asian woman.

## A Sample of Social Sexual Scripts: Loose Black Women, Big Black Men, and Other Dangerous Myths

In addition to the existing racialized, gendered, and sexualized controlling images of black women (i.e., the Mammy, Sapphire, Jezebel, etc.) that suggest they are asexual, emasculating, domineering, oversexual or hypersexual, and lazy or economically dependent on others (or more generally, animalistic, aggressive, subhuman), other just as dubious but arguably "more sexually explicit" images can be added to the list: freaks, gold diggers, divas, and dykes (Stephens and Phillips 2003: 3). These updated labels cast black women as sexually insatiable (and always

available), money-grubbing, high maintenance, and independent to a fault (so much so that they presumably do not need men). Such controlling images may color interracial attractions to black women.

In relation to black male sexuality, Bogle (2002) discovered comparable controlling images which depict black men in similarly unflattering ways, including as a brutish black buck: "a barbaric black out to raise havoc . . . subhuman and feral . . . the nameless characters setting out on a rampage full of black rage" [black brute]; and/or as "big, baaddd niggers, oversexed and savage, violent and frenzied as they lust for white flesh" [black buck] (Bogle 2002: 13–14). These characterizations linger in cultural productions and racial representations. Yet updated versions of these racialized myths about black masculinity continue to emerge, casting black men as hypermasculine, hypersexual, thuggish, and aggressive animals. For black men, these controlling images suggest much about their purported sexual proclivity, promiscuity, aggression, and inclination towards violence. Angela Y. Davis (1981) develops this line of critical inquiry in her work, arguing that the prevalence of images of black male rapists, and similarly racist and sexist depictions remain problematic and arguably adversely impact social and sexual interracial relationships.

Controlling images of Latinos/as proliferate as well, with the more prevalent ones relating their hypersexuality. Latinos get cast as pleasure-seeking, and villainous, characteristically "bad boys" oozing sexuality and constantly on the prowl. Similarly, Latinas are depicted as "lusty and hot-tempered," sexually titillating, and as nymphomaniacs who passionately pursue sexual activity and possess an "erotic combination of characteristics" such as "suavity and sensuality, tenderness and sexual danger." Latinas are represented as "mysterious, virginal, inscrutable, aristocratic—and alluring precisely because of these characteristics" (Berg 1997: 112–114).

Some controlling images of Asians include asexuality or a feminization of both women and men. More specifically, Asian men are effectively emasculated, neutered, castrated, or rendered sexually deviant, then disqualified for their supposed inability to sexually satisfy, especially in comparison to white men. Conversely, Asian women are seen as sexually skillful, mysterious, cunning, servile, erotic, exotic, "sensuous, promiscuous, but untrustworthy" (Espiritu 2000: 93). Their uberfemininity makes Asian feminized masculinity more noticeable and evident in its various media manifestations.

What controlling images of whites exist? As Patricia Hill Collins and others explicate, whites often construct these images, since they largely control their creation or production (Collins 2000). Conversely, in this control of the media, the number of racialized and gendered representations of whites remains high, so the different depictions operate more as competing, rather than controlling, images. This occurs because of the wide variation of whiteness that emerges in the media, variation that still favors, centers, and implicitly rewards a particular kind of whiteness, one that remains largely heteronormative and respects and reproduces the social expectations of homogeneity and homogamy. These hegemonic images cast white men as American, heterosexual, young, athletic, smart, and so forth, and white women are similarly American, heterosexual, often demure, pure, virginal, virtuous, and in need of appropriate male protection and security (Connell 1995).

The media also incorporates other images of whiteness, ones that compete for attention with and create contradictions when compared to more hegemonic and heteronormative images of whiteness. "Slutty white girls" and "goofy white guys" seemingly expand the characterizations of whites, but never to the degree of fully jeopardizing or compromising whiteness. The same may not be true for other racial groups, on the basis of the representations produced largely by the dominant group.

Nevertheless, other racial and ethnic groups have their own imagination about whites. As Es-

piritu (2000) and others have suggested, white women are seen as whores, sexually experimental and adventurous, not as virtuous as other dominant-group produced scripts suggest. However, because whites dominate and regulate the creation and dispersal of these controlling images, they may have more resources available to them to dismiss or counter any existing compromising images. Consequently, even when conflicting or competing images of whites exist, they seem to be less powerful and detrimental to whites in general, because of a racial hierarchy and social structures that generally privilege whites and position them at the top of society. The disparaging myths about all racial groups help us understand some of the obstacles to forming interracial relationships. Within the space of these racialized sexual scripts, however, the space for agency remains, where individuals can embrace or resist these narratives to some degree.

### Dating Exotic, Sleeping Erotic, Marrying Vanilla Plain Jane? The Bedroom Politics of Interracial Intimacy

*With reference to Brazil, as an old saying has it: "White woman for marriage, mulatto woman for f——, Negro woman for work," a saying in which, alongside the social convention of the superiority of the white woman and the inferiority of the black, is to be discerned a sexual preference for the mulatto. Gilberto Freyre,* The Masters and the Slaves

Sexual scripts and stereotypes inform people's views of others, and often enable them to fetishize others, or view them in special, unique, or exceptional ways. They motivate people to experiment or explore their curiosities about others without the sincerity to match or balance this misguided curiosity.

Many people want the freedom to fulfill their fetishes and find fun in the bedroom without the obligation of more permanent partnerships, commitments, or long-term relationship arrangements. This desiring of difference inspires individuals to "date exotic" (i.e., look liberal, progressive, and more interesting via the token person of color as a "different" date); "sleep erotic" (i.e., fulfill sexual fantasies with people society would otherwise frown on the individual being with); and finally "marry Vanilla Plain Jane" (i.e., settle down and follow the societal pattern of partnering long term with someone much like oneself). This typology of sorts exposes the ways we categorize people, placing them in sexually enjoyable and potentially exploitable positions, "fuckable not marriable," while proverbially putting others on a pedestal, preserving them as options for meeting mom and dad before wedding bells ring.

Kara Joyner and Grace Kao (2005) consider these differing articulations of commitment and highlight the importance of investigating single (dating) and cohabiting relationships, since rates of interracial marriage do not capture the complete picture of interracial intimacy. They posit that the social barriers to dating and cohabiting may be less intense than that to marriage. They also suggest that interracial fertility rates are increasing, even though interracial marriages are not. Interracial sex, then, does not undergo the sort of scrutiny that more public declarations and celebrations of intimacy and love, as expressed in marriage proposals and ceremonies, might. Quite possibly, a certain privacy (the bedroom) may protect interracial sexual intimacy from being directly policed in the way that more public displays of such intimacy might not enjoy, with pregnancy/mixed race babies being possible exceptions.

Interracial sex also seems to shape marital partner preferences, such that "women are more likely to select husbands across racial lines if they select first sex partners across these lines" (Joyner and Kao 2005: 564). Sadly, this lends credence to such sayings as, "Once you go black, you never go back," "Once you go white, you just might," or "Once you go Asian, you don't go Caucasian." Optimistically, though, these sayings suggest that sexually gratifying and otherwise rewarding, fulfilling dating and mating experiences may more likely result in marriage. Couples with this experience may develop long-lasting and meaningful relationships because of or in spite of their racial differences.

## Concluding Remarks

Although controlling images and prevailing stereotypes might expose and inform people's perceptions of one another, they may also positively influence the potential formation of interracial relationships in instances where people's sexual curiosities develop into more meaningful and sustained relationships. Although evidence of interracial intimacy of varying degrees continues to accumulate slowly, people's resistance to norms of racial relationship homogamy and homogeneity will continue to inspire others to challenge these expectations and date, sleep with, or marry someone who satisfies in a variety of ways. For me, this resistance comes in multiple forms, and gets expressed in my own interracial relationships and on the T-shirts I imagine wearing, ones with sayings like, "I'm his daughter, not his lover" (for those inevitable trips to Florida when visiting my parents); "Everybody loves a mixed race girl;" or the one I'll wear when hanging out with my white boyfriend to curb and calm any anxieties and satisfy any suspicions, "Yes, he's my boyfriend, and yes, the sex is great." Do you think people could handle that?

## REFERENCES

Bogle, Donald. (2002). *Toms, Coons, Mulattoes, Mammies, and Bucks: An Interpretive History of American Film* (4th ed.). New York: Continuum.

Bonilla-Silva, Eduardo. (2004). "From Biracial to Tri-Biracial: The Emergence of a New Racial Stratification System in the United States" in *Skin Deep: How Race and Complexion Matter in the "Color-Blind" Era* (pp. 224–239). Cedric Herring, Verna Keith, and Hayward Derrick Horton (Eds.). Urbana: University of Illinois Press.

Collins, Patricia Hill. (2000). *Black Feminist Thought: Knowledge, Consciousness, and the Politics of Empowerment* (2nd ed.). New York: Routledge.

Coltrane, Scott. (2000). *Gender and Families*. Lanham, MD: Rowman and Littlefield Publishers.

Connell, R. W. (1995). *Masculinities*. Berkeley: University of California Press.

Dalmage, Heather M. (2000). *Tripping on the Color Line: Black-White Multiracial Families in a Racially Divided World*. New Brunswick, NJ: Rutgers University Press.

Dalmage, Heather M. (Ed.) (2004a). *The Politics of Multiracialism: Challenging Racial Thinking*. Albany: State University of New York Press.

Dalmage, Heather M. (Ed.) (2004b). "Protecting Racial Comfort, Protecting White Privilege" in *The Politics of Multiracialism: Challenging Racial Thinking* (pp. 203–218). Albany: State University of New York Press.

Davis, Angela Y. (1981). *Women, Race and Class*. New York: Random House.

Davis, Angela Y. (2003). *Are Prisons Obsolete?* New York: Seven Stories Press.

Davis, F. James. (1991). *Who Is Black? One Nation's Definition*. University Park: The Pennsylvania State University Press.

Espiritu, Yen Le. (2000). *Asian American Women and Men*. Lanham, MD: Alta Mira Press.

Gans, Herbert J. (2003). "The Possibility of a New Racial Hierarchy in the Twenty-First Century United States" in *Rethinking the Color Line: Readings in Race and Ethnicity* (2nd ed., pp. 588–604). Charles A. Gallagher (Ed.). New York: McGraw Hill.

Gallagher, Charles A. (Ed.) (2003). *Rethinking the Color Line: Readings in Race and Ethnicity* (2nd ed.). New York: McGraw Hill.

Gallagher, Charles A. (2004). "Racial Redistricting: Expanding the Boundaries of Whiteness" in *The Politics of Multiracialism: Challenging Racial Thinking* (pp. 59–76). Heather Dalmage (Ed.). Albany: State University of New York Press.

Hacker, Andrew. (2003). *Two Nations: Black and White, Separate, Hostile, Unequal*. New York: Scribner.

Herring, Cedric, Verna Keith, and Hayward Derrick Horton. (Eds.) (2003). *Skin Deep: How Race and Complexion Matter in the "Color-Blind" Era*. Urbana: University of Illinois Press.

Hunter, Margaret L. (2005). *Race, Gender, and the Politics of Skin Tone*. New York: Routledge.

Joyner, Kara and Grace Kao. (2005). "Interracial Relationships and the Transition to Adulthood" in *American Sociological Review* 70(4): 563–581.

Kalmijn, M. (Sep. 1993). "Trends in Black/White Intermarriage." *Social Forces* 72(1): 119–146.

Massey, Douglas and Nancy Denton. (1993). *American Apartheid: Segregation and the Making of the Underclass*. Cambridge, MA: Harvard University Press.

Moran, Rachel F. (2001). *Interracial Intimacy: The Regulation of Race and Romance*. Chicago: University of Chicago Press.

Qian, Zhenchao. (Fall 2005). "Breaking the Last Taboo: Interracial Marriage in America" in *Contexts* (pp. 33–37). Berkeley: University of California Press/American Sociological Association.

Ramu, G. N. (1989). "Patterns of Mate Selection" in *Family and Marriage: Cross-Cultural Perspectives* (pp. 165–178). K. Ishwaran (Ed.). Toronto: Wall and Thompson.

Root, Maria P. P. (Ed.) (1992). *Racially Mixed People in America*. Thousand Oaks, CA: Sage Publications.

Root, Maria P. P. (Ed.) (1996). *The Multiracial Experience: Racial Borders as the New Frontier*. Thousand Oaks, CA: Sage Publications.

Spain, Daphne. (1999). *America's Diversity: On the Edge of Two Centuries*. Washington, D.C.: Population Reference Bureau.

Stephens, Dionne P. and Layli D. Phillips. (Winter 2003). "Freaks, Gold Diggers, Divas, and Dykes: The Sociohistorical Development of Adolescent African American Women's Sexual Scripts" in *Sexuality and Culture* 7(1): 3–48.

Tyson, A. S. (1997). "Young Love Bridges Race Divide" in *Christian Science Monitor* 90(6): 1–4.

U.S. Census Bureau. (1998). *Statistical Abstract of the United States, 1998* (118th ed.). Washington, D.C.: U.S. Government Printing Office.

U.S. Census Bureau. (2000). "Interracial Marriage in the United States, 1999." *Statistical Abstract of the United States, 2000* (p. 51, Table 54). Washington, DC: U.S. Government Printing Office.

Yancey, George A. (Spring 2002). "Who Interracially Dates: An Examination of the Characteristics of Those Who Have Interracially Dated." *Journal of Comparative Family Studies* 33(2): 179–190.

Yancey, George A. (2003). *Who Is White? Latinos, Asians, and the New Black/Nonblack Divide*. Boulder, CO: Lynne Rienner Publishers.

# Influences of Culture on Asian Americans' Sexuality

**Sumie Okazaki**

**W**hile sharing their Asian ancestry and vestiges of Asian cultural heritage to varying degrees, Asian Americans comprise an ethnic minority group that defies simple characterizations. Consisting of approximately 4% of the total U.S. population, Asian Americans trace their roots to one or more of 28 Asian countries of origin or ethnic groups. The largest proportions of Asian Americans in 1990 were Chinese (24%) and Filipino (20%), followed by Japanese, Korean, and Asian Indian at approximately 11% to 12% each and Vietnamese at 9% (U.S. Bureau of the Census, 1993). However, the continuing influx of new immigrants from Southeast Asia and South Asia as well as from China and Korea provide a backdrop for diversity among Americans of Asian ancestry on important dimensions such as national origin, language, nativity, generational status, religion, acculturation to the mainstream American values and customs, and so on. The majority (66%) of Asian Americans in 1990 were born in foreign countries (U.S. Bureau of the Census, 1993).

The present review concerning the impact of Asian and Asian American cultures on sexuality will first examine aspects of various Asian cultural traditions and values that influence sexual attitudes and behavior among Asian Americans, then examine the available scientific literature in several major areas. . . . Most studies that are reviewed here do not specifically test the link between aspects of Asian or Asian American culture and sexual variables but instead use Asian American ethnicity as a proxy for culture.

## Cultural Roots

Sexuality is linked to procreation in most Asian cultures. Gupta (1994) argues that sexuality was not a taboo subject in ancient Hindu culture granted that it was discussed within the context of marriage. Rather, sexuality was openly discussed in religious and fictional texts (e.g., the Kama Sutra) and depicted in paintings and sculptures, some with explicit erotic details. Japanese and Chinese erotica also date back to ancient times. On the other hand, sex is a taboo subject in contemporary Chinese culture, where sex education in schools is minimal and parents as well as health professionals are reluctant to discuss sexuality and sexual information (Chan, 1986). Traditional Cambodian society believed that a lack of knowledge regarding sexuality would prevent premarital sexual activity that would tarnish the family honor; consequently, discussions of information regarding sexual intercourse and sexuality were kept to a minimum (Kulig, 1994). Filipino culture, with the strong influence of Catholicism, tends to have a strong moral undercurrent that scorns premarital sex, use of contraceptives, and abortion (Tiongson, 1997).

Regardless of each Asian culture's degree of openness surrounding sexual discourse, expressions of sexuality outside of marriage are

From Okazaki, Sumie. 2002. "Influences of Culture on Asian American's Sexuality." *Journal of Sex Research* 39: 34–41. Reprinted by permission from the Society for the Scientific Study of Sexuality.

considered highly inappropriate in most Asian cultures. Most Asian cultures are highly collectivistic and patriarchical; thus, sexuality that is allowed open expression (particularly among women) would represent a threat to the highly interdependent social order as well as to the integrity of the family. Many Asian cultural traditions place emphasis on propriety and the observance of strict moral and social conduct, thus modesty and restrained sexuality are valued (Abraham, 1999). The sexually conservative beliefs and behavior that many Americans of Asian ancestry may exhibit may, in turn, be misinterpreted by the larger American society as asexual (Tsui, 1985).

### Sexual Knowledge, Attitudes, and Norms

Available data regarding the sexual knowledge, attitudes, and norms among Asian Americans reflect relative conservatism. In a 1993 study in British Columbia comparing 346 Asian Canadian and 356 non-Asian Canadian[1] university students enrolled in introductory psychology courses, Meston, Trapnell, and Gorzalka (1998) found that Asian Canadians held more conservative sexual attitudes and demonstrated less sexual knowledge than non-Asian Canadians. Among Asian Canadians, the more acculturated they were to the Canadian culture the more permissive their sexual attitudes. . . .

There are some data suggesting that Asian Americans' sexually conservative attitude may erode with higher degrees of exposure to the American culture. Abramson and Imai-Marquez (1982) . . . found that each subsequent younger generation of Japanese Americans and White Americans reported less guilty thoughts and feelings concerning sexual matters, although Japanese Americans still reported more sex guilt than White Americans within each age cohort group. However, in a different study of 18 Japanese American, 22 Mexican American, 20 African American, and 27 White American parents in Los Angeles regarding their attitudes toward sex

education, the attitudes of Japanese American parents were found not to differ from those of other ethnic group parents once father's education and mother's religiosity were controlled for (Abramson, Moriuchi, Waite, & Perry, 1983). Notably, all of the Japanese American parents were born in the U.S.

### Sexual Behavior

Most studies of sexual activity among Asian Americans have been conducted with adolescents and college students. The most comprehensive survey of American adults' sexual behavior, the National Health and Social Life Survey conducted in 1992, did not oversample Asian American individuals (Laumann, Gagnon, Michael, & Michaels, 1994). Consequently, only 2% of the total sample was Asian American, making it difficult to sufficiently characterize the sexual behavior of Asian American (particularly female) adults in the general population.

#### Adolescents

In a survey of 2,026 high school students in Los Angeles County, Asian American adolescents (*n* = 186) were more likely to be virgins (73%) than African American (28%), Latino (43%), and White Americans (50%) (Schuster, Bell, & Kanouse, 1996). Further analyses of the same data revealed that Asian American adolescents were less likely to have initiated a vaginal intercourse at an early age and were less likely to report having participated in other heterosexual genital sexual activities during the prior year than their non-Asian counterparts as well (Schuster, Bell, Nakajima, & Kanouse, 1998). The researchers found that Asian American nonvirgins also reported the lowest number of lifetime partners for vaginal intercourse, even though the reported frequency of sexual activity did not differ from those of other ethnic group adolescents. Asian American adolescents in homes where English is the primary language spoken were more likely than other Asian Americans to be nonvirgins and to have engaged in heterosexual genital sexual activities. Asian American adolescents were also more likely than non-Asian Americans to think that their parents and friends would disapprove if they had vaginal intercourse and that people their own age should not have vaginal intercourse.

Another study of an ethnically diverse sample of 877 Los Angeles County youths (Upchurch, Levy-Storms, Sucoff, & Aneshensel, 1998) found that Asian American males had the highest median age of first sex (18.1) and that Asian American females (as well as Hispanic females) had rates of first sex that was about half that of White females. Finally, an analysis of the national Youth Risk Behavior Survey data (total $N = 52,985$) collected by the Centers for Disease Control and Prevention (Grunbaum, Lowry, Kann, & Pateman, 2000) also found that Asian American high school students were significantly less likely than Black, Hispanic, or White students to have had sexual intercourse or to have had four or more sex partners. Only 28% of Asian American students reported lifetime experience of sexual intercourse compared to 77% of Black, 55% of Hispanic, and 48% of White students. However, among those who were currently sexually active, Asian American students were found to be as likely as other groups to have used alcohol or drugs during last sexual intercourse or to have used a condom at last intercourse. It should be noted that there is variability among Asian ethnic groups with respect to sexual behavior. Horan and DiClemente (1993) reported that among 11th and 12th grade students in San Francisco, only 13% of Chinese American students were sexually active but 32% of Filipino students were sexually active.

## College Students

The patterns found with Asian American adolescents also extend to college students. In a 1982 survey of 114 Chinese American college students in northern California (60% of whom were U.S.-born), Huang and Uba (1992) found that the majority (over 60%) approved of premarital sexual intercourse when partners are in love or engaged

to be married; however, only 37% of the men and 46% of the women surveyed had ever engaged in coitus. In this sample, Chinese American women were generally more sexually experienced than men, with more women having engaged in kissing, necking, and petting, although men ($M = 18.5$) and women ($M = 18.8$) did not differ in age of first vaginal intercourse experience. There was a positive correlation between the level of acculturation to the U.S. and engagement in premarital sexual intercourse, and those Chinese Americans dating only White Americans consistently had more sexual experience than those dating only Chinese Americans. Huang and Uba concluded that Chinese American college students were not avoiding premarital sex because they do not find it permissible. Rather, the authors speculated that Chinese Americans' sexual behavior and gender differences may reflect internalized racism (e.g., less positive body images), more conservative standards for engaging in premarital sexual relations, and racialized stereotypes of Asian American men as asexual and undesirable sexual partners.

In a 1987–1988 survey of 153 Asian American college students in Southern California (half of who were born in the U.S.), Cochran, Mays, and Leung (1991) found that 44% of the men and 50% of the women had engaged in heterosexual sexual intercourse at least once. The rate of Asian Americans who were sexually active (47%) was significantly lower than their age cohorts in other ethnic groups. Among those who were sexually active, the rates of engagement in oral sex was high (86% for women, 75% for men). In an analyses of their 1993 data on 346 Asian and 356 non-Asian Canadian college students, Meston, Trapnell, and Gorzalka (1996) found significant and substantive ethnic differences in all measures of interpersonal sexual behavior (i.e., light and heavy petting, oral sex, intercourse) and interpersonal sexual behavior (i.e., frequency of fantasies, masturbation incidence and frequency, and ideal frequency of intercourse), and all sociosexual restrictiveness measures (e.g., lifetime number of partners, number of partners in the past year, predicted number of partners, lifetime number of one-night stands). Overall, 35% of Asian Canadian college students in this survey reported having experienced intercourse. This study did not find any differences among Asian Canadians in their sexual behavior according to their length of residency in Canada.

A survey of 148 White American and 202 Asian American college students in Southern California (McLaughlin, Chen, Greenberger, & Biermeir, 1997) also found that Asian American men (over 55%) and women (60%) were significantly more likely than White American men (25%) and women (< 30%) to be virgins. Among those who were sexually experienced, Asian American men ($M = 2.3$) and women ($M = 2.2$) reported fewer lifetime sexual partners than White American men ($M = 5.5$) and women ($M = 3.5$). Within the Asian American sample, women from least acculturated families were more likely to be virgins (77%) than those from moderately or highly acculturated families (52% and 53%, respectively). This pattern did not hold for Asian American men. Of note, Asian Americans and White Americans endorsed casual sex to a similar degree even though the groups differed significantly in the number of partners. McLaughlin et al. interpreted this attitude-behavior inconsistency among Asian American college students as possibly reflecting the larger and more effective role that their parents play in controlling the adolescents' behavior.

In sum, the available data indicate that Asian Americans tend to be more sexually conservative than non-Asian Americans of the same age group, particularly with regard to the older age of initiation of sexual activity. One exception is a study by Sue (1982), who reported in a survey of 36 Asian American college students enrolled in a human sexuality course that rates of premarital sexual behavior did not differ from those of non-Asian students. However, Sue's anomalous data are likely the result of the selective nature of Asian American students who voluntarily enrolled in a human sexuality course. . . .

## Sexual Abuse and Aggression

The scope of sexual abuse in the Asian American community is unknown, as most state and national agencies that collect such data fail to segregate the data for Asian American victims. Where data are available, the reported incidence among Asian Americans appears relatively low compared to other ethnic groups, possibly due to their lack of access or reluctance to use mental health services and public agencies (Kenny & McEachern, 2000). However, many service providers assert that the actual incidence is much higher than reported (Okamura, Heras, & Wong-Kerberg, 1995). High rates of history of sexual victimization among Cambodian American refugees women and children, which they suffered during the Khmer Rouge reign of terror or at refugee camps, have been extensively documented (e.g., Mollica, Wyshak, & Lavelle, 1987; Rozée & Van Boemel, 1989; Scully, Kuoch, & Miller, 1995). In a study of abuse history among 102 Vietnamese Amerasian refugee young adults in the Philippine Refugee Processing Center who were awaiting placement in the United States, 12% of men and 9% of women reported having been sexually abused (McKelvey & Webb, 1995).

Those who work with Asian American communities speak of the Asian American victims' extreme reluctance to disclose or report sexual abuse or assault (Okamura et al., 1995; Tsuneyoshi, 1996). For example, most Southeast Asian refugees surveyed by Wong (1987) stated that they would respond to sexual abuse in their own family by keeping it a family secret. Further, sexual abuse within the context of marriage may be fatalistically tolerated among some Asian American communities. As, a result, immigrant Asian American women may be at a higher risk of marital sexual abuse than U.S.-born Asian American women because they may have been socialized to believe that they had fewer sexual rights than their husbands (Lum, 1998). An analysis of interviews with 25 South Asian immigrant women who were abused by their spouses found that

60% of the women reported being forced to have sex with their husbands against their will, and sexual abuse took many forms such as marital rape and violence and the husbands' control of women's reproductive choices (e.g., forcing the wife to get an abortion, refusal to allow the use of contraceptives, etc.) (Abraham, 1999). Similarly, an interview study with 150 immigrant Korean American women in Chicago revealed that 60% of the women reported being battered, and 37% of those who were physically abused also reported being forced to have sex by their partners (Song, 1996). . . .

Hall and Barongan (1997) noted that there appeared to be a lower prevalence of sexual aggression in Asian American communities. A national survey of sexual aggression found that fewer Asian American men perpetrate rape and fewer Asian American women are victims of rape than other ethnic groups (Koss, Gidycz, & Wisniewski, 1987). In their review of risk and protective factors for sexual aggression among Asian Americans, Hall, Windover, and Maramba (1998) argued that the patriarchical aspects of Asian culture, in which women hold subordinate status to men, may create a risk for, and a tolerance of, sexual aggression by Asian American men. On the other hand, Asian cultural emphases on self-control and interpersonal harmony may serve as protective factors for sexual aggressive behavior among Asian Americans. . . .

Other studies point to a possible role of Asian cultural factors in the attitudes toward sexual violence. For example, a study of 302 Asian American and White American college students (Mori, Bernat, Glenn, Selle, & Zarate, 1995) found that Asian Americans were more likely to endorse negative attitudes toward rape victims and greater belief in rape myths than their White counterparts. Moreover, less acculturated Asian Americans held more negative attitudes toward rape victims than more acculturated Asian Americans. A telephone survey about domestic violence attitudes with 262 Chinese Americans in Los Angeles County (Yick, 2000) found that although 89%

of the respondents agreed that sexual aggression constituted domestic violence, the respondents' gender role beliefs (traditional or egalitarian) emerged as a significant factor that shapes their definitions of abuse. In summary, certain facets of traditional Asian cultures (e.g., traditional gender roles, concerns about loss of face) appear to be implicated in Asian Americans' attitudes toward, reporting of, and perpetration of sexual abuse and aggression.

### Sexual Orientation

Little empirical research exists concerning sexual orientation and sexual identity among Asian Americans apart from the HIV-risk studies, although a body of scholarly work (largely in the humanities) regarding Asian American gay, lesbian, and bisexual identities and sexual orientation exists (e.g., Leong, 1994, 1996). One study of 13 Japanese American gay men revealed that only half of their respondents were open with their families regarding their gay identity (Wooden, Kawasaki, & Mayeda, 1983). In a survey of 19 women and 16 men (ages 21–36) who identified as both Asian American and lesbian or gay, Chan (1989) found that they tended to be more involved in social and political activities in the lesbian-gay community than in the Asian American community. More than half of the respondents (57%) reported being more comfortable in the lesbian/gay community than in the Asian American community and identified more strongly with the gay or lesbian aspects of their identity, although a minority of the respondents reported a synthesized ethnic and sexual identities. Although the majority (77%) had come out to a family member (e.g., sibling), only 26% had disclosed their gay identity to their parents because of fear of rejection.

Finally, in a study investigating whether cultural backgrounds moderate the relationship between sexual orientation and gender-related personality traits, Lippa and Tan (2001) found that participants from more gender-polarized cultural backgrounds (Hispanics and Asian Americans) showed larger homosexual-heterosexual differences in gender-related traits than White Americans for both men and women. That is, Hispanic and Asian American gay men assumed more feminine roles and Hispanic and Asian American lesbians assumed more masculine roles with respect to occupational and hobby preferences as well as self-ascribed masculinity and femininity. Hispanic and Asian American gays and lesbians were also found to fear social disapproval of their homosexuality more than their White counterparts. Taken together, the findings from the few existing studies on sexual orientation among Asian Americans suggest possible influences of cultural and community factors in their sexual identity, disclosure of homosexuality, and gender-related traits.

## Conclusion

Although there are significant gaps in the social science literature concerning Asian Americans' sexuality and sexual behavior, the existing data converge on notable differences between Asian Americans and other ethnic groups on major aspects such as sexual timetables and behaviors and attitudes surrounding sexuality, reproductive health, and sexual abuse. Many characteristics of the Asian Americans' sexual attitudes and behavior have significant implications for public health and clinical work. The next generation of empirical work must begin to test specific hypotheses regarding the Asian cultural characteristics as well as the impact of minority status on sexuality of Asian Americans.

### NOTES

Preparation of this manuscript was supported in part by a grant from the National Institute of Mental Health (MH-01506).

1. In this and all other studies conducted by Meston et al. (1996, 1997, 1999), individuals born in South Asia (India and Pakistan) were classified as non-Asians rather than Asians. (South Asians are considered in this review as Asians, following the convention in Asian American scholarship and the U.S. Census classification.) However, because South Asian Canadians typically constituted less than 3% of Meston et al.'s (1996, 1997, 1999) non-Asian samples, the results of their ethnic comparisons are likely to be reliable. The Asian Canadian group in their studies consisted primarily (70%) of ethnic Chinese.

### REFERENCES

Abraham, M. (1999). Sexual abuse in South Asian immigrant marriages. *Violence Against Women, 5,* 591–618.

Abramson, P. R., & Imai-Marquez, J. (1982). The Japanese-American: A cross-cultural, cross-sectional study of sex guilt. *Journal of Research in Personality, 16,* 227–237.

Abramson, P. R., Moriuchi, K. D., Waite, M. S., & Perry, L. B. (1983). Parental attitudes about sexual education: Cross-cultural differences and covariate controls. *Archives of Sexual Behavior, 12,* 381–397.

Chan, C. S. (1989). Issues of identity development among Asian-American lesbians and gay men. *Source Journal of Counseling & Development, 68,* 16–20.

Chan, D. W. (1986). Sex misinformation and misconceptions among Chinese medical students in Hong Kong. *Archives of Sexual Behavior, 19,* 73–93.

Cochran, S. D., Mays, V. M., & Leung, L. (1991). Sexual practices of heterosexual Asian-American young adults: Implications for risk of HIV infection. *Archives of Sexual Behavior, 20,* 381–391.

Grunbaum, J. A., Lowry, R., Kann, L., & Pateman, B. (2000). Prevalence of health risk behaviors among Asian American/Pacific Islander high school students. *Journal of Adolescent Health, 27,* 322–330.

Gupta, M. (1994). Sexuality in the Indian subcontinent. *Sexual & Marital Therapy, 9,* 57–69.

Hall, G. C. N., & Barongan, C. (1997). Prevention of sexual aggression: Sociocultural risk and protective factors. *American Psychologist, 52,* 5–14.

Hall, G. C. N., Sue, S., Narang, D. S., & Lilly, R. S. (2000). Culture-specific models of men's sexual aggression: Intra- and interpersonal determinants. *Cultural Diversity & Ethnic Minority Psychology, 6,* 252–267.

Hall, G. C. N., Windover, A. K., & Maramba, G. G. (1998). Sexual aggression among Asian Americans: Risk and protective factors. *Cultural Diversity & Ethnic Minority Psychology, 4*, 305–318.

Horan, P. F., & DiClemente, R. J. (1993). HIV knowledge, communication and risk behavior among White, Chinese-, and Filipino-American adolescents in a high-prevalence AIDS epicenter: A comparative analysis *Ethnicity & Disease, 3*, 97–105.

Huang, K., & Uba, L. (1992). Premarital sexual behavior among Chinese college students in the United States. *Archives of Sexual Behavior, 21*, 227–240.

Kenny, M. C., & McEachem, A. G. (2000). Racial, ethnic, and cultural factors of childhood sexual abuse: A selected review of the literature. *Clinical Psychology Review, 20*, 905–922.

Koss, M. P., Gidycz, C. A., & Wisniewski, N. (1987). The scope of rape: Incidence and prevalence of sexual aggression and victimization in a national sample of higher education students. *Journal of Consulting & Clinical Psychology, 55*, 162–170.

Kulig, J. C. (1994). Sexuality beliefs among Cambodians: Implications for health care professionals. *Health Cane for Women International, 15*, 69–76.

Laumann, E. O., Gagnon, J. H., Michael, R. T., & Michaels, S. (1994). *The social organization of sexuality: Sexual practices in the United States.* Chicago: The University of Chicago Press.

Leong, R. (Ed.) (1994). Dimensions of desire [Special issue]. *Amerasia Journal, 20*(1).

Leong, R. (Ed.) (1996). *Asian American sexualities: Dimensions of the gay and lesbian experience.* New York: Roudedge.

Lippa, R. A., & Tan, F. D. (2001). Does culture moderate the relationship between sexual orientation and gender-related personality traits? *Cross-Cultural Research, 35*, 65–87.

Lum, J. L. (1998). Family violence. In L. C. Lee & N. W. S. Zaire (Eds.), *Handbook of Asian American psychology* (pp. 505–525). Thousand Oaks, CA: Sage.

McKelvey, R. S., & Webb, J. A. (1995). A pilot study of abuse among Vietnamese Amerasians. *Child Abuse & Neglect, 19*, 545–553.

McLaughlin, C. S., Chen, C., Greenberger, E., & Biermeier, C. (1997). Family, peer, and individual correlates of sexual experience among Caucasian and Asian American late adolescents. *Journal of Research on Adolescence, 7*, 33–53.

Meston, C. M., Heiman, J. R., & Trapnell, P. D. (1999). The relation between early abuse and adult sexuality. *The Journal of Sex Research, 36*, 385–395.

Meston, C. M., Heiman, J. R., Trapnell, P. D., & Carlin, A. S. (1999). Ethnicity, desirable responding, and self-reports of abuse: A comparison of European- and Asian-ancestry undergraduates. *Journal of Consulting & Clinical Psychology, 67*, 139–144.

Meston, C. M., Trapnell, P. D., & Gorzalka, B. B. (1996). Ethnic and gender differences in sexuality: Variations in sexual behavior between Asian and non-Asian university students. *Archives of Sexual Behavior, 25*, 33–72.

Meston, C. M., Trapnell, P. D., & Gorzalka, B. B. (1998). Ethnic, gender, and length-of-residency influences on sexual knowledge and attitudes. *The Journal of Sex Research, 35*, 176–188.

Mollica, R., Wyshak, G., & Lavelle, J. (1987). The psychological impact of war trauma and torture on Southeast Asian refugees. *American Journal of Psychiatry, 144*, 1567–1571.

Mori, L., Bernat, J. A., Glenn, P. A., Selle, L. L., & Zarate, M. G. (1995). Attitudes toward rape: Gender and ethnic differences across Asian and Caucasian college students. *Sex Roles, 32*, 457–467.

Okamura, A., Heras, P, & Wong-Kerberg, L. (1995). Asian, Pacific Island, and Filipino Americans and sexual child abuse. In L. A. Pontes (Ed.), *Sexual abuse in nine North American cultures: Treatment and prevention* (pp. 67–93). Thousand Oaks, CA: Sage.

Rozée, P. D., & Van Boemel, G. (1989). The psychological effects of war trauma and abuse on older Cambodian refugee women. *Women & Therapy, 8*(4), 23–50.

Schuster, M. A., Bell, R. M., Nakajima, G. A., & Kanouse, D. E. (1998). The sexual practices of Asian and Pacific Islander high school students. *Journal of Adolescent Health, 13*, 221–231.

Schuster, M. A., Bell, R. M., Petersen, L. P., & Kanouse, D. E. (1996). Communication between adolescents and physicians about sexual behavior and risk prevention. *Archives of Pediatric and Adolescent Medicine, 150,* 906–913.

Scully, M., Kuoch, T, & Miller, R. A. (1995). Cambodians and sexual child abuse. In L. A. Fontes (Ed.), *Sexual abuse in nine North American cultures: Treatment and prevention* (pp. 97–127). Thousand Oaks, CA: Sage.

Song, Y. I. (1996). *Battered women in Korean immigrant families.* New York: Garland.

Sue, D. (1982). Sexual experience and attitudes of Asian American students. *Psychological Report, 51,* 401–402.

Tiongson, A. T., Jr. (1997). Throwing the baby out with the bathwater: Situating young Filipino mothers and fathers beyond the dominant discourse on adolescent pregnancy. In M. P. P. Root (Ed.), *Filipino Americans: Transformation and identity* (pp. 257–271). Thousand Oaks, CA: Sage Publications.

Tsui, A. M. (1985). Psychotherapeutic considerations in sexual counseling of Asian immigrants. *Psychotherapy, 22,* 357–362.

Tsuneyoshi, S. (1996). Rape trauma syndrome: Case illustration of Elizabeth, an 18-year-old Asian American. In F. H. McClure & E. Teyber (Eds.), *Child and adolescent therapy: A multicultural relational approach* (pp. 287–320). New York: Harcourt Brace College Publishers.

Upchurch, D. M., Levy-Storms, L., Sucoff, C. A., & Aneshensel, C. S. (1998). Gender and ethnic differences in the timing of first sexual intercourse. *Family Planning Perspectives, 30,* 121–127.

Urquiza, A. J., & Goodlin-Jones, B. L. (1994). Child sexual abuse and adult revictimization with women of color. *Violence & Victims, 9,* 223–232.

U.S. Bureau of the Census. (1993). *We the Americans: Asians.* Washington, DC: U.S. Government Printing Office.

Wong, D. (1987). Preventing child sexual assault among Southeast Asian refugee families. *Child Today, 16,* 18–22.

Wooden, W. S., Kawasaki, H., & Mayeda, R. (1983). Lifestyles and identity maintenance among gay Japanese-American males. *Alternative Lifestyles, 5,* 236–243.

Yick, A. G. (2000). Domestic violence beliefs and attitudes in the Chinese American community. *Journal of Social Service Research, 27,* 29–51.

# Sexual Desire in Later Life

John D. DeLamater

Morgan Sill

Human sexuality is generally an understudied area of scientific investigation, and researchers have been particularly neglectful of the study of sexuality in the aging population. Since the number of elderly persons in the U.S. doubled from nearly 17 million in 1960 to 35 million in 2000, and is projected to reach 53.7 million by 2020 (United States Bureau of the Census, 2002), this topic takes on particular importance.

Much of the prior research . . . assumes that as people age, physical changes, hormonal changes, or chronic illnesses reduce or eliminate sexual desire and sexual behavior. This literature reflects the general trend toward the medicalization of human sexual functioning, which has accelerated in the past 20 years (Tiefer, 2004). It overlooks psychological and social influences on sexuality. . . .

The purpose of this study is to examine how levels of sexual desire are associated with . . . biopsychosocial factors. . . . In particular, we wanted to determine whether sexual desire declines with age, and, if it does, identify which . . . factors are the main influences. We are especially interested in the impact of attitudes, which reflect the influence of cultural values and stereotypes.

## Sexual Desire

There is no universally accepted definition of sexual desire. Often it is confused with other as-

From DeLamater, John D. and Morgan Sill. 2005. "Sexual Desire in Later Life." *Journal* of *Sex Research* 42: 138–149. Reprinted by permission from the Society for the Scientific Study of Sexuality.

pects of human sexuality. In fact, sexual desire can be associated with sexual behavior but is simultaneously separate from it.

Theorists and researchers in the area of sexual desires have used two main frameworks. The first and most common assumes that sexual desire is an innate motivational force (i.e., an instinct, drive, need, urge, appetite, wish, or want). The second framework emphasizes the relational aspects of sexual desire, conceptualizing desire as one factor in a larger relational context. . . .

In this [reading], we have [defined] sexual desire in terms of cognitive events (sexual thoughts, sexual fantasies). Our concept of sexual desire is not associated with any overt sexual activity. We believe that thoughts and fantasies represent motivational aspects of sexual experience and therefore may serve as indirect measures of sexual desire (Sherwin, 1988).

## Biological Influences

*Age.* . . . Sexual behavior in women and men declines steadily from adolescence into older age, and to a lesser extent there is a [decline] in sexual desire (Maurice, 1999). Some researchers report that older adults continue to be interested in sex as long as poor health does not affect their sexual desire. . . .

*Hormones.* A second biological factor is sex hormones. It appears that sexual desire is influenced by androgens in men and by estrogens and androgens in women (American College of Obstetricians and Gynecologists, 2000). As one ages, there are many changes in the production and functioning of sex hormones (Morley, 2003). . . .

*Illness.* Chronic disorders, such as cardiovascular disease, diabetes, arthritis, and cancer, may have negative effects on sexual functioning and response (Maurice, 1999; Schiavi, 1999). These diseases impair sexual function both directly, by acting on physiological mechanisms . . . and reproductive structures, and indirectly, by limiting total body function.

Cardiovascular diseases . . . are commonly associated with sexual response problems (Schiavi, 1999). Many studies have reported a loss of sexual drive in as few as 10% to as many as 70% of patients after myocardial infarction (Papadopoulos, 1989). Studies on sexual behavior after a stroke report decreased levels in sexual desire (Angeleri, Angeleri, Foschi, Giaquinto, & Nolfe, 1993; Boldrini, Basaglia, & Calanca, 1991). . . .

Hypertension is prevalent among older adults, and it is also associated with peripheral vascular disease, myocardial infarction, and stroke (Schiavi, 1999). Although there are numerous studies on the sexual consequences of anti-hypertension treatment, there are few on sexual functioning in persons with these illnesses who are not receiving treatment (Schiavi).

Diabetes mellitus, which has vascular effects on blood vessels, is one of the most frequent systemic disorders associated with sexual problems in aging adults (Masters et al., 1994; Schiavi, 1999). . . .

Arthritis in aging adults is a major cause of discomfort and disability. It has often been assumed that those with arthritis have sexual difficulties, but this has seldom been systematically investigated (Schiavi, 1999). . . .

Prostate disease occurs frequently in aging men. It is the second most prevalent cancer, present in almost 90% of men ages 80 and older, and the second most common cause of death from cancer (Masters et al., 1994; Schiavi, 1999). Sexual dysfunction is a common complication of this disease and its treatment (Jakobsson, Loven, & Hallberg, 2001). . . .

*Medications.* Numerous prescription drugs have adverse effects on sexual functioning, including antidepressant and anti-hypertension medications. Moreover, adverse drug effects have been reported much more frequently in the aging population than in the general population (Wade & Bowling, 1986). . . .

Many prescription drugs cause sexual side effects. However, knowledge is limited by inadequate information on the specifics of drug action, such as how drugs are distributed, metabolized, excreted, and targeted in older persons, especially women. Medications may influence sexual responses, which include desire, by nonspecific effects on general well-being, energy level, and mood (Schiavi, 1999). . . .

## Psychological Influences

Psychological factors are major determinants of the intensity of sexual desire. Yura and Walsh (1983) state that attitudes, knowledge, and expectations of one's self and one's sexual partner impact personal behavior. Sexual attitudes, knowledge, and sexual experiences in earlier years are closely interwoven with sexual desire (Butler, Lewis, Hoffman, & Whitehead, 1994). Negative attitudes toward sex among older women and men are common (Story, 1989). In part, these attitudes reflect America's youth-oriented culture. American popular culture equates sex appeal with the characteristics of a youthful body, such as a firm body and smooth skin (Levy, 1994). Another contributor is the emphasis on reproduction. In populations where the primary purpose of sexual intimacy is seen as reproduction, it is considered inappropriate for a postmenopausal woman to continue to be sexually active (Deacon, Minichiello, & Plummer, 1995; Levy; Story). . . .

Sexuality is socially and culturally constructed (Irvine, 1990; Masters et al., 1994; Stock, 1984; Tiefer, 1991, 2004). Culture provides a set of expectations, beliefs, and attitudes about sexuality, and women and men draw on these to attach meaning to their experiences. In the U.S., aging women and men's sexuality is influenced by a cultural environment that is fraught with both ageism and sexism (Abu-Laban, 1981; Sanford, 1998; Shaw, 1994). Sociocultural factors work to minimize or deny the existence or value of sexuality for older persons (Gott & Hinchliff, 2003). . . .

The images available in U.S. society about sexuality and the aged are negative. Sex is seen as unseemly, even unnatural [for older people]. One elderly gentleman contended, "We're supposed to be asexual, and those who refuse to be so are branded dirty old men" (Stock, 1999, p. 51). The media bombards us with a plethora of sexual images, mainly those of young, energetic people. The sexuality of older women and men is rarely portrayed in a positive light (Brown, 1989; Levy, 1994). These images influence many older people's beliefs, leading to the conclusion that sex is only for the young and beautiful (Hillman & Stricker, 1994). These stereotypes and myths set in motion a self-fulfilling prophecy. Older people may withdraw from any form of sexual expression and ignore or suppress sexual desire because it is "sick," "unsuitable," or "wrong." According to Sloane (1993), many older women and men do feel asexual. . . .

Aging women and men with inadequate knowledge of sex and sexuality may be vulnerable to faulty expectations and concerns about performance (White & Catania, 1982). There is a widespread assumption that vaginal intercourse is the only "real sex" (Blank, 2000); therefore, if the person . . . is unable to have intercourse, he or she may lose interest in sex. To meet the challenge of maintaining sexual activity during the aging process, couples have to make love with what they have. Hands and mouths are reliable; penises and vaginas are not. However, it is common for couples to end their sexual lives together because one or both partners believe that an erection is necessary to "get the job done" or see non-coital sex as immoral or perverse (Blank; Cogen & Steinman, 1990; Levine, 1998).

## Relational Influences

The presence or absence of a sexual partner is an extremely important factor in understanding differing levels of sexual desire and activity among aging women and men. Many people consider sexual intimacy to be only or most appropriate in marriage (Levy, 1994). Many older persons are not married or no longer live with a spouse. . . .

Marriage is the most common social arrangement within which normative sexual activity takes place (Rossi, 1994; Schiavi, 1999). Thus, the death of a spouse usually leads to the cessation of sexual behavior (Rossi). Women tend to marry older men, which is a main reason that women are more likely to be widowed. Women outlive their mates, often by a decade or more (Sanford, 1998). . . .

Sex is important for many unmarried older adults, too (Masters et al., 1994). Some fulfill their desire for sexual intimacy within a long-term committed relationship. . . .

Household income is potentially an important social factor. Other things equal, an individual or couple with a higher income has access to health care and activities that may maintain general physical and mental health. Better health, in turn, is likely to be associated with sexual desire. . . .

## Method

### Study Population and Procedure

The American Association of Retired Persons' (AARP) *Modern Maturity* Sexuality Survey was a mail survey completed by 1,384 women and men ages 45 and older. . . . Potential respondents were told that "the purpose of the study is to better understand the role of sexuality in the lives of mid-life and older persons." . . .

The following research questions were addressed in this study:

1. What influences are related to low sexual desire in older women and men?

2. What biopsychosocial factors are the primary influences related to decreasing sexual desire? . . .

## Results

### Demographic Characteristics

. . . [In the sample, men] are more likely to be employed than women. The sample is primarily European-American. About 56% of the men and 64% of the women are married and living with a partner. . . .

### Sexual Desire

[M]en on average report slightly higher levels of desire than women. [Moreover, the] results show that there is a strong positive relationship between increasing age and low levels of sexual desire for both women and men. . . .

### Illness

High blood pressure is significantly related to low levels of sexual desire for both women and men. Nearly the majority of women and men who have been diagnosed with high blood pressure have [low] desire. . . .

Among men, we found that diagnosis of an enlarged prostate was related to low levels of desire. . . . Diagnoses of diabetes, arthritis, and depression were not significantly related to levels of sexual desire for women. A diagnosis of diabetes was not significantly related to levels of sexual desire for men.

### Medications

Regular use of four medications is significantly related to low levels of sexual desire in women. These prescription medications include anticoagulants, cardiovascular medications, medications to control elevated cholesterol, and medications for hypertension. . . . Among men, only reports of taking anticoagulants and medications for hypertension are significantly related to low levels of sexual desire. . . .

### Attitudes toward Sex

For women, . . . attitudes about sex in relationships are significantly correlated with desire; women who strongly agree that sexual activity is important to their quality of life and their relationships [have higher levels of] . . . desire. . . . [W]omen who . . . do not enjoy sex and . . . would be happy never having sex again have lower desire. . . . The results are similar for men. . . .

### Partner Presence/Marital Status

The survey included a [question on] marital status and a question asking whether the respondent had a sexual partner. . . .

For women, having a sexual partner is . . . related to [higher] level[s] of sexual desire. . . . For men the correlation is much smaller. . . . The impact of a partner on one's sexual desire depends in part on the characteristics of the partner. Each participant who reported having a partner was asked whether the partner had any physical or emotional limitations "which restrict your sexual activity." . . . The relationship [of partner limitations to reduced sexual activities] is much stronger for women . . . than for men. . . .

### Household Income

The data show that household income is [correlated] with [higher levels of] sexual desire . . . both in women . . . and in men. . . . Thus, older persons with greater income experience higher levels of desire.

In summary, the . . . results indicate that among women, age, high blood pressure, prescription medications, negative attitudes toward sexuality, absence of a sexual partner, and low household income are correlated with low sexual desire. . . .

Among men . . . age, high blood pressure, enlarged prostate, anticoagulants and medications for hypertension, presence of a sexual partner, negative attitudes toward sexual activity, and [low household] income were all . . . correlated with . . . [low levels of] sexual desire.

*Presence of a Sexual Partner by Age and Gender*

| AGE | % WOMEN (N = 737) | % MEN (N = 635) |
|---|---|---|
| 45–49 | 83.12 | 83.46 |
| 50–54 | 76.72 | 82.08 |
| 55–59 | 71.13 | 88.24 |
| 60–64 | 65.91 | 87.80 |
| 65–69 | 50.62 | 73.61 |
| 70–74 | 40.48 | 74.51 |
| 75–79 | 27.12 | 79.25 |
| 80–84 | 21.05 | 44.83 |
| 85–89 | 0.00 | 57.14 |
| 90–94 | 25.00 | — |

## Discussion

This study explored biopsychosocial factors, including age, illness, medication use, attitudes, marital status, presence or absence of a sexual partner, and household income, in relation to sexual desire in a representative sample of women . . . and men . . . over the age of 45.

### Age

The results indicate that age is significantly associated with desire. . . . Sexual desire decreases as women and men age. However, sexual desire does not decrease as fast as popular belief dictates. In our study, it is not until age 75 or older that the majority of women and almost a majority of men report a low level of sexual desire.

### Illnesses and Medications

Although being diagnosed with some illnesses and reports of taking medications to lower cholesterol were negatively correlated with desire, these predictors were not significant . . . for men. . . . Women who report taking a greater variety of medications in the two weeks prior to the survey have lower desire. . . . Women who report hav-

ing been diagnosed with more illnesses also have lower desire. . . . [R]elatively few participants report taking those medications thought to affect desire. Although these drugs, such as drugs for high blood pressure, may substantially affect those who take them, their use is not widespread. Thus, biological factors have a modest effect on female sexual desire.

### Attitudes toward Sex

Negative attitudes toward sex are correlated with low sexual desire. . . . [R]ating sex as important to one's self was associated positively and substantially with desire. . . . Rating sex as important to one's relationships was also a significant predictor of desire. . . . The effects of attitudes are larger than the effects of any other predictor included in our analyses except age.

### Education

Education was significantly related to desire for both men and women. . . . We believe that attitudes mediate much of the relationship between education and desire. Greater education may undermine the negative stereotypes of sexual expression by older persons.

## Presence of Partner

Even though sexual desire remains intact in healthy older persons, they need a partner, especially an interested partner, in order to continue partnered sexual activities, and for some, to continue having sexual desire. The absence of a partner or an interested partner can be an obstacle for many. In our study, having a partner is a significant predictor of desire among women but not among men. . . . What is surprising is that the majority of men with a low level of desire have a partner. Also, whether the partner has limitations that affect the respondent's sexual activity is related to reports of desire by women but not by men. These results suggest that a woman's desire is attuned to her relationship context, but a man's desire is not. . . .

Across this sample of persons 45 and older, the principal influences on sexual desire are age and the importance of sex to the person. For women, having a partner, taking medications and being diagnosed with illnesses also play a modest role. These results suggest that stereotypes of older persons as not interested in sexual intimacy are wrong. They also suggest that negative attitudes about sexual activity among older persons need to be challenged so that future cohorts are not influenced by such attitudes. It is particularly important that health care professionals not convey negative attitudes to older patients. Finally, we should scrutinize economic and residential arrangements for the elderly and structure them to facilitate rather than hinder intimate relationships. . . .

## NOTE

We gratefully acknowledge the American Association of Retired Persons for giving us access to the data from AARP/Modern Maturity Sexuality Survey, 1999, conducted for AARP by NFO Research, Incorporated.

## REFERENCES

Abu-Laban, S. (1981). Women and aging: A futurist perspective. *Psychology of Women Quarterly, 6,* 85–99.

American Association of Retired Persons. (1997). *A profile of older Americans: 1996.* Washington, DC: Author.

American College of Obstetricians and Gynecologists. (2000). Androgen treatment of decreased libido. *ACOG Committee Opinions, 96* (5 part 1), 1–2.

Angeleri, F., Angeleri, V., Foschi, N., Giaquinto, S., & Nolfe, G. (1993). The influence of depression, social activity, and family stress on functional outcome after stroke. *Stroke, 24,* 1478–1483.

Blank, J. (Ed.). (2000). *Still doing it. Women and men over 60 write about their sexuality.* San Francisco: Down There Press.

Boldrini, P., Basaglia, N., & Calatrca, M. (1991). Sexual changes in hemiparetic patients. *Archives of Physical Medicine and Rehabilitation, 72,* 202–207.

Brown, L. (1989). Is there sexual freedom for our aging population in long-term care institutions? *Journal of Gerontological Social Work, 13,* 75–90.

Butler, R., Lewis, M., Hoffman, E., & Whitehead, E. (1994). Love and sex after 60: How to evaluate and treat the sexually active woman. *Geriatrics, 49*(11): 33–42.

Cogen, R., & Steinman, W. (1990). Sexual function and practice in elderly men of lower socioeconomic status. *Journal of Family Practice, 31,* 162–166.

Deacon, S., Minichiello, V., & Plummer, D. (1995). Sexuality and older people: Revisiting the assumptions. *Educational Gerontology, 21,* 447–513.

Gott, M., & Hinchliff, S. (2003). Sex and aging: A gendered issue? In S. Arber, K. Davidson, & J. Ginn (Eds.), *Gender and aging: Changing roles and relationships.* Buckingham: Open University Press.

Hillman, J., & Stricken, G. (1994). A linkage of knowledge and attitudes toward elderly sexuality: Not necessarily a uniform relationship. *The Gerontologist, 34*(2), 256–260.

Irvine, J. (1990). *Disorders of desire: Sex and gender in modern American sexology.* Philadelphia, PA: Temple University Press.

Jakobsson, L., Loven, L., & Hallberg, I. (2001). Sexual problems in men with prostate cancer in comparison with men with benign prostatic hyperplasia and men from the general population. *Journal of Clinical Nursing, 10*(4), 573–592.

Levine, S. (1998). *Sexuality in mid-life.* New York: Plenum Press.

Levy, J. (1994). Sex and sexuality in later life stages. In A. S. Rossi (Ed.), *Sexuality across the life course* (pp. 287–309). Chicago: University of Chicago Press.

Masters, W., Johnson, V., & Kolodny, R. (1994). *Heterosexuality.* New York: Harper Collins.

Maurice. W. (1999). *Sexual medicine in primary care.* New York: Mosby.

Morley, J. (2003). Hormones and the aging process. *Journal of the American Geriatrics Society, 51*(7 Supplement), S333–S337.

Papadopoulos, C. (1989). Coronary artery disease and sexuality. In *Sexual medicine: Vol. 10. Sexual aspects of cardiovascular disease* (pp. 1–22). New York: Praeger.

Rossi, A. S. (Ed.). (1994). *Sexuality across the life course.* Chicago: University of Chicago Press.

Sanford, W. (Ed.). (1998). *Our bodies, ourselves for the new century.* New York: Simon & Schuster.

Schiavi, R. (1999). *Aging and male sexuality.* Cambridge: Cambridge University Press.

Shaw, J. (1994). Aging and sexual potential. *Journal of Sex Education and Therapy, 20,* 134–139.

Sherwin, B. (1988). A comparative analysis of the role of androgen in human male and female sexual behavior: Behavioral specificity, critical thresholds, and sensitivity. *Psychobiology, 16,* 416–425.

Sloane, E. (1993). *Biology of Women.* Milwaukee, WI: Delmar Publishers.

Stock, R. W. (1999, September-Octobtr). Lost and found. *Modern Maturity, 42*(5), 50–53.

Stock, W. (1984). Sex roles and sexual dysfunction. In C. S. Widom (Ed.), *Sex roles and psychopathology* (pp. 311–328). New York: Plenum.

Story, M. (1989). Knowledge and attitudes about the sexuality of older adults among retirement home residents. *Educational Gerontology, 15*(5), 515–526.

Tiefer, L. (1991). Historical, scientific, clinical and feminist criticisms of "The Human Sexual Response Cycle" model. *Annual Review of Sex Research, 2,* 1–24.

Tiefer, L. (2004). *Sex is not a natural act, and other essays,* 2nd ed. Boulder, CO: Westview Press.

United States Bureau of the Census. (2002). Current Population Report, P-20–547. Retrieved June 30, 2004 from http://www.census.gov/population/www/socdemo/hh-fam/cps2002.html.

Wade, B., & Bowling, A. (1986). Appropriate use of drugs by elderly people. *Journal of Advanced Nursing, 11,* 47–55.

White, C., & Catania, J. (1982). Sexual interest, attitudes, knowledge, and sexual history in relation to sexual behavior in the institutionalized aged *Archives of Sexual Behavior, 11,* 11–21.

Yura, H., & Walsh, M. (1983). *Human needs and the nursing process.* Norwalk, CT: Appleton-Century-Croft.

reading 37

# A Down Low
# Dirty Shame

Joshunda Sanders

Late in 2003, the Centers for Disease Control and Prevention released a study showing that black women accounted for 72 percent of all new HIV cases, and that they were most likely to contract the disease from heterosexual men. But additional data collected by the CDC also found that a "significant number" of black men who sleep with men identify as heterosexual, and that black women at risk "may not be aware of their male partners' possible risks for HIV infection such as . . . bisexuality."

While there have always been closeted gay men and men living so-called double lives, the supposed trend of black men who hide their homosexual encounters from unsuspecting wives and girlfriends—termed "living on the down low"—has recently [attracted considerable media attention].

In 1991, E. Lynn Harris published *Invisible Life,* a novel about a man on the DL [down low] who infects his girlfriend with HIV, and since then a smattering of articles on the topic have appeared, including a lengthy 2003 *New York Times Magazine* profile of the flourishing DL scene in Columbus, Ohio. It was in 2004, though, that mainstream forums from Oprah to *The New York Times* to *Essence* to the *Advocate* took on the topic in earnest; the subject even made it onto an episode of *Law & Order.* As a hot topic, the

From Sanders, Joshunda. 2005. "A Down Low Dirty Shame: The New Assault on Black Male Sexuality." *Bitch* 28(Spring): 33–35, 91. Reprinted by permission.

DL is tailor-made: Widespread publicizing of alarming disease statistics like the CDC's . . . , coupled with the timely emergence of a media-savvy DL poster boy and a generous sprinkling of Oprah's magic, have turned the down low into a downright phenomenon.

In April 2004, a convenient few months after the CDC's bombshell, Chicago native J. L. King released his first-person account of living on the DL. *On the Down Low: A Journey into the Lives of "Straight" Black Men Who Sleep with Men* not only positioned King—who for years had been an anonymous source on the DL lifestyle for mainstream media—as a bona fide expert, but inspired a full-blown media exploration of the trend. The book centers around King's [encounters] with men while he was married, and is peppered with CDC statistics and a dash of irresponsible assertions ("Women involved with DL men are being infected with HIV because these men do not believe in wearing condoms and they don't know their HIV status"). King also details how both his relationship with god and his concern for the type of man his daughter would marry led him to write the book, and then launches into flashback tales about sleeping with a married man from his church and hooking up with a (male) preacher.

King's tale of well-orchestrated deception, which quickly hit the bestseller list, was generally treated as a self-help book—and accepted as gospel, despite the lack of statistical information to back up his pronouncements about seemingly straight black men. When, in April 2004, the Queen of Talk herself tried to get some concrete answers from King, he dodged even her. Discussing the "secret fraternity" of men who sleep with men, Oprah asked:

*Winfrey:* How big is this fraternity?

*King:* This invisible population, if you just look at the numbers, if you look at 68 percent of all new cases, I'm even surprised sometimes when I meet a DL brother. It blows me away when a brother comes up to me or I find out that he's on the DL. We're like, "How—you're on the DL, too?"

*Winfrey:* Well, how does one know who is and who isn't?

*King:* We do it by the—we do it by the eyes.

*Winfrey:* You do it by the eyes.

*King:* We do it by the eyes. You know, I wrote a chapter about the signs.

*Winfrey:* Yes, you did. Yeah.

Though data from the *American Journal of Public Health,* among others, suggests that men of all ethnicities engage in DL sex, black men are the group most likely to live life on the down low. Because black men have been more marginalized in the economic, educational, and social spheres than other men, researchers say, they tend to be more hesitant to surrender what they may consider a crucial and defining element of their masculinity—heterosexual sex—by defining themselves as bisexual or homosexual. This behavior is nothing new, of course, but with the advent of HIV/AIDS it's taken on a different meaning.

In the '80s, as inner-city black neighborhoods were saturated with crack cocaine and President Reagan responded with a war on drugs, millions of young black men were sent to jail. It's suspected that, while serving harsh sentences, some men participated—willingly or not—in the don't-ask-don't-tell, sex-as-power-brokering culture of the prison-industrial complex. Since condoms aren't exactly placed on your pillow in the pen, it makes sense that at least some of the ubiquity of both DL behavior and HIV infection originated behind bars. Other significant contributing factors are the rampant—and for the most part accepted—homophobia in the black community,

the overwhelming silence of most black churches around HIV and sexuality, and widespread misinformation about HIV.

But rather than use the troubling CDC statistics and memoirs like King's as a chance to open up a potentially painful yet necessary dialogue about race, sexuality, and behavior, the media, as usual, seized upon the most sensationalistic aspects of the issue. The news stories that erupted in the wake of King's book resembled slipshod tabloid journalism far more than they did serious exploration of a social phenomenon: In most of the stories, men engaging in DL sex weren't characterized as complex human beings, but as sexual culprits and perpetrators of bad behavior; the women in their lives were presented as innocent pawns. The structure and substance of many articles centered around denial, the futility of prevention efforts, and the lack of sexual integrity in the black community. Many pieces focused on individual women who were shocked to discover, upon having blood rejected at the blood bank or being turned down for health insurance, that they had contracted HIV from their men. A lengthy 2003 *Orlando Sentinel* piece is a prime example: It profiled a woman who discovered she was HIV-positive during a blood test to determine her eligibility as a bone-marrow donor. When she realized she had contracted the virus from her husband, she became suicidal. The article suggested that the woman's husband was both a drug addict and on the down low. Though the article stated that the husband had no idea whether he'd contracted HIV from a man or a woman, the reporter went on to describe characteristic DL behavior in some detail. (Two weeks later, the paper ran a correction that would seem to nullify the whole story, saying the woman's husband had died in 1999 but had never tested positive for HIV.)

Many of these articles led with King's book, treating him as an HIV-prevention activist brave enough to come forward and tell his story. Taking their cues from King, journalists and TV producers pretty much agreed: Men on the DL—who were referred to mostly as "closeted bisexuals" and men who just had trouble coming out of the closet—were killing black women with their denial. "A New Kind of Brotherly Love" read one newspaper headline. Not juicy enough? *USA Today* got more specific, even if it missed the whole point: "The danger of living 'down low': Black men who hide their bisexuality can put women at risk." A two-part series in *Essence* was titled "Deadly Deception." It was never clear, in these . . . stories, whether the coverage was geared toward getting black women informed or simply preventing legions of men who have sex with men from ever telling the truth to anyone.

Still, a handful of publications—including *Newsweek, ColorLines,* and the *Village Voice*—turned out sensitive and respectable articles of their own on the subject, noting that many of King's claims were unsubstantiated. An April 2004 *New York Times* article profiled a group of black women who'd seen a musical about men on the DL and explored their resulting sense of urgency about it. Other pieces, including one in the *Denver Westword,* examined HIV-prevention classes or ways that information about the DL was changing the way black women felt about relationships.

The *ColorLines* article was one of the few to be penned by an out bisexual black man, without a pseudonym. In it, Juba Kalamka, a member of the queer hip hop group Deep Dickollective, shared a refreshingly astute view of black identity and sexuality:

> While gay and straight white academic communities and the popular media continued to engage in rote, inflammatory, sensational and racist demonizing of black sexuality, the black community, gay and straight, has not been able to get a handle on the discussion either. This failure is largely due to the dynamic overlap of homophobia and class privilege that has stunted most discussions of the way unchallenged patriarchy and sexism are integral to the experience of those on the DL and those they may infect.

Kalamka's article underscored two questions largely ignored in all the media coverage: Why hasn't the black community shed the idea of HIV as a gay white man's cross to bear, and why, even though blacks get the disease at a rate 11 times that of whites, do many still feel invincible in the face of it?

It's reasonable to conclude that the majority of media outlets aren't concerned with constructing a nuanced, ongoing dialogue about black sexuality and American culture. "It's just so irresistible for the press to have something to say about black men that is in some way demeaning or embarrassing," says Brenda Wade, a San Francisco-based psychologist and host of local TV show *Black Renaissance.* "One, it's about sex. But two, it's about the myth of the black man as a stud being blown apart. So people are saying, 'Ah ha! A lot of them are actually gay men.'" Black men—already vilified in the media and canonized in pop culture as immoral thugs, sexually insatiable mandingos, and big scary bogeymen—are easy targets when it comes to sensationalism. When those same black men are declared to be disease-infested vectors, the result is a psychoanalyst's playground. Wade, who wrote a practitioner's response to King's book for *Black Issues Book Review,* was one of the few levelheaded voices to emerge amidst the hysteria. She suggested that black folks [should] simply grow up, so that we can talk frankly about sexuality instead of sending men deeper into the closet.

What is lacking in all this coverage, according to Phill Wilson, executive director of the Black AIDS Institute in Los Angeles, is a real story, with real facts and numbers. Apart from Gary Dorsey's June 2004 article in the *Baltimore Sun,* which expressed some ambivalence about the tangible connection between the DL and HIV-infection rates in women, and the extent to which DL men were to blame for black women contracting the disease, few people have asked the important question: Just how many men are we talking about here? "No one has quantified this phenomenon," says Wilson. "We don't know if it's a big deal or a little deal; we don't know if it's 100 percent of black men or 1 percent of black men. And no one has done any research to ascertain whether men on the DL are indeed having unsafe sex with their male partners."

But lack of evidence hasn't stopped some publications from enhancing their arguments with shoddy reporting. *Jet* erroneously reported that 60 percent of black men who were having sex with newly infected black women were living on the DL. The *New York Times Magazine* article about the DL scene in Columbus, Ohio, devoted just two paragraphs to a connection between the DL and HIV in black women, and the statistics the reporter cited raise more questions than they answer:

> *While intravenous drug use is a large part of the problem, experts say that the leading cause of H.I.V. in black men is homosexual sex (some of which takes place in prison, where blacks disproportionately outnumber whites). According to the Centers for Disease Control, one-third of young urban black men who have sex with men in this country are H.I.V.-positive, and 90 percent of those are unaware of their infection.*

The most troubling aspect of the DL media frenzy is that it places the blame directly on men who sleep with men for a burden that is too big for any one group to carry. Can we be certain that black women are not contracting HIV by willingly having unprotected sex with genuinely heterosexual men? If women are socially programmed to have sex without insisting on condoms, whose fault is that? Instead of asking the hard questions, many articles have stuck to the same old easy-to-regurgitate story: Black men will do anything—even kill—for sex.

Still, there's hope for a more thoughtful exploration of black sexuality than what's been presented thus far. During the otherwise tepid vice-presidential debates of 2004, moderator Gwen Ifill asked candidates Cheney and Edwards to comment on the government's role in ending the AIDS epidemic in the U.S., specifically mentioning the high rates of HIV infection among black women. Predictably enough, neither was familiar with the statistics Ifill cited, and neither had an intelligent response. But it did give debate commentators a chance to present the DL as one of many factors related to the deaths of hundreds of thousands of black people from AIDS. And [in] February [2005], Keith Boykin published *Beyond the Down Low: Sex, Lies, and Denial in Black America,* which could bring some balance to what has been a very one-dimensional story.

Meanwhile, J. L. King [published] a new book . . . about the overwhelming response to his memoir, which he says sold over 200,000 copies. When asked about his first book and its exaggerations of the scope of the DL phenomenon as well as its connection to HIV and AIDS in black women, he responds, "I tell people to do their own research and find out what's going on in their state and go to the Centers for Disease Control. Don't take my word for it, I'm an activist, not a health educator. I'm just telling my story."

---

## *10 Things You Should Know about the DL*

**Keith Boykin**

It's coming again. Get ready for a new round of news stories about the down low. It started [in 2004] with a wave of media hype and sensationalism designed to scare black women about men on the DL. But now . . . it's important to separate fact from fiction in this delicate conversation.

Almost everything we've been told about the down low in recent years is wrong. That's why I've put together a quick list of ten things everyone should know about the down low.

**1. The down low is just a black version of "the closet."**

The down low is popularly used to refer to men who have sex with men but do not identify as gay or homosexual. Maybe you've heard that concept before. Long ago, we called it "the closet." The term "down low" is just a new way of describing a very old thing, but it's the hot new buzz word of the moment.

**2. The down low is not new.**

The phrase itself may be new, but the practice is as old as history. Men have been secretly sleeping with men since the beginning of time. And married men have been doing the same thing. The only thing new is what we call it.

**3. The down low is not just a black thing.**

When Jim McGreevey, the governor of New Jersey, announced [in 2004] that he had cheated on his wife with another man, no one bothered to make the obvious point—Governor McGreevey had been on the down low. When white men do it, we call it what it is and move on. When black men do the same thing, we want to pathologize it. Therein lies a double standard.

**4. The down low is not simply a gay thing.**

The term "down low" entered the mainstream of black popular culture in the early 1990s. In 1993, Salt-n-Pepa recorded a song called "Whatta Man" that mentioned the down low. In 1994, TLC recorded a song called "Creep" about a woman on the down low. In 1995, Brian McKnight recorded his song, "On the Down Low," about a woman named Maxine on the DL. Then in 1996 and 1998, R. Kelly recorded not one, but two songs about the down low.

We laughed about it when it was a heterosexual thing, but suddenly we became alarmed when we "discovered" that gay and bisexual men were on the down low too. There's another double standard. In reality, the down low is simply about cheating, whether heterosexual, homosexual or bisexual.

**5. The down low is not the cause of the black AIDS epidemic.**

In 2003 (the last year in which we have full CDC data available) there were more than 7,000 black female AIDS cases reported in the United States. Out of that number, only 118 reported "sex with a bisexual male" as the method of exposure. That's just 1.6 percent of all black female AIDS cases. Believe it or not, there are other ways to get infected besides having sex with a man on the down low. Many women are also becoming infected through injection drug use, sex with an injection drug user, and sex with a heterosexual (not down low) man.

Focusing on the down low misleads women to think that the down low is a health threat instead of HIV. That's a serious mistake. A man on the down low who is HIV negative cannot pass the virus to you, but a straight man who is not on the down low could easily give you HIV if he is infected with the virus. The down low does not cause AIDS. HIV causes AIDS.

**6. The down low discussion is a distraction from the real issues.**

All the time we've spent sensationalizing the down low in the past few years is time we could have spent talking about solutions to the AIDS epidemic in our communities.

On an individual level, we need to encourage men and women to exercise personal responsibility. On an institutional level, we need to mobilize our churches, fraternities, sororities and civic organizations so they can provide reliable safe sex information, HIV testing, and nonjudgmental counseling. And on a public policy level, we need to talk about free testing facilities, needle exchange programs, condoms in prison, targeted AIDS prevention funding, resources for low-income people living with AIDS, and safe sex education in public schools. That's the dialogue we should be having.

**7. There are no "signs" to tell if a man is on the down low.**

There are going to be a lot of people out there trying to tell you how to find out if your man is on the DL. Don't waste your time. The whole point of the down low is that these are people who do not want to be detected. The moment you come up with a "guidebook" to give you some warning signs is the moment when men on the down low will devise new strategies to elude you.

**8. Becoming a "down low detective" is not the answer.**

Log onto various Internet web sites about the down low, and you'll find lots of information about how to spy on your partner. Sure, you could hire a private investigator to follow him around when he goes to work, but what does that say about your relationship? If you do suspect something is fishy, you may be in for a shocking surprise. Your man may be cheating on you—with another woman!

A better solution is to confront the homophobia in our community that contributes to the down low. If we want to stop the down low, then we need to create a climate where men (and women) don't feel the need to be on the down low in the first place. Then we won't have as many men who feel forced into fake relationships to keep the parents, friends and nosey neighbors out of their lives.

**9. Demonizing men on the down low will not make them straight.**

One popular response to the down low is to demonize all down low men as villains. That may make us feel a little better for a moment, but it won't change the reality of who they are. In fact, demonizing men on the down low is more likely to push these men further into denial about their sexuality. People often ask, "Why don't these men simply come out and say they're gay?" That's a good question, but as long as we keep demonizing homosexu-

ality, don't expect any mass confessions to happen anytime soon.

**10. Stereotyping women as victims will not keep them safe.**

Much of the discussion about the down low recently has portrayed women as "victims" of black men. Framing the issue this way disempowers women from the ability to protect themselves, reinforces negative stereotypes about black men and encourages an unhealthy battle of the sexes in the black community.

The media machine behind the down low business (and it is a business) has tried to exploit women's fears about the DL in order to make a quick buck. But fear is not the answer. Education is. Knowledge is power, and all women and men need to know the truth.

*Source:* Boykin, Keith. 2005. "10 Things You Should Know About the DL." www.keithboykin.com. Reprinted by permission.

# Kink without Borders:
# Sexual "Deviance" across Cultures

Dinesh Bhugra

## Introduction

A range of . . . sexual behaviors is observed and reported in . . . Western industrialized societies. Deviance is behavior that [violates] the norms of society. Such deviance can be defined [in] a number of [ways]. . . .

Sexual deviance is often used as a term for individuals whose sexual preferences . . . do not fall into mainstream sexual behavior. However, this remains a pejorative term so that, by definition, a negative value is being expressed. Bancroft (1989) suggests using sexual minority behavior as a term. Paraphilia is the current preferred term in psychiatric literature and will be used in [this reading].

Gagnon and Simon (1967) classified sexual deviance as normal, subcultural or individual deviance. Normal deviance includes behavior like masturbation, oral sex and premarital intercourse which, while legally or socially proscribed in some parts of the world, is practiced by large numbers of people, thereby falling within the statistical norm. Subcultural deviance is associated with particular subcultures (for example, homosexual) and will include categories of fetishism, sadomasochism, transvestism and transsexualism. These are often consensual behaviors, and their incidence is difficult to establish. . . .

From Bhugra, Dinesh. 2000. "Disturbances in Objects of Desire: Cross-Cultural Issues." *Sexual and Relationship Therapy* 15: 67–78. Reprinted by permission of Taylor & Francis Ltd. www.tandf.co.uk/journals.

*Sex and Societies* by Bullough (1976) provides a classic account of sexual variance . . . across different time periods, religions and geographical areas. He argues that male and female patterns of sexual orientation and behavior (i.e. sex roles) are attributable to acquired learning, therefore, to social and cultural factors. . . . For example, [he found that] different societies have had widely different rules and attitudes about masturbation but, regardless of whether the attitude was one of approval or condemnation, at least some adults in all or nearly all societies appear to have masturbated. . . .

[Moreover,] in many societies, homosexuality [is] acceptable only in certain age groups and not others. In societies where women and men are not expected to be seen together or could appear in mixed company only under carefully controlled conditions, the need for companionship and entertainment was often served either by professional outcasts such as prostitutes or by men who acted the part of women. Some of these men–women were transvestites, others were homosexuals and, for others, the line was blurred. In addition, double standards often apply to the sexes. Men are encouraged to be promiscuous . . . whereas women are not expected to have any sexual desire at least till marriage. . . . This is by no means a universal view.

Some societies . . . were sex-positive . . . and others sex-negative. These attitudes . . . were not static and often changed in response to religion and changing political climates. For example, early Hinduism was strongly sex-positive because sex was seen as a mystic and magical activity. Contrary to prevalent beliefs elsewhere, the Hindus believed that women enjoyed sex much more than men and, in their sex manuals, considerable attention was devoted to other non-procreative purposes of sex, and a range of sexual behaviors was considered normal. The sexual act, according to various sex manuals, was to be seen as a refined form of combat. The male attacks, the woman resists and, amid the subtle interplay of advance, retreat, assault and defense, the desires are built up. However, the final result is a delightful victory for both parties. Women are said to be aroused by a show of strength and men by a show of resistance. At the height of passion, consciousness is enhanced by intensive stimulation, often through sadistic acts, because the senses have become so dulled to the unpleasantness of pain that they find sharp delight in it. During such a combat it is possible to bite, scratch, pull the hair of the partner and beat or slap with the palm of the hand, the back of the hand, the side of the hand, a half-open fist or a closed fist on the shoulders, back, bosom and buttocks (Kalyanamalla, 1964). Various types of nail marks and teeth marks are described with observations that certain kinds of marks on women are supposed to be responded to in return with only specific types of marks. . . . From such a liberal view of sex, sexual behavior and sexual activity, where temples were constructed for celebration and worship of activity, things changed with the invasions of Muslim rulers. Hindu women went into purdah and the openness of sexual mores started to change dramatically; over the past few centuries India has become relatively conservative.

. . . [I]n China, . . . sexual union of the male and female was like the intermingling of heaven and earth—essential to achieving harmony as well as a happy and healthy sex life. Several manuals described the secrets of intercourse, though most of them have been destroyed (Bullough, 1976). Of various sexual positions described, a few included a third party; thus polygamy or multi-partner sex-

ual activity was acceptable. Males were expected to satisfy more than one wife without ejaculating. For this purpose, clear guidelines were given on the frequency of intercourse as well as its timing. Initially, women were seen as superior or equal to men, but gradually their status was lowered. Foreplay was encouraged and oral sex was permitted. Sexual intercourse with prostitutes was accepted, although semen loss was not encouraged. Manipulation of sexual organs without orgasm was encouraged. Balls were placed inside the vagina to heighten the pleasures of sexual intercourse or masturbation. Special instruments, soaked mushrooms and other materials were also placed inside the vagina to achieve sexual pleasure.

Eunuchs fulfilled a valuable function in China, being allowed free access to the palaces and yet not being a threat because they were seen as incomplete men. They were also known to engage in homosexual activity, especially passive activity, because the anus was supposed to have a highly developed sense of touch which made the activity pleasurable. Women changing into men and men changing into women were described. It is difficult to say whether this change was anatomical or psychological. However, transvestitism was institutionalized on stage. From this relatively open and positive attitude [toward] sexual variations in ancient China, the country has certainly become less positive today: for example, in the Chinese diagnostic system, homosexuality is still recorded as a mental illness.

From these two illustrations it appears that attitudes [toward] sexual mores and norms develop and change with social, economic and cultural factors. . . .

Ford and Beach (1965) reported that, of 78 relatively primitive societies, 49 approved or tolerated homosexuality in some form. Of the total 190 societies studied, they observed that heterosexual coitus was the prevalent form of sexual behavior for the majority of adults in all human societies, but this is rarely the only sexual activity indulged in. Although the actual sexual position may be different in some societies, the initiation of sexual intercourse in some cultures is encouraged to be by the female partner.

There are several societies in Ford and Beach's sample where couples indulge in a minimum of sexual foreplay. Kissing is a ubiquitous item in the sex play in most societies. However, there are some peoples among whom kissing is unknown and it is equated with a dirty practice of eating saliva and dirt. Thus it would appear that some cultures pay little attention to foreplay which includes kissing. There were at least some cultures where penetration was the key factor and no foreplay or afterplay was described. These were largely preliterate societies where obviously sexual behavior was for the purposes of procreation only.

For nearly every human society, sexual intercourse is usually preceded by some degree of sensory stimulation and is often accompanied by stimulation, often visual or tactile. Visual stimulation is often of the individual partner, but sometimes this stimulation is related to a body part or part of clothing in achieving sexual excitement. . . . Within each culture and society there are variations too, both in pre-intercourse stimulation and foreplay. Some couples may well practice elaborate forms of genital manipulation, whereas others who may have bad feelings about sex or their partner may wish to skip the preliminaries. Breast stimulation and kissing as forms of sexual stimulation are more or less restricted to the human species, whereas preliminary stimulation of genital organs has more ancient . . . origin. (Ford & Beach, 1965).

The infliction of physical pain is often associated with sexual excitement, and this process is regular and characteristic in many human societies. In many cultures, individuals whose stereotype of intense lovemaking includes scratching, biting and pulling of the hair of the partner in sexual excitement are seen. There are also societies in which these forms of sexual stimulation are totally absent. . . .

In most societies, sexual intercourse takes place in seclusion, although in some cultures it could be in public but not in front of children and not in places where children might come across the copulating couple. Societies living in unpartitioned multiple dwellings are more likely to have outdoor sex.

Some societies will have sex only at night (irrespective of individuals' preferences) because to be seen copulating is a source of great shame and day time coitus is too risky. Only a few societies prefer sex only during the day because children conceived in darkness may be born blind. . . .

There are few, if any, universal standards of sexual attractiveness. The physical characteristics which are regarded as sexually stimulating vary appreciably from one society to another. In most societies, the physical beauty of the female receives more explicit consideration than that of the male. This may go some way towards explaining why men get turned on by objects. These selected female traits include plump body build, small ankles, elongated labia majora, large clitoris or pendulous breasts.

In some societies, bestiality is tolerated (even though seen as unnatural, silly and disgusting, and inferior to normal sexual activity) in the absence of more appropriate sexual behavior. Such contact is often seen as inadequate and is sometimes allowed for teenage males. There are at least four societies in which animal contacts are practiced and do not meet with condemnation (Ford & Beach, 1965). Such a variation reflects the influence of learning and social channelization.

Similarly, adult masturbation is tolerated in some societies and encouraged in others, but the double standards in response to male and female masturbation remain. The relative infrequency of adult masturbation in some societies is said to be the result of socialization (Ford & Beach, 1965). In societies which are restrictive in their attitudes [toward] sex, teenagers may suppress their sexual desire but it is unlikely that no sexual activity takes place. Where boys are less carefully watched than girls, it appears that youths are able to circumvent the barriers. In semi-restrictive societies, formal prohibitions exist but are apparently not very serious, and are not enforced. Sexual experimentation may take place in secrecy but without incurring punishment. Permissive societies have a permissive and tolerant attitude towards sex expression in childhood. Girls are expected to remain virgins until marriage in restrictive societies, whereas in the other two types, such expectations, if they exist at all, are not obvious. Actual sexual behavior develops somewhat more rapidly in certain societies than in others.

## Culture and Behavior

Intracultural and intercultural behaviors are affected to a degree by learning behaviors. With increasing globalization, industrialization and the spread of global media, very few societies and cultures have been left isolated. Attitudes of a society towards certain sexual activities and behaviors are key factors in the way individuals adopt and enjoy a passive or an active role in the sexual relationship. The emphasis on the feminine means that females are encouraged not to take the lead in sexual intercourse and to be passive; they are less likely to experience clear-cut sexual orgasm. . . .

## Paraphilias across Cultures

The field of paraphilias across cultures is severely limited. . . . Of the four paraphilias to be considered here, fetishism is probably quite common. . . . There is general agreement that fetishism is rare in women. . . . The determinants of fetishism are many, and social learning theory must be seen to play an important role. There is virtually no literature reporting fetishism from non-industrialized countries. . . .

Bancroft (1989) argues a majority of fetishes can be understood as an extension of the loved one which acquires special importance if there are other factors or causes of anxiety blocking the development of a more appropriate sexual relationship. Under these circumstances it makes

sense that, in societies where sexual love may have amorphous meaning and the individual's concept of the self is socio-centric rather than egocentric, the likelihood of being attracted to high heels, leather, rubber or boots may be low. In cases where fetishes are extremely bizarre and cannot be understood as extensions of the body, but are more likely to be associated with some neurological abnormality such as temporal lobe epilepsy, the stimulus may be random, and it is possible that cases may occur across cultures. . . . [S]adomasochistic behavior is more likely to occur across cultures especially if it develops as part of sexual foreplay and individuals accept it.

Of the remaining two paraphilias, transvestism and transexualism are quite interesting. Cross-dressing occurs in most societies and throughout history, and is also less likely to be a true paraphilia. Bhugra and de Silva (1996) postulate that for uniforms to work as fetish or individuals to dress in uniforms for sexual performance can be a reflection of fashion or fantasy. The sexual significance of cross-dressing is incredibly complex. Bancroft (1989) divides this group into four types; the fetishistic transvestite, the transsexual, the double-role transvestite and the homosexual transvestite. The sexual relationships of cross-dressers vary accordingly.

In their cross-cultural study of the sexual thoughts of children, Goldman and Goldman (1982) found that 50% of boys and 9.5% of girls expressed aversion to their biological sex. This reaction peaked in adolescence, with 30% of 13-year-old boys in Australia and 20% in the USA expressing such feelings which, by contrast, were virtually absent in Sweden. Bancroft (1989) suggests that the more rigid the sex role stereotypes in a society, the greater the likelihood of this gender dysphoria. Thus, rigid expectations could produce anxiety and insecurity about gender identity, for which transsexual ideas would offer one method of coping. . . .

The heterogeneity of sexual behavior and societies in which they occur suggests that males are more likely to have fetishistic tendencies and that the development of sexual identity is dictated by social and cultural factors, thereby producing variation in rates of different fetishistic behaviors.

Several authors (Caplan, 1987; Herdt, 1990a, 1990b; Herdt & Stoller, 1990) have argued that intersexes may not be discomfited by issues of sex and gender identity. Yet across cultures this identity may not conform to that coinciding with the Western binary mode of gender assignment. . . . Such an individual . . . is neither a man nor a woman, nor a man wanting to be a woman (or vice versa) but belongs to a distinct third category. . . .

It must be emphasized that gender identity may not bear any relation to sexual arousal. Sexual identity, cross-dressing and sexual orientation are not on a direct continuum but discrete independent categories (Callender & Kochens, 1986). . . . [T]he binary model is not necessarily applicable to many other societies.

### Culture-Bound Syndromes

. . . [T]hese syndromes have implications for understanding fertility concerns and concerns with sexual performance in certain cultures and certain ethnic groups. . . . [T]here is a danger inherent in . . . fascination with these exotic syndromes, through which clinicians and researchers alike reduce considerations of cultural sensitivity and turn these sexual disorders into colourful high-profile conditions, overlooking the extent to which all the sexual disorders . . . are culture-bound. . . .

Cultural constructionists insist that, to develop culturally sensitive understandings of human sexuality and sexual behavior, one must move beyond the simple assumptions and simplistic assessment of how select features of sexuality of other cultural and ethnic groups fit into or vary from that propounded by Western society . . . (Davis, 1996). It would therefore make sense to move away from a classificatory-based system to an emphasis on questioning and analyzing the constructions of these categories as culture-

bound. Foucault (1978) argues for a reassessment of the nature and applicability of these categories across historical, ethnic and ethnographic tenets. Thus sexuality has to be viewed not as a fixed or given biological or psychic entity—instead sexualities are constantly practiced, altered, modified and amended, as are the meanings and categories attributed to them. . . . [For example, in] Papua New Guinea, Herdt and Stoller (1990) found that man–boy sex was common and oral sex and swallowing of the semen were part of the rites of passage, and yet this concept does not reflect Western concepts of pedophilia. It has been argued that pedophilia is a Western culture-bound syndrome and reflects Western views of sex as an . . . individual personal responsibility . . . (Rubin, 1984). . . . Western sexualities are structured within an extremely punitive social framework, where an excess of significance is associated with differences in sexual acts and unfit forms of sexual desire (especially those that deviate from practices with reproductive potential). . . .

Davis (1996) argues that Krafft-Ebing was the person responsible for the categorization of paraphilias (and also for their medicalization). The search for cultural relativity among these norms and values may well have done a disservice to patients and those seeking help, [for] "paraphiliac" sexual disorders may not have a parallel in all countries (Kendell, 1991). Most standard paraphilias are unique to Western societies. They have been linked to the non-availability of sexual partners and the primacy of masturbatory behavior (Meikle, 1982; Weatherford, 1986). However we know masturbatory behavior is almost universal—as is the lack of sexual partners up to a certain age—so how is it that they are so common in Western societies. Gebhard (1971) explains this as a result of living in complex societies where individuals can evade social sanctions through anonymous behaviors. It is also likely that . . . social sanctions are few and far between and, where they exist, are part of a legal framework.

. . . The critique of the categories of paraphilias is wide and comes from a variety of sources such as feminists (Irvine, 1990; Teifer, 1998), historians (D'Emilio & Freedman, 1989; Weeks, 1985), social scientists (Reiss, 1996; Puieroba, 1988), and members of sexual minorities (Ullerstam, 1966; Weeks, 1985).

## Culture versus Biology

The interaction between culture and biology is important in [understanding] . . . paraphiliac behavior. . . .

For fetishism, one of the biological factors identified has been temporal lobe epilepsy. Other factors which play a role in the development of sexual preferences and are also likely to play some role in the development of paraphilias . . . include central nervous systems, hormones, chromosomal abnormalities, effects of exogenous hormones and steroids during pregnancy or puberty and other factors. These have been studied at some length in conjunction with the development of sexual characteristics and gender and sexual identity but have not been studied well in paraphilias.

## Conclusions

The interactions of social and cultural factors with biological factors need to be studied, even though social learning theorists have made a useful start in the field. Future research must focus on rates of paraphilias across different cultures and ethnic groups and then correlate these with social and cultural factors. . . .

There is little doubt that paraphilias are, by and large, a Western culture-specific syndrome. . . . Social, rather than biological, factors are more likely to play a key role in the [development] of paraphilias.

**REFERENCES**

Bancroft, J. (1989) *Human Sexuality and Its Problems* (Edinburgh, Churchill Livingstone).

Bhugra, D. & de Silvia, P. (1996) Uniforms: fact, fashion, fantasy and fetish, *Sexual and Marital Therapy*, 11, pp. 393–406.

Bullough V. I. (1976) *Sexual Variance in Society and History* (Chicago, IL, University of Chicago Press).

Callender, C. & Kochens, I. (1986) Men and non men: male gender mixing statuses and Homosexuality, in: E. Blackwood (Ed.) *Anthropology and Homosexual Behaviors* (New York, Haworth).

Caplan, P. (Ed.) (1987) *The Cultural Construction of Bisexuality* (London, Tavistock).

Davis, D. L. (1996) Cultural sensitivity and the sexual disorders of DSM-IV, in: J. E. Mezzich, A. Kleinman, H. Fabrega & D. L. Parson (Eds), *Culture and Psychiatric Diagnosis* (Washington, DC, APA Press).

Ford, C. F. & Beach, F. (1965) *Patterns of Sexual Behavior* (London, Eyre and Spottiswoode).

Foucault, M. (1978) *The History of Sexuality,* Vol. 1 (New York, Pantheon).

Gagnon, J. & Simon, W. (1967) *Sexual Deviance* (New York, Harper & Row).

Gebhard, P. H. (1971) Human sexual behavior, in: H. S. Marshall & R. C. Suggs (Eds) *Human Sexual Behaviors* (New York, Basic Books).

Herdt, G. H. (1990a) Mistaken gender, *American Anthropologist*, 92, pp. 433–446.

Herdt, G. H. (1990b) Development discontinuities and sexual orientation across cultures, in: D. McWhirter (Ed.) *Homosexuality/Heterosexuality* (New York, Oxford University Press).

Herdt, G. H. & Stoller, R. (1990) *Intimate Communications* (New York, Columbia University Press).

Irvine, I. M. (1990) *Disorders of Desire: Sex and Gender in Modern American Sexology* (Philadelphia, PA, Temple University Press).

Kalyanamalla (trans. T. Ray) (1964), *Ananga Raga.* (New York, Citadel Press).

Kendell, R. (1991) Relationship between DSM-IV and ICD-10, *Journal of Abnormal Psychology*, pp. 297–301.

Meikle, S. (1982) Culture and sexual deviation, in: I. Al-Issa (Ed.) *Culture and Psychopathology* (Baltimore, University Park Press).

Puieroba, J. (1988) Antropologia Sexual: *Lectuaros de Antropologi Sexual* (Madrid, Universidad Nacional de Education Distancia).

Reiss, H. (1996) *Journey into Sexuality* (Englewood Cliffs, NJ, Prentice Hall).

Rubin G., (1984) Thinking sex: Notes for a radical theory of the politics of sexuality, in: C. Vance (Ed.) *Pleasure and Danger* (Boston, MA, Routledge & Kegan Paul).

Teifer, I. (1988) A feminist critique of the sexual dysfunction nomenclature, in: E. Cole (Ed.), *Women and Sex Therapy* (New York, Haworth).

Ullerstam, I. (1966) *The Erotic Minorities* (New York, Grove Press).

Weatherford, J. M. (1986) *Porn Row* (New York, Arbor House).

Weeks, J. (1985) *Sexuality and Its Discontents* (London, Routledge).

**Sextistics**

## Did You Know?

- On average, 18 to 29 year olds have sex 112 times per year, 30 to 39 year olds have sex 86 times per year, and 40 to 49 year olds have sex 69 times per year.[1]
- Ninety-seven percent of men and 98 percent of women have had vaginal intercourse.[2]
- Nearly half of women admit faking an orgasm.[3]
- Forty percent of men and 35 percent of women have had heterosexual anal sex.[4]
- Twenty-two percent of sexually active girls report that their partners never perform oral sex on them, while only 5 percent of boys say the same.[5]
- Twenty-four percent of single men and 7 percent of single women reported engaging in some form of group sex.[6]
- Two percent of all married couples, mainly middle class couples with children, have shared mates at least once during their marriage.[7]
- Sadomasochism is pictured in the "Kama Sutra," an ancient Indian marriage manual from around 450 AD.[8]
- Fifty-four percent of men think about sex every day or several times a day. Only 19 percent of women say they think about sex every day or several times a day.[9]
- Fifty-three percent of men and 25 percent of women masturbated for the first time between the ages of 11 and 13.[10]
- Approximately 60 percent of men and 40 percent of women report masturbating in the past year. Eighty-five percent of men and 45 percent of women who were living with a sexual partner reported masturbating in the past year.[11]

—Compiled by Mikel Walters

**NOTES**

1. Piccinino, Linda J., and William D. Mosher. 1998. "Trends in Contraceptive Method Used in the United States: 1982–1994." *Family Planning Perspectives* 30:4–10.

2. Mosher, William D., Anjani Chandra, and Jo Jones. 2005. "Sexual Behavior and Selected Health Measures: Men and Women 15–44 Years of Age, United States, 2002." *CDC Advance Data From Vital and Health Statistics* 362 (September 15, 2005). Retrieved January 30, 2006 from www.cdc.gov/nchs/products/pubs/pubd/ad/361-370/ad362.htm.

3. Ibid.

4. Mosher et al.

5. NBC News. 2005. "NBC News, People Magazine Commission Landmark National Poll." MSNBC, January 19, 2005. Retrieved November 21, 2005 from www.msnbc.com.

6. Reinisch, June Machover. 1990. *The Kinsey Institute New Report on Sex* (p. 149). St. Martin's Press.

7. Ibid.

8. Vatsysayana. [450] 1964. *Kama Sutra.* Lancer Books.

9. Laumann, Edward O, John H. Gagnon, Robert T. Michael, and Stuart Michaels. 1994. *The Social Organization of Sexuality: Sexual Practices in the United States*. University of Chicago Press.

10. Ibid.

11. Ibid.

# chapter 7

# *Procreative Issues*

## Dorothy E. Roberts

Dorothy E. Roberts, J.D., is Kirkland & Ellis Professor at Northwestern University School of Law, with joint appointments in the Departments of African American Studies and Sociology, as faculty fellow of the Institute for Policy Research, and as a faculty affiliate of the Joint Center for Poverty Research. She has written extensively on the interplay of gender, race, class, and legal issues concerning reproduction and motherhood. Roberts is the author of *Killing the Black Body: Race, Reproduction, and the Meaning of Liberty* (Pantheon, 1997) and *Shattered Bonds: The Color of Child Welfare* (Basic Books, 2002), as well as the coauthor of casebooks on constitutional law and women and the law. She has published more than fifty articles and essays in books and scholarly journals.

### How did you become involved in your research for Killing the Black Body?

*I began researching the issues I discuss in* Killing the Black Body *in 1988, soon after I became a law professor, when I began reading articles in the newspaper about the prosecution of women for drug use during pregnancy. I suspected—and later confirmed—that most of these women were poor and black. Thinking about the criminalization of their childbearing led me to explore other ways in which the dominant society devalues and the state regulates black women's fertility and reproductive decision making. I realized that there was currently an explosion of policies and rhetoric that sought to punish poor black women's procreation and that it was connected to a history of racial oppression in America. I also felt that this history had been largely neglected in books about reproductive freedom and about racial inequality.*

### How did you decide on the title Killing the Black Body?

*I wanted to capture the brutal way in which punitive reproductive policies attempt to control black women's bodies and deny their humanity. "Killing" is often used metaphorically to signify a spiritual destruction and not a literal death. Some people emphasize the impact of population control policies on actual fertility rates. I believe that policies that devalue black reproduction are unjust because of the way they reinforce a racist social order.*

### How do you deal with negative reactions, or with resistance to the ideas you present in your work?

*First, I lay a strong foundation for my ideas that is difficult to refute. I try to make a well-reasoned argument about the injustice of the policies I criticize, and I document my arguments with numerous sources. Still, there are people who oppose my views on ideological grounds. I challenge their resistance by demonstrating the race, class, and gender disparities in policies and discourse concerning reproduction and the lack of justification for them. For example, when someone disagrees with my claim that the prosecution of maternal substance abuse is racially biased, I point out that there is no legitimate reason to single out poor, black mothers who smoke crack for punishment. Maternal substance abuse cuts across all racial and socioeconomic backgrounds, and there are other maternal behaviors (as well as social factors) that are more harmful to a fetus than smoking crack cocaine. I also ask them if they can imagine the police dragging dozens of white middle-class mothers from private maternity wards just after giving birth to a baby. Would they really support a racially neutral policy that punishes all women who use drugs or alcohol while pregnant? Many people who think honestly about these questions are forced to concede that punitive policies addressing maternal substance abuse depend on the devaluation of black mothers. I also realize, however, that people who firmly believe that we live in a fair and egalitarian society, and who are unwilling to acknowledge structural inequities based on race, class, and gender, may be incapable of accepting my arguments no matter how well I support them.*

**What do you see as the links between oppressive procreative policies and practices and ideology about sexuality and motherhood?**

*Ideologies that value women in relation to social norms about sexuality and motherhood help to produce oppressive procreative policies and practices and, in turn, are reinforced by these policies and practices. The state reinforces the norm that associates legitimate sex and motherhood with marriage, for example, by penalizing women who raise children without a husband. My work has explored the way a disparaging mythology about black women's sexuality and mothering legitimates policies that seek to regulate black women's reproductive decision making. The popular image of black women as irresponsible and deviant reproducers—both sexually licentious and careless as mothers—supports policies that seek to reduce their fertility and to punish them for bearing children.*

**If you could teach people one thing about the links between procreation, sexuality, and social control, what would it be?**

*The regulation of procreation and sexuality not only interferes with individual women's rights but also serves to reinforce social inequalities. One of the most powerful ways of masking group oppression is to pretend that oppressed people are the cause of their own problems and that the solution is to curb their sexuality and reproduction. Blaming disadvantaged groups for the effects of social injustice diverts attention away from the need for social change.*

—Interviewed by Denise Donnelly

# The Pleasures of Childbirth

Ina May Gaskin

Is childbirth always painful? Although at first thought it might seem easy to answer this straightforward question with a loud and unequivocal yes, the truth is less simple. It is true that many women who have given birth more than once answer in the affirmative. But I have given birth four times without pain or medication, so my answer is not always. There are exceptions, and from them we can gain important insights about labor and birth.

I am far from being alone in saying that birth is not always painful. In fact, under the right circumstances and with good preparation during pregnancy, labor and birth can even be pleasurable for many women. How do I know? I have worked as a midwife for over thirty years, and many of the women I have attended have told me so. I have been with them during these ecstatic experiences, virtually all of which occurred in women who took no pain-numbing medication. Just as compelling, my own body has informed me.

Let's start by looking at some of the written evidence that exists. Numerous reports of painless birth have been gathered over the last couple of centuries by missionaries, travelers, soldiers, and doctors. Ezra Stiles, an early American clergyman and educator, wrote during the period of 1755 to 1794: "I have often been told that a pregnant Squaw [sic] will turn aside and deliver herself, and take up the Infant and wash it in a Brook, and walk off" (Vogel cited in Speert, 1980, p. 1).

Judith Goldsmith, a modern-day writer, has gathered many reports from European observers of various cultures. Among them is the following account of Guyanese women of South America in 1791: "When on the march an Indian is taken with labor, she just steps aside, is delivered, wraps up the baby with the afterbirth and runs in haste after the others. At the first stream that presents itself she washes herself and the infant" (1990, p. 2). Another seemingly painless birth was that noted by a visitor to the island of Alor, near Java, who witnessed six births without seeing a mother show real signs of pain. Sweat and soft groans were noted, but each of the six women gave birth easily (2). Livingston Jones, a visitor among the Tlinget people of Alaska, remarked: "The vast majority of Tlinget women suffer very little and some not at all, when their children are born. They have been known to give birth while sleeping" (cited in Goldsmith, 1990, p. 2).

Giving birth while sleeping! How can this be? As unusual as this seems, it can and does occasionally happen. Dr. Alice Stockham describes a doctor's account of a birth that took place in 1828:

*On his arrival he found the house in the utmost confusion, and was told that the child had been born before the messenger was dispatched for the doctor. From the lady herself he learned that, about half an hour previously, she had been awakened from a natural sleep by the alarm of a daughter about five years old, who slept with her. This alarm was occasioned by the little girl feeling the movements, and hearing the cries of an infant in bed. To the mother's great surprise, she had brought forth her child without any consciousness of the fact. (1890, p. 3)*

Stockham's book *Tokology,* published late in the nineteenth century, quoted a world traveler who said, "I know of no country, no tribe, no class, where childbirth is attended with so much pain and trouble as in North America" (1890, p. 11). She believed that the reputed better performance of peasant or indigenous women in birth was largely due to their superior physical vigor from a healthy diet and regular exercise. European-American women could have healthy births, too, she argued, adding:

> *I attended a neighbour of mine in four different confinements. I never was able to reach her before the birth of the child, although I lived only across the street, and, according to her injunctions, always kept my shoes "laced up." She sent for me, too, at the first indication of labor. There was always one prolonged effort and the child was expelled. (1890, p. 15)*
>
> *Another lady patron had two children without a particle of pain. With the first she was alone with her nurse. During the evening she remarked that she felt weary and believed that she would lie down. She had been on the bed no more than twenty minutes when she called to her nurse, saying: "How strangely I feel! I wish you would see what is the matter," when to their astonishment the child was already born. (1890, p. 3)*

Even though it is possible to find an occasional reference in U.S. medical textbooks of the nineteenth and twentieth centuries to women of "civilized" cultures giving birth with little or no apparent pain, such accounts are usually the exception rather than the rule. In general, childbirth pain is viewed to be severe and intrinsic to the process of labor and birth. Even in texts written during the nineteenth century, when anesthetics and analgesics were not yet a normal feature of care giving, there is little recognition that childbirth pain can vary tremendously according to the position adopted (or required) by the mother during labor and birth.

In one of the exceptional works, *Labor among Primitive Peoples,* published in 1883, Dr. George Engelmann made a huge contribution by synthesizing knowledge drawn from obstetrics, cultural anthropology, and massage therapy. Renowned

as an accomplished biologist, archaeologist, and anthropologist, he corresponded regularly with a long list of scholars and explorers who also studied the medical practices of people who still lived according to "primal" ways. His book supports the general observations about the greater ease of birth-giving among indigenous women compared with their "civilized" sisters.

To Engelmann, the short, comparatively easy labors of women who lived in cultures untouched by civilization could be explained by several factors. He noted that these women typically led active lives right up to the time they went into labor. But his correspondence with physicians who knew about indigenous ways of giving birth convinced him that it was not just exercise during pregnancy that made birth easier for indigenous women. He thought their behavior in labor was at least as important a factor. Unlike European-American women, who stayed in their beds during the last weeks and months of pregnancy and in labor, indigenous mothers moved about freely and adopted various positions, many of them upright, during the different stages of labor. There was no supposedly superior class of women in these societies to sanction practices and positions that were obstetrically fashionable, and there was no prudery, so they behaved according to instinct. Equally important, the clothing they wore during pregnancy did not hamper free movement or full expansion of the lungs. The comfortable and practical clothes of indigenous women contrasted sharply with the clothing styles of prosperous civilized women of the nineteenth century, a period when corsets with whalebone or steel stays were typically worn laced so tightly that women wearing them sometimes suffered displacement of their kidneys, liver, and other organs. Fainting was common among corset-wearers because tight lacing kept them from breathing deeply.

To his great credit, Engelmann was one of the few North American doctors who took the view that civilized women had something to learn from women who were more in tune with nature. He was very frank about his opinion that women whose connection with their instincts had not been altered by civilization were far more able to give birth without complication, protracted labor, or unbearable pain, and that physicians, as well as European-American women, had much to learn from them. "The savage mother, the Negress, the Australian or Indian, still governed by her instinct, is far in advance of the ordinary woman of our civilization," he emphasized (1883, p. xvii).

Nineteenth-century feminist philosopher and writer Elizabeth Cady Stanton regarded pregnancy as a natural state rather than an illness, and she knew from her own experience that labor and birth could be painless. Instead of accepting physicians' advice to stay in bed from the seventh or eighth months of pregnancy until a month after giving birth, she kept on with her usual work until she went into labor with each of her seven children. She felt that confinement (restriction of movement by clothes or social custom) was the cause of women's difficult labors, as well as their numerous postpartum ailments. After the birth of her fifth child, she wrote:

> I never felt such sacredness in carrying a child as I have in the case of this one. She is the largest and most vigorous baby I have ever had, weighing twelve pounds. And yet my labor was short and easy. I laid down about fifteen minutes and brought forth this big girl. I sat up immediately, changed my own clothes, put on a wet bandage, and after a few hours' repose sat up again. Am I not almost a savage? For what refined, delicate, genteel, civilized woman would get well in so indecently short a time? Dear me, how much cruel bondage of mind and suffering of body poor woman will escape when she takes the liberty of being her own physician of both body and mind? (1971, p. 4)

Probably the best-known physician in the twentieth century to study the riddle of pain in childbirth (at least, in the English-speaking world) was Dr. Grantly Dick-Read. He included the story of the first pain-free birth he ever witnessed in *Childbirth without Fear* because it amazed him enough to change forever the way he thought about childbirth. The birth in question

took place in the Whitechapel district of London around 1913. Despite the fact that the mother was laboring in the poorest of hovels, with the rain pouring in through a broken window, Dick-Read remarked on the atmosphere of "quiet kindliness" in the room. The only note of dissonance during the entire experience stemmed from his attempt to persuade the laboring woman to let him put the chloroform mask over her nose and mouth as the baby's head was being born. Dick-Read (1972) wrote:

> She, however, resented the suggestion, and firmly but kindly refused to take this help. It was the first time in my short experience that I had ever been refused when offering chloroform. As I was about to leave some time later, I asked her why it was she would not use the mask. She did not answer at once, but looked from the old woman who had been assisting to the window through which was bursting the first light of dawn; then shyly she turned to me and said: "It didn't hurt. It wasn't meant to, was it, doctor?" (p. 5)

For months and years after that experience, Dick-Read thought about the woman's question and eventually came to realize that "there was no law in nature and no design that could justify the pain of childbirth" (1953, p. 39). Later experience in World War I in foreign lands gave him chances to witness many more apparently painless births. The sum of all these experiences plus his own battlefield experience of terror and loneliness led him to articulate his theory of why some women experience pain in birth while others do not. "It slowly dawned on me that it was the peacefulness of the relatively painless labor that distinguished it most clearly from the others. There was a calm, it seemed almost faith, in the normal and natural outcome of childbirth," he wrote (1953, p. 34).

Dick-Read was the first physician to write about birth as a spiritual experience and to discuss fear as a major contributing factor to pain in childbirth. He wrote that the pain of what he called "cultural childbirth" was caused by a combination of fear and muscle tension caused by ignorance of the birthing process, isolation during labor, and uncompassionate care received in hospital labor and delivery wards.

Remember the soft groans mentioned earlier, in reference to a Javanese birth that took place in the nineteenth century? It is worth noting that the only way one could write about orgasm during that period of U.S. history was to allude to soft moans or groans. By the 1970s times had changed, and a new group of people began to weigh in on the topic of painless birth: women who, in the tradition of Elizabeth Cady Stanton, had given birth themselves and had something to say about their experience. Among them were Raven Lang (1972), Jeannine Parvati Baker (1974), and myself (1975). Not only did these writers mention painless birth, they also mentioned the phenomenon of orgasm during labor or birth.

Since the appearance of these books, virtually nothing has been written on this subject. When I began hearing from young women that many were opting for elective cesarean as a way avoiding pain during labor and birth, I began to wonder why so many writers and childbirth educators never mentioned the possibility of it. Is it so rare that they simply can't conceive of it, or do they wish to avoid raising women's expectations given that many women would still experience pain even if they knew that orgasm was a possibility? I began asking young women if they had ever heard of women having ecstatic labors and births and found that most hadn't.

Curious about how many women I could find who had orgasmic experiences in labor or birth, I decided to conduct a small survey among some close friends. Of 151 women, I found 32 who reported experiencing at least one orgasmic birth. That is 21 percent—considerably higher than I had expected. Most of the women had their babies on The Farm (the community in Tennessee where my colleagues and I have been practicing midwifery for over a quarter-century), but interestingly, some said the orgasm occurred during a hospital birth. I have included some of the women's comments below, as they perhaps shed some light on what factors are present when women have birth experiences such as these. (I have changed the women's names out of respect for their privacy.)

*Julia:* I had an orgasm when I had my fourth child. It happened while I was pushing. We went to the hospital after I had been "stalled" at nine centimeters for a while, attempting a home birth with some midwives who made me nervous. I no sooner got inside the door than I began having overwhelming urges to push that baby OUT!!! I orgasmed as she was being born. They just barely got me onto the delivery table in time for her birth, but I was oblivious to all that because it was feeling so good to get her out.

*Margaret:* I had a cosmic union orgasm, a bliss-enhanced state. In a way, this has had a permanent effect. I can still go to that place.

*Vivian:* Being in labor felt like work; but giving birth, the actual process of passing the baby's entire body out of my womb (which did happen quite quickly), was indescribably incredible, particularly the first time.

*Marilyn:* My last birth was very orgasmic in a sustained sort of way, like I was riding on waves of orgasmic bliss. I knew more what to expect, was less afraid, and tried to meet and flow with the energy rather than avoid or resist as I had the first time. The effect was probably mostly psychological in that it gave me tremendous satisfaction just to have accomplished such a difficult passage safely. I felt great for months afterward, which helped me feel positive about myself in general. This, in turn, affected how I felt about myself sexually. I also think that, for me, learning to let go and let my body take over in labor (as opposed to thinking about it with my mind all the way through!) helped me tap into a part of me I never knew before and helped me feel more willing to let go while making love.

*Janelle:* Giving birth was like pre- and post-orgasm by the second or third birth but did not contain the pulsation felt at climax. Being in tune with rushes [contractions], pushing, deeply relaxing in between was a very sexual and powerful experience but higher than orgasm, because orgasm can seem more self-gratifying and is short-lived. Giving birth is such a spiritual experience, so miraculous, you are very in tune with God and seeing the divinity in everyone that the sexual part is not that important. You are totally immersed in selfless love and so the blissful and sexual feelings are a byproduct, a gift of allowing your body to do what it knows how to do while your consciousness is very expanded.

*Paula:* I have been pondering this question for some time. I have always felt that labor and birth were like one big orgasm. The contractions were like waves of pleasure rippling through the body. I only found the final few centimeters of dilation as extremely strong and slightly less pleasurable. But I felt like labor and birth were/are a continuous orgasm. I can't say that it is like the orgasm experienced during sexual intercourse, where I find myself being engulfed and lost in the wave of orgasm. The type I experienced during labor and birth was a more all-consuming feeling that required more of my attention than that experienced during sex. However, I do feel that it is an orgasm. The birth itself is very orgasmic as the baby comes through the birth canal—extremely pleasurable and rewarding.

*Maria:* I had to think about this one for a few days. At first I thought "no," but there certainly were sensations in the first stage during dilation that were incredibly intense when Ted would kiss me or I would bury my face in his neck during a rush. I did not have a particularly hard time during the first stage of any of my births and remember enjoying the birthing process for the most part. The general excitement, rushes of energy, and all the touching were very pleasurable. The sensations weren't the same as an orgasm exactly, but when the rushes would end, the total splash-out [relaxation] was very similar to how I feel after orgasm now (which I call the wet-noodle effect). For me, however, the second stage was another story. I remember not liking that part because of the intense stinging of the tissue stretching. I always thought I was weird since I liked the first stage and couldn't really get into the second stage. Anyway, it goes without saying that good energy rushes are enjoyable and, even though I don't know if my inner muscles were twitching rhythmically or not, having a baby was the greatest energy sweep ever. I think it is very probable that it is much larger than an orgasm rush, or certainly different. One other thing I think might be true—I think it is possible that I hadn't perfected the art of having superorgasms back then when I was so young and having the babies. Since then, over the years, I have become quite good at it, so I'm not sure if that lack of experience could have kept me from experiencing some of those sensations during labor and birth.

Some of the women described, instead of orgasm, a euphoria that had some similarities to the bliss they associate with sexual pleasure.

*Elayne:* I didn't have an orgasm, but I felt a little bit like it when I had my first baby. And that was only at the transition shortly before pushing. For a moment I felt like [I do] . . . shortly before orgasm—being high, having pain, and being afraid [of] what's coming next. And I felt all this at the same time.

*Alicia:* No, I can't say I would describe the experience as "orgasmic." Rather, it was "euphoric." To say it was orgasmic would describe the experience in almost a base way. Rather, it was spiritual.

*Nanette:* I wouldn't say I experienced orgasm either in labor or giving birth. However, I would say the sensation of out-of-controlledness (!) was comparable. My sister says that giving birth was "like" the biggest orgasm ever—but only "like" it—so it sounds like a qualitative difference. I remember you telling me that my brain had migrated to my pelvic area, which was where it was needed, and I think you were right—the births of all three children are a delightful blur that was so much just being there and experiencing it with my body and not my head.

To conclude, I'll speak from personal experience. It is easier to reach orgasm if one is not feeling violated, angry, frightened, distracted, or goal-oriented. I'm sure that it is easier when there is no one shouting at you when and how to push or counting. As I mentioned earlier, I haven't encountered any reports of orgasm in women who had received pain medication. Orgasm is more possible if one is touched in just the right way—at the right place, the right pace, the right amount of pressure, and the right time. The challenge for women and their caregivers during birth is to come up with a system of pregnancy preparation and birth care that is not inimical to orgasm during labor and birth.

## REFERENCES

Baker, Jeannine Parvati. 1974. *Prenatal Yoga & Natural Birth*. Berkeley, CA: North Atlantic Books.

Dick-Read, Grantly. 1953. *Childbirth without Fear* (2nd revised edition). New York: Harper & Row.

Engelmann, George. 1883. *Labor among Primitive Peoples*. St. Louis, MO: J. M. Chambers & Co.

Gaskin, Ina May. 1977. *Spiritual Midwifery*. Summertown, TN: The Book Company.

Goldsmith, Judith. 1990. *Childbirth Wisdom from the World's Oldest Societies*. Brookline, MA: East-West Health Books.

Lang, Raven. 1972. *The Birth Book*. Palo Alto, CA: Genesis Press.

Stanton, Elizabeth Cady. 1971. *Eighty Years and More: Reminiscences of Elizabeth Cady Stanton 1815–1987*. New York: Schocken.

Speert, Harold. 1980. *Obstetrics and America: A History*. Chicago: American College of Obstetricians and Gynecologists.

Stockham, Alice. 1890. *Tokology*. Melbourne, Australia: Butler & Tanner, Frome and London.

Vogel, V. J. 1970. *American Indian Medicine*. Norman: University of Oklahoma Press.

## *Sexuality and Childbirth*

**Sheila Kitzinger**

Almost universally woman is seen as having a threatening power which can weaken and emasculate men . . . her sexuality and the products of her body are considered potent and dangerous. She is like a bomb which can be defused only by denial of her sensuality, by carefully circumscribed behaviour on her part, by meticulous avoidance during those critical periods when her body opens up and its fluids and other substances emerge, or at any time when a man is engaged on some task which involves special skills and concentration. The shame which women feel in Eastern Mediterranean countries, the rituals offered by husband and wife during unclean time in Judaism and Hinduism, and the taboo on sexual intercourse before going into battle or on an important hunt, engaging in a community activity of great significance or making sacrifice to the ancestors, which is typical of tribal societies, all indicate that everywhere woman is at once the creator and the destroyer, the terrible goddess Kali, who bears life in her hands. Perhaps this is how all children feel at some time about their apparently omnipotent mothers. Girls grow up and start to menstruate themselves and develop the power to bear babies in their own bodies. But boys can never do this. Some psychoanalysts have explained frequently encountered male attitudes in terms of "uterine envy."[1]

The obstetrician, as distinct from the midwife who is traditionally far less interventionist, seeks to take control of childbirth. It is then almost as if he, and not the woman, gives birth to the baby. The intricate technology has defused the bomb; childbirth has been desexed. The previously mysterious power has been analysed, and he has harnessed it to a masculine purpose and according to a masculine design.

**NOTE**

1. Ian Surtie. *The Origins of Love and Hate.* Kegan Paul, 1935.

# Punishing Drug Addicts Who Have Babies:
# Women of Color, Equality, and the Right of Privacy

Dorothy E. Roberts

## The Devaluation of Black Motherhood

. . . The systematic, institutionalized denial of reproductive freedom has uniquely marked Black women's history in America. An important part of this denial has been the devaluation of Black women as mothers. A popular mythology that degrades Black women and portrays them as less deserving of motherhood reinforces this subordination. This mythology is one aspect of a complex set of images that deny Black humanity in order to rationalize the oppression of Blacks.[1]

In this [reading], I will discuss three manifestations of the devaluation of Black motherhood: the original exploitation of Black women during slavery, the more contemporary, disproportionate removal of Black children from their mothers' custody, and sterilization abuse. Throughout this [reading], I will also show how several popular images denigrating Black mothers—the licentious Jezebel, the careless, incompetent mother, the domineering matriarch, and the lazy welfare mother—have reinforced and legitimated their devaluation.

### The Slavery Experience

The essence of Black women's experience during slavery was the brutal denial of autonomy over reproduction. Female slaves were commercially valuable to their masters not only for

their labor, but also for their capacity to produce more slaves.[2] Henry Louis Gates, Jr., writing about the autobiography of a slave named Harriet A. Jacobs, observes that it "charts in vivid detail precisely how the shape of her life and the choices she makes are defined by her reduction to a sexual object, an object to be raped, bred or abused."[3] Black women's childbearing during slavery was thus largely a product of oppression rather than an expression of self-definition and personhood.

The method of whipping pregnant slaves that was used throughout the South vividly illustrates the slaveowners' dual interest in Black women as both workers and childbearers. Slaveowners forced women to lie face down in a depression in the ground while they were whipped.[4] This procedure allowed the masters to protect the fetus while abusing the mother. It serves as a powerful metaphor for the evils of a fetal protection policy that denies the humanity of the mother. It is also a forceful symbol of the convergent oppression inflicted on slave women: they were subjugated at once both as Blacks and as females.

From slavery on, Black women have fallen outside the scope of the American ideal of womanhood.[5] Slave owners forced slave women to perform strenuous labor that contradicted the Victorian female roles prevalent in the dominant white society. Angela Davis has observed: "judged by the evolving nineteenth-century ideology of femininity, which emphasized women's roles as nurturing mothers and gentle companions and housekeepers for their husbands, Black women were practically anomalies."[6] Black women's

From Roberts, Dorothy E. 1991. "Punishing Drug Addicts Who Have Babies: Women of Color, Equality, and the Right of Privacy." *Harvard Law Review* 104: 1419–1482. Reprinted by permission.

historical deviation from traditional female roles has engendered a mythology that denies their womanhood.

One of the most prevalent images of slave women was the character of Jezebel, a woman governed by her sexual desires.[7] As early as 1736, the *South Carolina Gazette* described "African Ladies" as women "of 'strong robust constitution' who were 'not easily jaded out' but able to serve their lovers 'by Night as well as Day.'"[8] This ideological construct of the licentious Jezebel legitimated white men's sexual abuse of Black women.[9] The stereotype of Black women as sexually promiscuous helped to perpetuate their devaluation as mothers.

The myth of the "bad" Black woman was deliberately and systematically perpetuated after slavery ended.[10] For example, historian Philip A. Bruce's book, *The Plantation Negro as a Freeman,* published in 1889, strengthened popular views of both Black male and Black female degeneracy.[11] Bruce traced the alleged propensity of the Black man to rape white women to the "wantonness of the women of his own race" and "the sexual laxness of plantation women as a class."[12] This image of the sexually loose, impure Black woman that originated in slavery persists in modern American culture.[13]

Black women during slavery were also systematically denied the rights of motherhood. Slave mothers had no legal claim to their children.[14] Slave masters owned not only Black women, but also their children. They alienated slave women from their children by selling them to other slaveowners and by controlling childrearing. . . .

Black women struggled in many ways to resist the efforts of slave masters to control their reproductive lives. They used contraceptives and abortives, escaped from plantations, feigned illness, endured severe punishment, and fought back rather than submit to slave masters' sexual domination.[15] Free Black women with the means to do so purchased freedom for their daughters and sisters.[16] Black women, along with Black men, succeeded remarkably often in maintaining the integrity of their family life despite slavery's disrupting effects.[17]

## The Disproportionate Removal of Black Children

The disproportionate number of Black mothers who lose custody of their children through the child welfare system is a contemporary manifestation of the devaluation of Black motherhood.[18] This disparate impact of state intervention results in part from Black families' higher rate of reliance on government welfare.[19] Because welfare families are subject to supervision by social workers, instances of perceived neglect are more likely to be reported to governmental authorities than neglect on the part of more affluent parents.[20] Black children are also removed from their homes in part because of the child welfare system's cultural bias and application of the nuclear family pattern to Black families.[21] Black childrearing patterns that diverge from the norm of the nuclear family have been misinterpreted by government bureaucrats as child neglect.[22] For example, child welfare workers have often failed to respect the longstanding cultural tradition in the Black community of shared parenting responsibility among blood-related and non-blood kin.[23] The state has thus been more willing to intrude upon the autonomy of poor Black families, and in particular of Black mothers, while protecting the integrity of white, middle-class homes.[24]

This devaluation of Black motherhood has been reinforced by stereotypes that blame Black mothers for the problems of the Black family. This scapegoating of Black mothers dates back to slavery, when mothers were blamed for the devastating effects on their children of poverty and abuse of Black women. . . .

The scapegoating of Black mothers has manifested itself more recently in the myth of the Black matriarch, the domineering female head of the Black family. White sociologists have held Black matriarchs responsible for the disintegration of the Black family and the consequent failure of Black people to achieve success in America.[25]

Daniel Patrick Moynihan popularized this theory in his 1965 report, *The Negro Family: The Case for National Action*.[26] According to Moynihan:

> At the heart of the deterioration of the fabric of the Negro society is the deterioration of the Negro family. It is the fundamental cause of the weakness of the Negro community. . . . In essence, the Negro community has been forced into a matriarchal structure which, because it is so out of line with the rest of the American society, seriously retards the progress of the group as a whole.[27]

Thus, Moynihan attributed the cause of Black people's inability to overcome the effects of racism largely to the dominance of Black mothers.

### The Sterilization of Women of Color

Coerced sterilization is one of the most extreme forms of control over a woman's reproductive life. By permanently denying her the right to bear children, sterilization enforces society's determination that a woman does not deserve to be a mother. Unlike white women, poor women of color have been subjected to sterilization abuse . . . for decades.[28] The disproportionate sterilization of Black women is yet another manifestation of the dominant society's devaluation of Black women as mothers.

Sterilization abuse has taken the form both of blatant coercion and trickery and of subtle influences on women's decisions to be sterilized.[29] In the 1970s, some doctors conditioned delivering babies and performing abortions on Black women's consent to sterilization.[30] In a 1974 case brought by poor teenage Black women in Alabama, a federal district court found that an estimated 100,000 to 150,000 poor women were sterilized annually under federally-funded programs.[31] Some of these women were coerced into agreeing to sterilization under the threat that their welfare benefits would be withdrawn unless they submitted to the operation.[32] Despite federal and state regulations intended to prevent involuntary sterilization, physicians and other health care providers continue to urge women of color to consent to sterilization because they view these women's family sizes as excessive and believe these women are incapable of effectively using other methods of birth control.[33]

Current government funding policy perpetuates the encouragement of sterilization of poor, and thus of mainly Black, women. The federal government pays for sterilization services under the Medicaid program . . . while it often does not make available information about and access to other contraceptive techniques and abortion.[34] In effect, sterilization is the only publicly-funded birth control method readily available to poor women of color.

Popular images of the undeserving Black mother legitimate government policy as well as the practices of health care providers. The myth of the Black Jezebel has been supplemented by the contemporary image of the lazy welfare mother who breeds children at the expense of taxpayers in order to increase the amount of her welfare check.[35] This view of Black motherhood provides the rationale for society's restrictions on Black female fertility. . . . It is this image of the undeserving Black mother that also ultimately underlies the government's choice to punish crack-addicted women.

### Prosecuting Drug Addicts as Punishment for Having Babies

Informed by the historical and present devaluation of Black motherhood, we can better understand prosecutors' reasons for punishing drug-addicted mothers. . . .

It is important to recognize at the outset that the prosecutions are based in part on a woman's pregnancy and not on her illegal drug use alone.[36] Prosecutors charge these defendants not with drug use, but with child abuse or drug distribution—crimes that relate to their pregnancy. Moreover, pregnant women receive harsher sentences than drug-addicted men or women who are not pregnant.[37]

The unlawful nature of drug use must not be allowed to confuse the basis of the crimes at issue.

The legal rationale underlying the prosecutions does not depend on the illegality of drug use. Harm to the fetus is the crux of the government's legal theory. Criminal charges have been brought against women for conduct that is legal but was alleged to have harmed the fetus.[38]

When a drug-addicted woman becomes pregnant, she has only one realistic avenue to escape criminal charges: abortion.[39] Thus, she is penalized for choosing to have the baby rather than having an abortion. In this way, the state's punitive action may coerce women to have abortions rather than risk being charged with a crime. Thus, it is the *choice of carrying a pregnancy to term* that is being penalized.[40]

There is also good reason to question the government's justification for the prosecutions—the concern for the welfare of potential children. . . .

When a society has always closed its eyes to the inadequacy of prenatal care available to poor Black women, its current expression of interest in the health of unborn Black children must be viewed with suspicion. The most telling evidence of the state's disregard of Black children is the high rate of infant death in the Black community. . . . The government has chosen to punish poor Black women rather than provide the means for them to have healthy children.

The cruelty of this punitive response is heightened by the lack of available drug treatment services for pregnant drug addicts.[41] Protecting the welfare of drug addicts' children requires, among other things, adequate facilities for the mother's drug treatment. Yet a drug addict's pregnancy serves as an *obstacle* to obtaining this treatment. Treatment centers either refuse to treat pregnant women or are effectively closed to them because the centers are ill-equipped to meet the needs of pregnant addicts.[42] Most hospitals and programs that treat addiction exclude pregnant women because their babies are more likely to be born with health problems requiring expensive care.[43] Program directors also feel that treating pregnant

addicts is worth neither the increased cost nor the risk of tort liability.[44]

Moreover, there are several barriers to pregnant women who seek to use centers that will accept them. Drug treatment programs are generally based on male-oriented models that are not geared to the needs of women.[45] The lack of accommodations for children is perhaps the most significant obstacle to treatment. Most outpatient clinics do not provide child care and many residential treatment programs do not admit children.[46]. . . Predominantly male staffs and clients are often hostile to female clients and employ a confrontational style of therapy that makes many women uncomfortable.[47] Moreover, long waiting lists make treatment useless for women who need help during the limited duration of their pregnancies. . . .

Finally, and perhaps most importantly, ample evidence reveals that prosecuting addicted mothers may not achieve the government's asserted goal of healthier pregnancies; indeed, such prosecutions will probably lead to the opposite result. Pregnant addicts who seek help from public hospitals and clinics are the ones most often reported to government authorities.[48] The threat of prosecution based on this reporting forces women to remain anonymous and thus has the perverse effect of deterring pregnant drug addicts from seeking treatment.[49] For this reason, the government's decision to punish drug-addicted mothers is irreconcilable with the goal of helping them.

Pregnancy may be a time when women are most motivated to seek treatment for drug addiction and make positive lifestyle changes.[50] The government should capitalize on this opportunity by encouraging drug-addicted women to seek help and providing them with comprehensive treatment. Punishing pregnant women who use drugs only exacerbates the causes of addiction—poverty, lack of self-esteem, and hopelessness.[51] Perversely, this makes it more likely that poor Black women's children—the asserted beneficiaries of the prosecutions—will suffer from the same hardships. . . .

### The Intersection of Privacy and Equality

. . . The singling out of Black mothers for punishment combines in a single government action several wrongs prohibited by constitutional doctrines. Black mothers are denied autonomy over procreative decisions because of their race. The government's denial of Black women's fundamental right to choose to bear children serves to perpetuate the legacy of racial discrimination embodied in the devaluation of Black motherhood. . . .

Poor crack addicts are punished for having babies because they fail to measure up to the state's ideal of motherhood. Prosecutors have brought charges against women who use drugs during pregnancy without demonstrating any harm to the fetus.[52] Moreover, a government policy that has the effect of punishing primarily poor Black women for having babies evokes the specter of racial eugenics, especially in light of the history of sterilization abuse of women of color. . . . These factors make clear that these women are not punished simply because they may harm their unborn children. They are punished because the combination of their poverty, race, and drug addiction is seen to make them unworthy of procreating. . . .

Denying someone the right to bear children—or punishing her for exercising that right—deprives her of a basic part of her humanity.[53] When this denial is based on race, it also functions to preserve a racial hierarchy that essentially disregards Black humanity.

The abuse of sterilization laws designed to effect eugenic policy demonstrates the potential danger of governmental standards for procreation. During the first half of the twentieth century, the eugenics movement embraced the theory . . . that intelligence and other personality traits are genetically determined and therefore inherited.[54] This hereditarian belief, coupled with the reform approach of the progressive era, fueled a campaign to remedy America's social problems by stemming biological degeneracy. Eugenicists advocated compulsory sterilization to prevent reproduction by people who were likely to produce allegedly defective offspring. Eugenic sterilization was thought to improve society by eliminating its "socially inadequate" members.[55] Many states around the turn of the century enacted involuntary sterilization laws directed at those deemed burdens on society, including the mentally retarded, mentally ill, epileptics, and criminals.[56]

In a 1927 decision, *Buck v. Bell*, . . . the Supreme Court upheld the constitutionality . . . of a Virginia involuntary sterilization law.[57] The plaintiff, Carrie Buck, was described in the opinion as "a feeble minded white woman" committed to a state mental institution who was "the daughter of a feeble minded mother in the same institution, and the mother of an illegitimate feeble minded child."[58] The Court approved an order of the mental institution that Buck undergo sterilization. Justice Holmes, himself an ardent eugenicist, . . . gave eugenic theory the imprimatur of constitutional law in his infamous declaration: "Three generations of imbeciles are enough."[59]

The salient feature of the eugenic sterilization laws is their brutal imposition of society's restrictive norms of motherhood. Governmental control of reproduction in the name of science masks racist and classist judgments about who deserves to bear children. It is grounded on the premise that people who depart from social norms do not deserve to procreate. . . . Carrie Buck, for example, was punished by sterilization not because of any mental disability, but because of her deviance from society's social and sexual norms. . . .

Fourteen years after *Buck v. Bell*, the Court acknowledged the danger of the eugenic rationale. Justice Douglas recognized both the fundamental quality of the right to procreate and its connection to equality in a later sterilization decision, *Skinner v. Oklahoma*. . . . *Skinner* considered the constitutionality of the Oklahoma Habitual

Criminal Sterilization Act . . . authorizing the sterilization of persons convicted two or more times for "felonies involving moral turpitude."[60] An Oklahoma court had ordered Skinner to undergo a vasectomy after he was convicted once of stealing chickens and twice of robbery with firarms. . . . The statute, the Court found, treated unequally criminals who had committed intrinsically the same quality of offense. For example, men who had committed grand larceny three times were sterilized, but embezzlers were not. The Court struck down the statute as a violation of the equal protection clause. Declaring the right to bear children to be "one of the basic civil rights of man,"[61] the Court . . . held that the government failed to demonstrate that the statute's classifications were justified by eugenics or the inheritability of criminal traits. . . .

Although the reasons advanced for the sterilization of chicken thieves and the prosecution of drug-addicted mothers are different, both practices are dangerous for similar reasons. Both effectuate ethnocentric judgments by the government that certain members of society do not deserve to have children. As the Court recognized in *Skinner,* the enforcement of a government standard for childbearing denies the disfavored group a critical aspect of human dignity. . . .

The history of compulsory sterilization demonstrates that society deems women who deviate from its norms of motherhood—in 1941, teenaged delinquent girls like Carrie Buck who bore illegitimate children, today, poor Black crack addicts who use drugs during pregnancy—"unworthy of the high privilege" of procreation. The government therefore refuses to affirm their human dignity by helping them overcome obstacles to good mothering. . . . Rather, it punishes them by sterilization or criminal prosecution and thereby denies them a basic part of their humanity. When this denial is based on race, the violation is especially serious. Governmental policies that perpetuate racial subordination through the denial of procreative rights, which threaten both racial

equality and privacy at once, should be subject to the highest scrutiny. . . .

### Conclusion

Our understanding of the prosecutions of drug-addicted mothers must include the perspective of the women whom they most directly affect. The prosecutions arise in a particular historical and political context that has constrained reproductive choice for poor women of color. The state's decision to punish drug-addicted mothers rather than help them stems from the poverty and race of the defendants and society's denial of their full dignity as human beings. Viewing the issue from their vantage point reveals that the prosecutions punish for having babies women whose motherhood has historically been devalued.

A policy that attempts to protect fetuses by denying the humanity of their mothers will inevitably fail.[62] We must question such a policy's true concern for the dignity of the fetus, just as we question the motives of the slave owner who protected the unborn slave child while whipping his pregnant mother. Although the master attempted to separate the mother and fetus for his commercial ends, their fates were inextricably intertwined. The tragedy of crack babies is initially a tragedy of crack-addicted mothers. Both are part of a larger tragedy of a community that is suffering a host of indignities, including, significantly, the denial of equal respect for its women's reproductive decisions.

It is only by affirming the personhood and equality of poor women of color that the survival of their future generation will be ensured. The first principle of the government's response to the crisis of drug-exposed babies should be the recognition of their mothers' worth and entitlement to autonomy over their reproductive lives. A commitment to guaranteeing these fundamental rights of poor women of color, rather than punishing them, is the true solution to the problem of unhealthy babies.

## NOTES

1. . . . For a discussion of the hegemonic function of racist ideology, see Crenshaw, *supra* note, at 1370–81 (1988). *See generally* G. Fredrickson, The Black Image in the White Mind 256–82 (1071) . . . ; J. Williamson, The Crucible of Race: Black-White Relations in the American South Since Emancipation 111–51 (1984). . . .

2. *See* A. Davis, Women, Race, and Class 7 (1981); J. Jones, Labor of Love, Labor of Sorrow: Black Women, Work and the Family from Slavery to the Present 12 (1985). Legislation giving the children of Black women and white men the status of slaves left female slaves vulnerable to sexual violation as a means of financial gain. *See* P. Giddings, When and Where I Enter: The Impact of Black Women on Race and Sex in America 37 (1984). . . .

   White masters controlled their slaves' reproductive capacity by rewarding pregnancy with relief from work in the field and additions of clothing and food, punishing slave women who did not give birth, manipulating slave marital choices, forcing them to breed, and raping them. *See* J. Jones, *supra,* at 34–35; We Are Your Sisters: Black Women in the Nineteenth Century 24–26 (D. Sterling ed. 1984); Clinton, *Caught in the Web of the Big House: Women and Slavery,* in The Web of Southern Social Relations 19, 23–28 (W. Raser, R. Saunders & J. Wakelyn eds. 1985).

3. Gates, *To be Raped, Bred or Abused,* N. Y. Times Book Rev., Nov. 22, 1987, at 12 (reviewing H. Jacobs, Incidents in the Life of a Slave Girl (J. Yellin ed. 1987)).

4. *See* J. Jones, *supra* note, at 20; Johnson, *supra* note 1, at 513.

5. *See* A. Davis, *supra* note 2, at 5; D. White, Ar'n't I a Woman? Female Slaves in the Plantation South 16, 27–29 (1985). . . .

6. A. Davis, *supra* note 91, at 7.

7. *See* D. White, *supra* note 5, at 28–29.

8. *Id.* at 30.

9. *See* E. Fox-Genovese, *supra* note, at 292; D. White, *supra* note 94, at 61.

10. *See* Black Women in White America 163–71 (G. Lerner ed. 1173); P. Giddings, *supra* note 91, at 85–89; B. Hooks, *supra* note 17, at 55–60.

11. *See* Gresham, *supra* note, at 117.

12. P. Bruce, The Plantation Negro as a Freeman 84–85 (1889).

13. *See* b. hooks, *supra* note, at 65–68; Omolade, *Black Women, Black Men and Tawana Brawley: The Shared Condition,* 12 Harv. Women's L. J. 12, 16 (1989).

14. *See* Allen, *Surrogacy, Slavery, and the Ownership of Life,* 13 Harv. J. L. & Pub. Pol'y 139, 140 n.9 (1990). . . .

15. *See* P. Giddings, *supra* note 2, at 46; We Are Your Sisters, *supra* note 2, at 25–26, 58–61; D. White, *supra* note 5, at 76–90.

16. *See* Black Women in White America, *supra* note 10, at 40–42 . . . Black Women in Nineteenth-Century American Life 329 (B. Loewenberg & R. Bogin eds. 1976).

17. *See generally* H. Gutman, The Black Family in Slavery and Freedom, 1790–1925 (1976) (describing the life of the Black family during slavery); Jones, *"My Mother Was Much of a Woman": Black Women, Work, and the Family Under Slavery,* 8 Feminist Stud. 235, 252–61 (1982). . . .

18. *See* Gray & Nybell, *Issues in African-American Family Preservation,* 69 Child Welfare 513, 513 (1990) (noting that about half of the children in foster care are Black); Hogan & Sin, *Minority Children and the Child Welfare System: An Historical Perspective,* 33 Soc. Work 493 (1988). Once Black children enter foster care, they remain there longer and receive less desirable placements than white children; they are also less likely than white children to be returned home or adopted. *See* B. Mandell, Where Are the Children? A Class Analysis of Foster Care and Adoption 36 (1973); Gray & Nybell, *supra,* at 513–14; Stehno, *Differential Treatment of Minority Children in Service Systems,* 27 Soc. Work 39, 39–41 (1982). These realities have led some Blacks to deem foster care a system of legalized slavery. *See* B. Mandell, *supra,* at 60. . . .

19. *See* Wald, *supra* note, at 629 n.22.

20. See Faller & Ziefert, *supra* note, at 47; Wald, *supra* note 53, at 629 n. 21. . . . Jenkins, *Child Welfare as a Class System,* in Children and Decent People 3–4 (A. Schorr ed. 1974).

21. *Cf.* Santosky v. Kramer, 455 U.S. 745, 763 (1982) (noting that termination proceedings "are often vulnerable to judgments based on cultural or class

bias"); Gray & Nybell, *supra* note 18, at 515–17; Stack, *Cultural Perspectives on Child Welfare*, 12 N. Y. U. Rev. L. & Soc. Change 539, 541 (1983–84) *See generally* A. Billingsley & J. Giovannoni, Children of the Storm (1972) (tracing the history of Black children in the American child welfare system).

22. *See* Gray & Nybell, *supra* note 18, at 515–17; Stack, *supra* note 21, at 541. . . .

23. *See* Stack, *supra* note 112, at 539–43.

24. *See id.* at 547.

25. *See* P. Giddings, *supra* note 2, at 325–35; b. hooks, *supra* note 17, at 70–83; R. Staples, The Black Woman in America 10–34 (1976); Bennett & Gresham, *supra* note, at 117–18.

26. Office of Planning & Policy Research, U.S. Dep't of Labor, The Negro Family: The Case for National Action (1965).

27. *Id.* at 5.

28. *See* A. Davis, *supra* note 2, at 215–21; Nsiah-Jefferson, *Reproductive Laws, Women of Color, and Low-Income Women,* in Reproductive Laws for the 1990s, at 46–47 (S. Cohen & N. Taub eds. 1988). One study found that 43% of women sterilized in 1973 under a federally funded program were Black, although only 33% of the patients were Black. . . . Spanish-speaking women are twice as likely to be sterilized as those who speak English. *See* Levin & Taub, *Reproductive Rights,* in Women and the Law § 10A.07[3][b], at 10A-28 (C. Lefcourt ed. 1989). The racial disparity in sterilization cuts across economic and educational lines, although the frequency of sterilization is generally higher among the poor and uneducated. Another study found that 9.7% of college-educated Black women had been sterilized, compared to 5.6% of college-educated white women. Among women without a high school diploma, 31.6% of Black women and 14.5% of white women had been sterilized. *See id.*

29. *See* Clarke, *Subtle Forms of Sterilization Abuse: A Reproductive Rights Analysis,* in Test-Tube Women 120, 120–32 (R. Arditti, R. Klein & S. Minden eds. 1984); Nsiah-Jefferson, *supra* note, at 44–45; Petchesky, *supra* note 124, at 32.

30. *See* Nsiah-Jefferson, *supra* note, at 46–47.

31. *See* Relf v. Weinberger, 372 F. Supp. 1196, 1199 (D.D.C. 1974), *on remand sub nom.* Relf v. Mathews, 403 F. Supp. 1235 (D.D.C. 1975), *va-* *cated sub nom.* Relf v. Weinberger, 565 F.2d 722 (D.C. Cir. 1977).

32. *See id.*

33. *See* Nsiah-Jefferson, *supra* note, at 47–48; . . . In contrast to the encouragement of minority sterilization, our society views childbearing by white women as desirable. . . . *See* Colker, *Feminism, Theology, and Abortion: Toward Love, Compassion, and Wisdom,* 77 Calif. L. Rev. 1011, 1067 n.196 (1989). . . .

34. *See* Nsiah-Jefferson, *supra* note 125, at 45–46; Petchesky, *supra* note, at 39; . . .

35. *See* Harrington, *Introduction* to S. Sheehan, A Welfare Mother at x–xi (1976); Milwaukee County Welfare Rights Org., Welfare Mothers Speak Out 72–92 (1972).

36. At Jennifer Johnson's sentencing, the prosecutor made clear the nature of the charges against her: "About the end of December 1988, our office undertook a policy to begin to deal with mothers like Jennifer Johnson . . . as in the status of a child abuse case, Your Honor. . . . *We have never viewed this as a drug case.*" Motion for Rehearing and Sentencing at 12, State v. Johnson, No. E89-890-CFA (Fla. Cir. Ct. Aug. 25, 1989) (emphasis added).

37. The drug user's pregnancy not only greatly increases the likelihood that she will be prosecuted, but also greatly enhances the penalty she faces upon conviction. In most states, drug use is a misdemeanor, while distribution of drugs is a felony. *See* Hoffman, *supra* note, at 44.

38. Pamela Rae Stewart, for example, was charged with criminal neglect in part because she failed to follow her doctor's orders to stay off her feet and refrain from sexual intercourse while she was pregnant. *See* People v. Stewart, No. M508197, slip op. at 4 (Cal. Mun. Ct. Feb. 26, 1987); Bonavoglia, *The Ordeal of Pamela Rae Stewart,* Ms., Jul./Aug. 1987, at 92, 92.

39. Seeking drug treatment is not a viable alternative. First, it is likely that the pregnant addict will be unable to find a drug treatment program that will accept her. . . . Second, even if she successfully completes drug counseling by the end of her pregnancy, she may still be prosecuted for her drug use that occurred during pregnancy before she was able to overcome her addiction.

40. I recognize that both becoming pregnant and continuing a pregnancy to term are not necessarily

real "choices" that women—particularly women of color and addicted women—make. Rape, battery, lack of available contraceptives, and prostitution induced by drug addiction may lead a woman to become pregnant without exercising meaningful choice. Similarly, coercion from the father or her family, lack of money to pay for an abortion, or other barriers to access to an abortion may force a woman to continue an unwanted pregnancy. . . .

Nevertheless, these constraints on a woman's choice do not justify the government's punishment of the reproductive course that she ultimately follows. While we work to create the conditions for meaningful reproductive choice, it is important to affirm women's right to be free from unwanted state intrusion in their reproductive decisions.

41. *See* Chavkin, *Drug Addiction and Pregnancy: Policy Crossroads,* 80 Am. J. Pub. Health 483, 485 (1990); McNulty, *supra* note, at 301–02. . . .

42. *See* Cusky, Berger & Densen-Gerber, *Issues in the Treatment of Female Addiction: A Review and Critique of the Literature,* 6 Contemp. Drug Probs. 307, 324–26 (1977); McNulty, *supra* note, at 301–02; Suffet, Hutson & Brotman, *Treatment of the Pregnant Addict: A Historical Overview,* in Pregnant Addicts and Their Children: A Comprehensive Care Approach 13, 21 (R. Brotman, D. Hutson & F. Suffet eds. 1984); Alters, *supra* note 30, at 1, col. 1; Freitag, *Hospital Defends Limiting of Drug Program,* N. Y. Times, Dec. 12, 1989, at B9, col. 1.

43. *See* McNulty, *supra* note, at 301; Teltsch, *supra* note 30, at A14, col. 1.

44. *See* Chavkin, *Drug Addiction and Pregnancy: Policy Crossroads, supra* note 147, at 485; McNulty, *Combatting Pregnancy Discrimination in Access to Substance Abuse Treatment for Low-Income Women,* 23 Clearinghouse Rev. 21, 22 (1989).

45. *See* Cuskey, Berger & Densen-Gerber, *supra* note 44, at 312–14; Alters, *supra* note, at 1, col. 1.

46. *See* McNulty, *supra* note 150, at 22; *Substance Abuse Treatment for Women: Crisis in Access, supra* note 147, at 9.

47. *See* Chavkin, *Drug Addiction and Pregnancy, Policy Crossroads, supra* note 41, at 485; *see also* National Institute on Drug Abuse, Drug Dependency in Pregnancy 46 (1978) (describing pervasive negative attitudes toward pregnant addicts).

48. *See* Berrien, *Pregnancy and Drug Use: The Dangerous and Unequal Use of Punitive Measures,* 2 Yale J. L. & Feminism 239, 247 (1990).

49. *See* American Medical Association, *Report of the Board of Trustees on Legal Interventions During Pregnancy: Court Ordered Medical Treatments and Legal Penalties for Potentially Harmful Behavior by Pregnant Women,* 264 J. A. M. A. 2663, 2669 (1990). The reaction of pregnant women in San Diego to the 1997 arrest of Pamela Rae Stewart for harming her unborn child illustrates the deterrent effect of prosecution. Health care professionals reported that their pregnant clients' fear of prosecution for drug use made some of them distrustful and caused others to decline prenatal care altogether. *See* Moss, *supra* note, at 1411–12.

50. . . . Chavkin, *Help, Don't Jail, Addicted Mothers, supra* note 147 at A21, col. 2.

51. *See* Escamilla-Mondanaro, *Women: Pregnancy, Children and Addiction,* 9 J. Psychedelic Drugs 59, 59– 60 (1977); *see also* Zuckerman, Amaro, Bauchner & Cabral, *Depressive Symptoms During Pregnancy: Relationship to Poor Health Behaviors,* 160 Am. J. Obstetrics & Gyn. 1107, 1109 (1989). . . .

52. In the *Johnson* trial, for example, the prosecution introduced no evidence that Johnson's children were adversely affected by their mother's crack use. Indeed, there was testimony that the children were healthy and developing normally. *See* Trial Transcript, *supra* note 4, at 46–47, 120 (testimony of Dr. Randy Tompkin and Clarice Johnson, Jennifer's mother). A law proposed in Ohio makes drug use during pregnancy grounds for sterilization. . . . Similarly, several states have enacted statutes that make a woman's drug use during pregnancy by itself grounds to deprive her of custody of her child. *See supra* note 50.

53. *See* Karst, *supra* note, at 32; Stefan, *Whose Egg Is It Anyway? Reproductive Rights of Incarcerated, Institutionalized and Incompetent Women,* 13 Nova L. Rev. 405, 454 (1989); . . . Asch, *Reproductive Technology and Disability,* in Reproductive Laws for the 1990s, *supra* note, at 106–07. . . .

I recognize that there are women who choose not to have children or are incapable of having children and that this choice or inability does not make them any less human. . . . It is not the act of having children that makes an individual fully human; it is society's view of whether she deserves to have children.

54. For a discussion of the eugenic sterilization movement in the early twentieth century, see Burgdorf & Burgdorf, *The Wicked Witch Is Almost Dead: Buck v. Bell and the Sterilization of Handicapped Persons,* 50 Temp. L.Q. 995, 997–1005 (1977); and Cynkar, Buck v. Bell: *"Felt Necessities" v. Fundamental Values?,* 81 Colum. L. Rev. 1418, 1425–35 (1981). . . .

The discrediting of eugenic theory, the development of the constitutional doctrine of reproductive autonomy, and the changing view of mental retardation spurred a major reform of sterilization law. . . . Reports of Nazi Germany's program of racial eugenics achieved through widespread sterilization precipitated the modern rejection of these laws. *See* Scott, *supra* note, at 811–12.

55. One report written by a leading scholar of the eugenic movement defined the "socially inadequate" as:

> "(1) feeble-minded; (2) insane (including the psychopathic); (3) criminalistic (including the delinquent and wayward); (4) epileptic; (5) inebriate (including drug-habitués); (6) diseased (including the tuberculous, the syphilitic, the leprous, and others with chronic, infectious and legally segregable diseases); (7) blind (including those with seriously impaired vision); (8) deaf (including those with seriously impaired hearing); (9) deformed (including the crippled); and (10) dependent (including orphans, ne'er-do-wells, the homeless, tramps and paupers)."

Cynkar, *supra* note 54, at 1428 (quoting H. Laughlin, The Legal Status of Eugenical Sterilization 65 (1929)).

56. As late as 1966, 26 states still had eugenic sterilization laws. . . . It has been estimated that over 70,000 persons were involuntarily sterilized under these statutes.

57. 1924 Va. Acts 394. For a discussion of the history of the Virginia sterilization law's enactment, see Lombardo, *Three Generations, No Imbeciles: New Light on* Buck v. Bell, 60 N.Y.U.L. Rev. 30, 34–48 (1985).

58. *Bell,* 274 U.S. at 205. Subsequent research has revealed that the Court's factual statement was erroneous. Although Carrie Buck became pregnant out of wedlock, the finding that she was "feeble minded" was based on insubstantial testimony. *See* Gould, *Carrie Buck's Daughter,* 2 Const. Commentary 331, 336 (1985); Lombardo, *supra* note 57, at 52.

59. *Bell,* 274 U.S. at 207.

60. *Id.* § 173.

61. *Id.* at 541.

62. I hear this false dichotomy in the words of Muskegon, Michigan, narcotics officer Al Van Hemert: " 'If the mother wants to smoke crack and kill herself, I don't care.' . . . 'Let her die, but don't take that poor baby with her.' " Hoffman, *supra* note 5, at 34.

# Imaging Bodies, Imagining Relations:
# Narratives of Queer Women and "Assisted Conception"

Jacquelyne Luce

For many years, Kiera's[1] favorite bedtime story was the story about her birth. Her moms, Susan and Tracy, took turns telling her about the first contractions, the many showers they took during labor, and Kiera's first appearance after her journey through her mom's birth canal into this world. Over and over again Kiera requested this story, able to recite it herself, but pleased to drift off to the sound of one of her mom's voices telling the tale of how her mom carried her in her uterus until it was time for her to be born. One late September evening, at the wise age of three and a half, Kiera interrupted the well-worn story with a question. "But," she said, "how did I get *in* Mommy's uterus in the first place?"

Kiera's question captures the focus of my ongoing research. I heard the story a few times from different women and eventually from Kiera's moms themselves. The story was used as a way of conveying children's interest in their own conception stories and, I propose, draws attention to disparate (yet not conflicting) stories about origins (conceptions) and the making of queer[2] families. Following the work of Sarah Franklin (1997) on the making of "new narratives of conception" in the age of assisted reproduction my research in this area began with a desire to focus on queer women's narratives of assisted conception. Now,

after years of commitment to this project, including 18 months of fieldwork and interviews with 80 lesbian, bisexual and queer women living in large and small communities of British Columbia, Canada, I still stumble when asked to define my project. Most often, and perhaps most accurately, I describe it as a project that explores lesbian, bi and queer women's experiences of trying to get pregnant. Sometimes, I say that the research is about how we bring children into our lives. I tell people that my research is about conception stories and how the meaning of conception is redefined by women's individual and collective experiences.

During the late-1990s, British Columbia emerged as a jurisdiction that supports lesbian and gay parents. In 1996, the B.C. government implemented the *Adoption Act,* which allows "any one or two persons to adopt." This legislation entitles lesbians and gay men to file adoption applications either as single or co-parents. In 1998, the *Family Relations Act* of B.C. was revised to include same-sex partners in the definition of spouse, thereby conferring the rights and obligations of spousal support and child custody, visitation rights, and financial support on same-sex partners and parents in the event of a break-up. In 1999 and 2000, I interviewed women about experiences that spanned two decades, from 1980 to 2000, a period characterized by the "lesbian baby boom." The stories of the women I interviewed and my own are most often set in British Columbia. Some of the tales women told took place in other Canadian provinces or U.S. states and were recounted by women now

From Luce, Jacquelyne. 2004. "Imaging Bodies, Imagining Relations: Narratives of Queer Women and 'Assisted Conception.' " *Journal of Medical Humanities* 25: 47–56. Reprinted with kind permission from Springer Science and Business Media.

living in British Columbia. The oldest child of one of the women I interviewed was born in 1983. Some women were pregnant at the time of the interview and some women were in the process of trying to conceive, adopt and foster. The stories I retell in this paper are defined by twenty years of awareness and knowledge of HIV and safer-sex campaigns, the normalization of reproductive technologies, changes to same-sex rights legislation, and the shifting visibility of single and partnered queer biological, adoptive and social parents. The availability of technology, the isolation and connectedness of lesbians living in urban centres, small cities and rural settings, and visions of lesbian bodies and queer sex and sexualities, all figure into the narratives told. Images, produced and read within the fields of visual arts, genetics, obstetrical sciences, and the imaginations of queers and straights alike are at the forefront of popular and personal dyke conception stories. This paper offers a series of snapshots produced at the intersection of queerness and reproduction, invoking images of dyke experiences and queer definitions and uses of technology, as a means of reimaging and reimagining the cultural landscape of reproduction.

"A very large category of users of human cloning might be lesbian couples." Bridging the columns of a 1999 article in *Scientific American,* these words are set above a photo of Dolly, the first successfully cloned mammal, and her "natural" offspring Bonnie. The author, Ronald Green, suggests that cloning technologies would offer lesbians a means of circumventing the legal complications present in the face of changing legislation regarding the rights of gamete donors. Here, he is referring to the practice of awarding donors custody and visitation rights in donor v. lesbian court cases. Furthermore, he states, the combination of genetic material from both women, "affords lesbian couples an approximation of sexual reproduction" (Green, 1999, p. 82). Cloning thus becomes the most recent addition to the ever-growing repertoire of "ideal" lesbian procreation methods.

"Affords lesbian couples an approximation of sexual reproduction." The advent of contraceptive technologies is the impetus for academic, religious and medical statements regarding the separation of reproduction from sexuality during the twentieth century. Sex without babies. The perceived removal of "sex" from procreative acts involving the use of reproductive technologies depicts assisted conception as asexual. Babies without sex. If reproduction (conception) can occur without sex, heteronormative logic suggests, it then becomes *possible* for lesbians (and gay men) to become parents. Furthermore, invasive, technological assistance such as cloning, or more realistically, the practice of transferring an embryo created using the egg of one woman into the uterus of her partner, is viewed as allowing lesbians to most closely approximate "sexual reproduction," and thus it would seem, "real" parenthood. What if you don't think about sexuality as intrinsically tied to reproduction? What if neither contraceptive nor conception technologies challenge your ideas about sexuality or how babies are made? Would employing an assisted reproductive technology still render assisted reproduction "asexual"? I suggested once, or perhaps more than once, that lesbian conceptions aren't necessarily asexual. Rather, such a definition rests on perceptions and meanings of both sex and sexuality.

Hmm. Dyke. Did you know that some dykes fuck boyz[3] to get pregnant? It can be planned. It can be accidental. It's inexpensive. It's risky. It's safe. "If inseminating. . . ." Finally, lesbian safe-sex literature is starting to include information about sex with men and inseminations with fresh sperm. "Live donors" they tend to be called. Note: Sexually transmitted diseases (STDs) can be transmitted with or without "the sex." Test first. Follow standard STD and HIV protocols. Then again, many dykes fuck grrls to get pregnant. Whether fresh or frozen, by body or by mail, one item of information that circulates is that orgasms are conducive to conception. At home, some women leave instructions for donors to leave when *they're* done "doing their thing" so that the women can continue doing theirs. "We figured we needed to prepare my body," one woman explains. At clinics, some nurses dim the lights, leave the room. "She gave us time to be together," comments a lesbian mom.

This is one of my stories, a "partial truth" tale about a dyke talking to lesbians, bi women, queer women, and listening to stories about how babies are made, how children are grieved, how we process life and loss. It is a partial tale reflecting the realities of partial truths and individual perspectives. It is partial in the sense that the stories are fragmented and identities are blurred. It is a reworking of words and images. It is a rewriting of voices to produce a dialogue through space and time. It is a tale told by a queer medical anthropologist. Oops. I've said it again. I hear that's academic suicide. "What perspective do you have?" The male voice questions me, finally agreeing to an interview. First thing, step into his office, sit down, hand him my consent form over the wide oak desk, "Are you heterosexual?" he asks. No. His voice fills the room as he explains to me—the lesbian body sitting in his space, asking questions about his practice—that he is *quite* heterosexual. Quite. Emphasis his. His mouth still moving, garbled noises, familiar. Questions of location. Different questions, different locations. "I was wondering if you were queer," says the lesbian prospective parent over fresh baked cookies and tea after an hour of talking about sperm, bodies and legal custody issues. "I mean, obviously you are." Obviously. October. At a Queer Families Workshop handing out flyers about my project a dyke looks at me, "Are you queer?" Wearing a femmy short sleeved purple turtleneck, I'm moving this weekend, don't have access to my clothes, and wouldn't have chosen to wear this in this space I answer, yes.

"You have to prove that you're out and then when you are pregnant, you have to prove that you're out all over again," comments the woman sitting across from me in a diner off a side road in a small town in the not-so-northern northern interior of British Columbia. "I told my doctor I was pregnant. That I sleep with women. She told me that I'm obviously straight. That it's confusing for the child when parents go back and forth all the time. She assumed that is what I do." A little while later, I ask, "How did you think about your sexuality when you got pregnant?" With a serious look, she answers, "It threw me for a loop. I thought, maybe I'm not a lesbian." Boxes. Labels. Behaviors. Bodies. Expectations.

I wrote about bisexuality and queerness during the first year of my Ph.D. studies. The year I came out. Or rather, the year I first identified as queer. The year I submitted proposals to do research on queer women and reproductive technologies. The year a faculty member suggested that I leave the word lesbian out of the project description. The year that I put quotes around queer followed by an author date citation . . . Butler, 1990. *Gender Trouble*. I wrote about where my sense of bisexual politics and queer identities fits within an historical body of medical literature that pathologizes "lesbianism" and scrutinizes our deviant bodies for evidence of biologically determined deviant desires.

Straight men? Gay men? Men with children? Men with partners? Choosing donors is a complicated process. "I think I'd choose a gay donor." She's already approached a few men, but nothing has worked out so far. "It would be like a gift for him, too, because gay men don't have many opportunities to have children. And anyway, what if it is genetic? Why shouldn't we try to up the odds of the gay gene?" Across town, a few years earlier, a lesbian couple sought their family physician's advice about the technical aspects of at-home donor insemination. "She always seemed nice, friendly. When we told her that we were planning to have a gay friend of ours act as our donor, the doctor asked, 'Are you not worried about it being hereditary?' Homosexuality being hereditary. Oh? And that would be a problem?"

Over email a straight man wanting to know how to put himself out on the donor market asks me about terminology—homosexual, bi, queer, dyke, gay. He saw one of my posters in a small town on Vancouver Island. He has a teenage daughter and he has always thought that being a donor would be a nice thing to do for someone. But, how do you know what language to use? How should I answer that question? How do we think through the idea that lesbians who sleep with men are not bisexual? How do we make sense of the idea that bi women may never sleep with men? One woman I interviewed cringes at the word "dyke." It is a word that has hurt her on several occasions. Another woman sees herself as a queer femme, but says she uses context dependent identity labels. Another woman identifies as trans; her girlfriend alternately refers to her/him as her girlfriend/boyfriend. Other women don't talk about sexual identity at all fearing the loss of their jobs, their homes, their children. Is it possible to understand that words and identities and behavior mean everything and nothing simultaneously? In order to talk about queer women's health and queer parenting we need to use language that has meaning in our everyday lives. "Lesbian health" literature often boxes people in obscuring the fluidity and flexibility of behaviors, desires and sometimes/often the pragmatics of living.

Anonymous. Known. Willing-to-be-known. With a photo. With a video. Without. Someone with the same cultural background. Somebody different. Someone who is smart. Someone who is creative. A construction worker. An engineer. Women's choices regarding donors are tied to histories, perspectives on genetics, and the politics of recognition by society. Who counts as a parent? What is considered risky? I'm back at the little café, my tape recorder on the table between us. The key issues are health, time and sexuality. "My straight friends are like, oh geez, it's not like you've never slept with guys . . . Because before I realized where I wanted to be I was supposed to be married. I had slept with men and what would it mean to do so one more time? But, it's not that healthy out there. I'd be worried about what I'd be conceiving. And having this male figure that would be coming back 10 months down

the road saying, that's my kid, too, and I want rights. There are too many things to consider. You have to go through all this testing. And even then some of the results, or symptoms, don't show up for 5 years. I don't have five years to wait."

Playing the odds of conception. Lesbians constantly weigh social against medical against legal risks. And costs. And emotions. Labeled "socially *infertile*" by the medical establishment, lesbians (lesbian bodies) are expected to seek out medically assisted conception. Labeled "*socially* infertile" justifies the exclusion of lesbians (lesbian bodies) from fertility programs. I'm surprised to hear myself arguing for the need to recognize lesbians' abilities to get pregnant without medical intervention just as often as I lobby for recognition of lesbians' experiences of pregnancy loss and difficulties conceiving.

"I thought about it a lot. Why not just go pick up a guy at a bar? A young straight man because around here HIV isn't as prevalent among heterosexuals. Maybe that's how I'd do it this time around." Her boots rest on the desk in the office I am using for the day. At thirty-nine she's tried twice. She talks about driving four hours from her small town home to a physician's office in the big city, sometimes paying to stay at a cheap motel while waiting to ovulate so that the sperm would be injected at the most opportune and cost-effective moment. Six months and no embryo. She wasn't comfortable putting hormones from horses in her body. She stopped trying. A couple of years later she started again. That time, six months taking Chlomid and, still, it didn't work. "Every month I had to say, 'I'm not pregnant.' I thought I was a disappointment to the group." The group of lesbians wanting to be moms, creating supportive environments for children not yet conceived.

"Why would lesbians want to have children anyway?" Excuse me? The woman asking the question stood by as a lesbian mom who just heard one of my papers told me about a court decision not to let gay sperm into New York State. Another woman shared that she and her partner are starting to think about trying and she'll want to follow my studies. Yet another woman handed me her card . . . she's done research in sperm banks, keep in touch. "I don't think I understand your question," I say. "Well, lesbians are supposed to be overthrowing the system. Why would they then want to have children?" I respond by asking her why straight women want to have children. "I don't want to have children," she says emphatically. "Well, some lesbians want to have children and some don't." I tell her that my partner never planned to have children. I have always wanted children. She looks at me. "Well, if all you are going to do is base this on your own experience. . . ." The safety of the space is gone. I'm queer. I'm not a feminist anthropologist well versed in the rhetoric of experience, the need to recognize one's own situatedness in research and the value of sharing knowledge. I'm just some dyke who stood at a podium and told a few stories about her "friends" (Anne Heche, Rachel Pepper, Noreen Stevens, Melissa Etheridge). And I've already decided she's straight, she thinks her questions are the critical ones and she's probably not even listening to my ideas about how we need to displace this strange heteronormative narrative of motherhood and gender and sexuality. That I'm not interested in doing a comparative study of queer women's and straight women's maternal desires is obviously not the correct response. The woman continues to reiterate the question I should be asking, makes some comment about how she can see that perhaps lesbians need families to take to corporate picnics, and walks away with the statement that she "gets it"—"The less aggressive one has the baby." Pause. Butch and femme aesthetics, play, and realities are not up for discussion. The same issues really do come up in my life . . . queers talking about nuclear and extended families, butches wearing maternity dresses, daughters growing up with four moms, lesbians discussing the differences between being mothers and being parents, jokes about feeling both comfortable and not with expanded networks of straight friends, having to constantly

come out as a lesbian single mom, thinking through the politics of getting pregnant, adoption, choosing donors, getting married, defining family, being out.

The sign on the door to the maternity unit reads, *Only Husbands Allowed*. A relic of the past, I'm told. Six hours southeast I am in another city that maintains these artifacts. In the living room a three-week-old baby boy is bundled in a blanket, resting in the crook of his mom's elbow. Sitting across from us, his other mom tells me about her first experience giving him a bath. Still in the hospital, she followed the nurse to the bathing room. The nurse was quiet. A bit aloof. "After a few minutes, I just looked at her and said, 'Well, we're not your conventional family, are we?' The nurse snorted back, 'You said it, not me!' 'Yeah, I nodded, 'but you thought it.'" Constant struggles for recognition. And, yet, people continue to tell me that it isn't important whom "I sleep with." They say it really doesn't matter.

I am heading to Prince George to do some interviews. The taxi driver picks me up outside of my apartment building on Commercial Drive in Vancouver. As we drive up Commercial and then Victoria, he comments about the change in the neighborhood, the differing degrees of diversity. "It used to be," he says, "that you wouldn't be caught in this area unless you were a screaming faggot." My stomach feels queasy. I am not exactly early for my flight. Taxis are hard to come by. "You're making me uncomfortable with your comments." I think that's what finally comes out of my mouth. "Oh, I don't mean anything by it. I have a lot of homosexual and transsexual clients. Why just last night . . . I didn't mean to offend you." When he drops me off at the airport he shakes my hand and thanks me for the chance to talk.

"The baby died inside her. She was bleeding hard inside. The doctor held my partner's shoulders and told her that the baby was gone; they needed to save her now. They told me to phone her next of kin—not me. They told me to phone her brother. Somebody would have to make decisions." I hold back tears. I haven't yet learned to be okay with crying during interviews. She's a good storyteller. Walked me through the experience of planning, conceiving, pregnancy. The pregnancy was going really well. And then at seven months pregnant, her then-partner started having cramps. . . .

"By the time we got to the hospital she was crashing. She was dying. The doctor repeatedly said that it looked like a botched abortion. We thought she had miscarried early. An unwanted pregnancy, the doctor said. Aborted. It wasn't. We were having this child together. She was still dying. Finally, a general surgeon—there were no obstetricians available—said the only thing left to do was open her up. The baby had started growing in her tube." This would have been their second child. The sibling of her son, now 16. Fourteen years ago, and as I hear the story sitting in her sun-filled kitchen, the details make it seem as though it might have happened just weeks ago.

For months I didn't want to do another interview. I had forgotten how to take care of myself during research. I'm second now as we go around the room introducing ourselves at a workshop for service providers working with clients experiencing pregnancy loss. I say that I am doing my research on lesbians' and bisexual women's experiences of conception and that, of course, means that a number of the women I speak with have experienced a loss. We spend the day watching videos, talking, doing role-plays, visiting the morgue, looking at tiny clay models of hands and feet no larger than the tip of my pinky. Life and Death. We so often think about them separately. This day was about seeing life and death in the same moment. . . .

Rayna Rapp, an anthropologist studying the social impact of amniocentesis, writes that we, the women who do research on pregnancy, prenatal testing and infertility are the *mavens* of reproductive grief (Rapp, 1999, p. 262). The word is Yiddish. I thought it might mean keepers. We are the ones who hear the stories of loss. The stories

about the dreams that were never realized. The stories about the babies conceived who were never born. The stories about those who experienced life for only a few brief hours. I didn't expect the translation to be "expert." What am I an expert in? Where do we talk about the losses we carry in our hearts, in our fieldnotes—the losses we are responsible for writing into public space?

"I was lying there, looking up at the ceiling. I felt her gaze on my body as she inserted the tubing through my cervix. 'My, you have a lot of tattoos.' The ring through my tongue felt heavy. I thought, yeah, what kind of mother am I going to make? I lay there with that sperm inside me and I prayed I wouldn't get pregnant. Please, don't let me get pregnant."

I'm exhausted. Ethnography is about everyday life. I do my research at home, in hospitals, on the street, at the park. We've made our professions personal and personalized our professions. As an anthropologist trained in the 1990s, I learned to question "anthropology in place." I became enticed by the multi-sitedness of studies that trace issues, follow people, track movement. Sometimes, it hurts too much. It is too emotionally draining to see "the field" as everything and everywhere. I start drawing boundaries. It's the homophobia and the heterosexism that gets pushed aside. Not for analysis. Not today. It takes too much energy to write. . . .

## NOTES

1. All names used in this paper are pseudonyms and identifying information has been blurred. The stories that appear in this essay do not necessarily represent verbatim quotations from interview transcripts. Rather, they represent a reconstruction of women's stories in order to produce a new narrative based on the intersecting experiences of the women I interviewed and myself.

2. In this paper I use the "labels" lesbian, bisexual, queer, straight, femme and dyke in ways that reflect how they were used by women I interviewed as well as how they appear in the broader sphere of contemporary popular culture. The particular meaning that each term holds is often context dependant and usage varies

according to individual experience, geographical location, education and class affinities, and the time and places in which women "come out" and live.

3. In 1997, the AIDS Committee of Toronto (Canada) launched a new brochure with information on lesbians and HIV. The brochure included the language "grrls on grrls" and "dykes do boyz" which is common today within alternative youth, 'zine and queer cultures. The campaign expanded the parameters of how "lesbian sexuality" is represented in public health discourse to include fluid exchanging sexual practices between women and women and women and men.

## REFERENCES

Green, R. (1999). I, clone. *Scientific American, 10(3),* 80–83.

Franklin, S. (1997). *Embodied progress: A cultural account of assisted conception.* London and New York: Routledge.

Rapp, R. (1999). *Testing the women, testing the fetus: The social impact of amniocentesis in America.* New York and London: Routledge.

# Current Reproductive Technologies:
# Increased Access and Choice?

Linda J. Beckman

S. Marie Harvey

. . . We define reproductive technologies as the drugs, medical and surgical procedures, and devices that facilitate conception, prevent or terminate pregnancy, and prevent the acquisition and transmission of sexually transmitted infections (STIs). It is important to note that these techniques separate sex from reproduction (Tangri & Kahn, 1993). Therefore, these technologies allow individuals to engage in sexual intercourse for purposes other than procreation and facilitate procreation without engaging in sexual intercourse.

Our approach . . . is grounded in our belief that for women to gain equality with men, nationally and internationally, requires that they have control over their bodies and are able to choose whether or not and when to have children. Reproductive health is defined by the World Health Organization (1998) as "complete physical, mental, and social well being in all matters related to the reproductive system" (p. 1). One important strategy for increasing reproductive health is to provide needed services and tools to women to help them overcome infertility; carry wanted pregnancies to term; avoid STIs and prevent unintended pregnancies; when desired, terminate a pregnancy; and enjoy physical and psychological

From Beckman, Linda J. and S. Marie Harvey. 2005. "Current Reproductive Technologies: Increased Access and Choice?" *Journal of Social Issues* 61: 1–20. Reprinted by permission of Blackwell Publishing and the authors.

health during and beyond the childbearing years. Our distinctive approach leads to a comprehensive analysis of issues involving reproduction with the goal of promoting more integrated reproductive health services for all women.

Over the last 25 years new reproductive technologies have emerged and extant techniques have been improved or rediscovered. Many new procedures that increase individuals' ability to build a family have led to scenarios previously only visualized in novels such as Huxley's (1998) *Brave New World*. The event that initially galvanized the field of infertility treatment in 1978 was the birth of the first child resulting from in vitro fertilization (IVF), the most popular of the assisted reproductive technologies (ARTs). ARTs are non-coital methods of conception that involve manipulation of both eggs and sperm. The most popular ART is IVF, used in over 70% of all ART procedures (Resolve of Minnesota, n.d.). IVF is a process that uses drugs to stimulate egg production in a woman. The ripened eggs from the ovary are then retrieved in the laboratory, and fertilized with semen. The resulting embryo or embryos are then transferred back into the uterus for implantation (Centers for Disease Control, 2003; Resolve of Minnesota, n.d.). ARTs are expensive, (averaging $8,000–10,000 per approximately two-week egg retrieval cycle [Resolve of Minnesota, n.d.] and ranging from $60,000 to over $150,000 per successful delivery [Neumann, Gharib, & Weinstein, 1994]). In addition, they are time consuming, involve multiple injections of drugs, and have a modest success rate. Less than 25% of cycles involving fresh, non-donor eggs result in a live birth (American Society for Reproductive Medicine, 2000; Centers for Disease Control, 2003).

Procedures that involve only the use of fertility drugs or intrauterine insemination (IUI), commonly known as artificial insemination (AI), typically are not considered ART. However, for purposes of this [reading] they are included as reproductive technologies. Both IUI and IVF allow a couple to contract with a third-party woman who carries a child that is genetically linked to one or both members of the couple and who relinquishes that child to the couple after birth. Third party contractual parenting (commonly know as surrogacy) challenges traditional views of what constitutes a family and the relative importance of social versus genetic ties to a child. . . . [U]se of methods such as surrogacy raises profound ethical and legal issues and varies in acceptability by culture. Moreover, because of high costs and lack of insurance coverage, many individuals have limited access to these methods.

In addition to technologies to overcome infertility problems, a host of technological advances are now available to prevent unintended pregnancies and limit unwanted births (Harvey, Sherman, Bird, & Warren, 2002; Schwartz & Gabelnick, 2002; Severy & Newcomer, [2005]). Methods to prevent or terminate unwanted pregnancy include female hormones delivered via injection, implant, or pill; mechanical devices placed in the uterus; devices that alert women about their fertile period; and surgical procedures. Moreover, not all methods must be used prior to or during sexual intercourse. Emergency contraception involves the use of hormones up to three to five days after unprotected intercourse to prevent conception. Voluntary termination of pregnancy may involve simple surgical techniques (e.g., electric vacuum aspiration, manual vacuum aspiration) or drug-induced techniques. Some drugs, such as mifepristone (also known as the abortion pill, Mifeprex, or RU 486), have been tested extensively in other countries; others such as methotrexate were originally developed and

used for other purposes. Procedures and methods to prevent conception and terminate pregnancies are not nearly as high-tech as those to overcome infertility. Yet, they raise similar types of problems and issues in terms of their acceptability to various cultural and religious groups and because of their limited accessibility. Such problems may be exacerbated by the use of technology for purposes not originally intended (e.g., the use of female hormones originally designed for contraception to control menopausal symptoms and reduce risk of disease in peri-menopausal and postmenopausal women).

Because of the world-wide AIDS pandemic (UNAIDS, 2003) and the high incidence of many other STIs such as chlamydia and gonorrhea nationally and internationally, women and men need methods to protect against Human Immunodeficiency Virus (HIV)/STIs (Eng & Butler, 1997; Rosenberg & Gollub, 1992; Stone, Timyan, & Thomas, 1999). The male condom is widely recognized as the most effective method of protecting against HIV and some other STIs for sexually active couples (Stone, Timyan, & Thomas, 1999). Some men may, however, be unwilling to use condoms and if women desire protection, they frequently must negotiate condom use with their male partners. Because of gender-based power inequities, some women may not be able to negotiate condom use to protect themselves against diseases (Amaro, 1995; Amaro & Raj, 2000; Blanc, 2001). There is, therefore, an urgent need for additional, preferably female controlled, methods for HIV/STI prevention. Of critical significance are devices and products still under development such as microbicides (for examples see Koo, Woodsong, Dalberth, Viswanathan, & Simons-Rudolph, [2005]; Severy & Newcomer, [2005]) that would protect women and their partners from HIV and other STIs. Although these devices and products are designed to prevent disease rather than to control fertility or overcome infertility, issues of acceptability are equally critical to their use. . . .

Taken together, the technologies—some old, some new, some still on the horizon—provide more options for women and their partners, theoretically making it possible for them to have greater control over their physical health and psychological well-being. The development of better, more sophisticated scientific technologies generally is viewed by couples and medical professionals as a benefit that could potentially improve physical health and well-being (Kailasam & Jenkins, 2004; Women's Health Weekly, 2004). That said, these technologies have engendered great controversy even among feminists (Henifin, 1993; Tangri & Kahn, 1993) as has their marketing (Kolata, 2002). Feminists have failed to achieve an integrated discourse about women's reproductive decision making across the various technologies (Cannold, 2002). While they support women's right to limit or terminate pregnancy, radical feminists generally oppose assisted reproductive technology. Feminists see women as independent rational decision makers when confronted with an unwanted pregnancy. In contrast, many of them believe that women may be coerced into procedures such an IVF and surrogacy and, therefore, they cannot make unconstrained, independent decisions about these procedures (Cannold, 2002).

Certain religious and cultural groups view some or most of these technologies as unacceptable, even immoral. For instance, the Catholic Church characterizes abortion and contraception as immoral and urges women to forgo these methods (Russo & Denious, [2005]; Watkin, 2003). Each of these reproductive technologies raises significant, social, ethical, and psychological issues for women and their sexual partners (e.g., Pasch & Christensen, 2000). Technologies at both ends of the fertility spectrum may be difficult to use and involve significant emotional, social, and/or economic costs (e.g., Pasch & Christensen).

The purpose of this [reading] is to provide a selective overview of [a few key] psychological, ethical, sociocultural, and political issues as they relate to reproductive technologies; to

consider the [political] implications of these issues; and to promote new research through [the] synthesis and integration of extant literature. . . . Although it is difficult to impose a strong theoretical framework that encompasses the diverse perspectives . . . we offer a general conceptual framework to help integrate the multitude of variables examined and issues raised. This framework emphasizes four sets of factors: situational context, relationship context, user characteristics and method characteristics, and their relationships to outcomes associated with reproductive technologies. . . .

## Reproductive Technologies: Key Issues

### Contextual and Personal Barriers to Use

Many factors restrict women's access to reproductive technology. All four sets of variables . . . may serve as barriers to use. . . . Moreover, barriers are not equitably distributed throughout the social structure (Henifin, 1993). They differentially affect women of certain cultures, race/ethnicities and sexual preferences. Poverty and lack of economic resources, in particular, may limit access to reproductive technology (Henifin, 1993). For example . . . many technologies, particularly those associated with reversing infertility, are expensive and not covered by medical insurance.

Equally as important as the situational context is the acceptability of a method or procedure to the individual user. New technologies will not be effective in increasing the availability of reproductive health services unless female consumers and providers find these methods acceptable and women are willing to use them. . . . In addition, the acceptability of technologies is shaped by factors such as culture, ethnicity, age, social class, and sexual preference. . . .

### Complexity of Decision Making

Even when women have ready access to reproductive methods and treatments, the decision to use them can be difficult and emotionally draining. Giving women and their partners more choices also increases the complexity and difficulty of decision making about reproductive issues and may raise painful, ethical, inter-personal, and emotional issues for them (Ciccarelli & Beckman, [2005]). In addition, reproductive health decisions frequently are couple decisions rather than individual decisions (e.g., Ciccarelli & Beckman, [2005]; Koo et al., [2005]; Severy & Newcomer, [2005]) which raise issues about power in intimate relationships, gender roles, and women's ability to negotiate outcomes with their partners.

Accurate, easily understood information is essential for informed choices and optimal decision making about reproductive options. In the present political climate, accurate information on certain controversial topics such as sexual behavior or abortion may be difficult to obtain. In some cases, curtailment of funding has led to gaps in the knowledge base (Woodsong & Severy, [2005]); in others, misinformation may be provided by groups with a specific social agenda or economic interest (Naughton, Jones, & Shumaker, [2005]; Russo & Denious, [2005]). . . .

In addition, culture is of great significance in individual and couple decision making about use of reproductive technology (Burns, 2003; Dagger, 1998; Erickson & Kaplan, 1998). What is acceptable differs depending on cultural values and beliefs (e.g., Harvey, Beckman, & Branch, 2002; Woodsong, Shedlin, & Koo, 2004). Women may desire to postpone or avoid childbearing in order to achieve educational and occupational goals or because they do not have the economic resources to support another child. However, pronatalist norms may propel them toward motherhood (Russo, 1976). Similarly, in part because of these norms and beliefs, women with fertility problems are willing to undergo stressful, painful, expensive, and inconvenient procedures that often are unsuccessful in order to attempt to bear a child of their own (Stanton, Lobes, Sears, & DeLuca, 2002). Still other women and their partners are willing to contract with a stranger in order to have a baby genetically connected to at least one

intended parent (Ciccarelli & Beckman, [2005]). Most cultural groups identify infertility as a major problem with especially strong stigma attached to infertility in women (Mabasa, 2002; Remennick, 2000; Whiteford & Gonzalez, 1995). It is ironic that the cultures that are most pronatalist also are ones that most often disapprove of infertility treatments, especially if donated gametes are involved.

## The Personal Is Political

Reproductive technologies frequently are acclaimed for increasing women's reproductive rights by providing new choices and options (Gollub, 2000; Gollub, French, Latka, Rogers, & Stein, 2001; Latka, 2001; Raphan, Cohen, & Boyer, 2001). Having choice is further extolled as empowering women. To the extent that these technologies allow women (and their partners) more control over the planning and spacing of children, women are more likely to achieve educational and career goals (Zabin & Cardona, 2002) and improve their quality of life and physical health (e.g., Beckman, in press; Murphy, 2003; Wingood & DiClemente, 2000). Moreover, female-controlled pregnancy and STI prevention methods will likely lead to greater feelings of control for the women who use them and provide women with greater ability to avoid unprotected sexual behavior (Stein, 1993, 1995).

We must acknowledge, however, another and darker side to this analysis that (a) suggests that only an elite group of privileged well-to-do non-Hispanic White women can have access to many of these new options, and (b) question whether even privileged women experience greater control and reproductive autonomy because of the availability of options to promote and prevent conception and birth. It is generally recognized that differential access, especially to costly infertility treatments, exists for privileged versus disadvantaged women (Henifin, 1993). The effects of access to fertility promoting reproductive technology on women's experienced control and empowerment have, however, been relatively ignored. In a recent book McLeod (2002) contends that women's reproductive autonomy in many cases may decline when new reproductive treatments become available. Insensitive treatment by providers, paternalism, and lack of social support may diminish self-trust and thereby threaten a woman's reproductive freedom (McLeod, 2002).

Unfortunately, political agendas and considerations abound as far as reproductive technology is concerned. The politics of reproductive technology often guide social policy, especially in the United States where bitter and sometimes violent struggles have characterized the abortion debate (Beckman & Harvey, 1998; Russo & Denious, [2005]; Sherman, [2005]). The political controversies, although not as vitriolic in other areas of reproductive technology, extend far beyond abortion and are rooted in differences in religious, moral, and personal values (Russo & Denious, 1998; Russo & Denious, [2005]). Characterizing the use of various reproductive technologies as moral issues by conservative religious groups has lead to the promotion of policies that attempt to limit women's access to these technologies. For instance, despite the recommendations provided by two panels of expert advisors, in May 2004 the Food and Drug Administration (FDA) again rejected a pharmaceutical company's application for over-the-counter access to one version of emergency contraceptive pills (ECPs) (Plan B). Although opponents claim that this action was in response to pressure from conservative and anti-abortion groups (American Civil Liberties Union, 2004), spokespersons for the FDA cite lack of research on the safety of ECPs for young adolescents (Food and Drug Administration, 2004).

On the other side of the political spectrum, feminists and advocates for women's rights lobby for social policies to increase access to reproductive technology. In addition, efforts to restrict certain groups' access to technology may be motivated by racist or homophobic beliefs. For instance, ethical questions about lesbians' rights to artificial insemination may be buttressed by homophobic attitudes (Erlichman, 1988; Jacob,

1997). On the other hand, cultural beliefs about government conspiracies can affect the willingness of some African Americans to use specific pregnancy or HIV/STI prevention methods (Bird & Bogart, [2005]).

The personal and the political are more deeply interwoven today than in past political landscapes. The executive branch of government in the United States has always used political processes to promote its social agenda. Regrettably, the current Republican administration has attempted to impose its social and moral values upon the American public by removing, withholding, or misrepresenting scientific information when it does not fit their social mandate (Russo & Denious, [2005]). Much of this information involves women and girls (National Council of Research on Women, 2004) and nowhere is this attempted embargo on scientific knowledge clearer than in the area of reproductive health issues. Concerned scientists throughout the country have indicated their opposition to both the distortion or withdrawal of scientific information from government reports and Web sites and attempts to subvert the scientific process of merit review in the pursuit of a social agenda (Consortium of Social Science Associations, 2004; Russo & Denious, [2005]; Union of Concerned Scientists, 2004). These attempts to limit access to information are detrimental to the mental and physical health of women and to their families and communities (National Council of Research on Women, 2004). . . .

## REFERENCES

Amaro, H. (1995). Love, sex, and power: Considering women's realities in HIV prevention. *American Psychologist, 50,* 437–443.

Amaro, H., & Raj, A. (2000). On the margin: Power and women's HIV risk reduction strategies. *Sex Roles, 42,* 723–749.

American Civil Liberties Union. (2004, May 12). *Food and Drug Administration puts politics before women's health; ACLU says investigation warranted.* Retrieved June 22, 2004, from http://www.

aclu.org/ReproductiveRights/ReproductiveRights. cfm?ID=15690&c=225

American Society for Reproductive Medicine. (2000). *Fact Sheet: In Vitro Fertilization (IVF)*. Retrieved May 20, 2003, from http://www.asrm.org/Patients/ FactSheets/invitro.html

Beckman, L. J. (in press). Women's reproductive health: Issues, findings and controversies. In C. Goodheart & J. Worell (Eds.), *Handbook of girls' and women's psychological health*. New York: Oxford University Press.

Beckman, L. J., & Harvey, S. M. (Eds.). (1998). *The new civil war: The psychology, culture and politics of abortion*. Washington, DC: American Psychological Association.

Bird, S. T., & Bogart, L. M. (2005). Conspiracy beliefs about HIV/AIDS and birth control among African Americans: Implications for the prevention of HIV, other STIs, and unintended pregnancy. *Journal of Social Issues, 61*, 109–126.

Blanc, A. K. (2001). The effect of power in sexual relationships on sexual and reproductive health: An examination of the evidence. *Studies in Family Planning, 32*, 189–213.

Burns, L. H. (2003). *Cross-cultural issues and the use of assisted reproductive technologies*. Unpublished manuscript.

Cannold, L. (2002). Understanding and responding to anti-choice women-centred strategies. *Reproductive Health Matters, 10*(19), 171–179.

Centers for Disease Control. (2003). *2000 Assisted Reproductive Technology success rates: Commonly asked questions about U.S. ART clinic reporting system*. Retrieved May 20, 2003, from the National Center for Chronic Disease and Prevention and Health Promotion Web site: http://www.cdc. gov/nccdphp/drh/ART00/faq.htm

Ciccarelli, J. C., & Beckman, L. J. (2005). Navigating rough waters: An overview of psychological aspects of surrogacy. *Journal of Social Issues, 61,* 21–43.

Consortium of Social Science Associations. (2004). *Coalition to protect research: Support scientific integrity*. Retrieved June 22, 2004, from http://www. cossa.org/CPR/scientificintegrity.html

Dugger, K. (1998). Black women and the question of abortion. In L. J. Beckman & S. M. Harvey, (Eds.), *The new civil war: The psychology, culture and politics of abortion.* (pp. 107–131).

Washington, DC: American Psychological Association.

Eng, T., & Butler, W. T. (1997). *The hidden epidemic: Confronting sexually transmitted diseases*. Washington, DC: National Academy Press.

Erickson, P. L., & Kaplan, C. P. (1998). Latinas and abortion. In L. J. Beckman & S. M. Harvey (Eds.), *The new civil war: The psychology, culture and politics of abortion* (pp. 133–155). Washington, DC: American Psychological Association.

Erlichman, K. L. (1988). Lesbian mothers: Ethical issues in social work practice. *Women and Therapy, 8,* 207–224.

Food and Drug Administration. (2004, May 7). *FDA issues not approvable letter to Barr Labs; Outlines pathway for future approval*. Retrieved June 22, 2004 from, http://www.fda.gov/bbs/topics/ news/2004/NEW01064.html

Gollub, E. L. (2000). The female condom: Tool for women's empowerment. *American Journal of Public Health, 90,* 1377–1381.

Gollub, E. L., French, P., Latka, M., Rogers, C., & Stein, Z. (2001). Achieving safer sex with choice: Studying a women's sexual risk reduction hierarchy in an STD clinic. *Journal of Women's Health & Gender-Based Medicine, 10,* 771–783.

Harvey, S. M., Beckman, L. J., & Branch, M. R. (2002). The relationship of contextual factors to women's perceptions of medical abortion. *Health Care for Women International, 23,* 654–665.

Harvey, S. M., Sherman, S. A., Bird, S. T., & Warren, J. (2002). *Understanding medical abortion: Policy, politics and women's health* (Policy Matters Paper 3). Eugene: University of Oregon, Center for the Study of Women in Society.

Henifin, M. S. (1993). New reproductive technology: Equity and access to reproductive health care. *Journal of Social Issues, 49,* 61–74.

Huxley, A. (1998). *Brave New World* (Perennial Classics ed.). New York: Harper Collins. (Original work published in 1932).

Jacob, M. C. (1997). Concerns of single women and lesbian couples considering conception through assisted reproduction. In. S. R. Leiblum (Ed.), *Infertility: Psychological issues and counseling strategies.* (pp. 189–206). Oxford, England: Wiley.

Kailasam, C., & Jenkins, J. (2004). Risks and benefits of assisted conception. *Pulse, 64*(5), 46–47.

Retrieved June 22, 2004, from the Health Source: Nursing/Academic Edition database.

Kolata, G. (2002, January 1). Fertility Inc: Clinics race to lure clients. *New York Times,* pp. D1, D7.

Koo, H. P., Woodsong, C., Dalberth, B. T, Viswanathan, M., & Simons-Rudolph, A. (2005). Context of acceptability of topical microbicides: Sexual relationships. *Journal of Social Issues, 61,* 67–93.

Latka, M. (2001). Female-initiated barrier methods for the prevention of STI/HIV: Where are we now? Where should we go? *Journal of Urban Health, 78,* 571–580.

Mabasa, L. F. (2002). Sociocultural aspects of infertility in a Black South African community. *Journal of Psychology in Africa, South of the Sahara, the Caribbean and Afro-Latin America, 12,* 65–79.

McLeod, C. (2002). *Self-trust and reproductive autonomy.* Cambridge, MA: MIT Press.

Murphy, E. M. (2003). Being born female is dangerous for your health. *American Psychologist, 58,* 205–210.

National Council for Research on Women. (2004). *Missing: Information about women's lives.* Retrieved May 12, 2004, from http://www.ncrw.org/misinfo/report.pdf

Naughton, M. J., Jones, A. S., & Shumaker, S. A. (2005). When practices, promises, profits, and policies outpace hard evidence: The post-menopausal hormone debate. *Journal of Social Issues, 61,* 159–179.

Neumann, P. J., Gharib, S. D., & Weinstein, M. C. (1994). The cost of a successful delivery with in vitro fertilization. *New England Journal of Medicine, 331,* 239–243.

Pasch, L. A., & Christensen, A. (2000). Couples facing fertility problems. In K. B. Schmaling & T. G. Sher (Eds.), *The psychology of couples and illness: Theory, research and practice* (pp. 241–267). Washington, DC: American Psychological Association.

Raphan, G., Cohen, S., & Boyer, A. M. (2001). The female condom, a tool for empowering sexually active urban adolescent women. *Journal of Urban Health, 78,* 605–613.

Remennick, L. (2000). Childless in the land of imperative motherhood: Stigma and coping among infertile Israeli women. *Sex Roles, 43,* 821–841.

Resolve of Minnesota. (n.d.). *Assisted reproductive technologies.* Retrieved May 20, 2003, from http://www.resolvemn.org/art.htm

Rosenberg, M. J., & Gollub, E. L. (1992). Commentary: Methods women can use that may prevent sexually transmitted disease, including HIV. *American Journal of Public Health, 82,* 1473–1478.

Russo, N. F. (1976). The motherhood mandate. *Journal of Social Issues, 32,* 143–154.

Russo, N. F., & Denious, J. E. (2005). Controlling birth: Science, politics, and public policy. *Journal of Social Issues, 61,* 181–191.

Schwartz, J. L., & Gabelnick, H. L. (2002). Current contraceptive research. *Perspectives on Sexual and Reproductive Health, 34,* 310–316.

Severy, L. J., & Newcomer, S. (2005). Critical issues in contraceptive and STI acceptability research. *Journal of Social Issues, 61,* 45–65.

Sherman, C. A. (2005). Emergency contraception: The politics of post-coital contraception. *Journal of Social Issues, 61,* 139–157.

Stanton, A. L., Lobel, M., Sears, S., & DeLuca, R. S. (2002). Psychosocial aspects of selected issues in women's reproductive health: Current status and future directions. *Journal of Consulting and Clinical Psychology, 70,* 751–770.

Stein, Z. (1993). HIV prevention: An update on the status of methods women can use. *American Journal of Public Health, 83,* 1379–1382.

Stein, Z. (1995). Editorial: More on women and the prevention of HIV infection. *American Journal of Public Health, 85,* 1485–1487.

Stone, K. M., Timyan, J., & Thomas, E. L. (1998). Barrier methods for the prevention of sexually transmitted diseases. In K. K. Holmes, P. Mardh, P. F. Sparling, S. M. Lemon, W. E. Stamm, & P. Piot (Eds.), *Sexually transmitted diseases.* New York: McGraw-Hill.

Tangri, S. S., & Kahn, J. R. (1993). Ethical issues in the new reproductive technologies: Perspectives from feminism and the psychology profession. *Professional Psychology: Research and Practice, 24,* 271–280.

Union of Concerned Scientists. (2004, March). *Scientific integrity in policymaking: An investigation into the Bush Administration's misuse of science.* Retrieved June 22, 2004, from http://www.ucsusa.org/publications/report.cfm?publicationid=730

Watkin, D. J. (2003, November 13). Bishops open a new drive opposing contraception. *New York Times,* pp. A20.

Whiteford, L. M., & Gonzalez, L. (1995). Stigma: The hidden burden of infertility. *Social Science and Medicine, 40,* 27–36.

Wingood, G. M., & DiClemente, R. J. (2000). Application of the Theory of Gender and Power to examine HIV-related exposures, risk factors, and effective interventions for women. *Health Education & Behavior, 27,* 539–565.

Woodsong, C., Shedlin, M., & Koo, H. (2004). Natural, normal and sacred: Beliefs influencing the acceptability of pregnancy and STI/HIV prevention methods. *Journal of Culture, Health and Sexuality, 6,* 67–88.

Woodsong, C., & Severy, L. J. (2005). Generation of knowledge for reproductive health technologies: Constraints on social and behavioral research. *Journal of Social Issues, 61,* 193–205.

Women's Health Weekly. (2004). Advances in fertility technology open new doors for couples. *Health Source—Consumer Edition Database.* Feb. 19, 98–99.

World Health Organization. (1998). *Division of reproductive health: Overall aims and goals.* Geneva, Switzerland: Author.

Zabin, L. S., & Cardona, K. M. (2002). Adolescent pregnancy. In G. Wingood & R. DiClemente (Eds.), *Handbook of women's sexual and reproductive health* (pp. 231–253). New York: Kluwer Academic/Plenum.

## Induced Abortion in the United States

**Alan Guttmacher Institute**

### Incidence of Abortion

49% of pregnancies among American women are unintended; $\frac{1}{2}$ of these are terminated by abortion.[1] 24% of all pregnancies (excluding miscarriages) end in abortion.[2]

In 2002, 1.29 million abortions took place, down from an estimated 1.36 million in 1996. From 1973 through 2002, more than 42 million legal abortions occurred.[3]

Each year, 2 out of every 100 women aged 15–44 have an abortion; 48% of them have had at least one previous abortion.[4]

### Who Has Abortions

52% of U.S. women obtaining abortions are younger than 25: Women aged 20–24 obtain 33% of all abortions, and teenagers obtain 19%.[5]

Black women are more than 3 times as likely as white women to have an abortion, and Hispanic women are $2\frac{1}{2}$ times as likely.[6]

43% of women obtaining abortions identify themselves as Protestant, and 27% identify themselves as Catholic.[7]

$\frac{2}{3}$ of all abortions are among never-married women.[8]

Over 60% of abortions are among women who have had 1 or more children.[9]

### Contraceptive Use

54% of women having abortions used a contraceptive method during the month they became pregnant. 76% of pill users and 49% of condom users reported using the methods inconsistently, while 13% of pill users and 14% of condom users reported correct use.[10]

8% of women having abortions have never used a method of birth control; nonuse is greatest among those who are young, poor, black, Hispanic or poorly educated.[11]

49% of the 6.3 million pregnancies that occur each year are unplanned [12]; 47% of these occur among the 7% of women at risk of unintended pregnancy who do not practice contraception.[13]

As much as 43% of the decline in abortion between 1994 and 2000 can be attributed to the use of emergency contraception.[14]

## Providers and Services

The number of abortion providers declined by 11% between 1996 and 2000 (from 2,042 to 1,819). 87% of all U.S. counties lacked an abortion provider in 2000. These counties were home to 34% of all 15–44-year-old women.[15]

97% of abortion facilities provide abortion at 8 weeks, and 86% provide services at 12 weeks, but provision drops off steeply after that, with only 13% of providers offering services at 24 weeks.[16]

A growing proportion of providers offer very early abortion (at 4 weeks gestation), an increase from 7% in 1993 to 37% in 2000.[17]

In 2000, the cost of a nonhospital abortion with local anesthesia at 10 weeks of gestation ranged from $150 to $4,000, and the average amount paid was $372.[18]

## Medication Abortion

In September, 2000, the U.S. Food and Drug Administration approved the abortion drug mifepristone to be marketed in the United States as an alternative to surgical abortion.

About 37,000 medication abortions were performed in the first half of 2001; these procedures involved the use of mifepristone or methotrexate.[19]

Approximately 600 providers offered medication abortion in the first half of 2001.[20]

In nonhospital facilities offering mifepristone for use in medication abortion in 2000, the average cost of a medical abortion was $490.[21]

## Safety of Abortion

The risk of abortion complications is minimal; less than 1% of all abortion patients experience a major complication.[22]

Eighty-eight percent of abortions occur in the first 12 weeks of pregnancy, 2001.

There is no evidence of childbearing problems among women who have had a vacuum aspiration abortion, the most common procedure, within the first 12 weeks of pregnancy.[23]

The risk of death associated with abortion increases with the length of pregnancy, from 1 death for every one million abortions at 8 or fewer weeks to 1 per 29,000 at 16–20 weeks and 1 per 11,000 at 21 or more weeks.[24]

The risk of death associated with childbirth is about 11 times as high as that associated with abortion.[25]

Almost half of the women having abortions beyond 15 weeks of gestation say they were delayed because of problems in affording, finding or getting to abortion services.[26]

Teens are more likely than older women to delay having an abortion until after 15 weeks of pregnancy, when medical risks associated with abortion increase significantly.[27]

## Law and Policy

In the 1973 Roe v. Wade decision, the Supreme Court ruled that women, in consultation with their physician, have a constitutionally protected right to have an abortion in the early stages of pregnancy—that is, before viability—free from government interference.

In 1992, the Court upheld the right to abortion in Planned Parenthood v. Casey. However, the ruling significantly weakened the legal protections previously afforded women and physicians by giving states the right to enact restrictions that do not create an "undue burden" for women seeking abortion.

33 states currently enforce parental consent or notification laws for minors seeking an abortion: AL, AR, AZ, CO, DE, GA, IA, ID, IN, KS, KY, LA, MA, MD, MI, MN, MO, MS, NC, ND, NE, OH, PA, RI, SC, SD, TN, TX, UT, VA, WI, WV, and WY. The Supreme Court ruled that minors must have the alternative of seeking a court order authorizing the procedure.[28]

45% of minors who have abortions tell their parents, and 61% undergo the procedure with at least one parent's knowledge. The great majority of parents support their daughter's decision.[29] . . .

## Public Funding

The U.S. Congress has barred the use of federal Medicaid funds to pay for abortions, except when the woman's life would be endangered by a full-term pregnancy or in cases of rape or incest.[30]

17 states (AK, AZ, CA, CT, HI, IL, MA, MD, MN, MT, NJ, NM, NY, OR, VT, WA and WV) do use public funds to pay for abortions for some poor women. About 14% of all abortions in the United States are paid for with public funds (virtually all from state governments).[31]

Without publicly funded family planning services, an estimated 1.3 million additional unplanned pregnancies would occur annually; about 632,300 would end in abortion.

## REFERENCES

1. Henshaw SK, Unintended pregnancy in the United States, *Family Planning Perspectives,* 1998, 30(1):24–29 & 46.
2. Finer LB and Henshaw SK, Estimates of U.S. Abortion Incidence in 2001 and 2002, The Alan Guttmacher Institute, 2005, <http://www.guttmacher.org/pubs/2005/05/18/ab_incidence.pdf>, accessed May 17, 2005.
3. Ibid.
4. Jones RK, Darroch JE and Henshaw SK, Patterns in the socioeconomic characteristics of women obtaining abortions in 2000–2001, *Perspectives on Sexual and Reproductive Health,* 2002, 34(5):226–235.
5. Ibid.
6. Ibid.
7. Ibid.
8. Ibid.
9. Ibid.
10. Jones RK, Darroch JE and Henshaw SK, Contraceptive use among U.S. women having abortions in 2000–2001, *Perspectives on Sexual and Reproductive Health,* 2002, 34(6):294–303.
11. Ibid.
12. Henshaw SK, 1998, op. cit. (see reference 1).
13. AGI, 2000, op. cit. (see reference [12]).
14. Jones RK, Darroch JE and Henshaw SK, 2002, op. cit. (see reference [10]).
15. Finer LB and Henshaw SK, Abortion incidence and services in the United States in 2000, *Perspectives on Sexual and Reproductive Health,* 2003, 35(1):6–15.
16. Henshaw SK and Finer LB, The accessibility of abortion services in the United States, 2001, *Perspectives on Sexual and Reproductive Health,* 2003, 35(1):16–24.
17. Ibid.
18. Ibid.
19. Finer LB and Henshaw SK, 2003, op. cit. (see reference [16]).
20. Ibid.
21. Ibid.
22. AGI, Abortion and Women's Health: A Turning Point for America? New York: AGI, 1990, p. 30.
23. Ibid.
24. Bartlett LA et al., Risk factors for legal induced abortion-related mortality in the United States, 2004, *Obstetrics and Gynecology,* 103(4):729–737.
25. Ibid.
26. Torres A and Forrest JD, Why do women have abortions? *Family Planning Perspectives,* 1988, 24(4): 169–176.
27. Centers for Disease Control and Prevention, Abortion surveillance—United States, 1999, *Morbidity and Mortality Weekly Report,* 2002, 51(SS09).
28. AGI, Parental involvement, State Policies in Brief, Dec. 2002.
29. Finer LB et al., Timing of steps and reasons for delays in obtaining abortions in the United States, *Contraception,* 2006 (forthcoming).
30. Strauss LT et al., Abortion surveillance—United States, 2002, 2005, 54(SS-7), p. 30, Table 16.
31. Guttmacher Institute, Parental Involvement, *State Policies in Brief,* April 2006, <http://www.guttmacher.org/statecenter/spibs/spib_PIMA.pdf>, accessed Apr. 28, 2006.

*Source:* Alan Guttmacher Institute. "Induced Abortion in the United States." *Facts in Brief.* Retrieved from www.agi-usa.org.

## From Contraception to Abortion: A Moral Continuum

**Wendy Simonds**

I've spent nearly two decades doing sociological research on procreative matters; I've focused mostly on investigating ways in which women seek to prevent procreation. These methods include abortion (both surgical and medical—with mifepristone, commonly known as RU-486), and emergency contraception (higher dosages of the same drugs in birth control pills, which, when taken within seventy-two hours of unprotected heterosex, can be 80 percent effective at preventing a pregnancy) (Simonds and Ellertson 2004, Simonds et al. 1998, Simonds 1996, Simonds 1991, Ellertson et al. 1999). I've become fascinated by the ways in which health care workers and the women they serve think and speak about abortion and contraception as a moral issue, within a politicized climate in which anti-abortionists and pro-choice activists do rhetorical battle over women's rights and fetal status.

Each side refutes the other's language: anti-abortionists call themselves "pro-life," and refer to their enemies as "pro-abortion," whereas those who support abortion rights counter with "pro-choice," and refer to their opponents as "anti-choice," or more simply, as "antis." Each side seeks to ally itself with what the general public defines as *truly* moral, offering judgments about what the opposing value system threatens. Pro-choice activists proclaim the endangerment of individual rights, especially those of women. Anti-abortionists predict the destruction of the patriarchal heterosexual family unit by selfish (or sadly misguided) aborting women and evil profit-mongering doctors and clinic workers—all of whom they label "baby killers" (see, e.g., Ginsburg's 1989 and Luker's 1984 ethnographies of activists on both sides of the issue).

Carole Joffe writes that early anti-abortionist rhetoric in the United States in the late nineteenth century included the views that "abortion represents a threat to male authority and the 'traditional role' of women; abortion is a symbol of uncontrolled female sexuality and an 'unnatural' act. Above all, the aborting woman is selfish and self-indulgent" (1995: 29). In 1871, the AMA Committee on Criminal Abortion wrote of "the" aborting woman: "She becomes unmindful of the course marked out for her by Providence. . . . She yields to the pleasures—but shrinks from the pains and responsibilities of maternity" (Joffe 1995: 29). Today, with the popularization of sonography, and high-tech enhanced medical photography techniques (like Lennart Nilsson's film, *The Miracle of Life*), embryonic and fetal images have become ubiquitous; anti-abortionists take advantage of this technology in their quest to personify the fetus. This relatively recent fetal fetish means that women are increasingly absent from quite a lot of anti-abortion visual rhetoric (see, e.g., Petchesky 1987), and their absence may well go unnoticed the more accustomed people become to this manner of seeing fetuses.

Pro-choice rhetoric and representations, in contrast, are distinctly woman centered. Legal framing of the issue is more neutral: defining the right to abortion as a right to privacy, though sexual privacy remains *another* deeply contested issue in our culture. Pro-choice rhetoric draws on both liberalism and capitalism: As Barbara Katz Rothman (1989) points out, women are portrayed as individual self-owners entitled to control over our bodies. If I "own" my body, it is mine; anything within it counts as my property, thus abortion becomes an exercise in unarguably justifiable individualism. This rhetoric sidesteps an overt discussion of sexuality, but viewing sexuality through this lens clearly means seeing women as free choosers of what they want.

Pro-choice rhetoric includes endorsements of motherhood as a *chosen* activity; the decision to abort serves as testimony to how seriously women take motherhood. As Elizabeth Karlin writes, "I am an abortion practitioner because of my utmost respect for motherhood, which I refuse to believe is punishment for a screw. I do what I do because I am convinced that being a mother is the hardest job there is" (1998: 287).

In years spent talking with health care workers and their clients, I've found that a particular moral continuum emerges that shows how anti-abortionist views of sex as shameful and women as frivolous shape aspects of the pro-choice view, too. This moral continuum is particular to our time: Bear in mind that it is only recently (the late twentieth century) that contraception has not shared the same stigma as abortion, and that abortion was not considered a moral issue until the mid-1800s.

On "our" current moral continuum, late abortion is the worst, and responsible heterosex is the best. (*No sex* is another matter altogether: the anti-abortionists' ultimate moral category for unmarried women, seen as unrealistic or nonsensical by pro-choice activists.) Women who have heterosex should be "responsible"—this means, basically, that they should use contraception. So an unanticipated pregnancy that happens because a condom breaks is morally superior to an unanticipated pregnancy that occurs without any contraception; using contraception during actual sex is better than using emergency contraception the next day or the day after that; having an abortion in the first trimester is better than having one later on; and so forth. Yet at least one dominant cultural script for sex endorses being carried away (especially for women wooed by men) and another discourages women from planning for sexual encounters, because to do so indicates slutty intent (according to the script, to be prepared equates being "loose").

Poll data show that people buy the moral dilemma approach promulgated by anti-abortionists. According to a recent *New York Times*/CBS News poll, "public support for legal abortion plummets from 61 percent" in the first trimester "to only 15 percent" in the second trimester (Goldberg 1998). A large majority supports abortion when a pregnant woman's life is endangered by the pregnancy, when her pregnancy resulted from rape or incest, or when the fetus is "defective." Support wanes (ranges from less than half to one quarter of those polled) if a woman "cannot afford any more children"; if she "does not want to marry the man"; and if the "pregnancy would interfere with [her] work or education." These poll data indicate the power of cultural attitudes about sexually active women as untrustworthy and immoral.

In sum, depending on societal attitudes about women's sexuality, the freedom to use contraception and abortion may be conceptualized as dangerous and immoral or as an essential aspect of individual liberty. Current political trends could exacerbate moral divisions on this matter. At this writing, two spots on the Supreme Court are in the process of being filled: The Bush administration is doing its best to ensure that these judges are anti-abortion. Both the legal and moral future of abortion—and other methods of limiting procreation—remain at stake.

## REFERENCES

Ellertson, Charlotte, Wendy Simonds, Kimberly Springer, and Beverly Winikoff. "Providing Mifepristone-Misoprostol Medical Abortion: The View from the Clinic." *Journal of the American Women's Medical Association* 54 (Spring, 1999): 91–96, 102.

Ginsburg, Faye D. *Contested Lives: The Abortion Debate in an American Community.* Berkeley: University of California Press, 1990.

Goldberg, Carey, with Janet Elder. "Public Still Backs Abortion, But Wants Limits, Poll Says." *New York Times* (January 16, 1998): A1, A16.

Joffe, Carole. *Doctors of Conscience: The Struggle to Provide Abortion before and after Roe v. Wade.* Boston: Beacon, 1995.

Karlin, Elizabeth. "'We Called it Kindness': Establishing a Feminist Abortion Practice." In *Abortion Wars: A Half Century of Struggle, 1950–2000,* Rickie Solinger, ed. Berkeley: University of California Press, 1998.

Luker, Kristin. *Abortion and the Politics of Motherhood.* Berkeley: University of California Press, 1984.

Petchesky, Rosalind Pollack. "Fetal Images: The Power of Visual Culture in the Politics of Reproduction." *Feminist Studies,* v. 13, no. 2 (Summer, 1987): 263–292.

Rothman, Barbara Katz. *Recreating Motherhood: Ideology and Technology in a Patriarchal Society.* New York: W.W. Norton, 1989.

Simonds, Wendy. *Abortion at Work: Ideology and Practice in a Feminist Clinic.* New Brunswick, NJ: Rutgers University Press, 1996.

———. "Abortion and Political Rhetoric." In *Historical and Multicultural Encyclopedia of Women's Reproductive Rights,* J. Baer, ed. Westport, CT: Greenwood, 2002: 9–11.

———. "At an Impasse: Inside an Abortion Clinic." In *Current Research on Occupations and Professions* 6, Helena Z. Lopata and Judith Levy, eds. Greenwich, CT: JAI Press, 1991: 99–116.

Simonds, Wendy, Charlotte Ellertson, Kimberly Springer, and Beverly Winikoff. "Abortion, Revised: Participants in the U.S. Clinical Trials Evaluate Mifepristone." *Social Science & Medicine* 46 (1998): 1313–1323.

Simonds, Wendy, and Charlotte Ellertson. "Emergency Contraception and Morality: Reflections of Health Care Workers and Clients." *Social Science & Medicine* 58 (2004): 1285–1297.

**Sextistics**

## *Did You Know?*

- Historians believe that the condom was invented in the 1700s by a doctor named "Condom" or "Condon" during the reign of King Charles II, with the goal of reducing the births of children to unmarried women.[1]
- Research shows that male condoms are one of the best methods of preventing unwanted pregnancy, with 98 percent effectiveness.[2] Female condoms prove approximately 79 percent effective in preventing pregnancy.[3]
- Currently the federal government spends over $205 million each year on abstinence-only education. Spending on abstinence-only education will likely increase to $270 million by 2008.[4] The Bush administration has spent no money on comprehensive sex education.[5]
- Women who are egg donors receive approximately $5,000 per donation,[6] whereas sperm donors receive $40 to $50 per "adequate" specimen.[7]
- The FDA recently advised sperm banks to bar gay men as donors, even though all sperm donors are extensively screened for HIV and other STDs.[8]
- In 1995, 14 percent of all sexually experienced males aged 15 to 19 had sex that resulted in a pregnancy.[9]
- Project Prevention, formally known as CRACK (Children Requiring a Caring Kommunity), will give women addicted to crack cocaine $200 for having a tubal ligation or using Norplant.[10] Both are relatively invasive methods of pregnancy prevention.
- In 1960, the FDA approved the first birth control pill in the United States. By 1963, 2.3 million American women were using the pill, even though eight states prohibited the sale of contraceptives.[11]
- In 1965, the Supreme Court of the United States legalized the sale of the pill to married women in the United States. It wasn't until 1972 that the pill was legalized for use by all women, regardless of marital status.[12]
- In 2004, unmarried mothers reached a record high of almost 1.5 million births, up 4 percent from 2003. Births to older women (35–39 years) continued to increase as well, up 4 percent from 2003.[13]

*—Compiled by Mikel Walters*

**NOTES**

1. Lewis, M. 2000. "A Brief History of Condoms." In *Condoms,* edited by Adrian Mindel. BMJ Books.

2. Sexuality Information and Education Council of the United States. 2004. "The Truth about Condoms." Retrieved November 21, 2005 from www.siecus.org/pubs/fact/fact0011.html.

3. Ibid.

4. Planned Parenthood. 2005. "President Bush Risks Teen Lives by Increasing Funding

for Dangerous Abstinence-Only Education." Retrieved January 20, 2006 from www.planned parenthood.org/pp2/portal/media/pressreleases/pr-050207-abstinence.xml.

5. Fields, Jessica and Celeste Hirschman. 2004. "Citizenship Lessons: Sexuality Education in the United States." *American Sexuality Magazine* 1:6. Retrieved January 30, 2006 from http://nsrc.sfsu.edu/MagArticle.cfm?Article=164&PageID=51&SID=A49BF5E7C46E29EF41B947C531C6C37F&DSN=nsrc_rev2.

6. Glazer, Ellen Sarasohn and Evelina Weidman Sterling. 2005. *Having Your Baby through Egg Donation.* Perspective Press.

7. Paul, Sudipta, Steve Harbottle, and Jane A. Stewart. 2004. "How Good Are We at Recruiting Sperm Donors?" Retrieved January 30, 2006 from http://ivf.net/content/index.php?page=out&id=305&PHPSESSID=6c891e31ce304e209d5dd594be296cef.

8. Stimola, Aubrey Noelle. 2005. "Wanted: Scientific Reasons for FDA's Gay Sperm Ban." American Council on Science and Health. Retrieved January 20, 2006 from www.acsh.org/factsfears/newsID.556/news_detail.asp.

9. Sexuality Information and Education Council of the United States. 2004. "Teen Pregnancy, Birth and Abortion." Retrieved November 21, 2005 from http://siecus.org/pubs/fact/fact0010.html.

10. Project Prevention. 2004. "How We Help the Children." Retrieved November 22, 2005 from www.projectprevention.org.

11. Public Broadcasting System. 2002. "Timeline: The Pill." Retrieved January 20, 2006 from www.pbs.org/wgbh/amex/pill/timeline/timeline2.html.

12. Ibid.

13. Hamilton, Brady E., Stephanie J. Ventura, Joyce A. Martin, and Paul D. Sutton. 2006. "Preliminary Births for 2004." Centers for Disease Control: National Center for Health Statistics. Retrieved January 20, 2006 from www.cdc.gov/nchs/products/pubs/pubd/hestats/prelim_births/prelim_births04.htm.

# chapter 8

# *Sexual Disease*

## Spotlight on Research

*An interview with . . .*

### Claire Sterk

Claire Sterk, Ph.D., is Charles Howard Candler Professor in Public Health in the Department of Behavioral Sciences and Health Education at the Rollins School of Public Health of Emory University in Atlanta, Georgia. Her research interests include HIV/AIDS, mental health and drug use, sexuality, and women's health. In addition to being the author of *Fast Lives: Women Who Use Crack Cocaine* (Temple University Press, 1999) and *Tricking and Tripping: Prostitution in the Era of AIDS* (Social Change Press, 1999), Dr. Sterk has written numerous journal articles about these issues.

**What led you to begin studying sexuality?**

*My initial interest was triggered less by scientific curiosity to learn more about the topic, and more by the way in which scholars interested in sexuality are viewed. When studying sexuality, researchers are expected to justify their interest, and if they don't, they may be accused of being "deviant" or even "perverse." Growing up in the Netherlands, a country where prostitution has been legalized, I frequently encountered challenges of why I, as a social scientist, would be interested in the sex industry. An answer often was not expected, as the persons asking the question also volunteered answers such as, "you must have been involved in the sex industry," or "you use scholarship to satisfy your own sexual curiosity."*

### Which of your projects have you found most interesting?

*Maybe because it was one of my first research endeavors in the area of sexuality, but a study of street prostitutes in the 1980s left an incredible impact on me. At that time, prostitution as a victimless crime was being challenged, the connection between prostitution and drug use was accentuated by the emerging crack cocaine epidemic, and the role of prostitution in the spread of HIV/AIDS was discussed. Prostitution reveals a society's views on gender and sexuality. In our society, prostitution traditionally was associated with social pathology and only in the last few decades have theories emerged that address the impact of gender role expectations, power differences, social constraints, and social policies on the lives of women. Through in-depth life history interviews with women involved in prostitution, I learned that their sexual behavior largely was determined by social, and not individual, factors. For example, trading sex for money or other material goods had little or no connection with the women's sexual desires. More important were factors such as economic opportunities, survival, and discrimination based on gender, race, and class.*

### Why is it important to do sex research?

*Sex is an important part of human behavior and it is much more complex than often assumed. For instance, sex serves more than reproductive purposes. Sex research also requires an interdisciplinary approach and it forces students and researchers to look beyond their own disciplinary boundaries. As Foucault pointed out, sexuality needs to be understood in its sociohistorical context and is socially constructed. Such a perspective allows for placing sex research in the larger context of the social and behavioral sciences and it forces a continued discussion of sex as well as gender and its influence on people's lives. More recently, sex research has gained popularity among public health scholars. This is largely driven by the HIV/AIDS epidemic. A key route of transmission for the virus causing AIDS is through unprotected sex. Not only has this interest made sex research more respectable, it also has shown the complexities of linking sexual identity and sexual behaviors.*

### What ethical dilemmas have you faced? How did you resolve them?

*When using a qualitative research paradigm, combined with a feminist orientation, studying sex and sexuality raises a multitude of ethical dilemmas. To mention a few: the woman who realizes that she has been prostituting herself without recognizing it; the man who describes his views on sex and in the process* starts realizing that he is homosexual; the woman who reflects on her first sexual encounter, which happened to have been abusive; or, the man who knows he has a sexually transmitted disease, maybe even AIDS, but who refuses to use a condom. There is no simple solution to such situations. When people encounter sexual discoveries, it is important to remain a researcher who is supportive and willing to assist, but who does not pretend to be a social worker or psychotherapist. When dealing with abuse situations, either with the person who was abused or the abuser, it is important to withhold judgment. At the same time, there is the legal obligation of having to report certain types of abuse. When discovering that a person might cause others to become sick, in the case of AIDS—a disease for which there is no cure—it might be difficult to adhere to the promise of confidentiality. The key is to be honest to yourself and the study participants.

### How do people react when they discover you are a sex researcher?

As I mentioned earlier, when presenting myself as a sexuality researcher, people assume there is some hidden reason. I can't count how many times I have been asked if I study prostitution because I am a prostitute, maybe was one in the past, or maybe want to become one. Typically, the more uncomfortable people feel with sex and sexuality, the more negatively they will react to the discovery of me doing sexuality research. A response that works well is to turn the tables and to indicate that the response reveals a lot about the person in question. It either creates silence or opens the door for a more constructive dialogue.

### If you could teach people one thing about sex, what would it be?

You need to look at it from an interdisciplinary perspective. It is biology, psychology, sociology, and much more.

—Interviewed by Denise Donnelly

# Tracking the

# Hidden Epidemics

**Centers for Disease Control and Prevention**

In the United States, more than 65 million people are currently living with an incurable sexually transmitted disease (STD). An additional 15 million people become infected with one or more STDs each year, roughly half of whom contract lifelong infections (Cates, 1999). Yet, STDs are one of the most under-recognized health problems in the country today. Despite the fact that STDs are extremely widespread, have severe and sometimes deadly consequences, and add billions of dollars to the nation's healthcare costs each year, most people in the United States remain unaware of the risks and consequences of all but the most prominent STD—the human immunodeficiency virus or HIV.

While extremely common, STDs are difficult to track. Many people with these infections do not have symptoms and remain undiagnosed. Even diseases that are diagnosed are frequently not reported and counted. These "hidden" epidemics are magnified with each new infection that goes unrecognized and untreated.

This document presents the latest available data on the status of the STD epidemics in the United States. By combining data on reported cases of disease with various studies of the level of infection in specific populations, researchers can compile a more complete picture of the magnitude of these diseases.

From Centers for Disease Control and Prevention. 2000. "Tracking the Hidden Epidemics: Trends in STDs in the United States, 2000." Retrieved from www.cdc.gov.

## Magnititude of the Epidemics Overall

More than 25 diseases are spread primarily through sexual activity, and the trends for each disease vary considerably, but together these infections comprise a significant public health problem.

The latest estimates indicate that there are 15 million new STD cases in the United States each year (Cates, 1999). Approximately one-fourth of these new infections are in teenagers. And while some STDs, such as syphilis, have been brought to all time lows, others, like genital herpes, gonorrhea, and chlamydia, continue to resurge and spread through the population.

Because there is no single STD epidemic, but rather multiple epidemics, discussions about trends over time and populations affected must focus on each specific STD. More is known about the frequency and trends of some STDs than others, since many of the diseases are difficult to track. Not including HIV, the most common STDs in the U.S. are chlamydia, gonorrhea, syphilis, genital herpes, human papillomavirus, hepatitis B, trichomoniasis and bacterial vaginosis. . . .

## Answers to the Most Frequently Asked Questions

### Are STDS Increasing or Decreasing in the United States?

It depends on the disease. The latest scientific data suggest that chlamydia has declined in areas with screening and treatment programs, but remains at very high levels. For the first time in nearly

**441**

two decades, gonorrhea is on the rise, increasing more than nine percent from 1997 to 1999, after a 72 percent decline from 1975 to 1997. An increase in drug-resistant gonorrhea has been seen in Hawaii and in small clusters in other states. Syphilis, in both adults and infants, has declined overall and is now at an all time low, presenting an opportunity for elimination of the disease. In October 1999, CDC launched the National Plan to Eliminate Syphilis in the United States. Chancroid also has declined steadily since 1987 (DSTDP, CDC, 2000).

Genital herpes continues to increase, spreading across all social, economic, racial and ethnic boundaries, but most dramatically affecting teens and young adults (Fleming, 1997). With an estimated 20 million people in the United States currently infected with human papillomavirus (HPV), this viral STD also continues to spread. An estimated 5.5 million people become newly infected with HPV each year (Cates, 1999).

## What Are the Most Serious STDs in Women?

By far, women bear the greatest burden of STDs, suffering more frequent and more serious complications than men. Ten to 20 percent of women with gonorrhea and chlamydia develop one of the most serious complications, pelvic inflammatory disease (PID). PID can lead to chronic pelvic pain, infertility, and potentially fatal ectopic pregnancy. Many different organisms can cause PID, but most cases are associated with gonorrhea and chlamydia.

HPV also can result in severe consequences for women. Infection with certain types of HPV place women at increased risk for cervical cancer.

In addition, women who are infected with an STD while pregnant can have early onset of labor, premature rupture of the membranes, or uterine infection before and after delivery. STD-related syndromes—like bacterial vaginosis—may cause harm to infants through their association with premature birth. Preterm birth is the leading cause of infant death and disability in the United States, and there has been no reduction in more

than 20 years. It is estimated that 30 to 40 percent of excess preterm births and infant deaths are due to STDs and bacterial vaginosis (Goldenberg, 1997).

## Can the Most Serious STDs Infect Babies?

Many STDs can be passed from an infected woman to fetus, newborn, or infant, before, during or after birth. Some STDs—like syphilis—cross the placenta and infect the fetus during its development. Other STDs—like gonorrhea, chlamydia, genital herpes, and genital HPV infection—are transmitted from mother to child as the infant passes through the birth canal. HIV infection can cross the placenta during pregnancy, can infect the newborn during the birth process, or unlike other STDs, can infect a child as a result of breast feeding.

If an STD in a pregnant woman is detected soon enough, precautions can often be taken so that the disease is not spread to the baby. Newborns infected with syphilis and herpes may suffer severe consequences not completely relieved by treatment, including neurologic damage and death. Gonorrhea and chlamydia can cause prematurity, eye disease, and pneumonia in infants.

## What Are the Most Common STDs among Teens?

Teens are at high behavioral risk for acquiring most STDs. Teenagers and young adults are more likely than other age groups to have multiple sex partners, to engage in unprotected sex, and, for young women, to choose sexual partners older than themselves. Moreover, young women are biologically more susceptible to chlamydia, gonorrhea and HIV.

Chlamydia and gonorrhea are the most common curable STDs among teens. Curable STDs are typically caused by bacteria that can be killed with antibiotics. However, if these diseases remain undetected and untreated, they can result in severe health consequences later in life. Among teens, it is not uncommon to see more than five percent of young men and five to 10 percent of young women infected with chlamydia (Mertz, CDC, 1998). Rates of gonorrhea are highest in females 15 to 19 years of age and in males 20 to 24 years of age.

The prevalence of herpes increases with age. Since this disease stays within the body once acquired, the older people are, the more likely they have been infected. The rate of new infections for herpes and HPV—both viral STDs—is typically highest during the late teens and early twenties. Among women under the age of 25, studies have found that 28 to 46 percent are typically infected with HPV. Between 15 to 20 percent of young men and women have become infected with herpes by the time they reach adulthood.

### What Are STD Trends in Teens?

Syphilis, hepatitis B, and chancroid are declining among teens and other age groups. Chlamydia is likely going down in areas where there is screening and treatment among teens at family planning clinics and school-based screening programs. In areas where these services are not available, the disease may be increasing. Herpes was increasing among teens through the early 1990s. Currently, the data are not available to tell us whether HPV, trichomoniasis, or bacterial vaginosis are increasing, but these diseases are extremely widespread.

### What Are the Most Common STDs among Men Who Have Sex with Men?

Researchers estimate that men who have sex with men (MSM) still account for 42 percent of new HIV infections annually in the United States and for 60 percent of all new HIV infections among men. Several recent studies have pointed to high, and increasing, levels of other STDs among MSM.

One 26-city study, the Gonococcal Isolate Surveillance Project, reported that from 1994 to 1999, the proportion of gonorrhea cases among MSM more than doubled from six to 13 percent. An STD clinic in Washington, D.C., serving a large number of gay and bisexual men reported that gonorrhea cases increased 93 percent from

1993 to 1996, with 82 percent of these cases among MSM.

In King County, Washington—which includes the city of Seattle—researchers reported marked increases in both gonorrhea and syphilis cases among MSM. Most notably, while the county had no cases of early syphilis in 1996, 88 cases were reported between 1998 and the first half of 1999, 85 percent of which were in gay and bisexual men. These men reported having multiple partners and frequently engaging in unprotected anal intercourse.

### What Areas of the Country Have the Greatest Problems with STDs?

Herpes and HPV are widespread throughout the nation, showing very little regional variation. Chlamydia is also extremely common across geographic boundaries, but is on the decline in regions where effective screening and treatment programs are in place. Chlamydia remains most widespread among women in the southern region of the country. The south also faces the highest rates of both gonorrhea and syphilis. The high rates of STDs in the south may be due to high rates of poverty and lack of access to quality health care.

### Are STDS More Common among Racial and Ethnic Minorities? If So, Why?

Although STDs like chlamydia, HPV, and herpes are widespread across racial and ethnic groups, STD rates tend to be higher among African Americans than white Americans. Reported rates of some STDs, like gonorrhea and syphilis, are as much as 30 times higher for African Americans than for whites. This disparity is due, in part, to the fact that African Americans are more likely to seek care in public clinics that report STDs more completely than private providers. However, this reporting bias does not fully explain these differences. Other important factors include the distribution of poverty, access to quality health care, health-seeking behaviors, the level of drug use, and sexual networks with high STD prevalence.

Moreover, the level of prevention education may vary widely across communities. In some areas, community-based efforts may be widespread across social, educational, and religious organizations, but in others, STD prevention may not yet be a high priority. Efforts are underway to increase both public and private sector HIV and STD prevention efforts in communities at risk throughout the nation. Yet, research demonstrates that some groups at very high risk still lack even basic information about STD prevention (Bunnell, CDC, 1998).

### What Are the Economic Costs of STDS in the United States?

STDs are associated with both direct and indirect costs. Direct costs include expenditures for medical and non-medical services and materials, such as physician services, laboratory services, hospitalization, transportation, and medical supplies. Indirect costs mainly include lost wages due to illness or premature death. STDs also result in intangible costs related to pain, suffering, and diminished quality of life. In 1994, the direct and indirect costs of the major STDs and their complications were estimated to total almost $17 billion annually.

**REFERENCES**

Bunnell R, Dahlberg L, Stone K, et al. Misconceptions about STD Prevention and Associations with STD Prevalence and Incidence in Adolescent Females in a Southeastern City [abstract]. In: Program and Abstracts of the 1998 National STD Prevention Conference; December 1998.

Cates W et al. Estimates of the Incidence and Prevalence of Sexually Transmitted Diseases in the United States. *Sex Trans Dis* 1999;26 (suppl):S2-S7.

Division of STD Prevention. Sexually Transmitted Disease Surveillance, 1999. U.S. Department of Health and Human Services, Atlanta: Centers for Disease Control and Prevention (CDC), September 2000.

Fleming DT, McQuillan GM, Johnson RE, et al. Herpes Simplex Virus Type 2 in the United States, 1976 to 1994. *N Engl J Med* 1997;337(16):1105-11.

Goldenberg RL, Andres WW, Yuan AC, et al. Sexually Transmitted Diseases and Adverse Outcomes of Pregnancy. *Clin Perinatal* 1997;March;2491:23-41.

Mertz KJ, McQuillan GM, Levine WC, et al. A pilot study of the prevalence of Chlamydial infection in a National household survey. *Sex Trans Dis* 1998; May:225-228.

## Preventing STIs

**Heather Boonstra**

In his [2004] State of the Union address . . . , President Bush expounded on the dangers that young people face from exposure to sexually transmitted infections (STIs). "Each year, [millions of] teenagers contract sexually-transmitted diseases that can harm them, or kill them, or prevent them from ever becoming parents," he said. His prescription was simple: "We will double federal funding for abstinence programs, so schools can teach this fact of life: Abstinence for young people is the only certain way to avoid sexually-transmitted diseases." . . .

As teenage pregnancy rates have continued to fall, STIs have largely replaced pregnancy in the drive for funding for abstinence-only education programs. Social conservatives dismiss sexual risk reduction strategies as ineffective. Instead, they advocate a risk elimination approach: a clear and simple message that the best means of preventing STIs is to avoid risk altogether.

### STIs in Perspective

[E]stimates published in the January/February 2004 issue of *Perspectives in Sexual and Reproductive Health* show that nearly 19 million new STIs occurred in the United States in 2000. Although they make up only a quarter of the sexually active population, young people aged 15–24 account for nearly half of new infections. This is not surprising, as most young people are not yet in a long-standing, stable relationship. According to the

U.S. Census Bureau, 78% of 20–24-year-olds in 2000 had never been married.

With the exception of HIV, STIs are not new; the diseases or their manifestations have been recognized for decades, even centuries. The impact of STIs on people's lives varies widely. At one end of the spectrum is HIV, which still must be considered inevitably fatal, although new drug regimens are helping many people with HIV/AIDS live longer. Many of the most common STIs, however, are either harmless or can be treated and cured. . . .

## Preventing STIs

Social conservatives' solution to the problem of STIs is simple: Young people should simply abstain from all sexual activity until they are married to a disease-free spouse. Organizations such as Focus on the Family and the Medical Institute for Sexual Health say we must stop promoting condoms, which are known to have high failure rates in actual use. Instead, they say we should be promoting abstinence, which is 100% effective, 100% of the time.

If the president's proposal to double funding for abstinence-only education is adopted, the federal government will spend almost a quarter of a billion dollars in the fiscal year beginning October 1 to promote abstinence for all unmarried people.* In accordance with the requirement that these programs have abstinence promotion as their "exclusive purpose," they may include instruction about the failure rates of condoms and other forms of contraception, but they may not provide any information about contraceptive methods that could be construed as promoting contraceptive use. The Bush proposal is sparking hope among abstinence-only proponents who are a key component of the president's political base of support. "This is a president who's finally putting his money where his mouth is," said LeAnna Benn, a pioneer in the abstinence-only movement, to the *Washington Times.* Benn went on to say that what is needed now is for abstinence-friendly government officials to structure grant programs so that an abstinence network can be built to match the powerful family planning network.

Meanwhile, . . . social conservatives hope that a warning label on condoms will dissuade people from having sex, but public health experts are skeptical. Because in the real world, abstinence can and does fail ("Understanding 'Abstinence': Implications for Individuals, Programs and Policies," *TGR,* December 2003, page 4), a more comprehensive and nuanced approach is needed, they say. "There is no magic bullet," says Ralph DiClemente, a researcher at Emory University who has been studying HIV prevention among adolescents. "That's why young people need a 'menu' of interventions, including information about condoms. There is no moral justification for withholding information or, worse yet, discouraging individuals from adopting behaviors that could save their life." Theresa Raphael, executive director of the National Coalition of STD Directors, agrees. "While abstinence is a public health message that we can all support, it cannot be the only message," she says in a February 5, 2004, press release. "Public health officials are obligated to dwell in the real world and support an approach . . . that reflects how Americans actually live."

Public opinion data have consistently shown that while American adults want abstinence to be promoted to young people, they also want those young people to have information about contraception and condom use. According to a 2003 poll conducted by NPR, the Kaiser Family Foundation and Harvard's Kennedy School of Government, 93% of adults support instruction in school-based sex education programs about waiting to have sexual intercourse until marriage. At the same time, overwhelming proportions also support giving teens information on how to use and where to obtain contraceptives (86%), how to put on a condom (83%) and how to get tested for HIV and other STIs (94%).

Even conservatives cannot avoid the inescapable conclusion that most Americans do not support abstinence-only sex education. According to a Heritage Foundation analysis of a survey conducted earlier this year by Zogby International for Focus on the Family, "Some 75 percent of parents want teens to be taught about both abstinence and contraception." . . .

*Author's Note:* FY05 funding for abstinence-only education was $167 million. In FY06, it was $176 million. The president requested $204 million for FY07 and promised to increase funding to $270 million by the end of his administration.

*Source:* Boonstra, Heather. 2004. "Comprehensive Approach Needed to Combat Sexually Transmitted Infections Among Youth." *The Guttmacher Report on Public Policy* 7(1): 3–5. Reprinted by permission.

# Venereal Disease:

# Sin versus Science

**Elizabeth Fee**

**W**ays of perceiving and understanding disease are historically constructed. Our social, political, religious, and moral conceptions influence our perceptions of disease, just as do different scientific and medical theories. Indeed, these different elements often cannot be easily separated, as scientists and physicians bring their own cultural ideas to bear in the construction of scientific theories. Because these cultural ideas may be widely shared, their presence within medical and scientific theory may not be readily apparent. Often, such cultural conceptions are more obvious when reviewing medical and scientific theories of the past than they are in contemporary medical practice.[1]

Just as cultural conceptions of disease may be embodied in the framing of scientific theories, so these theories also influence popular perceptions of disease. At times such scientific theories may reinforce, or contradict, other cultural conceptions, such as religious and moral ideas or racial stereotypes.

In the case of the venereal diseases, it is clear that our attitudes embody a fundamental cultural ambivalence: are venereal diseases to be studied and treated from a purely biomedical point of view—are they infectious diseases like any others—or are they to be treated as social,

moral, or spiritual afflictions?[2] As the name implies, venereal diseases are inevitably associated with sexuality—and therefore our perceptions of these diseases tend to be entangled with our ideas about the social meanings and moral evaluation of sexual behaviors. In the case of syphilis, a major killer in the first half of the twentieth century, health officials could decide that the true "cause" of syphilis was the microorganism *Treponema pallidum,* or they could define the "underlying cause" as "promiscuous sexual behavior." Each claim focuses on a different part of social reality, and each carries different messages of responsibility and blame. Each is part of a different language in which the disease may be described and defined. The first suggests the primacy of the medical clinic for treating disease; the second, the primacy of moral exhortation.

Throughout the twentieth century struggles have been waged over the meaning and definition of the venereal diseases. At times these diseases have been blanketed in silence, as though they belonged to a "private" realm, not open to public discussion. Wars, however, have tended to make venereal diseases visible, to bring them out of the private sphere and into the center of public policy discussions; this has highlighted the struggles over their proper definition and treatment. In World War I, for example, the American Social Hygiene Association consistently equated venereal disease with immorality, vice, and prostitution.[3] Its members thus tried to close down brothels and taverns, to arrest prostitutes, and to advocate continence and sexual abstinence for the soldiers. The

From Fee, Elizabeth. 1988. "Sin vs. Science: Venereal Disease in Baltimore in the Twentieth Century." *Journal of the History of Medicine and Allied Sciences* 43: 141–164. Reprinted by permission of Oxford University Press and the author.

Commission on Training Camp Activities tried to suppress vice and liquor and also to organize "good, clean fun": sports events, theatrical entertainments and educational programs.[4] The Army, however, quietly issued prophylactic kits to the soldiers and made early treatment after possible exposure compulsory. Any soldier who failed to get treatment could face trial and imprisonment for neglect of duty. . . .

When dealing with major disease problems, we often try to find some social group to "blame" for the infection. During the war, educational materials clearly presented the fighting men as the innocent victims of disease; prostitutes were the guilty spreaders of infection. Indeed, prostitutes were often presented as implicitly working for the enemy against patriotic American soldiers.[5] In many communities prostitutes would be the focus, and often the victims and scapegoats, of the new attention to venereal infections. Prostitutes— the women responsible for the defilement of the heroic American soldier—would be regularly rounded up, arrested, and jailed in the campaign against vice.

The end of the war, however, brought a waning of interest in venereal disease and a return to "normal life," freed of the restrictions and regulations of military necessity. The energetic public discussion of venereal disease again lapsed into a public silence. Prostitutes and their customers were again permitted to operate without much official harassment; health departments quietly collected statistics on venereal disease but avoided publicity on the subject.[6]

This essay will examine the subsequent history of venereal disease, and especially syphilis, by focusing on a major industrial city, Baltimore, to see how the struggle between the moral and biomedical views of disease was played out in the context of city politics in the 1930s and 1940s. Although syphilis is no longer a significant public health problem, this account should be useful in helping us to reflect on the . . . problem of AIDS (acquired immune deficiency syndrome) today.

## Treatment for Veneral Disease: The Public Health Clinics

In Baltimore in the 1920s a great social silence surrounded the problem of syphilis. Since venereal diseases carried such negative social stigma, only a small proportion of cases were ever reported. Deaths from syphilis were often attributed to other causes as physicians endeavored to save patients and their families from possible embarrassment. A social conspiracy of silence resulted: patients did not talk about their diseases, physicians did not report them, the health department did not publicize them, and the newspapers never mentioned them. The diseases were thus largely invisible. Most hospitals and some physicians refused to treat patients with venereal diseases; some physicians specialized in these diseases and made a great deal of money from private patients.[7] Many patients, however, could not afford private medical care.

In the aftermath of the war, the city health department began quietly to treat venereal diseases in its public clinics. The first such clinic, opened in 1922, had 13,000 patient visits in its first year of operation. The clinic population grew so fast that the city soon opened a second clinic, and then a third. These patients, brought to the public clinics through poverty, were recorded in health department files as venereal disease cases. Like all the diseases of the poor, these cases attracted little public attention.

The venereal disease problem in Baltimore was, however, made publicly visible by a survey conducted by the United States Public Health Service in 1931.[8] The survey defined syphilis as a major problem in Baltimore, and as a problem of the black population. The reported "colored" rate was 22 per 1,000 males and 10 per 1,000 women; this contrasted with a reported white rate of 4 per 1,000 men and 1.3 per 1,000 women. Of course, whites were more likely to be seeing private physicians and thus less likely to have their disease reported to the health department. Syphilis, originally perceived as a disease of vice and prostitution, was now a black disease. . . .

### The Depression: Restricting Treatment

During the Depression public clinics became more crowded than ever, with over 84,000 visits in 1932 alone. The city health department, already burdened with tight budgets and increasing health problems of every kind, complained that the hospitals in town were dumping poor patients on the city clinics.[9] . . .

In 1933 the problem of overcrowding became so acute that the city health department decided to treat only patients at the infectious stage of syphilis. They discontinued treatment to any patients who had received sufficient drugs to render them noninfectious to others, even though they had not been cured.[10] . . .

### Venereal Disease and Racism

In the 1930s as today, health statistics were gathered by race but not by income. The statistics on venereal diseases confirmed the definition of syphilis as predominantly a black or "colored" problem. In fact almost all infectious diseases were far more prevalent among blacks than whites, reflecting the effects of poverty, poor housing, and overcrowding. . . .

While [Ferdinard] Reinhard [the head of the bureau of venereal diseases] described the black venereal disease problem as an effect of economics and social conditions, most whites saw venereal disease simply as a question of sexual morality. Blacks were popularly perceived as highly sexual, uninhibited, and promiscuous. . . . White doctors saw blacks as "diseased, debilitated, and debauched," the victims of their own uncontrolled or uncontrollable sexual instincts and impulses. . . .[11] [H]ealth officials were certainly convinced that the main issue was sexual behavior, and they were equally convinced that it was the sexual behavior of the black population that had to be changed.

Since the problem was clearly understood as one of sexual behavior, the city health department began an energetic public education project aimed at changing sexual attitudes—by persuasion or by fear. In 1934 the department directed a new program on sex hygiene at the black population. They gave talks at the Colored Vocational School and the Frederick Douglass High School, and organized exhibits for Negro Health Week and for the National Association of Teachers in Colored Schools. They distributed nearly 14,000 pamphlets on venereal diseases. A "social hygiene motion picture" with the discouraging title *Damaged Lives* played in twenty-three theaters, thus reaching over 65,000 people, one-tenth of Baltimore's adult population.[12]

The main aim of this health propaganda was to stress the dangers of sexual promiscuity, but it also emphasized the need for early detection and treatment of disease. . . . Pamphlets distributed by the Social Hygiene Association and the city health department continued to urge chastity before marriage and sexual fidelity within marriage as the proper solutions to syphilis.

In 1935 syphilis was by far the most prevalent of the communicable diseases occurring in the city, with 5,754 reported cases; the next most prevalent disease was chickenpox—not a disease considered of much importance—with 3,816 reported cases.[13] . . . The facilities for actually treating syphilis were still completely inadequate.

Syphilis deaths were now running at between 110 and 150 per year. As Reinhard complained, "Any other group of diseases scattered throughout the community to this extent would be considered to have taken on epidemic proportions and would be cause for alarm on the part of health authorities.[14] . . .

Reinhard continued for several years to struggle against the partial treatment plan and to advocate extended clinic facilities, sufficient for all syphilis patients, and staffed with black physicians, nurses, and social workers. It seemed, at the time, to be a one-man campaign. Most physicians approved of the fact that the health department was not offering treatment, the proper domain of fee-for-service medicine. Particularly during the depression years, when many physicians found it difficult to make a living on patient fees, the medical profession was antagonistic to efforts by public health officers to offer free treatments to any patients, whatever their illness.

## Syphilis as Everyone's Disease: A National Campaign

In 1936 Reinhard's "one-man campaign" against syphilis in Baltimore suddenly became part of a major national effort. Thomas Parran, Surgeon General of the United States Public Health Service, now lent the full weight of his authority to a campaign against venereal diseases. A forceful and dynamic man, Parran decided to break through the wall of silence and make the public confront the magnitude of the problem. To do this, he redefined syphilis as a disease that struck "innocent" victims: the educated, respectable, white population. . . . Parran called syphilis "the great American Disease" and declared: "we might virtually stamp out this disease were we not hampered by the widespread belief that nice people don't talk about syphilis, that nice people don't have syphilis, and that nice people shouldn't do anything about those who *do* have syphilis."[15] Parran's point was that nice people *did* have syphilis; he never tired of pointing out that respectable physicians, innocent children, and heads of industry were among those infected.[16] . . .

Parran declared that half the victims of syphilis were "innocently infected": "Many cases come from such casual contacts as the use of [a] recently soiled drinking cup, a pipe or cigarette; in receiving services from diseased nursemaids, barber or beauty shop operators, etc., and in giving services such as those of a dentist, doctor or nurse to a diseased person."[17] Syphilis was just another contagious disease, although a highly threatening and dangerous one. The point was to find syphilis cases and to treat them; the state should be obliged to provide treatment, said Parran, and

the patient should be obliged to endure it. Syphilis would be the next great plague to go—as soon as the public broke with the old-fashioned and pre-scientific notion that syphilis was "the wages of sin." . . .

[W]hile the city health department was consolidating the new biomedical approach to syphilis, it was suddenly challenged with a resurgent moral crusade against vice and prostitution, led by none other than the redoubtable J. Edgar Hoover.

## Medical Treatment or Crusade against Vice?

"Captives Taken in Weekend Drive Against City's White Slave Traffic," declared the headlines of the Baltimore *Sun* on May 17, 1937.[18] . . . The raids generated great excitement and controversy, magnified when local prostitutes implicated a number of high level police officers and at least one state senator in Baltimore's "white slave trade."[19] The local newspapers took delight in reporting the activities of this organized racket, playing up Baltimore as a notorious center of vice and iniquity. . . .

State Senator Raymond E. Kennedy now implied that the city health department, like the police department, was implicitly involved in condoning vice. He demanded that all prostitutes being treated in city clinics be immediately incarcerated. Parran was called to appear as a witness before a Grand Jury investigation. On his arrival in Baltimore, however, Parran managed to turn this into a public relations coup for the health department. He announced a state survey of venereal diseases, suggested that Baltimore follow the successful Swedish model of disease control, including the provision of free drugs, and he declared to enthusiastic mass meetings that Maryland would take the lead in the fight against "social diseases."[20] . . .

Thanks to citywide publicity and political pressure on Mayor Jackson, Williams was able to expand his budget and open the Druid Hill Health Center for black patients in west Baltimore—the first time that adequate public health facilities had been available in this area of the city.[21]

The city health department now tackled the problem of syphilis in industry. At the time, industrial workers were being fired (or never hired in the first place) if they were found to have positive blood tests for syphilis. Employers fired infected workers on the grounds that they were more likely to be involved in industrial accidents, and thus would increase the costs of workmen's compensation and insurance premiums. The health department started to provide free laboratory blood tests for industrial workers; the test results were kept confidential and those infected were referred for appropriate therapy. The health department followed individual workers to make sure they were receiving treatment but, at least in theory, no worker who accepted treatment could be fired. The fact that no guarantees were offered workers refusing therapy meant, however, that syphilis treatment was essentially made compulsory for industrial workers participating in the plan.[22] . . .

## The Impact of War

In the late 1930s there were considerable grounds for optimism that the campaign against the venereal diseases was beginning to show results. The more open public health attitude toward syphilis as a problem of disease rather than of morality seemed to be successful. . . . The numbers of reported cases of syphilis were decreasing each year, despite increased screening efforts and more effective reporting mechanisms. In 1938, 8,236 new cases were reported; in 1939, 7,509; and in 1940, only 6,213. . . . These records of syphilis incidence and prevalence may have been quite unreliable from an epidemiological point of view, but this was the first time that syphilis rates had even seemed to be declining; it was a natural conclusion that health department efforts were finally showing demonstrable results.

In the midst of this optimism, however, came the prospect of war and, with it, the fear that war

mobobilization and an influx of 60,000 soldiers would upset all previous gain.[23] In 1941, with the institution of selective service examinations, reported venereal disease rates began to climb. In Baltimore that year, 1.7 percent of the white enlistees had positive blood tests for syphilis, as had twenty-four percent of the black recruits.[24] Baltimore City won the dubious distinction of having the second highest syphilis rate in the country, second only to Washington, D.C. Baltimore's rate was 101.3 cases per 1,000 men examined, more than twice the national rate.[25] In an effort to justify these statistics, the city health department blamed the situation on the nonwhite population: the relatively high proportion of blacks to whites "explained" why Baltimore had the second highest venereal disease rate among the country's largest cities.[26] . . .

Such justifications were hardly likely to be sufficient for a country at war. With the war mobilization had come renewed national attention to protecting the health and fighting efficiency of the soldiers. As during World War I, the first concern was with the control or suppression of prostitution in the vicinity of army camps and with "social hygiene" rather than treatment programs. The May Act passed by Congress made prostitution a federal offense in the vicinity of military camps. . . .

[T]he Baltimore police seemed determined to prove their dedication to the attack on prostitution. By early 1943 they claimed to have closed most of Baltimore's brothels and to have driven prostitutes from the streets.[27] Police Commissioner Stanton demanded statewide legislation to allow police officers to arrest prostitutes and force them to submit to medical examination and, if infected, medical treatment.[28]

Dr. Nels A. Nelson, head of the state venereal disease control program, declared that these arrests of prostitutes and compulsory medical examinations were completely ineffective: only a few prostitutes could be arrested at any one time, and as soon as they were treated and released, they would immediately return to the streets to become reinfected and to continue to spread infection until their next arrest. The only real control of venereal disease, concluded Nelson, depended on the complete "repression of sexual promiscuity."[29] Meanwhile, the reported cases of syphilis were rapidly increasing. In 1942 the selective service records showed that almost three percent of the white draftees and over thirty-two percent of the black soldiers had syphilis.[30] . . . Between 1940 and 1942 new cases of syphilis had almost doubled, from 6,213 to 11,293, and gonorrhea rates were also climbing. . . .

Nelson of the state health department had . . . abandoned the fight against prostitution. He was busily distributing free drugs for syphilis control to private physicians, while he publicly declared the city venereal disease clinics "little more than drug pumping stations in dirty, unattractive quarters."[31] Nelson told the press he was tired of hearing the VD rate discussed as though it were only a Negro problem: "Negroes are plagued by venereal diseases because of their economic and social position."[32] . . .

The Army was also under attack for failing to organize an effective VD program.[33] Its programs and policies were plagued by contradictions; publicly, it advocated chastity, while privately, it provided prophylactics for the men. . . . The Army finally adopted a pragmatic approach and attempted to reduce the sources of infection as much as possible. The pragmatic approach lacked the fervor of a purity crusade, but tried to steer some middle course between laissez-faire attitudes and moral absolutism.

In Baltimore the new acting directors of the city's venereal disease program, Ralph Sikes and Alexander Novey, shared this pragmatic position. . . . Under their leadership health officers cooperated with the armed services in distributing prophylactic kits throughout the city: in police stations, fire houses, transportation terminals, hospitals, and clinic.[34] Implicitly, the VD control officers had thus accepted the idea that this was a campaign *against* disease, rather than a campaign *for* sexual morality; they concentrated on a fairly

mechanical (if effective) approach to prevention while leaving the struggle around prostitution to social hygiene reformers, the police, and the courts.

## Sex Education during the War

During the war the city health department and a research group at the Johns Hopkins School of Hygiene and Public Health undertook a daring task—to teach "sex hygiene" in the public schools. They gave talks to groups of high school students, (separated by sex) showed plaster models of male and female reproductive systems, and gave simple explanations of "menstruation, conception, pregnancy, nocturnal emissions and masturbation, but omitting intercourse and childbirth."[35] . . .

Having been assured that sex was both exciting and dangerous, students were then given a brief description of male reproductive physiology, ending with a caution against masturbation. Masturbation was not dangerous, students were told, merely unnecessary and possibly habit-forming. . . . A brief description of the female reproductive system was followed by a discussion of morals and ethics, warning of the need for judgment, but avoiding specific advice. . . . Students were urged to discuss their questions with parents and teachers and to read a social hygiene pamphlet on "Growing Up in the World Today."[36]

The third part of the presentation, on venereal diseases, emphasized the dangers of sex. Intimacy brought the germs of syphilis: sexual intercourse was the most threatening, but even kisses could carry disease. The best strategy was to avoid any possible contact with these sexual germs:

> They can be caught only from an infected person and therefore, we should avoid intimate contact with an infected person. But we cannot tell by looking at a person whether he or she, is infected or not; the answer is to avoid intimate contact with all persons except in marriage. This is the only sure way of avoiding these diseases.[37]

At least for these high school students, the link between sexual morality and venereal disease was clear: sexual intimacy led to syphilis and was therefore to be avoided except in marriage. Why marital sex should be "safe" was never explained, nor was congenital syphilis ever mentioned.

## After the War: The New Penicillin Therapy

By the end of World War II, the problem of syphilis was beginning to recede, both in public consciousness and in statistical measures. Part of this was the normal relaxation in the immediate aftermath of war, the return to home and family, the desire for stability, and a reluctance to confront social and sexual problems or to dwell on their existence. Even more important, however, was the success of the new drug, penicillin: at last, venereal diseases could, it seemed, be quickly and effectively treated. Many felt it was only a matter of time before the venereal diseases were finally eliminated with the aid of modern medicine's "miracle cures."

By 1940 the new "miracle drug" penicillin had been discovered and purified; in 1943 it was first used against syphilis, but it was not yet generally available; supplies were still strictly rationed.[38] Soon, it would completely transform the old methods of treating venereal diseases. On December 31, 1944, the Baltimore City Hospitals opened the first Rapid Treatment Center for treating syphilis with penicillin. Penicillin doses for syphilis were given over eight days; since supplies of the drug were then very limited, only cases judged to be highly infectious were sent for "an eight-day cure, or what is for the present considered to be a cure."[39] From all initial reports the new experimental treatment was remarkably effective.

On June 20, 1945, Mayor Theodore R. McKeldin approved a new city ordinance making treatment for venereal diseases compulsory for the first time. Those suspected of having syphilis or gonorrhea were required to take penicillin therapy at the Rapid Treatment Center.[40] Those refusing treatment could be quarantined and isolated in the Baltimore City hospitals. . . .

The ordinance was, however, rarely invoked. Most patients were eager to go to the Rapid Treatment Center when diagnosed. In 1946 nearly 2,000 people with infectious syphilis received treatment; most were reported as completely cured. (Before penicillin, only an estimated twenty-five percent of patients completed the lengthy treatments considered necessary for a full cure.[41]) In 1947 the Baltimore *Sun* reviewed the city's experience with the new ordinance:

> On the basis of this experience (over the last 16 months), it is clear that the protection of the public against persons carrying the disease and refusing to be treated more than outweighs the sacrifice of individual rights by so small a number. . . . Under the circumstances, the enactment of a permanent ordinance seems fully justified.[42]

The state health department in 1947 announced that "for the first time in history any resident of Maryland who contracts syphilis can obtain treatment resulting in prompt and almost certain cure."[43]

## Conclusion: The End of the Struggle?

The biomedical approach to venereal diseases had apparently been stunningly successful. Diseases that only ten years before had been described as the most serious of all the infectious diseases had now been tamed by chemotherapy with a simple, safe, and effective cure. Diseases that twenty years previously had been guilty secrets, virtually unmentionable in the public press and quietly ignored by health departments, were now glorious examples of the triumph of modem medicine in overcoming ancient plagues. The ideological struggle between those who had seen the fight against venereal disease as a battle for sexual morality and those who had seen it as simply another form of bacteriological warfare was now over. The social hygiene reformers had to concede defeat to the public health officers, epidemiologists, and laboratory researchers. Or did they?

In 1947 the Maryland State Department of Health, announcing the success of the rapid treatment program, concluded its press bulletin with the warning: "To decrease the number of repeat patients and prevent venereal diseases it will be necessary to reduce sexual promiscuity. If fear of disease is a less powerful restraining factor the problem must be attacked more strongly through moral training and suppression of prostitution."[44] . . .

Even those most committed to the bacteriological view of disease seemed uneasy about the decoupling of venereal disease from sin and promiscuity: How would sexual morality be controlled if not by the fear of disease? Would "rampant promiscuity" defeat the best efforts of medical treatment?

A brief review of health statistics in the years since the discovery of penicillin suggests that syphilis has, in the main, been effectively controlled. New cases of syphilis are reported each year, and doubtless others go unreported, but the rates are relatively low. In 1986 a total of 373 cases of primary, secondary, and early latent cases were reported in Baltimore; in 1987, a total of 364 cases. Although these cases are of continuing concern to health department officials, at least from the perspective of the 1930s and 1940s, the miracle of control really has occurred. . . .

As we have since discovered, the fear and underlying ambivalence toward sexuality were only lying dormant. Public concern, horror, and fear about AIDS have recently reignited the older social hygiene movement in a new form. The once prevalent description of the black population as sexually promiscuous, sexually threatening, and a reservoir of disease has now been applied to the gay male population. AIDS is popularly seen as "caused" by gay promiscuity and, even more broadly, as a punishment for unconventional or unapproved sexual behavior, rather than simply as the result of infection by a microorganism. Venereal disease is again perceived as the "wages of sin," or, as the Reverend Jerry Falwell says: "A man reaps what he sows. If he sows seed in the field of his lower nature, he will reap from it a harvest of corruption." . . .

Both the biomedical and moral perspectives on venereal disease highlight specific aspects of a complex social reality. Venereal diseases, like all other diseases, are experienced and reproduced in a social context. We may separate the biological and social aspects for analysis, but any complete understanding of a disease problem must involve both, as interrelated parts of a single social reality.

Social and cultural ideas offer a variety of ways in which diseases can be perceived and interpreted. The germ theory provides an explanation of disease that largely—but not completely—isolates it from this social context, robbing it of some of its social (and in this case, moral) meaning. But the purely "scientific" interpretation is never wholly victorious, for social and cultural meanings of disease reassert themselves in the interstices of science and prove their power whenever the biomedical sciences fail to completely cure or solve the problem. Only when a disease condition is completely abolished do social and cultural meanings cease to be relevant to the experience and perception of human illness.

### NOTES

1. For a fascinating analysis of the history of cultural and scientific conceptions of syphilis, see Ludwig Fleck, *Genesis and Development of a Scientific Fact* (1935, rpt., Chicago: 1979).

2. For an excellent recent history of the controversies around venereal diseases in the United States, see Allan Brandt, *No Magic Bullet: A Social History of Venereal Diseases in the United States Since 1880* (New York: 1985).

3. National Academy of Sciences, *Scientific and Technical Societies of the United States and Canada*, 8th ed. (Washington, D.C.: 1968), 62.

4. Edward H. Beardsley, "Allied Against Sin: American and British Responses to Venereal Disease in World War I," *Medical History* 20 (1976): 194.

5. As one widely reprinted article, said to have reached eight million readers, described 'The Enemy at Home': "The name of this invisible enemy is Venereal Disease—and there you have in two words the epitome of all that is unclean, malignant and menacing. . . . Gonorrhea and syphilis are 'camp followers' where prostitution and alcohol are permitted. They form almost as great an enemy behind the lines as do the Huns in front." "V. D.: The Enemy at Home," as cited by William H. Zinsser, "Social Hygiene and the War: Fighting Venereal Disease a Public Trust," *Social Hygiene* 4 (1918): 519–20.

6. In 1920 William Travis Howard, a member of the city health department, complained: "The Baltimore health department has never inaugurated a single administrative measure directed at the control of the venereal diseases . . . the Baltimore health department has contented itself with receiving such reports as were made and with lending its power, when called upon, to force a few recalcitrant patients to appear at the venereal disease clinic established by the United States Government." Howard, *Public Health Administration and the Natural History of Disease in Baltimore, Maryland: 1797–1920* (Washington, D.C.:1924): 154–55.

7. Baltimore City Health Department, Annual Report (1930).

8. Taliaferro Clark and Lida Usilton, "Survey of the Venereal Diseases in the City of Baltimore, Baltimore County, and the Four Contiguous Counties," *Venereal Disease Information* 12 (Washington, D.C.:20 October 1931): 437–56.

9. Baltimore City Health Department, Annual Report (1932), 62.

10. Baltimore City Health Department, Annual Report (1933), 93.

11. James H. Jones, *Bad Blood. The Tuskegee Syphilis Experiment* (New York: 981), 16–29.

12. Baltimore City Health Department, Annual Report (1934), 107.

13. Baltimore City Health Department, Annual Report (1935), 115.

14. Ferdinand O. Reinhard, "The Venereal Disease Problem in the Colored Population of Baltimore City," *American Journal of Syphilis and Neurology* 19 (1935): 183–95.

15. Thomas Parran, "Why Don't We Stamp Out Syphilis?" *Reader's Digest* (July 1936), reprinted in Baltimore *Health News* (August 1936): 3.

16. *E.g.* Parran, *Shadow on the Land: Syphilis* (New York: 1937). 207, 230.

17. Parran, "Why Don't We Stamp Out Syphilis?" *Reader's Digest,* 65–73.

18. "G-Men's Haul in Vice Raids Totals 47," *Baltimore Sun,* 17 May 1937.

19. "Vice Witness Names Police Lieutenant," *Baltimore Sun,* 18 May 1937; "Vice Arrests May Total 100; Bierman Named," *Sunday Sun,* 19 May 1937.

20. "Starts to Survey Venereal Disease," *Baltimore Sun,* 29 July 1937; "Venereal Disease Fight is Planned," *Baltimore Sun,* 22 August 1937; "Fight Opens Here on Social Disease," *Baltimore Sun,* 25 August 1937; "Syphilis Control Unit Begins Work," *Baltimore Sun,* 21 October 1937; "Over 2,000 Attend Talks on Syphilis," *Baltimore Sun,* 26 October 1937.

21. Baltimore City Health Department, Annual Reports (1938), 159; (1939), 159.

22. Baltimore City Health Department, Annual Report (1938); 16; "21 Employers Asked in Drive on Syphilis," *Baltimore Sun,* 27 March 1938; "Syphilis Control is Under Way Here," *Baltimore Sun,* 22 May 1938; W. M. P., "We Join the Anti-Syphilis Crusade," *The Kalends* (June 1938), reprinted in *Baltimore Health News* 15 (July 1938): 53–54; Baltimore City Health Department, "Syphilis in Industry" (Baltimore: n.d.).

23. Baltimore City Health Department, Annual Report (1940), 149–51.

24. Baltimore City Health Department, Annual Report (1941), 139.

25. "City Shown Second in Syphilis Survey," *Baltimore Sun,* 22 October 1941.

26. "High Syphilis Rate Laid to Race Ratio," *Baltimore Sun,* 26 October 1941.

27. "Says Vice Control Has Improved Here," *Baltimore Sun,* 27 January 1943.

28. "State Law Held Needed in War on Vice," *Baltimore Sun,* 28 January 1943.

29. "Stanton Idea for Examination of Prostitutes Is Denounced," *Baltimore Sun,* 29 January 1943.

30. "Venereal Picture Dark: Dr. Huntington Williams Says No Improvement Is Expected for Some Time," *Baltimore Sun,* 21 January 1943.

31. "Clinics Here Under Fire," *Baltimore Sun,* 30 March 1943.

32. "Venereal Disease Rate High in State," *Baltimore Sun,* 15 June 1943.

33. Parran and Vonderlehr, *Plain Words About Venereal Disease,* especially 96–120.

34. Baltimore City Health Department, Annual Report (1943), 148.

35. C. Howe Eller, "A Sex Education Project and Serologic Survey in a Baltimore High School," *Baltimore Health News* 21 (November 1944): 83.

36. Emily V. Clapp, *Growing Up in the World Today* (Boston: n.d.).

37. *Ibid.,* 14.

38. For the development of penicillin therapy, see Harry F. Dowling, *Fighting Infection: Conquests of the Twentieth Century* (Cambridge: 1977): 125–57.

39. Baltimore City Health Department, Annual Report (1945), 29.

40. Baltimore City Health Department, Annual Report (1945), 145–46; "Venereal Law Made Specific," *Baltimore Sun,* 26 August 1945.

41. "End of VD—Cure Center Seen as Calamity," *Evening Sun,* 12 June 1946.

42. "A Temporary Power Made Permanent," *Baltimore Sun,* 9 January 1947.

43. "Rapid Treatment," Press Bulletin No. 1043, Maryland State Department of Health, (27 January 1947) Enoch Pratt Library, Maryland Room, Baltimore.

44. *Ibid.*

# Damaged Goods: Women Managing the Stigma of STDs

Adina Nack

The HIV/AIDS epidemic has garnered the attention of researchers from a variety of academic disciplines. In contrast, the study of other sexually transmitted diseases (STDs) has attracted limited interest outside of epidemiology and public health. In the United States, an estimated three out of four sexually active adults have human papillomavirus infections (HPV—the virus that can cause genital warts); one out of five have genital herpes infections (Ackerman 1998; Centers for Disease Control and Prevention [CDC] 1998a). In contrast, the nation-wide rate of HIV infection is approximately 1 out of 300 (CDC 1998b). Current sociological research on the interrelationships between sexual health, stigma, and the self has focused overwhelmingly on HIV/AIDS (Sandstrom 1990; Siegel and Krauss 1991: Weitz 1989). . . .

This article focuses on how the sexual self-concept is transformed when the experience of living with a chronic STD casts a shadow of disease on the health and desirability of a woman's body, as well as on her perceived possibilities for future sexual experiences. The term *sexual self* means something fundamentally different from *gender identity* or *sexual identity*. Invoking the term *sexual self* is meant to conjure up the innately intimate parts of individuals' self-concepts that encompass how they think of themselves

From Nack, Adina. 2000. "Damaged Goods: Women Managing the Stigma of STDs." *Deviant Behavior* 21(2): 95–121. Copyright 2000 from *Deviant Behavior* article by Adina Nash. Reproduced by permission of Taylor & Francis Group, LLC, www.taylorand francis.com.

with regards to their experienced and imagined sensuality. Components of a sexual self may include the following: level of sexual experience, emotional memories of sexual pleasure (or lack thereof), perception of one's body as desirable, and perception of one's sexual body parts as healthy. . . .

To understand the individual-level experience of living with a chronic STD, it is important to take into account how these infections are symbolically constructed in American culture. The meanings that Americans give to being infected with an STD are intersubjectively formed during interactions. Individuals' experiences of health, illness, and medical care "are connected to the particular historically located social arrangements and the cultural values of any society" (Conrad and Kern 1994:5). Present American social values reflect the longstanding connections between sexual health and morality: Interactions with medical practitioners and lay people are the conduit through which the stigma of STDs is reinforced (Brandt 1987). Pryce (1998) pointed to a critical gap—the "missing" sociology of sexual disease—and asserted that this application of sociology should focus on the social construction of the body as central in the medical and social iconography of STDs.

In answer to Pryce's (1998) challenge, this research . . . sociologically analyz[es] the impact of genital herpes and HPV on women's sexual selves. This study adds to this research area by examining sexual self-transformation, starting from the point of how individuals' sexual selves are transformed by the lived experiences of being diagnosed and treated for chronic STDs. Beginning from a premise that the majority of people grow up feeling sexually invincible, a variety of traumas have the capacity to disrupt a positive sexual self-concept (e.g., molestation, rape, and illness). Social–interactional traumas also transmit messages that can damage sexual selves: Some physical bodies are undesirable; some sexual preferences are unacceptable; some levels of sexual experience are immoral.

## Setting and Method

The motivation for this study stems from my personal experience with STDs. My "complete membership role" (Adler and Adler 1987) stems from legitimacy and acceptance by other women with STDs as a member of this unorganized and stigmatized group. At 20, sexual health became the center of my world when I was diagnosed with mild cervical dysplasia, the result of an HPV infection. I began an informal self-education process that helped me manage the stress of my treatments. My commitment to managing my sexual health status would become the foundation for this research project and provide me with the personal insights needed to connect with others facing STDs and the clinical knowledge necessary to be a sexual health researcher.

As a campus sexual health educator, I began to question what sexual health services were not provided. Seeing that women and men were being diagnosed and treated for STDs without receiving follow-up education and counseling, I developed a women-only support group for individuals dealing with STDs. Because of the topic's sensitive nature, I chose a gender-segregated approach to the support group and, ultimately, to the research. . . .

Unfortunately, only one woman used the support group. Initially disheartened, I began to question why people flocked to other support groups that were based on shared stigma (e.g., eating disorders and alcoholism) but failed to use this sexual health support group. Even persons living with HIV and AIDS used support groups to collectively manage their stigma. . . .

To investigate the failure of this support group, I conducted a survey among patients using a local women's health care clinic. During a month chosen at random, clinic staff gave each patient who came in for an appointment an anonymous survey about a new service being offered: a women's sexual health support group. In all, 279 completed surveys were collected. . . . Owing to the population from which the sample was drawn, generalizability is restricted to the population of women who receive women's health care services from this clinic. . . .

I performed a multiple regression analysis on the data, the results of which supported the hypothesis that a person who has been diagnosed with an STD is less likely to be interested in a sexual health support group. . . . One of the most revealing findings was that only 23.3 percent of the women were definitely interested ("yes") in a sexual health support group. . . .

I interpreted this finding to reflect that the stigma of having an STD is so severe that the perceived cost of disclosing this sexual health status to strangers outweighs the possible benefits. Because there has yet to be a moral entrepreneurial campaign to destigmatize STDs in our society, the norm remains secrecy (Brandt 1987). . . .

On the basis of these findings, I determined that in-depth interviews were my best chance for obtaining valid data. I constructed my research methods to reflect a reciprocal intention: As the women gave their stories to me, I would offer my support and resources as a sexual health educator. . . .

My first hurdle was to achieve approval from the campus Human Research Committee. . . . Because of the confidential nature of individuals' STD diagnoses, I was not allowed to directly recruit participants. Rather, they had to approach me, usually after hearing about my research project from other participants or women's health care practitioners with whom I had consulted. . . . I used snowball sampling to generate interviews.

I conducted 28 conversational, unstructured interviews with consensual participants, who ranged in age from 19 to 56. . . . I conducted the interviews in participants' preferred locations: their homes, my home, or other private settings. The interviews lasted from 1 to 2 hours and were tape recorded with the participants' permission. When appropriate, I concluded the interview with offers to provide sexual health information and resources, either in the form of health education materials or referrals to resources.

I then analyzed the data according to the principles of grounded theory (Glaser and Strauss 1967). . . . With each interview, I started to cluster participants' experiences around particular stages to check the validity of my initial model. The six stages of sexual self-transformation [that emerged from the interviews] in chronological order, are as follows: sexual invincibility, STD suspicion, diagnostic crisis, damaged goods, healing/treatment, and integration. . . .

### Stigma and the Sexual Self

For all but 1 of the 28 women, their STD diagnoses radically altered the way that they saw themselves as sexual beings. Facing both a daunting medical and social reality, the women used different strategies to manage their new stigma. Each stigma management strategy had ramifications for the transformation of their sexual selves.

### Stigma Nonacceptance

Goffman (1963) proposed that individuals at risk for a deviant stigma are either "the discredited" or "the discreditable." The discrediteds' stigma was known to others either because the individuals revealed the deviance or because the deviance was not concealable. In contrast, the discreditable were able to hide their deviant stigma. Goffman found that the majority of discreditables were "passing" as nondeviants by avoiding "stigma symbols," anything that would link them to their deviance, and by using "disidentifiers," props or actions that would lead others to believe

they had a nondeviant status. Goffman (1963) also noted that individuals bearing deviant stigma might eventually resort to "covering," one form of which he defined as telling deceptive stories. To remain discreditable in their everyday lives, 19 of the women used the individual stigma management strategies of passing and/or covering. In contrast, 9 women revealed their health status to select friends and family members soon after receiving their diagnoses.

### Passing

The deviant stigma of women with STDs was essentially concealable, though revealed to the necessary inner circle of health care and health insurance providers. For the majority, passing was an effective means of hiding stigma from others, sometimes even from themselves.

Hillary, a 22-year-old White college senior, recalled the justifications she had used to distance herself from the reality of her HPV infection and to facilitate passing strategies.

> At the time, I was in denial about it. I told myself that that wasn't what it was because my sister had had a similar thing happen, the dysplasia. So, I just kind of told myself that it was hereditary. That was kinda funny because I asked the nurse that called if it could be hereditary, and she said "No, this is completely sexually transmitted"—I really didn't accept it until a few months after my cryosurgery.

Similarly, Gloria, a Chicana graduate student . . . was not concerned about a previous case of gonorrhea she had cured with antibiotics or her chronic HPV "because the warts went away." Out of sight, out of her sex life: "I never told anybody about them because I figured they had gone away, and they weren't coming back. Even after I had another outbreak, I was still very promiscuous. It still hadn't registered that I needed to always have the guy use a condom."

When the women had temporarily convinced themselves that they did not have a contagious infection, it was common to conceal the health risk with partners because the women themselves did not perceive the risk as real. Kayla, a . . . White college senior, felt justified in passing as healthy with partners who used condoms, even though she knew that condoms could break. Cleo, a White 31-year-old . . . , had sex with a partner after being diagnosed with HPV.

> So at the time I had sex with him, yes, I knew but, no, I hadn't been treated yet. That gets into the whole "I never told him," and I didn't. Part of me thought I should, and part of me thought that having an STD didn't fit with my self-concept so much that I just couldn't disclose.

Francine, a White 43-year-old professional . . . , had never intended to pass as healthy, but she did not get diagnosed with herpes until after beginning a sexual relationship with her second husband.

> I think there was all the guilt: What if I bring this on you? So, I felt guilt in bringing this into the relationship. Because he had not been anywhere near as sexually active as I had. . . .

Similarly, Tasha, a White graduate student, found out that she might have inadvertently passed as healthy when her partner was diagnosed with chlamydia. "I freaked out—I was like, 'Oh my God! I gave you chlamydia. I am so sorry! I am so sorry!' I felt really horrible, and I felt really awful." . . . Even if the passing is done unintentionally, it still brings guilt to the passer.

The women also tried to disidentify themselves from sexual disease in their attempts to pass as being sexually healthy. Rather than actively using a verbal or symbolic prop or action that would distance them from the stigma, the women took a passive approach. Some gave nonverbal agreement to putdowns of other women who were known to have STDs. For example, Hillary recalled such an interaction.

> It's funny being around people that don't know that I have an STD and how they make a comment like "That girl, she's such a slut. She's a walking STD." And how that makes me feel when I'm confronted with that, and having them have no idea that they could be talking about me.

Others kept silent about their status and tried to maintain the social status of being sexually healthy and morally pure. . . . Putting up the facade of sexual purity, these women distanced themselves from any suspicion of sexual disease.

### Covering

When passing became too difficult, some women resorted to covering to deflect family and friends from the truth. Cleo summed up the rationale by comparing her behavior to what she had learned growing up with an alcoholic father. " . . . I learned that's what you do. Like you don't tell people those things that you consider shameful, and then, if confronted, you know, you lie."

Hillary talked to her parents about her HPV surgery, but never as treatment for an STD. She portrayed her moderate, cervical dysplasia as a precancerous scare, unrelated to sex. . . . When Tasha's sister helped her get a prescription for pubic lice, she actually provided the cover story for her embarrassed younger sister. "She totally took control, and made a personal inquiry: 'So, how did you get this? From a toilet seat?' And, I was like, 'a toilet seat,' and she believed me." . . . For Anne, a 28-year-old . . . graduate student, a painful herpes outbreak almost outed her on a walk with a friend. She was so physically uncomfortable that she was actually waddling. Noticing her strange behavior, her friend asked what was wrong. Anne told her that it was a hemorrhoid; that was only a partial truth because herpes was the primary cause of her pain. As Anne put it, telling her about the hemorrhoid "was embarrassing enough!"

### Deception and Guilt

The women who chose to deny, pass as normal, and use disidentifiers or cover stories shared more than the shame of having an STD—they had also told lies. With lying came guilt. Anne, who had used the hemorrhoid cover story, eventually felt extremely guilty. Her desire to conceal the truth was in conflict with her commitment to being an honest person. . . . Deborah, a 32-year old White professional . . . , only disclosed to her first sexual partner after she had been diagnosed with HPV; she passed as healthy with all other partners. Deborah reflected, "I think my choices not to disclose have hurt my sense of integrity." However, her guilt was resolved during her last gynecological exam when the nurse practitioner confirmed that after years of "clean" pap smear results Deborah was not being "medically unethical" by not disclosing to her partners. In other words, her immune system had probably dealt with the HPV in such a way that she might never have another outbreak or transmit the infection to sexual partners.

When Cleo passed as healthy with a sexual partner, she started "feeling a little guilty about not having told." However, the consequences of passing as healthy were very severe for Cleo:

> No. I never disclosed it to any future partner. Then, one day, I was having sex with Josh, my current husband, before we were married, and we had been together for a few months, maybe, and I'm like looking at his penis, and I said, "Oh, my goodness! You have a wart on your penis! Ahhh!" All of a sudden, it comes back to me.

Cleo's decision to pass left her with both the guilt of deceiving and infecting her husband.

Surprisingly, those women who had unintentionally passed as being sexually healthy (i.e., they had no knowledge of their STD status at the time) expressed a similar level of guilt as those who had been purposefully deceitful. Violet, a middle-class, White 36-year-old, had inadvertently passed as healthy with her current partner. Even after she had preventively disclosed to him, she still had to deal with the guilt over possibly infecting him.

> It hurt so bad that morning when he was basically furious at me thinking I was the one he had gotten those red bumps from. It was the hour from hell! I felt really majorly dirty and stigmatized. I felt like "God, I've done the best I can: If this is really caused by the HPV I have, then I feel terrible."

When using passing and covering techniques, the women strove to keep their stigma from tainting social interactions. They feared . . . rejection from their social circles of friends, family, and, most important, sexual partners. For most of the women, guilt surpassed fear and became the trigger to disclose. Those who had been deceitful in passing or covering had to assuage their guilt: Their options were either to remain in nonacceptance, disclose, or transfer their guilt to somebody else.

### Stigma Deflection

As the women struggled to manage their individual stigma of being sexually diseased, real and imaginary social interactions became the conduit for the contagious label of damaged goods. Now that the unthinkable had happened to them, the women began to think of their past and present partners as infected, contagious, and potentially dangerous to themselves or other women. The combination of transferring stigma and assigning blame to others allowed the women to deflect the STD stigma away from themselves.

#### *Stigma Transference*

. . . Stigma is neither an emotion nor an impulse; rather, it is a formal concept that captures a relationship of devaluation (Goffman 1963). Although the participants attributed their devalued relationship with sexual health ideals to real and imaginary others, they were not controlling unacceptable feelings. Rather, stigma transference manifests as a clear expression of anger and fear, and the women did not connect this strategy to a reduction in their levels of anxiety; in fact, several discussed it in relation to increased anxiety.

Cleo remembered checking her partner's penis for warts after her doctor told her that she could detect them by visual inspection. It became a habit for Kayla to check her partner for any visible symptoms of an STD. Gloria was more careful about checking future partners and asking if they had anything. Tasha explained, "I just felt like I was with someone who was dirty." In all four cases, the women were only sure of their own STD infections, yet in their minds these partners had become diseased.

Transference of stigma to a partner became more powerful when the woman felt betrayed by her partner. When Hillary spoke of the "whole trust issue" with her ex-partner, she firmly believed he had lied to her about his sexual health status and that he would lie to others. Even though she had neither told him about her diagnosis nor had proof of him being infected, she fully transferred her stigma to him. . . .

Kayla also transferred the stigma of sexual disease to an ex-partner, never confronting him about whether he had tested positive for STDs. The auxiliary trait of promiscuity colored her view of him: "I don't know how sexually promiscuous he was, but I'm sure he had had a lot of partners." Robin, a 21-year-old White undergraduate, went so far as to tell her ex-partner that he needed to see a doctor and "do something about it." He doubted her ability to pinpoint contracting genital warts from him and called her a slut. Robin believed that he was the one with the reputation for promiscuity and decided to trash him by telling her two friends who hung out with him. Robin hoped to spoil his sexual reputation and scare off his future partners. In the transference of stigma, the women ascribed the same auxiliary traits onto others that others had previously ascribed to them. . . .

In all cases, it was logical to assume that past and current sexual partners may also have been infected. However, the stigma of being sexually diseased had far-reaching consequences in the women's imaginations. The traumatic impact on their sexual selves led most to infer that future, as yet unknown partners were also sexually diseased. . . . They had already been damaged by at least one partner. Therefore, they expected that future partners, ones who had not yet come into their lives, held the threat of also being damaged goods.

For Hillary, romantic relationships held no appeal anymore. She had heard of others who also had STDs but stayed in non-acceptance and never changed their lifestyle of having casual, unprotected sex:

I just didn't want to have anything to do with it. A lot of it was not trusting people. When we broke up, I decided that I was not having sex. Initially, it was because I wanted to get an HIV test. Then, I came to kind of a turning point in my life and realized that I didn't want to do the one-night-stand thing anymore. It just wasn't worth it. It wasn't fun.

At this stage in her sexual self-transformation, Hillary imagined the world of possible partners having been polluted with contagion.

Anne's lesbian friends [told her] . . . future partners should be suspected of being dangerous. . . . Anne recalled [one] friend's reaction. "Those rotten men! You should just leave them alone. It's clear that you should be with women, and it's safer and better that way. Women don't do this kind of thing to each other." Her friends' guidance was an overt attempt to encourage Anne to believe that only potential male partners bore the stigma.

Instead of going by gender, Gloria, a self-identified Chicana, made a distinction based on ethnicity as a predictor of sexual health status:

Now, if it was a White man, I made 'em wear a condom because I got it from a White man, and so I assumed that there had to be something with their culture—they were more promiscuous. But, one thing I do know culturally and with the times is that Chicano men were more likely to have a single partner.

These women felt justified in their newfound attitudes about sexual partners. What was only supposed to happen to "bad" women had happened to them. Overall, these women transitioned from blaming their own naivete to blaming someone else for not being more cautious or more honest.

### Blame

The women's uses of stigma transference techniques were attempts to alleviate their emotional burdens. First, the finger of shame and guilt pointed inward, toward the women's core sexual selves. Their sexual selves became tainted, dirty, damaged. In turn, they directed the stigma outward to both real and fictional others. Blaming others was a way for all of the women to alleviate some of the internal pressure and turn the anger outward. This emotional component of the damaged goods stage externalized the pain of their stigma.

Francine recalled how she and her first husband dealt with the issue of genital warts. . . . Francine's husband had likely contracted genital warts from his wild fraternity parties: "We really thought of it as, that woman who did the trains [serial sexual intercourse]. It was still a girl's fault kind of thing." By externalizing the blame to the promiscuous women at fraternity parties, Francine exonerated not only herself but also her husband. . . .

For Violet, it was impossible to neatly deflect the blame away from both herself and her partner.

> I remember at the time just thinking, "Oh man! He gave it to me!" While he was thinking, "God, [Violet]! You gave this to me!" So, we kind of just did a truce in our minds. Like, OK, we don't know who gave it—just as likely both ways. So, let's just get treated. We just kind of dropped it.

Clearly, the impulse to place blame was strong even when there was no easy target.

Often, the easiest targets were men who exhibited the auxiliary traits of promiscuity and deception. Tasha wasn't sure which ex-partner had transmitted the STD. However, she rationalized blaming a particular guy. "He turned out to be kind of a huge liar, lied to me a lot about different stuff. And, so I blamed him. All the other guys were, like, really nice people, really trustworthy." Likewise, when I asked Violet from whom she believed she had contracted chlamydia, she replied, "Dunno, it could've been from one guy, because that guy had slept with some unsavory women, so therefore he was unsavory." . . .

The actual guilt or innocence of these blame targets was secondary. What mattered to the women was that they could hold someone else responsible.

### Stigma Acceptance

Eventually, every woman in the study stopped denying and deflecting the truth of her sexual health status by disclosing to loved ones. The women disclosed for either preventive or therapeutic reasons. That is, they were either motivated to reveal their STD status to prevent harm to themselves or others or to gain the emotional support of confidants.

### Preventive and Therapeutic Disclosures

The decision to make a preventive disclosure was linked to whether the STD could be cured. Kayla explained,

> Chlamydia went away, and I mean it was really bad to have that, but I mean it's not something that you have to tell people later 'cause you know, in case it comes back. Genital warts, you never know.

Kayla knew that her parents would find out about the HPV infection because of insurance connections. Before her cryosurgery, Kayla decided to tell her mom about her condition.

> . . . [I]t was kind of hard at first. But, she wasn't upset with me. Main thing, she was disappointed, but I think she blamed my boyfriend more than she blamed me.

. . . Preventive disclosures to sexual partners, past and present, were a more problematic situation. The women were choosing to put themselves in a position where they could face blame, disgust, and rejection. For those reasons, the women put off preventive disclosures to partners as long as possible. For example, Anne made it clear that she would not have disclosed her herpes to a female sexual partner had they not been about to have sex. After "agonizing weeks and weeks and weeks before trying to figure out how to tell," Diana, a 45-year-old African American professional, finally shared her HPV and herpes status before her current relationship became sexual. Unfortunately, her boyfriend had a negative reaction: "He certainly didn't want to touch me anywhere near my genitals." . . .

For Summer, a 20-year-old Native American administrative assistant, and Gloria, their preventive disclosures were actually a relief to their sexual partners. Summer decided to disclose her genital warts to a new boyfriend after they had been "getting hot n' heavy." Lying in bed together, she said, "I need to tell you something." After she disclosed, he lay there, staring at the ceiling for a couple of minutes before deeply exhaling, "I thought you were going to tell me you had AIDS." Similarly, one of Gloria's partners sighed in relief when she revealed that she had herpes; he thought she was going to say she was HIV positive.

Many of the therapeutic disclosures were done to family members. The women wanted the support of those who had known them the longest. . . . Tasha disclosed to her mother right after she was diagnosed with chlamydia.

> My family died—"Guess what, mom, I got chlamydia." She's like, "Chlamydia? How did you find out you got chlamydia?" I'm like, "Well, my boyfriend got an eye infection." [laughter] "How'd he get it in his eye?" [laughter] So, it was the biggest joke in the family for the longest time!

. . . The women often unburdened their feelings of shame and guilt onto their close friends. Cleo shared her feelings with her roommate: "I told her that I was feeling weird about having had sex with this second guy, knowing that I had an STD." Kayla's therapeutic disclosure was reciprocal with her best friend. "At that time, she was also going through a similar situation with her boyfriend, so I felt okay finally to talk about it." . . . In Anne's case, her therapeutic disclosure to a friend was twofold: both to seek support and to apologize for initially having used the hemorrhoid cover story. Anne explained to her friend that she had felt too uncomfortable to tell the truth. . . .

### Consequences of Disclosure

With both therapeutic and preventive disclosure, the women experienced some feelings of relief in being honest with loved ones. However, they still carried the intense shame of being sexu-

ally diseased women. The resulting emotion was anxiety over how their confidants would react: rejection, disgust, or betrayal. Francine was extremely anxious about disclosing to her husband. "That was really tough on us because I had to go home and tell Damon that I had this outbreak of herpes . . . I was really fearful—I didn't think that he would think I had recently had sex with somebody else—but, I was still really afraid of what it would do to our relationship." . . .

Overall, disclosing intensified the anxiety of having their secret leaked to others in whom they would never have chosen to confide. In addition, each disclosure brought with it the possibility of rejection and ridicule from the people whose opinions they valued most. For Gloria, disclosing was the right thing to do but had painful consequences when her partner's condom slipped off in the middle of sexual intercourse.

> I told him it doesn't feel right. "You'd better check." And, so he checked, and he just jumped off me and screamed, "Oh fuck!" And, I just thought, oh no, here we go. He just freaked and went to the bathroom and washed his penis with soap. I just felt so dirty.

The risk paid off for Summer, whose boyfriend asserted, "I don't ever want to be *that guy*—the one who shuns people and treats them differently." He borrowed sexual health education materials and spent over an hour asking her questions about various STDs. Even in this best-case scenario, the sexual intimacy in this relationship became problematized (e.g., having to research modes of STD transmission and safe-sex techniques). Disclosures were the interactional component of self-acceptance. The women became fully grounded in their new reality when they realized that the significant people in their lives were now viewing them through the discolored lenses of sexual disease.

### Conclusion

The women with STDs went through an emotionally difficult process, testing out stigma management strategies, trying to control the impact of STDs on both their self-concepts and on their relationships with others. . . .

Ironically, most of the women first tried to deny this deviant health status—one that was virtually secret through the protection of doctor–patient confidentiality laws. Although many used passing and covering techniques that relied on deceiving others, self-deception was impossible to maintain. The medical truth began to penetrate their sexual self-conceptions as soon as they fabricated their first lie. To strategize a successful ruse, it was necessary to know the scope of what they were trying to hide.

When guilt caught up with them, making it hard to pass as healthy, their goal shifted to stigma deflection. . . . However, this only delayed the inevitable—a deviant sexual self that penetrated the women's prior conceptions of their sexual selves.

After mentally transferring their stigma to real and imaginary others, all of the women finally accepted their tainted sexual health status through the reflexive dynamics of disclosure. . . . The women's sexual selves moved along a deviant career path by means of the interactive dynamics of their stigma management strategies.

. . . As the women made choices on which stigma management strategies to use, they grappled with the ramifications of internalizing this new label. Choosing passing and covering techniques meant they could remain in non-acceptance and put off stigma internalization. When they deflected the stigma onto others by means of stigma transference, the women glimpsed the severity of an STD stigma as reflected in the presumed sexual selves of real and imaginary others. Finally, the women's disclosures confirmed the new story of their tainted sexual selves.

. . . Unlike the stigma of HIV/AIDS—which carries the threat of life-changing illness, death, and contagion beyond the scope of sexual behaviors—the STD stigma lends itself to compartmentalization. The women were able to hide their shame, guilt, and fear (of further health complications, of contaminating others,

of rejection, etc.) in the sexual part of their self-concept. They recognized that this part of their self-concept did not have to affect their entire identity. . . . If the impact of the STDs on their sex lives ever became too emotionally painful, the women could always decide to distance themselves from this role: choosing temporary or permanent celibacy. . . .

A narrative model of the self proposes that personal myths create the self and become "the stories we live by" (McAdams 1996:266). I propose that we seek to understand the significance of the stories we choose not to live by. Personal STD "stories" are rarely told in American mass culture. McAdams (1996:22) proposed that "carrying on affairs in secret"—maintaining a discreditable stigma—is a way to keep stigmatizing stories from occupying center stage in people's personal myth. However, these data suggest that individuals manage identity transformations, especially transformations into deviant identities, by constructing and sharing self-narratives through disclosure interactions. Although the women do not maintain secrecy, they do keep their STD stories from center stage. . . .

## REFERENCES

Ackerman, Sandra J. 1998. "HPV: Who's Got It and Why They Don't Know." *HPV News* 8(2):1, 5–6.

Adler, Patricia A. and Peter Adler. 1987. *Membership Roles in Field Research*. Newbury Park, CA: Sage.

Brandt, Allan M. 1987. *No magic bullet: A social history of venereal disease in the United States since 1880*. New York: Oxford University Press.

Centers for Disease Control and Prevention. 1998a. "Genital Herpes." *National Center for HIV, STD & TB Prevention*. Retrieved from the World Wide Web February 4, 1998: URL.

———. 1998b. "HIV/AIDS Surveillance Report." *National Center for HIV, STD & TB Prevention*. Retrieved from the World Wide Web February 4, 1998: URL.

Conrad, Peter, and Rochelle Kern, eds. 1994. *The Sociology of Health & Illness: Critical Perspectives*. 4th ed. New York: St. Martin's Press.

Glaser, Barney G. and Anselm L. Strauss. 1967. *The Discovery of Grounded Theory: Strategies for Qualitative Research*. Chicago: Aldine.

Goffman, Erving. 1963. *Stigma*. Englewood Cliffs, N. J.: Prentice Hall.

McAdams, Dan P. 1996. *The stories we live by: Personal myths and the making of the self*. New York: Guilford Press.

Pryce, Anthony. 1998. "Theorizing the Pox: A Missing Sociology of VD." Presented to the International Sociological Association.

Sandstrom, Kent L. 1990. "Confronting Deadly Disease: the Drama of Identity Construction among Gay Men with AIDS." *Journal of Contemporary Ethnography,* 19(3):271–94.

Siegel, Karolynn and Beatrice J. Krauss. 1991. "Living with HIV Infection: Adaptive Tasks of Seropositive Gay Men." *Journal of Health and Social Behavior* 32(1):17–32.

Weitz, Rose. 1989. "Uncertainty and the Lives of Persons with AIDS." *Journal of Health and Social Behavior* 30(3):270–81.

## *Lesbian Women and Sexually Transmitted Infections*

**Kathleen Dolan and Phillip W. Davis**

Many people believe lesbian women are not at risk for sexually transmitted infections (STIs) and HIV, but several studies have found that, similar to heterosexual people, about one in four have a lifetime history of at least one STI.[1] Reported infections include herpes, gonorrhea, hepatitis A, genital warts, HIV, and bacterial vaginosis. Risk factors for lesbian women are similar to those for other groups. These factors include drug and alcohol use, having unprotected sex with men, and having sex with men who have sex with men. You may wonder why sex with men is a risk factor for lesbians. People are often surprised to learn that many lesbian women had sex with men prior to coming out, and that some of them continue to do so. This is important when discussing lesbian sexual health because women with infections such as herpes often say that they contracted them from a man, and it is possible to then transmit them to another woman. Transmission of herpes (and several other STIs) only requires skin to skin contact, and genital to genital rubbing (sometimes called *tribadism*) is common among lesbian women.

Other potentially risky behaviors include performing oral sex on a menstruating partner and sharing sex toys. Infections can also be transmitted if women have cuts on their fingers when they use their hands to stimulate their partner's genitals. One thing that can help is wearing latex gloves, although some women believe that gloves are cumbersome and offensive. Another thing that can help is the use of a dental dam during oral sex. Dams are sheets of latex about 8 inches square that can prevent or inhibit transmission. Some women prefer to use plastic kitchen wrap instead. Needless to say, taking these kinds of precautions can be a delicate and complex matter, especially in a community in which the risk of STIs is often unacknowledged and in which members often do not receive adequate sexual health information, treatment, and services.

To find out more about the topic, we surveyed an especially diverse sample of 162 self-identified lesbian women in a large southeastern city in 1998 and 1999. One third were African American, Latina, and Asian, and two thirds were white. Consistent with other studies, our participants reported an overall infection rate of 23 percent. Eight out of ten had had vaginal sex with a man at some point in their lives, and one out of three had had sex with a man in the last year. Our study found relatively high rates of fisting (placing the entire hand in a partner's vagina), which can tear the vaginal lining, leaving small abrasions where viruses or bacteria could enter the bloodstream (thirty percent had fisted, twenty-three percent had been fisted). Half of the women reported performing oral sex on a menstruating partner.

When it comes to subjective perceptions of risk, the women generally fell into three groups. One group viewed themselves as essentially invulnerable. In other words, they felt protected from infection by virtue of being lesbian, believing that only heterosexuals were at risk. Most participants fell into a second group that viewed lesbian women as "socially inoculated." This view was based on a woman's familiarity with her partner's sexual history and her faith in her partner's honesty. A third group viewed themselves as fundamentally vulnerable, or at least as vulnerable as anyone else. They were very cautious when having sex. They used dental dams for oral sex and they put condoms on their sex toys. These three views were not fixed and static, and over time many women shifted in their views in response to new information, to their partners' beliefs and preferences, and to their own infections. Many of these patterns, beliefs, and practices are likely to change as health care providers become more knowledgeable, as health activism spreads in the lesbian community, and as lesbian women's sexual health becomes a higher priority in research, medical, and policy arenas.

For more information on this topic, see our article, "Nuances and shifts in lesbian women's constructions of STI and HIV vulnerability," in *Social Science and Medicine* (2003).

**NOTE**

1. Solarz (ed.) *Lesbian health: Current assessment and directions for the future.* 1999. Washington, D.C.: National Academy Press.

# Showdown in Choctaw County

Jacob Levenson

**D**avid deShazo is chain-smoking Marlboros as he drives north out of Mobile on a bright November morning. A garbage bag stuffed with blankets, baby clothes, and toys takes up most of the backseat of the Pontiac. The car is chilly because deShazo's heater is busted, and he doesn't have the two hundred bucks it will cost to get it fixed. He's headed up to Choctaw County to find two sisters, Sara and Rebecca Jackson, who are infected with HIV. They live with their mother and their two baby sons down a dirt road somewhere outside of Gilbertown, near the Mississippi border. The girls haven't been heard from in seven months. He takes another draw off his cigarette, squints through his bug-smeared windshield at the two-lane highway, and tries to resist a flickering current of anxiety.

DeShazo hadn't really known what to expect when he was hired to work in the poor counties of southern Alabama to search out people infected with HIV, to convince the at-risk to get tested, and to warn community leaders about the threat of AIDS. In the 18 months since he took the job, he's driven more than 60,000 miles talking about the virus to just about anyone who will listen. He's caught hateful stares at general stores and gas stations. A county commissioner over in Wilcox attacked him verbally at a church meeting for talking about AIDS without permission. And he's heard comments that the "niggers" and "faggots"

are just getting what they deserve. None of these things has really surprised deShazo. What's unsettling is the silence that surrounds him in these towns. When he talks to people it often seems as though he is shouting across an unbridgeable chasm.

The Alabama that deShazo has been traveling for a year and a half ceased to exist in the minds of most Americans after the Civil Rights movement. Somehow it was never remade into the New South of Ted Turner, Emeril Live, and urban sprawl. There remains an expansive, aching beauty to these counties. The countryside, with its forests of hickory, oak, and pine, its cotton fields and tangles of green creeks and rivers, feels timeless. A procession of churches lines every road: NEW PROVIDENCE BAPTIST, JESUS IS LORD OLD ZION MISSIONARY, LITTLE ZION BAPTIST.

All of this lends the region a sense that it is somehow insulated from the perils of modern life. But now the greatest epidemic of recent times is spreading slowly and quietly through the black communities of rural Alabama. In the years since AIDS hit the headlines, the disease gradually has become a black epidemic. In 2000, according to the Centers for Disease Control, 54 percent of all new AIDS cases were African Americans. The disease is now the number-one killer of both black men and black women between the ages of 22 and 45. What's perhaps even more surprising is that the South is the new epicenter of AIDS in the United States. More people are living with AIDS in this region than in any other part of the country. And while the disease is still concentrated in

From Levenson, Jacob. 2002. "Showdown in Choctaw County." *Utne Reader* 111(May/June): 73–80. Reprinted by permission.

Southern cities, there are warning signs that it is creeping into the countryside. The number of rural cases in the South more than doubled in seven years.

DeShazo and his co-workers represent a thin line of defense against this brewing public health crisis. Impoverished patients already have overburdened Alabama's small network of AIDS agencies. Mobile AIDS Support Services (MASS), for which deShazo works, has five caseworkers for roughly 800 clients in Mobile and the surrounding six rural counties. Most of their patients don't have private insurance, Medicaid, or direct access to the new drug cocktails. The caseworkers spend the bulk of their time just trying to get medicine for their clients. MASS needs to hire more staff, but as it is can only afford to pay people like deShazo a salary of $23,000.

As deShazo crosses Choctaw County, a couple of logging trucks stacked with clear-cut pine trees rush by in the opposite direction. The last cotton plantations disappeared in the 1960s, and paper mills are pretty much the only industry now. The county is home to 16,000 people, roughly half of whom are black, with 22 percent of the population living in poverty. And there are no hospitals or infectious-disease doctors in Choctaw County.

DeShazo drives through Gilbertown, which isn't much more than a stoplight, a cemetery, a grocery, a pharmacy, and a dollar store, and makes a right turn down a narrow, unmarked dirt road. He saw the Jackson sisters once before, as a favor to the social worker in Selma who is supposed to be in charge of their case. A part of him is pissed off that they've dropped off the agency's radar since then. At the same time, he's not surprised, given the patchwork nature of AIDS care in Alabama. As worried as he is about these girls, he seems charged up about the case, confident that he has the skills to work through the welfare system so that the sisters can get the medications, doctors, and care that might save their lives. It's a sense of purpose that he has rarely felt in other social work jobs, which mostly left him feeling weak and hopeless.

DeShazo pulls over in front of a trailer home, steps out, climbs three rickety steps, and knocks. A female voice yells to come on in.

DeShazo opens the door and feels a wave of heat. The first person he sees is Sara, who is sitting on a couch changing a 2-year-old boy on her lap. She's wearing a Michael Jordan T-shirt and her hair is in long cornrows. He is relieved to see that she has full cheeks and looks healthy. Another child in blue pajamas is giggling and waddling back and forth on the floor. Piles of clothes, empty soda cans, and an overturned tricycle litter the living room. A raspy cough comes from the kitchen, where Sara's sister, Rebecca, is slumped over a chair facing an open oven, trying to keep warm. She must have fever chills because the trailer is stifling, almost too hot to breathe in. DeShazo sets his bag of clothes and toys down on the floor. "Hi, I'm David deShazo from Mobile AIDS Support Services," he says. "How y'all doing?"

Rebecca doesn't move. Sara looks up from the couch and says hi. He had been worried about how they would receive him. White men who work for the government aren't always greeted warmly around here. But there is a loose confidence to Sara's smile, and the casual way she continues changing her son's diaper puts him at ease. DeShazo says that he's brought some supplies and then sits down and asks Sara if she's got any income.

"Nothing but food stamps," she says, seemingly unfazed.

"How about Rebecca?"

"She got a disability check."

"How long has Rebecca been like that?" deShazo asks, nodding toward the kitchen.

"She's been real sick for three days now," Sara answers. "Something's messing with her eyes."

DeShazo feels a twinge of fear. He thinks that she probably has contracted CMV, normally a relatively benign virus, but one that can blind AIDS patients.

"You getting any medicine, Sara?" deShazo asks.

"I get medicine while I'm pregnant, but I save it," she says. "I ain't going to get no more when I have the baby."

DeShazo's head starts to spin. "You pregnant again, Sara?" he asks. He was so relieved to see her carrying weight.

Sara smiles, shakes her head as if she can't believe he couldn't tell, and says, "Seven months."

DeShazo's questions begin to tumble out faster and with more urgency. "Y'all still seeing those doctors in Waynesboro?" he asks.

"Yeah, but I missed my last two appointments because I didn't have no way to get there," she says.

Rebecca still hasn't uttered a word. She coughs again—a coarse hack. Sara tells deShazo that she was turned down for Medicaid before she got pregnant. He figured as much. In Alabama you have to be over 65 years old or prove you are blind or disabled. In his experience, most people aren't able to get the help they need unless a lawyer or a professional advocate is working their case. Rebecca stumbles into the room and collapses on a couch next to the door. She has white flecks of spittle on her mouth and chin.

Sara's pregnancy has deShazo worried that she might have infected others. He asks Sara if her boyfriend has been tested. He tested negative a year ago, she says, but he hasn't been retested since she got pregnant again. (He's now in prison.) And, as far as she knows, Rebecca's boyfriend hasn't been tested at all. "My boyfriend takes some of my medicine," Sara says, "just to be careful." DeShazo feels a flush of anger. He can't believe these sisters are having unprotected sex and that they think feeding them AZT is going to keep their boyfriends safe. They could be starting a small epidemic.

As for the toddlers, Benny and William, Sara tells deShazo that they were tested a few months ago. This is good news, but it doesn't mean they are all right. Small children need to be tested repeatedly before it can be absolutely determined that they didn't contract the disease from their mothers. . . .

DeShazo was hired along with seven community outreach workers to canvas 32 of Alabama's poorest rural counties, which based on their sexually transmitted disease and teen pregnancy rates appear most vulnerable for AIDS. A year and a half into the three-year project, deShazo estimates that he's approached 300 people for testing. Only two have agreed to get into his aging blue Pontiac and head down to the local health department. This isn't unusual. There is a long-standing shortage of doctors and health facilities in black Southern communities. And many blacks in the region distrust doctors—a legacy of the infamous Tuskegee Syphilis Study, in which black test subjects were denied treatment for decades as part of a long-term health experiment. What is mentioned less often is that, compared with gay communities, much of black America—and particularly the rural South—has been relatively ignored in the campaign to educate people about AIDS.

DeShazo was hired in part because he had an idea about how to navigate the socially conservative, religious, and racially fractured landscape of rural Alabama. He was raised in Clark County, 50 miles north of Mobile, where his father was a country doctor. His understanding of the culture, the spiritual convictions of the people, and even the subtle rhythms of their speech have allowed him to penetrate his territory more deeply than any of his fellow workers. But growing up in the segregated world of 1950s Alabama did not prepare him for the rural black world this job has allowed him to enter. . . .

Alabama, which has always had a relatively low rate of AIDS, now seems primed for a burgeoning epidemic. Crack—which often breeds a sex-for-drugs trade and seems inevitably to show up just ahead of AIDS—has moved in from Florida and Texas and made its way into even the most rural counties. Already black women in the South are 26 times more likely than white women to have HIV. DeShazo is armed with these facts, but they seem somehow abstract in places like Gilbertown. The threat of AIDS here feels deeply entwined with poverty and the lingering effects of segregation. . . .

Every spring, Sara and Rebecca Jackson's high school holds a blood drive. It's always been a popular event with the students. Giving a pint of blood helps the sick, and it's an easy excuse to get out of afternoon classes. At least that's how 16-year-old Sara and her 14-year-old sister, Rebecca, felt one afternoon when they volunteered to have their blood drawn.

Sara was the more rebellious of the two sisters. Always using her quick wit to get her way with her mother, she had declared her independence by marrying her boyfriend and moving out of the house. As soon as she graduated she planned to join the army so she could earn enough money to pay for college and become a lawyer. Rebecca, the baby of the family, was more sensitive and even as a youngster wanted to become a nurse. Their father—who had been in and out of prison for drug offenses when the girls were young—worked as a logger and was making enough money to allow their mom to stay home with Rebecca. On a warm Wednesday afternoon about two months after the blood drive, Sara came home for a visit and greeted her mother, who absently handed her a plain white envelope from the county health department. Simple and straightforward, the letter thanked her for her donation but said that her blood was contaminated with HIV. Sara was stunned. She didn't know anything about the disease except that it was deadly.

Three days later an identical letter arrived for Rebecca.

Sara and Rebecca dropped out of high school. Sara's marriage didn't last, and the girls' father was soon back in prison. . . . Their mother has tried to care for the girls and her grandsons as best she can but has avoided asking welfare workers or AIDS agencies for help.

DeShazo is talking to Rebecca and Sara's aunt in the kitchen. He has been at the trailer for about an hour now. He is worried that he is not going to be able to keep these girls alive without help. He wants to enlist family and neighbors who can drive Rebecca two hours to Mobile to see a specialist. That is going to be tough as long as the sisters keep their illness secret. When he comes back into the living room, he says to Sara, "I know the doctors in Waynesboro have been good to you, but it may be time for you guys to see a specialist. How do you feel about that?"

"I'll do anything that'll keep me healthy like I am 'cause I don't want to leave my children like this," Sara says. But when he asks if she would consider telling her grandparents or the host of cousins and in-laws who live in the area that she's infected with HIV, she is silent. All the MASS case workers have heard stories about clients getting discriminated against at their jobs, frozen out by their churches, and abandoned by their families. Occasionally, the social worker who handles the agency's rural cases must deliver medications to clients at "secret" locations like a grocery store parking lot. . . .

Needing a break, [deShazo] offers to go down to the pharmacy in Gilbertown and pick up Rebecca's medication. . . .

AIDS can move relatively quickly through a rural county. HIV spreads mainly through what epidemiologists call "sexual networks," social groups in which people are sleeping together. On paper they can be traced like genealogical trees. When HIV is introduced into a small town where a significant number of people belong to a single tree, there is a real risk of an epidemic. (When two girls in a rural Mississippi town were diagnosed with AIDS several years ago, the state health department found a heterosexual network of 44 people, of whom 34 were tested and seven were found to be HIV positive. When the Centers for Disease Control followed up several months later, only two of the seven were receiving medical care.)

When deShazo gets back to the trailer, Sara has put the place together: The tricycle has been righted, and the clothes that were on the floor have been put away. Rebecca is sitting up, talking on the phone. She flashes a smile and for an instant looks like any other teenager. DeShazo sits down in front of her. She puts down the phone and is holding William tightly in her arms on the couch.

"Do you ever feel like there's no reason to live, Rebecca?" deShazo asks.

William's head is buried in her breast, and she is rocking him back and forth. "Sometimes," she says and stares at the ground.

"Is there anybody you can go to when you feel like that?" he asks.

"There ain't nobody but myself," she says and clenches her jaw. Her eyes fill with tears, but she stops herself just short of crying. . . .

If Sara is denied benefits, deShazo says, he will apply for free medications from one of the pharmaceutical companies. He also wants to get the sisters on a program that will help pay for electricity and heat without exposing that they have HIV. He carries a generic business card that says he works for the United Way. Maybe he can use it to cut a deal with the local utility company. He would like to find a nurse in the area with some HIV experience who will check up on Rebecca, but that will involve getting Rebecca approved for Alabama's home health program, which requires a medical history from her doctor and the cooperation of the Choctaw County health department. She might be dead by then. . . .

The job of getting AIDS patients like Rebecca and Sara Jackson the drug cocktails that have been popularly heralded as a panacea will ultimately fall on the shoulders of community-based organizations like MASS. In 2000, MASS, which operates on an annual budget of $600,000, had to "professionally beg" pharmaceutical companies for $1.8 million in medications for uninsured clients. The Alabama legislature has been unwilling to fully match federal funds to help the poor pay for expensive drugs, which can cost anywhere from $10,000 to $18,000 a year. And during any given month, about 400 infected Alabamians—mostly black, all living below the poverty line—can be on a waiting list to get on the federal government's drug assistance program.

The next Tuesday morning deShazo drives out to see Rebecca and Sara. He has been thinking about them all weekend. "I wasn't going to cry, and then I had all this stuff dammed up inside and the tears just came," he says. "Then the anger started. I've got to channel that anger. This girl ain't going to die. She ain't going to die. These girls are going to have a chance."

When he arrives at the Jacksons' trailer, there is no sign of anyone. A late-'70s Chevrolet drives up the road. Sara is in the backseat with her son, Benny. "Where's Rebecca?" he asks. Sara says Rebecca collapsed on Saturday. Just stopped breathing. She's in the hospital in Waynesboro. . . .

Waynesboro is a city of around 6,000. DeShazo passes a cluster of single-story brown cinderblock buildings—a housing project that seems out of place in a small town. After a couple of wrong turns, he finds the hospital. In the elevator heading up to Rebecca's room, deShazo looks tired and stares nervously up at the blinking floor numbers.

He finds Rebecca's door. Inside, she is in the fetal position facing a single window. She's alone. A movie is playing on a television bolted to the wall. Rebecca has her arms pulled up close to her face. An IV is hooked up to her right arm, and she's clinging to her blanket like a small child. DeShazo walks around to the side of her bed. He leans up against the radiator next to the window. "How you feeling, Rebecca?" he asks. "I'm going to have surgery tomorrow," she says, her voice raspy.

"What for?" deShazo asks.

"My gallbladder," she says before being seized by a fit of heavy coughing.

"How old are you, Rebecca?" deShazo asks.

"Nineteen," she answers.

"You know, Rebecca," deShazo says, "there's a lady in Mobile who does nothing but check on children whose parents are infected."

"He ain't infected," Rebecca says. This is the strongest statement she has ever made to him.

"I know," he says, "but it may be wise for William to see her anyway."

"My mama's with him," Rebecca says softly.

"Yeah, I know your mama's there doing a real good job." Realizing that there's nothing he can do or say at this moment to make the situation better, he decides to leave.

In the coming month deShazo will dedicate almost all of his time to this case. Rebecca's doctor will drop her for failing to take her medications. It will turn out that the doctor never even prescribed protease inhibitors, the most powerful lifesaving drugs, because he didn't believe she would take them. DeShazo will drive Rebecca to a specialist two hours away in Mobile, who will diagnose her with pneumonia, CMV, and thrush. When he tries to get home health care for her, an anonymous caller will warn the Choctaw County health department not to send a nurse to the Jacksons' because Rebecca plans to bite and infect as many people as she can before she dies. Sara will go into labor a month prematurely. The hospital in Waynesboro, saying they don't have the facilities to handle a premature birth, will refuse to admit her and opt instead to drive her to Mobile. Forty-eight hours after she gives birth, the hospital in Mobile, citing policy for mothers on public assistance, will attempt to discharge her with a bus ticket back to Gilbertown. DeShazo will get her another day in the hospital. But when Sara gets back to her trailer, the electricity will be shut off.

All of this is still in front of them though. On the drive back from th hospital in Waynesboro, the harsh reality hits deShazo: Keeping Rebecca alive with what few resources are available is unlikely. He passes a hand painted sign for Pine Grove Cemeter on the corner of a dirt road leading into the forest. He is smoking another cigarette. Along the highway the sweet gum trees have turned flaming orange and the oaks a sunflower yellow, "She's going to die," he says. "She's going to die, and there ain't one goddamn f-ing thing I can do about it."

EPILOGUE: DeShazo angles the blue Pontiac in front of Rebecca Jackson's trailer and kills the engine. It's spring, 2002. Their wooden porch has collapsed. He's stopped by to see Rebecca. For the past year, his work and much of his life has been centered around keeping her alive. Gradually, he's seen Rebecca's own desire to survive grow. Last spring, her boyfriend, John, proposed. And as soon as Rebecca is strong enough, they plan to have a wedding. Officially, deShazo was supposed to hand off the case to another social worker months ago. But he can't. Rebecca needs him (especially since Sara had pneumonia over the summer). In a sense he's kin to the Jackson's now. DeShazo hears the sound of wheels on the gravel road. He turns. It's John and he has Rebecca in the car. She's thinner than deShazo has ever seen her. John helps her out of her seat. She's too weak to walk so John lifts her into his arms and carries her into the trailer. A few days later, she'll be back in the hospital.

## *Aging and HIV—The Changing Face of AIDS*

**David M. Latini and David W. Coon**

The face of HIV is changing. More older adults are becoming infected and more people who have become infected before their 50th birthdays are now aging with HIV/AIDS. These changing faces create new challenges for health educators, medical providers, and clinical researchers.

Even among Americans age 50 and older, the face of HIV is diverse. In San Francisco, the HIV epidemic has primarily impacted white men who have sex with men. In contrast, according to the Florida Department of Health, older Floridians diagnosed with HIV are primarily African-American (47.4%), with Latinos (16.1%) and women (18%) making up sizable proportions of the epidemic.

Older adults are more frequently diagnosed with HIV at a later stage of the disease and they are likely to die sooner than their younger counterparts. Among seniors, AIDS-related symptoms, such as fatigue, weight loss, and diminished appetite, are often misdiagnosed by health care professionals as age-related conditions rather than symptoms of HIV/AIDS. "It is difficult for me to think that HIV is why I feel old or have the problems of aging; and, it is difficult to think entirely otherwise," says Paul Quin, age 60 who was diagnosed with HIV 17 years ago. "I feel unable to track symptoms or monitor my health. I no longer understand what might be normal for a man my age and what might come with HIV—what might be a warning."

The picture is further complicated by the fact that there is little research regarding the safety and efficacy of AIDS medications in older adults, including accurate understandings of dosage and frequency. Medical providers also appear to have a limited understanding of how AIDS medications may interact with medications for other conditions common in older adults, such as diabetes, heart disease, and arthritis. All-too-common stereotypes about the sexuality of older adults persists among professionals and the public at large, making HIV prevention efforts more difficult. The myth that, "grandparents aren't interested in sex, and if they are interested in sex, no one is interested in them," continues to be a prevalent assumption in the general public. Debunking this myth is AARP's 1999 survey reporting that over 50% of 45–59 year olds, and over 25% of those 60–74, had sex at least once if not more, times a week.

Another common misperception is that older adults only have sex within the context of a heterosexual monogamous relationship. According to Florida's Senior HIV Intervention Project (SHIP), the ratio of men to women in South Florida is 1 to 7. This gender imbalance may make women more likely to have unprotected sex in order to secure a male partner. SHIP also reports that older males may frequent sex workers, particularly near the time that pension checks arrive.

It is also assumed that older adults do not use or abuse illicit drugs, or if they have used drugs, their use was so long ago that it does not carry any risk of HIV infection. Even the use of prescribed medications may carry HIV risk. Because seniors often live on a fixed income, they may be more likely to reuse and exchange needles for prescribed medications such as insulin. Healthcare providers may also share these misperceptions and may not assess older patients for sexual and drug use risks, or counsel them about safer sex practices. . . .

Seniors may hold their own misperceptions about their risk for HIV. In the early years of the HIV epidemic, research with at-risk groups such as heterosexual adolescents found that many teens who engaged in risky sexual practices did not believe themselves to be at risk because they saw HIV/AIDS as a gay man's disease. Some seniors still view HIV/AIDS as a younger person's disease and do not consider themselves to be at risk, regardless of their sexual behaviors.

"Post menopausal women and their sexual partners won't automatically consider using condoms, since they are past childbearing age," Dea reported. Even among older adults who would like to use condoms, the subject can be difficult to discuss. Because the reason for condom use would clearly be to prevent disease, the implication is that there is a lack of trust in a current partner. . . .

According to Dea, sexual behavior for seniors has also changed because of an increase in the use of Viagra. "Viagra is passed around like candy and middle-aged and older adults are continuing to get infected." Viagra has permitted men who have not been recently sexually active to reenter the dating and mating arena, perhaps in an environment of HIV/AIDS risk they do not understand and for which they are not prepared. . . .

Overcoming the taboos that older adults may hold about discussing their sexual behavior with their partners and healthcare providers, and dismantling ageist assumptions, are critical steps in effective HIV/AIDS education for older people. Among the stereotypes about older people, lies a particularly dangerous one—"You can't teach an old dog new tricks." This adage fuels the assumption that older adults are unwilling or unable to change their behavior. However, decades of gerontological research demonstrates that older adults can and will change their behavior when provided with appropriate education and interventions that target specific health concerns and provide support for skill development for seniors' real-world concerns. . . .

*Source:* Latini, David M. and David W. Coon. 2003. "Aging and HIV—The Changing Face of AIDS." *American Sexuality Magazine* 1(1). Copyright 2003, National Sexuality Resource Center/ San Francisco State University. Reprinted by permission.

## HIV/AIDS and People with Disability

**Nora Ellen Groce**

Although AIDS researchers have studied the disabling effects of HIV/AIDS on previously healthy people, little attention has been given to the risk of HIV/AIDS for individuals who have a physical, sensory, intellectual, or mental health disability before becoming infected. It is commonly assumed that disabled individuals are not at risk. They are incorrectly thought to be sexually inactive, unlikely to use drugs, and at less risk for violence or rape than their non-disabled peers. Yet a growing body of research indicates that they are actually at increased risk for every known risk factor for HIV/AIDS. For example, in a recent article, S Blumberg and W Dickey [1] analyze findings from the 1999 US National Health Interview Survey and show that adults with mental health disorders are more likely to report a medium or high chance of becoming infected with HIV, are more likely to be tested for HIV infection, and are more likely to expect to be tested within the next 12 months than are members of the general population. . . .

[D]espite the assumption that disabled people are sexually inactive, those with disability—and disabled women in particular—are likely to have more sexual partners than their non-disabled peers. Extreme poverty and social sanctions against marrying a disabled person mean that they are likely to become involved in a series of unstable relationships.[2] Disabled individuals (both male and female) around the world are more likely to be victims of sexual abuse and rape than their non-disabled peers. Factors such as increased physical vulnerability, the need for attendant care, life in institutions, and the almost universal belief that disabled people cannot be a reliable witness on their own behalf make them targets for predators.[3,4] In cultures in which it is believed that HIV-positive individuals can rid themselves of the virus by having sex with virgins, there has been a significant rise in rape of disabled children and adults. Assumed to be virgins, they are specifically targeted.[5] . . . Individuals with disability are at increased risk of substance abuse and less likely to have access to interventions. It is estimated that 30% of all street children have some type of disability and these young people are rarely reached by safe-sex campaigns.[6]

Furthermore, literacy rates for disabled individuals are exceptionally low (one estimate cites an adult literacy rate of only 3% globally[6]), thus making communication of messages about HIV/AIDS all the more difficult. Sex education programmes for those with disability are rare.[7–9] and almost no general campaigns about HIV/AIDS target (or include) disabled populations.[10] . . .

The future for disabled individuals who become HIV positive is equally grim. Although little is known about access to HIV/AIDS care, disabled citizens receive far fewer general health-services than others.[11,12] Indeed, care is not only often too expensive for impoverished disabled persons, but it can also be physically inaccessible . . .

Currently, little is known about HIV/AIDS and disability. Only a few studies have estimated prevalence [13,14] and no prevalence data exist for any disabled populations from sub-Saharan Africa, Asia, Europe, Central and South America, or the Caribbean. However, a growing number of stories from disability advocates worldwide point to significant unreported rates of infection, disease, and death.[15] Over the past decade there have be a handful of articles on HIV/AIDS pilot programmes and interventions for intellectually disabled adults or services for deaf adolescents.[16,17] Many of these projects are innovative but almost all are small and underfunded. There is a real need to understand the issue of HIV/AIDS in disabled people in global terms and to design and implement programmes and policy in a more coherent and comprehensive manner. The roughly 600 million individuals who live with a disability are among the poorest, least educated, and most marginalised of all the world's peoples. They are at serious risk of HIV/AIDS and attention needs to be focused on them. . . .

### NOTES

1. Blumberg SJ, Dickey WC. Prevalence of HIV risk behaviors, risk perceptions, and testing among US adults with mental disorders. *J Acquir Immune Defic Syndr* 2003; 32: 77–79.

2. Economic and Social Commission for Asia and the Pacific. Hidden sisters: women and girls with disabilities in the Asian Pacific region. New York: United Nations, 1995.

3. Nosek MA, Howland CA, Hughes RB. The investigation of abuse and women with disabilities: going beyond assumptions. *Violence Against Women* 2001; 7: 477–99.

4. Chenoweth L. Violence and women with disabilities: silence and paradox. *Violence Against Women* 1996; 2: 391–411.

5. UNICEF. Global survey of adolescents with disability: an overview of young people living with disabilities: their needs and their rights. New York: UNICEF Inter-Divisional Working Group on Young People, Programme Division, 1999.

6. Helander E. Prejudice and dignity: an introduction to community-based rehabilitation. New York: UNDP, 1993.

7. Collins P, Geller P, Miller S, Toro P, Susser E. Ourselves, our bodies, our realities: an HIV prevention intervention for women with severe mental illness. *J Urban Health* 2001; 78: 162–75.

8. Gaskins S. Special population: HIV/AIDS among the deaf and hard of hearing. *J Assoc Nurses AIDS Care* 1999; 35: 75–78.

9. Robertson P, Bhate S, Bhate M. AIDS: education and adults with a mental handicap. *J Mental Def Res* 1991; 35: 475–80.

10. UNAIDS. Report on the global HIV/AIDS epidemic 2002. New York: Joint UN Programme on HIV/AIDS, 2002.

11. Altman BM. Does access to acute medical care imply access to preventive care: a comparison of women with and without disabilities. *J Disabil Policy Stud* 1997; 8: 99–128.

12. Lisher D, Richardson M, Levine P, Patrick D. Access to primary health care among persons with disabilities in rural areas: a summary of the literature. *Rural J Health* 1996; 12: 45–53.

13. Van Biema D. AIDS and the deaf. *Time Magazine* 1994; 143: 76–78.

14. Cournos F, Empfield M, Howarth E, Schrage H. HIV infection in state hospitals: case reports and long-term management strategies. *Hosp Comm Psychiatry* 1990; 41: 163–66.

15. Moore D. HIV/AIDS and deafness. *Am Ann Deaf* 1998; 143: 3.

16. Gaskins S. Special population: HIV/AIDS among the deaf and hard of hearing. *J Assoc Nurses AIDS Care* 1999; 10: 75–77.

17. McGillivray J. Level of knowledge and risk of contracting HIV/AIDS amongst young adults with mild/moderate intellectual disability. *J Appl Res Intellect Disabil* 1999; 12: 113–26.

# The Global HIV/AIDS Pandemic, Structural Inequalities, and the Politics of International Health

Richard Parker

As the HIV/AIDS epidemic enters its third decade, much of the sense of urgency that accompanied discussions of AIDS only 10 or 15 years ago seems to be disappearing.[1] Thanks to the development of new antiretroviral treatments capable of transforming HIV infection into a chronic but manageable health condition, mortality rates due to AIDS have fallen throughout the industrialized or "developed" world, and even in some of the more privileged "developing" countries.[2]

The worst types of discrimination and human rights violation against people living with HIV and AIDS (or suspected to be at risk for HIV infection), which occurred regularly during the early years of the epidemic, seem to have declined as well. Legal systems and official structures have been pushed to respond to the epidemic by reaffirming the basic rights of all human beings, independent of serostatus. And both governmental and civil society organizations in countries around the world have gradually mobilized resources and developed programs to overcome what once was described as "AIDS exceptionalism,"[3] increasingly mainstreaming programmatic responses to the epidemic at international, national, and local levels. Indeed, as we have turned the page on the past century and entered the new millennium, and as we head into the third decade of the HIV/AIDS epidemic, the progress made in responding to AIDS over the past decade seems to give reason for guarded optimism.

## Structural Inequalities

When we turn our gaze beyond our own borders to focus on the HIV/AIDS pandemic in the most resource-poor countries of the developing world, however, the picture is considerably worse. The Joint United Nations Program on AIDS (UNAIDS) estimates that by the end of 2000 approximately 36.1 million people had been infected with HIV globally.[2] Of these, approximately 34.7 million are adults—16.4 million are estimated to be women—and 1.4 million are children. Since the beginning of the epidemic, 21.8 million people are estimated to have died—17.5 million adults (roughly 9 million women) and 4.3 million children. In 2000 alone, 3 million deaths were attributed to AIDS, and 5.3 million new infections are believed to have occurred—2.2 million among women and nearly 570,000 among children.[2]

These current estimates are enough to give us pause, but it is also important to remember that there is little likelihood that the situation will improve any time soon. On the contrary, UNAIDS and the World Bank predict that HIV, which was responsible for 8.6% of deaths from infectious disease in the developing world in 1990, will be responsible for 37.1% of such deaths among adults between the ages of 15 and 59 by 2020.[4] If treatment advances and other recent scientific advances give us reason for optimism, there is equally good reason for concern, as HIV/AIDS

From Parker, Richard. 2002. "The Global HIV/AIDS Pandemic, Structural Inequalities, and the Politics of International Health." *American Journal of Public Health,* 92(3): 343–346. Copyright © American Public Health Association. Reprinted by permission.

continues to stand as one of the most significant global health problems that must be confronted in the new millennium.

Beyond the sheer weight of the numbers, what is perhaps most important about the shape of the HIV pandemic is the fact that the global distribution of infection has been anything but equal. It is estimated that approximately 920,000 people have been infected in North America, for example, with 540,000 infections in Western Europe and another 15,000 in Australia and New Zealand.[2] In sub-Saharan Africa, by contrast, it is estimated that as many as 25.3 million persons have been infected by HIV. Another 5.8 million have been infected in South and Southeast Asia, and 1.4 million have been infected in Latin America.[2] In short, the vast majority of HIV infections can be found in the poorest regions of the world, in developing countries already facing a wide range of other serious public health problems.

This concentration of HIV infection in the countries of the developing world becomes even more worrisome if we look again at societies such as the United States, where disproportionate levels of HIV infection have been documented among racial and ethnic minority populations. Rates are especially high among gay and bisexual men in communities of color and among heterosexual women living in poverty in the inner cities.[5]

Indeed, if we bring together the available data on HIV/AIDS in the developing world with the most recent trends on HIV infection in countries such as the United States, it is impossible not to be impressed by the extent to which a range of structural inequalities intersect and combine to shape the character of the HIV/AIDS epidemic everywhere, both North and South, in developed as well as developing countries. In all societies, regardless of their degree of development or prosperity, the HIV/AIDS epidemic continues to rage—but it now affects almost exclusively the most marginalized sectors of society, people living in situations characterized by diverse forms of structural violence.[6]

It is in the spaces of poverty, racism, gender inequality, and sexual oppression that the HIV epidemic continues today—in large part unencumbered by formal public health and education programs, let alone by the advances in treatment that might otherwise convince us that the emergency has passed. The context in which the HIV/AIDS epidemic continues to expand in countries around the world is one of growing polarization between the very rich and the very poor, increasing the isolation of some segments of the population at a time when others are perversely integrated into the criminal economies of international drug smuggling and the like, and increasing social inequalities that seem to be an integral part of globalization based on neoliberal economic policies.[7]

These structural factors, which shape the HIV/AIDS epidemic within the contours of specific societies, even in the resource-rich industrialized countries, are the same factors that shape the global epidemic, particularly in the resource-poor and often economically dependent countries of the developing world. Indeed, perhaps no other major international public health problem so clearly reflects the social, political, and economic architecture of what has been described as the new world order: a post–Cold War international system in which, at least until very recently, the gravest threats to human security seemed to stem less from state-controlled and state-inflicted violence (such as the threat of nuclear war) than from the dismantling of previously existing health, education, and welfare systems in many of the most advanced industrial societies and from diverse forms of structural adjustment that have been imposed on many developing countries.[8]

### The Politics of International Health

Given these trends, . . . [it is unfortunate that] the initial response in terms of commitment of resources to the [Global Fund to Fight Aids] has been disappointing. Although [UN Secretary-General Kofi] Annan originally estimated that

US $7 to $10 billion would be needed by 2005 to meet expected demand, as of November 2001 only slightly more than US $1.5 billion had been committed by governments, nongovernmental organizations, and private donors. This amount includes only US $300 million committed thus far by the government of the United States.[9]

The relatively disappointing response of the United States should be cause for alarm for anyone concerned about HIV/AIDS or issues of international health more broadly. As the richest nation in the world—and as one of the chief beneficiaries of the current global economic order, which has done so much to shape the HIV/AIDS pandemic as a product of structural inequalities both within and between nations—the United States is unquestionably the key point of reference for other nations, as well as for private- sector organizations and individuals in evaluating their own contributions to the global effort to respond to HIV/AIDS and other major international health problems.

Without renewed and expanded commitment from the . . . US . . . , the likelihood is that the Global Fund to Fight AIDS, Tuberculosis and Malaria will fall far short of its goal, and one of the most innovative opportunities in the response to HIV/AIDS globally will be lost. At a time when health care around the world is increasingly privatized, and when banks have increasingly become the arbiters of international health policy, losing this chance to reaffirm a vision of health as a fundamentally public good would be a terrible loss—not only for those who are living with or vulnerable to HIV infection, but for all who understand that questions of health can never be separated from broader struggles for responsibility, fairness, and social justice.

### Maintaining Commitment

The risk of a lack of ongoing commitment to HIV/AIDS internationally, and to the Global Fund to Fight AIDS, Tuberculosis and Malaria in particular, has of course become all the more serious in the wake of the terrible terrorist attacks on September 11 and the ensuing military response of the United States. As the international system struggles to come to grips with the many changes that have been brought about by these events, public attention has understandably turned to questions of our immediate security in a world that now seems physically unsafe in a new and very different way, and our ability to maintain interest in the seemingly more long-term and distant security concerns of issues such as HIV/AIDS is threatened.

Although the United Nations leadership has stood firm in emphasizing the continued importance of the Global Fund and the high priority that must be given to struggles against infectious diseases, issues such as terrorism and bioterrorism have understandably taken precedence in many of the most recent debates about human well-being and safety within the broader context of international relations. Within this rapidly changing context, we can only hope that new concern will emerge, as well, with the fundamental inequities that have been such an integral part of recent processes of globalization—in particular, with the ways in which such inequities have contributed to the terrible new forms of risk and insecurity that confront us today in a world that often seems to be spinning out of control.[7]

Now, more than ever, it is crucial that we work to analyze and understand the social and economic processes that have not only produced extreme forms of physical violence, but that have exacerbated the health threats that face so much of the world's population on a daily basis. Clearly, public health research and analysis has a key role to play in building the intellectual bridges that will be necessary to understand the health consequences of the development models that have been pursued in recent decades—and the ways in which these models may have contributed to new forms of insecurity that are omnipresent in today's world.

In a policy context that is increasingly conditioned by fear—and, because of this fear, by urgent demands for immediate solutions—one of our greatest challenges is to build an understanding of the broader structural forces that have shaped not only the first epidemics of a truly globalized world, but also its most recent political and ideological challenges.[10] And in a historical moment in which our most pressing dangers have come so close to home, one of our most urgent priorities must be to keep alive, as well, the broad range of public health issues that must be confronted as we march into the new millennium. The future of the global HIV/AIDS epidemic, and of the millions of lives affected by it, will depend on the ways in which we confront these dilemmas.

## REFERENCES

1. Parker, R. Administering the epidemic, HIV/AIDS policy, models of development, and international health. In Global Health Policy, Local Realities: The Fallacy of the Level Playing Field. Boulder, Colo: Lynn Renner Publishers, 2000: 39–55.
2. UNAIDS. AIDS epidemic update—December 2000. Available at: http//www.unaids.org. Accessed November 15, 2001.
3. Kirp, D., Bayer, R., eds. AIDS in the Industrialized Democracies. New Brunswick, NJ: Rutgers University Press, 1992.
4. World Bank. Confronting AIDS: Public Priorities in a Global Epidemic. New York, NY: Oxford University Press, 1997.
5. Karon, J. M., Fleming, P. L., Steketee, R. W., DeCock, K. M. HIV in the United States at the turn of the century: an epidemic in transition. *Am J Public Health,* 2001, 91: 1060–1068.
6. Farmer, P., Connors, M., Summons J., eds. Women, Poverty and AIDS: Sex, Drugs and Structural Violence. Monroe, Me: Common Courage Press, 1996.
7. Castelis, M., End of Millennium. Oxford, England: Blackwell, 1998.
8. Beck, U. What Is Globalization? Cambridge, Mass: Polity Press, 2000.
9. Office of the Spokesman for the Secretary-General. Contributions pledged to the Global Fund to Fight AIDS, Tuberculosis and Malaria. Available at: http://www.un.org/News/ossg/aids.htm. Accessed November 15, 2001.
10. Castclis, M. The Power of Identity. Oxford England: Blackwell, 1997.

## The Feminization of AIDS

**New York Times Editorial Desk**

This year, once again, the annual report from the Joint United Nations Program on H.I.V./AIDS and the World Health Organization tragically documents the way the global AIDS epidemic is still killing millions of people and spawning hot spots in Asia and Eastern Europe. The most striking news is that AIDS is fast becoming a disease that strikes younger women disproportionately. Ignorance is part of the problem, but the laws and social customs that keep women powerless and poor—and subject to sexual exploitation—are far more insidious.

According to the new report's eye-opening analysis, AIDS is spreading quickly into the ranks of women—both single and married—in regions where AIDS is already well established. In sub-Saharan Africa, women 15 to 24 years old are three times as likely to be infected as men the same age. In Thailand, 90 percent of AIDS transmissions a decade ago occurred between sex workers and their clients. More recent estimates suggest that 50 percent of the new infections are occurring between spouses, as men who picked up AIDS from prostitutes pass it on to their wives.

The soaring infection rates among younger women are driven partly by social customs that require the women to remain ignorant of sex and sexuality until they marry. Indeed, UN AIDS researchers have found that a majority of young women in some nations have no idea how to protect themselves from H.I.V. The root problem, especially in many developing nations, is a pervasive gender inequality that keeps women from amassing capital, asserting their rights under the law or even deciding when to have sex. A staggering number of women reported that their first sexual experiences came as a result of rape.

Marginalized in the economy and under the law, women in developing nations are often left with sex as their only marketable resource. In some parts of Africa, older men who take young lovers commonly help the girl's family by paying for school fees and food. Young women who are bartered this way have no standing to refuse sex or ask their partners to use condoms. Marriage and fidelity offer little protection from disease for these women, who typically marry older men who have been sexually active for decades. In some areas, infection rates for young married women who remain faithful are actually higher than for single women not yet in permanent relationships.

AIDS education is crucial in fighting the epidemic. But information alone is not enough. Countries with entrenched epidemics need to enhance women's rights under the law and end retrograde traditions that make them second-class citizens. Only then can women hope to protect themselves.

*Source:* "The Feminization of AIDS." *New York Times,* December 13, 2004, p. A26. Copyright © 2004 by The New York Times Co. Reprinted by permission.

## *Did You Know?*

- Human papillomavirus (HPV) is transmitted by direct skin-to-skin contact. People with HPV may experience no visible signs of symptoms.[1] Nearly 75 percent of Americans aged 15 to 49 have been infected with the virus.[2]
- Fewer than 50 percent of adults aged 18 to 44 in the United States have been tested for a sexually transmitted infection (STI) other than HIV. However, adults are more likely to be infected with an STD other than HIV.[3]
- Using condoms reduces the chance of transmitting (and getting) STIs such as gonorrhea, chlamydia, herpes, trichomoniasis, and HIV. The main reason that condoms sometimes fail to prevent STIs or pregnancy is incorrect or inconsistent usage, not the failure of the condom itself.[4]
- When asked, 92 percent of whites Americans, 71 percent African Americans, and 73 percent of Latinos aged 15 to 17 agreed that "sex without a condom isn't worth the risk."[5]
- In the same report, white Americans, African Americans, and Latinos agreed that if a partner suggested using a condom they would feel "like the person cared about me."[6]
- A recent nationwide study found that one in six men who had sexual intercourse with men, recently had had sexual intercourse with women. Nearly a quarter of those men reported having had unprotected sexual intercourse with both men and women.[7]
- At the end of 2003, the Center for Disease Control estimated 1,039,000 to 1,185,000 persons in the United States were living with HIV/AIDS. Of these cases, an estimated 24 to 27 percent were either undiagnosed or unaware of their infection. Thirty-nine percent of people diagnosed with HIV in 2003 had AIDS within a year.[8]
- In 2003, men accounted for almost 75 percent of all new HIV/AIDS diagnoses. Of all new HIV/AIDS cases diagnosed, half were among African Americans.[9]
- The World Health Organization estimates that in 2005, 40.3 million people worldwide were living with HIV. Of those, 17.5 million were women and 2.3 million were children under the age of 15. Almost five million people worldwide were estimated to be newly infected with HIV in 2005.[10]
- Over three million people worldwide were estimated to have died from AIDS-related illnesses in 2005. More than one half million of those deaths were to children under the age of 15.[11] Over twenty-million people have died from AIDS-related illnesses since 1981.[12]

*—Compiled by Mikel Walters*

**NOTES**

1. Sexuality Information and Education Council of the United States. 2004. "The Truth about STDs." Retrieved November 21, 2005 from www.siecus.org/pubs/fact/fact0019.html.

2. Dailard, Cynthia. 2003. "HPV in the United States and Developing Nations: A Problem of Public Health or Politics?" *The Guttmacher Report on Public Policy* 6:3. Retrieved January 20, 2006 from www.guttmacher.org/pubs/tgr/06/3/gr060304.html.

3. Sexuality Information and Education Council of the United States. 2004. "The Truth about STDs." Retrieved November 21, 2005 from www.siecus.org/pubs/fact/fact0019.html.

4. Ibid.

5. Sexuality Information and Education Council of the United States. 2004. "Fact Sheet: Sexuality and Youth in Communities of Color." Retrieved March 1, 2005 from www.siecus.org/pubs/fact/fact0012.html.

6. Ibid.

7. Sexuality Information and Education Council of the United States. 2001. "Fact Sheet: Lesbian, Gay, Bisexual, and Transgender Youth Issues." Retrieved January 30, 2006 from www.siecus.org/pubs/fact/fact0013.html.

8. Centers for Disease Control and Prevention. 2005. "HIV/AIDS Surveillance Report, 2004, Volume 16. U.S. Department of Health and Human Services, Centers for Disease Control and Prevention. Retrieved January 30, 2006 from www.cdc.gov/hiv/stats/2004SurveillanceReport.pdf.

9. Ibid.

10. World Health Organization. 2005. "AIDS Epidemic Update." Retrieved January 30, 2006 from www.who.int/entity/hiv/epi-update2005_en.pdf.

11. Ibid.

12. World Health Organization. 2004. "A Global Overview of the AIDS Epidemic." Retrieved January 30, 2006 from www.unaids.org/bangkok2004/GAR2004_html/GAR2004_03_en.htm#P237_35114.

chapter 9

# Social Control of Sexuality

*An interview with . . .*

### Keith Boykin

Keith Boykin, J. D., a graduate of Harvard Law School, is one of America's leading commentators on issues of race and sexuality. He is author of the Lambda Literary Award-winning book *Respecting the Soul: Daily Reflections for Black Lesbians and Gays* (Avon Books, 1999) and *One More River to Cross: Black and Gay in America* (Doubleday, 1998), which was also a finalist for the Lambda Literary Award. To find out more about his work, visit his website at www.keithboykin.com.

**What led you to begin writing about sexuality?**

*I took a course on race relations and a course on sexual orientation at Harvard Law School and I saw similarities in the arguments that people use to justify racism and homophobia. Everyone seemed to approach race and sexuality as two disconnected and limited entities, as though race was entirely about blacks and sexual orientation entirely about gays. I wanted someone to acknowledge that not all gays are white and not all blacks are straight, so I decided to write about these issues myself.*

**Which of your projects have you found most interesting?**

*The most interesting part of my work has been the opportunity to travel the country and talk about sexuality. I often speak about what I call "the seven deadly lies of race and sexual orientation" and I'm amazed how pervasive those lies have become in our culture. I love exploding the myths that people have about these issues.*

**What is the most challenging issue when writing about sexual orientation?**

*The most difficult issue in writing about sexual orientation is getting people to think. So many people turn off their minds on sexuality issues and don't bother to think about them rationally. Many of us cannot see past our own experiences, and we automatically assume that if we are heterosexual, then everyone must be heterosexual. Or, if we are homosexual, everyone must be homosexual, at least secretly. The truth is that sexuality is a very personal experience and we don't help ourselves to understand it by projecting our biases on to everyone else.*

**Why is it important to educate people about sexuality?**

*People need to be liberated from the fear-based, confusing, and misleading information they've heard about sex, and particularly about homosexuality and bisexuality. Teaching people to open their minds is a very rewarding experience because you can see change take place when people are open to it. I like to think that my work helps people get beyond their fears and learn to love themselves.*

**Have you faced any ethical dilemmas in writing about sexuality? How did you solve them?**

*The only significant issue I've faced is the question of "outing" people who are not open about their sexual orientation. I don't believe in outing, so I don't disclose information that other people don't want revealed. For example, some people suggest that outing celebrities is a good thing because it shows the world well-known people who are gay or lesbian or bisexual. I disagree because what it really shows is that even prominent persons are still afraid to disclose their sexuality. That's a horrible message to send to a young person. If rich and famous people can't cope with being gay, how is a poor, unknown teenager supposed to deal with it? It's better to let celebrities come out when they are ready to come out, and the message that's communicated to others will be more powerful and affirming.*

**How do people react when they find that you write and speak on race and sexuality?**

*I travel to 25 to 30 schools a year to speak about race and sexuality, and there's a scenario that happens quite often in various cities I visit. I'm very open about my sexual orientation so that's not an issue on campus. But as soon as I step off campus into a waiting cab or car to take me to the airport, I know what's going to happen next. The driver will engage me in conversation, ask me what I was doing on campus, and ask me what I do for a living. At some point, it's bound to come out that I write and speak about issues related to homosexuality. It's never caused a scene with a cab driver, but I know some of them probably wish they'd never asked.*

**If you could teach people one thing about sexuality, what would it be?**

*I would encourage people to be comfortable with sex and sexuality. Parents don't always talk about sexuality issues, and when they do, they don't always give accurate information. A lot of young people have very primitive ideas about sex that they learned from their parents, which their parents learned from their parents, and so on. Despite all the sexual images in the media, sex is still not an issue that people want to discuss. Many of us are afraid to talk about sex at all. I suppose we feel this way because we've been conditioned to view sex as dirty or nasty. We've also been taught by some churches that sex should exist solely for procreative purposes. But if this is true, should married couples abandon sex after the woman has passed her childbearing age? Should young people stop using condoms when they have sex? Of course not. This is another example of why we need to think for ourselves about sex.*

—Interviewed by Denise Donnelly

# The Social Control of Adult–Child Sex

Jeffery S. Mullis and Dawn M. Baunach

In a New Jersey suburb, July 29, 1994, 7-year-old Megan Kanka was raped and strangled to death by Jesse Timmendequas, a 33-year-old twice-convicted sex offender who lived across the street from the Kanka residence. When questioned by police the next day, Timmendequas confessed and led them to a nearby park to show where he had hidden the body. The victim's mother told reporters that if she had known a sex offender lived nearby, her daughter would still be alive.

Three years later a jury found Timmendequas guilty and recommended the death penalty. In the three-year period between the crime and the sentencing, Megan Kanka's parents led a nationwide movement calling for local authorities to notify residents whenever a sex offender moves into the community. Their efforts were highly successful: today, every state in the United States has adopted some version of community notification—also known as "Megan's Law." Similar procedures designed to monitor the whereabouts of sex offenders, such as the requirement that offenders register their current addresses with local police, have also been implemented in Canada, England, Wales, and Australia (Lieb, Quinsey, and Berliner 1998; Plotnikoff and Woolfson 2000; Hinds and Daly 2001).

These and other recent developments in the handling of sex crimes against children are the impetus behind the present reading. Our main goals are, first, to place these developments in historical and cross-cultural perspective and, second, to identify underlying commonalities in the wide range of responses to adult–child sex in modern society.[1] Such responses can be understood as

*social control;* that is, they are part of a larger process by which deviant behavior is defined and counteracted and conformity is encouraged. Social control is ubiquitous in human groups, and it manifests itself in a complex variety of ways. Whenever people express any kind of disapproval over the actions of others—whether they do so informally or formally, individually or collectively, peacefully or violently—social control is present. People may even respond to their own actions with disapproval, a phenomenon known as "social control of the self" (Black 1993: 65). Social scientists study social control in order to better understand all its manifestations and effects. In this reading we use the theory of social control developed by Donald Black (1976, 1993) to classify responses to adult–child sex into four different categories of control—penal, therapeutic, compensatory, and preventive—each one a distinctive method of handling all manner of deviant behavior.

Unlike prior research on the regulation of sex crimes, we are not concerned here with whether the social response is disproportionately severe relative to the actual incidence of such crimes, nor do we focus on the functions of social control for maintaining moral boundaries in society. Excellent work has already been done along these lines. For example, Sutherland (1950) argues that the widespread passage of sexual psychopath laws between 1937 and 1949 was based on unfounded fears generated by the news media. And Jenkins (1998) shows how past "moral panics" over the welfare of children were defensive reactions against large-scale social changes such as those occurring in gender roles and sexual mores during the twentieth century. Although we recognize that the social construction of social problems is a process not always commensurate with objective conditions and that moral panics serve important functions for group solidarity, we set these issues aside and concentrate instead on simply describing and classifying variation in the social control of adult–child sex.[2] Although our purpose is mainly descriptive and classificatory, we also present some explanations of the observed variation. Finally, we examine the unintended consequences of the notification laws enacted in the wake of Megan Kanka's tragic death.

### Modern and Premodern Views

From the standpoint of contemporary Western norms, *child molester* is one of the most stigmatizing labels that can be applied to a person. Disgust and outrage are evoked in almost everyone at the mere contemplation of such people (Finkelhor 1984; Holmes 1991; Pryor 1996). Even in prisons—within a society of sinners, so to speak—other inmates single out the child molester as particularly depraved and deserving of punishment (e.g., see Siewers 1994).[3]

The wrath reserved for child molesters is a product of our cultural construction of childhood. We will return to this subject shortly; for now we note that despite the popularized views of Sigmund Freud, who saw even infants as highly sexual beings, and despite the wealth of research that documents the existence of childhood sexuality,[4] children are commonly seen as innocently devoid of sexual motivation. This image, by extension, casts sex offenders of children as exploitive, corruptive, and blameworthy. Modern law codifies this image by portraying children as mentally incapable of consenting to sexual relations and as guiltless in criminal procedures. Thus predisposed with these cultural directives, jurors find it difficult to be impartial in deciding the facts of child sexual assault cases: "[T]hat the defendant is charged with sexual assault against a child will cause the juror to consider the defendant probably guilty, or, at the very least, the burden will be placed on that defendant to prove his or her innocence" (Vidmar 1997: 6). Defendants themselves will sometimes report feeling guilty, angry, and shocked by their own actions, as indicated in the following statements from four convicted offenders (all male):[5]

*I realized that it was wrong. Normal people don't do these things. (O'Brien 1986: 46)*

*When I look into myself [I feel] anger, hatred for myself, sorrow, and hurt. . . . I feel disgustingly dirty, and wonder what makes me feel that I have the right to live after what I've caused. (Ingersoll and Patton 1990: 71)*

*I thought, oh God, all kinds of things. Like "God, what have I done?" . . . Before [the molestation] happened this was something I would read about. And the first thing that would come to my mind was, "They ought to take that sucker out and cut his nuts off and kill him. He doesn't deserve a trial." And that's the way I felt. Then it happened to me and that's what I thought about myself. I ought to be taken out and shot. . . . But that didn't stop me from doing it. (Pryor 1996: 166)*

*When I touched her the first time on her behind . . . almost every time I touched her, I said, "This isn't right." I knew it wasn't right. . . . After the first episode . . . I got mad. I picked a chair up and tossed it across the room. (Pryor 1996: 167)*

Whether these men are sincere or merely providing the socially desirable response is unknown. The more relevant point is that they echo in their sentiments the larger societal reaction—as if they realize their acts are indefensible and therefore require appropriate self-condemnation. It is interesting to note that not all sex offenders against children are similarly self-condemning. Indeed, some are adamantly unrepentant and deny that anything is wrong with the behavior. This contrary view is most clearly expressed by the handful of organizations, such as the North American Man/Boy Love Association and the René Guyon Society, dedicated to justifying and normalizing adult–child sex. The slogan of the latter organization is "Sex by year eight or else it's too late" (De Young 1988: 584).

Such views are, of course, extremely disreputable and rare. Even so, the negative reaction that currently prevails is far from a cross-cultural universal. Excluding cases of father–daughter and mother–son incest (prohibitions against which are found in almost all known societies), the world-historical evidence contains numerous examples of adult–child sex as part of normal cultural life; these examples include both same-sex and opposite-sex behaviors involving sexually mature and immature or maturing persons. But nowhere is adult–child sex the predominant form of sexual interaction, and in those times and places where it is accepted it tends to be, like all sexual behavior, highly regulated. Perhaps the best-known example is the ancient Greek system of *pederasty* ("love of boys"), in which sexual relationships between upper-class men and boys were embedded in an educational context designed to further the younger males' social and emotional development. The sexual component of these mentor–student relationships was socially accepted, but only under certain conditions. For example, the man was expected to always be the dominant partner (penetrator) and the boy the submissive partner (penetrated) in anal and intercrural (between the thighs) sex. In addition, the boy was not supposed to actually enjoy the sexual interaction because it was considered improper for a future Athenian leader to desire taking a submissive role in any dealings with other males (Dover 1978; Halperin 1990). The boy also needed to be pubescent, for grown men who pursued sex with prepubescent boys were potentially subject to harsh legal punishment (Tannahill 1992). The onset of puberty thus appears to have been an important boundary dividing the acceptable from the unacceptable in adult–child sex among Grecian males. This "puberty standard" extended to upper class Grecian girls as well, as evidenced by their average age at marriage being between 14 and 18 and usually to a male around age 30 (Blundell 1995).

Beyond Ancient Greece, sexual contact between adults and children has served developmental goals elsewhere, such as the South Pacific, where ethnographers in the twentieth century documented adult–child sex rituals in several island societies. For instance, the Sambian tribe, located in the eastern mountains of Papua New Guinea, believed as late as the 1970s that the fellated semen of an older male "masculinizes" a prepubescent boy, allowing the boy to mature into a fierce warrior. Thus, around age 7, boys would begin a prolonged rite-of-passage characterized by frequent oral-sexual contacts with older, sexually mature males. Again, a reversal of dominant/submissive roles here was forbidden, and fully mature men were expected to live a heterosexual existence (Herdt 1984).

On Kolepom, an island located on the south coast of Irian Jaya/West Papua, a prepubescent girl of the Kiman Papuan would engage in sexual intercourse with multiple men as part of an elaborate semen-centered ritual. The semen produced by the intercourse would be collected in a banana leaf and rubbed on the girl's future husband, himself either prepubescent or pubescent. The cultural meaning of this custom was two-fold: intercourse with several older men was intended to test the girl's suitability for marriage, and the rubbing of the semen helped facilitate the boy's entrance into manhood (Serpenti 1984).

On the Polynesian island of Mangaia, boys and girls both would be initiated into adulthood through explicit instruction and practical experience in how to sexually satisfy the opposite sex. A pubescent boy, for example, would first be instructed by an older man on such techniques as cunnilingus and how to achieve simultaneous mutual orgasm with a female partner. This formal instruction would be followed by a practical application in which the boy would have sex with a mature, sexually experienced woman. Of particular importance here was teaching the boy how to delay ejaculation. Emphasis was placed on the female orgasm, which was seen as a pleasurable end unto itself for Mangaian males. Failure to induce orgasm in a future female partner might also result in a loss of social status for men, as the news would spread through gossip. Consequently, for men (and presumably for women, too), the ideal ratio of female-to-male orgasms was at least two to one (Marshall 1971).

In addition to historical and ethnographic accounts, age of consent laws are another source of information on attitudes toward adult–child sex. The legal age of sexual consent is the minimum age at which a person is considered, by the particular government in question, to be capable of consenting to sexual activity. Although minimum age statutes may apply to both male and female children, such laws have tended to be written with specific reference to females only, reflecting the historical view of females as property in need of special protection (Oberman 1994) and also suggesting a greater tolerance of young male sexuality.

Following English common law, most jurisdictions in colonial America considered a 10-year-old girl to be old enough to give valid consent to sexual intercourse. If the girl was younger than 10, the act was defined as felony rape or carnal abuse (Jenkins 1998). A notable exception to the common law tradition was Delaware, which, curiously, set its age of consent at 7. Prepubescent ages such as these remained on the books in most U.S. states until the late 1800s, at which time a popular "social purity" movement began to pressure state legislatures and Congress to raise minimum ages. The moral justification for changing the laws was to prevent men from corrupting young girls and luring them into a life of prostitution, decried by purity activists as a major urban problem of the day. From 1886 to 1895, in response to the purity movement's campaign, the age of sexual consent was raised to between 14 and 18 years in the majority of states (Pivar 1973; D'Emilio and Freedman 1997).

At present, the age of sexual consent is 16 to 18 throughout most of the United States. Worldwide, whenever legislation specifies a minimum age, it is typically at least 14. Throughout contemporary Europe, for example, it tends to range from 14 to 16, although in a handful of European locales it is still as low as 12 (e.g., Malta, Spain, Vatican City) (Graupner 2000).[6] During the same time span that the legal age for sex has risen, the average age at puberty has fallen (see Jenkins 1998: 24), creating a category of people we might call *sexually mature legal minors*—youth in their mid-adolescent years caught in a limbo of hormonal urges and legal constraints.[7]

Why is adult–child sex taboo in the modern world? Why was it a culturally actionable option in earlier times and other places but not here and now? A number of factors have given shape to the current taboo, some more directly than others. Here we briefly sketch the influence of three historical developments: the spread of Christian thought, the "invention" and lengthening of childhood, and the advent of compulsory schooling. First and oldest among these is the spread of Christianity—now the leading religion of the Western world. Early Christian tenets strictly forbade all nonprocreative sex, a view that can still be found among many Christian moralists and one that clearly prohibits sexual intercourse with prepubescents at the same time that it prohibits masturbation and homosexuality. Christianity also has long emphasized the innocent and vulnerable nature of children and the need to protect them from "the harsh and sinful world" (see Conrad and Schneider 1992: 146). This view of childhood as an innocent, precious stage of life began to gain wider favor through the 1700s in Western Europe and the 1800s in the United States. Children increasingly became seen as "fragile creatures of God" (Ariès 1962: 133) who have special needs of their own, and parents increasingly became concerned with attending to those needs by applying appropriate childrearing practices, more benevolent and nurturing in style. Some scholars (e.g., Ariès 1962; Stone 1977) claim this general period of history marks a dramatic turning point in family life—the "invention" of childhood—the implication being that children prior to the Enlightenment were not recognized as fundamentally different from adults. This was certainly true in several key respects. For example, both adults and children were expected to make economic contributions to the family—most children in poorer families were put to work as early as age six. However, it is likely that there was more underlying continuity than dramatic change in attitudes toward and treatment of the very young in particular (Pollock 1983). For present purposes, the most important change from the eighteenth century onward is the gradual lengthening of that period of life referred to as "growing up," so that these ideas about the preciousness of childhood began to be applicable over a wider age range. Put differently, children remained *childlike*—relatively innocent and free from adult obligations—for a longer period of time than in earlier eras. We see this in the notion of the "teenager," which by the mid-1900s had become entrenched in popular thought and custom as a distinct age category characterized by continued development and dependency. A facilitating factor behind the lengthening of childhood was the expansion of laws requiring formal schooling during the late nineteenth and early twentieth centuries. Compulsory education from ages 6 to 16 helped solidify the separation of children from adults by creating a distinct role for children outside of the home economy and the paid labor market. Compulsory education also acted latently as an additional constraint on sexuality: Students were not supposed to have families of their own because of the heavy burden this would place on both the student and the educational system (Killias 1991).

These historical changes provide a normative backdrop against which the social purity agenda and other child-saving reforms become possible. To a greater degree than in centuries past, children and adults have come to live under separate social expectations, governmentally mandated and divinely ordained, with children as protected and adults as protector. Because adult–child sex, embodied by the child molester, defiles the sanctity of childhood, the child molester has become "the

most evil social type in our society" (Davis 1983: 110–111). How do we respond to this evil?

## Varieties of Social Control

Human societies have developed a diverse repertoire of responses to deviant behavior. Adult–child sex provokes a number of these responses. For example, it is prosecuted in criminal courts as statutory rape and treated in psychiatric hospitals as pedophilia. Drawing on Black's theoretical framework, we classify these and other examples according to the general method of social control they illustrate, whether penal, therapeutic, compensatory, or preventive. These represent different strategies for defining and handling deviant behavior. They are not necessarily mutually exclusive strategies, however. Some of the specific examples described next combine the different methods of control in ways that make our classification somewhat arbitrary. In such cases our decision to classify in one category and not another is based on the primary type of social control in evidence.

### Penal Control

In the application of penal control, the deviant is defined as an offender and punishment is seen as the logical response (Black 1976). The criminal justice system exemplifies the formal (i.e., governmental) variety of this type of social control. From the standpoint of criminal law, sexual contact between adults and minors may be prosecuted under any number of different sex offenses, including statutory rape, sexual assault, crimes against nature, defilement of a minor, carnal knowledge of a child, and indecent liberties with a child. In modern society it is the adult who is held accountable for these offenses. The minor is not charged with any crime and is in fact perceived as the victim of criminal wrongdoing, but the extent of perceived victimization will vary directly with situational characteristics such as the age difference between those involved and whether the act is mutually consensual versus coerced. Mutual consent, however, can have complex effects, sometimes absolving the older party of wrongdoing and sometimes resulting in a form of collective liability where both old and young are punished. For example, consider the following:

> *A priest by the name of Johann Arbogast Gauch, who for ten years (1735–1744), while serving as village parson in the former principality of Fürstenberg (Germany), had sexual relations with a number of boys and a few girls. The sexual acts were restricted to masturbation and, with the girls, displaying of the genitals. Some of the children were willing participants; many seem to have resisted at first but were compelled to give in. It seems that the whole village had been well aware of what had been going on, but for a long time nobody interfered. After ten years, i.e., after a change on the throne of Fürstenberg, however, Gauch was finally prosecuted and sentenced to death. The children were kept in a subterranean prison for several months and the boys, as accessories to the crimes, were beaten and whipped. The oldest of the boys barely escaped death sentences. The girls only received ecclesiastical penalty for unchaste behavior. Since the sexual activities in which they had been involved were heterosexual, they were thus not considered as being too serious. (Killias 1991: 42)*

Imprisonment and torture of the younger parties and capital punishment of the adult are evidenced in this example from eighteenth-century Germany. Today, in the United States, life imprisonment of the adult, without the possibility of parole, is the most severe formal punishment meted out for child sexual abuse.[8] But if murder is also committed, as in the case of Megan Kanka mentioned at the outset of this reading, then capital punishment may be imposed with the sexual act and the age of the victim regarded as aggravating circumstances justifying the harsher penalty.

In contrast to imprisonment and other officially authorized actions, ordinary citizens have been known to apply their own brand of punishment to child molesters. These informal measures vary from covert acts apparently perpetrated by lone individuals to more organized and collective responses, and they have become more common in the wake of community notification laws. For example, the home of a convicted child molester was burned to the ground after his name and address were released to the public (van Biema 1993). In another case, a convicted molester's car was firebombed within days of the community being notified of his release (Chiang, Gaura, and Lee 1997). In yet another case, five gunshots were fired at the home of a known molester, injuring no one but narrowly missing a woman in an upstairs room (Hajela 1999). In one community, 100 neighbors of a known molester protested outside his apartment building and collected signatures in a campaign to persuade his landlord to evict him (DelVecchio 1997). In some instances the actions of neighbors have forced molesters to move to a new location in the community or to move out of town altogether (see Anderson 1997).

It may seem incongruous to classify these informal and sometimes criminally violent acts together with official governmental sanctions. In particular, how can crimes such as arson and assault with a deadly weapon be equated with legitimate legal responses such as arrest and imprisonment? Although these acts would seem to be diametrically opposed—the difference between lawful and unlawful—Black's theory of social control leads us to consider the characteristics they share in common:

> *Far from being an intentional violation of a prohibition, much crime is moralistic and involves the pursuit of justice. . . . To the degree that it defines or responds to the conduct of someone else—the victim—as deviant, crime is social control. . . . This implies that many crimes belong to the same family as gossip, ridicule, vengeance, . . . and law itself. . . . In other words, for certain theoretical purposes we might usefully ignore the fact that crime is criminal at all. (Black 1993: 27, 41–42)*

Paradoxically, then, the molester might be both the perpetrator of crime and the victim of crime, depending on whether public officials or private citizens are acting against him. In either case, penal social control is present.

## Therapeutic Control

One of the most significant trends in the social control of deviance is the increasing use of a therapeutic model to understand behaviors that might otherwise be seen as immoral or criminal, a trend referred to as the *medicalization of deviance* (Conrad and Schneider 1992). Therapeutic social control entails viewing the deviant as a patient, sick and in need of help (Black 1976). The impulse behind therapy is not to punish but to treat and ideally cure the deviant, thereby restoring normalcy to the mind or body. Psychiatric treatment exemplifies this type of social control. In psychiatry and related mental health fields, sexual contact between an adult and a child (whether real or imagined contact) indicates a potential mental disorder in the adult, namely pedophilia, defined clinically as "recurrent, intense, sexually arousing fantasies, sexual urges or behaviors" involving a prepubescent child, in which the individual with the disorder is at least 16 years old and five years older than the child (American Psychiatric Association 1994: 527–528). Pedophilia is distinguished from ephebophilia, which refers to an adult's sexual attraction to pubescent children or young teenagers. Ephebophilia is not widely recognized in professional therapeutic doctrine as a mental disorder. This may reflect the well-documented preference among human and other primate males for sexually mature younger partners (Ames and Houston 1990; Okami 1990), making ephebophilia perhaps more readily comprehensible as a biocultural norm than as a psychiatric problem.

The therapeutic control of pedophilia includes such techniques as social skills training, victim role-taking, aversion therapy, orgasmic reconditioning, surgical castration, libido-reducing drugs, and a host of other behavioral, cognitive, and pharmacological treatments (Howitt 1995;

Stone, Winslade, and Klugman 2000). The sheer variety underscores the psychiatric belief that there is no single cause of pedophilia and that no single treatment is effective for all cases. Courts frequently order or provide such treatments as part of the criminal sentence, a practice that illustrates institutional cooperation between the criminal justice and mental health care systems in the control of deviant behavior (see Szasz 1963). This cooperation is further illustrated by U.S. Supreme Court rulings that allow states to confine "sexual predators" for psychiatric treatment *after* they have served their prison sentences (Greenhouse 2002).[9]

Of the different treatments for pedophilia, the most controversial are surgical castration and so-called *chemical castration*. Both reduce the level of testosterone in the body, which in turn reduces sexual desire. The controversy revolves around the ethics and efficacy of castration, some claiming it is simply barbaric (especially the surgical variety) and others questioning the validity of the theory that pedophilia is in fact caused by sexual desire. In surgical castration the testes are removed, permanently reducing testosterone. Chemical castration yields a temporary reduction in testosterone via the injection of antiandrogen drugs such as Depo-Provera. Historically, castration has served both penal and therapeutic ends. It has been used throughout history as punishment for sex crimes such as rape and adultery but is intended in modern society as a medical deterrent to sexual deviance. The first European country to legalize surgical castration was Denmark in 1929, followed by Germany, Iceland, Sweden, and other countries (Heim and Hursch 1979). A growing number of U.S. states authorize both surgical and chemical castration as a condition of parole for convicted child molesters. Because neither form has been shown to unambiguously reduce recidivism, some critics have speculated that therapists and lawmakers who advocate castration are actually seeking punishment by medical means (see Heim and Hursch 1979; Stone et al. 2000).

## Compensatory Control

In compensatory social control, the deviant is defined as a debtor who has failed to fulfill an obligation. Payment is the solution (Black 1976), though punishment may be a byproduct. Compensatory control is seen most clearly and familiarly in civil lawsuits, in which offenders are asked to pay damages to remedy the wrongs they allegedly committed. It is also seen in lesser-known victim compensation programs, in which the government provides payment to victims, a provision partly based on social welfare ideology and partly on the argument that the government is liable because it has failed to prevent crime (Henderson 1985; Greer 1994). Although both civil lawsuits and governmental funds are options available to victims of sex crimes, we focus here on lawsuits only, specifically, lawsuits against the Roman Catholic Church.

In recent years the Catholic Church has been embroiled in public scandal over pedophilic priests, who might be more aptly termed "ephebophilic priests" because most of their known sexual activities have involved adolescents (Jenkins 1998; Ripley 2002). Reliable statistics are lacking on the total number of lawsuits and amount of paid compensation, but a national survey of Catholic dioceses suggests that, since the early 1960s, over 850 priests in the United States have been accused of child sexual abuse, and an estimated one billion dollars has been paid to the accusers in court-ordered and out-of-court settlements (Cooperman and Sun 2002). Approximately 40 percent of the accused priests were removed from their ministerial positions. Only 6 percent of these were actually defrocked (removed from the priesthood altogether) (Cooperman and Sun 2002). The Church apparently failed to promptly remove all the priests that were known to be abusers, thus enabling them to become repeat offenders:

> *At the same time that Church officials denied that clergy engaged in sexual activities with children, they privately assured complainants that the "problem" would be investigated and resolved immediately. In actuality, the Church began to transfer perpetrators either to active ministry in other parishes or to church-affiliated treatment centers. The international scope of the Catholic Church allowed the official hierarchy to relocate offending individuals to distant geographical locations. For Church officials, such moves [temporarily] solved the problem. (Krebs 1998: 19, citation omitted)*

However, the accumulating claims of abuse and the accompanying media scrutiny eventually forced the Church to take additional steps—the drafting of a zero-tolerance policy, "Charter for the Protection of Children and Young People." This is a truly remarkable title considering that the protection being referenced is *protection from priests,* in other words, from the Church itself.

Despite the number of civil claims against wayward priests, very few criminal charges have been brought to date (Pfeiffer and Cullen 2002). Why? In some cases the statute of limitations has expired, while other cases may prove to be unfounded. But, in general, the high number of civil claims and the low number of criminal charges reflects the social structure of these cases: When the accused ranks relatively high in social status, as priests do as individuals and the Catholic Church does as an organization, then compensatory control becomes more likely and penal control becomes less likely (see Black 1993: 53–55).

## Preventive Control

In preventive social control deviants are defined in terms of past transgressions and the likelihood of future offending. Prevention might be attempted by placing deviants under closer surveillance or by restricting their freedom of movement, and by potential victims taking steps to reduce their vulnerability (see Black 1993: 8; Horwitz 1990). Corresponding examples in the preventive control of adult–child sex are registration and notification systems, electronic monitoring devices that alert authorities when the target has ventured beyond permitted boundaries, and the informal method of avoidance, curtailing interaction with the deviant. Next we describe registration and notification as implemented in the United States. We then address the unanticipated consequences of notification.

Beginning in the mid-1990s, all fifty states became federally required to maintain sex offender registries. On release into the community, offenders are ordered to provide local law enforcement with such data as their home address, photograph, criminal history, fingerprint identification, social security number, place of employment, vehicle registration, and DNA profile. The purpose is to maintain a record of the whereabouts and characteristics of offenders. If a sex crime occurs in the vicinity of a known offender, the police have an immediate suspect. Thus the lag between the commission of the crime and apprehension/arrest is potentially shortened (Finn 1997). Updated registries are needed for states to fulfill a second federal requirement of the 1990s, community notification (or Megan's Law), signed in 1996. Although roughly half of the fifty states had implemented notification systems before 1996, the federal version of Megan's Law required the remaining states to do so. All now have. States achieve notification in several ways, ranging from active to passive. For example, officers may distribute fliers with the offender's photo, address, and criminal history, or a centralized database may be made available to the public via the internet (Adams 1999). In some jurisdictions, the offender may be required to notify neighbors personally, going door-to-door. Judges have also required offenders to place warning signs in their yards and bumper stickers on their cars. As Jenkins notes, such procedures have seldom been seen in Anglo-American law, "at least not since the days when thieves, adulterers, and blasphemers were branded or otherwise mutilated in order that they be identifiable by their crimes" (1998: 199).

## Consequences of Community Notification

Notification transforms a "discreditable" neighbor into a "discredited" one (Goffman 1963; Pryor 1996), the secret stigma now publicly known. As a result, the neighborhood at large is placed in a heightened state of uneasy awareness:

> [W]hat few facts residents already had about their new neighbor—his chattiness, his bike rides, reports of his playing with children with water balloons—took on sinister implications after the police alert. (DelVecchio 1997)

As mentioned previously, the results of notification include vandalism, assault, protest demonstrations, and subsequent migration or banishment of the offender, none of which notification was intended to produce. Notification is premised on the "parents' right to know." The information is intended to be used as part of an avoidance-prevention strategy, with parents warning their children not to go near the offender's home or walk alone in the neighborhood. Vigilantism was an unintended consequence, but states are now fully aware of its possibility. In fact, many Internet-based registries now specifically warn citizens against using the information to commit a crime. The criminal actions of notified citizens may encourage child molesters to "go underground," not registering with local law agencies, thus thwarting notification. This in turn may allow them to continue molesting, only now with greater anonymity. In this sense, notification potentially creates the crime it is designed to control.

But how common are these informal responses? Are they in fact driving large numbers of child molesters underground? Even if uncommon, it plausibly takes only a few well-publicized incidents to get the attention of numerous molesters, who may read or watch the story with great interest and then choose to act upon it by moving, not registering, and so on. We investigated these issues by conducting a Lexis-Nexis search of incidents reported in newspapers nationwide during the years 1994 to 2001. The results are presented in Figure 48.1,

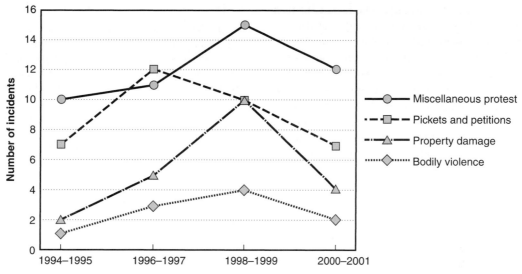

*Figure 48.1*    **What Happens When Sex Offenders Become Neighbors? Tracking the Consequences of Community Awareness, 1994–2001**

which shows the nature and extent of informal responses occurring before and after the federal notification statute.[10] As shown in Figure 48.1, the number of incidents increased from 1994 through 1999. This increase very likely reflects (a) the enactment of notification, as those states without it began to comply with the federal statute, and (b) the novelty of notification (i.e., people initially responded with greater outrage on learning that a pedophile lived nearby). Over time, however, as people across the country became accustomed to the laws (and perhaps resigned to their neighbors), outrage diminished, as suggested by the decrease in events from 1998 through 2001.

Perhaps the most striking finding in Figure 48.1 is the seemingly low number of incidents—115 in all—surely far fewer incidents than there were notifications in this time period. The low number, however, is consistent with the findings of other studies. For example, surveys of law enforcement specialists who routinely work with sex offenders find that name calling, verbal threats, graffiti, protest demonstrations, and minor vandalism sometimes do occur, but not nearly

as frequently as expected (see Finn 1997: 13–14 for an overview of these studies). In our data, the most common type of incident is what we call "miscellaneous protest," a category consisting mainly of scattered complaints to the police, landlords, and employers. There were forty-eight such incidents described in newspaper articles from 1994 through 2001. The second most common type of event is the comparatively organized protest demonstration (or picket), most of which occurred in front of offenders' homes. Overall, there were thirty-one pickets from 1994 through 2001. Also included in this second category are three instances of petitioning in 1996 through 1997 and two instances of petitioning in 2000 through 2001, in which individuals collected signatures supporting the ousting of offenders from their homes or jobs. We grouped these with picketing because of a tendency for petitioning and picketing to occur together. The third most common type of event is property damage, including firebombed cars, threats spray-painted on cars and lawns, homes set ablaze, and bricks and eggs thrown at homes. There were twenty-one instances of property damage. The least common event is actual physical violence inflicted on offenders. There were only ten such incidents reported in newspapers from 1994 through 2001. Two of these incidents were cases of mistaken identity in which residents beat the wrong man. In three of the ten cases the molester inflicted the violence on himself by committing suicide shortly after notification was made to the neighborhood. Finally, not shown in Figure 48.1 is the number of offenders evicted or otherwise compelled to relocate as a result of community actions. Overall, there were thirty-nine reported relocations, and these tended to occur during the height of the other activity, becoming less frequent from 1998 onward.

## Summary and Conclusion

A wide range of social control is directed toward adult–child sex in modern society: imprisonment, hospitalization, castration, drug treatment, civil litigation, surveillance, assault, banishment, and even suicide, a type of self-applied social control. Extreme deviance brings forth the extremes in social control. We have sought to place these modern responses to adult–child sex in a world-historical context. Ancient Greece was examined in this regard, together with South Pacific examples and the changing legal age of sexual consent. Further, we have attempted to identify Blackian commonalities among the different responses, focusing on penal, therapeutic, compensatory, and preventive social control.

Regarding the consequences of community notification, we anticipate a continued drop in confrontational and violent social control, at least until the next moral panic over child sexual abuse. Then it seems reasonable to expect an increase in violence against child molesters. Community notification laws, unlike many other laws, appear to be a written rule that actually has some consequence for the way people behave, for better or worse.

## NOTES

1. In the scientific literature and the news media alike, adult–child sex is often referred to as *child sexual abuse, child molestation,* and *pedophilia.* *Pedophilia* denotes a psychiatric disorder found in some, but not all, sex offenders of children (Freund, Watson, and Dickey 1991). Depending on the context, we use each of these alternative terms, but for general sociological purposes we prefer the more neutral term *adult–child sex* because contemporary evaluative notions of abuse, molestation, and disorder do not always fit the empirical record of this behavior. For discussion of the normative character of research on adult–child sex and how it impedes a scientific understanding of the subject, see Ames and Houston (1990), Okami (1990), and Rind, Tromovitch, and Bauserman (2000).

2. Unless otherwise indicated, what follows is intended to apply to both incestuous and nonincestuous adult–child sex.

3. The early French sociologist Emile Durkheim suggests that even within a perfect "society of saints," certain acts inevitably will be defined as deviant, albeit to the average person the acts in question would probably be considered trifling ([1895] 1938: 68–69). Likewise, even within a society of sinners (such as a prison), there exists a moral ranking of acts from bad to worse. The fact that child molestation is considered one of the more loathsome crimes within the prison subculture—where tolerance levels for deviance are comparatively high—indicates the gravity of the stigma attached to the act in ordinary society.

4. Most college textbooks on human sexuality provide overviews of this research, and most rightly caution against equating early childhood sexuality with adult sexuality. The pleasure-seeking behavior of young children is not the same thing, subjectively at least, as the learned eroticism experienced later in life (e.g., see Rathus, Nevid, and Fichner-Rathnus 2000: 386–392; Kelly 2001: 163–166. . .

5. Almost all convicted child molesters are male. Female offenders may be more prevalent, however, than the gender profile of the convicted would suggest. For example, compared to other offending scenarios, when an adult female sexually engages an underage male the event may be less likely construed as an unwelcome advance and hence less likely to be reported to the police. It can even become a source of pride and status

for the boy (see Pryor 1996: 36–37). If it is reported, others will consider it less serious than cases involving male offenders, with arrest, prosecution, and conviction being comparatively unlikely. In one case, a father remarked that his son "should consider himself lucky to have had a sexual experience with an older woman" (Holmes 1991: 34).

6. In the Philippines and in Thailand, where the child sex industry thrives, the ages of sexual consent are 12 and 15, respectively, except in cases of prostitution, whereupon it is raised to 18 in both countries in an attempt to curtail the exploitation of children (Graupner 2000).

7. This term has an analogue in the healthcare context, where the *mature minor doctrine* enables older adolescents to bypass parental consent and make their own decisions regarding medical treatment. The term *minor* in this doctrine refers to those under the age of full majority rather than those specifically under the age of sexual consent.

8. On sentencing outcomes and rates of incarceration, see Ross and Goldschmidt (1997).

9. In the most recent ruling, *Kansas v. Crane* (decided January 22, 2002), the Supreme Court specified that post-prison confinement is appropriate if offenders have a mental disorder that undermines their self-control.

10. We read newspaper articles with an eye toward counting the number of separate informal incidents resulting from notification. Newspapers tend to report more violent or organized incidents, hence minor insults and harassments are undoubtedly underrepresented. Considering the enormous media attention paid to the Kanka case and to notification legislation generally, when more visible events did occur (e.g., picketing), the news media probably were keen to report them (see Best and Horiuchi 1985 for a similar point regarding their newspaper analysis of Halloween sadism). Overall, from the period of January 1994 through December 2001, there were 1,401 articles generated by our inclusive keyword searches. The articles were generated from the Lexis-Nexis database of 219 different newspaper sources, including major city, regional, and national newspapers, and Associated Press and state/local wire reports. During the period observed, 128 separate incidents involving 85 different molesters were reported in these sources. Figure 48.1 presents a subset of these cases (n=115) classified according to the type of incident. The vast majority of

incidents were directed at child molesters even though notification applies to other kinds of sex offenders too. Some incidents received coverage in multiple papers and on multiple days; these were counted only once. In addition, some offenders were targets in multiple incidents; these were counted as separate events. The complete details of the analysis are available on request.

## REFERENCES

Adams, Devon B. 1999. *Summary of State Sex Offender Registry Dissemination Procedures.* Washington, D.C.: Department of Justice, Bureau of Justice Statistics.

American Psychiatric Association. 1994. *Diagnostic and Statistical Manual of Mental Disorders* (4th edition). Washington, D.C.: American Psychiatric Association.

Ames, M. Ashley, and David A. Houston. 1990. "Legal, Social, and Biological Definitions of Pedophilia." *Archives of Sexual Behavior* 19: 333–342.

Anderson, Nick. 1997. "Convicted Molester Will Find New Home." *Los Angeles Times*, March 13, p. B1.

Ariès, Philippe. 1962. *Centuries of Childhood: A Social History of Family Life.* New York: Vintage Books.

Best, Joel, and Gerald T. Horiuchi. 1985. "The Razor Blade in the Apple: The Social Construction of Urban Legends." *Social Problems* 32: 488–499.

Black, Donald. 1976. *The Behavior of Law.* New York: Academic Press.

———. 1993. *The Social Structure of Right and Wrong.* San Diego, CA: Academic Press.

Blundell, Sue. 1995. *Women in Ancient Greece.* Cambridge, MA: Harvard University Press.

Cheit, Ross E., and Erica B. Goldschmidt. 1997. "Child Molesters in the Criminal Justice System." *New England Journal of Criminal and Civil Commitment* 23: 267–301.

Chiang, Harriet, Maria Alicia Gaura, and Henry K. Lee. 1997. "Disclosure of Molesters Brings Fear of Vigilantism." *San Francisco Chronicle*, July 12, p. A1.

Conrad, Peter, and Joseph W. Schneider. 1992. *Deviance and Medicalization: From Badness to Sickness.* Philadelphia: Temple University Press.

Cooperman, Alan, and Lena H. Sun. 2002. "Crisis in the Church: Survey Finds 218 Priests Have Been Removed This Year." *Boston Globe,* June 9, p. A34.

Davis, Murray S. 1983. *Smut: Erotic Reality/Obscene Ideology.* Chicago: University of Chicago Press.

De Young, Mary. 1988. "The Indignant Page: Techniques of Neutralization in the Publications of Pedophile Organizations." *Child Abuse and Neglect* 12: 583–591.

DelVecchio, Rick. 1997. "Residents Want Molester Out of Santa Rosa." *San Francisco Chronicle,* July 7, p. A13.

D'Emilio, John, and Estelle B. Freedman. 1997. *Intimate Matters: A History of Sexuality in America* (2nd edition). Chicago: University of Chicago Press.

Dover, K. J. 1978. *Greek Homosexuality.* Cambridge, MA: Harvard University Press.

Durkheim, Emile. [1895] 1938. *The Rules of Sociological Method.* New York: Free Press.

Finkelhor, David. 1984. *Child Sexual Abuse: New Theory and Research.* New York: Free Press.

Finn, Peter. 1997. *Sex Offender Community Notification.* Washington, D.C.: Department of Justice, Office of Justice Programs.

Freund, Kurt, Robin Watson, and Robert Dickey. 1991. "Sex Offenses against Female Children Perpetrated by Men Who Are Not Pedophiles." *Journal of Sex Research* 28: 409–423.

Goffman, Erving. 1963. *Stigma: Notes on the Management of Spoiled Identity.* Englewood Cliffs, NJ: Prentice-Hall.

Graupner, Helmut. 2000. "Sexual Consent: The Criminal Law in Europe and Overseas." *Archives of Sexual Behavior* 29: 415–461.

Greenhouse, Linda. 2002. "Court Sets Limit on Detaining Sex Offenders after Prison." *New York Times,* January 23, p. A1.

Greer, Desmond S. 1994. "A Transatlantic Perspective on the Compensation of Crime Victims in the United States." *Journal of Criminal Law and Criminology* 85: 333–401.

Hajela, Deepti. 1999. "Linden Man Gets 10-Year Terms in Vigilante Shooting." *The Record,* February 20, p. A3.

Halperin, David M. 1990. "Why Is Diotima a Woman? Platonic Eros and the Figuration of Gender." In *Before Sexuality: The Construction of Erotic Experience in the Ancient Greek World,* edited by David M. Halperin, John J. Winkler, and Froma I. Zeitlin (pp. 257–308). Princeton, NJ: Princeton University Press.

Heim, Nikolaus, and Carolyn J. Hursch. 1979. "Castration for Sex Offenders: A Review and Critique of Recent European Literature." *Archives of Sexual Behavior* 8: 281–304.

Henderson, Lynne. N. 1985. "The Wrongs of Victim's Rights." *Stanford Law Review* 37: 937–1021.

Herdt, Gilbert H. 1984. "Semen Transactions in Sambian Culture." In *Ritualized Homosexuality in Melanesia,* edited by Gilbert H. Herdt (pp. 167–210). Berkeley: University of California Press.

Hinds, Lyn, and Kathleen Daly. 2001. "The War on Sex Offenders: Community Notification in Perspective." *Australian and New Zealand Journal of Criminology* 34: 256–276.

Holmes, Ronald M. 1991. *Sex Crimes.* Thousand Oaks, CA: Sage.

Horwitz, Allan V. 1990. *The Logic of Social Control.* New York: Plenum Press.

Howitt, Dennis. 1995. *Paedophiles and Sexual Offences against Children.* New York: Wiley.

Ingersoll, Sandra L., and Susan O. Patton. 1990. *Treating Perpetrators of Sexual Abuse.* Lexington, MA: Lexington Books.

Jenkins, Philip. 1998. *Moral Panic: Changing Concepts of the Child Molester in Modern America.* New Haven, CT: Yale University Press.

Kelly, Gary F. 2001. *Sexuality Today* (7th edition). New York: McGraw-Hill.

Killias, Martin. 1991. "The Historic Origins of Penal Statutes Concerning Sexual Activities Involving Children and Adolescents." *Journal of Homosexuality* 20: 41–46.

Krebs, Theresa. 1998. "Church Structures That Facilitate Pedophilia among Roman Catholic Clergy." In *Wolves within the Fold: Religious Leadership and Abuses of Power,* edited by Anson Shupe (pp. 15–32). New Brunswick, NJ: Rutgers University Press.

Lieb, Roxanne, Vernon Quinsey, and Lucy Berliner. 1998. "Sexual Predators and Social Policy." In Michael Tonry (ed.) *Crime and Justice: A Review of Research,* 23: 43–114.

Marshall, Donald S. 1971. "Sexual Aspects of the Life Cycle." In *Human Sexual Behavior: Variations in the Ethnographic Spectrum,* edited by Donald

S. Marshall and Robert C. Suggs (pp. 103–162). New York: Basic Books.

Oberman, Michelle. 1994. "Turning Girls into Women: Re-evaluating Modern Statutory Rape Law." *Journal of Criminal Law and Criminology* 85: 15–79.

O'Brien, Shirley J. 1986. *Why They Did It: Stories of Eight Convicted Child Molesters.* Springfield, IL: Thomas Books.

Okami, Paul. 1990. "Sociopolitical Biases in the Contemporary Scientific Literature on Adult Human Sexual Behavior with Children and Adolescents." In *Pedophilia: Biosocial Dimensions,* edited by J. R. Feierman (pp. 91–121). New York: Springer-Verlag.

Pivar, David J. 1973. *Purity Crusade: Sexual Morality and Social Control, 1868–1900.* Westport, CT: Greenwood Press.

Pfeiffer, Sacha, and Kevin Cullen. 2002. "Crisis in the Church: D. A. Seeks to Lift Time Limit on Rape Cases." *Boston Globe,* June 27, p. A23.

Plotnikoff, Joyce, and Richard Woolfson. 2000. *Where Are They Now: An Evaluation of Sex Offender Registration in England and Wales.* Police Research Series, Paper 126: Crown.

Pollock, Linda. 1983. *Forgotten Children: Parent–Child Relations from 1500–1900.* Cambridge: Cambridge University Press, 1983.

Pryor, Douglas W. 1996. *Unspeakable Acts: Why Men Sexually Abuse Children.* New York: New York University Press.

Rathus, Spencer A., Jeffrey S. Nevid, and Lois Fichner-Rathus. 2000. *Human Sexuality in a World of Diversity* (4th edition). Boston: Allyn and Bacon.

Rind, Bruce, Philip Tromovitch, and Robert Bauserman. 2000. "Condemnation of a Scientific Article: A Chronology and Refutation of the Attacks and a Discussion of Threats to the Integrity of Science." *Sexuality and Culture* 4: 1–62.

Ripley, Amanda. 2002. "Inside the Church's Closet." *Time,* May 20, p. 60.

Serpenti, Laurent. 1984. "The Ritual Meaning of Homosexuality and Pedophilia among the Kiman-Papuans of South Irian Jaya." In *Ritualized Homosexuality in Melanesia,* edited by Gilbert H. Herdt (pp. 292–317). Berkeley: University of California Press.

Siewers, Alf. 1994. "Prisoners Also Judge and Jury; Heinous Crimes Can Make Some Inmates a Special Target." *Chicago Sun-Times,* November 29, p. 7.

Stone, Lawrence. 1977. *The Family, Sex, and Marriage in England, 1500–1800.* New York: Harper and Row.

Stone, T. Howard, William J. Winslade, and Craig M. Klugman. 2000. "Sex Offenders, Sentencing Laws, and Pharmaceutical Treatment: A Prescription for Failure." *Behavioral Sciences and the Law* 18: 83–110.

Sutherland, Edwin H. 1950. "The Diffusion of Sexual Psychopath Laws." *American Journal of Sociology* 56: 142–148.

Szasz, Thomas. 1963. *Law, Liberty, and Psychiatry.* New York: Macmillan.

Tannahill, Reay. 1992. *Sex in History.* New York: Scarborough House.

van Biema, David. 1993. "Burn Thy Neighbor." *Time,* July 26, p. 58.

Vidmar, Neil. 1997. "General Prejudice and the Presumption of Guilt in Sex Abuse Trials." *Law and Human Behavior* 21: 5–25.

# The Sexual Politics
# of Black Womanhood

Patricia Hill Collins

*Even I found it almost impossible to let her say what had happened to her as she perceived it. . . . And why? Because once you strip away the lie that rape is pleasant, that children are not permanently damaged by sexual pain, that violence done to them is washed away by fear, silence, and time, you are left with the positive horror of the lives of thousands of children . . . who have been sexually abused and who have never been permitted their own language to tell about it.*

—*Alice Walker 1988, 57*

In *The Color Purple* Alice Walker creates the character of Celie, a Black adolescent girl who is sexually abused by her stepfather. Writing letters to God and forming supportive relationships with other Black women help Celie find her own voice, and her voice enables her to transcend the fear and silence of her childhood. By creating Celie and giving her the language to tell of her sexual abuse, Walker adds Celie's voice to muted yet growing discussions of the sexual politics of Black womanhood. But when it comes to other important issues concerning Black women's sexuality, U.S. Black women have found it almost impossible to say what has happened.

As Evelynn Hammonds points out, "Black women's sexuality is often described in metaphors of speechlessness, space, or vision; as a 'void' or empty space that is simultaneously ever-visible

(exposed) and invisible, where black women's bodies are already colonized" (1997, 171). In response to this portrayal, Black women have been silent. One important factor that contributes to these long-standing silences both among African-American women and within Black feminist thought lies in Black women's lack of access to positions of power in U.S. social institutions. Those who control the schools, news media, churches, and government suppress Black women's collective voice. Dominant groups are the ones who construct Black women as "the embodiment of sex and the attendant invisibility of black women as the unvoiced, unseen—everything that is not white" (Hammonds 1997, 171).

Critical scholarship also has approached Black women's sexuality through its own set of assumptions. Within U.S. Black intellectual communities generally and Black studies scholarship in particular, Black women's sexuality is either ignored or included primarily in relation to African-American men's issues. In Black critical contexts where Black women struggle to get gender oppression recognized as important, theoretical analyses of Black sexuality remain sparse (Collins 1993; 1998a, 155–83). . . . Everyone [else] has spoken for Black women, making it difficult for us to speak for ourselves.

But suppression does not fully explain African-American women's persistent silences about sexuality. U.S. Black women have been discouraged from analyzing and speaking out about a host of topics. Why does this one remain so difficult? In response, Paula Giddings identifies another important factor, namely, the "last taboo" of disclosing "not only a gender but a sexual discourse, unmediated by the question of racism" (Giddings 1992, 442). Within this taboo, to talk of White racist constructions of Black women's sexuality is acceptable. But developing analyses of sexuality that implicate Black men is not—it violates norms of racial solidarity that counsel Black women always to put our own needs second. Even within these racial boundaries, some topics are more acceptable than others—White men's rape of Black women during slavery can be discussed whereas Black men's rape of Black women today cannot. . . .

[C]ertain elements of Black women's sexuality can be examined, namely, those that do not challenge a race discourse that historically has privileged the experiences of African-American men. The cost is that other elements remain off-limits. Rape, incest, misogyny in Black cultural practices, and other painful topics that might implicate Black men remain taboo.

Yet another factor influencing Black women's silences concerns the potential benefits of remaining silent. . . . [W]here regulating Black women's bodies benefited systems of race, class, and gender alike, protecting the safe spaces for Black women's self-definitions often required public silences about seemingly provocative topics. This secrecy was especially important within a U.S. culture that routinely accused Black women of being sexually immoral, promiscuous jezebels. In a climate where one's sexuality is on public display, holding fast to privacy and trying to shut the closet door becomes paramount. Hine refers to this strategy as a culture of dissemblance, one where Black women appeared too outgoing and public, while using this facade to hide a secret world within. As Hine suggests, "only with secrecy, thus achieving a self-imposed invisibility, could ordinary black women accrue the psychic space and harness the resources needed to hold their own in the often one-sided and mismatched resistance struggle" (Hine 1995, 382). In contexts of violence where internal self-censorship was seen as protection, silence made sense.

The convergence of all of these factors—the suppression of Black women's voice by dominant groups, Black women's struggles to work within the confines of norms of racial solidarity, and the seeming protections offered by a culture of dissemblance—influences yet another factor shaping patterns of silence. In general, U.S. Black women have been reluctant to acknowledge the valuable contributions of Black lesbian feminist theory in reconceptualizing Black women's sexuality. Since the early 1980s, Black lesbian theorists and activists have identified homophobia and the toll it takes on African-American women as an important topic for Black feminist thought. "The oppression that affects Black gay people, female and male, is pervasive, constant, and not abstract. Some of us die from it," argues Barbara Smith (1983, xlvii). Despite the increasing visibility of Black lesbians as parents (Lorde 1984, 72–80; Williams 1997), as academics (Davenport 1996), as activists (Gomez and Smith 1994), within lesbian history (Kennedy and Davis 1993, 113–31), and who have publicly come out (Moore 1997), African-Americans have tried to ignore homosexuality generally and have avoided serious analysis of homophobia within African-American communities.

In this context, Black lesbian theorizing about sexuality has been marginalized, albeit in different ways, both within Black intellectual communities and women's studies scholarship. As a result, Black feminist thought has not yet taken full advantage of this important source of Black feminist theory. As a group, heterosexual African-American women have been strangely silent on the issue of Black lesbianism. Barbara Smith suggests one compelling reason: "Heterosexual privilege is usually the only privilege that Black women have. None of us have racial or sexual privilege, almost none of us have class privilege, maintaining 'straightness' is our last resort" (1982, 171). In the same way that White feminists identify with their victimization as women yet ignore the privilege that racism grants them, and that Black men decry racism yet see sexism as being less objectionable, heterosexual African-American women may perceive their own race and gender oppression yet victimize lesbians, gays, and bisexuals. Barbara Smith raises a critical point that can best be seen through the outsider-within standpoint available to Black lesbians—namely, that intersecting oppressions of sexuality, race, gender, and class produce neither absolute oppressors nor pure victims. . . .

Treating race, class, gender, and sexuality less as personal attributes and more as systems of domination in which individuals construct unique identities, Black feminist analyses routinely identify multiple oppressions as important to the study of Black women's sexualities. For example, Black feminist thinkers have investigated how rape as a specific form of sexual violence is embedded in intersecting oppressions of race, gender, and class (Davis 1978, 1981, 1989; Crenshaw 1991). Reproductive rights issues such as access to information on sexuality and birth control, the struggles for abortion rights, and patterns of forced sterilization require attention to how nation-state policies affect U.S. Black women (Davis 1981; Roberts 1997; Collins 1999). Black lesbians' work on homophobia investigates how heterosexism's impact on African-American women remains embedded in larger social structures (Lorde 1982, 1984; C. Clarke 1983; Shockley 1983; Barbara Smith 1983, 1998). This contextualization in power relations generates a particular kind of social constructionist argument, one that views Black women's sexualities as being constructed within an historically specific matrix of domination characterized by intersecting oppressions. In understanding these Black feminist contextualizations, it may be more appropriate to speak of the *sexual politics of Black womanhood*, namely, how sexuality and power become linked in constructing Black women's sexualities.

## Black Women, Intersecting Oppressions, and Sexual Politics

Due in large part to the politicized nature of definitions themselves, questions of sexuality and the sexual politics in which they participate raise special concerns. What is sexuality? What is power? Both of these questions generate widespread debate. Moreover, analyzing questions of sexuality and power within an interpretive framework that takes intersecting oppressions into account can appear to be a daunting task.

Whereas sexuality is part of intersecting oppressions, the ways in which it can be conceptualized differ. Sexuality can be analyzed as a freestanding system of oppression similar to oppressions of race, class, and gender. This approach views heterosexism as a system of power that victimizes Black women in particular ways. Within heterosexism as a system of oppression, African-American women find that their distinctive group placement within hierarchies of race, class, and gender shape the experiences of Black women as a collectivity as well as the sexual histories of individual Black women.

A second approach examines how sexualities become manipulated *within* class, race, nation, and gender as distinctive systems of oppression and draw upon heterosexist assumptions to do so. Regulating Black women's sexualities emerges as a distinctive feature of social class exploitation, of institutionalized racism, of U.S. nation-state policies, and of gender oppression. In essence, this approach suggests that both the sexual meanings assigned to Black women's bodies as well as the social practices justified by sexual ideologies reappears across seemingly separate systems of oppression.

Yet another approach views sexuality as a specific site of intersectionality where intersecting oppressions meet. Studying Black women's sexualities reveals how sexuality constitutes one important site where heterosexism, class, race, nation, and gender as systems of oppression converge. For Black women, ceding control over self-definitions of Black women's sexualities upholds multiple oppressions. This is because all systems of oppression rely on harnessing the power of the erotic. In contrast, when self-defined by Black women ourselves, Black women's sexualities can become an important place of resistance. Just as harnessing the power of the erotic is important for domination, reclaiming and self-defining that same eroticism may constitute one path toward Black women's empowerment.

## Heterosexism as a System of Power

One important outcome of social movements advanced by lesbians, gays, bisexuals, and transgendered individuals has been the recognition of heterosexism as a system of power. In essence, the political and intellectual space carved out by these movements challenged the assumed normality of heterosexuality (Jackson 1996; Richardson 1996). These challenges fostered a shift from seeing sexuality as residing in individual biological makeup, to analyzing heterosexism as a system of power. Similar to oppressions of race or gender that mark bodies with social meanings, heterosexism marks bodies with sexual meanings. Within this logic, *heterosexism* can be defined as the belief in the inherent superiority of one form of sexual expression over another and thereby the right to dominate.

When it comes to thinking about Black women's sexualities, what is needed is a framework that not only analyzes heterosexism as a system of oppression, but also conceptualizes its links to race, class, and gender as comparable systems of oppression. Such a framework might emphasize two interdependent dimensions of heterosexism, namely, its symbolic and structural dimensions. The symbolic dimension refers to the sexual meanings used to represent and evaluate Black women's sexualities. For example, via the "hoochie" image, Black women's sexualities are seen as unnatural, dirty, sick, and sinful. In contrast, the structural dimension encompasses how social institutions are organized to reproduce heterosexism, primarily through laws and social customs. For example, refusing to prosecute Black women's rapists because the women are viewed as sexual "freaks" constitutes a social practice that reinforces and shapes these symbolic structures.

While analytically distinct, in actuality, these two dimensions work together.

In the United States, assumptions of heterosexuality operate as a hegemonic or taken-for-granted ideology—to be heterosexual is considered normal, to be anything else is to become suspect. The system of sexual meanings associated with heterosexism becomes normalized to such a degree that they are often unquestioned. For example, the use of the term *sexuality* itself references *hetero*sexuality as normal, natural, and normative.

The ideological dimension of heterosexism is embedded in binary thinking that deems heterosexuality as normal and other sexualities as deviant. Such thinking divides sexuality into two categories, namely, "normal" and "deviant" sexuality, and has great implications for understanding Black women's sexualities. Within assumptions of normalized heterosexuality, two important categories of "deviant" sexuality emerge. First, *African* or *Black* sexuality becomes constructed as an abnormal or pathologized heterosexuality. Long-standing ideas concerning the excessive sexual appetite of people of African descent conjured up in White imaginations generate gender-specific controlling images of the Black male rapist and the Black female jezebel, and they also rely on myths of Black hypersexuality. Within assumptions of normalized heterosexuality, regardless of individual behavior, being White marks the normal category of heterosexuality. In contrast, being Black signals the wild, out-of-control hyperheterosexuality of excessive sexual appetite.

Within assumptions of normalized heterosexuality, *homosexuality* emerges as a second important category of "deviant" sexuality. In this case, homosexuality constitutes an abnormal sexuality that becomes pathologized as heterosexuality's opposite. Whereas the problem of African or Black sexual deviancy is thought to lie in Black hyperheterosexuality, the problem of homosexuality lies not in an excess of heterosexual desire, but in the seeming absence of it Women who lack interest in men as sexual partners become pathologized as "frigid" if they claim heterosexuality and stigmatized as lesbians if they do not.

Under Eurocentric ideologies, normalized heterosexuality thus becomes constructed in contrast to two allegedly deviant sexualities, namely, those attributed to people of African descent and those applied to lesbians and gays, among others. The binary fundamental to heterosexism, namely, that dividing alleged normal sexuality from its deviant other dovetails with binaries that underlie other systems of oppression. [Other] important binaries . . .—white/black, male/female, reason/emotion, and mind/body—now become joined by a series of sexual binaries: madonna/whore, real woman/dyke, real man/faggot, and stud/sissy. These sexual binaries in turn receive justification via medical theories (normal/sick), religious beliefs (saved/sinner), and state regulation (legal/illegal).

All of this influences the actual system of sexual regulation in the United States, where ideas about normalized heterosexuality permeate a range of social institutions. Despite the similarities that characterize constructions of African/Black sexuality and homosexuality, these sexualities differ in their characteristic modes of regulation. Black people experience a highly visible *sexualized racism,* one where the visibility of Black bodies themselves reinscribes the hypervisibility of Black men and women's alleged sexual deviancy. Because U.S. understandings of race rely on biological categories that, while renegotiated, cannot be changed—skin color is permanent—Black hypersexuality is conceptualized as being intergenerational and resistant to change.

The seeming intractability of the stigma of Blackness in turn shapes possible responses to this socially constructed yet highly visible deviancy. . . . Because biological traits are conceptualized as permanent, reformist strategies are unlikely to work. In this context, containment strategies of all sorts rise in importance. For example, racial segregation in housing, schools, employment, and public facilities not only benefit some groups of Whites economically—it also keeps allegedly hy-

persexual Blacks separated from Whites. Maintaining physical distance need not be the sole strategy. Blacks have long worked in close proximity to Whites, but Blacks and Whites alike were discouraged from seeing one another as friends, neighbors, lovers, and, most important, legal sexual partners. In a context where Black bodies signal sexual deviancy, laws against intermarriage and other components of racial segregation ensured that the deviancy could be simultaneously exploited yet contained.

Because the nature of the threat is deemed different, forms of control for lesbians, gays, and other sexually stigmatized groups differ from those of sexualized racism. *Homophobia* flourishes in a context where the invisibility of the alleged deviancy is perceived to be the problem. Whereas the fears associated with racism lie in ideas projected upon highly visible, objectified Black bodies, the fears underlying homophobia emerge from the understanding that *anyone* could be gay or lesbian. Reminiscent of the proximate racism of anti-Semitism, one where, for example, Nazi scientists spent considerable time trying to find ways to identify Jewishness, homophobia constitutes a proximate fear that anyone could at any time reveal himself or herself as gay or lesbian.

The panoply of responses to the alleged deviancy of homosexuality also match the nature of the perceived threat. Containment also operates, but differently. For example, the medical profession has been assigned the reformist strategy of counseling gays and lesbians to better cope with normalized heterosexuality. Hate crimes punish individuals, but such crimes make an example of a visible homosexuality in order to drive the rest back into the closet. Recognizing that homosexuality most likely cannot be eliminated, the intended effect is to remove it from public and thereby legitimated space. Laws forbidding gay and lesbian marriages coupled with resistance to gays and lesbians having and raising children seem designed to stop the "spread" of homosexuality. Within this logic of the proximate threat, efforts to keep gays, lesbians, and other sexual minorities "in the closet" and "hidden" seem designed to contain the threat within.

Making heterosexism as a system of oppression more central to thinking through Black women's sexualities suggests two significant features. First, different groups remain differentially placed within heterosexism as an overarching structure of power. . . . African-American women's group history becomes crafted in the context of the specificity of the U.S. matrix of domination. Black women's particular group history within heterosexism intersects with that of other groups. For example, constructions of Black male and female sexuality are linked—they are similar yet different. Similarly, middle-class White women's sexuality could not be constructed as it is without corresponding controlling images applied to U.S. Black women. Moreover, this collective U.S. Black women's history does not eliminate further specification of group histories within the larger collectivity of African-American women, e.g., Black lesbians, adolescent Black women, older Black women, Black women who must rely on social welfare programs, and so on. Instead, it specifies the contours of sexual meanings that have been attributed to Black women. Considerable diversity exists among U.S. Black women as to how the symbolic and structural dimensions of heterosexism will be experienced and responded to.

A second significant feature concerns the space created for Black women's individual agency. Because African-American women express a range of sexualities, including celibate, heterosexual, lesbian, and bisexual, with varying forms of sexual expression changing throughout an individual's life course, Black women's self-definitions become essential. It is important to stress that both the symbolic and structural dimensions of heterosexism are always contested. Individual African-American women construct sexual meanings and practices within this overarching structure of heterosexual power relations. Thus, the individual agency of any one U.S. Black woman emerges in the context of larger institutional structures and particular group histories that affect many others. For individual Black women, the struggle lies in rejecting externally defined ideas and practices, and claiming the erotic as a mechanism for empowerment.

## Sexuality within Distinctive Systems of Class, Race, Gender, and Nation

Analyzing how heterosexism as a system of oppression victimizes Black women constitutes one major approach to examining sexuality. A second approach explores how sexualities constructed in conjunction with an unquestioned heterosexism become manipulated within class, race, gender, and nation as distinctive systems of oppression. For example, the controlling image of jezebel reappears across several systems of oppression. For class oppression, the jezebel image fosters the sexual exploitation of Black women's bodies through prostitution. The jezebel image reinforces racial oppression by justifying sexual assaults against Black women. Gender ideology also draws upon the jezebel image—a devalued jezebel makes pure White womanhood possible. Overseeing these relationships are nation-state policies that because they implicitly see Black women as jezebels, deny Black women equal treatment under the law. Unmarried Black mothers have struggled to gain social welfare benefits long available to White women (Amott 1990), Black adolescents are more likely than White women to receive Norplant and other contraceptive methods that assume they cannot control their sexual libidos (Roberts 1997, 104–49), and as Anita Hill found out, Black women's claims of being sexually harassed and raped are often discounted. Thus, each system has a vested interest in regulating sexuality and relies on symbolic and structural practices to do so.

Examining how regulating Black women's sexuality functions to support each system constitutes one way of investigating these relationships. Controlling Black women's bodies has been especially important for capitalist class relations in the United States. When it comes to U.S. Black women's experiences, two features of capitalism remain noteworthy. First, Black women's bodies have been objectified and commodified under U.S. capitalist class relations. The objectification of Black women . . . and the subsequent commodification of those objectified bodies are closely linked—objectifying Black women's bodies turns them into commodities that can be sold or exchanged on the open market. Commodified bodies of all sorts become markers of status within class hierarchies that rely on race and gender. For example, healthy White babies are hot commodities in the U.S. adoption market, while healthy Black babies often languish in foster care. A second feature of U.S. capitalist class relations concerns how Black women's bodies have been exploited. Via mechanisms such as employment discrimination, maintaining images of Black women that construct them as mules or objects of pleasure, and encouraging or discouraging Black women's reproduction via state intervention, Black women's labor, sexuality, and fertility all have been exploited.

Not only are commodification and exploitation linked, patterns of exploiting Black women's sexuality have taken many forms. In some cases, the entire body itself became commodified. For example, slave auctions brokered the commodified bodies of both Black women and men—bodies could be bought and sold on the open market. In other cases, parts of the body could be commodified and sold for profitability. Barbara Omolade introduces this notion of specialized commodification where "every part of the black woman" was used by the White master. "To him she was a fragmented commodity whose feelings and choices were rarely considered: her head and her heart were separated from her back and her hands and divided from her womb and vagina" (Omolade 1994, 7). Black women's sexuality could be reduced to gaining control over an objectified vagina that could then be commodified and sold. The long-standing interest in Black women's genitalia within Western science seems apt here in that reducing Black women to com-

modified genitalia and vaginas effectively treats Black women as potential prostitutes. Similarly, current portrayals of Black women in popular culture—reducing Black women to butts—works to reinscribe these commodified body parts. Commodifying and exploiting Black women's wombs may be next. When a California judge rejected African-American Anna Johnson's claim that the White baby she had carried in her womb entitled her to some rights of motherhood, the message seemed clear—storage lockers and wombs constitute rental property (Hartouni 1997).

Regulating Black women's sexuality has certainly been significant within racist discourse and practice. In the United States, because race has been constructed as a biological category that is rooted in the body, controlling Black sexuality has long been important in preserving racial boundaries. U.S. notions of racial purity, such as the rule claiming that one drop of Black "blood" determines racial identity, required strict control over the sexuality and subsequent fertility of Black women, White women, and Black men. Although explicitly a means to prevent Blacks and Whites from associating in public accommodations, racial segregation in the South rested upon a deep-seated fear that "social mixing would lead to sexual mixing" (d'Emilio and Freedman 1988, 106). These mechanisms of control affected diverse population groups differently. Affluent White men typically enjoyed access to the bodies of all women and removed other men from sexual competition. The creation of a class of "angry White men" in the aftermath of social reforms of the 1960s and 1970s reflects, in part, the deterioration of White supremacist practices that gave White men such power (Ferber 1998). Wealthy White women were valued for a premarital virginity that when "lost" in the context of heterosexual marriage, ensured that all children would be biologically "White." Regardless of social class, Whites were encouraged to fear racial amalgamation, believing that it would debase them to the status of other races (d'Emilio and Freedman 1988, 86). In this context, Black men were constructed as sexually violent beasts, a view that not only justified their persecution by the state (Berry 1994), but was used to deny them access to White women's bodies. Black women's sexuality found no protections. Thus, notions of White supremacy relied on a notion of racial difference where "difference would be largely based on perceptions of sexual difference, and . . . the foundation of sexual difference lay in attitudes about black women" (Giddings 1992, 447).

Regulating Black women's sexuality also constituted a part of gender oppression. Dividing women into two categories—the asexual, moral women to be protected by marriage and their sexual, immoral counterparts—served as a gender template for constructing ideas about masculinity and femininity. The major archetypal symbols of women in Western thought construct women's sexuality via a tightly interwoven series of binaries. Collectively, these binaries create a sexual hierarchy with approved sexual expression installed at the top and forbidden sexualities relegated to the bottom. Assumptions of normal and deviant sexuality work to label women as good girls or bad girls, resulting in two categories of female sexuality. Virgins are the women who remain celibate before marriage, and who gain license to engage in heterosexual sexual practices after marriage. In contrast, whores are the unmarried women who are willingly "screwed." Whether a woman is an actual virgin or not is of lesser concern than whether she can socially construct herself as a "good" girl within this logic. Racializing this gender ideology by assigning all Black women, regardless of actual behavior, to the category of "bad" girls simplifies the management of this system.

It is important to remember that what appear to be natural and normal ideas and practices concerning sexuality are in fact carefully manufactured and promoted by schools, organized religions, the news media, and, most importantly, government policies. The local, state, and federal branches of the U.S. government may appear to be removed from issues of sexuality, but via their taxation, social welfare, and other policies, the U.S. nation-state in effect regulates which sexualities are deemed legitimate and which are not. For example, U.S. nation-state policies shape understandings of which citizens shall be afforded privacy. Affluent families living in suburban gated communities are provided with far more privacy and government protection than are poor families who live in urban public housing, where police intrude on family privacy more often than they protect it. In a similar fashion, Black women's sexuality has been constructed by law as public property—Black women have no rights of privacy that Whites must observe. As Barbara Omolade suggests, "White men used their power in the public sphere to construct a private sphere that would meet their needs and their desire for black women, which if publicly admitted would have undermined the false construct of race they needed to maintain public power. Therefore, the history of black women in America reflects the juncture where the private and public spheres and personal and political oppression meet" (Omolade 1994, 17).

### Regulating Black Women's Bodies

Sexuality can be conceptualized as a freestanding system of oppression similar to oppressions of race, class, nation, and gender, as well as part of each of these distinctive systems of oppression. A third approach views sexuality as one important social location that joins these distinctive systems of oppression. This conceptualization views sexuality as conceptual glue that binds intersecting oppressions together. Stated differently, intersecting oppressions share certain core features. Manipulating and regulating the sexualities of diverse groups constitutes one such shared feature or site of intersectionality.

In this context, investigating efforts to regulate Black women's bodies can illuminate the larger question of how sexuality operates as a site of intersectionality. Within this larger endeavor, Black women's experiences with pornography, prostitution, and rape constitute specific cases of how more powerful groups have aimed to regulate Black women's bodies. These cases emphasize the connections between sexual ideologies developed to justify actual social practices and the use of force to maintain the social order. As such, these themes provide a useful lens for examining how intersecting oppressions rely on sexuality to mutually construct one another.

### Pornography and Black Women's Bodies

. . . Contemporary pornography consists of a series of icons or representations that focus the viewer's attention on the relationship between the portrayed individual and the general qualities ascribed to that class of individuals. Pornographic images are iconographic in that they represent realities in a manner determined by the historical position of the observers and by their relationship to their own time and to the history of the conventions which they employ (Gilman 1985). The treatment of Black women's bodies in nineteenth-century Europe and the United States may be the foundation upon which contemporary pornography as the representation of women's objectification, domination, and control is based. Icons about the sexuality of Black women's bodies emerged in these contexts. Moreover, as race and gender-specific representations, these icons have implications for the treatment of both African-American and White women in contemporary pornography. . . .

One key feature about the treatment of Black women in the nineteenth century was how their bodies were objects of display. In the antebellum American South, White men did not have to look at pornographic pictures of women because they could become voyeurs of Black women on the auction block. A chilling example of this objectification of the Black female body is provided by the exhibition, in early-nineteenth-century Europe, of Sarah Bartmann, the so-called Hottentot Venus. Her display formed one of the original icons for Black female sexuality. An African women, Sarah Bartmann was often exhibited at fashionable parties in Paris, generally wearing little clothing, to provide entertainment. To her audience she represented deviant sexuality. At the time European audiences thought that Africans had deviant sexual practices and searched for physiological differences, such as enlarged penises and malformed female genitalia, as indications of this deviant sexuality. Sarah Bartmann's exhibition stimulated these racist and sexist beliefs. After her death in 1815, she was dissected, with her genitalia and buttocks placed on display (Gilman 1985). . . .

The pornographic treatment of the bodies of enslaved African women and of women like Sarah Bartmann has since developed into a full-scale industry. Within pornography, all women are objectified differently by racial/ethnic category. Contemporary portrayals of Black women in pornography represent the continuation of the historical treatment of their actual bodies (Forna 1992). African-American women are usually depicted in a situation of bondage and slavery, typically in a submissive posture, and often with two White men. A study of fifty-four videos found that Black women more often were portrayed as being subjected to aggressive acts and as submitting after initial resistance to a sexual encounter. Compared with White women, Black women were shown performing fellatio on their knees more often (Cowan and Campbell 1994). Russell (1993, 45–49) reports that Black women are equated with snakes, as engaging in sex with animals, as incestuous, and as lovers of rape, especially by White men. As Bell observes, these settings remind us of "the trappings of slavery: chains, whips, neck braces, wrist clasps" (1987, 59). White women and women of color have different pornographic images applied to them. The image of Black women in pornography is almost consistently one featuring them breaking from chains. The image of Asian women in pornography is almost consistently one of being tortured (Bell 1987, 161). . . .

This linking of views of the body, social constructions of race and gender, pornography's profitability, and conceptualizations of sexuality that inform Black women's treatment as pornographic objects promises to have significant implications for how we assess contemporary pornography. Pornography's significance as a site of intersecting oppressions promises new insights toward understanding social injustice. . . .

While the sexual and racial dimensions of being treated like an animal are important, the economic foundation underlying this treatment is critical. Under capitalist class relations, animals can be worked, sold, killed, and consumed, all for profit. As "mules," African-American women become susceptible to such treatment. The political economy of pornography meshes with this overarching value system that objectifies, commodifies, and markets products, ideas, images, and actual people. Pornography is pivotal in mediating contradictions in changing societies (McNall 1983). It is no accident that racist biology, religious justifications for slavery and women's subordination, and other explanations for nineteenth-century racism and sexism arose during a period of profound political and economic change. Symbolic means of domination become particularly important in mediating contradictions in changing political economies. The exhibition of Sarah Bartmann and Black women on the auction block were not benign intellectual exercises—these practices defended real material and political interests. Current transformations in international capitalists require similar ideological justifications. Contemporary pornography meshes with late-twentieth-century global transformations of postcolonialism in a fashion reminiscent of global changes associated with nineteenth-century colonialism (Dines 1998). . . .

The treatment of all women in contemporary pornography has strong ties to the portrayal of Black women as animals. In pornography women become nonpeople and are often represented as the sum of their fragmented body parts. Scott McNall observes:

> *This fragmentation of women relates to the predominance of rear-entry position photographs. . . .*

> *All of these kinds of photographs reduce the woman to her reproductive system, and, furthermore, make her open, willing, and available—not in control. . . . The other thing rear-entry position photographs tell us about women is that they are animals. They are animals because they are the same as dogs—bitches in heat who can't control themselves. (McNall 1983, 197–98)*

This linking of animals and women within pornography becomes feasible when grounded in the earlier debasement of Black women as animals.

Developing a comprehensive analysis of Black women's placement in pornography and of pornography itself as a site of intersecting oppressions offers possibilities for change. Those Black feminist intellectuals investigating sexual politics imply that the situation is much more complicated than that advanced within Western feminism in which "men oppress women" because they are men. Such approaches implicitly assume biologically deterministic views of gender and sexuality and offer few possibilities for change. In contrast, the willingness of Black feminist analyses of sexual politics to embrace intersectional paradigms provides space for human agency. Women are not hard-wired as victims of pornography, nor are men destined uncritically to consume it. . . .

A changed consciousness is essential to social change. If Black men can understand how pornography affects them, then other groups enmeshed in the same system are equally capable of similar shifts in consciousness and action. . . .

### Prostitution and the Exploitation of Black Women's Bodies

. . . All Black women are affected by the widespread controlling image that African-American women are sexually promiscuous. . . . Not just White men, but Black men have been involved in finding ways to profit from Black women's bodies. During an interview with Brother Marquis from the group 2 Live Crew, Black cultural critic Lisa Jones realizes that "hoochie mama" and other songs by this group actually constitute "soft porn." Jones's interview with Brother Marquis reveals the important links among pornography, the marketing of Black women's images, and the exploitation of Black women's bodies. In defending the misogynist lyrics of 2 Live Crew's music, Brother Marquis states:

> I'm not gonna try to disrespect you and call you all those names like I do on those records. I would never do that to a young lady, especially a sister. I'm degrading you to try to get me some money. . . . And besides, you let me do that. You got pimps out here who are making you sell your body. Just let me talk about you for a little while, you know what I'm saying? And make me a little money. (Jones 1994, 243)

Brother Marquis's explanation displays familiar rationalizations. He divided women into two categories of good girls and "hoochies." In his mind, if Black women are devalued within prostitution already, what harm can it do to *talk* about debasing Black women, especially if he can profit from such talk?

Within Brother Marquis's logic, images of Black women as jezebels and "hoochies" do little harm. Yet this controlling image has been vital in justifying the negative treatment that Black women encounter with intersecting oppressions. Exploring how the image of the African-American woman as prostitute has been used by selected systems of oppression illustrates how sexuality links the three systems. But Black women's treatment also demonstrates how prostitution operates as a site of intersectionality.

Yi-Fu Tuan (1984) suggests that power as domination involves reducing humans to animate nature in order to exploit them economically or to treat them condescendingly as pets. Domination may be either cruel and exploitative with no affection or may be exploitative yet coexist with affection. The former produces the victim—in this case, the Black woman as "mule" whose labor has been exploited. In contrast, the combination of dominance and affection produces the pet, the individual who is subordinate and whose survival depends on the whims of the more powerful. . . .

African-American women simultaneously embody the coexistence of the victim and the pet, with survival often linked to the ability to be appropriately subordinate. Black women's experiences as unpaid and paid workers demonstrate the harsh lives victims are forced to lead. While the life of the victim is difficult, pets experience a distinctive form of exploitation. . . . Pets are treated as exceptions and live with the constant threat that they will no longer be "perfect in his sight," that their owners will tire of them and relegate them to the unenviable role of victim.

Prostitution represents the fusion of exploitation for an economic purpose—namely, the commodification of Black women's sexuality—with the demeaning treatment afforded pets. Sex becomes commodified not merely in the sense that it can be purchased—the dimension of economic exploitation—but also in the sense that one is dealing with a totally alienated being who is separated from and who seemingly does not control her body: the dimension of power as domination (McNall 1983). Commodified sex can then be appropriated by the powerful. . . . Both pornography and prostitution commodify sexuality and imply . . . that all African-American women can be bought.

Prostitution under European and American capitalism thus exists within a complex web of political and economic relationships. Gilman's (1985) analysis of the exhibition of Sarah Bartmann as the "Hottentot Venus" suggests another intriguing connection between race, gender, and sexuality in nineteenth-century Europe—the linking of the icon of the Black woman with the icon of the White prostitute. While the Hottentot woman stood for the essence of Africans as a race, the White prostitute symbolized the sexualized woman. The prostitute represented the embodiment of sexuality and all that European society associated with it: disease as well as passion. . . . These connections between the icons of Black women and White prostitutes demonstrate the interdependence of race, gender, and sexuality in shaping European understandings of social class.

In the American antebellum South both of these images were fused in the forced prostitution of enslaved African women. The prostitution of Black women allowed White women to be the opposite; Black "whores" make White "virgins" possible. This race/gender nexus fostered a situation whereby White men could then differentiate between the sexualized woman-as-body who is dominated and "screwed" and the asexual woman-as-pure-spirit who is idealized and brought home to mother (Hoch 1979, 70). The sexually denigrated woman, whether she was made a victim through her rape or a pet through her seduction, could be used as the yardstick against which the cult of true womanhood was measured. Moreover, this entire situation was profitable.

The image of the lesbian can also be linked with that of the prostitute and with images of Black women as the embodiment of the Black "race." Christian notes that Black women writers broadened the physical image of lesbians: "The stereotypical body type of a black lesbian was that she looked mannish; . . . she was not so much a woman as much as she was a defective man, a description that has sometimes been applied to any Negroid-looking or uppity-acting black woman" (1985, 191). Note Christian's analysis of the links among gender, race, and sexuality. Lesbianism, an allegedly deviant sexual practice, becomes linked to biological markers of race and looking "mannish." These links also reinforce constructions of Black women's sexualities as deviant—the co-joining of Black heterosexual women's sexual deviancy as lying in their excess sexual appetite with the perceived deviancy of Black lesbians as lying in their rejection of what makes women feminine, namely, heterosexual contact with men.

### Rape and Sexual Violence

Force was important in creating African-American women's centrality to American images of the sexualized woman and in shaping their experiences with both pornography and prostitution. Black women did not willingly submit to their exhibition on Southern auction blocks—they were forced to do so. Enslaved African women could not choose whether to work—they were beaten and often killed if they refused. Black domestics who resisted the sexual advances of their employers often found themselves looking for work where none was to be found. Both the reality and the threat of violence have acted as a form of social control for African-American women (Collins 1998d).

Rape has been one fundamental tool of sexual violence directed against African-American women. . . . Rape and other acts of overt violence that Black women have experienced, such as physical assault during slavery, domestic abuse, incest, and sexual extortion, accompany Black women's subordination in intersecting oppressions. These violent acts are the visible dimensions of a more generalized, routinized system of oppression. Violence against Black women tends to be legitimated and therefore condoned while the same acts visited on other groups may remain nonlegitimated and non-excusable. Historically, this violence has garnered the backing and control of the state (James 1996). Specific acts of sexual violence visited on African-American women reflect a broader process by which violence is socially constructed in a race- and gender-specific manner. Thus Black women, Black men, and White women experience distinctive forms of sexual violence. As Angela Davis points out, "It would be a mistake to regard the institutionalized pattern of rape during slavery as an expression of white men's sexual urges. . . . Rape was a weapon of domination, a weapon of repression, whose covert goal was to extinguish slave women's will to resist, and in the process, to demoralize their men" (1981, 23).

Angela Davis's work (1978, 1981, 1989) illustrates this effort to conceptualize sexual violence against African-American women as a site of intersecting oppressions. Davis suggests that depicting African-American men as sexually charged beasts who desired White women created the myth of the Black rapist. Lynching emerged as the specific form of sexual violence visited on Black men, with the myth of the Black rapist as its ideological justification. The significance of this myth is that it "has been methodically conjured up when recurrent waves of violence and terror against the black community required a convincing explanation" (Davis 1978, 25). Black women experienced a parallel form of race- and gender-specific sexual violence. Treating African-American women as pornographic objects and portraying them as sexualized animals, as prostitutes, created the controlling image of jezebel. Rape became the specific act of sexual violence forced on Black women, with the myth of the Black prostitute as its ideological justification.

Lynching and rape, two race/gender-specific forms of sexual violence, merged with their ideological justifications of the rapist and prostitute in order to provide an effective system of social control over African-Americans. Davis asserts that the controlling image of Black men as rapists has always "strengthened its inseparable companion: the image of the black woman as chronically promiscuous. And with good reason, for once the notion is accepted that black men harbor irresistible, animal-like sexual urges, the entire race is invested with bestiality" (1978, 27). A race of "animals" can be treated as such—as victims or pets. "The mythical rapist implies the mythical whore—and a race of rapists and whores deserves punishment and nothing more" (Davis 1978, 28).

Black women continue to deal with this legacy of the sexual violence visited on African-Americans generally and with our history as collective rape victims. One effect lies in the treatment of rape victims. Such women are twice victimized, first by the actual rape, in this case the collective rape under slavery. But they are victimized again by family members, community residents, and social institutions such as criminal justice systems which somehow believe that rape victims are responsible for their own victimization. Even though current statistics indicate that

Black women are more likely to be victimized than White women, Black women are less likely to report their rapes, less likely to have their cases come to trial, less likely to have their trials result in convictions, and, most disturbing, less likely to seek counseling and other support services.

Another effect of this legacy of sexual violence concerns the significance of Black women's continued silences concerning rape. But Black women's silence about rape obscures an important issue: Most Black women [who are raped] are raped by Black men. While the historical legacy of the triad of pornography, prostitution, and the institutionalized rape of Black women may have created the larger social context within which all African-Americans reside, the unfortunate current reality is that many Black men have internalized the controlling images applied to Black women. Like Brother Marquis, they feel that if they as individuals do not rape women, they contribute little to the overall cultural climate that condones sexual violence. These beliefs allow them to ignore Black women's rape by other Black men, their own culpability in fostering Black women's objectification as pornographic objects, and, in some cases, their own behavior as rapists. For example, Black women and men often disagree as to whether Nola Darling, the sexually liberated heroine in Spike Lee's acclaimed film *She's Gotta Have It,* was raped. Men disbelieve Nola's protestations and see her protest as serving to heighten the sexual pleasure of her male partner. In contrast, many women see her reaction as typical for those of a rape victim. Recognizing that it is useless to protest, Nola Darling submits. Was Nola Darling raped? Do the sexual politics of Black womanhood that construct jezebels and "hoochies" have any grounding in reality? The answers to both questions may lie in who has the power to define.

## REFERENCES

Amott, Teresa L. 1990. "Black Women and AFDC: Making Entitlement Out of Necessity." In *Women, the State, and Welfare,* ed. Linda Gordon, 280–98. Madison: University of Wisconsin Press.

Bell, Laurie, ed. 1987. *Good Girls/Bad Girls: Feminists and Sex Trade Workers Face to Face.* Toronto: Seal Press.

Berry, Mary Frances. [1971] 1994. *Black Resistance, White Law: A History of Constitutional Racism in America.* New York: Penguin.

Christian, Barbara. 1985. *Black Feminist Criticism, Perspectives on Black Women Writers.* New York: Pergamon.

Clarke, Cheryl. 1983. "The Failure to Transform: Homophobia in the Black Community." In *Home Girls: A Black Feminist Anthology,* ed. Barbara Smith, 197–208. New York: Kitchen Table Press.

Collins, Patricia Hill. 1993. "It's in Our Hands: Breaking the Silence on Gender in African-American Studies." In *Understanding Curriculum as Racial Text,* ed. William F. Pinar and Louis Castenall, 127–41. Albany: SUNY Press.

———. 1998a. *Fighting Words: Black Women and the Search for Justice.* Minneapolis: University of Minnesota Press.

———. 1998d. "The Tie That Binds: Race, Gender and U.S. Violence." *Ethnic and Racial Studies* 21 (5): 918–38.

———. 1999. "Will the 'Real' Mother Please Stand Up?: The Logic of Eugenics and American National Family Planning." In *Revisioning Women, Health and Healing: Feminist, Cultural and Technoscience Perspectives,* ed. Adele Clarke and Virginia Olesen, 266–82. New York: Routledge.

Cowan, Gloria, and Robin R. Campbell. 1994. "Racism and Sexism in Interracial Pornography. *Psychology of Women Quarterly* 18: 323–38.

Crenshaw, Kimberle William. 1991. "Mapping the Margins: Intersectionality, Identity Politics, and Violence Against Women of Color." *Stanford Law Review* 43 (6): 1241–99.

Davenport, Doris. 1996. "Black Lesbians in Academia: Visible Invisibility." In *The New Lesbian Studies: Into the Twenty-First Century,* ed. Bonnie Zimmerman and Toni A. H. McNaron. New York: Feminist Press.

Davis, Angela Y. 1978. "Rape, Racism and the Capitalist Setting." *Black Scholar* 9(7): 24–30.

———. 1981. *Women, Race and Class.* New York: Random House.

———. 1989. *Women, Culture, and Politics.* New York: Random House.

D' Emilio, John, and Estelle Freedman. "Race and Sexuality." In *Intimate Matters. A History of Sexuality in America,* 85–108. New York: Harper and Row.

Dines, Gail. 1998. *Pornography: The Production and Consumption of Inequality.* New York: Routledge.

Ferber, Abby. 1998. *White Man Falling: Race, Gender, and White Supremacy.* Lantham, MD: Rowman & Littlefield.

Forna, Aminatta. 1992. "Pornography and Racism: Sexualizing Oppression and Inciting Hatred." In *Pornography: Women, Violence, and Civil Liberties,* ed. Catherine Itzin, 102–12. New York: Oxford University Press.

Giddings, Paula. 1992. "The Last Taboo." In *Race-ing Justice, En-gendering Power,* ed. Toni Morrison, 441–65. New York: Pantheon.

Gilman, Sander L. 1985. "Black Bodies, White Bodies: Toward an Iconography of Female Sexuality in Late Nineteenth-Century Art, Medicine, and Literature." *Critical Inquiry* 12 (1): 205–43.

Gomez, Jewell, and Barbara Smith. 1994. "Taking the Home Out of Homophobia: Black Lesbian Health." In *The Black Women's Health Book: Speaking for Ourselves,* ed. Evelyn C. White, 198–213, Seattle: Seal Press.

Hammonds, Evelynn M. 1997. "Toward a Genealogy of Black Female Sexuality: The Problematic of Silence." In *Feminist Genealogies; Colonial Legacies, Democratic Futures,* ed. M. Jacqui Alexander and Chandra Talpade Mohanty, 170–81. New York: Routledge.

Hartouni, Valerie. 1997. "Breached Birth: Anna Johnson and the Reproduction of Raced Bodies." In *Cultural Conceptions. On Reproductive Technologies and the Remaking of Life,* 85–98. Minneapolis: University of Minnesota Press

Hine, Darlene Clark. 1995. "For Pleasure, Profit, and Power: The Sexual Exploitation of Black Women." In *African American Women Speak Out on Anita Hill–Clarence Thomas,* ed. Geneva Smitherman, 168–77. Detroit: Wayne State University Press.

Hoch, Paul. 1979. *White Hero Black Beast: Racism, Sexism and the Mask of Masculinity.* London: Pluto Press.

Jackson, Stevi. 1996. "Heterosexuality and Feminist Theory." In *Theorising Heterosexuality,* ed. Diane Richardson, 21–38. Philadelphia: Open University Press.

James, Joy. 1996. *Resisting State Violence: Radicalism, Gender, and Race in U.S. Culture.* Minneapolis: University of Minnesota Press.

Jones, Lisa. 1994. *Bulletproof Diva: Tale of Race, Sex, and Hair.* New York: Anchor.

Kennedy, Elizabeth Lapovsky, and Madeline Davis. 1994. *Boots of Leather, Slippers of Gold: The History of a Lesbian Community.* New York: Penguin.

Lorde, Audre. 1982. Zami, *A New Spelling of My Name.* Trumansberg, NY: Crossing Press.

———. 1984. *Sister Outsider.* Trumansberg, NY: Crossing Press.

McNall, Scott G. 1983. "Pornography: The Structure of Domination and the Mode of Reproduction." In *Current Perspectives in Social Theory Volume 4,* ed. Scott McNall, 181–203. Greenwich, CT: JAI Press.

Moore, Lisa C., ed. 1997. *Does Your Mama Know? An Anthology of Black Lesbian Coming Out Stories.* Decatur: Red Bone Press.

Omolade, Barbara. 1994. *The Rising Song of African American Women.* New York: Routledge.

Richardson, Diane. 1996. "Heterosexuality and Social Theory." In *Theorising Heterosexuality,* ed. Diane Richardson, 1–20. Philadelphia: Open University Press.

Roberts, Dorothy. 1997. *Killing the Black Body: Race, Reproduction, and the Meaning of Liberty.* New York: Pantheon.

Russell, Diane E. H. 1993. *Against Pornography: The Evidence of Harm.* Berkeley: Russell Publications

*She's Gotta Have It.* 1986. Directed by Spike Lee. 40 Acres and a Mule Filmworks.

Shockley, Ann Allen. 1974. *Loving Her.* Tallahassee, FL: Naiad Press.

———. 1983. "The Black Lesbian in American Literature: An Overview." In *Home Girls: A Black Feminist Anthology,* ed. Barbara Smith, 83–93. New York: Kitchen Table Press.

Smith, Barbara. 1982. "Toward a Black Feminist Criticism." In *But Some of Us Are Brave,* ed. Gloria T. Hull, Patricia Bell Scott, and Barbara Smith, 157–75. Old Westbury, NY: Feminist Press.

———. 1983. "Introduction." In *Home Girls: A Black Feminist Anthology,* ed. Barbara Smith, xix–lvi. New York: Kitchen Table Press.

———. 1998. *The Truth That Never Hurts: Writings on Race, Gender and Freedom.* New Brunswick: Rutgers University Press.

Tuan, Yi-Fu. 1984. *Dominance and Affection: The Making of Pets.* New Haven, CT: Yale University Press.

2 Live Crew. 1995. "Hoochie Mama." Friday Original Soundtrack: Priority Records.

Walker, Alice. 1988. *Living by the Word.* New York: Harcourt Brace Jovanovich.

Williams, Rhonda. 1997. "Living at the Crossroads: Explorations in Race, Nationality, Sexuality, and Gender." In *The House That Race Built: Black Americans, U.S. Terrain,* ed. Wahneema Lubiano, 136–56. New York: Pantheon.

# Slut! Insult of Insults

**Leora Tanenbaum**

Women living in the United States are fortunate indeed. Unlike women living in Muslim countries, who are beaten and murdered for the appearance of sexual impropriety, we enjoy enormous sexual freedom.[1] Yet even we are routinely evaluated and punished for our sexuality. In 1991, Karen Carter, a twenty-eight-year-old single mother, lost custody of her two-year-old daughter in a chain of events that began when she called a social service hot line to ask if it's normal to feel sexual arousal while breast feeding. Carter was charged with sexual abuse in the first degree, even though her daughter showed no signs of abuse; when she revealed in court that she had had a lifetime total of eight (adult male) lovers, her own lawyer referred to her "sexual promiscuity."[2] In 1993, when New Mexico reporter Tamar Stieber filed a sex discrimination lawsuit against the newspaper where she worked because she was earning substantially less than men in similar positions, defense attorneys deposed her former lover to ask him how often they'd had sex.[3] In the 1997 sexual-harassment lawsuits against Mitsubishi Motor Manufacturing, a company lawyer asked for the gynecological records of twenty-nine women employees charging harassment, and wanted the right to distribute them to company executives.[4] And in 1997 a North Carolina woman sued her husband's secretary for breaking up their nineteen-year-marriage and was awarded $1 million in damages by a jury. During the seven-day trial the secretary was described as a "matronly" woman who deliberately began wearing heavy makeup and short skirts in order to entice the husband into an affair.[5]

It's amazing but true: Even today a common way to damage a woman's credibility is to call her a slut. Look at former CIA station chief Janine Brookner, who was falsely accused of being a drunken "slut" after she reprimanded several corrupt colleagues in the early 1990s.[6] Consider Anita Hill, whose accusation that Clarence Thomas sexually harassed her was dismissed by the Senate because, in the memorable words of journalist David Brock, she was "a bit nutty and a bit slutty."[7] Clearly, slut-bashing is not confined to the teenage years.

Nor is it a new phenomenon. If anything, it is the continuation of an old tradition. For girls who came of age in the 1950s, the fear of being called a slut ruled their lives. In that decade, "good" girls strained to give the appearance that they were dodging sex until marriage. "Bad" girls—who failed to be discreet, whose dates bragged, who couldn't get their dates to stop—were dismissed as trashy "sluts." Even after she had graduated from high school, a young woman knew that submitting to sexual passion meant facing the risk of unwed pregnancy, which would bar her entrée to the social respectability of the college-educated middle class. And so, in addition to donning cashmere sweater sets and poodle skirts, the 1950s "good" girl also had to hone the tricky talent of doling out enough sexual preliminaries to keep her dates interested while simultaneously exerting enough sexual control to stop before the point of no return: intercourse. The twin fears of pregnancy and loss of middle-class respectability kept her desires in check. The protagonist of Alix Kates Shulman's novel *Memoirs of an Ex-Prom Queen* summed up the prevailing attitude: "Between me and Joey already one thing had led to another—kissing had led to French kissing, French kissing to necking, necking to petting, petting to bare-titting, bare-titting to dry humping—but somehow, thank God, I had always managed to stop at that penultimate step."[8]

No wonder that obtaining a reputation was even more frightening than becoming pregnant. An unwanted pregnancy could be taken care of—somehow, somewhere. A reputation, however, was an indelible stamp. "Steve's finger in my cunt felt good," reminisced Erica Jong's alter ego, Isadora Wing, about her 1950s high school boyfriend in *Fear of Flying.* "At the same time, I knew that soft, mushy feeling to be the enemy. If I yielded to that feeling, it would be goodbye to all the other things I wanted. 'You have to choose,' I told myself sternly at fourteen. Get thee to a nunnery. So, like all good nuns, I masturbated . . . at fourteen all I could see were the disadvantages of being a woman. . . . All I could see was the swindle of being a woman."[9] The maneuvering was so delicate that pretty girls, the ones most sought after by the boys, sometimes secretly wished they were ugly just to avoid the dilemma altogether.

In the realm of sexual choices we are light-years beyond the 1950s. Today a teenage girl can explore her sexuality without getting married, and most do. By age eighteen over half of all girls and nearly three quarters of all boys have had intercourse at least once.[10] Yet at the same time, a fifties-era attitude lingers: Teens today are fairly conservative about sex. A 1998 *New York Times/ CBS News* poll of a thousand teens found that 53 percent of girls believe that sex before marriage is "always wrong," while 41 percent of boys agree.[11] Teens may be having sex, but they also look down on others, especially girls, who are sexually active. Despite the sexual revolution, despite three decades of feminism, despite the Pill, and despite legalized abortion, teenage girls today continue to

be defined by their sexuality. The sexual double standard—and the division between "good" girls and "bad" or "slutty" ones—is alive and well. Some of the rules have changed, but the playing field is startlingly similar to that of the 1950s.

Skeptical? Just take a look at teenage pop culture. On the TV show *Dawson's Creek,* which chronicles the lives of four hip, painfully self-aware teens, an episode is devoted to Dawson's discovery that his girlfriend Jen is not only not a virgin, she's had sex with a number of guys. Dawson is both disappointed and disapproving, and before long the relationship ends. An ad for Converse sneakers, appearing in a 1995 issue of *Seventeen,* depicts two girls, one white and the other black, sharing self-satisfied smirks as a busty girl in a short, tight dress lingers nearby. The caption reads, "Carla and Rachel considered themselves open-minded, nonjudgmental people. Although they did agree Brenda was a tramp." In the 1996 movie *Jerry Maguire* you just know that Tom Cruise's girlfriend is a good-for-nothing tramp the moment you lay eyes on her: She makes her first appearance in a torrid, sweaty sex scene. (If it were a horror movie, she'd be murdered within ten minutes.) Indeed, her heartlessness is later revealed when she berates Cruise for allowing conscience rather than greed to guide his career as a sports agent.

But forget about make-believe characters in TV shows, ads, and movies: real life has enough examples. In Kentucky in 1998, two high school students were denied membership in the National Honor Society because they were pregnant—even though boys who engaged in premarital sex faced no such exclusion.[12] One Georgia teen wrote anxiously to *Seventeen:* "A few months ago, when my mom saw me hugging my boyfriend outside my house, she called me a slut and said we were 'putting on a show for the whole neighborhood.' I've never been so hurt in my life. I had done nothing to be called such an awful word other than display affection for someone I love very much. The word 'slut' doesn't need a definition; it needs to be abolished."[13]

Teenage model Jamie Messenger sued *YM* magazine for $17.5 million because the magazine ran her photo, without her permission, alongside an advice-column letter that had no connection to her. The headline was I GOT TRASHED AND HAD SEX WITH THREE GUYS. After the magazine's two million readers received their issue in the mail, Messenger got a quick course in slut-bashing. The football team bet on who would sleep with her first; her best friend's parents wouldn't allow their daughter to visit anymore. Her brother was caught in a fight after someone called the model a whore. "She wanted to go to the prom, she wanted to go to the homecoming," her mother said. "She wanted to be part of that. But unfortunately, she couldn't."[14]

Jamie Messenger isn't the only girl who has turned to the courts. A number of high school students around the country have sued their school districts for sexual harassment because teachers and administrators allowed slut-bashing to flourish. In 1996 alone there were three well-publicized cases, all involving junior high school students. In upstate New York, Eve Bruneau was called "whore" and "dog-faced bitch" by the boys in her sixth-grade class and became so depressed that she transferred schools; her harassment complaint against the South Kortright School District was rejected.[15] But Tianna Ugarte, a fourteen-year-old girl living near San Francisco, won a $500,000 award from a jury that found school officials had ignored her complaints of verbal abuse from a male sixth-grade classmate.[16] And in another northern California case, a girl identified only as Jane Doe from Petaluma won a settlement of $250,000 because the faculty at Kenilworth Junior High did nothing to stop students from hounding her for a year and a half with rumors that she had sex with hot dogs. (It got so bad that one day a boy felt free to stand up in class and say, "I have a question. I want to know if Jane Doe has sex with hot dogs.")[17]

In 1988, educators Janie Victoria Ward and Jill McLean Taylor surveyed Massachusetts teenagers across six different ethnic groups—black, white,

Hispanic, Haitian, Vietnamese, and Portuguese—and found that the different groups upheld different sexual values. But one thing was universal: The sexual double standard. Regardless of race or ethnicity, "boys were generally allowed more freedom and were assumed to be more sexually active than girls." Ward and Taylor found that "sexual activity for adolescent males usually met cultural expectations and was generally accepted by adults and peers as part of normal male adolescence. . . . In general, women are often seen in terms of their sexual reputation rather than in terms of their personal characteristics."[18]

The double standard, we know, does not vaporize after high school. Sociologist Lillian Rubin surveyed six hundred students in eight colleges around the country in the late 1980s and found that 40 percent of the sexually active women said that they routinely understate their sexual experience because "my boyfriend wouldn't like it if he knew," "people wouldn't understand," and "I don't want him to think I'm a slut." Indeed, these women had reason to be concerned. When Rubin queried the men about what they expected of the women they might marry, over half said that they would not want to marry a woman who had been "around the block too many times," that they were looking for someone who didn't "sleep around," and that a woman who did was a "slut."[19]

Similarly when sex researcher Shere Hite surveyed over 2,500 college men and women, 92 percent of the men claimed that the double standard was unfair. Yet overwhelmingly they themselves upheld it. When asked, "If you met a woman you liked and wanted to date, but then found out she had had sex with ten to twenty men during the preceding year, would you still like her and take her seriously?," 65 percent of the men admitted that they would not take her seriously. At the same time only 5 percent said they would lose respect if a male friend had had sex with ten to twenty women in one year.[20]

Teenage girls who are called sluts today experience slut-bashing at its worst. Caught between the conflicting pressures to have sex and maintain a "good" reputation, they are damned when they do and damned when they don't. Boys and girls both are encouraged to have sex in the teen years—by their friends, magazines, and rock and rap lyrics—yet boys alone can get away with it. "There's no way that anyone who talks to girls thinks that there's a new sexual revolution out there for teenagers," sums up Deborah Tolman, a developmental psychologist at the Wellesley College Center for Research on Women. "It's the old system very much in place." It is the old system, but with a twist: Today's teenage girls have grown up after the feminist movement of the late 1960s and 1970s. They have been told their whole lives that they can, and should, do anything that boys do. But soon enough they discover that sexual equality has not arrived. Certain things continue to be the privilege of boys alone.

With this power imbalance, it's no wonder high school girls report feeling less comfortable with their sexual experiences than their male counterparts do. While 81 percent of adolescent boys say that "sex is a pleasurable experience," only 59 percent of girls feel the same way.[21] The statistical difference speaks volumes. Boys and girls both succumb to early sex due to peer and media pressures, but boys still get away with it while girls don't.

## Who Gets Picked On

Girls who are singled out for being "sluts" are by no means a monolithic group. And contrary to what most people think of when they visualize a "slut," many have no more sexual experience than their peers do, and some have no sexual experience at all. Whether or not a girl is targeted because of her sexual behavior, the effect is nonetheless to police her sexuality.

### "She's So Loose": The Sexual Girl

One type of girl is picked on because she appears to flaunt a casual attitude about sexuality: She is either sexually active or is perceived to be sexually active.

Pamela Spring, from Massachusetts, was a sexual girl who was taught a lesson. When she was discovered to have had intercourse with two different boys the summer before ninth grade, a girl on the basketball team called her over during lunch. "Pam," she asked before a packed table, "did you fuck Andy and John?" Everyone laughed. People talked about her in school and at parties. When she was a senior, someone spray-painted "Pam is a slut" on the school building.

On the other end of the spectrum, some girls who aren't sexually active at all are presumed to be so because of their physique. When everyone else in the class is wearing training bras, the girl with breasts becomes an object of sexual scrutiny. Yet when boys develop early, they are not similarly stigmatized. A girl with visible breasts becomes sexualized because she possesses a constant physical reminder of her sexual potential, whereas height, the marker of boys' development, does not carry sexual meanings, notes sociologist Barrie Thorne.[22] (Boys generally don't develop in build or grow facial hair until they're in high school.) In other words, a girl can become known as possessing a sexual persona simply because of the way she looks, not the way she behaves.

Eighteen-year-old Paula Pinczewski, from northwestern Wisconsin, got her period in the fifth grade and by seventh grade wore a 36C. In eighth grade, classmates called Paula, a virgin, a "five-cent whore," "hooker," and "slut." They took her notebook and wrote things in it like, "You're not worth shit" and "You're a bitch." "If I didn't get one of my daily insults," Paula tells me, "it was not worthy of being a school day." For her part, Julie, the girl who was raped when she passed out from drinking, was singled out as a "slut," she suspects, "because I was chesty. I was wearing a C bra in ninth grade. Even my girlfriends would make comments about my chest. It made the stories about me easier to believe. I fit into a stereotype."

### *"She Asked for It": The Raped Girl*

I never expected to find so many "sluts" who had been raped or attempted-raped. In fact, when I first thought about why certain girls might be singled out as "sluts," the issue of sexual coercion did not occur to me, nor did I ask a single interviewee if she had been assaulted or raped. And yet over and over again my interviewees volunteered that they had been raped by a date, acquaintance, or stranger, or that the boys in school assumed they were "easy" and therefore gang-raped or tried to gang-rape them. (Others mentioned that they had been sexually abused by a relative or baby-sitter.) Not one reported her assault to the police or school.

The parenthetical way some of the girls and women told me these stories made me wonder how reliable rape statistics are, especially for teenagers. According to a 1997 Commonwealth Fund survey, one in five high school girls has been physically or sexually abused, with nearly one in ten of the older girls reporting abuse by a date or boyfriend.[23] But I wouldn't be surprised if the real numbers are much higher. The fact is that most people refuse to believe that a teenage girl has been raped, especially if she knows her attacker. They assume that the sex was consensual, not forced.

The "slut" reputation protects rapists because it makes the victims believe that they are partly to blame. Julie, for instance, did not press charges against her rapist. "I knew no one would believe me," she explained to me. "And I didn't want to tell my parents because they'd be mad that I was out drinking." She did confide in a few of the girls at school, but as expected, they thought she was making the rape up. "They felt, 'Oh, she's just saying it because she has a bad reputation.'"

Two of Julie's friends heard from another friend that the sex was in reality a rape. But Julie sensed that they didn't really believe it. "They never came out and said they thought I was lying, but if we'd be talking about past boyfriends, they would bring up the rapist's name, as if he were a boyfriend. In their minds they believed the ru-

mors. My friend Liz, who had seen me passed out, would stand by me in those cases. She was like, 'Well, that was a different situation; Julie couldn't help that. She was raped.' But the group always liked to have someone to make fun of, and I was the butt of jokes at times. Even though they were my friends, it stopped being funny."

### *"Not One of Us": The Outsider*

Adolescents label everybody. When they are confronted with someone who doesn't fit their idea of how a girl should act or look, they grasp for an insulting label. Typically the girl with the "slut" reputation fails to conform in some way. "Slut" becomes an insult like any other, with sexual implications thrown in for added measure.

Jaclyn Geller is a tall, striking-looking woman with defined cheekbones and penetrating blue-green eyes. Born in 1963, she is currently an essayist and doctoral candidate in English literature. She was called a "slut" in junior high. "I didn't have sexual relations with people aside from playing Spin the Bottle," she says, "so I knew it was a crazy thing." Jaclyn was taller and older-looking than the other kids. She read books while everyone else went to football games. She always sensed that somehow she was different.

Jaclyn grew up in the leafy suburb of Scarsdale, New York, where "popularity did not necessarily mean wealth—everyone was affluent. Popularity meant conformity." During the seventh grade, boys called her a slut when she walked down the halls. The jokes turned into violence when she was in the eighth grade walking to the cafeteria: Five boys pushed her down on the ground and climbed on top of her; Jaclyn had to fight them off. They were all boys who lived in her neighborhood.

Janice, now thirty-six, was a new student when she entered seventh grade: her father was in the military and the family had just moved to town. Almost immediately the boys in her Illinois junior high school started a rumor that she stuffed her bra. "I was very embarrassed. I changed my seat to get away from the boys who were talking about me, but my teacher made me go back.

When my mother found out, she said, 'Don't you care about your reputation?'" This was already her third school, and in eighth grade she moved again. Each time she was a new student, the boys looked her over. Even though Janice was not sexually active, the boys reinforced the idea that she had no right to be sexual. Janice began to hunch her shoulders and wear a coat whenever possible. "I never really felt comfortable with my body," she says. "To this day I don't like people to hug me or feel my body."

### Girls Slut-Bashing Girls

A refrain throughout the interviews was how cruel girls could be. Nearly every "slut" told me that girls either had engineered the ostracism themselves or were more hurtful than boys. In some cases a girl spread a rumor about another girl whom she envied or resented.

Janet Jones, twenty-four, has radiant brown skin and deep brown eyes. In her South Carolina high school, she was captain of the cheerleading squad. "I don't mean to sound conceited," says Janet, now a student at a black women's college in Atlanta. "My immediate friends in my circle—I ain't gonna say they weren't *as* attractive—but they weren't. And girls can be extremely vengeful and extremely jealous when it comes to things like that. Friends that I thought were friends turned out not to be at all. That was my first important lesson in life. I found out that people I thought I could count on would turn on me."

One Sunday, Janet spent the afternoon with a close male friend, talking and hanging out. The next day everyone was buzzing about how the two of them had slept together. "What really hurt is that no one came back to me and asked me, 'Janet, is this true?' They just accepted it." It was girls, not boys, who made the rest of her high school years miserable. Even her best friend from elementary school stopped talking to her.

Boys and girls both can inflict emotional harm, but when girls are involved, the harassment tends to become more personal. Julie, the girl who was raped, says that it hurt more when girls judged

her than when guys did. "If a girl gets a reputation and then does something that gets on another girl's nerves, that girl is going to immediately mention the reputation. Like, 'Not only did she do better than me on that test but she's also a slut.'"

Because girls rather than boys are often on the front lines of slut-bashing, teachers rarely identify the behavior as a form of sexual harassment. Americans seem to care more about harassment when it involves a male and female than when both harasser and victim are the same gender. Yet, as we will see, girls can bring enormous pain to other girls, leading them to engage in a number of self-destructive behaviors. . . .

### Shame

Public humiliation is in vogue. Former independent Whitewater Counsel Kenneth Starr publicized all the details of Bill Clinton's sexual affair with Monica Lewinsky, it seems, mainly to embarrass the president. When a thirty-six-year-old Dallas woman was arrested recently for stealing three cartons of cigarettes, she was given a "shaming sentence": Judge Ted Poe of the 228th State District ordered her to stand before a supermarket carrying a sign reading, "I Stole From This Store. Do Not Steal! This Could Be You!" Judge Poe has similarly required welfare cheats to take out ads in local newspapers detailing their frauds.[24] In La Mesa, California, men convicted of soliciting prostitutes find their names and photos published in *The Daily Californian,* right next to the winning lottery numbers.[25] And in Kansas City, the television show *John TV* broadcasts on cable the names, mug shots, birth dates, and hometowns of men arrested for trying to buy sex and of women arrested for trying to sell it. The show is so popular that it runs four times every Wednesday.[26]. . .

In 1995 [Newt] Gingrich, then Speaker of the House, declared that he wanted to institute the public stigmatization of sexually active, unwed girls. Gingrich told Congress that in Victorian

England "they reduced the number of children born out of wedlock by almost 50 percent. They changed the whole momentum of their society. They didn't do it through a new bureaucracy. They did it by reestablishing values, by moral leadership, and by being willing to look at people in the face and say, 'You should be ashamed when you get drunk in public; you ought to be ashamed if you're a drug addict.' "[27]

But even without the intervention of Congress, girls who are sexually active (or believed to be sexually active) are disgraced every day. The "slut" label makes them feel very ashamed indeed. Over and over, girls and women told me about the disgust, guilt, and squeamishness they felt about sex for years. Some adult women, former "sluts," continue to feel uncomfortable with sex to this day. . . .

Abstaining from sex, hitting the books, and wearing loose-fitting clothes are common ways that girls try to molt their "slutty" image. But more often their shame leads them to self-destructive behavior. They become willing to do things that they wouldn't have dreamed of doing before they were scandalized because they now feel they have so little to offer. Some girls do drugs or drink to excess in an attempt to blot away their stigma. Others become depressed and anorexic. And others think so little of themselves that they date boys who insult or beat them.

Carmen, the daughter of Ecuadorian immigrants, felt it was important to study hard and be a "good" girl to make her parents proud. But in her school's hierarchy of popularity, her honor-student image placed her squarely at the bottom. She felt like an outsider. Longing both to fit in and let loose, she went on her school's senior ski trip in Vermont, intending to get drunk and fool around with the boys. Her best friend helped her pour vodka into empty shampoo bottles so that she wouldn't get caught. Over the course of the weekend, she did indeed get very drunk. And while she was still a virgin when she returned home, she had experimented sexually with several different classmates.

Back in school Monday morning, everybody was talking. "Behind my back I was called a slut and a sex maniac," she remembers. One classmate boasted that he had "fucked Carmen four times" the night before. The story spun so much out of control that Carmen was rumored to have had two abortions. Miserable and ashamed, she began to drink regularly, smoke, and cut classes. She failed two classes that semester.

Carla Karampatos, a high school senior in the Northeast, was always made fun of because of her Greek name and complexion. In seventh grade the girls seethed with resentment when twelfth-grade boys called Carla cute. When she turned down the advances of a tenth-grade boy, he called her a slut, an insult that pleased the girls. Before long the girls were picking fights with her. In the beginning of eleventh grade, Carla was so despondent that she ingested an entire bottle of sleeping pills. She would have died if her mother hadn't found her on the kitchen floor and rushed her to the hospital, where her stomach was pumped.

Jackie Garcia, twenty-four, was called a slut by black girls at her Queens public high school who were jealous that all the black guys liked her, a Latina. Even though she was not sexually active, girls broke into her gym locker and wrote "Jackie is a ho" on the cafeteria walls and in the girls' bathrooms. In response, Jackie stopped eating and lost twenty-five pounds. She explains that she was trying to reduce the size of her bust. (It didn't work.)

Julie dated guys who abused her emotionally and physically. "Like I was with one guy who used to hit me, and like I let him do it for a while. I was with him for four months. Eventually I was like, forget it. It wasn't fun always being on guard. I started to not see him as much, and then I just stopped. I always kind of assumed, 'I have this horrible reputation, I'm never going to get away from it, so I don't really have a choice about whether or not a guy treats me badly,' " she explains. Then she dated a guy who cheated on her. "I was definitely attracted to men who treated me badly, maybe because I thought I didn't deserve any better. Even in the relationship I'm in now, which is really good, there have been times where I've been like, 'Oh, I don't deserve you, you're too nice to me.'"

### Strength

While many girls crumble, some muster their strength to defy the slut label. Faced with rejection by their peers, they in turn reject the values of their peers. They come to believe that being known as a slut may not be so bad after all; it may even have liberating possibilities. These girls flaunt a proud, rebellious persona. Their attitude is: Why not flee the suffocation of conformity? Why not show everyone that being "good" is a farce? Why not be "bad"—and have fun with it?

"I'm a lot stronger now," says Paula Pinczewski, the young woman from Wisconsin who was called a "five-cent whore" in the eighth grade because of her breasts. "I can stand up for myself now where I couldn't before. If somebody stares at me, I think 'Go ahead, stare.' If somebody throws an insult my way, I'll throw one right back. I wear whatever I want to wear—clothes that are as baggy or as sexy as I want. I even dressed up as a Playboy bunny for Halloween last year, with the little tail."

Susan Houseman, thirty-one, reports that being known as a slut gave her the freedom to have a lesbian relationship during her senior year of high school—something she never would have had the courage to do, at least at that age, had she stayed on course as a "good" girl. After graduation, instead of getting married right away as many of her classmates did, Susan traveled for a few years before going to college.

Because of her own reputation, Janet Jones, the cheerleader from South Carolina, decided to go to college four and a half hours away from home, to start fresh without any of her highschool classmates. She was able to escape her small town, where "no one had any long-term goals. Everyone just wanted to stay there and do the same old thing. I felt like I grew up, but no one else did. So maybe the reputation stuff was a blessing in disguise."

None of the "sluts" I interviewed is a victim. Every one went through a painful experience, but each ultimately turned her experience into a positive thing. Having a "slut" reputation sharpened her thinking, gave her a sense of perspective about gender roles, and made her acutely aware of the small-mindedness of the sexual double standard. . . .

To tell you the truth, I began this book embarrassed about my research into slut-bashing. Whenever someone asked me what I was working on, I mumbled something vague about "sexual harassment" or "teen sexuality" without offering any specifics. This was a deliberate tactic: if I volunteered that I was writing about slut-bashing, inevitably, I knew, I would be asked how I became interested in the subject, and eventually I would be cornered into admitting that, yes, I was a high school "slut." But I've become an eager, sometimes almost Oprah-esque, confessor. I have come to appreciate the experience I went through. I have learned that once a person is labeled anything, she becomes a caricature rather than a full-fledged human being with both talents and flaws. I have learned about the subtleties of emotional cruelty and the enormities of biological difference. And I discovered all this with the help of girls and women around the country who shared their own experiences with me. Their strength proved to me that it's those who use the insult "slut" who should be embarrassed, not us. Definitely not us.

**NOTES**

1. In Jordan in 1993 a sixteen-year-old girl who had been raped by her older brother was killed by her family because, it was said, she had seduced him into sleeping with her. Kristen Golden, "Rana Husseini: A Voice for Justice," *Ms.*, July/August 1998, p. 36; Tali Edut, "Global Woman: Rana Husseini," *HUES*, Summer 1998, p. 41. In Afghanistan, where women must remain covered from head to toe in shrouds called

*burqas,* the General Department for the Preservation of Virtue and Prevention of Vice beats women for wearing white socks or plastic sandals with no socks, attire that is said to provoke "impure thoughts" in men. John F. Burns, "Sex and the Afghan Woman: Islam's Straitjacket," *The New York Times,* August 29, 1997, p. A4. And in Turkey in 1998 five girls attempted suicide by eating rat poison and jumping into a water tank to avoid a forced virginity examination. An unmarried woman discovered not to be a virgin risks being beaten or killed. The virginity tests were carried out as the girls recovered in their hospital beds; when one girl did succeed in killing herself, her father had the exam performed on her corpse. Kelly Couturier, "Suicide Attempts Fuel Virginity Test Debate," *The Washington Post,* January 27, 1998, p. A18.

2. Lauri Umansky, "Breastfeeding in the 1990s: The Karen Carter Case and the Politics of Maternal Sexuality" in Molly Ladd-Taylor and Lauri Umansky, eds., *"Bad" Mothers: The Politics of Blame in Twentieth-Century America* (New York: New York University Press, 1998), pp. 299–309. Karen Carter is a pseudonym.

3. Tamar Stieber, "Viewpoint," *Glamour,* August 1996, p. 138.

4. Stieber, p. 138.

5. Jon Jeter, "Woman Who Sued Ex-Husband's Mistress Is Awarded $1 Million," *The Washington Post,* August 7, 1997, p. A3.

6. Tim Weiner, "C. I. A. to Pay $410,000 to Spy Who Says She Was Smeared," *The New York Times,* December 8, 1994, p. A1; Tim Weiner, "Woman Who Was C. I. A. Chief Requests Criminal Investigation," *The New York Times,* July 18, 1995.

7. David Brock, "The Real Anita Hill," *The American Spectator,* March 1992, p. 27.

8. Alix Kates Shulman, *Memoirs of an Ex-Prom Queen* (Chicago: Cassandra Editions, 1985; first published 1972), p. 61.

9. Erica Jong, *Fear of Flying* (New York: New American Library, 1973), pp. 156–157.

10. *Sex and America's Teenagers* (New York and Washington: The Alan Guttmacher Institute, 1994), p. 20.

11. Laurie Goodstein with Marjorie Connelly, "Teen-Age Poll Finds a Turn to the Traditional," *The New York Times,* April 30, 1998, p. A20. The poll, of 1,048 teenagers ages thirteen to seventeen, was conducted by telephone in April 1998. The poll also found that only 18 percent of thirteen- to fifteen-year-olds said they had ever had sex, as against 38 percent of sixteen- and seventeen-year-olds.

12. Ethan Bronner, "Lawsuit on Sex Bias by 2 Mothers, 17," *The New York Times,* August 6, 1998, p. A14. A year later, however, after the American Civil Liberties Union sued on the students' behalf, the society was ordered to accept them. Michael Pollak, "Honored, a Year Later," *The New York Times,* May 19, 1999, p. C30.

13. "All in a Name" (Letters page), *Seventeen,* November 1995, p. 12.

14. Lorne Manly, "Off the Record," *The New York Observer,* June 23, 1997. (Messenger was ultimately awarded $100,000 by a jury that found that *YM* was "grossly irresponsible" for using the photo without "valid consent."—Greg B. Smith, " 'Trashed' Model Wins Mag to Cough Up $100,000," New York *Daily News,* March 28, 1998, p. 6.)

15. Tamar Lewin, "Kissing Cases Highlight Schools' Fears of Liability for Sexual Harassment," *The New York Times,* October 6, 1996; David Stout, "Schoolgirl's Harassment Complaint is Rejected," *The New York Times,* November 22, 1996.

16. "Girl, 14, Wins Case Charging Sex Harassment" (AP), *The New York Times,* October 4, 1996.

17. "School District in California Settles Sex Harassment Suit," *The New York Times,* December 27, 1996, p. A24; Tamar Lewin, "Students Seeking Damages for Sex Bias," *The New York Times,* July 15, 1994, p. B7.

18. Janie Victoria Ward and Jill McLean Taylor, "Sexuality Education for Immigrant and Minority Students: Developing a Culturally Appropriate Curriculum," in Janice M. Irvine, *Sexual Cultures and the Construction of Adolescent Identities* (Philadelphia: Temple University Press, 1994), p. 63.

19. Lillian B. Rubin, *Erotic Wars: What Happened to the Sexual Revolution?* (New York: HarperPerennial, 1991), p. 119.

20. Shere Hite, *Women and Love* (New York: St. Martin's Press, 1987), p. 205.

21. Tamar Lewin, "Boys Are More Comfortable With Sex Than Girls Are, Survey Finds," *The New York Times,* May 18, 1994.

22. Barrie Thorne, *Gender Play: Girls and Boys in School* (New Brunswick, NJ.: Rutgers University Press, 1993), p. 141.

23. The Commonwealth Fund Survey of the Health of Adolescent Girls, Washington, D.C., September 30, 1997. The survey included 6,748 girls and boys in grades 5 through 12 in public, private, and parochial schools.

24. Jennifer Wolff, "Named and Shamed," *Marie Claire*, March 1998, pp. 108–112.

25. Jonathan Alter and Pat Wingert, "The Return of Shame," *Newsweek*, February 6, 1995, p. 24.

26. Pam Belluck, "Forget Prisons. Americans Cry Out for the Pillory," *The New York Times*, October 4, 1998, Week in Review p. 5.

27. Katharine Q. Seelye, "Gingrich Looks to Victorian Age to Cure Today's Social Failings," *The New York Times*, March 14, 1995.

# In the Closet

Steven Seidman

Heterosexual domination may have a long history, but the closet does not.[1] As I use the term, the closet will refer to a life-shaping pattern of homosexual concealment. To be in the closet means that individuals hide their homosexuality in the most important areas of life, with family, friends, and at work. Individuals may marry or avoid certain jobs in order to avoid suspicion and exposure. It is the power of the closet to shape the core of an individual's life that has made homosexuality into a significant personal, social, and political drama in twentieth-century America.

The closet may have existed prior to the 1950s, but it was only in the postwar years that it became a fact of life for many gay people.[2] At this time, there occurred a heightened level of *deliberateness and aggressiveness* in enforcing heterosexual dominance. A national campaign against homosexuality grew to an almost feverish pitch in the 1950s and 1960s. . . .

The attack on gays accompanied their social visibility. After the war years, many gay individuals moved to cities where they expected to find other people like themselves and at least enough tolerance to put together something like a gay life. My sense is that gay visibility was less the cause than the justification of an anti-gay campaign. A growing public homosexual menace was invoked to fuel an atmosphere of social panic and a hateful politic. But why the panic around homosexuality?

Despite popular images of domestic tranquility on television and in the movies, the 1950s and early 1960s was a period of great anxiety for many Americans.[3] There was a feeling of change in the air that evoked new hopes as well as new dangers. For example, as the war ended America emerged as a true superpower. However, it now faced what many considered to be a growing Soviet threat. Hysteria around the red scare narrowed social tolerance. Dissent and nonconventional lifestyles were associated with political subversion. Communists and homosexuals were sometimes viewed as parallel threats to "the American way of life." As invisible, corrupting forces seducing youth, spreading perversion and moral laxity, and weakening our national will, communists and homosexuals were to be identified and ruthlessly suppressed. And ruthlessly suppressed they were.[4]

Moreover, though the war was over and America was victorious, this nation was changing in ways that were troubling to many of its citizens. For example, women now had some real choices. Their social independence during the war gave many women a sense of having options; some wanted only to return to being wives and mothers, but others wished to pursue a career or remain single. Set against the happy homemaker on television shows such as *I Love Lucy, Leave It to Beaver,* and *Ozzie and Harriet* was the "new woman" in *Cosmopolitan* or Helen Gurly Brown's *Sex and the Single Girl*. The Cosmo girl may have been heterosexual, but she was also educated, career-minded, and sexy.

Men were also restless. During the war they had been exposed to different types of people, places, and ideas. While many men wanted little more than a job, wife, and a home, the world they returned to offered them many choices—a bounty of well-paying jobs, free higher education, and "good" women who did not necessarily believe that sex had to lead to marriage. Hugh Hefner's playboy lifestyle may not have expressed men's actual lives, but it tapped into a reality and a wish for expanded sexual choice.

It was not just adults who were restless. There was a growing population of young people who were becoming downright unruly. The popularity of rock 'n' roll expressed something of their restless spirit. Many young people wished to fashion lives that expressed their individual desires and wants rather than the social scripts of their parents and society. The panic over "juvenile delinquents" and "loose girls" expressed Americans' fears that the family, church, and neighborhood community had lost control of their youth.

So, while changes in the postwar period created a sense of expanded choice for many Americans, it also stirred up fears of disorder and social breakdown. Many citizens looked to the government and cultural institutions like television and magazines such as *The Reader's Digest* to be reassured about what this nation stood for. On the global front, protecting what came to be thought of as "the American way of life" meant flexing our military muscle to ward off the communist threat. On the domestic front, moral order was thought to require stable families—and such families were to be built on the exclusive foundation of heterosexuality, marriage, monogamy, and traditional dichotomous gender roles. In this context, the homosexual stepped forward as a menacing figure, invoked to defend a narrow ideal of respectable heterosexuality. In popular culture and in the psychiatric establishment, the homosexual came to symbolize a threat to marriage, the family, and civilization itself; he or she was imagined as predatory, seductive, corrupting, promiscuous, and a gender deviant. The moral message of this campaign against homosexuality was clear: anyone who challenges dominant sexual and gender norms risks homosexual stigma and

social disgrace. The homosexual was not alone in symbolizing social disorder and deviance; there was also the "loose woman," "the delinquent," and "the sex offender." All these menacing figures served to reinforce a narrow norm of the respectable sexual citizen—heterosexual, married, monogamous, gender conventional, and family oriented.

By the end of the 1960s, the idea of a rigid division between the pure heterosexual and the polluted, dangerous homosexual began to take hold in American culture. The state and other institutions were given the moral charge to protect America from the homosexual menace. Gay men and lesbians were to be excluded from openly participating in respectable society. They were demonized, and any trace of them in public was to be repressed. The world of the closet was created.

### The Closet as Social Oppression

. . . If the concept of the closet is to be sociologically useful, it should not be used casually to cover any and all acts of homosexual concealment. The closet is a historically specific social pattern. This concept makes sense only if there is also the idea of homosexuality as a core identity. Viewed as an identity, homosexuality cannot be isolated and minimized as a discrete feeling or impulse; choosing to organize a public heterosexual life would create a feeling of betraying one's true self. The closet may make a respectable social status possible but at a high price: living a lie. Not surprisingly, the closet is often likened to "a prison," "an apartheid," "a coffin-world," or to "lives led in the shadows."[5] It is said to emasculate the self by repressing the very passions that give life richness and vitality. . . .

In short, the closet is about social oppression. Among its defining features are the following. First, to be in the closet means that individuals act to conceal who they are from those that matter most in their lives: family, friends, and sometimes spouses and children. Being in the closet will shape the psychological and social core of an individual's life. Second, the closet is about social isolation. Individuals are often isolated from other homosexually oriented individuals and are often emotionally distant from the people they are closest to—kin and friends.[6] Third, secrecy and isolation are sustained by feelings of shame, guilt, and fear. The closeted individual often internalizes society's hatred of homosexuals; if he or she manages to weaken the grip of shame, the fear of public disgrace and worse enforces secrecy and isolation. Finally, secrecy, isolation, shame, and fear pressure individuals to conduct a life involving much deception and duplicity.[7] To be in the closet is, then, to suffer systematic harm—to lack basic rights and a spectrum of opportunities and social benefits; to be denied respect and a feeling of social belonging; and more than likely to forfeit the kinds of intimate companionship and love that make personal happiness possible.

This notion of the closet makes sense only in relation to another concept: *heterosexual domination*.[8] The closet is a way of adjusting to a society that aggressively enforces heterosexuality as the preferred way of life. In the era of the closet, heterosexual dominance works not only by championing a norm of heterosexuality but also by demonizing homosexuality. The making of a culture of homosexual pollution is basic to the creation of the closet. Enforcing the exclusion of homosexuals from public life also involves aggressive institutional repression. Homosexuals are suppressed by means of laws, policing practices, civic disenfranchisement, and harassment and violence. The state has been a driving force in the making of the closet. To the extent that heterosexual privilege is enforced by keeping homosexuals silent and invisible, we can speak of a condition of heterosexual domination.

The closet does not, however, create passive victims. Too often, critics emphasize only the way the closet victimizes and strips the individual of any sense of integrity and purposefulness. But closeted individuals remain active, deliberate agents. They make decisions about their lives, forge meaningful social ties, and may manage somewhat satisfying work and intimate lives, even if under strained circumstances.

Passing is not a simple, effortless act; it's not just about denial or suppression. The closeted individual closely monitors his or her speech, emotional expression, and behavior in order to avoid unwanted suspicion. The sexual meaning of the things (for example, clothes, furniture) and acts (for example, styles of walking, talking, posture) of daily life must be carefully read in order to skillfully fashion a convincing public heterosexual identity. For closeted individuals, daily life acquires a heightened sense of theatricality or performative deliberateness. The discrete, local practices of "sexual identity management" that is the stuff of the closet reveals something of the workings of heterosexual domination but also of how gays negotiate this social terrain.

Accommodating to the closet is only part of the story. Rebellion is the other. For individuals to rebel against the closet they must be seen as active, thoughtful, and risk-taking agents. Passive victims do not rebel; they surrender to things as they are. To reject the closet, individuals must view the disadvantages and indignities of the closet as illegitimate and changeable. They must have the inner resources and moral conviction to contest heterosexual domination. As sociologists have put it, rebellion is propelled less by utter despair and victimization than by "relative deprivation." Individuals rebel when social disadvantages feel unjust but changeable—which is to say, when they don't feel only like victims.

Finally, it is perhaps more correct to speak of multiple closets. The experience and social pattern of being in the closet vary considerably depending on factors such as age, class, gender, race, ability or disability, region, religion, and nationality. In this [reading] I convey something of the negotiated and varied texture of the closet through a series of case studies. These examples are not intended to capture the full spectrum of closet experiences, but to show something of its oppressive, negotiated, and varied character. . . .

## Social Class and the Closet: Bill's Story

Bill (b. 1958) is a baby boomer. . . . He grew up in a small town. Bill recalls feeling sexual desire for boys at an early age. "I probably started thinking about my homosexuality around the time I was ten. I guess it was when other boys were becoming interested in girls and dating and I wasn't. That's when I started to see that I've got to hide who I am and I've got to pretend that I like girls.". . . Bill remembers being exposed to a public culture of homophobia. Family and friends referred to homosexuals in demeaning ways. Bill was very religious and quickly learned from his church minister that "God hates homosexuals.". . . Bill grew up in a culture that not only viewed heterosexuality as an ideal, but also aggressively enforced its compulsory status by defiling the homosexual.

Bill felt overwhelming pressure to be heterosexual. His parents encouraged dating and expected him to marry and have a family. Kin, friends, church, and the media likewise celebrated an adult life organized around heterosexuality. For virtually all Americans born after 1950, there was a clear, often explicit expectation that adults should marry and raise a family.

Bill didn't want to disappoint those who mattered to him. While being socialized into an ideal of heterosexuality motivated him to adopt a public heterosexual identity, fear drove Bill into the closet. "Fear is the biggest thing. Fear of the people that might find out, fear of what will happen if they did." Fear, for Bill, translated into an anxiety that he would lose his family, livelihood, and the respect of his community.

The closet provided Bill with a strategy to resolve the conflict between social expectations and his homosexuality. He decided to present a consistently heterosexual public identity. This entailed managing his homosexual feelings and negotiating a public identity that avoided suspicion. From the standpoint of being in the closet, Bill experienced social life as filled with risk, a world where others read the sexual meaning of

his behavior. To navigate this scary world, Bill had to learn the skills to successfully project a heterosexual identity. . . .

From childhood to his coming out in his mid-thirties, Bill relied on several strategies to sustain the closet. At the heart of the closet was self-control. At times, this meant that Bill simply had to suppress any homosexual feeling. "I didn't act on it at all for many years." At other times, Bill threw himself into work and his marriage to control his homosexuality. "I channeled my energies into work and our marriage. I wanted a family, a house. I just worked and worked. I was so closeted." Even after he was married, Bill describes a life of intense self-control to a point of self-estrangement. "I've always been aware of what I say and how I act, how I hold my cigarette, how I laugh, I mean anything. When I was living in the closet, I had a mask that I presented to anybody. It was tailored to the person or people that I was around. I didn't know who I was really." Self-control meant carefully regulating his behavior. Bill dressed to avoid homosexual suspicion. "I didn't wear anything that looked like it could be gay." Finally, self-control involved social distance. Bill had few friends after high school, and they were kept at arm's length to avoid possible exposure. Although his family was close, Bill kept aloof from his parents. "I couldn't be as open to them as I wanted to be."

In Bill's closet world, everyone potentially suspected. Despite his considerable efforts to avoid suspicion, including marriage, enlisting in the marines, and a seamless masculine self-presentation, Bill believed that his wife suspected. Perhaps, he thinks, she interpreted his lack of sexual passion symptomatically. Bill believes that his parents suspected as well. Asked why, Bill referred to a cluster of behaviors that might signal homosexuality. "The people I hung around with, the way I dressed, and [after marriage] the absence of a girl in my life." Bill thought that his mother suspected because he didn't date after his divorce. Bill threw himself into work and parenting in part to avoid suspicion. "I was hoping that my mother would figure that I didn't have time for a relationship, but I think that's when she started to question [my sexual identity]." In this world of pervasive suspicion, Bill began to suspect others. For example, he wondered about his father. "I always had an idea that he might be gay. He was very gentle. He tried real hard to get everybody to like him, and everybody did."

Bill described his closet world in theatrical terms. "My whole life until recently has been being the actor, pretending I'm somebody I'm not." Invoking the image of the actor to describe his life tellingly acknowledges that Bill had in fact acquired considerable social skill in order to succeed at passing. Of course, this heterosexual identity performance meant, as he says, living an inauthentic life. Bill passed successfully, but to do so he married, had children, joined the marines, became dependent on alcohol, and distanced himself from his own inner life as well as from family and friends. In short, the closet was a way to accommodate being the bearer of a polluted identity but at a considerable psychic and social cost. . . .

Homosexuality presented a real symbolic and economic threat. . . . In . . . working-class culture, family was the corner-stone of life. Getting married and having a family was expected and celebrated. Men were expected to present a more or less seamless masculine self. Homosexuality threatened humiliation—for themselves and their families. Exposure risked isolation from their kin and their blue-collar community of kin, peers, and neighbors. . . .

[His] fear of exposure was also economically based. The financial interdependence between the individual and family is central to working-class life. For example, as a wage earner Bill was economically independent. Yet he was aware that his material well-being was never secure. Growing up, he had seen adults lose jobs as industry migrated from his hometown. He saw kin sustaining their own when brothers, cousins, aunts, and uncles were out of work for long periods of time. Bill considered his family a potential source of material support; he also expected that at some point his family would ask for his financial help.

Class shapes closet patterns.[9] The extent of economic interdependence between the individual and his or her family varies between blue- and white-collar workers. This class difference shapes how individuals manage their homosexuality.

For the middle class, economic independence is valued and expected. This provides a material base for coming out and organizing a public gay life. At a minimum, middle-class individuals have options. They can move to avoid exposure; they can afford to establish a workable double life; and they can sustain themselves if estranged from their families. Moreover, because of the high value placed on individualism, middle-class individuals anticipate a considerable disengagement from their family and the community they were brought up in. They can also expect a relatively smooth integration into a middle-class gay life as compensation for any estrangement from family and friends resulting from coming out.

For working-class individuals, economic interdependence with kin is a lifelong expectation. Exiting the closet as a working-class lesbian or gay man carries serious economic risks—for themselves and their kin. Blue-collar workers expect that at some point they will either turn to kin for economic help or their family will turn to them. Additionally, estrangement from kin carries the threat of losing a primary source of community. There is no anticipation of an immediate compensation for lost community because of the middle-class character of the gay institutionalized world.

The closet is not, then, the same experience for all individuals. To understand its workings, we have to pay close attention to . . . social class.

### Race and the Closet: Robert's Story

Bill's . . . strong economic ties to [his family] made exiting the closet difficult and potentially more risky than for the economically independent middle class. But [his] white racial status made it relatively easy for [him] to identify as gay. The gay world—at least the institutionalized world of bars, social and political organizations, and cultural institutions (newspapers, magazines, publishers, theater groups)—was and still is overwhelmingly white. Moreover, American public cultures, both white and nonwhite, associate being gay with being white. Accordingly, race is a key factor shaping the dynamics of homosexuality, including the closet. . . .

To illustrate, consider the implications for blacks of an overwhelmingly white gay community. No matter how accepting some individuals may be, blacks often feel like outsiders in the gay community. The culture, the leadership, the organizations, and the political agenda of the institutionalized gay world have been and remain dominated by whites. Blacks often report encountering an inhospitable gay world, one that until recently participated in the racism of straight America. For example, through the early 1990s, black men tell of being carded at gay bars or objectified as exotic sexual selves; black women describe being silenced or ignored in decisions about social events and politics. Despite a deliberate commitment to a multicultural gay community, blacks continue to feel that they have to negotiate a somewhat foreign social terrain.

White privilege in the gay world means that blacks manage their homosexuality somewhat differently than whites. Whites may come out to an unfriendly world of kin and friends, but they anticipate an easy integration into a gay world that will affirm their sense of self and offer an alternative type of community. By contrast, if blacks exit from the closet they expect a struggle for acceptance not only in the straight but also in the gay world. To state the contrast sharply, whites expect a trade-off when they come out: estrangement from the straight world in exchange for social integration and acceptance in the gay community. Blacks do not expect such compensation for their anticipated disapproval and diminished status in the straight world. Given their

more ambivalent relationship to the gay community, blacks may be more likely than their white counterparts to manage their homosexuality within the framework of the closet.

If an inhospitable or at least uncertain reception in the gay world gives pause to blacks as they consider coming out, so too does the central role that a race-based community plays in their lives. Many blacks have a fundamental personal and social investment in maintaining integration into a race-based community. This community offers protection and material sustenance in the face of the bodily and economic threats of racism; it provides a positive culture of racial pride and solidarity. Maintaining strong ties with kin and a race-based community is a cornerstone of black identity in a way that is obviously not true for whites. If whites grow up with a sense of racial entitlement and a feeling that it is their America, many blacks experience and expect an inhospitable reception in the larger society. Experience and kin have taught them that their personal and social well-being depends on maintaining solidarity with a black community. For many blacks, America is two nations, and it's only in the black world that they feel a sense of integrity and social belonging.

In short, blacks—straight or gay—are heavily invested in their racial identity and in their membership in the black community in a way that is generally not true of whites. Coming out, then, risks not merely estrangement from kin and community but potentially the loss of a secure sense of identity and social belonging. In other words, leaving the closet threatens social isolation from both the straight and gay worlds. It risks being cast adrift in a society that does not recognize or value being black and gay; it jeopardizes a secure sense of belonging and protection (physical and economic) in exchange for an outsider status. . . .

The absence, at least until recently, of a politically assertive public gay and straight culture supporting black gay men and women has made the wager of coming out risky and potentially too costly for many individuals. Moreover, as black communities have continued to struggle with a sense of being under assault by racism, poverty, and family instability, tolerance for a public gay life is shaky. The closet presents a credible option, especially if, as some evidence suggests, a more relaxed or flexible closet pattern than that experienced by . . . Bill is possible in many black communities. Moreover, as black gay networks developed in the 1980s and 1990s, some blacks now have an alternative to the closet. However, to the extent that these networks remain small and institutionally insecure, establishing an independent gay life remains much more difficult for many blacks than for whites.

Some of these dynamics and dilemmas of being black and gay in America surface in Robert's story. His is a story of a black gay man trying to navigate between a black world that is not seen as particularly hostile nor especially friendly and a somewhat welcoming white-dominated gay world but one that doesn't feel quite like home. In the end, Robert tries to forge a satisfying life by becoming part of a small, fragile black gay world that is not solidly part of a gay or a black community. . . .

Anticipation of disapproval and rejection underpins Robert's emotional and social distancing from the straight world. Fear prevented Robert from disclosing to his family as a young person. Fear also shaped his public school experience. Although he grew up in a predominantly black community in Brooklyn, Robert went to high school in what he described as a small all-white town in upstate New York. He lived in an almost constant state of fear during these years. Negotiating his racial difference was hard enough. The prospect of being viewed as sexually deviant terrified him. Robert managed by maintaining social distance. He avoided any contact with classmates that might be suspected of being gay. He remained silent in the face of an openly homophobic school culture. Robert tried to fit in by lying about having a girlfriend back home. Despite excelling in sports and enjoying athletics, Robert refused to participate in any school team sports. He was afraid that he'd "get a hard-on in the shower.". . .

After high school, Robert joined the navy, where exposure would have meant a discharge as well as social disgrace. He managed to pass by being a loner and by excessive drinking during his years in the service.

After leaving the navy, Robert worked as an electrician in Los Angeles. Away from home, economically independent, and in a liberal social environment, Robert began to participate in gay life. He dated and soon had a boyfriend.

Robert did not, however, disclose his sexual identity to any of his coworkers. He preferred to keep personal matters out of his work life. Although his coworkers often talked about their boyfriends, girlfriends, marriages, and children, Robert never shared any of his personal life. Robert remained aloof. Although he worked at this job for six years, he did not become friends with any of his coworkers. In order to sustain social distance, Robert avoided any meaningful social ties with his coworkers. As a result of being closeted, Robert's workplace experience resembled the impersonal, dehumanizing world that Karl Marx and Max Weber described in their chilling portraits of modern industrial life.

At the age of twenty-three, Robert came out to his mother, who told his father and his siblings. Robert has never discussed specific aspects of his gay life with any family member. They all know, but it's not talked about. Robert interprets the absence of hostile behavior and rejection on the part of his family as indicating acceptance. Asked why he keeps his gay life separate from his family, Robert says that his homosexuality is personal and doesn't need to be shared. Accordingly, his family knew nothing of his boyfriend or any other aspect of his personal life. Much to his regret, but hardly surprising, Robert speaks of a weakening of his family bond. Today, he's not close to his mother or anyone in his family. His visits with his family are infrequent and lack the emotional spontaneity and richness of past family interactions. For these reasons, Robert has not told his family that he is HIV positive. . . .

Cheap housing led Robert to live in a predominantly black neighborhood. His contacts with his neighbors are formal and lack emotional depth. In fact, he has never come out to any straight black person, aside from his mother. Robert says matter-of-factly that no black person ever asked him if he was gay. He admits, though, that many blacks disparage being gay. "Many blacks think . . . it's already dangerous out there for a black man, why would you want to add another danger to your life? Besides, being gay was viewed for a long time as equivalent to having AIDS. So, most of the conversations [among blacks] about being gay . . . is about having sex and death. Because they perceive the lifestyle as being very painful . . . not many people are going to be accepting of the lifestyle." . . .

Today, Robert's life is divided between a gay and a straight world. The former provides emotional and social sustenance; the latter is a somewhat risky terrain he navigates to do what he has to do. He speaks, as is typical of those speaking from a closeted standpoint, of a heterosexual dictatorship. Robert's closetedness entails such a narrowing of his world that intimate expression and bonding are possible only within a very small social circle. His closet world is not built on pretense (as was true of Bill), but a fear and distrust so deeply felt that his social distancing has cost him his family, meaningful ties to a black community, a satisfying work life, and has resulted in a pervasive loneliness. . . .

### Gender and the Closet: Renee's Story

Despite their . . . differences, . . . Bill and Robert relied heavily on being more or less conventionally masculine men to avoid suspicion. Fortunately, a masculine self-presentation and social roles expressed their spontaneous sense of themselves. However, not all lesbians and gay men can manage a conventional gender presentation so effortlessly. For some individuals, their sense of self can

be poignantly at odds with gender norms. If these individuals are to avoid coming out, they must find ways to be gender nonconventional without eliciting suspicion.

These remarks highlight an obvious point: managing gender has been and still is at the heart of managing sexual identity. This is true for men and women. To the extent that men and masculinity are socially privileged, however, the dynamics of managing gender and sexual identity are somewhat different for men and women.[10]

For men, exhibiting the conventional signs of masculinity confers social authority and privilege. Although factors such as class, ethnicity, or ableness create inequalities among men, their masculinity establishes them as a privileged group in relation to women. Masculine men are also presumed to be heterosexual. Of course, if men fail to exhibit those behaviors that serve as conventional markers of masculinity, their dominant status is threatened. And if men depart considerably from masculine norms, they risk losing the privileges associated with being a man and being heterosexual. For men whose inner sense of self is emphatically feminine, passing presents a huge challenge because of the scarcity of acceptable social identities and roles for feminine men. Accordingly, gay men who wish to successfully pass must effectively manage a routine performance of masculinity. But—and here's the key point—when gay men pass by means of exhibiting a conventional masculine persona they share fully in men's gender privilege. Closeted gay men are given the same support straight men receive to conform to masculine gender roles and can claim its considerable social benefits.

For women, the gender managing of sexual identity is somewhat different. Although a conventional feminine self-presentation confers a status as normal and straight, it also positions women as subordinate to men. Respectable women are expected to take up social identities and roles that are consistent with feminine gender expectations. In contemporary America, these roles do not carry the authority, status, and material advantage of masculine roles. Women who wish to assume the social roles and claim the privileges associated with masculine men risk disapproval and may forfeit the benefits of being a normal woman. Lesbians who wish to pass but also to appropriate masculine roles that confer authority and material advantage risk exposure. This is a dilemma that men don't experience. Men who claim masculine power are rewarded as men, and as presumptively straight; women who claim the same privileges associated with masculinity are gender rebels and risk stigma and social harm.

One way that lesbians manage this dilemma is to take on social roles that may be considered masculine (for example, as an athlete, a member of the military service, an office manager) but are viewed as marginally legitimate for straight women. Although there are such roles, they are few and are not free of risk. The story of Renee illustrates this particular closet strategy.

Renee describes herself as a masculine woman. She was born in 1970 and grew up in a small southern town. Her Baptist family and community did not accept homosexuality. Growing up, she became aware of her strong feelings for women while learning that others considered homosexuality to be immoral. She was confused about what these feelings meant for her sense of self. She decided to keep them secret. "I was brought up hearing the statement that you can grow up to be anything you want except a faggot. And it was engrained in me that this was not an accepted lifestyle. It was sinful and it was a way that God was telling you that your life is not good." Renee "feared rejection. I mean, nobody wants to be rejected." Exposure would put her at risk of losing her family "emotionally and financially. . . . The biggest thing that I feared was they wouldn't love me anymore because it was so engrained that this [homosexuality] was not an acceptable lifestyle."

It was not only the homophobia of her family and community that worried Renee. The world of her kin, neighbors, and church was heterosexual— it was both the reality and the unquestioned ideal.

Renee was expected to marry and have a family. "My father talked all the time about how much he was looking forward to walking me down the aisle and that I should have lots of children so that they could have lots of grandchildren." Renee retreated into the closet to avoid social rejection and to manage the conflict between what was expected of her and her desires.

Because Renee is not a feminine woman, the closet has been a difficult adjustment. As long as she can remember, Renee felt more comfortable as part of a masculine male culture. As a young person, she was thought of as a tomboy. She says that in the town where she grew up in the 1970s and early 1980s, the tomboy did not evoke homosexual suspicion. Girls could be tomboys but only, as she came to learn, as a young person. The same masculine self-presentation in an adult would evoke suspicion. . . .

Renee felt that a masculine-gendered self was basic to who she was. It could not be denied or changed, but perhaps its social meaning could be managed. As the tomboy identification lost credibility in high school, she tried to fashion a public identity as an athlete. Renee thought that participating in school sports might minimize suspicion or at least create ambiguity around the sexual meaning of her masculine presentation. It was as if being identified as a female athlete, like her earlier identity as a tomboy, would allow Renee to safely express her masculinity. In short, as Renee moved closer to an adult world, it was harder to control the social meaning of her masculine self-presentation; it became difficult to avoid being read, by herself and others, as a lesbian.

In a last-ditch effort to find a legitimate social role for her masculinity Renee joined the military. She encountered a fairly open network of lesbians. She came to accept herself as a lesbian in the course of her military duty.

She believes that today people look at her and see a lesbian. "There's no doubt in my mind that because of my masculine way of dress and look that this signals to people that I am a lesbian. . . . The way I walk, dress, wear my hair. . . . I look like a dyke." Renee feels the weight of a society that collapses gender and sexual nonconformity. Indeed, since Renee believes that her masculinity expresses something basic to who she is, the choice she confronted was stark: to be spontaneous and honest, and therefore to be read as a lesbian; or to pass, which would require a considerable effort at refashioning her public persona. Because gender nonconventionality was at the core of her sense of self, the closet proved a tough accommodation. For a time, the availability of social roles for masculine but presumed straight women (tomboy, athlete, soldier) allowed Renee to avoid exposure. However, as she became an adult civilian, the lack of such roles put pressure on her to either escalate gender management in order to pass or come out. Renee eventually came out.

While there are no unambiguous markers of sexual identity in contemporary America, gender has served as perhaps the chief sign. Masculine men and feminine women are typically assumed to be heterosexual. Emphatically feminine men and masculine women would likely surrender this presumption. As one twenty-four-year-old gay man told me, "You assume straight men are more masculine, a little rough looking, hair's not perfect. So when you see a guy whose dress is perfect, the hair's perfect, everything is, you know, picture perfect, that's gay." Managing gender presentation has then been at the heart of managing sexual identity. To the extent, moreover, that gender is thickly coded, passing may entail considerable effort. Describing herself as having a forceful, take-charge personality as well as preferring a no-makeup, jeans-and-sweatshirt look, Rachel, a forty-three-year-old lesbian, says that passing required a virtual makeover of her public self. She groomed and dressed in a self-consciously feminine style and crafted a public persona that deemphasized her masculine personality. "I try to look and act very feminine so people won't look at me or take notice."

Gender is not, however, an unambiguous sign of sexual identity. Albert is a twenty-six-year-old

gay black man. His soft and high-pitched voice and the meticulous attention he pays to grooming and dress could have marked him as gay during high school. However, Albert thinks that his high profile as an athlete and the absence of explicit homosexual disclosure created ambiguity around his sexual identity. Being black reinforced uncertainty about the sexual meaning of his gender nonconformity. "A lot of people see being gay as a white issue."

The indeterminate character of a homosexual sign system is in sharp contrast to the way racial and gender identities are socially coded. In the United States, race is in most instances unambiguously conveyed by skin color. And gender is so thickly coded by the sexed body and by our behaviors that it's almost impossible to avoid publicly flagging a clear gender identity.[11] Sexual identity, however, is thinly and ambiguously coded. In the age of the closet, there were efforts to thicken the code by identifying specific behaviors as marking heterosexual and homosexual identities. In particular, gender served as a master code of sexual identity, but it remained somewhat ambiguous as a sexual signifier. A prolonged single status, a lack of interest in the opposite sex, a steady gaze at a person of the same sex, or a fastidiousness about grooming (men) or the lack thereof (women) have also functioned as part of a historically specific grammar of sexual identity.

### Neither Victims nor Heroes

The closet is a condition of social oppression. To be in the closet is to live with shame, guilt, and fear. Individuals carefully manage daily life in order to avoid suspicion. Some individuals may make life-shaping decisions about love and intimacy, or work and friends, that are motivated by the wish to avoid detection. The closet makes integration possible but at a considerable personal cost: passionless marriages, loveless lives, estrangement from family and peers, and, sometimes, a paralyzing isolation that leaves individuals depressed and suicidal.

The closet didn't just happen. The aggressive enforcement of heterosexuality as an identity and way of life produced it. Specifically, the closet took shape in response to a culture that polluted homosexuality and policed behavior by stigmatizing gender nonconformity as a sign of homosexuality. And, through the repressive (censoring, criminalizing, and disenfranchising) practices of the state, the homosexual was driven from public life. By the 1950s the closet had become the defining reality for many gay Americans.

The closet is a strategy of accommodating to heterosexual domination. Individuals choose the closet to manage what is considered a deviant identity; it makes possible social respect and integration, even if it may cost the individual his or her sense of personal integrity and well-being. There is enormous variation in closet patterns. . . .

[The] shift in the emotional, moral, and social texture of the closet after Stonewall is evident in the stories of Bill, Robert, and Renee. . . . They each grew up in a world organized around heterosexuality. But there was a well-organized visible movement and gay subcultures in many cities that celebrated being gay as good. Despite the weight of society pressuring them to live heterosexually, the decision to live as a "heterosexual" wasn't a foregone conclusion. Individuals coming of age after the 1970s had a sense of choice that was for all practical purposes absent [before]. But the flip side was that choosing to be closeted was likely much more anguished and difficult for these later generations. . . . Being in the closet was now associated with living a false, inauthentic life. . . .

Stonewall likely had the effect of driving many individuals deeply into the closet. Indeed, many homosexuals who came of age in the 1950s and early 1960s thought that this new social assertiveness and visibility would bring about greater social repression; it would also create considerable turmoil for many homosexuals who had managed a more or less comfortable social adjustment in the closet. They were in some ways right. While the closet doors may have tightened for some, they were loosened, even unhinged, for many others. "Out of the closet" became the slogan of the new gay liberationist movement.

The closet is an unstable social condition. While its purpose is to keep homosexuals silent and invisible, its very creation causes a heightened public awareness of homosexuality. Laws criminalizing homosexuality, police harassing and arresting homosexuals, and newspapers publishing their names in order to shame them have the effect of both enforcing heterosexual domination and heightening public awareness of the pervasive presence of homosexuals. The closet may expel real, living homosexuals from visible public life, but it makes this sexual personage into a haunting symbolic presence.[12] The status of the closeted homosexual as both omnipresent but unseen shapes a culture of homosexual suspicion. In principle, no one is to be spared. No matter how impeccable an individual's heterosexual credentials, he or she is not entirely free of suspicion. A flawless heterosexual presentation may, after all, be taken as masking a latent homosexual self.

The closet has another ironic effect. It creates a heightened self-awareness on the part of homosexually oriented individuals. The social pressure to methodically conceal rivets attention precisely on that which is proscribed: homosexuality. For some closeted individuals, homosexuality becomes a core self-identity as daily life centers on either avoiding suspicion of homosexuality or coming out. And the fashioning of homosexuality into a core social identity makes rebellion against the closet possible—and likely. At an individual level, rebellion often meant coming out, affirming a gay self, and becoming part of a gay community. At a political level, a movement took shape—gay liberationism and lesbian feminism—that challenged the institutional and cultural supports of the closet; that is, the culture of pollution and the state-backed policy of repression. This movement has, by all accounts, been enormously successful even if so many battles have been lost and so many remain to be waged.

The era of the closet is hardly over. Yet the present is a world apart from that of just one or two decades ago. The universe of the butch, the queen, the normal straight, the culture of camp, the seamless and open homophobic culture, and uniform state and institutional repression are taking on the character of a historical era. The closet has not disappeared, but there are today more people choosing to live beyond the closet.

## NOTES

1. Consider this description of the world of a middle-class lesbian living in the late 1920s and 1930s: "During the 1920s and 1930s Boyer Reinstein was an active lesbian within a community of lesbian friends. She had few, if any, negative feelings about being a lesbian, and she was 'out' to her immediate family. . . . Yet, she did not publicly disclose being gay. She was always discreet." The author, Elizabeth Kennedy, cautions against using the concept of the closet to depict Reinstein's social world. "I am afraid using the term 'closet' to refer to the culture of the 1920s and 1930s might be anachronistic." Elizabeth Kennedy, " 'But We Would Never Talk about It': The Structures of Lesbian Discretion in South Dakota, 1928–1933," in *Inventing Lesbian Cultures in America,* ed. Ellen Lewin (Boston: Beacon Press, 1996). Similarly, George Chauncey describes a working-class gay culture in which gays and straights openly mingle in saloons, cafeterias, rent parties, and speakeasies. The gay world before World War I is said to be very different from the era inaugurated by the Stonewall rebellions. For example, the language and concept of "coming out of the closet" was foreign to this gay world. "Gay people in the prewar years . . . did not speak of coming out of what we call the gay closet but rather of coming out into what they called homosexual society or the gay world, a world neither so small, nor so isolated, nor . . . so hidden as closet implies." George Chauncey, *Gay New York Gender, Urban Culture, and the Making of the Gay Male World, 1890–1940* (New York: Basic Books, 1994).

2. For descriptions of homosexual life in the 1950s and 1960s, *The Mattachine Review* and *The Ladder,* respectively published by the Mattachine Society and the Daughters of Bilitis, are superb sources. For examples of personal testimony, see Peter Nardi, David Sanders, and Judd Marmor, eds., *Growing up before Stonewall: Life Stories of Some Gay Men* (New York: Routledge, 1994); Donald Vining, A *Gay Diary,* 5 vols.

(New York: Pepys Press, 1979–93); Martin Duberman, *Cures: A Gay Man's Odyssey* (New York: Dutton, 1991); Robert Reinhart, *A History of Shadows: A Novel* (Boston: Alyson, 1986); Audre Lorde, *Zami: A New Spelling of My Name* (New York: Crossing Press, 1982); Andrea Weiss and Greta Schiller, *Before Stonewall; The Making of the Gay and Lesbian Community* (New York: Naiad Press, 1988); Jonathan Ned Katz, *Gay American History* (New York: Meridian, 1976) and *Gay/Lesbian Almanac* (New York: Harper and Row, 1983); and Eric Marcus, *Making History: The Struggle far Gay and Lesbian Equal Rights: An Oral History* (New York: HarperCollins, 1992). For informative popular and academic work of the time, see Daniel Webster Cory [psuedonym Edward Sagarin], *The Homosexual in America* (New York: Peter Nevill, 1951); Evelyn Hooker, "Male Homosexuals and Their Worlds," in *Sexual Inversion,* ed. J. Marmor (New York: Basic Books, 1965); Martin Hoffman, *The Gay World* (New York Basic Books, 1968); Del Martin and Phyllis Lyon, *Lesbian/Woman* (San Francisco: Bantam, 1972); Sidney Abbott and Barbara Love, *Sappho Was a Right-On Woman: A Liberated View of Lesbianism* (New York: Stein and Day, 1972); John Gagnon and William Simon, "The Lesbians: A Preliminary Overview," in *Sexual Deviance,* ed. William Simon and John Gagnon (New York Harper and Row, 1967). For some current scholarly perspectives on gay life in the immediate postwar years, see John D'Emilio, *Sexual Politics, Sexual Communities: The Making of a Homosexual Minority in the United States, 1940–1970* (Chicago: University of Chicago Press, 1983); Lillian Faderman, *Odd Girls* and *Twilight Lovers: A History of Lesbian Life in Twentieth-Century America* (New York: Columbia University Press, 1991); Elizabeth Kennedy and Madeline Davis, *Boots of Leather, Slippers of Gold: The History of a Lesbian Community* (New York: Roudedge, 1993); Leila J. Rupp, " 'Imagine My Surprise': Women's Relationships in Mid-Twentieth-Century America," in *Hidden from History,* ed. M. Duberman, M. Vicinus and G. Chauncey Jr. (New York: Meridian, 1990); Rochella Thorpe, " 'A House where Queers Go': African-American Lesbian Nightlife in Detroit, 1940–1975," in *Inventing Lesbian Cultures in America,* ed. Ellen Lewin (Boston: Beacon Press, 1996); and Marc Stein, *City of Sisterly and Brotherly Loves: Lesbian and Gay Philadelphia, 1945–72* (Chicago: University of Chicago Press, 2000).

3. To understand the social context of the 1950s as a time of both change and anxiety, especially regarding gender and intimate life, I have drawn on the following: Wini Breines, *Young, White, and Miserable: Growing up Female in the Fifties* (Boston: Beacon Press, 1992); Stephanie Coontz, *The Way We Never Were: American Families and the Nostalgia Trap* (New York: Basic Books, 1992); Barbara Ehrenreich, *Hearts of Men: American Dreams and the Flight from Commitment* (Garden City, N.Y.: Anchor Books, 1983); Elaine Tyler May, *Homeward Bound: American Families in the Cold War Era* (New York: Basic Books, 1988); Jessica Weiss, *To Have and to Hold: Marriage, the Baby Boom, and Social Change* (Chicago: University of Chicago Press, 2000); Cynthia Enloe, *The Morning after: Sexual Politics and the End of the Cold War* (Berkeley: University of California Press, 1993); and Robert Corber, *In the Name of National Security: Hitchcock, Homophobia, and the Political Construction of Gender in Postwar America* (Durham, N.C.: Duke University Press, 1993).

4. On the making of the closet in the 1950s, see John D'Emilio, "The Homosexual Menace: The Politics of Sexuality in Cold War America," in *Making Trouble: Essays on Gay History, Politics, and the University* (New York: Routledge, 1992), and *Sexual Politics, Sexual Communities;* Allan Berube and John D'Emilio, "The Military and Lesbians during the McCarthy Years," *Signs* 9 (Summer 1984): 759–75; Barbara Epstein, "Anti-Communism, Homophobia, and the Construction of Masculinity in the Postwar U.S." *Critical Sociology* 20 (1994): 21–44; Faderman, *Odd Girls;* Robert Corber, *Homosexuality in Cold War America: Resistance and the Crisis of Masculinity* (Durham, N.C.: Duke University Press, 1997); and Gerard Sullivan, "Political Opportunism and the Harassment of Homosexuals in Florida, 1952–1965," *Journal of Homosexuality* 37 (1999): 57–81.

5. Chauncey, *Gay New York*, p. 6; William Eskridge Jr., *Gaylaw: Challenging the Apartheid of the Closet* (Cambridge, Mass.: Harvard University Press, 1999), p. 13; Paul Monette, *Becoming a Man: Half a Life Story* (New York: HarperCollins, 1992), p. 2; Joseph Beam, "Leaving the Shadows Behind," in *In the Life: A Black Gay Anthology*, ed. Joseph Beam (Boston: Alyson, 1986), p. 16.

6. In his memoir, Mel White, the former ghostwriter for Billy Graham and Jerry Falwell, movingly describes his experience of isolation: "I was isolated, not by bars or guards in uniforms, but by fear. I was surrounded by my loving family and close friends, but there was no way to explain to them my desperate, lonely feelings even when we were together. I wasn't tortured by leather straps or cattle prods, but my guilt and fear kept me in constant torment. . . . I was starving for the kind of human intimacy that would satisfy my longing, end my loneliness." White says that this isolation made him "feel like an alien who had been abandoned on a strange planet. . . . Living rooms and dining rooms, restaurants and lobbies, became foreign, unfriendly places. [I grew] weary of pretending to be someone I was not, tired of hiding my feelings. . . . My once lively spirit was shriveling like a raisin in the sun. . . . Desperation and loneliness surged. . . . I felt trapped and terrified." Mel White, *Stranger at the Gate: To Be Gay and Christian in America* (New York: Plume, 1995), pp. 123, 177–78.

7. Allan Berube describes the closet as a "system of lies, denials, disguises, and double entendres—that had enabled them to express some of their homosexuality by pretending it didn't exist and hiding it from view." Berube, *Coming Out under Fire*, p. 271.

8. My research suggests that the category of the closet initially appeared in the writing of gay liberationists. The earliest reference I've found was an "editorial" statement in the short-lived newspaper *Come Out!* in 1969. By the early 1970s the concept of the closet was widely circulating in liberationist writings; e.g., Signo Canceris, "From the Closet," *Fag Rag* 4 (January 1973); Bruce Gilbert "Coming Out," *Fag Rag* 23/24 (1976); Morgan Pinney, "Out of Your Closets," *Gay Sunshine* 1 (October 1970); Ian Young, "Closet Wrecking," *Gay Sunshine* 28 (Spring 1976); Jennifer Woodhul, "Darers Go First," *The Furies* 1 (June/July 1972); and Allen Young, "Out of the Closets, into the Streets," in *Out of the Closets*, ed. Karla Jay and Allen Young. The closet underscored a condition of oppression. Gays were not merely discriminated against but dominated. And the closet was not a product of individual ignorance or prejudice but a social system of heterosexual domination. The core institutions and culture of America were said to be organized to enforce the norm and ideal of heterosexuality. In short, the closet underscored the way a system of compulsory heterosexuality creates a separate and oppressed homosexual existence. By arguing that the very organization of American society compels homosexuals to live socially isolated, inauthentic lives, the category of the

closet served both as a way to understand gay life and as a critique of America.

By the mid-1970s, as liberationism gave way to a politics of minority rights, the concept of the closet was in wide use. However, its meaning began to change. Within the minority rights discourse that triumphed in the late 1970s, the closet was viewed as an act of concealment in response to actual or anticipated prejudice; it was seen as a matter of individual choice. By, the late 1970s and 1980s, some gays were arguing that America had become a much more tolerant nation; the risks of coming out were greatly diminished. Being in or out of the closet was now seen as an individual choice rather than an adjustment to heterosexual domination. In fact, gays began to feel considerable pressure to come out, as many came to believe that visibility was both more possible and a key to challenging prejudice. For example, David Goodstein, the owner and editor of *The Advocate* from roughly the mid-1970s through the mid-1980s, gravitated to a view of the closet as almost self-imposed, as a product of "low self-esteem" or "cowardice." "I truly believe that there is no reason for you to be closeted and hide who you are" (*The Advocate*, 1983, p. 6). Goodstein blamed social intolerance in part on the cowardice of those who choose to be closeted. "I take a dim view of staying in the closet. . . . What brings up my irritation at this time . . . is the price we uncloseted gay people pay for the cowardice and stupidity of our [closeted] brothers and sisters" ("Opening Spaces," *The Advocate*, 1981, p. 6).

I have stated my preference for a liberationist approach. If the concept of the closet is to help us to understand changes in gay life, it should be used in a way that indicates more than an act of concealment. In this regard, the liberationist idea of the closet as a condition of social oppression is persuasive. Explaining gay subordination, at least from the 1950s through the 1980s, as a product of individual prejudice or ignorance makes it hard, if not impossible, to understand its socially patterned character. It was not simply that gays were disadvantaged in one institution or only by isolated acts of discrimination or disrespect, but gay subordination occurred across institutions and culture. Heterosexual privilege was aggressively enforced by the state, cultural practices, daily acts of harassment and violence, and by institutions such as marriage, the wedding industry, and a dense network of laws covering taxes, family, immigration, military policy, and so on. At least during the heyday of the closet, the social risks

of exposure were so great that it is naive to speak of the closet as an individual choice. In short, the concept of the closet helps us to understand the way heterosexuality functioned as an "institution" or a "system" that oppressed gay people.

A liberationist approach requires, however, some modification. In particular, the closet should be approached as a product of historically specific social dynamics; in particular, a culture of homosexual pollution and state repression. Furthermore, liberationists tend to read heterosexual domination as so closely and deeply intertwined with a whole system of gender, racial, economic, and political domination that America is viewed as irredeemably repressive. Such totalizing views are not credible.

9.   Class is absent from much of queer social analysis. There are theoretical and rhetorical appeals to the importance of class, but little social research that addresses class patterns of concealment and coming out, gay and lesbian identification, and workplace dynamics. I have made use of the following work: Nicole Field, *Over the Rainbow: Money, Clans, and Homophobia* (London: Pluto Press, 1995); Steve Valocchi, "The Class-Inflected Nature of Gay Identity," *Social Problems* 46 (1999): 207–44; Katie Gilmartin, "We Weren't Bar People: Middle Class Identities and Cultural Space," *Gay and Lesbian Quarterly* 3 (1996): 1–5; Roger Lancaster, *Life Is Hard: Machismo, Danger, and the Intimacy of Power in Nicaragua* (Berkeley: University of California Press, 1992); and David Evans, *Sexual Citizenship: The Material Construction of Sexualities* (London: Routledge, 1993). Joshua Gamson's *Freaks Talk Back: Tabloid Talk Shows and Sexual Nonconformity* (Chicago: University of Chicago Press, 1998) and Chrys Ingraham's *White Weddings: Romancing Heterosexuality in Popular Culture* (New York: Routledge, 1999) weave class into an analysis of sexual identities in interesting ways. Lillian Faderman's *Odd Girls, Twilight Lovers* and Kennedy and Davis's *Boots of Leather, Slippers of Gold* are indispensable sources for understanding the role of class in early postwar lesbian life.

10.   There is a substantial theoretical and research literature on the role of gender in shaping patterns of sexual identification and dynamics of the closet and coming out. The literature of gay liberationism and lesbian feminism is crucial. On the tradition of lesbian feminism, see Nancy Myron and Charlotte Bunch, eds., *Lesbianism and the Women's Movement.* (Baltimore: Diana Press, 1975). For gay liberationism, see Karla

Jay and Allen Young, eds., *Out of the Closets: Voices of Gay Liberationism*, (New York: New York University Press, 1992 [1972]). For more recent theoretical and empirical statements, see Judith Butler, *Gender Trouble: Feminism and the Subversion of Gender* (New York: Routledge, 1990); Biddy Martin, "Sexualities without Genders and Other Queer Utopias," *Diacritics* 24 (Summer 1994): 104–21; Chrys Ingraham, "The Heterosexual Imaginary: Feminist Sociology and Theories of Gender," in *Queer Theory/Sociology*, ed. Steven Seidman (Cambridge: Blackwell, 1996); Peggy Reeves Sanday, *Fraternity Gang Rape: Sex, Brotherhood, and Privilege on Campus* (New York: New York University, 1990); Christine Williams and Arlene Stein, eds., *Sexuality and Gender* (Maiden, Mass.: Blackwell, 2002); and Kath Weston, *Render Me, Gender Me: Lesbians Talk Sex, Class, Color, Nation, Studmuffins* (New York: Columbia University Press, 1996).

It is interesting to note that the term *the closet* was initially developed in liberationist texts, which, though a mid-gender movement, was shaped considerably by men. By contrast, the chief architects of lesbian feminism such as Charlotte Bunch, Rita Mae Brown, Ti Grace Atkinson, the Furies Collective, and New York Radicalesbians did not place the concept of the closet at the center of their thinking and politics. To the extent that being a lesbian was understood as a political act of resistance to male dominance and compulsory heterosexuality, it was the struggle against sexism and the development of a women-centered culture that was the political focus. With the decline of lesbian feminism, along with the gradual development of a gender-integrated gay movement, the closet and issues of coming out became more prominent in lesbian writing as well.

11. For a wonderful illustration of the thickness of gender codes in contemporary America, see Deirdre McCloskey's description of gender passing in her memoir, *Crossing* (Chicago: University of Chicago Press, 1999), pp. 160–62.

12. For approaches to the closet that emphasize dynamics of knowledge/ignorance, presence/absence and its haunting power, see Sedgwick, *The Epistemology of the Closet*, Diana Fuss, "Inside/Out," in *Inside/Out: Lesbian Theories, Gay Theories* (New York: Routledge, 1991); Michael Moon, "Flaming Closets," in *Out in Culture: Gay, Lesbian, and Queer Essays on Popular Culture*, ed. Corey Creekmur and Alexander Doty (Durham, N.C.: Duke University Press, 1995); and Lee Edelman, "Tearooms and Sympathy, or, The Epistemology of the Water Closet," in *The Lesbian and Gay Studies Reader*, ed. Henry Abelove, Michele Aina Barale, and David Halperin (New York: Routledge, 1993).

## LGBTQ Politics in America: An Abbreviated History

### Chet Meeks

The lesbian, gay, bisexual, transgender, queer (LGBTQ) community has been the target of systematic, institutionalized forms of regulation in American society since at least the middle of the 20th century. This means that LGBTQ people are not merely discriminated against by particular individuals, but that a social norm making heterosexuality superior is embedded in and informs the logics of all of America's core social institutions: the state, the criminal justice system, the media, education, and the family. American social institutions have worked to make any sexuality deviating from the heterosexual norm criminal and deviant. When a group of individuals is systematically regulated in such a way, they sometimes organize to create social changes in the areas of law, public opinion, or social policy. Sometimes they try to revolutionize how we think of and practice sex itself. This is what we mean by "sexual politics," and here I offer an abbreviated history of LGBTQ politics in America.

The first rumblings of LGBTQ resistance could be felt in the 1950s. Harry Hay and Rudi Gernreich organized a group called the Mattachine Society. Del Martin and Phyllis Lyon organized the Daughters of Bilitis at almost the same time. Some others were ONE, and The Society for Individual Rights. These early groups called themselves "homophile" organizations. They emerged in response to the state-sponsored harassment and criminalization of homosexuality in America. America in the 1950s was a place where homosexuality, like communism, had come to be associated with evil and moral bankruptcy. Homophile organizations were fledgling groups, and only ever partially visible in the mainstream public sphere. They spoke through heterosexual proxies, like tolerant doctors or lawyers, in order to make their case about a given issue. Homophile groups had some successes, though. For example ONE sued the American postal service in 1958 for refusing to mail their monthly magazine. But in reality, a strong, vocal, and truly organized LGBTQ politics did not really get underway until the late 1960s.

On June 28, 1969, a brawl broke out between New York City police officers and some drag queens at a Greenwich Village bar called the Stonewall. The Stonewall riots marked the beginning of a new era in LGBTQ politics. From the spirit of rebellion at Stonewall, two LGBTQ organizations were born: The Gay Liberation Front and The Gay Activist Alliance. Although these organizations are no longer around, the spirit and worldview that animated their respective political actions remain very much present in contemporary forms of LGBTQ struggle.

The Gay Liberation Front was organized by Martha Shelley, Craig Rodwell, and Jim Fourrat three weeks after the Stonewall riots. As their name suggests, the Gay Liberation Front espoused a liberationist worldview. According to liberationists, America is a society that systematically demonizes, criminalizes, and ghettoizes all forms of sexual and gender expression that do not conform to a very narrow standard of heterosexual "normality." Struggle and resistance, in a world like this, cannot be limited to demanding civil rights, reform, or tolerance. Rather, revolution—sexual revolution in particular—is the only viable option. Borrowing an idea from feminism, liberationists argued that "the personal is political," and they believed that only by transforming sexuality could the broader social fabric be revolutionized. They encouraged their members to experiment with new forms of "liberated" sexuality and social relationships—like nonmonogamy and communal living. Liberationists, moreover, viewed the plight of LGBTQ people as indelibly linked to the problems faced by black Americans, third world people and refugees, the victims of American and European military aggression, and the working classes. They struggled alongside the Black Panthers and critics of the Vietnam War demanding justice for all oppressed people.

Although the Gay Activist Alliance emerged at nearly the same time and in the same political climate as the Gay Liberation Front, they possessed a worldview that was very different than that of the liberationists. They did not believe that the plight faced by lesbians and gay men was necessarily linked to other forms of oppression, like race or class status. Neither did they believe that American society was systematically anti-queer, in the way suggested by liberationists. Rather, they believed that, at bottom, America was a tolerant and just society, one that had successfully integrated a large number of minority groups. American institutions, they argued, are copious and open to change. The problem was that this tolerance had not yet reached lesbians, gay men, transgender people, and bisexuals.

Sexual revolution was not the answer, according to the Gay Activist Alliance. They were not liberationists, but reformists. They believed that tolerance and respect for LGBTQ people had to be won through the slow, incremental reform of existing institutions. They believed that, just as black Americans and women had fought to gain civil rights reforms in the 1960s and 1970s, lesbians and gay men must fight to be recognized as respectable Americans. They fought to pass civil rights ordinances in cities like New York. Unlike the liberationists, they focused much less on the sexual lives of activists themselves, and they eschewed attempts to connect lesbian and gay justice to the struggles of other groups.

Although the Gay Liberation Front and the Gay Activist Alliance have long since disbanded, the worldviews that animated their activism are very much alive. The liberationist worldview was reborn in the radical sexual politics of the 1980s and 1990s, in groups like Act-Up and Queer Nation. The Reagan Administration of the 1980s had completely ignored the growing AIDS epidemic, largely because gay men were the most visible victims of the disease. Also, large pharmaceutical companies were making the drugs used to treat AIDS symptoms so expensive that only the very wealthy could afford them. Against this stifling climate, Act-Up shouted "Silence equals Death," and against the growing stigmatization of gay and queer people due to AIDS, Queer Nation shouted "We're Here, We're Queer, Get Used to It!" Like liberationists, Act-Up and Queer Nation linked notions of social revolution to self-transformation. And they believed that nothing would ever truly change until queer people had put an end to "straight tyranny." More recently, the National Lesbian and Gay Task Force took a vocal stance against the Bush Administration's decision to declare war on Iraq. Echoing the earlier liberationist worldview, they argued that the heightened patriotism and nationalism of wartime often results in heightened violence toward minorities, including gays and lesbians, who are perceived to be "anti-American."

As for the Gay Activist Alliance, their reformist spirit remains central to many of the most visible contemporary LGBTQ organizations. Coming to power largely in the 1990s, the Human Rights Campaign, the Lambda Legal Defense and Education Fund, and the Gay and Lesbian Alliance Against Defamation all borrow from the worldview of the Gay Activist Alliance. The Human Rights Campaign has become an extremely successful lobbying organization in Washington, DC. It has over 600,000 members, and they lobby Congress continually for Federal hate crimes legislation and other legal reforms to make LGBTQ people safe and equal citizens. Both the Human Rights Campaign and the Lambda Legal Defense and Education Fund have been slowly but surely making inroads in the fight toward lesbian and gay equality in the arena of marriage. Lambda was the first organization to successfully take a marriage lawsuit to a state Supreme Court in the famous *Baehr v. Lewin* case in Hawaii in 1993. GLAAD was declared by *Entertainment Weekly* to be one of the most successful media organizations in the country. GLAAD came into existence in an era when LGBTQ people were only vilified on television and in the media, when they were represented at all. Today, the GLAAD awards (given for fair, accurate, and positive portrayals of LGBTQ people) are coveted by many of Hollywood's most elite actors, actresses, directors, and producers.

A lot has changed in American society since the 1950s and 1960s, when the postal service refused to carry LGBTQ publications, when cities like New York still had laws requiring that everyone wear at least "three articles of gender appropriate clothing," and when police would frequently raid bars like the Stonewall in order to harass their patrons. We live in the world of *Will and Grace*, *Queer as Folk*, and *Lawrence v. Texas*.[1] LGBTQ inequality nonetheless persists, as does the norm of heterosexuality, even if in more subtle forms. LGBTQ people still face violence in their everyday lives, and second-class status in most areas of social policy. It will be up to tomorrow's LGBTQ political organizations to tackle these problems—but in doing so, they will likely borrow from the tactics and worldviews of their historical predecessors.

## NOTE

1. *Lawrence v. Texas* was decided in 2003. This case struck down the ruling in an earlier case, *Bowers v. Hardwick,* decided in 1986, in which the Supreme Court ruled that homosexuals had no Constitutional protections against laws that criminalized sodomy. With *Lawrence v. Texas,* an era where homosexuality could be made officially criminal was finally over. The case was remarkable because the Supreme Court very rarely goes against its previous decisions, and because it provides LGBTQ people with a new legal precedent when battling for other rights such as marriage.

# The Pentagon's Gay Ban Is Not
# Based on Military Necessity

Aaron Belkin

As I first started to delve into the issue of gays and lesbians in the military several years ago, I became familiar with the work of the Servicemembers Legal Defense Network in Washington. The Servicemembers Legal Defense Network is in the business of reporting abuses of gays and lesbians in the military, abuses that are tolerated by military officials and that include a widespread pattern of violent harassment such as beatings and rapes (Sobel, Westcott, Benecke & Osburn, 2000).

And as I read about these events, I wondered what had happened to the policy known as "Don't-Ask, Don't-Tell." I thought that the President and the Congress and the Pentagon had reached a compromise that allowed gay people to serve honorably in the military and to be left alone as long as they did not reveal their sexual orientation (Halley, 1999, pp. 19–26). And as I learned more and more about the evidence, I became more and more appalled. And I came to realize that literally, there is no intellectually honest position from which to argue that lifting the ban on gays and lesbians would harm the military.

I realize that such an extreme statement may cause discomfort given that our entire political system is based on compromise and gradual reform. However, whether one is a Republican or a Democrat, whether one likes gay people or dis-

likes them, whether one is a donor to Bob Jones University or not, I want to claim that there is no possibility for making an argument based on evidence that lifting the ban would harm the military.

Before walking through the evidence, I would like to review the basics of the military ban, the policy known as "Don't-Ask, Don't-Tell." What is this policy that the Pentagon has violated over 5,000 times in the last few years alone? "Don't-Ask, Don't-Tell" is a policy that says that gays and lesbians are allowed to serve in the military as long as they do not reveal their sexual orientation. The military imagines that coming out of the closet is like spreading contagious fluid, almost like the AIDS virus (Butler, 1997, p. 116). For a soldier to admit that he or she is gay, to say the words "I am gay," is so bad that other people in the soldier's unit would be socially infected and the unit no longer would be able to function. Hence the compromise: we will not ask you if you are gay, but you are not allowed to tell us if you are gay. Don't-Ask, Don't-Tell.

Is "Don't-Ask, Don't-Tell" reformable? Recently there have been initiatives to try to improve the implementation of this policy, to stop harassment, to stop gay bashing, to stop the beatings of gay people in the military ("Harassment of Gays," 2000). But I like to think about the reformability of "Don't-Ask, Don't-Tell" in terms of a poll tax. Consider a poll tax that charges some group of people, say Chinese people, ten dollars to vote. One could introduce a reform initiative and say "well, we are going to reform our poll tax, and we are going to charge only five

From Belkin, Aaron. 2001. "The Pentagon's Gay Ban Is Not Based on Military Necessity." *Journal of Homosexuality* 41: 103–119. Reprinted by permission of The Haworth Press.

dollars for Chinese people to vote." But a poll tax is a poll tax is a poll tax. And the same is true with "Don't-Ask, Don't-Tell." Why? Because as long as gay and lesbian people are not allowed to admit who they are, there is no way for them to complain about harassment. They cannot complain about harassment, of course, because doing so could get them kicked out of the military for being gay. And the fact that they are not allowed to complain about harassment provides a green light to anyone thinking of tormenting them or beating them.

What is the justification behind "Don't-Ask, Don't-Tell"? One might guess that this policy has ten justifications or five or three. But in fact, the official policy as articulated in congressional statute and Pentagon implementing regulations specifies only one official rationale for the "Don't-Ask, Don't-Tell" policy. And that rationale is called the "unit cohesion" rationale. The unit cohesion rationale is the idea that if gays and lesbians revealed their sexual orientation, then units no longer would be able to function. Heterosexual soldiers hate gays and lesbians and cannot trust them with their lives and unit performance and cohesion would fall apart.

Consider a *60 Minutes* report that was broadcast in December, 1999. In the broadcast, Lieutenant Colonel Robert McGinnis, who also happens to be a staff member of the Family Research Council, provides a very clear articulation of the unit cohesion rationale (*Don't Ask*, 1999; U.S. Congress, 1993). He says:

> *Cohesion is the glue that holds small units together. In ranger school we would wrap a poncho liner around us when we were cold. So you're sharing body heat. If there is any perception of inappropriate behavior that you think might result from that, you have to have total trust that not only are they going to pull your wounded body off the battlefield but that they won't do any thing untoward.*

Ed Bradley follows, "so if you were under that poncho sharing body heat with that gay soldier, that would make you uncomfortable?" Mc-

Ginnis responds "It definitely would make me uncomfortable."

This is the rationale for the gay ban. And this rationale depends on a funny assumption. It depends on the assumption that most people in the military, most days of their lives, spend time in foxholes. Now we could start to pick apart the unit cohesion rationale by noting that of the 400,000 or so people in the Air Force, I am not aware of a single one who spends any time in a foxhole. In fact, most people in the military work together in the same way the people of corporate America work together in offices. Given that much if not most of the military looks like an office, and given that gays and heterosexuals can work together at Microsoft and Boeing and the Marriott Corporation, one starts to wonder why they cannot work together in the military.

People who support the gay ban provide two pieces of evidence to show that known gays and lesbians undermine military performance. The first kind of evidence they cite is anecdotal evidence. And most anecdotes take the following form: "Well, I served for twenty years in the military, and I was in a unit once where we had a gay guy and something bad happened" (U.S. Senate, 1993). And that something bad might have been that the gay person did something bad, or something bad was done to the gay person, or the gay person had sex when he or she was not supposed to have sex. It is anecdotal evidence, and the specific content of the anecdote does not matter. The critical point to consider is that anecdotes are not a sound basis for policy. If we did base policy on anecdotes, certainly we could come up with anecdotes of chubby people who have caused problems in the military and left-handed people and Chinese people and African American people and heterosexual people who have caused problems. But anecdotes are not a sound foundation for law because official policies should not be based on inferring the attributes of an individual from stereotypes about his or her class. And even if one could identify thousands of anecdotes about gay people causing problems, that would not mean that any particular gay person is problematic. Gays and lesbians should be judged by their own record in the same way that everyone else is judged on their individual record.

In addition, anecdotes do not constitute scientifically valid evidence. The question is not whether one or ten or one hundred or even one thousand gays and lesbians have undermined their units' cohesion. Rather, the question is whether *on average* gays and lesbians tend to undermine cohesion. For every anecdote that advocates of discrimination use to show that gays and lesbians undermine cohesion, others can be identified to show that they do not undermine cohesion. So the anecdotal evidence that supporters of discrimination cite is not something that can be taken seriously.

However, there is another type of evidence that advocates of discrimination cite to support the unit cohesion rationale. This second piece of evidence consists of statistical surveys that show that heterosexual soldiers do not like gay soldiers (Miller & Williams, 1999). And therefore an equation is made in which straight soldiers' dislike of gay soldiers is said to be the same as unit cohesion falling apart.

There are three reasons why surveys do not count as evidence for the unit cohesion rationale. First, dislike has no impact on organizational performance. I am not citing one study or ten studies here. Literally there are hundreds of studies from sports theory, organization theory and military theory that show that whether group members like each other has no bearing on how well organizations perform (Kier, 1998). One can think of sports teams in which the quarterback and the wide receiver hate each other. Whether or not those teams do well has nothing to do with hatred. Performance depends, rather, on whether team members are committed to the same goals.

Indeed, in the military itself one can point to numerous groups whose members have been at each other's throats. Yet the armed forces have served as a socialization engine that lets them serve together. Imagine someone from Bob Jones University in a unit with someone who is in an interracial romantic relationship. Those people would learn to work together because dislike has no impact on organizational performance. Again, that is the result of hundreds of studies summarized most recently in the Harvard University journal *International Security* (Kier, 1998). It is not a gay journal. It is not even a liberal journal. It is the most prestigious journal in the field of international security and it summarized these hundreds of studies.

The second reason why these statistical surveys do not support the idea that the presence of known gays in the military would undermine performance or cohesion is that bigoted attitudes are not the same as bigoted behavior. As described in the well-known Lapiere study (1934), a white man toured the country with two Chinese people and logged over 10,000 miles on his car. They visited 251 hotels and restaurants and trailer parks. And before arriving at each establishment, Lapiere called and said "I have very important Chinese visitors with me. Would you mind if we stay in your hotel or would you mind if we eat in your restaurant?" Every single establishment said, "No, we do not accept Chinese people in our restaurant or our hotel." Then Lapiere and his Chinese friends visited the establishment and 250 out of 251 of them served the Chinese couple without a problem. The evidence shows that bigoted attitudes are not the same as bigoted behavior.

One could claim that the Lapiere study has nothing to do with homosexuality. But then I would point to an entire literature that has been produced in the last fifteen years that shows that even when people dislike homosexuals, as soon as they have contact with an actual gay or lesbian person, in most cases the dislike goes away, and in all cases people are able to work together (Herek & Capitanio, 1996).

One could respond that those studies do not reflect the military. In that case, I would point to a study of the Canadian military that my research center sponsored. In 1985, the Defense Department in Canada did a survey of 6,500 soldiers. At the time, Canada prohibited known gays and lesbians from serving in the military. And of those 6,500 soldiers, 62% said they would not shower with a gay person, that they would not bunk with a gay person, and that they would not undress with a gay person. Now fast-forward to 1992. Canada lifted its gay ban. Now fast-forward to 1995, when the Canadian military did another survey and found no problems whatsoever with discipline. The Canadians found that the majority of soldiers were satisfied with the fact that gays could serve openly (Belkin & McNichol, 2000; Zuliani, 1986; Wenek, 1995). The bottom line is that bigoted attitudes are not the same as bigoted behavior. Even though supporters of discrimination can point to surveys that show that heterosexual soldiers do not like gays and lesbians, this does not mean that known gays undermine unit cohesion.

The third reason why statistical surveys are not evidence is that heterosexual soldiers' dislike of gays and lesbians is less extreme than supporters of the gay ban suggest. According to people who oppose lifting the ban, heterosexuals in the armed forces hate gays and lesbians. A close reading of the evidence shows that this is not true. From 1992 to 1998, the percentage of U.S. Army men who strongly oppose gays and lesbians in the military dropped from 67% to just 36%. The percentage of Army women who strongly oppose gays and lesbians in the military dropped from 32% to 16% (Miller, 1994; Kier, 1999, p. 196).

Armando Estrada, a psychologist at the University of Texas, administered a feeling thermometer to a sample of male U.S. marines in a 1999 study (Estrada & Weiss, 1999). On this particular feeling thermometer, a score of zero reflects total hatred of gay people and a score of one hundred signals complete acceptance. Estrada found that the Marines' average result on the feeling thermometer was 47.52. The specific number is not important but it is meaningful that the average score fell roughly in the middle of the scale, thus indicating mild dislike rather than widespread ha-

tred. Some people in the military hate gays and lesbians but on average one finds mild dislike. Another finding from the Estrada study is that 47% of male Marines say that if there is a draft, gays should be drafted just like everybody else. If gays should be drafted like everybody else, then how can it be true that they undermine unit cohesion when we have a volunteer military?

So, for two reasons I would argue that there is no evidence to support the unit cohesion rationale. Neither statistical surveys nor anecdotes show that gays and lesbians undermine military cohesion.

Before addressing the evidence on the other side of the coin that shows that gays can serve in military organizations without causing problems, it makes sense to consider whether or not the gay ban has any costs. I would argue that there are at least four costs associated with "Don't-Ask, Don't-Tell."

First, the policy is expensive and the most conservative estimate of the cost of kicking out gay people from the military is that over the last five years, the Pentagon has spent $130 million dollars in lost training. And over the course of the Cold War, the U.S. spent about $500 million dollars kicking out gay and lesbian people (Shilts, 1993, p. 476; Sobel, Westcott, Benecke & Osburn, 2000, p. 74). These are conservative figures because they do not include soldiers who were forced to resign and they do not include the cost of investigations. They include only the cost of the lost training of people who were fired.

The second problem associated with the gay ban is brain drain and talent loss. The U.S. military fires about one thousand people each year for being gay. Many of the soldiers who have been fired or who have left the military as a result of the gay ban are very talented people such as Andrea Hollen, a Rhodes scholar. These are people who should be using their talents to serve their country as they choose and who enter the private sector and pursue successful careers.

Ruined lives and psychological casualties constitute the third problem with this policy. The tactics and techniques of military investigators leave psychological scars on their victims that last for years. To take one of many examples, consider the case of Loren Loomis who was fired from the military just five days short of his twenty-year eligibility for retirement (Egan, 1998, p. 30).

A fourth and final problem with this policy is that it leads to violence against women. During a debate on *Catholic Family Radio,* I faced an extreme right-wing pundit who claimed that the military ban does not lead to violence against women and that complaints about this issue come from "a few whining lesbians." Perhaps this pundit was not aware of a recent Veterans Administration study that found that 23% of women in the military experience actual physical violence or the threat of physical violence during their military careers. While the Pentagon has not released recent data, figures show that between 1987 and 1991 there were 484 rapes of women serving in the military (Chema, 1993).

What does this pattern of violence against women have to do with the gay ban? The link is that in many cases women cannot report their harassers and even their rapists because if they do they can be investigated for homosexuality. Perpetrators know that women are unlikely to report them and this knowledge serves as a green light for would-be abusers. For example, after Canada lifted its gay and lesbian ban, sexual harassment against women dropped 46% (Belkin & McNichol, 2000, pp. 25–26; Beneck & Dodge, 1990). While there were several reasons why sexual harassment dropped 46%, one factor was that women were free to report their harassers, thus deterring potential perpetrators.

A final point to consider is whether any evidence shows that gays and lesbians can serve openly without undermining cohesion. I would like to present six pieces of evidence that show that known gays and lesbians can serve in the military without causing any problems.

First, known gays and lesbians already do serve openly in the American military without causing problems. In a recent debate on *National*

*Public Radio,* Charles Moskos, the architect of "Don't-Ask, Don't-Tell," said that "there are no open gays in the U.S. military." If you consult the *University of Missouri-Kansas City Law Review,* Fall 1995, however, you will find an eight-page list of gays who have served openly in the military (Osburn, 1995, pp. 215–223). And, a recent study found that 39.1% of enlisted naval personnel know a gay sailor (Bicknell, 2000).

Second, gays and lesbians serve openly in police departments without causing problems. San Diego is a conservative city but the gay-lesbian liaison officer of the San Diego police department reports that about fifty known gays and lesbians serve on the force. Police work requires daily exposure to violence, and unit cohesion and trust of fellow officers are very important. And yet the many American police departments that have lifted their gay bans continue to function properly (Koegel, 1996).

Advocates of military discrimination note that police officers do not live or shower in shared quarters. While this is true, they should consider a third piece of evidence that gays can serve openly without causing problems. Gays and lesbians are allowed to serve openly in fire departments and this has not caused a problem for unit cohesion. They are allowed to live in fire houses and to take showers with their peers in Seattle, Chicago, New York and elsewhere (Koegel, 1996).

A fourth piece of evidence that gays and lesbians can serve openly without causing any detriment to unit cohesion is that they are allowed to serve in the CIA, in the FBI and in the Secret Service (on President Clinton's security detail). It is not possible to claim that the President's security detail does not require unit cohesion.

The fifth piece of evidence is that gays and lesbians are allowed to serve openly in foreign militaries. Every original NATO country except Turkey allows known gays and lesbians to serve in the armed forces ("Gay Troops," 2000). People who support discrimination respond that there are variations in policy, that in some countries gays and lesbians cannot be promoted past a certain level and that in others they are denied security clearances. These variations do not matter. The fact is that despite the variations, known gays and lesbians are allowed to serve and they do not undermine unit cohesion. Another response is that cultural differences underscore the irrelevance of foreign military experiences for determining whether known gays and lesbians would undermine cohesion in the U.S. armed forces. While no two cultures are the same, twenty-three different countries allow known gays and lesbians to serve. Given that there is no evidence that any of these countries have suffered a decline in military performance despite their cultural differences, one has to wonder why a more tolerant policy would fail in the United States. Advocates of discrimination respond that most people do not come out of the closet in foreign militaries. If gay soldiers prefer to serve on a discreet basis, however, then there is even less reason to fear lifting the ban. Advocates of discrimination seem to assume that there is something different about American gays and lesbians that would make them disclose their sexual orientation at a higher rate than gays and lesbians in other militaries.

After Canada lifted its gay ban in 1992, Britain sent an investigative team to Canada to study the effects of the new policy. At the time, Britain had not yet lifted its ban and the British team was looking for evidence to show that the new Canadian policy was a failure. After they visited the Canadian forces, however, the British investigators changed their minds because they saw that lifting a gay ban does not undermine military performance (Belkin & McNichol, 2000, p. 29).

The sixth and final piece of evidence that gays and lesbians can serve openly without causing problems involves American wartime experience. The rate of discharges of gays and lesbians in the American military always declines during wartime. The World War II rate of discharge was ten times lower that the post-war rate. During the Korean and Vietnam Wars, the Pentagon kicked out about half as many gays and lesbians as was the case during peacetime. During the Persian

Gulf Crisis, the Pentagon issued a stop-loss order that directed commanders to refrain from firing gays and lesbians. General Bill Nash, who is against letting known gays and lesbians serve in the military, admitted on National Public Radio that when he was in Bosnia, he did not have time to kick several known gays out of his unit.

If gays and lesbians can serve during wartime, and indeed if the Pentagon tries to make them serve during wartime because it wants more bodies available for service, how can one claim that gays undermine cohesion in peacetime? Advocates of military discrimination say that the Pentagon reduces gay discharges during wartime to prevent straight soldiers from trying to escape service by pretending to be homosexual. If military leaders are worried about straight people trying to get out of the military during wartime by pretending to be gay, however, they should lift the gay ban.

Recall that according to the unit cohesion rationale, known gays make it impossible for their units to survive in combat. Let us take the most conservative estimate of the number of gay people in the military. Let us say that 2% of the American military consists of gay soldiers. This is a conservative estimate given that 3.5% of the Canadian military is gay. But let us say that only 2% of the U.S. military is gay or lesbian. That would mean that there are 30,000 gays and lesbians serving. Now let us say that just 10% of these soldiers are known by their peers to be gay and that the other 90% remain in the closet. Again, this is a conservative estimate because it is difficult for soldiers who share quarters, who do not have wedding rings, and who do not discuss romantic partners to hide sexual orientation. And, recall that 39.1% of enlisted naval personnel know a gay sailor. So let us just say conservatively that 10% or 3,000 people in the military are known by their peers to be gay. According to the Pentagon's own logic, each one of these 3,000 soldiers undermines his or her unit's ability to survive. If the Chairman of the Joint Chiefs of Staff believed the unit cohesion rationale, he would kick these 3,000 known gays and lesbians out of the military during wartime to prevent them from destroying their units. When wars occur, however, the Pentagon retains gay and lesbian soldiers. Do military leaders actually expect us to believe that they are willing to permit 3,000 soldiers to destroy their units in order to prevent straight soldiers from pretending to be homosexual? Clearly, even the Pentagon knows that the unit cohesion rationale is not true.

What are the sources for this evidence? Are these points based on gay propaganda? One source is a 518-page RAND Corporation study of the impact of known gays on fire departments, foreign militaries, and police departments. The RAND study includes a 53-page bibliography and it was written by 30 Ph.D. authors. Other sources include a General Accounting Office study of 1993 and a Harvard University study of 1998. These comprehensive reviews of the literature reach the same conclusion: There is no evidence to show that gays and lesbians undermine cohesion (National Defense Research Institute, 1993; U.S. General Accounting Office, 1993; Kier, 1998; Belkin & McNichol, 2000).

To conclude, the military's ban on known gay and lesbian soldiers seems to be an instance of willful ignorance, a situation in which powerful people prefer to be blind to evidence (Sedgwick, 1990, pp. 4–8). The policy known as "Don't-Ask, Don't-Tell" is proud of its ignorance and its refusal to see. The media has framed the debate on gays in the military as if there is evidence on both sides of the question, as if there are data on both sides of the issue. One does not have to like gay people or be a liberal, however, to see that the media and the talking heads and the pundits have framed this debate on an assumption that is not true.

General Colin Powell and ex-Senator Sam Nunn and Professor Charles Moskos and the other architects of this policy should answer the following questions: If gays undermine unit cohesion, why are they allowed to serve in Canada without causing problems? Why are there fifty of them serving on the San Diego police department without causing problems? Why are they in the

Australian navy? Why are they on the Seattle fire department? Why are they in the Israeli military? Why are they in the U.S. secret service without causing problems? Why are they in the British military without causing problems? The architects of this policy should have the integrity to admit that "Don't-Ask, Don't-Tell" is not based on data. It is not based on military necessity. It is based on prejudice and bigotry and nothing else. . . .

## REFERENCES

Belkin, A. & McNichol, J. (2000). *Effects of the 1992 lifting of restrictions on gay and lesbian service in the Canadian Forces: Appraising the evidence.* Santa Barbara, CA: Center for the Study of Sexual Minorities in the Military. Available: http://www.gaymilitary.ucsb.edu. (July 22, 2000)

Benecke, M. M. & Dodge, K. (1990). Military women in nontraditional job fields: Casualties of the armed forces' war on homosexuals. *Harvard Women's Law Journal, 13,* 215–250.

Bianco, D. A. (1996). Echoes of prejudice: The debates over race and sexuality in the armed forces. In C. A. Rimmerman (Ed.), *Gay rights, military wrongs; Political perspectives on lesbians and gays in the military* (pp. 47–70). New York: Garland Publishing, Inc.

Bicknell, Jr., J. W. (2000). *Study of naval officers' attitudes toward homosexuals in the military.* Monterey, CA: Naval Postgraduate School.

Butler, J. (1997). Contagious word: paranoia and "homosexuality in the military." In *Excitable speech: A politics of the performative* (pp. 103–126). New York: Routledge.

Chema, J. R. (1993). Arresting "tailhook": The prosecution of sexual harassment in the military. *Military Law Review, 140.*

Don't ask, don't tell. (1999, December 12). *Sixty Minutes.*

Egan, J. (1998, June 28). Uniform in the closet. *New York Times Magazine.*

Estrada, A. X. & Weiss, D. J. (1999). Attitudes of military personnel toward homosexuals. *Journal of Homosexuality, 37,* 83–97.

Gay troops in Europe. (2000, January 15). *New York Times.*

Halley, J. E. (1996). The status/conduct distinction in the 1993 revisions to military anti-gay policy. *GLQ, 3*, 159–252.

Halley, J. E. (1999). *Don't; A reader's guide to the military's anti-gay policy.* Durham: Duke University Press.

Harassment of gays in the military. (2000, March 28). *New York Times.*

Harris interactive election 2000 study. (2000, January 19–26).

Herek, G. M. & Capitanio, J. P. (1996). Some of my best friends–Intergroup contact, concealable stigma, and heterosexuals' attitudes toward gay men and lesbians. *Personality and Social Psychology Bulletin, 22*, 412–424.

Hertzog, M. (1996). *The lavender vote.* New York: New York University Press.

Kier, E. (1998). Homosexuals in the U.S. military: Open integration and combat effectiveness. *International Security, 23*, 5–39.

Kier, E. (1999). Rights and fights: Sexual orientation and military effectiveness. *International Security, 24*, 194–201.

Koegel, P. (1996). Lessons learned from the experience of domestic police and fire departments. In G. M. Herek, J. B. Jobe, & R. M. Carney (Eds.), *Out in force; sexual orientation and the military* (pp. 131– 153). Chicago: University of Chicago Press.

Lapiere, R. T. (1934). Attitudes versus actions. *Social Forces, 13*, 230–237.

Miller, L. L. (1994). Fighting for a just cause: Soldiers' attitudes on gays in the military. In W. J. Scott & S. C. Stanley (Eds.), *Gays and lesbians in the military* (pp. 69–85). New York: Aldine de Gruyter.

Miller, L. L. & Williams, J. A. (1999). Combat effectiveness vs. civil rights? U.S. military culture, cohesion, and personnel policies in the 1990s. Paper prepared for the Triangle Institute for Security Studies Project on the Gap Between the Military and Civilian Society.

National Defense Research Institute. (1993). *Sexual orientation and U.S. military personnel policy: Options and assessment.* Santa Monica, CA: RAND.

Osburn, C. D. (1995). A policy in desperate search of a rationale: The military's policy on lesbians, gays, and bisexuals. *University of Missouri-Kansas City Law Review, 64*, 215–223.

Sedgwick, E. (1990). *Epistemology of the closet.* Berkeley: University of California Press.

Shawver, L. (1995). *And the flag was still there: Straight people, gay people, and sexuality in the U.S. military.* New York: Harrington Park Press.

Shilts, R. (1993). *Conduct unbecoming; Gays and lesbians in the U.S. military.* New York: Fawcett Columbine.

Sobel, S. L., Westcott, K. S., Benecke, M. M., & Osburn, C. D. (2000). *Conduct unbecoming; The sixth annual report on "don't ask, don't tell, don't pursue, don't harass."* Washington, DC: Servicemembers Legal Defense Network. Available: http://www.sldn.org. (July 22, 2000)

U.S. Congress. (1993). *10 United States code 654.* (Pub.L. 103–160 571, 107 Stat., 1547). Washington, DC: U.S. Government Printing Office.

U.S. General Accounting Office. (1993). *Homosexuals in the military: Policies and practices of foreign countries* (GAO/NSIAD-93-215). Washington, DC: U.S. Government Printing Office.

U.S. Senate. (1993). *Policy concerning homosexuality in the armed forces.* (Hearings before the Committee on Armed Services, U.S. Senate, 103d Congress, 2d Sess). Washington, DC: U.S. Government Printing Office.

Wenek, K. (1995). *Briefing note for director of public policy.* Ottawa: Canadian Forces.

Zuliani, R. A. (1986). *Canadian Forces survey on homosexual issues.* Ottawa: Department of National Defence.

# Sexuality and Globalization

Dennis Altman

## Sexuality and Globalization

During the 2002 Gay Games in Sydney a number of meetings were organized by Asia/Pacific Rainbow, a group of self-consciously gay, lesbian, and bisexual activists from across south and east Asia and Australasia. Many would question whether these identities are meaningful in Asia, arguing either that there is no room for homosexuality in traditional Asian morality, or alternatively that traditional Asian arrangements of sexuality and gender allow for a far richer diversity than is suggested by the Western terms of (homo)sexual identity politics. Preliminary discussions in the planning of Rainbow stressed the need to avoid these sorts of arguments in favor of a pragmatic stress on organizing around homosexual advocacy using the language of international human rights.

One of the Indian participants wrote of his experiences at the opening ceremony of the Games:

> I could see the distance we have to travel back home before we get to a point of celebrating our sexuality without fear or repression. I could also feel the euphoria of freedom where it exists, and the desirability of it, for it is inherently good. But most of all I could feel a validation of what I do back home, for unfolding before my eyes was an ideal that could be had, and playing at the back of my mind was the actual oppression I witness every day I live and work in India. (Bondyopadhay, 2002)

From Altman, Dennis. 2004. "Sexuality and Globalization." *Sexuality Research & Social Policy* 1(1): 63–68. Copyright 2004, National Sexuality Resource Center/San Francisco State University. Reprinted by permission.

This quote illustrates the complexities involved in applying universal norms of both freedom and sexual identity to societies with very different cultural and social structures from those which produced the particular construction of "gay" and "lesbian" identities. Arguments around the tensions have taken place in recent years in most non-western countries, often with a conflation of "tradition" and the legacy of colonialism, with the result that post-colonial states such as India, Zimbabwe, and Malaysia defend the retention of anti-homosexual laws that are in fact legacies of colonialism (Phillips, 2001; Reddy, 2002). At the same time gay and lesbian groups are emerging in most countries with sufficient political space for any sort of political organizing, and gay pride parades are now held in cities as different as Manila, Johannesburg, and Sao Paulo. Are we to understand this as a product of globalization, in all the ways that term is currently understood?

If by globalization we understand the range of shifts in the social, economic, and cultural spheres which are part of the growing movement of peoples, ideas, trade, and money across the world (Held & McGrew, 2002; Soros, 2000), then globalization affects sexuality in a number of interconnected ways. The common thread is perhaps the growth of consumerism and individualism, features which seem more easily transferred with economic growth than specific political values. It is important to recognize that similar rhetoric and appearances may mask significant differences: it is easier to globalize fashion than underlying attitudes. The music, the clothes, and the hairstyles in the discos may be the same, but the meanings are likely to vary.

As young people pour into the rapidly growing cities across the third world, they are exposed to new media images, through cinema, television, and above all the Internet, which offer radically different ways of imagining sex and gender arrangements and identities. Increasingly people live in a world rich in conflicting and hybrid imagery. Young Saudi and Egyptian men studying the Koran also see images of sexuality on television which they are taught are evil, while young people flock to discos in Shanghai, Jakarta, and Lima to dance to music and video images from the United States (Farrar, 2002). While the current U.S. administration fosters a conservative position on reproductive rights and sexual education, the images of the dominant U.S. film and video industry offer new ways of constructing lives, along with identities based upon sexuality and gender. Of course not all electronic images come from the United States, and globalization implies a greater degree of international imagery, as through the popularity of Latin American telenovelas (Allen, 1995; Sinclair, 1996) or the films of Bollywood.

Such "new ways" are only possible because of massive social and economic changes that create the conditions to break away from old ways of doing things, much as the Industrial Revolution reshaped personal relations in nineteenth century Europe. In the past thirty years there have been enormous shifts in China, as tens of millions of people have moved from the countryside to booming metropolitan centers, where there is a freedom to experiment in "personal life" unimaginable in their villages (Brownell & Wasserstrom, 2002; Dutton, 1998). Out of these shifts people are creating new forms of sexual behavior and norms, which in his discussion of contemporary Mexico Hector Carrillo terms a "new hybridity" (Carrillo, 2002). As he points out, older forms of acting out homosexual behavior coexist with imported identities, so that one finds in Mexico, as in most other parts of the world, what some writers have termed a "global gay" identity. For many people sexual desire coexists with a "desire for modernity," that is, a desire to be part of the

affluence and freedom associated with images of the rich world.

As a consequence of these shifts, the "traditional" ways of regulating and controlling sexuality decline. These shifts are perhaps most obvious in much of East Asia, where there has been a rapid collapse in the last thirty years of arranged marriages in favor of marriages entered into through the free choice of the couple concerned. Evidence for shifts in sexual behavior are harder to establish, though one can find a range of examples from different parts of the world. In Thailand there are claims of a declining use of sex workers by young men, paralleled by a greater degree of premarital sex as young women become less likely to postpone intercourse until marriage (Perrin, 2002). In Zimbabwe there are reports of "kissing and smooching" in nightclubs, to the dismay of older Zimbabweans (Runganaga & Aggleton, 1998). Perhaps most significant, if hardest to measure, are ways in which a stress on female pleasure as legitimate is spreading with the diffusion of a mixture of Western feminism and consumerism. Certainly reports from a number of societies speak of the growth of "dating" as social conditions change and unmarried girls are no longer subject to the total surveillance of their families.

I do not want to suggest that the changes in the regulation and experience of sexuality are always liberatory. The greater mobility and (in some cases) affluence associated with globalization mean traditional family and community ties are weakened, while allowing for new patterns of private life to develop. This is most obvious for women, who often carry a disproportionate burden of the consequences of rapid economic change. On the one hand economic "development" means that millions of women become economically independent and are able to imagine new ways of living (thus the quick spread of marriage by choice, of women controlling their own reproduction, of single women building lives for themselves, of extensive changes in dating and extra-marital sex). Others are far less lucky, as economic shifts leave them destitute and without either communal or state support to look after themselves and their children. The "feminization of poverty" has become an international phenomenon as a result of pressure to adopt neo-liberal economics policies that have thrown millions of women into the search for poorly paid and badly protected jobs (Parrenas, 2001).

Globalization is leading to new forms of inequality, as people differ radically in the opportunities they have to benefit from rapid change. While many people have been able to move into middle class lifestyles, many more, especially since the financial crashes in countries as far apart as Indonesia, Argentina, Russia, and Turkey, have been pauperized, and at a time when the state's ability to provide basic services is declining. For some, globalization means the ability to emulate the lives portrayed in U.S. movies and television. For many, it means increasing struggles for survival, through petty crime, begging, and sex work. It is not surprising that two influential books on the meanings of globalization share the title *Globalization and Its Discontents* (Sassen, 1998; Stiglitz, 2002).

Critiques of globalization along these lines have become increasingly mainstream, as even institutions like the World Bank acknowledge the failures of too rapid an imposition of market economies and too precipitous a withdrawal of government services (Milanovic, 2003). In the case of sexuality one might point to a corresponding gap as increasing numbers of people in non-Western societies become aware of the possibilities for far greater individual autonomy elsewhere through their exposure to Western societies and media. The tensions between the local and the global are reflected in developing movements such as that among homosexuals or sex workers (Altman, 2003; Berry, Martin, & Yue, 2003; Drucker, 2000; Kempadoo & Doezema, 1998), where models derived from images of the first world are blended with very different social and cultural environments. In turn such movements confront a strong backlash to what their

opponents characterize as Western decadence and social collapse (this rhetoric, similar to that of the religious right, infuses critiques of Western liberalism expressed by exponents of "Asian values"). It is safe to predict that just as globalization is sharpening a sense of economic inequality in the world, so too it is ensuring that very different conceptions of the sexual will become politically contested.

## Mobility, Health, and Human Rights

The mobility associated with globalization is as much between as within states, and few countries remain unaffected by the influx of large numbers of migrants, often unwanted and marginalized (Martin, 2000). This huge movement of peoples creates considerable social tension as large numbers of people move to societies with very different regimes of sexuality and gender. Thus there is considerable conflict between, say, South Asian immigrants to Britain, who seek to maintain communal cohesion by arranging marriages through contacts "back home," and their British-educated children who often resist such moves.

Prostitution is certainly not the invention of globalization, but it is being reshaped by increasing population movements and collapsing social cohesion. While it is not clear that prostitution is expanding, it is certainly being globalized, as large scale trafficking in young women and men means that most major world cities have an extremely cosmopolitan sex work force, often through the organized smuggling of people—from Moldova and Albania to Western Europe; from Nepal to India; from Mozambique and the Congo to South Africa. One recent report talks of the importation of "gigolos" from Jamaica and Nigeria for "high society" women in Bangkok ("Rising Demand," 2002). Most dramatic has been the huge movements of young people from the former Soviet Union into the international sex industry in the past ten years, with estimates of perhaps half a million young women and men moving west as sex workers since the end of the Cold War.

Not for nothing was the Iron Curtain described as "the world's largest condom." "Sex tourism" underlies part of the growth of prostitution, but is probably less significant than sometimes claimed. Except in a few holiday destinations the majority of customers are local. Nor, of course, is all sex tourism based on prostitution: the term might also be deployed to describe the many lesbians and gay men who travel to events such as the Gay Games or Sydney's Mardi Gras, or the wholesale exodus of American college students for spring break vacations (Josiam, Hobson, Dietrich, & Smeaton, 1998; Maticka-Tyndale, 1998).

The most dramatic examples of the effect of globalization on sexuality come through the rapid growth of the HIV/AIDS pandemic. In many senses AIDS is an epidemic of globalization, both in terms of its spread and its response. It is symbolic that the epidemic, first identified in the hospitals of the United States, is most prevalent in the poorest countries of the world, and there are effectively now two epidemics, a small one in rich countries, which is growing slowly, and a rapidly expanding one in much of the poor world where the huge advances in medical therapies are largely unavailable. The epidemic is spread by the relentless movement of people, the breakdown of old sexual restraints, increasing needle use, and the unwillingness of authorities, both governmental and religious, to confront the real needs of prevention (Barnett & Whiteside, 2002; Farmer, 1998). But the growing international mobilization to counter HIV/AIDS is also a sign of globalization, and as part of this response, development resources are made available to groups working with "men who have sex with men" and sex workers, which is extremely politically controversial.

In part because of HIV/AIDS, questions of sexuality are becoming more central to debates about international human rights. International meetings on population (Cairo 1994), women (Beijing 1995), human rights (Vienna 1993) (Desai, 1999; Smith & Pagnucco, 1998), and AIDS (the General Assembly Special Session in 2001) have all seen major debates about sexual rights, and human rights organizations, led by Amnesty International, have started considering cases related to sexuality. Some scholars are developing theories of "sexual rights" as a way of prioritizing the protection of individual autonomy over the claims of culture, religion, and tradition (Petchesky, 2000; Stychin, 1998).

War crime prosecutions for rape in former Yugoslavia and Rwanda, along with considerable publicity surrounding "traditional" punishments for adultery and homosexuality, are altering the language of human rights law to encompass what was once regarded as private, and beyond the reach of law. Similar to the assertions of the gay/lesbian groups in Rainbow is international support for the rights of women to choose when and with whom to have sex, and to have access to the technologies of reproduction and sexual health. In the last few years the brutal gang rape of a woman in Pakistan, accused of sex with someone outside her caste, and the sentencing to death by stoning of a Nigerian woman found guilty of adultery, became international causes celebres, with few people prepared to defend the unlimited right of states to ignore the protection of basic human rights in the name of custom and religion.

As arguments around sexuality move from the private into the public realm, strange parallels emerge in very different social, cultural, and political settings. The bitter battles over attitudes to sexual diversity in American schools were matched in an attempt a few years ago to ban homosexuals from entering Thai teachers' colleges. The concept of gay marriage has become a political issue in South Africa, the Philippines, and most of Europe as well as the United States. Restrictions on condom advertising are contested in Malaysia, Chile, and the United States. Almost all authoritarian regimes are repressive around matters sexual: the punitive ways of the Taliban are well known, but the Hindu Tamil Tigers are said to have imposed ten years imprisonment in underground jails for prostitution.

Because every society has its own particular hypocrisies over sexuality, it is sometimes difficult to understand the extent to which a more universal set of sexual norms and behaviors are emerging. Clearly the extent to which women are subordinated is a crucial variable—one would not expect the same attitudes to sexuality in Sweden as in Indonesia—but the differences are not absolute. Sweden has criminalized anyone who seeks the services of prostitutes (Kulick, 2003), while the Suharto regime created a whole set of rules governing the "proper" behavior of women. In both cases the state saw its role as protecting innocent and vulnerable women, even though one was a liberal social democracy and the other an authoritarian regime committed to defending "Asian values" against Western excesses.

While most liberal Western countries have moved towards a more interventionist approach on matters of sexual rights, other parts of the world have sought to resist these moves as part of a general reaction against "modernization" and "Westernization." The old Communist language of "bourgeois decadence" is today echoed in the ways in which leaders such as Robert Mugabe and Mohammed Mahathir attack sexual "permissiveness," often defined by tolerance of homosexuality, which becomes defined, however ahistorical this may be, as a Western import. The United States, as so often, seems the exception. The Bush Administration has reversed much of Clinton's support for international family planning programs, and forced the United Nations Population Fund to cut back on a number of its programs by withholding $34 million, following claims that the Fund supported abortions in China.

Some might argue that governments should seek to remain neutral in matters of personal behavior and morality, enforcing neither a liberal humanist view of human rights or positions derived from particular religious or cultural backgrounds. Yet the AIDS epidemic illustrates graphically that the line between private and public is increasingly blurred. While some countries have adopted prevention programs advocating abstinence outside of, and postponement of sexual relations until and fidelity within marriage, the realities of human sexuality mean that such programs can only be partially successful. In the long term, effective prevention means access to and knowledge of condoms, acknowledgement of sex work and homosexuality, and cooperation with those involved in such behaviors, stigmatized or not.

The state inevitably affects sexuality through a myriad of laws and regulation, and the choice is not whether it should intervene but what forms its interventions should take. Support for "family planning" and reproductive health technology can be used to enforce top-down population planning, as was the case in very different ways in China and Romania in the 1990s, or it can be used to enhance women's choices and empowerment. The United States has backed various forms of reproductive policies for half a century, and any American administration will face strong and conflicting domestic pressures on how foreign aid is used in such programs.

With some reluctance governments and international organizations are coming to accept that they cannot avoid matters to do with the "private" and basic arrangements of sexuality and gender. The battle lines that divided those supporting "traditional" strictures on sex at the 1994 Cairo conference, where the Vatican and the Reagan Administration found themselves allied with fundamentalist Islamic states, are repeated today, for example at the U.N. Conference on Sustainable Development in Johannesburg in 2002. Claims by feminist, gay, and human rights organizations for particular positions to be adopted by international bodies are prefiguring a debate which will become more central, and places otherwise bitterly antagonistic governments—e.g. the United States and Iran—on the same side.

Defenders of globalization claim that it is ensuring an increase in individual freedoms and affluence. An analysis of whether such an increase is apparent at the level of sexuality and gender is a significant test of these claims, and a reminder that massive social change almost always has both victors and casualties. It also reminds us that globalization does not necessarily mean homogenization. To end where I began: in Thailand, as in most Asian countries, one can find men who identify as "gay," and there are numerous venues in Bangkok which are immediately recognizable as part of a global gay world. At the same time many other Thai men identity as *kathoey,* a particular sort of effeminate man who approximates, but is not the same as a "nelly queen," as depicted in the very successful Thai film *Iron Ladies.* Globalization means greater diversity within as well as between nations, but it certainly does not eliminate cultural differences.

## REFERENCES

Allen, R. (Ed.). (1995). *To be continued. . . . : Soap operas around the world.* London: Routledge.

Altman, D. (2001). *Global sex.* Chicago: University of Chicago Press.

Altman, D. (in press). Queer centres and peripheries. *Cultural Studies Review.*

Barnett, T., & Whiteside, A. (2002). *AIDS in the twenty-first century.* Basingstoke, England: Macmillan.

Berry, C., Martin, F., & Yue, A. (2003). *Mobile cultures: New media in queer Asia.* Durham, NC: Duke University Press.

Bondyopadhay, A. (2002, November 3). Message posted to ap-rainbow (Asia Pacific Rainbow) electronic mailing list, archived at http://groups.yahoo.com/group/ao-rainbow/

Brownell, S., & Wasserstrom, J. (Eds.). (2002). *Chinese femininities/Chinese masculinities.* Berkeley, CA: University of California Press.

Carrillo, H. (2002). *The night is young.* Chicago: University of Chicago Press.

Desai, M. (1999). From Vienna to Beijing. In P. van Ness (Ed.), *Debating human rights* (pp. 184–196). London: Rutgers University Press.

Drucker, P. (Ed.). (2000). *Different rainbows.* London: GMP.

Dutton, M. (1998). *Streetlife China.* Melbourne, Australia: Cambridge University Press.

Farmer, P. (1998). *Infections and inequalities.* Berkeley, CA: University of California Press.

Farrar, J. (2002). Opening up: Youth sex culture and market reform in Shanghai. Chicago: Chicago University Press.

Held, D., & McGrew, A. (2002). *Globalization/anti-globalization.* Cambridge, England: Polity.

Josiam, B. M., Hobson, J. S. P., Dietrich, U. C., & Smeaton, G. (1998). An analysis of the sexual, alcohol, and drug-related behavioral patterns of students on spring break. *Tourism Management, 19,* 501–513.

Kempadoo, K., & Doezema, J. (Eds.). (1998). *Global sex workers.* New York: Routledge.

Kulick, D. (2003). Sex in the new Europe. *Anthropological Theory, 3*(2), 199–218.

Martin, S. (2000). An era of international migration. *World Migration Report.* Geneva, Switzerland: International Organization for Migration.

Maticka-Tyndale, E., Herold, E., & Mewhinney, D. (1998). Casual sex on spring break: Intentions and behavior of Canadian students. *Journal of Sex Research, 35,* 254–62.

Milanovic, B. (2003). The two faces of globalization. *World Development, 31*(4), 667–683.

Parrenas, R. (2001). *Servants of globalization.* Palo Alto, CA: Stanford University Press.

Perrin, A. (2002, December 19). Thailand overwhelmed by runaway AIDS. *San Francisco Chronicle.*

Petchesky, R. (2000). Sexual rights: Inventing a concept, mapping an international practice. In R. Parker, R. Barbosa, & P. Aggleton (Eds.), *Framing the sexual subject* (pp. 81–103). Berkeley, CA: University of California Press.

Phillips, O. (2001). Constituting the global gay. In C. Stychin, & D. Herman (Eds.), *Law and sexuality: The global arena* (pp. 17–34). Minneapolis, MN: University of Minnesota Press.

Reddy, V. (2002). Perverts and sodomites: Homophobia as hate speech in Africa. *South African Linguistics and Applied Language Studies, 20,* 163–175.

Rising demand for black gigolos. (2002, July 13). *The Nation,* Bangkok.

Runganaga, A., & Aggleton, P. (1998). Migration, the family and the transformation of a sexual culture. *Sexualities, 1*(1), 73.

Sassen, S. (1998). *Globalization and its discontents.* New York: New Press.

Sinclair, J. (1996). Mexico, Brazil and the Latin world. In J. Sinclair, L. Jacka, & S. Cunningham (Eds.),

*New patterns in global television.* Oxford, England: Oxford University Press.

Smith, J., & Pagnucco, R. (1998). Globalizing human rights: The work of transnational human rights NGOs. *Human Rights Quarterly, 20*(2), 379–412.

Soros, G. (2000). Open society: Reforming global capitalism. London: Little Brown.

Stiglitz, J. (2002). *Globalization and its discontents.* New York: Norton.

Stychin, C. (1998). *A nation by rights.* Philadelphia: Temple University Press.

## Did You Know?

- As of January 2006, seventeen states ban discrimination based on sexual orientation or sexual identity.[1]
- In Arizona, Alabama, Mississippi, South Carolina, Texas, and Utah, public school teachers cannot portray homosexuality as acceptable.[2]
- Even though the U.S. Constitution ensures that women have the right to access safe and legal abortion, women who are serving in the Armed Forces, as well as spouses and dependants of service members, are prohibited from exercising this right. [3]
- Under certain conditions, "virginity pledges" have been shown to delay the onset of sexual intercourse for an average of eighteen months. However, those who delay tend to be less effective in their use of contraception when they do become sexually active.[4]
- In the state of Texas it is illegal to purchase or sell dildos, artificial vaginas or vibrators. If sold, vibrators must be marketed as "personal massagers" and dildos as "educational models." Customers must sign a legal statement indicating they will not use the devices for any lewd or lascivious purpose.[5] If a private individual owns more than seven of such devices, they are presumed to intend to "promote." Texas penal code, Section 43.23, considers this a misdemeanor punishable by up to one year in prison and a $4,000 fine.[6]
- Seventeen states allow the use of public funds to pay for abortions for some poor women. [7]
- In the 2003 U.S. federal budget, $50 million was devoted to funding programs that promote the idea that a "mutually faithful monogamous relationship in the context of marriage is the expected standard of human sexual activity."[8]
- In 2003, the Episcopal church made history by electing the first openly gay bishop, Rev. V. Gene Robinson.[9]
- As of January 2006, Massachusetts is the only state in the U.S. that issues marriage licenses to same-sex couples.[10] Other countries that allow same sex marriage are the Netherlands, Belgium, Canada, and Spain.[11]
- In June 2006, the U.S. Supreme Court ruled in a five-to-three decision (*Lawrence v. Texas*) that state sodomy laws were unconstitutional.[12]
- On June 12, 1967, the U.S. Supreme Court overturned Virginia's miscegenation laws, which prohibited the recognition of interracial marriage. The couple, Mildred and Richard Loving, pleaded guilty in 1959 to a Virginia court for violating the law. They received a suspended sentence of one year in prison and were banned from entering the state together for twenty-five years. In 1963, the Lovings filed a motion in a state trial court to vacate the judgment against them, which brought the case to the United States Supreme Court. [13]

*—Compiled by Mikel Walters*

## NOTES

1. Human Rights Campaign. 2006. "Washington State Bans Discrimination against Gay, Lesbian, Bisexual, and Transgender Citizens." Retrieved January 30, 2006 from www.hrc.org/Template.cfm?Section=Press_Room&CONTENTID=30797&TEMPLATE=/ContentManagement/ContentDisplay.cfm.

2. Sexuality Information and Education Council of the United States. 2006. "Lesbians, Gay, Bisexual, Transgender, and Questioning (LGBTQ) Youth." Retrieved January 30, 2006 from www.siecus.org/policy/LGBTQ_FS.pdf.

3. Center for Reproductive Rights. 2003. "Penalized for Serving Their Country: The Ban on Abortion for Women in the Military." Retrieved November 11, 2005 from www.crlp.org/pub_fac_military.html.

4. Sexuality Information and Education Council of the United States. 2001. "Issues and Answers: Fact Sheet on Sexuality Education." Retrieved November 21, 2005 from www.siecus.org/pubs/fact/fact0007.html.

5. Scott, Meghan. "Second Sex #1: Outlaw." Society for Human Sexuality. Retrieved November 21, 2005 from www.sexuality.org/l/mscott/ssex01.html.

6. Texas Penal Code, Chapter 43, Section 43.23. Retrieved January 28, 2006 from www.capitol.state.tx.us/statutes/docs/PE/content/htm/pe.009.00.000043.00.htm#43.23.00.

7. Guttmacher Institute. 2005. "Facts in Brief: Incidence of Abortion." Retrieved January 30, 2006 from www.guttmacher.org/pubs/fb_induced_abortion.html

8. Rothschild, Cynthia. 2004. "Abstinence Goes Global: The U.S., the Right Wing, and Human Rights." *American Sexuality* 1:6. Retrieved January 30, 2006 from http://nsrc.sfsu.edu/HTMLArticle.cfm?Article=165&PageID=51&SID=D7CEC2B77A4F3E98266EC0B09E7F5D2E&DSN=nsrc_rev2.

9. Human Rights Campaign. 2004. "Religions' and Denominations' Positions on LGBT Issues: The Episcopal Church." Retrieved January 28, 2006 from www.hrc.org/Template.cfm?Section=Home&Template=/ContentManagement/ContentDisplay.cfm&ContentID=21757.

10. Human Rights Campaign. 2006. "Relationship Recognition in the U.S." Retrieved January 30, 2006 from www.hrc.org/Template.cfm?Section=Center&CONTENTID=26860&TEMPLATE=/ContentManagement/ContentDisplay.cfm.

11. Human Rights Campaign. 2006. "Marriage/Relationship Recognition Laws: International." Retrieved January 30, 2006 from www.hrc.org/Template.cfm?Section=Center&CONTENTID=26546&TEMPLATE=/TaggedPage/TaggedPageDisplay.cfm&TPLID=70.

12. Lambda Legal Defense and Education Fund. 2003. "*Lawrence v. Texas.*" Retrieved January 30, 2006 from www.lambdalegal.org/cgi-bin/iowa/cases/record?record=93.

13. U.S. Supreme Court. 1967. "*Loving v. Virginia,* 388 U.S. 1." Retrieved January 30, 2006 from http://caselaw.lp.findlaw.com/scripts/getcase.pl?court=US&vol=388&invol=1.

# chapter 10

# *Sexual Violence*

*An interview with . . .*

## Diana E. H. Russell

Diana E. H. Russell, Ph.D., is one of the foremost experts on sexual violence against women and girls in the world. For the last thirty-five years she has been engaged in research and activism on this massive social problem. She has authored, co-authored, edited, or co-edited seventeen books, which have become authoritative sources on rape (including wife rape), incest, femicide (the misogynist murder of women), and pornography.

### What led you to begin studying rape and sexual assault?

*In 1971, I was outraged by a typically sexist rape trial that occurred in San Francisco in which it appeared that the victim, not the accused, was on trial. After participating in a feminist protest outside the courthouse, I realized how little I knew about women's experiences of rape. A review of the rape literature revealed that it too was riddled with sexist woman-blaming, so I decided to embark on an interview-based study of rape survivors. My book,* The Politics of Rape *(1975), which includes twenty-one of these interviews, was among the first feminist analyses of this woman-hating crime.*

*I was not aware at the time that I was also motivated by my own experiences of childhood incestuous abuse and an attempted rape when I was 20 years old. I am now convinced that the most traumatic of these experiences (the incestuous abuse) caused me to dedicate my life to research and writing about many different forms of sexual violations perpetrated by males on females, including incestuous abuse.*

### How do people react when they find [out] that you study this topic?

*Most women praise me for working on such important but painful topics as rape and child sexual abuse. However, I believe it has counted heavily against me in academia because so many male academics in my field (sociology) consider rape and other forms of sexual victimization to be unimportant topics. In addition, women who conduct research on male violence—particularly those of us who are radical feminists—threaten many of them. When I started working on rape in 1971, followed by [work on] woman battery, wife rape, incestuous abuse, extrafamilial child sex abuse, femicide, and pornography, many of the faculty members at my college (Mills College, Oakland) were shocked by these topics—despite the fact that Mills is a women's school.*

### Which of your projects have you found most interesting? Why?

*I found working on incestuous abuse to be most interesting. My research on this topic culminated in my book,* The Secret Trauma: Incest in the Lives of Girls and Women *(1986), which was a co-recipient of the 1986 C. Wright Mills Award for books that exemplify outstanding social science research on a significant social problem. Completing this book was cathartic for me, particularly as it revolutionized people's understanding of incestuous abuse in the United States and other countries. It was also helpful to many incest survivors.*

### What ethical dilemmas have you faced in studying rape and sexual assault?

*One of my ethical dilemmas was caused by my being a white South African (South Africa is the country of my birth) who wanted to study rape and incest there, so as to raise awareness about the shocking magnitude of these problems in that country. Despite the tremendous need for research on sexual violence against women and girls in South Africa, particularly in the black community, the long history of apartheid has resulted in very few black women researchers having the time, motivation, or qualifications to tackle this form of terrorism against females. Since approximately 85 percent of the South African population was black (Africans, Indians, and "Coloreds") when I conducted my study, this meant that the majority of my informants would be black (the term used for all people of color in South Africa) had my research reflected the racial composi-*

*tion of that country. Some black people in South Africa, as here in the United States, resent white people doing research on their lives. In addition, accounts about black men's violence toward black women and children would likely have reinforced many white people's racist stereotypes about black men. I would probably have been considered racist had 85 percent of my respondents been black. Therefore, I limited my research for a book on incestuous abuse to white South Africans (see* Behind Closed Doors in White South Africa: Incest Survivors Tell Their Stories *[1997]). However, in my effort to avoid contributing to racist stereotypes, I again risked being viewed as racist for confining my research to the white ruling class minority in South Africa. I was literally caught between a rock and a hard place whatever decision I made about the racial composition of my respondents.*

### What do you think is the most challenging thing about studying [researching, writing, speaking about] rape and sexual assault?

*I am most challenged by the fact that—as a researcher and author on rape and other sexual assault—I am often unable to have an impact on those whom I most want to effect. For example, I, and other feminist rape researchers, have made several determined efforts to point out the appalling inadequacies in the research methodology of the National Crime Victimization Surveys (NCVS) conducted annually by the Federal Government's Bureau of Justice Statistics (BJS). Their severely flawed survey methods result in a massive underestimation of the incidence of rape, thus resurrecting the old myth that rape is a rare crime. Even when the BJS undertook a revision of their methodology, they totally ignored our criticisms, instead introducing methodological changes that rendered their findings about the incidence of rape even more inaccurate than before.*

### Why is it important to do this kind of research?

*Choosing from several different research studies that I have conducted on rape and child sexual abuse, I will focus here on the importance of conducting rigorous scientific studies on the prevalence of different forms of violence against women and girls. By prevalence, as distinct from incidence, I am referring to the percentage of women who were victims of rape or child sexual abuse at some time in their lives, or during [a particular] specified period of time. (The incidence of rape typically refers to the number of rapes that occurred within the prior year.) It is vital to know the approximate magnitude of a problem before theorizing about it or trying to ascertain the most effective ways to combat it. For example, before my study of the prevalence of incestuous abuse, there was no scientific basis for estimating the prevalence of this mostly hidden crime. One psychiatrist estimated that only one in a million females had been so victimized. However, my study found that 16 percent of a probability sample of adult women in San Francisco had been the victims of completed or attempted incestuous abuse before they turned 18, and 4.5 percent of them had been sexually abused by a biological, step-, or adoptive father. These findings—still an underestimate—revolutionized the contemporary understanding of incestuous abuse in the United States.*

**If you could teach people one thing about sexuality, what would it be?**

*I would teach people that sexuality is socially constructed. In our patriarchal society, sexuality is shaped by male domination and sexism: For example, many men view having sex with women as conquest—a notch on their belts. They see it as proof of their "manhood." The more notches they have on their belts, the more status they have among their male peers. They brag with their male friends about whether or not they "got to first base" or made a "home run." For such men, sex is often devoid of caring, respect, love, or tenderness—as is the pornography they use. Sexual equality cannot be achieved without gender equality.*

—Interviewed by Denise Donnelly

# "I Wasn't Raped, but . . .": Revisiting Definitional Problems in Sexual Victimization

Nicola Gavey

When a woman says she wasn't raped but describes an experience of forced, unwanted sexual intercourse, what are we to think? Was she "really" raped, despite disowning that label for her experience? Or does her refusal of the label suggest that her interpretation of the experience as other than rape makes it so? And what does it say about our culture(s) that there can be so much ambiguity over the differential diagnosis of rape versus sex? How should we conceptualize and judge the myriad coercive sexual acts that lie somewhere between rape and consensual sex? Finally, is being the object of violence or coercion always the same thing [as] being the *victim* of such violence or coercion?

In this chapter I begin to explore some of the convoluted layers of issues in which such questions are embedded. . . . In thinking through and around these questions, I find I can't settle comfortably into a straightforward, unitary position from which to craft an argument. . . . I have concluded . . . that there are indeed murky issues at the interface between (hetero)sex and sexual victimization. Even at the most basic level, I want to talk about and against rape and sexual victimization (as though these are straightforward terms) at the same time as I destabilize these categories,

in the belief that this is an important part of the same fight at a different level.

I trace some of the changes in research on rape and sexual victimization over the past two decades and consider some of the implications of the new feminist social science approach. In particular, I consider three points that raise the need to revisit current conventions for conceptualizing sexual victimization. These points concern the concept of the unacknowledged rape victim, the loose distinction between rape and attempted rape, and the use of the term *sexual victimization* to refer to a broad range of arguably normative coercive heterosexual practices. . . .

## A Starting Point

In the title of this [reading], I refer back to Martha Burt and Rhoda Estep's 1981 paper "Who Is a Victim? Definitional Problems in Sexual Victimization." In their . . . article, Burt and Estep mapped the nascent influence of 1970s feminism on a redefinition and reconceptualization of sexual assault. They endorsed the more inclusive definition of sexual assault that was emerging from feminism at the time, drawing attention to the similarity between rape and other coercive sexual practices. Moreover, they argued strongly for the benefits for all women who have been sexually assaulted to claim the victim role. Although aware of what they called the "negative social value" and the "obligations" of the victim role, they proposed that the benefits would include "the right to claim assistance, sympathy, temporary relief from other role responsibilities,

From Gavey, Nicola. 1999. " 'I Wasn't Raped, but . . .': Revisiting Definitional Problems in Sexual Victimization." In *New Versions of Victims: Feminists Struggle with the Concept* (pp. 57–81), edited by Sharon Lamb. Reprinted by permission of New York University Press.

legal recourse, and other similar advantages."
(p. 16).

. . . [Using] the language of victimization was
imposed as a way of making sense of and opposing the moral injustice of women's oppression in
the forms of violence and harassment.

## The "New" Feminist Research on Sexual Victimization

Since 1981, . . . both feminist activism and
feminist social science have been instrumental in
promoting a major rethinking of rape—and sexual victimization in many western societies. . . .
In a very short time we moved from a climate in
which rape was widely regarded as rare to one
in which rape is regarded as a widespread social
problem. . . .

[F]eminist empirical research was specifically
designed to overcome the limitations of previous
estimates of rape prevalence (which relied on reports of rape to the police or reports in national
crime surveys). . . . This work introduced an important methodological point of departure from
any previous attempts to measure the scope of
rape. Women were asked not whether they had
been raped[1] but rather whether they had had any
experiences that matched behavioral descriptions
of rape. For example, they were asked whether
they had ever had sexual intercourse when they
didn't want to because a man threatened or used
some degree of physical force to make them do so
(e.g., Koss et al. 1987). Moreover, this question
was one among many such specific questions that
women would be asked about a range of coercive
sexual experiences. Such methodological refine-
ments were designed to be sensitive to women's
reluctance to report rape. They were seemingly
successful, and the body of research produced
shocking new data showing widespread rape and
sexual victimization.

At the same time, two other important changes
to the picture of rape emerged from this research.
First, Diana Russell (1982; 1984)—and later,
others—showed that women were far more likely

to be raped by husbands, lovers, boyfriends, and
dates than by strangers. Not only were the cultural blinkers that had enabled this to be regarded
as "just sex" lifted, but it was found that such
rapes were far more common than the stereotypical rape by a stranger. Second, . . . while rape
[was] the extreme act, it [was] regarded as being
on a continuum with more subtle forms of coercion, from an unwanted kiss to unwanted sexual
intercourse submitted to as a result of continual
verbal pressure. . . .

[These changes] have two important effects:
(1) They construe experiences that would have
previously fallen within the realm of sex as forms
of sexual *victimization;* and 2) they implicitly invite a critical examination of the whole realm of
normal heterosexual practice. . . .

Against a backdrop where rape was considered
to be rare—and where complaints of rape were
commonly regarded to be lies, distortions of normal sex, harmless, or provoked by the victim—
the call to broaden the definition of sexual assault
and victimization has been an important feminist
move. Similarly, the way in which we have elabo-
rated on the understanding of rape as a form of
*victimization* has arguably contributed to more
widespread concern about rape as a serious social problem. These moves [were] one part of increased focus during the 1980s on many forms of
victimization, and of widespread social concern
for understanding their extent and dynamics and
for ameliorating and preventing their harm.

## "Victimization" in Crisis

[By] the late 1990s, the concept of victimization [was] arguably in crisis. Joel Best (1997)
opened a . . . *Society* commentary with the un-
favorable verdict that "victimization has become fashionable" (p. 9). As Richard Feldstein
(1997) . . . observed, the term *victim* . . . has been
targeted for critique by neoconservatives in the
United States. . . . As part of more general conservative campaigns against research and services
relating to victimization, there has been critical

dispute over the new feminist research on rape—especially that on "date rape." It has been claimed that the issue has been exaggerated or that it has no validity as a concept (e.g., Gilbert 1994; Paglia 1992; Roiphe 1993 see also Denfeld 1995; Sommers 1994; Newbold 1996). . . .

### Are Victims Created by a Victimization Framework?

*There are many ways to victimize people. One way is to convince them that they are victims.*

—(Hwang 1997, p. 41)

One strand of public concern at the moment is the fear that talk about victimization is needlessly creating victims. Moreover, critics of the movement against date rape have implied that it violates "assumptions of women's basic competence, free will, and strength of character" (Roiphe 1993, p. 69; see also Paglia 1992). . . .

There are various ways in which the language of sexual victimization can have material cultural effects. . . . For example, it may reinforce and perpetuate images of women as weak, passive, and asexual and images of men as sexually driven, unstoppable, and potentially dangerous. These gendered ways of being may be further enhanced by the exacerbation of women's fears about rape through media reportage and through warnings about violent sexual attacks that emphasize women's vulnerability to rape over their potential for resistance. . . . A rapist's moral infringement prescribes an experience of victimization for the rape *victim* . . . [and a] particular psychological outcome is preconfigured by calling the violence "victimization."

. . . [H]ow valid is the sort of seductive public warning in Karen Hwang's point? Are victims really created out of thin air? When feminists and other social critics name certain practices as victimization, they are drawing attention to the relationships of power that systematically privilege the experiences of some groups of people over those of others. Is the hysterical anxiety behind the suggestion that talking about victimization creates victimization a sort of head-in-the-sand approach to unpleasant social conditions—a naive hope that if a phenomenon is not seen and not heard, then it does not exist? . . . [C]ommentators such as Katie Roiphe suggest that "prior to the discourse of date rape, the experience itself did not occur, or at least not with such traumatizing after-effects as we now associate with rape" (p. 16). . . .

In light of the backlash crisis of representation of victimization . . . , it is perhaps time to revisit Martha Burt and Rhoda Estep's (1981) contention that it is in a woman's best interests to be perceived as a victim when she has experienced sexual coercion or violence. It is difficult to know how to evaluate this claim, and our attempts may benefit from some empirical analysis of women's accounts of their experiences of coercion, abuse, and violence. Few would deny that what we refer to as rape, sexual assault, sexual coercion, and sexual abuse can be victimizing. That is, they can be horrific events that traumatize women[2] and produce victims. Moreover, abusive and coercive practices can produce victims in a more subtle and less horrific ways, through undermining a woman's confidence and eroding her agency over time. In the fight against rape, public feminist rhetoric has tended to privilege one of the many contradictory broader cultural meanings of rape—that is, its power to cause severe and irrevocable psychological harm to the victim. Those of us drawn to activism against rape often have firsthand knowledge of the effects of rape on friends, family members, women we have worked with, or ourselves. The potential trauma and devastating harm of rape, silenced and hidden for so many years, has now come to be almost automatically signified by the term *rape* (although not without exceptions). . . .

### Unacknowledged Rape Victims

As discussed earlier, the new research on rape has tended not to rely on asking women whether or not they have ever experienced "rape." Some studies have included this direct question along with the more specific behavioral questions about forced, unwanted sex. It has been found that only around 30 to 50 percent of women who affirm they have had an experience that meets a narrow definition of rape identify that they have experienced "rape" (e.g., Koss 1988; Gavey 1991a; 1991b). . . . [T]his research paradigm has . . . categorize[d] women as victims of rape if they report having had an experience consistent with the predetermined behavioral description that researchers define as rape when the questionnaires or structured interview data are analyzed. If these women do not report that they have experienced "rape" (when asked directly), then they are considered "unacknowledged" rape victims by the researchers (e.g., Koss 1985). . . .

[S]ocial critics have targeted this feature of the feminist empirical work on rape prevalence as a major weakness of the whole body of research.[3] Neil Gilbert (1994), for example, cites as a problem of Koss's rape prevalence estimates that "almost three-quarters of the students whom Koss defined as victims of rape did not think they had been raped" (p. 23). . . . Ironically, this methodological approach is totally consistent with the positivist conventions of social and behavioral psychology . . . , where it is considered good research practice to use operational definitions for specifying precise categories of behavior that can be reliably measured. . . . For instance, it would be considered valid to classify a person as "depressed" if he or she answered a range of questions on a depression inventory in the predicted ways, even if the individual did not affirm the statement "I am depressed."

Let us consider an example of the sort of experience that could be described as an unacknowledged rape. One woman I interviewed described an experience, which occurred when she was nineteen, of waking to find her thirty-year-old male apartment mate in her bed, "groping" her (Gavey 1990; 1992). She had no prior

sexual or romantic relationship with this man, but on this night he got into her bed while she was asleep and had intercourse with her, with no apparent consideration of her lack of interest. She explained:

*Ann:* . . . it all happened quite quickly really, but I remember thinking quite clearly, "Well if I don't—If I try and get out of the bed, perhaps if I run away or something . . . he might rape me [pause] so I had better just . . ."
*Nicola:* If you try and run away you mean?
*Ann:* If I tried it, if I'd resisted, then he might rape me, you know. So he did anyway, sort of thing, really, when you think about it, when I look back.

This man was rough and left her bleeding. Later, she was frightened, "confused," "nervous within the house," and hypervigilant about making sure she was never asleep before he'd gone to bed. . . . Nevertheless, Ann did not conceptualize this event as rape at the time.

Technically, this encounter may not count as rape in a narrow legal sense, because it is unclear how explicitly Ann communicated her nonconsent. Most feminist analyses, however, would point out the restraints on her being able to do this, such as being only just awake and fearing that her resistance might lead to worse treatment. Feminists would also highlight the absence of reasonable grounds for this man assuming consent (e.g., Pineau 1989). That is . . . it [is not] reasonable for a man to assume that a woman approached when she is asleep in her own bed by a man with whom she had no prior sexual or romantic relationship would be consenting to sex, in the absence of some active communication of this consent. Consequently, many feminists would describe this incident as rape or, at the very least, sexual assault. Clearly, in spite of Ann's resistance to the identity of rape victim, the experience had a negative psychological impact on her. It is impossible to know how, if at all, the effects would have been different had she viewed what happened as rape. There is some indication in her account that to have had an experience she would have called "rape" would have been worse—"if I'd resisted, then he might rape me." Indeed, it would have been a different experience and one that may have more powerfully signaled her lack of control and her vulnerability. Psychologically, she perhaps maintained more control (a meager but significant amount) and risked losing less by choosing not to "run away or something" than if she had resisted as hard as she could and been raped anyway.

During our interview several years after this incident, Ann moved toward retrospectively understanding it as rape—after explaining that she did not resist because "he might rape me," she said "So he did anyway, sort of thing . . . when I look back." . . . I . . . struggle with the validity and ethics of labeling Ann a "rape victim" at the time when she did not choose this label herself. However, . . . ambiguity . . . arises in talking about Ann's experience and how to make sense of it in the research context. . . . If this woman's experience is not considered to be rape or some form of sexual assault very close to rape (by her *or* by the man involved *or* by police, judges, and juries *or* by researchers and social theorists), then what is it? Sex? If it can be accepted as just part of the realm of sex, then it redirects a critical spotlight onto heterosexuality itself.

It is worth noting that although Ann "resisted" seeing herself as a rape victim, this did not enable her to resist the assault physically. This illuminates how it would be misleading to assume that *not* being positioned in an overt discourse of rape or victimization somehow protects a woman from sexual assault. In a situation such as that Ann faced, the mark of gender difference imposed on what is a physical contest of sorts already incites certain responses, such as immobility and fear, that aid a rapist in his attack. . . . [T]his suggests that [we need] . . . ways of understanding heterosex that don't leave room for ambiguity over a woman's entitlement to refuse unwanted sex.

## A Feminist Response—The Methodology

With critical reflection on the research strategy of classifying some women as unacknowledged rape victims, what do we want to say in response to the critics but also as part of ongoing . . . research practice? There is probably no straightforward answer, but I think it is important that we approach it as an open question rather than with formulaic answers. Why do so many women who have bad experiences consistent with a legal definition of rape label resist the label of "rape victim" (e.g., Koss 1985)? And how should feminist research respond to these women's rejection of the "rape" label? These questions raise complicated issues that are at the heart of feminist theory about research practice. If we see our role as giving women voice, then it may not be legitimate to "put words in their mouths," to describe experiences as rape that women themselves do not describe in that way. However, feminist research increasingly seeks to go beyond giving women voice and reporting on women's experiences, to offer analyses and critiques that help make sense of women's experiences as they are shaped and constrained by power relations in social contexts. When women's voices don't always tell "our story," it can be troubling to know how to proceed. (See also Fine 1992; Kitzinger and Wilkinson 1997.)

Evaluated in this light, the feminist empirical research on rape prevalence occupies an interesting position. In its use of traditional methods to produce conventional data dressed in the language of science rather than that of feminist politics, this research has been an important part of wider feminist action. This action has had some important successes—most notably, changes to rape laws, in many English-speaking countries and in portions of the United States, to recognize rape within marriage as a crime. Widespread publicity about date rape has also led to rape prevention programs on many university campuses. Despite the limited effectiveness of these changes so far (for instance, convictions for wife rape are extremely rare), this body of research has nevertheless had a subversive and transformative role in the changing representations of rape. It has generated a profound shift in the meaning of rape, to the extent that it is no longer impossible to think of man raping his wife or a sporting hero raping a woman he dated (although this possibility is still more likely to be readily accepted if the man is black). . . .

## Research and Complexity

. . . [R]esearch . . . has yielded the findings discussed above at a cost. It has forced closure on definitions of various forms of victimization and classified women's experiences into readymade categories of victims. This style of methodology necessitates disregard for nuanced and possibly contradictory meanings. Moreover, researchers seem to find it reasonably unproblematic that answers to such basic questions as whether or not a particular experience counts as "rape" are constructed through the research process. The resulting certainty that can be projected about the extent and nature of rape and sexual victimization may eventually undermine the authority of the findings, when it is found that the reductive and universalizing features of this style of research don't "speak to" the experience of all women whom it ostensibly represents. Not only are decisions about who is and who is not a rape victim not always straightforward, but the partiality of new truths about the effects of rape is sometimes overlooked.

In some instances, women's reactions may be contradictory and not consistent with either dominant traditional or dominant feminist constructions of rape. One woman participating in my research (Gavey 1990) described a situation with her boyfriend, whereby she said she wanted to say to him, "The very first time we had sex you raped me." However, she didn't always view the forced sex as rape, and she continued her relationship with this man for more than two years. She detailed a complex set of contradictory, ambivalent, and changing reactions to this and other coercive

sexual experiences in the relationship. She also discussed how the usual feminist analyses of rape, such as those she later encountered at a rape crisis center, were not entirely helpful. Her reactions were not consistent with what she was hearing about how women, respond to rape—because she loved the man who raped her, remembered some of their sex as "wonderful," and so on—she went through a stage of feeling that she must be a "sick" and "masochistic" person. . . .

Feminist accounts of rape need to be able to take account of such women's experiences without, in effect, dismissing them as the result of false consciousness. Carefully listening to and theorizing such ambivalent and confusing experiences may illuminate the complex relationship between heterosexuality and rape. Moreover, it may produce feminist analyses of rape that are sympathetic to all women who are raped, no matter how they experience it.

Although there may be short-term political costs, embracing a more complex and less certain position on the ways in which rape can and does affect women may ultimately be an effective political strategy. By this I mean that psychologists, therapists, and activists should continue to work on understanding, helping, and speaking about the trauma of rape but at the same time be open to accepting, for example, that not all women are traumatized by rape. . . . The notion that it may be possible to experience rape and suffer no lasting devastating psychological effects is less often articulated than is the discourse of harm. But this "finding" about the effects of rape begs the question of whether such research, which once again must compress and order experience into finite categories, is adequate to perceive more subtle, idiosyncratic, and unpredictable psychological effects of rape. . . .

## Is Attempted Rape Sometimes Very Different from Completed Rape?

While some experiences of sexual coercion (and presumably most, if not all, experiences of sexual coercion that fit a narrow definition of rape) are surely victimizing, some possibly are not. Is it possible that our framework for conceptualizing *all* instances of sexual assault, and many instances of unwanted sex, as victimization actually helps constitute some of these experiences as victimizing, when they might otherwise have had effects that were less disabling? Although this question shares the anxiety typical of the backlash positions, it is an important question for feminists. In particular, are experiences of attempted rape and attempted sexual assault *sometimes* very different from actual experiences of rape and sexual assault?

I can think of a personal experience, when I was sixteen, that was probably attempted rape. This episode involved being tricked into stopping at an older male co-worker's place on the way to a party after we had finished work past midnight on New Year's Eve. I was thrown onto a bed that was just across from the front door of the flat, and he proceeded to jump on top of me and attempt to remove my pants. He was a relatively small man, and I was relatively physically strong from sports, and I remember having to struggle as hard as I could to prevent him [from] removing my pants, with the intention (it seemed to me at the time) of having intercourse with me. (This point also reminds me how it is difficult to judge when a man's actions become "attempted rape" when a man and woman are acquainted and, at some stretch of the imagination, a mutual sexual encounter could be appropriate.) Despite the fact that both of us had been drinking alcohol with other workers at the restaurant where we worked before we left, I was never in any doubt as to my lack of sexual interest in this man—at all, let alone on this occasion. I was not ambivalent in my communication with him and told him clearly, verbally, that I did not want to have sex with him, and I resisted him physically as hard as I could. Yet he seemed to have one goal on his mind, which was unchanged by my refusal. I think it was my relative physical strength that enabled me to resist him vigorously and successfully, to the point that he possibly decided not to keep trying.

Ten years later, when I was working at a sexual abuse counseling agency, the subcultural milieu encouraged me to think back on and identify this experience as attempted rape and to wonder about its negative effects on me. While this was not a totally new way of interpreting this experience, it did sediment it with more certainty. And it did induce me to scrutinize my past to look for psychological effects of this experience. I recall that I was subsequently worried about this man's "interest" in me and arranged for my mother to pick me up from work on some of the following nights. I also recall that being able to successfully prevent a forceful attempt at unwanted sex left me feeling strong, determined, and invulnerable. Although I can't remember enough of the detail of what followed to be sure there were not also subtle negative effects on my identity and sexuality, it strikes me that such experiences of attempted rape that is successfully repelled are extremely different from experiences of completed rape, in terms of their effect on women. In my case, I did not feel like a victim. I despised his actions, but I did not feel I had been harmed. To the contrary, the effects of his attempt had probably been as empowering as they were disempowering. Was what happened "victimization"? Or is there a better way of describing it that recognizes and celebrates the power of this kind of physical resistance, of fighting back . . . ?

. . . [A]t the time I was imagining the possibility of identifying as an attempted rape victim, it seemed important to join together with women who had been sexually victimized by men, in part to make a political show of solidarity in the face of oppressive acts of male sexuality. However, I never really felt like I properly "belonged," in the sense that I didn't share the legacy of pain that some of the women around me had suffered. Moreover, it backed me into a speaking position that did not fully represent my recollected experience. That adopting an identity as an attempted rape victim would have silenced my different kind of story, which included traces of empowerment, seemed (and still seems) a relatively trivial concern in relation to the political and interpersonal importance of standing alongside women who *had* been harmed. However, perhaps there is more at stake here than some notion of making room for the "authenticity" of experiences like my own. Perhaps there is some political advantage in being able to tell lots of different stories about diverse experiences of sexual violence. In making room for a respectful plurality, we may be able to acknowledge the oppressiveness and potential pain of rape at the same time as igniting discourses that disrupt the possibilities of rape. . . .

Clearly, not all attempted rapes are the same. Some experiences will involve violent and terrifying attacks, where a woman may literally fear for her life. However, the use of behavioral descriptions in surveys to measure the extent of sexual victimization does not distinguish these discrepant possibilities.

## Emphasizing Women's Strength

. . . [T]he normative practices of therapy for rape and sexual abuse victims may inadvertently help reinforce some of the effects of victimization through their concern with trauma, recovery, and healing. Again, a particular kind of psychological subject is assumed by such therapy approaches, and arguably, this "recovering" subject is always already constituted as lacking and in need of "betterment."

. . . Sharon Marcus (1992) considers how particular constructions of rape affect the very possibility of rape. . . . Marcus argues that in order to resist rape culture, we need to deny a necessary conflation between the act of rape and irrevocable harm. Marcus's feminist approach to rape is radically different from the approach of Susan Brownmiller's (1975) classic feminist analysis of rape. Marcus (1992) considers that "such a view takes violence as a self-explanatory first cause and endows it with an invulnerable and terrifying facticity which stymies our ability to challenge and

demystify rape" (p. 387). She, in contrast, argues that

> *in its efforts to convey the horror and iniquity of rape, such a view often concurs with masculinist culture in its designation of rape as a fate worse than, or tantamount to, death; the apocalyptic tone which it adopts and the metaphysical status which it assigns to rape implies that rape can only be feared or legally repaired, not fought. (p. 387)*

Marcus instead argues for the need to "envision strategies which will enable women to sabotage men's power to rape, which will empower women to take the ability to rape completely out of men's hands" (p. 388). It is sometimes difficult to understand exactly how this sort of transformation could take place, but Marcus's . . . argument is at least suggestive that it may be possible to conceptualize rape differently, in a way that somehow renders it less powerful without trivializing it.

I suggest that a small step in this sort of transformative direction would be the opening up of all sorts of narratives of resistance—by making room for stories about how potential rape was successfully fought, about how some women who are raped do not experience overwhelming psychological despair, and so on. As I suggested earlier, the potential cost of this strategy is that it may do violence to the experience of women who are victimized and traumatized by rape. Sensitivity to this possibility is necessary so that stories of particular kinds of resistance don't come to be privileged in ways that contribute once again to a silencing of women's experiences of victimization.

Apart from concern about the . . . effects of the language of victimization, there are other questions that should be on the minds of feminists. . . . [W]e may need to observe critically the effects of backlash discourse around "victimization." In the ensuing battle over the meaning of victimization, we may need to question which sorts of tactics are most likely to be effective in the political fight against rape. For instance, will the . . . strategy of simply speaking a victim-advocacy position more loudly be sufficient, or will we need to . . . contest the very terms of the debate? . . . [Moreover,] I suggest that an unwanted kiss or touch doesn't always make a *victim,* and the effect of this rhetorical excess in the context of backlash activity may be to weaken the whole struggle against rape by acquaintances, dates, husbands, and so on. . . . [We must recognize that we live in] a culture of heterosexuality in which power is allowed to infuse sex in different ways for women and men—ways that consistently foreground men's rather than women's rights and desires. . . .

Another problem with the way the framework of victimization is used is that it may implicitly require us to establish psychological harm in order to take a moral stand against violence and against heterosexual practice that is offensive or disrespectful without necessarily being violent (in the usual sense). That is, the injustice of sexual coercion and sexual violence may become too closely tied with the "proof" of psychological damage. . . .

### Supplementing the Language of Victimization

The new feminist research has come a long way, since Burt and Estep's article (1981), in describing the widespread problem of sexual victimization. But has it both gone too far and not gone far enough? Positivist methodologies have required us to iron out complexity, ambivalence, and contradiction. Public expectations of science have reinforced this drive for certainty in the form of concrete, definitive "findings." But when we peep behind the positivist mask, all sorts of discomforting questions arise: Are all instances of sexual coercion always victimizing? Do they always cause harm? For instance, in the arena of attempted sexual assaults, are women sometimes warriors, fighters, heroes? What are the effects of using these different kinds of language? Are the more subtle forms of sexual coercion, argued to be contiguous with rape by some feminists, best

conceptualized on a continuum of sexual victimization? Or are there other ways of critiquing heterosexual practice, which routinely privileges men's sexual interests over women's? Or should both strategies be adopted simultaneously?

In case I've overstated my concerns about the language of victimization, I emphasize that I am not arguing for an abandonment of the victimization framework. Rather, I am suggesting that we need to question whether it is always appropriate or wise to talk about all the different forms and occasions of sexual coercion, sexual assault, sexual abuse, and sexual violence as *victimization.* Making connections between everyday sexual practices (such as sexual pressure in a marriage) and sexual violence has been important for highlighting the role of normative culture in sustaining problems such as rape. However, we have not always maintained a distinction between the theorization of, say, a continuum of sexual victimization and the implications for how we then understand men's and women's actions and experiences at the more normative end of the continuum. Using the language of victimization to discuss this territory of the continuum may be theoretically valid yet at the same time (wrongly?) give the impression that we believe every act that falls along the continuum is an act of "victimization," that it makes "victims." I don't think I want to insist every time a woman experiences some unwanted sexual contact, it is an experience of victimization. But far from dismissing such experiences, it seems to me the challenge is to find different ways of critiquing the ways in which our culture(s) can tolerate all sorts of injustices, inequalities, and plain unfairness in the name of normative heterosexuality.

I close this [reading] in a mood of uncertainty. I worry that my questions could lead to unnecessary and undermining problems for the feminist analyses of rape and sexual coercion that I value. Yet I raise these points in a desire to help strengthen and sharpen our critique of victimizing forms of sexual coercion, in ways that help prevent victimization and ameliorate the effects of potentially victimizing acts for individual women. If we don't ask these questions about the victimization framework, I sense we may risk leaving a fertile gap for backlash discourse to take hold. At the same time, this kind of move should create spaces for developing supplementary ways to critique both normative and violent forms of heterosexual practice—without losing sight of the possibility for both rape and more normative forms of sexual coercion to be victimizing. That is, it may enable us to issue new and more varied moral arguments against the cultural acceptance of a form of heterosexual practice in which it can be hard to tell the difference between "just sex" and rape.

## NOTES

1. In some of Koss's studies women were asked this direct question in addition to many more of the specific behavioral questions.

2. Of course, men are also raped and sexually abused, but not usually by women. As I am writing largely about the rape and sexual coercion of women in heterosexual relationships, I refer to those who rape as men and those who are raped as women.

3. Another common criticism of this work centers on the ambiguity of questions about unwanted sexual intercourse and unwanted attempts that occurred "because a man gave you alcohol or drugs." Due to the ambiguity of the question, the validity of scoring affirmative responses as "rape" has been questioned. Discussion of this problem with the research is beyond the scope of this chapter.

## REFERENCES

Best, J. May/June 1997. Victimization and the victim industry. *Society,* 9–17.

Brownmiller, S. 1975. *Against our will: Men, women and rape.* Harmondsworth: Penguin.

Burt, M. R., and Estep, R. E. 1981. Who is a victim? Definitional problems in sexual victimization. *Victimology: An International Journal* 6, 15–28.

Denfeld, R. 1995. *The new Victorians: A young woman's challenge to the old feminist order.* New York: Warner Books.

Feldstein, R. 1997. *Political correctness: A response from the cultural left.* Minneapolis: University of Minnesota Press.

Fine, M. 1992. *Disruptive voices: The possibilities of feminist research.* Ann Arbor: University of Michigan Press.

Gavey, N. 1990. Rape and sexual coercion within heterosexual relationships: An intersection of psychological, feminist, and postmodern inquiries. Unpublished doctoral thesis, University of Auckland.

———. 1991a. Sexual victimization prevalence among Auckland university students: How much and who does it? *New Zealand Journal of Psychology* 20, 63–70.

———. 1991b. Sexual victimization prevalence among New Zealand university students. *Journal of Consulting and Clinical Psychology* 59, 464–466.

———. 1992. Technologies and effects of heterosexual coercion. *Feminism and Psychology* 2, 325–351.

Gilbert, N. 1994. Miscounting social ills. *Society* 31 (3), 18–26.

Hwang, K. 1997. Excerpt from *The Humanist,* July/August 1997. Cited in Talking stick. *Utne Reader,* (84), 41.

Kitzinger, C., and Wilkinson, S. 1997. Validating women's experience? Dilemmas in feminist research. *Feminism and Psychology* 7, 566–574.

Koss, M. P. 1985. The hidden rape victim: Personality, attitudinal, and situational characteristics. *Psychology of Women Quarterly* 9, 193–212.

———. 1988. Hidden rape: Sexual aggression and victimization in a national sample of students in higher education. In A. W. Burgess (ed.), *Rape and sexual assault,* Vol. 2 (pp. 3–25). New York and London: Garland.

Koss, M. P., Gidycz, C. A., and Wisniewski, N. 1987. The scope of rape: Incidence and prevalence of sexual aggression and victimization in a national sample of higher education students. *Journal of Consulting and Clinical Psychology* 55, 162–170.

Marcus, S. 1992. Fighting bodies, fighting words: A theory and politics of rape prevention. In J. Butler and J. W. Scott (eds.), *Feminists theorize the political* (pp. 385–403). New York: Routledge.

Newbold, G. 1996. Commentary on Professor Mary Koss's keynote address: Redefining rape. In J. Broadmore, C. Shand, and T. Warburton (eds.),

*The proceedings of 'Rape: Ten years' progress? An interdisciplinary conference,'* Wellington, New Zealand, 27–30 March 1996 (pp. 144–146). Doctors for Sexual Abuse Care.

Paglia, C. 1992. Sex, art, and American culture. New York: Vintage Books.

Pineau, L. 1989. Date rape: A feminist analysis. *Law and Philosophy* 8, 217–243.

———. 1996. A response to my critics. In L. Francis (ed.), *Date rape: Feminism, philosophy, and the law* (pp. 63–107). University Park, PA: Pennsylvania State University Press.

Roiphe, K. 1993. *The morning after: Sex, fear, and feminism.* London: Hamish Hamilton.

Russell, D. E. H. 1982. *Rape in marriage.* New York: Macmillan.

———. 1984. *Sexual exploitation: Rape, child sexual abuse, and workplace harassment.* Beverly Hills: Sage.

Sommers, C. H. 1994. *Who stole feminism? How women have betrayed women.* New York: Simon & Schuster.

## BDSM or Intimate Violence: How Do You Tell the Difference?

### Denise Donnelly

What if I told you that a neighbor of yours had bitten, slapped, pinched, or verbally demeaned their partner? Would you be shocked? Outraged? Would you conclude that this person had committed intimate violence or partner abuse? Careful . . . what seems so simple at first glance may not be. What if I then told you that these actions took place during sex and with the consent of the partner? Would you still think of it as intimate violence?

Those who practice BDSM (bondage, discipline, dominance, submission, and/or sadomasochism) note that pain, humiliation, and dominance can be powerful sexual aphrodisiacs, and if practiced by two or more consenting adults, they are viable sexual choices. They argue that so long as consent is present, rules are agreed on beforehand, and safe sex is practiced, no abuse has taken place. They go on to point out that unlike most abusive relationships (in which a woman is victimized), often it is the male partner who is dominated, bound, humiliated, or made to feel pain in a BDSM relationship.

Advocates for battered women, on the other hand, argue that abusive relationships often masquerade as "al-ternative sexuality," allowing the batterers to justify the abuse and elude arrest. They note that battered women (and men) may go along with this explanation—all the while insisting the actions are consensual—because of reasons as diverse as love, fear of losing the other person, or the risk of being seriously injured or killed. Finally, they also point out that adults abused as children may be acting out old familiar scenarios where violence masquerades as love, and that they may not be able to recognize "healthy" sexual and intimate relationships.

So, how does one tell the difference between BDSM and intimate violence? It's not that easy. One writer[1] offered this suggestion: If it leaves one or both partners feeling trapped, used, angry, or afraid, then it is probably coercive and exploitive. If, on the other hand, it leaves them feeling free, creative, valued, and trusting, it is likely consensual sex play.

### NOTE

1. Eckhart, T. J. (2005). "BDSM and Feminism: An Insider's View." Retrieved October 27, 2005 from www.columbia.edu/cu/sister/BDSM.html.

# The Knockout Punch

# of Date Rape Drugs

**Melissa Abramovitz**

Rohypnol, GLIB, and ketamine are known as date rape drugs or acquaintance rape drugs. Here's what you should know to protect yourself from becoming a victim. . . .

## The Dangers

[Date rape] has been happening more frequently . . . since Rohypnol and the other so-called date rape drugs (GHB and ketamine) were introduced into the United States in the early 1990s. Not only are these drugs themselves extremely dangerous, but the people who use them knowingly or unknowingly are subject to rape and other forms of abuse because of the powerful sedative effects. It's also difficult to prosecute those who commit rape after forcing their victims to ingest the drugs because these substances tend to erase the victim's memory of what happened. The drugs also move quickly through the body and often cannot be detected in blood or urine tests by the time the person gets to a hospital.

## Physically and Emotionally Devastating

Date rape doesn't always involve drugs, but it is always physically and emotionally devastating for its victims. It is part of the wider category of "acquaintance rape" cases that involve someone

being forced to have sex by a person he or she knows.

Most rape cases involve a female being attacked by a male, but males have been victims too. The legal definition of rape includes instances in which the victim is physically forced, verbally threatened, or under the influence of drugs that make her or him incapable of making a decision or resisting the attack.

In 1996 the federal government passed a law called the Drug-Induced Rape Prevention and Punishment Act. . . . This law makes it a felony to give an unsuspecting person a date rape drug with the intent of committing violence, including rape, against him or her. The law also imposes penalties of large fines and up to 20 years in prison for importing or distributing more than one gram of these drugs. However, even with this law in effect, the use of date rape drugs is growing.

## Club Drugs

Date rape drugs are also known as club drugs because of their use at dance clubs, fraternity parties, and all-night raves. Because in the United States Rohypnol and GHB are illegal and ketamine is tightly regulated, most users get them from dealers who import them from Mexico, Europe, or South America, where they are legal. Sometimes the drugs are manufactured illicitly in the United States using highly toxic ingredients. This exposes users to the risk of being poisoned or overdosing on nonstandardized drug concentrations.

From Abramovitz, Melissa. 2001. "The Knockout Punch of Date Rape Drugs." *Current Health 2* 27(7): 18–23. Reprinted by permission.

In one well-publicized case, a 15-year-old boy died from an overdose of GHB at a rave in Joshua Tree, California. A 30-year-old man allegedly made the drug out of engine degreaser, drain cleaner, and water and distributed it to teens at the party. The man is being tried for second-degree murder.

This case is only one of thousands in which club drugs have killed people. While many users think these drugs are safe, they are actually extremely dangerous for several reasons. Users never really know what dosage they're getting and are exposed to the risk that poisons like drain cleaner are likely to be part of the package.

### Lasting Effects on the Brain

Consider, too, these facts about club drugs:

- Recent research shows that some club drugs can have lasting effects on the brain, resulting in memory loss, impaired motor skills, and distorted sensations.
- They make people less aware of what's going on around them and unable to fully control or protect themselves or drive safely.
- The drugs can be fatal when combined with alcohol and other drugs.
- The drugs are addictive.

### A Drug with Many Names

The most prevalent date rape drug is Rohypnol, also known as roofies, forget pills, the drop drug, rope, LaRocha, ropies, Mexican valium, R-2, row-shay, rib, ruffies, roachies, ruffles, roche, wolfies, and rophies. The chemical name is flunitrazepam. Rohypnol is a powerful central nervous system depressant prescribed in Europe as a sleeping pill or as a pre-anesthetic for surgery. It is illegal in the United States

The drug comes in pill form as a white tablet that quickly dissolves in liquid with no odor, taste, or color. It is also found in liquid form. Because of its widespread abuse as a date rape drug, the manufacturer now makes a new Rohypnol tablet that dissolves more slowly and turns a drink blue. There are also new "copycat" versions made in Africa and South America that are reddish-brown.

Rohypnol can be taken orally, injected, or crushed and inhaled through the nose. It begins acting 10 to 30 minutes after ingestion, causing muscle relaxation, sleepiness, dizziness, hot or cold feelings, nausea, trouble speaking or moving, a drop in blood pressure, vision problems, and difficulty urinating. It sometimes causes aggression, anger, or hallucinations. Users often pass out and wake up six to eight hours later feeling shaky, with no memory of anything that happened. Blackouts can last up to 24 hours. When combined with alcohol or other drugs, Rohypnol has an even more powerful effect that can be fatal.

Repeated use can lead to physical and psychological dependence and withdrawal if the drug is stopped. Withdrawal can include headache, muscle pain, anxiety, restlessness, confusion, numbness, tingling, irritability, convulsions, and shock.

### GHB: Danger at Any Dose

GHB, or gamma hydroxybutyrate, is also called liquid ecstasy, somatomax, scoop, grievous bodily harm, liquid x, Georgia home boy, goop, gamma-oh, and G. The drug was once sold legally in the United States as a body-building food supplement. But the government made GHB illegal after doctors warned of its lethal dangers.

The drug comes as an odorless, colorless liquid that tastes salty or as a white powder or in capsule form. It is generally taken orally. The strength of the drug varies from batch to batch, leading to frequent overdoses.

The effects of GHB begin within 10 minutes to one hour after ingestion. Low doses produce euphoria, an out-of-body high, sleepiness, increased sex drive, memory loss, hallucinations, headache, loss of reflexes, sweating, and lowered blood pressure. Higher doses can cause nausea, vomiting, difficulty breathing, seizures (especially when GHB is combined with methamphetamine), unconsciousness, coma (especially when combined with alcohol), and even death. Repeated use is associated with mood swings, liver tumors, violent behavior, dependence, and withdrawal if the drug is stopped.

### "Entering a K-Hole"

Ketamine, the third date rape drug, has the chemical name ketamine hydrochloride. It is known by users as Special K, K, vitamin K, Kit Kat, Keller, super acid, and super C. Developed in the 1970s as a surgical anesthetic for humans and animals, it is now illegal to use in the United States except under a doctor's supervision.

Ketamine is in a class of drugs called dissociative anesthetics that act on the central nervous system to separate perception and sensation. It comes as a white powder, tablet, or liquid and can be snorted, taken orally, or injected. The powder form is sometimes sprinkled on tobacco or marijuana and smoked.

When injected, the effects begin very quickly; in fact the person often loses control of his or her muscles during the injection. Taken orally, ketamine begins working in 10 to 20 minutes, and when snorted, in five to 10 minutes. The effects peak in one to six hours and can last up to 48 hours.

At lower doses of 10 to 100 milligrams, ketamine causes hallucinations, memory loss, decreased oxygen to the brain, slurred speech, increased blood pressure, muscle rigidity, dreaminess, numbness, paralysis, paranoia, aggressive behavior, and feelings of being outside the body. Users call these out-of-body feelings "entering a K-hole." Frequent use of ketamine is linked to severe mental illness and psychological addiction. Higher doses of one gram or more lead to unconsciousness and even death. Combining ketamine with other drugs can be fatal.

### Beware the Dangers

It's obvious that date rape drugs can be very dangerous, whether taken voluntarily or given without someone's knowledge. [People] who use these drugs may try to get others to try them by touting the quick euphoric high and hallucinations they bring. But the memory loss, unconsciousness, and lasting physical and mental effects make them a dangerous choice for anyone. Add this to the risk of being raped or otherwise harmed when under the influence, and it's obvious why authorities are so concerned about the way these drugs are endangering many young people.

There are a variety of ways you can protect yourself from these drugs. Staying away from parties where they are being used and saying no if someone offers them to you are the first steps toward keeping yourself safe. . . .

### Protecting Yourself against Date Rape Drugs

- Always keep your eye on your drink at any party or on a date. Don't put the drink down and leave it unattended, even to go to the restroom or to greet a friend on the other side of the room.
- Don't accept a drink of any sort from someone else, particularly if you don't know the person well.
- Never drink anything from an open container unless you yourself opened it.
- Don't drink anything from a punch bowl or other communal container like a keg.
- Go to parties with close friends and watch out for each other. If you leave the party, tell a friend where you're going and with whom.
- If you think someone drugged you, call 911 and get someone to take you to the hospital to be tested for drugs—and for treatment and counseling if needed.

## Linking Sexual Aggression and Fraternities

**Mindy Stombler**

*"It was her first fraternity party. The beer flowed freely and she had much more to drink than she had planned. It was hot and crowded and the party spread out all over the house, so that when three men asked her to go upstairs, she went with them. They took her into a bedroom, locked the door and began to undress her. Groggy with alcohol, her feeble protests were ignored as the three men raped her. When they finished, they put her in the hallway, naked, locking her clothes in the bedroom."[1]*

This scenario is more typical than you might think, regularly repeated on college and university campuses across the country. Why do fraternity membership and sexual aggression seem to be related? Researchers have explored these connections, using qualitative studies of predominantly white fraternities,[2] and have come up with some interesting findings.[3] They describe a fraternity context in which the structure, culture, and the nature of rushing and pledging often encourage sexual aggressiveness and even gang rapes. Researchers also suspect that fraternity men's narrow conceptualizations of masculinity, comprising "competition, athleticism, dominance, winning, conflict, wealth, material possessions, willingness to drink alcohol, and sexual prowess vis-à-vis women," play a major role in sexual aggression. Alcohol and drugs, combined with intense pressure to have sex with women, create a "party rape" culture in which these substances are used as "weapons against sexual reluctance."[4] The ultimate goal is to "work out a yes"[5] with available young women (who often lack power to escape the situation because of social pressure, brute force, and/or their own alcohol or drug use).

However, not all fraternities and their members buy into this culture or engage in sexual exploitation or assault.[6] Much depends on their traditions, guiding ideologies, relative level of prestige, and interpersonal dynamics. In addition, some fraternity men have tried to change fraternity culture by attending rape prevention programs and rethinking what it means to be a man. Universities and colleges have also begun to crack down on sexual offenses, and to require that fraternities be educated on sexual assault and familiar with the laws in their particular areas. In the process, fraternities are changing the ways in which they treat women and are revising traditional fraternity versions of masculinity.

## NOTES

1. Sanday, Peggy Reeves. 1990. *Fraternity Gang Rape: Sex, Brotherhood, and Privilege on Campus.* New York: New York University Press, p. 3.

2. Researchers have not yet produced in-depth analyses of predominantly black fraternities and rape behaviors.

3. Martin, Patricia Yancey, and Robert A. Hummer. 1989. "Fraternities and Rape on Campus." *Gender & Society* 3(4): 457–473.; Sanday; Stombler, Mindy. 1994. "'Buddies' or 'Slutties': The Collective Sexual Reputation of Fraternity Little Sisters." *Gender & Society* 8(3): 297–323.

4. Martin and Hummer, 460, 464.

5. Koss, Mary P., and Hobart H. Cleveland III. 1996. "Athletic Participation, Fraternity Membership, and Date Rape." *Violence Against Women* 2(2): 180–190.; Martin and Hummer, 464; Sanday.

6. Humphrey, Stephen E., and Arnold S. Kahn. 2000. "Fraternities, Athletic Teams, and Rape: Importance of Identification with a Risky Group." *Journal of Interpersonal Violence* 15(2): 1313–1322.

# Raped: A Male Survivor Breaks His Silence

Fred Pelka

The man who raped me had a remarkable self-assurance which could only have come from practice. He picked me up just outside Cleveland, heading east in a van filled with construction equipment. That early morning in May I'd already spent a sleepless 24 hours trying to hitchhike from Oxford, Mississippi, to Buffalo, New York, so it felt good when I was offered a ride through the western fringe of Pennsylvania. First, though, the driver told me he needed to stop along the way, to pick up some building supplies. We drove to a country club undergoing renovation, where I hung out with his co-workers while he signed for several boxes of equipment which we carried back to his van. Getting back onto the turnpike he told me about one more stop he had to make.

As a man, I've been socialized never to admit to being vulnerable, to discuss those moments when I wasn't in control. I know also how women and children are routinely punished when they speak out about abuse, how they are blamed for their own victimization. The examples are endless: Witness the contempt with which Anita Hill was treated. For these reasons and more I'm still reticent, years after it happened, to recount what happened to me that day in Ohio. This article

marks the first time in 15 years I have publicly discussed it under my own name.

The second building seemed deserted. We went up a flight of stairs, down a corridor into a side room. I looked around for the equipment he'd mentioned, and noticed him locking the door behind us. He slugged me before I could react, forced me down with his hands around my throat. As I began to lose consciousness I heard him say, "If you scream, if you make one wrong move, I'll kill you."

The police told me later that the man who raped me was a suspect in the rapes of at least six other young men. During the assault his mood swung from vicious, when he promised to strangle me or break my neck, to self-pity, when he wept because we were both among "the wounded ones." In that enormous calm that comes after the acceptance of death, I wondered who would find my body.

Most rapes don't happen like this. Most victims know their attacker(s)—he is a neighbor, friend, husband, or father, a teacher, minister or doctor. The vast majority of rapes are committed by men against women and children, and the FBI estimates that anywhere from 80 to 90 percent go unreported. Rape is an integral part of our culture, and fully one third of all women in this country will be raped at some point in their lives. But this sexist violence does occasionally spill over onto boys and men. The National Crime Survey for 1989 estimated that one in 12 rape survivors is male.

For all this, nobody really knows how many men are raped each year, or how many boys are sexually abused. One study at the University of

From Pelka, Fred. 1995. "Raped: A Male Survivor Breaks His Silence." In *Rape and Society: Readings on the Problem of Sexual Assault* (pp. 250–256), edited by Patricia Searles. Copyright © 1995. Reprinted by permission of Westview Press, a member of Perseus Books, LLC.

New Hampshire found that one in 11 young men surveyed had been sexually abused before their 18th birthday. I've seen articles which speculate that anywhere from one in nine to one in seven men will be raped or sexually abused in their lifetime, most often by other males, but these are little more than guesses.

"Since rape is generally misconstrued to be a sexually motivated crime," write Dr. A. Nicholas Groth and Anne Wolbert Burgess, "it is generally assumed that males are unlikely targets of such victimization, and then when it does occur, it reflects a homosexual orientation on the part of the offender. However, the causes of male rape that we have had an opportunity to study do not lend much support to either assumption." Groth and Burgess interviewed men in the community who had been raped, and men who admitted to raping other men, and published their findings in the *American Journal of Psychiatry*. In half the cases they studied, the gender of the victim "did not appear to be of specific significance" to the rapist. "Their victims included males and females, adults and children," and "may symbolize . . . something they want to conquer or defeat. The assault is an act of retaliation, an expression of power, and an assertion of their strength or manhood."

In their article, Burgess and Groth dispute some of the prevalent myths about male rape. The first is that men simply don't get raped, at least not outside prison. Of course, if men don't get raped then what happened to me either wasn't rape (the police asking, "Did you come?"), or I'm not a man (my male friends wanting to know how I could "let something like this" happen to me). The second myth—that all men who are raped or rape other men are gay—is a product of our culture's homophobia, and our ignorance of the realities of sexual violence. Most people find it difficult to understand why a straight man would rape another straight man. But if you see rape as a way of exerting control, of confirming your own power by disempowering others, then it makes perfect sense. If it makes you feel powerful and

macho to force sex on a woman or child, think of how much more powerful you feel raping another man.

"I have a special place," the man who raped me said after a long while. "It's out in the country, where we can make all the noise we want." It seemed obvious what would happen to me once we arrived at "his special place," but I knew there was no hope for my survival as long as we stayed in that room. So I agreed to go with him to "the country." I promised not to try to escape. It is perhaps an indication of his fragile hold on reality that he believed me.

We walked back to his van and drove away. I waited until I saw some people, then jumped as we slowed to make a turn, rolling as I hit the pavement. I ran into the nearest building—a restaurant—just as patrons were finishing their lunch. Conversation stopped, and I was confronted by a roomful of people, forks raised in mid-bite, staring.

"I think you'd better call the police," I told the waitress. This was all I could say, placing my hands flat on the counter between us to control their trembling. She poured me a cup of black coffee. And then the police arrived.

The two detectives assigned to my case conformed to the standard good cop/bad cop archetype. The good cop told me how upset he'd seen "girls" become after being raped. "But you're a man, this shouldn't bother you." Later on he told me that the best thing to do would be to pull up my pants "and forget it ever happened." The bad cop asked me why my hair was so long, what was I doing hitchhiking at seven o'clock in the morning? Why were my clothes so dirty? Did I do drugs? Was I a troublemaker?

I used to be puzzled at how the bad cop obviously didn't believe me, in spite of the fact that, by his own account, in the months before my assault six other men had come to him with similar stories. Then I heard of the Dahmer case in Milwaukee, how in May 1991 Dahmer's neighbors saw him chasing a naked 19-year-old boy, bleeding from the anus, through the alley behind their building. The responding officers returned the boy to Dahmer's apartment, where Dahmer explained that this was just a lover's spat, which the police believed in spite of the youth's apparent age, and the photos scattered on Dahmer's floor of murdered and mutilated boys and men. The police reassured a neighbor who called again, saying that everything was all right—this at the very moment Dahmer was murdering Konerak Sinthasomphone. Afterwards Dahmer dismembered Sinthasomphone's body.

Sinthasomphone was one of at least 17 boys and men raped and murdered by Dahmer, their body parts stored in vats and freezers in his apartment. It was reported that his first assaults were committed in Ohio, so I had to brace myself before I could look at Jeffrey Dahmer's photo in the paper. At first I was relieved to find that he was not the man who raped me. Then I thought how this meant my assailant is likely still out there, looking for more "wounded ones."

Because I gave them such detailed information—the country club, the name painted on the side of his van—the detectives were able to locate my assailant not too many hours after I was brought into their precinct. The good cop asked, after I identified the rapist, whether I wanted to press charges. He explained how I'd have to return to Ohio to appear before a grand jury, and then return again for the trial, how the newspapers would publish my name, how little chance there was of a conviction.

"He says you seduced him," the good cop said. "So it's your word against his."

The bad cop glared at me when I told them there was no way I wanted any of this to be made public. "You mean," he fumed, "I wasted my whole afternoon on this shit?" Standing in front of me with an expression of disgust, he asked, "How do you think this makes me feel?"

By then it was getting dark. I hitchhiked the remaining 200 miles home, studying every movement of every man who offered me a ride. I arrived at my apartment after midnight, walking the last 10 miles.

In the weeks that followed the assault, every stupid, insensitive thing I'd ever said about rape came back to haunt me. A friend of mine had been attacked several months earlier, also while hitchhiking. She told me just a few hours after it happened how she'd missed her bus, and didn't want to be late to work. She said the man offering her a lift seemed normal enough, even "nice."

"You should've waited for the next bus," I lectured. Today I cringe at my arrogance. Hitchhiking, like walking alone after dark, or feeling safe on a date, at work, at home, is another perquisite to which only men are entitled. How dare she not understand the limits of her freedom?

While women tell me that the possibility of rape is never far from their minds, most men never give it a first, let alone a second, thought. This may explain why they react so negatively to accounts by male survivors. To see rape as "a women's issue" is a form of male privilege most men would prefer not to surrender. They would rather believe that they can move with immunity through the toxic atmosphere of violence and fear they and their compatriots create. Being a male survivor meant I'd lost some of that immunity. No wonder I felt as if I'd been poisoned, as if I were drowning.

For years I pretended, as per the good cop's recommendation, that nothing had happened, secretly feeling that I was somehow less masculine. The turning point came with the media storm that swirled up around the Big Dan rape in New Bedford, Massachusetts. The movie "The Accused" is based on that incident—a woman assaulted in a bar while other men looked on and cheered. Naive as I was, I figured this was a pretty clear-cut case. Where the police might have doubted my will to resist (no broken bones, no massive lacerations), here was a victim overpowered by half a dozen men. How could anyone doubt that she had been brutalized? Yet, during the trial, *The Boston Herald* ran the front page headline "SHE

LED US ON!" I realized then that, even had I been murdered, someone would have inevitably questioned my complicity: "He probably liked rough sex."

It's just this sort of victim-blaming that discourages survivors from reporting their trauma, or seeking treatment, but there are other factors which may discourage males in particular. Homophobia for one: The sort of gender McCarthyism that labels any man a faggot who cannot or will not conform to accepted norms of masculine feeling or behavior. Men who rape other men capitalize on this, knowing that straight victims don't want to appear gay, and gay victims might fear coming out of the closet. Groth and Burgess report, for instance, that "a major strategy used by some offenders . . . is to get the victim to ejaculate." This "strategy" was attempted in roughly half the cases they studied, and in half of those the rapist succeeded in ejaculating his victim. This confuses the victim, who often misidentifies ejaculation with orgasm. It confirms for the rapist the old canard about how victims "really want it." And, as Groth and Burgess say, it leaves the survivor "discouraged from reporting the assault for fear his sexuality may be suspect."

For male survivors of child sexual abuse there is also the unfortunate theory that boys who are abused inevitably grow up to be men who rape. One survivor told me it was for this reason he had decided never to be a father. Not that he'd ever wanted to abuse children, nor was there any evidence he ever would. He eventually came to realize that because some rapists are themselves survivors doesn't mean that all male survivors of child sexual abuse turn out to be rapists.

Finally, rape crisis centers, the only institutions in our society founded expressly to help rape survivors, are identified by some men as hotbeds of feminism, and many men take "feminist" to mean "man-hating." It's true that the vast majority of rape crisis counselors are women, that the entire stop-rape movement is an extension of the women's movement. For the record, though, I have never felt any hostility in response when calling a rape crisis center, this in spite of the fact that RCCs are often plagued by "hotline abusers"—men who call to masturbate to the sound of a female voice.

On the other hand, I've run across a good deal of hostility toward women from male survivors with whom I've talked. One man told me how certain he was that the counselors at his local RCC hated men, even though, by his own admission, he'd never called, and knew no one who had. A while back I attended a survivors' conference organized by a Boston women's group, attended by several hundred women and maybe a dozen men. One of these men stood up during a plenary session to shout at the women on the podium. As an incest survivor, he said, he felt "marginalized" and "oppressed" by the way the conference was run, despite the fact that a number of the workshops were specifically geared toward males, and that a keynote speaker received a standing ovation when he described his work with boys and men. Some male survivors even blame women for the denial and homophobia they encounter after their assault. They openly resent the (pitifully few) resources available to female survivors, as if any help women receive is at the expense of men. Even Geraldo has picked up this theme: His show on male survivors ended with an attack on rape crisis centers for their alleged refusal to acknowledge male victimization.

This hostility has been exacerbated by the so-called men's movement, the Robert Bly/mythopoetic crowd, with their "Wild Man" and "Inner Warrior" archetypes. These men say a lot of absurd things about sexual violence, not the least of which is that "just as many men get raped as women." This last statement is often repeated by Chris Harding, editor of *Wingspan,* which *The Boston Globe* calls "the bible of the new men's movement." Harding is generally quick to add that most of these rapes "occur in prison"—a statement which is as inaccurate as it is pernicious, assuming as it does that a disproportionate number of male rapes are committed by working-class and minority men. The men's movement claims that rape is a "gender-neutral issue," and thus has nothing to do with sexism.

What is ironic about all this is that what little acknowledgement there is of male victimization generally comes from the *women's* stop-rape movement. To the extent that male survivors *can* tell their stories, it is because of the foundation laid by feminists. So this women-bashing is as ungrateful as it is gratuitous.

One source of confusion appears to be the distinction between victimization and oppression. Male survivors charge that feminists see rape as a "man vs. woman" issue, emphasizing the central role male violence plays in stunting and destroying women's lives, and they're right. The distinction is that while many women, and some men, are victimized by rape, all women are oppressed by it, and any victimization of women occurs in a context of oppression most men simply do not understand. Rape for men is usually a bizarre, outrageous tear in the fabric of reality. For women, rape is often a confirmation of relative powerlessness, of men's contempt for women, and its trauma is reinforced every day in a thousand obvious and subtle ways.

For myself, I don't need for rape to be gender neutral to feel validated as a male survivor. And I certainly don't need to denigrate women, or to attack feminists, to explain why I was abused by the (male) police, ridiculed by my (male) friends, and marginalized by the (male dominated) society around me. It is precisely because we have been "reduced" to the status of *women* that other men find us so difficult to deal with. It was obvious to me at the police station that I was held in contempt because I was a *victim*—feminine, hence perceived as less masculine. Had I been an accused criminal, even a rapist, chances are I would have been treated with more respect, because I would have been seen as more of a man. To cross that line, to become victims of the violence which works to circumscribe the lives of women, marks us somehow as traitors to our gender. Being a male rape survivor means I no longer fit our culture's neat but specious definition of masculinity, as one empowered, one always in control. Rather than continue to deny our experience, male survivors need to challenge that definition.

As Diana E. H. Russell says in *The Politics of Rape,* "Women must start talking about rape: Their experiences, their fears, their thoughts. The silence about rape must be broken."

The same must be true for men. And so I offer this article as my first contribution to that effort.

---

## Women Raping Men

**Denise Donnelly**

In their article entitled "Sexual Molestation of Men by Women," P. M. Sarrel and W. H. Masters recount this story of a 27-year-old male, 178-pound truck driver, who was held captive for more than 24 hours. When he was released, he did not tell others about his experience, fearing ridicule. He experienced erectile dysfunction following the rape.

"[Sam] had been drinking and left a bar with a woman companion he had not known previously. They went to a motel where he was given another drink and shortly thereafter fell asleep. He awoke to find himself naked, tied hand and foot to a bedstead, gagged, and blindfolded. As he listened to voices in the room, it was evident that several women were present. When the women realized that he was awake, he was told to "have sex with all of them." He thinks that during *his period of captivity four different women used him sexually, some of them a number of times. Initially he was manipulated to erection and mounted. After a very brief period of coitus, he ejaculated. He was immediately restimulated to erection and the performance was repeated . . . it became increasingly difficult for him to maintain an erection. When he couldn't function well, he was threatened with castration and felt a knife held to his scrotum. He was terrified that he would be cut and did have some brief improvement in erectile quality."[1]*

**NOTE**

1. Sarrel, P. M., and W. H. Masters. 1982. "Sexual Molestation of Men by Women." *Archives of Sexual Behavior,* 11(2): 117–181.

# The Problem

# of Prison Rape

Daniel Brook

. . . Spike Lee's recent film *25th Hour* follows a busted New York City drug dealer named Monty Brogan on his last day of freedom before he's to be sent upstate. Brogan, played by Edward Norton, rues having to leave behind his friends, his girlfriend, and his father, but his uneasiness about losing them is matched by his dread of what awaits him in prison—rape. Near the end of the film, just hours before he's to depart, he goads his best friend Frank into beating him. "I need you to make me ugly," he says. "If they get one look at me looking like this I'll be finished." Frank obliges and beats him bloody.

Many other films and books have also invoked the specter of prison rape; to say that it is an unacknowledged problem in American culture is clearly inaccurate. Yet while our culture may not be bashful about discussing prison rape, it has, for the most part, portrayed it as a problem with no solution. Evocations like the one in *25th Hour* aren't meant to inspire outrage in the moviegoer; they're meant to stir up fear. In films like Lee's, or Curtis Hanson's *L.A. Confidential,* rape is a fixture of prison life as unavoidable as lights out. In Hanson's film, it's a convenient shorthand for all the potential horrors of prison that can be used by detectives to extract confessions—from innocent suspects, no less.

The prevalence of rape in prison *is* fearsome. Line officers recently surveyed in one southern

state estimated that one in five male prisoners were being coerced into sex; among higher-ranking officials, the estimate was one in eight. Prisoners themselves estimated one in three. (Female prisoners are the victims of rape as well, though they are usually assaulted by male guards, not other inmates; the phenomenon of male-on-male prison rape is generally studied separately.)

Compiling statistics on prison rape involves the same pitfalls as compiling conventional rape statistics. Male rape victims may be even more likely than female victims to underreport out of intimidation or shame. . . . Even without taking this reticence into account, the numbers are staggering. The most authoritative studies of the problem, conducted by the University of South Dakota professor Cindy Struckman-Johnson, found that over 20 percent of prisoners are the victims of some form of coerced sexual contact, and at least 7 percent are raped. Extrapolating from Struckman-Johnson's findings suggests that some 140,000 current inmates have been raped. The corrections industry itself estimates that there are 12,000 rapes per year, which exceeds the annual number of reported rapes in Los Angeles, Chicago, and New York combined.

Despite its prevalence, prison rape has generally been treated by courts and corrections officials as it has by novelists and filmmakers—as a problem without a solution. Prison rape is rarely prosecuted; like most crimes committed in prison, rapes aren't taken on by local district attorneys but left to corrections officials to handle. When inmates seek civil damages against the prison system, as Johnson has done, they must prove not merely that prison officials should have done more to prevent abuse but that they showed "deliberate indifference"—that is, that they had actual knowledge that an inmate was at risk and disregarded it. Showing that a prison guard should have known is not enough, no matter how obvious the signs of abuse.

This standard was established by the Supreme Court in the 1994 case *Farmer v. Brennan,* in which a transsexual inmate imprisoned for credit card fraud sued federal prison officials for ignoring his rape behind bars. While the court affirmed that prison rape is a violation of an inmate's constitutional rights and stated plainly that sexual assault is "not part of the penalty that criminal offenders pay for their offenses," it set up formidable barriers to establishing the culpability of corrections staff. At the cellblock level, the "deliberate indifference" standard discourages prison guards from shining a light into dark corners. What they don't know can't hurt them. . . .

Many people on the outside, including some within the criminal justice system, believe that prison rape is committed by "predatory homosexuals," a term used repeatedly in federal circuit court decisions. While inmate-on-inmate rape is in the most basic sense homosexual—both participants are male—researchers who have studied it have found that gay men are actually far more likely to be its victims than its perpetrators.

The feminist mantra that "rape isn't about sex, it's about power" may be even more applicable in the prison context, where it is common for men who would have never engaged in sexual contact with other men on the outside to become rapists when incarcerated. What's more, the relationship between rapist and victim in prison is often more than just a sexual one—it can devolve into out-and-out servitude. Victims are given women's names and made to perform household tasks such as cooking food, washing clothes, and cleaning the living space. . . .

The traditional rationale for prison rape is the lack of women, but most psychologists consider this facile. They see prison rape mainly as a means by which people who have been stripped of control over the most basic aspects of their lives—when to eat a meal, take a shower, or watch TV—can reclaim some sense of power. As one Louisiana prisoner, Wilbert Rideau, wrote, "the psychological pain involved in such an existence creates an urgent and terrible need for reinforcement of [a prisoner's] sense of manhood and personal worth." Others believe that prisoners become rapists out of fear of becoming victims themselves; it's a choice between becoming predator or prey. The psychologist Daniel Lockwood, in his study *Prison Sexual Violence,* calls this strategy "pre-emptive self-defense."

County Jail No. 3 sits on a landscaped hill in San Bruno, Calif., and when the sun shines on its Art Deco façade, you can see what a proud accomplishment it must have been for California law enforcement back in the *Dragnet* era. On the inside, however, the prison is crumbling. I traveled to the prison's fourth floor in its manually operated elevator, a harrowing experience I shared with Eileen Hirst, the chief of staff for the San Francisco County sheriff, and with a sheriff's deputy who trailed along to ensure our safety.

When we arrived at the night guard's post, Hirst issued a polite order. "Stand here," she said, putting me in the spot where the guard would keep watch. "Can you see anything that's going on in any cell?" Looking down the narrow whitewashed corridor, I couldn't even say for sure that there were cells in this cellblock, and I certainly couldn't see any of the prisoners sitting inside then. Anything could have been happening behind the bars.

Hirst was willing to show off this obvious rape trap because a 1994 federal court decision had ordered that the out-of-date facility be closed. County Jail No. 3 will be decommissioned by the end of [2004], replaced by a new, state-of-the-art facility. The changes were brought about by *Besk v. City and County of San Francisco,* a case that originated with an allegation of prison rape and eventually turned into a broader class-action suit about overcrowding. In its decision, a federal court mandated that the county build new state-of-the-art prisons, essentially ordering the San Francisco Board of Supervisors to come up with the necessary funds.

Even before *Besk,* however, San Francisco County had been a leader in trying to reduce sexual assaults in prison. . . . [In the current system,] after new inmates are booked, they're interviewed, sometimes for as long as 45 minutes. Inmates are sorted into three classification levels—minimum, medium, and maximum—based on their likelihood of harming fellow inmates. The levels do not correspond to the crimes these people committed but to the amount of jail time they have under their belt.

San Francisco's first attempt at a classification system separated gays from straights and violent offenders from nonviolent offenders, but [they] found that sorting prisoners by their vulnerability is more effective. . . . San Francisco's classification system has not eliminated rapes in the county's jails, but the city has found ways to drastically reduce the rate of sexual assault in a corrections facility. The efforts have also demonstrated, however, that such reforms do not come cheap. . . .

County Jail No. 8, which sits on a city block in San Francisco's South of Market neighborhood once home to dot-com start-ups, is one of the new jails built with money from *Besk.* Eileen Hirst and I stood at the elevated guard station in one of the pods. The station, decked out with controls, monitors, and a swivel chair, felt a bit like the bridge of the Starship Enterprise. With the cells arrayed in a semicircle, from the guard's chair I could see into each cell, just as an actor on an amphitheater stage can make eye contact with every audience member. Instead of bars, the cell doors had large glass windows. Overcrowding remains a problem, and some inmates in County Jail No. 8 are double-celled. But according to Lt. Sonny Bruno, who is in charge of classification at the new jail, overcrowding has not yet led to rape. "I don't have knowledge of anyone who's reported a sex assault in these pods," she said.

In 1826, in what was likely the first published mention of prison rape in the history of the republic, the Rev. Louis Dwight wrote that "Boys are Prostituted to the Lust of old Convicts" throughout the institutions he surveyed from Massachusetts to Georgia. Dwight, the founder of the Prison Discipline Society of Boston, a prison reform group, wrote that "Nature and humanity cry aloud for redemption from this dreadful degradation." It was not until the 21st century, however, that the nation saw its first anti-prison-rape legislation.

[In 2003,] Congress passed the Prison Rape Reduction Act, which allocates $60 million to support rape-prevention programs run by federal, state, and local corrections staff and to aid investigations and punishment of perpetrators. The bill, which enjoyed bipartisan support in the House and the Senate, also requires states to collect statistics on prison rape. Backers of the legislation hope federal oversight will make sexual assault prevention a priority for jail and prison systems across the nation. . . .

A higher hurdle, however, is the task of changing the way Americans think about prison rape. While San Francisco was honing its rape-prevention protocols, the state's attorney general, Bill Lockyer, was joking that he "would love to personally escort" Enron CEO Ken Lay "to an 8-by-10 cell that he could share with a tattooed dude who says, 'Hi, my name is Spike, honey.'"

While humor about conventional rape has always been taboo, jokes about prison rape remain common. A recent 7-Up ad, eventually pulled from the air, depicted a spokesman handing out 7-Up in prison. When he accidentally drops a can, he says, "I'm not picking that up." Later, the spot shows the spokesman sitting in a cell, being hugged by an inmate. "When you bring the 7-Up, everyone is your friend," he says nervously. "Okay, that's enough being friends," he adds as the cell door slams. The insinuation of what's going to happen next is clear—and it's played for a laugh.

Commercials like this one might merely be examples of corporate tastelessness, but there is ample evidence that they are symptoms of a more disturbing phenomenon: an indifference to the rights of prisoners or perhaps even an acceptance of rape as a de facto part of the punishment. It may be unseemly to admit finding solace in the thought that a convicted child molester or rapist will get a taste of his own medicine behind bars, but who hasn't had such a thought or heard such an idea expressed by another? . . .

## The Prison Rape Elimination Act of 2003

### Denise Donnelly

On September 4, 2003, President Bush signed the Prison Rape Elimination Act (PREA) into law. This bill, which had bipartisan support, passed unanimously in both houses of Congress. According to Human Rights Watch, "[This] legislation to address prison rape represents a major step forward in national efforts to protect the rights of prisoners. . . . [It] marked a turning point in how prison rape is viewed and discussed in the United States."[1]

Specifically, the PREA provided funding of $60 million annually for the years 2004 through 2010. It contained provisions for conducting research and collecting annual data on prison rape; establishing a national commission to study prison rape and recommend standards; creating a national clearing house on prison rape; training/educating federal, state, and local prison authorities on the issue; and making grants to state and local governments for establishing more effective programs to prevent, investigate, and prosecute prison rape.[2]

In July of 2005, the Department of Justice (DOJ) released its first statistical report on prison rape, as required by the PREA. Using a sample of 2,730 local and state facilities, they estimated that there were over 8,000 reported allegations of sexual violence in 2004. This averages out to just over three allegations per 1,000 inmates nationally. The DOJ notes that this is probably a huge underestimate of the actual amount of rape that occurs in our nation's correctional institutions, because few people—inside or outside of jail—ever report rape. Interestingly enough, while female corrections officers were more likely to assault male inmates than the reverse, 90 percent of the persons involved in sexual assaults involving two or more inmates were male. [3, 4]

In conclusion, although most experts agree that the PREA represents a solid step in the right direction, they also note that prison rape is a problem that will not be easily solved. Widespread beliefs—that inmates "deserve" to be raped, that men can't be raped by women, and that men who are raped are gay—help to support a prison rape culture that will not easily be legislated away.

### NOTES

1. Human Rights Watch. *No Escape: Male Rape in U.S. Prisons.* Copyright 2005 by Human Rights Watch. www.hrw.org/reports/2001/prison/learn.html.

2. Congressional Budget Office. *H. R. 1707, Prison Rape Reduction Act of 2003.* www.cbo.gov/showdoc.cfm?index=4425&sequence=0.

3. *Economist.* The Silent Horror. Vol. 376, Issue 8438, p. 25 (8/5/2005).

4. Bureau of Justice Statistics, 2005. *Sexual Violence Reported by Correctional Authorities, 2004.* Washington, DC: U.S. Department of Justice.

# Rape and War: Fighting Men and Comfort Women

Joane Nagel

[S]exuality has always been an important, though often disregarded aspect of all militaries and military operations. Throughout history women have been among "camp followers" providing services such as laundry, nursing, companionship, and sex to soldiers on military missions during peace and war.[1] Sometimes these women have been wives, relatives, or girlfriends, but always among their ranks have been prostitutes as well. Women who have had sex with servicemen around the world, however, have not always been volunteers. Throughout history local women have been involuntarily "drafted" in the sexual service of militaries as rape victims and sexual slaves.[2]

Rape in war is at its core an ethnosexual phenomenon. Whether a war is fought across national borders or inside state boundaries, the military front is typically an ethnosexual frontier. Differences in nationality, race, or ethnicity separate the combatants and identify the targets of aggression in military operations. Whether violence in war is from combat or sexual attack, and whether it is guns or bodies that are used as weapons, those who are physically or sexually assaulted almost always are different in some ethnic way. Men at war do not, as a rule, rape their "own" women unless, of course, those women are sus-pected of disloyalty, especially sexual disloyalty or "collaboration."

Sexual exploitation and abuse are important weapons of war, and rape is perhaps the most common component of war's sexual arsenal. Susan Brownmiller documents the routine practice of rape, especially gang rape, in war.[3] Moving or occupying armies use the rape of "enemy" women and girls as both a carrot and a stick: raping local women is a spoil of war for the troops to enjoy, and rape is also a technique of terror and warfare designed to dominate and humiliate enemy men by sexually conquering their women. Rape in war, as in many other ethnosexual settings, is best understood as a transaction between men, where women are the currency used in the exchange. Sexually taking an enemy's women amounts to gaining territory and psychological advantage. In countries around the world, rape often is defined as a polluting action, a way to soil the victim, her kin, and her nation physically and symbolically. Sexual warfare can extend beyond the moment of violation in situations where victims are reputationally smeared, physically mutilated, or when pregnancies or births result from sexual assaults. For instance, the widespread rape of mainly Muslim and some Croatian women by Serbian men in Bosnia in the early 1990s was partly intended to impregnate the women so that they would bear Serbian babies, "little Chetniks."[4] In order to guarantee that these rape victims could not obtain abortions, the Serbs set up concentration camps where pregnant women were imprisoned until they gave birth.[5]

Probably the best-known instance of rape in war is the so-called Rape of Nanking that occurred during the Japanese invasion of China in the winter and spring of 1938–1939, when Japanese soldiers raped an estimated eighty thousand Chinese women and girls.[6] A less well-known instance of Japanese wartime sexual exploits was the sexual enslavement of thousands of mainly Asian women by the Japanese Imperial Army during World War II. Sexual slavery in war is a variation on the theme of wartime rape. Slavery extends the tactic of rape as a short-term strategy of a military mission into a permanent feature of military operations. The Japanese military established camps of so-called military comfort women *(Jugun Ianfu)* in Japan and other countries where Japanese troops were stationed. While there were some mainly lower-class Japanese women forced into sexual slavery, most of the estimated 200,000 women enslaved by the Japanese army were ethnic or national. Others were brought from Korea, China, Taiwan, Indonesia, Malaysia, and the Philippines to sexually service the troops.[7] Kazuko Watanabe reports that in such settings a woman's worth as a sexual commodity was based on her class and her ethnicity:

> *The Japanese Imperial Army divided comfort women into a hierarchical order according to class, race, and nationality. . . . Korean and most other Asian women were assigned to lower-class soldiers. Japanese and European women went to high-ranking officers. Most of the European women were Dutch [often of mixed ancestry] who were imprisoned in a prisoner of war camp in the Netherlands East Indies.*[8]

Soldiers' rankings of and preferences for women of particular races and nationalities enslaved in rape camps were not unique to the Japanese military.[9] Japan was not the only country that established large-scale organized operations of forced sexual servitude during World War II. The Nazis used concentration camps in Germany and other occupied countries for more than industrial and war-related labor, their program of genocide against the Jews, and the mass deportation and killing of Roma (gypsies) and other "non-Aryan" peoples. Sexual labor was also demanded of women internees, and both men and women prisoners were used for sexual experimentation by Nazi scientists and physicians. German concentration camps were sites of forced prostitution and sexual assault, and as was the case with Japan, not all women in the German camps were treated as "equal" when it came to sexual abuse. A woman's age, youth, and physical appearance made her more or less likely to be the target of Nazi sexual aggression.[10] And, as in so many areas of social life, even (especially) in wartime concentration camps, ethnicity mattered. There were official prohibitions against German soldiers having sex with Jewish women, though these rules often were not enforced. Many Jewish women survivors reported extensive sadistic sexual torture, as well as rape, and these assaults often were accompanied by a barrage of racial and anti-Semitic verbal abuse.[11]

The Allies also were involved in sexual violence and exploitation during World War II. Some was in the form of mass rapes, such as those committed against German women by the Soviet army.[12] In other cases, sexual abuse and exploitation resulted when military personnel capitalized on the vulnerability of women who faced economic hardship, malnourishment, or starvation because of the war's disruption of local economies and food production. Many women in occupied or liberated countries found sexual liaisons or prostitution preferable to the grim alternatives available for themselves and their dependent families. U.S. troops also committed rapes during the war and the occupation that followed. In her examination of U.S. Army records, Brownmiller found 947 rape *convictions*, not simply charges or trials of American soldiers in Army general courts-martial during the period from January 1942 to July 1947.[13]

Wartime rape did not stop at the end of World War II, nor did its ethnosexual character change after 1945. The practice of rape in war extended into major and minor conflicts during the second half of the twentieth century—in civil wars, wars of independence, and military invasions, interventions, and operations in countries and regions around the world including Bangladesh, Vietnam, Iraq, Kuwait, Bosnia, Croatia, Serbia, Rwanda, Liberia, Kashmir, and Sierra Leone.[14] The logic of rape in war is always the same: rapes are committed across ethnosexual boundaries, and rape is used by both sides for the familiar time-honored reasons—to reward the troops, to terrorize and humiliate the enemy, and as a means of creating solidarity and protection through mutual guilt among small groups of soldiers. Ethnic loyalty and ethnic loathing join hands in rape in war.

In the post-Soviet era East European nationalist conflicts, the use of rape as a weapon of war has begun to move from the shadows more fully into view. For instance, during the 1990s warfare occurred along a number of ethnic and national borders in the former Yugoslavia—between Croats and Serbs, Christians and Muslims, and against Roma, among others. The most notorious of these ethnic conflicts was in Bosnia; the conflict's notoriety stemmed in part from its sexual character, especially the mass rape of Bosnian Muslim women by Orthodox Christian Serbian men. Many of these men and women were former neighbors. Muslims and Christians had lived side by side in the city of Sarajevo and elsewhere in Bosnia for decades and many had intermarried. That peace was shattered in 1992 when "ethnic cleansing" began.

Ethnic cleansing, or the removal of one ethnic group from a territory claimed by another, followed a common pattern across the region. Groups of armed Serbian men (sometimes uniformed troops and sometimes "irregulars" who were not officially in the military and not in uniform) roamed Bosnian towns and villages in groups, opportunistically looting and pillaging houses and businesses, raping and killing mainly unarmed Muslims they encountered along the way. Survivors reported that the Serbs came through the same towns several times in waves. During the first wave, typically, some of the Mus-

lim men were killed and the rest were rounded up to be killed later or to be interned in concentration camps. Muslim women, children, and the elderly were left behind. It was during the next waves of Serbs passing through the towns that they raped local non-Serbian girls and women.

Munevra was a forty-eight-year-old widow with three sons ranging in age from fourteen to twenty-four, ages that made them targets for the Serbs to kill or deport to concentration camps. She kept the young men hidden in the cellar as small groups of armed Serbian men repeatedly came through the town. In the spring of 1992, two men came to her house and sexually assaulted her. . . .

> *I was afraid my sons would hear me. I was dying of fear 'cause of my sons. They're decent people. . . . Then this man touched my breasts. He pulled up my blouse and took out my breasts. . . . He said, "For a woman your age your breasts aren't bad." Then they brought me to the other room. . . . I begged him and cried, and I crossed my legs. Then he took out his thing, you know, and he did it and sprayed it on me. When he was done the other one came and did the same thing. . . . When they left, my sons came out and . . . they asked me what happened: "What'd they do to you?" I said, "Nothing." I couldn't tell them about it. . . . I'd rather die than have them find out about it.[15]*

Women's and families' shame about such incidents were part of the process of victimization and violations.[16] Munevra's experience occurred relatively early in the nationalist conflict; far worse sexual violations were in store for women as the war escalated.

The scene in Serbian so-called rape camps was a longer, more brutal nightmare for Muslim and other non-Serbian women and girls. Twenty-six-year-old Ifeta was arrested by Serbian soldiers, most of whom she knew, and taken to a women's camp in Doboj:

> *Three drunken [Serbian army] soldiers . . . dragged her into a classroom . . . here she was raped by all three men "at the same time," says Ifeta, pointing to her mouth and backside. "And while they were doing it they said I was going to have a baby by*

*them". . . . After that the rapes were a part of Ifeta's daily life. . . . It was always a gang rape, they always cursed and humiliated her during it, and the rapists very frequently forced her to have oral sex with them.*[17]

Another camp internee, Kadira, described the weeks she spent at Doboj:

*"They pushed bottle necks into our sex, they even stuck shattered, broken bottles into some women. . . . Guns too. And then you don't know if he's going to fire, you're scared to death". . . . Once she was forced to urinate on the Koran. Another time she and a group of women had to dance naked for the Serbian guards and sing Serbian songs. . . . She has forgotten how many times she was raped.*[18]

The same pattern of sexual terror, torture, and rape used by the Serbs in their campaigns of ethnic cleansing and warfare in Bosnia was repeated in Kosovo, Yugoslavia, in 1998–1999. Once again groups of Serbian men—police, soldiers, irregulars—swept through villages invading homes and raping Kosovar Albanian (mainly Muslim) female occupants, sexually attacking Kosovar Albanian women refugees fleeing combat zones, and sexually assaulting Kosovar Albanian women who were being held hostage or detained. The Kosovo conflict ended when NATO troops entered Kosovo in June 1999.[19]

In spring 2000, the UN convened the *International Criminal Tribunal for the Former Yugoslavia* in The Hague, Netherlands, to investigate and prosecute those ordering mass killing and mass rape in the various ethnic conflicts in the former Yugoslavia.[20] This investigation raised the issue of whether rape and sexual slavery are "crimes against humanity." Enloe argues that this question reflects a new awareness and public airing of what has been a long hidden history of sexual assault, torture, and exploitation of women during war:

*[T]he rapes in Bosnia have been documented by women's organizations . . . [that] have helped create an international political network of feminists who are making news of the Bosnian women's victimization not to institutionalize women as*

*victims, not to incite men to more carnage, but to explain anew how war makers rely on peculiar ideas about masculinity. . . . [F]eminist reporters are using news of wartime sexual assaults by male soldiers to rethink the very meanings of both sovereignty and national identity. . . . If they succeed, the construction of the entire international political arena will be significantly less vulnerable to patriarchy.*[21]

As the reports of human rights hearings and organizations document every year, it is not only enemy women who are the targets of sexual abuse and torture in war. I have not seen reported the establishment of rape camps with men as sexual slaves, however, men often are assaulted sexually as part of intimidation, torture, and combat in international conflicts and wars, as well as in military or paramilitary operations against internal political or ethnic insurgents. For instance, in Bosnia, there were numerous reports of cases in which Muslim and Croatian men were castrated or forced to castrate one another:

*In villages, towns, cities, the countryside, and concentration camps, male and female adults and children are raped as part of more extensive torture. Many of the atrocities committed are centered on the genitalia. . . . [T]estimonies of castrations enforced on Bosnian-Herzegovinian and Croatian prisoners, and in particular of orders under threat of death that they castrate each other with various instruments and at times with their teeth, are widely available, as the [United Nations] Bassiouni Report makes clear.*[22]

Men also can be vulnerable to sexualized warfare in more indirect ways. In her critique of Japan's patriarchal Confucianist view of all women and racist treatment of non-Japanese men and women, Kazuko Watanabe also identifies a danger for men. She argues that in many countries men are trapped in masculinist roles, and forced to act out patriarchal and sexual scripts that commodify and endanger them as well as the women they victimize:

*Men's bodies and sexualities are also victims of militarist and consumerist capitalist societies. Men are, supposedly, unable to control their sexual impulses and are in need of prostitutes. [In World War II] Male soldiers were dehumanized to make them good fighters then stimulated by sexual desire that was fulfilled by comfort women. . . . Both the soldiers who were forced to die for the emperor on the battlefields and today's businessmen who die for their companies from* karoshi *(overwork) have often been rewarded with prostitutes.*[23]

Watanabe's analysis suggests that although they are perpetrators of the rape and sexual abuse of both women and other men in times of war, men pay a psychological, social, and physical price for their complicity in patriarchal masculinist systems of sexual and ethnosexual violence. For instance, many soldiers display varying degrees of post-traumatic stress or "shell shock" following combat. Michael Kimmel reports that during World War I officers and doctors tended to view such disorders as "failures to conform to gender demands":

> *Most psychiatric treatments for shell shock involved treating the disease as the result of insufficient manliness. T. J. Calhoun, assistant surgeon with the Army of the Potomac, argued that if the soldier could not be "laughed out of it by his comrades" or by "appeals to his manhood," then a good dose of battle was the best "curative."*[24]

Although modern-day soldiers suffering from post-traumatic stress are viewed with more sympathy than their historical counterparts, many, including those working in the health care industry, still view soldiers exhibiting symptoms arising from combat and military operations with some suspicion, as malingerers, frauds, or weaklings.[24] . . .

## NOTES

1. See for instance, Butler, *Daughters of Joy, Sisters of Misery*.

2. For a recent overview see Barstow, *War's Dirty Secret*.

3. Brownmiller, *Against Our Will*.

4. Allen, *Rape Warfare*, 96.

5. Ibid., 96.

6. See Iris Chang, *The Rape of Nanking: The Forgotten Holocaust of World War II* (New York: Basic Books, 1997); James Yin and Shi Young, *The Rape of Nanking: An Undeniable History in Photographs* (Chicago: Innovative Publishing Group, 1997).

7. Japan has yet to make satisfactory restitution to Korean and Filipina "comfort women" who were sexually enslaved during World War II, and some former victims have come forward to demand a public apology and accounting for their treatment; see Seth Mydans, "Inside a Wartime Brothel: The Avenger's Story," *New York Times*, November 12, 1996:A3; Maria Rosa Henson, *Comfort Woman: A Filipina's Story of Prostitution and Slavery under the Japanese Military* (Lanham, MD: Rowman and Littlefield Publishers, 1999); Sangmie Choi Schellstede, *Comfort Women Speak: Testimony by Sex Slaves of the Japanese Military* (New York: Holmes and Meier, 2000); for discussions of Japan's system of brothels, see George L. Hicks, *The Comfort Women: Japan's Brutal Regime of Enforced Prostitution in the Second World War* (New York: W.W. Norton, 1995); Keith Howard, *True Stories of the Korean Comfort Women* (London: Cassell, 1995); Sayoko Yoneda, "Sexual and Racial Discrimination: A Historical Inquiry into the Japanese Military's 'Comfort' Women System of Enforced Prostitution," in *Nation, Empire, Colony: Historicizing Gender and Race*, ed. Ruth Roach Pierson and Nupur Chaudhuri (Bloomington: Indiana University Press, 1989), 237–50; for a discussion of restitution in general and specifically as it relates to the women enslaved by Japan during World War II, see Elazar Barkan, *The Guilt of Nations: Restitution and Negotiating Historical Injustices* (New York: W.W. Norton, 2000), especially chapter 3.

8. Watanabe, "Trafficking in Women's Bodies," 503–504.

9. Both sexual and nonsexual labor were also demanded of women enslaved by the Japanese (ibid., 503); the Japanese also used rape as an instrument of terror and domination, most infamous is the "rape of Nanking" in which thousands of women were raped and killed; see Brownmiller, *Against Our Will*, 53–60.

10. Brownmiller, *Against Our Will*, 61–62.

11. For firsthand accounts of women's treatment in the camps, see Sarah Nomberg-Przytyk, *Tales from a Grotesque Land* (Chapel Hill: University of North Carolina Press, 1985), 14–20; Livia E. Bitton Jackson, *Elli: Coming of Age in the Holocaust* (New York: Times Books, 1980) 59–61; Cecile Klein, *Sentenced To Live* (New York: Holocaust Library, 1988), 73–77; Lore Shelley, *Auschwitz: The Nazi Civilization* (Lanham, MD: University Press of America, 1992).

12. See Cornelius Ryan, *The Last Battle* (New York: Simon and Schuster, 1966); Barstow, *War's Dirty Secret.*

13. Brownmiller, *Against Our Will,* 76–77; these 947 convictions are only part of a much greater universe of sexual assault by U.S. troops for several reasons: most rape is not reported and when it is, convictions are relatively rare even today, much less back in the 1940s during a state of war and/or military occupation; further, these were *convictions* where the soldier was found guilty, and did not include what could only have been a much larger number of charges filed and trials conducted; further still, these records were only for convictions of Army and Air Force personnel, and did not include data on the U.S. Navy or Marine Corps; finally, these records did not include information on charges, trials, or convictions for lesser sexual crimes than rape, such as sodomy or assault with the intent to commit rape or sodomy.

14. See Americas Watch and the Women's Rights Project, *Untold Terror: Violence against Women in Peru's Armed Conflict* (New York: Americas Watch, 1992); Asia Watch and Physicians for Human Rights, *Rape in Kashmir: A Crime of War* (New York: Asia Watch, 1993); Ximena Bunster, "Surviving beyond Fear: Women and Torture in Latin America," in *Women and Change in Latin America,* ed. June Nash and Helen Safa (South Hadley, MA: Bergin & Garvey, 1986), 297–325; Samir al-Khalil, *Republic of Fear: The Politics of Modern Iraq* (Berkeley: University of California Press, 1989).

15. Stiglmayer, "The Rapes in Bosnia-Herzegovina," 101.

16. See Elizabeth Bumiller, 'Deny Rape or Be Hated: Kosovo Victims' Choice," *New York Times,* June 22, 1999:1; Peter Finn, "Signs of Rape Sear Kosovo; Families' Shame Could Hinder Investigation," *Washington Post,* June 27, 1999:1.

17. Stiglmayer, "The Rapes in Bosnia-Herzegovina," 117–18.

18. Ibid., 118–19.

19. Human Rights Watch reports that although both sides committed sexual assault during the conflict, rates of rape by Serbian men far outnumbered instances of sexual abuse by Kosovar Albanian men during the conflict; see Human Rights Watch Report, "Kosovo: Rape as a Weapon of 'Ethnic Cleansing' " (March 21, 2000); my thanks to Hsui-hua Shen, Department of Sociology, University of Kansas, for bringing this report to my attention.

20. For early reports on the hearings and judgments of that tribunal, see Marlise Simons, "Bosnian Serb Trial Opens: First on Wartime Sex Crimes," *New York Times,* March 21, 2000:3; John-Thor Dahlburg, "Bosnian Witness Says She Endured Series of Rapes; Courts: Victim No. 50 Testifies in The Hague," *Los Angeles Times,* March 30, 2000:1; Chris Bird, "UN Tribunal Told of Bosnian Rape Camp Horrors," *Guardian,* April 21, 2000:1; Roger Thurow, "A Bosnian Rape Victim Suffers from Scars that Do Not Fade," *Wall Street Journal,* July 17, 2000:18.

21. Cynthia Enloe, "Afterword: Have the Bosnian Rapes Opened a New Era of Feminist Consciousness?" in *Mass Rape,* 219–30; progress continues to be made, slowly, in the shift toward defining rape as a human rights violation and in the prosecution of those responsible for the sexual assaults in the former Yugoslavia: on June 29, 2001, the Serbian government turned over former Yugoslavian president Slobodan Milosevic to the United Nations war crimes tribunal in The Hague, Netherlands; Marlise Simons with Carlotta Gall, "Milosevic Is Given to U.N. for Trial in War-Crime Case," *New York Times,* June 29, 2001:1; it is important to note that at about the same time the rapes and killings were happening in Yugoslavia and Bosnia, millions of men, women, and children were being raped, mutilated, and murdered in Rwanda; while Western governments dithered and delayed responding to both the Yugoslavian and Rwandan massacres and atrocities, and while an international tribunal was established in 1994 to prosecute Rwandans for their war crimes, the issue of rape as a war crime came to the fore in Yugoslavia, but not in the much larger-scale Rwandan case; perhaps it required reports of the mass rapes and sexual enslavement of white women, albeit Muslim white women, for the "civilized" world to take notice of ethnosexual violence in war.

22. Allen, *Rape Warfare*, 78; the "Bassiouni Report" is the result of an October 1992 decision by the Secretary-General of the United Nations to appoint a commission of experts "to examine and analyze information gathered with a view to providing the Secretary-General with its conclusions on the evidence of grave breaches of the Geneva Conventions and other violations of international humanitarian law committed in the territory of the former Yugoslavia" (ibid., 43).

23. Watanabe, "Trafficking in Women's Bodies," 506–507.

24. Kimmel, *Manhood in America*, 133–34.

## Did You Know?

- One in six women have experienced an attempted or completed rape. One in ten sexual assault victims are men.[1]
- Almost two-thirds of all rapes are committed by someone the victim knows.[2] Ninety percent of rape victims under age 13 knew their attackers.[3]
- Only 36 percent of all rapes and sexual assaults are reported to the police.[4]
- In a survey of 11 to 14 year olds, 51 percent of the boys and 41 percent of the girls said forced sex was acceptable if the boy "spent a lot of money" on the girl.[5]
- Sixty-one percent of all female sexual assault victims are under the age of 18.[6]
- In cases of date rape, 75 percent of male students and 55 percent of female students had been drinking or using drugs when the assault occurred.[7]
- One in twenty college women are the victims of sexual assault every year.[8]
- Over 50 percent of all reported rapes and incidents of sexual assault took place at or within one mile of victims' homes.[9]
- Seventy percent of rape victims report they were too intoxicated at the time of the assault to give their consent or refuse sex.[10]
- In cases of reported rape, only about half result in an arrest. Eighty percent of arrested alleged perpetrators are prosecuted.[11]
- Including all unreported rapes, about 5 percent of rapists will serve time in jail.[12]
- The average sentence for rapists is 128 days of incarceration.[13]
- Persons with disabilities are one and a half to five times more likely to be sexually abused and assaulted than are non-disabled persons.[14]
- Rape Shield laws make victims' sexual history or conduct inadmissible in court.[15]
- Hate crimes based on sexual orientation made up approximately 15.6 percent of all hate crimes in 2004, following only those based on racial and religious biases. Of these crimes based on sexual orientation, 60.8 percent resulted from anti-male homosexual bias, 21.1 percent from an anti-homosexual bias, 14.3 percent from an anti-female homosexual bias, 2.5 percent from an anti-heterosexual bias and 1.3 percent from an anti-bisexual bias.[16]
- Data from the FBI show that transgendered people are particularly at risk for being targets of violent hate crimes. The agency found that transgendered people have a one in twelve chance of being murdered, compared to the one in 18,000 chance for "average Americans."[17]

*—Compiled by Mikel Walters*

**NOTES**

1. Bureau of Justice Statistics. 2005. "Criminal Victimization, 2004." U.S. Department of Justice.

2. Ibid.

3. Bureau of Justice Statistics. 1997. "Sex Offenses and Offenders Study," U.S. Department of Justice.

4. Ibid.

5. White, Jacqueline W. and John A. Humphrey. 1991. "Young People's Attitudes towards Acquaintance Rape." *Acquaintance Rape: The Hidden Crime,* edited by Andrea Parrot and Laurie Bechhofer. John Wiley and Sons.

6. Beach, Roberta K. and Suzanne Boulter. 1994. "Sexual Assault and the Adolescent." *Pediatrics* 94:761–755.

7. Student Life. 2004. "Alcohol and Sexual Assault on Campus: New Findings." *Administrator* 23(6):8.

8. Ibid.

9. Bureau of Justice Statistics. 1997.

10. Ibid.

11. Bureau of Justice Statistics. 2004. "National Crime Victimization Report, 2003." U.S. Department of Justice.

12. Ibid.

13. National Center for Policy Analysis. 1999. "Crime and Punishment in America: 1999." Retrieved January 30, 2006 from www.ncpa.org/studies/s229/s229.html.

14. Sobsey, Dick. 1994. *Violence and Abuse in the Lives of People with Disabilities: The End of Silent Acceptance?* Brooks Publishing Company.

15. Anderson, Michelle J. 2002. "From Chastity Requirement to Sexuality License: Sexual Consent and a New Rape Shield Law." *George Washington Law Review* 70:51. Retrieved January 30, 2006 from www.vawnet.org/Sexual Violence/PublicPolicy/Chastity.pdf.

16. Department of Justice, Federal Bureau of Investigation. 2004. "Crime in the United States 2004: Hate Crime." Retrieved January 30, 2006 from www.fbi.gov/ucr/cius_04/offenses_reported/hate_crime/index.html.

17. Human Rights Campaign. "Transgender Basics." Retrieved January 30, 2006 from www.hrc.org/Content/NavigationMenu/HRC/Get_Informed/Issues/Transgender_Issues1/Transgender_Basics/Transgender_Basics.htm.

# chapter 11

# Commercial Sex

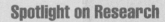

**Spotlight on Research**

*An interview with . . .*

### Jacqueline Boles

Jacqueline Boles, Ph.D., is a professor emeritus of sociology at Georgia State University in Atlanta, Georgia. Her research interests include sex work and sex workers, prostitution and HIV transmission, and deviant behavior. Dr. Boles is the author of over 40 articles and book chapters.

#### How did you get involved in the study of sexuality?

*My dissertation advisor said, "Why don't you study strippers?" He knew my husband and I had been in show business and that I knew people familiar with the business. I thought, "Why not?" The great fan dancer, Sally Rand, was in town. I interviewed her and then began interviewing strippers in Atlanta clubs. About a year after I finished my dissertation, the police asked me to find out why so many prostitutes were coming to Atlanta. A colleague and I started interviewing prostitutes in the vice squad office, hooking bars, massage parlors, and on the street. That's how it all got started.*

### Which of your projects have you found most interesting?

*In 1987, Kirk Elifson and I received a grant from the CDC to investigate HIV risk factors among male prostitutes (hustlers). We interviewed and drew blood from over 300 male prostitutes. We found that hustlers self-identified as heterosexual, homosexual, and bisexual. A hustler's self-identification was a strong predictor of HIV seropositivity. For example, heterosexual identified hustlers refused to engage in anal receptive sex, which is a major risk factor for contracting HIV. Consequently, heterosexual identified sex workers had the lowest rate of HIV seropositivity.*

### What have you found most challenging about studying sexuality?

*A person can be HIV seropositive for 10 years without exhibiting any symptoms. When we began our research, we needed to look at the sexual history of the hustlers over a 10-year period. How do you ask these men to account for all their sex acts over 10 years? We needed to know how many partners they had, the gender of the partners, what kinds of sex acts were performed, and whether a condom was used. We faced a similar problem with drug use. Intravenous drug use is a risk factor for HIV, so we needed a history. We had to develop a workable strategy for getting accurate histories, and this took a great deal of experimentation and pre-testing of our instruments.*

### What have you learned from your years of research?

*Too bad that sexual behavior in humans is not instinctive. If it were, we would all behave similarly, and life would be less complicated. Unfortunately, behaving sexually (or not) is associated with a number of problems: low self-esteem, jealousy and rage, sexually transmitted diseases, psychosocial adjustment issues, etc. We cannot help solve these problems unless we understand sexual behavior: what people do and how they feel about what they do. Simply asserting that a behavior is "wrong" or "immoral" will not prevent the behavior from occurring.*

### Have you encountered any ethical dilemmas in your research? How did you resolve these?

*In our hustler study, we guaranteed the anonymity of all our study participants. They were given a patient identification number that they could use to receive their HIV serostatus from the health department. Even though we knew their serostatus, we were not allowed to inform them. Many times we knew that an HIV-positive hustler was living with an HIV-negative lover. We could not warn the uninfected person; all we could do is stress to lovers that they "get their test results." When we started our study, we did not want any thing we did to have a negative impact on our study participants. We declined interviews with the media so that our results would not be sensationalized. The sex workers we studied were constantly harassed by police, and we did not want to do anything that would increase that harassment.*

### How do people react when they find that you are a sex researcher?

*A few years ago, I was asked to substitute for a well-known prostitute/activist on a panel. After the program ended, a woman (who had come late and did not know that I was not a sex worker) came up to me and gushed, "I always wanted to meet one; now I can say I have finally met a woman of the night." I did not have the heart to disappoint her! Most people are curious about the people I have met and interviewed. They enjoy hearing about the strip clubs, massage parlors, hooking bars, and other disreputable places I frequent. I try to humanize sex workers by sharing favorite stories.*

### If you could teach people one thing about sex, what would it be?

*I may be swimming against the current, but I would like to suggest that we are asking sex to carry too big a burden. "Good sex will make me happy; if I'm not successful sexually, then I'm a failure; there's nothing worse than a sexual loser." Sex is designed to give pleasure, but so are swimming in a clear lagoon, viewing Monet's garden, eating an ice-cream cone, and cuddling one's child. Good sex (whatever that means) is but one component of a life well lived.*

—Interviewed by Denise Donnelly

# Naked Capitalists

Frank Rich

. . . The $4 billion that Americans spend on video pornography is larger than the annual revenue accrued by either the N.F.L., the N.B.A. or Major League Baseball. But that's literally not the half of it: the porn business is estimated to total between $10 billion and $14 billion annually in the United States when you toss in porn networks and pay-per-view movies on cable and satellite, Internet Web sites, in-room hotel movies, phone sex, sex toys and that archaic medium of my own occasionally misspent youth, magazines. Take even the low-end $10 billion estimate (from a 1998 study by Forrester Research in Cambridge, Mass.), and pornography is a bigger business than professional football, basketball and baseball put together. People pay more money for pornography in America in a year than they do on movie tickets, more than they do on all the performing arts combined. As one of the porn people I met in the industry's epicenter, the San Fernando Valley, put it, "We realized that when there are 700 million porn rentals a year, it can't just be a million perverts renting 700 videos each."

Yet in a culture where every movie gross and Nielsen rating is assessed ad infinitum in the media, the enormous branch of show business euphemistically called "adult" is covered as a backwater, not as the major industry it is. Often what coverage there is fixates disproportionately on Internet porn, which may well be the only Web business that keeps expanding after the dot-com collapse but still accounts for barely a fifth of American porn consumption. . . .

Size matters in the cultural marketplace. If the machinations of the mainstream TV, movie and music industries offer snapshots of the American character, doesn't this closeted entertainment behemoth tell us something as well? At $10 billion, porn is no longer a sideshow to the mainstream like, say, the $600 million Broadway theater industry—it *is* the mainstream.

And so I went to the San Fernando Valley, aka Silicone Valley, on the other side of the Hollywood Hills to talk with the suits of the adult business. . . . I wanted to find out how some of the top players conduct their business and how they viewed the Americans who gorge on their products.

Among other things, I learned that the adult industry is in many ways a mirror image of Hollywood. Porn movies come not only in all sexual flavors but also in all genres, from period costume dramas to sci-fi to comedy. . . . Adult has a fabled frontier past about which its veterans wax sentimental—the "Boogie Nights" 70s, when porn was still shot only on film and seen in adult movie theaters. (The arrival of home video revolutionized porn much as sound did Hollywood.) Adult also has its own Variety (Adult Video News), its own star-making machinery (the "girls" at Vivid and Wicked are promoted like bygone MGM contract players), its own prima donnas and cinéastes. It has (often silent) business partners in high places: two of the country's more prominent porn purveyors, Marriott (through in-room X-rated movies) and General Motors—(though its ownership of the satellite giant DirecTV now probably to be sold to Rupert Murdoch), were also major sponsors of the Bush-Cheney Inaugural. Porn even has its own Matt Drudge—a not-always-accurate Web industry gossip named Luke Ford, who shares his

From Rich, Frank. 2001. "Naked Capitalists."
*New York Times Magazine* May 20:51–56, 81–82.
© 2001, Frank Rich. Reprinted by permission.

prototype's political conservatism and salacious obsessiveness. . . .

If the people who make and sell pornography are this "normal"—and varied—might not the audience be, too? It can't be merely the uneducated and unemployed who shell out the $10 billion. And it isn't. Porn moguls describe a market as diverse as America. There's a college-age crowd that favors tattooed and pierced porn performers; there's an older, suburban audience that goes for "sweeter, nicer, cuter girls," as Bill Asher of Vivid Pictures puts it. There is geriatric porn (one fave is called "Century Sex"), and there's a popular video called "Fatter, Balder, Uglier." Oral sex sells particularly well in the Northeast, ethnic and interracial videos sell in cities (especially in the South), and the Sun Belt likes to see outdoor sex set by beaches and pools. . . .

"Porn doesn't have a demographic—it goes across all demographics," says Paul Fishbein, 42, the compact and intense man who founded Adult Video News. "There were 11,000 adult titles last year versus 400 releases in Hollywood. There are so many outlets that even if you spend just $15,000 and two days—and put in some plot and good-looking people and decent sex—you can get satellite and cable sales. There are so many companies, and they rarely go out of business. You have to be really stupid or greedy to fail."

He points me toward the larger producers whose videos top AVN's charts and have the widest TV distribution. There are many successful companies, but some of them cater to niche markets (like gay men) that as of yet haven't cracked the national mass market of TV, where pay-per-view pornographic movies, though priced two or three times higher and not promoted, often outsell the Hollywood hits competing head to head. In a business with no barrier to entry—anyone with a video camera can be a director or star—there are also countless bottom feeders selling nasty loops on used tape. Whatever the quality or origin of a product, it can at the very least be exhibited on one of the 70,000 adult pay Web sites, about a quarter of which are owned by a few privately held companies that slice and dice the same content under different brands. . . .

Russell Hampshire, who owns one of the biggest companies, VCA Pictures, . . . is also a graduate of McDonald's Hamburger U., which he attended while running McDonald's franchises in El Paso in the 70s. It's business training that came in handy in the porn biz. "I learned about inventory, buying the proper insurance, doing everything by the book, not taking shortcuts," he says. . . .

He has been in the business since 1978 and waxes nostalgic for the early video days, when you could transfer a prevideo Marilyn Chambers classic to cassette and sell it wholesale for up to a hundred bucks. Now his top movies wholesale for $18 or $19, sometimes lower. "There used to be only 10 to 12 titles to choose from in a video store," he says. "Now there are thousands of titles." A typical release may sell only 2,000 units or less—7,500 would be a modest hit—but thanks to TV and international sales, Hampshire says he makes money "on every title." Though the total income from a hit is pocket money by Hollywood standards, Hollywood should only have such profit margins. An adult film that brings in $250,000 may cost only $50,000 to make—five times the original investment. Production locations are often rented homes, shooting schedules run less than a week, and most projects are not shot on the costly medium of film. There are no unions or residuals. Marketing costs are tiny, since quote ads run in AVN and skin magazines, not in national publications or on TV. Most economically of all, porn movies don't carry the huge expense of theatrical distribution: video killed off adult movie theaters far more effectively than it did regular movie theaters. . . .

Almost every adult company is pursuing innovative media, preparing for Internet broadband and interactive hotel-room TV. At Wicked Pictures' newly revamped Web site, for instance, a visitor can cross-index a particular porn star with a sexual activity, then watch (and pay for) just those scenes that match. Digital Play-ground's "Virtual Sex" DVD's resemble video games in how they allow the user to control and inject himself into the "action."

As in nonadult video, DVD is cutting into videocassette sales—even more so in adult, perhaps, because DVD's have the added virtue of being more easily camouflaged on a shelf than cassettes. Hampshire is particularly proud of VCA's DVD technology. With his vast catalog, he is following the model of Hollywood studios by rereleasing classics—"The Devil in Miss Jones 2," "The Opening of Misty Beethoven"—in "Collectors Editions," replete with aural commentaries from original stars like Jamie Gillis. As with Hollywood's DVD rereleases, they are pitched at nostalgic consumers in the "boomer-retro" market. "These aren't 'adult'—they're pop culture now," says Mischa Allen. . . .

Veronica Hart, 44, is one of the business's most prominent female executives and, before that, a leading porn star of the late 70s and early 80s. . . .

"The difference between us and Hollywood," she elaborates, "is money and ego. We deal with thousands of dollars, not millions. In mainstream, people are more cutthroat and pumped up about themselves. We're just like regular people—it has to do with exposing yourself. If you show something this intimate, there isn't a lot you can hide behind. You're a little more down to earth. We're not curing cancer. We're providing entertainment." . . .

Hart has been in adult longer than anyone I met and has done "everything" in it, she jokes, "including windows." She warns me that "any blanket statement about the business is meaningless" because it's so big that "every conceivable type of person" can be found in it. . . . "You'll find everyone who fits the stereotype and everyone who goes against the stereotype. . . . What ticks me off is that all of adult is classified according to the lowest that's out there. We've always been legal.

Child molestation has never been in mainstream adult. We've always policed ourselves. There's no coerced sex. But there are little pipsqueaks who get their disgusting little videos out there. There's a trend in misogynistic porn, and it's upsetting. I've been in the business for more than 20 years, and I helped make it possible for these guys to make these kinds of movies. I don't believe that's what America wants to see."

As for her own movies, Hart, like many of her peers, is preoccupied with the industry's biggest growth market—women and couples. The female audience was thought to be nearly nil when consuming pornography required a visit to a theater, an adult book store or the curtained adult section of a video store. But now hard core is available at chains like Tower (though not Blockbuster), through elaborate Web sites like Adultdvdempire that parallel Amazon and by clicking a pay-per-view movie on a TV menu (where the bill won't specify that an adult title was chosen). . . .

Today's porn stars can be as temperamental as their Hollywood counterparts, or more so. . . . Some porn directors have similar pretensions. They can receive grandiose billing—"A Brad Armstrong Motion Picture"—and are sometimes grudgingly indulged with a "big budget" project ($250,000 tops) made on film, even though sex scenes are far harder to shoot on film (with its trickier lighting and shot setups) than on video—and even though adult films are almost never projected on screens. . . . Performers are paid at fairly standardized rates—by the day or sex scene, as much as $1,000 per day for women, as little as $200 for men. The contract girls at Vivid and Wicked sign for $100,000 and up a year, in exchange for which they might make nine movies, with two sex scenes each, over that time, along with any number of brand-boosting promotional appearances at consumer conventions and video stores. The top stars double or triple that figure by running their own subscription Web sites, marketing autographs (along with less innocent mementos) and most lucratively, dancing in the nation's large circuit of strip clubs at fees that can top $10,000 a week. . . .

No wonder the porn industry has its finger on the pulse of American tastes. Not only do its players have a lifestyle more middle class than that of their Beverly Hills counterparts, but in their desire to keep their porn careers camouflaged in a plain brown wrapper, they connect directly with their audience's shame and guilt. Still, the next generation of porn consumers and producers alike may break with that puritan mind-set. The teenagers who grew up with cable and the VCR "come to the table already saturated with sex," says Bryn Pryor. "They've never known a time without Calvin Klein ads and MTV. By the time they see porn, they've already seen so many naked people they're pre-jaded."

This may explain why Americans are clamoring for ever more explicit fare. In mainstream TV, sex is no longer sequestered on late-night public access shows like "Robin Byrd." At HBO, Sheila Nevins, the highly regarded executive in charge of its nonfiction programming, has been stunned by the success of sexual documentaries like "Real Sex," now in its 11th year, and "Taxicab Confessions." Focus groups complain to HBO that another hit series, "G-String Divas," doesn't go far enough. "They know what really happens in a strip club," Nevins says, and find HBO's version "too R-rated." . . . "At first we were embarrassed by the sex shows, and producers didn't want their names on them. Now we have Academy Award producers, and their names can't be big enough."

At Playboy, Jim English, the head of its TV division, and his boss, Christie Hefner, have felt the heat. Its Playboy and Spice channels have been squeezed from both sides in the cable-satellite marketplace. . . . Meanwhile, erotic networks like Hot and Ecstasy, which run XX films, are cannibalizing Playboy's audience from the other end of the erotic spectrum. The result: This summer Playboy plans to start "Spice Platinum Live," which edges toward XXX. . . .

Even in an economic downturn, everything's coming up porn. Newly unemployed dot-com techies who can't find jobs in Silicon Valley are heading to Silicone Valley, where the work force is expanding, not contracting. "Vivid overall has doubled, tripled revenues and profits in the past couple of years," says Bill Asher. While he says there's no such thing as a Hollywood-style "home run" in porn—unless another celebrity like Pamela Anderson turns up in a sex video, intentionally or not—he sees potentially "a tenfold jump" in profits as distribution increases through broadband and video-on-demand. . . . There are opportunities here that Paramount will never have in terms of growth," Asher says. "Our product travels well internationally and is evergreen. Five-year-old product is still interesting to someone; it's not yesterday's news like a five-year-old Hollywood blockbuster. Our costs are relatively fixed. As there's more distribution, 90 cents of a dollar hits the bottom line." The absence of adult retail stores in conservative pockets of the country is no longer a barrier. "You can get a dish relatively anywhere," Asher says, "and get whatever you want."

When Vivid took over and expanded the Hot Network in 1999, Asher says, "there was no outcry. We got thank-you letters and sales boomed. We put up two more channels in months. Cable companies were begging for them. It doesn't take a genius to do this. Literally the customers say, I like what you've got—give me some more of it." Entertainment-industry executives not directly involved in the adult business confirm its sunny future. Satellite and cable companies have found that the more explicit the offerings, the more the market grows. AVN reports that TV porn may actually be increasing videostore sales and rentals rather than cannibalizing them—by introducing new customers to the product. Though some cable companies say they don't want adult, only one of the country's eight major cable providers, Adelphia, forbids it. The others are too addicted to the cash flow to say no. . . . And despite a rumor that one porn mogul keeps a Cessna waiting at Van Nuys airport to escape to Brazil if there's a government crackdown, the odds of that look slim. Too many Fortune 500 corporations with Washington clout, from AT&T to AOL Time Warner, make too much money on porn—whether through phone sex, chat rooms or adult video. At the local level, the Supreme Court's 1973 "community standard" for obscenity may be a non sequitur now that there's a XX national standard disseminated everywhere by satellite and the Web. A busted local video retailer in a conservative community can plead that his product is consistent with what the neighbors are watching on pay-per-view.

Pryor envisions a day when adult and Hollywood will converge, but in a sense that's al-ready the case. If much of porn ranges from silly to degrading, what's the alternative offered on the other side of the hills? The viewer who isn't watching a mediocre porn product is watching—what? "Temptation Island"? W.W.F.?

Moralists like to see in pornography a decline in our standards, but in truth it's an all-too-ringing affirmation of them. Porn is no more or less imaginative than much of the junk in the entertainment mainstream—though unlike much of that junk, it does have an undeniable practical use. In that regard, anyway, there may be no other product in the entire cultural marketplace that is more explicitly American.

---

## Sex Cells!

**Matt Richtel and Michel Marriott**

The cellphone, which already plays music, sends and receives e-mail and takes pictures, is adding a steamier offering: pornography. With the advent of advanced cellular networks that deliver full-motion video from the Internet—and the latest wave of phones featuring larger screens with bright color—the pornography industry is eyeing the cellphone, like the videocassette recorder before it, as a lucrative new vehicle for distribution.

In recent months, that prospect has produced a cadre of entrepreneurs in the United States hoping to follow the lead of counterparts in Europe, where consumers already spend tens of millions of dollars a year on phone-based pornography. The major American cellular carriers have so far been adamant in their refusal to sell pornography from the same content menus on which they sell ring tones and video games. But there are signs that they may soften their stance.

The cellular industry's major trade group is drafting ratings for mobile content—akin to those for movies or video games—signaling that phones, too, will be a subject of viewer discretion. For now, the Web-based video available on many cellphones is crude. Images take time to load and appear grainy, and video feeds are often interrupted by inconsistent wireless signals. . . .

For the carriers, it is a tricky proposition. Offering pornography would stir a tempest over indecency and possible pressure from regulators or Congress. But conceding the field to third parties would leave millions of dollars on the table. At present, sales of pornography over mobile phones in this country amount to virtually nothing. But cellphone commerce is on the rise, with sales of ring tones alone expected to reach $453 million this year, according to the Yankee Group, a research firm. The company estimates that by 2009, sales of pornography for phones will hit $196 million, still meager compared with a projected $1.2 billion for ring tones.

But the likelihood that pornography will be increasingly accessible by phone has children's advocacy groups mobilizing. This month, the National Coalition for the Protection of Children and Families, a nonprofit group that seeks to promote "biblical morality," met with leaders of the wireless industry to voice concern that phones could provide minors with all-too-easy access to inappropriate material. . . .

The Federal Communications Commission, meanwhile, has its own concerns, said David Fiske, a spokesman. "The commission takes very seriously the issue of inappropriate material reaching cellphones that are in the hands of children," he said. Mr. Fiske declined to comment on what actions the commission might take. To some extent, though, the agency's hands are tied in that mobile phone carriers, like other telecommunications companies, are not responsible for what Internet sites consumers visit. But the carriers could be held accountable, experts said, if they take part in selling pornography to minors.

In the past, pornography has helped to drive the popularity of new technologies, including the videocassette recorder, cable television and the Web itself, and it is a source of revenue for many major media companies, including cable giants like Time Warner and Comcast, which have pay-per-view channels devoted to pornography.

Many of those in the business of pornography are not deterred by today's technical difficulties in delivering cellphone video. Harvey Kaplan, director of mobile operations for xobile.com, a company in Charlotte, N.C., that sells two-minute hard-core video clips for download over phones, said he believed that thirst for sex-related content would drive the popularity of Internet-enabled phones. . . . Xobile started in April, and Mr. Kaplan said that each month the company was adding 6,000 customers, who pay around 44 cents to see a two-minute video clip. To use the service, a customer signs up and enters a credit card number at the company's Web site from a computer or a mobile phone. . . .

The bigger purveyors of pornography are looking to become involved, too. "We look very forward to being one of the leaders in the business here," said Steven Hirsch, founder and chairman of Vivid Entertainment, the largest maker of sexually explicit movies, noting that wireless content could earn as much as 30 percent of the company's $100 million annual revenues. "We are perfectly positioned with the amount of content we have."

While some of Vivid's hard-core materials can be found "off network" (that is, not through the major cellphone carriers), he said his company was focusing on getting "on the deck"—available directly from the carriers' cellphone menus, as ring tones are. He said it was only a matter of time before the carriers resolved what he termed the fundamental roadblock: age verification. . . .

In England, for example, age verification is handled at the point of sale for cellphones. A buyer provides proof of age. If buyers are of the age of consent, they can stipulate that their phones have access to sexually explicit material. . . .

The major carriers have said that for now they do not intend to include sexually explicit content on their menus. In a statement, for instance, Cingular Wireless said the company "does not provide adult content to its customers." But Cingular, the largest wireless company, also said it would not and could not stop people from using their phones to obtain such content directly from the Internet. . . .

John Walls, spokesman for CTIA, the mobile phone trade group, said that it expected to have content ratings in place early next year. Such ratings, he predicted, would include a category for people 18 or older, allowing carriers to feel more comfortable selling sex-oriented content—at least of the soft-core variety. "If there's a demand for service or product, then just from a business standpoint you'd like to find a way to serve that demand," he said.

*Source:* Richtel, Matt and Michel Marriott. 2005. "Ring Tones, Cameras, Now This: Sex Is the Latest Cellphone Feature." *New York Times,* September 17, pp. A1. Copyright © 2005 by The New Tork Times Co. Reprinted with permission.

# Sex and Tourism

Joane Nagel

Growth in travel and tourism are hallmarks of the post–Cold War period, and ethnosexuality is a feature of the marketing of tourist destinations and products. . . . Depictions of distant lands as libidinous locales run through centuries of travel narratives, such as those of Columbus and Vespucci or Lewis and Clark. . . . The earliest travelogues written by Westerners visiting the Asia Pacific region contain vivid depictions of peoples and places as erotic and exotic, carnal and carnival—sexualized spectacles of Others and Otherness.[1] For instance, George Forster traveled with his father, Johann Reinhold Forster, on Captain James Cook's second voyage to the Pacific from 1772 to 1775. They described the Polynesian women they encountered in their 1777 and 1778 travel memoirs:

> a beautifully proportioned shape, an irresistible smile, and eyes full of sweetness and sparkling with fire . . . . [and] a charming frankness. . . . The view of several of these nymphs swimming nimbly all around the sloop, such as nature had formed them was perhaps more than sufficient entirely to subvert the little reason which a mariner might have left to govern his passions.[2]

. . . Margaret Jolly notes the historical continuity in images of Pacific Island women presented by the Forsters and those who followed in their wake. Enthusiastic chroniclers of the charms of "native beauties" included women travelers as well, such as journalist Beatrice Grimshaw, who visited Tahiti in the 1890s and early 1900s:

> One exceedingly pretty girl, with a perfect cataract of black hair overflowing her pale green gown, and a pair of sparkling dark eyes that never could be matched outside the magic lines of Cancer and Capricorn . . . has half a dozen French officers around her, enjoying breakfast and flirtation.[3]

The Pacific Islands thus were personified in the imaginations of women and men and in the descriptive discourses of Europeans and Americans as lovely, bare-breasted, beflowered, and deflowered young women.

. . . [T]hese early accounts of the ethnosexual delights of distant lands resonate with contemporary imaginings of exotic locales and raise an interesting set of issues and questions about the place of ethnicity and sexuality in tourism. What is the role of ethnosexuality in the development of tourist sites, in the marketing of tourist destinations, and in the experience and definition both of being a tourist and of living in and being part of a tourist destination? How do patterns of ethnosexual consumption in tourist markets and the international sex industry mirror and reproduce patterns of domination, inequality, colonization, and imperialism among nations and peoples in the global system? How does consuming the exotic Other through tourism facilitate racial, ethnic, and national self-imaginings and constructions?

## Sex and Economic Development

Researchers have noted a number of parallels between sex tourism and other forms of tourism, noting the importance of sex tourism in economic development and the role of commercially organized tours in delivering consumers to sex tourism destinations. Julie Scott identifies a gendered, sexualized side to tourism in general, not just sexual tourism. In her study of the roles of Turkish Cypriot and migrant women in the Cyprus tourist industry, she finds that "[w]hile the participation of Turkish Cypriot women in the tourism labor force has increased in recent years, migrant women are employed primarily in those occupations that are considered 'unsuitable' for local women."[4] She reports, for instance, that the employment of Rumanian women migrants as croupiers in Cyprus' gambling industry is seen as a way to protect local women from being polluted in what is defined as a sexualized work setting.

While it may pose a threat to the virtue of national women and thus require the importation of Other women to work in sexually hazardous occupations, in many developing countries tourism is a major employer and source of foreign revenues.[5] In Third World countries struggling with international debt, such as Tunisia, Puerto Rico, Haiti, Nepal, or the Gambia, tourism has become a larger industry than many traditional exports. While all tourist destinations also are sites of sex commerce, in major sex tourist destinations such as Thailand, the Philippines, Belize, Jamaica, or Sri Lanka, selling local and imported sexuality is an important component of economic development, and some governments even advertise sex tourism.[6] Cofounder of the Coalition Against Trafficking in Women Kathleen Barry links the economics of the sex trade to the economics of development, and Patrick Larvie agrees, arguing, for instance, that "Brazil's tourist industry promotes the country as one which offers sexual attractions as part of the nation's natural and cultural resources."[7]

It is not only government and private tourism promoters who publicize sex tourism, major publishers of tour books such as *Fodor's*, *Frommer's*, *Rough Guide*, and *Lonely Planet* have entered the market, and include sections on night life and gay tourism that refer to the sex trade and offer various bits of advice. For instance, the 1988 and 1991 editions of *Insight Guide* to Thailand explained "how to negotiate the transactions in a massage parlor and how to buy a bar dancer out for the night, advising against taking a prostitute to a first-class hotel."[8] Bishop and Robinson make a connection between sex tourism and tourism in general when they liken sex workers in sex tourist destinations to wildlife and other exotic attractions. They point out that sex tourism produces a "consumer approach to local natural and cultural resources including—semiotically and literally—the sexuality of local women."[9]

Ethnic similarity *and* diversity both are hallmarks of the sex industry and sex tourism. Ethnic similarities can work to facilitate the recruitment of sex workers through ethnic networks that aid in communication and trust and can provide cover for illegal activities by keeping them "in the [ethnic] family." Ethnic differences that separate sex workers and sex industry managers and owners can make exploitation more palatable since it is not one's own people who are being mistreated or coerced. Ethnic differences also characterize the sex worker/client relationship, since sex with an exotic Other is one of the chief attractions for sex tourists, just as dreams of being rescued from poverty is a central fantasy of sex workers. Siriporn Skrobanek and associates interviewed a number of sex workers in Thailand, many of whom walked parallel paths into the sex industry and shared similar dreams of the way out. For instance,

> *Noy is 33 and living in Pattaya with an Englishman. She left her village in Roi-et with her sister. . . . They began as go-go girls in a bar. They had no intention of becoming sex workers, but changed their minds because they wanted gold jewelry like other girls there. Noy's sister went to live in Switzerland with her boyfriend, and she sent money home. Noy will take her English boyfriend to visit her home in Roi-et, in the hope he will build her a new house there.[10]*

Male sex customers also have dreams and fantasies, often imagining that women sex workers find them especially attractive or exceptionally skilled sexual technicians:

> It's funny, but in England, the girls I fancy don't fancy me and the ones that do fancy me, I don't fancy. They tend to be sort of fatter and older, you know, thirty-five, but their faces, they look forty. But in Cuba, really beautiful girls fancy me. They're all over me. They treat me like a star. My girlfriend's jet black, she's beautiful. . . . Cuban girls don't expect so much. . . . English girls . . . don't want someone like me. . . . If you take a Cuban girl out for dinner, she's grateful.[11]

Kamala Kempadoo's study of the sex trade in Curacao, where the government suspended local laws against brothels and pimping, locates definitions of desire and desirability in longstanding racial hierarchies of superiority and subordination that are rearticulated in contemporary ethnosexual class formations:

> [W]omen who command the better working conditions and pay on the island work as escorts for "VIP's" and are more often than not white European women, mainly Dutch. . . . Migrant sex workers from Colombia and the Dominican Republic are predominantly "light-skinned," mulatto (mixed African-European) women, while "local" prostitutes who invariably work the streets and ill-paid sectors, are far more likely to be of Afro-Caribbean descent. . . . As one man simply put it, "if she's light-colored, then she is sexually attractive to the population."[12]

Kempadoo links the presence of Curacao's extensive sex industry to global processes—first to colonialism: "[i]n 1944 this island was established by the [Dutch] colonial government as a center in the region for prostitution by migrant women";[13] and more recently to World Bank and International Monetary Fund economic restructuring programs under which both migrating and local "women are increasingly more active in informal economies, which includes sex industries."[14] For some workers, sex work offers wages unmatched in other employment sectors;[15] even when their wages do not meet their expectations, the promise of high wages and the need of many workers

to support their entire families draw sex workers from around the world. For instance, Pasuk Phongpaichit argues that "the economic boom in Thailand in the 1980s and early 1990s led to a rapid increase in demand for skilled and unskilled labor" which was filled poorer neighboring countries, especially Burma, Southern China, Laos.[16] It is not only women, however, who are employed as exotic suppliers of ethnosex in the global sex trade, it is also men.

## Men at [Sex] Work

Male sex workers share some of the same motivations, desires, and desperation as women and children working in the sex trade, though they are much less often reported to be enslaved.[17] Like their female counterparts, most male sex workers are poor, and many are hoping for a better life through the money they make hustling or in a rescue relationship. There are also some important differences between men and women working in the sex industry. Unlike their female counterparts—"daughters of joy, sisters of misery"[18]—male sex workers sometimes report using prostitution to gain access to same-sex sexual contact in a local context of forbidden homosexual desire. Male sex workers not engaged in survival sexwork speak of combining "cruising" and recreational sex with prostitution much more frequently than do female sex workers. Dennis Altman interviewed a self-defined gay man in Lima who said he mixed business with pleasure: "When I'm there it's to meet people, and when I meet them I don't think about whether they will pay me or not. . . . If they give me a tip, it's very welcome."[19]

Like women sex workers who may define themselves as straight, bisexual, or lesbians, the reported sexual orientation of male sex workers is not always consistent with their clientele. The issue of *male* sex workers' *real* sexual orientation arises more often in research reports, however, although it is not entirely clear if it is a preoccupation only of the researchers or if the men themselves bring up the subject. In either case, many self-identified straight men have male clients, and gay and bisexual men have sex with women.[20] . . .

Jacob Shifter and Peter Aggleston report that in Costa Rica, although many male sex workers also tend to define themselves as heterosexuals *(cacheros)*, they have sex with men for money; the rule seems to be: "as long as sexual desire continues to be shown towards the opposite sex and behavior is masculine at all times, one is still a [heterosexual] man."[21] Sometimes the attribution of homosexuality is made on the basis of who is the active (penetrator, i.e., heterosexual) and who is the passive (penetrated, i.e., homosexual) partner in the sex act, rather than whether a man is selling sex to a woman or another man.[22]

The distinction between sexual behavior and sexual desire stands in contrast to the essentialist, all or nothing, either gay or straight conception of sexuality characteristic of Western sexual epistemologies. In fact, Shivananda Khan raises questions about the whole hetero/homosexual binary's applicability to non-Western cultures and the extent to which many researchers might simply be finding sexual binaries that exist in their own minds and cultures rather than in the minds of the men they are interviewing.[23] . . .

Some aspects of male sex work parallel findings in studies of women sex workers, not about the issue of sexual orientation, but about workers' interpretations of the meaning of the sex work. It is common to hear both male and female sex workers refer to a paid sexual interlude as a friendship, dating relationship, or something less commercial and more intimate. Fantasies of living a better life or of paid sex developing into a friendship or loving relationship characterize both male and female sex work. One French transvestite *gigolo*[24] reported a long-term intimate relationship with a client:

> He's married. He's a grandfather and lives in the countryside. He's very well known. He comes up once a month to Paris in order to see me. He pays the rent, he pays for the telephone, he gives me 4000 francs a month, jewellery, things like that. He's good luck for me, there's an emotional relationship between us of course. . . . I love him a lot and if we ever broke up, it would make me very upset. . . . He's the father I never had.[25]

Crossing ethnosexual boundaries is a common feature of male sex work as it is for women and children. The racial, ethnic, and national differences between male sex workers and their clients are most clearly revealed by the international character of the sex trade and sex tourism. For instance, Boushaba and associates report that 67 percent of the 172 male sex workers they interviewed in Morocco "sold sex primarily to a non-Moroccan clientele.[26] . . . [W]hile many male sex workers have male clients, not all men sell sex to men. Some sex consumers are women, and their transactions also are likely to involve rendezvous in ethnosexual frontiers.

## "Romance" Tourism

Women's sexual touristic encounters with local Other men most certainly are planted in much earlier sands than those on the beaches of the modern global system. Like all things associated with contemporary globalization, however, the scale and commercialization of women's sexual consumption has increased. Like sex, ethnosex sells, and early in the marketing of Hawaii as a tourist destination, for instance, Jane Desmond notes that "Hawaiian Tourist Bureau ads from the 1920s set up an explicit connection between white women and Native Hawaiian men."[27] She cites a scene at the Royal Hawaiian Hotel described in a 1937 travel book, *Isles of Enchantment:*

> Here an eastern lady of fashion lies prone beneath the sun while a smiling Hawaiian youth anoints her back and legs with coconut oil. . . . Near-by another bronze boy kneels over another fair visitor, kneading and manipulating the muscles in the soothing and relaxing Hawaiian massage.[28]

This quaint depiction of the attractive, attentive, courteous native man servicing the white woman seems much less an explicit hard sell than one would expect in the marketing of contemporary sex tourism, especially that targeting men. Researchers have found, nonetheless, that this image of a safe, but exotic vacation affair has remained a stable feature of women's sex tourism. Although the attitudes and behavior of today's women sex consumers often challenge traditional passive female sexual stereotypes, many contemporary women sex tourists are looking more to be swept away by men than to assert strong control over their paid male partners. These women "romance tourists" are interested in more than a quick sexual encounter; they often establish relationships with the men they "date" while on holiday. For instance, researchers find that it is not uncommon for women romance tourists to establish long-term liaisons with the men they meet on vacation and to correspond, send money, and return year after year to spend time with their offshore "boyfriends."[29]

De Moya and associates studied male sex workers in Puerto Plata, Dominican Republic, in the early 1990s, and found that, like male tourists, female tourists viewed local men through a racialized and sexualized lens, as exotic Others. Many Dominican male sex workers "claimed that for foreign women 'black skin color is the most relevant feature,'" and "long, kinky, and trenched hair, as well as youth, fitness, manliness, and sexiness" were the most sought-after traits of popular male sex workers.[30] Cabezas summarized this view: "The men capitalize on the demand for racialized fantasies of erotic encounters."[31]

Deborah Pruitt and Suzanne LaFont's study of Western women's romance tourism in Jamaica noted the same exoticization of male sex workers, where Jamaican men, especially "Rasta" men wearing dreadlocks, are constructed [by both white and black women tourists] as more passionate, more emotional, more natural, and sexually tempting" than the men back home.[32] Jamaican men had special appeal for white women since, "Stereotypes of black men and their sexuality" combined with Jamaican "men's displays of machismo drawn from their cultural gender scripts" to lead white women to see Jamaican men as "ar-

chetypical masculine" men.[33] Pruitt and LaFont also found that Western women, especially white women, occupied a complementary niche as exotic Others for some Jamaican men.

> *Light skin, straight hair and caucasian facial features are highly valued, and women who are considered overweight in their own cultures are appreciated by many Jamaican men. Thus, foreign women who may not satisfy standards of beauty at home find themselves the object of amorous attention by appealing to local men.*[34]

Although I refer to the local men with whom women tourists enter into sexual liaisons as "male sex workers," research suggests that this label would be challenged by many of these working men, just as women sex workers might argue that they were simply "dating" men who paid them for their sexual company. Kempadoo finds that

> *male sex workers in the Caribbean do not necessarily self-define in the same way as women who are in the same position. Instead of being identified . . . as prostitute . . . the men tend to be identified as "beach boy," "island boy," "player," "gigolo.". . . Sex with a female tourist who holds the economic dominant position in the relationship appears not to threaten or disrupt this culturally approved expression of masculinity but rather to enable feelings of personal worth and self-confidence.*[35]

Nandasena Ratnapala observed a similar definition of the situation in Sri Lanka among men who offer sex for money to women tourists: "[s]uch men are found in or near tourist hotels, often operating as tour guides or such innocent-looking jobs . . . in the hotels as bell-boys, waiters. . . . taxi drivers . . . they often conceal their real work beneath a more socially acceptable role."[36] And in Peru and the Philippines women find sex for sale not in the typical venues frequented by male sex customers (e.g., in brothels or massage parlors), but in more "legitimate" spaces such as ballroom dancing studios or discotheques.[37]

Kempadoo argues that not only do the social and sexual transactions between male prostitutes and women clients tend to uphold the gender order, but that sex commerce between First World consumers and Third World suppliers reproduces hegemonic racialized and sexualized views of those with dark skin as hypersexualized and subordinate. . . .

Instances of these racialized/sexualized North/South narratives can be heard in Vron Ware's recounting of a spate of reports in 1990 in a British tabloid newspaper and women's magazine about the "seduction" of European women by African men. The stories centered on white women traveling to tourist destinations in West Africa, falling in love with local men, and leaving their English husbands. Under the headlines, "Mud-Hut Rat Stole My Wife!" "Gambian Rat Stole My Wife, Too!" and "Love at First Sight," Britain's *Sun* newspaper ran a three-day series, beginning with the saga of thirty-nine-year-old Sandra Anderson who "set up home in a mud hut with a tribal prince after husband Frank took her on a Gambian holiday." The *Sun* articles were accompanied by photos, including one of "eight black men, with dreadlocks, guitars and cheerful smiles, supporting the weight of a horizontal young white woman, all bare legs and arms and smiling happily."[38] The stories detailed a competition that invited the reader to "Test your Marriage in Africa," and promised the winner seven nights in a top Gambian hotel.[39] . . .

[E]thnosexual frontiers are nuanced settings where interracial, interethnic, and international gender definitions and sexual contact rules complicate and confound long-standing and emergent cultural patterns and interpersonal relationships. Even when ethnosexual contacts in tourist settings are not specifically sexual business transactions, they trouble ethnic, gender, and sexual status quos and reveal the tensions between power based in gender systems and power based on wealth and class.

## Sex and Slavery in the New World Order

The new world order of the twenty-first century with its opening of international borders, increasing international business and leisure travel, and rapidly growing international communication, has expanded both the supply of and demand for sex and romance. Many commercial sex providers are migrant workers who enter the industry through a variety of routes, some legal and some illegal. Women often knowingly become sex workers, although they may not be aware of the conditions under which they will labor. Others are more naive or perhaps too willing to believe recruiters' promises that they will be simply hostesses, waitresses, or entertainers, and will not be asked to have sex with clients. Still others are promised jobs outside the sex industry, presumably in factories or as domestic workers, but then find sex work is the only way they can settle large debts to recruiters or pay off loans their families obtained when they essentially were sold into service. Finally, some sex workers are coerced by "traffickers" in human beings who locate and force into sexual servitude migrants or refugees trying to escape poverty or repression.[40] . . .

Sex traffickers often charge fees for transport and then deliver their human cargo to staff the massage parlors, clubs, and brothels of countries around the world. The trafficked workers then are required to do sex work to repay sex industry managers who have paid off their transport fees. Once they have become sex workers, these migrants are "soiled" symbolically or as a result of contracting diseases such as AIDS, and thus become unfit for other work even after their fees are paid. As Enloe summarizes:

> To succeed, sex tourism requires Third World women to be economically desperate enough to enter prostitution; having done so it is made difficult to leave. The other side of the equation requires men from affluent societies to imagine certain women, usually women of color, to be more available and submissive than the women of their own countries. Finally the industry depends on an alliance between local governments in search of foreign currency and local and foreign businessmen willing to invest in sexualized travel.[41]

Sex work, sex tourism, sex workers, and human trafficking are not only features of Third World and postcolonial landscapes. Gillian Caldwell and associates report that since the break up of the Soviet Union, "Russia and the

Newly Independent States, including Ukraine and Latvia, have become primary countries of origin [for sex workers] supplementing and sometimes replacing previously significant sources of women from Asia and Latin America."[42] Eastern European and Russian women's destinations are sex industries in Europe, the Middle East, Asia, and the United States. Their entry into the sex industry is the result of the same combination of forces pushing and pulling women of color into sex work—economics, exploitation, and exoticness, the latter because these white women are "a relative novelty in the sex market.[43] These new sex workers' economic motivations stem from the economic collapse in many former Soviet republics, the consequences of which have been especially harsh for women. Researchers report that in the mid-1990s nearly two-thirds of Russia's unemployed were women, including 70 percent of women graduating from institutions of higher learning.[44]. . .

The United States is also a destination for sex workers from the former Soviet Union and from countries around the world. In a 2001 report on "Trafficking in Persons," the U.S. State Department estimated that

> at least 700,000 persons, especially women and children, are trafficked each year across international borders . . . and within countries. . . . The U.S. is principally a transit and destination country for trafficking in persons. It is estimated that 45,000 to 50,000 people, primarily women and children, are trafficked to the U.S. annually. . . . Our understanding is that the problem has broadened [since monitoring began in 1994].[45]. . .

A 1995 case illustrates the ethnic and international character of sex trafficking.

> In conjunction with Thai traffickers, Ludwig Janak, a German national who operated a tour guide service in Thailand, recruited Thai women to come to the United States to work. Several of the women were told they would have good jobs working in restaurants. Once in the US, Thai traffickers and a Korean madam forced the women into prostitu-

tion. . . . A total of 18 defendants were indicted on charges of kidnapping, alien smuggling, extortion, and white slavery.[46]

Many of the cases recounted in the CIA report ["International Trafficking in Women to the United States: A Contemporary Manifestation of Slavery and Oganized Crime"] involved promises of work outside the sex industry.

> From about February 1996 to March 1998, some 25–40 Mexican women and girls, some as young as 14 years old, were trafficked from the Veracruz state in Mexico to Florida and the Carolinas in the United States. The victims had been promised jobs in waitressing, housekeeping, landscaping, childcare and elder care. Upon their arrival, the women and girls were told they must work as prostitutes in brothels serving migrant workers or risk harm to themselves and/or their families. Besides enduring threats, women who attempted to escape were subjugated to beatings. . . . One woman was locked in a closet for 15 days as punishment for trying to escape.[47]

### Child Sex Labor

The involvement of children in the commercial sex trade raises questions not obvious when considering adults. While both adult men and women might be enslaved or coerced into sex work, they are capable of informed consent. Children, by definition and international convention those under eighteen, are not considered legally or morally capable of making the decision to sell their bodies. For instance, Heather Montgomery notes the difficulty of determining even what to call children involved in the sex trade: child prostitutes, child sex workers, children exploited by the sex industry. This is because of the volitional assumptions imbedded in the terms *sex worker* or *prostitute*. She cites Ireland's definition of child prostitution as a situation

> where the person selling or hiring their sexuality is under eighteen years of age. . . . All children under the age of eighteen who are in prostitution are considered, de facto, to be sexually exploited.[48]

The United Nations Convention on the Rights of the Child also specifies the age of eighteen as the end of childhood, places the responsibility and guilt for child prostitution or pornography squarely on the shoulders of adults involved in any sexual transaction involving children, and defines child prostitution as:

> [T]he act of obtaining, procuring, or offering the services of a child or inducing a child to perform sexual acts for any form of compensation or reward (or any acts that are linked with that offence) (even with the consent of the child).[49]

Montgomery distinguishes between children in the sex industry who are deceived or coerced into situations of forced prostitution from those who "choose" prostitution to escape abusive family situations or to support them selves and their families in situations of economic desperation. Montgomery does not resolve the question of whether it makes sense to talk about "free choice" for those facing extreme poverty. Her question about whether all children must be "saved" and stopped from sex work, however, resonates with the discourse of the prostitutes' rights movement and organizations such as COYOTE (Call Off Your Old Tired Ethics) or those who attended the World Whores' Summit in San Francisco in 1989. Prostitutes' rights discourse emphasizes the hypocrisy present in the simultaneous demand for sex by consumers on the one hand, and the stigmatizing of sex work on the one hand, as well as demands for sex workers' rights to use their bodies as they wish.[50] Scholars are by no means in agreement that children should be included in this logic— that children should have the right to sell their sexuality—because of children's relative vulnerability compared to adults, and because of children's developmental differences from adults. In fact, children are generally seen as a separate and special class needing protection, perhaps at the expense of their rights to be sex workers.

Whatever their sexual rights are or should be, children are reported to be a growing segment of the sex trade because of consumers' fears of AIDS and their often mistaken beliefs that children are less likely to be infected. Williams provides an overview of the illegal global traffic in children for commercial sex, estimating that "the number of child prostitutes world-wide could easily exceed five million."[52] He finds that the same ethnosexual boundaries operate for children as for women in the sex trade generally, and in sex tourism in particular:

> Children are increasingly sold and trafficked across frontiers—between developing and developed countries, among developing countries, and among developed countries. The spread of child prostitution worldwide is part and parcel of the less positive aspects of globalization. The main child trafficking pipelines include those from Nepal to India and from Burma to Thailand. In addition, girls and young women from India and Pakistan are frequently sold to wealthy Middle Eastern men. Abduction, false documentation and sham marriages are all used to facilitate this movement.[53]

Lin Lim also links the sexual exploitation of children to the sex tourism industry, as does the tourism industry itself.[54] For instance, in 1996 the World Tourism Organization passed a resolution condemning organized sex tourism that "denounces and condemns in particular child sex tourism, considering it a violation of Article 34 of the [UN] Convention on the Rights of the Child and requiring strict legal action by tourist sending and receiving countries."[55] The 1999 CIA report on slavery and illegal international trafficking of women and children into the United States describes similar ethnosexual border crossing in the obtaining and moving of children forced into sex work:

> Girls from Asian and African countries, some as young as 9, were essentially sold to traffickers by their parents, "for less than the price of a toaster," one government official said. This mainly happens in cultures where female children are not valued. The girls are smuggled into the United States where, in a typical case, they are forced to work "in an indentured sexual-servitude arrangement."[56]

## Conclusion

Gender, class, and politics organize sexual exchanges in macro, international, commercial arenas as well as in micro, national, personal settings. The sex industry today is a lucrative local, national, and international business attracting labor and capital, consumers and workers, entrepreneurs and gangsters. As Watanabe notes, the new warlords of ethnosexuality are less likely to be soldiers than businessmen, less likely to be ethnosexual invaders than ethnosexual traffickers. . . . The sex industry, like other major commercial enterprises, has gone global, with businesses and managers moving from country to country in search of the highest profits, and with workers migrating from villages to cities, from poorer to richer countries in search of the highest wages.

The phenomena of forced sexual slavery and the trafficking of children for sexual exploitation whether in times of war or peace, stand in contrast to the almost festive label, *sex tourism,* or the more neutral term, *sex work.* A reading of summaries of the some of the origins, destinations, and methods of child entry into the sex industry illustrates the ethnosexual character of the trade: girls from Latin America, Asia, Eastern Europe, and Africa are moved to the United States, children are moved from Nepal to India, from Burma to Thailand, from India and Pakistan to the Middle East. These national borders crossed in the trafficking of children parallel the racial and ethnic boundaries that frequently divide those who work in the sex trade from their clients. For both children and adults, race, ethnicity, and nationality are the marks of exploitable and expendable ethnosexual Others.[57]

## NOTES

1.  See Chris Rojek and John Urry, *Touring Cultures: Transformations of Travel and Theory* (New York: Routledge, 1997).

2.  Quoted in Jolly, "From Point Venus to Bali Ha'i," 100–101; see also Johann Reinhold Forster, *Observations Made During a Voyage Round the World on Physical Geography, Natural History and Ethic Philosophy* (London: G. Robinson, 1778); George Forster, *George Forster's Werke—Band 1 [A Voyage Round the World in his Britannic Majesty's Sloop, Resolution],* ed. Robert L. Kahn (London: B. White, [1777], 1968).

3.  Jolly, "From Point Venus to Bali Ha'i," 106; for a discussion of sexuality in travel literature, see Ian Littlewood, *Sultry Climates: Travel and Sex since the Grand Tour* (London: John Murray, 2001).

4.  Julie Scott, "Sexual and National Boundaries in Tourism," *Annals of Tourism Research* 22 (1995): 385–403, 385.

5.  See John Urry, *Consuming Places* (New York: Routledge, 1995); Martin Mowforth and Ian Munt, *Tourism and Sustainability: New Tourism in the Third World* (New York: Routledge, 1998).

6.  Martin Opperman, *Sex Tourism and Prostitution: Aspects of Leisure, Recreation, and Work* (New York: Cognizant Communications, 1998).

7.  Patrick Larvie, "Natural Born Targets: Male Hustlers and AIDS Prevention in Urban Brazil," in *Men Who Sell Sex: International Perspective on Male Prostitution and HIV/AIDS,* ed. Peter Aggleton (Philadelphia: Temple University Press, 1999), 163; Enloe, *Bananas, Beaches and Bases,* 32; Kempadoo, *Sun, Sex, and Gold.*

8.  Bishop and Robinson, *Night Market,* 82–91; Bishop and Robinson report that by the 1993 edition of *Insight Guide,* the AIDS epidemic had led editors to moderate the enthusiastic tone of their advice about sex tourism, and to include admonitions such as, "do not be foolish; there is a drugstore just down the street" (84); see also Thiesmeyer, "The West's 'Comfort Women' and the Discourses of Seduction," 73–74.

9.  Bishop and Robinson, *Night Market,* 109.

10.  Skrobanek et al., *The Traffic in Women,* 40.

11.  Davidson, *Prostitution, Power, and Freedom,* 169; for a brief discussion of the resurgence of the sex trade in recent years in postrevolutionary Cuba, see Smith and Padula, *Sex and Revolution,* 178–80; researchers find that a central fantasy for many sex tourists and for some sex workers is that they are "friends" and "dating" rather than engaged in a commercial transaction; sex workers try to establish quick friendships with a returning client in the hopes of developing into a more steady relationship and perhaps something more permanent; for sex customers, there is the illusion of being chosen or special to the sex worker, or of satisfying her sexually; for instance, Davidson quotes a student who was backpacking in Thailand and his explanation of

the money he gave to a Thai woman with whom he had sex:

> Basically the thing was, she basically said to me, "I'm going to have to go and sleep with somebody because I need the money." So we were left in this awful situation where . . . she was going to have to sleep with somebody unless I paid her not to. . . . So we talked about it and we agreed, I would give her money. . . . But I'm fairly certain that's not the reason she went off with me. I just don't believe it was. I'm a reasonable judge of character and I wouldn't have gone off with just an out and out girl that was going to be with me just for money. (Davidson, *Prostitution, Power and Freedom*, 177).

12. Kamala Kempadoo, "The Migrant Tightrope: Experiences from the Caribbean," *in Global Sex Workers: Rights, Resistance, and Redefinition*, ed. Kamala Kempadoo and Jo Doezema (New York: Routledge, 1998), 131; see also Safa, *The Myth of the Male Breadwinner*.

13. Kempala, "The Migrant Tightrope," 124.

14. Ibid., 129.

15. For instance, Bishop and Robinson interviewed sex industry workers in Bangkok; a dancer there reported making four times her monthly salary as a maid, and prostitutes could earn ten times that amount and more; Bishop and Robinson, *Night Market*, 157, 165.

16. Pasuk Phongpaichit, "Trafficking in People in Thailand," in *Illegal Immigration and Commercial Sex*, 89; such international migration into Thailand complicated the ethnosexual landscape of the local sex industry; not only were sex consumers and sex workers from a variety of countries, sex workers from the same country were often an ethnically diverse group; for instance, Phongpaichit reports that many refugees from Burma who become sex workers in Thai border towns or in big Thai cities such as Bangkok were Burmese ethnic minorities fleeing discrimination and slavery in Burma: "Mon, Karen, and Shan people [who] prefer to come to Thailand to escape forced labor and other repressive policies imposed on them by the [majority] Burmese government" (ibid., 90); see also Pasuk Phongpaichit, *From Peasant Girls to Bangkok Masseuses* (Geneva: International Labour Organization, 1982); Pasuk Phongpaichit and Chris Baker, *Thailand: Economy and Politics* (Kuala Lampur: Oxford University Press, 1995); see also Yayori Matsui, *Women in the New Asia: From Pain to Power* (New York: Zed Books, 1999).

17. An exception is Ratnapala's discussion of male children who are procured

> by local pimps catering for European Paedophiles. Houses are rented out and children are brought there by cheating them, or by using force. In 1995–96, an estimated 1500 children were involved in this kind of work. Of them, nearly two-thirds were boys. . . . Local pimps provide boys according to the particular client's taste. Sometimes, drugs are given to these children in order to arouse them. (Nandasena Ratnapala, "Male Sex Work in Sri Lanka," in *Men Who Sell Sex*, 216–17).

18. Butler, *Daughters of Joy, Sisters of Misery*.

19. Dennis Altman, "Foreword," in *Men Who Sell Sex*, xv; Wim Zuilhof, "Sex for Money between Men and Boys in the Netherlands: Implications for HIV Prevention," in *Men Who Sell Sex*, 23–39.

20. Amine Boushaba, Oussama Tawil, Latefa Imane, and Hakima Himmich, "Marginalization and Vulnerability: Male Sex Work in Morocco," in *Men Who Sell Sex*, 269–70; in 1991 G. Kruks found that 72 percent of males engaging in "survival sex" (for money, food, shelter, protection) in Los Angeles identified themselves as gay or bisexual; G. Kruks, "Gay and Lesbian Homeless/Street Youth: Special Issues and Concerns," *Journal of Adolescent Health* 12 (1991): 515–18; Edward Morse and associates reported that 60 percent of their U.S. sample of male sex workers identified themselves as gay or bisexual; Edward V. Morse, Patricia M. Simon, and Kendra E. Burchfiel, "Social Environment and Male Sex Work in the United States," in *Men Who Sell Sex*, 88.

21. Jacobo Schifter and Peter Aggleston, "*Cacherismo* in a San Jose Brothel: Aspects of Male Sex Work in Costa Rica," in *Men Who Sell Sex*, 143; see also Jacobo Schifter, *Lila's House: Male Prostitution in Latin America* (New York: Harrington Park Press, 1998).

22. Roger Lancaster observes this distinction in Nicaragua as well where *cochon* refers to the male recipient of anal intercourse:

> [T]he dominant Anglo-American rule would read as follows. A man gains sexual status and honor among other men through and only through his sexual transactions with women. Homosexuals appear as the active refuseniks of that system. In Nicaragua, the rule is built around different principles. A man gains sexual status and honor among other men through his active role in sexual intercourse

(either with women or with other men). Cochones are passive participants in that system. (Roger N. Lancaster, *Life Is Hard: Machismo, Danger, and the Intimacy of Power in Nicaragua* [Berkeley: University of California Press, 1992], 250)

23. Shivananda Khan, "Through a Window Darkly: Men Who Sell Sex to Men in India and Bangladesh," in *Men Who Sell Sex*, 195; even this distinction can be unstable; Ana Louisa Liguori and Peter Aggleton found that although male sex workers in Mexico City made the distinction between heterosexuals and homosexuals, somewhere between 20 and 30 percent of men working any given shift in a brothel might allow themselves to be penetrated; interestingly, penetration was reported by respondents about *other* sex workers, not about the respondents themselves; Ana Luisa Liguori and Peter Aggleton, "Aspects of Male Sex Work in Mexico City," in *Men Who Sell Sex*, 116; see also Gutmann, *The Meanings of Macho;* Carolyn Sleightholme and Indrani Sinha, *Guilty without Trial: Women in the Sex Trade in Calcutta* (New Brunswick, NJ: Rutgers University Press, 1997), 151–53; Dede Octomo, "Masculinity in Indonesia: Genders, Sexualities, and Identities in a Changing Society," in *Framing the Sexual Subject: The Politics of Gender, Sexuality, and Power,* Richard Parker, Regina Maria Barbosa, and Peter Aggleton (Berkeley: University of California Press, 2000), 46–59.

24. A category unlike Moroccan *gigolos* who do not cross-dress, but similar in that both French and Moroccan *gigolos* considered themselves primarily heterosexuals, see Lindinalva Laurindo da Silva, *"Travestis* and *Gigolos:* Male Sex Work and HIV Prevention in France," in *Men Who Sell Sex*, 51.

25. Ibid.; this respondent's closing line suggests that although they were having sex, he chose to emphasize the paternal rather than the sexual aspects and attributes of the relationship, perhaps to include the heterosexual component of his identity

26. Boushaba et al., "Marginalization and Vulnerability," 266.

27. Desmond, *Staging Tourism,* 125.

28. Ibid., 126; see also Clifford Gessler, *Isles of Enchantment* (New York: Appleton-Century, 1937).

29. See Deborah Pruit and Suzanne LaFont, "For Love and Money: Romance Tourism in Jamaica," *Annals of Tourism Research* 22 (1995): 421–40, 437; Beverly Mullings, "Fantasy Tours: Exploring the Global Consumption of Caribbean Sex Tours,"

in *New Forms of Consumption: Consumers, Culture, and Commodification* (Lanham, MD: Rowman and Littlefield, 2000), 227–50; Davidson, *Prostitution, Power, and Freedom;* Kempadoo, *Sun, Sex, and Gold;* Rory O'Merry reports that men get involved in long-term fantasy relationships with women sex workers as well:

> Some men send money to the girl of their dreams in Thailand. These were the women they had the time of their life with, and were easy to love. They don't feel as if they're sending money to a prostitute, but to a friend who was poor and who lives in a developing country, to help her and her family financially. . . . When he is in town he can have all the sex he can handle—No "I have a headache." The exchange rate makes him a millionaire. Paradise. (Rory O'Merry, *My Wife in Bangkok* [Berkeley: Asia Press, 1990], 139)

30. De Moya et al.'s research is cited and quoted in Cabezas, "Women's Work Is Never Done," 101; see also E. Antonio de Moya, Rafael Garcia, Rosario Fadul, and Edward Herold, *Sosua Sanky-Pankies and Female Sex Workers* (Santo Domingo: Instituto de Sexualidad Humana, Universidad Autonoma de Santo Domingo, 1992).

31. Cabezas, "Women's Work Is Never Done," 101.

32. Pruit and LaFont, "For Love and Money," 437.

33. Ibid.

34. Ibid., 426.

35. Kempadoo, *Sun, Sex, and Gold,* 24.

36. Ratnapala, "Male Sex Work in Sri Lanka," 217.

37. Carlos F. Caceres and Oscar G. Jimenez, *"Fletes* in Parque Kennedy: Sexual Cultures among Young Men Who Sell Sex to Other Men in Lima," in *Men Who Sell Sex*, 190; Tan, "Walking the Tightrope," 244.

38. Vron Ware, "Purity and Danger: Race, Gender and Tales of Sex Tourism," in *Back to Reality: Social Experience and Cultural Studies,* ed. A. McRobbie (Manchester: Manchester University Press, 1997), 139; the Sun article's author reported that she was "one woman who did not fall under the black magic spell . . . the photographer and I had a job to do."

39. Ibid., 140.

40. See Sietske Altink, *Stolen Lives: Trading Women into Sex and Slavery* (London: Scarlet Press, 1995).

41. Enloe, *Bananas, Beaches and Bases,* 36–37.

42. Gilliam Caldwell, Steve Galster, Jyothi Kanicks, Nadia Steinzor, "Capitalizing on Transition Economies: The Role of the Russian Mafiya in Trafficking

Women for Forced Prostitution," 42–73 in *Illegal Immigration and Commercial Sex*, 44–47.

43. Ibid., 44.

44. Ibid., 48; see also *Human Rights Country Reports, Russia* (Washington, DC: U.S. Department of State, 1997); Human Rights Watch, "Neither Jobs nor Justice: Discrimination against Women in Russia" (March 1995): 6.

45. U.S. Department of State, *Trafficking in Persons Report* (Washington, DC: Government Printing Office, 2001), 1; Caldwell and associates provide a similar definition of trafficking as "the recruitment or transportation of persons within or across borders [involving] deception, coercion or force, abuse of authority, debt bondage, or fraud for the purpose of placing persons in situations of abuse or exploitation such as forced prostitution, sweatshop labor, or exploitative domestic servitude"; Caldwell et al., "Capitalizing on Transition Economies," 42.

46. Amy O'Neill Richard, "International Trafficking in Women to the United States: A Contemporary Manifestation of Slavery and Organized Crime," Central Intelligence Agency, Center for the Study of Intelligence (Washington, DC: Government Printing Office, 1999), 49.

47. [O'Neill Richard, "International Trafficking in Women to the United States,"] 47; the CIA report prompted the introduction of federal legislation and the U.S. House of Representatives also approved extension of federal witness protection programs to the victims of human smuggling and sex slavery; see *The Humanitarian Times* (May 11, 2000):1; my thanks to Norman R. Yetman, University of Kansas for bringing this report to my attention.

48. Heather Montgomery, "Children, Prostitution, and Identity: A Case Study from a Tourist Resort in Thailand," in *Global Sex Workers, 146;* see also, Kevin Ireland, Wish You *Weren't Here* (London: Save the Children, 1993), 3.

49. Lin Lean Lim, "Child Prostitution," in *The Sex Sector: The Economic and Social Bases of Prostitution in Southeast Asia,* ed. Lin Lean Lim (Geneva: International Labor Office, 1998), 171.

50. See Shannon Bell, *Reading, Writing, and Rewriting the Prostitute Body* (Bloomington: Indiana University Press, 1995); Cleo Odzer, *Patpong Sisters* (New York: Blue Moon-Arcade, 1994).

51. See Kane, *Sold for Sex.*

52. Williams, "Trafficking in Women and Children," 160.

53. Ibid., 162–63.

54. Lim, "Child Prostitution."

55. Ibid., 199.

56. *New York Times,* "Once-hidden Slave Trade: A Growing U.S. Problem."

57. It is important to note that most prostitution and sex work by both adults and children do not involve international trafficking, but rather workers and their clients are local; it is the case, however, that much sex work is characterized by racial, ethnic, or class differences between clients and workers; see Kevin Bales, *Disposable People: New Slavery in the Global Economy* (Berkeley: University of California Press, 1999); Kamala Kempadoo and Jo Doezema, eds., *Global Sex Workers: Rights, Resistance, and Redefinition* (New York: Routledge, 1998).

## *Sexuality and Militarism*

**Cynthia Enloe**

. . . Through wartime mobilization, postwar demobilization, and peacetime preparedness maneuvers, sexuality and militarism have been intertwined. They have been constructed and reconstructed together, usually with the help of deliberate policy decisions. *Together,* ideologies of militarism and sexuality have shaped the social order of military base towns and the lives of women in those towns. . . .

Conditions that promote organized prostitution:

1. When large numbers of local women are treated by the government and private entrepreneurs as second-class citizens, a source of cheapened labor, even while other women are joining the newly expanded middle class. . . .

2. When the foreign government basing its troops on local soil sees prostitution as a "necessary evil" to keep up their male soldiers' fighting morale

3. When tourism is imagined by local and foreign economic planners to be a fast road to development

4. When the local government hosting those foreign troops is under the influence of its own military men, local military men who define human rights violations as necessary for "national security.". . .

The [Status of Forces Agreement] (SOFA) is a major vehicle for cementing and sustaining a military alliance between the U.S. government and its international partners. A SOFA spells out in minute detail the conditions under which American troops can be stationed on the host government's territory. Health, surveillance, policing, finances—all are subjects of the intense government-to-government negotiations that result in these formal diplomatic agreements. The fine print of these alliance agreements is not open to public scrutiny. In behind-closed-door negotiations over a SOFA, governments' officials hammer out the sexual politics of militarization.

The actual implementation of any SOFA is left to American base commanders. Anyone wanting a realistic sense of how a government-to-government alliance works needs to keep an inquisitive eye on base commanders. A base commander for a U.S. force overseas is not merely an instrument of the policy makers in the White House or the State Department. He (rarely have U.S. women officers been promoted to base commander) is not even simply a cipher for Defense Department senior officials' designs. A base commander has his own concerns and his own career aspirations. Typically, he is a colonel. That is, he (and now occasionally, on some small bases, she) is at a very delicate point in his military career. In all militaries there are fewer slots for generals (or admirals) than there are for colonels. Not all colonels will be promoted. A colonel is a person who hopes to be a general. So much depends on how his superiors assess his performance as a base commander. A base commander has his own sources of information, his own social circles.

The base commander and his deputy commander (in the 1990s more American women officers are gaining assignments as deputy base commanders) are likely to have a stake in creating smooth working relationships with local host-country officials and with local business owners. It is standard procedure for American base commanders in South Korea, for example, to develop mutual relationships with the local Korean Chamber of Commerce, many of whose members are the proprietors of the bars and discos that are at the heart of the prostitution industry. Some American military officers, women and men, have reported feeling quite uneasy with this part of their jobs as deputy base commanders. On the other hand, their performance—and thus their own chances for future promotion—will depend on how trouble-free they can keep these base–local business relations. . . .

## Prostitution and Peacekeeping. . . .

Many future military peacekeeping operations will look like the peacekeeping missions launched in Cambodia in 1992–1994, in Bosnia in 1996–1998, and in Kosovo in 1999: "victory" will be elusive; a variety of governments will contribute soldiers of their own, many of them trained to be combat troops; the UN Secretariat's own Peace Keeping Organization (UNPKO) will be able to run military training programs, but only for officers and only for those officers whose governments have the funds and the will to pay for their officers' UNPKO training; coordination between governments and the UN will be delicate; NATO will be directly involved; civilian businesses will win contracts to provide support services for the troops; humanitarian aid agencies will be trying to operate without being too reliant on militaries and too deeply sucked into militarized cultures; rival domestic politicians will be competing in the rearranged public arena; local residents will be trying to recover from war-produced trauma while at the same time creating political organizations to compete in the postwar public space; pro-democracy activists will be seeking lasting reforms. Each of these processes will be gendered, will be shaped by how femininity and masculinity are imagined and deployed.

There is nothing inherent in international peacekeeping operations as currently structured that makes their soldiers immune to the sort of sexism that has fueled military prostitution in wartime and peacetime. As in every other military operation conducted by every other government, the extent of future military peacekeeping operations' reliance on the prostitution of some women will be determined by decisions made at the top and in the middle of military organizations. . . .

*Source:* Enloe, Cynthia. 2000. "The Prostitute, the Colonel, and the Nationalist." In *Maneuvers: The International Politics of Militarizing Women's Lives* (pp. 49–107). Reprinted by permission of the University of California Press.

# Human Rights, Sex Trafficking, and Prostitution

Alice Leuchtag

**D**espite laws against slavery in practically every country, an estimated twenty-seven million people live as slaves. . . .

## A Life Narrative

Of all forms of slavery, sex slavery is one of the most exploitative and lucrative with some 200,000 sex slaves worldwide bringing their slaveholders an annual profit of $10.5 billion. Although the great preponderance of sex slaves are women and girls, a smaller but significant number of males—both adult and children—are enslaved for homosexual prostitution. The life narrative of a Thai girl named Siri . . . illustrates how sex slavery happens to vulnerable girls and women. Siri is born in northeastern Thailand to a poor family that farms a small plot of land, barely eking out a living. Economic policies of structural adjustment pursued by the Thai government under the aegis of the World Bank and the International Monetary Fund have taken former government subsidies away from rice farmers, leaving them to compete against imported, subsidized rice that keeps the market price artificially depressed.

Siri attends four years of school, then is kept at home to help care for her three younger siblings. When Siri is fourteen, a well-dressed woman visits her village. She offers to find Siri a "good job,"

From Leuchtag, Alice. 2003. "Human Rights, Sex Trafficking, and Prostitution." *Humanist* 63(1): 10–15. Reprinted by courtesy of Alice Leuchtag and *The Humanist*.

advancing her parents $2,000 against future earnings. This represents at least a year's income for the family. In a town in another province the woman, a trafficker, "sells" Siri to a brothel for $4,000. Owned by an "investment club" whose members are business and professional men—government bureaucrats and local politicians—the brothel is extremely profitable. In a typical thirty-day period it nets its investors $88,000.

To maintain the appearance that their hands are clean, members of the club's board of directors leave the management of the brothel to a pimp and a bookkeeper. Siri is initiated into prostitution by the pimp who rapes her. After being abused by her first "customer," Siri escapes, but a policeman—who gets a percentage of the brothel profits—brings her back, whereupon the pimp beats her up. As further punishment, her "debt" is doubled from $4,000 to $8,000. She must now repay this, along with her monthly rent and food, all from her earnings of $4 per customer. She will have to have sex with three hundred men a month just to pay her rent. Realizing she will never be able to get out of debt, Siri tries to build a relationship with the pimp simply in order to survive.

The pimp uses culture and religion to reinforce his control over Siri. He tells her she must have committed terrible sins in a past life to have been born a female; she must have accumulated a karmic debt to deserve the enslavement and abuse to which she must reconcile herself. Gradually Siri begins to see herself from the point of view of the slaveholder—as someone unworthy and deserving of punishment. By age fifteen she no longer protests or runs away. Her physical enslavement has become psychological as well, a common occurrence in chronic abuse.

Siri is administered regular injections of the contraceptive drug Depo-Provera for which she is charged. As the same needle is used for all the girls, there is a high risk of HIV and other sexual diseases from the injections. Siri knows that a serious illness threatens her and she prays to Buddha at the little shrine in her room, hoping to earn merit so he will protect her from dreaded disease. Once a month she and the others, at their own expense, are tested for HIV. So far Siri's tests have been negative. When Siri tries to get the male customers to wear condoms—distributed free to brothels by the Thai Ministry of Health—some resist wearing them and she can't make them do so.

As one of an estimated 35,000 women working as brothel slaves in Thailand—a country where 500,000 to one million prostituted women and girls work in conditions of degradation and exploitation short of brothel slavery—Siri faces at least a 40 percent chance of contracting the HIV virus. If she is lucky, she can look forward to five more years before she becomes too ill to work and is pushed out into the street.

### Thailand's Sex Tourism

Though the Thai government denies it, the World Health Organization finds that HIV is epidemic in Thailand, with the largest segment of new cases among wives and girlfriends of men who buy prostitute sex. Viewing its women as a cash crop to be exploited, and depending on sex tourism for foreign exchange dollars to help pay interest on the foreign debt, the Thai government can't acknowledge the epidemic without contradicting the continued promotion of sex tourism and prostitution.

By encouraging investment in the sex industry, sex tourism creates a business climate conducive to the trafficking and enslavement of vulnerable girls such as Siri. In 1996 nearly five million sex tourists from the United States, Western Europe,

Australia, and Japan visited Thailand. These transactions brought in about $26.2 billion—thirteen times more than Thailand earned by building and exporting computers.

In her 1999 report *Pimps and predators on the internet: Globalizing the sexual exploitation of women and children,* published by the Coalition Against Trafficking in Women (CATW), Donna Hughes quotes from postings on an Internet site where sex tourists share experiences and advise one another. The following is one man's description of having sex with a fourteen-year-old prostituted girl in Bangkok:

> *Even though I've had a lot of better massages . . . after fifteen minutes, I was much more relaxed. . . . Then I asked for a condom and I fucked her for another thirty minutes. Her face looked like she was feeling a lot of pain. . . . She blocked my way when I wanted to leave the room and she asked for a tip. I gave her 600 bath. Altogether, not a good experience.*

Hughes says, "To the men who buy sex, a 'bad experience' evidently means not getting their money's worth, or that the prostituted woman or girl didn't keep up the act of enjoying what she had to do . . . one glimpses the humiliation and physical pain most girls and women in prostitution endure."

Nor are the men oblivious to the existence of sexual slavery. One customer states, "Girls in Bangkok virtually get sold by their families into the industry; they work against their will." His knowledge of their sexual slavery and lack of sensitivity thereof is evident in that he then names the hotels in which girls are kept and describes how much they cost!

As Hughes observes, sex tourists apparently feel they have a right to prostitute sex, perceiving prostitution only from a self-interested perspective in which they commodify and objectify women of other cultures, nationalities, and ethnic groups. Their awareness of racism, colonialism, global economic inequalities, and sexism seems limited to the way these realities benefit them as sex consumers.

## Sex Traffickers Cast Their Nets

According to the *Guide to the new UN trafficking protocol* by Janice Raymond, published by the CATW in 2001, the United Nations estimates that sex trafficking in human beings is a $5 billion to $7 billion operation annually. Four million persons are moved illegally from one country to another and within countries each year, a large proportion of them women and girls being trafficked into prostitution. The United Nations International Children's Emergency Fund (UNICEF) estimates that some 30 percent of women being trafficked are minors, many under age thirteen. The International Organization on Migration estimates that some 500,000 women per year are trafficked into Western Europe from poorer regions of the world. According to *Sex trafficking of women in the United States: International and domestic trends,* also published by the CATW in 2001, some 50,000 women and children are trafficked into the United States each year, mainly from Asia and Latin America.

Because prostitution as a system of organized sexual exploitation depends on a continuous supply of new "recruits," trafficking is essential to its continued existence. When the pool of available women and girls dries up, new women must be procured. Traffickers cast their nets ever wider and become ever more sophisticated. The Italian Camorra, Chinese Triads, Russian Mafia, and Japanese Yakuza are powerful criminal syndicates consisting of traffickers, pimps, brothel keepers, forced labor lords, and gangs which operate globally.

After the breakdown of the Soviet Union, an estimated five thousand criminal groups formed the Russian Mafia, which operates in thirty countries. The Russian Mafia traffics women from African countries, the Ukraine, the Russian Federation, and Eastern Europe into Western Europe, the United States, and Israel. The Triads traffic women from China, Korea, Thailand, and other Southeast Asian countries into the United States and Europe. The Camorra traffics women from Latin America into Europe. The Yakuza traffics women from the Philippines, Thailand, Burma, Cambodia, Korea, Nepal, and Laos into Japan.

## A Global Problem Meets a Global Response

Despite these appalling facts, until recently no generally agreed upon definition of trafficking in human beings was written into international law. In Vienna, Austria, during 1999 and 2000, 120 countries participated in debates over a definition of trafficking. A few nongovernmental organizations (NGOs) and a minority of governments—including Australia, Canada, Denmark, Germany, Ireland, Japan, the Netherlands, Spain, Switzerland, Thailand, and the United Kingdom—wanted to separate issues of trafficking from issues of prostitution. They argued that persons being trafficked should be divided into those who are forced and those who give their consent, with the burden of proof being placed on persons being trafficked. They also urged that the less explicit means of control over trafficked persons—such as abuse of a victim's vulnerability—not be included in the definition of trafficking and that the word exploitation not be used. Generally supporters of this position were wealthier countries where large numbers of women were being trafficked and countries in which prostitution was legalized or sex tourism encouraged.

The CATW—140 other NGOs that make up the International Human Rights Network plus many governments (including those of Algeria, Bangladesh, Belgium, China, Columbia, Cuba, Egypt, Finland, France, India, Mexico, Norway, Pakistan, the Philippines, Sweden, Syria, Venezuela, and Vietnam)—maintains that trafficking can't be separated from prostitution. Persons being trafficked shouldn't be divided into those who are forced and those who give their consent because trafficked persons are in no position to give meaningful consent. The subtler methods used by traffickers, such as abuse of a victim's vulnerability, should be included in the definition of trafficking and the word exploitation be an essential part of the definition. Generally supporters of this majority view were poorer countries from which large numbers of women were being trafficked or countries in which strong feminist, anti-colonialist, or socialist influences existed. The United States, though initially critical of the majority position, agreed to support a definition of trafficking that would be agreed upon by consensus.

The struggle—fed by the CATW to create a definition of trafficking that would penalize traffickers while ensuring that all victims of trafficking would be protected—succeeded when a compromise proposal by Sweden was agreed to. A strongly worded and inclusive UN Protocol to Prevent, Suppress, and Punish Trafficking in Persons—especially women and children—was drafted by an ad hoc committee of the UN as a supplement to the Convention Against Transnational Organized Crime. The UN protocol specifically addresses the trade in human beings for purposes of prostitution and other forms of sexual exploitation, forced labor or services, slavery or practices similar to slavery, servitude, and the removal of organs. The protocol defines trafficking as:

> *The recruitment, transportation, transfer, harboring or receipt of persons, by means of the threat or use of force or other forms of coercion, of abduction, of fraud, of deception, of the abuse of power or of a position of vulnerability or of the giving or receiving of payments or benefits to achieve the consent of a person having control over another person, for the purpose of exploitation.*

While recognizing that the largest amount of trafficking involves women and children, the wording of the UN protocol clearly is gender and age neutral, inclusive of trafficking in both males and females, adults and children.

In 2000 the UN General Assembly adopted this convention and its supplementary protocol; 121 countries signed the convention and eighty countries signed the protocol. For the convention and protocol to become international law, forty countries must ratify them.

## *Highlights*

Some highlights of the new convention and protocol are:

- For the first time there is an accepted international definition of trafficking and an agreed-upon set of prosecution, protection, and prevention mechanisms on which countries can base their national legislation.
- The various criminal means by which trafficking takes place, including indirect and subtle forms of coercion, are covered.
- Trafficked persons, especially women in prostitution and child laborers, are no longer viewed as illegal migrants but as victims of a crime.
- The convention doesn't limit its scope to criminal syndicates but defines an organized criminal group as "any structured group of three or more persons which engages in criminal activities such as trafficking and pimping."
- All victims of trafficking in persons are protected, not just those who can prove that force was used against them.
- The consent of a victim of trafficking is meaningless and irrelevant.
- Victims of trafficking won't have to bear the burden of proof.
- Trafficking and sexual exploitation are intrinsically connected and not to be separated.
- Because women trafficked domestically into local sex industries suffer harmful effects similar to those experienced by women trafficked transnationally, these women also come under the protections of the protocol.
- The key element in trafficking is the exploitative purpose rather than the movement across a border.

The protocol is the first UN instrument to address the demand for prostitution sex, a demand that results in the human rights abuses of women and children being trafficked. The protocol recognizes an urgent need for governments to put the buyers of prostitution sex on their policy and legislative agendas, and it calls upon countries to take or strengthen legislative or other measures to discourage demand, which fosters all the forms of sexual exploitation of women and children. . . .

## Refugees, Not Illegal Aliens

In October 2000 the U.S. Congress passed a bill, the Victims of Trafficking and Violence Protection Act of 2000, introduced by New Jersey republican representative Chris Smith. Under this law penalties for traffickers are raised and protections for victims increased. Reasoning that desperate women are unable to give meaningful consent to their own sexual exploitation, the law adopts a broad definition of sex trafficking so as not to exclude so-called consensual prostitution or trafficking that occurs solely within the United States. In these respects the new federal law conforms to the UN protocol.

Two features of the law are particularly noteworthy:

• In order to pressure other countries to end sex trafficking, the U.S. State Department is to make a yearly assessment of other countries' anti-trafficking efforts and to rank them according to how well they discourage trafficking. After two years of failing to meet even minimal standards, countries are subject to sanctions, although not sanctions on humanitarian aid. "Tier 3" countries—those failing to meet even minimal standards—include Greece, Indonesia, Israel, Pakistan, Russia, Saudi Arabia, South Korea, and Thailand.

• Among persons being trafficked into the United States, special T-visas will be provided to those who meet the criteria for having suffered the most serious trafficking abuses. These visas will protect them from deportation so they can testify against their traffickers. T non-immigrant status allows eligible aliens to remain in the United States temporarily and grants specific non-immigrant benefits. Those acquiring T-1 non-immigrant status will be able to remain for a period of three years and will be eligible to receive certain kinds of public assistance—to the same extent as refugees. They will also be issued employment authorization to "assist them in finding safe, legal employment while they attempt to retake control of their lives."

## A Debate Rages

A worldwide debate rages about legalization of prostitution fueled by a 1998 International Labor Organization (ILO) report entitled *The sex sector: The economic and social bases of prostitution in Southeast Asia*. The report follows years of lobbying by the sex industry for recognition of prostitution as "sex work." Citing the sex industry's unrecognized contribution to the gross domestic product of four countries in Southeast Asia, the ILO urges governments to officially recognize the "sex sector" and "extend taxation nets to cover many of the lucrative activities connected with it." Though the ILO report says it stops short of calling for legalization of prostitution, official recognition of the sex industry would be impossible without it.

Raymond points out that the ILO's push to redefine prostitution as sex work ignores legislation demonstrating that countries can reduce organized sexual exploitation rather than capitulate to it. For example, Sweden prohibits the purchase of sexual services with punishments of stiff fines or imprisonment, thus declaring that prostitution isn't a desirable economic and labor sector. The government also helps women getting out of prostitution to rebuild their lives. Venezuela's Ministry of Labor has ruled that prostitution can't be considered work because it lacks the basic elements of dignity and social justice. The Socialist Republic of Vietnam punishes pimps, traffickers, brothel owners, and buyers—sometimes publishing buyer's names in the mass media. For women in prostitution, the government finances medical, educational, and economic rehabilitation.

Raymond suggests that instead of transforming the male buyer into a legitimate customer, the ILO should give thought to innovative programs that make the buyer accountable for his sexual exploitation. She cites the Sage Project, Inc. (SAGE) program in San Francisco, California, which educates men arrested for soliciting women in prostitution about the risks and impacts of their behavior.

Legalization advocates argue that the violence, exploitation, and health effects suffered by women in prostitution aren't inherent to prostitution but simply result from the random behaviors of bad pimps or buyers, and that if prostitution were regulated by the state these harms would diminish. But examples show these arguments to be false.

In the pamphlet entitled *Legalizing prostitution is not the answer: The example of Victoria, Australia,* published by the CATW in 2001, Mary Sullivan and Sheila Jeffreys describe the way legalization in Australia has perpetuated and strengthened the culture of violence and exploitation inherent in prostitution. Under legalization, legal and illegal brothels have proliferated, and trafficking in women has accelerated to meet the increased demand. Pimps, having even more power, continue threatening and brutalizing the women they control. Buyers continue to abuse women, refuse to wear condoms, and spread the HIV virus—and other sexually transmitted diseases—to their wives and girlfriends. Stigmatized by identity cards and medical inspections, prostituted women are even more marginalized and tightly locked into the system of organized sexual exploitation while the state, now an official party to the exploitation, has become the biggest pimp of all.

The government of the Netherlands has legalized prostitution, doesn't enforce laws against pimping, and virtually lives off taxes from the earnings of prostituted women. In the book *Making the harm visible* (published by the CATW in 1999), Marie-Victoire Louis describes the effects on prostituted women of municipal regulation of brothels in Amsterdam and other Dutch cities. Her article entitled "Legalizing Pimping, Dutch Style" explains the way immigration policies in the Netherlands are shaped to fit the needs of the prostitution industry so that traffickers are seldom prosecuted and a continuous supply of women is guaranteed. In Amsterdam's 250 officially listed brothels, 80 percent of the prostitutes have been trafficked in from other countries and 70 percent possess no legal papers. Without money, papers, or contact with the outside world, these immigrant women live in terror. Instead of being protected by the regulations governing brothels, prostituted women are frequently beaten up and raped by pimps. These "prostitution managers" have practically been given a free hand by the state and by buyers who, as "consumers of prostitution," feel themselves entitled to abuse the women they buy. Sadly and ironically the "Amsterdam model" of legalization and regulation is touted by the Netherlands and Germany as "self-determination and empowerment for women." In reality it simply legitimizes the "right" to buy, sexually use, and profit from the sexual exploitation of someone else's body.

## *A Human Rights Approach*

As part of a system of organized sexual exploitation, prostitution can be visualized along a continuum of abuse with brothel slavery at the furthest extreme. All along the continuum, fine lines divide the degrees of harm done to those caught up in the system. At the core lies a great social injustice no cosmetic reforms can right: the setting aside of a segment of people whose bodies can be purchased for sexual use by others. When this basic injustice is legitimized and regulated by the state and when the state profits from it, that injustice is compounded.

In her book *The prostitution of sexuality* (New York University Press, 1995), Kathleen Barry details a feminist human rights approach to prostitution that points the way to the future. Ethically it recognizes prostitution, sex trafficking, and the globalized industrialization of sex as massive violations of women's human rights. Sociologically it considers how and to what extent prostitution promotes sex discrimination against individual women, against different racial categories of women, and against women as a group. Politically it calls for decriminalizing prostitutes while penalizing pimps, traffickers, brothel owners, and buyers.

Understanding that human rights and restorative justice go hand in hand, the feminist human rights approach to prostitution addresses the harm and the need to repair the damage. As Barry says:

> Legal proposals to criminalize customers, based on the recognition that prostitution violates and harms women, must . . . include social-service, health and counseling and job retraining programs. Where states would be closing down brothels if customers were criminalized, the economic resources poured into the former prostitution areas could be turned toward producing gainful employment for women.

With the help of women's projects in many countries—such as Buklod in the Philippines and the Council for Prostitution Alternatives in the United States—some women have begun to confront their condition by leaving prostitution, speaking out against it, revealing their experiences, and helping other women leave the sex industry.

Ending the sexual exploitation of trafficking and prostitution will mean the beginning of a new chapter in building a humanist future—a more peaceful and just future in which men and women can join together in love and respect, recognizing one another's essential dignity and humanity. Humanity's sexuality then will no longer be hijacked and distorted.

# Naked Profits

Tad Friend

San Francisco has led the sexual revolution since 1964, the year a teenage dancer named Carol Doda caused a sensation by appearing onstage at the Condor night club in a Rudi Gernreich swimsuit that lacked a top. In subsequent months, the sensation grew, as Doda pioneered the silicone-injection craze and ballooned to a size 44-DD. Before long, a sailor in North Beach could buy a cone at a topless ice-cream stand, eat it while getting a topless shoe shine, then take in a show starring "a topless mother of eight."

Feminism came to San Francisco early, too. In the Nixon era, women of evolved consciousness picketed the Condor, claiming that Doda was being exploited. "They said, 'Burn your bra!'" Doda recalls. "I said, 'I'm not even wearing a bra!'"

Today, Carol Doda is marketing lingerie and the Condor is a sports bar, but a new sexual experiment is in progress at the Lusty Lady Theatre, around the corner from the Condor. Last year, the Lusty, as it is known, became the first employee-owned strip club in the country. It has been the thinking woman's strip club since it was founded, in 1984; its dancers, rather than taking the usual stage names of Barbie or Angel, called themselves Virginia Dentata or Attila the Honey. (At their request, the dancers mentioned in this story are identified only by their stage names.) Lili Marlene is currently using her experience with customers

to refine her thinking on the socialization of male sexuality; Donna Delinqua is writing a doctoral thesis, "Narrative and the Production of Lesbian Identity," between shifts. The dancers respect one another's sensitivities by avoiding "scented or perfumed grooming products," and Cayenne, who has a master's degree in social work and a shaved head, says that part of her work is "to model self-respecting behavior for the customers." In other words, she explains, "I won't put up with shit."

In 1997, the dancers took their polemics outside, picketing for the right to have a union. Chants such as "Two, four, six, eight, don't go here to masturbate!" and "No contract, no pussy!" made their point, and the Lusty became the only one of the country's twenty-five hundred strip clubs to unionize. "Those dancers are our most functional chapter," Lawanna Preston, the staff director of Local 790 of the Service Employees International Union, says. "They alone negotiated the majority of their last contract"—in January, 2003, resulting in a three-dollar-an-hour raise for some employees.

A month later, the club's manager, Darrell Davis, announced that the owners had asked him to close down the Lusty. In May, however, the dancers bought the business for four hundred thousand dollars—all borrowed from the old owners—and reorganized it as a cooperative: dancers, janitors, and cashiers pay a three-hundred-dollar fee to become co-owners and share in the profits. They sought business advice from the Rainbow Grocery and Good Vibrations, two local cooperatives that market organic produce and sex toys, respectively. A dancer named Havana incorporated the club as

From Friend, Tad. 2004. "Naked Profits: The Employees Take Over a Strip Club." *The New Yorker* 80(19). Reprinted by permission of International Creative Management, Inc. Copyright © 2004 by Tad Friend.

the Looking Glass Cooperative, after consulting the "Co-Op Incorporation Sourcebook," and another dancer, Miss Muffy, a high-school graduate, drew up the co-op's buy-sell agreement, promissory note, and membership paperwork with the help of sample forms downloaded from the Internet.

Traditionally, stripping is capitalism at its most explicit: men sell women's bodies to other men. The idea behind the new Lusty Lady was that capitalism would give way to the Utopian glories of self-ownership. Rather than capital (the owner) renting labor and forcing it to do dull and repetitive tasks, labor would rent capital (borrow money) and be free to reinvent not only the notion of tasks but also the master-slave dynamic inherent in sex work. "We extinguish the concept of hierarchy," the clubs new mission statement declared; everyone would take turns hiring and firing, debating corporate strategy, and maintaining client relations (an executive function previously viewed as mere entry-level wiggling around in the nude).

Morale at the club improved after the takeover, and a wave of new customers—a more respectful, less drunk sort of customer—came in to support employee ownership. But some observers remained dubious. A manager at Roaring 20s, a club up the street, who identified himself only as Anthony, snickered when he was asked about the Lusty Lady's prospects. "I've been working here for three years and I don't know how to run a club, so how could they?" he said.

"Workers always believe management is full of shit," Darrell Davis told me. A soft-spoken man, Davis had spent the past twenty years in the sex business, and was relieved to be getting out of it. He hopes to become a teacher. "That antagonism was much more powerful at the Lusty, because the women were nude, and vulnerable, and from San Francisco," he continued. "During the first union negotiations, the dancers told me I was 'raping' new dancers by paying them less than more senior dancers. I offered to start everyone at the highest wage and cut their salary by a dollar every few

months, but they didn't want that, either. The real problem was that some of the dancers felt that any profit the company made was immoral." He added, "But they are now what they never wanted to be: corporate owners."

The façade of the Lusty Lady Theatre testifies to the sex industry's peculiar faith in alliteration: the "Lovely Lusty Ladies" inside are billed as not only "Hot Hard Horny" but also "Naked Naughty Nasty." Should these traditional enticements fail, an "Under New Management!" banner flaps from the building's marquee, and a sandwich board proclaims that the club is "Worker Owned." Inside the club, however, the Barbary Coast-style décor remains unrefreshed. Shabby velvet curtains droop from the entrance, blocking out any ambient light. Rules are posted by the cashier's desk "No loitering! One guy per booth! Don't tap booth glass! Clean up after yourself!"

At a conventional strip club, a dancer gyrates on a stage ornamented with a pole and a disco ball and, often, dry-ice vapor, while other strippers work the room looking for lap-dance customers; the Lusty Lady, by contrast, is a peep show. After navigating a dim hallway, customers enter one of twelve small booths that surround a stage covered in red carpet. Inside, when they drop a quarter into a slot, a shutter rises, and for seventeen seconds they can gaze through a glass window at three women, naked except for high heels, who strut and grind.

On the other side of the hallway are private video booths, and around the corner is the Private Pleasures booth, where, for ten or twenty dollars, a solitary dancer behind glass will take requests; for a customer, it's the equivalent, one dancer says, of "having your car valet-parked."

Downstairs, behind a locked door, is the dancers' lounge and changing room, and off the lounge there is a windowless office that contains three battered metal desks and a vintage poster of Rosie the Riveter that declares, "We Can Do It!" The Lusty Lady has seven board members, who meet here every Monday afternoon. Although an atmosphere of good humor prevails, the business's problems have proved to be as incessant as the solutions are makeshift. The cooperative's work-in-progress bylaws, for instance, explain that share ownership is "pursuant to subsection (b) of Bylaw Section 8.03 (of the Rainbow Grocery Co-operative Bylaws, which we have yet to fully understand)."

A board meeting in mid-November began when Pepper, a thirty-three-year-old blonde with two piercings curling up from her lower lip, said, "O.K., I'm going to do my usual bullish facilitation, because, remember, in high school I was on student council." . . .

The board listened to a status report on the club's negotiations with its landlord, Roger Forbes, who, in the past three years, had more than doubled the rent, to $13,442 a month. The dancers had requested a new lease at a lower rate, but Forbes had initially demanded a sixty-thousand-dollar security deposit. . . .

Forbes finally gave the cooperative a new lease at the same rate—with no security deposit required. "It would behoove them, after they get the lease set, to spend some money sprucing up their facility," he told me. "As far as I can tell, no one's spent a dime on that place in twenty years."

Forbes has an ownership stake in several of the properties owned by Déjà Vu, Inc., the country's largest strip-club chain. Déjà Vu has taken over seven clubs in the Lusty Lady's neighborhood, including Roaring 20s and the Hungry i, where Lenny Bruce developed his act in the nineteen-fifties. At Déjà Vu clubs (and at most clubs in San Francisco), dancers have to pay the management "stage fees," as high as two hundred and forty dollars a night, for the privilege of working a shift as an "independent contractor." On a good night, a dancer at a conventional strip club can make far more money than a dancer at the Lusty Lady—as much as a thousand dollars. But because they begin each shift in debt, and know that they can be fined for chewing gum or for clapping out of time onstage, strippers at other clubs often feel pressure to use the private lap-dancing booths to engage in "dirty dancing" or "extras."

Sex work is as subject to the iron laws of economics as any other form of labor. The advent of the Internet has given strip-club patrons the opportunity to post reviews of individual dancers, often in the raunchiest language imaginable, on Web sites; this dissemination of information has, as the Chicago School of economists would have predicted, led to increased competition and falling prices. A "bareback blow job"—that is, oral sex performed without a condom—which local call girls charged three hundred dollars for in the mid-nineties, can now routinely be had at a strip club for twenty dollars, or no more than a lap dance. "Things are so bad in other clubs that the Lusty Lady is a great ray of hope," says Daisy Anarchy, a stripper who has worked at numerous clubs and is attempting to unionize the city's erotic dancers and legalize prostitution. "It's, like, 'You haven't got all of us!'"

The Lusty Lady's board went on to discuss plans for a fund-raiser that would feature a spanking booth and an auction of the dancers' underwear. Havana, a slim strawberry blonde, said, "We'll make more money if a dancer takes off her underwear for the winner right there." . . .

Pepper steered the meeting back to the agenda: the Lusty Lady was broke. When the employees bought the club, they knew that revenues from the live shows, buffeted by the rise in Internet porn and the soft local economy, had fallen forty per cent since 1996, when the club grossed nearly three million dollars. But they suspected that Darrell Davis had underplayed the club's profitability all along, and hoped that incentives and new ideas would invigorate the business.

The new management tried ladies' nights, but it turns out that women aren't as eager as men are to look at naked women. A plan to blanket the city with ads was scotched when the dancers discovered that they didn't have the money to do it, even though Davis had given them twelve thousand dollars in cash to get started, and had suspended their debt payments for five months. The co-op's most profitable innovation had turned out to be the installation of a Pepsi machine.

The situation was such, Pepper reminded everyone, that they would have to close if they didn't cut costs by two thousand dollars a week "We need to think outside the box," she said. . . .

The board had polled the workers to learn which of fifteen possible cuts had the greatest support. Health insurance and pay for the dancers' prep time were being eliminated, late shifts would be curtailed, and the workers also strongly favored reducing the top dancers' wage, from twenty-six dollars an hour to twenty-three. . . .

"Do we still believe in additional money for seniority?" Havana asked, returning to the radical issue that had so vexed Davis.

"I do," Pepper said. End of subject. "But we also have to make sure it all seems super-super-democratic and everyone feels super-super-heard," she continued. Pepper and Donna are union shop stewards, positions that—until a few dancers volunteered to serve as temporary union reps—would have required them to negotiate salary cuts with themselves.

"We have to have the illusion of two different parties with different ideas," Pepper continued, "although, ultimately, I'm going to make the whole fucking thing happen in half an hour by just"—she made a sound of chewing through flesh.

"That's so Darrell," Tony, another support staffer, said.

"You've learned," Aesop said. "You've learned from the best."

A few weeks later, the dancers voted to cut their pay by between one and three dollars an hour, with the highest paid among them taking a larger hit. "In our last contract discussions with Darrell," Pepper told me, "he couldn't negotiate us to the position that we have to accept from ourselves now. Nobody could be more shocked and unhappy about that fact than me." . . .

Most dancers at other clubs are young, blond, and voluptuous. At the Lusty, some dancers are slight, some are heavy, some are hairy, some are bald, and one, Calipso, recently became a grandmother. The "madams"—dancers elected to replace the previous regimes shift supervisors—still hire according to the old personnel policy, which requires dancers to have a "trim stomach," "a minimum of cellulite," and "clean, healthy teeth," but they no longer classify dancers by body type. "Under old management, I was hired as a 'blond, small-breasted, slim, tall,' and if I needed to have someone fill my shift it could only be another body type like mine," Vega, a madam, says. "You were just a piece of meat, filling their quota." . . .

"In the Private Pleasures booth, every man's greatest anxiety is penis size," Cayenne says. "You can play that and make money off it—'You're so big!'—and sustain the anxiety. But I myself don't measure up to the female ideal. So I find something else to affirm in men, without playing into that insecurity." Still, she acknowledges, "It's hard to have a humanitarian cooperative in an environment where you need to make money. So many things that save money just suck. It sucks that you save by having high turnover and paying new employees less. It sucks that regular customers want you to work your shifts at different times so they keep seeing new dancers. It sucks that eventually your tits are going to sag and you won't be able to do the job anymore. And, most of all, it sucks that, even working with other women, it's hard to ameliorate the nature of the business we're in, which is the commodification of an image produced by a white, supremacist, capitalist patriarchy."

As their responsibilities sink in, a few of the new owners are growing weary of theory. "I totally support the performers—they're amazing women," Aesop told me. "But some of the men feel we need to look at this more as a business and less as a sociology experiment. I mean, I know it's controversial, but I do think the women should be attractive and the place should be kept somewhat clean."

At the November board meeting, Ruby, who had changed for work into a skimpy maroon dress and a string of pearls, mentioned that no one was getting enough shifts. Suddenly, everyone was talking at once. Havana pointed out, to general agreement, that three shifts a week—about two hundred and forty dollars for the average dancer—was just enough to not quite live on. (Most of the dancers have at least one other job.)

In years past, dancers often became dissatisfied and left; now that they're staying, there are too many of them. Many laid the blame for this state of affairs not on the law of unintended consequences but on the new madams. They used to grumble about the old shift supervisors, too, calling them "Aunty Toms." Like many low-wage workers, the club's dancers are accustomed to the politics of resentment, to resisting whatever management—even a management that they have elected—suggests.

Miss Muffy said, "A lot of people who complain about shifts aren't doing their fucking jobs and shouldn't get shifts." Penny, a madam, gave Miss Muffy a high five. After the takeover, revenues from the live shows dropped, and customers complained that the dancers were just standing around—or, worse, just standing around discussing "sex-positive" feminism. So Miss Muffy put in everyone's pay envelope a note that began, "Yo, we need to check ourselves before we wreck ourselves." For two weeks, revenues rose by more than ten per cent, before levelling off again.

"If Miss Muffy was dictator," Miss Muffy continued, "she would hire new dancers and replace fifteen of the people here now." . . .

"I've been reading a book about creative organizational management," she said. "I'm proposing we have an Employee of the Week and give her a five-dollar coupon to Vesuvio's"—a local bar.

Several of the board members snapped their fingers approvingly. The longest discussion of the afternoon ensued, with a vocal constituency arguing for an Employee of the Month, who would receive twenty dollars in cash. Tony pointed out that the janitors and cashiers had already chosen the Pepsi machine as the Employee of the Month. A vote determined that three members favored creating an Employee of the Week, three favored an Employee of the Month, and one was so deeply ambivalent that she abstained. With Lyndon Johnson-like instincts for the expedient compromise, Miss Muffy proposed that the award be biweekly. By a unanimous vote, the board approved the creation of an Employee of the Fortnight.

The last serious piece of business concerned payroll. When Penny, who had been doing payroll for years, left the room, Miss Muffy said, "Lots of people want her job. And when we started doing the cooperative we were all about people learning new skills and getting the chance to move into management."

"That's kind of good in theory," Tony began. Pepper interjected, "Whenever anyone who isn't Penny does payroll, it's all fucked up." The vote to keep Penny in place was six for, Miss Muffy against. "What about our original ideas?" she said. "What is this cooperative all about?"

"Staying in business," Pepper said. "Let's move on."

Another iron rule that the owners have discovered—one as familiar to the Bolsheviks as it became to the American colonists—is that the needs of the collective soon trump those of its members, even though those individual needs were the reason that the collective had formed in the first place. "What we have here now is the closest I can get to a matriarchy," Havana told me. "But it's hard to take it further." She understands that self-ownership alone cannot mitigate the fact that you can make money off women in a glass cage. "In a perfect world," Havana said, "we would make a little more money and the work would be intellectually stimulating—it's very monotonous. And, in a truly perfect world, I could put the job on my résumé."

## Forty Reasons Why Whores Are My Heroines

**Annie Sprinkle**

1. Whores have the ability to share their most private, sensitive body parts with total strangers.
2. Whores have access to places that other people do not.
3. Whores challenge sexual mores.
4. Whores are playful.
5. Whores are tough.
6. Whores have careers based on giving pleasure.
7. Whores are creative.
8. Whores are adventurous and dare to live dangerously.
9. Whores teach people how to be better lovers.
10. Whores are multicultural and multigendered.
11. Whores give excellent advice and help people with their personal problems.
12. Whores have fun.
13. Whores wear exciting clothes.
14. Whores have patience and tolerance for people that other people could never manage to put up with.
15. Whores make lonely people less lonely.
16. Whores are independent.
17. Whores teach people how to have safer sex.
18. Whores are a tradition.
19. Whores are hip.
20. Whores have a good sense of humor.
21. Whores relieve millions of people of unwanted stress and tension.
22. Whores heal.
23. Whores endure despite the fact that many people have prejudices against them.
24. Whores make good money.
25. Whores always have a job.
26. Whores are sexy and erotic.
27. Whores have special talents that other people do not have. Not everyone has what it takes to be a whore.
28. Whores are interesting people with lots of exciting life stories.
29. Whores get laid a lot.
30. Whores help people explore their sexual desires.
31. Whores explore their own sexual desires.
32. Whores are not afraid of sex.
33. Whores hustle.
34. Whores sparkle.
35. Whores are entertaining.
36. Whores have the guts to wear very big wigs.
37. Whores are not ashamed to be naked.
38. Whores help the handicapped.
39. Whores make their own hours.
40. Whores are rebelling against the absurd, patriarchal, sex-negative laws affecting their profession and fighting for the legal right to receive financial compensation for their valuable work.

*Source: Prostitution: On Whores, Hustlers, and Johns,* edited by James A. Elias, Vern L. Bullough, Veronica Elias, and Gwen Brewer, "Forty Reasons Why Whores Are My Heriones," pp. 114–115 (1998). (Amherst, NY: Prometheus Books). Copyright © 1998 by James A. Elias, Vern L. Bullough, Veronica Elias, and Gwen Brewer. Reprinted with permission.

## Strip Clubs and their Regulars

**Katherine Frank**

Sexual services and products have long been a part of the U.S. entertainment and leisure industries. In a 1997 article for *U.S. News & World Report,* Eric Schlosser reported that in the prior year Americans spent "more than $8 billion on hard-core videos, peep shows, live sex acts, adult cable programming, sexual devices, computer porn, and sex magazines." The number of major strip clubs catering to heterosexually identified men nearly doubled between 1987 and 1992, and an estimate for late 1998 puts the number of clubs at around 3000 with annual revenues ranging from $500,000 to more than $5 million.

While some men dislike strip clubs or find them boring, there is a significant population of heterosexual American males who are willing to spend their money on the kind of public, voyeuristic (although interactive) fantasy available in a no-contact strip club. Despite popular beliefs to the contrary, strippers are generally not selling sex to their customers in this type of club—although they are selling sexualized and gendered services. Rather than fulfilling a biological need for sexual release, as some pop sociobiological accounts suggest, or serving a masculine need for domination, strip clubs provide a kind of intermediate space (not work and not home, although related to both) in which men can experience their bodies and identities in particular pleasurable ways. . . .

Strip clubs are stratified in terms of luxury, status, and other distinguishing features. Whereas strip clubs were once primarily located in "red light" areas of towns and cities associated with crime and prostitution, the upscale clubs are now often quite visible and work to develop reputations for safety, comfort, and classiness. Drawing on cultural markers of status—such as luxury liquors, fine dining, valet parking, and private conference rooms—upscale clubs advertise themselves as places for businessmen to entertain clients or for middle class professionals to visit after work. Dancers may be advertised as refined, well-educated women. Sophisticated sound and lighting equipment, multiple stages, large video screens, and multi-million dollar construction budgets make many contemporary strip clubs into high-tech entertainment centers. This is not to say that smaller or "seedier" clubs have disappeared. The clubs in any locale, however, are categorized through their relationships to one another and this system of relationships helps inform both the leisure experiences of the customers and the work experiences of the dancers.

The proliferation and upscaling of strip clubs during the 1980s needs to be situated in late capitalist consumer culture as well as within a variety of social changes and developments. In many ways it makes sense that strip clubs should multiply during the last several decades, along with the panic about AIDS and fears about the dissolution of "the family." The process of upscaling in strip clubs, with a promise of "clean" and respectable interactions, alleviated fears about contamination and disease. The fact that sexual activity is not generally expected or offered in strip clubs also fit well with a growing emphasis on monogamy and marriage for heterosexuals after the sexual experimentation (and ensuing disillusionment for many) of the 1970s. There are other social changes which may be influencing this rapid increase in strip clubs as well: women's increased presence in the workforce, continuing backlashes against feminism, on-going marketing efforts to sexualize and masculinize particular forms of consumption ("sports, beer, and women," for example), changing patterns of mobility which influence dating practices and intimate relationships, and increased travel for businessmen and more anonymous opportunities to purchase commodified sexualized services, to name just a few.

Despite their prevalence and popularity, strip clubs are still often the subject of intense public scrutiny. Local ordinances have been drafted across the nation to harass, limit or eradicate strip clubs—often citing "adverse secondary effects" such as increased crime and decreased property values in neighborhoods that house such venues as justifications for these legislative actions. Many such ordinances seem to be based on conjectures about just what the men (and women) are up to when they set foot in a strip club. There is endless speculation about drug use, prostitution, and crime—by customers, lawmakers, and people who have never even entered a strip club. . . . While these activities surface at times, in often scandalous ways—as they do in many industries—I came away from my research with a belief that most of the customers were in search of something completely different through their interactions.

Media and scholarly attention to the customers of strip clubs has been far less pervasive than that focused on the dancers or the clubs themselves. But what is it, exactly, that the customers are seeking in these venues? After all, without enough men willing to open their wallets each night the industry would cease to exist. As a cultural anthropologist dedicated to participant observation—that is, becoming immersed in the community you study—I selected five strip clubs in one city, sought employment as an entertainer, and interviewed the regular male customers of those clubs. For regulars, visits to strip clubs are a significant sexualized and leisure practice; these are not men who have wandered into a club once or twice or visit only for special occasions like bachelor parties. The majority of the regulars were men middle-aged or older with enough disposable income and free time that they could engage in this relatively private and often expensive leisure practice. I also interviewed dancers, club managers and other club employees, advertisers, and men who preferred other forms of adult entertainment.

Most of the regular customers claimed that they knew where to get sex if they wanted it, and that they chose no-contact strip clubs (or clubs that offered table-dancing rather than lap dancing) precisely because they knew that sex would not be part of the experience. While watching the dancers perform on the stages was certainly appealing, many of the regulars were also interested in the conversations that they could have with dancers. Unlike burlesque performers of years past, contemporary exotic dancers "perform" not just on-stage but individually for the customers as they circulate amongst the crowd selling table-dances. Dancers are thus also selling their personalities, their attentions, and conversation to the customers. Some of the regulars returned repeatedly to see a particular dancer; others enjoyed briefer interactions with a number of dancers. Either way, talk was one of the important services being provided and conversations would focus on work, family, politics, sports, sexual fantasies, or any number of other topics.

Whether visiting a small neighborhood bar or a large, flashy gentleman's club, the customers repeatedly told me that they visited strip clubs to relax. Part of the allure of strip clubs for their patrons lies in part in their representation as somewhere out of the ordinary, somewhere proscribed and perhaps a bit "dangerous"—yet as a safe space of play and fantasy where the pressures, expectations and responsibilities of work and home can be left behind.

In many ways, then, strip clubs were seen as relaxing because they provided a respite from women's demands or expectations in other spheres, as well as the possibility (not always actualized) of avoiding competition with other men for women's attention. Strip clubs also offered the customers an opportunity for both personal and sexual acceptance from women, a chance to talk about their sexual desires without reproach or to fantasize that they were attractive enough to gain the interest of a dancer regardless of whether or not they paid her. Some customers wanted an ego boost. As one man said: "It's just absolutely an ego trip because you go in there, and if you're a warthog, bald, and got a pot belly, some good looking girl's gonna come up and go, 'Hey, do you want me to dance for you?' Seducing women is something all men wish they were better at . . . this seems like you're doing it, and it's easy!"

Strip clubs were also relaxing because they provided a safe space in which to be both married or committed and interacting with women in a sexualized setting, and the services offered fit well with these particular men's desires to remain sexually monogamous. Customers are also not expected to perform sexually or to provide any pleasure to the dancer (beyond paying her for her time), and this was also seen as relaxing by many of the men. . . .

However, because they provided a space in which many everyday expectations are inverted (by featuring public nudity, for example), the clubs were still seen as "taboo," as dangerous and exciting, by the regulars as well as safe and predictable. Many of the interviewees discussed their experiences in the language of "variety," "travel," "fun," "escape" and "adventure" and described themselves as "hunters" or "explorers" despite the fact that their experiences in the clubs were highly regulated by local ordinances, club rules, and club employees. Some customers enjoyed the fact that their visits to strip clubs took them to marginal areas of the city. Further, visits to the clubs often were unacceptable to the married regulars' more "conservative" wives or partners. Significantly, then, strip clubs are also dangerous enough to be alluring, a bit "less civilized" and rowdier than the places these middle-class customers would ordinarily enter. This balance between safety and excitement was very important, for if strip clubs lose their edge for a particular customer, or conversely, become too transgressive, he may lose interest and seek a different form of entertainment.

Understanding the motivations of the men who frequent no-contact strip clubs can help quell some of the fears that tend to drive oppressive regulation. There are indeed problems with strip clubs as they currently exist, often rooted in material inequalities between different classes of laborers, in the poor working conditions found in many clubs, in the stigma that surrounds sex work, and in double standards for men's and women's sexualities, for example. However, eradicating or more tightly regulating strip clubs does little to combat these problems, which are related to the organization of labor in late capitalism, to systemic inequalities and prejudices, and to the stigmatization and fear that still surrounds issues of sex and sexuality in the United States.

*Source:* Frank, Katherine. 2003. "Strip Clubs and Their Regulars." *American Sexuality Magazine* 1(4). Copyright 2003, National Sexuality Resource Center/San Francisco State University. Reprinted by permission.

## *Did You Know?*

- It is often claimed that four out of ten people using the Internet have visited a pornographic adult site within the last week.[1]
- Porn can be downloaded directly to your iPod.[2]
- Annual profits from pornography are estimated to be $10 billion.[3] Microsoft earned just over $8 million in annual profits in 2004.[4]
- According to one estimate, one million people in the United States have worked as prostitutes (approximately 1% of all American women).[5]
- Ninety percent of average prostitution arrests are of the sex workers themselves (70% women sex workers, 20% men sex workers). Only 10% of prostitute arrests are customers. Street work accounts for only around 20 percent of prostitution yet 85 to 90 percent of sex workers who are arrested work on the street.[6]
- The sex trade industry accounts for between 2 and 14 percent of the gross domestic product (GDP) of Malaysia, Indonesia, the Philippines, and Thailand.[7]
- A 1949 United Nations resolution recommended the decriminalization of prostitution. This resolution has been ratified by fifty nations (excluding the United States).[8]
- In Thailand a third of foreign sex workers are less than 18 years old.[9]
- Many sex workers in Asia do not see themselves as sex workers nor at risk for HIV, therefore, they do not use condoms.[10]
- *Deep Throat,* a pornographic film released in 1977, was shot in six days for $25,000 but grossed in excess of $600 million. The main character's clitoris was supposedly located in her throat and therefore only stimulated by oral sex.[11]
- Prostitution became legal in Nevada in 1971.[12]
- Heidi Fleiss, the former Hollywood Madam, is planning to open Heidi's Stud Farm, in Nevada. If successful, this will be the country's first legal brothel serving female customers.[13]

—*Compiled by Mikel Walters*

**NOTES**

1. Caslon Analytics Profile. "Adult Content Industries." Retrieved January 30, 2006 from www.caslon.com.au/xcontentprofile1.htm.

2. Harris, Ron. 2005. "iPod Gets Eye-Opener in Adult Entertainment: Already Big Business Online, Porn Makes Way to Small Screens." *Austin American-Statesman,* November 5. Retrieved January 30, 2006 from www.statesman.com/business/content/business/stories/11/5portableporn.html.

3. Richard, Emmanuelle. 2002. "The Naked Untruth." Retrieved November 30, 2005 from www.alternet.org/story/13212.

4. Fortune 500. 2005. "Fortune's Annual Ranking of America's Largest Corporations." CNN Money. Retrieved January 30, 2006 from

www.money.cnn.com/magazines/fortune/fortune 500.

5. Alexander, Priscilla. 1987. "Prostitution: A Difficult Issue for Feminists." In *Sex Work: Writings by Women in the Sex Industry* (pp. 184–214), edited by Frédérique Delacoste and Priscilla Alexander. Cleis Press.

6. Ibid.

7. World Health Organization. "Press Release: Sex Trade Expanding in Asia." Retrieved January 30, 2006 from www.wpro.who.int/media_centre/press_releases/pr_20010813.htm.

8. Prostitutes' Education Network. "Prostitution in the United States—The Statistics." Retrieved January 30, 2006 from http://bayswan.org/stats.html.

9. World Health Organization. "Press Release: Sex Trade Expanding in Asia."

10. Ibid.

11. Roth, Kim (Executive Producer), Fenton Bailey (Director and Writer), and Randy Barbato (Director and Writer). 2005. *Inside Deep Throat* [documentary film]. HBO Documentary Films.

12. Minster, Tovah. 2003. "One out of Fifty: Legalized Prostitution in the State of Nevada." *Georgetown Law Review.* Retrieved January 30, 2006 from www.law.georgetown.edu/glh/minster.htm.

13. Friess, Steve. 2005. "Betting on the Studs." *Newsweek.* Retrieved January 30, 2006 from www.msnbc.msn.com/id/10313009/site/newsweek.

# Name Index

# Subject Index